MODERN AMERICAN REMEDIES

ASPEN CASEBOOK SERIES

MODERN AMERICAN REMEDIES
CASES AND MATERIALS

Fifth Edition

Douglas Laycock
Robert E. Scott Distinguished Professor of Law
and Professor of Religious Studies
University of Virginia

Alice McKean Young Regents Chair in Law Emeritus
The University of Texas at Austin

Richard L. Hasen
Chancellor's Professor of Law and Political Science
University of California-Irvine

Published by Wolters Kluwer in New York.

Wolters Kluwer Legal & Regulatory U.S. serves customers worldwide with CCH, Aspen Publishers, and Kluwer Law International products. (www.WKLegaledu.com)

To contact Customer Service, e-mail customer.service@wolterskluwer.com, call 1-800-234-1660, fax 1-800-901-9075, or mail correspondence to:

Wolters Kluwer
Attn: Order Department
PO Box 990
Frederick, MD 21705

Printed in the United States of America.

1 2 3 4 5 6 7 8 9 0

ISBN 978-1-4548-9127-7

Library of Congress Cataloging-in-Publication Data

Names: Laycock, Douglas, author. | Hasen, Richard L., author.
Title: Modern American remedies : cases and materials / Douglas Laycock,
  Robert E. Scott Distinguished Professor of Law and Professor of Religious
  Studies, University of Virginia, Alice McKean Young Regents Chair in Law
  Emeritus, The University of Texas at Austin; Richard L. Hasen,
  Chancellor's Professor of Law and Political Science, University of
  California-Irvine.
Description: Fifth edition. | New York : Wolters Kluwer, [2019] | Series:
  Aspen casebook series | Includes bibliographical references and index.
Identifiers: LCCN 2018042686 | ISBN 9781454891277
Subjects: LCSH: Remedies (Law)–United States. | LCGFT: Casebooks (Law)
Classification: LCC KF9010 .L394 2019 | DDC 347.73/77–dc23 LC record available at https://lccn
  .loc.gov/2018042686

About Wolters Kluwer Legal & Regulatory U.S.

Wolters Kluwer Legal & Regulatory U.S. delivers expert content and solutions in the areas of law, corporate compliance, health compliance, reimbursement, and legal education. Its practical solutions help customers successfully navigate the demands of a changing environment to drive their daily activities, enhance decision quality and inspire confident outcomes.

Serving customers worldwide, its legal and regulatory portfolio includes products under the Aspen Publishers, CCH Incorporated, Kluwer Law International, ftwilliam.com and MediRegs names. They are regarded as exceptional and trusted resources for general legal and practice-specific knowledge, compliance and risk management, dynamic workflow solutions, and expert commentary.

For Joe and Natasha and John and Hannah
Great couples, great kids, great young adults
—D.L.

For Doug Laycock,
Who dragged the field of Remedies kicking and screaming
into the 21st century (making us all considerably better off)
—R.H.

SUMMARY OF CONTENTS

CONTENTS

CHAPTER 3

PUNITIVE REMEDIES   223

CHAPTER 4

PREVENTING HARM: THE MEASURE OF INJUNCTIVE RELIEF   273

CHAPTER 5

CHOOSING REMEDIES   381

CHAPTER 6

REMEDIES AND SEPARATION OF POWERS	**521**

CHAPTER 7

PREVENTING HARM WITHOUT COERCION: DECLARATORY REMEDIES   591

CHAPTER 8

BENEFIT TO DEFENDANT AS THE MEASURE OF RELIEF: RESTITUTION   641

CHAPTER 9

ANCILLARY REMEDIES: ENFORCING THE JUDGMENT · 787

CHAPTER 10

MORE ANCILLARY REMEDIES: ATTORNEYS'
FEES AND THE COSTS OF LITIGATION   919

CHAPTER 11

REMEDIAL DEFENSES   975

CHAPTER 12

FLUID-CLASS AND CY PRES REMEDIES   1043

APPENDIX

PRESENT VALUE TABLES   1061

PREFACE TO THE FIFTH EDITION

A NEW CO-AUTHOR

The biggest change in this edition is the addition of a second author, Richard L. Hasen of the University of California-Irvine. Rick is a long-time user of the book who has made many helpful suggestions over the years and is the author of *Examples and Explanations: Remedies* (4th ed. Wolters Kluwer 2017). It has been a true collaboration. There are no Laycock chapters or Hasen chapters; we have each reviewed every line of every chapter. We will spare readers our mutual respect and admiration, except to say that we are both very happy with the new arrangement.

THE GOALS OF THE BOOK

We hope and believe that the implementation has improved with each edition, but the book's basic goals remain the same. Most important, this book reflects our belief that a course in remedies should not be a series of appendices to the rest of the substantive curriculum. This book contains no chapters on remedies for particular wrongs. Such chapters are important, but their place is in the substantive courses to which they pertain. This book attempts to explore general principles about the law of remedies that cut across substantive fields and that will be useful to a student or lawyer encountering a remedies problem in any substantive context. It attempts to give the law of remedies an intellectual structure of its own, based on remedies concepts rather than concepts from other fields.

Second, the book tries to integrate the study of public-law and private-law remedies. Public-law remedies are built on traditional private-law remedies. If we study public-law remedies alone, we tear them from their roots and from a set of principles that can help guide the vast discretion that courts exercise in public-law cases.

Third, as the title suggests, the book emphasizes problems of contemporary importance. We have tried to place contemporary issues in historical context, and we have retained some classic cases that are still good law today, but we have not devoted much ink to issues that have been largely mooted by modern developments. We take as givens the merger of law and equity, the ambitious reach of modern American equity, and a generally applicable law of restitution.

Fourth, the book explores and tests the claims of the Chicago school of law and economics. It tries to do so in a way that is accessible to students who lack backgrounds in economics, that is fair to both sides, and that doesn't dominate the book. We believe that doctrine and corrective justice are as important as economics, and we have tried to give all these values equal treatment. But we think that the course in remedies is an especially important place to test the economic theory. If law is or should be mostly about adjusting incentives, then remedies is where much of the adjusting must occur.

Finally, this book tries to teach students as much as possible before class, so that class discussion has a stronger base. Most of the rest of this preface explains that pedagogical choice.

SOME NOTES ON PEDAGOGY

This book is designed to teach basic principles and to help students think about difficult problems. We have tried to supply memorable cases, lots of structure, and lots of information. The book is principally designed for a survey course that covers the full range of remedies, but we hope the material is rich enough to support more detailed treatment of particular remedies for teachers so inclined.

The book's pedagogical theory is pragmatic. Sometimes the notes ask questions, sometimes they provide explanation, sometimes they summarize related cases, and sometimes they offer our own speculations. The style of the notes depends on the material available. When there are settled rules, we try to explain them. When doctrine is unsettled or when it presents hard problems at the margins, we are more likely to ask leading questions. We never deliberately hide the ball. The law has plenty of real difficulties to grapple with; it is never necessary to create artificial ones.

We have collected illustrations, but not citations. There are no string cites in this book; we have generally taken the view that if the facts are not worth developing, the case is not worth citing. But we do try to provide one good citation, a citation that will lead to others, for each important point. Readers who want more citations for research purposes should follow up on those leads, look at the principal cases in the original reporters to see what the court cited for the points in the opinion, and of course, check the standard reference sources in the field.

What are the standard reference sources in the field? There are two treatises: Dan B. Dobbs & Caprice L. Roberts, *Law of Remedies* (3d ed., West Hornbook Series 2018), and James M. Fischer, *Understanding Remedies* (3d ed., LexisNexis 2014). The Dobbs treatise was foundational to the field and has now been fully updated by Professor Roberts.

There is no treatise on damages since 1935, and no treatise on injunctions for longer than that. There is a treatise on restitution: George E. Palmer, *The Law of Restitution* (Little Brown 1978 & Supp.) (four volumes). The supplement has grown to the equivalent of a fifth volume. A more current and more valuable resource on restitution is the *Restatement (Third) of Restitution and Unjust Enrichment* (Am. Law Inst. 2011).

Finally, there is Douglas Laycock, *The Death of the Irreparable Injury Rule* (Oxford Univ. Press 1991). This is not a standard source, but it does collect and classify hundreds of injunction cases and documents how judges actually decide whether to grant injunctions.

A Note to Teachers

You may occasionally fear that a set of notes has left you nothing to talk about in class—that the notes have given too much away. That is not the students' view, and that has not been our experience. Laycock has taught many of these cases in drafts without notes, then with skeletal and incomplete notes, and finally with full notes. With no exception that he can remember, the more the students knew at the beginning of class, the better the class discussion. If we want students to be thoughtful in class, we have to give them some advance notice of what to think about.

A colleague who read the first edition in manuscript knew all the basic issues in damages, but little of injunctions. She thought the book had given too much away in the chapter on compensatory damages, but she thought she didn't quite understand the chapter on injunctions. She came to the injunctions chapter with a student's perspective instead of a teacher's.

One other important piece of advice: If you are new to the book, you should *look at the teacher's manual*, even if you have never used one. We have tried to make it possible for you to tailor your own course the first time through the book, in the way you would tailor it the second or third time through. The book is organized in daily units of material of roughly uniform length. These units are laid out in the teacher's manual, with a menu of daily assignments for courses of different lengths and with different emphases. There is advice on what to teach and what to skip if you want to sample more chapters than you can cover thoroughly. We also give you the benefit of our own trials and errors in teaching individual cases.

A Note to Students

Most of our students have been enthusiastic about the notes, and we hope that you will be too. The notes provide much information and raise many questions. They are designed to help you learn a lot before you come to class. This allows class to start from a higher base; unprepared students will be at a greater disadvantage. There won't be time to discuss in class every issue raised in the notes; you will be expected to think about some things on your own.

There is a lot of information packed into the notes. No sensible teacher will expect you to memorize that information; that is not the point. Part of our goal is to answer questions that might reasonably arise as you discuss the principal cases. Part of our goal is to immerse you in context. Each principal case arises out of a doctrinal context, and sometimes an historical context or a practical, commercial, or policy context. The more contextual information you get surrounding each case, the better you will understand the case. Some of that information will stick in your memory, and some of it won't, but it will all help you understand the case. And if you return to the book in later years, you can retrieve the information that you don't actually remember.

Take the questions in the notes seriously. They are all questions that you can answer or begin to answer with the information in the book. Where you need facts, we have given them to you; where there is a settled rule, we have told you about it. If a series of leading questions seems to suggest inconsistent answers, all the suggested answers are fairly arguable, and you need to think about the choices.

Finally, the headings in this book *are* part of the text. Chapters and sections and subsections all have headings; every set of notes has a heading; every individual note has a heading; some subdivisions of notes have headings. Those headings organize the material for you and signal the main focus of each unit of material, from chapters down to paragraphs. Read the headings and use them; don't ignore them.

Editing the Cases

The selection and editing of the cases also reflect the decision to direct student attention to central issues. We have tried to select opinions with memorable facts and that focus squarely on an important issue. To the extent possible, we have tried to select cases that are clearly written or can be made so with enough editing. We have edited the cases aggressively in places, always with the goal of making them more readable. We have been careful not to change substance, but we have deleted extraneous issues and excess verbiage.

We have deleted citations in opinions and excerpts, except for the sources of direct quotations and citations to cases the students are likely to recognize. We have standardized citation form inside cases and excerpts, and we have substituted full citations in places where the court used a short form referring back to an earlier citation that has been deleted. We have deleted many footnotes, but those that remain retain their original numbers. We have corrected obvious typos, and sometimes removed internal quotation marks. These changes have been made without notation.

All other editorial changes are identified as such. Inserted or substituted material is in brackets; deletions are indicated with ellipses. We have uniformly used three dots, either following a period or following a word that was originally in the middle of a sentence, without regard to the length or paragraphing of the deleted material. We have occasionally inserted paragraph breaks for judges who didn't do it on their own; these insertions are marked with a paragraph sign in brackets: [¶].

Ellipses and bracketed changes in quotations within principal opinions, or in quotations within quotations in the notes, might have been made either by your editors or by the judge or the quoted author. We have generally not inserted bracketed explanations to explain which it was. Added emphasis in such cases is always by the court or the quoted author; bracketed changes are usually by the court or the author; deletions may be either by us or by the court or the author. We have attributed such editorial changes only in rare cases where we made the change and someone might reasonably think the change is substantively important.

We have omitted dates and publishers from citations to statutes in the notes. Unless otherwise indicated, those citations are always to the statute as it existed in early summer 2018.

Before you quote from any source excerpted in this casebook, you would be wise to confirm the exact quotation with the original source.

CHANGES IN THIS EDITION

Apart from a new co-author, what else is new? The organizational structure of the fourth edition has been brought forward with only modest tweaks at the subunit level. Two units, on school desegregation and on initiating criminal and administrative remedies, have been omitted. The school cases were receding ever further into the past, and the Supreme Court and the D.C. Circuit had largely ended any private right to force prosecutors or administrative agencies to act. Those materials are available on the book's website for teachers who still want them.

There are nine new principal cases, and we think that each is a clear improvement over the case that it replaces. Older cases that clearly illustrate their central point and work well in the classroom have been retained.

Most of the changes are in the notes, which we have reviewed and updated line by line. We have added many recent illustrations, including cases from the first half of 2018. We have given substantial attention to major new developments, including the rise to prominence of nationwide injunctions that protect persons who were never parties to the litigation, litigation with and about President Trump, and the Supreme Court's intervention in the dispute over cy pres remedies. We have made offsetting cuts, so that the book has not gotten much longer.

We find the continuing flow and development of remedies issues a source of endless fascination. We can only hope that teachers and students find it as interesting to teach and study as we found it to write and revise.

Douglas Laycock   *Richard L. Hasen*
Austin   Irvine
September 2018   September 2018

ACKNOWLEDGMENTS

A great many people contributed to this book, many of them in ways they little guess. We have benefited from careers spent at excellent law schools with great colleagues—5 years at Chicago, 25 at Texas, 4 at Michigan, and now 8 at Virginia for Laycock as he followed his bride's career in university administration; 4 at Chicago-Kent, 14 at Loyola Law School, Los Angeles, and now 7 at UC Irvine for Hasen. At every stop, our colleagues patiently answered questions as we tried to figure out how remedies interacts with the various other substantive fields of law. And at every stop we have learned from hearing about the many interesting projects our colleagues were working on and the many things they knew.

We have especially benefited from the work of Professor Andrew Kull, now at the University of Texas, who served as Reporter for the *Restatement (Third) of Restitution and Unjust Enrichment* (Am. Law Inst. 2011).

Laycock took Owen Fiss's Injunctions course at Chicago before Owen moved to Yale and later taught the course from Owen's book for several years. Materials to supplement that book, initially ill conceived, eventually evolved into this casebook. And Laycock remains grateful to three tenacious litigators who mentored him as a young attorney and taught him something of litigation and remedies in the real world—Robert Plotkin and Aram Hartunian of the Chicago bar, and Glen Wilkerson of the Austin bar—and to Jack Taurman, a partner in the D.C. office of Vinson & Elkins, who actually specialized in remedies issues.

Hasen did not take a Remedies course as a student and thinks he passed the California bar exam despite, not because of, his answer on a constructive trusts question. Hasen quickly learned in practice, and then as a law professor teaching Torts and Election Law, that understanding how to use and choose among remedies is one of the most important skills a lawyer can possess. It is certainly the only thing many clients will care about.

Hasen began teaching Remedies as a visiting professor at Loyola Law School, Los Angeles, where then-associate dean Laurie Levenson gave Hasen a path back to Los Angeles through the teaching of the course. It is now one of his favorite courses to teach. Hasen learned Remedies the way you will—from (an earlier version of) this casebook and from the wisdom of Doug Laycock. Laycock was patient and cheerful in answering myriad questions from a new law teacher, and Hasen considers it a great privilege to get to collaborate on this fine book.

Updating a book that covers so much territory would be impossible without the help of excellent student research assistants. We give them protocols that cast a wide net, and we work mostly with what survives their screening and with what we save from our own current-awareness reading between editions. We are grateful to John Boyle, John Dao, Kain Day, David Gremling, James Hasson, John Melcon, Trina Rizzo, Colin Snyder, and Cheryl Wang at the University of Virginia and to Julia Jones, Makenna

Miller, and Laura Wertheimer at the University of California-Irvine. We also thank Hasen's faculty assistant Stacy Tran for excellent administrative help.

Finally, we are grateful to copyright holders for permission to reprint excerpts from the following items:

Diver, Colin, The Judge as Political Power Broker: Superintending Structural Change in Public Institutions, 65 Virginia Law Review 43 (1979). Copyright © 1979 by the Virginia Law Review Association.

Laycock, Douglas, The Death of the Irreparable Injury Rule (Oxford University Press 1991). Copyright © 1991 by Oxford University Press. Reprinted by permission of Oxford University Press.

————, The Triumph of Equity, 56 L. & Contemp. Probs. No. 3 at 53 (Spring 1993). Copyright © 1993 by Law and Contemporary Problems.

Posner, Richard A., Economic Analysis of Law (9th ed., Wolters Kluwer 2014). Copyright © 2014 by Richard A. Posner. Reprinted by permission.

Wixon, Rufus, ed., Accountants' Handbook (4th ed. 1960). Copyright © 1946 by the Ronald Press Company. Reprinted by permission of John Wiley & Sons, Inc.

Wright, Scott W., Living with Pain, Austin American-Statesman A1, A12 (Sept. 21, 1990).

MODERN AMERICAN REMEDIES

CHAPTER

1

Introduction

THE ROLE OF REMEDIES

A remedy is anything a court can do for a litigant who has been wronged or is about to be wronged. The two most common remedies are judgments that plaintiffs are entitled to collect sums of money from defendants (damages) and orders to defendants to refrain from their wrongful conduct or to undo its consequences (injunctions). The court decides whether the litigant has been wronged under the substantive law that governs primary rights and duties; it conducts its inquiry in accordance with the procedural law. The law of remedies falls somewhere in between procedure and primary substantive rights. Remedies are substantive, but they are distinct from the rest of the substantive law, and sometimes their details blur into procedure. For long periods in our past, remedies were casually equated with procedure.

Remedies give meaning to obligations imposed by the rest of the substantive law. Suppose Owner discovers that Neighbor claims the timber in Owner's forest and plans to cut it. Remedies law does not determine who owns the land; neither does it create the law's prohibitions of theft, conversion, and trespass. But remedies law does determine the consequences of violating those prohibitions. Remedies law determines whether Owner can enforce the law in advance through an order to Neighbor to stay off the land, or whether he must wait until after his timber has been cut. If the timber is cut, remedies law determines whether Owner gets money and how much he gets. Owner might get a sum based on the value of the uncut trees, or the value of the finished lumber, or the difference between the value of the land with and without the trees, or a sum not based on value at all, such as nominal damages or punitive damages. If Neighbor disobeys the order to stay off the land, or fails to pay the judgment, remedies law determines what Owner can do about that.

Remedies law can thus determine whether Owner gets $1, or $100,000, or an order that saves him from being harmed at all. Such a body of law is not sensibly thought of as procedural. But remedies law does not change Neighbor's underlying obligation to leave Owner's trees alone, so it is distinct from the law that creates the obligation. Remedies are the means by which legal obligations are given effect.

John Norton Pomeroy (pronounced Pŭm-roy), one of the giants of nineteenth-century American law, had a vocabulary for this distinction. Borrowing from the English legal theorist John Austin, he called the rules that regulate human behavior and impose liability "primary rights and duties," and he distinguished these primary rights and duties from the remedies and procedure designed to enforce them. John Norton Pomeroy, *Remedies and Remedial Rights by the Civil Action, According to the Reformed American*

1

Procedure §1 at 1 (Little Brown 1876). The phrase has been largely forgotten, and H.L.A. Hart used "primary and secondary rules" to describe a more elaborate distinction with a different focus. H.L.A. Hart, *The Concept of Law* 79-99 (2d ed., Oxford Univ. Press 1994). Either way, the idea of "primary" rights, duties, or rules describes something important. This book will sometimes use such phrases to refer to all the substantive law other than remedies. But inevitably, we will also use "substantive" or "substance" in contrast to remedies. These phrases are less precise, but they are shorter and more familiar.

The category historically contrasted with primary rights and duties has been more variable and less helpful. Pomeroy certainly knew the difference between remedies and procedure. But he did not attend to vocabulary for describing the distinction, and *Remedies* was the first word in the title of his treatise on *Reformed American Procedure.* In the wake of that treatise, lawyers and law professors often used the word *remedies* to mean what we would now call "civil procedure." This usage finally faded away after the emergence of the modern remedies course in the 1950s and 60s.

Courts are required to classify remedies as either substantive or procedural when state claims are tried in federal court and when federal claims are tried in state court. In these contexts, the law that creates the claim governs substantive issues, and the law of the forum governs procedural issues. Erie Railroad Co. v. Tompkins, 304 U.S. 64 (1938). For this purpose, it is well settled that the measure of damages is substantive. Gasperini v. Center for Humanities, Inc., 518 U.S. 415, 437-438 n.22 (1996); Monessen Southwestern Railway Co. v. Morgan, 486 U.S. 330, 335 (1988). The same principle would seem to apply to the availability and scope of injunctions, but there seems to be more uncertainty about that, and the issue is often neglected.

However we categorize it, remedies law is of immense practical importance. In the litigation over the 2000 presidential election, the anonymous author of the Supreme Court's per curiam opinion tried to minimize the decision by saying it was "only" a dispute about remedies. "Seven Justices of the Court agree that there are constitutional problems with the recount ordered by the Florida Supreme Court that demand a remedy. The only disagreement is as to the remedy." Bush v. Gore, 531 U.S. 98, 111 (2000).

The problem with the Florida recount, as seven justices saw it, was that different counties were applying different standards to distinguish valid and invalid ballots. This treated different voters unequally. For the dissenters, the remedy should have been to complete the recount under a uniform statewide standard. For the majority, the remedy was to reinstate the original count, because the time for counting had run out. This disagreement over remedy was as important as any issue in the case, and more important than most. The choice of remedy may have determined who became President of the United States. Remedies are like that. They are the difference between big wins and little wins, between empty wins and practical wins. Remedies are essential to any practical benefit for your client. Clients are more interested in the bottom line than in the principle of the thing.

This book is about the bottom line. In every case, we will assume that defendant's conduct is unlawful and ask what the court can do about it: What does plaintiff get? How much does he get? Why does he get that instead of something more, or less, or entirely different?

CLASSIFYING REMEDIES

Anglo-American law has developed a rich inventory of remedies. Most remedies fit rather easily into a small number of categories, and it is helpful to label those categories as a way of organizing thought and providing a common vocabulary. The most important categories of remedies are:

1. Compensatory remedies
2. Preventive remedies
   a. Coercive remedies
   b. Declaratory remedies
3. Restitutionary remedies
4. Punitive remedies
5. Ancillary remedies

Remedies can be categorized by their function (what they do) or by their form (how they are worded). We have tried so far as possible to classify remedies functionally, but sometimes form dominates, especially in the distinction between coercive and declaratory remedies. In part because of discrepancies between form and function, some remedies are hard to classify. The important question is always which remedies are available and what they offer, not where they fit in somebody's classification scheme.

Compensatory remedies are designed to compensate plaintiffs for harm they have suffered. The most important compensatory remedy is compensatory damages, a sum of money designed to make plaintiff as well off as he would have been if he never had been wronged. In the example of Owner and Neighbor, payment of the value of Owner's trees would be compensatory damages. Payment for plaintiff's court costs and attorneys' fees might also seem compensatory. But for historical and doctrinal reasons, these are thought of as ancillary remedies and not as compensatory damages.

Preventive remedies are designed to prevent harm before it happens, so that the issue of compensation never arises. Preventive remedies come in two forms, coercive and declaratory.

The most important *coercive remedy* is the injunction. An *injunction* is a personal command from a court to litigants, ordering them to do or to refrain from doing some specific thing. A typical example is an order directing Neighbor to stay off Owner's land, or to quit cutting Owner's trees. A *specific performance decree*, ordering defendants to perform their contract, is a specialized form of injunction. Courts also issue a variety of specialized coercive orders that for one reason or another are not traditionally thought of as injunctions, such as writs of mandamus, prohibition, and habeas corpus. These too are designed to prevent harm to the plaintiff.

A defendant who violates a direct order from a court is guilty of contempt. The court may impose escalating punishments until defendant obeys, or a fixed punishment for past disobedience. It is the direct order and the potential for punishing disobedience that distinguish coercive remedies from declaratory remedies.

Declaratory remedies authoritatively resolve disputes about the parties' rights, but they do not end in a personal command to defendant. For example, Owner might sue Neighbor, asking the court to decide who owns the forest. If the court formally declared that Owner owned the forest, that would decide the matter, and Neighbor would probably honor the decision. If so, the declaration would prevent harm to Owner as effectively as an injunction. In general, declaratory remedies prevent harm to litigants by resolving uncertainty about their rights before either side has been harmed by erroneously relying on its own view of the matter. If Neighbor really thinks he has a right to the trees, he might be as eager as Owner to get a declaration of ownership; without it, he can cut trees only at the risk of incurring liability to Owner. The most important declaratory remedy is the declaratory judgment, but there are also older, more specialized declaratory remedies, such as bills to quiet title.

It is not exactly true to say that declaratory remedies are noncoercive. It is more accurate to say that the coercive threat is implicit rather than explicit. If either party ignores a declaratory judgment, the court will enforce its declaration with sterner measures. If a personal command backed by coercion turns out to be necessary, it will be available as supplemental relief following the declaratory judgment. So the distinction between declaratory and coercive remedies is largely one of form.

Restitutionary remedies are designed to restore to plaintiff all that defendant gained at plaintiff's expense. In some cases, restitution and compensation are identical. If the court holds Neighbor liable for the market value of Owner's timber, it compensates Owner and simultaneously deprives Neighbor of what he gained at Owner's expense. In many applications, restitutionary remedies reverse mistaken or voidable transactions, restoring both sides to their original position. In such applications, restitutionary remedies differ from compensatory remedies conceptually, in their focus on defendant's side of the transaction, and sometimes practically, because they may reverse the transaction in kind, restoring possession of specific property where it is practical to do so.

In their most ambitious applications, restitutionary remedies award to plaintiff the profits defendant earned by conscious wrongdoing, even if those profits exceed plaintiff's damages. In the timber example, the court would probably measure Owner's loss by the value of the standing timber. It might measure Neighbor's gain the same way, but it might also measure Neighbor's gain by the higher value of the finished lumber. If Neighbor could retain a profit that he was able to earn only because he stole Owner's timber, then he has an incentive to steal timber. There are difficult allocation problems here; Neighbor's profit is partly the product of Owner's forest, and partly the product of Neighbor's own labor and investment in logging equipment and a sawmill. But at least if Neighbor were a conscious wrongdoer, most courts would allow Owner to recover Neighbor's profits from the finished timber.

Punitive remedies are designed to punish wrongdoers. Criminal prosecution, not civil liability, is the usual route to punishment. But there are punitive civil remedies: The best known is punitive damages. If Neighbor deliberately stole Owner's timber, a jury could award punitive damages in addition to compensatory damages. If Neighbor erroneously thought the forest belonged to him, even if he were negligent in locating the boundary or checking title to the land, punitive damages would not be available.

A variety of statutes authorize minimum recoveries in excess of actual damages, or recovery of double or triple plaintiff's actual damages; timber-producing states often provide triple damages for knowingly cutting another's timber. See, e.g., Or. Rev. Stat. Ann. §105.810. Such statutes may also be thought of as punitive remedies.

Ancillary remedies are designed in aid of other remedies. Court costs and attorneys' fees are one important set of ancillary remedies. Another is the means of enforcing the primary remedy against a recalcitrant defendant, or securing the possibility of later enforcement when recalcitrance is anticipated. Thus, punishment for contempt is ancillary to coercive remedies. Various means of collecting money are ancillary to all remedies that end in money judgments. Under a writ of execution, a sheriff will seize defendant's property, sell it, and use the proceeds to pay plaintiff's judgment. In garnishment, the court will order people who owe money to defendant to pay plaintiff instead; these payments will be applied to the judgment. More extraordinary collection devices are available if defendant has concealed his assets or removed them from the jurisdiction. Despite these remedies, many money judgments go uncollected. One should not assume that plaintiff wins when she gets a money judgment.

A more unusual ancillary remedy is the receivership. Sometimes it is necessary for the court to manage assets pending litigation. If the court could not trust either side to manage the forest pending litigation, it might appoint a receiver to manage the forest until the rights of Owner and Neighbor could be determined. Receivership is also sometimes used as an extraordinary collection device after judgment.

SUBSTITUTIONARY AND SPECIFIC REMEDIES

Remedies may be divided into two more basic categories:

> The most fundamental remedial choice is between substitutionary and specific remedies. With substitutionary remedies, plaintiff suffers harm and receives a sum of money. Specific remedies seek to avoid this exchange. They aspire to prevent harm, or undo it, rather than let it happen and compensate for it. They seek to prevent harm to plaintiff, repair the harm in kind, or restore the specific thing that plaintiff lost. Substitutionary remedies include compensatory damages, attorneys' fees, restitution of the money value of defendant's gain, and punitive damages. Specific remedies include injunctions, specific performance of contracts, restitution of specific property, and restitution of a specific sum of money.
>
> The essence of the difference is illustrated by the closest case, restitution of a specific sum of money. Consider the choice of remedies for sale of defective goods. Plaintiff's substitutionary remedy is damages, measured by the difference between the value of the goods as promised and the value of the goods as delivered. His specific remedy is either specific performance or cancellation. Specific performance, if it is available, will give him goods that fully conform to the contract in exchange for his payment of the price. Cancellation will give him a full refund of the price—restitution of the sum of money—in exchange for his returning the goods.
>
> This example illustrates the two hallmarks of substitutionary relief. First, [a plaintiff who recovers damages] gets neither what he started with—his money—nor what he was promised—goods conforming to the contract. Instead, he gets defective goods and money to compensate for the defect. Second, the sum of money he receives is based on a fact finder's valuation of his loss. The relief is substitutionary both in the sense that the sum of money is substituted for plaintiff's original entitlement, and in the less obvious sense that the fact finder's valuation of the loss is substituted for plaintiff's valuation. Specific relief aspires to avoid both these substitutions, giving plaintiff the very thing he lost if that is what he wants.

Douglas Laycock, *The Death of the Irreparable Injury Rule* 12-13 (Oxford Univ. Press 1991).

This and related distinctions are thoroughly explored in Colleen P. Murphy, *Money as a Specific Remedy*, 58 Ala. L. Rev. 119 (2006). Professor Murphy shows that these distinctions are messier, and more prone to exceptions, than we usually assume. For example, lawyers think of injunctions as granting specific relief. But an injunction ordering Neighbor to restore Owner's land and plant new trees would not give Owner the mature trees he had before the wrong. Such an order would substitute new trees for those that were lost.

These distinctions help lawyers communicate, but usually not much turns on precise categorization of cases near the line. When legislatures use such categories to specify available remedies, the stakes can be much higher. For example, the Administrative Procedure Act waives the sovereign immunity of the United States in any suit to review an action of an administrative agency and "seeking relief other than money damages." 5 U.S.C. §702. And the Employee Retirement Income Security Act, 29 U.S.C. 1132(a)(3), authorizes "appropriate equitable relief," but no legal remedies.

LEGAL AND EQUITABLE REMEDIES

Remedies may also be classified as legal or equitable. For half a millennium or so, England had two separate sets of courts functioning side by side: courts of law and courts of equity. Each set of courts devised its own body of substantive rules, its own procedures, and its own remedies; there was a separate set of rules for determining which cases went to which set of courts. The most general of these rules was that plaintiff cannot have an equitable remedy if a legal remedy would be adequate. But the equity courts got to decide whether legal remedies were adequate.

The United States inherited separate courts of law and equity and their separate bodies of law. By now, the separate courts have been merged in nearly all the states. The merged courts have largely combined the two sets of substantive rules and adopted a single set of procedures, except that the right to jury trial is generally guaranteed only in cases that would have been legal before the merger. Remedies are still classified as legal or equitable, and the rule that plaintiff cannot have an equitable remedy if a legal remedy would be adequate is still on the books everywhere, but it no longer has much bite.

The line between law and equity is largely the result of a fight for turf; each set of courts took as much jurisdiction as it could get. Consequently, the line is jagged and not especially functional; it can only be memorized. Damages are the most important legal remedy; in general, compensatory and punitive remedies are legal. Injunctions and specific performance decrees are the most important equitable remedies; some of the specialized coercive remedies, such as mandamus, prohibition, and habeas corpus, are legal. Declaratory judgments were created by statute after the merger, so they are not classified either way; most of the older, more specialized declaratory remedies are equitable. Restitution was developed independently in both sets of courts; some restitutionary remedies are legal, some equitable, and some both. Receiverships are equitable. Most legal remedies are substitutionary, and most equitable remedies are specific, but there are important exceptions in both directions. The law/equity distinction is not a proxy for the substitutionary/specific distinction.

Where the law/equity distinction is especially murky, as in restitution, lawyers and judges tend to overlook it, and the distinction becomes less and less important. Where the distinction is written into substantive law, judges have trouble applying it. The Supreme Court tends to simplify the question, substituting modern proxies for historical inquiries. "[A]s memories of the divided bench, and familiarity with its technical refinements, recede further into the past," the Court has said, it becomes less and less likely that Congress drafts precisely when it refers to legal or equitable remedies. Mertens v. Hewitt Associates, 508 U.S. 248, 256 (1993). This is no doubt true, and perhaps the lesson should be to quit using law and equity as doctrinal or statutory categories. But Anglo-American lawyers have been talking about those categories for centuries; they are hard to eliminate.

NOTE ON THE NATURE OF REMEDIES

The first section of this introduction suggests that remedies law is distinct from the rest of the substantive law—different from the law that creates primary rights and duties. That suggestion is not entirely uncontroversial. To the extent that the argument is purely definitional, it is not worth pursuing. But the argument that remedies are the essence of substance casts light on the nature of remedies and of substance and the relationship between them.

There is a sense in which the remedy ultimately defines the substantive obligation. This suggestion requires a choice between two ways of looking at the law. The first view says that we expect people to comply with the law that creates primary rights and obligations, whatever the remedy for violation might be. In French v. Dwiggins, 458 N.E.2d 827 (Ohio 1984), the court retroactively applied a statute that substantially expanded the measure of damages in wrongful death cases. The court reasoned that the substantive rule governing defendant's conduct had not been changed, and that he "could not reasonably be expected to conduct his affairs differently" depending on the measure of damages. Returning to the example of Owner and Neighbor, this first view says that the substantive law forbids the cutting of other people's trees, and that the usual remedy for a violation is a money judgment for the value of the trees.

The second view says that the law forbids nothing; it merely specifies the consequences of various choices. Thus, the law says that if Neighbor cuts Owner's trees, he will suffer a money judgment for their value; Neighbor has a free choice. Justice Holmes sometimes talked in these terms, and so do some of the modern scholars who analyze legal problems in economic terms. Most law-and-economics scholars fundamentally reject the Ohio Supreme Court's view; they think the measure of damages is mostly about adjusting the incentives of potential defendants.

This second view effectively highlights the importance of remedies. It is certainly true that some individuals will obey the law only if the consequences of violation are more painful than obedience. The potential victims of such individuals have substantive rights, but those rights are not worth much unless the rights are backed up by effective remedies.

Even so, we find the attempt to define primary rights in terms of remedies unpersuasive. To do so denies the normative function of the law. To say that the law forbids Neighbor to cut Owner's trees is a meaningful statement, a statement with moral force, whether the remedy is an injunction or damages or criminal punishment or a slap on the wrist. That some individuals are unmoved does not eliminate the statement's moral force for the rest of us.

Moreover, once one says that prohibitions are no more than a choice between alternatives, there is no reason to stop with the first such choice. What does it mean to say that Neighbor must leave Owner's trees alone or suffer a money judgment? Not that Neighbor must leave the trees alone or pay, but only that if he does not pay, Owner can ask the sheriff to seize Neighbor's assets to pay the judgment. Neighbor then has a further choice: He may surrender his assets, or attempt to conceal them, or in some circumstances, discharge Owner's judgment in bankruptcy. The enactment of generous bankruptcy laws says something about the comparative importance a society attaches to the rights of plaintiffs and the distress of insolvent defendants. But such laws do not mean that if Neighbor is insolvent, cutting Owner's trees does not violate the substantive law.

Carrying the point further, Neighbor is forbidden to conceal his assets, but that means only that he can choose between concealing assets or going to jail for contempt of court if Owner and the authorities are sufficiently diligent in their efforts to enforce the judgment. But again, if nothing is forbidden, his choice is not between concealing assets or going to jail but between going to jail or going into hiding or beyond the reach of the jurisdiction. We find it implausible to say that all this is merely the process of defining Neighbor's substantive obligation—that if the government will not go to war to retrieve Neighbor from the Cayman Islands, Neighbor does not violate the law when he cuts Owner's trees and flees the jurisdiction.

We chose the example of Owner and Neighbor because it can be used to illustrate all sorts of remedies without too much straining. But the example may stack the deck in favor of the view that substantive law has moral force independent of the remedies provided. If we assume it is clear that Owner owns the forest, then Neighbor is an intentional wrongdoer. It is easy to agree that theft is wrong, and forbidden, even though most thefts go unremedied because thieves are too hard to catch.

The case of Owner and Neighbor may look different if we assume that ownership is genuinely disputed, and that the court is still in doubt even when it makes its decision based on the preponderance of the evidence. And there may be other legal rules with less independent moral force than the rules against theft. Some scholars who take an economic view of law believe that parties to contracts should have an option to perform or pay compensatory damages, and they believe that people should be allowed or even encouraged to act in ways that will foreseeably injure others, so long as they compensate their victims. But only a few of them believe that people should be allowed or encouraged to engage in intentional torts so long as they are willing to compensate their victims.

A course in remedies is a good place to test these views, and we will explore them intermittently throughout the book. We do not mean to prejudge them here when we say that the substantive rules that create primary rights and duties are analytically distinct from the remedies available to enforce those rights and duties. Whether we design remedies that encourage profitable violations, or remedies that seek to minimize violations, or remedies that serve some other purpose altogether, we are making choices distinct from the choices we make when we design the rest of the substantive law.

THE MODERN REMEDIES COURSE

The modern Remedies course was created by combining older courses in Damages, Equity, and Restitution, and by dropping those parts of the Equity and Restitution courses that dealt with primary rights and duties. The resulting package seemed obvious once it caught on, but it was a long time coming. Such a course might have been conceptually impossible before the abolition of the writ system and the merger of law and equity.

The modern Remedies course appears to have been independently invented three times: by Edgar Durfee and John Dawson at Michigan about 1936, by the Minnesota curriculum committee and Charles Alan Wright about 1951, and by John Wilson at Baylor about 1952. It was Professor Wright who fully developed the modern course, condensed it to one semester, and published the first modern casebook, *Remedies*, in 1955. He also promoted the course in an article. Charles Alan Wright, *Remedies as a Social Institution*, 18 U. Detroit L.J. 376 (1955). Then he abandoned the field and moved on to become the dominant figure in the law of federal courts and federal procedure. This history is told in considerable detail, based on archival materials and interviews with the surviving founders of the field, in Douglas Laycock, *How Remedies Became a Field: A History*, 27 Rev. Litig. 161 (2008).

The old sequence of Damages, Equity, and Restitution took three or four semesters. The first Remedies courses were also spread over three semesters or even more.

Of course, these multi-semester courses were much more detailed than any one-semester course taught from a modern remedies book.

This book is necessarily more conceptual than a book designed for a three-semester sequence. This book aims for a balance of theory and practice, for reasonably complete coverage of broad principles, and for a sample of the more important rules that implement those broad principles. It tries to offer a base of information and a set of intellectual tools that students can use to approach the novel remedies issues they will encounter in a lifetime in the law.

The abandoned parts of the old Equity course — trusts, mortgages, servitudes, and all the rest — were mostly distributed around the rest of the curriculum. But some parts of the old Equity course slipped through the cracks, and no one picked up the abandoned parts of the old Restitution course. The law of restitution offers more than just remedies; it also creates causes of action and imposes liabilities. This body of substantive law has dropped out of the curriculum at most American law schools, and that is a serious loss. In Chapter 8, when we study restitutionary remedies, we will also take a peek at the restitutionary liability rules and at some of the equity rules about competing claims to property.

CHAPTER
2

Paying for Harm: Compensatory Damages

A. THE BASIC PRINCIPLE: RESTORING PLAINTIFF TO HIS RIGHTFUL POSITION

UNITED STATES v. HATAHLEY
257 F.2d 920 (10th Cir. 1958)

[Plaintiffs are eight families of Navajo Indians who have lived for generations on open range land owned by the United States. Plaintiffs' livestock grazed on the public lands along with livestock owned by whites who held grazing permits. The United States and these white stockmen considered the Indians to be trespassers, and in separate litigation sought to have them ordered off the public lands.

While those lawsuits were pending, government agents rounded up plaintiffs' horses and burros and sold them for nominal prices, some to a horse-meat plant and some to a glue factory. Federal law required that alleged trespassers be given notice and an opportunity to remove their animals before such a roundup; no such notice was given. The Supreme Court held that the roundup was a trespass under Utah law, actionable against the United States under the Federal Tort Claims Act. Hatahley v. United States, 351 U.S. 173 (1956). The Court remanded to the district court for further findings on the amount of damages. This is an appeal from the district court's decision on remand.]

Before BRATTON, Chief Judge, and MURRAH, PICKETT, LEWIS and BREITENSTEIN, Circuit Judges.

PICKETT, Circuit Judge. . . .

Upon remand, the District Court took additional evidence on the issue of consequential damages, and without an amendment of the complaint, entered a judgment against the United States for the total sum of $186,017.50. The value of each horse or burro taken was fixed at $395; each plaintiff was awarded $3,500 for mental pain and suffering; and damages were given for one-half of the value of the diminution of the individual herds of sheep, goats and cattle between the date the horses and burros were taken in 1952, and the date of the last hearing in 1957. . . .

The fundamental principle of damages is to restore the injured party, as nearly as possible, to the position he would have been in had it not been for the wrong of the other party. Applying this rule, the plaintiffs were entitled to the market value, or replacement cost, of their horses and burros as of the time of taking, plus the use value of the animals during the interim between the taking and the time they, acting prudently, could have replaced the animals.

11

The plaintiffs did not prove the replacement cost of the animals, but relied upon a theory that the animals taken were unique because of their peculiar nature and training, and could not be replaced. The trial court accepted this theory, and relying upon some testimony that a horse or a burro could be traded among Indians for sheep, goats or cattle worth a stated price, together with the owner's testimony of the value, arrived at a market value of $395 per head. No consideration was given to replacement cost. The court rejected evidence of the availability of like animals in the immediate vicinity, and their value. This, we think, was error. It is true that animals of a particular strain and trained for a special purpose are different from animals of another strain and not so trained, but that does not mean that they cannot be replaced by animals similarly developed and trained, or which may be trained after acquisition. Ordinarily every domestic animal is developed and trained for the purpose to which the owner intends to use it. This development and training adds to its usefulness and generally increases the market value of the animal. In arriving at a fair market value of destroyed animals, the court should consider evidence of the availability of like animals, together with all other elements which go to make up market value. . . .

Likewise, we think the court applied an erroneous rule, wholly unsupported by the evidence, in arriving at the amount of loss of use damage. There was testimony by the plaintiffs that because of the loss of their horses and burros they were not able to maintain and look after as much livestock as they had been able to before the unlawful taking; consequently the size of their herds was reduced. If the unlawful taking of the animals was the proximate cause of the herd reductions, the measure of damages would be the loss of profits occasioned thereby.

Applying the same formula to all plaintiffs, the court, without giving consideration to the condition, age or sex of the animals, found the value of the sheep and goats in 1952 to be $15 per head, and cattle to be $150 per head. The number of sheep, goats and cattle which each plaintiff had in 1952, as well as the number which each had at the date of the last hearing was established. This difference was multiplied by $15, in the case of sheep and goats and by $150 in the case of cattle, and judgment was entered for one-half of the amount of the result. No consideration was given to the disposition of the livestock by the plaintiffs in reducing the herds. For example, the plaintiff Sakezzie had 600 sheep and goats and 101 head of cattle when his horses and burros were taken in 1952. At the date of the last hearing in 1957, he had 160 head of sheep and goats and 39 head of cattle. The dollar value of the difference at $15 per head for the sheep and goats, and $150 per head for the cattle, amounted to $15,900. The court found "that approximately fifty percent of this amount represents damages to the plaintiff proximately caused by deprivation of the use of plaintiff's horses, and on this basis plaintiff is entitled to recover $7,950.00 as consequential damages resulting from such deprivation." The result, insofar as it related to use damage, was arbitrary, pure speculation, and clearly erroneous. In United States v. Huff, 175 F.2d 678 (5th Cir. 1949), a case where the method of computing damages for loss of sheep and goats was strikingly similar to that used here, the court said:

> Moreover, there has been no sufficient showing of how much of the damage from the loss of the sheep and goats was proximately caused by the Government's failure to maintain and repair the fences under the lease, and how much of the damage resulted from the various other causes. There is no testimony whatever as to the specific dates of loss of any of the sheep and goats, or as to their age, weight, condition and fair market

value at the time of the alleged losses. It therefore becomes patent that the evidence as to the loss of these animals in each case fails to rise above mere speculation and guess.

Id. at 680.

Plaintiffs' evidence indicated that the loss of their animals made it difficult and burdensome for them to obtain and transport needed water, wood, food, and game, and curtailed their travel for medical care and to tribal council meetings and ceremonies. Plaintiffs also testified that because of the loss of their animals they were not able to grow crops and gardens as extensively as before. These were factors upon which damages for loss of use could have been based. This does not exclude the right to damages for loss of profits which may have resulted from reduction of the number of livestock, or actual loss of the animals, if the unlawful acts of the defendant agents were the proximate cause of the loss and were proved to a reasonable degree of certainty.

But the right to such damages does not extend forever, and it is limited to the time in which a prudent person would replace the destroyed horses and burros. The law requires only that the United States make full reparation for the pecuniary loss which their agents inflicted.

The District Court awarded each plaintiff the sum of $3,500 for mental pain and suffering. There is no evidence that any plaintiff was physically injured when his horses and burros were taken. There was evidence that because of the seizure of their animals and the continued activity of government agents and white ranchers to rid the public range of trespassers, the plaintiffs and their families were frightened, and after the animals were taken, they were "sick at heart, their dignity suffered, and some of them cried." There was considerable evidence that some of the plaintiffs mourned the loss of their animals for a long period of time. We think it quite clear that the sum given each plaintiff was wholly conjectural and picked out of thin air. The District Court seemed to think that because the horses and burros played such an important part in the Indians' lives, the grief and hardships were the same as to each. The equal award to each plaintiff was based upon the grounds that it was not possible to separately evaluate the mental pain and suffering as to each individual, and that it was a community loss and a community sorrow.[5]

Apparently the court found a total amount which should be awarded to all plaintiffs for pain and suffering, and divided it equally among them. There was no more justification for such division than there would have been in using the total value of the seized animals and dividing it equally among the plaintiffs. Pain and suffering is a personal and individual matter, not a common injury, and must be so treated. While damages for mental pain and suffering, where there has been no physical injury, are allowed only in extreme cases, they may be awarded in some circumstances.

Any award for mental pain and suffering in this case must result from the wrongful taking of plaintiffs' animals by agents of the United States, and nothing else.

---

5. The court's finding on this subject is as follows:

28. It is not possible for the extent of the mental pain and suffering to be separately evaluated as to each individual plaintiff. It is evident that each and all of the plaintiffs sustained mental pain and suffering. Nor is it possible to say that the plaintiffs who lost one or two horses sustained less mental pain and suffering than plaintiffs who lost a dozen horses. The mental pain and suffering sustained was a thing common to all the plaintiffs. It was a community loss and a community sorrow shared by all. On this basis, the Court finds and awards the sum of $3,500.00 to each of the plaintiffs as a fair and reasonable approximation of the mental pain and suffering sustained by each, as a proximate result of the taking of the horses by the defendant.

As the case must be remanded for a new trial as to damages, we are confronted with the contention of the United States that it cannot obtain a fair and impartial trial before the same Judge because of his personal feelings in the matter. . . .

A casual reading of the two records leaves no room for doubt that the District Judge was incensed and embittered, perhaps understandably so, by the general treatment over a period of years of the plaintiffs and other Indians in southeastern Utah by the government agents and white ranchers in their attempt to force the Indians onto established reservations. This was climaxed by the range clearance program, with instances of brutal handling and slaughter of their livestock, which the Court, during trial, referred to as "horrible," "monstrous," "atrocious," "cruel," "coldblooded depredation," and "without a sense of decency." The Court firmly believed that the Indians were being wrongfully driven from their ancestral homes, and suggested Presidential and Congressional investigations to determine their aboriginal rights. He threatened to conduct such an investigation himself. A public appeal on behalf of the plaintiffs was made for funds and supplies to be cleared through the Judge's chambers. From his obvious interest in the case, illustrated by conduct and statements made throughout the trial, which need not be detailed further, we are certain that the feeling of the presiding Judge is such that, upon retrial, he cannot give the calm, impartial consideration which is necessary for a fair disposition of this unfortunate matter, and he should step aside. . . .

[W]e suggest that when the case is remanded to the District Court, the Judge who entered the judgment take appropriate preliminary steps to the end that further proceedings in the case be had before another Judge.

Reversed, and remanded for a new trial as to damages only.

NOTES ON THE BASIC PRINCIPLE

1. The but-for principle. The name is pronounced Hah-Tah-Lay, with equal emphasis on all three syllables. *Hatahley*'s rule—that the fundamental principle of damages is to restore the injured party as nearly as possible to the position he would have been in but for the wrong—is the essence of compensatory damages. "[T]he purpose of damages is to put the aggrieved party in the position, as near as possible, as he or she would have been without the injury or damage." MCI Communications Services v. CMES, Inc., 728 S.E.2d 649, 652 (Ga. 2012). Tort cases stating this principle are collected in Heidi Li Feldman, *Harm and Money: Against the Insurance Theory of Tort Compensation*, 75 Tex. L. Rev. 1567, 1578-1579 nn.52-59 (1997). The law does not always succeed in achieving this goal; maybe it rarely succeeds. Many plaintiffs will recover too little, and some will recover too much. But plaintiff's position but for the wrong is the most basic guide to compensatory damages.

2. The rightful position. We need a shorter phrase than "the position plaintiff would have been in but for the wrong." "Plaintiff's original position" is not quite right, because often, defendant interfered with some pending improvement in plaintiff's position. Lost earnings are an obvious case: Personal injury defendants are liable for earnings plaintiff would have earned, even though plaintiff never had that money before. A better shorthand is "plaintiff's rightful position"—the position he rightfully would have come to but for defendant's wrong. We intend "rightful position" to mean substantially the same thing as the more cumbersome "position plaintiff would have been in but for the wrong."

What does it mean to restore plaintiffs to their rightful position? The court cannot resurrect their dead horses or undo their mental pain. The remedy must be in dollars, and the court's disagreement with the district judge is over how many dollars and how the number is to be determined. Damage remedies are often described as "substitutionary," because they substitute dollars for what plaintiff lost. Sometimes dollars are exactly what plaintiff lost, as in a suit for lost income. Sometimes dollars can be used to replace what was lost; the court assumed that plaintiffs in *Hatahley* could use their damage award to buy new horses. For losses like these, the substitution is quite direct, and a mandate to restore plaintiffs to their rightful position gives real guidance. What does it mean to restore plaintiffs to their rightful position with respect to mental pain and suffering?

3. More facts in *Hatahley*. Professor Threedy reviewed the trial record and other public documents about the dispute. Debora Threedy, *United States v. Hatahley: A Legal Archaeology Case Study in Law and Racial Conflict*, 34 Am. Indian L. Rev. 1 (2010). The trials were complicated by deep differences in language, culture, and economic organization. At the first trial, Judge Ritter made findings of fact totaling 39 pages, mostly devoted to the value of the horses. It is hard to see where his ultimate finding of $395 per horse came from, but it appears to have been a conservative compromise, closer to the government's evidence than to the plaintiffs'.

There was no cash market for Navajo horses; the Navajo wouldn't sell them and the whites didn't want them. Nor did the Navajo buy horses from the whites; they lacked the cash, and their own horses were bred and trained to survive on scarce forage and scarce water. The Navajo would trade a good horse for five cattle or 25 to 35 sheep. Cattle could be sold for $200 a head, sheep for $30 a head, which implies a value of $750 to $1,050 for a horse. The judge also found that replacing the horses would cost $1,000 per horse. The basis of this finding was not entirely clear, but the method of replacement was to buy mares from the whites, and buy hay to feed them (apparently because they could not survive on what Navajo horses ate) until their foals could be raised and trained to life in Navajo conditions. None of the Navajo had the cash to follow this strategy without first collecting a judgment.

As against this evidence of a value in the $1,000 range, horses were bought and sold in the white community for $300, and one Navajo testified that if he were ever to sell a horse for cash, which he had never done, he would accept $300. The rental value of a horse in the white community was $5 per day.

The other damage items were the focus of the second trial. Professor Threedy believes that the emotional loss really was communal and that this finding reflected the realities of Navajo culture. But she thinks that Judge Ritter's attribution of 50 percent of the losses of sheep and cattle to the theft of the horses was "pulled out of the air"; there were too many factors at work in the decline of the herds and not enough evidence to apportion losses among the various causes.

The case eventually settled in the early 1960s for $45,000; $9,000 went to the lawyers for nearly ten years of litigation, and the plaintiffs divided the rest in proportion to the number of animals they had lost. The litigation did not resolve their right to the land, but the government ultimately traded much of the land in dispute to the Navajo in exchange for Navajo land inundated by the Glen Canyon Dam. Professor Threedy believes that the liability judgment in *Hatahley* is the first time that Native Americans prevailed against the federal government on a claim of intentional wrongdoing.

4. Why the rightful position? Assuming we know what it means to restore plaintiffs to their rightful position, is it self-evident that that should be the standard? In part, the disagreement between the trial and appellate court is over how precisely damages must be proven and found. The district judge would restore plaintiffs to their rightful position, but he would use average losses and approximations of loss to determine that position. At times, the court of appeals implies that the district judge thought his task was simply to require the payment of a sum of money that would be fair. In the first trial, despite his detailed findings on the value of the horses, the judge ultimately awarded a lump sum of $100,000, the amount requested in the complaint, with little explanation of how that number was calculated. And at times, the court of appeals implies that the district judge took the complaint about the slaughter of the horses as an occasion to remedy all the Navajos' grievances against the United States and the white population of Utah. Is there anything to be said for either of these approaches?

Until fairly modern times, the standard jury instruction on damages was to give a fair or appropriate sum. Professor Goldberg argues that, at least in tort, the rule of make-whole or rightful-position damages is a nineteenth-century innovation. John C.P. Goldberg, *Two Conceptions of Tort Damages: Fair v. Full Compensation*, 55 DePaul L. Rev. 435 (2006).

5. Corrective justice. The traditional argument for restoring plaintiff to her rightful position is based on corrective justice. Plaintiff should not be made to suffer because of wrongdoing, and if we restore plaintiff to her rightful position, she will not suffer. To do less would leave part of the harm unremedied; to do more would confer a windfall gain.

6. Efficiency. More recently, a quite different justification has been offered for the rightful-position rule. Proponents of the economic analysis of law argue that in most contexts the purpose of law is to maximize the value of conflicting activities. Economists view individual profit as a good proxy for social value, because a seller or investor can make a profit only by persuading someone else to pay more for his product, service, or capital than he has spent to produce it.

Those who apply this view to law believe that the law should generally encourage profitable activity, even activity that harms others and incurs liability for breach of contract or unintentional torts, so long as breachers and tortfeasors pay for the damage they cause. Activity that is profitable even after payment of all the costs it imposes on others is said to be efficient or economical; other activity is inefficient or uneconomical. The law is said to be efficient to the extent it encourages efficient activity and discourages inefficient activity. The classical school of law and economics believes that the law should always be efficient, and that the common law usually is efficient. Other scholars who apply economics to law make less sweeping claims. Some of them are concerned about the distribution of wealth as well as the creation of wealth; still others view economics as simply one tool among many for analyzing legal problems. Some law-and-economics scholars assume that all humans are rational profit maximizers; others, in a subfield known as behavioral economics, take more account of how real humans actually behave.

In the classical economic view, the function of compensatory damages is to force law violators to take account of the harm they inflict. If damage liability is less than the harm inflicted, potential defendants will violate the law when it is inefficient to do so. If damage liability exceeds the harm inflicted, potential defendants will obey the law when it is inefficient to do so. Damages should be set exactly equal to harms inflicted, and then, if the expected profit from a tort or breach of contract exceeds the expected damages, the actor should go ahead. But for reasons to be considered later, intentional torts are generally placed outside this account.

Compensation and corrective justice have nothing to do with this view of damages; the point is to manipulate incentives of potential defendants. The incentives to defendants would be just as effective if damages were paid to the state instead of to victims, or if damages were paid in cash to be run through a paper shredder. The economic reason for paying damages to victims is so that they will have a reason to sue and enforce the rules against defendants. See Richard A. Posner, *Economic Analysis of Law* §6.10 at 223 (9th ed., Wolters Kluwer 2014). There is an apparently serious academic proposal to randomly divide all newly filed cases into two groups. The first group would be automatically dismissed without regard to the merits; in the second group, any defendants who lost would have to pay double damages. Incentives would be unaffected, but we would save the cost of litigating half the cases. David Rosenberg and Steven Shavell, *A Simple Proposal to Halve Litigation Costs*, 91 Va. L. Rev. 1721 (2005).

Compensation and corrective justice may be irrelevant, or at best secondary, from an economic perspective. But are they irrelevant from a legal perspective? From a moral perspective? In the minds of voters who elect legislators and judges to create and enforce rules of law? For the argument that noneconomic considerations should never matter, see Louis Kaplow and Steven Shavell, *Fairness Versus Welfare* (Harvard Univ. Press 2002). Professors Kaplow and Shavell argue that any consideration of fairness or corrective justice necessarily reduces social welfare, and that while such "notions" might suggest crude rules of thumb for the unsophisticated populace, serious legal analysts should rigorously exclude them from consideration.

7. Proving damages. There is no right to jury trial in tort suits against the United States. *Hatahley* was therefore tried before a judge, and judges must give reasons for their decisions. Juries do not have to give reasons, and the imponderable difficulties illustrated in *Hatahley* can often be buried in general verdicts. Judges tend to uphold jury determinations of damages, even when the amount is unusually large or small and in round numbers. But even general verdicts require some evidentiary theory that enables judges to explain how the jury might have calculated its number. The following tirade about sloppy lawycring is from an opinion sharply reducing a jury verdict in a case where police officers beat the plaintiff in the course of an arrest. They also failed to tell him how to reclaim the property in his possession at the time of the arrest, with the consequence that the property was subsequently destroyed. The property included the only copy of manuscripts he had written.

> No proof concerning the value of the manuscripts to Taliferro was presented. His lawyer pulled the figure of $50,000 out of his hat at closing argument.
>
> The other figures are equally fanciful. We have criticized the casual attitude of many tort plaintiffs toward proof of damages . . . . A plaintiff is not permitted to throw himself on the generosity of the jury. If he wants damages, he must prove them. The only effort at proof here . . . was Taliferro's testimony that he was distraught and humiliated by his mistreatment at the hands of the police, as well as suffering physical pain.

Taliferro v. Augle, 757 F.2d 157, 162 (7th Cir. 1985).

8. The one-satisfaction rule. A corollary of the rightful-position standard is the one-satisfaction rule. The phrase has more than one meaning, but the settled core is that plaintiff cannot recover the same item of damage more than once. Thus in Tony Gulla Motors I, L.P. v. Chapa, 212 S.W.3d 299 (Tex. 2006), where plaintiff recovered for fraud, breach of contract, and violation of the state's Deceptive Trade Practices Act, all for failure to deliver the promised model of SUV, plaintiff could recover under only one theory. Similarly, if plaintiff collects a judgment from one defendant, he cannot collect it again from any other.

Both halves of the rule were at issue in Janusz v. City of Chicago, 832 F.3d 770 (7th Cir. 2016). An unconstitutional search led to a criminal prosecution, which was later dropped; the criminal prosecution caused plaintiff to lose his job. He sued his employer in state court for employment discrimination and defamation; he sued the city and the police officers in federal court for violating the Constitution; and he alleged his loss of employment as the principal source of damages. His settlement with the employer was credited against the liability of the city and the police officers, because he was alleging the same harm in both cases.

As this example illustrates, partial settlements and separate trials add complexity and controversy. The parties may dispute whether the settlement and the verdict cover the same damage or different damage, and of course the settlement amount is likely to be different from what a judge or jury would have awarded. The competing solutions are beyond the scope of this note; they are thoroughly explored in *Restatement (Third) of Torts: Apportionment of Liability* §16 (Am. Law Inst. 2000).

B.   VALUE AS THE MEASURE OF THE RIGHTFUL POSITION

IN RE SEPTEMBER 11TH LITIGATION
590 F. Supp. 2d 535 (S.D.N.Y. 2008)

ALVIN K. HELLERSTEIN, District Judge:

In April 2001, the Port Authority of New York and New Jersey, Inc. accepted the bid of a New York real estate developer, Larry Silverstein, to purchase . . . four of the World Trade Center towers. In July 2001, the Port Authority . . . conveyed . . . Towers One, Two, Four and Five to corporations formed by Silverstein. . . .

Two months after Silverstein took possession, the towers became rubble, destroyed by the terrorist-related aircraft crashes of September 11, 2001. Towers One and Two were turned into raging infernos and collapsed, bringing down and destroying Tower Four, Tower Five, and additional buildings and properties in and around the World Trade Center. Silverstein's . . . companies . . . (collectively, "WTCP") filed suit against [the airlines, the airport security companies, and the operator of Boston's Logan Airport] alleging that, but for [their] negligence, the terrorists would not have gained entrance into the aircrafts they hijacked. . . . WTCP's lawsuit seeks recovery of $16.2 billion, the alleged replacement value of Towers One, Two, Four and Five. . . .

FACTUAL BACKGROUND

I. THE SALE OF WORLD TRADE CENTER BUILDINGS
ONE, TWO, FOUR AND FIVE . . .

The [sale of the buildings] culminated a worldwide competitive bidding process that the Port Authority had initiated to implement a decision, reached several years earlier, to privatize the World Trade Center. . . . [For our purposes, WTCP paid $2.8 billion for the four buildings. The deal was structured as a 99-year lease, which spread out the payments on the $2.8 billion. We can mostly disregard that complication.]

II. A BRIEF HISTORY OF THE WORLD TRADE CENTER

In 1962, New York and New Jersey, through coordinated legislation, directed that the World Trade Center be built . . . for "the single object of preserving . . . the economic well-being of the northern New Jersey-New York metropolitan area [which] is found and determined to be in the public interest." N.Y. Unconsol. Law §6601(9) (2000). The Port of New York was suffering economically and the complex's construction was seen as a way to revitalize the area. Specifically, the legislators intended through building the World Trade Center to improve transportation between New York and New Jersey; centralize, enable, and attract port-related activity; and provide an optimal platform upon which to conduct international trade. . . .

Construction commenced in 1965 and cost approximately one billion dollars. . . .

During the 1970s, the World Trade Center struggled to fill its space, relying heavily on government tenants. By the early 1980s, the towers began to enjoy commercial success, replacing government tenants with a variety of higher paying commercial tenants. . . .

By September 11, 2001, the World Trade Center had become a profit center. Forty thousand workers, and many more tourists, came into the towers daily. . . . The towers were a symbol of the city and an integral part of its skyline. New York City's downtown area flourished. . . .

DISCUSSION . . .

II. FAIR MARKET VALUE IS THE PROPER MEASURE OF DAMAGES. . . .
A. The "Lesser of Two" Rule

New York courts follow the "lesser of two" rule: a plaintiff whose property has been injured may recover the lesser of the diminution of the property's market value or its replacement cost. This rule applies even when the property in question has been completely destroyed.

The New York Court of Appeals recently affirmed the lesser of two rule in Fisher v. Qualico Contracting Corp., 779 N.E.2d 178 (N.Y. 2002). In *Fisher*, plaintiff's Long Island home, an 8,000 square foot Victorian residence on 1.5 acres of land, was destroyed in a fire negligently started by defendant, a contractor hired by plaintiff to do work on the home. . . . In the damages phase of the trial, the parties proved that the replacement cost was $1,033,000, but that the diminution in the property's market value was $480,000. The jury was instructed to award $480,000, the lesser of the two amounts. On appeal, the Court of Appeals affirmed, holding that "[r]eplacement cost and diminution in market value are simply two sides of the same coin." *Id.* at 181-182. "Each is a proper way to measure lost property value, the lower of the two figures affording full compensation to the owner" yet "avoiding uneconomical efforts." *Id.*

B. Specialty Property Exception

WTCP acknowledges that the lesser of two rule generally applies to property damage cases. However, WTCP argues that there is an exception for specialty properties, and that the World Trade Center towers, because of their history and purpose, fit that exception.

In most cases, WTCP acknowledges, damages for destroyed or "taken" property will be fixed by market value. However, in some cases where the property is of a type "seldom traded" and for which there is no "market price," a different kind of valuation must be used. In such a circumstance where the market value cannot be measured, the property is considered "specialty property" and replacement cost is considered the proper measure of fixing damage. Commonly falling within this category are churches, hospitals, clubhouses and spaces held by nonprofit organizations for use as community centers. . . .

WTCP argues that, because the World Trade Center buildings were unique and served a public function, they should be considered specialty properties, . . . and that their replacement value should therefore be considered the proper measure of damages for their destruction. WTCP contends that the World Trade Center's unique and special nature flows from its history, from the reasons that caused the New York and New Jersey legislatures to establish it, and from the Port Authority's mission to use the towers to promote local commerce and industry, public transportation, and the surrounding regions of New Jersey and New York.

However, the time for measuring damages is not the 1960s, as WTCP's argument proposes, but September 11, 2001. By then, the World Trade Center buildings had been privatized. They were flourishing profit centers—offices and retail spaces filled with tenants paying market rates. A world-wide public auction established prices for the towers' privatization[,] and the bids that private companies presented, and that they were ready, willing, and able to pay, fully reflected the symbolic, as well as the commercial character, of the buildings. Unlike a clubhouse or church, which "may be regarded by the organization that owns and utilizes it as worth everything that it cost to construct it and more, yet . . . may not be 'marketable' because no similar group would have sufficient need for the property to be willing to purchase it even at its reproduction value," Rochester Urban Renewal Agency v. Patchen Post, Inc., 379 N.E.2d 169, 171 (N.Y. 1978), the World Trade Center towers had a determinable and verifiable value in the marketplace. [New York's] test for specialty properties is not satisfied. . . .

[T]he test for specialty properties is not whether there are, or were, special or unique aspects to the property, but rather whether the *use* to which the property is put at the time of the tort is a unique use, suitable only to the owner, and without a fair market value.

Clearly, the price WTCP paid . . . reflected a full and fair market price for the property. If WTCP is entitled to recover, recovery of the properties' market value would fully compensate it. WTCP is not entitled to recover the larger value of replacement cost.

C. The Covenants of WTCP's Net Leases Do Not Authorize a Larger Recovery.

[Structuring the deal as a lease had one consequence that we cannot entirely ignore. WTCP had continuing contractual obligations to the Port Authority, including the obligation to "rebuild, restore, repair and replace" the buildings if they were damaged or destroyed. WTCP argued that it was entitled to recover the cost of performing this obligation to rebuild.] The Aviation Defendants argue, in opposition, that they cannot be held responsible in tort for WTCP's contractual undertakings, and that, even if they could be held responsible, the new buildings that are envisioned as replacements for the destroyed buildings represent radical improvements and differences and cannot be considered replacement structures within the meaning of the contract.

When a party commits a tort that results in damage to property, the wronged party may recover damages for injuries which flow directly from that tort and are its natural and probable consequences. The tortfeasor is not responsible for damages which are remote from the wrong or indirectly related to it. Stated differently, the tortfeasor is responsible only for injuries that are the direct, natural and proximate result of the tortfeasor's actions, and that the parties would have foreseen, contemplated or expected. Palsgraf v. Long Island Railroad Co., 162 N.E. 99 (N.Y. 1928).

If proved at trial, the direct, natural and proximate cause of the Aviation Defendants' alleged negligence . . . would be the destruction of the two towers, and the related destruction of Towers Four and Five. The market value of the towers is the measure of recovery for their destruction. If WTCP bears a special or different burden, it flows directly from WTCP's contract clauses, not the Aviation Defendants' negligence. The particular features of WTCP's contracts cannot be made the special responsibility of the Aviation Defendants, nor the natural and probable result of their negligence, nor the foreseeable consequence of their acts and omissions. . . .

III. WTCP MAY NOT RECOVER DAMAGES IN ADDITION TO DESTROYED MARKET VALUE. . . .
A. Lost Rental Payments

WTCP argues that its tenants stopped paying their rents because the four buildings were destroyed. WTCP alleges that the present value of its lost rentals since September 11, 2001 is $3.9 billion. It seeks this amount over and above the value of the destroyed buildings, whether measured by market value or replacement value.

WTCP's claim is without merit. The price that WTCP paid to the Port Authority included the value of anticipated rentals. . . . The price it paid fully reflected the present value of those rental streams. If it recovers that market value, it necessarily regains the present value of the rental streams that were destroyed. WTCP cannot recover twice, once in the form of the property's market value, which fully includes the rental streams reasonably expected from the property, and again for the separate value of the rental streams. . . .

IV. WTCP WILL HAVE AN OPPORTUNITY TO MAKE A SHOWING REGARDING THE FAIR MARKET VALUE OF ITS LEASES.

The Aviation Defendants ask me to rule that the $2.8 billion consideration that WTCP paid . . . on July 16, 2001 also should be considered the September 11, 2001 market value, and the limit of WTCP's potential recovery. The fair market value of a property is "the price at which the property would change hands between a willing buyer and a willing seller, neither being under any compulsion to buy or to sell and both having reasonable knowledge of relevant facts." United States v. Cartwright, 411 U.S. 546 (1973). Generally, "a recent sale price for the subject asset, negotiated by the parties at arm's length, is the 'best evidence' of its market value." Schonfeld v. Hilliard, 218 F.3d 164, 178 (2d Cir. 2000).

The parties, as ready, willing and able buyers and sellers, agreed to a $2.805 billion consideration . . . on April 26, 2001, when their contract was signed and delivered. They conveyed the [buildings] on July 16, 2001, when the transactions closed. The time lapse to September 11, 2001 is short enough to be entitled to a presumption of equivalence as the "best evidence" of market value. However, the parties may introduce proof to overcome the presumption, for market values can fluctuate rapidly, and . . . property privately owned and managed by an experienced real estate developer may enjoy a different market value than property owned and managed by a governmental bureaucracy. . . .

NOTES ON MARKET VALUE

1. The appeal. The World Trade Center's appeal, which had to await a final judgment resolving all the issues in the case, was finally decided in In re September 11 Litigation, 802 F.3d 314 (2d Cir. 2015). The court agreed that the measure of damages is the loss of value and not replacement cost. The court thought it clear that an outright owner would not recover the cost of replacing the towers, and it said that the plaintiff's contractual obligation to rebuild should not change the result.

Judge Straub would have certified the issues concerning replacement cost to the New York Court of Appeals. The state had filed an amicus brief arguing that the towers were special purpose property, more valuable to the public than to the market. And there were New York tort cases awarding consequential damages arising out of the plaintiff's contractual obligations. Of course the stakes were radically different, and the issue was not replacement cost. For example, a plaintiff whose leased car was destroyed in a collision recovered the value of the car plus the early termination fees on the lease. Plouffe v. Rogers, 534 N.Y.S.2d 731 (App. Div. 1988).

The Second Circuit vacated and remanded for the district court to apply a more precise method of valuing the 99-year lease, a method that does not concern us and seems unlikely to change the bottom line. Litigation surprises are always possible, but we still expect the damages to be about $2.8 billion. Because the buildings were insured for more than that, and because New York has largely repealed the collateral-source rule, WTCP will likely recover nothing from the airlines.

2. Damages based on value. Determinations based on value are pervasive in damage measures. Familiar damage measures include the value of property taken or destroyed, the difference between the value of property before damage and the value after damage, and the difference between the contract price and the market value of property promised but not delivered. In well-functioning markets, giving plaintiffs the value of what they lost implements the rightful position by enabling plaintiffs to replace the thing they lost. Plaintiffs may choose to spend the money some other way, but so long as the choice is theirs, there is no reason to doubt that they have been made whole.

3. Determining value. Value measures of damage are unproblematic in many routine contexts. Value may be proved by price quotations in an active market for the same or similar property, by the estimates of experts, or even by the estimate of the owner. If the property is unique or if there is no active market, these different witnesses may give very different estimates. Courts tend to view such disparities as simply a proof problem.

Many things have a market value even though they are irreplaceable. If defendant destroys a one-of-a-kind painting, damages will be based on the painting's value in the art market. Plaintiff cannot use the damages to replace the painting, but if he receives the painting's value in cash, he is as close to his rightful position as it is possible to put him. Plaintiff may not have been interested in selling at that price, but courts will not try to identify the higher price at which he might have sold—that number is too speculative, and plaintiff's testimony would be too self-serving and too untestable. The usual measure of damages is therefore market value, not value to plaintiff.

4. WTCP's rightful position. The World Trade Center presents a more problematic application of value. The position WTCP would have occupied but for the wrong is ownership of four thriving and iconic office towers full of high-rent tenants. Replacement was entirely possible, but recovery of market value was not nearly enough to pay for replacement. Should replacement cost be irrelevant to judicial definition of the rightful position?

Would WTCP be made more than whole if defendants had to pay for towers that are more valuable than the ones it lost? The replacement towers will be 40 years younger, with more modern technology. What if the replacement cost were adjusted to take account of these differences? What if plaintiff offered evidence of what it would cost to reproduce the original towers with no improvements? And what if it allowed for 40 years' depreciation? Should WTCP be entitled to replacement cost measured that way? The Supreme Court once suggested that such a calculation might be prone to error, and "if it is calculated correctly, the entire process may amount to nothing more than a roundabout method of arriving at the market value" of the original property.

United States v. Fifty Acres of Land, 469 U.S. 24, 35 (1984). Often that will be true; sometimes it will not. It depends on why market value is less than replacement cost.

5. Disparities between value and replacement cost—real property. Powerful market forces tend to cause construction costs and market values to converge. Builders could not stay in business if construction costs generally exceeded what people were willing to pay for buildings. So why might replacement cost and market value sometimes be greatly different? The Supreme Court was thinking about differences in age, quality, and size. Other reasons are a bad location, overbuilding and excessive supply, or a financial panic.

Another set of reasons is special features that may be important to the owner but cannot be rebuilt at prices the market is willing to pay. The owner may put the property to a unique use, in which profit is not a motive. Or the owner may value aesthetic features more than the market does. The owner might have paid to build such features, or he might have bought them at the market price. Why was the 8,000-square-foot Victorian home in Fisher v. Qualico Contracting (discussed in the principal opinion) worth less than half its replacement cost? Perhaps because it was 100 years old, but perhaps also because 8,000-square-foot Victorian homes cost more to build than buyers are willing to pay, so no one builds them anymore. Yet if you live in such a home, and it is wrongfully destroyed, a remedy that leaves you unable to rebuild your house will not feel like the rightful position.

Damages based on market value might enable plaintiff to buy another set of office towers, or another large Victorian home, but perhaps not, and certainly not in the same location. Equitable remedies—specific performance of real estate contracts and injunctions against interfering with real estate—are based in part on the premise that every parcel of land is unique, so that a substitute parcel somewhere else is not an adequate remedy. But once the building has been destroyed, the choice between measures of damage looks rather different from the choice between preventing the damage from happening or letting it happen and then compensating for it.

6. Disparities between value and replacement cost—personal property. The gap between market value and replacement cost also arises with respect to depreciated personal property, but the list of causes is different. If Professor crashes into Student's reliable old jalopy, Professor's insurer, or a court if Student sues him, may tell Student that her car's value is only $1,000. Repairs may cost far more than that; a new car of the same model may cost $25,000; and a reliable used car may cost $5,000 or more. When the insurer says Student's car is totaled, or a total loss, that does not mean it cannot be repaired, but only that repair would cost more than the car is worth. A court in that situation would say Student's damages are $1,000, because that is all she lost.

Part of the anomaly comes from the difference between used goods and new goods. Part of the anomaly comes from serious imperfections in the market for used goods. If Student could buy for $1,000 a used car identical to her own, she would be made whole. But she cannot. The $1,000 cars on the used car lot are not equivalent to the one she lost. At least they are not equivalent to Student, for a reason of general importance: She knows everything about her old car and almost nothing about the cars on the used car lot. Suppose her car is old and beat up, but still reliable. Only she knows that; potential buyers will be reluctant to take her word for it. Buyers will generally assume that the car is at least as unreliable as the average for its age. They may even assume that it is especially unreliable; maybe that's why Student is selling it. These sorts of fears on the part of buyers are what hold the market value of her car down to $1,000.

When Student goes to the used car lot, the tables are turned. She can see that the $1,000 cars are old and beat up; she has no way to know whether they are reliable. She can spend $1,000 and take a chance, or she can spend more to get a car more likely to be as reliable as what she lost. Economists call this imbalance in information about used goods the lemon effect: Buyers assume the worst about used goods, so they pay low prices, so sellers won't sell used goods of high quality, so the used goods on the market tend to be of low quality, so buyers are justified in assuming the worst, and so on in a downward spiral until lemons are a large part of inventory on the used market. The effect is strongest for goods of modest value or short useful life, where it is not feasible to pay an expert to inspect each item offered for sale, but the effect persists even when buyers can inspect. The classic article is George Akerlof, *The Market for Lemons*, 84 Q.J. Econ. 488 (1970). Akerlof won the Nobel Prize in Economics for this and other work on the economics of asymmetric information.

7. Value in which market? There are separate markets along any chain of distribution; consumers, retailers, wholesalers, and manufacturers all pay different prices. WTCP paid $2.8 billion, but the total of all the rent it charged its tenants would have been much higher—enough to pay the purchase price and the expense of operating the buildings and make a profit. Why not calculate value based on what WTCP would have collected instead of on what it paid?

The usual rule is that plaintiffs recover value in the market in which they would have bought, which has the effect of excluding the profit plaintiff would have earned by selling the destroyed property. If the property is replaceable, the same profits from sale can be earned with replacement goods. But a comment to the *Restatement* says that if the destroyed property was already under contract to be sold, and plaintiff cannot acquire replacement goods in time to perform the contract, she is entitled to her profit on the lost sale. *Restatement (Second) of Torts* §911 cmt. *d* (Am. Law Inst. 1979).

8. Loss of use. Recall that in *Hatahley*, the court of appeals approved an award of damages from loss of use of the horses. Loss-of-use damages did not run forever, but for a reasonable period of time in which the horses could be replaced. Loss of use was measured by the loss of sheep and cattle and by an attempt to value inconvenience; another common measure of loss of use is rental value.

The equivalent to loss of use in *September 11th* is loss of the rental value of the towers during the time reasonably required to replace them. Why shouldn't plaintiff recover that? Partly because of political and regulatory obstacles, and partly because of the enormous scale of the project, the towers did not reopen to tenants until November 2014; WTCP did not collect rent for 13 years.

Courts routinely award loss of use during the time it takes to repair damaged property. But when the property is destroyed, courts divide. In theory, the value of the property includes the present value of all the income it would ever produce. Market value of the building plus lost rent for the life of the building would plainly be a double recovery. This leads some courts—most courts until fairly recently—to conclude that any lesser amount of rent is also included in market value. But does that assume that replacement is instantaneous?

Assume that WTCP could create precisely equivalent replacements for the towers—40-year-old buildings of the same size, condition, and function, and with exactly the same value. Plainly, the right to own such a building beginning in 2014 is not equal to the right to own such a building beginning in 2001. Plaintiff is not made whole by an identical building that appears 13 years after the loss. The loss of net rental income is a good measure of the difference. But if inability to replace is not relevant to the measure of damages, why would delay in replacement be relevant? To a court convinced that the market value in 2001 is all that WTCP lost, lost rent during the construction period is not part of the rightful position.

Most courts would now award prejudgment interest on the award of market value. See section 2.F.2. Interest is commonly viewed as an alternate measure of the value of loss of use, and because the litigation took even longer than the construction, this would provide some compensation, usually much less generous than lost rent, for the long delay in rebuilding.

Compare J & D Towing, LLC v. American Alternative Insurance Corp., 478 S.W.3d 649 (Tex. 2016), unanimously allowing loss-of-use damages for the time reasonably needed to replace a destroyed tow truck. That time turned out to be more than two months, because the plaintiff could not afford to replace the truck until it received an initial payment from defendant's insurer. The opinion finds a clear trend to compensating loss of use when replacement takes time, and it says that refusing compensation for the two months without a truck would be "nonsensical and inequitable." *Id.* at 663. It collects similar cases from 27 other jurisdictions in notes 180-182. This opinion is focused on personal property, but it is hard to see any reason why chattels should be treated differently from real estate; the operating income from a truck has the same economic relation to the value of the truck as the rental income from a building has to the value of the building.

9. Scope of liability. The court says that WTCP's contractual obligations to the Port Authority are irrelevant. Why is that? Such contractual obligations to rebuild are hardly unusual, and they were publicly recorded in the real estate records. Are plaintiff's contractual obligations just definitionally outside the scope of defendant's liability?

NOTES ON "VALUE TO THE OWNER"

1. The lesser-of-two rule. What New York calls the lesser-of-two rule says that plaintiff is entitled to be made whole, but only in the least expensive way: market value or replacement cost, whichever is less. The rule is well settled, but it is not entirely uncontroversial, and there are exceptions around the edges. And many courts apply a less restrictive rule when property is damaged but repairable instead of totally destroyed.

Louisiana appears to reject the rule outright. See Roman Catholic Church v. Louisiana Gas Service Co., 618 So. 2d 874 (La. 1993), awarding full replacement cost, without allowance for depreciation, for destruction of 16 units of a low-income housing complex. The court did not say that low-income housing is special-purpose property. Rather, it said that for a plaintiff that wants to use its property rather than sell it, awarding less than replacement cost forces plaintiff to finance premature replacement and fails to make plaintiff whole.

2. Special-purpose property. The exception for special-purpose property is widely accepted. Property designed for a particular use, especially if that use is a not-for-profit use, may have little value to anyone other than the owner. Yet someone valued that use highly enough to have paid the cost of building the property in the first place. Such owners are entitled to continue their use of the property, even if no market value can be determined, and even if, in some formulations of the rule, the cost of replacement exceeds a small market value that can be determined.

WTCP tried to fit itself into the rule for special-purpose property by emphasizing the public purpose of the towers and their symbolic value to the city and the nation. This purpose and value justified rebuilding even if the cost exceeded market value.

Defendants and the court responded that the towers had been successfully operated for profit, so there was no reason to doubt the market value evidenced by the recent arm's-length purchase and sale.

3. Personal items and used consumer goods. The *Restatement (Second) of Torts* defines value to mean "exchange value or the value to the owner if this is greater than the exchange value." *Id.* §911. "Exchange value" is a synonym for market value. Value to the owner includes the special-purpose property cases, but the concept is broader than just real estate that is rarely bought or sold:

> [A] personal record or manuscript, an artificial eye or a dog trained to obey only one master, will have substantially no value to others than the owner. The same is true of articles that give enjoyment to the owner but have no substantial value to others, such as family portraits. Second-hand clothing and furniture have an exchange value, but frequently far less than its use value to the owner.
>
>   Real property may also have a value to the owner greater than its exchange value. Thus a particular location may be valuable to an occupant because of a business reason, as when he has built up good will in a particular neighborhood.

Id. cmt. *e.*

Courts disagree about how to calculate value to the owner. For loss of consumer items that are functional and replaceable, courts can award replacement cost minus depreciation based on the age of the item and its expected useful life. Thus in Concord General Mutual Insurance Co. v. Gritman, 146 A.3d 882 (Vt. 2016), plaintiffs recovered $100,541 for personal property destroyed by trespassing teenagers. The teens gathered at plaintiffs' vacation home, partied in the yard and on the deck, and left too big a fire in the outdoor fireplace, destroying the house. An insurance adjuster testified to replacement cost, less depreciation, of the furniture and other items in the house. Defendants unsuccessfully objected to the methodology but did not introduce any alternative evidence, such as value in the market for second-hand consumer goods.

Much of the problem here is the lemon effect: Used consumer goods are far more valuable to the owner, who knows their quality and chose them because they fit his needs, than to potential buyers who may expect the worst but cannot afford better. There is objective evidence that consumers generally value their goods more highly than the market: They typically sell in the secondhand market only when they no longer need the goods or when they are desperate for cash.

4. Sentimental value. Items that are irreplaceable and idiosyncratic present harder questions. For the loss of irreplaceable family photographs and videotapes, the Alaska court said that damages could be based on the original cost of the film, developing, and tapes. Landers v. Municipality of Anchorage, 915 P.2d 614, 618-620 (Alaska 1996). But where sentimental value is the principal or only value at issue, some courts allow recovery of usual or reasonable sentimental value, whatever that might mean, but not mawkish or excessive sentimental value. An apparently larger number of courts allow special value to the owner but not sentimental value. Edmonds v. United States, 563 F. Supp. 2d 196 (D.D.C. 2008). It seems likely that special value and reasonable sentimental value come out to about the same thing, allowing modest but more than trivial recoveries. The *Edmonds* judge, in a bench trial, awarded $2,500 for each of two irreplaceable photographs of plaintiff's father as a high-school student.

5. Commercial examples. Consider King Fisher Marine Service, Inc. v. The NP Sunbonnet, 724 F.2d 1181 (5th Cir. 1984). Plaintiff bought a used barge for $30,000, planning to convert it into a base for a dry dock. Two days later, the barge was sunk due to the negligence of the company hired to tow it to the dry dock site. The court awarded replacement cost of $232,996.75. There was uncontradicted expert testimony that the first barge was ideally suited as a dry dock platform, that there were only six similar barges in the world, and that none of the others were for sale. On petition for rehearing, the court said:

> [T]he choice between awarding mere exchange value and, on rare and appropriate occasions, "value to the owner" is one of policy—not of ineluctable accounting. Logic compels neither. But where one who has arrived at a bargain of unique value to him is deprived of it by the fault of another, and where he can convince the trial court that its value to him was real and not speculative or later devised, he should recover it.

729 F.2d 315, 316 (5th Cir. 1984).

And plaintiffs recovered the replacement cost of a specialized truck in Sawyer Brothers, Inc. v. Island Transporter, LLC, 887 F.3d 23 (1st Cir. 2018). The court found that market value could not be determined. Defendant's expert testified to a market value of $38,000, based on the insurance company's efforts to sell the truck in its damaged condition. That was obviously no evidence of the value of the truck before the damage. It appears that defense counsel had not attended to the most basic steps of preparing an expert witness; the witness didn't understand the facts.

One of the plaintiffs testified that the truck was worth $80,000 to $90,000, but when asked the basis for that opinion, he appeared not to understand the question. He was then questioned at length about the search for a replacement. The business had very specialized needs for the equipment on its truck, and it searched for months before finding a truck in Wisconsin that it could modify to meet those needs. The maritime law test for market value is based on sales of like property; the court concluded that there were no sales of like property, and it dismissed the owner's testimony (normally admissible) as not based on the proper test. The Wisconsin truck, plus the cost of modifying it, came to nearly $207,000, and the court affirmed an award of that amount.

6. A professional example. Jafar Vossoughi was an engineer who taught courses and maintained a research lab at the University of the District of Columbia. In the course of a dispute over his continued employment, the university evicted him from his lab. His property was supposed to be securely stored, but the jury found that most of it was just trashed. He lost the notes for 21 courses, 10 ongoing research projects, 19 scientific instruments that he had fabricated himself and were not commercially available, and 98 pieces of commercially available equipment.

He valued the course notes at $25,000 apiece, on the theory that it took half a semester to develop a new course and the average engineering professor made $100,000 per year. He valued the research projects at $50,000 each, based in part on the average size of the government grants that had supported them. He valued the hand-made scientific instruments individually, based on how long he thought it would take to replace them. He testified to the original purchase price of the commercially available equipment (and offered receipts for most of it), and he testified that wear and tear was offset by the steadily increasing price of scientific equipment. Two colleagues testified and supported his valuations. The jury awarded $1,650,000 in a general verdict. The court affirmed, emphasizing that "this property had great use value to Dr. Vossoughi but no comparable (if any) market value." Trustees of University of District of Columbia v. Vossoughi, 963 A.2d 1162, 1176 (D.C. 2009).

7. Value to the owner less than market? Usually, value to the owner is greater than market value. But what if it's the other way around? Consider United States v. Crown

Equipment Corp., 86 F.3d 700 (7th Cir. 1996), where a defective forklift started a fire that destroyed a million pounds of surplus butter, stored in a government warehouse to keep it off the market. The government recovered $1.01 a pound, the price of butter on the Chicago Mercantile Exchange on the day of the fire. But the only reason the government owned the butter was to artificially support the price. Judge Manion, dissenting, thought the government had reaped a windfall from the fire.

A similar issue reached the Supreme Court in Horne v. Department of Agriculture, 135 S. Ct. 2419 (2015). To support the price of raisins, the government confiscated much of each year's crop. The Court held that this was a taking of private property requiring just compensation, and that plaintiffs should recover the government-supported market price. Three dissenters argued that without the government's price-support program, plaintiff's raisins would have been much less valuable. Plaintiff was getting the benefits of government price support without bearing any of the costs.

TRINITY CHURCH v. JOHN HANCOCK MUTUAL LIFE INSURANCE CO.

502 N.E.2d 532 (Mass. 1987)

Before WILKINS, LIACOS, ABRAMS, LYNCH and O'CONNOR, JJ.

LYNCH, Justice.

This case arises out of property damage sustained by the plaintiff, Trinity Church in the City of Boston, during construction of the John Hancock Tower Building in Copley Square. . . .

Following jury verdicts for the plaintiff on three counts in the sum of $4,170,300, Hancock appealed.[3] . . . We affirm.

There was evidence from which the jury could have found the following facts. Trinity Church was designed by Henry Hobson Richardson in 1872 and completed in 1876. . . . Today, Trinity Church is a national historic landmark as well as a functioning church.

Trinity Church is constructed almost entirely of stone masonry. Stone masonry is heavy and very brittle compared to other construction materials; when placed under stress it does not deform, but it cracks. When stone masonry cracks, it characteristically breaks throughout its entire thickness, and its strength diminishes significantly. Ordinarily it cannot be repaired except by disassembly, resetting, and reconstruction. . . .

During construction of the Hancock tower, the foundation of the church was undermined by a failure of the excavation system at the Hancock site. As work was being performed on the excavation system, the ground immediately surrounding the construction site moved inward toward the excavation. This caused the foundation of the church to settle unevenly, most dramatically on the south side closest to the tower site, and to migrate horizontally toward the Hancock tower excavation. This settlement produced a spray of cracks up through the masonry walls of the church which affected the structural integrity of the church. [The cracks broke the church into several parts that were no longer structurally connected to each other.] . . .

---

3. . . . Approximately $3.6 million of the verdicts represents compensation for structural damages. The addition of interest more than doubles the award.

I. DAMAGES. . . .

This appeal only involves the church's claim for structural damages.

Trinity based its structural damage claim on the changes which took place within the church during the time the Hancock tower was being constructed. Trinity quantified these changes in terms of a percentage of the church's ultimate "takedown" condition.

A. THE "TAKEDOWN" THEORY OF DAMAGE ASSESSMENT

The plaintiff introduced evidence to show that the level of structural damage within a masonry structure such as the church can be related directly to the amount of distortion in its foundations caused by differential settlement. The degree of differential settlement can be expressed in terms of "angles of distortion," which can be calculated directly from the settlement survey data. At a certain angle of distortion, the structural damage to a building reaches a point where disassembly and reconstruction become necessary. This ultimate level of damage is referred to as the "takedown" level of damage.

For the purpose of calculating its damage claim, angles of distortion were calculated for the years 1968 and 1972, for each section of the church for which sufficient data were available. . . . The percentage difference before and after the tower construction was taken to represent the amount of damage caused to the building during the construction period. The final dollar value of the claim was established by applying the change in physical damage from 1968 to 1972, expressed as a percentage of the over-all takedown condition, to the estimated cost of takedown and reconstruction for each affected section.

The general rule for measuring property damage is diminution in market value. However, "market value does not in all cases afford a correct measure of indemnity, and is not therefore 'a universal test.'" Wall v. Platt, 48 N.E. 270, 273 (Mass. 1897). For certain categories of property, termed "special purpose property" (such as the property of nonprofit, charitable, or religious organizations), there will not generally be an active market from which the diminution in market value may be determined. The parties agree that Trinity Church falls within the definition of special purpose property and that the damage to the church could not be measured on the basis of fair market value.

In such cases, this court . . . has provided:

> [s]pecial opportunities for proof of value . . . where it is felt that there is no market value. . . . The courts in these cases . . . may be doing no more than recognizing that more complex and resourceful methods of ascertaining value must be used where the property is unusual or specialized in character and where ordinary methods will produce a miscarriage of justice.

Newton Girl Scout Council v. Massachusetts Turnpike Authority, 138 N.E.2d 769, 773-774 (Mass. 1956).

In a number of situations involving special purpose property, the cost of reproduction less depreciation has been utilized as an appropriate measure of damages [citing cases of eminent domain takings of a church, an armory, and a Girl Scout camp, and tax assessment of a harness-racing track].

Replacement or restoration costs have also been allowed as a measure of damages in other contexts where diminution in market value is unavailable or unsatisfactory as a measure of damages [citing cases of replacing trees and vegetation and restoring land affected by an oil spill]. Where expenditures to restore or to replace to pre-damage condition are used as the measure of damages, a test of reasonableness is imposed. Not only must the cost of replacement or reconstruction be reasonable, the replacement or reconstruction itself must be reasonably necessary in light of the damage inflicted by a particular defendant. In some cases, "to make such a restoration would be an uneconomical and improper way of using the property" and "might involve a very large and disproportionate expense to relieve from the consequences of a slight injury." Hopkins v. American Pneumatic Service Co., 80 N.E. 624, 624 (Mass. 1907).

Trinity is entitled to be compensated for the reasonable costs of restoring the church to the condition it was in prior to the Hancock excavation. Trinity's method of damage assessment meets the test of reasonableness by quantifying the amount of the incremental damage sustained between 1968 and 1972. For example, in the south transept, the most heavily damaged section of the church, Trinity estimated a total takedown and reconstruction cost of $1,724,457. By 1972, the south transept had reached a level of damage equivalent to 65 percent of its takedown condition, compared to a 1968 level of damage of 26 percent. Multiplying the increase of 39 percent by the total reconstruction cost of the south transept, Trinity arrived at its claim of $672,538 for structural damages in this section of the church.

It is useful to consider Trinity's method with a view toward the impact of future damage. If at some time in the future another construction project damaged the church causing it to reach its "total loss" or takedown point, the church would clearly be entitled to recover the depreciated reconstruction cost. Depreciation at that point, however, would include all the damage sustained up to that time, including that related to the Hancock tower construction. For this reason, unless Trinity is compensated for the Hancock related damages now, these damages will forever pass into the realm of nonrecoverable depreciation.

The plaintiff's method of damage assessment, based upon a percentage of reconstruction cost, is consistent with the depreciated-cost-of-reconstruction standard applicable to special purpose property cases. We conclude that Trinity's method of proving damages is an acceptable measure of the amount of damage reasonably attributable to the defendant's acts. . . .

C. PRESENT VALUE

Over Hancock's objection, the judge refused to admit any evidence on or to instruct the jury regarding reducing the award of future damages to their present value. Hancock claims that it was reversible error to preclude the jury from considering the application of present value reduction to the plaintiff's claim.

In Chesapeake & Ohio Railway v. Kelly, 241 U.S. 485, 489 (1916), the Supreme Court recognized that, unless an award for future damages is reduced to present value, the award will, with interest, exceed the sum of the plaintiff's future damages . . . .

Trinity's theory was that all of the structural damages had occurred. . . . The fact that . . . the repairs will not be done until some time in the future does not compel the conclusion that it is seeking recovery for future damages. The theory attempts to set a present dollar value for damages which have occurred but which will not be repaired until some time in the future. An injured party is not required to perform repairs in order to recover for diminution in market value of its property. . . .

Judgments affirmed.

O'CONNOR, Justice (dissenting in part). . . .

Damages are not appropriate simply to respond to an unsolicited alteration of real property, but are appropriate only as compensation for actual loss. In appropriate circumstances, diminution in the market value of real property constitutes compensable loss. Also, in appropriate circumstances, the loss of use of special purpose property, being rationally susceptible of measurement in terms of money, is compensable. Loss of use fairly encompasses a reduction in the "life expectancy" of a building, and, therefore, such a reduction, if it results from a defendant's tortious conduct, ought to be compensable. But, the record contains no evidence of a diminution in the church's market value, or of a present loss of use or enjoyment of the church, or of even a minute shortening of its usable life. There is no evidence that the church will ever be less usable or less enjoyable than it is now, or that it ever will have to be taken down and reconstructed. . . . Therefore, Trinity has not sustained its burden of proving a loss based on structural damage. . . .

[T]he court assumes without discussion that the distortion of the church's foundation and the resulting wall cracks have resulted in a loss. . . . [T]he award does not purport to put the plaintiff in position to restore the church to its condition prior to the excavation, but rather it is designed to require Hancock to pay now what is deemed to be Hancock's equitable share of the cost of restoration sometime in the future should restoration ever become reasonably necessary. The award misses the mark, however, because costs of restoration, in whole or in part, are not a proper method of measuring damages unless restoration either is, or is likely to become, reasonably necessary, and there is no such evidence in this case. . . .

If, as I argue, Trinity has not sustained a loss as a result of the Hancock excavation, its building has not depreciated, for loss is depreciation and depreciation is loss. If [a second nearby construction project should cause the church to reach its takedown point], the wrongdoer will not be entitled to deduct from the reconstruction cost any depreciation attributable to Hancock because there will not be any. It is not unusual for a court to conclude in a tort case that the defendant must take the plaintiff as he finds him . . . .

The court's holding causes a windfall to Trinity and an injustice to Hancock. . . . I would remand the case to the Superior Court for the entry of a new judgment consistent with this opinion.

NOTES ON SPECIAL-PURPOSE PROPERTY

1. Was the church damaged? Can it really be that the church has suffered no damage? The church is quite literally broken in pieces, but each piece is still standing and usable. What if the church never has to be taken down and rebuilt? What if, when it is taken down, the congregation decides to replace it with a much smaller and more modern church? What if it decides to sell the land to a developer and rebuild in the suburbs? Is the judgment a windfall on these scenarios?

Whether a plaintiff actually replaces his damaged property is normally irrelevant. But when damages are based on replacement cost, courts are more likely to ask whether the property will actually be replaced, and whether the replacement is reasonable.

The takedown theory of damages is a factual theory, not a legal theory. The south transept had reached 26 percent of its takedown point in the first century of existence, and the Hancock tower had moved it 39 percent further toward the takedown point in only four years. Maybe that implies a shorter useful life, but maybe not. There was apparently no evidence to that effect, and we cannot assume that settling or angles of distortion proceed in continuous fashion or at anything like a constant rate. And even if settling continued, it seems likely that the takedown point would still be far in the future. Is any theory of what might happen in 50 or 100 years too speculative to support a damage award?

Early in the new millennium, the church did substantial restoration work, and its website discussed the foundations. The church said of the cracks created by the Hancock tower construction: "Fortunately, those cracks haven't grown since then. This kind of crack is different than—and unrelated to—deterioration of the structural piling system." That page has been taken down. Today the website touts the building's architectural significance but says nothing about the foundation.

2. Does the church have a value? *Trinity Church* is hard because it's not clear what to make of the damage. The court tries to measure that damage with a fraction of replacement cost. But replacement cost might be irrelevant were it not for a second problem in the case: The church has little or no market value. There are few if any potential buyers for this building, before or after the structural damage. Any congregation large enough to need such a church building probably already has one, and there are few other uses to which such a building could be converted. Somebody might buy it for the prestige of owning and preserving a famous landmark, but it would be hard to predict the price in such a transaction, where the buyer is acting on non-economic motives.

What damages if the Hancock tower had destroyed the church entirely? It would still be true that the building had no market value. Should the church recover nothing? Or should it recover replacement cost?

Is it reasonable to build another expensive structure with no market value on expensive land in the heart of the city? Or should the church be required to mitigate damages by taking the opportunity to sell the land and build a less expensive church on less expensive land elsewhere? The rule that destruction of special-purpose property is compensated by replacement cost depends on the judgment that the congregation is entitled to this church building on this land if that is what it wants. The owners of the church have demonstrated its value to them by spending the money to build it in the first place—although there may be little correlation between original cost and replacement cost—and by spending money to preserve and maintain it.

NOTES ON REPAIR COSTS

1. The lesser-of-two rule in repair cases. The lesser-of-two rule applies to the choice between repair costs, on the one hand, and the difference in the value of the property before and after the damage, on the other. But the choice is not so stark in repair cases as in replacement cases. There may be no active market in damaged property, and if the repair is one that most buyers would be likely to make, repair costs may be the best evidence of the decline in market value. So in Rexam Beverage Can Co. v. Bolger, 620 F.3d 718 (7th Cir. 2010), the court affirmed a finding that the value of a building was reduced by the anticipated cost of replacing the roof. The Kentucky court went further in Ellison v. R & B Contracting, Inc., 32 S.W.3d 66 (Ky. 2000), where defendants dumped tons of road-construction debris on plaintiffs' undeveloped land. The court adhered to the lesser-of-two rule, but it held that the jury could have inferred a loss of value equal to the cost of removing the debris, even though plaintiffs had offered no more direct evidence of lost value and defendant's appraiser had testified that there had been no loss of value.

Many courts have been willing to compensate repair costs viewed as reasonable, even if the repairs cost more than what they add in value. The Nebraska court thought that an owner is "entitled to have his building without the broken bricks and windows even though the total value remains unchanged." L Investments, Ltd. v. Lynch, 322 N.W.2d 651, 656 (Neb. 1982). A federal opinion takes the Nebraska rule to be that plaintiff is entitled to repair costs unless defendant proves that those costs would "greatly outweigh" the benefits of repair. BLB Aviation South Carolina, LLC v. Jet Link Aviation, LLC, 808 F.3d 389, 393 (8th Cir. 2015). Defendant met that burden in *BLB*, where plaintiff sued to recover the cost of completely redoing all the maintenance work on two jets because of deficiencies in defendant's paperwork documenting the original maintenance.

Courts are more willing to view expensive repairs as reasonable when the property is a residence or there is some other indication that the owner is personally attached to that very property. Where a city had repeatedly and negligently flooded a residential neighborhood, the West Virginia court allowed the cost of raising the foundations above the recurring flood line, even though that cost more than the houses were worth. Brooks v. City of Huntington, 768 S.E.2d 97 (W. Va. 2014). The *Restatement* authorizes repair or restoration costs "reasonably incurred," but not costs that are "disproportionate" to the loss in value, "unless there is a reason personal to the owner for restoring the original condition." *Restatement (Second) of Torts* §929(1)(a) cmt. *b*.

2. Environmental restoration. Many applications of the *Restatement* section have been to restoration costs for environmental damage. See Sunburst School District No. 2 v. Texaco, Inc., 165 P.3d 1079 (Mont. 2007), where the court affirmed a judgment for $15 million in restoration costs in a case of benzene contamination, where the contaminated property—several houses and a school—was worth only $2 million. The court feared that strictly limiting damages to the decline in market value would give tortfeasors "a power akin to a private right of eminent domain." *Id.* at 1090.

Compare Poffenbarger v. Merit Energy Co., 972 So. 2d 792 (Ala. 2007), a case of oil contamination of an undeveloped wood lot, where the court limited recovery to the $6,000 decline in market value. Remediation costs were variously estimated at $15,000, $56,000, and $2.6 million; if remediation were the measure of damage, the court would have to decide what quality of remediation supplied the measure.

This issue was famously presented in Peevyhouse v. Garland Coal & Mining Co., 382 P.2d 109 (Okla. 1963), where defendant promised to restore plaintiffs' land after strip-mining the coal. There the issue was contract damages, not tort; the fact that the parties expressly bargained for restoration of the land might be thought a reason to award restoration costs rather than a reason to measure damages more conservatively. Relying on the disproportion between restoration costs and decline in value, and on its dubious view that the restoration clause was not a principal purpose of the contract, the court reduced the judgment to what it (mistakenly) thought to be the loss of market value. But *Peevyhouse* represents only one side of a deeply divided body of cases.

3. Trees. Trees grown commercially for timber, fruit, or nuts generally have a determinable market value. But courts have struggled with how to value trees grown for the landowner's enjoyment. Courts may start with the difference in the value of the land with and without the trees, but that often seems undercompensatory. So courts have also awarded the cost of replacement, if not unreasonably excessive, or the "intrinsic value" of the trees. Cases and competing approaches are collected in Evenson v. Lilley, 282 P.3d 610, 616-617 (Kan. 2012).

Intrinsic value may just be a label for choosing a number that seems reasonable. Or it may be much more. Arborists will sometimes testify to rules of thumb for valuing healthy trees by species and size. The Texas court affirmed a jury verdict of $288,000 for the intrinsic value of trees destroyed along "several hundred feet" of pipeline right of way; defendant had wholly ignored a contractual obligation to tunnel under the trees. Gilbert Wheeler, Inc. v. Enbridge Pipelines (East Texas), L.P., 449 S.W.3d

474, 477 (Tex. 2014). The court did not explain what evidence supported the jury's number, but it equated intrinsic value with ornamental and utilitarian value, with the principal utilitarian value specified as shade. The market value of the entire 153-acre property, heavily wooded and used as a family retreat, was only $383,000. The court rejected an award of $300,000 in restoration costs as unreasonably disproportionate to the nominal decline in the value of the tract, which was estimated to be $3,000 at most.

4. Pets. The general rule is that the owner of a pet that is killed can recover only the market value of the pet as property. The supreme courts of Georgia and Texas have each unanimously reaffirmed the traditional rule; the Texas opinion is substantial and wide-ranging. Barking Hound Village, LLC v. Monyak, 787 S.E.2d 191 (Ga. 2016); Medlen v. Strickland, 397 S.W.3d 184 (Tex. 2013).

But if the pet is injured, owners can recover the costs of medical care. A handful of cases are collected in Kimes v. Grosser, 126 Cal. Rptr. 3d 581 (Ct. App. 2011), where defendant shot plaintiff's cat with a pellet gun, and plaintiff spent $6,000 on veterinary care and $30,000 on other expenses related to the cat's care. Plaintiff conceded that the cat had no market value. But the court said he was entitled to go to the jury on whether it was reasonable to spend $36,000 to save the cat. The court applied *Kimes* to a negligence case (veterinary malpractice) in Martinez v. Robledo, 147 Cal. Rptr. 3d 921 (Ct. App. 2012).

Another line of cases allows emotional distress damages against persons who intentionally kill or injure a pet. Plotnik v. Meihaus, 146 Cal. Rptr. 3d 585, 600-601 (Ct. App. 2012) (collecting cases). The ABA Journal reports a series of six-figure settlements, and a $1.2 million jury verdict (reduced to $207,500 under a statute limiting liability for local governments) in suits against police officers who shoot and kill dogs. Arin Greenwood, *Pet Threat*, ABA J. 16 (April 2018). None of these cases are reported; a less dramatic reported example is Thomas v. Cannon, 289 F. Supp. 3d 1182 (W.D. Wash. 2018), upholding a $10,000 jury verdict. (Defendants' appeal is No. 18-35040 in the Ninth Circuit.) Emotional distress is often recoverable in intentional tort, but generally not in negligence or in breach of contract.

NOTES ON PROPERTY THAT FLUCTUATES IN VALUE

1. The problem. The standard rule is to value property at the time and place of the loss in tort cases, or at the time and place for delivery in contract cases. That usually produces sensible results, but any fixed time may produce arbitrary results when values are subject to rapid change. Contracts are often intended to allocate the risk of such fluctuations. The problem of fluctuating values is greater in tort, and it has been most frequently litigated in cases involving investment securities.

A few states value the loss at the time of the wrong even in the context of rapidly fluctuating values, but modern decisions of this type tend to find escape routes from the rule. A larger group of states resolves doubts against defendant by awarding the highest value between the time of the wrong and the time of trial, the time of filing suit, or some similar date. Perhaps most sensibly, the New York rule, also followed in the federal courts and a number of other states, gives plaintiff the highest value between the time he learned of the loss and a reasonable time thereafter in which he could have replaced the property. The approaches and their variations are reviewed in Roxas v. Marcos, 969 P.2d 1209, 1266-1270 (Haw. 1998), applying the New York rule to gold bars and a large golden Buddha that had been confiscated by the corrupt dictator of the Philippines.

2. Stock in a start-up. Compare Miga v. Jensen, 96 S.W.3d 207 (Tex. 2002), where the principal owner of a privately held telecom company refused to honor the stock options of a key employee who had resigned. The options entitled the employee to buy at 8 cents a share (adjusted for splits); the value at the time, December 1994, was $2 a share. The stock went public in 1996 at $12; it peaked at $45 in October 1997, and was trading at $35 at the time of trial in November 1997. The jury awarded damages based on value at the time of trial, but the court measured damages as of the date of breach, for reasons that are less than clear. The court emphasized that this was a simple breach of an executory contract. Perhaps more important, it was unwilling to assume that the employee would still have held the stock at the time of trial, and to award damages based on the $35 value would give plaintiff the benefit of that extraordinary appreciation without his having been subject to the risks of owning the stock.

3. Growing crops. Growing crops are typically valued as of the time of harvest, even if a litigant can show with some reliability that plaintiff would have held the harvest for sale at a later time and at a different price. A good example is Decatur County Ag-Services v. Young, 426 N.E.2d 644 (Ind. 1981), where a negligent crop sprayer destroyed nearly half of plaintiff's soybeans. Plaintiff sold the surviving half in the spring, as he had always done, at $10.38 a bushel, but he recovered only $7.00 a bushel, the price at harvest time. The court thought that if he wanted to speculate in beans, he should have bought more when his crop failed. This may be harsh on a small farmer, but it is a modest variation on the New York rule of giving plaintiff a reasonable opportunity to replace.

C.   EXPECTANCY AND RELIANCE AS MEASURES OF THE RIGHTFUL POSITION

NERI v. RETAIL MARINE CORP.
285 N.E.2d 311 (N.Y. 1972)

GIBSON, Judge. . . .

The plaintiffs contracted to purchase from defendant a new boat of a specified model for the price of $12,587.40, against which they made a deposit of $40. They shortly increased the deposit to $4,250 in consideration of the defendant dealer's agreement to arrange with the manufacturer for immediate delivery on the basis of "a firm sale," instead of the delivery within approximately four to six weeks originally specified. Some six days after the date of the contract plaintiffs' lawyer sent to defendant a letter rescinding the sales contract for the reason that plaintiff Neri was about to undergo hospitalization and surgery, in consequence of which, according to the letter, it would be "impossible for Mr. Neri to make any payments." The boat had already been ordered from the manufacturer and was delivered to defendant at or before the time the attorney's letter was received. Defendant declined to refund plaintiffs' deposit and this action to recover it was commenced. Defendant counterclaimed, alleging plaintiffs' breach of the contract. . . . [D]efendant had summary judgment on the issue of liability tendered by its counterclaim; and Special Term directed an assessment of damages. . . .

[T]he boat ordered and received by defendant in accordance with plaintiffs' contract of purchase was sold some four months later to another buyer for the same price as that negotiated with plaintiffs. From this proof the plaintiffs argue that defendant's loss on its contract was recouped, while defendant argues that but for plaintiffs' default, it would have sold two boats and [would] have earned two profits instead of one. Defendant proved, without contradiction, that its profit on the sale under the contract in suit would have been $2,579 and that during the period the boat remained unsold incidental expenses aggregating $674 for storage, upkeep, finance charges and insurance were incurred. . . .

The issue is governed in the first instance by §2-718 of the Uniform Commercial Code which provides, among other things, that the buyer, despite his breach, may have restitution of the amount by which his payment exceeds: (a) reasonable liquidated damages stipulated by the contract or (b) absent such stipulation, 20 percent of the value of the buyer's total performance or $500, whichever is smaller. . . . [T]he trial court awarded defendant an offset in the amount of $500 under paragraph (b) and directed restitution to plaintiffs of the balance. [This judgment was affirmed without opinion. 326 N.Y.S.2d 984 (App. Div. 1971).] Section 2-718(a)(3), however, establishes an alternative right of offset in favor of the seller, as follows: "(3) The buyer's right to restitution under subsection (2) is subject to offset to the extent that the seller establishes (a) a right to recover damages under the provisions of this Article other than subsection (1)."

Among "the provisions of this Article other than subsection (1)" are those to be found in §2-708, which the courts below did not apply. Subsection (1) of that section provides that:

> the measure of damages for non-acceptance or repudiation by the buyer is the difference between the market price at the time and place for tender and the unpaid contract price together with any incidental damages provided in this Article (Section 2-710), but less expenses saved in consequence of the buyer's breach.

However, this provision is made expressly subject to subsection (2), providing:

> (2) If the measure of damages provided in subsection (1) is inadequate to put the seller in as good a position as performance would have done then the measure of damages is the profit (including reasonable overhead) which the seller would have made from full performance by the buyer, together with any incidental damages provided in this Article (Section 2-710), due allowance for costs reasonably incurred and due credit for payments or proceeds of resale.

. . . The conclusion is clear from the record—indeed with mathematical certainty—that "the measure of damages provided in subsection (1) is inadequate to put the seller in as good position as performance would have done," UCC §2-708(2), and hence—again under subsection (2)—that the seller is entitled to its "profit (including reasonable overhead) . . . together with any incidental damages . . . , due allowance for costs reasonably incurred and due credit for payments or proceeds of resale." . . .

[T]he last sentence of subsection (2), . . . referring to "due credit for payments or proceeds of resale[,]" is inapplicable to this retail sales contract.[2] Closely parallel to

---

2. The concluding clause, "due credit for payments or proceeds of resale," is intended to refer to "the privilege of the seller to realize junk value when it is manifestly useless to complete the operation of manufacture." Supp. No. 1 to the 1952 Official Draft of Text and Comments of the Uniform Commercial Code, as Amended by the Action of the American Law Institute and the National Conference of Commissioners on Uniform Laws 13 (1954). . . .

the factual situation now before us is that hypothesized by Dean Hawkland as illustrative of the operation of the rules:

> Thus, if a private party agrees to sell his automobile to a buyer for $2,000, a breach by the buyer would cause the seller no loss (except incidental damages, i.e., expense of a new sale) if the seller was able to sell the automobile to another buyer for $2,000. But the situation is different with dealers having an unlimited supply of standard-priced goods. Thus, if an automobile dealer agrees to sell a car to a buyer at the standard price of $2,000, a breach by the buyer injures the dealer, even though he is able to sell the automobile to another for $2,000. If the dealer has an inexhaustible supply of cars, the resale to replace the breaching buyer costs the dealer a sale, because, had the breaching buyer performed, the dealer would have made two sales instead of one. The buyer's breach, in such a case, depletes the dealer's sales to the extent of one, and the measure of damages should be the dealer's profit on one sale. Section 2-708 recognizes this, and it rejects the rule developed under the Uniform Sales Act by many courts that the profit cannot be recovered in this case.

William D. Hawkland, *Sales and Bulk Sales* 153-154 (ALI-ABA 1958).

The record[,] which in this case establishes defendant's entitlement to damages in the amount of its prospective profit, at the same time confirms defendant's cognate right to "any incidental damages provided in this Article (Section 2-710)."[3] UCC §2-708(2). . . . [I]t is too clear to require discussion that the seller's right to recover loss of profits is not exclusive and that he may recoup his "incidental" expenses as well. . . .

It follows that plaintiffs are entitled to restitution of the sum of $4,250 paid by them on account of the contract price less an offset to defendant in the amount of $3,253 on account of its lost profit of $2,579 and its incidental damages of $674. . . .

Fuld, C.J., and Burke, Scileppi, Bergan, Breitel and Jasen, JJ., concur. . . .

NOTES ON §2-708(2) AND ATTEMPTS TO CODIFY REMEDIES

1. Seller's remedies under the UCC. The Uniform Commercial Code was promulgated and is kept current by the American Law Institute and the Uniform Law Commissioners; it has been adopted (sometimes with modifications) in every state but Louisiana. Article 2 of the UCC codifies remedies for buyers and sellers of goods. This codification parallels, but is not always identical to, the common law of contracts. When a buyer repudiates the contract or refuses to accept goods that conform to the contract, the seller can recover the difference between the contract price and the market price, §2-708(1), or resell the goods and recover the difference between the contract price and the resale price, §2-706. In either case, seller can also recover any incidental damages, §2-710, such as the cost of reselling, reshipping, or repackaging the rejected goods, less any expenses saved in consequence of the buyer's breach. If buyer keeps the goods but fails to pay, seller can sue for the price. §2-709. If seller discovers that buyer is insolvent, seller can stop delivery or reclaim the goods, §§2-702, 2-704, subject to stringent limitations in the federal Bankruptcy Code. Of course, there is more detail, but that is the basic structure of seller's remedies.

---

3. "Incidental damages to an aggrieved seller include any commercially reasonable charges, expenses or commissions incurred in stopping delivery, in the transportation, care and custody of goods after the buyer's breach, in connection with return or resale of the goods or otherwise resulting from the breach." UCC §2-710.

2. The glitch in §2-708(2). *Neri* addresses a special case, badly codified in §2-708(2). As the facts appeared to the court, it is plain that the award of lost profits plus incidental damage was necessary to put Retail Marine in the position it would have been in had the contract been performed. It is also relatively clear that the framers of the UCC intended this remedy for the volume seller. But it is almost impossible to get that result from the statute.

Are you persuaded by the court's efforts to explain away the last clause of §2-708(2)? A credit for the proceeds of resale makes perfect sense when a seller agrees to sell something he has only one of. Any resale is a sale he would not have made but for the first buyer's breach. But in that case, isn't the seller fully compensated under §2-708(1) or §2-706?

In *Neri*, a credit for the proceeds of resale renders §2-708(2) absurd and futile. Subsection 2 does not come into effect at all unless subsection 1 is "inadequate to put the seller in as good a position as performance would have done." Subsection 1 does not put the seller in that position on these facts, because the market price is equal to the contract price and that measure of damages does not allow for the fact that the seller could have made two sales instead of one. But subsection 2 appears to produce the identical result. The resale price is also equal to the contract price, and crediting plaintiff for proceeds of resale leaves seller in exactly the same inadequate position. Does it help to note that plaintiff is entitled only to "due credit" for proceeds of resale? Does that leave to the court the power to decide how much credit is "due" on any set of facts?

No such argument can avoid the central problem: In the cases where the "due credit for proceeds of resale" clause makes sense, it never comes into effect; in cases where it comes into effect, it makes no sense. Are courts free to never apply part of a statute that seems to be a mistake? Compare Robbins v. Chronister, 402 F.3d 1047 (10th Cir. 2005), collecting cases where courts departed from the literal language of statutes to avoid "absurd" results.

Would the UCC drafters have done better to enact a general damages principle instead of detailed damages rules? They did enact a broad interpretive principle: "The remedies provided by [the Uniform Commercial Code] must be liberally administered to the end that the aggrieved party may be put in as good a position as if the other party had fully performed[.]" UCC §1-305(a). Won't there always be unforeseen situations in which detailed rules designed to implement such a principle fail to do so? When you encounter a mechanical damage rule, make sure you understand what it is trying to accomplish and how it relates to the rightful position.

The particular glitch in §2-708(2) applies to more than just a few oddball cases. Retailers, wholesalers, and manufacturers of mass-produced products, and of many specialty products, are very commonly lost-volume sellers. A prolific UCC scholar has said that the lost-volume remedy "is truly the dominant damage remedy" for "aggrieved sellers" when a buyer breaches before delivery. Roy Ryden Anderson, *Damages for Sellers Under the Code's Profit Formula*, 40 Sw. L.J. 1021, 1063 (1988).

3. Lost-volume sellers and the common law. The *Restatement (Second) of Contracts* §347 cmt. *f* (Am. Law Inst. 1981) adopts the lost-volume seller theory for contracts governed by the common law. Cases are collected in Bitterroot International Systems, Ltd. v. Western Star Trucks, Inc., 153 P.3d 627 (Mont. 2007), where the buyer repudiated a contract for logistical services in the management and routing of its trucking fleet. The court approved a jury instruction requiring plaintiff to prove by a preponderance of the evidence that it had the capacity to perform additional contracts, that those contracts would have been profitable, and that it would have entered into those contracts even if defendant had not breached.

4. Litigating plaintiff's lost-volume status. Even sellers of standardized goods must be put to their proof on the lost-volume issue. Assuming they can get an effectively unlimited supply of goods, it doesn't follow that they can attract an effectively unlimited supply of buyers and supply them all at a profit. The boat Neri ordered was "a very slow mover," and the next year's models had already come out. "[E]very sales person at our location was offered an additional commission to sell that boat." Retail Marine specially advertised the boat, and it offered the second buyer an extra trade-in allowance, recorded on its books as $988. These facts from the record are reported in Stewart Macaulay, John Kidwell, and William Whitford, *Contracts: Law in Action — The Concise Course* 56-58 (2d ed., Matthew Bender 2003). These facts suggest that the second sale did not fully recoup the loss of the first sale, but they tend to undermine the claim that Retail Marine was a lost-volume seller with respect to Neri's boat. Maybe the second buyer would have bought some other boat if he had not bought Neri's boat; maybe he would have bought it at closer to full price. Or maybe that customer would not have bought any boat at all without the special trade-in allowance. The case appears to have been badly litigated, and these facts were not brought to the court's attention.

5. The opposite problem. What if a general damage formula seems to put plaintiff in a better position than if the contract had been performed? This issue has arisen in a series of cases involving claims for contract-market damages where, for one reason or another, plaintiff was not exposed to the risk of changes in the market price. Consider Westlake Petrochemicals, L.L.C. v. United Polychem, Inc., 688 F.3d 232 (5th Cir. 2012), involving a contract for the sale of 60 million pounds of ethylene, a petroleum product used in plastics, for 54 cents a pound. The market price plummeted to 27 cents a pound, and the buyer repudiated the contract. Seller had not yet acquired the ethylene from its suppliers, so it was not stuck with millions of pounds of ethylene worth much less than its original cost. Contract/market damages were $16.3 million, but the court limited damages to seller's lost profit, an amount to be determined on remand. The court appeared to believe that this would be a much smaller number. But if the price at which seller could acquire ethylene had also plummeted, which seems likely, lost profits might have approached contract/market.

The court relied on an earlier case with similar facts, Nobs Chemical, U.S.A., Inc. v. Koppers Co., 616 F.2d 212 (5th Cir. 1980). But there, the seller had locked in its purchase price as well as its sales price to defendant, so its lost profit could be determined precisely. And it had the right to cancel its contract to buy from its supplier, so it was not stuck with a supply of product in a declining market.

The same issue can arise on the buyer's side — if the market price soars, seller refuses to deliver, buyer had a contract to resell at a price lower than the new market price, and buyer can get out of that contract. An example that limits seller to its lost profit is NHF Hog Marketing, Inc. v. Pork-Martin, LLP, 811 N.W.2d 116 (Minn. Ct. App. 2012); the reasoning parallels that in *Westlake* and *Nobs*. One that goes the other way is Tongish v. Thomas, 840 P.2d 471 (Kan. 1992). The Kansas court awarded contract-market damages, holding that the UCC unambiguously authorizes them and that there is no provision like §2-708(2) authorizing smaller damages if contract-market damages put plaintiff in a position better than if the contract had been performed.

Courts that limit recovery to the lost profit on the aborted transaction seem to concede that plaintiff could recover contract-market damages if she had not already locked in a price for purchase (if buyer breaches) or resale (if seller breaches). The *Westlake* court appeared to miss this issue; presumably it remained open on remand. And it appears to be essential to these cases that the plaintiff is not going to be sued on its other contract; otherwise, contract-market damages would be a good approximation of plaintiff's liability on that contract. Plaintiff's contractual arrangements in other transactions are thus treated as central to measuring—and limiting—damages on the contract that was breached. Compare the *September 11th Litigation*, where the court held that plaintiff's contractual obligation to rebuild the towers was not proximately caused by defendants and was irrelevant to the measure of damages.

These and similar cases are discussed at length in Roy Ryden Anderson, *A Look Back at the Future of UCC Damages Remedies*, 71 SMU L. Rev. 185 (2018). Professor Anderson comes down firmly on the side of rejecting contract-market damages whenever plaintiff's loss can be measured by some actual transaction.

NOTES ON EXPECTANCY AND RELIANCE

1. The three "interests" in contract remedies. If the Neris paid Retail Marine its $674 in incidental expenses, then as the court understood the facts, Retail Marine would be as well off as if the contract had never been made. Awarding expected profits involves a choice. In remedies terms, the question is what we mean by rightful position: the position plaintiff would have occupied if she had never made the contract (compensating only the reliance interest), or the position plaintiff would have occupied if the contract had been performed (compensating the expectancy interest).

There is a third option: We could try to restore *defendant* to the position *defendant* occupied before the contract. The general principle of *Hatahley* commits us to a focus on the plaintiff's position, at least if she seeks compensatory damages. But restitutionary measures of recovery sometimes give plaintiff the option of focusing on defendant's position. This option can be attractive, but it has been the subject of much confusion.

Neri illustrates all three interests, but not as neatly as editors might hope. Retail Marine's $674 in expenses is its reliance loss, and the $2,579 in lost profits is its expectancy loss. Retail Marine has no restitution interest at issue; it has not paid or delivered anything to the Neris. But the Neris have a restitutionary interest in recovering their $4,250 deposit, which conferred an unearned benefit on Retail Marine. The Neris have no claim in contract—Retail Marine did not breach—so their right to restitution is not a restitution interest arising *from the contract*. Rather, it is a claim in unjust enrichment of the sort we will examine in Chapter 8. Even though the Neris breached, Retail Marine would be unjustly enriched if it kept the whole deposit. The Neris' breach inflicted $3,253 damage on Retail Marine, but the court says they are still entitled to restitution of the difference—$997.

2. Fuller and Perdue. The vocabulary of expectancy, reliance, and restitution interests comes from a famous article by L.L. Fuller and William R. Perdue, Jr., *The Reliance Interest in Contract Damages*, 46 Yale L.J. 52 (1936). Fuller and Perdue's substantive contribution has been challenged from multiple directions, but their vocabulary continues to dominate.

The expectancy interest is the value of plaintiff's entitlement under the contract. Plaintiff has a gross expectancy, measured by the full payment or performance she was promised under the contract, and which she expected would cover the full cost of her own payment or performance plus a profit margin. Plaintiff also has a net expectancy, measured by her expected profit on the contract—that is, her gross expectancy less the cost of her own payment or performance.

The reliance interest includes everything plaintiff gave up in reliance on the contract. This includes expenditures necessary to perform the contract, which Fuller and Perdue called "essential reliance." They called all other reliance "incidental reliance," and in their original theoretical conception, this was quite broad. Foregone opportunities are a form of reliance, as when plaintiff turns down a proffered new contract that would require time or resources she has already committed to an existing contract.

But reliance of this sort is difficult to prove. The result has been a tendency to think of the reliance interest as the interest in recovering out-of-pocket losses, and of the expectancy interest as the interest in recovering the benefit of the bargain, including any expected profit. Professor Kelly has charged that by the end of their article, Fuller and Perdue had reduced the reliance interest in practice "to a tool with no greater purpose than to produce the smallest plausible damage award." Michael B. Kelly, *The Phantom Reliance Interest in Contract Damages*, 1992 Wis. L. Rev. 1755, 1759.

3. Lost volume and the reliance interest. The $674 reliance interest in *Neri* consists only of out-of-pocket expenses, the narrow and practical measure of reliance damages that Professor Kelly attacks. But in *Neri*, the $674 also fully implements the theoretical definition of the reliance interest: As the court understood the facts, $674 would restore Retail Marine to the position it would have occupied if it had never made a contract with the Neris. Retail Marine's claim to be a lost-volume seller is a claim that it could get as many boats as it could sell. Unlimited supply maximizes Retail Marine's expectancy recovery: It could have sold two boats instead of one. But unlimited supply minimizes its reliance recovery: It did not have to forgo any other contract in reliance on its contract with the Neris.

4. The limit on reliance damages. The first-level statement of the rule is that plaintiff may elect recovery based on expectancy, reliance, or restitution. In fact, clear examples of reliance recoveries are rare; they consist almost entirely of cases where neither side could prove the expectancy. From plaintiff's perspective, reliance damages are "a second-best option, selected only where expectation damages are difficult or impossible to prove." Spring Creek Exploration & Production Co., LLC v. Hess Bakken Investment, II, LLC, 887 F.3d 1003, 1025 (10th Cir. 2018).

To see why, suppose that plaintiff spends $30,000 preparing to perform the contract, and then defendant breaches. If plaintiff can prove she would have made a $10,000 profit, she will recover $40,000. This is her gross expectancy; it covers her expenses and leaves her with her $10,000 net expectancy. If defendant can prove that plaintiff would have lost $10,000, the rule is that this expected loss must be subtracted from any reliance recovery. *Restatement (Second) of Contracts* §349. After paying her expenses, she winds up $10,000 in the hole, and that was her net expectancy. In *Spring Creek*, with millions of dollars at stake and large law firms on both sides, the court said that plaintiffs "have not cited a single case in which a plaintiff was allowed to pursue—let alone recover—reliance damages in excess of ascertainable expectation damages." 887 F.3d at 1027. The logic of this rule is that damages for breach should not make plaintiff better off than if the contract had been fully performed. Under this rule, our hypothetical plaintiff recovers only $20,000: $30,000 reliance less her $10,000 expected loss. So despite talk of an option to recover reliance, the rules actually produce an expectancy recovery whenever either side can prove the expectancy.

5. The restitution interest. The restitution interest has been the subject of much confusion over the years, and unraveling that confusion is best saved for section 8.B.3. But the basics go here, because most applications of the restitution interest in contract have more to do with contract damages than with restitution of unjust enrichment. The best explanation of the difference, and of what the restitution interest means in contract, is Andrew Kull, *Rescission and Restitution*, 61 Bus. Law. 569 (2006).

In Fuller and Perdue's explanation, the reliance interest included all expenditures reasonably made in reliance on the contract; the restitution interest included only expenditures in reliance that had directly benefited the defendant. So the restitution interest was a subset of the reliance interest. In *Neri*, Retail Marine has a $674 reliance interest, but a zero restitution interest, because the boat was never delivered, and consequently, none of the expenses of storing and insuring the boat conferred any benefit on the Neris.

The *Restatement (Third) of Restitution and Unjust Enrichment* §38 (Am. Law Inst. 2011) states rules of contract damages that roughly correspond to what Fuller and Perdue called the reliance and restitution interests. It does not address the expectancy interest at all, leaving that to the *Restatement (Second) of Contracts*. It expressly rejects the formulations of the reliance and restitution interests in the first and second *Restatements of Contracts*, which are the source of much of the confusion.

The newly stated rule is that a victim of breach "may recover damages measured by the cost or value" of his performance. §38(1). Elaborating further, a contract plaintiff may recover either his expenditures made in reasonable reliance on the contract, capped at his provable expectancy as described in note 4. Or he may recover the value of what he delivered, or the value of any other performance that actually benefited defendant, capped at the portion of the contract price allocable to plaintiff's partial performance. This limit on the second measure disapproves a line of cases holding that recovery of the restitution interest is *not* limited by plaintiff's expectancy or even by the contract price. These cases made the restitution interest a way to escape the limits on the reliance interest, but it is hard to think of any good reason why expectancy should limit reliance recoveries but restitution recoveries should be wholly unlimited.

Whether the courts will accept this new formulation remains to be seen. But it draws substantial support from a line of decisions in the Court of Federal Claims and the Federal Circuit. Those courts heard scores of cases in which the government promised special tax and accounting rules for as long as 40 years to sound financial institutions that would take over failed financial institutions. Then Congress passed a statute that took away the special tax and accounting rules. The statute was valid and enforceable, but it was also a breach of contract. United States v. Winstar Corp., 518 U.S. 839 (1996).

The Federal Circuit generally held expectancy damages—what would have happened over 40 years—too speculative to be proved, an issue examined in the notes following Bigelow v. RKO Radio Pictures in section 2.E.5. That holding forced these cases to focus on the reliance and restitution interests. In their treatment of the facts, some of these opinions just seem determined to minimize the government's liability. But in their treatment of the law, they arrived after some trial and error at substantially the same rules as the *Restatement (Third)*. A good example is LaSalle Talman Bank, F.S.B. v. United States, 317 F.3d 1363, 1376 (Fed. Cir. 2003), which treats the value of plaintiff's part performance (the restitution interest, in Fuller and Perdue's terms) as just another way to measure the reliance interest:

> When restitution damages are based on recovery of the expenditures of the non-breaching party in performance of the contract, the award can be viewed as a form of reliance damages, wherein the non-breaching party is restored to its pre-contract position by returning as damages the costs incurred in reliance on the contract. . . .
>
> The principle of restitution damages is to return the costs incurred in performing the contract, costs sometimes conveniently measured by the benefits conferred on the breaching party. . . .

NOTES ON COMPENSATING EXPECTANCIES

1. Why the expectancy? *Neri* presents the pure choice between reliance and expectancy, with all numbers proved to the court's satisfaction. Why are Retail Marine's damages $3,253 instead of $674? That is, why does the law protect expectancies? The rule is well settled. It is fundamentally premised on the view that the contract creates rights to which the plaintiff becomes entitled, and this contractual entitlement is what the plaintiff loses when defendant breaches. The rightful position is the position plaintiff would have occupied if the contract had been performed.

But the rule is the subject of continued controversy among academics. This section examines that debate—why contract damages try to put plaintiff in the position defendant would have put him in instead of the position he would have occupied on his own; whether that is true only in contract; and if so, what is so special about contract. This section also asks a closely related question of more immediate practical importance: Are there exceptional cases where plaintiff cannot recover the expectancy even in contract?

2. Academic alternatives. Professor Wolcher believes that expectancy damages unfairly penalize promisors' right to change their minds. Louis E. Wolcher, *The Accommodation of Regret in Contract Remedies,* 73 Iowa L. Rev. 797 (1988). Law-and-economics scholars increasingly take the view that neither compensation nor any conception of the rightful position should matter; they tend to think that the purpose of remedies for breach of contract should be to adjust incentives for performance or breach. Some of them suggest that damages should be continuously adjustable if need be to get incentives right. Richard Craswell, *Against Fuller and Perdue,* 67 U. Chi. L. Rev. 99 (2000). Others suggest that default rules should be clear, simple, and even a bit one sided, to encourage contracting parties to include explicit remedies provisions in the contract. Robert E. Scott & George G. Triantis, *Embedded Options and the Case Against Compensation in Contract Law,* 104 Colum. L. Rev. 1428 (2004). Professor Goldberg views protection of seller's expectancy in the lost-volume seller remedy as absurd, but that appears to be principally because he believes that no buyer ever contracts to buy anything; contracts merely give buyers an option to buy if they choose to perform. Victor P. Goldberg, *The Lost Volume Seller, R.I.P.,* 2 Criterion J. Innovation 205 (2017).

Such proposals do not appear to have had much influence on courts: Expectancy damages remain the basic rule, and Professor Craswell's continuously adjustable measures of damage would be wholly unworkable in real litigation. Professor Eisenberg has argued that all the proposals for remedies based on goals other than making the promisee indifferent between performance and compensation—goals such as adjusting the incentives of the parties or maximizing the joint value of the contract—are wrongheaded, inadministrable, underdeveloped, mutually inconsistent, and incapable of being made consistent. Melvin A. Eisenberg, *Actual and Virtual Specific Performance, the Theory of Efficient Breach, and the Indifference Principle in Contract Law,* 93 Cal. L. Rev. 975, 981-989 (2005).

Even so, contracting parties often negotiate alternative rules. Consumers are often permitted to cancel even after performance, by returning the goods for a refund. Many contracts include limitation-of-remedies or liquidated-damage clauses, or options, buyout fees, and other sophisticated provisions that may be remedies terms disguised to look like substantive contract terms. We will consider some basic examples of these clauses in section 2.E.1. Courts will generally enforce such terms, with some limits and exceptions. The question is what remedy the law should provide in the many contracts that simply say what the parties promise to do for each other.

3. Expectancy in a credit economy. One reason for compensating expectancies is that in a credit economy, an expectation of future income has present cash value. This is the reason emphasized by Fuller and Perdue:

> The essence of a credit economy lies in the fact that it tends to eliminate the distinction between present and future (promised) goods. Expectations of future values become, for purposes of trade, present values. In a society in which credit has become a significant and pervasive institution, it is inevitable that the expectancy created by an enforceable promise should be regarded as a kind of property, and breach of the promise as an injury to that property. . . . That the promisee had not "used" the property which the promise represents (had not relied on the promise) is as immaterial as the question whether the plaintiff in trespass . . . was using his property at the time it was encroached upon. . . .
>
> The law measures damages by the expectancy *in part* because society views the expectancy as a present value; society views the expectancy as a present value *in part* because the law . . . gives protection to the expectancy.

46 Yale L.J. at 57-63.

4. Efficiency, in general. Judge Posner, a prominent founder of the law-and-economics movement, still defends the expectancy measure as the best approximation of plaintiff's economic loss, even if imperfect. He would probably not disagree with the credit explanation, but he offers other practical reasons:

> In long-run competitive equilibrium, the total revenues of the sellers in a market are equal to their total costs; there is no "profit" in an economic sense but merely reimbursement of the costs of capital, of entrepreneurial effort, and of other inputs, including the marketing efforts that led up to the contract. All these items of cost are excluded by the reliance measure of damages, which will tend, therefore, to understate the social costs of breach. Even if the breach occurs before the victim has begun to perform, he may have incurred costs (especially precontractual search costs, but these are not recoverable as damages—they are difficult for the other party to estimate in advance and often difficult to assign to a specific contract). Suppose the victim has not incurred any costs before performance begins, so that until then his reliance costs are zero. Then if reliance costs were the exclusive measure of damages, parties could walk away from their contracts whenever a contract was still executory. Except in special situations, it is unclear what the social gain would be from such a "cooling off" period, and there may be a social loss as a result of uncertainty and the need to make additional transactions.

Richard A. Posner, *Economic Analysis of Law* §4.10 at 133 (9th ed., Wolters Kluwer 2014).

5. Efficient breach? Judge Posner also offers another reason, better known but more controversial. Recall the economic view that profitable violations of law, not including intentional torts, should be encouraged so long as violators compensate their victims. In contract, this view leads to a concept that its supporters call "efficient breach." Suppose a contract to sell custom widgets for $10,000, and that the buyer will use the widgets in his factory and make a $1,000 profit. Now suppose that before the widgets are delivered, some third party offers seller $10,500 for the same widgets. Or suppose the third party offers $12,000 for the widgets. Should the seller breach his contract and sell to the third party in either case? How do we know whether the third party's use for the widgets is more valuable than the original buyer's use for the same widgets?

The only way to get the seller to take account of the value of the buyer's use for the widgets is to make the seller liable for the value of that use. If seller knows that he must pay buyer's $1,000 expectancy if he breaches, then he won't breach unless the third party offers more than $11,000. If seller's liability were limited to buyer's reliance, seller might breach even when breach is inefficient. See *id.* at 131.

This is a plausible explanation where it applies. But how wide a range of cases is that? Does this example help explain why Retail Marine recovers its expectancy? If Neri can't use the boat, it is inefficient to make him accept delivery. An unwanted boat in Neri's driveway would be a waste. The law prevents this result with the rule of no recovery for avoidable consequences (perhaps better known as the duty to mitigate damages): Retail Marine cannot deliver the boat and demand full payment despite Neri's cancellation of the order. *That* is an efficiency-protecting rule.

But whether Retail Marine recovers reliance or expectancy seems to be more about distribution of gains and losses than about allocation of scarce resources. No rule will deprive anyone of a boat; Retail Marine successfully claimed that it could get as many boats as it could sell. And its distributional services will not be reallocated to anyone else, whatever the rules governing Neri's lawsuit. We can say that Neri must pay full expectancy damages to ensure that he takes account of the cost to Retail Marine before he decides that he values medical care more highly than a boat. There may be some value to thus deterring frivolous changes of mind, although Professor Wolcher might view this as a cost. But any effect on resource allocation is attenuated at best. Professor Triantis seems fully committed to economic analysis, but he appears to think efficient breach is as obsolete as expectancy damages are in his view.

6. A duty to keep promises? The simplest explanation of expectancy damages may be the widespread moral belief that people should keep their promises. If the right thing to do is to perform the contract, but for some reason performance must be commuted to payment of a sum of money, then isn't the expected value of performance the right amount of money? Compensation based on the reliance interest would assume that it is equally acceptable to perform or withdraw the promise, and that the promisee's only right is not to be made worse off than if the promise had never been made. Of course, an explanation based on a moral duty to keep promises will never satisfy critics who believe that promisors are entitled to change their mind or that contracts are merely options. But might it still be an important explanation for many judges and ordinary citizens? Does it matter whether Neri really got sick or simply found another boat he liked better?

Posner's concept of efficient breach assumes that breach of contract is often a good thing that should be encouraged. He would deal harshly with "opportunistic" breachers—people who accept and retain the other side's performance and then refuse to pay or perform in return. *Id.* at 129. But he thinks that most breaches result from inability to perform, from inability to perform at reasonable cost, or from changed circumstances that make performance wasteful rather than beneficial. Doctrines such as impossibility, frustration of purpose, and mitigation of damages take account of such obstacles to performance.

More controversially, Posner and many other economically minded scholars approve breach to pursue a better deal that comes along after the contract is signed. Such scholars tend to dismiss claims of a duty to keep promises as based on a morality that is obsolete or irrelevant. Each side tends to assume that its own view of promise keeping reflects a cultural consensus.

Small-scale surveys cast some light on relevant subsets of public opinion. One survey asked 119 businesspeople in North Carolina about cases where performance was possible but the obligor breached because prices changed or he got a better offer elsewhere, as distinguished from cases where unforeseen events made performance difficult or impossible. David Baumer & Patricia Marschall, *Willful Breach of Contract for the Sale of Goods: Can the Bane of Business Be an Economic Bonanza?*, 65 Temple L. Rev.

159 (1992). Eighty-eight percent of businesspeople said such a breach was unethical; 81 percent said they would withhold future business from such a breacher.

A series of small-scale social psychology experiments are harder to describe and interpret, but highly suggestive. Subjects were given a series of breach scenarios and, in some cases, tort scenarios that caused identical harm. On average, respondents found breach of contract more immoral than negligence; they awarded greater damages for breach than for negligence. They found breach to take advantage of a better offer elsewhere more immoral than breach because of some unforeseen cost or difficulty, and they awarded damages accordingly. Tess Wilkinson-Ryan & Jonathan Baron, *Moral Judgment and Moral Heuristics in Breach of Contract*, 6 J. Empirical Legal Stud. 405 (2009). A related study with similar experiments concludes that victims of deliberate breach react so strongly because they feel betrayed; they trusted their contractual partner, and he played them for a sucker. Tess Wilkinson-Ryan & David A. Hoffman, *Breach Is for Suckers*, 63 Vand. L. Rev. 1003 (2010).

CHATLOS SYSTEMS, INC. v. NATIONAL CASH REGISTER CORP.
670 F.2d 1304 (3d Cir. 1982)

Before ALDISERT, ROSENN and WEIS, Circuit Judges.

PER CURIAM. . . .

Chatlos Systems initiated this action . . . alleging . . . breach of warranty regarding an NCR 399/656 computer system it had acquired from defendant National Cash Register Corp. . . . Following a nonjury trial, the district court determined that defendant was liable for breach of warranty and awarded $57,152.76 damages for breach of warranty and consequential damages in the amount of $63,558.16. 479 F. Supp. 738 (D.N.J. 1979). Defendant appealed and this court affirmed the district court's findings of liability, set aside the award of consequential damages, and remanded for a recalculation of damages for breach of warranty. 635 F.2d 1081 (3d Cir. 1980). On remand, applying the "benefit of the bargain" formula of N.J. Stat. Ann. §12A:2-714(2) (UCC §2-714(2)),[1] the district court determined the damages to be $201,826.50,[2] to which it added an award of prejudgment interest. Defendant now appeals. . . .

Waiving the opportunity to submit additional evidence as to value on the remand which we directed, appellant chose to rely on the record of the original trial and submitted no expert testimony on the market value of a computer which would have performed the functions NCR had warranted. Notwithstanding our previous holding that contract price was not necessarily the same as market value, appellant faults the district judge for rejecting its contention that the [$46,020] contract price for the NCR 399/656 was the only competent record evidence of the value of the system as warranted. The district court relied instead on the testimony of [plaintiff's] expert, Dick Brandon, who, without estimating the value of an NCR model 399/656, presented his estimate of the value of a computer system that would perform all of

---

1. Section 2-714(2) states:

The measure of damages for breach of warranty is the difference at the time and place of acceptance between the value of the goods accepted and the value they would have had if they had been as warranted, unless special circumstances show proximate damages of a different amount.

2. The district court found the fair market value of the system as warranted to be $207,826.50; from this is subtracted its determination of the value of the goods delivered, $6,000.

the functions that the NCR 399/656 had been warranted to perform. Brandon did not limit his estimate to equipment of any one manufacturer; he testified regarding manufacturers who could have made systems that would perform the functions that appellant had warranted the NCR 399/656 could perform. He acknowledged that the systems about which he testified were not in the same price range as the NCR 399/656. Appellant likens this testimony to substituting a Rolls Royce for a Ford. . . .

Appellee did not order, nor was it promised, merely a specific NCR computer model, but an NCR computer system with specified capabilities. The correct measure of damages, under §2-714(2), is the difference between the fair market value of the goods accepted and the value they would have had if they had been as warranted. Award of that sum is not confined to instances where there has been an increase in value between date of ordering and date of delivery. It may also include the benefit of a contract price which, for whatever reason quoted, was particularly favorable for the customer. Evidence of the contract price may be relevant to the issue of fair market value, but it is not controlling. . . . Appellee developed evidence of the worth of a computer with the capabilities promised by NCR, and the trial court properly credited the evidence.

Appellee was aided, moreover, by the testimony of Frank Hicks, NCR's programmer, who said that he told his company's officials that the "current software was not sufficient in order to deliver the program that the customer . . . required. . . ." Hicks recommended that Chatlos be given an NCR 8200 but was told, "that will not be done." Gerald Greenstein, another NCR witness, admitted that the 8200 series was two levels above the 399 in sophistication and price. This testimony supported Brandon's statement that the price of the hardware needed to perform Chatlos' requirements would be in the $100,000 to $150,000 range.

Essentially, then the trial judge was confronted with the conflicting value estimates submitted by the parties. . . . Although we might have come to a different conclusion on the value of the equipment as warranted had we been sitting as trial judges, we . . . may reverse the district court only if its factual determinations were clearly erroneous. . . .

The judgment of the district court will be affirmed.

ROSENN, Circuit Judge, dissenting. . . .

II

A . . .

Chatlos presented its case under a theory that although, as a sophisticated purchaser, it bargained for several months before arriving at a decision on the computer system it required and the price of $46,020, it is entitled, because of the breach of warranty, to damages predicated on a considerably more expensive system. . . . [E]ven if it bargained for a cheap system, i.e., one whose low cost reflects its inferior quality, because that system did not perform as bargained for, it is now entitled to damages measured by the value of a system . . . of far superior quality and accordingly more expensive.

The statutory measure of damages for breach of warranty specifically provides that the measure is the difference at the time and place of acceptance between the value "of the goods accepted" and the "value they would have had if they had been as warranted." The focus of the statute is upon "the goods accepted"—not other hypothetical goods which may perform equivalent functions. "Moreover, the value to be considered is the reasonable market value of the *goods delivered*, not the value of the goods to a particular purchaser or for a particular purpose." KLPR-TV v. Visual Electronics Corp., 465 F.2d 1382, 1387 (8th Cir. 1972) (emphasis added). . . .

Although NCR warranted performance, the failure of its equipment to perform, absent any evidence of the value of any NCR 399 system on which to base fair market value, does not permit a market value based on systems wholly unrelated to the goods sold. . . . NCR rightly contends that the "comparable" systems on which Brandon drew were substitute goods of greater technological power and capability and not acceptable in determining damages for breach of warranty under §2-714. Furthermore, Brandon's hypothetical system did not exist and its valuation was largely speculation.

III

The purpose of . . . §2-714 is to put the buyer in the same position he would have been in if there had been no breach. See §1-106(1) [now UCC §1-305(a)]. . . . The buyer may not receive more than it bargained for; it may not obtain the value of a superior computer system which it did not purchase even though such a system can perform all of the functions the inferior system was designed to serve. . . .

NOTES ON EXCESSIVE EXPECTANCIES

1. Buyer's remedies under the UCC. A seller might repudiate the contract or fail to deliver the goods, or deliver nonconforming goods that the buyer rightfully returns. These are breaches that leave the buyer without the goods he was promised under the contract. In that event, the buyer has two choices: (1) recover the difference between the contract price and the market price, §2-713(1); or (2) buy replacement goods and recover the difference between the contract price and the cost of replacement (usually called the cover price, §2-712). In either case, the buyer may also recover incidental damages. §2-715(1). She may also recover consequential damages that the seller had reason to know about at the time of contracting and that the buyer could not reasonably avoid. §2-715(2)(a). These remedies largely parallel the seller's remedies, but doing without the promised goods can cause harms to buyers—consequential damages—that have few parallels for sellers. In addition, if the goods are unique or the buyer is otherwise unable to cover, the buyer may seek specific performance of the contract. §2-716.

Chatlos deals with a different form of breach by the seller; the goods are delivered, and accepted, but are not as warranted. For this, plaintiff can recover the difference between the value of the goods as delivered and the value of the goods if they had been as warranted, §2-714(2), plus any incidental or consequential damages under §2-715.

2. Excessive expectancies? Did Chatlos recover too much? Don't make the legal issue go away by rejecting the findings of fact. The legal issue could be presented quite unambiguously. Suppose NCR made specific written representations that the computer would do X, and no computer under $207,000 would do X. Chatlos's expectancy was that it would get a computer that would do X for $46,000. That's a great deal, but it's what Chatlos was promised. Does NCR's foolish promise entitle Chatlos to something it never could have gotten otherwise? If you don't like the result, suppose the computer had done what that model was supposed to do, so that it was worth $46,000. Should Chatlos recover nothing? No matter what NCR warranted?

Most puzzling are cases where plaintiff consciously expected far more than she paid for. Suppose a contract to sell a Stradivarius violin for $100,000. If it's a fake, and a real Stradivarius is worth $3 million (not a hypothetical number), can plaintiff recover $3 million less the actual value of the fake? The question is posed but not answered in Smith v. Zimbalist, 38 P.2d 170 (Cal. Ct. App. 1934). If a patent medicine man sells a "cancer cure" for $2, does he become liable for whatever a jury decides a cancer cure is worth? Isn't that what UCC §2-714(2) says? Should plaintiffs be limited to *reasonable* expectancies? Or is reasonableness just evidentiary on the question whether plaintiff really expected what she now claims? Should frauds who breach unbelievable warranties have less liability than honest businesspeople who commit minor breaches? Keep in mind that one way to overcome a victim's resistance is to offer a bargain.

Chatlos involved a federal court in diversity jurisdiction interpreting New Jersey law. A federal district judge in New Jersey has expressed "some doubt" that the New Jersey Supreme Court would have reached the same result. Boyce v. Greenwich Boat Works, Inc., 27 F. Supp. 2d 543, 553 (D.N.J. 1998).

3. An incredible bargain on oil? The limits of compensation for expectancies were tested in Texaco, Inc. v. Pennzoil Co., 729 S.W.2d 768 (Tex. Ct. App. 1987). Whether any contract ever existed was hotly disputed, but the jury found that Pennzoil had a contract to buy three-sevenths of Getty Oil for $3.4 billion. Less than 48 hours later, the Getty interests reneged and sold to Texaco. Because Pennzoil's share of Getty would have included a billion barrels of oil, the jury plausibly valued Pennzoil's expectancy at $7.5 billion. (There is more about this valuation in section 2.D.) Do any of the explanations for compensating expectancies explain why we compensate this one?

> Pennzoil's expectancy was very large, very short-lived, and contingent on a factual dispute about intent. . . .
>
> There is no pretense that Pennzoil conferred some social benefit deserving of a billion barrels of oil as compensation, and there is no basis to claim that the oil would be more valuable in Pennzoil's hands than in Texaco's, or vice versa. Economic efficiency is not at issue here except in marginal and attenuated ways. This was high stakes poker for distributional gains. The conflict within Getty created an opportunity for someone to reap a windfall, and Pennzoil seized the opportunity.
>
> The reason for compensating Pennzoil's expectancy is simply that it falls within the general rule that we compensate contractual expectancies. All rules have boundaries, and some cases fall close to the line. . . . But once the jury found a binding contract, the case fell within the rule, and Pennzoil was entitled to full compensation for its expectancy. . . .
>
> The traditional rule makes it possible for parties to know when they are bound. . . . If the right to an expectancy were subject to review by judge or jury to determine whether the plaintiff really deserved the expectancy, . . . [n]o amount of planning would enable parties to know exactly when they entered into a full contractual relationship with full contractual remedies.

Douglas Laycock, *The Remedies Issues: Compensatory Damages, Specific Performance, Punitive Damages, Supersedeas Bonds, and Abstention*, 9 Rev. Litig. 473, 491-492 (1990).

Compare Mark P. Gergen, *The Texaco-Pennzoil Affair and the Economic Analysis of Remedies for Mistakes in Contract Formation*, 9 Rev. Litig. 441, 446-452 (1990). Gergen argues that the Getty-Pennzoil contract resulted from a mistake—Getty sold too cheap. This is classically not the sort of mistake for which a court will relieve a party from its contract. But Gergen argues that it is a mistake nonetheless, and that the best remedy for a mistake in contract formation is reliance damages. Pennzoil's inability to acquire Getty at a mistakenly low price is not a real economic loss, but merely a failure to collect a windfall. The risk of being held liable for such a mistaken expectancy increases the risk of contract and makes parties unduly cautious about contracting in the first place.

4. Impossible expectancies? Similarly in *Chatlos*, Professor Gergen would say that the loss of Chatlos's expectancy was not a real loss, because it was never possible that a $46,000 computer could do what Chatlos expected. Gergen sees no societal interest in compensating the gullible for impossible dreams not realized. Is there a societal interest in holding promisors responsible for what they promised, so they will not promise the moon and then defend on the ground that it was never possible anyway?

Compare Gergen and *Chatlos* with Overstreet v. Norden Laboratories, Inc., 669 F.2d 1286 (6th Cir. 1982). Defendant warranted that a vaccine would prevent a disease that causes miscarriages in pregnant mares. Plaintiff used the vaccine, but his mares miscarried anyway. The court held that plaintiff could not recover the value of the lost foals unless he could show causation in the sense that the warranty induced him not to use some other product that would have prevented the miscarriages. *Id.* at 1295-1297. This is Gergen's principle of no recovery for impossible expectancies.

Doctrinally, the case fell in a different niche than *Chatlos*. The court did not treat the value of the foals as going to the value of the product if it had been as warranted, but as consequential damages from the breach. That moved the case from UCC §2-714 to §2-715, and that introduced causation as an express element of plaintiff's claim.

5. Efficiency again. Consider another of Judge Posner's examples distinguishing efficient from inefficient breaches. Seller agrees to build and deliver a machine for $100,000. The next day she repudiates the contract, having realized that it will cost $105,000 to perform. Buyer has incurred no reliance costs and can still get the machine from the second lowest bidder for $112,000. Buyer's expectancy damages are the difference between the contract price and the cover price, or $12,000. Posner says that Seller's breach is inefficient—it inflicts a $12,000 loss on Buyer to achieve a $5,000 gain for Seller. Limiting damages to reliance would encourage this inefficient breach. Posner, *Economic Analysis of Law* §4.10 at 131-132.

Is Posner's hypothetical just *Chatlos* and *Pennzoil*, with only the proportions changed? NCR bid $46,000; its cost to perform is something over $200,000; and if a second bid had been obtained, that bid would also be something over $200,000. Should NCR be liable for Chatlos's expectancy so that it will have adequate incentive to perform as long as no one else can do it cheaper?

SMITH v. BOLLES
132 U.S. 125 (1889)

The Court in its opinion, stated the case as follows:

Richard J. Bolles [sued] Lewis W. Smith . . . to recover damages for alleged fraudulent representations in the sale of shares of mining stock. . . . [P]laintiff [bought] four thousand shares . . . at $1.50 per share . . . . Plaintiff then alleged that . . . "said stock and mining property was then, and still is, wholly worthless; and that had the same been as represented by defendant it would have been worth at least ten dollars per share. . . ." . . .

Chief Justice FULLER delivered the opinion of the Court. . . .
   [T]he court charged the jury . . . that

> the measure of recovery is generally the difference between the contract price and the reasonable market value, if the property had been as represented to be, or in case the property or stock is entirely worthless, then its value is what it would have been worth if it had been as represented by the defendant . . . .

In this there was error. . . . What the plaintiff might have gained is not the question, but what he had lost by being deceived into the purchase. The suit was not brought for breach of contract. The gist of the action was that the plaintiff was fraudulently induced by the defendant to purchase stock upon the faith of certain false and fraudulent representations. . . . If the jury believed from the evidence that the defendant was guilty of the fraudulent and false representations alleged, and that the purchase of stock had been made in reliance thereon, then the defendant was liable to respond in such damages as naturally and proximately resulted from the fraud. He was bound to make good the loss sustained, such as the moneys the plaintiff had paid out and interest, and any other outlay legitimately attributable to defendant's fraudulent conduct; but this liability did not include the expected fruits of an unrealized speculation. The reasonable market value, if the property had been as represented, afforded, therefore, no proper element of recovery.

Nor had the contract price the bearing given to it by the court. What the plaintiff paid for the stock was properly put in evidence, not as the basis of the application of the rule in relation to the difference between the contract price and the market or actual value, but as establishing the loss he had sustained in that particular. If the stock had a value in fact, that would necessarily be applied in reduction of the damages. . . .

For the error indicated, the judgment is reversed and the cause remanded with a direction to grant a new trial.

NOTES ON EXPECTANCY IN TORT

1. Expectancies in fraud. The conventional wisdom is that expectancy damages are recoverable only in contract, not in tort. That is why Chatlos recovers its expectancy and Bolles does not. What sense does that make? Why should plaintiff's right to recover his expectancy depend on whether he frames his complaint in fraud or breach of warranty? The anomaly is heightened by the difference between the mental element of the two wrongs—fraud requires deliberate misrepresentation or reckless disregard of the truth, but one is liable for breach of warranty even if his failure to deliver the goods as warranted is innocent and not even negligent.

Many states have responded to the anomaly by allowing plaintiffs to recover the value of what was promised whether they sue in fraud or in warranty. An example is Formosa Plastics Corp. U.S.A. v. Presidio Engineers & Contractors, Inc., 960 S.W.2d 41, 49 (Tex. 1998), recognizing plaintiff's right to choose between the out-of-pocket measure and the benefit-of-the-bargain measure in Texas fraud cases. With respect to the sale of goods, the UCC provides that "[r]emedies for material misrepresentation or fraud include all remedies available under this Article for non-fraudulent breach." §2-721.

2. The federal rule. The federal courts did not follow this trend; they have adhered to the out-of-pocket rule of Smith v. Bolles: "Under that measure, damages are calculated as the difference between the actual—fraud-tainted—transaction price and the true value of the security measured on the date of the transaction." Michael J. Kaufman, *Securities Litigation: Damages* §3.13 (West 2001 & Supp.). A plaintiff who buys a stock in January for $15 a share on the basis of a fraudulent misrepresentation, and sells it in December for $10 a share, has not necessarily suffered $5 in damages. The price might have declined for many reasons: the truth came out, the general market went down, the company suffered some misfortune unrelated to the fraud. Plaintiff's damages were the difference between $15 a share and the true value of the stock when purchased in January. Of course there were variations and exceptions, and the price of the stock after the truth came out often had evidentiary value on the stock's true value at the time of the fraud.

3. "Loss causation." Simply alleging that "the price on the date of purchase was inflated because of the misrepresentation" is no longer enough to state a cause of action for securities fraud. Dura Pharmaceuticals, Inc. v. Broudo, 544 U.S. 336, 340 (2005). The Court said that plaintiff has suffered no loss at that instant, because he could immediately resell the stock at the same fraud-inflated price. And if he sells later at a loss, that loss might have been caused by the misrepresentation or by any other factor affecting the market price. Plaintiff must both plead and prove "loss causation"—that his loss was caused by the misrepresentation.

There is nothing new about taking account of the possibility that a subsequent decline in price might be caused by factors unrelated to the fraud. And it is not new to recognize that an investor who buys at a price inflated by fraud, and quickly resells at a price equally inflated by fraud, has an offsetting benefit from the fraud and no net damage. The real change in *Dura* may be to make these issues part of plaintiff's obligation to plead and prove as part of his prima facie case. Surveys of the early cases implementing *Dura* suggest that plaintiffs have generally been able to meet this burden. See Kaufman, §§11A:14 and 11A:15.

When the truth came out in *Dura* itself, the stock's price "temporarily fell but almost fully recovered within one week." 544 U.S. at 339. So it is quite plausible that plaintiffs were not damaged—except for those who joined in the panic selling immediately after the disclosure. The Court might have read this price history as evidence that the stock price was never actually inflated by the earlier misrepresentation. The Court appears to have read it instead, or also, as evidence that few class members were damaged even if the price had been inflated.

4. Expectancies not derived from defendant. Tort plaintiffs routinely recover losses of future wages or future profits—money that they expected to acquire but never had before the tort. But there is an important difference between the tort cases and the contract cases. In the contract cases, plaintiff is seeking to recover an expectancy that is itself a product of defendant's promise—an expectancy that never would have existed but for defendant. In the typical tort case, plaintiff's expectancy is not derived from defendant. Plaintiff expected wages or profits from her own efforts, and defendant's wrong disrupted that expectancy. In that context, there can be no doubt that full compensation requires defendant to restore what plaintiff would have earned. The argument about expectancy versus reliance has real bite only when plaintiff seeks to collect on an expectancy that would never have existed at all but for the defendant's promise. That argument typically arises in contract cases, but also in torts such as fraud and misrepresentation, where the tort includes a promise. See generally Michael B. Kelly, *The Phantom Reliance Interest in Tort Damages*, 38 San Diego L. Rev. 169 (2001), arguing that tort law generally compensates lost expectancies.

D.   CONSEQUENTIAL DAMAGES

BUCK v. MORROW
21 S.W. 398 (Tex. Civ. App. 1893)

STEPHENS, J.

On the 1st day of May, 1886, H.C. Morrow leased to A.C. Buck a certain pasture in Wise county, for a term of five years, commencing with that date, for the sum of $125 per year, with the provision that after the second year, should Morrow have occasion to sell the land, he should compensate Buck for any or all losses occasioned by the sale. It was understood between the parties at the time that the land was being leased by Buck to graze cattle thereon.

[¶] At the expiration of two years the land was sold, and appellant, Buck, dispossessed. He offered to prove on the trial, by the witness J.L. Campbell, that, at the time he was dispossessed, he had 140 head of cattle in the pasture, under the charge and control of said Campbell, and that he and Campbell had made diligent inquiry and search for another pasture for the cattle, but failed to find one; that said cattle were turned out of the pasture on the commons, and ran at large on the range for a period of five months before another could be procured; that during the time the cattle were on the range it required an extra hand to look after and keep them rounded up, at a cost of $1.50 per day, which was a reasonable charge; that all reasonable diligence was used to prevent said cattle from straying off, but during said time 15 of them were lost, reasonably worth $15 per head, and, after diligent search, could not be found. Further evidence was offered as to the expense of pasturing the cattle in another pasture thereafter procured. This testimony was all excluded, on the ground that it was immaterial, the measure of damages being the difference, if any, between the contract price and the rental value of the pasture for the unexpired term.

[¶] The rule followed by the trial court in excluding this evidence is undoubtedly the correct rule for measuring the general damages incident to the breach of a covenant for quiet enjoyment in a lease. In addition to the difference between the rent to be paid and the actual value of the unexpired term, the tenant may also recover as special damages such extra expense and damage, if any, as are the natural and proximate result of the breach. The rule which confines the general damage to the difference between the rental value and the stipulated rent seems to rest upon the assumption that the tenant can go at once into the market and obtain like property. Where the reason of the rule does not exist, it would seem that the rule itself should not apply to the exclusion of all other considerations in estimating the damages. Special damages, in addition, have been allowed in many instances. It was held in De la Zerda v. Korn, 25 Tex. 188, 194 (Supp. 1860), that injury to the tenant's goods or stock in trade, in addition to the value of the use and occupation of the premises, should be considered in estimating the damages.

[¶] Whatever special damage naturally and proximately resulted to appellant from the sale of the land and termination of the lease—whatever may reasonably be supposed to have entered into the contemplation of the parties at the time of the contract—he should recover. The items of expense which he sought to prove for pasturage elsewhere, we think, should be included in the general damages, measured by the difference between the market value of the residue of the term and the contract price, and that part of the evidence was perhaps properly excluded.

As to the extra expense and loss incident to a temporary holding of his cattle on the commons pending a diligent effort to secure another pasture, if the proof should show that these items were the proximate result of the sale of the land and termination at that time of the lease, and that thereby a loss was sustained, which otherwise would not have occurred, and that it was not the result of the want of proper care and diligence on the part of appellant, we think he would be entitled to recover the amount of loss thus sustained, as special damages. . . .

HEAD, J., disqualified, and not sitting.

NOTES ON GENERAL AND SPECIAL DAMAGES

1. The facts in Buck v. Morrow. Plaintiff has expended $1.50 per day for five months, or $225. He has also lost 15 cattle worth $15 per head, for another $225. In addition, his rent will be higher for the two years and seven months between the time he was able to rent alternative pasture and the time his original lease would have expired. The opinion does not indicate what the higher rent was, but the original rent was only $125 per year. Even if there had been substantial inflation in the intervening two years, plaintiff's losses from the difference in rent would likely be a small fraction of the $450 in extra wages and lost cattle. Assuming plaintiff acted reasonably and could not have found alternative pasture any sooner than he did, is there any theory under which he is restored to his rightful position without being compensated for the extra wages and lost cattle? What purpose is served by distinguishing the increase in rent (general damages) from the extra wages and lost cattle (special damages)? And why would the trial court say the special damages cannot be recovered?

2. Other examples. We have already encountered a number of cases in which the court awarded special or consequential damages, without noting any particular difficulty. In United States v. Hatahley, in section 2.A, the court authorized recovery for plaintiffs' loss of sheep, goats, and cattle that resulted from the loss of their horses and burros. In Neri v. Retail Marine Corp., in section 2.C, the seller recovered $674 for incidental expenses of storage, insurance, and maintenance of the unsold boat, and most lawyers would characterize the profits from the lost sale as consequential damages. It seems clear that such losses result from defendant's wrongdoing, and that plaintiff must recover them if he is to be restored to his rightful position. Yet there is a long-standing suspicion of such damages, reflected in the trial court's judgment in Buck v. Morrow. The suspicion lingers even today, although the trend is certainly to award consequential damages more freely.

3. Lingering hostility to consequentials. Consider §1-305(a) of the UCC:

> The remedies provided by [the UCC] must be liberally administered to the end that the aggrieved party will be put in as good a position as if the other party had fully performed but neither consequential or special damages nor penal damages may be had except as specifically provided in [the UCC] or by other rule of law.

The contrast between the two halves of this provision is sharp, and is made even sharper in the Official Comment:

> Subsection (a) is intended to . . . make it clear that compensatory damages are limited to compensation. They do not include consequential or special damages. . . .

Could the drafters really have believed that compensation is complete even though plaintiff is not reimbursed for his consequential losses? Perhaps not; the UCC frequently provides for consequential damages. Examples are §2-715 (Buyer's Incidental and Consequential Damages) and §4-402 (Bank's Liability to Customer for Wrongful Dishonor).

Another manifestation of suspicion of consequential damages is the pleading rule in Federal Rule of Civil Procedure 9(g) and similar state rules: "If an item of special damage is claimed, it must be specifically stated." A whole area in which consequential damages are almost never awarded is eminent domain. The rule was reaffirmed in United States v. Fifty Acres of Land, 469 U.S. 24, 33 (1984).

4. Why the historic hostility? The traditional reasons for hostility to consequential damages are that such damages are more speculative, less certain, more remote, and more likely to have been avoidable if the plaintiff had been more diligent. There are doctrines for dealing with each of these concerns; we will take them up in section 2.E. But there is a sense in many of the cases, especially the older cases, that such doctrines are not enough and must be supplemented by a general hostility to consequential damages, even at the cost of failing to achieve the goal of compensation. Here is a statement of the traditional view:

> For a wrong, the law's ideal, not always realized, is compensation, neither more nor less. Theoretically the loss to an injured party because of a broken contract is its value to him. Yet this rule may not always be safely applied. He may have in mind or claim that he had in mind some special object which would make the contract of extraordinary value. It is well to avoid temptation. It is well to have some theory applicable to the majority of cases. The rule is, therefore, limited. As such value, for such loss, he may recover as damages only those that would naturally arise from the breach itself, or those that might reasonably be supposed to have been contemplated by the parties when the contract was made. True this is an arbitrary rule. By it full justice is not always done. But it has seemed a politic one.

Orester v. Dayton Rubber Manufacturing Co., 126 N.E. 510, 511 (N.Y. 1920).

5. Should the hostility continue? You are not yet in a position to assess the adequacy of the doctrines that deal directly with certainty, remoteness, and avoidable consequences. But you can begin to think about whether those problems are avoided by emphasizing general measures of damage. How would you prove "the market value of the residue of the term" of the lease in Buck v. Morrow? Outside the special context of organized exchanges, market value is an abstraction. And note that the court says that the price plaintiff agreed to pay for alternate pasture elsewhere is not admissible on the question of market value. That startling proposition is no longer good law, although it was a long time dying. Plaintiff's rent elsewhere may now be admitted as evidence of market value, or even as the general measure of damage. But defendant could still argue that plaintiff paid too much, or that the alternative pasture was better and more expensive than the pasture covered by the broken lease, just as the airlines in the *September 11th Litigation* argued that the replacement towers would be newer, better, and more expensive than the destroyed towers. Are these issues different in kind from whether plaintiff's extra wages and lost cattle could have been avoided through greater diligence?

NOTES ON THE VOCABULARY OF DAMAGES

1. General, special, direct, and consequential damages. General damages are sometimes called "direct" damages; special damages are commonly called "consequential" damages. Lawyers use these terms; contracts use these terms. But their meaning is often unclear, and customary usage does not match up very well with customary definitions.

2. Judicial definitions. Courts use verbal formulas to suggest differences in degree. "Direct damages are the necessary and usual result of the defendant's wrongful act; they flow naturally and necessarily from the wrong. . . . Consequential damages, on the other hand, result naturally, but not necessarily, from the defendant's wrongful acts." Arthur Anderson & Co. v. Perry Equipment Corp., 945 S.W.2d 812, 816 (Tex. 1997). Responding to such a definition in Georgia law, the Eleventh Circuit said:

> So stated, however, the rule does little to further one's understanding of the type of damages that may "arise naturally from the contract" as opposed to the type that may be the "probable result of the breach." The Court finds it helpful to consider general (i.e., direct) damages as those damages that compensate for "the value of the very performance promised" and consequential damages as those damages that "seek to compensate a plaintiff for additional losses (other than the value of the promised performance) that are incurred as a result of the defendant's breach." Schonfeld v. Hilliard, 218 F.3d 164, 175-176 (2d Cir. 2000).

Silverpop Systems, Inc. v. Leading Market Technologies, Inc., 641 Fed. Appx. 849, 855-856 (11th Cir. 2016). This helpful clarification was immediately muddied in application. The court said that the promised performance was to provide targeted e-mail marketing, and that the contractual promise to keep plaintiff's data safe was not the promised performance, but just "a specific term" of the contract. The alleged destruction of the data's market value was held to be consequential damages.

A California formulation may have combined elements of necessity with the Eleventh Circuit's idea of being a step beyond the very thing promised: "General damages are often characterized as those that flow directly and necessarily from a [wrong], or that are a natural result. . . . [S]pecial damages are . . . secondary or derivative losses arising from circumstances that are particular to the . . . parties." Lewis Jorge Construction Management, Inc. v. Pomona Unified School District, 102 P.3d 257, 261 (Cal. 2004).

3. Usage based on formulas. The bench and bar developed standardized measures of general damages. The difference between contract price and market value, the difference between the value of the goods as delivered and as warranted, and interest on detained money were such measures. Many lawyers mean only such standardized measures when they refer to general damages; in that usage, all other damages are consequential or special. But these standard formulas have only an attenuated relationship to definitions based on foreseeability; consequential damages not reducible to a formula are often readily foreseeable.

4. The usage of personal injury lawyers. A quite different definition is that special damages are damages that are reduced to a sum certain before trial. Thus, in the customary usage of personal injury lawyers, pain and suffering are general damages, and medical expenses and lost earnings are special damages. Note how this usage flips the usual prejudices: special damages are real, provable, and reliably measurable; general damages are speculative and suspect.

5. More analytic definitions. If there is any useful content to these terms, it is that "general damages" should refer to the value of what plaintiff lost from the initial impact of defendant's wrongdoing, such as the value of the property destroyed or not delivered, or the reduction in the value of property that was damaged or defective. Consequential damages should refer to everything that happens to plaintiff as a consequence of this initial loss. Perhaps "initial" or "nonconsequential" damages would be a better term than "general" or "direct," but neither is used.

Professors Dobbs and Roberts have offered a similar definition, with a secondary distinction between losses to capital and losses to income:

> Judicial definitions of general damages are usually vague or almost tautological, but the actual decisions make it clear that the courts hold a fairly precise idea about general damages. General damages are market-measured damages. They value plaintiff's entitlement by looking at its value on some real or supposed market. . . .
>
> While general or market damages attempt to protect the plaintiff's net worth by valuing the asset loss resulting from tort or contract breach, the consequential measure attempts to protect plaintiff's income by awarding damages for losses of that income or, what is the same thing, for increases in expenses. General damages measures the losses in the very thing to which the plaintiff is entitled (an undamaged plane [in a case of tortious damage to a plane], a horse in the stable [in a case of breach of a contract to sell a horse]). Consequential damages measures something else; not the very thing the plaintiff was entitled to but income it can produce or losses it can avoid.

Dan B. Dobbs & Caprice L. Roberts, *Law of Remedies* §3.3(3), (4) at 228, 233 (3d ed., West 2018).

6. Lost profits. Lost profits are usually thought of as consequential damages and obviously so. But occasionally courts find even lost profits to be direct damages. An example is Biotroniks A.G. v. Conor Medsystems Ireland, Ltd., 11 N.E.3d 676 (N.Y. 2015). Plaintiff agreed to distribute defendant's products outside the United States. Defendant retained substantial control over plaintiff's sales efforts, and the price paid to defendant was determined by a formula based on the price plaintiff could obtain in the market. The court said that this "was not a simple resale contract, where one party buys a product at a set price to sell at whatever the market may bear." *Id.* at 678. The key distinction "is whether the lost profits flowed directly from the contract itself or were, instead, the result of a separate agreement with a nonparty" *Id.* at 681. The court concluded, four to three, that the lost profits on this contract were direct damages.

7. The UCC definitions—buyer's damages. The UCC defines the buyer's consequential and incidental damages from contracts for the sale of goods in §2-715:

> (1) Incidental damages resulting from the seller's breach include expenses reasonably incurred in inspection, receipt, transportation and care and custody of goods rightfully rejected, any commercially reasonable charges, expenses or commissions in connection with effecting cover and any other reasonable expense incident to the delay or other breach.
>
> (2) Consequential damages resulting from the seller's breach include
>
> (a) any loss resulting from general or particular requirements and needs of which the seller at the time of contracting had reason to know and which could not reasonably be prevented by cover or otherwise; and
>
> (b) injury to person or property proximately resulting from any breach of warranty.

What is the difference between "incidental" and "consequential" damages in this definition? Aren't incidental damages just a subset of consequential damages—a subset of consequences so universally foreseeable that the drafters thought it unnecessary to require a showing that defendant had reason to anticipate them?

8. The UCC definitions—seller's damages. When the buyer breaches, more may turn on the distinction; the UCC says that sellers can recover incidental damages. §§2-706, 2-708. It does not mention consequential damages, but seller's incidental damages are arguably defined more broadly than buyer's incidental damages. Section 2-710 provides:

> Incidental damages to an aggrieved seller include any commercially reasonable charges, expenses or commissions incurred in stopping delivery, in the transportation, care and custody of goods after the buyer's breach, in connection with return or resale of the goods or otherwise resulting from the breach.

What are the limits of "commercially reasonable . . . expenses . . . otherwise resulting from the breach"? Could there ever be damages that are not incidental damages within this definition? See Nobs Chemical, U.S.A., Inc. v. Koppers Co., 616 F.2d 212 (5th Cir. 1980), where buyer's breach forced seller to reduce orders from its own supplier, with the consequence that seller lost a quantity discount. The court denied recovery for the lost quantity discount, stating that §2-710 applies only to expenses "contracted by the seller after the breach and occasioned by such things as the seller's need to care for, and if necessary, dispose of the goods in a reasonable manner." Doesn't that read "otherwise resulting from the breach" right out of the statute? But if "otherwise resulting from the breach" is read literally, that would seem to eliminate the traditional contract rule that buyer have reason to anticipate the consequence at the time of contracting. Is "otherwise resulting from the breach" another drafting glitch?

You have seen *Nobs Chemical* before, in note 5 immediately following Neri v. Retail Marine. The court refused to award contract-market damages to the seller, on the ground that seller had locked in a much smaller profit margin—the difference between its contractual purchase price and its contractual sales price—and that it could get out of its purchase contract by reducing its order. But that same purchase contract specified the quantity discount. Is there any justification for the court to consider terms of the purchase contract that tend to limit seller's damages but to ignore terms of that same purchase contract that tend to increase seller's damages? The statutory text is not much of an explanation, because the statutory text authorizes contract-market damages without exception.

9. Consequential damages and expectancy and reliance. These UCC provisions, and also *Buck, Neri,* and many other contracts cases, illustrate that the distinction between general or direct and special or consequential damages is independent of the distinction between expectancy and reliance. One of the things you rely on when you sign a contract, and one of the things you expect, is that your contractual partner will not breach the contract in a way that causes you to suffer consequential damages. So freedom from consequential damages is part of both the expectancy and the reliance interests, although the UCC assumes that consequential damages to sellers are so rare that they can be ignored.

10. Actual damages. Another term that is occasionally used, especially in statutes, is "actual" damages. The term might be helpful if it were consistently used in its ordinary English sense to exclude punitive damages and presumed damages. Plaintiff could recover for any losses she suffered, but she would have to prove that they were actually suffered. But the term is often construed to exclude more than that.

The Supreme Court has held that "actual" damages as used in the Privacy Act, 5 U.S.C. §552a(g)(4)(A), excludes all liability for emotional distress or loss of reputation. Federal Aviation Administration v. Cooper, 566 U.S. 284 (2012). The majority collected cases interpreting "actual damages" in a remarkable variety of ways. Emphasizing that the Privacy Act creates a cause of action against the United States, and invoking the principle that waivers of sovereign immunity must be narrowly construed, the Court concluded that "actual damages" means "special damages for proven pecuniary loss." *Id.* at 298. Therefore, "actual damages" do not include emotional distress and apparently do not include loss of reputation unless the harm to reputation causes a loss of income or the like. Three dissenters argued that "actual damages" simply means no presumed damages. Justice Kagan did not participate.

There are lengthy discussions of the meaning of special damages and general damages, both generally and in the special context of defamation and privacy torts, responding in part to a congressional decision not to authorize "general damages" in the Privacy Act. The majority argued that emotional distress is a form of general damages, which is generally true; the dissenters argued that general damages for defamation can be presumed, and that it is that meaning of general damages—presumed damages—that Congress declined to authorize.

The Federal Deposit Insurance Corporation Act limits contract damages against the FDIC to "actual direct compensatory damages." This time Congress provided a definition; these damages do not include punitive damages, pain and suffering, or "damages for lost profits or opportunity." 12 U.S.C. §1821(e)(3)(B)(ii).

11. Summing up. Should any rule of law depend on whether damages are characterized as general or special, direct or consequential? The importance of these distinctions is declining, and our own sense is that little remains of the traditional hostility to special or consequential damages. This is especially true in tort, but consequential damages are now much more likely to be awarded in contract as well. Of course, courts are hostile to claims that seem exaggerated or speculative, but as *Nobs Chemical* illustrates, they sometimes find general damages (contract/market damages there) more exaggerated than consequentials (lost profits there). And the large recovery in *Chatlos* for the value of the computer if it had been as warranted was a general damages recovery; consequential damages had been disclaimed. But cases like *Chatlos* and *Nobs Chemical* are exceptional. Consequential damages are more likely to raise issues of causation, foreseeability, remoteness, and the like, and rules for dealing with these issues are often stated as limits on consequential damages. The one place where the meaning of "consequential damages" can be dispositive is contract interpretation; form contracts routinely disclaim liability for consequential damages, often without defining the term.

MEINRATH v. SINGER CO.
87 F.R.D. 422 (S.D.N.Y. 1980)

WEINFELD, District Judge.

Plaintiff Leopold Meinrath is a Belgian entrepreneur engaged in the marketing and distribution of computers and computer-related products principally in the Benelux countries and France. He commenced this suit to recover payments of "bonus compensation" allegedly due under an Agreement of Purchase and Sale . . . entered into among him, the four "Unicard companies" in which he had controlling interests, and the defendant, The Singer Company. . . .

[H]is first claim is for $300,000—the difference between the amount he received in bonus compensation and the maximum allowable amount, to which he claims entitlement. . . .

Meinrath claims "consequential damages" in the amount of U.S. $770,000. This claim is based upon allegations that Singer knew at the time it entered into the contract that Meinrath had substantial subsisting business ventures that would survive the

Agreement; that Meinrath repeatedly apprised Singer and its representatives of the necessity for prompt payment of the bonus compensation as it became due in order to provide working capital for his Unicard ventures; and that as a direct, foreseeable result of Singer's failure to make timely payments to which he claims he was entitled but defendant denies, Meinrath's other businesses suffered substantial losses. . . .

[Singer moved for summary judgment on the claim for consequential damages.]

Meinrath's claim for consequential damages consists of (1) losses of approximately $648,000 in invested capital suffered as a result of the liquidation of Unicard France in 1975, and of the forced sale of all assets of Unicard Nederland in 1974 for the nominal sum of $2, and (2) a $122,000 decline in the net worth of Unicard Belgique which Meinrath continues to own and operate, due to operating and tax losses allegedly attributable to the losses suffered by the other two Unicard companies. . . .

The essence of each of these claims is that at the time of the signing of their Agreement and even prior thereto, Singer had a special awareness of the Unicard companies' financial plight and their dire need for funds with a consequent obligation upon Singer to make timely payments of bonus compensation. In essence, plaintiff seeks to parlay Singer's knowledge of his and his companies' financial predicament into a claim that Singer was required to provide them with necessary financial capital by making prompt payment of all amounts due under the Agreement. The Agreement contains no such explicit or implicit undertakings. . . .

Singer does not dispute that for purposes of this motion, both before and after September 7, 1973, it had actual knowledge of Meinrath's other business ventures, and of his and their need for funds to finance these other enterprises. Moreover, Singer acknowledges that Meinrath made several unsuccessful demands for payment of bonus compensation he alleged was due him. We assume for purposes of this motion that in fact the payments were wrongfully withheld when due. Nonetheless, under these facts Singer is not liable for consequential damages for the failure of Meinrath's other business ventures, unrelated to the contract. Meinrath's essential claim is one for payment withheld although due; the consequential damages stemming from such a claim are not compensable. Almost one hundred years ago the Supreme Court in Loudon v. Taxing District, 104 U.S. 771 (1881), resolved the precise issue now before the Court and in the process formulated a rule which survives today. . . . "[A]ll damages for delay in the payment of money owing upon contract are provided for in the allowance of interest, which is in the nature of damages for withholding money that is due." *Id.* at 774. . . .

Moreover, all of the commentators have held that where the alleged breach of contract consists only of a failure to pay money, remedy for the breach is limited to the principal owed plus damages in the form of interest at the prevailing legal rate. As Professor Williston has noted:

> In an action by a creditor against his debtor for the non-payment of the debt, no other damages [than the sum of money itself with interest at the legal rate from the time when it was due] are ever allowed.
>
> When a large order of goods is bought on credit from a seller known to have but little capital, it may be plainly foreseeable by the buyer when he enters into the transaction that failure to pay the price when it is due may ruin the seller financially, and such a consequence is both proximate and natural.
>
> The universality of the rule limiting damages to interest is, therefore, based on the policy of having a measure of damages of easy and certain application, even though occasionally leading to results at variance with the general principle of compensation.

11 Samuel Williston, *Contracts* §1410 at 605-606 (3d ed., Baker Voorhis 1968).

In opposing the motion, plaintiff has not cited a single authority that supports the award of damages other than interest where the claim is for payment withheld. Our own independent search reveals none either. Instead, plaintiff strains to analogize this case to Spang Industries, Inc. v. Aetna Casualty, 512 F.2d 365 (2d Cir. 1965), in which our Court of Appeals upheld the award of consequential damages to a construction company which incurred emergency expenses in completing construction of a bridge after its subcontractor had breached its obligation timely to deliver steel girders before the onset of winter. That case is distinguishable from the instant case. In *Spang* the contract was for the provision of a specialty item not easily replaceable or found elsewhere. Moreover, the damages suffered, which flowed from plaintiff's crash program to complete the bridge, were a natural outgrowth of the breach. They related solely to plaintiff's efforts to complete the breached contract and thereby mitigate damages. Likewise, in For Children, Inc. v. Graphics International, Inc., 352 F. Supp. 1280 (S.D.N.Y. 1972), a case also cited by Meinrath, plaintiff recovered lost profits when the defendant failed to provide a unique article (children's "pop-up pictures") unobtainable elsewhere; the damages were suffered by the same enterprise that was injured by the breach. Those cases cannot be analogized to the facts of the instant case. Here the plaintiff's claim is not for a unique article, but only for payments withheld although allegedly due. Moreover, the claimed loss was not related to the completion of the contract; instead, it was incurred in other, wholly unrelated ventures. Plaintiff's argument that his injury was foreseeable to Singer at the time of the contract is unavailing; if he wanted to impose liability upon Singer for the failure of his business empire because of non-payment of amounts allegedly due under their contract, he could have bargained for that result by fixing liquidated damages for a breach. Accordingly, we hold that as a matter of law plaintiff's consequential loss is too remote from the main injury to be compensable and too speculative to be ascertainable; plaintiff is barred from recovering such damages.

As Professor Williston has noted, there are sound policy reasons for limiting recovery in cases such as this to lost interest. If allowed to assert the consequential damages claim, plaintiff would infuse the trial of a simple contract dispute with a vast array of evidence concerning his far-flung business empire.[12] To permit him to do so upon a claim of payments withheld is only one step less extreme than permitting him to prove that, had he received timely payments, he would have invested his money wisely and profited thereby. If such were the case every contract dispute would be rendered complex, limited only by counsel's imagination and conceptual theories of unrealized profits and opportunities.

Singer's motion for summary judgment on the issue of consequential damages is granted. . . .

NOTES ON CONSEQUENTIAL DAMAGES FROM FAILURE TO PAY MONEY

1. The rule in *Meinrath*. *Meinrath* presents the pure case of a court refusing to award consequential damages. Defendant's motion for summary judgment was decided on the basis of the undisputed facts and plaintiff's version of all disputed facts. On that

---

12. The parties appear to agree that the consequential damages claim, if permitted, would swallow the main claim of an alleged unpaid $300,000 bonus compensation and would extend the trial a period of a full month. . . .

view of the facts, is there any ordinary sense in which plaintiff's losses were remote and speculative? Even if there were, what about the usual rule that defendant is liable for unusual consequences if he had actual notice that his breach would cause them? The court says the damages were too "remote" and "speculative," but more fundamentally, it says no consequential damages are available for failure to pay money, without regard to remoteness.

Does the court's flat rule make sense on a cover theory—that plaintiff could have borrowed the $300,000 to keep his business going until defendant paid? That rationale might explain the cases where plaintiff claims that if he had been paid promptly he would have invested the money shrewdly. But a plaintiff like Meinrath, who claims that defendant's failure to pay drove him over the brink of insolvency, might have had great difficulty finding someone to lend him $300,000. And if he found such a loan only at exorbitant rates, Loudon v. Taxing District (quoted in *Meinrath*) says he could not even recover the extra interest he paid. Would there be anything remote or speculative about that?

Are you persuaded by the court's fear that a trial on Meinrath's consequential damage claim would dwarf the trial on the merits? Does it matter that in cases where plaintiff could not borrow elsewhere, causation would always be murky because of the risk that plaintiff's business would have failed anyway? Even so, why an absolute rule? There will be cases in which causation is clear: Williston's example of a solvent small seller who borrows heavily to fill a very large order. If the buyer fails to pay, seller will be ruined; if buyer pays, or if buyer had never placed the order at all, seller would have been financially comfortable.

Suppose you conclude that we need an absolute rule that interest is the only measure of damage for failure to pay money. Do the traditional distinctions between direct and consequential damages, or general and special damages, make it any easier to reach or explain that rule?

2. Exceptions to the rule? On its facts, *Meinrath* would probably be good law everywhere. But there is some erosion in the rule in cases where causation is clear and the amount is certain. The simplest extension is to award unpaid plaintiffs the actual interest they paid or failed to earn, instead of the legal rate. The Tenth Circuit awarded an employee the interest and tax penalties incurred when he borrowed from his retirement funds while awaiting promised reimbursement of relocation expenses from his employer. O'Toole v. Northrop Grumman Corp., 305 F.3d 1222 (10th Cir. 2002), and 113 Fed. Appx. 314 (10th Cir. 2004). A further step appears in Lyons v. Montgomery, 701 S.W.2d 641, 643-644 (Tex. 1985), where plaintiff bought a house subject to seller's mortgage, and seller failed to pay the mortgage when due. Plaintiff lost the house and her down payment; she got a judgment for the down payment.

The Tenth Circuit in *O'Toole* was applying New York law; it relied on a New York loan commitment case and a New York insurance case. But most jurisdictions have treated these as special cases.

3. Loan commitments. Some cases have also denied consequential damages for breach of a contract to lend money. But the majority rule allows such damages where they are sufficiently foreseeable. A striking example is Basic Capital Management, Inc. v. Dynex Commercial, Inc., 348 S.W.3d 894 (Tex. 2011). Dynex promised to lend $160 million to entities that Basic would create to invest in real estate. Interest rates rose, Dynex reneged, and Basic was priced out of some deals when it had to pay the new and higher interest rates to borrow elsewhere. A jury awarded $2 million in increased financing costs and $256 million in lost profits on the lost deals. The court held that these damages were recoverable if there was sufficient evidence to support them, an issue to be determined on remand.

A more conventional example, with out-of-pocket losses rather than missed investment opportunities, is Anuhco, Inc. v. Westinghouse Credit Corp., 883 S.W.2d 910 (Mo. Ct. App. 1994). A trucking company struggling with cash shortages was forced into bankruptcy when Westinghouse refused to honor a $65 million loan commitment. The court affirmed a judgment for $70 million, based on a conservative estimate of the difference between the value of the company with the Westinghouse loan and the value of the company in bankruptcy.

Why is a promise to pay money on condition that it be repaid so different from a promise to pay money absolutely? The answer may lie in the purpose of loan commitments. If plaintiff could borrow elsewhere, he should mitigate damages by doing that. But if he cannot, the inability to borrow is the very risk he tried to avoid by paying for a loan commitment. And his financial need has been fully disclosed to the lender in the process of getting the loan commitment. In both *Basic* and *Anuhco*, the courts emphasized that the damages suffered were in the lender's contemplation when it committed to the loan.

4. Insurers. Another exception flourishes in suits against insurers for bad-faith refusal to settle. The insured has no claim merely for failure to pay or delay in payment. But if the insurer refuses or delays in bad faith, knowing that it is liable, plaintiff can sue not only for interest but also for consequential damages and, in many states, punitive damages. Cases from many jurisdictions are collected in Acquista v. New York Life Insurance Co., 730 N.Y.S.2d 272 (App. Div. 2001). The court said that awarding only the money due with interest "presumes that a plaintiff has access to an alternative source of funds," and that this "is frequently an inaccurate assumption." *Id.* at 276. Another example is Bell v. Zurich American Insurance Co., 156 F. Supp. 3d 884 ((N.D. Ohio 2015), where defendant egregiously mishandled the claim and failed to pay on an accidental death policy. The plaintiff widow recovered $10,000 in borrowing costs, $100,000 for emotional distress, $33,240 in attorneys' fees, nearly $293,000 in punitives, and $3,700 in interest, all in addition to the $166,200 policy proceeds.

These cases typically involve consumers or small businesses, in desperate straits from their original loss, seemingly at the mercy of huge insurance companies. It is easy to understand why courts think there must be some remedy beyond collecting the amount due with interest. But the usual arguments against consequential damages for failure to pay money apply; it is no easier to measure damage or trace causation in these cases. Many insureds will be in desperate straits after a loss, but some won't be, and in a society that lives on credit, most people will be in bad shape if expected money doesn't arrive, whether it's insurance money or any other kind of money.

5. Deterring defenses? One argument for the general rule does not appear in *Meinrath*. If any delay in paying money triggered liability for consequential damages, the risks of negotiating or litigating disputed claims would be increased. Everyone who lost a lawsuit would potentially be liable for additional consequential damages caused by his failure to pay as soon as the claim was made. The $450,000 remedy in Bell v. Zurich American cannot be for ordinary disputes. Even liability for tangible consequentials, excluding emotional distress and punitives, would give creditors another bargaining chip with debtors. Our law encourages litigation; courts have been reluctant to deter disputes by imposing liability for asserting one's assumed rights.

TEXACO, INC. v. PENNZOIL CO.

729 S.W.2d 768 (Tex. Ct. App. 1987)

Before WARREN, JACK SMITH and SAM BASS, JJ.

WARREN, Justice.

This is an appeal from a judgment awarding Pennzoil damages for Texaco's tortious interference with a contract between Pennzoil and . . . Getty Oil Co., the Sarah C. Getty Trust, and the J. Paul Getty Museum. . . .

The jury found, among other things, that:

(1) At the end of a board meeting on January 3, 1984, the Getty entities intended to bind themselves to an agreement providing for the purchase of Getty Oil stock, whereby the Sarah C. Getty Trust would own 4/7 of the stock and Pennzoil the remaining 3/7; and providing for a division of Getty Oil's assets, according to their respective ownership if the Trust and Pennzoil were unable to agree on a restructuring of Getty Oil by December 31, 1984;

(2) Texaco knowingly interfered with the agreement between Pennzoil and the Getty entities;

(3) As a result of Texaco's interference, Pennzoil suffered damages of $7.53 billion. . . .

DAMAGES . . .

In a cause involving a tortious interference with an existing contract, . . . plaintiff is not limited to the damages recoverable in a contract action, but instead is entitled to the damages allowable under the more liberal rules recognized in tort actions. . . .

Section 774A of the *Restatement (Second) of Torts* (Am. Law Inst. 1977), reads in pertinent part:

> (1) One who is liable to another for interference with a contract . . . is liable for damages for
>   (a) the pecuniary loss of the benefits of the contract . . . ; [and]
>   (b) consequential losses for which the interference is a legal cause. . . .

. . .

Pennzoil relied on two witnesses to prove the amount of its damages: Dr. Thomas Barrow and Dr. Ronald Lewis. . . .

Dr. Barrow prepared three damages models, as follows:

(1) a replacement cost model,
(2) a discounted cash flow model, and
(3) a cost acquisition model.

Because the jury based its award of damages on the replacement cost model, the other two models will not be discussed. By Dr. Barrow's testimony, Pennzoil showed that because of Texaco's interference with its Getty contract, it was deprived of its right to acquire 3/7 of Getty's proven reserves, amounting to 1.008 billion barrels of oil equivalent (B.O.E.), at a cost of $3.40 a barrel. Pennzoil's evidence further showed that its cost to find equivalent reserves (based on its last five years of exploration costs) was $10.87 per barrel. Therefore, Pennzoil contended that it suffered damages equal to 1.008 billion B.O.E. times $7.47 (the difference between $10.87, the cost of finding equivalent reserves, and $3.40, the cost of acquiring Getty's reserves) or $7.53 billion. The jury agreed.

Texaco first alleges that the trial judge should have instructed the jury that the measure of Pennzoil's damages was the difference between the market value of Getty Oil stock and its contract price at the time of the breach. We reject this contention. The Getty/Pennzoil agreement contemplated something more than a simple buy-sell stock transaction. Pennzoil's cause of action against Texaco was in tort, not in contract, and Pennzoil's measure of damages was the pecuniary loss of the benefits it would have been entitled to under the contract. There was ample evidence that the reason Pennzoil (and later, Texaco) wanted to buy Getty was to acquire control of Getty Oil's reserves, and not for any anticipated profit from the later sale of Getty stock. There was evidence that such fluctuations in market price are primarily of interest to holders of small, minority share positions.

The court in Special Issue No. 3 correctly instructed the jury that the measure of damages was the amount necessary to put Pennzoil in as good a position as it would have been in if its agreement, if any, with the Getty entities had been performed. . . .

Texaco next contends that the replacement cost theory is based on the speculative and remote contention that Pennzoil would have gained direct access to Getty's assets. Texaco strongly urges that Pennzoil had a "good faith" obligation under its alleged contract to attempt to reorganize and restructure Getty Oil rather than to divide its assets. We agree. Under New York law, a duty of fair dealing and good faith is implied in every contract. But a duty of good faith and fair dealing does not require that Pennzoil completely subordinate its financial well-being to the proposition of reorganization or restructuring.

The directors of Pennzoil would have had a duty to the company's shareholders to obtain the greatest benefit from the merger assets, by either restructuring, reorganizing, or taking the assets in kind. If taking the assets in kind would be the most advantageous to Pennzoil, its directors would, in the absence of a great detriment to Getty, have a duty to take in kind. So the acquisition of a pro rata share of Getty Oil's reserves would be more than a mere possibility, unless the restructuring or reorganization of Getty would be just as profitable to Pennzoil as taking the assets in kind.

Next, Texaco urges that the jury's use of the replacement cost model resulted in a gross overstatement of Pennzoil's loss because [of multiple errors].

Our problem in reviewing the validity of these Texaco claims is that Pennzoil necessarily used expert testimony to prove its losses by using three damages models. In the highly specialized field of oil and gas, expert testimony that is free of conjecture and speculation is proper and necessary to determine and estimate damages. Texaco presented no expert testimony to refute the claims but relied on its cross-examination of Pennzoil's experts to attempt to show that the damages model used by the jury was flawed. Dr. Barrow testified that each of his three models would constitute an accepted method of proving Pennzoil's damages. It is inevitable that there will be some degree of inexactness when an expert is attempting to make an educated estimate of the damages in a case such as this one. Prices and costs vary, depending on the locale, and the type of crude found. The law recognizes that a plaintiff may not be able to prove its damages to a certainty. But this uncertainty is tolerated when the difficulty in calculating damages is attributable to the defendant's conduct.

In his replacement cost model, Dr. Barrow estimated the cost to replace 1.008 billion barrels of oil equivalent that Pennzoil had lost. Dr. Barrow admitted that some of Getty's reserves consisted of heavy crude, which was less valuable than lighter crude, and that he had made no attempt to determine whether there was an equivalency between the lost Getty barrels and the barrels used to calculate Pennzoil's exploration costs. Dr. Barrow also testified that there was no way to determine what grade of reserves Pennzoil would find in its future exploration; they could be better or worse than the Getty reserves. Finally Dr. Barrow testified that in spite of his not determining the value equivalency, the replacement cost model was an accepted method of figuring Pennzoil's loss. Dr. Lewis testified that with improved refining technology, the difference in value between light and heavy crude was becoming less significant.

Texaco next urges that Pennzoil should have calculated replacement cost by using a longer time period and industry wide figures rather than using only its own exploration costs, over a five year period. Dr. Lewis admitted that it might have been more accurate to use a longer period of time to estimate exploration costs, but he and Dr. Barrow both testified that exploration costs had been consistently rising each year and that the development cost estimates were conservative. Dr. Barrow testified that in his opinion, Pennzoil would, in the future, have to spend a great deal more than $10.87 a barrel to find crude. Dr. Lewis testified that industry wide exploration costs were higher than Pennzoil's, and those figures would result in a higher cost estimate than the $10.87 per barrel used by Pennzoil. . . .

Texaco also claims that Pennzoil should have used post-tax rather than pre-tax figures in figuring its loss calculations. First, it contends that there are large tax incentives for exploration and development that are not applicable to acquisition of reserves. Second, it contends that there was a $2 billion tax penalty attached to the Pennzoil/Getty agreement, and Pennzoil's $900 million share of that penalty would have increased its $3.40 pre-tax acquisition cost by nearly a dollar.

Dr. Barrow testified that the fact that Pennzoil included $997 million as recapture tax in its costs of acquiring the Getty reserves . . . made the pre-tax comparison between the $3.40 per barrel to acquire Getty reserves and the $10.87 per barrel for Pennzoil to find new oil, "apples and apples"; in other words, the $997 million tax adjustment compensated for the tax benefits reaped when discovering, as compared with purchasing, reserves. Further, there was no conclusive proof that the Internal Revenue Service would have assessed a $2 billion penalty to Getty's purchase of the Museum's shares under the Pennzoil/Getty agreement, as alleged by Texaco. Several witnesses, familiar with tax law, testified that it was unlikely that such a tax would be imposed; therefore it was for the jury to decide when assessing damages, whether Pennzoil's pro rata share of the speculative tax penalty should reduce the amount of its damages.

Texaco's contention that Pennzoil's cost replacement model should be discounted to present value ignores the fact that Pennzoil's suit is not for future damages but for those already sustained. Pennzoil would have had an interest in the Getty reserves immediately if the agreement had been consummated, and it did not seek damages for reserves to be recovered in the future. The cases cited by Texaco are inapposite here because all involve damages that the plaintiff would incur in the future, such as lost wages or future yearly payments. Also, Texaco requested no jury instruction on a discount or a discount rate; therefore, any complaint of the court's failure to submit the issue or instruction is waived. . . .

Texaco claims that the court erroneously applied New York law when it allowed prejudgment interest, because most of the damages are to compensate for expenses to be incurred over the next 25 years. We have previously considered and rejected Texaco's contention that Pennzoil's recovery, or any part thereof, was for future damages.

Under New York law, a plaintiff in an action for inducing a breach of contract is entitled as a matter of right to interest on the amount of recovery, measured from the date of the accrual of the cause of action. . . .

Because we are of the opinion that the evidence supports the jury's award of compensatory damages, we do not consider a remittitur of those damages appropriate. . . .

NOTES ON AN 11-FIGURE VERDICT

1. The facts in *Pennzoil*. The jury also awarded $3 billion in punitive damages, which the court of appeals remitted to $1 billion. The Texas Supreme Court refused a writ of error. While a petition for certiorari was pending, the case settled for $3 billion. The difference between the contract price of the Getty stock and the highest estimate of the market value of the stock (based on the higher price that Texaco actually paid) was about $500 million.

2. What kind of damages was the cost of replacing the oil? Isn't Texaco right that the billion barrels of oil does not replace the stock, and that the cost of finding oil cannot be the basis for contract-market damages? But isn't the court right that loss of the oil is consequential damage that flows directly from loss of the stock?

The court relies in part on Pennzoil's claim being in tort rather than contract. But wouldn't Pennzoil's argument work just as well in a contract suit against Getty? Recall from first-year Contracts the rule of Hadley v. Baxendale, 156 Eng. Rep. 145 (1854): Plaintiff is entitled to recover for those consequences of breach that were within the contemplation of the parties when they made the contract. Can there be any doubt that Pennzoil was after the oil reserves, and that every competent person on both sides knew that?

The usual measure of contract damages is the difference between the contract price and the market price (or the difference between the contract price and the cover price), plus consequential damages that defendant had reason to know about. That formula would give Pennzoil the $500 million difference between the contract price and the market price of the stock, *plus* the $7.53 billion cost of replacing the oil.

That can't be right, because the stock has little value apart from the oil. Compensation for both the stock and the oil would be a double recovery. But that makes the oil an odd sort of consequential damages. Does it mean the oil is not really consequential damages at all? If the value of the stock and the value of the oil are two measures of the same thing, should Pennzoil have been limited to the lesser of two? But if the oil reserves are the main point of the contract, how can a damage calculation ignore them? Wouldn't a damage measure based on the stock market ignore economic reality? Didn't Pennzoil's rightful position include a billion barrels of oil?

3. Pennzoil's damage models. Pennzoil witnesses said the oil could not be replaced by purchase, and Texaco did not identify any other company with a billion barrels of oil that was willing to sell or vulnerable to a takeover by Pennzoil. It was cheaper to replace the oil than do without; at the time of the contract, oil sold for $30 a barrel, far more than Pennzoil's historic exploration and development costs plus a reasonable estimate of production costs.

Pennzoil's replacement-cost model is explained in the opinion; Texaco's objections and the responses of Pennzoil's experts illustrate the kinds of fact issues that can arise with respect to such models. Pennzoil's discounted-cash-flow model projected the profits from producing the billion barrels of oil over a period of 40 years and discounted those profits to present value at an interest rate of 12 percent. This produced a damage figure of $6.68 billion. Probably the verdict should have been based on this lower figure, but it is not enough lower to make much difference to Texaco or to critics of the judgment. We could not find a clear account of the cost-acquisition model.

4. Net present value. The discounted-cash-flow model produced a result in the same range as the replacement-cost model, even though one was discounted to present value and the other was not. Here is the solution to that puzzle: The replacement-cost model used historic exploration costs, and those costs were rising more rapidly than the general inflation rate. To ignore future increases in the cost of exploration was a rough-and-ready way of discounting future costs to present value, and probably just as accurate, because future exploration costs are notoriously unpredictable. We will consider the relationship between inflation and present value in section 2.F.3.

5. The source of Pennzoil's bargain. Much of the problem with the case is the sheer size of Pennzoil's expectancy. It is an extraordinary bargain, seemingly too good to be true, to buy $30 billion worth of oil (a billion barrels at $30 per barrel) for $3.4 billion. How could the value of the oil be so different from the value of the stock that controlled the oil? No one is entirely sure, but there was little serious dispute about any of the key numbers: the number of shares and barrels and the price of each. Such enormous value discrepancies seem to be pervasive in natural resource companies.

Texaco relied on a similar discrepancy in its own valuation at a later stage in the litigation. Texaco's stock was worth $9.5 billion, but its net assets were worth $22 billion. See Texaco v. Pennzoil Co., 626 F. Supp. 250, 253 (S.D.N.Y.) (stock value), *rev'd in part*, 784 F.2d 1133, 1155 (2d Cir. 1986) (asset value), *rev'd on other grounds*, 481 U.S. 1 (1987). Because it owned net assets more than twice the size of Pennzoil's judgment, Texaco argued that there was no need for a bond to secure the judgment. But if asset valuations are real for purposes of collecting Pennzoil's damages, aren't they equally real for purposes of measuring those damages?

To buy oil by buying stock, you have to buy control of the company. Hardly any investors can do that, so oil reserves and oil company stock generally trade in separate markets. Pennzoil could trade in both markets, buying enough stock to control the company and thus the oil. Such a buyer can offer a premium price to stockholders who trade only in the stock market, and still get an enormous bargain in terms of the oil market. But incumbent managements also control the oil; they are rarely willing to sell that control at a bargain price. Thus, most takeovers in the oil industry are hostile; the buyer goes over the heads of management and buys directly from the widely dispersed stockholders. Getty was closely held but vulnerable to a takeover because the controlling shareholders were deadlocked in a power struggle that neither side could win. This analysis of oil company valuations is based on John C. Coffee, *Shareholders Versus Managers: The Strain in the Corporate Web*, 85 Mich. L. Rev. 1 (1986). It is applied to Pennzoil's damages in Douglas Laycock, *The Remedies Issues: Compensatory Damages, Specific Performance, Punitive Damages, Supersedeas Bonds, and Abstention*, 9 Rev. Litig. 473 (1990). For a vigorous defense of Texaco's contract-market measure, see Richard A. Epstein, *The Pirates of Pennzoil: A Comic Opera Made Possible by a Grant from the Texaco Corporation*, 32 Law School Record 3 (Univ. of Chicago 1986).

E. LIMITS ON DAMAGES

Many rules limit damages, often in ways that limit plaintiff to less than her rightful position. These limits are closely related to distinctions between direct and consequential damages. The primary tools for restricting recovery of consequential damages are (1) contractual limitations on remedies, and (2) rules about avoidable consequences, remoteness, and uncertainty.

1. The Parties' Power to Specify the Remedy

KEARNEY & TRECKER CORP. v. MASTER ENGRAVING CO.
527 A.2d 429 (N.J. 1987)

STEIN, J.

The critical issue posed by this appeal is whether the Uniform Commercial Code, N.J. Stat. Ann. §§12A:1-101 to 10-106, . . . permits the enforcement of a contractual exclusion of consequential damages where the buyer's limited remedy authorized in the contract of sale has failed to achieve its essential purpose. . . .

I

Kearney & Trecker Corp. (K & T) is the manufacturer of the Milwaukee-Matic 180 (MM-180), a computer-controlled machine tool capable of performing automatically a series of machining operations on metal parts. . . . Master Engraving Co. . . . is engaged in the manufacture and engraving of component parts for industrial application. . . .

In the fall of 1978, the parties began discussions about Master's purchase of an MM-180. K & T furnished Master with a sales brochure describing the MM-180: "The new Milwaukee-Matic 180 combines simplicity with efficiency. It was designed using fewer parts. It is this simplicity of design that does much to explain the MM 180's amazing low maintenance requirements."

In response to a proposal from K & T, Master issued its purchase order for the MM-180 in December 1978, and the order was promptly acknowledged and accepted by K & T. The purchase price was $167,000. The written proposal included the following provision:

> WARRANTY, DISCLAIMER, LIMITATION OF LIABILITY AND REMEDY: Seller warrants the products furnished hereunder to be free from defects in material and workmanship for the shorter of (i) twelve (12) months from the date of delivery . . . or (ii) four thousand (4,000) operating hours. . . .
>
> UNDER NO CIRCUMSTANCES WILL SELLER BE LIABLE FOR ANY INCIDENTAL OR CONSEQUENTIAL DAMAGES, OR FOR ANY OTHER LOSS, DAMAGE OR EXPENSE OF ANY KIND, INCLUDING LOSS OF PROFITS ARISING IN CONNECTION WITH THIS CONTRACT OR WITH THE USE OF OR INABILITY TO USE SELLER'S PRODUCTS FURNISHED UNDER THIS CONTRACT. SELLER'S MAXIMUM LIABILITY SHALL NOT EXCEED AND BUYER'S REMEDY IS LIMITED TO EITHER (i) REPAIR OR REPLACEMENT OF THE DEFECTIVE PART OF PRODUCT, OR AT SELLER'S OPTION, (ii) RETURN OF THE PRODUCT AND REFUND OF THE PURCHASE PRICE, AND SUCH REMEDY SHALL BE BUYER'S ENTIRE AND EXCLUSIVE REMEDY.

. . . According to Master's witnesses, the machine malfunctioned frequently during the first year of operation, and was inoperable from 25 percent to 50 percent of the time available for its use. . . . Over K & T's objection, testimony was introduced estimating lost profits on customer orders allegedly unfilled because of the inoperability of the machine. . . .

[T]he trial court instructed the jury that it could award consequential damages notwithstanding the contractual exclusion if it found that K & T failed "to make the machine as warranted." . . .[1]

The jury returned a verdict in favor of Master for $57,000. . . . In affirming, the Appellate Division interpreted the jury verdict to mean that the limited remedy of repair and replacement had failed of its essential purpose. §2-719(2). 511 A.2d 1227 (N.J. Super. Ct. App. Div. 1987). . . .

II . . .

Under the Code, consequential losses constitute a recoverable item of damages in the event of a breach by the seller. §2-714(3). However, the potential significance of liability for consequential damages in commercial transactions undoubtedly prompted the Code's drafters, consistent with the Code's endorsement of the principle of freedom of contract, to make express provision for the limitation or exclusion of such damages. §2-719.[3] . . . As one commentator has observed:

> As a general matter, consequential damages exclusions are hands down the most significant limitation of liability in a contract for the sale of goods. Potential liability for consequential damages in commercial contexts, usually in the form of the buyer's lost profits from the use or resale of the goods in its business, is enormous in comparison to the contract price of the goods. On the other hand, the general or direct damages that a buyer may suffer upon a seller's breach are finite and can be gauged at a maximum amount either in terms of the contract price or market price of the goods to be sold. . . .

Roy Ryden Anderson, *Failure of Essential Purpose and Essential Failure on Purpose: A Look at Section 2-719 of the Uniform Commercial Code*, 31 Sw. L.J. 759, 774 (1977). In a commercial setting, the seller's right to exclusion of consequential damages is recognized as a beneficial risk-allocation device that reduces the seller's exposure in the event of breach.

An equally fundamental principle of the Code, comparable in importance to the right of parties to limit or exclude consequential damages, is the Code's insistence that . . . :

> [I]t is of the very essence of a sales contract that at least minimum adequate remedies be available. If the parties intend to conclude a contract for sale within this Article they must accept the legal consequence that there be at least a fair quantum of remedy for breach of the obligations or duties outlined in the contract. Thus any clause purporting to modify or limit the remedial provisions of this Article in an unconscionable manner is subject to deletion and in that event the remedies made available by this Article are applicable as if the stricken clause had never existed. Similarly, under subsection

---

1. The trial court also instructed the jury to consider the representation in the sales brochure about the MM-180's "amazing low maintenance requirements" as constituting an express warranty of the machine's performance. . . . K & T does not challenge this ruling. . . .

3. §2-719(3) provides:

> Consequential damages may be limited or excluded unless the limitation or exclusion is unconscionable. Limitation of consequential damages for injury to the person in the case of consumer goods is prima facie unconscionable but limitation of damages where the loss is commercial is not.

(2), where an apparently fair and reasonable clause because of circumstances fails in its purpose or operates to deprive either party of the substantial value of the bargain, it must give way to the general remedy provisions of this Article.

Comment 1, §2-719.

These competing policies—freedom of contract, including the right to exclude liability for consequential damages, and the insistence upon minimum adequate remedies to redress a breach of contract—frame the issue before us. If a limitation or exclusion of consequential damages is not unconscionable when the contract is made, must it be held unenforceable if the limited remedies provided in the contract do not achieve their intended purpose?

To the extent that the UCC addresses this issue, its response is inconclusive. The Code provides merely that when a limited remedy fails of its essential purpose, "remedy may be had as provided in this Act." §2-719(2). . . . [C]onsequential damages is a buyer's remedy "provided in this Act," §2-714(3), but the Code is silent as to whether that remedy survives if the sales contract excludes it.

A related question concerns the extent of the remedies other than consequential damages that are available to a buyer relegated to a limited remedy that has failed to achieve its essential purpose. Typically, the limited remedy most often offered by sellers is the repair and replacement warranty found in the sales contract in this case. When a repair and replacement warranty is combined, as here, with an exclusion of consequential damages, the commercial objectives of the contracting parties are reasonably evident. As summarized in Beal v. General Motors Corp., 354 F. Supp. 423, 426 (D. Del. 1973):

> The purpose of an exclusive remedy of replacement or repair of defective parts . . . is to give the seller an opportunity to make the goods conforming while limiting the risks to which he is subject by excluding direct and consequential damages that might otherwise arise. From the point of view of the buyer the purpose of the exclusive remedy is to give him goods that conform to the contract within a reasonable time after a defective part is discovered. When the warrantor fails to correct the defect as promised within a reasonable time he is liable for a breach of that warranty.

The commonly-applied formula to compute a buyer's damages for breach of any warranty, including the repair or replacement warranty, is the difference "between the value of the goods accepted and the value they would have had if they had been as warranted." §2-714(2). . . .

The Code also affords to the buyer the right to recover incidental damages, §2-714(3), as well as the right to revoke acceptance of the goods within a reasonable time after discovery of a nonconformity that substantially impairs the value of the goods to the buyer, §2-608. A buyer who revokes his acceptance of goods may also seek damages for the seller's breach. §2-608; §2-711(1).

Courts that have considered the validity of an exclusion of consequential damages in the context of a repair or replacement warranty that has not fulfilled its purpose have reached significantly different results. A substantial number of courts seem to have adopted the view that there is an integral relationship between the exclusion of consequential damages and the limited remedy of repair or replacement, so that the failure of the limited remedy necessarily causes the invalidation of the exclusion of consequential damages. Characteristic of the rationale employed by these courts is this excerpt:

> It is the specific breach of the warranty to repair that plaintiff alleges caused the bulk of its damages. This Court would be in an untenable position if it allowed the defendant

to shelter itself behind one segment of the warranty when it has allegedly repudiated and ignored its very limited obligations under another segment of the same warranty, which alleged repudiation has caused the very need for relief which the defendant is attempting to avoid.

Jones & McKnight Corp. v. Birdsboro Corp., 320 F. Supp. 39, 43-44 (N.D. Ill. 1970).

In sharp contrast, a number of other courts have concluded that an exclusion of consequential damages is to be viewed independently of a limited warranty of repair or replacement, so that if the warranty fails to fulfill its purpose, the validity of the consequential damages exclusion depends upon the specific circumstances and the probable intention of the parties.

The Third Circuit's opinion in *Chatlos I* is typical of the reasoning articulated in these cases. Chatlos Systems, Inc. v. National Cash Register Corp. 635 F.2d 1081 (3d Cir. 1980). [It is *Chatlos II* that is reprinted in section 2.C.] In *Chatlos I*, . . . [t]he sales agreement warranted that the system would be free from defects for twelve months, excluded liability for consequential damages, and limited NCR's responsibilities to the correction of any errors or defects within sixty days. . . .

The Third Circuit agreed that the limited repair remedy had failed of its essential purpose, but reversed the trial court's award of consequential damages, concluding that the contractual exclusion of consequential damages should be enforced:

> It appears to us that the better reasoned approach is to treat the consequential damage disclaimer as an independent provision, valid unless unconscionable. . . .
>
> The limited remedy of repair and a consequential damages exclusion are two discrete ways of attempting to limit recovery for breach of warranty. The Code, moreover, tests each by a different standard. The former survives unless it fails of its essential purpose, while the latter is valid unless it is unconscionable. We therefore see no reason to hold, as a general proposition, that the failure of the limited remedy provided in the contract without more, invalidates a wholly distinct term in the agreement excluding consequential damages. . . .
>
> Whether the preclusion of consequential damages should be effective in this case depends upon the circumstances involved. The repair remedy's failure of essential purpose, while a discrete question, is not completely irrelevant to the issue of the conscionability of enforcing the consequential damages exclusion. . . . [T]he question here narrows to the unconscionability of the buyer retaining the risk of consequential damages upon the failure of the essential purpose of the exclusive repair remedy. . . .

635 F.2d at 1086-1087. . . .

We are also persuaded that many routine business transactions would be dislocated by a rule requiring the invalidation of a consequential damage exclusion whenever the prescribed contractual remedy fails to operate as intended. . . . [T]he commercial reality is that for many sellers, immunity from liability for their customers' consequential damages may be indispensable to their pricing structure and, in extreme cases, to their solvency.

Nor do we find that enforcement of a consequential damages limitation when a limited remedy has failed of its essential purpose is necessarily inequitable to the buyer. As noted earlier, the Code affords remedies other than consequential damages when a warranty is breached. . . .

Accordingly, we conclude that §2-719 does not require the invalidation of an exclusion of consequential damages when limited contractual remedies fail of their essential purpose. It is only when the circumstances of the transaction, including the seller's breach, cause the consequential damage exclusion to be inconsistent with the intent and reasonable commercial expectations of the parties that invalidation of the exclusionary clause would be appropriate under the Code. For example, although a buyer may agree to the exclusion of consequential damages, a seller's wrongful repudiation of a repair warranty may expose a buyer to consequential damages not contemplated by the contract, and other Code remedies may be inadequate. In such circumstances, a court might appropriately decline to enforce the exclusion.

III

In this case, a sophisticated buyer purchased for $167,000 a complex, computer-controlled machine tool. The sales agreement allocated to Master the risk of consequential damages. K & T's responsibility was to repair or replace the machine or any defective parts in order that the machine would be "free from defects in material and workmanship" for the shorter of twelve months or four thousand operating hours. The testimony at trial demonstrated that the MM-180 was a complex piece of equipment and that its normal operation could be adversely affected by a wide variety of factors, including deficiencies in maintenance or in computer-programming for which Master's employees were responsible. . . . ". . . [W]e are not dealing with a piece of equipment that either works or does not, or is fully repaired or not at all. On the contrary, the normal operation . . . spans too large a spectrum for such simple characterizations." American Electric Power Co. v. Westinghouse Electric Corp., 418 F. Supp. 435, 458 (S.D.N.Y. 1986). . . .

Nor was there any contention by Master that K & T did not make service calls when requested. . . . What was sharply disputed was Master's claim that the machine was defective during the first year, since K & T's witnesses testified that most of the problems encountered during this period were the fault of Master's employees. . . .

In our view, the facts in this record do not justify invalidation of the consequential damage exclusion, a risk allocation agreed to by both parties. . . .

Master could have offered evidence, although it did not, that the value of the MM-180 was less than the contract price because of the erratic performance during the first year. . . . We are fully satisfied that the availability of damages for breach of the repair and replacement warranty under §2-714(2), combined with the return and refund provision in the contract of sale not invoked by Master, adequately fulfills the UCC's mandate that "at least minimum adequate remedies be available" when a limited remedy fails to achieve its purpose.

For the reasons stated, the judgment . . . is reversed and the matter is remanded to the Law Division for a new trial.

NOTES ON LIMITATION-OF-REMEDY CLAUSES

1. The Code. Section 2-719 provides that contracts for the sale of goods may limit or modify the remedies that would otherwise be available:

> (1) Subject to the provisions of subsections (2) and (3) of this section and of the preceding section on liquidation and limitation of damages,
>   (a) the agreement may provide for remedies in addition to or in substitution for those provided in this Article and may limit or alter the measure of damages recoverable under this Article, as by limiting the buyer's remedies to return of the goods and repayment of the price or to repair and replacement of non-conforming goods or parts; and

(b) resort to a remedy as provided is optional unless the remedy is expressly agreed to be exclusive, in which case it is the sole remedy.

(2) Where circumstances cause an exclusive or limited remedy to fail of its essential purpose, remedy may be had as provided in this Act.

Section 2-719(3) is set out in footnote 3 of the opinion.

2. The "essential purpose" of a limited remedy. *K & T* treats the jury verdict as deciding that the repair-and-replace remedy failed of its essential purpose, and it recites the common understanding of the purpose of such remedies: The repair-and-replace remedy fails of its essential purpose when seller is unable or unwilling to repair or replace in a reasonable time.

What if the contract recited that the essential purpose of the remedy was to leave the entire risk of loss on buyer except that seller would try in good faith to repair? What if the contract said that whether the product worked depended almost entirely on how buyer took care of it, and consequently, seller would have no liability at all, not even to repair and replace? How could that clause fail of its essential purpose? But might that clause be unconscionable, even in a commercial setting, if its essential purpose is to leave one side with no remedy at all? Isn't that the point of the Official Comment to §2-719, quoted in *K & T*?

Why must there be some "minimum quantum of remedy"? Why can't the seller deliver a machine with absolutely no further obligation if that is what the parties want? Despite the implications of the Comment, he probably can if he sells an existing machine "as-is" and effectively disclaims all warranties. But any description of the product can give rise to express warranties; note the reliance on the sales brochure in *K & T*.

3. A purpose to put the risk on plaintiff? Consider Rheem Manufacturing Co. v. Phelps Heating and Air Conditioning, Inc., 746 N.E.2d 941 (Ind. 2001). Rheem sold furnaces; Phelps was a local contractor that installed them. Rheem's warranty and limitation of remedy were inside the box with each furnace. Rheem warranted parts for one year, but it said that the exclusive remedy was replacement parts. It disclaimed any liability for service or repair costs. The court said that the essential purpose of this remedy was to distinguish the local installer from the distant manufacturer, and to put the cost of repairs on the installer, or on the consumer if the installer also disclaimed liability. And it didn't matter that Rheem had been unable to furnish reliable parts, leaving many furnaces unrepaired for up to four years. The form in the box also disclaimed any liability for incidental or consequential damages.

4. Limiting remedies vs. disclaiming warranties. There is more than one way to limit liability under a contract. A party can limit his substantive obligation or limit his liability for breach. Should we apply the same standards to both kinds of disclaimers? The UCC implies warranties of merchantability and fitness of purpose, and for the most part, it requires that disclaimers of these warranties be conspicuous. If a seller can achieve substantially the same result by making the warranties and limiting liability for their breach, why don't limitation-of-remedy clauses have to be conspicuous?

On the other hand, if the only substantive constraint on disclaiming warranties and otherwise limiting the scope of the substantive obligation is the general unconscionability section, why is there a detailed section regulating limitation of remedies? Maybe it is easier to communicate a limited promise than an unlimited promise that is illusory for lack of a remedy.

5. When the limited remedy fails of its essential purpose, what's left? If the limited remedy fails of its essential purpose, "remedy may be had as provided in this Act."

UCC §2-719(2). Did Master get remedy as provided in the Act, or only as provided in the contract?

What result if the contract simply said, "Buyer's only remedy is that seller will repair or replace the machine"? If that sentence of the contract is enforced, there can be no consequential damages. But if that sentence is not enforced, because the repair-or-replace remedy fails of its essential purpose, would consequential damages become available? Is it essential to *K & T* that the contract had two sentences, seemingly redundant on first reading? One says that the only remedy is repair or replace, and another says that buyer cannot recover consequentials. The clause disclaiming consequentials is still there even after the repair-or-replace clause is eliminated.

Courts remain deeply divided on whether disclaimers of consequentials survive the failure of repair-or-replace remedies, but *K & T* appears to state the majority rule, at least in disputes between businesses. Courts are more likely to knock out the disclaimer of consequentials in consumer cases.

6. General damages under §2-714(2). Did Master's lawyers snatch defeat from the jaws of victory by failing to offer evidence of the value of the machine as delivered? How much would the damages under §2-714(2) be? What was the machine worth "at the time and place of acceptance"? The value of a machine that partly works part of the time is a theoretical construct; there is probably no market for such machines. But note that the jury's award for consequentials was only about one-third of the sales price. If Master had tried to sell the machine with full disclosure of its alleged problems, isn't it likely that the price would have to be discounted more than that? The lawyers were naturally drawn to consequentials, perhaps because they seemed larger, but mostly because they were more tangible.

Note that Chatlos got a large recovery under §2-714(2) after an identical holding excluding consequentials. This was partly because Chatlos had received such extraordinary warranties, but also because Chatlos proved that the computer system actually delivered was nearly worthless.

But might the *K & T* court have misread the clause? Does it disclaim direct damages under §2-714(2) as well as consequential damages under §2-714(3)?

7. Bargaining over remedies. The courts in these cases tend to emphasize the parties' equal bargaining power. What does that mean? Should we suppose that in a deal of this size, buyer could have gotten its remedy clause for a higher price? Sellers routinely disclaim liability for consequentials, or for anything other than repair or replacement. It is impossible to bargain for changes in small transactions, and very often impossible even in large transactions. In S.M. Wilson Co. v. Smith International, Inc., 587 F.2d 1363 (9th Cir. 1978), involving the sale of a $550,000 machine, seller flatly rejected buyer's attempt to renegotiate the limitation-of-remedy clause, and buyer abandoned the effort. In *Rheem Manufacturing*, in note 3, the court treated the form, enclosed in the box and addressed to the ultimate consumer, as if it had been negotiated between two sophisticated businesses.

If few sellers will consider liability for consequential damages at prices buyers are willing to pay—or at any price at all—does that show that sellers have unfair bargaining power? Or simply that it is not cost effective to shift these losses to sellers?

8. Gross negligence? In Severn Peanut Co. v. Industrial Fumigant Co., 807 F.3d 88 (4th Cir. 2015), defendant applied a pesticide in a way that violated state and federal safety regulations and appears to have been—the issue was not adjudicated— seriously negligent. The result was a fire that destroyed 20 million pounds of peanuts and did major structural damage to the storage facility. The court enforced a disclaimer of consequential damages.

Judge Wilkinson's opinion said that the litigated cases "often necessarily involve bargains that look like raw deals in retrospect," but that enforcing limitations of remedies protects liberty of contract, lets parties allocate risks to the party best able to bear them, and often lowers prices. Defendant's contract recited that its $8,600 price was based on the value of its services, not on the value of plaintiff's property, and that the price was "not sufficient to warrant [seller] assuming any risk of incidental or consequential damages." *Id.* at 92.

9. Unconscionable limits on remedies. Section 2-719(3) makes it prima facie unconscionable to exclude liability for personal injury caused by consumer goods. Tort law also addresses personal injuries and often refuses to enforce exculpatory agreements.

Decisions holding limitation-of-remedy clauses unconscionable in other contexts are rare and largely unpredictable. One recurring example is defective seeds sold to farmers. By the time the defect is revealed by a failed crop, the farmer has invested substantial money and labor, and repair-and-replace has become impossible. Cases going both ways are collected in Harris Moran Seed Co. v. Phillips, 949 So. 2d 916, 926-931 (Ala. Civ. App. 2006).

COMMERCIAL REAL ESTATE INVESTMENT, L.C. v. COMCAST OF UTAH II, INC.

285 P.3d 1193 (Utah 2012)

[The plaintiff, referred to in the opinion as CRE, bought a lot and built a building to the design specifications of Comcast's predecessor in interest, a company called TCI. The building was in a mostly undeveloped industrial park, and CRE bought the lot next door, but CRE did not tell TCI that it intended further development in the area. TCI drafted the lease, in which it promised to continuously occupy and operate the building, promised to pay the rent, and promised to pay as liquidated damages an additional amount equal to the rent—in total, double rent—for each day of any breach. The court does not explain why the tenant drafted such a clause. Perhaps it was based on oral negotiations. Perhaps it was copied from a form.

The lease began in 1995, and TCI performed until 2001. Then it vacated the building. Comcast acquired TCI and assumed its obligations under the lease in 2002. Comcast listed the building with a real estate agent, and a new tenant took possession in 2006. TCI and Comcast paid the rent for the five years the building stood empty, but they refused to pay any liquidated damages.]

Justice DURHAM delivered the opinion of the Court. . . .

A. LIQUIDATED DAMAGES CLAUSES HAVE BEEN SUBJECT TO VARYING STANDARDS OF REVIEW

. . . [O]ur case law reflects several competing approaches to evaluating the enforceability of liquidated damages clauses. . . .

1. Disfavoring Penalties

One line of reasoning focuses on whether a contractual provision providing for liquidated damages constitutes a penalty. "It is an elementary principle of law that a provision in a contract between private individuals for a penalty in case of breach of such contract is void." Croft v. Jensen, 40 P.2d 198, 202 (Utah 1935). . . . When parties specify liquidated damages in "contracts for the payment of money only," the damages generally are treated as a penalty. *Id.* "The general rule is that, where an agreement imposes several distinct duties or obligations of different degrees of importance, and the same sum is named as damages for the breach of either indifferently, the sum is to be regarded as a penalty." Western Macaroni Manufacturing Co. v. Fiore, 151 P. 984, 985-986 (Utah 1915). . . . [I]f "whether a contract provides a penalty or liquidated damages is in doubt, the contract ordinarily will be regarded as providing a penalty" and thus unenforceable. *Id.* at 986. . . .

2. The Shock the Conscience Test

Another line of cases compares the amount of liquidated versus actual damages. The key inquiry concerns whether "the amount of liquidated damages bears no reasonable relationship to the actual damage or is so *grossly excessive* as to be entirely disproportionate to any possible loss that might have been contemplated that it *shocks the conscience*." Warner v. Rasmussen, 704 P.2d 559, 561 (Utah 1985) (emphases added). . . . [T]his court has repeatedly noted that courts should focus on what the contracting parties knew at the time of contracting. In practice, however, the court seems to have engaged frequently in post hoc weighing [quoting four cases that compared the proven actual damages to the liquidated damages, some of which were held to shock the conscience despite quite modest disproportions between liquidated and actual damages].

3. The Restatement of Contracts Test

The first *Restatement of Contracts* lays out the following test for evaluating liquidated damages clauses:

> An agreement, made in advance of breach, fixing the damages therefor, is not enforceable as a contract and does not affect the damages recoverable for the breach, unless
>
> (a) the amount so fixed is a reasonable forecast of just compensation for the harm that is caused by the breach, and
>
> (b) the harm that is caused by the breach is one that is incapable or very difficult of accurate estimation.

Restatement of Contracts §339(1) (Am. Law Inst. 1932). These two factors are evaluated as of the time of contract formation, not breach. *But see id.* cmt. *e* (noting that a liquidated damages clause is not enforceable if the breach "causes no harm at all," even if the parties believed at the time of contract formation that the harm was "incapable or very difficult of accurate estimation").* . . .

4. Deference to Contracting Parties

Another line of cases defers to parties' freedom to contract where the parties have fairly bargained for liquidated damages. . . .

---

* [The *Restatement (Second)* recast this provision but focused on the same two factors:

> Damages for breach by either party may be liquidated in the agreement but only at an amount that is reasonable in the light of the anticipated or actual loss caused by the breach and the difficulties of proof of loss. A term fixing unreasonably large liquidated damages is unenforceable on grounds of public policy as a penalty.

Restatement (Second) of Contracts §356(1) (Am. Law Inst. 1979). Comment *b* to this section says that a liquidated-damage clause is enforceable if the amount is reasonable either in light of the damages actually suffered or in light of the damages anticipated at the time of contracting. Illustration 4 says, somewhat inconsistently, that if the actual damages are easy to determine, a liquidated-damage clause providing for greater damages is an unenforceable penalty. –EDS.]

Cases employing this approach have at times emphasized unconscionability as the primary check on liquidated damages provisions. . . .

This court has on several occasions explicitly noted the tension between focusing on the right to contract and subjecting liquidated damages clauses to stricter scrutiny. . . .

B. LIQUIDATED DAMAGES CLAUSES SHOULD BE REVIEWED LIKE OTHER CONTRACTUAL PROVISIONS . . .

The direct determination whether a liquidated damages clause appears to be a penalty imposes an unnecessary additional check on the enforceability of such clauses. First, it improperly reverses the general presumption that contractual provisions are enforceable. Second, the penalty inquiry is motivated by "the interest of justice and fairness," *Western Macaroni*, 151 P. at 986 (Frick, J., concurring), which can be adequately protected through general contractual remedies. Prior cases' framing of the penalty inquiry as a search for unconscionability reinforces this point.

The "shock the conscience" standard similarly is problematic for a number of reasons. First, cases employing this approach have tended to evaluate the enforceability of liquidated damages clauses with the benefit of hindsight, rather than as of the time of contract formation. The opinions thus tend to contain conclusory statements that the court's conscience was shocked. Additionally, cases using this approach have frequently resulted in split opinions in which the majority and dissent sharply disagree regarding the post hoc weighing. . . .

The *Restatement* test raises similar concerns. . . . The first part of the *Restatement* test requires a "reasonable forecast" of actual damages, yet the second part requires actual damages to be "incapable or very difficult of accurate estimation." *Restatement of Contracts* §339. It is hard to comprehend how courts can evaluate the reasonableness of a forecast made when actual damages are nearly impossible to estimate at the time of contract formation. As the comments to the *Restatement* note, enforcement of liquidated damages clauses is intended to "save[ ] the time of courts, juries, parties, and witnesses and reduce[ ] the expense of litigation." *Id.* cmt. *c.* The *Restatement* test, however, actually *encourages* litigation regarding the reasonableness of the forecast and the difficulty of estimating the harm. . . .

We now hold that liquidated damages clauses should be reviewed in the same manner as other contractual provisions. . . . Courts should invalidate liquidated damages clauses "only with great reluctance and when the facts clearly demonstrate that it would be unconscionable to decree enforcement of the terms of the contract." Perkins v. Spence, 243 P.2d 446, 451 (Utah 1952).

Comcast argues that, by reviewing liquidated damages clauses only for unconscionability, this court would allow parties to "effectively stipulate to permit punitive damages in the event of breach." We disagree. Reviewing liquidated damages clauses for unconscionability still preserves challenges to penalty clauses. . . . Furthermore, our case law employing the penalty approach looks at "the circumstances surrounding the parties at the time of [the contract's] execution," *Croft*, 40 P.2d at 202 — the same inquiry we engage in for claims of unconscionability.

Thus we clarify that liquidated damages clauses are not subject to any form of heightened judicial scrutiny. Instead, courts should begin with the longstanding presumption that liquidated damages clauses are enforceable. A party may challenge the enforceability of a liquidated damages clause only by pursuing one of the general contractual remedies, such as mistake, fraud, duress, or unconscionability.

C. THE LIQUIDATED DAMAGES CLAUSE IN THIS CASE IS ENFORCEABLE . . .

[T]he burden properly rests on the party challenging the clause's enforceability because "the purpose of a liquidated damages provision is to obviate the need for the nonbreaching party to prove actual damages." Bair v. Axiom Design, L.L.C., 20 P.3d 388, 394 (Utah 2001).

"In determining whether a contract is unconscionable, we use a two-pronged analysis." Ryan v. Dan's Food Stores, Inc., 972 P.2d 395, 402 (Utah 1998). . . .

"Procedural unconscionability focuses on the negotiation of the contract and the circumstances of the parties." Id. at 403. . . . We have laid out six factors bearing on procedural unconscionability. . . . Comcast does not allege procedural unconscionability. Nor could it, as Comcast (through its predecessor) drafted the contract in its entirety. . . .

"Substantive unconscionability focuses on the contents of an agreement, examining the relative fairness of the obligations assumed." Id. at 402. It is not sufficient for the liquidated damages clause to be "unreasonable or more advantageous to one party." Id. Instead, "we consider whether a contract's terms are so one-sided as to oppress or unfairly surprise an innocent party or whether there exists an overall imbalance in the obligations and rights imposed by the bargain according to the mores and business practices of the time and place." Id.

There are no signs of substantive unconscionability with respect to the liquidated damages clause in this contract. Although the clause may be "more advantageous" to CRE, it is not "so one-sided as to oppress" Comcast—particularly where Comcast stands in the shoes of the party that drafted the clause in the first instance. Nor do we find the contractual amount of liquidated damages unreasonable as compensation for a breach of the contractual duty to continuously operate the building. Although Comcast now argues that over $1.7 million in liquidated damages is "grossly disproportionate" to CRE's actual damages, this type of post hoc weighing does not bear on the question of substantive unconscionability, which focuses on the "relative fairness of the obligations assumed" at the time of contracting. . . .

[The court also rejected Comcast's argument that CRE had failed to mitigate its damages. It rejected CRE's argument that Comcast was a unique and irreplaceable tenant. But assuming that Comcast could be replaced, the burden of persuasion was on Comcast, and while it repeatedly asserted that CRE had not done enough to find a new tenant, it had offered no evidence of what more CRE should have done.]

NEHRING and PARRISH, J.J., join the opinion of the court.

DURRANT, C.J., and FRATTO, J., not participating.

Justice LEE, concurring in part and concurring in the judgment:

. . . I am . . . in full agreement with a threshold course-correction charted by the majority—its repudiation of the hindsight-based approach followed in some of our cases and clarification that the reasonableness evaluation must be made from the standpoint of the parties at the time they entered into the contract. But I see no reason to take the additional step of abandoning the timeworn Restatement test in its entirety. That test, informed by a wealth of precedent in this state and the many others that have embraced it, provides needed predictability for contracting parties . . . .

The problem is not the Restatement test; it is . . . post-hoc evaluation of reasonableness. . . .

The supposed internal inconsistency in the Restatement standard is also no reason to abandon it. . . .

The reasonable forecast inquiry is the core standard under the *Restatement*; the difficulty of estimation element is subsidiary and explanatory. . . . When damages are difficult to estimate at the time of contract formation, a liquidated sum is more likely to be deemed reasonable (and vice-versa). That's the whole point of the *Restatement*'s two-part inquiry; it's a sliding scale . . . .

[E]ven if I were of a mind to jettison this test, I would not replace it with the undefined standard of "unconscionability" . . . . I am, of course, on board with the general principle of freedom of contract. . . . But those general principles are subject to limited exceptions, which are necessary . . . to foreclose the availability of "'punitive damages'" for breach of contract, which would have the troubling effect of deterring efficient breach. So the question before us is not whether to recognize a general rule favoring the freedom of contract; it is how to define the exception to the general rule in the liquidated damages context. . . .

The majority never explains how the substantive unconscionability or fairness of a liquidated damages clause is to be evaluated going forward. It offers only its bottom-line conclusion that "the contractual amount of liquidated damages" is not "unreasonable as compensation for a breach of the contractual duty to continuously operate the building." That fuzzy fairness analysis is an invitation for arbitrariness in judicial decisionmaking. Contracting parties . . . deserve a workable standard they can rely on and contract around. I see the *Restatement* standard as providing that predictability and workability. In rejecting it, the court revives the muddle it so helpfully resolved in the first part of its opinion. . . .

Under the *Restatement* standard that I would apply, the judgment entered by the majority would still obtain. . . . Comcast bore the burden of demonstrating that the damages liquidated by the parties in this case were [not] a reasonable forecast of the damages they anticipated at the time of the execution of the contract. . . . [B]ecause Comcast failed to present any evidence of the nature of the damages anticipated by the parties or of the relationship the liquidated damages bore to those damages, its challenge to the liquidated damages clause in this case fails as a matter of law. I would affirm on that basis instead of altering our standard in a way that seems sure to undermine predictability . . . and to inject arbitrariness into the judicial evaluation of liquidated damages clauses.

NOTES ON LIQUIDATED-DAMAGE AND PENALTY CLAUSES

1. Reducing inconsistency? Complaints about confusion and inconsistency in liquidated-damage cases are widespread and longstanding. One can find authority to support nearly any proposition. How much is too much is inherently a question of degree, which courts try to decide as a matter of law. Is the court likely to do any better asking whether the liquidated damages are unconscionable than by asking whether they are an unreasonable estimate? Maybe it is just signaling that review is henceforth to be more deferential.

There is a similar opinion in Arrowhead School District No. 75 v. Klyap, 79 P.3d 250 (Mont. 2003), reviewing inconsistent decisions and announcing that liquidated damage clauses are presumed to be enforceable and that they are to be reviewed for unconscionability. This was in the teeth of a statute providing that liquidated-damage clauses are void, except where "it would be impractical or extremely difficult to fix the actual damage." Mont. Code Ann. §28-2-721(2). The court said that it need not confront the statute because *Klyap* fit within the exception.

2. The facts in *Comcast*. Why should the court conclude, without explanation, that double rent for five years is not unconscionably one-sided and not an unreasonable estimate of the possible damages? In a passage omitted above, the court says that in Utah substantive unconscionability, found in excessively one-sided terms, can make a contract unconscionable even without any procedural unconscionability, typically found in deception or lack of choice in contract negotiations. But its discussion of substantive unconscionability returns to the fact that the tenant drafted the contract. Substantive and procedural unconscionability are further explored in section 11.A.

3. The majority rule. Variations on the *Restatement* approach are by far the majority rule in the United States. But the cases are inconsistent, often within the same jurisdiction, about whether the liquidated amount should be compared to what was reasonably estimated at the time of contracting or to the damages actually suffered, about who bears the burden of proof, and many other issues. Spotting trends in these circumstances is not easy, but the trend appears to be toward greater deference to these clauses.

Two decisions under Texas law can illustrate at least how federal courts understand Texas's adherence to the *Restatement* rule. In the first, plaintiff provided billing services for two cellphone providers. The liquidated damages clause said that if the cell companies terminated the contract, they had to pay the full price per customer for the remaining term of the contract. Defendants said that gross revenue could not possibly be a reasonable estimate of damages, which would be based on lost net profits. Plaintiff said that its business was just data processing, and that the marginal cost of an additional customer was zero, so that gross revenue *was* net profit. The court said that was possible and enforced the clause. RSA 1 LP v. Paramount Software Associates, Inc., 793 F.3d 903 (8th Cir. 2015). Not only that, but the court said that "Paramount intended the prospect of these liquidated damages to dissuade the RSAs from terminating the contract early." *Id.* at 905. That sounds like the definition of a penalty instead of an attempt to estimate damages. But the court recited that fact without comment.

A case at the other end of the continuum is Caudill v. Keller Williams Realty, Inc., 828 F.3d 575 (7th Cir. 2016). The parties had entered into a confidential settlement of earlier litigation; the settlement agreement provided liquidated damages of $10,000 for each violation of the obligation not to disclose its terms. But federal law required that the agreement be disclosed to some potential franchisees, and Keller Williams, either in confusion or excessive compliance, disclosed it to 2,000 existing and renewing franchisees as well. Plaintiff said that $10,000 per violation times 2,000 violations meant $20 million in liquidated damages. The district court found that the disclosures had done no damage, and the court of appeals said that at most they had done modest damage. Neither $20 million total nor $10,000 per disclosure was a reasonable estimate of actual damages; the clause was an unenforceable penalty.

4. Codification. UCC §2-718(1), which applies to the sale of goods, enacts a variation on the *Restatement* rule:

> Damages for breach by either party may be liquidated in the agreement but only at an amount which is reasonable in the light of the anticipated or actual harm caused by the breach, the difficulties of proof of loss and the inconvenience or nonfeasibility of otherwise obtaining an adequate remedy. A term fixing unreasonably large liquidated damages is void as a penalty.

Montana has enacted this provision for the sale of goods while retaining its much more stringent provision, copied from California and enacted in 1895, for all other contracts. California retains its stringent provision for consumer cases. Cal. Civ. Code §1671(d). But for all other cases, it provides that liquidated damages clauses are presumed to be reasonable and the party attacking the clause has the burden of showing that it "was unreasonable under the circumstances existing at the time the contract was made." §1671(b). The state's UCC provision, Cal. Com. Code §2718, has been rewritten to conform to the Civil Code. So in Roodenburg v. Pavestone Co., 89 Cal. Rptr. 3d 558, 565-566 (Ct. App. 2009), the court held that plaintiff has no burden to present any evidence either of actual or anticipated injury until and unless defendant proves that the clause was unreasonable.

No criteria for reasonableness are stated. The courts continue to emphasize the relationship between the liquidated damages and the damages that could reasonably have been anticipated. They at least say that they refuse to consider actual damages or anything else that happened after the making of the contract, and they appear not to require that the actual damages be hard to calculate. The leading case is Ridgley v. Topa Thrift & Loan Ass'n, 953 P.2d 484 (Cal. 1998), holding that a charge of six months interest for one late payment was unreasonable. Another example is Vitatech International, Inc. v. Sporn, 224 Cal. Rptr. 3d 691 (Ct. App. 2017), where a contract to settle litigation provided that if defendant failed to make a one-time payment of $75,000 on time, he would be liable for the amount plaintiff had demanded in the underlying litigation—$300,000. The court said this was a liquidated damage clause and the amount was unreasonable.

5. Another confidentiality agreement. Compare the contract that Donald Trump—or maybe just his lawyer—attempted to enter into with pornographic film actress Stormy Daniels in 2016, in which she agreed never to reveal an affair conducted shortly after the birth of his youngest son. She agreed to pay $1 million for each breach of the agreement, in addition to disgorging any profits from the breach (such as sums the tabloid press might pay for her story). Is $1 million per breach a reasonable estimate of the damages anticipated by a presidential candidate trying to keep an affair secret from the voters? By a wealthy husband trying to keep an affair secret from his wife? If California law applies (as it might), is the $1 million per breach "unreasonable under the circumstances existing" shortly before the election? If Utah law were to apply, is $1 million per breach unconscionable? Should it matter that Stormy Daniels probably does not have $1 million—and certainly does not have $20 million, the amount demanded in a Trump complaint alleging 20 violations? If the liquidated damages vastly exceed her ability to pay, does that show that the number was intended for deterrence rather than compensation? The contract is available at http://msnbcmedia.msn.com/i/TODAY/z_Creative/Filed%20 Complaint.pdf [https://perma.cc/EG6P-DYW7].

6. How much do we need to know about expected or actual damages? Some opinions, as in *Comcast*, find the liquidated-damage clause enforceable with only cursory attention to what items of potential damage the parties might have contemplated. Other opinions give far closer scrutiny to the reasonableness of the estimate. At the extreme, parties have sometimes felt obliged to prove their actual damages in order to show the reasonableness of the liquidated-damage clause. The only fully accepted purpose of liquidated-damage clauses is to avoid litigation over difficult damage issues. If the parties feel obliged to prove actual damages in order to show the reasonableness of liquidated damages, what has been gained? On the other hand, if the court is too accepting of the number in the contract, the rule against penalty clauses (or unconscionable clauses) becomes illusory.

7. Parties with equal bargaining power. Why should the courts second-guess the parties' contract at all? If the parties are free to agree on their own contract, why aren't they free to agree on the remedy? Is it likely that enforcing penalty clauses would lead to the "most terrible oppression," as suggested in Truck Rent-A-Center, Inc. v. Puritan Farms 2nd, Inc., 361 N.E.2d 1015, 1018 (N.Y. 1977)? *Keller Williams* in note 3 suggests that maybe sometimes, the answer is yes.

Is oppression likely in negotiations between large businesses? Liquidated-damages clauses sometimes recite that the clause is a reasonable estimate and not a penalty, negotiated at arms' length between sophisticated parties with equal bargaining power, and that the party subject to the clause agrees not to argue otherwise. Courts inclined to scrutinize liquidated damages generally give such clauses little weight. If courts are serious about not enforcing penalties, then they cannot change the result when the parties agree that this penalty is not really a penalty. And such recitals are likely to be fictional: If one party can force the other to accept a penalty clause, it can probably also force that party to agree that it is not a penalty clause. Such a clause appears in the contract in In re Trans World Airlines, 145 F.3d 124 (3d Cir. 1998). But this clause was inserted when TWA was unable to pay the rent on an aircraft lease, asking for a reduced payment schedule, and sliding into bankruptcy. Just because it was a big company did not mean that it had anything like equal bargaining power. Stormy Daniels no doubt had some leverage, but she agreed that $1 million per breach was a reasonable estimate of damages and not a penalty.

8. Consumers. Oppression may be a greater risk for consumers and for entities much smaller than their contractual partners.

a. Speeding in a rented car. Consider American Car Rental, Inc. v. Commissioner of Consumer Protection, 869 A.2d 1198 (Conn. 2005). American put global positioning systems in its cars and charged renters $150 each time their speed continuously exceeded 79 miles per hour for two minutes or more. If their speed dropped below 79 and then went above 79 for another two minutes, a new fee was triggered. A driver cruising at about 80, slowing down for traffic as necessary, could incur many separate fees of $150 each; the court didn't say whether the clause was enforced literally in such cases. The hearing officer calculated the cost of the extra wear and tear of driving 80 miles an hour for two minutes at 37 cents.

The court threw the clause out as a penalty for speeding and not as a reasonable estimate of damages. "A contractual provision for a penalty is one the prime purpose of which is to prevent a breach of the contract by holding over the head of a contracting party the threat of punishment for a breach. . . . A provision for liquidated damages, on the other hand, is one the real purpose of which is to fix fair compensation to the injured party for a breach of the contract." *Id.* at 1205-1206.

b. Cell phone termination fees. A California court held that the termination fee in Sprint's cell phone contracts was a penalty, designed to deter customers from changing carriers, and not a reasonable estimate of damages. In re Cellphone Fee Termination Cases, 122 Cal. Rptr. 3d 726 (Ct. App. 2011). Sprint argued that the fees helped cover the cost of the phone, which was spread through the price of the monthly service contract to minimize the upfront cost to consumers. But the court relied on evidence that in setting the fee, Sprint considered competitive impact, resulting revenue, and customer acceptance, but did no analysis of the cost of early terminations.

9. Employees. The defendant in *Arrowhead School District*, in note 1, was a teacher and coach who left in August to take another job. The liquidated-damage clause required him to pay 20 percent of a year's salary. The school hired a less experienced teacher at lower pay, but it said that this was not a real savings and that athletic programs and planning for the new school year had been disrupted. The school had 80 applicants for teaching positions in the spring, but only 2 remained available when defendant resigned. The court enforced the clause as not unconscionable.

It is worse when the employer fires the employee for cause and sues for liquidated damages. In Ashcroft & Gerel v. Coady, 244 F.3d 948 (D.C. Cir. 2001), a law firm fired the managing partner of its Boston office and got a judgment for $400,000 in liquidated damages. There is a similar judgment against a terminated insurance agent, who then solicited his former clients in violation of his contract with the insurer. American Family Mutual Insurance Co. v. Graham, 792 F.3d 951 (8th Cir. 2015). That judgment was for more than $1.3 million, based on "forfeiture" of the amount in a deferred-compensation account at the time of the breach. The court was skeptical that this amount bore any relationship to the expected damages from breach of the no-solicitation clause. But the agent had offered little evidence of how the actual damages might have been estimated, and the court enforced the clause. And it said that calling this remedy a "forfeiture" did not necessarily mean that it was not a liquidated-damage clause.

10. Compare with limitation-of-remedy clauses. One of the reasons offered for invalidating penalty clauses is that the remedy for breach of contract is compensation and the parties cannot deviate from that. But courts have generally been much more sympathetic to clauses limiting remedies to less than full compensation. Why is an undercompensatory remedy more acceptable than an overcompensatory remedy?

One answer might be that contracts are intended to allocate risk. In *K & T*, the risk that the machine won't work is inherent in the transaction, and a disclaimer of liability allocates that risk to the buyer. The risk of paying double rent, or of a large penalty for driving 80 miles per hour, is not inherent in the transaction; these risks are artificially created by the liquidated-damage clause. But it may also be that courts just don't view undercompensation as a significant problem.

11. The economic debate. Restrictions on liquidated damages have provoked debate among law-and-economics scholars. On the one hand, they fear that damages in excess of lost expectancy will deter efficient breaches; that is a reason not to enforce penalty clauses. On the other hand, they think that voluntary transactions are better than court decisions at moving resources to their most valuable use. If one side is willing to pay for a penalty clause (perhaps because it is worried about unprovable or noncompensable damages), and the other side is willing to grant a penalty clause (perhaps in exchange for a better price or to beat out the competition), both sides are presumably better off.

Early literature focused on whether penalty clauses distorted incentives to breach or provoke breach. These and a range of other arguments, pro and con, are summarized in Richard A. Posner, *Economic Analysis of Law* §4.12 at 140-144 (9th ed., Wolters Kluwer 2014). A later body of literature tends to focus on whether liquidated-damage and penalty clauses are peculiarly vulnerable to cognitive errors and the limits of human rationality. This literature is much influenced by behavioral economics, which considers how humans actually behave instead of assuming that we are all rational profit maximizers. If parties entering into a deal tend to be optimistic and greatly underestimate the risk of breach, or if they think only of the most obvious breaches and overlook the great variety of ways their deal can go bad, they may not think enough about the liquidated-damage clause or anticipate all the ways it might operate. A good example of this literature is Melvin Aron Eisenberg, *The Limits of Cognition and the Limits of Contract*, 47 Stan. L. Rev. 211 (1995). Wouldn't that argument apply to any contract clause about remedies? How does it distinguish liquidated-damage clauses from limitation-of-remedy clauses?

It may be that efficiency effects can be debated for so long without reaching a conclusion because they are so modest in practice. In civil law countries, the rule is generally the opposite. There is no distinction between liquidated-damage clauses and penalty clauses; either is enforceable. But courts have discretion to reduce a penalty that is grossly excessive, and parties generally cannot contract out of that power. Code provisions from some of the major European countries are collected in Aristides N. Hatzis, *Having the Cake and Eating It Too: Efficient Penalty Clauses in Common and Civil Contract Law*, 22 Intl. Rev. L. & Econ. 381 (2003).

12. Alternative-performance clauses. One way to draft around the problem is with an alternative-performance clause. Instead of saying that if a party breaches, he must pay liquidated damages, say that the party may perform the contract either by doing what the contract contemplates or by paying a sum of money. The *Restatement* says that courts must examine such clauses to ensure that they are not penalty clauses in disguise.

The Supreme Court of Washington held that paying a cellphone termination fee is an alternative way of performing the contract and not a penalty for breach. Minnick v. Clearwire US LLC, 275 P.3d 1127 (Wash. 2012). The Washington court viewed the distinction as more than a drafting trick dependent on "a form of words"; it said that to qualify as an alternative-performance clause, the two options must "give the promisor a real choice between reasonably equivalent choices," viewed as of the time of contracting. *Id.* at 1131. But there did not seem to be much content in the court's enforcement of this criterion. The court said the termination fee was not significantly different in amount from paying the monthly charge for the remaining term of the contract, so the choices were reasonably equivalent. But as the four dissenters pointed out, consumers got nothing for the termination fee; they would have gotten cellphone service for paying the remaining monthly charges.

NOTES ON UNDERLIQUIDATED-DAMAGE CLAUSES

1. Two different questions. In the typical case, defendant claims that the liquidated damages are too large. But sometimes, plaintiff complains that the liquidated damages are too small. In Northern Illinois Gas Co. v. Energy Cooperative Inc., 461 N.E.2d 1049 (Ill. App. Ct. 1984), the buyer repudiated a long-term contract for the purchase of naphtha, a hydrocarbon that can be converted into natural gas. The price of natural gas had fallen and the price of naphtha had gone up. The liquidated-damage clause provided for one cent per gallon, which came out to $13 million. Seller's actual damages, according to the jury, were $305 million. Is a clause that eliminates 96 percent of the damages a liquidated-damage clause, or a limitation-of-remedy clause?

In the overliquidated-damage cases, courts ask whether the clause is void or unenforceable. In the underliquidated-damage cases, the question is not whether the clause is void; plaintiff could ask for the liquidated amount even if that's unconscionably low. The question is whether the liquidated-damage clause is exclusive: Can plaintiff sue only for liquidated damages, or can she sue for actual damages in the alternative?

2. UCC §2-719(1). Section 2-719(1)(b) says that when a contract for the sale of goods provides for a remedy different from those provided in the Act, the contractual remedy is "optional unless the remedy is expressly agreed to be exclusive." If the contractual remedy was intended as a limitation-of-remedy clause, it is likely to say that it is exclusive. But if it was intended as a liquidated-damage clause, it may say no such thing. The clause in *Northern Illinois Gas* did not say it was exclusive.

3. UCC §2-718. Section 2-718 says that "unreasonably large liquidated damages" are void as a penalty, but it also says more generally that the liquidated amount must be "reasonable." The Official Comment notes that an "unreasonably small amount would be subject to similar criticism and might be stricken under the section on unconscionable contracts or clauses." There is a similar statement in the *Restatement (Second) of Contracts* §356 cmt. *a.* Is $13 million per se unreasonable when compared to $305 million? Or does the court have to know who was to bear the risk of an unexpectedly large swing in the price of naphtha? If so, how is the court supposed to figure that out?

One cent per gallon doesn't sound like much; buyer might have drafted it as a get-out-of-jail-free card. Or maybe it was expected to cover routine price fluctuations and no one anticipated a much bigger price change. Or maybe it was supposed to cover occasional gaps in performance and no one anticipated repudiation. With both sides taking adversarial positions after the fact, how can the court decide? If drafters do have a purpose in mind, their clause is more likely to be enforced if they recite that purpose in the contract.

4. UCC §2-719(2). Does a liquidated-damage clause "fail of its essential purpose" if it is grossly undercompensatory? Is that another way of asking whether the clause reasonably estimates damages?

5. *Northern Illinois Gas.* Decisions involving underliquidated damages are scattered and inconsistent. In *Northern Illinois Gas*, the court said that the clause was a liquidated-damage clause governed by §2-718, and that it was not a limitation-of-remedy clause and thus not subject to §2-719. And without much analysis, the court said that the clause implicitly precluded any claim for actual damages.

2. Avoidable Consequences, Offsetting Benefits, and Collateral Sources

S.J. GROVES & SONS CO. v. WARNER CO.
576 F.2d 524 (3d Cir. 1978)

Before ALDISERT, VAN DUSEN and WEIS, Circuit Judges.

WEIS, Circuit Judge. . . .

[T]he Pennsylvania Department of Transportation undertook the erection of the Girard Point Bridge in Southwest Philadelphia and selected American Bridge Company as the prime contractor. Plaintiff-appellant Groves was awarded a subcontract for the placement of the bridge's concrete decks and parapets and contracted with the defendant Warner for the delivery of ready-mixed concrete for use at the Girard Point site. Groves filed this lawsuit claiming extensive losses because of Warner's failure to deliver adequate supplies at scheduled times. The case was tried to the court. . . . Dissatisfied with the denial of a large part of its claimed damages, Groves appealed.

The contract at issue provided that Warner would supply approximately 35,000 cubic yards of ready-mixed concrete at a rate of 40 cubic yards per hour and at times specified by Groves. . . .

Groves expected to pour concrete for the decks of the bridge in the mornings and then to use some of the crew to construct parapets in the afternoons. This general plan was frustrated by Warner's frequent failures to make deliveries in compliance with Groves' instructions. As a result, deck pours originally scheduled for the mornings often extended into the afternoons and evenings and created overtime labor expense.

Concerned with its lagging progress, Groves considered securing other sources of concrete as early as 1971 but found no real alternatives. It was too expensive to build its own batching plant at the site and the only other source of ready-mixed concrete in the area was the Trap Rock Company, located near the Warner plant. Trap Rock, however, was not certified to do state work in 1971 and its price was higher than Warner's. Moreover, the production facilities at Trap Rock were limited, as was the number of trucks it had available. Meanwhile, Warner continued to assure Groves that deliveries would improve.

Despite its promises, Warner's performance continued to be erratic and on June 21, 1972, the . . . Department of Transportation ordered all construction at Girard Point halted until the quality of Warner's service could be discussed at a conference. . . . Based on Warner's renewed assurances of improved performance, state officials allowed work to resume on June 26, 1972. From that date until July 20, 1972, Warner's delivery service improved significantly, although it still did not consistently meet Groves' instructions. In the months following and until completion in October of 1972, Warner's performance continued to be uneven and unpredictable.

On June 14, 1972, when Groves again approached Trap Rock, that firm maintained that it could service the job at the desired delivery rate but did not reduce its price. On July 11, 1972, Trap Rock was certified by the state and the next day agreed to accept the same price as Warner. Groves, nevertheless, decided to continue with Warner as its sole supplier.

The district judge found that Warner had acted in bad faith by deliberately over-committing its ability to manufacture and deliver enough concrete, providing an inadequate number of trucks to service Groves' project, and following a policy of providing delivery at only 75 percent of the ordered rate. On that basis, the court stripped Warner of the protection offered by the no-claim-for-delay clause in its contract and awarded damages. In the court's view, on June 15, 1972, Groves had no reasonable expectation that Warner's performance would improve to "totally satisfactory levels" and by July 11, 1972, "there were no practical impediments to employing Trap Rock as a supplemental supplier." The court therefore concluded that "as of July 12, 1972, Groves had an obligation to utilize Trap Rock as a supplemental supplier . . . in order to mitigate any possible 'delay damages' resulting from Warner's service." Accordingly, the court did not award Groves all the delay damages it sought, allowing only $12,534 for overtime which had been paid on days when Warner's deliveries were late before, but not after, July 12, 1972. . . .

Section 2-715 [of Pennsylvania's Uniform Commercial Code] provides that the consequential damages a buyer may recover are those which "could not reasonably be prevented by cover or otherwise." Thus, generally, when a seller refuses to deliver goods, the buyer must attempt to secure similar articles elsewhere as a prerequisite to receiving consequential damages. "Cover" is defined in §2-712(1): "After a breach . . . the buyer may 'cover' by making in good faith and without unreasonable delay any reasonable purchase of or contract to purchase goods in substitution for those due from the seller." . . .

The requirement of cover or mitigation of damages is not an absolute, unyielding one, but is subject to the circumstances. Comment 2 to §2-712 says:

> [t]he test of proper cover is whether at the time and place the buyer acted in good faith and in a reasonable manner, and it is immaterial that hindsight may later prove that the method of cover used was not the cheapest or most effective.

Essentially the cover rules are an expression of the general duty to mitigate damages and usually the same principles apply. The burden of proving that losses could have been avoided by reasonable effort and expense must be borne by the party who has broken the contract. . . .

In July 1972, Groves found itself confronted with a breach by Warner and the consequent necessity to choose among a number of alternative courses of action. In the circumstances, Groves could have:

1. Declared the contract breached, stopped work, and held Warner liable for all damages. This was not a realistic alternative.
2. Set up its own cement batching plant at the job site. Time and expense made this impractical.
3. Accepted Warner's assurances that it would perform satisfactorily in the future. The court, however, found that it would have been unreasonable to have any faith in continued assurances from Warner.
4. Substituted Trap Rock for Warner for the remainder of the contract. The court made no finding on the reasonableness of this choice but it appears questionable whether Trap Rock had the resources to meet all of Groves' requirements.
5. Engaged Trap Rock as a supplemental supplier; or
6. Continued dealing with Warner in the belief that though its performance would not be satisfactory, consequential damages might be less than if the other alternatives were adopted.

Of the six alternatives, Groves was seemingly faced with three practical ones—all subject to drawbacks. Groves had to: allow Warner to continue in the hope of averting even greater losses; substitute Trap Rock for all of Warner's work—a choice made doubtful by Trap Rock's ability to handle the project; or, lastly, use Trap Rock as a supplemental supplier.

The last choice—the option chosen by the district court—was subject to several difficulties which the court did not discuss. Even if Trap Rock supplied part of the contract with perfect scheduling, there would be no guarantee that Warner would do so. The element of erratic deliveries by Warner would not necessarily be cured, nor would the problems with the quality of concrete it delivered to the site. The presence of two independent suppliers acting separately might indeed pose problems more severe than those which existed before. Moreover, the record reveals that Trap Rock received some of its raw material from Warner, and Groves suspected that Warner might not have been too cooperative if part of the Girard Bridge contract were taken away by Trap Rock.

Confronted with these alternatives, Groves chose to stay with Warner, a decision with which the district court did not agree. The court's preference may very well have been the best; that, however, is not the test. As Judge Hastie wrote in In re Kellett Aircraft Corp., 186 F.2d 197, 198-199 (3d Cir. 1950):

> Where a choice has been required between two reasonable courses, the person whose wrong forced the choice can not complain that one rather than the other was chosen.
> The rule of mitigation of damages may not be invoked by a contract breaker as a basis for hypercritical examination of the conduct of the injured party, or merely for the purpose of showing that the injured person might have taken steps which seemed wiser or would have been more advantageous to the defaulter. One is not obligated to exalt the interest of the defaulter to his own probable detriment.

There are situations in which continuing with the performance of an unsatisfactory contractor will avoid losses which might be experienced by engaging others to complete the project. In such a setting, mitigation is best served by continuing existing arrangements. As the troubled Prince of Denmark once observed we "rather bear those ills we have, Than fly to others that we know not of."

There is another unusual feature in this case. Engaging Trap Rock as an additional source of supply was a course of action open to Warner as well as Groves. Indeed, on other commercial work Warner *had* used Trap Rock as a supplemental supplier. When the . . . Department of Transportation approved Trap Rock, Warner could have augmented its deliveries to Groves by securing extra trucks and concrete from Trap Rock as needed. Such an arrangement by Warner would have had the distinct advantage of having one subcontractor directly answerable to Groves for proper delivery, timing and quality.

Where both the plaintiff and the defendant have had equal opportunity to reduce the damages by the same act and it is equally reasonable to expect the defendant to minimize damages, the defendant is in no position to contend that the plaintiff failed to mitigate. Nor will the award be reduced on account of damages the defendant could have avoided as easily as the plaintiff. . . .

Here, where the alternative the court imposed upon Groves was available to Warner as well, Warner may not assert Groves' lack of mitigation in failing to do precisely that which Warner chose not to do. Particularly is this so in light of the finding that Warner breached the contract in bad faith.

Thus, either upon the ground that Groves should not be faulted for choosing one of several reasonable alternatives or upon the basis that Warner was bound to procure an additional supplier, we hold that the district court erred in imposing on Groves as a matter of law a duty to engage Trap Rock. Accordingly, we vacate that portion of the court's judgment which allowed damages for delay only until July 12, 1972. We remand for assessment of damages from that point to completion of the contract on the same basis as that used for the . . . delay damages [incurred prior to July 12].

NOTES ON AVOIDABLE CONSEQUENCES

1. Vocabulary. The rule that defendant is not liable for avoidable consequences of his wrongdoing is closely related to doctrines of contributory and comparative negligence. But the avoidable-consequences doctrine applies in contract and to non-negligent torts as well. It is often discussed in terms of plaintiff's duty to mitigate damages. There is nothing inaccurate about the phrase "mitigation of damages," but it is not quite accurate to say that plaintiff has a "duty" to mitigate. He can mitigate or not, as he chooses, but he cannot recover for losses he could have avoided.

2. Burden of proof. Avoidable consequences is generally treated as an affirmative defense, with the burden of proof on defendant. For a whole opinion on the burden-of-proof issue, see Carnation Co. v. Olivet Egg Ranch, 229 Cal. Rptr. 261 (Ct. App. 1986). But avoidable-consequences cases can slip imperceptibly into cases on the basic measure of damage. Recall the cases in section 2.B, where defendant says plaintiff should have abandoned his property instead of spending so much to repair it. Is that an argument that plaintiff should have mitigated damages, so that defendant must prove the value of the property? Or is it an argument that plaintiff has not proved an essential element of damages until he offers evidence of value? For the mitigation theory, see Jenkins v. Etlinger, 432 N.E.2d 589, 590-591 (N.Y. 1982). For the element-of-damage theory, see O'Brien Brothers v. The Helen B. Moran, 160 F.2d 502, 504-505 (2d Cir. 1947).

3. Repudiation of contracts. The classic avoidable-consequences case is Rockingham County v. Luten Bridge Co., 35 F.2d 301, 307-309 (4th Cir. 1929), where the county cancelled a contract to build a bridge because it had decided not to build a road. The bridge company kept working, constructing a bridge from nowhere to nowhere in the middle of a forest. Not surprisingly, plaintiff's recovery was limited to what had been spent before the notice of cancellation and the profit that would have been earned by completing the work. Note that this is an uncontroversial example of efficient breach: The bridge is not needed, and it is far more efficient to pay the contractor's lost profits than to waste resources building the bridge.

Compare *Luten Bridge* with St. Clare Center, Inc. v. Mueller, 517 N.E.2d 236, 239 (Ohio Ct. App. 1986), where defendant refused to pay any further expenses of her mother's care in a nursing home: "We are not persuaded that the rule requiring mitigation of damages applies against a rest home so as to require it to evict an elderly woman with minimal resources and unknown ability to cope by herself the moment her daughter denies liability for her support."

More generally, Professor Gergen argues that any obligation to avoid consequences is rather weak, and that even the rule of *Luten Bridge* has exceptions. He collects several cases where plaintiff recovered for continued performance of a repudiated contract where stopping performance would have been difficult or would have caused damages that might not have been recoverable. Mark P. Gergen, *A Theory of Self-Help Remedies in Contract*, 80 B.U. L. Rev. 1397 (2009). Some of these examples amount to de facto specific performance. In Bomberger v. McKelvey, 220 P.2d 729 (Cal. 1950), plaintiff agreed to demolish a building and clear a lot in exchange for a cash price and the right to use salvaged materials in another project. Some of the salvaged materials were in short supply and could be purchased only with a delay. Defendant tried to cancel the contract; plaintiff completed the demolition and successfully sued for the cash part of the price.

4. How much must plaintiff do? How vigorous must plaintiff be in avoiding the consequences of defendant's wrongdoing? It is generally said that he need not take steps that are unreasonable.

a. Finding a new job. The question is most frequently litigated in employment discharge cases, where plaintiff must look for other employment. Some of the cases turn on the diligence of her search. These blend into cases about what kind of work she must search for and what offers she must accept. Must she leave the geographic area if there are better opportunities elsewhere? Must she accept work outside her field, or inferior to the job she was discharged from? Most courts answer each of these questions in the negative. The Supreme Court summarized the law as follows:

> This duty, rooted in an ancient principle of law, requires the claimant to use reasonable diligence in finding other suitable employment. Although the un- or underemployed claimant need not go into another line of work, accept a demotion, or take a demeaning position,[16] he forfeits his right to backpay if he refuses a job substantially equivalent to the one he was denied.

Ford Motor Co. v. Equal Employment Opportunity Commission, 458 U.S. 219, 231-232 (1982). So a plaintiff fired as an executive chef did not have to accept work as a line cook to mitigate damages. Shahata v. W Steak Waikiki, LLC, 721 F. Supp. 2d 968, 988 (D. Haw. 2010).

An illustration with more room for debate is Ford v. Nicks, 866 F.2d 865, 873-875 (6th Cir. 1989), involving an assistant professor of education discharged from a state college. The court held that she did not have to seek high school teaching jobs, even though she had high school teaching experience. She had taken real estate courses

---

16. Some lower courts have indicated, however, that after an extended period of time searching for work without success, a claimant must consider taking a lower-paying position. . . .

and gotten a broker's license, which she did not have to do; she did not follow up and begin work as a broker. Without deciding whether it was unreasonable not to go to work as a broker once she had a license, the court held that there was no evidentiary basis for estimating her possible earnings as a broker. But the court did find it unreasonable to turn down a comparable college job 70 miles away; she and her husband could have lived halfway between the two cities. The court emphasized that the couple had applied for jobs in other states, so they were willing to relocate. It distinguished an earlier case holding that a waitress did not have to take a job 25 miles away when she could not afford to repair her car, and another case holding that plaintiff did not have to interview for a job 223 miles away.

b. Medical treatment. Another recurring fact pattern is personal injury litigation in which plaintiff refuses some recommended medical treatment. The principle in *Groves* should enable you to decide these cases. Isn't it a matter of deciding if the treatment's likely benefits outweigh its risks and discomforts? Although many standards have been announced, most are variations of this basic approach.

An example with a twist is Small v. Combustion Engineering, 681 P.2d 1081 (Mont. 1984). Plaintiff refused low-risk knee surgery that had a 92 percent chance of restoring his ability to walk. The court found that choice objectively unreasonable, but reasonable for plaintiff. Plaintiff was manic-depressive, and because of his mental disorder, he considered only the risks and ignored the benefits. The court felt obliged to take the plaintiff's view. Is that the right result? There is a similar result in Botck v. Mine Safety Appliance Corp., 611 A.2d 1174 (Pa. 1992). And consider Badeux v. State, 690 So. 2d 203 (La. Ct. App. 1997), where plaintiff's obesity aggravated her pain and disability, but the court held that she was unable to lose weight, and thus had done as much as she could to mitigate her damages.

Cases involving injured Jehovah's Witnesses (who refuse blood transfusions), Christian Scientists (who often refuse all medical treatment), or members of other faith-healing groups go both ways. A Michigan court held that refusing a blood transfusion was a failure to mitigate damages, and that the court could not consider whether the religious belief was reasonable. Braverman v. Granger, 844 N.W.2d 485 (Mich. Ct. App. 2014). A Missouri court held that it is not unreasonable to practice one's religion; the Missouri dissenter thought it unconstitutional even to consider plaintiff's religion. Wilcut v. Innovative Warehousing, 247 S.W.3d 1 (Mo. Ct. App. 2008). The majority cited a case in which an illiterate plaintiff with limited English had refused a tetanus shot because he didn't understand the risk; that was held not unreasonable under the circumstances. Doesn't the constitutional right to free exercise of religion deserve at least as much deference as the other idiosyncratic personal traits in this note?

c. Financial inability. Another recurring issue is financial inability to mitigate, illustrated in Persinger v. Lucas, 512 N.E.2d 865 (Ind. Ct. App. 1987), where defendant rear-ended plaintiffs' car. The car was towed to a repair shop, but it turned out to be a total loss. Plaintiffs were on welfare and couldn't pay the towing bill, so the car sat in the shop accruing storage charges. The court awarded the storage charges as damages, holding that it was impossible for plaintiffs to mitigate these damages. It was also impossible for plaintiffs to replace their car, but the court cut off damages for loss of use after 30 days. Are the two holdings consistent? The court apparently feared speculative or inflated damages if loss of use could accrue indefinitely; the opinion collects conflicting cases from other jurisdictions.

There were no such fears in Geoscience Engineering & Testing, Inc. v. Allen, 2004 WL 2475280 (Tex. Ct. App. 2004), where the court awarded loss-of-use damages for 15 months. In *Geoscience,* plaintiff was injured in a car wreck, unable to work, and thus unable to repair or replace his car. To cut off loss-of-use damages "would be penalizing him for his lack of financial resources, denying him recovery of the damages he suffered . . . , and allowing the insurance company to reap the benefit of its refusal to pay the meritorious claim." *Id.* at *4.

d. Mitigation on defendant's terms. Plaintiff need not avoid loss by submitting to defendant's illegitimate demands. An example is Adenariwo v. Federal Maritime Commission, 808 F.3d 74 (D.C. Cir. 2015). Plaintiff purchased equipment that had to be shipped by sea from the United States to Nigeria. The shipping company refused to release the first shipment because of a problem with the bill of lading, an essential document prepared by the seller. Then it refused to release the second shipment because plaintiff had not paid the accruing storage charges on the first shipment. Eventually, both shipments were auctioned off to pay the storage charges. The court emphatically rejected the argument that plaintiff should have mitigated damages by paying the disputed charges.

Similarly, plaintiff is not required to surrender his claim in exchange for defendant's offer to do something that would mitigate plaintiff's damages. That is, refusal to settle is not failure to mitigate. Rolison v. Fryar, 204 So. 3d 725 (Miss. 2016).

e. Investment strategies. What is a reasonable damage-mitigating investment strategy? In Prusky v. ReliaStar Life Insurance Co., 532 F.3d 252 (3d Cir. 2008), plaintiffs negotiated special rights to trade daily, by fax, in defendant's mutual funds. Five years later, in a climate more resistant to the costs imposed by such frequent trading, defendant reneged. The court found a breach of contract, but it held that it was unreasonable for plaintiffs to park their entire $7 million balance in a money market fund for more than three years of litigation. If they could not implement their desired trading strategy, reasonable mitigation efforts required a next-best strategy. The litigation on liability extended from 2003 to 2007, a period of rising stock prices and low interest rates, so assuming that they should have been in the stock market instead of in a money market fund wiped out 90 percent of their damages. On one damage model, not selected by the district court, mitigation would have wiped out all their damages, because buy and hold performed better than their proposed daily trades. Judge Hardiman, concurring, voted to affirm only because the trial court's findings were not clearly erroneous. The standard for mitigation is reasonable, not next best, and had it been up to him, he thought it reasonable to pursue a low-risk investment strategy once plaintiffs were barred from their preferred strategy.

5. The seat-belt cases. Does plaintiff fail to avoid the consequences of an auto accident when he fails to use a seat belt? The admission of seat-belt evidence has always been a minority rule. Many of the cases are collected in Annotation, 62 A.L.R.5th 537 (1998 and Supp.), and Estep v. Mike Ferrell Ford Lincoln-Mercury, Inc., 672 S.E.2d 345, 353 n.5 (W. Va. 2008). Statutes in many states bar the admission of seat-belt evidence or limit the reduction of damages for failure to wear seat belts to token sums. Seat-belt evidence is offered on many different theories—avoidable consequences, contributory or comparative negligence, assumption of risk, product misuse, and to show that a vehicle was crashworthy when all its features are considered. Results can vary with the theory. In states that impose no liability for damages that would have been prevented by seat belts, there has been anecdotal evidence of jury nullification.

Texas now holds seat-belt evidence admissible on comparative fault. Nabors Well Services, Ltd. v. Romero, 456 S.W.3d 553 (Tex. 2015). The court said that the longstanding rule excluding such evidence arose at a time when any contributory negligence completely barred recovery, when no law required seat belt use, and when most Texans didn't use them. All those things had changed, and tort reformers had repealed a statute that had codified the exclusion of seat-belt evidence. The vast majority of drivers and passengers now wear seat belts, but half of all people killed in auto accidents were not using a seat belt. There is no sign so far that this opinion is the beginning of a trend. But if auto manufacturers are responsible for injuries suffered when seat belts fail to work, why are plaintiffs not responsible for injuries suffered when working seat belts are not used?

6. Mitigation by defendant? What about the alternative holding in *Groves*—that defendant could have avoided the damages as effectively as plaintiff? Why should that matter? Doesn't the avoidable-consequences doctrine assume that defendant is a wrongdoer and go from there?

The Ohio court distinguished *Groves* and one of its own similar decisions in Stacy v. Batavia Local School District, 829 N.E.2d 298 (Ohio 2005). Stacy was a wrongfully discharged employee; after he won his case on the original issue, the school board refused to reinstate him on the ground that in the meantime, he had retired. He appealed again and won on that issue. But he had refused to accept similar work during the years of litigation, so most of his lost pay was unrecoverable under the avoidable-consequences rule.

Stacy argued that the school board could have mitigated as easily as he could by reinstating him after the first decision in the Ohio Supreme Court. The court had several responses. The school board's retirement defense was a legitimately litigable issue. *Groves* was a case in which defendant could have mitigated by performing the *same* act that plaintiff could have performed; the court would not extend it to cases where defendant could have mitigated by performing some other act. And the court questioned the whole idea of mitigation by defendants: Stacy's theory "would relieve every plaintiff of the duty to mitigate because the defendant could have mitigated by not breaching in the first place." *Id.* at 311. The court thought that under Stacy's theory, employees could mitigate damages by requesting reinstatement, however futile the request, and making no effort to find work elsewhere.

The *Groves* rule is frequently stated, but very infrequently applied. Professor Kelly reports that the exception exists mostly in dicta; he would repudiate it as a potential source of mischief. Michael B. Kelly, *Defendant's Responsibility to Minimize Plaintiff's Loss: A Curious Exception to the Avoidable Consequences Doctrine*, 47 S.C. L. Rev. 391 (1996). Perhaps the exception's application depends on some notion of who is responsible for particular efforts to mitigate. Consider Travelers Indemnity Co. v. Maho Machine Tool Corp., 952 F.2d 26, 30-31 (2d Cir. 1991), holding that neither buyer nor its insurer had to pay the expenses of sending seller's engineer to Singapore to inspect a defective machine. The court said that mitigation did not require anyone to "relieve the seller of *the seller's* expenses," a formulation that might fit in note 4d, and in the alternative, if this inspection trip were necessary to mitigate damages, "it was *at least* as reasonable" for seller to pay as for buyer to pay, citing *Groves*.

7. Failed efforts to mitigate. Uncertainty is resolved against the wrongdoer. Groves recovers because it made a reasonable choice not to attempt an available means of mitigating damages. The opposite choice is also protected: Expenses incurred in reasonable but unsuccessful efforts to mitigate are recoverable as damages. So where a railroad tried to repair a damaged locomotive before concluding that it was beyond repair, it could recover both the value of the locomotive and the cost of the attempted repairs. This and several other examples are collected in Anderson v. Hannaford Brothers Co., 659 F.3d 151 (1st Cir. 2011).

Hannaford held that plaintiffs had stated a claim for recovery of the cost of closing accounts, credit monitoring, and identity-theft insurance after hackers got their credit-card information from defendant and unauthorized charges appeared on the accounts of many members of the putative class. The court characterized these damages as the cost of mitigating damages from unauthorized use of the credit cards. This would seem to be successful mitigation, but the court wanted to show that these costs were reasonable even for class members who acted before any unauthorized use of their own accounts. So it collected cases on reasonable mitigation efforts that turned out to be unsuccessful or to cost more than the damages avoided.

8. Sexual harassment. Avoidable consequences played a key role in the Supreme Court's development of the law of sexual harassment. Faragher v. City of Boca Raton, 524 U.S. 775 (1998); Burlington Industries, Inc. v. Ellerth, 524 U.S. 742 (1998). Both cases held that where the harasser takes "no tangible employment action" (such as discharge, discipline, reassignment, or refusing a raise or promotion), the employer has an affirmative defense to vicarious liability for the acts of the harasser. The defense has two elements: that the employer exercised reasonable care to prevent and promptly correct harassing behavior, and that the victim "unreasonably failed to take advantage of any preventive or corrective opportunities provided by the employer or to avoid harm otherwise." *Faragher* at 807; *Ellerth* at 765. The second element, as Justice Souter's opinion in *Faragher* recognized most explicitly, is an application of the avoidable-consequences doctrine.

NOTES ON OFFSETTING BENEFITS

1. The basic idea. We have already encountered cases in which plaintiff's damages were reduced by some offsetting benefit that resulted from the wrong. The argument about lost-volume sellers in Neri v. Retail Marine, in section 2.C, presupposes that damages should be reduced if defendant's breach of contract created an opportunity to make an otherwise impossible sale to someone else. Any claim to lost wages, whether for personal injury, wrongful discharge, or employment discrimination, will be offset by the wages plaintiff earns in other jobs that could not have been held if he had not lost the first job. The offsetting-benefit rule is closely related to the avoidable-consequences rule, because often the benefit conferred is an opportunity that plaintiff must take advantage of to avoid some of the consequences of the wrong.

If the goal is to restore plaintiff to her rightful position, it is clear that offsetting benefits must be taken into account. The arguments tend to be about valuation of the benefit and occasionally over whether it is really a benefit. Some of the cases are collected in Ariel Porat & Eric Posner, *Offsetting Benefits*, 100 Va. L. Rev. 1165 (2014).

2. The medical cases. Medical treatments may be tortious because of malpractice, failure to get informed consent, or failure to warn of risks. But such medical treatments often confer benefits as well as harms. An example is Guenther v. Novartis Pharmaceutical Corp., 2013 WL 4456505 (M.D. Fla. 2013) & 990 F. Supp. 2d 1299 (M.D. Fla 2014), where a patient with bone cancer took defendant's drug to protect her bones from breaking. She was not warned that the drug could also cause serious dental and jaw problems, which it did. Instructed to consider the drug's benefits as well as its harms, the jury awarded medical expenses plus $1 million for pain and suffering.

3. The same-interest requirement in tort. The tort cases commonly say that only benefits to the same interest that was harmed should be offset. Thus the *Restatement* says that if a defamation plaintiff alleges lost income, defendant may show that the publicity enabled plaintiff to earn large lecture fees. *Restatement (Second) of Torts* §920 illus. 5. But if the defamation plaintiff alleges only emotional distress and loss of reputation, the lecture fees are irrelevant. Illustration 4. These examples faithfully illustrate what the courts say, but it is not clear how much this rule matters. It is not easy to find recent cases squarely refusing an offset because the benefit was to a different interest, and as some of the following notes suggest, there may be better explanations when the offset is refused.

There is no comparable limitation on the statement of the offsetting-benefit rule in the *Restatement (Second) of Contracts*. See §§347 and 349.

4. The wrongful-birth cases. When parents sue for negligent performance of sterilization operations, some courts set off the presumed benefits of parenthood against the costs of childrearing. Dissenters have argued that parents who sought sterilization do not view the additional child as a benefit. But assuming that most of them come to love and value the extra child, don't the emotional benefits accrue to a different "interest" than the financial harm? Should that matter? Are judgments about the intrinsic value of human life a better guide to these cases? For the competing approaches, see Chaffee v. Seslar, 786 N.E.2d 705 (Ind. 2003).

5. Benefits too outrageous to consider? One might be reluctant to allow offsets in some of the *Restatement* illustrations on the ground that defendant's conduct is reprehensible and the offsetting benefit is a windfall that should be awarded to the victim rather than the wrongdoer. Consider United States v. House, 808 F.2d 508 (7th Cir. 1986), where defendant murdered a fellow prisoner and the sentencing judge ordered him to reimburse the government for the victim's funeral and burial costs. Defendant unsuccessfully argued that he had saved the government the much larger costs of feeding and housing the victim for the rest of his sentence.

6. Remarriage. One much-argued benefit is the remarriage of a plaintiff spouse in wrongful death cases. Under the usual measure of damages, remarriage may eliminate all subsequent damage. Remarriage provides a new source of financial support, companionship, society, services, etc. It does nothing for plaintiff's grief, but in most states, that is not compensable anyway. No state denies recovery to plaintiffs who do not remarry or make reasonable efforts to do so. Most conceal the fact of remarriage from the jury, or instruct the jury to ignore it. But England and a small minority of states instruct juries to consider any actual remarriage and also the possibility of remarriage in assessing damage. Some of the cases are collected in Addair v. Bryant, 284 S.E.2d 374, 379-380 (W.Va. 1981). What is the possibility of remarriage worth? If juries took that instruction seriously, wouldn't it be nearly equivalent to instructing that prolonged widowhood is an avoidable consequence for plaintiffs who could attract another mate? Is remarriage within the reasonableness limit of the avoidable-consequences rule?

Jurisdictions that consider remarriage have not necessarily assumed that marriages are fungible. See Jensen v. Heritage Mutual Insurance Co., 127 N.W.2d 228 (Wis. 1964), rejecting an argument that the damages awarded were excessive in light of plaintiff's remarriage: "It is pure speculation that the new husband will be able to provide plaintiff with the same amount of support that the deceased husband would be likely to have provided. . . . Likewise there is no assurance that plaintiff will be as happy in her new marriage as allegedly in the prior one." *Id.* at 234. The court did not seem interested in evidence on these questions. Do we really want plaintiff testifying how her new husband is inferior to the old?

Tort reformers in Ohio secured a statute making evidence of remarriage admissible and directing triers of fact to consider it, although not telling them what to do with it. Ohio Rev. Code §2125.02(A)(3)(b)(iii). The state court upheld the law against constitutional challenge, and permitted defendant to cross-examine plaintiff about how quickly he had remarried, what services the new wife performed, and whether she worked outside the home. Peña v. Northeast Ohio Emergency Affiliates, Inc., 670 N.E.2d 268 (Ohio 1995).

The rule in Illinois seems to be that the remarriage of a wrongful death plaintiff is admissible to offset loss of consortium but not to offset loss of financial support. Pfeifer v. Canyon Construction Co., 628 N.E.2d 746 (Ill. App. Ct. 1993). Does that distinction make any sense?

7. Takings of property. The Court summarily rejected a seemingly straightforward offsetting-benefits argument in Horne v. Department of Agriculture, 135 S. Ct. 2419 (2015), summarized in note 7 in Notes on Value to the Owner in section 2.B.

ODEN v. CHEMUNG COUNTY INDUSTRIAL DEVELOPMENT AGENCY
661 N.E.2d 142 (N.Y. 1995)

TITONE, Judge. . . .

The present action arises out of a December 1988 incident in which plaintiff, a 48-year-old ironworker, was injured when he was struck by a falling steel column that was apparently dislodged by a small hydraulic crane. . . .

Following a bifurcated jury trial, plaintiff was awarded damages as follows: $5,752.75 for past medical expenses, $20,000 for pain and suffering, $27,550 for lost past earnings, $66,000 for lost pension benefits and $80,000 for future lost earnings and health and welfare benefits. . . . Following a hearing pursuant to N.Y. C.P.L.R. §4545(c), the court ordered that the total award for future economic loss ($146,000) be reduced by . . . $141,330, the value of the disability retirement benefits that plaintiff expected to receive over his lifetime.

On plaintiff's appeal, the Appellate Division modified by restoring the full amount of the $80,000 award for future lost earnings and benefits and adjusting the total damages award upward accordingly. . . . 621 N.Y.S.2d 744, 746 (App. Div. 1995). The Court impliedly determined that only the award for lost pension benefits was sufficiently related to the collateral disability retirement benefits to qualify for the offset permitted by §4545(c). . . .

Under traditional common-law principles, a personal injury award may not be reduced or offset by the amount of any compensation that the injured person may receive from a source other than the tortfeasor. The collateral source rule, which is both a rule of evidence and a rule of damages, is based on the premise that a negligent defendant should not, in fairness, be permitted to reduce its liability by the proceeds of insurance or some other source to which that defendant has not contributed. Although the rule has been criticized, it was not modified or curtailed by the courts of this State.

[The rule was limited by the Legislature. The statute applies to any claim for "damages for personal injury, injury to property or wrongful death, where the plaintiff seeks to recover for the cost of medical care, dental care, custodial care or rehabilitation services, loss of earnings or other economic loss." The issue is not entrusted to juries; compensation from collateral sources is to be deducted from damages by the court: "If the court finds that any such cost or expense was or will, with reasonable certainty, be replaced or indemnified from any collateral source, it shall reduce the amount of the award by such finding." This was §4545(c) in 1995; it has since been relettered as §4545(a).]

Relying on its view of the language and purposes of the statute, appellant . . . argues that §4545(c) requires the court to reduce the total award for economic loss by the total amount of collateral source payments for economic loss that the plaintiff has or will receive as a result of the incident that led to the lawsuit. In contrast, plaintiff contends that the award for economic loss should be broken down into categories and the reductions for collateral source payments should then be made only in those categories that correspond to analogous collateral source categories. We conclude that plaintiff has the better of the argument.

We note at the outset that §4545(c) is a statute enacted in derogation of the common law and, as such, is to be strictly construed. . . . "[R]ules of the common law must be held no further abrogated than the clear import of the language used in the statute absolutely requires." N.Y. Stat. Law §301(b).

These principles and a close analysis of the statutory text provide support for plaintiff's position. The statute first refers to actions to recover for enumerated and other economic losses and then authorizes the trial court to consider that any "such" losses were or will be replaced from a collateral source. This use of the term "such," which serves as a grammatical echo for its immediate antecedent, suggests that a direct correspondence between the item of loss and the type of collateral reimbursement must exist before the required statutory offset may be made.

The statute's provision for the offset of "*any* such cost or expense" by a payment from "*any* collateral source" (emphasis added) does not contradict this conclusion. The statute's dual reference to "any" cost or expense and "any" collateral source was evidently a legislative effort to establish that, apart from the express statutory reservations, there are to be no limitations on the types of economic losses or the types of collateral benefits that the offset is intended to reach. Nothing in the use of that inclusive adjective negates the separate implication arising from the statute's other operative language that only those collateral source payments that actually replace a particular category of awarded economic loss may be used to reduce the injured's judgment.

The statutory requirement that the court make a finding that the awarded cost or expense "was or will . . . *be replaced or indemnified*" (emphasis added) from a collateral source belies the contention that the statute's juxtaposition of "*any* . . . cost or expense" with "*any* collateral source" was intended as a direction to treat all collateral source payments as fungible. . . . A disability annuity received as a result of an accident cannot be said to "replace" an out-of-pocket medical expense that the plaintiff incurred as a result of accident-related injuries. The proposition that a payment from "any" collateral source "replace[s] or indemnifie[s]" "any" accident-related cost or expense thus cannot be sustained.

The correctness of this construction of the statute is also supported by the policy considerations underlying the common-law collateral source rule and its recent legislative modifications. The chief criticism of the common-law rule was that it permitted double recovery. While the resulting windfalls to plaintiffs were deemed a necessary and acceptable "evil" when the primary aim of tort law was to punish and deter wrongdoers, the collateral source rule's doctrinal underpinnings were seriously eroded by the law's shift in focus to the considerably different goal of compensating injured individuals. If just compensation is the main end toward which tort law is directed, it makes little sense to perpetuate a damages rule that tolerates two or more recoveries for the same injury. It was this perception, along with rising insurance costs, that motivated the Legislature to take steps to modify the common-law rule.

The Legislature's goal of eliminating plaintiffs' duplicative recoveries is served by subtracting from the total award those collateral source payments that duplicate or correspond to a particular item of economic loss. The broader rule that appellant . . . advocates—which would mandate subtraction of all collateral source payments arising from the incident regardless of whether they duplicate an awarded item of pecuniary loss—would *over*compensate and produce results beyond those necessary to remedy the "evil" at which the legislation was aimed. Indeed, the rule appellant advances would confer an undeserved windfall on tort defendants and their insurers by permitting them to obtain a credit for collateral source payments that do not correspond to the items of economic loss that they are being called upon to reimburse.

In this instance, appellant . . . seeks to have plaintiff's award reduced by the entire amount he is expected to realize from his disability retirement pension. However, contrary to [appellant's] argument, plaintiff's retirement pension benefits have not been shown to replace the lost future earnings and health and welfare benefits for which the jury awarded him $80,000. Rather, those benefits are paid in lieu of ordinary pension benefits and do not necessarily correspond to any future earning capacity plaintiff might have had. Indeed, it is undisputed that, notwithstanding his retirement as an ironworker, plaintiff would have been free to earn income from his labor in other capacities without loss of his disability retirement pension benefits. Thus, it cannot be said that the disability pension benefits plaintiff expects to receive are duplicative of the award he received for lost future earnings. Accordingly, the Appellate Division properly limited the operation of §4545(c) in this case by applying plaintiff's anticipated $141,330 disability pension benefits to reduce to zero the $66,000 award for lost ordinary pension benefits which the disability pension benefits did replace.

We note that, despite [appellant's] expressed concerns about the practicality of requiring a close correspondence between the collateral source payment and the item of pecuniary loss to be replaced, we see no insurmountable difficulty in establishing the necessary linkage in appropriate cases. C.P.L.R. §4111(f), which requires a detailed itemization of the elements included in the jury's damage award, will operate to facilitate the task. The problem of matching up a collateral source to an item of loss is simply a matter of proof and factual analysis. The burden of establishing the requisite correspondence rests, of course, on the party seeking the §4545(c) offset. Where that burden is not sustained because the connection between the item of loss and the collateral source payment is tenuous or because the necessary correspondence between their essential elements is lacking, the purposes of the statute would not be served by applying the mandatory offset. . .

Accordingly, the order of the Appellate Division should be affirmed, with costs.

KAYE, C.J., and SIMONS, BELLACOSA, SMITH, LEVINE and CIPARICK, JJ., concur. . . .

NOTES ON THE COLLATERAL-SOURCE RULE

1. The debate over the traditional rule. The common-law collateral-source rule held that the compensation plaintiff received from other sources was not admissible in evidence and did not reduce the damages owed by defendant. Critics charged that the collateral-source rule allowed double recoveries to plaintiffs; plaintiff could recover medical expenses, say, first from her medical insurer and then again from a tortfeasor. The rule's defenders responded in three ways.

First, collateral sources were often entitled to subrogation—a right to be reimbursed out of the tort recovery. When subrogation worked as it should, there was no double recovery. Plaintiff recovered once; her insurers recovered once; and the loss was placed on the wrongdoer, where it belonged. But some academic critics said it was wasteful to litigate whether defendant's liability insurer should reimburse plaintiff's medical insurer; either insurer could spread the loss. And for the defense-side interests that set out to change tort law, the goal was to reduce their liability, a goal that would not be achieved if first-party insurers retained subrogation rights.

Second, even when subrogation was not sought, the rule's defenders thought it better that plaintiff get a double recovery than that defendant be off the hook. Plaintiff had first-party insurance only because she had paid insurance premiums, often for many years; the benefit of her thrift and foresight should not go to defendant. From a law-and-economics perspective, potential tortfeasors would have inadequate incentives to take care if they could ignore all losses covered by first-party insurance. Evidence of medical expenses, lost income, and other insured losses was necessary to help show the seriousness of the injury.

Third, the apparent double recovery often merely offset losses that went uncompensated, or undercompensated, elsewhere in the litigation process. Personal injury plaintiffs never recover their attorneys' fees (see section 10.A), some damages are hard to quantify, and most cases settle for less than plaintiff's full damages. All three lines of argument are nicely canvassed in Helfend v. Southern California Rapid Transit District, 465 P.2d 61 (Cal. 1970). Whatever one thinks of these arguments, the rule was well settled and reasonably uniform across the country, at least in its broad outlines.

2. Legislative amendment and repeal. The insurance industry's drive to revise tort law targeted the collateral-source rule and resulted in a bewildering variety of legislative compromises. The law of collateral sources now depends on the details of each state's statute, and the meaning of those details is often the subject of litigation. Much less is settled, and almost nothing is uniform. The variations are sampled and illustrated in Ellen S. Pryor, *Part of the Whole: Tort Law's Compensatory Failures Through a Wider Lens,* 27 Rev. Litig. 307, 319-325 (2008). Statutes and decisions from all 50 states are collected in Andrew F. Popper, *The Affordable Care Act Is Not Tort Reform,* 65 Cath. U.L. Rev. 1, 12-15 (2015). The details of the New York statute are not our concern here; it is simply an illustration. The details of each state's statute are now essential to collateral-source issues in much of the country.

3. What counts as a collateral source? Both collateral sources and many of the sources of offsetting benefits are third parties that pay money to plaintiff (or for her benefit) — money that, but for the wrong, plaintiff would never have received. Under the traditional rule, the courts had a clear intuitive sense, rarely articulated, of what counted as a collateral source and what counted as an offsetting benefit. In the collateral-source cases, the payments were made gratuitously or in fulfillment of a promise made in exchange for consideration paid earlier; in the offsetting-benefit cases, the payments were made for fresh consideration. So plaintiff's insurers; her employer's sick-pay plan; family members who chip in to pay medical bills; a government agency that pays emergency subsistence, disability, or Medicaid benefits; or a doctor or hospital that provides free care — all are acting to help the plaintiff and to compensate or ameliorate her injuries. All these people are out of pocket because of defendant's conduct and have a plausible claim to reimbursement. They are collateral sources.

By contrast, if plaintiff loses one job and finds another or suffers a breach of contract and sells her property to a new buyer, the new job and the new sale are offsetting benefits. The new employer or the new buyer is acting at arm's length and in his own self-interest. He receives fresh consideration, suffers no loss, and has no plausible claim to reimbursement.

The same intuition underlies the statutes limiting the collateral-source rule. But many of these statutes now list, or try to list, the specific sources that they mean to target. Delaware includes only government benefits. Del. Code Ann. tit. 18, §6862. Rhode Island includes medical insurance but omits Medicaid. Esposito v. O'Hair, 886 A.2d 1197 (R.I. 2005). Arizona includes life insurance. Ariz. Rev. Stat. Ann. §12-565(A). New York and several other states expressly exclude life insurance, and even critics of the collateral-source rule tend to concede that the investment feature of whole life insurance makes it different. What about term life insurance, which is paid for year by year like medical or accident insurance and has no investment value?

The New York statute in *Oden* originally tried to list categories of collateral sources and exceptions. Now it applies to "any collateral source, except for life insurance and those payments as to which there is a statutory right of reimbursement." N.Y. C.P.L.R. §4545(a). Collateral source is undefined. The legislature has not done anything to change the matching requirement announced in *Oden*.

4. Charitable contributions? In an early case under the New York statute, defendant negligently caused a fire that destroyed a landmark synagogue. Insurance was inadequate, but the synagogue raised $20 million in charitable donations to replace and modernize the building. Defendants sought to reduce any judgment by $20 million. The donors clearly were collateral sources; it was much less clear whether they were sources "such as" those that were then listed in the New York statute. The case settled. Diana B. Henriques & Leslie Eaton, *Once and Future Issue: Subtracting Donations from Damage Awards*, N.Y. Times (Nov. 18, 2001). The publicity arising from this case, at about the same time as the outpouring of donations for the relief of victims of September 11, led the legislature to provide that "[v]oluntary charitable contributions received by an injured party shall not be considered to be a collateral source of payment that is admissible in evidence to reduce the amount of any award, judgment or settlement." N.Y. C.P.L.R. §4545(b).

5. Accounting for premiums. Under the New York statute, plaintiff gets credit for the last two years of premiums paid for any insurance or other benefits that are applied to offset the tort judgment, plus the cost of keeping such benefits in effect for as long as they are applied to future damages. Other statutes address this issue in less detail, or not at all. Defendants say that only the premiums in the policy period for which benefits are collected paid for those benefits. Plaintiffs say they paid premiums for years, on that policy and similar policies in the past; they had to pay for all the years to be insured, because they could not know which year they would be hurt.

6. Matching the collateral source with the damage. Are you convinced that the New York statute requires the collateral source to replace a specific item of damage? Are you convinced that "disability retirement benefits" replace lost pension benefits but do not replace lost wages? The Second Circuit, applying New York law, held that Social Security disability benefits do replace lost earnings. Turnbull v. USAir, Inc., 133 F.3d 184 (2d Cir. 1998). Connecticut adopted a similar "matching" interpretation of its collateral-source statute. Jones v. Kramer, 838 A.2d 170 (Conn. 2004). The statutes are generally ambiguous on this issue.

7. Constitutionality. The new statutory restrictions on the collateral-source rule have been challenged on state constitutional grounds. Most states have upheld them, but a significant minority has struck them down; some of the cases are collected in Reid v. Williams, 964 P.2d 453, 458 n.9, 460 nn.15-16 (Alaska 1998).

8. Subrogation. Many of the new statutes do not apply to collateral sources with subrogation rights. This results in little effective change, because insurers are increasingly assertive about their subrogation rights. If the collateral-source rule is repealed only with respect to sources with no right to subrogation, it is hardly repealed at all. By contrast, Montana's statute expressly repeals all subrogation rights except those "specifically granted by state or federal law." Mont. Code Ann. §27-1-308(4). Subrogation rights are created by contract, by judge-made rules derived from equity (see section 8.C.3), and by statute. The legislature likely thought that only statutory subrogation rights were "specifically granted by . . . law."

Some statutes, including New York's, are silent on the subject. The New York courts have interpreted silence to mean that §4545 does not repeal or modify subrogation rights. The cases are collected in In re September 11 Litigation, 649 F. Supp. 2d 171 (S.D.N.Y. 2009), holding that the World Trade Center's property insurers are entitled to assert the owners' claims against the airlines and airport security companies. The court reached this conclusion over the united objections of the plaintiffs, who wanted a double recovery, and of the defendants, who wanted to pay nothing because the property insurers had already paid.

9. Subrogation in practice. Subrogation in these cases isn't simple either. Consider Arkansas Department of Health and Human Services v. Ahlborn, 547 U.S. 268 (2006). Ahlborn was a college student who suffered permanent brain damage in an auto accident; the resulting disability and large medical expenses made her eligible for Medicaid. Arkansas stipulated that her personal injury claim was worth more than $3 million, even though she settled for $550,000, apparently because the tortfeasors had inadequate liability insurance. Arkansas had expended about $215,000 on her medical care, and under Arkansas law, the state was entitled to recover the full $215,000 out of her $550,000 recovery. So the state would recover all of its losses, and she would be left with a total net recovery (from the settlement plus the earlier medical payments less the reimbursement of those medical payments) of about one-sixth of her losses.

The Supreme Court held that the federal Medicaid law that funded much of Arkansas's program precluded the state's claim. Ahlborn and the state had to share pro rata; the state recovered about $35,000, the same fraction of its claim that Ahlborn had recovered of hers. Private insurance policies often have clauses that work the same way as Arkansas's law, with no federal preemption to protect the policyholder. Some state insurance laws permit these clauses; some do not.

The stipulation about the value of Ahlborn's claim makes this allocation seem easy, but of course the state might have vigorously disputed the value of her personal injury claim. Or her settlement agreement with the tortfeasors might have purported to allocate the settlement, allocating high values to lost earnings and pain and suffering and minimizing the recovery allocated to medical expenses. Insurers say they need full recovery of all the benefits they pay to avoid being victimized by such manipulations; lawyers for personal injury claimants say they need the full protection of the collateral-source rule to avoid overreaching by insurers. Where Ahlborn's pro rata approach applies, the court must often hold a hearing after any settlement, determine the full value of the claim, and apportion the claim among the various elements of damage. Of course, the settlement was supposed to avoid such issues, but the first-party insurer is usually not party to the settlement. The Supreme Court required such a process in Medicaid cases in Wos v. E.M.A., 568 U.S. 627 (2013). It believed that such hearings had not been burdensome in states that held them, and suggested, without holding, that rebuttable presumptions might be permissible.

10. The problem of undercompensation. The problem of undercompensation illustrated by *Ahlborn* is widespread. Coverage limits, litigation risks, difficulties of proof, attorneys' fees, statutory caps on damages, and other problems often cause plaintiff's net recovery to be less than the reasonable value of her injuries — sometimes dramatically less. Many judgments and some settlements are never fully collected. In all these cases, there is no double recovery in the absence of subrogation, and subrogation aggravates the plaintiff's undercompensation. Some of these sources of undercompensation can be identified and measured; some are hard to address.

Many states addressed at least what could be measured with a make-whole rule: No insurer could claim subrogation rights unless the injury victim was fully compensated. An example is Fischer v. Steffen, 797 N.W.2d 501 (Wis. 2011). But the make-whole rule is undermined by statutes and contract provisions like the Arkansas Medicaid law in *Ahlborn*, providing that the subrogated insurer gets paid first and in full before the injury victim keeps anything.

11. Federal preemption cutting the other way. Federal preemption has protected personal-injury victims in the Medicaid cases, but more often it protects the insurers. Many health-insurance policies are provided by employers and are subject to the Employee Retirement Income Security Act. 29 U.S.C. §1001 *et seq.* ERISA gives employers power to write employee-benefit plans, makes those plans enforceable, and allows the terms of the plan to preempt most contrary state law. The plans typically provide for subrogation. But the insurer has to identify the proceeds of the tort settlement and collect from those proceeds before its insured spends the money. Board of Trustees of the National Elevator Industry Health Benefit Plan v. Montanile, 136 S. Ct. 651 (2016). The insurance program for federal employees contains a similar preemption provision, which overrides a state-law ban on subrogation clauses in insurance contracts. Coventry Health Care v. Nevils, 137 S. Ct. 1190 (2017).

In US Airways, Inc. v. McCutchen, 569 U.S. 88 (2013), a personal injury victim was left with a recovery of zero after paying his attorneys' fees and the subrogation claim of his employer's insurance plan. That plan did pay his medical expenses. Justice Kagan managed to avoid this result by interpreting the plan to require the insurer to bear a pro rata share of the attorneys' fees. But plans can easily draft around this result, and presumably will.

12. Coordination of benefits. Subrogation and the collateral-source rule are the principal tort-law elements of the broader problem of coordinating tort damages with other benefits. Good data are hard to find and verify, and they depend on important definitional questions, but tort damages appear to be a relatively small fraction of the total compensation package. Professor Pryor estimated annual tort damages for personal injury at $80 billion, workers' compensation payments at $55 billion, and various government social insurance programs at just over $200 billion. Ellen S. Pryor, *Part of the Whole: Tort Law's Compensatory Failures Through a Wider Lens*, 27 Rev. Litig. 307, 311-313 (2008). Privately owned and supplied first-party medical insurance, disability insurance, accident insurance, and property insurance would add many billions more to the total picture.

13. The collateral-source rule in contract. Contract damages are much less likely to be covered by first-party insurance, and when the issue arises in contract, courts are likely to be unfamiliar with it, and they sometimes decide it too quickly. The arguments for giving defendant the benefit of plaintiff's insurance are often no better in contract than in tort. Plaintiff's insurance may be the product of her own thrift; her insurer may be entitled to subrogation, etc. Cases going both ways are collected in Joseph M. Perillo, *The Collateral Source Rule in Contract Cases*, 46 San Diego L. Rev. 705 (2009). Professor Perillo clearly thought that the cases applying the collateral-source rule in contract were better reasoned and gave the issue more attention.

3. The Scope of Liability

PRUITT v. ALLIED CHEMICAL CORP.
523 F. Supp. 975 (E.D. Va. 1981)

MERHIGE, District Judge.

Plaintiffs bring the instant action against Allied Chemical Corp. . . . for Allied's alleged pollution of the James River and Chesapeake Bay with the chemical agent commonly known as Kepone. [Kepone was an insecticide that has since been banned, partly as a result of the events at issue in this case. Fishing was closed for thirteen years on a hundred miles of the James River.]

Plaintiffs allegedly engage in a variety of different businesses and professions related to the harvesting and sale of marine life from the Chesapeake Bay . . . . All claim to have suffered economic harm from defendant's alleged discharges of Kepone into the James River and thence into the Bay. . . .

Defendant moves to dismiss [nine] counts . . . of the complaint as they apply to all plaintiffs other than those directly engaged in the harvesting of the Bay's marine life. That is, defendant would dismiss these nine counts as to all plaintiffs except those classified in paragraph 6.A of the complaint (generally, fishermen, shellfishermen, and lessors of oysterbeds.) All plaintiffs subject to defendant's motion claim . . . lost profits resulting from their inability to sell seafood allegedly contaminated by defendant's discharges, and from a drop in price resulting from a decline in demand for seafood coming from areas affected by Kepone. These plaintiffs can generally be described as parties suffering only indirect harm to their property or businesses as the result of Kepone pollution. They or their possessions have not been caused direct, physical damage by defendant. Instead, plaintiffs allege that the stream of profits they previously received from their businesses or employment has been interrupted, and they seek compensation for the loss of the prospective profits they have been denied. . . .

Counts I, II and V allege that negligence, of some degree, by defendant entitles plaintiffs to recover. Count III alleges that the effluents released by defendant were "defective and unreasonably dangerous," and that defendant should be strictly liable for any harm caused by its discharges. All of these counts arise from the Court's diversity jurisdiction and rely on theories of state tort law.

The Virginia Supreme Court has . . . never directly considered the question of recovery for loss of prospective economic benefits. It is commonly stated that the general rule both in admiralty and at common law has been that a plaintiff cannot recover for indirect economic harm. The logical basis for this rule is obscure. Although Courts have frequently stated that economic losses are "not foreseeable" or "too remote," these explanations alone are rarely apposite. As one well-respected commentator has noted, "the loss to plaintiff in each case . . . would be readily recoverable if the test of duty—or remoteness—usually associated with the law of negligence were applied." Fleming James, Jr., *Limitations of Liability for Economic Loss Caused by Negligence: A Pragmatic Appraisal*, 25 Vand. L. Rev. 43 (1972).

The Court frankly acknowledges the fact that there exist a substantial number of cases that may be construed to establish a general rule favorable to [defendants]. As noted by the Ninth Circuit in Union Oil Co. v. Oppen, 501 F.2d 558 (9th Cir. 1974), the general rule has found application in a wide variety of contexts:

> [T]he negligent destruction of a bridge connecting the mainland with an island, which caused a loss of business to the plaintiff who was a merchant on the island, has been held not to be actionable. A plaintiff engaged in commercial printing has been held unable to recover against a negligent contractor who, while engaged in excavation pursuant to a contract with a third party, cut the power line upon which the plaintiff's presses depended. A defendant who negligently injures a third person entitled to life-care medical services by the plaintiff is liable to the third person but not to the plaintiff. The operators of a dry dock are not liable in admiralty to charterers of a ship, placed by its owners in the dry dock, for negligent injury to the ship's propeller where the injury deprived the charterer of the use of the ship.

Id. at 563-564.

Nevertheless, there also exist cases that conflict with this broadly recognized general rule. At least two of the minority cases deal with precisely the case present here: the loss of business opportunities due to pollution of streams adjoining a plaintiff's property. Moreover, even defendant concedes that a third case, *Union Oil*, that provided compensation for fishermen for losses caused by pollution from oil spills, is correctly decided. Although defendant would distinguish *Union Oil* as limited solely to those who labor on the water (but not at its edge) the rationale for creation of this particular distinction is unclear.

Given the conflicting case law from other jurisdictions, together with the fact that there exists no Virginia law on indirect, economic damages, the Court has considered more theoretical sources in order to find a principled basis for its decision. There now exists a considerable amount of literature on the economic rationale for tort law. In general, scholars in the field rely on Judge Learned Hand's classic statement of negligence[11] to argue that a principal purpose of tort law is to maximize social utility: where the costs of accidents exceeds the costs of preventing them, the law will impose liability.

The difficulty in the present case is how to measure the cost of Kepone pollution. In the instant action, these costs were borne most directly by the wildlife of the Chesapeake Bay. The fact that no one individual claims property rights to the Bay's wildlife could arguably preclude liability. The Court doubts, however, whether such a result would be just. Nor would a denial of liability serve social utility: many citizens, both directly and indirectly, derive benefit from the Bay and its marine life. Destruction of the Bay's wildlife should not be a costless activity.

In fact, even defendant in the present action admits that commercial fishermen are entitled to compensation for any loss of profits they may prove to have been caused by defendant's negligence. The entitlement given these fishermen presumably arises from what might be called a constructive property interest in the Bay's harvestable species. These professional watermen are entitled to recover despite [the lack of] any direct physical damage to their own property. Presumably, sportfishermen share the same entitlement to legal redress for damage to the Bay's ecology. The Court perceives no valid distinction between recognition of commercial damages suffered by those who fish for profit and personal harm suffered by those who fish for sport.

The claims now considered by the Court, however, are not those of direct users of the Bay, commercial or personal. Instead, defendant has challenged the right of those who buy and sell to direct users of the Bay, to maintain a suit. . . .

None of the plaintiffs here—including commercial fishermen—has suffered any direct damage to his private property. All have allegedly suffered economic loss as a result of harm to the Bay's ecology. Apart from these similarities, the different categories of plaintiffs depend on the Bay in varying degrees of immediacy. The commercial fishermen here fit within a category established in *Union Oil*: they "lawfully and directly make use of a resource of the sea." 501 F.2d at 570. The use that marine and charterboat owners make of the water, though hardly less legal, is slightly less direct. (And indeed, businesses in similar situations have been held entitled to recover in other courts.) Still less direct, but far from nonexistent, is the link between the Bay and the seafood dealers, restauranteurs, and tackle shops that seek relief (as do the employees of these establishments).

___

11. *See* United States v. Carroll Towing Co., 159 F.2d 169, 173 (2d Cir. 1947), in which Judge Hand stated that a person's duty to prevent injuries from an accident "is a function of three variables: (1) The probability that [the accident will occur]; (2) the gravity of the resulting injury, if [it] does; (3) the burden of adequate precautions."

One meaningful distinction to be made among the various categories of plaintiffs here arises from a desire to avoid doublecounting in calculating damages. Any seafood harvested by the commercial fishermen here would have been bought and sold several times before finally being purchased for consumption. Considerations both of equity and social utility suggest that just as defendant should not be able to escape liability for destruction of publicly owned marine life entirely, it should not be caused to pay repeatedly for the same damage.

The Court notes, however, that allowance for recovery of plaintiffs' lost profits here would not in all cases result in double-counting of damages. [Seafood wholesalers, retailers, processors, distributors, and restauranteurs] allegedly lost profits when deprived of supplies of seafood. Those profits represented a return on the investment of *each* of the plaintiffs in material and labor in their businesses, and thus the independent loss to each would not amount to double-counting. Conversely, defendants could not be expected to pay, as a maximum, more than the replacement value of a plaintiff's actual investment, even if the stream of profits lost[,] when extrapolated into the future, would yield greater damages.

Tracing the stream of profits flowing from the Bay's seafood, however, involves the Court in other complexities. The employees of the [affected businesses] had no physical investment in their employers' businesses. Yet if plaintiffs' allegations are proven, these employees undoubtedly lost wages and faced a less favorable job market than they would have, but for defendant's acts, and they have thus been harmed by defendant. What is more, the number of parties with a potential cause of action against defendant is hardly exhausted in plaintiffs' complaint. In theory, parties who bought and sold to and from the plaintiffs named here also suffered losses in business, as did their employees. In short, the set of potential plaintiffs seems almost infinite.

Perhaps because of the large set of potential plaintiffs, even the commentators most critical of the general rule on indirect damages have acknowledged that some limitation to liability, even when damages are foreseeable, is advisable. Rather than allowing plaintiffs to risk a failure of proof as damages become increasingly remote and diffuse, courts have, in many cases, raised an absolute bar to recovery.

The Court thus finds itself with a perceived need to limit liability, without any articulable reason for excluding any particular set of plaintiffs. Other courts have had to make similar decisions.[22] The Court concludes that plaintiffs who purchased and marketed seafood from commercial fishermen suffered damages that are not legally cognizable, because insufficiently direct. This does not mean that the Court finds that defendant's alleged acts were not the cause of plaintiffs' losses, or that plaintiffs' losses were in any sense unforeseeable. In fact, in part because the damages alleged by plaintiffs here were so foreseeable, the Court holds that [owners of fishing boats, tackle and bait shops, and marinas] have suffered legally cognizable damages. The Court does so for several reasons. The . . . Fourth Circuit has held, in admiralty, that a defendant should "pay . . . once, but no more" for damages inflicted. Venore Transportation Co. v. M/V Struma, 583 F.2d 707, 710 (4th Cir. 1978). While commercial fishing interests are protected by allowing the fishermen themselves to recover, it

---

22. *See, e.g.,* Judge Kaufman's opinion in Petition of Kinsman Transit Co., 388 F.2d 821, 824-825 (2d Cir. 1968), where the court noted that "in the final analysis, the circumlocution whether posed in terms of 'foreseeability,' 'duty,' 'proximate cause,' 'remoteness,' etc. seems unavoidable" and then turned to Judge Andrews' well-known statement in Palsgraf v. Long Island Railroad, 162 N.E. 99, 104 (N.Y. 1928): "It is all a question of expediency . . . of fair judgment, always keeping in mind the fact that we endeavor to make a rule in each case that will be practical and in keeping with the general understanding of mankind."

is unlikely that sportsfishing interests would be equally protected. Because the damages each sportsman suffered are likely to be both small[25] and difficult to establish, it is unlikely that a significant proportion of such fishermen will seek legal redress. Only if some set of surrogate plaintiffs is entitled to press its own claims which flow from the damage to the Bay's sportfishing industry will the proper balance of social forces be preserved. . . .

NOTES ON THE SCOPE OF LIABILITY

1. The rest of *Pruitt*. The court reached substantially similar conclusions with respect to the admiralty and nuisance counts. Defendants did not move to dismiss the intentional tort counts.

2. Multiple theories for limiting liability. There are a welter of doctrines for limiting damages that seem too remote from, or too unrelated to, the defendant's conduct or responsibility. These doctrines are conceptually distinct but often overlapping in practice. Courts may say that a negligent defendant owed no duty to plaintiff, or that defendant did not cause plaintiff's harm, or that defendant did not proximately cause plaintiff's harm, or that plaintiff's harm was not foreseeable, or that defendant is not liable for purely "economic loss," or that plaintiff contributed to causing his own injury. In contract, they may say that defendant had no reason to contemplate plaintiff's harm when the contract was made. These doctrines are often treated as part of the substantive law of tort and contract, but their practical function (sometimes, for some of them; always, for most of them) is to make some elements of damage unrecoverable. We cannot explore all these doctrines here, but we can consider illustrative applications of the doctrines most closely related to the determination of damages.

3. The economic-loss rules—postponed briefly. One argument in *Pruitt* is that no one had suffered physical damage to person or property, so no one could recover. This is a variant of the economic-loss rule, considered in the next set of notes. Even defendants agreed that this was too draconian, although they conceded only a narrow exception for people who directly harvested the damaged wildlife. The court refused to apply the economic-loss rule and looked for some other way to limit liability.

4. Expanding circles of liability. Once the court rejected the economic-loss rule, *Pruitt* became an example of harm that expands in ever-widening circles and eventually seems, to most judges, to reach further than liability should go. What is the source of the "perceived need to limit liability"? The court found that damages to businesses in the chain of distribution for seafood were foreseeable and not duplicative of the damages to fishers, boat and marina owners, and bait and tackle shops. Yet it cut off liability at the water's edge. Doesn't it follow that the court failed to achieve the goal of encouraging defendant to spend as much to avoid pollution as the pollution would cost?

Despite the inability to draw sensible lines or even to articulate a rationale, the feeling that liability must end somewhere has been widespread. Tests have been formulated in terms of foreseeable and unforeseeable, proximate and remote, and direct and indirect. As *Pruitt* illustrates, these labels are not interchangeable. Here, the damages are found to be foreseeable but indirect. Presumably they are also remote. But why does that matter?

---

25. The net loss to any sportsman would have to take into account any enjoyment received from natural areas visited as a substitute to the Chesapeake Bay.

5. The *Restatement*'s new vocabulary. The problem has most often been discussed in terms of *proximate cause*, a phrase that has long been criticized as confusing. Proximate cause cases are not about causation; rather, they hold that defendants are not liable for some harms that they undoubtedly caused. The American Law Institute has proposed discussing proximate cause in terms of the *scope of liability. Restatement (Third) of Torts: Liability for Physical and Emotional Harm* ch. 6 (Am. Law Inst. 2010). It seems unlikely that this improved usage will displace talk of proximate cause, but the Supreme Court of Iowa has adopted it. Thompson v. Kaczinski, 774 N.W.2d 829 (Iowa 2009).

6. Cause in fact and proximate cause. It is inherent in the rightful-position principle that defendant is liable only for harm she caused—for changes from the position plaintiff would have occupied but for the wrong. (This generalization requires modification in cases of multiple sufficient causes—the occasional cases of two fires, two shooters, and the like.) But causation in the but-for sense is not always enough, and courts are not always clear about the line between no causation and causal links that are too remote. Consider IHS Cedars Treatment Center v. Mason, 143 S.W.3d 794 (Tex. 2004), where plaintiff and her roommate asked defendants to release them early, before completion of their treatment plans and despite an absence of progress, from the mental health facility where they were being treated. The next day, the roommate had a psychotic episode while driving and lost control of the car; plaintiff was paralyzed and another passenger was killed. The court said that "cause in fact is not established where the defendant's negligence does no more than furnish a condition that makes the injuries possible." *Id.* at 799. What if defendants should have known that the roommate—the driver—was a danger to herself or others? Do they have to have known that she might be dangerous as a driver? The opinion collects several Texas cases, with disparate facts, decided on a similar rationale.

The Texas court said that cause in fact requires that defendant's conduct must be a "substantial factor" in bringing about the harm. Other courts and commentators have used this formulation as part of the meaning of proximate cause. The *Restatement (Third)* has abandoned it as "confusing" and "misused." §26 cmt. *j.* In the new *Restatement* formulation, *cause in fact* simply means "but-for cause" (§26), or one of multiple sufficient causes (§27).

7. Foreseeability and the *Restatement*. The new *Restatement* proposes two rules to do most of the work of limiting the scope of liability. First, negligent defendants are liable only for "those harms that result from the risks that made the actor's conduct tortious." §29. Is the risk of an auto accident one of the risks that makes a bad prognosis of a mental illness negligent? Second, "An actor is not liable for harm when the tortious aspect of the actor's conduct was of a type that does not generally increase the risk of that harm." §30. Does releasing mental health patients increase the risk that they might be in an auto accident? Intentional and reckless tortfeasors are liable for a broader but ill-defined range of consequences, with the scope of liability adjusted in light of culpability. §33.

The reporters for the new *Restatement* acknowledge that most courts define the scope of liability in terms of foreseeability, although a variety of other formulations are used instead or in addition. They say that their proposed language is broadly consistent with a foreseeability standard: The risks that make an actor's conduct tortious do not include risks that are unforeseeable. They think their language is more precise, and they offer a variety of examples in which the choice of language might matter.

8. Do the verbal formulations matter? One especially clear example comes from an English case, Darby v. National Trust, [2001] EWCA (Civ.) 189, 2001 WL 98075

(Ct. App. 2001). A pond at defendant's historic house was contaminated with the bacteria that cause Weil's disease, which is serious and occasionally fatal. Defendant failed to warn visitors not to swim in the pond; plaintiff's husband swam in the pond and was not infected. But he drowned. Drowning in a pond is certainly foreseeable; the court said the risk was so obvious to any adult that there was no duty to warn. The risk that made defendant negligent was the risk of Weil's disease, but that was not the risk that came to fruition.

The change in usage led to a reversal and remand in Thompson v. Kaczinski, the Iowa case in note 5. Parts of defendants' disassembled trampoline blew away in a high wind, landed in the road, and sometime later, caused an accident. The trial court held as a matter of law that there was no duty and no proximate cause; the supreme court held that an auto accident was within the risk that made it negligent to leave trampoline parts lying in the front yard.

The change made no difference in Asher v. Ob-Gyn Specialists, P.C., 846 N.W.2d 492 (Iowa 2014), a medical-malpractice case in which the court held that a substantial-factor instruction was harmless error. "[I]n most cases the alleged tortfeasor's scope of liability will not be an issue and this case provides a good example of that." *Id.* at 499. The cases where proximate cause or scope of liability is at issue are unusual almost by definition. There are some recurring patterns, but in many of these cases, the court's intuitive reaction to unique facts may matter more than any formal statement of a rule.

Neither *Restatement* formulation seems to help in *Pruitt*, where all the harm flowed from the harm to the wildlife, which was certainly part of the risk that made defendant's conduct tortious and a risk that defendant's conduct greatly increased.

9. Intervening negligence. Another consideration that courts sometimes invoke is the intervening negligence of a third party. In Baumann v. Zhukov, 802 F.3d 950 (8th Cir. 2015), two large trucks collided and blocked an interstate highway. Even at 4:00 a.m., traffic backed up for nearly a mile. An 18-wheeler plowed into the cars at the end of the line, killing a family of four and their unborn baby. Applying Nebraska law, the court held that the drivers who caused the accident at the front of the line were not responsible for the accident at the back of the line. Many other drivers had stopped without incident; the truck driver at the end of the line was fatigued and had not braked; he was the legal cause of the deaths, and his negligence was not foreseeable. The dissenter collected several cases from other states that had treated foreseeability on similar facts as a jury issue.

In a similar Mississippi case, the court said that the negligence that caused the original accident "only furnished the condition or occasion from which [plaintiff's] injuries were received, but it did not put in motion the negligence and wrongful agency that caused [his] injuries." Ready v. RWI Transportation, LLC, 203 So. 2d 590 (Miss 2016). Compare the reasoning of the Texas court in note 6.

10. Eggshell skulls? The classic eggshell skull rule of first-year torts is a specific rule about the scope of liability. One way to think about it is that the plaintiff's preexisting condition or vulnerability "only furnished the condition or occasion" for more severe injuries, but "did not put in motion" the wrongful conduct that caused those injuries. An example is Darden v. City of Fort Worth, 880 F.3d 723 (5th Cir. 2018), where police tasered and held down a morbidly obese man with a heart condition. He died of a heart attack. The court determined that if the jury found their actions unreasonable, the officers would be liable for the wrongful death. And of course the rule applies in negligence and not just in intentional torts.

11. "Directness" in the Supreme Court. The Supreme Court has rendered a series of proximate cause decisions in statutory cases, mostly under RICO, the Racketeer

Influenced and Corrupt Organizations Act, 18 U.S.C. §1964(c). The Court started from common-law premises, but it wound up in a very different place. The thrust of these decisions is that foreseeability is largely—perhaps entirely—irrelevant, and that "the focus is on the directness of the relationship between the conduct and the harm." Hemi Group, LLC v. City of New York, 559 U.S. 1, 12 (2010) (plurality opinion). The directness of harm has been an idea in the common-law cases as well, but the Court seems to be making it the exclusive idea in these statutory cases.

Hemi Group sells cigarettes over the internet. It has no obligation to pay or collect state or local cigarette or sales taxes in New York, and New York has no authority to regulate it. The Jenkins Act, now 15 U.S.C. §375 *et seq.*, requires it to report each of its customers and the quantity of their purchases to the state where each customer resides. The state of New York is contractually obligated to pass this information on to New York City. Hemi Group did not provide the information to the state, and it advertised that fact to potential customers; tax evasion seemed to be at the heart of its business model. New York City claimed that Hemi Group had deprived it of the revenue it could have collected by pursuing the customers that Hemi Group should have reported.

At least in the common-law cases, the scope of liability is usually expanded for intentional torts. Hemi Group was engaged in intentional wrongdoing. But Chief Justice Roberts said that Hemi Group owed a statutory duty only to the state, not to the city, and that the harm was caused by the customers who owed the taxes, not by Hemi Group. The Court noted that "the general tendency of the law, in regard to damages at least, is not to go beyond the first step." *Id.* at 10, quoting Justice Holmes in Southern Pacific Co. v. Darnell-Taenzer Lumber Co., 245 U.S. 531, 533 (1918). The Chief seemed to think that the causal chain leading to this harm required three steps. Congress promptly responded by amending the Jenkins Act, authorizing city, state, and tribal governments to sue for money damages. 15 U.S.C. §378(c)(1)(A).

12. Beyond RICO. The Court's directness rule is not confined to RICO. The Court unanimously applied it to a fair-housing case in Bank of America Corp. v. City of Miami, 137 S. Ct. 1296 (2017). Miami alleged that defendant banks discriminated on the basis of race in the terms of loans, in refinancing, and in foreclosures, causing many homes in minority neighborhoods to stand empty, lowering property values and tax revenues, and requiring additional expenditures for public safety. The Court said that the foreseeability of Miami's harms was not enough to show proximate cause; the housing market is connected to the larger economy and to social life, and many remote harms are foreseeable. Rather, there must be "some direct relation between the injury asserted and the injurious conduct alleged," and once again, "the general tendency . . . is not to go beyond the first step." *Id.* at 1306. It is hard to see how Miami's claims can survive this emphasis on "the first step," but the Court remanded to the Eleventh Circuit to apply its test in the first instance.

What result if the one-step rule were applied in *Pruitt?* Would recovery be limited to those who actually catch fish, eliminating all who either buy the fish or serve or supply the fishers?

13. A corollary. A corollary of the one-step idea is that "a plaintiff who complained of harm flowing merely from the misfortunes visited upon a third person by the defendant's acts was generally said to stand at too remote a distance to recover." Holmes v. Securities Investor Protection Corp., 503 U.S. 258, 268-269 (1992). This rule appears to be widely accepted in the common-law and state-law cases as well. Many cases fit this pattern—*A* injures *B*, either physically or economically, and *B* is then unable to perform obligations to *C*, but *C* does not thereby get a claim against *A*. In *Holmes*, fraudsters caused the insolvency of two brokerage houses. SIPC, which insures brokerage accounts, had to reimburse their customers. The brokerage houses had a claim against the fraudsters, but SIPC and the customers did not.

NOTES ON THE ECONOMIC-LOSS RULES

1. The basics. The defendant in *Pruitt* initially relied not on what was traditionally called "proximate cause" but on a variant of the economic-loss rule. In its broadest formulation, this rule says that a plaintiff in negligence or products liability who suffers no injury to her person and no physical damage to her property cannot recover for other losses. These other losses have come to be called "economic loss" in this context. The economic-loss rule is not just a factor to be considered in resolving questions of degree. In its usual application, it is much more mechanical. If plaintiff did not suffer damage to person or property, she cannot recover, no matter how foreseeable the harm or how direct the causation.

2. More than one rule. Various courts state the economic-loss rule in a wide variety of ways. Stating it as broadly as in note 1 requires more exceptions, and it conflates distinct contexts in which the rule serves very different purposes. Sometimes the rule limits the scope of liability in tort. Sometimes it confines the liability of contracting parties to claims on the contract. Sometimes it functions like the rule of no liability to third parties, which the Supreme Court treated as part of proximate cause in the preceding set of notes.

More careful courts have therefore subdivided the broad formulation. The *Restatement* formulation says, "Except as provided elsewhere in this Restatement, there is no liability in tort for economic loss caused by negligence in the performance or negotiation of a contract between the parties." *Restatement (Third) of Torts: Liability for Economic Harm* §3 (Am. Law Inst. Tent. Draft 1, 2012). The *Restatement*, and a fair number of courts, say that this, and only this, is the economic-loss rule.

That formulation requires a separate rule for cases like *Pruitt*: there is no liability in tort for economic loss resulting from damage to the person or property of someone other than the plaintiff (or as in *Pruitt*, from damage to things that are the property of no one). This rule has no widely accepted name. Professor Dobbs suggested calling it the stranger rule, because plaintiff and defendant in these cases generally have no legal relationship with each other. Dan B. Dobbs, *An Introduction to Non-Statutory Economic Loss Claims*, 48 Ariz. L. Rev. 713 (2006). The reach and rationale of these two rules—the contract and stranger variants of the economic-loss rule—are nicely summarized in Ward Farnsworth, *The Economic Loss Rule*, 50 Val. U. L. Rev. 545 (2016).

3. Expanding circles of liability again. There is a full review of the stranger variant as it applies to admiralty cases in American Petroleum and Transport, Inc. v. City of New York, 737 F.3d 185 (2d Cir. 2013). The city opened a drawbridge to let plaintiff's boats go upstream. Then the bridge malfunctioned and couldn't be opened; the boats were stranded upstream for two and a half days. The court thought it obviously foreseeable that a commercial vessel going upstream on a short river would soon return downstream, and it doubted the wisdom and provenance of the rule refusing recovery for economic loss without physical damage. But it deferred to precedent and the advantages of a bright-line rule, and denied recovery.

An earlier reevaluation of the rule better illustrates what courts are worried about. Louisiana ex rel. Guste v. M/V Testbank, 752 F.2d 1019 (5th Cir. 1985) (en banc). A chemical spill near the mouth of the Mississippi River caused losses to the fish and shellfish industry, similar to those in *Pruitt*. In addition, the mouth of the Mississippi was closed to navigation for two weeks. Traffic was backed up throughout the system, causing losses in distant ports.

Here too the majority wanted a bright-line rule. They also said that it was more efficient for firms to insure against disruption of their own business than to buy liability insurance for all the economic loss that might result from a single act of negligence. And they said that unlimited liability was not needed to optimally deter negligence, because at some point additional liability would "lose meaning" and have no additional deterrent effect. Doesn't additional liability have meaning until defendant's assets are exhausted?

4. The minority view. New Jersey and West Virginia reject the stranger variant of the economic-loss rule. People Express Airlines, Inc. v. Consolidated Rail Corp., 495 A.2d 107 (N.J. 1985); Aikens v. Debow, 541 S.E.2d 576 (W. Va. 2000). *People Express* was a chemical spill on land; in *Aikens*, a truck with a high load damaged an exit ramp and cut off convenient access to plaintiff's motel for 19 days. These courts said they would constrain liability with a requirement of particularly foreseeable harm to an identifiable plaintiff or class of plaintiffs. So in *People Express*, the airline with its offices next to the railroad track could recover; delayed travelers on highways near the spill could not. Probably the motel could recover under this standard, but that was left to the trial court on remand.

These opinions do not appear to have led to unmanageable liability in New Jersey or West Virginia. The minority rule mattered in In re Paulsboro Derailment Cases, 2015 WL 3545247 (D.N.J. 2015), and Sigman v. CSX Corp., 2016 WL 2622007 (S.D. W. Va. 2016). Both involved plaintiffs with physical locations near the site of a chemical spill.

5. Environmental exceptions. Some legislatures have enacted exceptions to the stranger variant of the rule. The Oil Pollution Act, 33 U.S.C. §2701 *et seq.*, imposes statutory liability for oil spills in navigable waters. A similar Rhode Island statute applies to any violation of Rhode Island pilotage or water pollution laws. Environmental Injury Compensation Act, R.I. Gen. Laws. ch. 46-12.3-4.

The federal act would not apply to *Pruitt* or to most of the cases discussed in notes 3 and 4, because except for *Sigman*, none of those cases involved oil spills. The Rhode Island act would apply to *Pruitt*, *Testbank*, *Sigman*, and possibly *Paulsboro*, but not to *People Express* or *Aikens*, because the latter cases did not involve water pollution. The ambiguity in *Paulsboro* is that the pollutant was a gas; some of it went in the water but much of it went in the air and into nearby buildings. Legislators address specific problems that capture their attention; they rarely search for all analogous problems.

Pruitt illustrates a widely accepted judge-made exception. Wildlife, especially seafood, may be of enormous economic importance, yet nobody owns it until it is harvested. Literally applied, the stranger variant of the economic-loss rule would allow polluters to destroy wildlife with no fear of tort liability for the resulting harm. Most courts faced with this issue have created enough of an exception to ensure that somebody will be able to sue.

6. The BP oil spill. In 2010, a BP oil rig exploded in the Gulf of Mexico. Oil poured into the Gulf for three months while BP struggled to cap the broken pipe. The Oil Pollution Act requires a party responsible for an oil spill in navigable waters to "establish a procedure for the payment or settlement of claims for interim, short-term damages." 33 U.S.C. §2705(a). These payments do not preclude later recovery for "damages not reflected in the paid or settled partial claim." *Id.* This provision is the underlying basis for the Gulf Coast Claims Facility, a $20-billion fund administered outside the courts. The Gulf Coast fund paid more than $6 billion in interim and permanent settlements.

Many plaintiffs took their permanent claims to court, and in 2013, the court approved class settlements of most claims of individuals and businesses for property damage, economic loss, or medical harms. The medical settlement created a matrix of objective criteria of injury linked to specified cash awards. Class members had to show where they fit on the matrix, and prove the objective criteria for eligibility, but all issues of liability, causation, and measurement of damages were reduced to these objective criteria. The property-damage and economic-loss settlement was structurally similar; most class members had to prove only that their business was in a defined geographic area and that it took in less revenue after the spill than before. These formulas made compensation possible at manageable expense, but they no doubt compensated some marginal or undeserving claims. The formulas turned out to be much more generous than BP anticipated, but the court rejected its objections to how the settlement fund was administered. "There is nothing fundamentally unreasonable about what BP accepted but now wishes it had not." In re Deepwater Horizon, 744 F.3d 370, 377 (5th Cir. 2014).

BP also agreed to a $20 billion settlement with the United States, the five Gulf Coast states, and more than 400 local governments along the coast, covering civil penalties and compensation for economic and environmental damage. *Judge Approves Settlement of $20 Billion in BP Oil Spill*, N.Y Times (April 5, 2016). BP estimates its total costs related to the spill at more than $61 billion. Steven Mufson, *BP's Big Bill for the World's Largest Oil Spill Reaches $61.6 Billion*, Washington Post (July 14, 2016). This includes criminal fines; clean-up costs; civil settlements with individuals, businesses, and governments; money paid through the Gulf Coast Claims Facility; and settlements with BP investors misled about the magnitude of the disaster.

7. Policing the boundary of tort and contract. The other principal variant of the economic-loss rule says that there is no liability for negligence in the negotiation or performance of a contract. The same limitation to physical injury or property damage is built into the usual statements of strict liability for defective products. These rules police the boundary between tort and contract.

The original leading case is Seely v. White Motor Co., 403 P.2d 145 (Cal. 1965). Seely bought a truck for his business; the truck was defective. He sued in products liability for the price of the truck and the profits he would have earned if the truck had not been defective. The court denied recovery in tort, holding that he must sue in contract for his economic losses. This contract variant of the economic-loss rule (also not a phrase that judges use) prevents plaintiff from evading limitations of liability in the contract, the UCC, or other relevant contract law. If plaintiff has a good claim on the contract for breach of warranty, then all is well. But if consequential damages have been disclaimed, or if the contract claim fails for any other reason, plaintiff cannot rescue his claim by suing in tort.

8. Damage to what property? In *Seely*, the truck simply didn't work. It didn't damage any other tangible property. But what if the truck caught fire and damaged the truck parked next to it, or burned down the garage? What property counts for identifying damage to property?

There is a surprising range of answers to that question. Some of the cases are collected in the majority and dissenting opinions in Arena Holdings Charitable, LLC v. Harman Professional, Inc., 785 F.3d 292 (8th Cir. 2015), trying to predict North Dakota law. In *Arena*, a defective amplifier caused a fire that did $5 million in damage to a concert venue. The majority applied the "foreseeability rule," which in this context is counterintuitive. It says that there is no tort liability for property damage if damage to that property was a foreseeable consequence of a defective product. This rule appears to exclude liability for damage even to clearly separate property if it would normally be physically close to the defective product.

At the other extreme is Jiminez v. Superior Court, 58 P.3d 450 (Cal. 2002), where defective windows, installed in a house, caused damage to everything around and under the window—stucco, insulation, drywall, wall and floor coverings, and baseboard. The court held that if a component part does damage to the rest of the product in which it is installed, that property damage is recoverable in tort. It is only damage to the window itself that is confined to contract claims by the economic-loss rule. New Jersey applied this rule to insulation and siding applied to the outside of a house. Dean v. Barrett Homes, Inc., 8 A.3d 766 (N.J. 2010).

In between, many courts apply an "integrated product" rule: has the defective component been integrated into a larger product? The Wisconsin court held that homeowners buy a house as an integrated whole; they do not buy its components separately. Any damage to the house is therefore subject to the economic-loss rule. Linden v. Cascade Stone Co., 699 N.W.2d 189 (Wis. 2005).

The federal admiralty rule distinguishes between those parts of the product supplied by the seller and those added by the owner; damage to the latter can be can be recovered in tort. In CHMM, LLC v. Freeman Marine Equipment, Inc., 791 F.3d 1059 (9th Cir. 2015), a defective door let sea water into the interior of a 60-meter luxury yacht and caused $18 million in damage. (Luxury yachts have fancy interiors.) All the interior furnishings had been provided and installed by the plaintiff owner, not by the ship builder. So the yacht was not separate property from the door, but the interior was separate property from the yacht.

9. Third-party cases. The economic-loss rule also reinforces the rule of not going beyond the "first step" in the proximate-cause cases. *A* can contract with *B* without incurring a duty to others who have contracted with *B*. If a wholesaler negligently fails to deliver promised goods to a retailer, he is liable to the retailer for breach of contract, but he is not liable to the retailer's disappointed customers.

One can view such decisions as channeling liability and the allocation of risks into a series of contracts: between the wholesaler and the retailer and then between the retailer and each customer. If both contracts permit it, liability can be passed up the chain to the party at fault. If one of the contracts disclaims the liability, perhaps (at least in theory) the other side was compensated for bearing the risk. But these cases do not always work out so neatly. Consider In re New England Fish Co., 749 F.2d 1277 (9th Cir. 1984), where a fish processor's negligence drove a fishing company into bankruptcy. A fish broker who had paid the fishing company for spoiled fish was left without a remedy against anyone. The broker's contract claim against the bankrupt fishing company was worthless, and its negligence claim against the processor was barred by the economic-loss rule.

10. The scope of the rule. The economic-loss rule is generally said to apply to negligence and products liability claims. Intentional torts such as fraud and interference with contract are outside the rule; these torts typically cause only economic loss. At least a few jurisdictions apply the rule to commercial cases but not to consumer cases. Florida applies it only to products liability cases and not to other kinds of contracts. Tiara Condominium Association, Inc. v. Marsh & McLennan Cos., 110 So. 2d 399 (Fla. 2013). Most jurisdictions recognize an exception for professional malpractice. An example is Hydro Investors, Inc. v. Trafalgar Power, Inc., 227 F.3d 8 (2d Cir. 2000), applying New York law to malpractice by an engineering firm.

SUNNYLAND FARMS, INC. v. CENTRAL NEW MEXICO ELECTRIC COOPERATIVE, INC.

301 P.3d 387 (N.M. 2013)

CHÁVEZ, Justice. . . .

[Sunnyland Farms purchased its electricity from defendant, which the court calls CNMEC.] On September 8, 2003, CNMEC shut off electrical service to Sunnyland. Prior to disconnecting electricity for nonpayment, CNMEC ordinarily gives its customers notice that they have fifteen days to pay their overdue bills before service is suspended. It did not give Sunnyland this fifteen-day notice. The trial court record indicates a confusing array of possible billing irregularities, but it is not necessary to address them here because CNMEC does not contest the trial court's findings that it was negligent and that it breached its duty to Sunnyland.

On the morning of September 9, 2003, before electrical service was restored, several Sunnyland employees engaged in arc welding near flammable materials, including cardboard boxes. In doing so, they started a fire that ultimately consumed Sunnyland Farms' packhouse and operations building. When Sunnyland's employees initially discovered the fire, they attempted to put it out using ordinary hoses, but without electricity, the Sunnyland facility had no running water, and the fire grew. Sunnyland does not contest that its employees were negligent both in starting the fire and in reacting to it, for example, by failing to use a fire extinguisher.

Someone living on Sunnyland's property called the fire department. Fire trucks arrived, but they were unable to access well water for firefighting because there was no electricity to power the pumps. Sunnyland had also failed to make alternative arrangements for emergency water in the event that power failed. Firefighters attempted to contact CNMEC to restore electricity to the water sources, but CNMEC employees expressed reservations to the emergency dispatcher, and the firefighters interpreted their statements as a threat that the fire department would have to assume liability. [Liability for what was never made clear. The electric bill for one day?] Firefighters attempted to use reservoir water and to preserve water by using foam and smaller hoses, but the buildings were nonetheless destroyed.

Sunnyland sued CNMEC in contract and tort, among other causes of action, for damages resulting from the fire, alleging that if CNMEC had taken adequate care prior to disconnecting Sunnyland's electrical service, firefighters and Sunnyland employees would have had access to water and the fire could have been contained. The trial court found CNMEC liable both in contract and in tort. It calculated total consequential damages of over $21 million, of which $13.7 million was the net value of lost crops that the facility would have been able to grow in the absence of the fire. The trial court reduced the damages in tort by 80% to account for Sunnyland's comparative fault; however, in contract, the trial court awarded the entire almost $21.4 million. The trial court allowed plaintiffs to elect a remedy in contract or tort after the resolution of their appeals. . . .

A. CONTRACT DAMAGES

1. HADLEY V. BAXENDALE AND *RESTATEMENT (SECOND) OF CONTRACTS* STATE THE PROPER TEST FOR CONSEQUENTIAL DAMAGES IN NEW MEXICO

This Court has previously stated that in an action for breach of contract, the breaching party "is justly responsible for all damages flowing naturally from the breach." Camino

Real Mobile Home Park Partnership v. Wolfe, 891 P.2d 1190, 1197 (N.M. 1995). Damages "that arise naturally and necessarily as the result of the breach" are "general damages," which give the plaintiff whatever value he or she would have obtained from the breached contract. In some circumstances, the plaintiff can also recover for "consequential damages" or "special damages," which "are not based on the capital or present value of the promised performance but upon benefits it can produce or losses that may be caused by its absence." *Id.*, quoting 3 Dan B. Dobbs, *Law of Remedies* §12.2(3) at 41 (2d ed. 1993).

The classic test for whether a plaintiff may recover consequential damages comes from Hadley v. Baxendale, 156 Eng. Rep. 145 (Ex. 1854). In that case, a mill was temporarily shut down due to a broken crankshaft. The defendants were common carriers who were supposed to ship the broken crankshaft to an engineering company to have a new one built, but the defendants "wholly neglected and refused so to do for the space of seven days," and the mill was shut down for five days longer than should have been necessary. *Id.* at 146. The jury awarded the mill damages for the profits it lost due to the delay. The appellate court reversed, holding that in an action for breach of contract, recovery was permitted for consequential damages only "such as may reasonably be supposed to have been in the contemplation of both parties, at the time they made the contract, as the probable result of the breach of it." *Id.* at 151.

The *Hadley* standard has been interpreted as an objective foreseeability test: A defendant is liable for losses that were foreseeable at the time of contracting, regardless of whether the defendant actually contemplated or foresaw the loss. *Restatement (Second) of Contracts* §351 cmt. *a* (Am. Law Inst. 1981). This foreseeability standard is more stringent than "proximate cause" in tort law; the loss must have been foreseeable as the *probable* result of breach, not merely as a possibility. The *Restatement* asks whether there were "special circumstances, beyond the ordinary course of events, that the party in breach had reason to know." *Id.* §351(2)(b); *see also* UCC §2-715(2)(a) (allowing buyers consequential damages for "any loss resulting from general or particular requirements and needs of which the seller at the time of contracting had reason to know and which could not reasonably be prevented by cover or otherwise"). In the absence of such circumstances, the breaching party is liable only for general damages. *Restatement* §351 cmt. *b* ("If loss results other than in the ordinary course of events, there can be no recovery for it unless it was foreseeable by the party in breach because of special circumstances that he had reason to know when he made the contract.").

This Court has cited the *Hadley* standard approvingly and described it as the appropriate rule of analysis in New Mexico cases dealing with consequential damages. However, we have also stated that "the foreseeability . . . rule anticipates an explicit or tacit agreement by the defendant" that he or she will assume particular damages if he or she breaches. *Camino Real*, 891 P.2d at 1200. . . .

We now abandon the "tacit agreement" test. While we suspect that there may not, in fact, be much space between a "tacit agreement" and the special circumstances required to render a defendant liable for consequential damages, our previous emphasis on the tacit agreement test is confusing and antiquated. We hold that the proper test for consequential damages in New Mexico is the *Hadley* standard as interpreted in *Restatement* §351. In a contract action, a defendant is liable only for those consequential damages that were objectively foreseeable as a probable result of his or her breach when the contract was made. To the extent our earlier cases suggest a different standard, they are overruled.

2. THERE WERE NO SPECIAL CIRCUMSTANCES IN THIS CASE WARRANTING CONSEQUENTIAL DAMAGES

. . . The trial court in this case issued very limited conclusions of law regarding the issue of foreseeability and consequential damages. The trial court made one finding of fact stating that "the damages suffered by Plaintiff were foreseeable and a proximate cause [sic—should probably be "result"] of Defendant's Breach of Contract, negligence and negligence per se." However, in its findings, the trial court did not distinguish between the proximate cause required for tort liability and the more stringent foreseeability required for consequential damages in contract. . . .

To support the conclusion that Sunnyland's damages were foreseeable to CNMEC at the time of contracting, we would expect the trial court to find "special circumstances, beyond the ordinary course of events." *Restatement* §351(2)(b). Despite the voluminous findings of fact by the trial court, there were no findings that special circumstances of this type existed.

Sunnyland suggests that it was sufficient that CNMEC knew that Sunnyland was a for-profit enterprise and it depended on electricity. . . . The trial court found that "CNMEC [e]mployees . . . testified that it was well known within the community that [the Sunnyland] facility was a hydroponic tomato facility." . . .

Taking these findings of fact to indicate the presence of special circumstances is problematic for three reasons. First, although this Court indulges reasonable inferences in favor of the trial court's judgment, this is simply too speculative. This Court does not speculate about what the fact-finder might have meant to say but did not.

Second, Sunnyland's injury was not directly caused by the lack of electricity. The actual harm was more attenuated: the lack of electricity interrupted Sunnyland's water supply, which, in conjunction with Sunnyland's lack of backup firefighting options, made it difficult for Sunnyland to respond to the fire its employees negligently started. There were no findings that CNMEC should have known that Sunnyland was likely to start fires or was depending on electricity in order to fight any fires that occurred. Even if some damage to the tomato crop was foreseeable from the disconnection of electricity, the particular damage that occurred was not, and consequential damages are only permissible if the particular damage that actually occurred was foreseeable. "The mere circumstance that some loss was foreseeable, or even that some loss of the same general kind was foreseeable, will not suffice if the loss that actually occurred was not foreseeable." *Restatement* §351 cmt. *a.*

Third, even if CNMEC had reason to know that Sunnyland depended on its electricity to power water in the event of a fire, CNMEC would still not be liable without the presence of additional special circumstances. *Hadley* provides a good example of what does and does not qualify as "special circumstances." In *Hadley,* the defendant knew that the crankshaft it was carrying was a broken part of a for-profit mill. However, the plaintiff never told the defendant exactly what was at stake, *i.e.,* that there was no backup shaft or other alternative plan to keep the mill running. Similarly, in this case, CNMEC would have needed to know not only that Sunnyland depended on its electricity for access to water, but that there was no backup power source, or that there was a particularized need for uninterrupted water or power. There is no evidence that CNMEC had reason to know any of this. In particular, CNMEC could not have been expected to know that Sunnyland did not have a separate power source, independent of the power for the main building, for the well that was to be used in the event of a fire. A firefighter's trial testimony agreed that "if it's going to be an approved firefighting source of water, it has to have two separate sources of electricity . . . [a]nd one of them cannot come through the building that's being . . . protected by the pump," and the trial court found that "Sunnyland Farms was negligent in having only one source of power which ran through the support building to energize the exterior well pump." CNMEC cannot have been expected to anticipate Sunnyland's negligence in this regard.

Langley v. Pacific Gas & Electric Co., 262 P.2d 846 (Cal. 1953), provides an instructive example of what a utility company would need to know to render it liable for consequential damages in the event of a power shutoff. The plaintiff ran a trout hatchery that required electricity to oxygenate the water and keep the trout alive. If power was shut off, the fish could survive for only three and a half hours. The plaintiff purchased electricity from the utility and explained his situation to its employees, asking whether the utility had 24-hour monitoring and would always be able to tell him before power was shut off. [The plaintiff installed a backup pump that he could activate if he knew that the power was off.] The utility's employees assured the plaintiff that he would be notified any time the power was shut off. Several years later, power to the fish hatchery was shut off for several hours, and the utility failed to warn or inform the plaintiff. Nearly all of the plaintiff's fish died. The plaintiff sued the utility for breach of contract, and the California Supreme Court upheld a jury verdict in his favor, apparently including full consequential damages. *See id.* at 850 (stating that the measure of the damages was identical under tort and breach of contract theories). The court found that the utility "knew that a continuous supply of electric current to plaintiff was imperative," and the utility had an obligation either to provide it or to give the plaintiff notice . . . .

The facts in *Langley* are starkly different from the facts in the present case. In *Langley,* the plaintiff had an unusual and pressing need for uninterrupted service, and he took steps to notify the utility of that need. . . . Unlike in *Hadley* and the present case, the utility in *Langley* understood the particular consequences that would result from a breach, and it accepted the contract anyway.

There were no findings in this case that CNMEC should have known of a particular vulnerability to fire on Sunnyland's part, or that Sunnyland had no backup source of power or water. With neither findings nor evidence of special circumstances, we cannot uphold a judgment for consequential damages. Accordingly, we affirm the Court of Appeals' reversal of the trial court's award of contract damages to Sunnyland.

MORE NOTES ON THE SCOPE OF LIABILITY

1. The tort claim. *Sunnyland* would be a better case for our purposes if defendant had also appealed the tort damages on proximate-cause or scope-of-liability grounds. It did not.

New Mexico says that intervening causes arising from plaintiff's negligence are to be addressed as issues of comparative fault, rather than as causation or proximate cause. Torres v. El Paso Electric Co., 987 P.2d 386 (N.M. 1999). With 80 percent of the fault apportioned to Sunnyland, CNMEC may have felt that it had won on that issue. New Mexico has pure comparative negligence, so CNMEC still had to pay 20 percent of the tort damages. The economic-loss rule did not apply, because there was physical damage to property.

Beyond that, New Mexico's understanding of proximate cause in tort appears to be friendly to plaintiffs. The Uniform Jury Instruction on causation says:

> An act or omission is a "cause" of harm if it contributes to bringing about the harm, and if the harm would not have occurred without it. It need not be the only explanation for the harm, nor the reason that is nearest in time or place. It is sufficient if it occurs in

combination with some other cause to produce the result. To be a "cause," the act or omission, nonetheless, must be reasonably connected as a significant link to the harm.

N.M. Unif. Jury Instruction 13-305. There is no further instruction on proximate cause. Foreseeability is part of the instruction defining negligence and ordinary care; the degree of care required depends on the foreseeable risks. But foreseeability is not mentioned in connection with causation. And the court has said that "[f]oreseeability does not require that the particular consequence should have been anticipated, but rather that some general harm or consequence be foreseeable." *Spencer v. Health Force, Inc.*, 107 P.3d 504, 511 (N.M. 2005). None of these formulations is unique to New Mexico, but they are towards the pro-plaintiff end of the continuum.

Suppose the fire was started by a lightning strike. And suppose that Sunnyland had a backup generator that also failed, through no fault of Sunnyland. Suppose, in short, that comparative fault were out of the picture and that the accident were even more freakish than what actually happened. CNMEC could surely foresee "that some general harm or consequence" might flow from cutting off the power without notice. Does that mean that it should be responsible in tort for "the particular consequence" of a fire that started while the power was off?

And how, if at all, would the New Mexico formulation limit liability in *Pruitt*?

2. Tort and contract. Comparative fault was not available on the contract claim; breach of contract is strict liability. But some torts are also strict liability, and often there is negligence or worse, or misrepresentation, in a breach of contract. How much should the limits of liability depend on whether the claim is in contract or tort?

One rationale for insisting on more specific foreseeability in contract is that contract liability is based on agreement, and defendants are entitled to know what liabilities they are potentially incurring. This is one explanation for Hadley v. Baxendale's requirement that contracting parties be notified of the risk of unusual damages. This leads to a difference in the time at which foreseeability is assessed. The question is not what defendant should have foreseen when he breached, but what he should have foreseen when he made the contract. In tort, but not in contract, the question is what defendant should have foreseen when he did the thing he is being sued for.

Sunnyland says, and many other cases and commentators say, that tort defendants have more extensive liability than contract defendants. And there is some truth to that; *Sunnyland* is an example. But it might be more broadly accurate to say that defendants have more extensive liability for causing injuries to the person than for causing what courts now call economic loss. Negligence defendants are broadly liable for personal injury and property damage but generally not liable for economic loss. Contract defendants can disclaim most damages but are significantly limited in their ability to disclaim damages for personal injury. Physical damage to property appears to be an intermediate case, placed more on the personal injury side in tort law but more subject to exclusion in contract.

In *Sunnyland*, wouldn't it be implausible to say that CNMEC was liable for 20 percent of the damages in tort but 100 percent of the damages in contract? Didn't the court have to make *Hadley* do the work that comparative negligence did in tort?

3. Hadley v. Baxendale in tort. Judge Posner applied Hadley v. Baxendale to a tort case in Evra Corp. v. Swiss Bank Corp., 673 F.2d 951 (7th Cir. 1982). Swiss Bank lost track of a $27,000 wire transfer, with the result that Evra lost the lease of a ship and $2.1 million in profits. Evra had no contract or banking relationship with Swiss Bank; it initiated the transfer through its own bank in Chicago. Evra sued for negligence.

The case could have been decided under the economic-loss rule, but the contract variant of that rule had a much lower profile in 1982, and perhaps there were not yet any Illinois cases. Today it could be decided under UCC §4A-305, which protects the banks from liability. But Article 4A had not yet been enacted. Finding no controlling authority under Illinois law, Posner took the occasion to explore the limits of liability in tort and contract and the relationship between the two.

Hadley applied even to negligent breaches of contract, and the court held that it also applied to negligence in a transaction without contract. "[T]he animating principle of *Hadley* . . . is that the costs of the untoward consequence of a course of dealings should be borne by that party who was able to avert the consequence at least cost and failed to do so." 673 F.2d at 957. Posner thought the lowest-cost avoider was Evra, which (because interest rates were high) had waited until the last minute to initiate its wire transfer, leaving no time to make the payment if anything went wrong. Evra was held responsible for foreseeing that banks sometimes make mistakes—general foreseeability—but Swiss Bank was not held responsible for foreseeing that some wire transfers are part of very large deals and that some of those deals are shaky. And no one had told Swiss Bank that Evra's lease was both highly profitable to Evra and a disastrous loss for the ship owner receiving the payment, who was looking for an excuse to repudiate the deal.

Posner also analogized *Hadley* to avoidable consequences. He thought that Evra had failed to respond aggressively enough to the lost wire, when its charter might still have been saved, and that it had acted recklessly before the lost wire by waiting to the last minute despite the fragility of its deal. Most courts would treat plaintiff's pre-accident negligence as going to comparative fault, but he thought it could also go to avoidable consequences and bar recovery of damages that reasonable pre-accident precautions would have avoided.

4. What kind of notice is enough? Should *Evra* come out the other way if the instructions for the wire transfer included a sentence explaining (to the clerk who monitored the fax machine) that the Chicago bank's customer might lose a multimillion-dollar deal if this payment were delayed? Compare Compania Anonima Venezolana de Navegacion v. American Express International Banking Corp., 1985 WL 1898 (S.D.N.Y. 1985), refusing summary judgment for defendant in a similar case, because the parties had a banking relationship and American Express knew enough about its customer's business to raise an issue of material fact on whether it should have known the consequences of failing to complete the transfer. The court distinguished *Evra*, and it cited a Cardozo opinion stating that a telegraph company could be liable if the contents of the telegram disclosed enough about a transaction to effectively disclose the risk if the telegram is lost. But the contents of telegrams were read only by rank-and-file employees, and not by management.

Or consider Langley v. Pacific Gas & Electric Co., discussed in *Sunnyland*, where plaintiff carefully explained his special needs to defendant's "employees." Does it matter which employees? The chief executive officer? A senior management official? A sales rep? The clerical employee who answered the phone that day?

5. Lowest-cost avoider? Talk of putting responsibility on the party that could avoid the harm at lowest cost is appealing in theory, but identification of the lowest-cost avoider is often intuitive. It costs very little to send a notice before cutting off the power. It is certainly cheaper than a backup power system. Is that the right question? Or is the question what it would cost to create a system that would never make a mistake and fail to send the notice?

Who was the lowest-cost avoider in *Evra*? Did the court have any way of knowing whether it is cheaper overall for banks to install more safeguards or buy liability insurance than for customers to surround every important transaction with hedges against the banks' negligence? The court's paragraph on lowest-cost avoiders did not address that question; it immediately slipped into a discussion of the ways in which Evra was at fault.

How would the lowest-loss-avoider formulation apply to *Pruitt?* Could anyone but the chemical company have avoided that harm?

4.   *Substantive Policy Goals*

BRUNSWICK CORP. v. PUEBLO BOWL-O-MAT
429 U.S. 477 (1977)

Justice MARSHALL delivered the opinion of the Court. . . .

I

Petitioner is one of the two largest manufacturers of bowling equipment in the United States. Respondents are three of the ten bowling centers owned by Treadway Companies. Since 1965, petitioner has acquired and operated a large number of bowling centers, including six in the markets in which respondents operate. Respondents instituted this action contending that these acquisitions violated various provisions of the antitrust laws.

In the late 1950's, the bowling industry expanded rapidly, and petitioner's sales of lanes, automatic pinsetters, and ancillary equipment rose accordingly. Since this equipment requires a major capital expenditure—$12,600 for each lane and pinsetter—most of petitioner's sales were for secured credit.

In the early 1960's, the bowling industry went into a sharp decline. . . . [P]etitioner experienced great difficulty in collecting money owed it; by the end of 1964 over $100,000,000, or more than 25%, of petitioner's accounts were more than 90 days delinquent. Repossessions rose dramatically, but attempts to sell or lease the repossessed equipment met with only limited success.

To meet this difficulty, petitioner began acquiring and operating defaulting bowling centers when their equipment could not be resold and a positive cash flow could be expected from operating the centers. During the seven years preceding the trial in this case, petitioner acquired 222 centers, 54 of which it either disposed of or closed. These acquisitions made petitioner by far the largest operator of bowling centers, with over five times as many centers as its next largest competitor. Petitioner's net worth in 1965 was more than eight times greater, and its gross revenue more than seven times greater, than the total for the 11 next largest bowling chains. Nevertheless, petitioner controlled only 2% of the bowling centers in the United States.

At issue here are acquisitions by petitioner in the three markets in which respondents are located: Pueblo, Colo., Poughkeepsie, N.Y., and Paramus, N.J. . . .

Respondents initiated this action in June 1966, alleging . . . that these acquisitions might substantially lessen competition or tend to create a monopoly in violation of §7 of the Clayton Act, 15 U.S.C. §18. Respondents sought damages, pursuant to §4 of the Act, 15 U.S.C. §15, for three times "the reasonably expectable profits to be made [by respondents] from the operation of their bowling centers." Respondents also sought a divestiture order, an injunction against future acquisitions, and such "other further and different relief" as might be appropriate under §16 of the Act, 15 U.S.C. §26. . . .

To establish a §7 violation, respondents sought to prove that because of its size, petitioner had the capacity to lessen competition in the markets it had entered by driving smaller competitors out of business. To establish damages, respondents attempted to show that had petitioner allowed the defaulting centers to close, respondents' profits would have increased. . . . The jury returned a verdict in favor of respondents in the amount of $2,358,030, which represented the minimum estimate by respondents of the additional income they would have realized had the acquired centers been closed. As required by law, the District Court trebled the damages. It also awarded respondents costs and attorneys' fees totaling $446,977.32, and, sitting as a court of equity, it ordered petitioner to divest itself of the centers involved here. 389 F. Supp. 996 (D.N.J. 1974). Petitioner appealed.

The Court of Appeals, while endorsing the legal theories upon which respondents' claim was based, reversed the judgment and remanded the case for further proceedings. 523 F.2d 262 (3d Cir. 1975). . . . [T]he court decided that the jury had not been properly charged and that therefore a new trial was required. It also decided that since "an essential predicate" for the District Court's grant of equitable relief was the jury verdict on the §7 claim, the equitable decree should be vacated as well. And it concluded that in any event equitable relief "should be restricted to preventing those practices by which a deep pocket market entrant harms competition. . . . [D]ivestiture was simply inappropriate."

Both sides petitioned this Court for writs of certiorari. . . . We granted Brunswick's petition.

II

The issue for decision is a narrow one. Petitioner does not presently contest the Court of Appeals' conclusion that a properly instructed jury could have found the acquisitions unlawful. Nor does petitioner challenge the Court of Appeals' determination that the evidence would support a finding that had petitioner not acquired these centers, they would have gone out of business and respondents' income would have increased. Petitioner questions only whether antitrust damages are available where the sole injury alleged is that competitors were continued in business, thereby denying respondents an anticipated increase in market shares.

To answer that question it is necessary to examine the antimerger and treble-damages provisions of the Clayton Act. Section 7 of the Act proscribes mergers whose effect "*may be* substantially to lessen competition, or *to tend to* create a monopoly." (Emphasis added.) It is, as we have observed many times, a prophylactic measure, intended "primarily to arrest apprehended consequences of intercorporate relationships before those relationships could work their evil." United States v. E.I. du Pont de Nemours & Co., 353 U.S. 586, 597 (1957).

Section 4, in contrast, is in essence a remedial provision. It provides treble damages to "[a]ny person who shall be injured in his business or property by reason of anything forbidden in the antitrust laws." Of course, treble damages also play an important role in penalizing wrongdoers and deterring wrongdoing, as we also have frequently observed. It nevertheless is true that the treble-damages provision, which makes awards available only to injured parties, and measures the awards by a multiple of the injury actually proved, is designed primarily as a remedy.

Intermeshing a statutory prohibition against acts that have a potential to cause certain harms with a damages action intended to remedy those harms is not without difficulty. Plainly, to recover damages respondents must prove more than that petitioner violated §7, since such proof establishes only that injury may result. Respondents contend that the only additional element they need demonstrate is that they are in a worse position than they would have been had petitioner not committed those acts. The Court of Appeals agreed, holding compensable any loss "causally linked" to "the mere presence of the violator in the market." Because this holding divorces antitrust recovery from the purposes of the antitrust laws without a clear statutory command to do so, we cannot agree with it.

Every merger of two existing entities into one, whether lawful or unlawful, has the potential for producing economic readjustments that adversely affect some persons. But Congress has not condemned mergers on that account; it has condemned them only when they may produce anticompetitive effects. Yet under the Court of Appeals' holding, once a merger is found to violate §7, all dislocations caused by the merger are actionable, regardless of whether those dislocations have anything to do with the reason the merger was condemned. This holding would make §4 recovery entirely fortuitous, and would authorize damages for losses which are of no concern to the antitrust laws.

Both of these consequences are well illustrated by the facts of this case. If the acquisitions here were unlawful, it is because they brought a "deep pocket" parent into a market of "pygmies." Yet respondents' injury—the loss of income that would have accrued had the acquired centers gone bankrupt—bears no relationship to the size of either the acquiring company or its competitors. Respondents would have suffered the identical "loss"—but no compensable injury—had the acquired centers instead obtained refinancing or been purchased by "shallow pocket" parents as the Court of Appeals itself acknowledged.[12] Thus, respondents' injury was not of "the type that the statute was intended to forestall," Wyandotte Co. v. United States, 389 U.S. 191, 202 (1967).

But the antitrust laws are not merely indifferent to the injury claimed here. At base, respondents complain that by acquiring the failing centers petitioner preserved competition, thereby depriving respondents of the benefits of increased concentration. The damages respondents obtained are designed to provide them with the profits they would have realized had competition been reduced. The antitrust laws, however, were enacted for "the protection of *competition* not *competitors*," Brown Shoe Co. v. United States, 370 U.S. 294, 320 (1962). It is inimical to the purposes of these laws to award damages for the type of injury claimed here.

Of course, Congress is free, if it desires, to mandate damages awards for all dislocations caused by unlawful mergers despite the peculiar consequences of so doing. But because of these consequences, "we should insist upon a clear expression of a congressional purpose," Hawaii v. Standard Oil Co., 405 U.S. 251, 264 (1972), before attributing such an intent to Congress. We can find no such expression in either the language or the legislative history of §4. To the contrary, it is far from clear that the loss of windfall profits that would have accrued had the acquired centers failed even constitutes "injury" within the meaning of §4. And it is quite clear that if respondents were injured, it was not "by reason of anything forbidden in the antitrust laws": while respondents' loss occurred "by reason of" the unlawful acquisitions, it did not occur "by reason of" that which made the acquisitions unlawful.

We therefore hold that for plaintiffs to recover treble damages on account of §7 violations, they must prove more than injury causally linked to an illegal presence in the market. Plaintiffs must prove *antitrust* injury, which is to say injury of the type the antitrust laws were intended to prevent and that flows from that which make

---

12. Conversely, had petitioner acquired thriving centers—acquisitions at least as violative of §7 as the instant acquisitions—respondents would not have lost any income that they otherwise would have received.

defendants' acts unlawful. The injury should reflect the anticompetitive effect either of the violation or of anticompetitive acts made possible by the violation. It should, in short, be "the type of loss that the claimed violations . . . would be likely to cause." Zenith Radio Corp. v. Hazeltine Research, Inc., 395 U.S. 100, 125 (1969).

III

We come, then, to the question of appropriate disposition of this case. At the very least, petitioner is entitled to a new trial, not only because of the instructional errors noted by the Court of Appeals that are not at issue here, but also because the District Court's instruction as to the basis for damages was inconsistent with our holding as outlined above. Our review of the record, however, persuades us that a new trial on the damages claim is unwarranted. Respondents based their case solely on their novel damages theory which we have rejected. While they produced some conclusory testimony suggesting that in operating the acquired centers petitioner had abused its deep pocket by engaging in anticompetitive conduct, they made no attempt to prove that they had lost any income as a result of such predation. Rather, their entire proof of damages was based on their claim to profits that would have been earned had the acquired centers closed. Since respondents did not prove any cognizable damages and have not offered any justification for allowing respondents, after two trials and over 10 years of litigation, yet a third opportunity to do so, it follows that . . . petitioner is entitled, in accord with its motion made pursuant to Rule 50(b), to judgment on the damages claim notwithstanding the verdict.

Respondents' complaint also prayed for equitable relief, and the Court of Appeals held that if respondents established a §7 violation, they might be entitled to an injunction against "those practices by which a deep pocket market entrant harms competition." Because petitioner has not contested this holding, respondents remain free, on remand, to seek such a decree.

The judgment of the Court of Appeals is vacated, and the case is remanded for further proceedings consistent with this opinion. . . .

NOTES ON REMEDIAL IMPLICATIONS OF SUBSTANTIVE POLICY

1. **Antitrust injury and scope of liability.** Is the reasoning in *Brunswick* any different from the *Restatement*'s definition of the scope of liability in personal injury cases? Recall the suggestion that negligent defendants are liable only for "those harms that result from the risks that made the actor's conduct tortious." *Restatement (Third) of Torts: Liability for Physical and Emotional Harm* §29, discussed in the notes following *Pruitt* in section 2.E.3. In the wake of *Brunswick*, the courts have developed a large body of law on antitrust injury.

The point is not limited to damages. A plaintiff seeking an injunction to prevent a merger must show that is threatened with antitrust injury as defined in *Brunswick*. Cargill, Inc. v. Montfort, Inc., 479 U.S. 104 (1986).

2. **Remedies that affirmatively undermine substance.** *Brunswick* holds that plaintiff cannot use the antitrust laws to preserve a local monopoly or get compensated for the loss of one. This is a dramatic illustration of a pervasive point. Remedies implement substantive policies, and any remedial principle, no matter how well settled, may have to be adapted or limited when applied in the context of a particular substantive violation.

3. Copyright injury. An actress's brief performance at a casting call was inserted into an anti-Muslim propaganda video, with the result that a Muslim cleric in Egypt issued a fatwa—a religious ruling—calling for her death. She received death threats that she believed to be credible, and suffered emotional distress and disruption to her acting career. Garcia v. Google, Inc., 786 F.3d 733 (9th Cir. 2015). She asserted a copyright in her own performance and sought an injunction ordering YouTube to delete the video. The court refused relief for multiple reasons, one of which was that emotional distress and death are not the kind of injuries that the copyright laws are designed to prevent. Copyright is about encouraging expression by enabling authors and performers to profit from their work. The court cited a few similar holdings on less dramatic facts.

4. The loss of illegal employment. Consider Hoffman Plastic Compounds, Inc. v. National Labor Relations Board, 535 U.S. 137 (2002). Hoffman laid off some of its employees in retaliation for their union organizing activities. One of the victims was an immigrant not authorized to work in the United States. Hoffman had violated the immigration laws by employing him, and it had violated the labor laws by laying him off. The NLRB awarded $66,000 in back pay for the labor-law violation.

The Supreme Court refused to enforce the award. The majority thought that any back pay or reinstatement would reward the *employee's* violation of the immigration laws; four dissenters thought that immunity from the labor laws rewarded and encouraged the *employer's* violations of both the labor laws and the immigration laws. Hoffman was ordered to comply with the labor laws in the future, and to post notices explaining its employees' right to unionize and detailing its past violations.

Hoffman set off a round of litigation about its reach. Employers and others responsible for workplace injuries began to argue that an immigrant who was illegally in the country and was injured on the job could not recover lost wages, or that he could recover only at the wage rates prevailing in his home country. Many of these cases are collected in Balbuena v. IDR Realty LLC, 845 N.E.2d 1246, 1256 n.5 (N.Y. 2006). *Balbuena* holds that the injured employee can recover lost wages; the dissenters would have said that he was trying to recover the benefit of an illegal bargain, and that, even if New York permitted such a recovery, it would be preempted by federal immigration law.

Hoffman has gotten a generally hostile reception in the lower courts. Employers have invoked it in all sorts of employment litigation, but just 5 percent of those cases find an employer substantively liable but refuse monetary relief because of the plaintiff's immigration status. Michael H. LeRoy, *Remedies for Unlawful Alien Workers: One Law for the Native and for the Stranger Who Resides in Your Midst? An Empirical Perspective*, 28 Geo. Immigration L.J. 623 (2014). *Hoffman* has largely been confined to its original context, the National Labor Relations Act.

5. Plaintiff misconduct, discovered only because of defendant misconduct. An employee's suit against an employer prompts the employer to more carefully investigate the employee's behavior. These investigations sometimes reveal résumé fraud or on-the-job misconduct that would have caused an employer, if it had only known, to refuse to hire or to discharge the employee for entirely lawful reasons. In McKennon v. Nashville Banner Publishing Co., 513 U.S. 352 (1995), a discharged secretary alleging age discrimination had copied her employer's confidential financial records and taken the copies home. The Court held that the presumptive remedy should be back pay from the time of the unlawful discharge to the time at which the employer discovered the facts that would have resulted in a lawful discharge. The National Labor Relations Board has followed this lead in the illegal immigrant cases, awarding back pay up to the point at which the employer discovered the worker's immigration status. The Colorado court has applied a more stringent rule to state-law claims; if the employer discovers résumé fraud such that he would not have hired the plaintiff in the first place if he had known the truth, the employee's claim for breach of the employment contract is entirely barred. Crawford Rehabilitation Services, Inc. v. Weissman, 938 P.2d 540 (Colo. 1997).

6. The exclusionary rule. The most important recurring example of the victim as wrongdoer is illegal searches and seizures. Suppose the police conduct two flagrantly illegal searches. In the first, they find no evidence of crime. In the second, they find evidence of murder, and that evidence ultimately leads to the victim of the search, not previously a murder suspect, being sentenced to life in prison. Suppose both victims sue the police for violating their Fourth Amendment rights. Should the murderer recover much more than the innocent citizen? Both suffered the same damage at the time of the search. But in addition, the murderer suffered life in prison. But for the illegal search, he wouldn't be there. Should he get compensation for that? Or is the murder, rather than the search, the legal cause of his imprisonment? Is imprisonment not "Fourth Amendment damage," in the same sense that the lost profits in *Brunswick* were not "antitrust damage"?

No plaintiff can recover damages in federal court "for allegedly unconstitutional conviction or imprisonment, or for other harm caused by actions whose unlawfulness would render a conviction or sentence invalid," unless the conviction or sentence is first reversed or expunged on appeal, on habeas corpus, or by executive clemency. Heck v. Humphrey, 512 U.S. 477, 486-487 (1994). Suppose our murderer serves six years before his conviction is vacated because the state relied on inadmissible evidence found in the search, and suppose that without that evidence, the state decides not to retry him. Can he recover for the six years in prison as damages for the illegal search?

If your intuition is that the murderer cannot recover compensation for the six years in prison, why should he escape the remaining years in prison altogether because of the exclusionary rule? The exclusionary rule prevents the harm of imprisonment from happening, so that compensation is unnecessary. The exclusionary rule is based more on grounds of deterring the police than of providing a remedy for the victims of illegal searches. Maybe it gives the victim of the search more than he deserves, but without it the Fourth Amendment would be almost wholly unenforceable. Damage actions tend to be worthless, because criminal suspects make unsympathetic plaintiffs, police officers make sympathetic defendants and often have immunity, and the real damages from the search itself are often dignitary rather than tangible.

7. Remedial defenses. The examples in notes 4 through 6 involve wrongdoing by plaintiffs. Another approach to that problem is to create a defense that bars recovery. Unclean hands is such a defense in equity, and *in pari delicto* at law. The uncertain content of these defenses is taken up in section 11.B.

8. An example without wrongdoing. Courts have limited the contract liability of clients who discharge attorneys without cause. They hold that the attorney can recover only the reasonable value of her services performed up to the time of breach, and not the expectancy she would have earned by completing the services. The Supreme Court of Florida explained that "there is an overriding need to allow clients freedom to substitute attorneys without economic penalty as a means of accomplishing the broad objective of fostering public confidence in the legal profession." Rosenberg v. Levin, 409 So. 2d 1016, 1021 (Fla. 1982).

That rule appears to be widely followed. But there is a sharp split in how to implement and measure the claim for the reasonable value of discharged lawyer's services in a contingent fee case. Some states say the lawyer cannot sue until the former client gets a judgment or a settlement; if the client abandons the case, or goes to trial and loses, the discharged attorney is out of luck, as she would have been if the contract had been performed. Other states say the discharged lawyer has an immediate claim for the value of her services to the date of discharge, typically measured by an hourly rate. That is consistent with general contract principles, but it does little to protect clients' economic freedom to change lawyers. The cases are collected in Salmon v. Atkinson, 137 S.W.3d 383 (Ark. 2003).

5.　*The Requirement of Reasonable Certainty*

BIGELOW v. RKO RADIO PICTURES
327 U.S. 251 (1946)

Chief Justice STONE delivered the opinion of the Court.

Petitioners brought this suit in the District Court for Northern Illinois under §§1, 2 and 7 of the Sherman Act and §§4 and 16 of the Clayton Act, for an injunction and to recover treble damages. Petitioners, who are owners of the Jackson Park motion picture theatre in Chicago, alleged . . . that respondents . . . entered into a conspiracy which continued from some date prior to November 1, 1936 to the date the suit was brought, July 28, 1942, pursuant to which film was distributed among moving picture theatres in the Chicago district in such a manner that theatres owned by some of the conspirators were enabled to secure and show feature pictures in advance of independent exhibitors, not affiliated with respondents, such as petitioners. . . .

Petitioners charged that in consequence they had been subjected to loss of earnings in excess of $120,000 during the five year period from July 27, 1937 to July 27, 1942. The matter of the injunction was reserved and the case went to trial solely on the question of damages. The jury returned a verdict for $120,000 in petitioners' favor. The trial court gave judgment for treble that amount, as prescribed by §4 of the Clayton Act. The Circuit Court of Appeals . . . reversed on the sole ground that the evidence of damage was not sufficient for submission to the jury, and directed the entry of a judgment for respondents *non obstante veredicto* [notwithstanding the verdict]. 150 F.2d 877 (7th Cir. 1945). . . .

Petitioners have been since November 1, 1936 the owners in partnership of the Jackson Park Theatre, located on the south side of Chicago. Respondents RKO Radio Pictures, Inc., Loew's, Inc., Twentieth Century-Fox Film Corporation, Paramount Pictures, Inc., and Vitagraph, Inc., are distributors of motion picture films. . . . Respondent Balaban & Katz Corporation is a motion picture exhibitor, which operates a chain of some fifty theatres in Chicago and its suburbs, including the Maryland Theatre and others on the south side of Chicago which compete with the petitioners' Jackson Park Theatre. Balaban & Katz is a subsidiary of Paramount. [Each of the other distributors (movie studios) also owned multiple exhibitors (movie theaters) in Chicago.]

Rental contracts between distributors and exhibitors undertake to furnish films to the exhibitors for stipulated rentals. . . . In Chicago, these contracts uniformly provide that the larger theatres in the Chicago Loop [downtown Chicago], all owned, leased, or operated by one or more of the respondents, shall have the right to the "first run" of the motion pictures distributed by the respondents, for one week or such longer period as they may desire to exhibit them. Following the "first run," the motion picture may not be shown in any Chicago theatre outside the Loop for three weeks, a period known as "clearance." In the fourth week following the end of the Loop run, the film is released for exhibition in theatres outside the Loop for successive runs in various theatres, for periods known as the "A", "B" and "C" "pre-release weeks," followed by weeks of "general release." . . .

There was evidence that respondent distributors and exhibitors conspired to give to the distributor-controlled or affiliated theatres preferential playing positions in the release system . . . with the result that petitioners' theatre was unable to obtain feature films until the first week of "general release," or ten weeks after the end of the Loop run. By that time most of respondent exhibitors' theatres, with several of which petitioners' theatre competes, and which enjoyed the prior "A", "B" or "C" pre-release runs, had finished their showings. Regardless of the price offered for rental of film, the respondent exhibitors [sic; "distributors" apparently intended], in execution of the conspiracy, refused to release films to petitioners' theatre except for the first week of "general release." . . .

Two classes of evidence were introduced by petitioners to establish their damage. One was a comparison of earnings during the five year period of petitioners' Jackson Park Theatre with the earnings of its competitor, the Maryland Theatre, the two being comparable in size, the Jackson Park being superior in location, equipment, and attractiveness to patrons. Under the discriminatory release system, the Maryland had been allowed to exhibit pictures in the C pre-release run, one week ahead of petitioners' first week of general release. The evidence showed that during the five year period, the Maryland's net receipts after deducting film rentals paid to distributors exceeded petitioners' like receipts by $115,982.34.

The second was a comparison of petitioners' receipts from the operation of the Jackson Park Theatre less cost of film for the five year period following July 1937, with the corresponding receipts for the four years immediately preceding, after making an allowance for the elimination of "Bank Night" receipts. The comparison shows a falling off of petitioners' receipts during the five year period aggregating $125,659.00, which was more than $5,000 in excess of the $120,000 damage demanded by petitioners' complaint. The significance of the comparison lies in the fact that during most of the four year period, and despite the operation of the release system as described, petitioners' theatre had been able to procure some films which had not already been shown in respondents' theatres, whereas petitioners were not able to procure such films during the five year period which followed, although there is evidence that they made diligent efforts to do so. The change is attributable to the introduction of the practice of "double features" (the showing of two films at a single performance) in theatres in the Chicago district. The evidence tended to show that when single features were being shown, exhibitors who had playing positions ahead of petitioners' . . . did not exhibit all of the films distributed, so that, despite their inferior playing position, petitioners were able to exhibit pictures which had not been shown elsewhere. With the advent of double featuring, theatres with playing positions ahead of petitioners' used nearly all of the films distributed, and the pictures which petitioners were able to exhibit in the first week of general release, by reason of the distribution system, had had prior showing in nearly every case. . . .

The circuit court of appeals concluded that the jury accepted the comparison of plaintiffs' earnings before and after the adoption of double billing as establishing the measure of petitioners' damage. But it held that this proof did not furnish a proper measure of damage for the reason that, while petitioners' earnings were known and proved for both the four and five year periods in question, it could not be proved what their earnings would have been during the five year period in the absence of the illegal distribution of films. It thought that the mere fact that earnings of the Jackson

Park Theatre were greater before the adoption of double billing did not serve to show what petitioners' earnings would have been afterwards, in the absence of the release system.

Similarly, the court of appeals rejected the comparison between petitioners' receipts and those of the Maryland Theatre during the five years in question, since, as it thought, the comparison would not tend to prove what the earnings of either theatre would have been during the critical period under any system other than that which was the product of the unlawful conspiracy.

Upon the record in this case it is indisputable that the jury could have found that during the period in question a first or prior run theatre possessed competitive advantages over later run theatres, because of its greater capacity to attract patronage to pictures which had not been shown elsewhere, and its ability to charge higher admission prices than subsequent run theatres, and that, other things being equal, the establishment of the discriminatory release system was damaging to the petitioners, who were relegated by it to a playing position inferior to that of their competitors.

Each of the two classes of evidence introduced by petitioners tended to show damage. They were not mutually exclusive, as the courts below seem to have thought, since each, independently of the other, tended to show that petitioners' inability to obtain films for exhibition before they had been shown elsewhere adversely affected their receipts, in the one case by showing that those receipts decreased when petitioners could no longer purchase such films following the introduction of double features, and in the other, that petitioners' receipts from its theatre were less by substantially the same amount than receipts of its competitor, the prior-run Maryland Theatre, operated under conditions in other respects less favorable than those affecting petitioners.

Respondents' argument is . . . that notwithstanding the force of this evidence, it is impossible to establish any measure of damage, because the unlawful system which respondents have created has precluded petitioners from showing that other conditions affecting profits would have continued without change unfavorable to them during the critical period if that system had not been established, and petitioners had conducted their business in a free competitive market. . . .

[W]hen petitioners acquired their theatre, it was possible for them . . . to secure films which had not had prior showing and to exhibit them in competition with theatres having preferred playing positions. Whatever restraints respondents' distribution system may then have imposed, and whether the later adopted practice of showing double features was or was not itself a product of an unlawful conspiracy, petitioners were entitled, as of right, to continue to purchase and show films which had not had prior showing free of the restraints of the unlawful distribution system. The fair value of petitioners' right thus to continue their business depended on its capacity to make profits. And a fair measure of the damage to that right by respondents' unlawful distributing system was the loss of petitioners' admission receipts resulting from the application of that system to petitioners.

Respondents' only answer is that, without the conspiracy, the conditions of purchase of films might not have been the same after as they were before July, 1937; that in any case it is not possible to say what those conditions would have been if the restraints had not been imposed, and that those conditions cannot be ascertained, because respondents have not removed the restraint. Hence, it is said, petitioners' evidence does not establish the fact of damage, and that further, the standard of comparison which the evidence sets up is too speculative and uncertain to afford an accurate measure of the amount of the damage.

The case in these respects is comparable to Eastman Kodak Co. v. Southern Photo Co., 273 U.S. 359 (1927), and Story Parchment Co. v. Paterson Co., 282 U.S. 555 (1931), in which precisely the same arguments now addressed to us were rejected. . . .

In each case we held that the evidence sustained verdicts for the plaintiffs, and that in the absence of more precise proof, the jury could conclude as a matter of just and reasonable inference from the proof of defendants' wrongful acts and their tendency to injure plaintiffs' business, and from the evidence of the decline in prices, profits and values, not shown to be attributable to other causes, that defendants' wrongful acts had caused damage to the plaintiffs. In this we but followed a well-settled principle. The tortious acts had in each case precluded ascertainment of the amount of damages more precisely, by comparison of profits, prices and values as affected by the conspiracy, with what they would have been in its absence under freely competitive conditions. Nevertheless, we held that the jury could return a verdict for the plaintiffs, even though damages could not be measured with the exactness which would otherwise have been possible.

In such a case, even where the defendant by his own wrong has prevented a more precise computation, the jury may not render a verdict based on speculation or guesswork. But the jury may make a just and reasonable estimate of the damage based on relevant data, and render its verdict accordingly. In such circumstances "juries are allowed to act upon probable and inferential, as well as direct and positive proof." *Story Parchment*, 282 U.S. at 561-564. Any other rule would enable the wrongdoer to profit by his wrongdoing at the expense of his victim. It would be an inducement to make wrongdoing so effective and complete in every case as to preclude any recovery, by rendering the measure of damages uncertain. Failure to apply it would mean that the more grievous the wrong done, the less likelihood there would be of a recovery.

The most elementary conceptions of justice and public policy require that the wrongdoer shall bear the risk of the uncertainty which his own wrong has created. That principle is an ancient one, and is not restricted to proof of damage in antitrust suits, although their character is such as frequently to call for its application. . . . [I]n cases where a wrongdoer has incorporated the subject of a plaintiff's patent or trademark in a single product to which the defendant has contributed other elements of value or utility, and has derived profits from the sale of the product, this Court has sustained recovery of the full amount of defendant's profits where his own wrongful action has made it impossible for the plaintiff to show in what proportions he and the defendant have contributed to the profits.

"The constant tendency of the courts is to find some way in which damages can be awarded where a wrong has been done. Difficulty of ascertainment is no longer confused with right of recovery" for a proven invasion of the plaintiff's rights. *Story Parchment*, 282 U.S. at 565.

The evidence here was ample to support a just and reasonable inference that petitioners were damaged by respondents' action, whose unlawfulness the jury has found, and respondents do not challenge. The comparison of petitioners' receipts before and after respondents' unlawful action impinged on petitioners' business afforded a sufficient basis for the jury's computation of the damage, where the respondents' wrongful action had prevented petitioners from making any more precise proof of the amount of the damage. . . .

The judgment of the district court below will be affirmed and the judgment of the court of appeals is reversed.

Justice JACKSON took no part in the consideration . . . of this case.

Justice FRANKFURTER, dissenting. . . .

[O]ur real question is whether the respondents' violation of the Sherman Law illegally injured the petitioners. This necessarily involves substantial proof that the petitioners' business would have been more profitable if the distribution of movie films in Chicago had been a free-for-all and if no factor of the scheme that constituted an illegal conspiracy had been in operation, than it was under the conditions that actually prevailed. . . . The record appears devoid of proof that, if competitive conditions had prevailed, distributors would not have made rental contracts with their respective exhibiting affiliates to the serious disadvantage of independents like the petitioners. They might individually have done so and not have offended the Sherman Law.

I agree that *Eastman Kodak* and *Story Parchment* should guide the disposition of this case. But I do not find that the decisive distinction made in those cases has been observed in deciding this case. The distinction is between proving that some damages were "the certain result of the wrong" and uncertainty as to the dollars and cents value of such injuring wrong. Such difficulty in ascertaining the exact amount of damage is a risk properly cast upon the wrong-doing defendant. But proof of the legal injury, which is the basis of his suit, is plaintiff's burden. He does not establish it merely by proving that there was a wrong to the public nor by showing that if he had been injured ascertainment of the exact amount of damages would have had an inevitable speculative element to be left for a jury's conscientious guess. This basic distinction was thus formulated in *Story Parchment*: "The rule which precludes the recovery of uncertain damages applies to such as are not the certain result of the wrong, not to those damages which are definitely attributable to the wrong and only uncertain in respect of their amount." 282 U.S. at 562. In the *Eastman* and *Story* cases the plaintiffs established what their profit was when competitive conditions prevailed and that the subsequent loss properly became exclusively attributable to restraint of such conditions. Such a comparison is not revealed by this record. It was wholly speculative, as the Circuit Court of Appeals properly held in applying the rule in the *Story Parchment* case, whether the intake of petitioners would have been more profitable if the distribution of films in Chicago had been left wholly to the haggling of a free market. . . .

NOTES ON THE REQUIREMENT OF REASONABLE CERTAINTY

1. What was wrong with the proof in *Bigelow*? There are two levels to Justice Frankfurter's dissent in *Bigelow*. The first, of more general importance, is that plaintiff has no evidence of what profits she would have earned in a competitive market. The second is that because it would be lawful for each of the movie studios to prefer its own chain of theaters, even a market that complied with the antitrust laws would not have been fully competitive; independents like plaintiff would still have been at a disadvantage.

2. Resolving uncertainty against the wrongdoer, but requiring reasonable certainty. The majority treats Frankfurter's defense as going to the amount of damages rather than to whether there was any damage at all. That brings the case within the rule that wrongdoers must bear the risk of uncertainty in the amount of damages. The principle is sound — *Bigelow* is still the leading federal case on uncertain damages, and most states have a similar rule — but it is not the whole story.

The cases also say that the amount of special or consequential damages must be proved with reasonable certainty and that damage verdicts cannot be based on speculation. And sometimes, courts say that plaintiff has not met that standard; his proof of damages is rejected as speculative. Sometimes they say this even when it seems clear that plaintiff suffered some damages. Are the two principles consistent? Attempting to combine them, we can make a fair generalization that plaintiff must prove damages with as much certainty as is reasonably possible under the circumstances, and that, occasionally, that might not be good enough. A common formulation in tort is that plaintiff must prove damages "with as much certainty as the nature of the tort and the circumstances permit." *Restatement (Second) of Torts* §912.

"Circumstances" vary. Commercial damages must generally be proved with more certainty than personal injury damages. It was a relevant circumstance in *Bigelow* that defendant's conspiracy had long prevented a competitive market from existing and had thus precluded anyone from having actual experience of profits in such a market. Evidence of the value of property is rarely rejected as uncertain, even though appraisers and experts often disagree. But lost profits are a fertile ground of litigation over uncertain damages. Past damages can usually be proved with greater certainty than future damages. Some of the California cases say that the certainty requirement "cannot be strictly applied where prospective damages are sought, because probabilities are really the basis for the award." Castro v. County of Los Angeles, 797 F.3d 654, 675 (9th Cir. 2015).

3. Failure of proof. An example where the proof failed is Glendale Federal Bank, FSB v. United States, 43 Fed Cl. 390 (Ct. Fed. Cl. 1999), *vacated in part on other grounds*, 239 F.3d 1374 (Fed. Cir. 2001). Savings and loans institutions were similar to banks; they took deposits and concentrated on real-estate lending. In the early 1980s, when many savings and loans were insolvent and the government insurance funds had nowhere near enough money to pay all the depositors, the government asked healthy savings and loans to acquire insolvent ones. The executive branch promised to honor an accounting fiction that would conceal the fact that adding the acquired institution's liabilities to the acquirer's balance sheet would instantly render the acquirer insolvent too, at least as a matter of regulatory accounting. The acquirers selected would have sufficient cash to keep operating, and they would be permitted to do so, despite their weak balance sheets. After Glendale and many others acquired insolvent savings and loans in such transactions, Congress reneged on the accounting fiction. Some of the acquirers were forced to close; Glendale survived by selling many of its assets to raise cash and by raising new capital in the investment markets.

A bench trial lasted 150 days, mostly devoted to Glendale's claim of $1.6 billion in expectancy damages. Glendale projected a 1.1 percent annual return, over the promised 40-year life of the accounting fiction, on the assets it was forced to sell. The judge awarded no expectancy damages. "While the court believes that there were indeed significant lost profits, plaintiff's model does not adequately prove the amount. [Many facts] support a strong inference of substantial profits in a non-breach scenario. The problem is quantification." 43 Fed. Cl. at 399.

Glendale's expert offered a model of its projected operations at the larger size achieved before the government's breach. But the court disagreed with key assumptions of that model, and Glendale had offered no evidence of other models that the court found more plausible. Glendale "would have done very well with its foregone assets, just not in the manner that Dr. Baxter's model predicts." *Id.* at 401 n.3. Given that finding, was it consistent with *Bigelow* to award no damages? If the court was sure there were substantial damages but unsure of the amount, why not reduce the projected rate of return? Wouldn't half a percent be more accurate than zero? Or is that too speculative, too much like awarding half the lost livestock in *Hatahley*?

Glendale did not appeal on expectancy, and a judgment of $798 million in restitution was reversed. The case was remanded for further consideration of reliance damages of about $380 million. Glendale's difficulty in sustaining a fully compensatory remedy partly reflects the uncertainty inherent in the scale of the enterprise and the 40-year term of the contract. It may also reflect ambivalence about the government contracting away its power to regulate, an unspoken sense that reliance is a more appropriate remedy if Congress overrules the agency, and fear that the government's potential liability in these cases was just too great.

4. An example where proof succeeded. Compare Brink's Inc. v. City of New York, 717 F.2d 700 (2d Cir. 1983). New York hired Brink's to retrieve change from parking meters. Brink's employees were caught stealing coins. When the city replaced Brink's with another company, collections went up a million dollars in the first ten months. Brink's argued that the comparison was useless, because several other things had changed about the same time: Gas rationing ended, a transit strike began, some meters were relocated, the number of snow emergency days varied, and there was evidence of an upward trend in collections anyway. Because all of these other factors were unmeasurable, Brink's argued that the comparison was more prejudicial than probative: It conveyed a delusion of precision when in fact the compensatory damages were speculative and unknowable. The city's expert witness claimed to have controlled for all the other factors to within a standard error of 10 percent; he apparently used some sort of sampling technique. The court upheld the evidence and the jury's million-dollar verdict.

5. Tort and contract. *Glendale* was a contract case; *Brink's* was a tort case. (It was not an intentional tort case, at least not formally; Brink's was held liable only for its negligent supervision of the thieves.) "Courts have traditionally required greater certainty" in contract than in tort, but even in contract, "[d]oubts are generally resolved against the party in breach." *Restatement (Second) of Contracts* §352 cmt. *a.*

6. The underlying dilemma. Professor Chiang sees the courts in these cases as struggling with a dilemma arising from incentives to produce information. Tun-Jen Chiang, *The Information-Forcing Dilemma in Damages Law*, 59 Wm. & Mary L. Rev. 81 (2017). Judges want plaintiffs to do the work of quantification and produce reasonably certain evidence of damages. The mechanism available to enforce such a requirement is an award of zero damages for failure to carry the burden of proof. But that penalty is too harsh in cases where it is clear that plaintiff suffered significant damages and the uncertainty is about the amount. To avoid that harsh result, courts take their best guess (or let juries do so) at the amount of damages, resolving uncertainty against the wrongdoer. But the prospect that courts will do that greatly reduces plaintiff's incentives to provide more and better evidence in the first place. Faced with this dilemma, it is hardly surprising that the cases are inconsistent, sometimes seeming to require too much evidence and sometimes too little. Professor Chiang collects examples of inconsistent cases from many areas of law.

7. Missing evidence. The dilemma is more easily resolved when the court can point to evidence that should have been readily available but that plaintiff failed to introduce. Consider Post and Beam Equities Group, LLC v. Sunne Village Development Property Owners Association, 124 A.3d 454 (Vt. 2015), where defendant blocked an easement that was the most convenient access to plaintiff's restaurant. Plaintiff showed that its revenues sharply declined, but it introduced no evidence of costs or profit margins. The court reversed the damage award as unproven. Motion Medical Technologies, L.L.C. v. Thermotek, Inc., 875 F.3d 765 (5th Cir. 2017), applying Texas law, goes a modest step further. Plaintiff proved changes in gross receipts and in the cost of goods sold, an accounting term for the direct production costs of labor and raw materials, but omitting all overhead or indirect costs. That was not reasonably certain evidence of lost net profits, which would take account of all receipts and all costs.

And in Licudine v. Cedars-Sinai Medical Center, 208 Cal. Rptr. 3d 170 (Ct. App. 2016), the court threw out a jury's award for lost earning capacity in a medical-malpractice case. Plaintiff proved that she had been admitted to law school, and that she was now too disabled to attend. But she offered no evidence of her likelihood of graduating, of passing the bar, or of finding a job, and no evidence of what lawyers earn. The court affirmed the trial court's decision to grant defendants a new trial on damages, instead of a judgment notwithstanding the verdict, and there were problems with how the case was tried that justified that decision. But the court emphasized that plaintiffs generally do not get a second chance if they fail to prove their damages the first time.

8. Assets of fluctuating value. One special case of uncertain damages, for which special rules have developed, is the problem of conversion, destruction, or damage of assets of fluctuating value, discussed in section 2.B.

9. Inflicting the same damage legally? Return to the second level of Frankfurter's argument. The antitrust laws preclude horizontal conspiracies between competing movie studios or competing theaters, but they are much more permissive with respect to large businesses under common ownership and with respect to vertical integration, as when a movie studio owns some of the theaters that show its films. So each defendant could have preferred its own theaters, and this might have meant that defendants could have inflicted all the same damage on plaintiff without violating any law. Should that be a defense? Is that defense repulsive to your sense of justice? Or does it indicate that defendants are being held liable on a technicality? If the ability to have inflicted the same harm legally is to be a defense, shouldn't it at least be an affirmative defense, with the burden of persuasion on defendants?

The majority's holding made it unnecessary to explore the facts of the defense that persuaded Frankfurter. But there is good reason to believe that defendants could not have inflicted the same harm legally. Paramount Pictures owned the Maryland Theatre, and undoubtedly the Maryland would get all Paramount movies before plaintiff. But in the absence of a conspiracy, the plaintiff would have been able to compete with the Maryland for movies from all the other studios. It may be that cases in which all the same harms could have been inflicted legally are quite rare. Some cases say that the fact that defendants "might have accomplished legally what they did illegally does not in any way lessen their liability." West Plains, L.L.C. v. Retzlaff Grain Co., 870 F.3d 774, 786 (8th Cir. 2017).

NOTES ON LITIGATING COMMERCIAL DAMAGES

1. Damage models. Damage issues in commercial litigation of any complexity often depend on expert models of what would have happened but for the wrong—what the facts would have been in plaintiff's "but-for world." In cases with smaller stakes, the plaintiff herself, or her accountant or a key employee, may offer evidence that is conceptually similar to a formal model but usually much simpler and based on the witness's first-hand experience with the business. An example is Lord & Taylor, LLC v. White Flint, L.P., 849 F.3d 567 (4th Cir. 2017), where plaintiff's long-time employee, who managed construction and renovation of its department stores, testified to the construction costs likely to result from defendant's redesign of a mall. An earlier opinion in this case appears in section 5.B.2 on the choice between damages and specific performance in contract.

We first encountered damage models in Texaco v. Pennzoil, in section 2.D, where experts offered three models of the expected value to Pennzoil of acquiring a share of Getty's oil fields. Despite the enormous stakes, the value of the oil in *Pennzoil* was a fairly simple model. Other models may be much more complex. The Seventh Circuit expected Florence Bigelow to prove how she would have fared in the marketplace if more competitive conditions had prevailed. In the absence of any real experience, but with sufficient stakes to support high-powered experts, it might have been possible to persuasively model competitive conditions. Or it might not.

If the wrong affected plaintiff's pricing structure, damages may require estimating the volume of sales if plaintiff had sold at a different price. In other cases, experts may have to project the positive and negative cash flows of disrupted investments over a period of years, and then discount these projections to present value at an interest rate appropriate to the investment and its risks. If the projections are too speculative, the case may fail for lack of proof. Models may rely on sophisticated statistical analysis. All models depend on assumptions about the but-for world, and each assumption must be justified and defended. But the models must be presented in a way that a jury and trial judge can understand.

2. Going-concern value or lost profits. Abstracting from all the detail of varied fact patterns, there are two main methods of valuing damages to a business's ability to earn profits: the going-concern method and the lost-profits method, sometimes called the ex ante method and the ex post method, respectively. The two methods can yield significantly different damage estimates in the same case.

The going-concern method conceives of all the damages as happening simultaneously with the wrong. What was the value of the business just before the wrong, and what was the value of the business just after the wrong? Damages are that difference in value. In a strict application of the ex ante method, all evidence and calculations must be based on facts known at the time of the wrong; actual experience after the wrong is irrelevant. Damages in the *September 11th Litigation* are a simple example of the ex ante method: the value of the towers before destruction less their value (presumably zero) after destruction. Some courts say that if the business is totally destroyed, plaintiff must use the ex ante method; this leads some plaintiffs to claim that their business is only seriously damaged, not destroyed, if the lost-profits method would support higher damages.

The lost-profits method attempts to calculate the stream of lost profits over time. Actual profits can be proved directly; what profits would have been but for the wrong must be modeled. Developments through the date of trial affect both numbers. Lost profits through the date of trial earn prejudgment interest; lost profits that would have been earned after the trial must be discounted to present value. The two methods are analyzed, with many illustrative cases, in George P. Roach, *Correcting Uncertain Prophecies: An Analysis of Business Consequential Damages*, 22 Rev. Litig. 1 (2003).

3. Before-and-after or a yardstick. *Bigelow* illustrates two of the most common methods of proving lost profits. Plaintiff may compare profits while the wrong continued to profits before it began or after it ended. In *Bigelow*, the wrong had lasted for decades and still continued at the time of trial; plaintiff compared profits when there were still ways to partially evade the conspiracy to profits when there were no escape routes left. The proof in *Brink's*, in the previous set of notes, is another example of before-and-after evidence.

Bigelow's comparison to the Maryland Theatre is an attempt to compare to a business unaffected by the wrong; litigators sometimes call the comparable business the yardstick. The Maryland was not unaffected by the wrong; it had actually benefited from the wrong. The Maryland was inferior in most other ways; its comparative disadvantages tended to offset its benefit from the conspiracy. But to assume that those offsetting effects were of roughly equal magnitude is rough-and-ready speculation;

there was no evidence of that and no particular reason to think it true. A real-world comparison, if it works, is less speculative and usually more persuasive than a more abstract model. But the yardstick is almost never exactly the same as plaintiff's but-for situation that the yardstick is supposed to measure.

4. Direct modeling. If no direct comparison is available, plaintiff has to directly model what would have happened but for the wrong. But each step in this model has to be based on something; it cannot just be a cloud of assumptions. Often the basis for assumptions is some narrower or partial comparison, such as plaintiff's prior experience in the industry or evidence of similar businesses with respect to particular steps in the model. Sometimes the model relies on careful calculations of plaintiff's own situation, as in *Pennzoil* or the example in note 5. Expected costs may be proved by witnesses who know how to build the needed facilities or carry out the planned activity; their knowledge will often be based on prior experience with comparable situations. The prospects of future business may be proved by contracts in hand, or market surveys, or customers who have used some related business owned by plaintiff. A summary of the Texas cases said:

> While the test is a flexible one in order to accommodate the myriad circumstances in which claims for lost profits arise, at a minimum, opinions or estimates of lost profits must be based on objective facts, figures, or data from which the amount of lost profits can be ascertained. In other words, "reasonable certainty" is not demonstrated when the profits claimed to be lost are largely speculative or a mere hope for success, as from an activity dependent on uncertain or changing market conditions, on chancy business opportunities, or on promotion of untested products or entry into unknown or unproven enterprises.

Toshiba Machine Co. v. SPM Flow Control, Inc., 180 S.W.3d 761, 777 (Tex. Ct. App. 2005).

5. An illustrative model. Here's an example of a direct model of the disrupted activity, and one with multiple pieces. In re Burlington Northern, Inc., 822 F.2d 518 (5th Cir 1987), was an antitrust case in which plaintiff alleged that railroads conspired to prevent construction of a pipeline to carry coal slurry from Wyoming to Texas. Plaintiff's effort to prove the lost profits that would have been earned by operating the pipeline required seven witnesses:

1. An engineer testified to the project's design.
2. A former vice president of a large global engineering firm estimated annual construction expenditures and operating costs.
3. One of plaintiff's vice presidents testified to revenue assumptions.
4. A Wharton School business professor, who specialized in transportation, projected revenue, cost, and inflation.
5. A partner at a major national accounting firm testified to accounting and tax assumptions.
6. A partner at a major investment bank testified to financing assumptions and to the but-for value of the project as of the date of trial.
7. Finally, the chief financial officer of the global engineering firm testified to a bottom-line damages number, subtracting the costs from the but-for value and converting the net amount to a pre-tax basis.

The plaintiff's lawyers made an elaborate chart diagramming how all this testimony fit together. They didn't offer this chart in evidence; they used it to keep track of their own case.

Plaintiff's evidence showed lost profits of just over a billion dollars; the verdict was $345 million. That number came from a relatively obscure defense exhibit designed to show that plaintiff's numbers were sensitive to its experts' choice of assumptions. Interviews with jurors revealed that they were unsure about damages but figured that defendants' number would be conservative. This suggests why some defense lawyers say that if they can't produce a model showing damages to be very small or zero, they shouldn't offer any model at all.

We owe the example to Jack Taurman, now retired from a partnership at Vinson & Elkins. No reported opinion in the case touches on the damage issues.

6. The new-business rule. Courts historically said that it was impossibly speculative to decide whether a new business, or a new project like the coal-slurry pipeline, would ever make money. So lost profits to a new business were unrecoverable as a matter of law. This version of the new-business rule has been abandoned in most jurisdictions. But courts give closer scrutiny to lost-profits evidence proffered by new businesses; they are quicker to say that such evidence is too speculative or insufficiently detailed. "What was once a rule of law has been converted into a rule of evidence." 1 Robert L. Dunn, *Recovery of Damages for Lost Profits* §4.3 at 378 (6th ed., Lawpress 2005).

An example of this approach is Tri-G, Inc. v. Burke, Bosselman & Weaver, 856 N.E.2d 389, 406-408 (Ill. 2006), finding that lost profits from a new real estate development were sufficiently proved by evidence of profits in a similar development that plaintiff had managed successfully. Compare Norris v. Causey, 869 F.3d 360 (5th Cir. 2017), where plaintiff offered evidence of several successful earlier projects, but offered little evidence of how his new project was similar to the earlier ones. It was not enough that they all involved real estate development; the court held the damages too uncertain and awarded nothing.

In *Sunnyland* (in section 2.E.3), New Mexico repudiated its rule barring recovery for new businesses, and it held that Sunnyland had sufficiently proved its lost profits. There was a battle of experts over the expected yield of the tomato plants, and defendant argued that Sunnyland's expert testimony on that point was exaggerated and not credible. But the trial judge found it credible, and the supreme court affirmed.

Even an unprofitable business can be damaged. Its losses can be greater than they would have been but for the wrong, a point emphasized in Post and Beam Equities Group, LLC v. Sunne Village Development Property Owners Association, 124 A.3d 454 (Vt. 2015).

F.   TAXES, TIME, AND THE VALUE OF MONEY

1.   The Impact of Taxes

NORFOLK & WESTERN RAILWAY v. LIEPELT
444 U.S. 490 (1980)

Justice STEVENS delivered the opinion of the Court.

In cases arising under the Federal Employers' Liability Act, 45 U.S.C. §51 *et seq.*, most trial judges refuse to allow the jury to receive evidence or instruction concerning the impact of federal income taxes on the amount of damages to be awarded. Because the prevailing practice developed at a time when federal taxes were relatively insignificant, and because some courts are now following a different practice, we decided to answer the two questions presented by the certiorari petition in this wrongful death action: (1) whether it was error to exclude evidence of the income taxes payable on the decedent's past and estimated future earnings; and (2) whether it was error for the trial judge to refuse to instruct the jury that the award of damages would not be subject to income taxation.

In 1973 a fireman employed by petitioner suffered fatal injuries in a collision caused by petitioner's negligence. Respondent, as administratrix of the fireman's estate, brought suit under the FELA to recover the damages that his survivors suffered as a result of his death. . . .

The decedent, a 37-year-old man, was living with his second wife and two young children and was contributing to the support of two older children by his first marriage. His gross earnings in the 11 months prior to his death on November 22, 1973 amounted to $11,988. Assuming continued employment, those earnings would have amounted to $16,828.26 in 1977.

The expert estimated that the decedent's earnings would have increased at a rate of approximately five percent per year, which would have amounted to $51,600 in the year 2000, the year of his expected retirement. The gross amount of those earnings, plus the value of the services he would have performed for his family, less the amounts the decedent would have spent upon himself, produced a total which, when discounted to present value at the time of trial, amounted to $302,000.

Petitioner objected to the use of gross earnings, without any deduction for income taxes, in respondent's expert's testimony and offered to prove through the testimony of its own expert, an actuary, that decedent's federal income taxes during the years 1973 through 2000 would have amounted to about $57,000. Taking that figure into account, and making different assumptions about the rate of future increases in salary and the calculation of the present value of future earnings, petitioner's expert computed the net pecuniary loss at $138,327. . . . [T]he jury returned a verdict of $775,000. [The verdict was affirmed. 378 N.E.2d 1232 (Ill. App. Ct. 1978).]

Petitioner argues that the jury must have assumed that its award was subject to federal income taxation; otherwise, it is argued, the verdict would not have exceeded respondent's expert's opinion by such a large amount.[4] For that reason, petitioner contends that it was prejudiced by the trial judge's refusal to instruct the jury that "your award will not be subject to any income taxes, and you should not consider such taxes in fixing the amount of your award." . . .

I

In a wrongful death action under the FELA, the measure of recovery is "the damages . . . [that] flow from the deprivation of the pecuniary benefits which the beneficiaries might have reasonably received." Michigan Central Railroad v. Vreeland, 227 U.S. 59, 70 (1913). The amount of money that a wage earner is able to contribute to the support of his family is unquestionably affected by the amount of the tax he must pay to the Federal Government. It is his after-tax income, rather than his gross income before taxes, that provides the only realistic measure of his ability to support his family. It follows inexorably that the wage earner's income tax is a relevant factor in calculating the monetary loss suffered by his dependents when he dies.

---

4. Respondent argues that the excess is adequately explained by the jury's estimate of the pecuniary value of the guidance, instruction and training that the decedent would have provided to his children.

Although federal courts have consistently received evidence of the amount of the decedent's personal expenditures, and have required that the estimate of future earnings be reduced by "taking account of the earning power of the money that is presently to be awarded," they have generally not considered the payment of income taxes as tantamount to a personal expenditure and have regarded the future prediction of tax consequences as too speculative and complex for a jury's deliberations.

Admittedly there are many variables that may affect the amount of a wage earner's future income tax liability. The law may change, his family may increase or decrease in size, his spouse's earnings may affect his tax bracket, and extra income or unforeseen deductions may become available. But future employment itself, future health, future personal expenditures, future interest rates, and future inflation are also matters of estimate and prediction. Any one of these issues might provide the basis for protracted expert testimony and debate. But the practical wisdom of the trial bar and the trial bench has developed effective methods of presenting the essential elements of an expert calculation in a form that is understandable by juries that are increasingly familiar with the complexities of modern life. We therefore reject the notion that the introduction of evidence describing a decedent's estimated after-tax earnings is too speculative or complex for a jury.

Respondent argues that if this door is opened, other equally relevant evidence must also be received. For example, she points out that in discounting the estimate of future earnings to its present value, the tax on the income to be earned by the damage award is now omitted. Logically, it would certainly seem correct that this amount, like future wages, should be estimated on an after-tax basis. But the fact that such an after-tax estimate, if offered in proper form, would also be admissible does not persuade us that it is wrong to use after-tax figures instead of gross earnings in projecting what the decedent's financial contributions to his survivors would have been had this tragic accident not occurred. . . .[10]

II

Section 104(a)(2) of the Internal Revenue Code provides that the amount of any damages received on account of personal injuries is not taxable income. . . .

Although the law is perfectly clear, it is entirely possible that the members of the jury may assume that a plaintiff's recovery in a case of this kind will be subject to federal taxation, and that the award should be increased substantially in order to be sure that the injured party is fully compensated. . . .

In this case the respondents' expert witness computed the amount of pecuniary loss at $302,000, plus the value of the care and training that decedent would have provided to his young children; the jury awarded damages of $775,000. It is surely not fanciful to suppose that the jury erroneously believed that a large portion of the award would be payable to the Federal Government in taxes and that therefore it improperly inflated the recovery. . . .

---

10. . . . [W]e see nothing in the language and are aware of nothing in the legislative history of §104(a)(2) to suggest that it has any impact whatsoever on the proper measure of damages in a wrongful death action. Moreover, netting out the taxes that the decedent would have paid does not confer a benefit on the tortfeasor any more than netting out of the decedent's personal expenditures. Both subtractions are required in order to determine "the pecuniary benefits which the beneficiaries might have reasonably received." *Michigan Central*, 227 U.S. at 70.

We hold that it was error to refuse the requested instruction in this case. That instruction was brief and could be easily understood. It would not complicate the trial by making additional qualifying or supplemental instructions necessary. It would not be prejudicial to either party, but would merely eliminate an area of doubt or speculation that might have an improper impact on the computation of the amount of damages.

The judgment is reversed and the case is remanded to the Appellate Court of Illinois for further proceedings consistent with this opinion. . . .

Justice BLACKMUN, with whom Justice MARSHALL joins, dissenting. . . .

In my view, by mandating adjustment of the award by way of reduction for federal income taxes that would have been paid by the decedent on his earnings, the Court appropriates for the tortfeasor a benefit intended to be conferred on the victim or his survivors. And in requiring that the jury be instructed that a wrongful death award is not subject to federal income tax, the Court opens the door for a variety of admonitions to the jury not to "misbehave," and unnecessarily interjects what is now to be federal law into the administration of a trial in a state court.

In this day of substantial income taxes, one is sorely tempted, in jury litigation, to accept the propriety of admitting evidence as to a tort victim's earnings *net* after estimated income taxes, and of instructing the jury that an award will be tax-free. This, it could be urged, is only common sense and a recognition of financial realities.

Ordinarily, however, the effect of an income tax upon the recipient of a payment is of no real or ultimate concern to the payer. Apart from required withholding, it just is not the payer's responsibility or, indeed, "any of his business." . . .

I

The employer-petitioner argues, and the Court holds, that federal income taxes that would have been paid by the deceased victim must be subtracted in computing the amount of the wrongful death award. Were one able to ignore and set aside the uncertainties, estimates, assumptions and complexities involved in computing and effectuating that subtraction, this might not be an unreasonable legislative proposition in a compensatory tort system. Neither petitioner nor the Court, however, recognizes that the premise of such an argument is the nontaxability, under the Internal Revenue Code, of the wrongful death award itself.

By not taxing the award, Congress has bestowed a benefit. Although the parties disagree over the origin of the tax-free status of the wrongful death award, it is surely clear that the lost earnings could be taxed as income. In my view, why Congress created this benefit under one statute is relevant in deciding where the benefit should be allocated under another statute enacted by Congress.

While Congress has not articulated its reasons for not taxing a wrongful death award, it is highly unlikely that it intended to confer this benefit on the tortfeasor. Two more probable purposes for the exclusion are apparent. First, taxing the award could involve the same uncertainties and complexities noted by respondent and the majority of the courts of this country as a reason for not taking income taxes into account in computing the award. Congress may have decided that it is simply not worthwhile to enact a complex and administratively burdensome system in order to approximate the tax treatment of the income if, in fact, it had been earned over a period of time by the decedent. Second, Congress may have intended to confer a humanitarian benefit on the victim or victims of the tort. . . .

Whichever of these concerns it was that motivated Congress, transfer of the tax benefit to the FELA tortfeasor-defendant is inconsistent with that purpose. If Congress felt that it was not worth the effort to estimate the decedent's prospective tax liability on behalf of the public fisc, it is unlikely that it would want to require this effort on behalf of the tortfeasor. And Congress would not confer a humanitarian benefit on tort victims or their survivors in the Internal Revenue Code, only to take it away from victims or their survivors covered by the FELA. I conclude, therefore, that any income tax effect on lost earnings should not be considered in the computation of a damages award under the FELA.

II

The Court concludes that, as a matter of federal law, the jury in a FELA case must be instructed, on request, that the damages award is not taxable. . . .

The required instruction is purely cautionary in nature. It does not affect the determination of liability or the measure of damages. It does nothing more than call a basically irrelevant factor to the jury's attention, and then directs the jury to forget that matter. Even if federal law governed such an admonition to the jury not to misbehave, the instruction required by the Court seems to me to be both unwise and unjustified, and almost an affront to the practical wisdom of the jury.

It also is "entirely possible" that the jury "may" increase its damages award in the belief that the defendant is insured, or that the plaintiff will be obligated for substantial attorney's fees, or that the award is subject to state (as well as federal) income tax, or on the basis of any number of other extraneous factors. Charging the jury about every conceivable matter as to which it should not misbehave or miscalculate would be burdensome and could be confusing. Yet the Court's decision today opens the door to that possibility. There certainly is no evidence in this record to indicate that the jury is any more likely to act upon an erroneous assumption about an award's being subject to federal income tax than about any other collateral matter. . . .

In any event . . . I cannot conclude . . . that a purely cautionary instruction to the jury not to misbehave implicates any federal interest. This issue truly can be characterized as one of the "ordinary incidents of state procedure," Dickinson v. Stiles, 246 U.S. 631, 633 (1918), which should be governed by state law. . . .

NOTES ON TAXES

1. Nontaxable judgments. There was much litigation about the scope of §104's exemption of compensation for personal injuries. Did it exempt compensation for emotional or dignitary harms? For employment discrimination? Did it exempt punitive damages?

Congress finally resolved these disputes, largely in favor of the IRS. The exemption now applies only to amounts received on account of "personal physical injuries or physical sickness." "Emotional distress shall not be treated as a physical injury or physical sickness," except that "the amount paid for medical care attributable to emotional distress" is exempt. I.R.C. §104(a). Punitive damages are now taxable, except in Alabama, where punitive damages are the only remedy for wrongful death.

2. Payroll taxes. Does *Liepelt* apply to Social Security taxes? They would have been payable on the decedent's wages, and they are not payable on the judgment. But they probably would also have generated increased Social Security benefits. There is a similar dispute about railroad retirement taxes, which are usually at issue in FELA cases and are also linked to individual benefits. But the tax that funds railroad retirement benefits applies to compensation for lost earnings even in personal injury cases, so railroad retirement taxes appear to be treated differently from Social Security taxes. Conflicting cases are collected in Liberatore v. Monongahela Railway Co., 140 A.3d 16 (Pa. Super. Ct. 2016).

3. The dissent. What about Justice Blackmun's argument that courts should not try to outwit congressional allocation of tax burdens? At one level, that is an argument that Congress should take judgments into consideration in writing tax laws, rather than have courts take tax laws into consideration in entering judgments. That doesn't seem very realistic as a general matter. Is he on stronger ground when he says that in the specific case of personal injury judgments, Congress did consider the problem and deliberately conferred a tax subsidy on plaintiffs? Is he treating the tax exempt status of personal injury judgments as a collateral source of compensation for tort victims?

4. The state reaction. *Norfolk & Western* announces two rules of federal law; only a small minority of states appears to have been persuaded of either. The decisions are collected in Annotation, 16 A.L.R.4th 589 (1982 & Supp.). More than one state court has said that "[t]o inject the incidence of the ever changing tax scheme . . . into a jury damage trial would lead the jury into a hopeless quagmire of confusion and conjecture." Blake v. Clein, 903 So. 2d 710, 730 (Miss. 2005).

The two federal rules apply to cases controlled by federal substantive law, whether tried in state or federal court; similarly, state rules on calculating damages and the substance of jury instructions about those calculations apply to cases controlled by state substantive law, whether tried in state or federal court. The FELA applies only to injured railroad workers; there are somewhat similar federal statutes for injured sailors and injured longshore workers.

Plaintiff normally has the burden of proving his damages under whatever rules apply. But several courts have held, and we suspect that many more have acted on the view, that it is defendant's burden to introduce evidence of plaintiff's tax liability, and that in the absence of such evidence, it is not error to calculate damages on the basis of gross income. Some of these cases are collected in CSX Transportation, Inc. v. Moody, 313 S.W.3d 72, 86 n.49 (Ky. 2010). The court also held that failure to instruct the jury that the judgment was not taxable was harmless error where the verdict did not appear to be excessive. That would seem to be a bit of state-court resistance to federal law.

5. Taxable judgments. Would the effect of taxes matter if personal injury awards were not tax exempt? Suppose plaintiff recovered five years' salary in a suit for breach of contract, or five years' lost profits in an antitrust suit. If you told the jury to figure losses on the basis of after-tax income, you would plainly have to tell it that its verdict would be taxable. Wouldn't it be easier to figure damages on the basis of gross income and assume that the taxes on the judgment would balance out the taxes on the lost income? That was the Court's solution in an antitrust case, even though tax rates had been cut sharply in the interim. Hanover Shoe v. United Shoe Machinery Corp., 392 U.S. 481 (1968).

Should plaintiff be compensated for the effect of being pushed into a higher tax bracket in the year he collects the judgment? A variety of approaches to this problem are collected in Sonoma Apartment Associates v. United States, 127 Fed. Cl. 721 (2016), where if plaintiff prevailed, more than 20 years of rental profits would be collected in a single year and taxed to the plaintiff's partners. A majority of these cases appear to say that plaintiff can recover the extra taxes if he can prove them; some claims fail because proof is difficult. The D.C. Circuit has flatly rejected the whole idea, most recently in Fogg v. Gonzales, 492 F.3d 449 (D.C. Cir. 2007), an employment discrimination case where several years of pay were recovered in a single year.

Sometimes defendant argues that plaintiff saved on taxes by getting her money through a judgment instead of in ordinary course. A few cases holding that these tax benefits are to be ignored (apart from the personal injury cases controlled by *Liepelt*) are collected in Osborn v. Griffin, 865 F.3d 417, 453 (6th Cir. 2017).

6. Tax shelters. Taxes loom large in suits for fraud or negligence in the sale of tax shelters. A tax-shelter plaintiff might have received substantial tax savings, even though the underlying investment turns out to be worthless. Should the tax savings be deducted from his damages as an offsetting benefit?

The Supreme Court said no in a narrow opinion that turned on the language of a statutory remedy that let plaintiff rescind the whole transaction. Randall v. Loftsgaarden, 478 U.S. 647 (1986). Rescission is a restitutionary remedy taken up in section 8.B.3.b; the Court did not decide whether it would consider tax benefits in a suit for damages. On that issue, plaintiffs argued that the judgment would be taxable, the earlier tax savings remained subject to audit, and but for the fraud, they would have gotten tax benefits plus investment profits.

7. Bad tax advice. For malpractice in giving tax advice, plaintiff can generally recover any extra taxes, interest, and penalties paid as a result of the malpractice, and the costs of dealing with the Internal Revenue Service to resolve the matter. Cases are collected in Jacob L. Todres, *Tax Malpractice Damages: A Comprehensive Review of the Elements and the Issues,* 61 Tax Law. 705 (2008). New York is a notable exception; it has disallowed recovery of either the extra taxes or the interest. The Seventh Circuit has held that the taxpayer's suicide is not a foreseeable consequence of bad tax advice. Cleveland v. Rotman, 297 F.3d 569 (7th Cir. 2002).

An interesting example of tax losses is Oddi v. Ayco Corp., 947 F.2d 257 (7th Cir. 1992), where the entire damage calculation focused on taxes—taxes due as a result of defendant's advice, less taxes that would have been due but for defendant's advice, plus taxes due on the judgment. Damages were enormously affected by predictions about future tax rates. Plaintiff argued that the court had to use current tax rates and could not speculate about future tax increases; defendant argued that the then-current 28 percent top rate was an historical anomaly that could not last long. Defendant turns out to have been right about the politics, but the court ruled for plaintiff. Did it have a workable alternative?

8. Defendant's taxes. Damages paid for liability incurred in operation of a business are generally a deductible business expense. Timing issues can make defendant's tax liability different from what it would have been if the money had been paid out in the ordinary course of business, but neither the tax law nor the law that creates the liability can do much about that. Consider United States v. Cleveland Indians Baseball Co., 532 U.S. 200 (2001). Fourteen players filed successful grievances for additional salary that should have been paid in 1986 and 1987; by the time they collected the money in 1994, none of them were still employed by the Indians. If the additional salary had been paid in 1986 and 1987, it would not have been subject to payroll tax, because the Indians had already paid the maximum on each player. But in 1994, this money was all the Indians paid to these players. So the team had to pay the maximum payroll tax on each player all over again. Employees get a refund to account for excess payroll taxes withheld by two employers in the same year, but there is no such break for the employers.

2. *Interest on Past Damages*

CITY OF MILWAUKEE v. CEMENT DIVISION, NATIONAL GYPSUM CO.

515 U.S. 189 (1995)

Justice STEVENS delivered the opinion of the Court.

This is an admiralty case in which the plaintiff's loss was primarily attributable to its own negligence. The question presented is whether that fact, together with the existence of a genuine dispute over liability, justified the District Court's departure from the general rule that prejudgment interest should be awarded in maritime collision cases.

I

Respondents are the owner and the insurers of the *E.M. Ford,* a ship that sank in Milwaukee's outer harbor on Christmas Eve 1979. At the time of this disaster, the *Ford* was berthed in a slip owned by the city of Milwaukee . . . . In the course of a severe storm, she broke loose from her moorings, battered against the headwall of the slip, took on water, and sank. She was subsequently raised and repaired.

In 1980 the *Ford's* owner, . . . National Gypsum . . . , brought suit against the City, invoking the District Court's admiralty and maritime jurisdiction. The complaint alleged that the City had breached its duty as a wharfinger by assigning the vessel to a berthing slip known to be unsafe in heavy winds and by failing to give adequate warning of hidden dangers in the slip. . . . The City denied fault and filed a $250,000 counterclaim for damage to its dock. The City alleged that National Gypsum was negligent in leaving the ship virtually unmanned in winter, with no means aboard for monitoring weather conditions or summoning help. . . . [After a three-week trial and an interlocutory appeal,] the Court of Appeals apportioned liability two-thirds to National Gypsum and one-third to the City. 915 F.2d 1154 (7th Cir. 1990).

Thereafter the parties entered into a partial settlement fixing respondents' damages, excluding prejudgment interest, at $1,677,541.86.[3] The parties agreed that any claim for interest would be submitted to the District Court for decision. A partial judgment for the stipulated amount was entered and satisfied.

Respondents then sought an award of over $5.3 million in prejudgment interest.[4] The District Court denied respondents' request. It noted that "an award of prejudgment interest calculated from the date of the loss is the rule rather than the exception

3. In arriving at this sum, the parties agreed that respondents' damages were slightly more than $5.4 million, while the City's damages were just over $192,000. The parties multiplied respondents' damages by one-third, resulting in a subtotal of $1,805,829.98 for which the City was responsible. From this subtotal, the parties subtracted two-thirds of the City's damages, or $128,288.12, as an offset because that was the amount of National Gypsum's responsibility. The difference was the City's obligation to respondents.

4. This figure was based on respondents' assertion that prejudgment interest should be compounded continuously, from the time of the sinking of the *Ford,* at the commercial prime rate of interest averaged over the period of assessment. The District Court did not express any view on the correctness of this analysis, nor do we. We merely note in passing that the discrepancy between the damages award and the interest sought by National Gypsum is in some measure attributable to the delays that have plagued this litigation—a factor that does not appear to be traceable to the fault of any party.

in cases brought under a district court's admiralty jurisdiction," but held that special circumstances justified a departure from that rule in this case. The court explained:

> In the instant case the record shows that from the outset there has been a genuine dispute over [respondents'] good faith claim that the City of Milwaukee was negligent for failing to warn the agents of [National Gypsum] (who were planning to leave the *Ford* unmanned during the Christmas holidays) that a winter storm could create conditions in the outer harbor at Milwaukee which could damage the ship. The trial court and the court of appeals both found mutual fault for the damage which ensued to the ship and to the [City's] dock. The court of appeals ascribed two-thirds of the negligence to [National Gypsum]. Thus, in this situation the court concludes that [National Gypsum's] contributory negligence was of such magnitude that an award of prejudgment interest would be inequitable.

The Court of Appeals reversed. 31 F.3d 581 (7th Cir. 1994). . . .

The Court of Appeals' decision deepened an existing Circuit split regarding the criteria for denying prejudgment interest in maritime collision cases. . . .

II

Although Congress has enacted a statute governing the award of postjudgment interest in federal court litigation, see 28 U.S.C. §1961 (1994), there is no comparable legislation regarding prejudgment interest. Far from indicating a legislative determination that prejudgment interest should not be awarded, however, the absence of a statute merely indicates that the question is governed by traditional judge-made principles. Those principles are well developed in admiralty, where "the Judiciary has traditionally taken the lead in formulating flexible and fair remedies." United States v. Reliable Transfer, 421 U.S. 397, 409 (1975).

Throughout our history, admiralty decrees have included provisions for prejudgment interest. . . .

The Courts of Appeals have consistently and correctly construed decisions such as these as establishing a general rule that prejudgment interest should be awarded in maritime collision cases, subject to a limited exception for "peculiar" or "exceptional" circumstances.

The essential rationale for awarding prejudgment interest is to ensure that an injured party is fully compensated for its loss.[7] Full compensation has long been recognized as a basic principle of admiralty law, where "*[r]estitutio in integrum* [restoration to the previous condition] is the leading maxim applied by admiralty courts to ascertain damages resulting from a collision." Standard Oil Co. v. Southern Pacific Co., 268 U.S. 146, 158 (1925). By compensating "for the loss of use of money due as damages from the time the claim accrues until judgment is entered," West Virginia v. United States, 479 U.S. 305, 310-311 n.2 (1987), an award of prejudgment interest helps achieve the goal of restoring a party to the condition it enjoyed before the injury occurred.

Despite admiralty's traditional hospitality to prejudgment interest, however, such an award has never been automatic. In The Scotland, 118 U.S. 507, 518-519 (1886), we stated that the

---

7. We have recognized the compensatory nature of prejudgment interest in a number of cases decided outside the admiralty context.

allowance of interest on damages is not an absolute right. Whether it ought or ought not to be allowed depends upon the circumstances of each case, and rests very much in the discretion of the tribunal which has to pass upon the subject, whether it be a court or a jury.

Although we have never attempted to exhaustively catalog the circumstances that will justify the denial of interest, and do not do so today, the most obvious example is the plaintiff's responsibility for "undue delay in prosecuting the lawsuit." General Motors Corp. v. Devex Corp., 461 U.S. 648, 657 (1983). Other circumstances may appropriately be invoked as warranted by the facts of particular cases.

In this case, the City asks us to characterize two features of the instant litigation as sufficiently unusual to justify a departure from the general rule that prejudgment interest should be awarded to make the injured party whole. First, the City stresses the fact that there was a good-faith dispute over its liability for respondents' loss. In our view, however, this fact carries little weight. If interest were awarded as a penalty for bad-faith conduct of the litigation, the City's argument would be well taken. But prejudgment interest is not awarded as a penalty; it is merely an element of just compensation.

The City's "good-faith" argument has some resonance with the venerable common-law rule that prejudgment interest is not awarded on unliquidated claims (those where the precise amount of damages at issue cannot be computed). If a party contests liability in good faith, it will usually be the case that the party's ultimate exposure is uncertain. But the liquidated/unliquidated distinction has faced trenchant criticism for a number of years. Moreover, that distinction "has never become so firmly entrenched in admiralty as it has been at law." Moore-McCormack Lines, Inc. v. Richardson, 295 F.2d 583, 592 (2d Cir. 1961). Any fixed rule allowing prejudgment interest only on liquidated claims would be difficult, if not impossible, to reconcile with admiralty's traditional presumption. Yet unless we were willing to adopt such a rule—which we are not—uncertainty about the outcome of a case should not preclude an award of interest.

In sum, the existence of a legitimate difference of opinion on the issue of liability is merely a characteristic of most ordinary lawsuits. It is not an extraordinary circumstance that can justify denying prejudgment interest.

The second purportedly "peculiar" feature of this case is the magnitude of the plaintiff's fault. Leaving aside the empirical question whether such a division of fault is in fact an aberration, it is true in this case that the owner of the *E.M. Ford* was primarily responsible for the vessel's loss. As a result, it might appear somewhat inequitable to award a large sum in prejudgment interest against a relatively innocent party. But any unfairness is illusory, because the relative fault of the parties has already been taken into consideration in calculating the amount of the loss for which the City is responsible.

. . . [B]efore prejudgment interest even entered the picture, the total amount of respondents' recovery had already been reduced by two-thirds because of National Gypsum's own negligence. The City's responsibility for the remaining one-third is no different than if it had performed the same negligent acts and the owner, instead of also being negligent, had engaged in heroic maneuvers that avoided two-thirds of the damages. The City is merely required to compensate the owner for the loss for which the City is responsible.

. . . [W]e are [therefore] unmoved by the City's contention that an award of prejudgment interest is inequitable in a mutual fault situation. Indeed, the converse is true: a denial of prejudgment interest would be unfair. As Justice Kennedy noted while he was sitting on the Ninth Circuit, "under any rule allowing apportionment of liability, denying prejudgment interest on the basis of mutual fault would seem to penalize a party twice for the same mistake." Alkmeon Naviera, S.A. v. M/V Marina L, 633 F.2d 789, 798 n.12 (9th Cir. 1980). Such a double penalty is commended neither by logic nor by fairness . . . .

Accordingly, we hold that neither a good-faith dispute over liability nor the existence of mutual fault justifies the denial of prejudgment interest in an admiralty collision case. Questions related to the calculation of the prejudgment interest award, including the rate to be applied, have not been raised in this Court and remain open for consideration, in the first instance, by the District Court.

The judgment of the Court of Appeals is

Affirmed.

Justice BREYER took no part in the consideration or decision of this case.

NOTES ON INTEREST

1. The common-law rule. The traditional common-law rule was that prejudgment interest would be awarded only when damages were liquidated or "ascertainable," and then only simple interest at the legal rate. The meaning of "ascertainable" varied widely among the jurisdictions. Almost all jurisdictions agreed that personal injury and wrongful death damages were not ascertainable; states that now award prejudgment interest in those cases have abandoned the ascertainability requirement. A majority now hold that damages for damaged or destroyed property are ascertainable.

Why should ascertainability matter in a modern economy? One answer in the cases is that defendant should not be penalized by the assessment of interest unless he could have paid and failed to do so, and that he could not have paid unless the amount he owed was ascertainable. This rationale suggests that the test should be whether *defendant* could ascertain the damages. Another rationale, offered in a case involving mental and emotional injury, is that "retroactive interest on such damages adds uncertain conjecture to speculation." Greater West Chester Home Association v. City of Los Angeles, 603 P.2d 1329, 1338 (Cal. 1979). Is either of these rationales persuasive? Does an assessment of interest really penalize the defendant? Or does it merely adjust for what he gained and plaintiff lost during the delays of litigation?

2. Changes in the common law. The traditional rules came under enormous pressure during the period of high interest rates in the 1970s and 1980s. The prime interest rate was in double digits for nearly eight years, peaking at 21.5 percent in December 1980. No prejudgment interest at all in many cases, interest well below the market rate in most of the remaining cases, and compound interest in hardly any cases added up to a substantial deviation from the general rule that plaintiff is to be restored to the position he would have occupied but for the wrong. Rules restricting the award of interest date from a time when wealth was held in land and tangible property, when income could not always be immediately reinvested, and when medieval religious prohibitions on interest were a recent memory. They became obsolete in an era of money market funds and continuous compounding. High interest rates focused attention on the problem and made it less tolerable.

By statute or decision, many jurisdictions have changed the traditional rules, but others have not. For a good review of the transition and careful treatment of the underlying issues, see Michael S. Knoll, *A Primer on Prejudgment Interest*, 75 Tex. L. Rev. 293 (1996). The trend to liberalize the award of prejudgment interest was always uneven, and it lost momentum as interest rates declined and as it bumped into the countervailing movement to limit tort recoveries.

3. Compound interest. The most persistent of the traditional rules was the unavailability of compound interest. If any interest was awarded, it was simple interest. Most cases simply cited the well-settled rule against compounding. On tracing that rule back to its origins, one usually finds some statement like this one from Chancellor Kent:

> Interest upon interest, promptly and incessantly accruing, would, as a general rule, become harsh and oppressive. Debt would accumulate with a rapidity beyond all ordinary calculation and endurance. Common business cannot sustain such overwhelming accumulation. It would tend also to inflame the avarice and harden the heart of the creditor. Some allowance must be made for the indolence of mankind, and the casualties and delays incident to the best-regulated industry.

Connecticut v. Jackson, 1 Johnson's Chancery 13, 17 (N.Y. Ch. 1814).

Even under the traditional rules, compounding was occasionally allowed where an established course of dealing included compound interest, e.g., Ma v. Community Bank, 686 F.2d 459, 466 (7th Cir. 1982), and in certain cases involving fiduciaries, *Restatement (Second) of Trusts* §207 and cmt. *d* (Am. Law Inst. 1959). Today, in contrast to Chancellor Kent's world, the litigant in possession of the funds can immediately get compound interest at any bank, money market fund, or bond fund. The result is that even the rule against compound interest is starting to succumb to economic reality, although Professor Knoll concluded that simple interest was still the majority rule as of 1996. Texas recommitted to simple interest in 1998, following a legislative policy enacted for tort cases and applying it to contract cases as well. Johnson & Higgins, Inc. v. Kenneco Energy, Inc., 962 S.W.2d 507 (Tex. 1998). For a judgment-debtor who does not have the money, Chancellor Kent's description is still apt.

4. The new and mixed regime. Many jurisdictions now presumptively award prejudgment interest, but the revolution remains incomplete. A mix of new and old rules has produced inconsistent rules and decisions, sometimes issuing simultaneously from the same court. Compare Monessen Southwestern Railway v. Morgan, 486 U.S. 330 (1988), with Loeffler v. Frank, 486 U.S. 549 (1988). *Monessen* held that prejudgment interest cannot be awarded to injured railroad workers under the Federal Employers' Liability Act. The majority reasoned that the common-law rule at the time the statute was enacted denied interest in personal injury cases, that the lower courts had long denied interest under the statute, and that Congress had not expressly changed this rule.

A week later, the Court in *Loeffler* approved the award of prejudgment interest in employment discrimination suits under the Civil Rights Act of 1964, a statute that authorizes back pay and other appropriate relief but does not mention interest. The Court commented that "[p]rejudgment interest, of course, is 'an element of complete compensation.'" *Monessen*, 486 U.S. at 558. *National Gypsum* creates a strong presumption in favor of interest in admiralty cases, where the old common-law rules never applied. And the Court has said that "[o]ur cases since 1933 have consistently acknowledged that a monetary award does not fully compensate for an injury unless it includes an interest component." Kansas v. Colorado, 533 U.S. 1, 10 (2001).

In Gianetti v. Norwalk Hospital, 43 A.3d 567 (Conn. 2012), the trial court denied both prejudgment and postjudgment interest, and the state supreme court found no abuse of discretion. The court found that defendant litigated in good faith, and that the damages could not be calculated until a lost-volume-seller issue was finally resolved after extremely long litigation delays; this was the third decision in the case in the state supreme court. Connecticut appears to take a rather narrow view of when to award interest.

5. Legislation. Legislative intervention has also produced a variety of rules with little pattern. A Texas statute tolls the accrual of interest in tort cases on the amount of any settlement offer for the period the settlement offer is open, forbids the award of compound interest, and provides that no interest accrues for the first 180 days after defendant receives notice of a claim (unless plaintiff files suit sooner). Correcting an earlier legislative blunder, the statute prohibits prejudgment interest on damages that will accrue in the future. Tex. Fin. Code Ann. §304.1045. California mandates interest in contract cases where the damages can be fixed by calculation, and allows interest in the discretion of the fact finder in other contract cases and some tort cases, but generally not in personal injury cases. But if a personal-injury plaintiff obtains a judgment more favorable than a settlement offer rejected by defendant, plaintiff is entitled to interest from the day of the first such offer. Cal. Civ. Code §§3287, 3288, 3291.

Some courts have proceeded under their rule-making power instead of by decision. Pennsylvania's rule calls interest "damages for delay"; interest accrues at the prime rate plus 1 percent, not compounded, beginning one year after defendant is served, but it does not accrue during any period in which plaintiff "caused delay of the trial," or for any period after defendant makes a settlement offer if plaintiff does not obtain a judgment greater than the offer. Pa. R. Civ. Proc. 238. The rule does not apply where some other body of law provides for interest.

6. Rates. In the absence of legislation, many courts award prejudgment interest at the prime rate, as in *National Gypsum* on remand. Prime is generally 3 percent above the federal funds rate, which is the rate at which banks borrow overnight from the Federal Reserve. Banks sometimes lend to their most qualified borrowers at prime, but most borrowers pay more, and many borrowers pay much more. Prime bottomed out at 3.25 percent from 2008 to 2015; as of June 2018, prime is 5 percent and expected to continue rising.

The Ninth Circuit generally awards the rate on 52-week Treasury bills as prejudgment interest, relying on the postjudgment interest statute by analogy. The Treasury bill rate—the rate at which the United States can borrow for a year—is very low, typically just slightly above the federal funds rate. But a different line of Ninth Circuit cases awards a higher rate in takings cases. The Constitution requires just compensation for property taken for public use, and some courts have read that to require a fully compensatory interest rate. The Ninth Circuit defines that rate as the rate that could be earned by a reasonably prudent investor investing in a "wide range of government and private obligations with both short term and long term maturities." United States v. 429.59 Acres of Land, 612 F.2d 459, 465 (9th Cir. 1980). Both lines of cases are collected in Schneider v. County of San Diego, 285 F.3d 784, 791-794 (9th Cir. 2002).

Some legislatures enacted fixed rates when interest rates were high, and have not revisited the issue. The prejudgment interest rate is 12 percent in Vermont and Rhode Island, 10 percent in California, 9 percent in New York, and 8.75 percent in New Mexico. These rates have been attacked as unconstitutional, bearing no rational relationship to any legislative purpose. Cases that rejected these constitutional arguments are collected in Concord General Mutual Insurance Co. v. Gritman, 146 A.3d 882 (Vt. 2016). These rates are very high compared to prime or the federal funds rate; they are not high compared to what consumers or many small or risky businesses actually pay.

7. Postjudgment interest. This debate has always been about prejudgment interest, which was at issue in *National Gypsum*. A judgment, once entered, bears interest at what is often called the "legal rate," and that rate is specified by statute. Some statutes specify interest rates that float up and down with changes in prime or some other index interest rate; others specify a fixed rate.

The federal statute on postjudgment interest now specifies "the weekly average 1-year constant maturity Treasury yield" for the week preceding the judgment, compounded annually. 28 U.S.C. §1961(c)(1). This is an artificial rate, calculated by the Federal Reserve, designed to match the average rate on one-year Treasury securities. Texas specifies the prime rate published by the Federal Reserve, with a floor of 5 percent and a cap of 15 percent, Tex. Fin. Code §304.003, except in judgments on a contract that specifies an interest rate, in which case the postjudgment interest rate is the lesser of the contract rate or 18 percent a year. *Id.* §304.002.

8. Incentives to delay. The traditional rules gave defendants substantial incentive to delay in cases where damages were large and interest rates were high. These incentives are not entirely eliminated even by market interest rates. The indexes tend to be at the low end—the prime rate, one-year Treasury bills—and often not compounded. Except for the strongest borrowers, a business's cost of capital is higher than these rates, and a successful business figures its own internal rate of return on investment at much higher rates. So business plaintiffs still view prejudgment interest as undercompensatory, and business defendants often view prejudgment interest as a cheap way to borrow money.

9. The remand in *National Gypsum*. The award of interest in *National Gypsum* was so large because the litigation was long delayed and interest rates were very high. With so much interest at stake, it became worthwhile to fully litigate issues that are often given short shrift. On remand, the district court awarded compound interest at the prime rate, not the municipal bond rate that would have been charged to defendant. Plaintiff got substantial gains from tax deferral, in the same way that retirement accounts and pension funds do: interest compounded tax free over the years, with a big tax bill due when the total was finally collected. If the judgment had been paid at the beginning, plaintiff would have paid taxes on each year's interest and could have compounded only the residue. But there was no precedent for making such an adjustment and the evidence needed to make it was not in the record. And the court held that prejudgment interest at the prime rate continued until it entered a judgment resolving the disputes over interest calculations; only then did postjudgment interest kick in at the lower statutory rate. The court of appeals affirmed on all three points, emphasizing that district courts are not required to engage in "refined rate-setting." Cement Division, National Gypsum Co. v. City of Milwaukee, 144 F.3d 1111, 1114 (7th Cir. 1998).

10. Procedure. Interest calculations are usually not submitted to juries, and interest is often awarded on post-trial motion. In federal court, a motion for prejudgment interest is a motion to alter or amend the judgment under Rule 59(e). Osterneck v. Ernst & Whinney, 489 U.S. 169 (1989). Such motions must be filed within ten days of the judgment, and they delay the time for filing a notice of appeal until they are disposed of.

11. Substance and procedure. The Second Circuit has held that prejudgment interest is substantive for *Erie* purposes, so that state law controls interest on state law claims. In re September 11 Litigation, 802 F.3d 314 (2d Cir. 2015). This seems clearly right; the award or denial of interest and the interest rate directly affect the amount of compensation for plaintiff's state-law injuries. But it does not appear to be a settled rule.

The federal statute on postjudgment interest, which also affects the amount of compensation, has generally been treated as procedural in diversity cases. Cappiello v. ICD Publications, Inc., 720 F.3d 109 (2d Cir. 2013). Courts have said that the statute controls the effect of a federal judgment and, at least when interest rates are high, tends to deter frivolous appeals in federal courts.

3. *The Net Present Value of Future Damages*

JONES & LAUGHLIN STEEL CORP. v. PFEIFER
462 U.S. 523 (1983)

Justice STEVENS delivered the opinion of the Court.

Respondent was injured in the course of his employment as a loading helper on a coal barge. As his employer, petitioner was required to compensate him for his injury under §4 of the Longshoremen's and Harbor Workers' Compensation Act, 33 U.S.C. §901 *et seq.* As the owner *pro hac vice* [for this occasion only] of the barge, petitioner may also be liable for negligence under §5 of the Act. . . .

The District Court found in favor of respondent and awarded damages of $275,881.31. . . .

The District Court's calculation of damages was predicated on a few undisputed facts. At the time of his injury respondent was earning an annual wage of $26,065. He had a remaining work expectancy of 12-1/2 years. On the date of trial (October 1, 1980), respondent had received compensation payments of $33,079.14. If he had obtained light work and earned the legal minimum hourly wage from July 1, 1979 until his 65th birthday, he would have earned $66,350.

The District Court arrived at its final award by taking 12-1/2 years of earnings at respondent's wage at the time of injury ($325,312.50), subtracting his projected hypothetical earnings at the minimum wage ($66,352) and the compensation payments he had received under §4 ($33,079.14), and adding $50,000 for pain and suffering. The court did not increase the award to take inflation into account, and it did not discount the award to reflect the present value of the future stream of income. The Court instead decided to follow a decision of the Supreme Court of Pennsylvania, which had held "as a matter of law that future inflation shall be presumed equal to future interest rates with these factors offsetting." Kaczkowski v. Bolubasz, 421 A.2d 1027, 1038-1039 (Pa. 1980). Thus, although the District Court did not dispute that respondent could be expected to receive regular cost-of-living wage increases from the date of his injury until his presumed date of retirement, the Court refused to include such increases in its calculation, explaining that they would provide respondent "a double consideration for inflation." For comparable reasons, the Court disregarded changes in the legal minimum wage in computing the amount of mitigation attributable to respondent's ability to perform light work.

It does not appear that either party offered any expert testimony concerning predicted future rates of inflation, the interest rate that could be appropriately used to discount future earnings to present value, or the possible connection between inflation rates and interest rates. Respondent did, however, offer an estimate of how his own wages would have increased over time, based upon recent increases in the company's hourly wage scale.

The Court of Appeals affirmed. 678 F.2d 453 (3d Cir. 1982). . . .

It is useful at the outset to review the way in which damages should be measured in a hypothetical inflation-free economy. We shall then consider how price inflation alters the analysis. Finally, we shall decide whether the District Court committed reversible error in this case.

I

In calculating damages, it is assumed that if the injured party had not been disabled, he would have continued to work, and to receive wages at periodic intervals until retirement, disability, or death. An award for impaired earning capacity is intended to compensate the worker for the diminution in that stream of income. The award could in theory take the form of periodic payments, but in this country it has traditionally taken the form of a lump sum, paid at the conclusion of the litigation. The appropriate lump sum cannot be computed without first examining the stream of income it purports to replace.

The lost stream's length cannot be known with certainty; the worker could have been disabled or even killed in a different, non-work-related accident at any time. The probability that he would still be working at a given date is constantly diminishing. Given the complexity of trying to make an exact calculation, litigants frequently follow the relatively simple course of assuming that the worker would have continued to work up until a specific date certain. In this case, for example, both parties agreed that the petitioner would have continued to work until age 65 (12-1/2 more years) if he had not been injured.

Each annual installment[11] in the lost stream comprises several elements. The most significant is, of course, the actual wage. In addition, the worker may have enjoyed certain fringe benefits, which should be included in an ideal evaluation of the worker's loss but are frequently excluded for simplicity's sake. On the other hand, the injured worker's lost wages would have been diminished by state and federal income taxes. Since the damages award is tax-free, the relevant stream is ideally of *after-tax* wages and benefits. See Norfolk & Western Railway v. Liepelt, 444 U.S. 490 (1980). Moreover, workers often incur unreimbursed costs, such as transportation to work and uniforms, that the injured worker will not incur. These costs should also be deducted in estimating the lost stream.

In this case the parties appear to have agreed to simplify the litigation, and to presume that in each installment all the elements in the stream would offset each other, except for gross wages. However, in attempting to estimate even such a stylized stream of annual installments of gross wages, a trier of fact faces a complex task. The most obvious and most appropriate place to begin is with the worker's annual wage at the time of injury. Yet the "estimate of loss from lessened earnings capacity in the future need not be based solely upon the wages which the plaintiff was earning at the time of his injury." Charles T. McCormick, *Handbook on the Law of Damages* §86 (West 1935). Even in an inflation-free economy—that is to say one in which the prices of consumer goods remain stable—a worker's wages tend to "inflate." The "real" wage inflation reflects a number of factors, some linked to the specific individual and some linked to broader societal forces.

With the passage of time, an individual worker often becomes more valuable to his employer. His personal work experiences increase his hourly contributions to firm

---

11. Obviously, another distorting simplification is being made here. Although workers generally receive their wages in weekly or biweekly installments, virtually all calculations of lost earnings, including the one made in this case, pretend that the stream would have flowed in large spurts, taking the form of annual installments.

profits. To reflect that heightened value, he will often receive "seniority" or "experience" raises, "merit" raises, or even promotions. Although it may be difficult to prove when, and whether, a particular injured worker might have received such wage increases, they may be reliably demonstrated for some workers.

Furthermore, the wages of workers as a class may increase over time. Through more efficient interaction among labor, capital, and technology, industrial productivity may increase, and workers' wages may enjoy a share of that growth. Such productivity increases—reflected in real increases in the gross national product per worker-hour—have been a permanent feature of the national economy since the conclusion of World War II. Moreover, through collective bargaining, workers may be able to negotiate increases in their "share" of revenues, at the cost of reducing shareholders' rate of return on their investments. . . .

Of course, even in an inflation-free economy the award of damages to replace the lost stream of income cannot be computed simply by totaling up the sum of the periodic payments. For the damages award is paid in a lump sum at the conclusion of the litigation, and when it—or even a part of it—is invested, it will earn additional money. It has been settled since our decision in Chesapeake & Ohio Railway v. Kelly, 241 U.S. 485 (1916), that "in all cases where it is reasonable to suppose that interest may safely be earned upon the amount that is awarded, the ascertained future benefits ought to be discounted in the making up of the award." *Id.* at 490.

The discount rate should be based on the rate of interest that would be earned on "the best and safest investments." *Id.* at 491. Once it is assumed that the injured worker would definitely have worked for a specific term of years, he is entitled to a risk-free stream of future income to replace his lost wages; therefore, the discount rate should not reflect the market's premium for investors who are willing to accept some risk of default. Moreover, since under *Liepelt*, the lost stream of income should be estimated in after-tax terms, the discount rate should also represent the after-tax rate of return to the injured worker.[21]

Thus, although the notion of a damage award representing the present value of a lost stream of earnings in an inflation-free economy rests on some fairly sophisticated economic concepts, the two elements that determine its calculation can be stated fairly easily. They are: (1) the amount that the employee would have earned during each year that he could have been expected to work after the injury; and (2) the appropriate discount rate, reflecting the safest available investment. The trier of fact should apply the discount rate to each of the estimated installments in the lost stream of income, and then add up the discounted installments to determine the total award.[22]

---

21. The arithmetic necessary for discounting can be simplified through the use of a so-called "present value table," such as those found in Rufus Wixon, *Accountants' Handbook* 29.58-29.59 (Ronald Press 4th ed. 1956), or Stuart M. Speiser, *Recovery for Wrongful Death 2d* §8:4 at 713-718 (Lawyers Co-op 1975). These tables are based on the proposition that if i is the discount rate, then "the present value of $1 due in n periods must be $1 / (1 + i)^n$." Wixon at 29.57. In this context, the relevant "periods" are years; accordingly, if "i " is a market interest rate, it should be the effective *annual* yield.

22. At one time it was thought appropriate to distinguish between compensating a plaintiff "for the loss of time from his work which has actually occurred up to the time of trial" and compensating him "for the time which he will lose in the future." McCormick, *Damages* §86. This suggested that estimated future earning capacity should be discounted to the date of trial, and a separate calculation should be performed for the estimated loss of earnings between injury and trial. *Id.* at §§86-87. It is both easier and more precise to discount the entire lost stream of earnings back to the date of injury—the moment from which earning capacity was impaired. The plaintiff may then be awarded interest on that discounted sum for the period between injury and judgment, in order to ensure that the award when invested will still be able to replicate the lost stream.

II

Unfortunately for triers of fact, ours is not an inflation-free economy. Inflation has been a permanent fixture in our economy for many decades, and there can be no doubt that it ideally should affect both stages of the calculation described in the previous section. The difficult problem is how it can do so in the practical context of civil litigation under §5(b) of the Act.

The first stage of the calculation required an estimate of the shape of the lost stream of future income. For many workers, including respondent, a contractual "cost-of-living adjustment" automatically increases wages each year by the percentage change during the previous year in the consumer price index calculated by the Bureau of Labor Statistics. Such a contract provides a basis for taking into account an additional societal factor—price inflation—in estimating the worker's lost future earnings.

The second stage of the calculation requires the selection of an appropriate discount rate. Price inflation—or more precisely, anticipated price inflation—certainly affects market rates of return. If a lender knows that his loan is to be repaid a year later with dollars that are less valuable than those he has advanced, he will charge an interest rate that is high enough both to compensate him for the temporary use of the loan proceeds and also to make up for their shrinkage in value.

At one time many courts incorporated inflation into only one stage of the calculation of the award for lost earnings. In estimating the lost stream of future earnings, they accepted evidence of both individual and societal factors that would tend to lead to wage increases even in an inflation-free economy, but required the plaintiff to prove that those factors were not influenced by predictions of future price inflation. No increase was allowed for price inflation, on the theory that such predictions were unreliably speculative. In discounting the estimated lost stream of future income to present value, however, they applied the market interest rate.

The effect of these holdings was to deny the plaintiff the benefit of the impact of inflation on his future earnings, while giving the defendant the benefit of inflation's impact on the interest rate that is used to discount those earnings to present value. Although the plaintiff in such a situation could invest the proceeds of the litigation at an "inflated" rate of interest, the stream of income that he received provided him with only enough dollars to maintain his existing *nominal* income; it did not provide him with a stream comparable to what his lost wages would have been in an inflationary economy. This inequity was assumed to have been minimal because of the relatively low rates of inflation.

In recent years, of course, inflation rates have not remained low. There is now a consensus among courts that the prior inequity can no longer be tolerated. There is no consensus at all, however, regarding what form an appropriate response should take.

Our sister common law nations generally continue to adhere to the position that inflation is too speculative to be considered in estimating the lost stream of future earnings; they have sought to counteract the danger of systematically undercompensating plaintiffs by applying a discount rate that is below the current market rate. . . . [I]n Australia, the High Court has adopted a 2% rate, on the theory that it represents a good approximation of the long-term "real interest rate."

In this country, some courts have taken the same "real interest rate" approach as Australia. They have endorsed the economic theory suggesting that market interest rates include two components—an estimate of anticipated inflation, and a desired "real" rate of return on investment—and that the latter component is essentially constant over time. They have concluded that the inflationary increase in the estimated lost stream of future earnings will therefore be perfectly "offset" by all but the "real" component of the market interest rate.[26]

Still other courts have preferred to continue relying on market interest rates. To avoid undercompensation, they have shown at least tentative willingness to permit evidence of what future price inflation will be in estimating the lost stream of future income. . . .

Finally, some courts have applied a number of techniques that have loosely been termed "total offset" methods. What these methods have in common is that they presume that the ideal discount rate—the after-tax market interest rate on a safe investment—is (to a legally tolerable degree of precision) completely offset by certain elements in the ideal computation of the estimated lost stream of future income. They all assume that the effects of future price inflation on wages are part of what offsets the market interest rate. . . .

The litigants and the amici in this case urge us to select one of the many rules that have been proposed and establish it for all time as the exclusive method in all federal trials for calculating an award for lost earnings in an inflationary economy. We are not persuaded, however, that such an approach is warranted. For our review of the foregoing cases leads us to draw three conclusions. First, by its very nature the calculation of an award for lost earnings must be a rough approximation. Because the lost stream can never be predicted with complete confidence, any lump sum represents only a "rough and ready" effort to put the plaintiff in the position he would have been in had he not been injured. Second, sustained price inflation can make the award substantially less precise. Inflation's current magnitude and unpredictability create a substantial risk that the damage award will prove to have little relation to the lost wages it purports to replace. Third, the question of lost earnings can arise in many different contexts. In some sectors of the economy, it is far easier to assemble evidence of an individual's most likely career path than in others.

These conclusions all counsel hesitation. Having surveyed the multitude of options available, we will do no more than is necessary to resolve the case before us. . . .

III . . .

In calculating an award for a longshoreman's lost earnings caused by the negligence of a vessel, the discount rate should be chosen on the basis of the factors that are used to estimate the lost stream of future earnings. If the trier of fact relies on a specific forecast of the future rate of price inflation, and if the estimated lost stream of future earnings is calculated to include price inflation along with individual factors and other societal factors, then the proper discount rate would be the after-tax market interest rate. But since specific forecasts of future price inflation remain too unreliable to be

---

26. What is meant by the "real interest rate" depends on how one expects the plaintiff to invest the award. If one assumes that the injured worker will immediately invest in bonds having a variety of maturity dates, in order to ensure a particular stream of future payments, then the relevant "real interest rate" must be the difference between (1) an average of short-term, medium-term, and long-term market interest rates in a given year and (2) the average rate of price inflation in *subsequent* years (i.e., during the terms of the investments).

It appears more common for "real interest rate" approaches to rest on the assumption that the worker will invest in low-risk short-term securities and will reinvest frequently. Under that assumption, the relevant real interest rate is the difference between the short-term market interest rate in a given year and the average rate of price inflation during that same year.

However one interprets the "real interest rate," there is a slight distortion introduced by netting out the two effects and discounting by the difference.

useful in many cases, it will normally be a costly and ultimately unproductive waste of longshoremen's resources to make such forecasts the centerpiece of litigation under §5(b). As Judge Newman has warned, "The average accident trial should not be converted into a graduate seminar on economic forecasting." Doca v. Marina Mercante Nicaraguense, 634 F.2d 30, 39 (2d Cir. 1980). For that reason, both plaintiffs and trial courts should be discouraged from pursuing that approach.

On the other hand, if forecasts of future price inflation are not used, it is necessary to choose an appropriate below-market discount rate. As long as inflation continues, one must ask how much should be "offset" against the market rate. Once again, that amount should be chosen on the basis of the same factors that are used to estimate the lost stream of future earnings. If full account is taken of the individual and societal factors (excepting price inflation) that can be expected to have resulted in wage increases, then all that should be set off against the market interest rate is an estimate of future price inflation. This would result in one of the "real interest rate" approaches described above. Although we find the economic evidence distinctly inconclusive regarding an essential premise of those approaches,[30] we do not believe a trial court adopting such an approach in a suit under §5(b) should be reversed if it adopts a rate between one and three percent and explains its choice.

There may be a sound economic argument for even further set-offs. . . . Professor Carlson of the Purdue University Economics Department contend[s] that in the long run the societal factors excepting price inflation—largely productivity gains—match (or even slightly exceed) the "real interest rate." John A. Carlson, *Economic Analysis v. Courtroom Controversy,* 62 A.B.A.J. 628 (1976). He thus recommended that the estimated lost stream of future wages be calculated without considering either price inflation or societal productivity gains. All that would be considered would be individual seniority and promotion gains. If this were done, he concluded that the entire market interest rate, including both inflation and the real interest rate, would be more than adequately offset.

Although such an approach has the virtue of simplicity and may even be economically precise,[31] we cannot at this time agree with the Court of Appeals for the Third

30. The key premise is that the real interest rate is stable over time. It is obviously not perfectly stable, but whether it is even relatively stable is hotly disputed among economists. In his classic work, Irving Fisher argued that the rate is not stable because changes in expectations of inflation (the factor that influences market interest rates) lag behind changes in inflation itself. Irving Fisher, *The Theory of Interest* 43 (Macmillan 1930). He noted that the "real rate of interest in the United States from March to April, 1917, fell below minus 70 percent!" *Id.* at 44. Consider also the more recent observations of Justice Stephen of the High Court of Australia:

> Past Australian economic experience appears to provide little support for the concept of a relatively constant rate of "real interest." Year by year a figure for "real interest" can of course be calculated, simply by subtracting from nominal interest rates the rate of inflation. But these figures are no more than a series of numbers bearing no resemblance to any relatively constant rate of interest which lenders are supposed to demand and borrowers to pay after allowing for estimated inflation. . . . [F]rom 1950 to 1979, the average "implicit real interest rate" is a negative rate of –.7 percent, with 4 percent as the greatest positive rate in any year and –20.2 percent as the greatest negative annual rate. *Interim Report of the Campbell Committee of Inquiry,* Table 9.1 (Australian Government Publication Service 1980).

Pennant Hills Restaurants v. Barrell Insurance, 55 A.L.J.R. 258, 267 (1981).

31. We note that a substantial body of literature suggests that the Carlson rule might even *under* compensate some plaintiffs. *See* Stuart M. Speiser, *Recovery for Wrongful Death, Economic Handbook* 36-37 (Lawyers Co-op 1970) (average interest rate 1% below average rate of wage growth). *But see* Comment, *Inflation, Productivity, and the Total Offset Method of Calculating Damages for Lost Future Earnings,* 49 U. Chi. L. Rev. 1003, 1023 & n.87 (1982) (noting "apparent congruence" between government projections of 2% average annual productivity growth and real interest rate, and concluding that total offset is accurate). . . .

Circuit that its use is mandatory in the federal courts. Naturally, Congress could require it if it chose to do so. And nothing prevents parties interested in keeping litigation costs under control from stipulating to its use before trial. But we are not prepared to impose it on unwilling litigants, for we have not been given sufficient data to judge how closely the national patterns of wage growth are likely to reflect the patterns within any given industry. . . .

As a result, the judgment below must be set aside. In performing its damages calculation, the trial court applied the theory of *Kaczkowski* as a mandatory federal rule of decision, even though the petitioner had insisted that if compensation was to be awarded, it "must be reduced to its present worth." . . .

IV

We do not suggest that the trial judge should embark on a search for "delusive exactness." See Feldman v. Allegheny Airlines, 524 F.2d 384, 392 (2d Cir. 1975) (Friendly, J., concurring dubitante), quoting Truax v. Corrigan, 257 U.S. 312, 342 (1921) (Holmes, J., dissenting). It is perfectly obvious that the most detailed inquiry can at best produce an approximate result. And one cannot ignore the fact that in many instances the award for impaired earning capacity may be overshadowed by a highly impressionistic award for pain and suffering. But we are satisfied that whatever rate the District Court may choose to discount the estimated stream of future earnings, it must make a deliberate choice, rather than assuming that it is bound by a rule of state law.

The judgment of the Court of Appeals is vacated and the case is remanded for further proceedings consistent with this opinion. . . .

NOTES ON THE SEPTEMBER 11 CALCULATIONS

1. The choice of remedies. The terrorist attacks of September 11, 2001, inflicted nearly 3,000 wrongful deaths and a comparable number of nonfatal injuries. Congress responded with an extraordinary remedy, funded by the federal government and administered outside the courts by an official with the title Special Master. This remedy was enacted on September 22, in Title IV of Pub. L. 107-42; it is strangely codified as a note to 49 U.S.C. §40101. Alternatively, victims could file civil suits in the Southern District of New York, but total damages for all claims would be capped at the amount of defendants' liability insurance. About 98 percent of the families of deceased victims, and 4,400 surviving personal injury victims, filed administrative claims. Ninety-six wrongful-death and personal-injury plaintiffs, and all the property-damage plaintiffs, sued the airlines and other defendants in federal court; thousands of cleanup workers also filed personal injury claims and eventually, Congress created an administrative fund for them too. Seven families, too depressed or grief stricken to take any action, failed to file either a lawsuit or an administrative claim, despite repeated personal appeals from senior officials responsible for the administrative remedy.

The press reported that total payments in the wrongful death cases were about $500 million. Benjamin Weiser, *Judge's Approval Is Sought in 2 Lawsuits From 9/11*, N.Y. Times (Mar. 4, 2010). This is more than $5 million per case, and more than double the average award in the administrative remedy. These cases also required greater expense, the risks of litigation, and a much longer delay before payment.

2. The administrative remedy as another example. The lost-income calculations in the administrative remedy are a good guide to the complexities of calculating lost income and offer creative solutions to those complexities. On the one hand, these calculations were more sophisticated than what is reasonably possible in a typical jury trial. On the other hand, the Special Master applied the same calculations to all victims, with no attempt to individualize beyond recent income and basic demographic data. The formula is summarized in volume I of the *Final Report of the Special Master for the September 11th Victim Compensation Fund of 2001*; the regulations are reprinted in volume II. Both volumes are available at *https://permanent.access.gpo.gov/lps55611/ lps55611.html.* These calculation methods were upheld against a broad range of legal attacks in Schneider v. Feinberg, 345 F.3d 135 (2d Cir. 2003).

3. Base earnings. The calculation started with age and the last three years of after-tax income, plus fringe benefits. The formula ignored income above the 98th percentile, or about $231,000. The Special Master heard individualized evidence in cases of higher income, but apparently did not give full weight to that income. A judge could not authorize this in an individual tort trial, but defendant could argue that such a high income might not have lasted a lifetime.

4. Future earnings. Annual increases in income were projected forward assuming 2 percent inflation, 1 percent productivity gain, and an additional component for "life-cycle or age-specific increase." This last component varied with age, so that the projected earnings growth rate for an 18-year-old was 9.7 percent annually, declining gradually to 3 percent for workers 52 and over. That is, workers 52 and over were presumed to have exhausted their life-cycle gains and to experience only general inflation and productivity gains. This is roughly consistent with *Jones & Laughlin*, because the decedent there was old enough, and the skill levels in his job were modest enough, that inflation and general productivity gains would have been the principal source of his salary increases. But for a younger worker, the life-cycle component adds far more than inflation and general productivity. The life-cycle component tends to be greater in more skilled occupations, and in an individual trial, evidence of expected earnings increases can be offered on an individual basis.

All projected earnings were reduced by 3 percent to allow for the risk of unemployment.

5. Working life. Working-life expectancy was based on actuarial data from a study done in 1997-1998; it assumed that an employed 25-year-old will work another 33.6 years, and that this number declines gradually to 4.2 years for an employed 65-year-old. Working-life expectancy for women is somewhat lower than for men, if the data are tabulated separately, but the male data were used for both sexes.

6. Consumption. The decedent's share of household consumption was subtracted, using average data by income and family size derived from the Consumer Expenditure Survey of the Bureau of Labor Statistics. The percentage attributed to personal consumption declined with income, and declined sharply with dependents. Thus a single adult earning $10,000 per year was presumed to spend 76.4 percent of his income on his own consumption, a figure that gradually declined to 48 percent as income rose to $90,000. If he were married with two dependent children, he was presumed to spend only 13.6 percent of his income on his own consumption at $10,000 per year, declining to 6.7 percent as his income rose to $90,000. "For lower income categories where total expenditures exceed income, expenditures were scaled to income, so as not to reduce income for expenses potentially met by other forms of support," such as help from relatives, welfare, food stamps, subsidized housing, and the like. The percentage attributed to the decedent's personal consumption was applied to after-tax income, although the Bureau of Labor Statistics apparently calculated it on the basis of before-tax income, and it was applied only to decedent's earnings, although defendants often offer evidence of decedent's personal consumption as a percentage of family income. On each of these points, the Special Master's formula is more favorable to claimants than legal doctrine; it is much harder to compare these calculations to the actual calculations or estimates of a typical jury.

7. Discounting. Future lost income was discounted to present value using discount rates based on current after-tax yields on "mid- to long-term U.S. Treasury securities," using "a mid-range effective tax rate." It was assumed that the survivors of younger victims would invest in longer term securities, so the discount rates varied with age: 5.1 percent for victims under age 36 (4.2% after presumed tax), declining to 4.2 percent (3.4% after presumed tax) for victims over 54. Using mid- to long-term securities increased the discount rate as compared to short-term securities, and thus favored defendant (the government here). To make these market interest rates comparable to the 1 to 3 percent range of real interest rates suggested in *Jones & Laughlin*, subtract the 2 percent annually that the Special Master had used to adjust future earnings for projected future inflation.

As it happened, interest rates continued declining and were at historic lows for much of victims' expected working lives. If their survivors invested in medium-term government bonds, they had to reinvest the principal at much lower interest rates than the Special Master predicted.

8. Other assumptions. The Special Master made other simplifying assumptions "to facilitate analysis on a large scale." Although he projected substantial salary growth over time, he used for each decedent the income-tax rate at the date of death and the personal consumption figures imputed at the date of death. "It was determined that the net effect of these and other facilitating assumptions was to increase the potential amount of presumed economic loss to the benefit of the claimant."

9. Collateral sources. Congress directed the Special Master to subtract "all collateral sources, including life insurance, pension funds, death benefit programs, and payments by Federal, State, or local governments." Some families feared that this might leave them with no recovery from the fund. The Special Master responded by deciding that contributions from private donors, 401(k) plans, and the large special tax exemptions enacted for victims would not be treated as collateral sources. He also announced his "expectation" that when the individual needs of each family were considered, "it will be very rare that a claimant will receive less than $250,000." This expectation appears to have required some creative statutory interpretation, but in fact, no claimant received less than $250,000 for a wrongful death.

10. Pain and suffering and emotional distress. The Special Master awarded $250,000 for the "noneconomic loss" of each decedent, plus $100,000 for the "noneconomic loss" of each spouse and each dependent of a decedent. Recognizing that "each person experienced the unspeakable events of that day in a unique way," he found these circumstances generally unknowable for decedents.

11. Net awards. Wrongful death awards ranged from the $250,000 minimum to $7.1 million—and this with no jury and a fixed amount for "noneconomic" loss. The variation resulted from income, age, dependents, and the subtraction of collateral sources. Because the affluent were more likely to be well insured, income did not make as much difference as might have been expected. There were minimum awards even at the highest income levels. The mean award was $2.1 million; the median was $1.7 million.

12. A de facto cap? The Special Master denied putting any cap on awards, but he also indicated reluctance to give full weight to extremely high incomes. He argued that such incomes might not continue for a lifetime, and that in any event, the families did not need the huge awards that would be produced by projecting such incomes over a lifetime. Families of deceased investment bankers, claiming economic losses of up to $52 million, claimed that the Special Master was applying a de facto cap.

The court let the Special Master do it his way. Schneider v. Feinberg, 345 F.3d 135 (2d Cir. 2003). It was not fully persuaded by his interpretation of the statute. But the statute protected his awards from judicial review after they were made, and in effect, the court held them equally unreviewable before they were made.

13. The personal injury awards. Personal injury awards ranged from $500 to $8.6 million, averaging about $1.85 million. Of course the injuries were much more variable than the deaths.

14. Lessons learned? The Special Master's process show that the large variations in wrongful death awards do not result merely from the vagaries of juries, and that choices about the collateral-source rule may have different average consequences at different income levels. The process suggests that it is possible to calculate damages with a sophisticated schedule, to process large numbers of claims quickly and efficiently, and to distribute substantial sums in compensation. But nothing about the process suggests that it is politically possible to implement more generally any lessons we might learn from it.

NOTES ON DISCOUNTING TO PRESENT VALUE

1. The problem. The common-law practice has been to include all damages in a single judgment, even though some damages will not be suffered until far into the future. In personal injury cases, this requires difficult predictions about future actual earnings, future medical expenses, and what future earnings would have been but for the injury. These predictions presuppose a more basic prediction: How long and how severely will plaintiff be disabled? Her recovery may be quicker or slower or more or less complete than any doctor or jury can predict.

Awarding damages in a lump sum also requires that these future damages be discounted to present value. Determining the present value of a stream of future wages is mathematically identical to determining the present value of a stream of future profits or the value of an income-producing property by the present value of its future earnings (known as the capitalized earnings method). Both the "capitalized value" and the "present value" refer to the amount of money that, if invested today, would produce the future stream of earnings. In either context, it is erroneous to ignore the effect of inflation on interest rates.

2. Inflation and interest rates. In addition to the "real" interest rate and the expected inflation rate, nominal interest rates are traditionally thought to include a premium for the risk of default. The Court can ignore that component because disabled plaintiffs are entitled to avoid that risk by investing in government bonds or government-insured certificates of deposit. That rule meets the needs of families without investment experience, who are likely to put any unspent portion of a large judgment or settlement in a bank. More financially sophisticated plaintiffs would do better to put the money into a well diversified array of investments with higher returns. In business litigation, the appropriate discount rate is rarely the interest rate on the safest investments; it is usually chosen based on the plaintiff's cost of capital or the riskiness of the investment from which the profits were lost.

Inflation tends to make plaintiff's future wage increases larger and thus to increase his recovery. Inflation also tends to make interest rates higher and thus to reduce plaintiff's recovery. Netting out these two effects of inflation avoids the need to predict the inflation rate; it is like subtracting *x* from both sides of an equation without having to know a numerical value for *x*. This procedure also reduces a potential credibility problem for the plaintiff. Consider the case of a semiskilled worker, age 29, earning $40,000 per year. If inflation persists at 2 percent, he would make about $80,000 at age 65, before any allowance for productivity gains or any other source of wage increase; if inflation went back up to 3 percent, he would make about $115,000 at age 65, and at 6 percent inflation, he would make $325,000 at age 65. Some juries may find such claims hard to believe.

Even if inflation is netted out, difficult predictions remain. Economists dispute the stability of the real interest rate, and those who consider it stable argue about its level. The real interest rate fluctuates notoriously in the short term; most claims of stability relate only to the long term. Yet most courts that have discussed the issue have assumed that plaintiff will make short-term investments. Minor differences in the estimate of the real interest rate can make enormous differences in judgments. *Jones & Laughlin* sanctions any estimate between 1 and 3 percent. For our 29-year-old worker earning $40,000 per year, a 1 percent discount yields $1,204,300 for the present value of lost wages. A 2 percent discount yields $1,019,554; a 3 percent discount yields $873,290.

3. Total offset. Some arguments for a total offset rule say that overall productivity gains, which vary from year to year, have usually been within the range of estimates for the real interest rate. See the Court's discussion of the Carlson article, and footnote 31, in *Jones & Laughlin*. The claim is that productivity gains plus inflation roughly equal market interest rates. It is not unreasonable to expect this coincidence to continue, although there is no reason in theory that it should.

Pennsylvania's total offset rule is different. The court assumed that inflation alone equals the market interest rate on safe investments, so that the real interest rate is zero. Productivity gains and any other source of wage increases were to be considered separately. Kaczkowski v. Bolubasz, 421 A.2d 1027 (Pa. 1980). Interest rates depend in part on predictions of future inflation, which are of course inaccurate, but it seems more likely that errors are random than that they are systematically on the low side. But see the negative average-real-interest rate for nearly 30 years in Australia, in footnote 30. Pennsylvania has adhered to the total offset method, but its decision to apply that method to compensation lost due to employment discrimination and breach of contract was four-three. Helpin v. Trustees of the University of Pennsylvania, 10 A.3d 267 (Pa. 2010).

4. Real wage increases. Litigants and juries who net out inflation, or inflation plus average productivity gains, must still predict what plaintiff's real wages would have been — her wage at the time of injury plus all increases from sources other than those that are netted out against the interest rate. Some wage increases result from increases in the employee's personal productivity, and some from productivity gains in the employer's work force, in the industry, or in the economy generally. Some are rewards for long service. The expected long-term earnings of a second-year law student far exceed her summer clerk's salary. Her productivity will increase vastly with education and experience, and her firm's compensation structure will be designed to reward those productivity increases as well as to reward partners with a share of the income produced by associates and staff. Of course, she may never make partner, but the job she goes to instead is also likely to pay well. A middle-aged loading helper such as Pfeifer will have less spectacular gains, but he will have some. He should at least share in overall productivity gains that arise from improved technology and similar factors.

Any sort of offset formula, total or otherwise, can deal only with average gains. It will always be necessary to take evidence on individual variations. For younger workers with even modest skills, it has long seemed likely that real wage gains would exceed the real interest rate. The Special Master in the September 11 proceedings assumed that this would be true for all younger workers. These assumptions may no longer hold; real wage increases have been quite modest in much of the economy for many years now. But low unemployment is finally putting some upward pressure on wages as we write this in early 2018. Our inability to predict wage growth through the production schedule for this book suggests the difficulty of predicting wage growth over the lifetime of an injured worker.

For an employee who has been getting regular pay increases, it may seem easier to project those pay increases forward without separating inflation from other sources of pay increase. If you do it this way, then you would discount to present value at market interest rates, not the real interest rate.

5. Medical expenses. The focus in *Jones & Laughlin* is on wages, but medical expenses present the same problem. They may be incurred over a long time; the cost will undoubtedly increase, probably much faster than general inflation; and the predicted cost must be reduced to present value. In Calva-Cerqueira v. United States, 281 F. Supp. 2d 279 (D.D.C. 2003), medical expenses were discounted at a negative real interest rate (that is, they were inflated rather than discounted), based on a finding about medical inflation. *Calva-Cerqueira* is a very careful opinion in a bench trial, with descriptions of conflicting expert testimony, illustrating how *Jones & Laughlin* works in practice when carefully applied.

6. Compounding. The formula in *Jones & Laughlin*—$1 / (1 + i)^n$—is the discount formula for compound interest. Is there any reason why plaintiff's future losses should be discounted to present value at compound interest rates, while plaintiff is compensated for his past losses with simple interest, or with no interest at all? In Monessen Southwestern Railway v. Morgan, 486 U.S. 330 (1988), decided under the Federal Employers' Liability Act, the Court refused interest on plaintiff's past losses but required that his future losses be discounted to present value. Justices Blackmun and Marshall said the two holdings were inconsistent. Weren't they right?

7. Procedure. One wonders about the capacity of jurors to handle discount calculations, with or without allowances for inflation and productivity. Witnesses can illustrate the calculations, but that may be little help if the jury does not accept all the witness's assumptions. One argument in favor of the total offset rule is that it simplifies calculations; the Pennsylvania court claimed that it could "reflect the impact of inflation in these cases without specifically submitting this question to the jury." *Kaczkowski*, 421 A.2d at 1039. In 1980, with inflation at 12 percent a year and a major political issue, it seems unlikely that an uninstructed jury would have ignored inflation.

Courts have disagreed over how to submit these issues to juries. Astonishingly, some courts simply tell juries to reduce future damages to present value, without telling them what that means or how to do it. An example is Castro v. County of Los Angeles, 833 F.3d 1060, 1066 n.2 (9th Cir. 2016). The Florida Supreme Court held that no particular method is required under the Florida Wrongful Death Act and that expert testimony is not required, but that the parties may offer expert testimony that "employs any recognized method." Delta Air Lines v. Ageloff, 552 So. 2d 1089, 1093 (Fla. 1989). A court subject to this rule has complained that "it is unrealistic to direct a jury to perform an economic calculation which the Florida Supreme Court candidly recognizes is beyond its reach." Milam v. Yenke, 752 So. 2d 1, 1 (Fla. Dist. Ct. App. 1999), *withdrawn*, 763 So. 2d 342 (Fla. Dist. Ct. App. 1999).

The Fifth Circuit held that judges may submit these cases on special verdicts and interrogatories, asking the jury to find how much plaintiff would have earned in each succeeding year and asking what discount rate to apply. The court or parties would then do the arithmetic. Culver v. Slater Boat Co., 722 F.2d 114, 122 (5th Cir. 1983). The Second Circuit urged parties to stipulate to such a procedure but held that it cannot be required. Oliveri v. Delta Steamship Lines, Inc., 849 F.2d 742, 751 (2d Cir. 1988). Other possibilities and conflicting cases are collected in Lewin Realty III, Inc. v. Brooks, 771 A.2d 446, 470-477 (Md. Ct. Spec. App. 2001), *aff'd*, 835 A.2d 616 (Md. 2003).

Courts are also split on who bears the burden of introducing evidence of an appropriate interest rate and method of discount. Several courts have held that defendant must introduce such evidence if it wants future damages reduced to present value. An example is Kay v. Menard, 754 A.2d 760, 771 (R.I. 2000). Other courts have held that because plaintiff bears the burden of proving his damages, a judgment entered without evidence of present value cannot stand. Watkins Co. v. Storms, 272 P.3d 503 (Idaho 2012). The Second Circuit once suggested a 2 percent discount rate, with the burden of proof apparently on the party that wants a higher or lower rate. *Oliveri*, 849 F.2d at 745-749.

The variety of methods for handling this issue means that trial lawyers simply must understand net present value well enough to reason through the various methods. Lawyers who do not understand it are at the mercy of those who do. There is potential for mixing inconsistent elements of different methods, with a risk of results that are disastrous for one side or the other. Even if you assume that instructions won't matter because the jury won't understand them, you still have to deal with any expert testimony offered by the other side. The lawyers in a case may tacitly agree to ignore the issue, and they often do, but either side may disrupt such a tacit agreement at any time before the argument has been irretrievably forfeited.

8. Arithmetic. It is a mistake to be put off by the arithmetic of present value calculations. The arithmetic is really rather simple; it can be done with a present value table like the one in the appendix, with the calculator on your personal computer or laptop, or with a preprogrammed function on a computer spreadsheet. The real intellectual work is in arguing for the most advantageous choice on each of the many assumptions required to do the calculation.

9. Current interest rates. Interest rates are just beginning to recover from historic lows; the *nominal* interest rate on the safest short-term investments was below the Supreme Court's assumption of a 1 to 3 percent *real* interest rate for years. A plaintiff who invested his judgment in low-risk, short-term securities at any time in the new millennium would have earned very little, and he would earn only a little more doing that in 2018. Inflation is also low, productivity gains are low, but age-cycle gains are probably in their normal range. Discounting to present value at current interest rates is likely to offset only a portion of projected future wage gains.

NOTES ON RACE- AND SEX-BASED DATA

1. The litigation. Demographic and social science data are often reported separately by race and sex, and such data have apparently been introduced in tort trials, often without objection. Such data may be used because the data are readily available, because the data seem more precise, or because defendant wants to show that a female or minority plaintiff would have had lower earnings and a shorter working life, or that a minority plaintiff will die sooner and thus have fewer future medical expenses. In G.M.M. v. Kimpson, 116 F. Supp. 3d 126 (E.D.N.Y. 2015), Judge Weinstein held it unconstitutional to reduce damages on the basis of race or ethnicity. His extensive opinion collects a growing literature and a smattering of cases. Data on the population, combining all racial and sexual groups into one category, are nearly always available. But testifying experts will generally use race- and sex-based data unless challenged on the point.

Professors Avraham and Yuracko find the use of race- and sex-based data extremely widespread, even in discrimination cases under the civil rights laws! Ronen Avraham & Kimberly Yuracko, *Torts and Discrimination*, 78 Ohio St. L.J. 661 (2017). Three states have banned race-based tables by statute, and one of these also bans sex-based tables. But three other states seem to require such tables by statute, and ten embed such tables in pattern jury instructions.

2. The insurance analogy. The insurance industry generally abandoned race-based premiums and benefits early in the twentieth century. Sex-based premiums and benefits remain pervasive where the industry is allowed a choice; women pay more for medical and disability insurance, but less for life and auto insurance, and women get smaller pensions and annuities than men. Life and auto insurance are the least expensive policies on this list, so taken as a whole, this industry practice costs women much more than it costs men. Such disparities are illegal in employer-sponsored insurance, because they violate the federal employment discrimination laws. Arizona Governing Committee v. Norris, 463 U.S. 1073 (1983). For a defense of the line of cases culminating in *Norris*, and a collection of sources criticizing it, see Lea Brilmayer, Richard W. Hekeler, Douglas Laycock, & Teresa A. Sullivan, *Sex Discrimination in Employer-Sponsored Insurance: A Legal and Demographic Analysis*, 47 U. Chi. L. Rev. 505 (1980).

3. The central question. It is one thing to project lower earnings based on an individual's skills, education, or work history. But should we give smaller awards for future damages to injured women and minorities on the basis of the average past experience of their race and sex?

Problem 2-1

Plaintiff was a 50-year-old industrial worker when he was injured on his birthday in 2018. His disability is permanent and total; he will never be able to earn a salary again.

At the time of his injury, plaintiff was earning $40,000 per year. His factory is not unionized.

Had plaintiff continued working, he could have taken early retirement at age 55. Few workers in his factory actually retire that early. The average retirement age in the factory is 62. Thirty-five percent of the workers in the plant continue to age 65. There is no mandatory retirement age, and two workers have continued past age 70. The later a worker retires, the larger his pension. Plaintiff was in good health prior to the injury.

Plaintiff's expert testified that the rate of productivity gain in plaintiff's industry has been 1 percent per year. Defendant's expert testified that plaintiff's wages have not kept up with inflation, so that his real wages are actually lower now than in 1990. Plaintiff had no plans to get additional training.

The annual rate of inflation at the time of trial is 2 percent. Interest rates are listed below.

One-year tax-exempt municipal notes	1.5%
52-week Treasury bills	2.25%
Money-market funds	0.5%
One-year government-insured certificates of deposit	2.25%
One-year investment-grade corporate notes	2.5%
One-year corporate junk bonds	6.0%
Ten-year Treasury bonds	3.0%
Ten-year government-insured certificates of deposit	3.5%
Ten-year investment-grade corporate bonds	4.0%
Ten-year tax-exempt municipal bonds	3.5%
Ten-year corporate junk bonds	8.0%

Calculate plaintiff's lost wages from the injury. There is a present value table in the appendix.

NOTES ON PERIODIC PAYMENTS AND STRUCTURED SETTLEMENTS

1. Periodic payment or determination of damages. One way to substantially reduce the difficulties of predicting future losses and economic events is to determine and pay damages periodically. That is the practice in some foreign countries, and it is authorized in this country in administrative schemes such as workers' compensation laws. We do it in court for child support and alimony, which are derived from equity, and before that, from ecclesiastical courts, rather than from common law. Fiduciaries can be required to periodically account to the court, in a procedure also derived from equity.

For an example of the potential breadth of redeterminations in administrative proceedings, see Metropolitan Stevedore Co. v. Rambo, 515 U.S. 291 (1995). Rambo was an injured longshoreman receiving compensation under a federal workers' compensation program. His disability was permanent and his physical condition did not change. But when he went to crane school and got a better-paying job, the employer successfully moved to end compensation for lost wage-earning capacity.

On remand, the Court of Appeals ordered nominal compensation to keep the case open, so that if Rambo lost his crane job and was unable to find another because of his disability, he would be eligible for another modification. The case returned to the Supreme Court, which approved this procedure for cases in which there is "a significant possibility" of a future decline in earning capacity. Metropolitan Stevedore Co. v. Rambo, 521 U.S. 121, 123 (1997). But it said that the administrative law judge, not the court of appeals, should decide whether this standard was met.

The Court emphasized the difficulties of the tort practice of assessing all damages at once. It noted that widely disparate outcomes were possible in *Rambo*: He might keep the crane job, but if he lost it, he might be unemployable. In such a case, awarding the weighted average of the possibilities would yield a number in the middle that would be wrong no matter what happened.

Why don't we wait and see what really happens in personal injury litigation? Is it just habit and tradition? Avoiding an administrative burden on the courts? Protecting the right to jury trial? Fear of creating incentives to malinger? Or assuring the lawyer quicker payment of her contingent fee? Does it matter that administrative schemes for periodic payment often make much less individualized determinations of damage? Whatever the reason, once-and-for-all judgments are deeply embedded in the system. In litigation derived from or modeled on the common law, damages are calculated and awarded in a lump sum and are immediately payable in a lump sum. Courts generally say that, absent statutory authorization, they have no power to award damages any other way. Some of the cases are collected in Reilly v. United States, 863 F.2d 149, 168-170 (1st Cir. 1988). There is an exception in patent law, where lump-sum damages for future infringement are so difficult to assess that courts (when they do not enjoin the infringement) have ordered infringers to pay periodic royalties instead. Paice LLC v. Toyota Motor Corp., 504 F.3d 1293, 1313-1316 (Fed. Cir. 2007), discussed in the notes following eBay v. MercExchange in section 5.A.4.

2. The "tort reform" proposals. A number of states have enacted mandatory provisions for periodic *payment* of judgments, mostly in medical-malpractice cases. Some of these proposals provide for periodic *determination* of the rate of inflation and of whether plaintiff is still alive. But no one has undertaken any periodic determinations that would require periodic hearings.

Some of these provisions have been upheld against constitutional attack, often without much difficulty. An example is Garhart ex rel. Tinsman v. Columbia/HealthOne, L.L.C., 95 P.3d 571 (Colo. 2004).

Opinions invalidating such provisions reveal some of the problems. The Arizona court struck down that state's periodic payment provision, Smith v. Myers, 887 P.2d 541 (Ariz. 1994), under a clause in the state constitution forbidding any law "limiting the amount of damages to be recovered for causing the death or injury of any person." Ariz. Const. art. 2 §31. The court found multiple reasons why periodic payments are less valuable than a lump sum, including the risk that the insurer would become insolvent and an asymmetry in dealing with future events that is common to these statutes. In the Arizona version, payments for medical care were cut off if plaintiff died prematurely, but they were not increased if plaintiff lived longer or required more medical care than originally expected. The court also cited an article arguing that lump sums are more valuable because they give plaintiff a choice: A plaintiff who collects a lump sum can buy an annuity, but a plaintiff who gets periodic payments cannot convert them into a lump sum. Actually she can, but the discount rate is likely to be ruinous. See note 4.

The Missouri court struck down a statute providing that future damages may be paid, "in whole or in part," in installments over the plaintiff's life expectancy, plus interest at the 52-week Treasury-bill rate. That rate has been extremely low for years; in May 2011, when judgment was entered, it was 0.26 percent. The court held that it was an abuse of discretion to pay any part of the damages for future medical expenses over 50 years at that interest rate. Watts v. Lester E. Cox Medical Center, 376 S.W.3d 633 (Mo. 2012). The court noted that medical inflation would be much greater, and that the judgment guaranteed that plaintiff would not have adequate funds for medical care.

3. Structured settlements. A *structured settlement* provides for a stream of payments or for an annuity that pays a guaranteed and inflatable sum for as long as the victim lives. Advertising from insurance companies claims that 90 percent of plaintiffs who recover a lump sum over $100,000 have spent the entire judgment within five years. Whatever the precise number, it is surely true that many lump-sum payments are quickly dissipated. Structured settlements can preserve the plaintiff's judgment; they can also make it difficult or impossible to pay the many bills that accumulated before the judgment was paid. It is in the industry's interest to highlight the benefits, because an insurer either makes or guarantees the payments in a structured settlement.

Structured settlements have a significant tax advantage: If the settlement complies with IRS rules, all payments to plaintiff are compensation for personal injury, tax exempt under §104 of the Internal Revenue Code. Suppose that defendant promises to pay $60,000 per year for 40 years. To keep the example simple, suppose defendant invests $1,000,000 at 6 percent to earn the annual payments under the settlement. This income is taxable to the defendant, but defendant's payments to plaintiff are deductible as a business expense. The income and the deduction net out for defendant, and the payment is not taxable to plaintiff because of §104. But if the million dollars were paid to plaintiff in a lump sum, plaintiff's subsequent investment income would not be compensation for personal injury. The investment income would be taxable to plaintiff, and plaintiff would have no offsetting deduction. Instead of getting $60,000 after tax, he would be left with about $46,800. Thus, the structured settlement lets the parties effectively exempt the investment income from tax. Congress has approved this device in 26 U.S.C. §104(a)(2). For a much more sophisticated explanation of how these settlements are structured and of their tax treatment, see Gregg D. Polsky and Brant J. Hellwig, *Taxing Structured Settlements*, 51 B.C. L. Rev. 39 (2010).

4. Selling your structured settlement. An industry has grown up to buy structured settlements from plaintiffs who want or need immediate cash. The settlement agreement often prohibits such sales; in those cases, plaintiffs and buyers try to conceal their transactions from the insurance companies. Most states now require court approval of such sales; an example is 215 Ill. Comp. Stat. §153/15. But many courts do little or nothing to protect personal injury victims in this process; for illustrative abuses, see Karen Czapanskiy, *Structured Settlement Sales and Lead-Poisoned Sellers: Just Say No*, 36 Va. Envtl. L.J. 1 (2018). The industry leader's continued aggressive advertising suggests that this business is very profitable. See *www.jgwentworth.com*. If Wentworth can buy a stream of payments from a well-capitalized insurance company, and pay a price based on discounting the stream of payments to present value with an interest rate appropriate for consumer debtors, it has a formula for making very large amounts of money with very little risk. Professor Czapanskiy would ban the sale of structured settlements.

NOTES ON DAMAGES IN FOREIGN CURRENCY

1. Foreign currency debts. Changes in the value of money are even more problematic in international litigation. Consider a U.S. suit by a Swiss seller against a U.S. buyer for a purchase price stated in Swiss francs. Courts have traditionally rendered judgment in their own currency, converting foreign currency obligations as of the day of breach or the day of judgment. Conversion as of the day of breach more nearly places plaintiff in the position she would have occupied had she been paid on time. Conversion as of the day of judgment more nearly places her in the position she would have occupied had she sued and collected in Switzerland. Which is preferable? Does it matter whether the franc is appreciating or depreciating against the dollar? Would it matter if the buyer were deliberately speculating on a decline in the value of francs? Should the seller have to know about that?

A creditor with a foreign judgment rendered in foreign currency can sue in the United States to enforce that judgment. Remarkably, how to treat that foreign judgment is mostly a matter of state law. Most courts convert the foreign currency to dollars using the exchange rate on the date of the U.S. judgment; some use the rate on the date of the foreign judgment. Some of the cases are collected in *Restatement*

(Fourth) of the Foreign Relations Law of the United States—Jurisdiction §420, reporter's note 5 (Am. Law Inst. 2017).

2. More complicated cases. The foreign currency debt is the simplest possible foreign currency case. For a taste of the possible complexities, suppose a German seller defaults on a contract to deliver machinery to a U.S.-owned factory in Mexico. The buyer might have made partial payments in euros and suffered consequential damages in pesos; both losses will show up on the bottom line in dollars, and the litigation may be before an arbitrator in London. There is no contract stating an obligation in a specific currency; seller's obligation was to deliver machinery. What currency should buyer's losses be valued in? If that is not the currency of judgment or collection, as of what date should currency be converted?

3. Matching interest rates with currency. One of the few things that should be clear in this area is that the choice of currency should control the choice of interest rate. If Swiss interest rates are low because Swiss inflation is low, and if British interest rates are high because British inflation is high, plaintiff should not be able to collect British interest rates on a loss compensated in the more stable Swiss currency.

G.   DAMAGES WHERE VALUE CANNOT BE MEASURED IN DOLLARS

1.   *Personal Injuries and Death*

DEBUS v. GRAND UNION STORES
621 A.2d 1288 (Vt. 1993)

JOHNSON, Justice. . . .

Plaintiff was injured while shopping at defendant's store on August 23, 1985, when a pallet of boxes, piled high and imbalanced, toppled over and fell upon her. The boxes, containing cans of pet food, tumbled off the pallet and onto plaintiff when a store clerk . . . , attempted to move the overloaded pallet. Plaintiff suffered injuries resulting in a 20% permanent disability. The jury awarded plaintiff damages of $346,276.23.

I.

During closing argument, plaintiff suggested that the jury think about plaintiff's injury in terms of daily pain and suffering, and then determine what amount of damages would be appropriate compensation for each day of suffering. An average daily figure was suggested to the jury, which it could then multiply by the number of days plaintiff would live, counting from the day of the accident until the end of her life expectancy, some thirty-five years. The jury was told to consider the figure only if it found the calculations useful in quantifying plaintiff's damages. Defendant contends that such per diem arguments are unduly prejudicial and should have been disallowed by the trial court. Defendant further contends that if per diem arguments are permissible, the court should give cautionary instructions.

A per diem argument is a tool of persuasion used by counsel to suggest to the jury how it can quantify damages based on the evidence of pain and suffering presented.

Other jurisdictions are divided as to whether to allow such arguments. The principal reason advanced against per diem arguments is that a jury's verdict must be based on the evidence before it, and a per diem figure, which is not in evidence, allows the jury to calculate damages based solely on the argument of counsel. Further, courts have reasoned that a per diem argument unfairly assumes that pain is constant, uniform, and continuous, and that the pain will prevail for the rest of plaintiff's life. Therefore, it creates an "illusion of certainty" in a disability that is more likely to be subject to great variation. Finally, some courts conclude that the jury will be too easily misled by the plaintiff's argument.

On the other hand, jurisdictions that have allowed per diem arguments counter that sufficient safeguards exist in the adversarial system to overcome the objections to its use. They point out that a plaintiff's hypothesis on damages, even if presented on a per diem basis, must be reasonable or suffer serious and possibly fatal attack by opposing counsel; further, the notion that pain is constant and uniform may be easily rebutted by reference to the evidence or the jury's own experience. Most importantly, they note that juries are entitled to draw inferences from the evidence before them and that the extent of damages attributable to pain and suffering is a permissible inference.

After review of the arguments and authorities, we are persuaded that there is nothing inherently improper or prejudicial about per diem arguments if they are made under the ordinary supervision and control of the trial court. In cases where claims for pain and suffering are made, juries are forced to equate pain with damages. The jury can benefit by guidance offered by counsel in closing argument as to how they can construct that equation. We permit counsel reasonable latitude in this phase of the trial to summarize the evidence, to persuade the jury to accept or reject a plaintiff's claim, and to award a specific lump sum. If a lump sum is to be suggested to the jury,* it cannot be impermissible to explain how the lump sum was determined.

Nor do we agree with defendant that per diem arguments must be accompanied by specific instructions. Juries are routinely instructed that arguments and suggestions by counsel are not evidence, whether or not a party makes a per diem argument. It may well be that other instructions may be required when per diem arguments are used, but we leave to the trial courts the fashioning of instructions and controls appropriate to the cases before them.

Our holding should not be taken to grant the plaintiff carte blanche [unlimited discretion; literally, a blank card] to depart from any reasonable view of the evidence. Rather, it reflects our confidence that the defendant's opportunity to refute the plaintiff's closing argument will ensure that an absurd hypothesis will be rejected. Even if it is not, and a verdict is excessive, the trial court has adequate mechanisms, such as remittitur, to deal with it.

The question remains as to whether the per diem argument in the present case was improper. In closing argument, plaintiff's counsel told the jury the per diem figure was only a suggestion for its consideration, and that determining a fair amount would be entirely up to the jury. He did not argue that plaintiff's pain was constant, uniform, and easy to quantify on a daily basis. In fact, counsel told the jury that pain fluctuates and that he was only suggesting an average figure for their consideration, and told them to "[d]isregard it if it is not helpful." Defendant had a full opportunity

---

* Counsel's request that the jury award a lump sum amount is not error per se. Although the lump sum may be more consistent with counsel's hope than with the reality of the evidence, use of a lump sum, like a per diem damages argument, is not reversible error unless shown to be prejudicial.

to rebut the per diem argument and did so. We cannot conclude that this argument invaded the province of the jury.

The case was submitted to the jury with appropriate instructions. The trial court cautioned the jury that "the arguments of the attorneys and any statements which they made in their arguments or in their summation is not evidence and will not be considered by you as evidence," and that "it is your recollection of the witness's testimony and not the attorney's statements which shall control you in reaching your decision." The court made it clear to the jury that the final determination of damages was to be made on the evidence alone and not on persuasive arguments for any particular formulas. That the jury was able to make this distinction between presented evidence and suggested formulas is demonstrated by their arriving at a total damages award $166,194 below the figure suggested by plaintiff's counsel, which figure counsel calculated in part by using the per diem formula. There was no error. . . .

Affirmed.

ALLEN, Chief Justice, dissenting.

The majority reasons that if a lump sum award may be suggested to a jury, it cannot be impermissible to explain how the lump sum was determined. The difficulty with this rationale, however, is that, until today, it has been improper in Vermont to mention to the jury the lump sum being sought. . . . [T]he amount which the plaintiff hopes to recover is not evidence, proof of the amount due, or a standard for estimating the damages.

It is unnecessary here to set forth the various arguments in favor of or against per diem arguments as they have been thoroughly and exhaustively discussed in opinions from virtually every other jurisdiction over the past thirty years. I believe the better answer is to permit counsel to argue to the trier of fact the appropriateness of employing a time-unit calculation technique for fixing damages for pain and suffering, but to prohibit any suggestion by counsel of specific monetary amounts either on a lump sum or time-unit basis. This approach was suggested in King v. Railway Express Agency, 107 N.W.2d 509, 517 (N.D. 1961), and adopted by rule in New Jersey. Rule 1:7-1(b), New Jersey Rules of Court.

The ultimate objective should be to aid the jury in determining what sum of money will reasonably compensate the plaintiff for the pain and suffering endured. The attainment of this goal is not enhanced by counsel arguing the dollar amounts that they desire to have a jury return. The fair and practical solution is to permit the jury to hear about the methodology and to apply its dollar amounts from the evidence rather than sums suggested in argument.

I further disagree with the majority in its reluctance to require a specific cautionary instruction, beyond the general language offered that "the arguments of the attorneys and any statements which they made in their arguments or in their summation [are] not in evidence and will not be considered by you as evidence." The instruction approved by the majority may be adequate to deal with remarks of an attorney that are plainly argumentative. The difficulty is that remarks regarding numbers or dollar amounts may not appear to be argument, but rather evidence itself. Hence, an instruction not to consider argument as evidence does not cure the problem. . . .

The majority relies on the proposition that "[i]n closing argument, plaintiff's counsel told the jury the per diem figure was only a suggestion for its consideration, and that determining a fair amount would be entirely up to the jury." The majority is overly generous. Counsel's remarks are at best ambiguous and come at the beginning of a lengthy and detailed mathematical presentation. That presentation, stated in part, follows:

> What award will it take to tell Grand Union what accountability means and that this is what the people in Bennington County think a human life and human suffering is worth[?]
>
> Now, let's just take one element. We have talked about pain and suffering. What would be fair compensation for pain and suffering? *Entirely up to you.* I have a suggestion. If you think about what it is like for Susanne to go through one day with the pain that she has and think about what would be fair compensation for that one day, what do you think it would be? Would it be $100 to go through that in a day? Would it be $75? Would it be $50, $40?
>
> Ladies and gentlemen, we want to be scrupulously fair about our request to you. So I am going to suggest to you that you award Susanne $30 a day for the loss of those three elements: pain and suffering, mental anguish, and loss of enjoyment of life. That is $10 a day for each one. *I put it to you for your consideration to follow that through.*
>
> You would do it this way, there are 365 days a year. I am just going to put here pain and suffering, mental anguish, loss of enjoyment of life. Now there are 365 days in a year. And Susanne's six years she has already suffered in these ways and 29 more, that is 35 years total that she should be compensated for. And if you multiply 35 times 365, there are 12,775 days. And if you multiply that figure by the $30 per day I just suggested, it comes out to $383,250 — sorry. $383,250.
>
> Now, another way of thinking of that is if you divide 35 years into this figure of $383,250 it comes out to slightly under $11,000 a year. Maybe that would be a help to think for you $11,000 a year to live the way she lives, to lose what she has lost. *Perhaps that would be a help for you; I don't know.* (Emphasis added.)

The caveats in this argument are nearly invisible, and an additional statement in rebuttal is no better. The residue is a set of specific numbers that are, by the majority's holding, proper, but which at least deserve a specific cautionary instruction. Yet the majority would substitute counsel's at best ambiguous message for a clear instruction from the bench about the use of the numbers.

I would not, and I dissent.

NOTES ON PAIN AND SUFFERING

1. A persistent split. The most detailed survey of jurisdictions is reported in John Campbell, Bernard Chao, & Christopher Robertson, *Time Is Money: An Empirical Assessment of Non-Economic Damages Arguments*, 95 Wash. U. L. Rev. 1 (2017). They report that 23 states and the District of Columbia allow a total demand supported by a per diem calculation. Nine states allow a lump sum demand but do not allow a per diem calculation. Two states allow plaintiff to argue for per diem calculations without assigning a value to the unit of time suggested. Four states allow neither a per diem argument nor the mention of a total demand. The remaining states either leave these issues to the discretion of the trial judge or have no identifiable rule. Of course the cases are clear in some states and fuzzy in others. The federal circuits are also split; they treat the issue as procedural and apply federal law in diversity cases. More cases are collected in Annotation, 3 A.L.R.4th 940 (1981 & Supp.).

2. Another example. For an example with a much more detailed description of plaintiff's injuries, consider Westbrook v. General Tire & Rubber Co., 754 F.2d 1233 (5th Cir. 1985). Injuries to plaintiff's back and knee made it impossible for him to bend or lift or sit for long periods without pain. He was unable to hold any of the semiskilled jobs at which he had worked. He was unable to ride horses, water ski, follow his coon dogs through the woods, or participate in any other active recreation. His wife had to help him in and out of the car, and she had to do most of the lifting and pulling around the house. When he did have a job, he often came home too tired to do anything but lie down. He was often irritable and frustrated; his relationship with his children suffered. The couple had sex two or three times a week before the accident, but less than once a week after the accident.

Plaintiff's counsel suggested a dollar per waking hour for pain, suffering, and mental anguish, another dollar per waking hour for loss of leisure activities and capacity to enjoy life, and $25 a week for the wife's loss of consortium. With a life expectancy of 45.6 years (and apparently assuming 18-hour days), this produced a total of $597,000 for the husband and $59,000 for the wife. Plaintiff also claimed $328,000 in lost earning capacity. The jury awarded the exact sum requested, $984,000 in all. That would be about $2.3 million today.

The court of appeals commented that the verdict was "at or above the maximum permissible award," but it did not reverse on the ground that the verdict was excessive. It reversed because of improper jury argument, including the per diem argument, and relied on the size of the verdict only to show that the improper argument had been prejudicial.

Westbrook was not the last word in the Fifth Circuit. In Foradori v. Harris, 523 F.3d 477, 510-514 (5th Cir. 2008), a 15-year-old plaintiff was permanently paralyzed from the neck down. His lawyer suggested that less than $1,100 per day would yield $25 million; the jury awarded $10 million for pain and suffering and loss of enjoyment of life. The court said counsel's argument did not present the dangers of per diem arguments, partly because the jury obviously had not accepted the argument, but also because the argument was very short, and presented orally, without charts, graphs, or written calculations. The court seemed to think that the jury might mistake a lawyer's chart for evidence, but that it would recognize an oral closing argument as argument.

3. One hour, one day, or one lifetime? How can the court know or decide that $597,000 for pain and suffering and loss of enjoyment of life is at or above the maximum permissible? And how can it be more confident in its valuation of a lifetime of pain and suffering than in its (or the jury's) valuation of an hour of pain and suffering? An earlier Fifth Circuit opinion, disingenuously distinguished in *Westbrook*, said that "there is little logic in prohibiting the discussion of large units of time in terms of their smaller mathematical equivalents." Baron Tube Co. v. Transport Insurance Co., 365 F.2d 858, 868 (5th Cir. 1966).

If the minimum wage law says that even the least skilled form of labor is worth $7.25 an hour, isn't it pretty conservative to say that Westbrook's suffering is worth only $2.00 an hour, or that Debus's is worth only $30 a day? Why does $2.00 an hour or $10 or $30 a day sound like so little, and $597,000 and $383,000 sound like so much? One reason is that jurors are familiar with one- and two-digit numbers and have no experience at all with six-digit numbers. The difference in most people's subjective reactions to the different formulations is why the per diem argument sometimes works. Is that a reason to permit it or to forbid it?

4. Emotional adaptation. The award for a short-term injury is nearly always far more per unit of time than the award for a similar long-term injury. Juries award large sums for minutes or seconds of conscious terror in plane crashes or in fatal accidents where death comes quickly but not instantly. Plaintiffs do not want per diem reasoning in these cases. Partly these verdicts reflect the jurors' sense that a serious wrong requires a serious verdict. But they may also reflect how victims experience pain and suffering.

There is a large and controversial literature on emotional adaptation. Most victims of permanent injury eventually become partially adapted to their new situation; they do not remain as unhappy over time as they were at the beginning. Some of this literature is collected in John Bronsteen, Christopher Buccafusco, and Jonathan S. Masur, *Hedonic Adaptation and the Settlement of Civil Lawsuits*, 108 Colum. L. Rev. 1516 (2008). Bronsteen and his coauthors may present this literature with undue optimism; for example, they claim as favorable a study showing that victims of severe disability eventually recover 30 percent of their initial loss in happiness. *Id.* at 1529. That's not much, but it's something. Is it a reason to reject per diem arguments?

The more aggressive argument from this literature is that pain and suffering, and loss of capacity to enjoy life, should not be compensated at all. The claim is that victims adapt, so these damages soon end, and that juries cannot imagine adapting to such injuries, so these damages are wildly overvalued. There is a powerful response to these arguments in Rick Swedloff and Peter H. Huang, *Tort Damages and the New Science of Happiness*, 85 Ind. L.J. 553 (2010). The methodology in the happiness studies, which consists largely of asking people to rate their mood at intervals, does not seem nearly robust enough to support the conclusion that victims of serious injuries are as happy as they were before they were hurt. And a second generation of studies has seriously undermined the earlier studies and caused some proponents of the theory to confess error. One study asked victims of permanent injury or chronic illness how many years of their remaining life they would give up in exchange for a cure. There are obvious problems with this methodology too, but the answers were that they would give up substantial fractions of their remaining life expectancy to be healthy in the years that remained.

5. Present value. A promise to pay $30 a day for 35 years is not really worth $383,000, because the promise of $30 in 35 years is not worth anything like $30 today. Discounted to present value at 2 percent, that stream of payments would be worth only about $250,000 instead of $383,000.

A minority of jurisdictions reduce pain-and-suffering awards to present value. Some of the cases are collected in Annotation, 28 A.L.R. 1177 (1924 & Supp.). An example is Delano v. United States, 859 F. Supp. 2d 487, 507, 509 (W.D.N.Y. 2012), applying New York law. Does it make any sense to pick a round number out of the air for a lifetime of pain and suffering, and then subject it to precise calculations of present value? Does it make more sense if the original number is carefully calculated at the rate of so much per hour or day?

6. Monstrous verdicts? Compare another court's remark that "no amount of money per day could compensate a person reduced to plaintiff's position, and to attempt such evaluation . . . leads only to monstrous verdicts." Ahlstrom v. Minneapolis, St. Paul & Sault Ste. Marie Railroad, 68 N.W.2d 873, 891 (Minn. 1955). Should the fear of "monstrous verdicts" play any role in assessing these issues? Or should we expect monstrous verdicts only in cases of monstrous injuries?

7. Suggesting a lump sum. The majority and dissenter in *Debus* disagree about whether Vermont had permitted counsel to suggest a lump sum figure. Whoever had the better of that argument in Vermont, the overwhelming majority rule is that counsel may suggest a total number for pain and suffering and tell the jury how much is requested in the complaint. But four states forbid even this. Does it make any sense to leave the jury utterly without guidance on the amount? But how much guidance does the jury really get from the argument of counsel? There is evidence that counsel's suggestion of a number "anchors"—becomes the starting point for—the jury's deliberations.

8. The Golden Rule? Another approach to pain and suffering is the Golden Rule argument, which asks jurors how much they would want if they had suffered plaintiff's injuries. This argument has been consistently disallowed. The appeal to put themselves in plaintiff's shoes is an appeal to abandon neutrality; defendant might as plausibly urge jurors to imagine how much they would want to pay if they had inflicted these injuries.

9. Market value? One other argument on pain and suffering is that jurors should give the market value of the injuries, or the amount it would cost to hire someone to suffer these injuries. So far as your editors are aware, no state permits that argument. Why should that be? Isn't that the measure most analogous to the measure in property-damage cases and other cases we have read? If we are serious about making plaintiff as well off as she would have been but for the wrong, don't we have to think about what people would actually view as an even trade?

Of course the analogy has problems. There is no market in pain and suffering. One can imagine hiring persons to undergo modest pain and suffering, in medical experiments, for example, but such experimental subjects are generally people with very few other options. It is hard to imagine hiring a person to suffer permanent paralysis or serious brain damage for any sum of money. Is the jury better off with no guidance, or with the guidance of trying to imagine an unimaginable transaction? People undergo substantial risks of serious injury, partly for money, but more for thrill, fame, glory, or patriotism. Think about football players, stunt car drivers, and members of the military. It would be hard to build a compensation scale from those transactions.

10. An experiment. Experimenters asked law students and lay people to award damages for a series of significant but not catastrophic personal injuries. Some respondents were simply told to award "appropriate" compensation; this is roughly equivalent to the standard jury instruction in most states. Some were told to award the amount that would be required to make them whole if they had suffered these injuries. And some were told to award the amount they would demand to suffer these injuries in a voluntary transaction. The results are not very clearly explained, but the basic pattern is unmistakable. After controlling for outliers, the make-whole instruction roughly doubled the awards, and the selling-price instruction roughly doubled them again. Edward J. McCaffery, Daniel J. Kahneman, and Matthew L. Spitzer, *Framing the Jury: Cognitive Perspectives on Pain and Suffering Awards*, 81 Va. L. Rev. 1341 (1995).

The team also got interesting responses in a survey of lawyers and judges. All recognized that the Golden Rule argument was prohibited in their jurisdiction, and most thought the selling-price argument prohibited, absurd, or both, but a large minority said they had seen plaintiffs' lawyers subtly slip elements of these approaches into their jury argument, and some offered ways to do it without creating reversible error.

11. More experiments. Campbell, Chao, & Robertson, cited in note 1, created a 40-minute video of the high points of a medical-malpractice trial: expert testimony, jury instructions, and opening and closing argument. The case was designed to be close on liability. They created four variations with and without a per diem argument and with or without a lump sum demand.

The per diem calculation increased awards modestly; suggesting $5 million increased awards much more dramatically. The mean award in the versions with the lump sum anchor were $2,042,006 and $1,887,500. The mean awards in the versions without the lump sum were $714,317 and $473,489. The medians were $1 million, $1 million, $275,000, and $225,000. These were the awards of individual mock jurors; there was no opportunity for deliberation with others. The authors collect other studies also suggesting that plaintiffs get more when they ask for a big lump sum. This is the anchoring effect.

A similar study tested high and low anchors and alternatives for how defense counsel might respond. John Campbell, Bernard Chao, Christopher Robertson and David V. Yokum, *Countering the Plaintiff's Anchor: Jury Simulations to Evaluate Damages Arguments*,

101 Iowa L. Rev. 543 (2016). Half the plaintiff's counsel asked for $250,000; half asked for $5 million, which the experimenters thought was unrealistically high on the facts. One-third of defense counsel ignored the lump sum demand; one-third countered, arguing that there was no liability but if the jury disagreed, damages should not exceed $50,000; and one-third ridiculed plaintiff's demand and argued that it showed that the jury could not trust anything the plaintiff and his lawyer said. And this time, the authors used sophisticated statistical methods to simulate jury deliberation, which tended to moderate the responses of individual mock jurors.

The $5 million demand increased damages from a mean of $65,000 to a mean of $278,000 in the simulated jury deliberations. But the high demand did affect plaintiff's credibility; it significantly reduced the percentage of verdicts for plaintiff. The effect on the magnitude of damages was much bigger than the effect on winning or losing, so the $5 million demand increased the expected value of the case. That makes the unrealistically high demand clearly in the interest of the lawyer, who can average out his experience over many cases. The interests of the client are different. He has only one case, and recovering nothing is a disaster. How to balance the risk of losing against the chance of increasing the verdict is a more complex choice than simply calculating expected values.

When plaintiff asked for $250,000, countering with $50,000 appeared to reduce the size of verdicts and reduce the number of plaintiff verdicts, and most of the differences were statistically significant. Many defense lawyers fear that suggesting a number will be taken to concede liability; this experiment suggests otherwise.

12. Loss of capacity to enjoy life. What if plaintiff is comatose or otherwise incapable of feeling pain? Many courts award substantial damages in such cases, either as part of pain and suffering or separately under the label "loss of capacity to enjoy life." Cases going both ways are collected in Alexandra Preece, Comment, *Joyless Life and Lifeless Joy: The Recovery of Hedonic Damages by Plaintiffs in a Persistent Vegetative State*, 50 San Diego L. Rev. 721 (2013). "Hedonic" damages, from the same root as hedonism, is used in multiple ways but most commonly refers to loss of capacity to enjoy life.

In McDougald v. Garber, 536 N.E.2d 372 (N.Y. 1989), New York's highest court held that there can be no compensation under either label unless plaintiff had "some level of awareness" of her loss. Two dissenters thought that loss of capacity to enjoy life was an objective fact, like loss of a leg, not dependent on plaintiff's subjective awareness, and distinct from pain and suffering. Disagreeing with the *McDougald* majority, a New Jersey court in Eyoma v. Falco, 589 A.2d 653 (N.J. Super. Ct. App. Div. 1991), held that a plaintiff put in a comatose state through a nurse's post-surgery medical malpractice could recover damages for loss of capacity to enjoy life but not damages for pain and suffering. "It would be fallacious to sever loss of enjoyment of life from disability and impairment by equating it with the anxiety suffered as a result of being aware of that loss. As stated, anxiety is compensable only if it is consciously suffered. However, the actual loss of enjoyment of life is not a function of pain and suffering. Rather, it is an element of the permanent injury plaintiff has suffered." *Id.* at 662.

Conscious plaintiffs who experience pain also experience reduced capacity to enjoy life. More generally, thinking through exactly what a victim of serious injury loses has led to a proliferation of categories and labels that inevitably overlap. The Texas court collected cases struggling with such distinctions in Golden Eagle Archery, Inc. v. Jackson, 116 S.W.3d 757 (Tex. 2003). In many states, these difficulties present questions of how to craft jury instructions; in states that ask juries to separately value distinct items of damage, they present questions of how to review awards for overlapping categories. The *Golden Eagle* jury awarded separate sums for physical pain and mental anguish, disfigurement, loss of vision, and other physical impairment. The court upheld an award of zero for other physical impairment. None of these terms were defined in a jury instruction, and the court thought the jury might reasonably have included physical impairment in pain and suffering.

NOTES ON WRONGFUL DEATH

1. The basic elements of recovery. Wrongful death cases raise equally intractable valuation problems. All American jurisdictions award funeral expenses and some measure of compensation for the financial support that decedent would have provided to dependents. Most permit recovery for the monetary value of services the decedent would have provided. Compensation for such "services" began with household chores and homemaking; it now usually includes the nurture, training, education, and guidance that children would have received from their parents or that one spouse would have received from the other.

2. Loss of society vs. grief. A smaller majority permits dependents to recover for loss of "society," which may include love, affection, care, attention, companionship, comfort, and protection. Society is limited to the positive benefits plaintiffs would have received if decedent had lived. Most jurisdictions do not allow recovery for grief, mental anguish, emotional distress, or other negative experiences resulting from the death. One may wonder how juries understand this distinction between failure to experience positive emotions and the much more obvious experience of negative emotions, but that has come to be the law in many jurisdictions.

A growing minority of jurisdictions now permit, by statute or judicial decision, compensation for grief and emotional distress. Cases with respect to grief over the loss of children are collected in Annotation, 45 A.L.R. 4th 234 (1986 & Supp.). Plaintiffs in these jurisdictions sometimes offer the testimony of "grief experts" or "thanatologists" to help the jury understand or value grief. Conflicting cases on whether to admit such testimony are collected in Carter v. United States, 2014 WL 3895751 (E.D Va. 2014).

3. Lives without value? The emphasis on financial support as the principal measure of recovery left three classes of persons whose deaths caused little recoverable damage: children, retired persons, and adults without dependents. These decedents provide no financial support to others, and their cases have driven the expansion of recoverable damages to include loss of society and intangible services. Whether the parents or other relatives of an unmarried adult may recover for loss of society often depends on the details of each state's wrongful death act. Compare Crowl v. M. Chin Realty Trust, 700 F. Supp. 2d 171 (D. Mass. 2010) ("next of kin" under Massachusetts law) with Armantrout v. Carlson, 214 P.3d 914 (Wash. 2009) ("dependent for support" under Washington law).

4. Loss of inheritance. An additional measure of recovery, in most states that have considered the issue, is loss of inheritance. If decedent's earnings are large enough to accumulate a surplus beyond what would be spent on self and dependents, that surplus cannot be recovered as loss of support, but it may be recoverable as loss of inheritance. States that deny recovery for loss of inheritance tend to do so on the ground that it is too speculative. Many Americans never save, and many others begin saving late in life. How can a jury decide whether a decedent who never saved a dime would have begun saving when his children were grown and his retirement approached, and that he would have died naturally before exhausting his savings, leaving an inheritance and leaving all of it to the plaintiffs? A Louisiana court found this too much to speculate about even in a case where decedent was regularly putting 16 percent of his pay into a tax-sheltered retirement plan. Hollingsworth v. State, 663 So. 2d 357 (La. 1996).

Assuming some savings, how much? Even a modest rate of saving can produce huge sums if one assumes sound investments, steady additions, and no withdrawals. A good example is In re Air Crash Disaster, 795 F.2d 1230 (5th Cir. 1986), where an expert testified that plaintiffs would have inherited nearly $1.8 million if their parents had lived. The court said the witness used "assumptions without basis in the real world" of the parents, and set aside the verdict. But there are also cases where decedent was plainly accumulating an estate and adding to it every year. So most courts treat the speculative nature of prospective inheritance as a matter of proof instead of a per se barrier. In Gardner v. State, 24 N.Y.S.3d 805 (App. Div. 2015), the court split the difference between competing experts on how much decedent was consuming and how much he was saving, and then for unexplained reasons awarded half the projected savings as loss of inheritance.

5. The value of decedent's life to himself. Connecticut, New Mexico, and Georgia allow recovery for the value of decedent's life to himself. Romero v. Byers, 872 P.2d 840, 845-846 (N.M. 1994); Anderson v. Steve Snyder Enterprises, 491 A.2d 389, 397 n.12 (Conn. 1985); Ga. Code §51-4-2(a) (surviving relatives "may recover the full value of the life of the decedent"). This is the most obvious loss in a wrongful death case, wholly excluded from all traditional measures of recovery. The obvious difficulties of valuation are considered in section 2.G.2. The Georgia statute has been on the books since 1887; speaking only impressionistically, it does not seem to have made any great difference in the size of wrongful death judgments.

But it may have mattered to the jury verdict in Chrysler Group, LLC v. Walden, 792 S.E.2d 754 (Ga. Ct. App. 2016), *aff'd on other grounds,* 812 S.E.2d 244 (Ga. 2018). An SUV with a plastic gas tank mounted behind the rear axle burst into flame in a rear-end collision; a four-year-old boy was burned to death. The jury awarded $30 million for the boy's pain and suffering and $120 million for the value of his life. Punitive damages were not at issue, but the jury found that Chrysler acted with reckless disregard for human life. This finding mattered to application of a ten-year statute of repose, and the verdict may have contained a large punitive element.

Chrysler's motion for new trial said that the wrongful death award was more than 11 times the largest award previously upheld in Georgia, and that the largest previous pain and suffering award was $7 million for a plaintiff who was hospitalized for months, paralyzed, and in severe pain. It argued that $30 million for one minute of suffering, however intense, is irrational. The trial judge reduced the award to $10 million for pain and suffering and $30 million for the value of the child's life. He refused to grant a new trial, calling the evidence at the first trial "overwhelming." The court of appeals affirmed. The appeal to the state supreme court did not further challenge the amount of damages.

6. Valuing loss of society. What is the value of society, services, companionship, and similar elements of damage? In Norfolk & Western Railway v. Liepelt, 444 U.S. 490 (1980), reprinted in section 2.F.1, decedent was a railroad fireman. He was survived by a wife, two young children, and two older children from an earlier marriage. Plaintiff's expert estimated the decedent's lost earnings, plus the value of the services he would have performed for his family, less the amounts he would have spent on himself, to be $302,000. Defendant's estimate was substantially less. The jury returned a verdict for $775,000. Plaintiff argued "that the excess is adequately explained by the jury's estimate of the pecuniary value of the guidance, instruction and training that the decedent would have provided to his children."

What does it mean to say that "guidance, instruction and training" is worth $473,000? That the father's guidance and training would have enabled the children to earn that much more during their lifetime? That the children would spend that much to purchase substitute guidance and training? That being fatherless increases the risk of a wide range of social ills, from delinquency and drug addiction to an earlier end to formal education, and that those substantial risks must have some substantial value? Or does this verdict simply illustrate that juries will find a way to compensate for grief and emotional distress even though they are told not to?

7. Why not grief? Is there any reason to pretend that we do not compensate for grief and emotional distress in wrongful death cases? In Carey v. Piphus, reprinted in section 2.G.3, the Supreme Court said that "distress is a personal injury familiar to the law." Why do we allow recovery for emotional distress in constitutional and dignitary torts but not for the death of a loved one? Is it the fear of monstrous verdicts again? The mere accident that wrongful death law was codified in the nineteenth century, when the understanding of proper compensation was less generous? The general pattern of different damage rules for negligence and intentional tort?

Large verdicts like the one in *Liepelt* suggest that jurors compensate for grief even when they are told not to. But there are also small verdicts; some juries do as they are told and not as they are expected. And consider Green v. Bittner, 424 A.2d 210 (N.J. 1980), where, with liability established, a jury found no damages for the wrongful death of a high school senior. The state supreme court commented on the "conscientious" jury. But it ordered a new trial on damages, and it slightly expanded New Jersey's restrictive measure of damages for the deaths of children. Another jury awarded zero for the wrongful death of a wife and mother with a three-year-old conviction for welfare fraud; the court held the conviction inadmissible because decedent's general character was not at issue. Johnson v. Dobrosky, 902 A.2d 238 (N.J. 2006).

An Arizona jury awarded $1 million to the widow and zero to the children in the wrongful death of the husband/father. Walsh v. Advanced Cardiac Specialists Chartered, 273 P.3d 645 (Ariz. 2012). This may have just been confusion about whether it mattered how the verdict was divided. The court said such verdicts were permissible even when the evidence was uncontested, but it directed the trial court to consider the children's motion for a new trial. Some jurisdictions hold that a verdict for plaintiff with a finding of zero damages is inconsistent and must be resubmitted to the jury or retried. Cases going both ways are collected in Stevens v. Allen, 536 S.E.2d 663 (S.C. 2000).

These are not the only zero verdicts, and verdicts in the low five digits are fairly common. Verdicts that are small but not zero are much less likely to result in new trials. The denial of recovery for grief must be defended on the ground that it is just, not on the ground that it is ineffective. But why is it just?

8. Variation in verdicts. Compare the damage assessments in Tables 2-1 and 2-2, all of which were quickly culled from a single annual volume of *Verdicts, Settlements, and Tactics.* Variations in awards for adult decedents may be partly explained by differences in earning capacity and life expectancy, but most of the variation appears in elements of damage unrelated to earning capacity. In the children's cases, earning capacity and life expectancy make little difference, and all the plaintiffs are parents. What explains the differences there? The law of the jurisdiction? Whether the death was especially painful or lingering? Whether the defendants were especially culpable? Or especially appealing? The credibility of the competing lawyers? Can any list of factors legitimate such extraordinary variations in the valuation of human lives?

The awards for adult decedents range from $110,000 to $72,000,000, but the variations can be even greater. A similar table of close-in-time verdicts in an earlier edition of this casebook ranged from $200,000 to $268,000,000.

9. Variation in relationships. Perhaps the variation in jury verdicts reflects not the value of human life, but the value of the relationships between decedents and their survivors. Consider Woodbury v. Nichols, 797 P.2d 556 (Wyo. 1990), where the jury found liability for the wrongful death of an 18-year-old son and awarded zero damages, in a state that authorizes recovery for "loss of companionship, society, and comfort." The state supreme court affirmed:

> Although each of the family members testified to the essentially loving and close relationship that existed between them all, on cross-examination it was revealed: that the father had virtually never paid child support to Michael's mother . . . ; that Michael was sent by his mother to Wyoming to live with his father and complete high school because she was unable to keep him in school and out of trouble; and that there had been only infrequent contact between Michael and his brother during the years just preceding Michael's death.

Id. at 558. Michael was killed in a one-car crash in his own car, with a friend driving; both boys were drunk, and the car's speed was estimated at 134 miles per hour. The jury dealt separately with Michael's comparative fault, holding him 45 percent responsible for the accident. *Id.* at 557. Fifty-five percent of nothing is nothing. Was there a better way for plaintiffs' lawyer to present this case?

Compare Gamble v. Hill, 156 S.E.2d 888 (Va. 1967), holding that evidence of the dead child's moral delinquencies was inadmissible, because it had no tendency to prove that the parents suffered a smaller loss. "[T]he parents of a wayward child may have a deep affection for it. If authority for this position be needed, it is found in the parable of the Prodigal Son." *Id.* at 894. (In this Christian story, a younger son asks for his inheritance in advance, squanders it in riotous living, and returns home in disgrace. His father greets him warmly and celebrates his return: "For this my son was dead and is alive again; he was lost, and is found." Luke 15:24.)

For conflicting cases on evidence of decedent's bad character, see Annotation, 99 A.L.R.2d 972 (1965 & Supp.). Many cases admit such evidence; many of those that exclude it do so on the ground that the particular evidence offered is not recent or otherwise not probative. It also matters whether the evidence is offered to show that decedent was not a reliable source of financial support, or that decedent's moral guidance had little value, or, as in *Woodbury* and *Gamble*, that plaintiffs suffered little grief or loss of society. A Louisiana case excluded evidence of drug use on the ground that its prejudicial effect outweighed its probative value. Williams v. Board of Supervisors, 135 So. 3d 804 (La. Ct. App. 2014). Plaintiff's attorney can open the door to evidence that would otherwise be excluded by commenting on the decedent's good moral character. An example is Sanchez v. City of New York, 949 N.Y.S.2d 368 (App. Div. 2012), admitting evidence of a recent conviction for shoplifting. The jury still brought in a substantial verdict.

The quality of marriages may be even more variable than the quality of children. An Ohio jury brought in a zero verdict for the wrongful death of a wife and stillborn child, where there was some evidence that the marriage had had "difficulties," and the husband remarried only three months later. Peña v. Northeast Ohio Emergency Affiliates, Inc., 670 N.E.2d 268 (Ohio 1995). The court granted a new trial, in part because the husband was not the only plaintiff; two minor children were also entitled to recover.

Most trial lawyers believe, undoubtedly with good reason, that damages are affected by any personal characteristic that affects the attractiveness of the decedent, or her survivors, or of the plaintiff in a personal injury case. Such factors may be positive or negative character traits that are formally irrelevant to damages, or they may be wholly illegitimate factors such as race and sex.

10. The human situation. Money can replace the decedent's financial support, and some of decedent's services may be replaceable in the market. But it is obvious that money

Table 2-1

Representative Assessments of Damage for Wrongful Death of Children

Case	Decedent	Damages	Special Facts	Elements of Damage
Messick v. Chesapeake Women's Care, P.A., 36 VST No. 2, NL 17 (Maryland 2015)	Baby, 2 days	$250,000	Failure to take steps to prevent premature delivery; liability evidence appears to have been weak.	$150,000 to mother; $100,000 to father; not further described. Maryland allows recovery for grief and loss of society, both broadly defined.
Wilson v. Swanson, 36 VST No. 7, NL 1 (Pennsylvania 2016)	Boy, 2 weeks	$1,300,000	Administered fatal overdose of drug during surgery.	$300,000 for child's lost future earnings; $1,000,000 for wrongful death; not further described. Pennsylvania does not compensate loss of society, except for spouses.
Hughes v. Niedens, 36 VST No. 7, NL 11 (Missouri 2016)	Stillborn infant	$2,500,000	Diagnosed but failed to monitor growing blood clot in mother, resulting in cutting off oxygen to baby.	$875,000 for personal injury to baby; $1,625,000 for wrongful death; neither further described. Missouri compensates loss of companionship.
Pointer v. Franciscan Alliance, Inc., 36 VST No. 6, NL 8 (Illinois 2016)	Boy, 7	$4,000,000	Irreversible brain damage during 12 hours of transfers among 3 hospitals during acute asthma attack.	Settlement. Damages not described. Illinois compensates grief and loss of society.
Haig v. Mayor, 36 VST No. 9, NL 7 (Illinois 2015)	Boy, 2 months	$5,072,030	Baby had congenital heart condition with 50% chance of survival; immediate cause of death was medication that baby was too dehydrated to tolerate.	$2,500,000 loss of society to parents; $2,500,000 grief, sorrow, and mental suffering to parents; $50,000 loss of society to sister; $10,000 pain and suffering to baby; $12,030 funeral expenses. Also $275,000 in settlements with other defendants.

Table 2-1 *(continued)*

Case	Decedent	Damages	Special Facts	Elements of Damage
Fils-Aime v. Marante, 36 VST No. 3, NL 5 (Florida 2015), *aff'd mem.*, 228 So. 3d 571 (Fla. Dist. Ct. App. 2017)	Boy, 15	$7,011,000	Admitted to hospital with acute respiratory distress; quit breathing when anesthetic administered. Earlier recommendation to transfer to university hospital had not been acted on.	Not described. Undisclosed settlements with two additional defendants. Florida compensates grief and loss of society.
Bethea v. Infantino, LLC, 36 VST No. 3, NL 43 (New Jersey 2015)	Boy, 25 days	$7,250,000	Baby suffocated in defective infant carrier on mother's back. Not the first such death.	Settlement. Damages not described. New Jersey compensates "pecuniary injuries," including lost services and advice of the sort available in the market, but not loss of society or grief.
Karow v. Evenflo Co., 36 VST No. 5, NL 51 (California 2016)	Girl, 7 months	$8,000,000	Baby suffocated while napping on defective mattress.	"Non-economic" damages. $1,000,000 past and $3,000,000 future to each parent, not further described. California compensates loss of society.
King v. Whirlpool Corp., 36 VST No. 9, NL 47 (Illinois 2016)	Girl, 1	$10,713,601	Died from third-degree burns in bathtub, caused by defective hot-water heater. Lived with burns for nearly 2 months.	$1,800,000 for grief, sorrow, and mental suffering; $1,800,000 for loss of society; $1,800,000 for child's loss of normal life; $1,800,000 for child's pain and suffering; $1,800,000 for child's emotional distress; $1,000,000 for loss of benefit child would have contributed in future; $713,601 medical expenses.

Table 2-1 (continued)

Case	Decedent	Damages	Special Facts	Elements of Damage
Nash v. VHS Physicians of Michigan, 36 VST No. 11, NL 2 (Michigan 2016)	Girl, 3 months	$19,000,000	Failure to diagnose pneumonia in baby known to have serious respiratory problems.	Loss of society. Damage cap reduced this to $900,000 range.
Hotchkiss v. Ng-Wagner, 36 VST No. 4, NL 16 (Maryland 2016)	Girl, 3 weeks	$44,105,000	Baby died after extremely premature birth to surrogate mother. Surrogate's previous pregnancy had ended in similarly premature birth from same cause, but fertility doctor had failed to check her records.	$42,000,000 "non-economic" damages; $2,100,000 to baby's estate, presumably for pain and suffering. Maryland compensates grief and loss of society, both broadly defined. But damage cap reduced combined recovery to about $900,000.

Table 2-2
Representative Assessments of Damage for Wrongful Death of Adults

Case	Decedent	Plaintiffs	Damages	Special Facts	Elements of Damage
Franklin/King v. Penn Presbyterian Medical Center, 36 VST No. 11, NL 14 (Pennsylvania 2016).	Elderly woman	Not identified	$110,000	Patient with multiple serious medical problems shuttled between hospital and nursing home. Trial appeared to focus on infected bed sores. Jury verdict for hospital but against nursing home and its doctor.	$40,000 for patient, presumably pain and suffering; $70,000 for wrongful death; $200,000 settlement with another defendant. Damages not further described. Pennsylvania does not compensate loss of society, except for spouses.
Burkhart v. Emergency Medicine Assoc., P.A., 36 VST No. 12, NL 5 (Maryland 2016)	Woman	Husband, 4 adult children	$428,410	Failure to diagnose internal bleeding. Basic diagnostic steps not taken. Patient had multiple pre-existing conditions.	$125,000 "non-economic" damages to husband; $127,000 loss of household services; $30,000 "non-economic" damages to each child; $38,610 medical expenses; $8,900 funeral expenses; $8,900 "non-economic" damages to patient, presumably pain and suffering.
Larkin v. Regents of Univ. of California, 36 VST No. 8, NL 34 (California 2016)	Woman, 44	Children, 10 and 11	$1,750,000	Failure to diagnose and treat gastric leak after hernia surgery.	"Non-economic" damages, not further described. California compensates loss of society. Reduced to $250,000 by damage cap.
Sobo v. Hayes, 36 VST No. 2, NL 14 (Maryland 2015)	Woman	Husband, 2 Children	$2,600,000	Failure to diagnose urinary tract infection.	$1,100,000 economic damages; $1,500,000 "non-economic" damages. Neither is further described. Maryland compensates grief and loss of society, both broadly defined. Damage cap reduced the "non-economic" damages to about $800,000.

Table 2-2 (continued)

Case	Decedent	Plaintiffs	Damages	Special Facts	Elements of Damage
Wickersham v. Ford Motor Co., 36 VST No. 9, NL 45 (South Carolina 2016)	Man	Wife	$4,650,000	Airbag deployed late, breaking bones in face, destroying one eye, and causing chronic pain. Driver, who had history of mental illness, committed suicide a year later, allegedly because of the pain. Ford held 70% responsible.	$1,250,000 for pain and suffering; $650,000 for pre-death loss of consortium; $1,375,000 for post-death loss of consortium; $1,375,000 for wrongful death, not further described. South Carolina compensates loss of society and lost services and training.
Tong-Summerford v. Abington Memorial Hospital, 36 VST No. 6, NL 29 (Pennsylvania 2016)	Man, 88	Not identified	$5,000,000	Feeding tube inserted into lung instead of stomach; patient drowned in feeding solution over 14-hour period.	$1,500,000 for wrongful death; $3,500,000 for survival action; $1,500,000 for patient, presumably pain and suffering. Pennsylvania does not compensate loss of society, except for spouses.
Britt v. Northrop Grumman Systems Corp., 36 VST No. 12, NL 37 (Florida 2016), *aff'd on other grounds*, 2017 WL 7790130 (Fla. Dist. Ct. App. 2017)	Benefits manager	Wife	$9,019,266	Mesothelioma from asbestos at defendant's work site.	$8,500,000 for loss of companionship, protection, and mental pain and suffering; $507,381 medical expenses; $11,885 funeral expenses.

Table 2-2 (*continued*)

Case	Decedent	Plaintiffs	Damages	Special Facts	Elements of Damage
Gonzalez v. Atlas Construction Supply, Inc., 36 VST No. 9, NL 53 (California 2016)	Construction worker, 30	Not identified	$26,953,170	Killed when 30-foot wall collapsed at work site.	$3.5 million economic damages; $23.5 million "non-economic" damages. Neither is further described. California compensates loss of society. 45% of this allocated to employer and thus unenforceable. Employer is immune in tort and liable only in worker's compensation for much smaller sums.
Marion v. Little, 36 VST No. 1, NL 35 (Georgia 2015)	Female school bus driver, 37	7 children	$36,000,000	Surgeon mistakenly tied off descending aorta after kidney surgery. By the time mistake was discovered, catastrophic damage to lower half of body. 19 months of continuous hospitalization before death from these causes.	$11,000,000 for wrongful death, not further described. Georgia compensates value of decedent's life to herself. $25,000,000 for pain and suffering, medical expenses, and funeral expenses.
Estate of Fox v. Johnson & Johnson, 2016 WL 799325 (Mo. Cir. Ct. 2016), *rev'd on other grounds*, 539 S.W.3d 48 (Mo. Ct. App. 2017)	Woman, 62	Not identified	$72,000,000	Decedent contracted ovarian cancer from use of talcum powder. Defendant had known of risk since 1980s.	$10,000,000 compensatory, not described; $62,000,000 punitive. Missouri compensates loss of companionship.

cannot replace the decedent. Some insight into the human situation of wrongful death plaintiffs comes from press coverage of a school bus accident in which 21 children drowned and 60 others survived. The death cases were promptly settled for amounts ranging from $1.5 to $4.5 million. (Why a 300 percent range for essentially identical cases? Informal reports in legal circles say that those families who hired the best-known and most fearsome personal injury lawyer in the county got the big settlements; those who hired lesser lawyers got lesser settlements.) The following account is from a newspaper story on the first anniversary of the accident:

> For several months after the wreck, the community drew together to comfort the families of the victims, who for the most part remain withdrawn and refuse to speak with reporters. . . .
> Now, however, in the aftermath of what was considered an unspeakable tragedy, many have begun to whisper about ill-gotten wealth, causing some residents to believe the accident has caused wounds that will never heal.
> "The families are building brand new homes, their kids are driving brand new cars. Some of them are even wearing diamond rings," said one man. "All that money went to those people's heads." . . .
> Several families are constructing spacious new homes that jut upwards like skyscrapers among the mostly shabby-looking houses of this poverty-stricken Hidalgo County town where many residents are former migrant workers.
> "The money. Everybody talks about the money," says Ruben Buentello, who is building one of the homes. "The money doesn't help any of us. The money can't give us back what we lost." . . .
> Myrta Cardona, a social worker at the Mission school who was hired to help students and family members cope, said rumors about how families are spending money from the settlements has caused only more pain and suffering.
> "They feel guilty about the money," she said. "They've heard the rumors, and they worry about how others perceive them. Most of them were very poor, and now suddenly they have money.
> "But I can tell you that none of them is flaunting it or bragging about it," Cardona added. "Most of them still live right here. Their kids still go to the same school."

Scott W. Wright, *Living With Pain*, Austin American-Statesman (Sept. 21, 1990). One of your editors once had a student from the community affected by this accident. She thought that Wright's story unfairly emphasized the negative, and that the money did more good and caused less resentment than the story suggests.

For these plaintiffs, all the money seems like new wealth, because financial support is not what they lost. What they lost is utterly irreplaceable and made a fundamental change in their lives; the money they received was otherwise utterly unobtainable and also made a fundamental change in their lives. Is that as close to even as we can come? Does anyone think it would be better to leave them uncompensated?

2. The Controversy over Tort Law

ARBINO v. JOHNSON & JOHNSON
880 N.E.2d 420 (Ohio 2007)

[Melisa Arbino sued Johnson & Johnson in federal court, alleging that she suffered blood clots and other serious side effects caused by the Ortho Evra Birth Control Patch. The federal judge certified to the Ohio Supreme Court the question whether the limit on "noneconomic" damages in Ohio Rev. Code Ann. §2315.18 (LexisNexis 2005) violates the Ohio Constitution.]

MOYER, C.J. . . .

II. TORT REFORM IN OHIO AND STARE DECISIS . . .

Since 1975, the General Assembly has adopted several so-called tort-reform acts . . . .

[In Morris v. Savoy, 576 N.E.2d 765 (Ohio 1991), we held that a $200,000 cap on general damages, in medical malpractice cases not involving death, with no exceptions for the most severe injuries,] violated the due-process protections of the Ohio Constitution. We specifically noted that "[i]t is irrational and arbitrary to impose the cost of the intended benefit to the general public solely upon a class consisting of those most severely injured by medical malpractice." *Id.* at 771. . . .

In Sorrell v. Thevenir, 633 N.E.2d 504 (Ohio 1994), we . . . held that . . . mandatory deduction of collateral [source] benefits violated the right to a jury trial, due process, equal protection, and the right to a remedy.

In Galayda v. Lake Hospital System, Inc., 644 N.E.2d 298 (Ohio 1994), we [invalidated a] statute [that] required trial courts to order awards of future damages in excess of $200,000 in medical-malpractice actions to be paid in a series of periodic payments upon the motion of any party. . . .

[I]n Zoppo v. Homestead Insurance Co., 644 N.E.2d 397 (Ohio 1994), . . . [the] statute required a trial judge to determine the amount of punitive damages to be awarded in a tort action, even when the trier of fact was a jury. We struck this section as a violation of the right to a jury trial. . . .

[In 1997, the legislature passed a wide-ranging bill to limit tort recoveries. This bill changed] over 100 sections of the Revised Code contained in 18 titles and 38 chapters. . . .

[We held that this act violated] the separation of powers and the single-subject clause of the Ohio Constitution. State ex rel. Ohio Academy of Trial Lawyers v. Sheward, 715 N.E.2d 1062 (Ohio 1999). . . .

The protracted interbranch tension on this subject establishes at least two key points. First, tort reform has been a major issue of concern in this state over the past several decades and remains one today. . . . State legislatures and judiciaries have differed widely in their responses to this issue. . . .

Second . . . [o]ur prior review has focused on certain unconstitutional facets of the prior tort-reform laws that can be addressed to create constitutionally valid legislation. . . .

III. STANDARD OF REVIEW . . .

A. LIMITS ON NONECONOMIC DAMAGES . . .

The statute [does not apply to tort actions against government entities, or to actions for wrongful death, medical or dental malpractice, or breach of contract. In all other tort actions, it requires the finder of fact to] specify both the total compensatory damages recoverable by the plaintiff and the portions of those damages representing economic and noneconomic losses. [Economic loss is defined as lost income, medical expenses, and "any other expenditures incurred," not including attorneys' fees. Noneconomic loss is defined as "nonpecuniary harm . . . including, but not limited to, pain and suffering, loss of society, consortium, companionship, care, assistance, attention, protection, advice, guidance, counsel, instruction, training, or education, disfigurement, mental anguish, and any other intangible loss." §2315.18(A)(4).]

The court must enter judgment for the plaintiff for the amount of economic damages, without limitation, as determined by the trier of fact. For noneconomic damages, the court must limit recovery to the greater of (1) $250,000 or (2) three times the economic damages up to a maximum of $350,000 [per person], or $500,000 per single occurrence. However, these limits on noneconomic damages do not apply if the plaintiff suffered "[p]ermanent and substantial physical deformity, loss of use of a limb, or loss of a bodily organ system," or "[p]ermanent physical functional injury that permanently prevents the injured person from being able to independently care for self and perform life-sustaining activities." §2315.18(B)(3). . . .

1. Right to a Trial by Jury . . .

[T]he right to trial by jury protects a plaintiff's right to have a jury determine all issues of fact in his or her case. Because the extent of damages suffered by a plaintiff is a factual issue, it is within the jury's province to determine the amount of damages to be awarded. . . .

Any law that prevents the jury from completing this task or allows another entity to substitute its own findings of fact is unconstitutional. We reaffirmed this principle in *Sorrell* by striking down a statute that required a court to determine any collateral benefits received by a plaintiff and deduct them from a jury award, regardless of whether those benefits were duplicated in the award. This statute was unconstitutional because it allowed courts to ignore the jury's finding of facts on collateral benefits. . . .

So long as the fact-finding process is not intruded upon and the resulting findings of fact are not ignored or replaced by another body's findings, awards may be altered *as a matter of law.* . . . Thus, without violating the Constitution, a court may apply the law to the facts determined by a jury.

We have recognized several ways in which a court may apply the law to change a jury award of damages without running afoul of the Constitution. For example, courts have the inherent authority to order remittiturs to reduce jury awards when they deem the amount to be excessive. . . .

[N]umerous statutes . . . treble jury damages awards in certain causes of action. . . . We have never held that the legislative choice to *increase* a jury award as a matter of law infringes upon the right to a trial by jury; the corresponding *decrease* as a matter of law cannot logically violate that right. . . .

Section 2315.18 . . . is distinguishable from those allowing courts to substitute their own findings of fact on collateral benefits or requiring repayment plans that "further reduce the jury's award of damages already once reduced to present value." *Galayda*, 644 N.E.2d at 301. Courts must simply apply the limits as a matter of law to the facts found by the jury; they do not alter the findings of facts themselves, thus avoiding constitutional conflicts.

Such limitations are also permissible under the analogous Seventh Amendment right to a jury trial in the federal system. "Federal courts uniformly have held that statutory damages caps do not violate the Seventh Amendment, largely because a court does not 'reexamine' a jury's verdict or impose its own factual determination regarding what a proper award might be. . . ." Estate of Sisk v. Manzanares, 270 F. Supp. 2d 1265, 1277-1278 (D. Kan. 2003).

Because §2315.18 follows these principles, it does not offend the right to a trial by jury under the Ohio Constitution.

2. Open Courts and Right to a Remedy . . .

The Constitution provides: "*All courts shall be open*, and every person, for an injury done him in his land, goods, person, or reputation, *shall have remedy* by due course of law, and shall have justice administered without denial or delay." Ohio Const. art. I, §16 (emphasis added). . . .

We have interpreted this provision to prohibit statutes that effectively prevent individuals from pursuing relief for their injuries. *See, e.g.*, Brennaman v. R.M.I. Co., 639 N.E.2d 425 (Ohio 1994) (finding a statute of repose unconstitutional because it deprived certain plaintiffs of the right to sue before they were aware of their injuries). . . .

Although §2315.18 does limit certain types of noneconomic damages, those limits do not wholly deny persons a remedy for their injuries. Injured persons not suffering the catastrophic injuries in §2318.18(B)(3) (for which there are no damages limits) may still recover their full economic damages and up to $350,000 in noneconomic damages, as well as punitive damages. These available remedies are "meaningful" ones under the Constitution. While the statute prevents some plaintiffs from obtaining the same dollar figures they may have received prior to the effective date of the statute, it neither forecloses their ability to pursue a claim at all nor "completely obliterates the entire jury award." *Sorrell*, 633 N.E.2d at 513. . . .

3. Due Course of Law/Due Process

Arbino's next challenge to §2315.18 also arises from §16, specifically, the "due course of law" provision. We have recognized this provision as the equivalent of the "due process of law" protections in the United States Constitution.

When reviewing a statute on due-process grounds, we apply a rational-basis test unless the statute restricts the exercise of fundamental rights. Because we have already concluded that §2315.18 violates neither the right to a jury trial nor the right to a remedy, we must find it valid under the rational-basis test "[1] if it bears a real and substantial relation to the public health, safety, morals or general welfare of the public and [2] if it is not unreasonable or arbitrary." Mominee v. Scherbarth, 503 N.E.2d 717, 720-721 (Ohio 1986). . . .

a. Real and substantial relation to the general welfare of the public

The record here reveals that the General Assembly reviewed several forms of evidence and made numerous findings relative to §2315.18. In an uncodified section of S.B. 80, it found that the current state of the civil litigation system "represents a challenge to the economy of the state of Ohio." This finding was supported by (1) a National Bureau of Economic Research study showing that states adopting tort reforms experienced growth in employment, productivity, and total output, (2) a 2002 White House Council on Economic Advisors study equating the cost of tort litigation to a 2.1 percent wage and salary tax, a 1.3 percent personal-consumption tax, and a 3.1 percent capital-investment-income tax, (3) a Harris Poll of 928 senior corporate attorneys showing that the litigation environment in a state greatly affected the business decisions of their companies, (4) a Tillinghast-Towers Perrin study showing that the tort system failed to return even 50 cents for every dollar to injured plaintiffs and that the cost of the national tort system grew at a record rate in 2001, with a cost equivalent to a five percent tax on wages, and (5) testimony from Ohio Department of Development Director Bruce Johnson on the rising costs of the tort system, which he believed were putting Ohio businesses at a disadvantage and hindering development.

In addition to these general economic concerns, the General Assembly noted that noneconomic damages are difficult to calculate and lack a precise economic value.

It further concluded that such damages . . . are inherently subjective and susceptible to influence from irrelevant factors, such as the defendant's wrongdoing. It also recognized that inflated damages awards were likely under the then current system and that the cost of these awards was being passed on to the general public.

Viewing these findings as a whole, we conclude that §2315.18 bears a real and substantial relation to the general welfare of the public. . . .

Arbino . . . challenges the persuasiveness of these findings and argues that the crisis proposed by the evidence is nonexistent. In doing so, she asks us to evaluate the information relied upon by the General Assembly and come to our own conclusions as to whether §2315.18 was warranted.

Such an intensive reexamination is beyond the scope of our review. . . . "[W]e are to grant substantial deference to the predictive judgment of the General Assembly" under a rational-basis review. State v. Williams, 728 N.E.2d 342, 360 (Ohio 2000). . . . Finding that the General Assembly's review of the evidence yielded a statute that bears a real and substantial relation to the general welfare of the public, we need not cross-check its findings to ensure that we would agree with its conclusions.

b. Neither arbitrary nor unreasonable

The second prong of the rational-basis test asks whether the statute is arbitrary or unreasonable. In *Morris*, we found that the damages caps violated this prong because they imposed the cost of the intended benefit to the public solely upon those most severely injured. . . .

Section 2315.18 alleviates this concern by allowing for limitless noneconomic damages for those suffering catastrophic injuries. Arbino suggests that even with this exception for catastrophic injuries, the noneconomic-damages limitations remain unreasonable and arbitrary. She argues further that it is irrational to strike a statute for imposing the costs of a public benefit on the most severely injured, but not the "second-most severely injured."

At some point, though, the General Assembly must be able to make a policy decision to achieve a public good. Here, it found that the benefits of noneconomic-damages limits could be obtained without limiting the recovery of individuals whose pain and suffering is traumatic, extensive, and chronic, and by setting the limits for those not as severely injured at either $250,000 or $350,000. Even Arbino acknowledges that the vast majority of noncatastrophic tort cases do not reach that level of damages. The General Assembly's decision is tailored to maximize benefits to the public while limiting damages to litigants. The logic is neither unreasonable nor arbitrary. . . .

4. Equal Protection . . .

The Ohio Constitution states: "All political power is inherent in the people. Government is instituted for their equal protection and benefit." Ohio Const. art. I, §2. We have interpreted this provision as the equivalent of the federal Equal Protection Clause.

a. Standard of review . . .

In arguing for strict scrutiny, Arbino alleges that §2315.18 infringes on both a fundamental right (the right to a jury trial) and the rights of suspect classes (she specifically claims that damages caps disproportionately affect women, children, minorities, the elderly, and people with low incomes). We rejected the fundamental-right argument in Section III.A.1 above. Further, even if we accepted Arbino's contention that the noneconomic-damages caps disproportionately affect certain classes, facially neutral laws that may have such an impact do not violate the Equal Protection Clause.

Finding §2315.18 to be facially neutral, we apply the rational-basis test. . . .

b. Rational relationship to a legitimate government purpose

The limitations on noneconomic-damages awards in certain tort actions in §2315.18 certainly create distinctions between different groups of people. In setting a cap of either $250,000 or $350,000 on noneconomic damages for certain injuries and no caps on others, the statute treats those with lesser injuries, i.e., those not suffering the injuries designated in §2315.18(B)(3), differently from those most severely injured. . . .

[W]e cannot say that the General Assembly's action lacked all rational relation to the legitimate state interest of improving the state's civil justice system and its economy. The limitations were aimed at reducing the uncertainty associated with the existing tort system and the negative consequences resulting from it. The distinctions the legislature drew in refusing to limit certain injuries were rational and based on the conclusion that catastrophic injuries offer more concrete evidence of noneconomic damages and thus calculation of those damages poses a lesser risk of being tainted by improper external considerations. That reasoning withstands scrutiny under the rational-basis test. . . .

5. Separation of Powers . . .

The argument that §2315.18 infringes on the judicial power to decide damages lacks merit. It is certainly a judicial function to decide the facts in a civil case, and the amount of damages is a question of fact. However, that function is not so exclusive as to prohibit the General Assembly from regulating the amount of damages available in certain circumstances. . . .

IV. Conclusion

The decision in this case affirms the General Assembly's efforts over the last several decades to enact meaningful tort reforms. It also places Ohio firmly with the growing number of states that have found such reforms to be constitutional. However, the issue remains a contentious one across the nation, with several states finding such statutes unconstitutional. . . .

Using a *highly deferential* standard of review appropriate to a *facial challenge* to these statutes, we conclude that the General Assembly has responded to our previous decisions and has created constitutionally permissible limitations. . . .

Lundberg Stratton, O'Connor, and Lanzinger, JJ., concur.

Cupp, J., concurring. . . .

It is long-settled constitutional law that it is within the power of the legislature to alter, revise, modify, or abolish the common law as it may determine necessary or advisable for the common good.

The power to alter or abolish a common-law cause of action necessarily includes the power to modify any associated remedy. . . .

[T]he legislature's [substantive] law-making power is not . . . limited [by the right to jury trial], provided the litigant retains the right to have the jury determine the amount of damages to the extent the damages are legally available. Legislative action, however, may alter or limit what damages the law makes available and legally recoverable. . . .

Lundberg Stratton, O'Connor, and Lanzinger, JJ., concur in the foregoing opinion.

O'Donnell, J., dissenting in part. . . .

[A] remittitur . . . differs fundamentally from the cap on noneconomic damages imposed by §2315.18. [A remittitur is based on a judicial determination that a particular verdict is excessive, and plaintiff must be offered a choice of remittitur or a new trial.]

Section 2315.18 does not resemble remittitur in any of these respects, as it arbitrarily establishes, without the consideration of any facts in any particular case, that a jury's award for noneconomic damages is excessive when it exceeds the statutory limit. More important, the statute reduces such a verdict without the consent of the party in whose favor the verdict was returned. . . .

[A] statutory damages multiplier . . . increases the damages found by a jury with respect to a *statutory* cause of action in keeping with the *punitive* nature of the legislation. This has no similarity . . . to §2315.18, which applies to *common-law* causes of action and precludes a court from [entering] judgment [on] a jury finding regarding *compensatory* damages. . . .

"[The court] essentially [is] saying that the right to trial by jury is not invaded if the jury is allowed to determine facts which go unheeded when the court issues its judgment. *Such an argument pays lip service to the form of the jury but robs the institution of its function.*" Sofie v. Fibreboard Corp., 771 P.2d 711, 721 (Wash. 1989) (emphasis added). . . .

Pfeifer, J., dissenting.

I. §2315.18

A. RIGHT TO TRIAL BY JURY . . .

The members of the majority profess to believe that because the findings of fact are ignored, not changed, the requirements of the Constitution have been observed. . . . Ignoring factual findings is the equivalent of changing them. Ignoring factual findings is the equivalent of rendering those findings impotent. . . .

If a damages cap of $250,000 is constitutional . . . why can't the General Assembly limit damages for claims they do not favor to $100,000? Or $1,000? Or $10? . . . [T]he power to cap noneconomic damages is the power to eliminate them. . . .

B. DUE PROCESS AND EQUAL PROTECTION . . .

[The court should apply strict scrutiny, because the right to jury trial is a fundamental right, but §2315.18 fails even the rational basis test.

The legislative findings claim to "balance . . the rights of those who have been legitimately harmed and the rights of those who have been unfairly sued, . . while curbing the number of frivolous lawsuits."] The rights of people who have been harmed and who prove the legitimacy of their case by prevailing in a trial cannot be balanced against the rights of the unfairly sued. They are mutually exclusive groups—people harmed by the tortious conduct of others don't *unfairly* sue. In imposing caps, §2315.18 decreases the protection afforded to legitimate plaintiffs yet does nothing to protect the unfairly sued. . . .

[N]othing in the statutory scheme addresses frivolous lawsuits, and damages caps are not even remotely related to frivolous lawsuits. The caps imposed by the statutory scheme can affect only those plaintiffs with meritorious claims, plaintiffs who have prevailed in a trial and who have suffered significant damages. . . .

There is no rational reason to "improve" the tort system in Ohio at the sole expense of a small group of people who are able to prove that they suffered damage significant enough to exceed the damages caps imposed by the General Assembly. . . .

None of the General Assembly's findings are reliable with respect to addressing Ohio-specific problems. First, the findings do not relate specifically to Ohio. Second, all of the proffered evidence is the product of biased sources with political agendas. Third, the studies contain serious flaws, relying either on information that they do not provide or on information (medical-malpractice awards) that is not relevant to §2315.18. [These charges were backed by several pages of detailed analysis.] In short, these findings do not support a conclusion that §2315.18 is rationally related to a legitimate government purpose in Ohio. . . .

The statutory scheme creates two classes of tort victims: those with catastrophic or minor injuries, who are able to recover the full measure of their damages, and those with significant but not catastrophic injuries, who are able to recover only a portion of their damages. . . . [T]he classification in this case is not rationally related to anything, let alone a legitimate governmental interest. . . .

Section 2315.18 is purportedly . . . designed to encourage businesses to move to or expand in Ohio. But the statutory caps imposed . . . would benefit any business located anywhere in the world. . . . Johnson & Johnson, a New Jersey-based multinational corporation, will be protected by the caps, whether or not it has business operations in Ohio. . . . This is a further example of how little rational relationship there is between §2315.18 and its purported rationale and the general welfare of Ohioans. . . .

NOTES ON THE CONSTITUTIONALITY OF LIMITING TORT REMEDIES

1. The "tort reform" agenda. Fixed limits on recovery for pain and suffering and other intangible damages are a centerpiece of the national movement for statutory limits on tort liability. The dispute has pitted the insurance industry and frequent defendants against the plaintiffs' personal injury bar, consumer organizations, and labor unions. The defendants' side has coined the phrase "noneconomic damages," which appears, with a definition, in the Ohio statute. The phrase is in common use. But "noneconomic" is not an economic term; an economist would attach economic significance to anything that humans value.

Much of the industry's argument is based on horror stories from individual cases, and many of these emphasize liability rather than damages. But few of the legislative proposals address liability. Most of the proposals deal with remedies issues, probably because it is easier to legislate bright-line restrictions on remedies than to redefine "negligence," "defect," "cause," or "proximate" in a way that would actually guide results in individual cases. Some of the common proposals are:

1. to limit recovery for "noneconomic" damages, or for total damages;
2. to limit or abolish the collateral-source rule;
3. to limit or abolish punitive damages;
4. to provide that judgments be paid over the life of the person injured;
5. to limit or abolish joint and several liability;
6. to let defendants recover attorneys' fees from plaintiffs who file frivolous claims or simply unsuccessful claims;
7. to limit the rates charged in contingent fee agreements; and
8. to shorten statutes of limitations or accelerate the point at which the statute begins to run.

Every state has enacted at least part of this agenda. Many state supreme courts have struck down at least some of these provisions. Each state's combination of statute and judicial reaction is different; a plaintiff's attorney with a choice of states in which to file must check both the statutes and the state constitutional law before filing. Enacted tort reform measures in every state, and decisions upholding or invalidating them, are collected in Ronen Avraham, *Database of State Tort Law Reforms (5th)*, https://ssrn.com/abstract=902711 (2014). Cases are organized more thematically in Chapter 6 of Jennifer Friesen, *State Constitutional Law* (4th ed., Matthew Bender 2006 & Supp.) and Chapter 19 of Jacob A. Stein, *Stein on Personal Injury Damages* (3d ed., West 1997 & Supp.).

2. Damage caps. Many states have enacted caps on "noneconomic" damages, first in medical malpractice cases and then, in some of these states, in all or most personal-injury cases. When legislatures began enacting these statutes in the mid-1970s, tort reformers settled on $250,000 as a nice round number. Most states with caps have increased them over the years, but some have not. And many tort reformers are still pushing for $250,000, which is now worth just over $50,000 in 1975 dollars.

3. Catastrophic injuries. Consider Atlanta Oculoplastic Surgery, P.C. v. Nestlehutt, 691 S.E.2d 218 (Ga. 2010). Plaintiff was a married woman, permanently disfigured by a facelift gone bad. She recovered $115,000 for medical expenses and $900,000 for pain and suffering; there was no lost income. How does that case fit with Ohio's attempt to statutorily define the most severe injuries?

Most damage-cap statutes enact a single cap for all cases. But Ohio and a few other states have responded to the criticism that it is irrational to extract all the savings from a small number of people who were the most seriously injured. Florida addressed the problem with a standard instead of a rule: a $500,000 cap on "noneconomic" damages in medical malpractice cases, raised to $1 million in cases of death, permanent vegetative state, or where the trier of fact finds that the injury was "catastrophic" and the trial court finds that the injury was "particularly severe" and determines that the lower cap would cause "a manifest injustice." The court struck these caps down in a case where a mother, left unattended despite serious complications, died in child-birth. Estate of McCall v. United States, 134 So. 2d 894 (Fla. 2014).

4. Caps on total damages. Only a few states have enacted caps on total damages in cases against private defendants, and many of those were struck down. A total cap can mean that plaintiff doesn't even recover her medical expenses. Nebraska's cap on total damages in medical malpractice cases was upheld against state constitutional challenges in Gourley ex rel. Gourley v. Nebraska Methodist Health System, Inc., 663 N.W.2d 43 (Neb. 2003), and against federal constitutional challenges in Schmidt v. Ramsey, 860 F.3d 1038 (8th Cir.), *cert. denied*, 138 S. Ct. 506 (2017). Both cases involved babies severely brain damaged at birth. The cap, which has since been raised to $2,250,000, took away 80 percent of the verdict in *Gourley* and 90 percent in *Schmidt*.

Total caps are common in suits against government entities, where they are generally upheld on the ground that the state can attach conditions when it waives sovereign immunity. But the Oregon Supreme Court applied the state jury-trial and right-to-a-remedy clauses, without relying on sovereign immunity, in upholding a $3 million cap in suits against the state. Horton v. Oregon Health & Science University, 376 P.3d 998 (Or. 2016). The jury had awarded just over $12 million, half of it for "economic" damages.

5. The impact of caps. The argument in *Arbino* that damages caps "disproportion-ately affect women, children, minorities, the elderly, and people with low incomes" is straightforward. Plaintiffs not in the labor force, or working for low pay, are dispropor-tionately affected because their damages based on lost earning capacity are relatively small, and "noneconomic" damages are a larger proportion of their recovery. If such a person is killed, there may be no significant medical expenses and no provable loss of earning capacity; "noneconomic" damages are all the damages. A child who is permanently injured will have trouble proving what her adult income would have been; she also will have many more expected years of pain and suffering. Studies have confirmed that caps take large sums from a few people, disproportionately children and most of them severely injured. In states like Ohio that exclude some of the most objectively serious injuries from the cap, the impact is less clear.

The limits of insurance policies are a more pervasive, and generally lower, de facto cap on recovery. Scholars studying fields as diverse as medical malpractice and securities fraud have found that settlements in excess of policy limits and payment out of personal assets are extremely rare even for affluent defendants. Tom Baker, Eric Holland, & Jonathan Klick, *Everything's Bigger in Texas: Except the Medmal Settlements*, 2 Conn. Ins. L.J. 1 (2016). Collecting out of personal assets is difficult at best and impossible at worst. See Chapter 9.

6. Counting jurisdictions. A fair number of courts and commentators have attempted to collect the state supreme court cases upholding or invalidating damage caps. Most of these lists contain cases that others missed. Some courts distinguish different kinds of caps, as in *Arbino*, and some courts have overruled earlier decisions. So no simple count of cases will ever be entirely accurate. But for a general indication, we compiled the cases cited in several recent sources. The most recent decision in 20 states upheld caps; the most recent decision in 12 states struck down caps. Five other state constitutions expressly prohibit damage caps, sometimes with an exception for workers' compensation cases. In two more states, the state constitution expressly prohibits caps in wrongful death cases.

7. Jury trial. Do damage caps set aside the jury's findings of fact? Or do they enact a legal rule about the effect of those findings?

8. Right to a remedy. Most state constitutions guarantee a right to a remedy, but these clauses remain inscrutable. The Oregon court in *Horton* (in note 4) exhaustively reviewed their history, from Magna Carta through Coke and Blackstone to early American constitutions and the cases from the founding to the present. It reached a conclusion, but no one would say it identified a clear meaning, originalist or otherwise. The right to a remedy must mean something, but it cannot mean that the legislature can never amend tort law.

Might the right to a remedy combine with the right to jury trial to mean that each plaintiff is entitled to a remedy for her injury as found by the jury?

9. How low can it go? Is it true that if the legislature can set a cap, it can set the cap at arbitrarily low levels? The Maryland court invalidated, under a right-to-a-remedy clause, a statute granting immunity to landlords for damages caused by lead-based paint. Jackson v. Dackman Co., 30 A.3d 854 (Md. 2011). The court said that the legislature could abolish common law remedies and substitute statutory remedies, but that here, the statutory remedy was "totally inadequate and unreasonable." *Id.* at 868. The plaintiff child had suffered permanent brain damage; the statutory remedy could provide a maximum of $17,000 in compensation if it applied, and in this case, it appeared not to apply. Maryland had upheld a $350,000 cap on "noneconomic" damages against challenges based on equal protection and the right to jury trial. Murphy v. Edmonds, 601 A.2d 102 (Md. 1992).

10. Separation of powers. The Illinois court held that a cap on "noneconomic" damages in medical malpractice cases violates the separation of powers by interfering with the judiciary's responsibility for remitting excessive jury verdicts. Lebron v. Gottlieb Memorial Hospital, 930 N.E.2d 895 (Ill. 2010).

11. Equal protection. There are a great variety of equal-protection theories. Plaintiffs argue that the medical malpractice statutes discriminate between victims of medical malpractice and victims of other torts. Plaintiffs argue, as in *Arbino*, that all these statutes discriminate between the most seriously injured and the less seriously injured, favoring the latter. The Florida court invalidated the state's medical malpractice cap on that ground and on the ground that it discriminated against plaintiffs in cases with multiple victims. Estate of McCall v. United States, 134 So. 3d 894 (Fla. 2014). There were three survivors in that wrongful death case; if any one of them had been the sole survivor, he would have been more fully compensated.

NOTES ON THE EMPIRICAL DEBATE: HOW BIG IS THE PROBLEM?

1. Legislative findings and judicial reactions. Tort reformers argue that tort liability has become a significant drag on the economy and that it often makes liability insurance unavailable or unaffordable. Legislators often rely on studies from lobbyists and advocacy groups. But an ever growing body of empirical research by academics and government statisticians disproves the tort reformers' claims. Studies are collected in Herbert M. Kritzer, Guangya Liu, & Neil Vidmar, *An Exploration of "Noneconomic" Damages in Civil Jury Awards*, 55 Wm. & Mary L. Rev. 971 (2014), and David A. Hyman & Charles Silver, *Medical Malpractice and Compensation in Global Perspective: How Does the U.S. Do It?*, 87 Chi.-Kent L. Rev. 163 (2012). This casebook remained neutral on tort reform through four editions, but the evidence has become more and more one-sided.

2. The insurance cycle. Defendants have pushed to limit tort remedies since the mid-1970s. Much of the actual legislation has come in waves, following a series of crises in the cost and availability of liability insurance. Each time, insurers and defendants blamed a "tort crisis."

These periodic crises have more to do with cycles in the insurance industry than with changes in tort claims. For a sophisticated explanation of the insurance cycle, see Tom Baker, *Medical Malpractice and the Insurance Underwriting Cycle*, 54 DePaul L. Rev. 393 (2005). Changes in claims do not explain the history of sudden and sharp changes in premiums and availability. When insurers are making money, they compete hard for market share, which leads to lower premiums and excess capacity, which eventually leads to insurers losing money. When insurers are losing money, they drop coverage for some risks and sharply raise premiums for the rest, which causes a "crisis" and eventually leads to insurers making money again. The effect is amplified in insurance lines with long tails—that is, long lags between collecting the premiums and paying the last of the claims. The insurance cycle is especially violent in medical malpractice, because medical malpractice claims have an especially long tail.

3. Games people play with statistics. The largest reliable data sets on tort trials are a series of studies by the Bureau of Justice Statistics (BJS) and the National Center for State Courts. Both agencies are staffed by career statisticians and reasonably insulated from politics. They gathered large samples of civil trials in 1992, 1996, 2001, and 2005.

The big picture, in these and other studies, is that there is little change and no evidence of crisis in routine personal injury cases. But verdicts are much larger in products liability and medical malpractice cases, and there have been unpredictable surges of liability in mass tort cases involving latent injuries from dangerous substances. Because the routine cases are the great bulk of all cases, data on all cases show little change over time. So one side cites all cases, and the other side cites medical malpractice and products cases.

Writers sympathetic to plaintiffs usually cite *median* verdicts. Writers sympathetic to defendants usually cite *mean* verdicts. The difference can be huge. In the 2001 BJS study, the median verdict was $27,000; the mean was $565,000. For medical malpractice, the median was $422,000; the mean was $1,932,000. Thomas H. Cohen & Steven K. Smith, *Civil Trial Cases and Verdicts in Large Counties, 2001*, table 6 (NCJ 202803 2004), available at *http://bjs.ojp.usdoj.gov/content/pub/pdf/ctcvlc01.pdf*.

Such differences arise because the most extreme verdicts sharply increase the mean without affecting the median. The median is the middle verdict; half of all verdicts are larger and half are smaller. The mean is the sum of all the verdicts divided by the number of verdicts. So if there are verdicts of $1,000, $10,000 and $1 million, the median is $10,000 but the mean is $337,000. Means tend to exceed medians in any distribution that has no upper limit.

Medians better reflect the experience of most plaintiffs; half of all plaintiffs get less than the median. Means better reflect what insurers have to pay; they pay the big verdicts as well as the small ones. But the largest verdicts are the most likely to be reduced, so reversals, remittiturs, and settlements pending appeal mean that insurers actually pay much less than the mean *verdict*. A study using insurance industry claims data, further described below, found that out of 311 wrongful death cases tried to verdict, only 48 were paid based on the verdict; 263 were paid pursuant to a subsequent settlement. Frank Cross & Charles Silver, *In Texas, Life Is Cheap*, 59 Vand. L. Rev. 1875, 1902 table 2 (2006). Of course the biggest verdicts are reduced the most. In a study of Texas medical malpractice cases, insurers actually paid 56 percent of the total amount of verdicts. David A. Hyman, Bernard Black, Kathryn Zeiler, Charles Silver, & William M. Sage, *Do Defendants Pay what Juries Award? Post-Verdict Haircuts in Texas Medical Malpractice Cases, 1988-2003*, 4 J. Empirical Legal Studies 3 (2007).

4. Data on trials. No doubt there was real and substantial growth in important elements of tort liability over the course of the twentieth century, much of it concentrated in the period after World War II. There is a broad survey in Philip L. Merkel, *Pain and Suffering Damages at Mid-Twentieth Century: A Retrospective View of the Problem and the Legal Academy's First Responses*, 34 Cap. U. L. Rev. 545 (2006). Perhaps from a long-run perspective, the movement to limit liability is a response to this long-run change in the liability regime.

But the tort reform movement claims much more than that. For tort claims to cause a series of crises in liability insurance over the last 40-some years, claims must have continued to grow sharply over that period, and the explanation would work best if claims grew in a series of sudden spurts. There is not much evidence of either.

The 2005 BJS study sampled the 75 largest counties, to maintain comparability with earlier studies, and also sampled all the remaining counties, creating the first truly national sample of civil trials. Lynn Langton & Thomas H. Cohen, *Civil Bench and Jury Trials in State Courts, 2005* (NCJ 223851, 2008), available at *http://bjs.ojp.usdoj. gov/content/pub/pdf/cbjtsc05.pdf*. Some 7.4 million cases were filed in state courts of general jurisdiction in 2005. *Id.* at 1. About 26,948 were tried, including 16,397 tort trials. *Id.* table 1. (The apparent precision of these numbers is illusory; for the statistical margins of error, see *id.* appendix table 1.) Tort plaintiffs won 51 percent of jury trials and 56 percent of bench trials, with a median verdict of $21,000 and a median judgment in bench trials of $24,000; neither difference between jury trials and bench trials was statistically significant. *Id.* table 2.

The range of awards was very large, and there were substantial differences by the kind of tort. BJS no longer reports data from which means can be calculated, but it does report information about the distribution of awards. See Table 2-3. These data include only cases won by plaintiff, and they include both compensatory and punitive damages.

Table 2-3
State-Court Tort Awards in 2005
Nationwide

Case Type	No. of Cases	Median Award ($)	<$10K (%)	$10K-$50K (%)	$50K-$250K (%)	$250K-$1 million (%)	>$1 million (%)
All torts	8,455	24,000	33	31	21	10	5
Asbestos	47	682,000	2	0	19	53	26
Products liability	99	567,000	4	17	13	35	30
Other	52	500,000	6	33	8	17	36
Medical malpractice	584	400,000	1	5	29	44	21
False arrest or imprisonment	8	259,000	38	0	12	12	38
Other professional malpractice	63	129,000	3	32	22	29	14
Premises liability	666	98,000	6	31	33	23	7
Other; unknown	305	83,000	36	9	27	13	15
Intentional tort	429	38,000	29	24	36	7	4
Conversion	148	27,000	24	32	37	4	3
Slander/libel	80	24,000	22	40	3	22	12
Animal attack	107	21,000	37	33	29	1	0
Motor vehicle	5,964	15,000	40	35	18	5	2

Langton & Cohen, table 6.

The 2005 study did not include federal courts, but in earlier studies, means and medians in federal courts were much larger than in state courts. For example, in 2001, the state median for all torts was $27,000, but the federal median was $179,000. Cohen & Smith, tables 6 and 8. This difference reflects the exclusion of modest claims; federal courts have no jurisdiction over diversity cases with less than $75,000 in controversy. 28 U.S.C. §1332(a).

Data on trends over the four BJS studies are confined to the 75 largest counties. The number of trials had dropped sharply in all categories; the size of verdicts had dropped in the routine cases but increased in products liability and medical-malpractice cases:

Table 2-4
Median State-Court Jury Verdicts in Tort Cases, 1992-2005
75 Most Populous Counties

Case Type	1992 ($)	1996 ($)	2001 ($)	2005 ($)
All torts	71,000	37,000	31,000	33,000
Products liability	154,000	409,000	597,000	749,000
Medical malpractice	280,000	315,000	474,000	682,000
Premises liability	81,000	70,000	67,000	94,000
Automobile	41,000	22,000	18,000	17,000

Langton & Cohen, table 11.

These data are consistent with widespread anecdotal evidence that jurors are responding to defense-side advertising about the tort system. See Stephen Daniels & Joanne Martin, *Texas Plaintiffs' Practice in the Age of Tort Reform: Survival of the Fittest — It's Even More True Now*, 51 N.Y.L. Sch. L. Rev. 285 (2007). This response appears to be concentrated in smaller cases with less serious injuries; the *mean* jury award in tort cases won by plaintiffs increased slightly faster than inflation, from $430,000 in 1996 to $565,000 in 2001.

Why would the size of verdicts continue to increase in the problem areas of products liability and medical malpractice? The simple answer is that that's where the crisis is, and the crisis continues. But an equally plausible answer is that smaller claims are no longer going to trial and that only the big cases remain. To choose between these explanations, we need more detailed data.

5. Data on claims. The vast majority of cases settle. But not only that. The vast majority of injuries, even serious injuries, never result in a claim. Studies are collected, and the reasons victims don't sue are explored, in David M. Engel, *The Myth of the Litigious Society: Why We Don't Sue* (Univ. Chicago 2016). The largest of these studies found that only 10 percent of injured persons took any kind of action, only 4 percent hired a lawyer, and only 2 percent filed a lawsuit. And propensity to take action did not correlate with the potential merits of the claim: Victims pursued weak claims as well as strong, and took no action on strong claims as well as weak.

Because personal injury lawyers get paid only out of what they recover, they screen out claims that are weak on liability, or short on damages, or where the defendant is inadequately insured. And because medical malpractice and products liability cases are much more expensive to try than an auto accident or a slip and fall, the threshold for a case worth pursuing is also much higher. A damage cap that is set too low makes many more cases not worth pursuing.

6. Data on settlements. Data on settlements are mostly scattered and nonpublic; insurance industry claims data are generally inaccessible. But a few states require insurers to disclose claims data in exchange for limits on liability; these data include both settlements and judgments. And the federal government has created a large database of medical malpractice claims, with mandatory reporting. The most detailed of these data sets, and the only one regularly audited for accuracy, covers medical malpractice claims in Texas. So much of this research has been conducted there, but there are also studies from other states, the BJS data, and the federal medical malpractice data base.

Mean and median settlements are smaller than verdicts, especially in the big cases, because compromise requires each side to give up some of what it expects from a trial. The *mean* medical-malpractice settlement in claims arising from 1991 to 1998—and mostly settled much later—was just under $250,000. This is considerably less than the *median* jury verdict. Ronen Avraham, *An Empirical Study of the Impact of Tort Reforms on Medical Malpractice Settlement Payments*, 36 J. Legal Stud. S183, S192 table 1 (2007) (using the federal database). But a New York study that was able to include all contingent-fee cases, including the small and routine cases, found no difference between the average settlement and the average judgment. Eric Helland, Daniel M. Klerman, & Yoon-Ho Alex Lee, *Maybe There Is No Bias in the Selection of Disputes for Litigation*, 174 J. Institutional & Theoretical Econ. 143 (2018). The data base was a document that contingent-fee lawyers are required to file in every case, even those that settle before filing a complaint, accounting for their fees.

Texas data are reviewed in Bernard Black, Charles Silver, David A. Hyman, and William M. Sage, *Stability, Not Crisis: Medical Malpractice Claim Outcomes in Texas, 1988-2002*, 2 J. Empirical Legal Stud. 207 (2005). The number of small claims declined sharply, driven out of the system by litigation costs and the tort reform movement. It is essential to control for inflation and the relative disappearance of small claims; without that, raw numbers can suggest a large but illusory growth in payments.

Payments per large claim paid rose very slightly in real dollars. This was the experience *before* Texas enacted its $250,000 damage cap and other restrictions on medical malpractice cases in 2003. Both the number of claims and payments per claim plummeted after that. Hyman & Silver, cited in note 1. Many claims, especially for children, the elderly, and those not employed outside the home, became not worth filing. And many personal injury lawyers closed their practices or shifted to a new specialty. Stephen Daniels & Joanne Martin, *Tort Reform, Plaintiffs' Lawyers, and Access to Justice* 205-239 (Univ. Press of Kansas 2015).

A study of Florida data found similar stability in the number of claims, and a similar squeezing out of small claims, but somewhat greater growth in mean and median payments, as compared to the pre-2003 Texas data. Neil Vidmar et al., *Uncovering the "Invisible" Profile of Medical Malpractice Litigation: Insights from Florida*, 54 DePaul L. Rev. 315 (2005).

Studies using the federal database of medical-malpractice payouts found substantial declines in the number of claims and stability or modest decline in the size of payments. From 1992 to 2012, annual malpractice payments per physician declined by half in constant dollars, to 0.11 percent (11/100 of one percent) of total spending on health care. Myungho Paik, Bernard Black, & David A. Hyman, *The Receding Tide of Medical Malpractice Litigation: Part 1—National Trends*, 10 J. Empirical Legal Stud. 612 (2013).

Cross and Silver, cited in note 3, reviewed Texas insurance-claim data on more than 11,000 wrongful death claims closed from 1988 to 2003. These data include only commercial liability policies, so most claims against individuals are excluded.

The median payment was only $200,000; the mean payment was $413,000; the variation around these numbers was enormous. There was no trend of either increasing or decreasing payments over time. They collect similar results from elsewhere, and studies showing much larger average *verdicts*.

7. Predictability and variability. The problem that remains is outlier verdicts—unusually large or small awards in individual cases. The problem is real, but damages are not as unpredictable as the outliers might suggest. Studies consistently show high levels of agreement on the relative severity of injuries. Agreement collapses over how to convert severity of injury into dollars. Even so, severity is the most important single influence on the size of damage awards.

The National Association of Insurance Commissioners created a nine-level scale for grading severity of injuries. A regression equation using this scale explained 40 percent of the variance in a sample of verdicts reported in jury verdict reporters; this scale and plaintiff's age explained 62 percent. Randall R. Bovbjerg, Frank A. Sloan, and James F. Blumstein, *Valuing Life and Limb in Tort: Scheduling "Pain and Suffering,"* 83 Nw. U. L. Rev. 908 (1989). These are remarkably high percentages in social science research. For levels two through eight, the mean and median verdicts increased steadily at each level. The mean and median death verdicts were smaller than those for the most serious permanent injuries. Despite the clear pattern in the results, they found enormous variation within each category. The Vidmar team, cited in note 6, got similar results when it applied the scale to Florida medical-malpractice claims. And Professor Sharkey got similar results applying the scale to medical malpractice cases in the BJS data. Catherine M. Sharkey, *Unintended Consequences of Medical Malpractice Damages Caps*, 80 N.Y.U. L. Rev. 391 (2005).

The Texas wrongful death study found that age and employment affected payments just as the legal rules say they should. But defendant's industry, litigation in a small number of plaintiff-friendly counties, and insurance policy limits—all legally irrelevant—also had statistically significant effects.

8. The merits? How many of the very large verdicts were fair responses to very serious injuries, and how many were runaway juries? No systematic study gets deep enough into case files to answer that question.

Why are verdicts in medical malpractice and products liability many times the size of verdicts for other torts? Much of the answer is that those cases are so expensive to litigate that lawyers don't file them unless the damages are large. Another part of the answer is that juries assess damages differently when the defendant is a doctor or a corporation than when the defendant is a driver who appears to be no better off than plaintiff. Defendant's apparent wealth is legally irrelevant, but in practice, it is highly significant.

This tension was at issue in Hand v. Howell, Sarto & Howell, 131 So. 3d 599 (Ala. 2013). Hand claimed that it was legal malpractice to sue only the driver who injured him and not that driver's corporate employer. The case against the driver settled for $625,000, which was less than Hand's medical expenses and lost income. His second set of lawyers estimated the settlement value of the claim against the employer at $1 to $1.2 million. Both potential defendants were covered by the same insurance policy. The new lawyers simply said that a claim against an individual was worth far less than the same claim against a large corporation. The court said that was irrelevant even if true. The court "must presume that juries will follow the law," and under the law, the identity, wealth, and corporate status of the defendant are all irrelevant. *Id.* at 603. Three dissenters voted for reality over theory.

NOTES ON VALUING PAIN AND SUFFERING AND HUMAN LIFE

1. The impossibility of compensation. Neither of the two traditional theories of damages can explain personal injury damages without an enormous exception for the most serious cases. The corrective justice model says that plaintiff should receive the full value of his injuries, so that he is placed, as nearly as may be, in the position he would have occupied if he had never been injured. The classical economic model also says that plaintiff should receive the full value of his injuries, so that defendants will take account of the cost of the injuries they inflict. One model focuses on fairness to plaintiff, the other on incentives to defendant, but both yield the same conclusion—damages should equal the full value of the harm to plaintiff.

At this point, both theories encounter the same problem, summarized by Judge Posner:

> Damage awards for pain and suffering, even when apparently generous, may well under-compensate victims crippled by accidents. Since the loss of vision or limbs reduces the amount of pleasure that can be purchased with a dollar, a very large amount of money will frequently be necessary to place the victim in the same position of relative satisfaction that he occupied before the accident. The problem is most acute in a death case. Most people would not exchange their lives for anything less than an infinite sum of money if the exchange were to take place immediately. . . . Yet it cannot be correct that the proper award of damages in a death case is infinite. Apart from the impossibility of such an award, it would imply that the optimum rate of fatal accidents was zero . . . . Obviously people are unwilling, individually or collectively, to incur the costs necessary to reduce the rate of fatal accidents so drastically.

Richard A. Posner, *Economic Analysis of Law* §6.12 at 229 (9th ed., Aspen 2014).

The corrective justice model also backs away from the problem. As we have seen, the doctrinal answer is to award some partial measure of loss to survivors in death cases, wholly ignoring the value of decedent's life to herself, and to award "reasonable compensation" for pain and suffering. The rule of reasonable compensation leaves courts and juries without a standard, not even an abstract and conceptual standard. This departure from full compensation leaves both the corrective justice and economic models in considerable disarray.

2. The value of a statistical life. Many law and economics scholars would infer the value of life (and presumably of serious injury) from the premiums that people charge to incur very small risks of death or injury. *Id.* at 230-233. Such studies have been done on workers in hazardous occupations and on the prices that consumers are willing to pay for safety devices. If workers must be paid an extra $5 an hour to take a job in which a worker is killed once every 100,000 person-hours, Judge Posner would say the workers have implicitly valued their lives at $500,000. Everyone agrees that this valuation is valid, if at all, only for low-level risks; valuations would rise toward infinity as the risks rise toward certainty. Risk premiums are also distorted by bargaining power and the lack thereof, by workers' and consumers' lack of good information about risk levels, and by cognitive difficulties in assessing such information when it is available. Posner now recognizes some of these difficulties. But supporters of the method argue that valuations produced in this way would yield the right level of deterrence, encouraging potential defendants to take precautions equivalent to those potential plaintiffs would be willing to pay for themselves.

This theory seems great wisdom to some and utter nonsense to others. There is an excellent discussion, which collects much of the literature, in Cross and Silver,

59 Vand. L. Rev. at 1878-1885. The value of a statistical life is one of the most heavily studied empirical questions in economics, and these studies have found a vast range of values. A survey of just the studies based on labor markets, which is the largest group, and excluding the most extreme 5 percent of results at each end, reported values ranging from negative $4.9 million to positive $63.2 million. W. Kip Viscusi, *Best Estimate Selection Bias of Estimates of the Value of a Statistical Life*, https://ssrn.com/abstract=2919555 (2017). The negative numbers, which were not rare, presumably reflect disadvantaged workers who have little choice about accepting low pay to do dangerous jobs. Professor Viscusi's highly technical paper applies statistical techniques to the whole set of studies and concludes that the best estimate is $9.5 to $11.5 million—or about 25 times the mean payment for wrongful death in Texas.

Professors Cooter and DePianto report a smaller survey, in a more readable paper. The central tendency of the studies they collect appears to be about $4 to 7 million. Robert Cooter & David DePianto, *Community Versus Market Values of Life*, 57 Wm. & Mary L. Rev. 713, 736-738 (2016). They propose using a subset of these studies, based on valuations implicit in community norms about safety, which they say yields a value of $2 to $3 million.

Most courts have excluded testimony based on the theory as unscientific and unreliable. Some of the major cases are reviewed in Richman v. Burgeson, 2008 WL 2567132, at *2-5 (N.D. Ill. 2008). But the method is widely used by regulatory agencies, which must assume some value for human lives saved when they compare the costs and benefits of proposed regulations. Viscusi reports that most federal agencies are using numbers in the range of $8 to $10 million.

3. The insurance theory. A related theory is based on an analogy to first-party insurance. A typical elaboration of this theory is Alan Schwartz, *Proposals for Products Liability Reform: A Theoretical Synthesis*, 97 Yale L.J. 353 (1988). Following Professor Pryor, we will call this the insurance theory. Ellen Smith Pryor, *The Tort Law Debate, Efficiency, and the Kingdom of the Ill: A Critique of the Insurance Theory of Compensation*, 79 Va. L. Rev. 91 (1993).

a. The basic idea. Insurance theorists would explicitly abandon any concept of rightful position or make-whole relief. They would ask what insurance coverage potential tort victims would buy if they were rational and if they had to insure against tortious injury at their own expense. This eliminates the possibility of infinite damages by limiting payments to what the class of potential victims would fund out of their own pockets. This limitation is sometimes said to reflect reality, because sellers of goods and services will attempt to recoup damage payments in their prices. But surely the cost is shared by consumers and producers, because the lowest-cost seller limits the capacity of other sellers to pass their excess cost through to consumers. If all the costs were freely passed to consumers, the tort-reform movement would have no reason to fight so hard to limit recoveries. The assumption that victims should pay for their own compensation is normative, not empirical.

b. Marginal utility or total utility. A central premise of the insurance theory is that in buying insurance, consumers seek to equalize their marginal utility before and after the injury. That is, the alternative pleasure that could have been purchased with the last dollar spent on insurance should equal the pleasure that can be purchased with the last dollar collected from insurance benefits.

The goal of equal marginal utility before and after the accident assumes a certain form of risk neutrality, but the whole practice of buying insurance is strong evidence that people are risk averse. Perhaps consumers seek to equalize their *total* utility before and after injury; that is, they may seek as nearly as may be to ensure that they are as well off after the injury as before—the rightful position standard. This formulation probably comes closer to capturing most consumers' commonsense view of insurance than formulations based on marginal utility. But consumers do often balk at the cost of insurance premiums, which shows that at least short-term choices about marginal utility play a role in their decisions.

c. The marginal utility of money after injury. The insurance theory also assumes that money does not buy much pleasure for the seriously injured. It is better to have a dollar when you are healthy and able to enjoy it than to spend it on insurance and get it back when you are injured and unable to enjoy it. It is principally this premise that leads the theory to propose eliminating compensation for pain and suffering.

Professor Pryor argues that serious injury so changes the things that plaintiff values that it is meaningless to compare utility curves before and after injury. She sees in the insurance-theory literature a pervasive bias of the healthy and a devaluing of the lives of the injured.

d. Evidence of consumer preferences. A secondary argument for the insurance theory is that consumers do not buy first-party insurance for "noneconomic" losses. Insurers don't offer such policies in any straightforward way. Perhaps that is for lack of demand, but more fundamentally, it seems to be about fear of claims that are hard to value or verify. Uninsured motorist coverage, accident insurance, double indemnity clauses, and airport flight insurance all cover nonpecuniary losses, and that may be their principal function for customers who already have health and disability insurance.

Many consumers lack medical insurance, and most fail to buy disability income insurance, although Social Security provides a modest level of coverage. Does it follow from the insurance theory that we should not compensate medical costs and lost income either? The insurance theorists say it doesn't, because it is irrational not to insure those losses, but quite rational not to insure pain and suffering. So their theory ultimately depends not on consumer sovereignty but on the assumptions that drive their definition of rationality.

4. Trading incommensurables and the feasible level of safety. The actual practice of judges and jurors has no such organized theory. Juries value pain and suffering intuitively, and judges review verdicts intuitively, each trying to do what seems reasonable. Can we say anything more than that?

Start with Judge Posner's insight that the amount of compensation needed to fully compensate a wrongful death or a serious injury is enormous, but unaffordable in terms of all the technology and activities we would have to give up to fully compensate all the injuries. Inevitably, we are trading lives and injuries for technology and convenience. But the values to be traded are incommensurable, and at least one side of the trade is not measurable in dollars. There is no reason the trade has to be made at any particular (and inevitably arbitrary) valuation of life. Plaintiff must be compensated in dollars, but the trade need not be conceptualized in dollars at all. We can think directly about how careful we want the managers of technology to be or about how much technology we are willing to give up to prevent how many serious injuries.

Such themes are explored in Gregory C. Keating, *Is Cost-Benefit Analysis the Only Game in Town?*, 91 S. Cal. L. Rev. 195 (2018). Professor Keating notes three distinct standards in direct safety regulation: cost-justified levels of safety, feasible levels of safety, and safe levels of safety. Cost-justified (or cost-benefit) regulation puts a dollar value on deaths and injuries and then seeks to minimize the sum of safety costs and accident costs. Feasibility regulation, as in the Clean Air Act and the Occupational Safety and Health Act, aspires to prevent as many injuries as possible without shutting down the industry or pricing its products beyond the means of ordinary Americans. Safe-level regulation, as in the Food Quality Protection Act, aspires to prevent all significant risk of serious injury. Note that the feasible level of safety does not assume any particular value of a human life. It will require greater expenditures per life saved in some industries than in others, depending on what safety expenditures each industry can absorb.

Juries will not articulate these distinctions as cleanly as Professor Keating. But it may well be that many juries think that defendants should achieve something like the feasible level of safety and that verdicts should be large enough to make that happen.

Critics oppose feasibility analysis in part because it is standardless; how much loss of technology or production is too much is left to a judgment call with no formal standard. Jonathan S. Masur and Eric A. Posner, *Against Feasability Analysis*, 77 U. Chi. L. Rev. 657 (2010). Cost-benefit analysis seems more precise, but only because it hides the judgment call in the artificially precise values placed on life and health. Critics also oppose feasibility analysis because they think it is irrational to spend more preventing injuries than the injuries are worth. But that too depends on treating the numbers placed on life and health as though they were real values and not arbitrary estimates.

5. Scheduling. Bovbjerg, Sloan, and Blumstein (in note 7 of the preceding set of notes) propose a variety of ways that courts possibly, and legislatures certainly, could use age and severity-of-injury categories to fix awards for pain and suffering. Juries could simply be asked to categorize the injury in a special verdict, with compensation determined by a statutory schedule indexed to inflation. Or juries could be given ten or so descriptions of representative cases based on the age and severity categories, with a statutory award attached to each description, and told to award damages in light of comparable cases as reflected in the descriptions. They propose minimum and maximum awards to deal with extreme verdicts.

Seeking to simplify further, Ronen Avraham proposes age-adjusted multipliers of medical expenses. Ronen Avraham, *Putting a Price on Pain-and-Suffering Damages: A Critique of the Current Approaches and a Preliminary Proposal for Change*, 100 Nw. U. L. Rev. 87, 110-117 (2006). The greater your medical expenses and the younger your age, the bigger your award for pain and suffering. These multipliers would be nonbinding guidelines for settlement negotiations and for juries. Juries would have power to deviate, because the correlation between pain and suffering and medical expenses is imperfect. It may be much cheaper to amputate a leg than to save it, yet the amputation victim has a greater loss.

Wrongful death cases could be scheduled on the model of the administrative remedy for September 11 victims: pecuniary losses narrowly conceived plus some number, indexed for inflation, for everything else. Is it a sufficient objection to such uniformity that families vary greatly in their closeness? That the amounts may be set at unreasonably low (or high) levels?

England and Wales, which no longer use juries in civil cases, have adopted detailed *Guidelines for the Assessment of General Damages in Personal Injury Cases*. The Guidelines are updated frequently, and administrative personnel apply them to individual cases.

6. What rightful position? Debates over pain and suffering tend to assume that medical expenses and lost income are fully compensatory. But of course, compensation for these more tangible damages is reduced by litigation delays, settlement discounts, insurance policy limits, and attorneys' fees. Professors Goldberg and Zipursky plausibly argue that in practice, compensation for pain and suffering makes up only part of the shortfall in compensation for medical expenses and lost income. John C.P. Goldberg and Benjamin C. Zipursky, *The Easy Case for Products Liability: A Response to Professors Polinsky and Shavell*, 123 Harv. L. Rev. 1919, 1939-1940 (2010).

3.   Dignitary and Constitutional Harms

LEVKA v. CITY OF CHICAGO
748 F.2d 421 (7th Cir. 1984)

Before BAUER, Circuit Judge, PELL, Senior Circuit Judge, and DUPREE, Senior District Judge.

PELL, Senior Circuit Judge. . . .

Plaintiff brought this suit pursuant to 42 U.S.C. §1983, claiming that . . . the City of Chicago violated her civil rights when Chicago police officers subjected her to a strip search after her arrest for a misdemeanor offense. As we have held previously, defendant's former policy searching female arrestees violated both the Fourth Amendment right to be free from unreasonable searches and the Fourteenth Amendment right to equal protection. . . . Following the jury's award of $50,000 as compensation for emotional injuries, defendant moved for judgment notwithstanding the verdict or, in the alternative, for a new trial or the entry of a remittitur. The district court denied the motion, and defendant appeals.

I. FACTS . . .

At the time of this incident, the City of Chicago enforced a policy of subjecting every arrestee at [the women's] lockup to a strip search regardless of the nature of the charge brought against her and regardless of whether reason existed to believe that she carried drugs or concealed weapons. Defendant stipulated that, pursuant to this policy: "The Arrestee was required to lift up her blouse and brassiere. A visual inspection was made. The Arrestee was then told to pull down her pants and pull down her underpants, then to squat several times, stand up and bend over. Again a visual inspection was made." . . .

According to plaintiff, . . . the matron returned to plaintiff's cell with another matron. The first matron asked plaintiff to pull up her sweater and turn her bra inside-out. After asking "why" and being informed "just do it," plaintiff complied. The matrons conducted a visual inspection from a distance of a couple of feet, and then told plaintiff that she could replace her bra and sweater. Then, one of the matrons asked her to lift up her skirt, pull down her underpants and pantyhose, bend over, and spread her buttocks. Again, plaintiff protested and was told "just do it." Plaintiff complied. Following the search, plaintiff testified, "I felt debased and humiliated and degraded, abused, misused. . . . I was absolutely shocked and stunned and horrified. I was sickened."

Plaintiff was released from jail about an hour or an hour and one-half after the strip search, approximately forty-five minutes after her daughter [Swenson] arrived at the lockup. When she saw her mother, Swenson testified, plaintiff looked pale and upset, as if she had been crying. . . . Plaintiff recounted the details of the strip search to her daughter and the others [the court never identifies these "others;" presumably they were friends] while they were in the car and again when they stopped for coffee on the way home. Swenson testified that plaintiff told them that she was very frightened and humiliated by the search and that she cried on and off and seemed very upset. After breakfast, plaintiff returned home where she tried to sleep. She did not fall asleep until about 9:00 A.M. . . .

[P]laintiff testified that in the weeks following the strip search she continued to be frightened and became afraid to go out alone at night. She testified that if she tried to go out alone, she would return home and fall apart. According to plaintiff, her fears became so pronounced that she consulted a psychiatrist one month after the search. She did not return for further consultation. As a result of the search, plaintiff claims that she continues to be afraid and that even now she will not go out alone at night. In fact, she testified that she no longer sees movies or attends parties, the ballet, or the theatre. Admittedly, plaintiff cannot separate the impact of her arrest from the impact of her strip search.

At trial, plaintiff produced four witnesses to corroborate her testimony that she has suffered continuous and deep emotional trauma as a result of her strip search. First, her daughter testified that during the two to three weeks following the search, she talked to her mother two to three times a week. Often during these conversations, plaintiff expressed to her daughter that she felt humiliated and afraid, and that she was frightened of the police and fearful for her own safety. Swenson testified that plaintiff does go out alone during the day, but will not go out at night unless accompanied by an escort. Second, Bonnie Deutsch, a neighbor of plaintiff's for the last thirteen years, testified that she noticed a change in plaintiff's behavior in 1976, and that she no longer sees plaintiff outdoors anymore. . . . On cross-examination, she admitted that she has no knowledge of whether plaintiff is employed or married.

At the time of the strip search, plaintiff worked as a booking agent for various musicians. As a part of her job, plaintiff visited various nightclubs during the night and early morning hours to listen to musicians. Plaintiff offered the testimony of her third and fourth witnesses to corroborate her claim that she could not maintain her job as a booking agent because of her fear of going out alone at night. Lynn Roeder, a professional musician, . . . testified that plaintiff refused her request to act as her agent in 1976. . . . According to Roeder, after inquiring for almost a year, she learned that plaintiff would not act as her agent because she was afraid to go out at night. On cross-examination, however, defendant impeached Roeder's credibility by pointing out that in an earlier deposition she had testified differently as to the date when plaintiff stopped booking her. Finally, Oett Mallard, a member of the Chicago Musicians Union and its examining board . . . , testified that plaintiff continued to bring clients to the board for auditions through 1977 or 1978. While he stated that plaintiff brought in fewer musicians in 1977, he admitted that the booking agent business suffered a general slowdown in 1978 or 1979.

To refute plaintiff's claim that the strip search caused her to become a "prisoner in [her] own home," defendant put witnesses on the stand who testified that they have seen plaintiff outside her home on a number of occasions since December 1975. John Danek, a police officer, testified that . . . he had seen plaintiff alone at night on some occasions.

James Shelton . . . stated that he saw plaintiff alone at [a] church function at night, but did not know whether she left alone.

Casimir and Barbara Krasuski, neighbors of the plaintiff for over twenty-five years, testified that they have not noticed any change in plaintiff's behavior after 1975. . . . Barbara Krasuski has seen plaintiff . . . coming and going at night both before and after 1975. . . . Additionally, she testified that plaintiff . . . recently . . . told her that she was beginning work . . . at Roosevelt Hospital from 3:00 P.M. until 11:00 P.M. She does not know whether plaintiff actually worked those hours.

Finally, defendant's last witness, E.H. Trisko, the secretary-treasurer of the Chicago Federation of Musicians, testified that . . . plaintiff paid dues to the union at least as late as December, 1976, one year after her strip search. . . .

[T]he jury returned a verdict in favor of the plaintiff in the amount of $50,000. The full amount of the award constituted compensation for "[e]motional trauma and distress, mental and physical suffering, anguish, fear, humiliation and embarrassment." With respect to plaintiff's claims for both lost earnings and loss or impairment of earning capacity, the jury . . . award[ed] no damages to plaintiff on either of those claims.

II. THE DAMAGE AWARD

In reviewing a jury verdict . . . to determine whether it is excessive, we must defer to the judgment of the jury unless the award is "monstrously excessive" or "so large as to shock the conscience of the court." Mary Beth G. v. City of Chicago, 723 F.2d 1263, 1275 (7th Cir. 1984) *(as modified)*. . . . One factor we must consider in determining whether to set aside an award is whether the award is out of line compared to other awards in similar cases.

In the nine damage suits brought against the City of Chicago by women who were subjected to unconstitutional strip searches, the juries have awarded compensatory damages ranging from $3,300 to $112,000. More particularly, the juries returned the verdicts in the following amounts: one for $3,300, two for $15,000, two for $25,000, one for $30,000, one for $45,000, and, one for $112,000. [Later the court discusses a $60,000 verdict that is omitted from this list.] Comparing the $50,000 award in this case with the awards in the other strip search cases, this award stands out as remarkably high. We are persuaded further of its inconsistency with prior awards by reviewing the facts of the three cases in which the juries returned verdicts over $30,000. In those cases, aggravating circumstances existed. . . .

In *Mary T.*, the case in which the jury returned a verdict . . . of $45,000, . . . plaintiff was subjected to a cavity search. [A cavity search includes physical probing of body cavities, typically the mouth, rectum, and vagina.] . . . [P]laintiff also alleged that the matron felt her breasts and threatened that if she did not comply with the strip search male officers would be called in to assist with the search. . . . [T]he jury attributed 75% of the $45,000 award to damages arising out of the cavity search.

Similarly, the presence of aggravating circumstances in *Joan W.* throws light on the jury's award of $112,000. . . . Judge Getzendanner noted that the matrons were hostile towards plaintiff when conducting the search, that they "ridicul[ed], shout[ed], taunt[ed], and threaten[ed]," that they referred to plaintiff's body in foul and vulgar terms, and they "forced her repeatedly to squat and to push her fingers into her vagina and rectum, all the time yelling to her that she was not doing it good enough, forcing her to weep and bend to their will." In upholding the jury's award, Judge Getzendanner emphasized that plaintiff possessed certain frailties prior to the strip search that caused her to be particularly susceptible to the damaging effects of the strip search.

In the only case in which this court has addressed the issue of excessiveness of damages arising from unconstitutional strip searches, we upheld two awards in the amount of $25,000, one award in the amount of $30,000, and one award of $60,000. *Mary Beth G.*, 723 F.2d 1263. . . . In reviewing the $60,000 award to Hinda Hoffman, we first ordered a remittitur reducing the award to $35,000 in order to bring it in line with the other awards. . . . [W]e subsequently modified our first opinion and affirmed the $60,000 award. We based our modification, in part, on the presence of aggravating circumstances. . . . Hoffman alleged that she was strip searched in front of a camera and in the presence of two male officers and a group of jeering prostitutes. Although this court allowed the award to stand, we reaffirmed the principle that an award may be set aside or reduced if it is "out of line with a clear trend of awards of lesser amounts." *Id.* at 1275.

Comparing the facts of this case to the facts of the three cases in which juries returned awards exceeding $30,000, we find that the award of $50,000 in this case is grossly excessive and must be reduced. . . . Here, no comparable aggravating circumstances exist. Plaintiff was not subjected to a cavity search, nor was she forced to probe herself. . . . [T]he matrons conducted the search in private, out of the presence of male officers, other arrestees, or a camera. Unlike the matrons in some of the other cases, the matrons in this case were pleasant and matter-of-fact, never threatening to plaintiff. In fact, fewer aggravating circumstances existed in this case than in two of the cases in which juries returned lesser damage awards. In *Susan B.*, the jury awarded $15,000 to a woman who was ordered to squat five times despite her objections that she had not recovered from a recent hysterectomy and that a strip search would cause her substantial pain and create a threat of injury. In *Stella S.*, the jury awarded $15,000 to a woman who was subjected to probing by a police officer of her vaginal and rectal openings.

Whatever the extent of our review of trial evidence may be ordinarily, the Supreme Court has mandated that when we are called upon to determine whether a jury award is excessive we must "make a detailed appraisal of the evidence bearing on damages." Grunenthal v. Long Island Railroad, 393 U.S. 156, 159 (1968). The plaintiff simply has not offered any evidence to suggest that the strip search to which she was subjected was performed in any aggravated manner. . . . While we believe that the particular frailties which some plaintiffs possess prior to being subjected to a strip search may make those women more susceptible to emotional damage than other women, we are not persuaded that plaintiff's age [53] is such a frailty in this case. . . .

Not only does defendant's evidence refute any suggestion of the presence of aggravating circumstances, but it also controverts plaintiff's testimony that she has become a prisoner in her own home as a result of the strip search. . . .

[T]he jury . . . reflected its opinion that her emotional distress and mental suffering was not such as to have been the cause of her claimed loss or impairment of earning capacity. We are left with the distinct impression from all the evidence that the jury was in fact assessing punitive rather than compensatory damages. . . .

While we do not belittle the distress that plaintiff sustained as a result of her strip search, we think that the evidence simply does not support a damage award of this magnitude. Although plaintiff testified that she visited a psychiatrist about one month after the strip search, one isolated visit to the psychiatrist is inconsistent with plaintiff's contention that she was suffering from severe and continuing trauma. Thus, in light of all the evidence and in light of the awards rendered in other strip search cases, we are of the opinion that a remittitur of $25,000 would be appropriate. . . .

III. Conclusion . . .

The district court's order is reversed . . . and this case is remanded . . . with directions to hold a new trial unless plaintiff accepts the entry of a remittitur reducing the award to $25,000.

NOTES ON VALUING EMOTIONAL DISTRESS

1. The strip-search cases. The $112,000 award in *Joan W.* was reduced on appeal to $75,000. Joan W. v. City of Chicago, 771 F.2d 1020 (7th Cir. 1985). The court said that the aggravating circumstances in *Joan W.* were no different in kind from the other cases, but that "a jury could rationally find some differences in degree." *Id.* at 1025.

Judgments like those in *Levka* are supposed to deter illegal policies, but bureaucracies are slow to get the word and sometimes stubborn when they do. Professor Schlanger found "nearly a hundred jail strip-search class actions, and . . . hundreds more individual cases." Margo Schlanger, *Jail Strip-Search Cases: Patterns and Participants,* 71 L. & Contemp. Probs. 65, 73 (Spring 2008). These policies apply to women's jails more often than men's jails, allegedly because women have more places to hide things.

The law had long been against the jailers in these cases, but that has changed. Florence v. Board of Chosen Freeholders, 566 U.S. 318 (2012), upheld routine strip searches of all arrestees who are placed in the jail's general population, no matter how trivial the offense. There were four dissents.

The Court reserved judgment on whether arrestees held briefly and separately from the general population (which appear to have been the facts in *Levka*) could be strip searched without reasonable suspicion. And nothing in *Florence* suggests that it would be lawful to strip search women but not men, as in *Levka.* So *Levka* may still be good law even on liability. However that turns out, the opinion is still a great vehicle for exploring the difficulties of proving, rebutting, and measuring damages for emotional distress.

2. Other examples. The constitutional nature of the claims in *Levka* did not affect the measure of damages. Plaintiff invoked common-law measures of damage developed for common-law dignitary torts. Dignitary torts—including assault, false imprisonment, malicious prosecution, intentional infliction of emotional distress, libel, slander, invasion of privacy, and batteries that are offensive but not physically harmful—present valuation problems comparable to those of pain and suffering. The amounts involved are generally smaller, but the valuations are no more reliable. As in the pain and suffering cases, juries are given no more precise instruction than to do what is reasonable. Consider the valuation problems in the following cases:

a. Police officers entered a house in the middle of the night, without a warrant or consent, but after one of the owners had opened the door. They awoke the owners' teenage son, who they say resisted, probably before coming fully awake. They punched him in the face, tasered him, handcuffed him, and took him out to squad car; at some point fairly early in this process, they realized that he was not the person they were looking for. They apologized. This case involves physical as well as emotional injuries, but none of the physical injuries were lasting. A jury found a Fourth Amendment violation and awarded $6 to the son and his parents against six defendants. Franklin v. Mentz, 2016 WL 7111993 (N.D. Ind. 2016).

b. A jury awarded $16,500 for the emotional distress of an innocent man jailed for 13 days. This was not a claim against those who prosecuted him, but a legal malpractice claim against his public defender, who lost a document that unambiguously exonerated him, and neglected to set his case for hearing. The document was a restoration of plaintiff's civil rights, entitling him to carry a firearm despite a felony conviction in the 60s. Rowell v. Holt, 850 So. 2d 474 (Fla. 2003).

c. Plaintiff and defendant broke up after a brief sexual relationship, and plaintiff married someone else. Defendant spread the word around town, including to plaintiff's family and employer, that he had gotten her pregnant before dumping her. She later claimed to have had a miscarriage; she apparently had never been pregnant. The town was Shell Rock, Iowa—population 1,300. Plaintiff testified that his sister and some of defendant's friends had shunned him, that he had lost sleep, and that he felt depressed. But his marriage was still happy, he still had his job, and he had not sought counseling. The trial judge awarded $2,500 for intentional infliction of emotional distress. Weaver v. Garner, 2016 WL 2941591 (Iowa Dist. Ct. 2016).

In North Carolina, one of the few states to retain and occasionally enforce the tort of alienation of affections, a trial judge awarded $50,000 for emotional distress and $50,000 in punitive damages against a woman who had seduced plaintiff's husband. King v. Harris, 2015 WL 13237467 (N.C. Super. Ct. 2015).

d. A judge sent a deputy sheriff to buy coffee. Both the judge and the deputy thought that the coffee tasted "putrid," and the judge told the deputy to get the coffee vendor and bring him "in front of me in cuffs." Plaintiff was handcuffed and marched through the courthouse in full view of dozens of people. The judge interrogated, threatened, and screamed at plaintiff for 20 minutes. Plaintiff testified that he was very upset by the incident, that he could not sleep, that he started to stutter and get headaches, that he required treatment at a hospital, that he could not work, and that his wife asked him to move out of the house. The jury awarded $80,000 compensatory damages and $60,000 punitive damages. The compensatory award was not challenged, and the punitive award was upheld. Zarcone v. Perry, 572 F.2d 52, 53 (2d Cir. 1978).

e. A security guard mistakenly accused a black woman of shoplifting, emptied her purse on a counter, and inspected the receipts for all her purchases. Hampton v. Dillard Department Stores, Inc., 247 F.3d 1091 (10th Cir. 2001). She was not arrested or expelled from the store.

> [P]laintiff gave eloquent and emotionally moving testimony that [the guard] disgraced and humiliated her, in front of her children, that she was too emotionally distraught to drive, and that she had to call her husband for a ride home. Immediately after the incident she was crying and she was so upset that she could not write out a customer comment card, and a Dillard's employee filled it out for her. She testified that "I don't feel my life will ever be the same."

Id. at 1115. Plaintiff also offered evidence of a pattern and practice of subjecting black customers to disparate security practices. The court upheld a jury verdict of $56,000 in compensatory damages and $1.1 million in punitive damages.

Compare Elrod v. Wal-Mart Stores, Inc., 737 So. 2d 208 (La. Ct. App. 1999), where a store manager mistakenly accused Elrod of harassing a female employee of the store. The conversation escalated until Elrod was shouting obscenities and bumped the store manager in the rear with his shopping cart. Wal-Mart then detained him in a back room, where the female employee promptly said that Elrod was not the man who had harassed her. Wal-Mart had Elrod charged with battery for the shopping cart bump; after being held in the back room from 4:00 to 5:00 P.M., he was escorted through the store in handcuffs and taken to jail. His wife bailed him out about 8:00 P.M., and they went home to a badly delayed family dinner celebrating Christmas Eve. He pled no contest to the battery and paid a small fine.

Elrod testified that he suffered stomach upset, diarrhea, and nervousness in the days following the incident and got medication from his doctor. His wife testified that he was upset during those days and that now he wants to stay home all the time. In a bench trial, the judge awarded $3,500. The appellate court rejected Wal-Mart's argument that this was excessive.

f. The court affirmed jury awards of $275,000 to the father, and $475,000 to the mother, against a crematorium that gave them ashes that were not those of their deceased son. Akers v. Prime Succession of Tennessee, Inc., 387 S.W.3d 495 (Tenn. 2012). There was evidence of widespread misconduct and scattering of uncremated bodies by defendant. This evidence went to show that what happened to plaintiffs was intentional infliction of emotional distress and not just a negligent mistake, but no doubt it also influenced the jury's assessment of damages. A Florida jury awarded $1 million for emotional distress and $2.5 million in punitive damages in a similar incident, apparently with much less evidence of widespread misconduct. Mitchell v. Stinson Industries, 2016 WL 6124224 (Fla. Cir. Ct. 2016).

A student on Staten Island was killed in an auto accident. The medical examiner for the county performed an autopsy and then released the body to the family for burial. Two months later, forensic-science students from decedent's high school took a field trip to the county morgue. One of them saw decedent's brain, labeled with his name, sitting in a jar on a shelf. It was soon revealed that the county had retained the brain and parts of other internal organs for later examination. The family's priest said that the burial was not proper without the brain; the family attended a second funeral and burial.

A jury awarded each parent $500,000 for violation of their common-law right to have the body for burial. The Appellate Division reduced this to $300,000 each—$600,000 in all—with little explanation. Shipley v. City of New York, 963 N.Y.S.2d 692 (App. Div. 2013). The facts are taken from the opinion of the Court of Appeals, which reversed on the ground that no rights had been violated. 37 N.E.3d 58 (N.Y. 2015).

g. The Second Circuit upheld $1,320,000 in compensatory damages for management's failure to protect a black employee from a three-year campaign of unusually severe racial harassment; many examples are set out in the opinion. Turley v. ISG Lackawanna, Inc., 774 F.3d 140 (2d Cir. 2014). The emotional damage may be permanent. The victim had once been happy and confident, but at the time of trial, he suffered from panic attacks, depression, and post-traumatic stress disorder; one witness described him as a "broken" man. The court said the award "tests the boundaries," but under the "exceptional and egregious facts of this case," it was "fair and reasonable." *Id.* at 163. The opinion collects somewhat similar cases from elsewhere.

h. A federal judge refused to set aside a verdict of $5 million for emotional distress and $10 million in punitive damages in an age discrimination case. Rawson v. Sears Roebuck & Co., 615 F. Supp. 1546 (D. Colo. 1985), *rev'd on other grounds*, 822 F.2d 908 (10th Cir. 1987). Plaintiff was a 60-year-old store manager discharged in a "callous and demeaning manner;" his reputation in the community was "destroyed;" and he "contemplated suicide." 615 F. Supp. at 1552-1553. Defendant argued that emotional distress could not rationally be worth several times as much as permanent quadriplegic paralysis. The court found that comparison "inapposite," in part because other sources of treatment and compensation were available to victims of paralysis. How convincing is that?

i. An Arizona jury awarded $22.8 million against a wealthy ex-husband who hired a hit man to kill his ex-wife, her sister, and her parents. The scheme failed, and the ex-husband was sentenced to life imprisonment. Rozenman v. Rozenman, 2015 WL 7008396 (Ariz. Super. Ct. 2015).

j. A novelist sued when a magazine incorrectly stated that she was one of the nude women in photographs of an orgy. An all-female jury in New York City awarded her $7 million for invasion of privacy, plus $33 million in punitive damages. The court of appeals found both awards "grossly excessive;" it noted that plaintiff had not sought counseling or suspended her writing and that other juries in similar cases had awarded $1,500 and $25,000. Lerman v. Flynt Distributing Co., 745 F.2d 123, 141 (2d Cir. 1984).

3. Punitive damages in disguise? Defendants' motives and the nature of their conduct, usually relevant only to punitive damages, become relevant to compensatory damages in these cases. The more outrageous the defendant's behavior, the more outraged and distressed the victim will be.

NOTES ON JUDICIAL REVIEW OF JURY VERDICTS

1. Remittitur. The procedure by which the verdict is reduced in *Levka* is called remittitur, because the court grants a new trial unless plaintiff remits part of the verdict. This is generally held to be consistent with the right to jury trial, because plaintiff is given a choice, and because the court is not supposed to remit down to what the court would have awarded, but only to the highest amount a jury could have awarded without triggering a new trial. The Seventh Amendment precludes federal courts from simply entering judgment for the lower amount. Hetzel v. Prince William County, 523 U.S. 208 (1998). Responsibility for federal remittiturs is principally vested in trial judges, whose decisions are reviewable only for abuse of discretion. Gasperini v. Center for Humanities, 518 U.S. 415 (1996). State practice varies but is generally similar.

2. Plaintiff's choice. Most plaintiffs accept remittiturs rather than the risk and expense of a new trial. A plaintiff who elects a new trial gambles both that the second jury will come in with a higher verdict than the court left after remittitur, and that the court will change its mind and let that higher verdict stand. Occasionally the court does change its mind in light of a better marshalling of the evidence on retrial or the concurrence of two juries. An example is Weinberg v. Johnson, 518 A.2d 985 (D.C. 1986), where the trial judge held that $800,000 was excessive and granted a new trial, and then upheld a second verdict of $2 million.

3. Additur? In federal court, the only remedy for an unreasonably low verdict is a new trial. The Supreme Court held that additur, or conditionally increasing the verdict, would violate the right to jury trial by adding damages that no jury had ever found. Dimick v. Schiedt, 293 U.S. 474 (1935). In states that permit it, it works like remittitur; defendant must be given a choice of a new trial or paying the increased amount. Rash v. Moczulski, 153 A.3d 719 (Del. 2016).

4. Comparative review. The *Levka* court evaluates the verdict by comparing it to other verdicts in similar cases. The traditional position—in all cases, not just emotional distress cases—has been that other verdicts are irrelevant. Facts and juries vary, and if you go to trial, you take your chances. The traditional view is illustrated in Chrysler Group, LLC v. Walden, 792 S.E.2d 754 (Ga. Ct. App. 2016), *aff'd on other grounds*, 812 S.E.2d 244 (Ga. 2018). But the traditional rule is under pressure; since *Levka*, several federal circuits have begun comparing verdicts. New York's experience with comparative review of verdicts is favorably assessed in David Baldus, John C. MacQueen, & George Woodworth, *Improving Judicial Oversight of Jury Damages Assessments: A Proposal for the Comparative Additur/Remittitur Review of Awards for Nonpecuniary Harms and Punitive Damages*, 80 Iowa L. Rev. 1109 (1995).

The Fifth Circuit experience is harshly criticized in Lawrence James Madigan, *Excessive Damage Review in the Fifth Circuit: A Quagmire of Inconsistency*, 34 Tex. Tech L. Rev. 429 (2003). Some panels compare verdicts and some don't; those that do have evolved a mechanical jurisprudence that can be manipulated by the choice of analogous verdicts. The whole concept is harshly criticized as arbitrary, and as operating in effect only to lower verdicts, in JoEllen Lind, *The End of Trial on Damages? Intangible Losses and Comparability Review*, 51 Buff. L. Rev. 251 (2003). For a Second Circuit example, upholding $115,000 for a false arrest and one night in jail after briefly reviewing several judgments in similar cases, see Dancy v. McGinley, 843 F.3d 93, 113-115 (2d Cir. 2016).

5. Judicial attitudes. Judicial aggressiveness in granting remittiturs or new trials varies over time and with political shifts and among jurisdictions. The deferential

view is captured in Rawson v. Sears, the case of the callously discharged manager summarized in the previous set of notes:

> [T]he constant exposure to death, injury and outrage which confronts judges neces-
> sarily jades our vision and immures our emotions. The genius of the jury system is the
> deliverance of judgment by collective response from members of the community who
> have ordinary experience. . . .
>   [M]y judicial conscience is not shocked—though my acquired cynicism has received
> a rather sharp blow.

615 F. Supp. at 1553.

Compare the very different judicial attitude in this excerpt from a personal injury
case:

> [T]his court takes note of the increasing willingness of the appellate courts to review
> damage awards. There is no doubt that this trend is a response to the increasingly out-
> rageous amounts demanded by plaintiffs and awarded by juries. A jury has very broad
> discretion in measuring damages; nevertheless, a jury may not abandon analysis for
> sympathy for a suffering plaintiff and treat an injury as though it were a winning lottery
> ticket.

Gumbs v. Pueblo International, 823 F.2d 768, 773 (3d Cir. 1987). The jury in *Gumbs*
awarded $900,000 in a slip and fall case, the trial judge reduced it to $575,000, and
the court of appeals reduced it again to $235,000. All three numbers appear to have
come out of thin air. The court of appeals emphasized that plaintiff had not been
hospitalized and lost no work; plaintiff emphasized that she suffered chronic pain
and sexual dysfunction that led to divorce, and that she missed no work only because
she worked as an accountant in her own house. Wasn't she hurt a lot worse than the
manager in *Rawson*?

Compare *Gumbs* with a remarkable European case. A botched operation left a
50-year-old woman with pain, incontinence, and inability to have sex. The trial court
awarded €96,000. Portugal's Supreme Administrative Court reduced that to €64,000,
partly on the ground that sex is less important to women over 50! Public opinion
was outraged, and the European Court of Human Rights reversed the reduction of
damages, attributing the decision to age and sex discrimination and "prejudices prevailing in the judiciary in Portugal." Morais v. Portugal, Application No. 17484/15
(Eur. Ct. Human Rights July 25, 2017), available at http://hudoc.echr.coe.int/
eng?i=001-175659.

NOTES ON RECOVERING FOR EMOTIONAL DISTRESS

1. In tort. Emotional distress is recoverable in intentional tort, but not in negligence without some additional threshold showing. A plaintiff who suffers physical injury can generally recover for associated emotional distress. About half the
states permit recovery for emotional distress by bystanders who see their loved one
injured, and another quarter permit recovery for persons within the zone of physical
danger created by defendant's negligence. There is occasional movement among
these rules; Oregon has abandoned its requirement of physical impact and allowed
recovery for plaintiffs who see a loved one killed or injured. Philibert v. Kluser, 385
P.3d 1038 (Or. 2016).

Many states also permit recovery for specific categories of negligence that are especially likely to inflict emotional distress; the traditional categories were sending false news of a death, mishandling a corpse, or leaving disgusting foreign matter in a food product. This list can expand; the Florida court imposed emotional distress liability on a marriage counselor who revealed confidences without permission. Gracey v. Eaker, 837 So. 2d 348 (Fla. 2002). The court relied on statutory protection for psychotherapeutic confidences and on cases holding that physical impact is not required when emotional distress is the principal harm to be expected from a tort. Cases on all these rules are collected in *Restatement (Third) of Torts: Liability for Physical and Emotional Harm* §§45-47 (Am. Law Inst. 2010).

Collectively, these rules are analogous to the stranger variant of economic-loss rule in section 2.E.3. To recover in tort for either economic loss or emotional distress, plaintiff must show something more than negligence: intentional tort, negligence plus physical impact, or negligence plus one of these other options for emotional distress. The restrictions on liability for emotional distress flow from persistent judicial fear of fraudulent claims and expansive liability for minor social frictions.

2. Objective manifestations. A few states say it is enough that plaintiff's emotional distress showed objective physical manifestations. In Bass v. Nooney Co., 646 S.W.2d 765, 772-773 (Mo. 1983), plaintiff suffered a "severe anxiety reaction" and was hospitalized for 5 days as a result of being trapped in an elevator for 30 minutes. The court allowed recovery, announcing that it will allow recovery for negligently inflicted emotional distress if it is "diagnosable" and "medically significant" and suffered by a "direct victim" of the negligence.

The reach of *Bass* was at issue in Jarrett v. Jones, 258 S.W.3d 442 (Mo. 2008). Plaintiff was a professional truck driver; defendant's car crossed the median of I-44 and crashed into his truck. Plaintiff stopped his truck and ran to the car, where he found a two-year-old girl dead. He suffered post-traumatic stress disorder and couldn't return to work for four months. So his distress was significant and medically diagnosable, and he was a direct victim of the accident. The court upheld his claim for negligent infliction of emotional distress against the driver of the car, who was the little girl's father.

3. Severity. Quite apart from objective manifestation as a possible plus in the requirement of negligence-plus, there is an ill-defined requirement that emotional distress be severe or substantial. In negligence, courts often require medically demonstrable emotional distress. Plaintiff's testimony has traditionally been enough in intentional tort cases, but that rule is encountering resistance. The Fifth Circuit has reversed emotional distress awards based only on the facts of what happened and plaintiffs' testimony about how bad they felt, in the absence of any corroborating evidence of physical symptoms, medical or psychological treatment, or testimony from others who observed the plaintiffs. "While the district court could infer that being referred to as a 'porch monkey' and 'nigger' would cause one emotional distress, Brown has not presented evidence with the specificity required . . . nor has Brown testified as to any manifestations of harm." Patterson v. P.H.P. Healthcare Corp., 90 F.3d 927, 939 (5th Cir. 1996). Why wasn't the district court's inference enough? Subsequent cases rejected the argument that *Patterson* requires medical testimony or other corroborating evidence in every case. Migis v. Pearle Vision, Inc., 135 F.3d 1041 (5th Cir. 1998).

Courts in New York and the Second Circuit now categorize emotional distress as "garden variety," "significant," or "egregious." It is not clear where these distinctions originated, but they are laid out in some detail in Parris v. Pappas, 844 F. Supp. 2d 271 (D. Conn. 2012). Garden variety emotional distress does not require medical treatment and can be proved by the plaintiff's own testimony, which may be "vague and conclusory." "Garden variety emotional distress claims generally merit $30,000 to $125,000 awards."

> Significant emotional distress claims . . . are based on more substantial harm or more offensive conduct, are sometimes supported by medical testimony and evidence, evidence of treatment by a healthcare professional and/or medication, and testimony from other, corroborating witnesses. Finally, egregious emotional distress claims generally involve either outrageous or shocking discriminatory conduct or a significant impact on the physical health of the plaintiff. In significant or egregious cases, where there is typically evidence of debilitating and permanent alterations in lifestyle, larger damage awards may be warranted.

Id. at 278.

The Eighth Circuit has said that an award for emotional distress must be supported by "competent evidence of 'genuine injury,'" but that the trial judge need not tell the jury that, and that it might be misleading if she does. A jury might take that to mean that medical or other expert evidence is required, but the "plaintiff's own testimony, along with the circumstances of the particular case, can suffice to sustain the plaintiff's burden." Blackorby v. BNSF Railway Co., 849 F.3d 716, 723 (8th Cir.), *cert. denied*, 138 S. Ct. 264 (2017).

4. Fear of disease. A recurring issue is whether plaintiffs exposed to toxic substances with long latency periods can recover for the fear of eventually contracting the disease. There is a good debate on these issues in Norfolk & Western Railway v. Ayers, 538 U.S. 135 (2003), a railroad case under the Federal Employers' Liability Act, 45 U.S.C. §51 *et seq.* The majority held that plaintiffs with asbestosis have suffered physical injury and can therefore sue for associated emotional distress, including the fear of later contracting cancer, provided that plaintiff must "prove that his alleged fear is genuine and serious." *Id.* at 157. Asbestosis patients have a higher risk of cancer, but even so, only about 10 percent eventually get cancer. Four dissenters thought that asbestosis supported only a claim for emotional distress from asbestosis, not distress based on fear of a cancer that would probably never happen. They thought the requirement of genuine and serious fear illusory.

In CSX Transportation, Inc. v. Hensley, 556 U.S. 838 (2009), the Court summarily reversed a judgment for plaintiff, because the trial court had not instructed the jury on the "genuine and serious" standard. Justice Ginsburg agreed that *Ayers* would support a "plain and simple instruction" that plaintiff must prove that his fear of cancer is genuine and serious. But she dissented on the ground that it was not error to refuse the "far more elaborate" and "defense-oriented instructions" the railroad had requested. CSX would have had the judge tell the jury that, in deciding whether plaintiff's fear of cancer is genuine and serious,

> you may take into account whether or not the Plaintiff has voiced more than a general concern about his future health, whether or not he has suffered from insomnia or other stress-related conditions, whether or not he has sought psychiatric or medical attention for his symptoms, whether he has consulted counselors or ministers concerning his fear, whether he has demonstrated any physical symptoms as a result of his fear, and whether he has produced witnesses who can corroborate his fear.

Id. at 843 n.1 (Stevens, J., dissenting). The reach of the Court's opinion is unclear, but we don't think it requires this instruction. We think it holds that it is error not to instruct on the "genuine and serious" issue, and that in the absence of any alternative from plaintiff or the court, it was error to refuse the instructions proffered by CSX.

5. In contract. Emotional distress is generally not compensable in contract. But most courts treat bad-faith breach of an insurance contract as a tort; this opens the door to emotional distress and punitive damages. The exception has not spread to other categories of one-sided contracts. Common-law claims for wrongful discharge are just a specialized breach-of-contract claim in most states. But emotional distress is often recoverable in statutory claims for employment discrimination, and is expressly contemplated in 42 U.S.C. §1981a(b)(3).

Erlich v. Menezes, 981 P.2d 978 (Cal. 1999), reversed an award for emotional distress in a suit by homeowners against their builder. The builder's gross negligence resulted in their dream house being saturated with water—rotting the ceiling, pouring in streams down the walls, and standing three-inches deep on the living room floor. No doubt they suffered emotional distress, but the court said their claim was for breach of contract, and to allow tort damages for a negligent breach would destroy the rule. The court surveyed exceptions, which it characterized as all involving personal injury, intentional wrongdoing, or insurance contracts. Two commentators add to this list unusually personal contracts, such as contracts about marriage, funerals, and the handling of bodies. David A. Hoffman & Alexander S. Radur, *Instructing Juries on Noneconomic Contract Damages*, 81 Fordham L. Rev. 1221 (2012). All of these exceptions appear to be narrowly construed.

CAREY v. PIPHUS
435 U.S. 247 (1978)

Justice POWELL delivered the opinion of the Court. . . .

[Piphus was a high school freshman. The school's principal saw Piphus with what the principal believed, by shape and smell, was a marijuana cigarette. Without recovering the joint or giving Piphus a chance to explain himself, the principal suspended Piphus for 20 days. Piphus sued, alleging that he had been suspended without an adequate hearing to determine his guilt or innocence, in violation of the Due Process Clause. He was readmitted to school under a temporary restraining order after 8 days.

Plaintiff sought a declaratory judgment, an injunction deleting the suspension from his record, and $3,000 in damages. The trial court held that the suspension without a hearing violated due process, but that plaintiff had offered no evidence of damages. The court said that plaintiff was entitled to declaratory and injunctive relief, but inexplicably dismissed the complaints without granting that relief. The court made no finding about Piphus's guilt or innocence. The court of appeals reversed on the remedial issues, holding that plaintiff was entitled to declaratory judgment, injunction, and damages. 545 F.2d 30 (7th Cir. 1976).]

II

Title 42 U.S.C. §1983 provides:

Every person who, under color of any statute, ordinance, regulation, custom, or usage, of any State or Territory, subjects, or causes to be subjected, any citizen of the United States or other person within the jurisdiction thereof to the deprivation of any rights, privileges, or immunities secured by the Constitution and laws, shall be liable to the party injured in an action at law, suit in equity, or other proper proceeding for redress.

The legislative history of §1983 demonstrates that it was intended to "[create] a species of tort liability" in favor of persons who are deprived of "rights, privileges, or immunities secured" to them by the Constitution. Imbler v. Pachtman, 424 U.S. 409, 417 (1976).

Petitioners contend that the elements and prerequisites for recovery of damages under this "species of tort liability" should parallel those for recovery of damages under the common law of torts. In particular, they urge that the purpose of an award of damages under §1983 should be to compensate persons for injuries that are caused by the deprivation of constitutional rights; and, further, that plaintiffs should be required to prove not only that their rights were violated, but also that injury was caused by the violation, in order to recover substantial damages. Unless respondents prove that they actually were injured by the deprivation of procedural due process, petitioners argue, they are entitled at most to nominal damages.

Respondents seem to make two different arguments in support of the holding below. First, they contend that substantial damages should be awarded under §1983 for the deprivation of a constitutional right *whether or not* any injury was caused by the deprivation. This, they say, is appropriate both because constitutional rights are valuable in and of themselves, and because of the need to deter violations of constitutional rights. . . . Second, respondents argue that even if the purpose of a §1983 damages award is, as petitioners contend, primarily to compensate persons for injuries that are caused by the deprivation of constitutional rights, every deprivation of procedural due process may be *presumed* to cause some injury. . . .

A

Insofar as petitioners contend that the basic purpose of a §1983 damages award should be to compensate persons for injuries caused by the deprivation of constitutional rights, they have the better of the argument. Rights, constitutional and otherwise, do not exist in a vacuum. Their purpose is to protect persons from injuries to particular interests, and their contours are shaped by the interests they protect. . . .

To the extent that Congress intended that awards under §1983 should deter the deprivation of constitutional rights, there is no evidence that it meant to establish a deterrent more formidable than that inherent in the award of compensatory damages.[11]

B

It is less difficult to conclude that damages awarded under §1983 should be governed by the principle of compensation than it is to apply this principle to concrete cases. But over the centuries the common law of torts has developed a set of rules to implement the principle that a person should be compensated fairly for injuries caused by

---

11. This is not to say that exemplary or punitive damages might not be awarded in a proper case under §1983 with the specific purpose of deterring or punishing violations of constitutional rights. . . . [T]here is no basis for such an award in this case. The District Court specifically found that petitioners did not act with malicious intention to deprive respondents of their rights or to do them other injury. . . .

We also note that the potential liability of §1983 defendants for attorney's fees, 42 U.S.C. §1988, provides additional—and by no means inconsequential—assurance that agents of the State will not deliberately ignore due process rights. *See also* 18 U.S.C. §242, the criminal counterpart of §1983.

the violation of his legal rights. These rules, defining the elements of damages and the prerequisites for their recovery, provide the appropriate starting point for the inquiry under §1983 as well. . . .

In order to further the purpose of §1983, the rules governing compensation for injuries caused by the deprivation of constitutional rights should be tailored to the interests protected by the particular right in question—just as the common-law rules of damages themselves were defined by the interests protected in the various branches of tort law. . . .

C

The Due Process Clause of the Fourteenth Amendment provides: "[N]or shall any State deprive any person of life, liberty, or property, without due process of law." . . . Procedural due process rules are meant to protect persons not from the deprivation, but from the mistaken or unjustified deprivation of life, liberty, or property. . . .

In this case, the Court of Appeals held that if petitioners can prove on remand that "[respondents] would have been suspended even if a proper hearing had been held," then respondents will not be entitled to recover damages to compensate them for injuries caused by the suspensions. The court thought that in such a case, the failure to accord procedural due process could not properly be viewed as the cause of the suspensions. . . . We do not understand the parties to disagree with this conclusion. Nor do we.

The parties do disagree as to the further holding of the Court of Appeals that respondents are entitled to recover substantial—although unspecified—damages to compensate them for "the injury which is 'inherent in the nature of the wrong,'" even if their suspensions were justified and even if they fail to prove that the denial of procedural due process actually caused them some real, if intangible, injury. Respondents, elaborating on this theme, submit that the holding is correct because injury fairly may be "presumed" to flow from every denial of procedural due process. Their argument is that in addition to protecting against unjustified deprivations, the Due Process Clause also guarantees the "feeling of just treatment" by the government. Joint Anti-Fascist Refugee Committee v. McGrath, 341 U.S. 123, 162 (1951) (Frankfurter, J., concurring). They contend that the deprivation of protected interests without procedural due process, even where the premise for the deprivation is not erroneous, inevitably arouses strong feelings of mental and emotional distress in the individual who is denied this "feeling of just treatment." They analogize their case to that of defamation per se, in which "the plaintiff is relieved from the necessity of producing any proof whatsoever that he has been injured" in order to recover substantial compensatory damages. Charles T. McCormick, *Handbook on the Law of Damages* §116 at 423 (West 1935).

Petitioners do not deny that a purpose of procedural due process is to convey to the individual a feeling that the government has dealt with him fairly, as well as to minimize the risk of mistaken deprivations of protected interests. They go so far as to concede that, in a proper case, persons in respondents' position might well recover damages for mental and emotional distress caused by the denial of procedural due process. Petitioners' argument is the more limited one that such injury cannot be presumed to occur, and that plaintiffs at least should be put to their proof on the issue, as plaintiffs are in most tort actions.

We agree with petitioners in this respect. As we have observed in another context, the doctrine of presumed damages in the common law of defamation per se "is an oddity of tort law, for it allows recovery of purportedly compensatory damages without evidence of actual loss." Gertz v. Robert Welch, Inc., 418 U.S. 323, 349 (1974). The doctrine has been defended on the grounds that those forms of defamation that are actionable per se are virtually certain to cause serious injury to reputation, and that this kind of injury is extremely difficult to prove. Moreover, statements that are defamatory per se by their very nature are likely to cause mental and emotional distress, as well as injury to reputation, so there arguably is little reason to require proof of this kind of injury either. But these considerations do not support respondents' contention that damages should be presumed to flow from every deprivation of procedural due process.

First, it is not reasonable to assume that every departure from procedural due process, no matter what the circumstances or how minor, inherently is as likely to cause distress as the publication of defamation per se is to cause injury to reputation and distress. Where the deprivation of a protected interest is substantively justified but procedures are deficient in some respect, there may well be those who suffer no distress over the procedural irregularities. Indeed, in contrast to the immediately distressing effect of defamation per se, a person may not even know that procedures *were* deficient until he enlists the aid of counsel to challenge a perceived substantive deprivation.

Moreover, where a deprivation is justified but procedures are deficient, whatever distress a person feels may be attributable to the justified deprivation rather than to deficiencies in procedure. But . . . the injury caused by a justified deprivation, including distress, is not properly compensable under §1983. This ambiguity in causation . . . provides additional need for requiring the plaintiff to convince the trier of fact that he actually suffered distress because of the denial of procedural due process itself.

Finally, we foresee no particular difficulty in producing evidence that mental and emotional distress actually was caused by the denial of procedural due process itself. Distress is a personal injury familiar to the law, customarily proved by showing the nature and circumstances of the wrong and its effect on the plaintiff.[20] In sum, then, although mental and emotional distress caused by the denial of procedural due process itself is compensable under §1983, we hold that neither the likelihood of such injury nor the difficulty of proving it is so great as to justify awarding compensatory damages without proof that such injury actually was caused. . . .

III . . .

Common-law courts traditionally have vindicated deprivations of certain "absolute" rights that are not shown to have caused actual injury through the award of a nominal sum of money. By making the deprivation of such rights actionable for nominal damages without proof of actual injury, the law recognizes the importance to organized society that those rights be scrupulously observed; but at the same time, it remains true to the principle that substantial damages should be awarded only to compensate actual injury or, in the case of exemplary or punitive damages, to deter or punish malicious deprivations of rights.

---

20. We use the term "distress" to include mental suffering or emotional anguish. Although essentially subjective, genuine injury in this respect may be evidenced by one's conduct and observed by others. Juries must be guided by appropriate instructions, and an award of damages must be supported by competent evidence concerning the injury.

Because the right to procedural due process is "absolute" in the sense that it does not depend upon the merits of a claimant's substantive assertions, and because of the importance to organized society that procedural due process be observed, we believe that the denial of procedural due process should be actionable for nominal damages without proof of actual injury. We therefore hold that if, upon remand, the District Court determines that respondents' suspensions were justified, respondents nevertheless will be entitled to recover nominal damages not to exceed one dollar from petitioners.

The judgment . . . is reversed, and the case is remanded for further proceedings consistent with this opinion. . . .

Justice MARSHALL concurs in the result.

Justice BLACKMUN took no part in the consideration . . . of this case.

NOTES ON VALUING CONSTITUTIONAL RIGHTS

1. The value of constitutional rights. Does the Court ever answer plaintiff's argument that "constitutional rights are valuable in and of themselves"? Does one dollar really "vindicate" the importance of constitutional rights?

Some courts of appeals confined *Carey* to procedural due process, holding it inapplicable to substantive constitutional rights. That issue was resolved in Memphis Community School District v. Stachura, 477 U.S. 299 (1986). Stachura was a discharged school teacher. He claimed violations of his rights to free speech and procedural due process, and both claims were submitted to the jury. The judge instructed that the jury could compensate lost income and earning capacity, out-of-pocket expenses, mental anguish, emotional distress, and the value of the right to free speech. He then gave the following instruction:

> The precise value you place upon any constitutional right which you find was denied to plaintiff is within your discretion. You may wish to consider the importance of the right in our system of government, the role which this right has played in the history of the republic, the significance of the right in the context of the activities which the plaintiff was engaged in at the time of the violation of the right.

The jury returned a verdict of $275,000 compensatory damages and $46,000 punitive damages. The Supreme Court reversed, holding that *Carey* applies to substantive constitutional rights. Did the trial court in *Stachura* allow sentiment to justify excessive compensation? Or does the Supreme Court err in denying that constitutional rights have intrinsic value?

The Court distinguished older cases about damages for loss of the right to vote as awarding "presumed damages for a non-monetary harm that cannot easily be quantified." 477 U.S. at 311 n.14. This exception has had at least some life in the lower courts. Some of the cases are collected in King v. Zamiara, 788 F.3d 207 (6th Cir. 2015), affirming modest damages to a prisoner placed in a more restrictive unit in retaliation for the exercise of other rights.

2. Proving the damages. *Carey* does not necessarily preclude substantial verdicts. In Contract Design Group, Inc. v. Wayne State University, 635 F. App'x 222 (6th Cir. 2015), the court affirmed a jury award of $100,000 for the emotional distress of the individual owner of a business that, without due process of law, was barred from contracting with the university. The court emphasized that the jury had not found the bar to be justified, that it had been handled in an abrupt and embarrassing way, that plaintiff's business and his personal and business relationships suffered, and that he sought professional counseling.

Suppose the jury had found that the bar was actually justified, but that it had been imposed without due process. What are the ethical obligations of an attorney questioning his client about the sources of his emotional distress?

If you represented plaintiff in *Carey*, how would you prove the value of plaintiff's emotional distress? Assuming that a fair hearing would not have resulted in a suspension, how would you prove the value of eight days in the Chicago public schools? How would you approach these issues if you represented defendants?

3. The value of a hearing. Plaintiff in *Carey* argued that he was entitled to recover the value of his lost hearing just as he would be entitled to recover the value of a stolen bicycle. He wouldn't have to show that he would have ridden the bicycle if it hadn't been stolen. Is that the right analogy? Or is the right to a hearing like the right to have the people around you exercise due care to avoid injuring you? If someone is negligent, but no one gets hurt, the people who might have been hurt do not get to sue for the value of their right to due care.

A hearing before plaintiff was suspended was a specific entitlement that belonged only to plaintiff. Why not ask the jury to determine the value of a hearing? Is it a persuasive answer here, as in the pain and suffering cases, that there is no market in hearings? Plaintiff could not sell his right to a hearing to another student. But plaintiff could conceivably sell his right to the school. Theoretically, although almost never in practice, the school might pay to save the expense of a hearing, and the plaintiff might accept the suspension in exchange for such a payment, especially if he expected to be suspended at the hearing anyway. Could the court ask the jury to imagine that transaction and determine the sale value of plaintiff's right to a hearing? Would such a verdict be too speculative? Or is the whole idea offensive, contrary to public policy and notions of "unalienable rights?"

In the plea bargaining process, criminal defendants regularly exchange their right to trial for reductions in charge or sentence. Citizens rarely sell constitutional rights to the government for money. But consider the case of Clifford Olson, as reported in the Wall Street Journal (Jan. 27, 1982). Canadian police were convinced Olson was guilty of a series of rapes and murders of children. Surveillance officers saw him pick up two female hitchhikers. They arrested him to protect the hitchhikers, but they still didn't have enough evidence to convict him. Olson eventually concluded an apparently unprecedented bargain. The government paid $90,000 to Olson's wife and infant son; in exchange, Olson provided the evidence needed to convict himself of 11 rapes and murders.

The Attorney General of British Columbia authorized the payment. He and other officials connected with the deal offered several justifications: It ensured a life sentence for Olson; it assured the people of Vancouver that there was only one murdering child molester at work; it ended the uncertainty of the victims' parents and gave their children "a Christian burial;" it prevented Olson from selling his information to the press; and it saved hundreds of thousands of dollars in police work. Some members of the public supported the transaction; others characterized it as a "reward for murder" and demanded the discharge of the responsible officials. The police inspector called it "probably the most difficult decision I have ever made."

4. The value of jail time. Does Olson's transaction prove that the privilege against self-incrimination is worth $90,000? Or does it prove only that imprisonment for life is worth $90,000? If life in prison is worth only $90,000 in an arm's-length transaction, how can 20 minutes in handcuffs be worth $80,000 in the coffee vendor case? Is it $90,000 per lifetime or $240,000 per hour? One imprisoned unjustly suffers far more distress than one imprisoned justly; the difference lies also in the fact that juries do not value short-term losses on a per diem basis. And note that in Rowell v. Holt, in note 2.b after *Levka*, a short-term unjust imprisonment was worth only a little more than $1,000 a day.

Wrongful imprisonment cases are collected in Limone v. United States, 497 F. Supp. 2d 143 (D. Mass. 2007), a remarkable case in which FBI agents and their superiors framed four men for a murder they did not commit. Three were sentenced to death, later reduced to life in prison. Two died in prison; two served 29 and 33 years, respectively, before their release. Based largely on a review of comparable verdicts, the judge in a bench trial awarded $1 million per year in prison to each of the four men, plus $1 million to three of the wives for loss of consortium, plus $200,000 to each child for loss of consortium, plus $50,000 to each wife and each child for emotional distress immediately resulting from the conviction. The fourth wife, whose marriage had been deeply troubled before the conviction and who abandoned her husband shortly after, got the emotional distress award but nothing for loss of consortium. The court of appeals said that the $1 million per year of incarceration was "extremely generous" and "troubling," but it affirmed. 579 F.3d 79, 106 (1st Cir. 2009).

5. Remedies are granted in judgments. Note that the district judge in *Carey* dismissed the complaints without granting the declaratory and injunctive relief to which he found plaintiff entitled. This highlights a simple but important point: Remedies are given in judgments, not in opinions. Whatever a judge says in her opinion, the prevailing party must make sure that appropriate relief appears in the judgment. Typically, both sides will be asked to submit proposed drafts of any important orders.

NOTE ON DEFAMATION DAMAGES

In defamation cases, the common law presumed substantial general damages without proof, but the Court refused to extend that practice to constitutional cases. The Court had already held that the Free Speech and Free Press Clauses of the First Amendment limit the liability that can be imposed on negligent defamers to proven compensatory damages. It said that presumed damages and punitive damages are unconstitutional except with respect to defendants who publish defamatory material with knowledge of its falsity or reckless disregard for the truth. Gertz v. Robert Welch, Inc., 418 U.S. 323, 338-350 (1974).

The Court limited *Gertz* in Dun & Bradstreet v. Greenmoss Builders, 472 U.S. 749 (1985). Holding *Gertz* inapplicable to speech that is "of no public concern," the Court affirmed a judgment for $50,000 in presumed damages and $300,000 in punitive damages in a case that apparently had no actual damages whatsoever. Dun & Bradstreet sent a seriously inaccurate credit report to five recipients; it sent a correction one week later. The opinion cites no evidence that the correction was not fully effective, or that plaintiff suffered any damages in the intervening week.

If the defamation plaintiff is a public official or a public figure, the speaker is not liable unless he knowingly lied or spoke with reckless disregard of truth and falsehood. New York Times Co. v. Sullivan, 376 U.S. 254 (1964). This protection is a rule about liability, not a rule about remedy, but it is prerequisite to understanding what the Court has done to defamation remedies.

CHAPTER
3

Punitive Remedies

Punitive remedies are unlike any other kind of remedy. They are measured neither by the plaintiff's rightful position nor by the defendant's, and they do not directly restore anyone to her rightful position or maintain anyone in it. They are justified in part by deterrence, and deterrence can be thought of as protecting other potential victims—victims who are not before the court and whose identities are unknown, but who will be maintained in *their* rightful positions if the class of potential defendants is deterred from violating the law. Deterrence is relevant to all remedies, but it is usually incidental. Most remedies focus on the rightful position of the litigants, not on other people who might be indirectly affected.

In terms of the logic of remedies, therefore, punitive remedies belong near the back of the book. We take them up at this point for a practical reason rather than a logical one: The debate over punitive damages is closely related to the debate over tort reform considered in section 2.G.

A. PUNITIVE DAMAGES

1. Common Law and Statutes

EXXON SHIPPING CO. v. BAKER
554 U.S. 471 (2008)

[The supertanker *Exxon Valdez* ran aground in Prince William Sound, spilling millions of gallons of crude oil. Joseph Hazelwood, the ship's captain, was a relapsed alcoholic who had dropped out of treatment. There was evidence that his superiors knew this. There was also evidence that before coming on board the night of the disaster, Hazelwood drank five double vodkas.

The ship left the normal channel to avoid ice. Two minutes before reaching the last point for turning back to the channel, Hazelwood put the ship on autopilot, left the bridge, and went to his cabin, leaving instructions for the third mate and the helmsman to make the turn. Both regulations and universal practice required his presence on the bridge for this turn; among other things, he was the only officer licensed to navigate in Prince William Sound. The autopilot setting increased the difficulty of the turn. For reasons unknown, the mate and the helmsman missed the

223

turn and ran aground. Hazelwood then tried to rock the ship off the reef; had he succeeded, much more oil would have been spilled.

Eleven hours after the spill, Hazelwood's blood-alcohol level was measured at .06; Exxon disputed the validity of the test. Extrapolating backwards, an expert testified that his blood-alcohol level would have been about .24 at the time of the spill.

Exxon spent $2.1 billion on cleanup efforts, paid a $25 million criminal fine, and paid $100 million in restitution in the criminal case. Criminal "restitution" is a form of compensation to victims. Exxon paid $1.3 billion in restoration costs and compensatory damages in civil settlements with the United States, Alaska, and private plaintiffs who sued in other cases.

This case consolidated class actions under the general maritime law on behalf of commercial fishermen, Native Alaskans, and local land owners. Exxon paid about $500 million in compensatory damages to these three classes, mostly in partial settlements, and some pursuant to the jury verdict.

Instructed to consider the reprehensibility of defendants' conduct, their financial condition, the magnitude of the harm, and any mitigating facts, the jury awarded $5 billion in punitive damages against Exxon and $5,000 against Hazelwood. The Ninth Circuit twice vacated and remanded on constitutional grounds, but the district judge thought the verdict justified and entered judgments for $4 billion on the first remand and $4.5 billion on the second. On the third appeal, the Ninth Circuit reduced the award to $2.5 billion.

The Supreme Court unanimously rejected Exxon's argument that the Clean Water Act preempts a claim for punitive damages under the general maritime law. It was evenly divided with respect to Exxon's argument that it could not be held vicariously liable in punitives for Hazelwood's reckless conduct. The result was to affirm on that issue without precedential effect.

Exxon also argued that the punitive damages were excessive, even as reduced by the Ninth Circuit. The general maritime law is federal law, made by judges in the manner of a common law court, subject to congressional authority to legislate when it chooses. So this is not a constitutional law case; rather, the Supreme Court functioned much like the supreme court of a state, reviewing a verdict in common law terms. Because the Court rarely does this, it had to select or create the standards it would apply.]

Justice SOUTER delivered the opinion of the Court. . . .

IV . . .

A

The modern Anglo-American doctrine of punitive damages dates back at least to 1763, when a pair of decisions by the Court of Common Pleas recognized the availability of damages "for more than the injury received." Wilkes v. Wood, 98 Eng. Rep. 489, 498 (K.B. 1763). In *Wilkes*, one of the foundations of the Fourth Amendment, exemplary damages awarded against the Secretary of State, responsible for an unlawful search of John Wilkes's papers, were a spectacular £4,000. . . .

Awarding damages beyond the compensatory was not, however, a wholly novel idea even then, legal codes from ancient times through the Middle Ages having called for multiple damages for certain especially harmful acts. But punitive damages were a common law innovation untethered to strict numerical multipliers, and the doctrine promptly crossed the Atlantic, to become widely accepted in American courts by the middle of the 19th century.

B

Early common law cases offered various rationales for punitive-damages awards, [commonly including punishment for the past and deterrence for the future].

A third historical justification . . . was the need "to compensate for intangible injuries, compensation which was not otherwise available under the narrow conception of compensatory damages prevalent at the time." Cooper Industries, Inc. v. Leatherman Tool Group, Inc., 532 U.S. 424, 437 n.11 (2001). But see Anthony Sebok, *What Did Punitive Damages Do?*, 78 Chi.-Kent L. Rev. 163, 204 (2003) (arguing that "punitive damages have never served the compensatory function attributed to them by the Court in *Cooper*"). . . .

[T]he consensus today is that punitives are aimed not at compensation but principally at retribution and deterring harmful conduct. This consensus informs the doctrine in most modern American jurisdictions, where juries are customarily instructed on twin goals of punitive awards. See, e.g., Cal. Jury Instr., Civil, No. 14.72.2 (2008) ("You must now determine whether you should award punitive damages against defendant[s] . . . for the sake of example and by way of punishment"); N.Y. Pattern Jury Instr., Civil, No. 2:278 (2007) ("The purpose of punitive damages is not to compensate the plaintiff but to punish the defendant . . . and thereby to discourage the defendant . . . from acting in a similar way in the future"). The prevailing rule in American courts also limits punitive damages to cases . . . where a defendant's conduct is "outrageous," *Restatement (Second) of Torts* §908(2) (Am. Law Inst. 1977), owing to "gross negligence," "willful, wanton, and reckless indifference for the rights of others," or behavior even more deplorable.

Under the umbrellas of punishment and its aim of deterrence, degrees of relative blameworthiness are apparent. Reckless conduct is not intentional or malicious, nor is it necessarily callous toward the risk of harming others, as opposed to unheedful of it. Action taken or omitted in order to augment profit represents an enhanced degree of punishable culpability, as of course does willful or malicious action, taken with a purpose to injure.

Regardless of culpability, however, heavier punitive awards have been thought to be justifiable when wrongdoing is hard to detect (increasing chances of getting away with it), or when the value of injury and the corresponding compensatory award are small (providing low incentives to sue). And, with a broadly analogous object, some regulatory schemes provide by statute for multiple recovery in order to induce private litigation to supplement official enforcement that might fall short if unaided.

C

State regulation of punitive damages varies. A few States award them rarely, or not at all. Nebraska bars punitive damages entirely, on state constitutional grounds. Four others permit punitive damages only when authorized by statute: Louisiana, Massachusetts, . . . Washington . . . , and New Hampshire. . . . Michigan courts recognize only exemplary damages supportable as compensatory, rather than truly punitive, while Connecticut courts have limited what they call punitive recovery to the "expenses of bringing the legal action, including attorney's fees, less taxable costs," Larsen Chelsey Realty Co. v. Larsen, 656 A.2d 1009, 1029 n.38 (Conn. 1995).

As for procedure, in most American jurisdictions the amount of the punitive award is generally determined by a jury in the first instance, and that "determination is then reviewed by trial and appellate courts to ensure that it is reasonable." Pacific Mutual Life Insurance Co. v. Haslip, 499 U.S. 1, 15 (1991). Many States have gone further by imposing statutory limits on punitive awards, in the form of absolute monetary caps [$350,000 in Virginia], a maximum ratio of punitive to compensatory damages

[2:1 in Ohio], or, frequently, some combination of the two [greater of 3:1 ratio or $500,000 in Alaska]. The States that rely on a multiplier have adopted a variety of ratios, ranging from 5:1 to 1:1.

Despite these limitations, punitive damages overall are higher and more frequent in the United States than they are anywhere else. . . .

And some legal systems not only decline to recognize punitive damages themselves but refuse to enforce foreign punitive judgments as contrary to public policy.

D

American punitive damages have been the target of audible criticism in recent decades, but the most recent studies tend to undercut much of it. A survey of the literature reveals that discretion to award punitive damages has not mass-produced runaway awards, and although some studies show the dollar amounts of punitive-damages awards growing over time, even in real terms, by most accounts the median ratio of punitive to compensatory awards has remained less than 1:1. Nor do the data substantiate a marked increase in the percentage of cases with punitive awards over the past several decades. The figures thus show an overall restraint and suggest that in many instances a high ratio of punitive to compensatory damages is substantially greater than necessary to punish or deter.

The real problem, it seems, is the stark unpredictability of punitive awards. Courts of law are concerned with fairness as consistency, and evidence that the median ratio of punitive to compensatory awards falls within a reasonable zone, or that punitive awards are infrequent, fails to tell us whether the spread between high and low individual awards is acceptable. The available data suggest it is not. A recent comprehensive study of punitive damages awarded by juries in state civil trials found a median ratio of punitive to compensatory awards of just 0.62:1, but a mean ratio of 2.90:1 and a standard deviation of 13.81. Theodore Eisenberg, et al., *Juries, Judges, and Punitive Damages: Empirical Analyses Using the Civil Justice Survey of State Courts 1992, 1996, and 2001 Data*, 3 J. Empirical Legal Stud. 263 (2006). Even to those of us unsophisticated in statistics, the thrust of these figures is clear: the spread is great, and the outlier cases subject defendants to punitive damages that dwarf the corresponding compensatories. The distribution of awards is narrower, but still remarkable, among punitive damages assessed by judges: the median ratio is 0.66:1, the mean ratio is 1.60:1, and the standard deviation is 4.54. *Id.* Other studies of some of the same data show that fully 14% of punitive awards in 2001 were greater than four times the compensatory damages, Thomas H. Cohen, *Punitive Damage Awards in Large Counties, 2001*, at 5 (Dept. of Justice, Bureau of Justice Statistics 2005), with 18% of punitives in the 1990s more than trebling the compensatory damages, Brian Ostrom, et al., *A Step Above Anecdote: A Profile of the Civil Jury in the 1990s*, 79 Judicature 233, 240 (1996). . . .

[T]hese ranges of variation might be acceptable or even desirable if they resulted from judges' and juries' refining their judgments to reach a generally accepted optimal level of penalty and deterrence in cases involving a wide range of circumstances, while producing fairly consistent results in cases with similar facts. But anecdotal evidence suggests that nothing of that sort is going on. One of our own leading cases on punitive damages, with a $4 million verdict by an Alabama jury, noted that a second Alabama case with strikingly similar facts produced "a comparable amount of compensatory damages" but "no punitive damages at all." See BMW v. Gore, 517 U.S. 559, 565 n.8 (1996). . . . We are aware of no scholarly work pointing to consistency across punitive awards in cases involving similar claims and circumstances.

E

The Court's response to outlier punitive damages awards has thus far been confined by claims at the constitutional level. . . .

Today's enquiry differs from due process review because the case arises under federal maritime jurisdiction, and . . . we are examining the verdict in the exercise of federal maritime common law authority, which precedes and should obviate any application of the constitutional standard. . . .

Whatever may be the constitutional significance of the unpredictability of high punitive awards, this feature of happenstance is in tension with the function of the awards as punitive, just because of the implication of unfairness that an eccentrically high punitive verdict carries in a system whose commonly held notion of law rests on a sense of fairness in dealing with one another. Thus, a penalty should be reasonably predictable in its severity, so that even Justice Holmes's "bad man" can look ahead with some ability to know what the stakes are in choosing one course of action or another. See Oliver Wendell Holmes, *The Path of the Law*, 10 Harv. L. Rev. 457, 459 (1897). And when the bad man's counterparts turn up from time to time, the penalty scheme they face ought to threaten them with a fair probability of suffering in like degree when they wreak like damage. The common sense of justice would surely bar penalties that reasonable people would think excessive for the harm caused in the circumstances.

F

1

With that aim ourselves, we have three basic approaches to consider, one verbal and two quantitative. As mentioned before, a number of state courts have settled on criteria for judicial review of punitive-damages awards that go well beyond traditional "shock the conscience" or "passion and prejudice" tests. Maryland, for example, has set forth a nonexclusive list of nine review factors under state common law that include "degree of heinousness," "the deterrence value of [the award]," and "[w]hether [the punitive award] bears a reasonable relationship to the compensatory damages awarded." Bowden v. Caldor, Inc., 710 A.2d 267, 277-284 (Md. 1998). Alabama has seven general criteria, such as "actual or likely harm [from the defendant's conduct]," "degree of reprehensibility," and "[i]f the wrongful conduct was profitable to the defendant." Green Oil Co. v. Hornsby, 539 So. 2d 218, 223-224 (Ala. 1989).

These judicial review criteria are brought to bear after juries render verdicts under instructions offering, at best, guidance no more specific for reaching an appropriate penalty. In Maryland, for example, which allows punitive damages for intentional torts and conduct characterized by "actual malice," U.S. Gypsum Co. v. Mayor & City Council of Baltimore, 647 A.2d 405, 424-425 (Md. 1994), juries may be instructed that "An award for punitive damages should be: (1) In an amount that will deter the defendant and others from similar conduct. (2) Proportionate to the wrongfulness of the defendant's conduct and the defendant's ability to pay. (3) But not designed to bankrupt or financially destroy a defendant." Md. Pattern Jury Instr., Civil, No. 10:13 (4th ed. 2007). In Alabama, juries are instructed to fix an amount after considering "the character and degree of the wrong as shown by the evidence in the case, and the necessity of preventing similar wrongs." 1 Ala. Pattern Jury Instr., Civil, No. §23.21 (Supp. 2007).

These examples leave us skeptical that verbal formulations, superimposed on general jury instructions, are the best insurance against unpredictable outliers. Instructions can go just so far in promoting systemic consistency when awards are not tied to specifically proven items of damage . . ., and although judges in the States that take this approach may well produce just results by dint of valiant effort, our experience with attempts to produce consistency in the analogous business of criminal sentencing leaves us doubtful that anything but a quantified approach will work. A glance at the experience there will explain our skepticism. . . .

[I]n the last quarter century federal sentencing rejected an "indeterminate" system, with relatively unguided discretion to sentence within a wide range, under which "similarly situated offenders were sentenced [to], and did actually serve, widely disparate sentences." Ilene H. Nagel, *Structuring Sentencing Discretion: The New Federal Sentencing Guidelines*, 80 J. Crim. L. & Criminology 883, 895-899 (1990). Instead it became a system of detailed guidelines tied to exactly quantified sentencing results, under the authority of the Sentencing Reform Act of 1984, 18 U.S.C. §3551 *et seq.* (2000 & Supp. V).

The importance of this for us is that in the old federal sentencing system of general standards the cohort of even the most seasoned judicial penalty-givers defied consistency. Judges and defendants alike were "[l]eft at large, wandering in deserts of uncharted discretion," Marvin E. Frankel, *Criminal Sentences: Law Without Order* 7-8 (Hill & Wang 1973), which is very much the position of those imposing punitive damages today, be they judges or juries, except that they lack even a statutory maximum; their only restraint beyond a core sense of fairness is the due process limit. This federal criminal law development, with its many state parallels, strongly suggests that as long "as there are no punitive-damages guidelines, corresponding to the federal and state sentencing guidelines, it is inevitable that the specific amount of punitive damages awarded whether by a judge or by a jury will be arbitrary." Mathias v. Accor Economy Lodging, Inc., 347 F.3d 672, 678 (7th Cir. 2003).

2

This is why our better judgment is that eliminating unpredictable outlying punitive awards by more rigorous standards than the constitutional limit will probably have to take the form adopted in those States that have looked to the criminal-law pattern of quantified limits. One option would be to follow the States that set a hard dollar cap on punitive damages, a course that arguably would come closest to the criminal law, rather like setting a maximum term of years. The trouble is, though, that there is no "standard" tort or contract injury, making it difficult to settle upon a particular dollar figure as appropriate across the board. And of course a judicial selection of a dollar cap would carry a serious drawback; a legislature can pick a figure, index it for inflation, and revisit its provision whenever there seems to be a need for further tinkering, but a court cannot say when an issue will show up on the docket again.

The more promising alternative is to leave the effects of inflation to the jury or judge who assesses the value of actual loss, by pegging punitive to compensatory damages using a ratio or maximum multiple. . . .

Although the legal landscape is well populated with examples of ratios and multipliers expressing policies of retribution and deterrence, most of them suffer from features that stand in the way of borrowing them as paradigms of reasonable limitations suited for application to this case. While a slim majority of the States with a ratio have adopted 3:1, others see fit to apply a lower one [1:1 in Colorado, 2:1 in Ohio], and a few have gone higher [5:1 in Missouri]. . . . With a few statutory exceptions, generally for intentional infliction of physical injury or other harm, the States with . . . ratios apply them across the board. . . . That is, the upper limit is not directed to cases like this one, where the tortious action was worse than negligent but less than malicious, exposing the tortfeasor to certain regulatory sanctions and inevitable damage actions;[23] the . . . ratio . . . also applies to awards in quite different cases involving some of the most egregious conduct, including malicious behavior and dangerous activity carried on for the purpose of increasing a tortfeasor's financial gain. We confront, instead, a case of reckless action, profitless to the tortfeasor, resulting in substantial recovery for substantial injury. Thus, a legislative judgment that 3:1 is a reasonable limit overall is not a judgment that 3:1 is a reasonable limit in this particular type of case.

For somewhat different reasons, the pertinence of the 2:1 ratio adopted by treble-damages statutes (offering compensatory damages plus a bounty of double that amount) is open to question. Federal treble-damages statutes govern areas far afield from maritime concerns (not to mention each other); the relevance of the governing rules in patent or trademark cases, say, is doubtful at best. . . . Congress devised the treble damages remedy for private antitrust actions with an eye to supplementing official enforcement by inducing private litigation, which might otherwise have been too rare if nothing but compensatory damages were available at the end of the day. That concern has no traction here, in this case of staggering damage inevitably provoking governmental enforcers to indict and any number of private parties to sue. . . . All in all, the legislative signposts do not point the way clearly to 2:1 as a sound indication of a reasonable limit.

3

There is better evidence of an accepted limit of reasonable civil penalty, however, in several studies mentioned before, showing the median ratio of punitive to compensatory verdicts, reflecting what juries and judges have considered reasonable across many hundreds of punitive awards. We think it is fair to assume that the greater share of the verdicts studied in these comprehensive collections reflect reasonable judgments about the economic penalties appropriate in their particular cases.

These studies cover cases of the most as well as the least blameworthy conduct triggering punitive liability, from malice and avarice, down to recklessness, and even gross negligence in some jurisdictions. The data put the median ratio for the entire gamut of circumstances at less than 1:1, meaning that the compensatory award exceeds the punitive award in most cases. In a well-functioning system, we would expect that awards at the median or lower would roughly express jurors' sense of reasonable penalties in cases with no earmarks of exceptional blameworthiness within the punishable spectrum (cases like this one, without intentional or malicious conduct, and without behavior driven primarily by desire for gain, for example) and cases (again like this one) without the modest economic harm or odds of detection that have opened the door to higher awards. It also seems fair to suppose that most of the unpredictable outlier cases that call the fairness of the system into question are above the median; in theory a factfinder's deliberation could go awry to produce a very low ratio, but we have no basis to assume that such a case would be more than a sport, and the cases with serious constitutional issues coming to us have naturally been on the high side. On these assumptions, a median ratio of punitive to compensatory damages of about 0.65:1 probably marks the line near which cases like this one largely should be grouped. Accordingly, given the need to protect against the possibility (and the disruptive cost to the legal system) of awards that are

---

23. We thus treat this case categorically as one of recklessness, for that was the jury's finding. But by making a point of its contrast with cases falling within categories of even greater fault we do not mean to suggest that Exxon's and Hazelwood's failings were less than reprehensible.

unpredictable and unnecessary, either for deterrence or for measured retribution, we consider that a 1:1 ratio, which is above the median award, is a fair upper limit in such maritime cases.

The provision of the Clean Water Act respecting daily fines confirms our judgment that anything greater would be excessive here and in cases of this type. Congress set criminal penalties of up to $25,000 per day for negligent violations of pollution restrictions, and up to $50,000 per day for knowing ones. 33 U.S.C. §1319(c)(1), (2). Discretion to double the penalty for knowing action compares to discretion to double the civil liability on conduct going beyond negligence and meriting punitive treatment. And our explanation of the constitutional upper limit confirms that the 1:1 ratio is not too low. In State Farm Mutual Automobile Insurance Co. v. Campbell, 538 U.S. 408 (2003), we said that a single-digit maximum is appropriate in all but the most exceptional of cases, and "[w]hen compensatory damages are substantial, then a lesser ratio, perhaps only equal to compensatory damages, can reach the outermost limit of the due process guarantee." *Id.* at 425.[28]

V

[The district judge calculated] the total relevant compensatory damages at $507.5 million. A punitive-to-compensatory ratio of 1:1 thus yields maximum punitive damages in that amount.

We therefore vacate the judgment and remand the case for the Court of Appeals to remit the punitive damages award accordingly. . . .

Justice ALITO took no part in the consideration or decision of this case.

Justice SCALIA, with whom Justice THOMAS joins, concurring.

I join the opinion of the Court, including the portions that refer to constitutional limits that prior opinions have imposed upon punitive damages. While I agree with the argumentation based upon those prior holdings, I continue to believe the holdings were in error.

Justice STEVENS, concurring in part and dissenting in part. . . .

II . . .

[B]oth caps and ratios of the sort the Court relies upon . . . are typically imposed by legislatures, not courts. . . . [I]t is telling that the Court fails to identify a single state *court* that has imposed a precise ratio, as the Court does today, under its common-law authority. . . . Congress is far better situated than is this Court to assess the empirical data, and to balance competing policy interests, before making such a choice. . . .

---

28. The criterion of "substantial" takes into account the role of punitive damages to induce legal action when pure compensation may not be enough to encourage suit, a concern addressed by the opportunity for a class action when large numbers of potential plaintiffs are involved: in such cases, individual awards are not the touchstone, for it is the class option that facilitates suit, and a class recovery of $500 million is substantial. In this case, then, the constitutional outer limit may well be 1:1.

The Court concludes that the real problem is large *outlier* awards, and the data seem to bear this out. But the Court never explains why abuse-of-discretion review is not the precise antidote to the unfairness inherent in such excessive awards. . . .

On an abuse-of-discretion standard, I am persuaded that a reviewing court should not invalidate this award. . . .

Justice GINSBURG, concurring in part and dissenting in part. . . .

While recognizing that the question is close, I share Justice Stevens' view that Congress is the better equipped decisionmaker. . . .

The 1:1 ratio is good for this case, the Court believes, because Exxon's conduct ranked on the low end of the blameworthiness scale: Exxon was not seeking "to augment profit," nor did it act "with a purpose to injure." What ratio will the Court set for defendants who acted maliciously or in pursuit of financial gain? Should the magnitude of the risk increase the ratio and, if so, by how much? Horrendous as the spill from the *Valdez* was, millions of gallons more might have spilled as a result of Captain Hazelwood's attempt to rock the boat off the reef. Cf. TXO Production Corp. v. Alliance Resources Corp., 509 U.S. 443, 460-462 (1993) (plurality opinion) (using potential loss to plaintiff as a guide in determining whether jury verdict was excessive). In the end, is the Court holding only that 1:1 is the maritime-law ceiling, or is it also signaling that any ratio higher than 1:1 will be held to exceed "the constitutional outer limit"? . . .

Justice BREYER, concurring in part and dissenting in part. . . .

Like the Court, I believe there is a need, grounded in the rule of law itself, to assure that punitive damages are awarded according to meaningful standards that will provide notice of how harshly certain acts will be punished and that will help to assure the uniform treatment of similarly situated persons. Legal standards, however, can secure these objectives without the rigidity that an absolute fixed numerical ratio demands. . . .

In my view, a limited exception to the Court's 1:1 ratio is warranted here. . . . [T]his was no mine-run case of reckless behavior. The jury could reasonably have believed that Exxon knowingly allowed a relapsed alcoholic repeatedly to pilot a vessel filled with millions of gallons of oil through waters that provided the livelihood for the many plaintiffs in this case. Given that conduct, it was only a matter of time before a crash and spill like this occurred. And as Justice Ginsburg points out, the damage easily could have been much worse. . . .

I can find no reasoned basis to disagree with the Court of Appeals' conclusion that this is a special case, justifying an exception from strict application of the majority's numerical rule. The punitive damages award before us already represents a 50% reduction from the amount that the District Court strongly believed was appropriate. I would uphold it.

NOTES ON PUNITIVE DAMAGES

1. Why punitive damages? If deterrence is the rationale, why don't compensatory damages provide sufficient deterrence? The dignitary tort cases provide one answer: Sometimes the law systematically underestimates damages. Emotional distress is now generally compensable in intentional tort cases, but it is hard to measure, and outrageous conduct sometimes inflicts little measurable harm. More controversially, few people would submit to serious and permanent personal injuries for any amount of money. If there is a widespread sense that victims of serious personal injury are not really made whole by compensatory damages, then we may want punitives to get more deterrence.

Many claims for compensatory damages go unenforced. Some wrongs are hard to detect; fraud is the classic example. Some cases are too expensive to litigate; some plaintiffs choose not to sue for other reasons. Not all suits are successfully prosecuted. Most cases settle, and most settlements are for less than what plaintiff would get if he succeeded at trial. Even if one believes that profitable violations of law should be encouraged, paying compensatory damages only in cases successfully prosecuted does not provide deterrence equal to the social cost of the prohibited conduct.

Some intentional tortfeasors may value the harm they inflict on their enemies, but the law does not recognize that value as legitimate. Most plausible examples of this source of underdeterrence are appropriate for criminal prosecution. But the criminal justice system is badly overloaded, and prosecutors may ignore minor crimes or treat them lightly.

Judge Richard A. Posner, one of the founders of the law-and-economics movement, sets out the economic rationale for punitive damages in Kemezy v. Peters, 79 F.3d 33 (7th Cir. 1996), emphasizing that damages are sometimes undercompensatory, that not all torts are detected, and that the criminal justice system is overloaded. Carried to its logical conclusion, economic analysis suggests that reprehensibility is irrelevant, and that underdeterrence is all that matters. Even a "'morally innocent' tortfeasor" should be subject to punitive damages equal to the inverse of his chances of escaping liability. Steve P. Calandrillo, *Penalizing Punitive Damages: Why the Supreme Court Needs a Lesson in Law & Economics,* 78 Geo. Wash. L. Rev. 774, 802 (2010). On that theory, punitive damages should be pervasive, although Professor Calandrillo does not draw that implication. He and other scholars filed an amicus brief presenting this economic argument in *Exxon,* but the Supreme Court appears not to have been interested.

2. Why in *Exxon*? What is the rationale for punitive damages in *Exxon*? There was little risk that the injury would go undetected, and no reason to think Exxon derived illicit satisfaction from destroying the environment. But the case was expensive to litigate, and despite the enormous incentives to successful litigation, such complex cases are often lost, or settled for less than the full amount of damages. And the risk of enormous liability had plainly not induced Exxon to respond more effectively to Hazelwood's drinking problem. Calandrillo adds that much environmental harm went uncompensated because of the economic-loss rule or because it was not yet provable at the time of trial, and that much cultural harm and severe emotional distress went uncompensated. Calandrillo, *id.* at 809-815.

3. The fear that compensatories will not deter. One recurring theme in the cases is that compensatory damages — or even punitive damages that are too small — may not deter. "[T]he manufacturer may find it more profitable to treat compensatory damages as a part of the cost of doing business rather than to remedy the defect." Grimshaw v. Ford Motor Co., 174 Cal. Rptr. 348, 382 (Ct. App. 1981). Defendants might decide that paying modest damages and a modest criminal fine is "more profitable than obeying the law." Jacque v. Steenberg Homes, Inc., 563 N.W.2d 154, 161 (Wis. 1997). "Punitive damage awards should not be a routine cost of doing business that an industry can simply pass on to its customers through price increases, while continuing the conduct the law proscribes." Seltzer v. Morton, 154 P.3d 561, 597 (Mont. 2007), quoting a California case.

And consider Brown v. Missouri Pacific Railroad, 703 F.2d 1050 (8th Cir. 1983), where a driver had been killed at an unprotected railroad crossing. The town had lobbied for a crossing gate for some time, but the railroad said that gates were too expensive. A citizen testified to the following exchange when a railroad employee spoke to the local Kiwanis Club:

> *The Witness*: I made the statement that it would be safer and cheaper in the long run to put gates on all the crossings in Prescott, instead of having so many people suing the railroad.
> *Question*: What was his response?
> *The Witness*: His response was, the way I understood, is that it was cheaper to have the suits than to put up the gates.

Id. at 1053.

The railroad denied such a policy and denied that the local employee knew its policy. The employee denied making the statement. But the jury awarded $62,000 in punitive damages. The court upheld the verdict, relying largely on this testimony.

The striking thing about such comments in accident cases is their square rejection of the economic view of accident law. (Economists would not disagree with respect to truly intentional torts.) The basic effort to compare the cost of prevention to the cost of the accidents is exactly what law-and-economics scholars think potential defendants should do. The law's response is not just that such calculations are no defense but that they are especially reprehensible and deserving of punitive damages. Anecdotal evidence suggests that juries are especially likely to punish defendants who omit a safety precaution on the basis of explicit cost-benefit analysis; such analysis seems to confirm that defendant deliberately decided that it would be cheaper to inflict the injuries.

Addressing the point more conceptually, the Supreme Court has said that "citizens and legislators may rightly insist that they are willing to tolerate some loss in economic efficiency in order to deter what they consider morally offensive conduct, albeit cost-beneficial morally offensive conduct; efficiency is just one consideration among many." Cooper Industries, Inc. v. Leatherman Tool Group, Inc., 532 U.S. 424, 439-440 (2001), quoting Marc Galanter & David Luban, *Poetic Justice: Punitive Damages and Legal Pluralism*, 42 Am. U. L. Rev. 1393, 1450 (1993). Courts that write such opinions do not expect defendants to prevent all injuries. The safety standards they expect are not always clearly articulated (which may be a problem if we are punishing defendants for noncompliance), but the implicit standard seems to be something like feasibility: Juries are allowed to impose punitive damages when defendants knowingly or recklessly allow serious injuries to happen that could have been prevented at affordable cost. Feasibility analysis is briefly considered in note 4 of Notes on Valuing Pain and Suffering and Human Life, in section 2.G.2.

The economic view traces its roots to Judge Learned Hand's famous balancing test for negligence set forth in United States v. Carroll Towing Co., 159 F.2d 169, 173 (2d Cir. 1947) — that liability depends on whether the burden of preventing the accident exceeds the harm to be prevented times the probability that it will happen. Professor Keating thinks the law-and-economics scholars mangled Hand's proposal. Keating views it not as a mathematical definition of negligence, but as "a heuristic device that isolates the elements of due care and the relations among them." Gregory C. Keating, *Must the Hand Formula Not Be Named?*, 163 U. Pa. L. Rev. Online 367, 373 (2014-2015). Does that help reconcile the tort approach with jury reactions to evidence of balancing the costs of safety devices against the costs of liability?

4. How bad must defendant be? Courts have struggled to define the level of culpability that juries may punish. California requires "willful and conscious disregard of the rights and safety of others." Simon v. San Paolo U.S. Holding Co., 113 P.3d 63, 76 (Cal. 2005). Doesn't the ordinary driver who knows that he's five miles an hour over the speed limit act in conscious disregard of the rights and safety of others? Auto manufacturers know to a virtual certainty that selling cars at all will result in injury to others; they build cars anyway. Compare Calmes v. Goodyear Tire & Rubber Co., 575 N.E.2d 416, 419 (Ohio 1991), requiring "conscious disregard for . . . a *great* probability of causing *substantial* harm." (emphasis added) and West Virginia, which allows punitives for "extremely negligent conduct that is likely to cause serious harm." Harris v. Norfolk Southern Railway Co., 784 F.3d 954, 970 (4th Cir. 2015).

Some courts have tried to require intent or actual knowledge, but they nearly always allow for the possibility of implied intent, which defeats their quest for a bright line and often results in a confused jumble of mental states. Thus the Arkansas court requires that the defendant "likely knew or ought to have known . . . that his conduct would naturally or probably result in injury, and that he continued such conduct in reckless disregard of the consequences from which malice could be inferred." Union Pacific Railroad Co. v. Barber, 149 S.W.3d 325, 343 (Ark. 2004). The Maine court requires clear and convincing evidence of "'express' or 'actual' malice," defined as an actual motivation of "ill will" toward the victim, or conduct "so outrageous that malice toward a person injured as a result of that conduct can be implied." Tuttle v. Raymond, 494 A.2d 1353, 1361 (Me. 1985). The court insisted that malice could not be inferred from reckless disregard of the circumstances. But if malice is to be inferred and does not depend on actual subjective intent, what else could it be inferred from?

There is an older tradition of describing the standard with epithets: fraud, malice, oppression, willful, wanton, outrageous, gross. Such terms aren't very precise, but they don't pretend to be. Is that the best we can do?

5. Vicarious liability. Whatever the standard, what does it mean when applied vicariously? About half the states—probably more than half since the tort-reform movement—require that managerial employees be implicated in the outrageous conduct. The remaining states apply ordinary respondeat superior rules to punitive damages: The employer is liable for punitives if any employee acting within the course and scope of his employment did something deserving of punitives. Many of the cases on both sides are collected in Bierman v. Aramark Refreshment Services, Inc., 198 P.3d 877, 883-884 (Okla. 2008), in which a delivery-truck driver was drunk.

In states that require managerial employees, rank or title is usually not dispositive. In California, plaintiff must show that "the employee exercised substantial discretionary authority over significant aspects of a corporation's business." White v. Ultramar, Inc., 981 P.2d 944, 954 (Cal. 1999). It was enough in *White* that the culpable manager supervised eight convenience stores; the most recent case held that supervising four employees at one location is not enough. Roby v. McKesson Corp., 219 P.3d 749, 767 (Cal. 2009). The parties in *Exxon* argued over what the federal rule should be and whether the captain of the *Exxon Valdez* was a managerial employee. He had sole command of an enormous seagoing vessel, but corporate headquarters could reach him by radio any time it chose. The Eleventh Circuit appears to require in employment discrimination cases that the discrimination be committed or approved not just by a managerial employee, but by "higher management" or an employee "high up in the corporate hierarchy." A "General Manager" who supervised only 25 employees, a trivial fraction of defendant's workforce, was not high enough. Equal Employment Opportunity Commission v. Exel, Inc., 884 F.3d 1326 (11th Cir. 2018). An earlier case held that a plant manager who supervised 1,400 employees was not high enough where that was only 1.5 percent of the employer's workforce and there were six levels of management above the plant managers. Ash v. Tyson Foods, Inc., 664 F.3d 883 (11th Cir. 2011).

Corporations cannot act except vicariously; if punitive damages make sense, they must be imposed for vicarious conduct. What about live human employers? Should they be immune from punitive damages for the acts of their employees?

6. Immune defendants. Punitive damages are unavailable against municipalities in civil rights suits, City of Newport v. Fact Concerts, Inc., 453 U.S. 247 (1981), and against unions in duty of fair representation suits, International Brotherhood of Electrical Workers v. Foust, 442 U.S. 42 (1979). The Court relied heavily on the vicarious nature of the liability, and on the fear that the burden would fall on innocent taxpayers and union members. Should we be equally concerned about corporate shareholders? Or should they suffer the risks of investing in a badly run company? What about other customers, if punitives drive up the price of goods?

Punitive damages traditionally were not available against fiduciaries sued for breach of trust, because trust beneficiaries traditionally sued trustees in equity courts where remedies such as constructive trusts (described in section 8.C.1) were allowed, but punitive damages were not. Increasingly courts recognize the availability of punitive damages against fiduciaries in the "egregious case." Samuel L. Bray, *Punitive Damages Against Trustees,* in Research Handbook on Fiduciary Law 201 (D. Gordon Smith & Andrew S. Gold, eds., Edward Elgar 2018).

7. Jury trial. Punitive damages are a major target of the campaign to change tort law, and many states have responded by tightening the substantive standard, by requiring clear and convincing evidence (beyond a reasonable doubt in Colorado, Colo. Rev. Stat. §13-25-127(2)), by capping recoveries, and in other ways.

State constitutional challenges to these restrictions have occasionally succeeded. The Ohio court struck down caps on punitive damages under the state right to jury trial. State ex rel. Ohio Academy of Trial Lawyers v. Sheward, 715 N.E.2d 1062, 1090-1091 (Ohio 1999). The Kansas court upheld a statute providing that the jury should determine only whether punitive damages should be awarded, and if the jury answered yes, then the court would determine the amount. The court reasoned that the Kansas right to jury trial does not apply to punitive damages, because plaintiffs had no right to them at common law. Smith v. Printup, 866 P.2d 985, 992-998 (Kan. 1993).

The federal right to jury trial, which applies to cases tried in federal court whether based on state or federal law, has two distinct clauses:

> In Suits at common law, where the value in controversy shall exceed twenty dollars, the right of trial by jury shall be preserved, and no fact tried by a jury, shall be otherwise re-examined in any Court of the United States, than according to the rules of the common law.

U.S. Const. amend. VII. The Supreme Court has held that the Re-examination Clause does not apply to punitive damages, because "the jury's award of punitive damages does not constitute a finding of 'fact.'" *Cooper,* 532 U.S. at 437 & n.11. It may follow that this nonfact need not be found by a jury in the first place. But it may not; the principal standard under the Preservation Clause is historical, and historical practice has been to submit punitive damages to juries. Justice Ginsburg disagreed with the Court's characterization, finding punitive damages indistinguishable from intangible compensatory damages for this purpose: "One million dollars' worth of pain and suffering does not exist as a 'fact' in the world any more or less than one million dollars' worth of moral outrage. Both derive their meaning from a set of underlying facts as determined by a jury." *Id.* at 446.

8. The empirical debate. Tort reformers won a major doctrinal victory in *Exxon*, but they suffered a major loss on the propaganda front. A very conservative court reviewed the data and concluded, in accord with all the serious empirical studies, that punitive damages are *not* out of control. The Eisenberg team's study cited in the opinion is based on a combined analysis of the first three of the four large data sets generated by the Bureau of Justice Statistics, more fully described in the notes following Arbino v. Johnson & Johnson in section 2.G.2. Out of 11,610 trials with a plaintiff win, the Eisenberg team found 551 awards of punitive damages, or 4.75 percent of plaintiff wins. 3 J. Empirical Legal Stud. at 268. Plaintiffs win about half of all cases, so that's about 2.4 percent of cases tried. The 2005 Bureau of Justice Statistics study reports punitive damages in 2.5 percent of cases tried, or less than 1 in 10,000 cases filed in state courts of general jurisdiction. Lynn Langton & Thomas H. Cohen, *Civil Bench and Jury Trials in State Courts, 2005* at 1 n.1, 2 table 1, & 6 table 7 (NCJ 223851, Oct. 2008), available at https://www.bjs.gov/content/pub/pdf/cbjtsc05.pdf.

Of the punitives awarded in the three earlier studies cumulated by the Eisenberg team, 24 percent of awards were under $10,000, and 60 percent were under $100,000; just under 11 percent were over $1 million. 3 J. Empirical Legal Stud. at 269 table 1. There was a strong correlation between the amount of compensatories and the amount of punitives, *id.* at 272-275, with little change over time, *id.* at 276-278.

McMichael and Viscusi unsurprisingly found that state tort reforms, especially caps on the amount of damages, reduced the amount of punitive damages, and that lowering the standard for bad conduct to a standard like "gross negligence" increased the chances of juries awarding punitive damages. Benjamin J. McMichael & W. Kip Viscusi, *The Punitive Damages Calculus: The Differential Incidence of State Punitive Damages Reforms,* 84 Southern Econ. J. 82 (2017). The authors conducted a follow-up examination of 137 "blockbuster" punitive awards of at least $100 million, and found that the Supreme Court's constitutional ratio analysis, and particularly *Exxon*'s 1:1 suggested ratio, "reduce both the frequency and size of blockbuster awards, while state punitive damages caps reduce only the frequency—most likely by preventing awards that would otherwise have qualified as blockbusters from crossing the $100 million threshold." Benjamin J. McMichael & W. Kip Viscusi, *Taming Blockbuster Punitive Damages Awards,* U. Ill. L. Rev. (forthcoming), https://ssrn.com/abstract=3124542 (2018 draft).

NOTES ON MEASURING PUNITIVE DAMAGES

1. The problem. What should we tell juries about how to measure punitive damages? And what criteria should judges apply in reviewing verdicts? Courts commonly mention the amount of compensatory damages and the reprehensibility of defendant's conduct; most mention defendant's wealth. *Exxon* also mentions whether the wrong was likely to be detected and to provoke a lawsuit. None of these is a measure; they are at most factors to be considered, and they leave a vast range of discretion. Of course punitive damages should be higher if conduct is more reprehensible. But it is hard to agree on a scale. Should juries think in hundreds, thousands, or millions?

2. A hard ratio? *Exxon*'s decision to adopt a hard mathematical ratio as the basis for appellate review has no antecedent in the common law. It is binding only in cases where federal law controls the substantive law of punitive damages; this is not a large number of cases. State courts do not appear to be following the Supreme Court's lead in limiting punitive damages to a 1:1 ratio. Bullock v. Philip Morris U.S.A., Inc., 131 Cal. Rptr. 3d 382, 403 (Ct. App. 2011) (rejecting defendants' argument of an "emerging consensus" to use a one-to-one ratio in cases involving six-figure damage awards). The overwhelming majority of favorable citations to *Exxon* are in federal courts.

3. This particular type of case. The one-to-one ratio applies only to "this particular type of case." What type is that? All cases of reckless conduct that is not motivated by hope of financial gain and that causes serious and obvious injury inevitably leading to large liability for compensatory damages? Or is the "type" broader or narrower than that? How many relevant "types" are there likely to be? The discretion that common law courts have exercised in reviewing individual verdicts may just be diverted into arguments over where to classify a case and when to recognize a new "type" of case.

4. Why so much emphasis on ratios? If punitive damages must be in a reasonable ratio to compensatory damages, that implies that the smaller the compensatories, the smaller the punitives. Might ratios be backwards? If part of the rationale for punitives is to deter wrongful conduct that does little measurable harm, and to express and channel outrage at such conduct, aren't small compensatories an argument for larger punitives? Exxon had already paid $3.5 billion in settlements, fines, and cleanup costs; were punitives needed to deter? What about Texaco v. Pennzoil, reprinted in section 2.D, where compensatories were $7.5 billion? Texaco was a very large company, but it was much smaller than Exxon. The Court appears to address this problem in its comment that "a lesser ratio" is justified when compensatories are large, which of course implies that larger ratios may be justified when compensatories are small.

Many states say that there can be no punitive damages without at least some compensatory damages. Cases illustrating a range of rules on this question are collected in Cush-Crawford v. Adchem Corp., 271 F.3d 352 (2d Cir. 2001). *Cush-Crawford* upheld $100,000 in punitives, with no compensatories, in a statutory sexual harassment case. For an opinion squarely rejecting both the relevance of ratios and the need for compensatories, see Kirkbride v. Lisbon Contractors, Inc., 555 A.2d 800 (Pa. 1989). Applying Pennsylvania law, the Third Circuit has held that although a district court could award punitive damages in a class action even absent provable compensatory damages, a punitive award against a government defendant should be "reasonable and proportionate to the wrong committed." Taha v. City of Bucks, 862 F.3d 292, 308 (3d Cir. 2017). How should courts judge reasonableness and proportionality when compensatory damages cannot be proven with reasonable certainty?

Many cases award nominal damages and punitive damages—most of them in jurisdictions that reject the relevance of ratios. Such cases are collected in Ross-Simons, Inc. v. Baccarat, Inc., 182 F.R.D. 386, 399-402 (D.R.I. 1998), a commercial distribution dispute in which plaintiff alleged that its damages were large but unquantifiable. In Givens v. O'Quinn, 447 F. Supp. 2d 593 (W.D. Va. 2006), the court upheld $1.00 in nominal damages and $15,000 in punitives against a prison supervisor who participated in "a misguided joke" against a guard. The perpetrators bound plaintiff with handcuffs and leg irons, pulled down his pants, taped his genitals to his leg, and took his picture. Are punitives a better solution than requiring plaintiff to hype his emotional distress?

5. Considering defendant's wealth. If the jury is to figure out how large an award is necessary to punish and deter the defendant, it surely must know something of his wealth. Judgments that would bankrupt the average citizen many times over would have no effect on Exxon. Presumably the verdict should be high enough that the defendant feels it. But is that point reached at 10 percent, 1 percent, or .1 percent of net worth? What about 100 percent? See State Farm Mutual Insurance Co. v. Brewer, 191 So. 3d 508 (Fla. Ct. App. 2016), where a jury awarded over $700,000 in compensatory damages in a personal injury case. It was undisputed that the defendant, a physician, fell asleep while driving, and plaintiffs presented evidence that the defendant had taken prescription sleeping medication before setting out on the fateful three-hour drive. The jury heard evidence that defendant's net worth was $284,000 and it awarded exactly that amount in punitive damages. The appellate court instructed the trial court to remit the punitive amount to "a reasonable proportion" of defendant's net worth, unless plaintiffs preferred a new trial on the amount of punitive damages.

Earlier in Florida, a jury awarded $145 billion in a tobacco class action, which was many times defendants' net worth. In upholding the verdict, the trial court relied on defendants' value in the stock market, and on their ability to earn cash and pay the judgment over time. It rejected corporate net worth as an artifact of conservative accounting conventions. Engle v. RJ Reynolds Tobacco, 2000 WL 33534572, at *28-*30 (Fla. Cir. Ct. 2000). Judge Posner has also argued that net worth "is an accounting artifact," because a firm financed with debt may have the same size and resources as a firm financed with equity, but its net worth will be very different. Mathias v. Accor Economy Lodging, Inc., 347 F.3d 672, 677-678 (7th Cir. 2003).

The Florida trial judge was reversed on this and other grounds. Liggett Group, Inc. v. Engle, 853 So. 2d 434 (Fla. Dist. Ct. App. 2003), *aff'd*, 945 So. 2d 1246 (Fla. 2006). The court of appeals said that judgments can be collected immediately and that it is prejudicial to tell a jury that a judgment might be paid in installments. 853 So. 2d at 463. The state supreme court said that punitive damages cannot exceed ability to pay, and it treated net worth as at least a relevant measure. 945 So. 2d at 1265 n.8.

6. Should wealth matter? The trial judge in *Exxon* instructed the jury to consider defendants' wealth, but the Supreme Court does not mention wealth as a relevant consideration. Some scholars and judges have argued that wealth should be irrelevant, because rational defendants are deterred if the liability for conduct exceeds the gains from the conduct. Kenneth S. Abraham & John C. Jeffries, Jr., *Punitive Damages and the Rule of Law: The Role of Defendant's Wealth*, 18 J. Legal Stud. 415 (1989). Judge Posner thought that wealth matters only because it empowers a tenacious and even frivolous defense, thus increasing the difficulty of finding a plaintiff's lawyer. *Mathias*, 347 F.3d at 677. Compare the reaction of the Utah Supreme Court that large awards are "necessary to attract the attention" of large organizations. Campbell v. State Farm Mutual Automobile Insurance Co., 65 P.3d 1134, 1147 (Utah 2001), *rev'd on other grounds*, 538 U.S. 408 (2003). An earlier $100 million judgment had not even been reported to corporate headquarters, and the regional vice president had no plans to report the $145 million judgment under review, even though it had been substantially based on evidence of national corporate policy.

Admitting evidence of defendant's wealth is surely prejudicial; we would not allow it in any other context. In most states, such evidence is admissible if either side chooses to offer it. A routine example is Flippo v. CSC Associates III, L.L.C., 547 S.E.2d 216, 222 (Va. 2001). California requires plaintiff to prove defendant's net worth as a prerequisite to punitives. Adams v. Murakami, 813 P.3d 1348 (Cal. 1991). An increasing number of states have bifurcated trials, excluding evidence of defendant's financial condition from the trial on liability and compensatories, or from the trial on liability for punitives or even the amount of punitives, but allowing or requiring such evidence at a separate hearing on the amount of punitive damages or on post-trial motions to review the jury's award of punitive damages. Courts also disagree on how much plaintiff must show, and how far along the case must be, before she can get discovery of defendant's financial situation. Conflicting cases on the discovery issue, and examples of bifurcation requirements, are collected in In re Jacobs, 300 S.W.3d 35 (Tex. Ct. App. 2009).

For a spectacular example, see Motorola Credit Corp. v Uzan, 509 F.3d 74 (2d Cir. 2007), applying Illinois law and affirming $1 billion in punitive damages against a family with net worth estimated at $5 billion. Defendants were found to have defrauded plaintiffs of $2 billion and to have obstructed justice throughout the litigation. Illinois puts on defendants the burden of proving their lack of wealth; defendants claimed the judgment was an economic death sentence but refused to offer any evidence about their finances. The court relied on published sources and on the inference that the evidence withheld would have been adverse to defendants. The judgment in *Motorola* remains uncollected; for an update, see section 9.B.1.

Punitive damages paid by business defendants are tax deductible, making them less punitive than they might otherwise appear to be. Professors Polsky and Markel argue that juries should be made aware of the tax consequences, so that they would adjust their awards upward. Gregg D. Polsky & Dan Markel, *Taxing Punitive Damages*, 96 Va. L. Rev. 1295 (2010).

7. The absence of wealth. It is hard to argue with the relevance of wealth at the other end of the economic continuum. Consider Stroud v. Lints, 790 N.E.2d 440 (Ind. 2003), where the court vacated $500,000 in punitive damages awarded against a drunk driver. Compensatories were $1.4 million (for a permanent disability), so the ratio was modest. But defendant had no assets and no financial prospects. The court said that punitive damages are excessive if defendant has no hope of ever paying them. But it is the defendant's burden to produce such evidence. Sims v. Pappas, 73 N.E.3d 700 (Ind. 2017). Ronen Perry and Elena Kantorowicz-Reznichenko, *Income-Dependent Punitive Damages*, 95 Wash. U. L. Rev. 835 (2018), suggest a formula for punitive damages based upon the severity of the wrong and the wrongdoer's daily income.

8. Other federal claims. Punitive damages are available for federal constitutional claims and for some statutory claims. *Exxon*'s general approach applies to these claims unless there is some more specific statutory provision. An example is Turley v. ISG Lackawanna, Inc., 774 F.3d 140 (2d Cir. 2014), a racial-harassment case more fully described in note 2.g of Notes on Valuing Emotional Distress, in section 2.G.3. The claims were based on state and federal civil rights laws and intentional infliction of emotional distress. The jury awarded $24 million in punitives, which the trial court reduced to $5 million. Reviewing this amount first under "federal common law," and then under the Constitution, the court of appeals ordered a further remittitur to two times compensatories, or $2.5 million against the corporate defendants. *Id.* at 164. The court said a 2:1 ratio was appropriate, despite the very large and ill-defined compensatories, because of "the extreme nature of defendants' conduct." *Id.* at 167. An award of $1,250 against a supervisor was not disturbed.

Claims of race discrimination can be brought under 42 U.S.C. §1981, which has no damages cap. Claims of discrimination based on sex, religion, national origin, or disability can be brought under 42 U.S.C. §1981(a), which caps compensatory and punitive damages combined at $300,000 for large employers and various smaller amounts for smaller employers. Plaintiffs in these categories can often join a claim under a state civil rights law with their federal claims, and many of the state laws have no caps.

Where the $300,000 combined cap applies, the Ninth Circuit held that it displaces the Supreme Court's analysis of ratios. The combined cap reverses the logic of ratios; the larger the compensatories, the smaller the possible punitives. The injuries are sometimes emotional and hard to value, and if the jury awards nominal damages plus punitives, the nominals do not attempt to measure the actual damages. The jury in a sexual-harassment case awarded $1 in nominal damages and $868,750 in punitives, which the trial court reduced to the $300,000 cap. Finding defendant's conduct sufficiently reprehensible to justify a maximum award, the court of appeals affirmed. Arizona v. ASARCO LLC, 773 F.3d 1050 (9th Cir. 2014) (en banc).

2. *The Constitution*

STATE FARM MUTUAL AUTOMOBILE INSURANCE CO. v. CAMPBELL
538 U.S. 408 (2003)

[In 1981, Curtis Campbell tried to pass six vans on a two-lane highway in Utah. He caused an accident that killed one driver (Ospital) and permanently disabled another (Slusher). Campbell's liability insurance with State Farm covered only $25,000 per person, but State Farm refused offers to settle for policy limits. The jury found Campbell 100 percent at fault and rendered verdicts totaling nearly $186,000. State Farm refused to pay the part of the judgment that exceeded policy limits and refused to post a supersedeas bond to delay collection of the judgment while Campbell appealed.

Campbell then hired his own lawyer, who negotiated a settlement. Slusher, and Ospital's estate, agreed not to collect from Campbell. Campbell agreed to sue State Farm, to be represented in that suit by Slusher and Ospital's lawyers, and to pay 90 percent of any recovery to Slusher and Ospital.

The Utah Supreme Court denied Campbell's appeal in the original tort suits, Slusher v. Ospital ex rel. Ospital, 777 P.2d 437 (Utah 1989), and State Farm belatedly paid the entire judgment. The Campbells then sued State Farm, alleging bad-faith refusal to settle, fraud, and intentional infliction of emotional distress.

The evidence showed that State Farm set corporate financial goals that required capping the amounts it would pay on claims, without regard to the number of claims or their merit. To meet these caps, State Farm often refused to pay claims on behalf of unsophisticated insureds who were thought unlikely to complain effectively. In pursuit of this scheme, State Farm put false documents in claim files, removed documents that suggested liability, and destroyed claims-handling manuals that might reveal the scheme. Former State Farm employees testified to the scheme, and one former employee provided a copy of the 1979 manual in which the scheme had originated.]

Justice KENNEDY delivered the opinion of the Court. . . .

I

The jury awarded the Campbells $2.6 million in compensatory damages and $145 million in punitive damages, which the trial court reduced to $1 million and $25 million respectively. Both parties appealed.

The Utah Supreme Court sought to apply the three guideposts we identified in BMW, Inc. v. Gore, 517 U.S. 559 (1996), and it reinstated the $145 million punitive damages award. [These "guideposts" were "the degree of reprehensibility of the defendant's conduct," the ratio "between the punitive damages award and *the harm likely to result* from the defendant's conduct as well as the harm that actually has occurred," and "the civil or criminal penalties that could be imposed for comparable misconduct." *Id.* at 575, 581, 583. The Utah court concluded that] State Farm's conduct was reprehensible. The court also relied upon State Farm's "massive wealth" and on testimony indicating that "State Farm's actions, because of their clandestine nature, will be punished at most in one out of every 50,000 cases as a matter of statistical probability," 65 P.3d 1134, 1153 (Utah 2001), and concluded that the ratio between punitive and compensatory damages was not unwarranted. Finally, the court noted that the punitive damages award was not excessive when compared to various civil and criminal penalties State Farm could have faced, including $10,000 for each act of fraud, the suspension of its license to conduct business in Utah, the disgorgement of profits, and imprisonment. . . .

II . . .

While States possess discretion over the imposition of punitive damages, it is well established that there are procedural and substantive constitutional limitations on these awards. The Due Process Clause . . . prohibits the imposition of grossly excessive or arbitrary punishments on a tortfeasor. The reason is that "[e]lementary notions of fairness enshrined in our constitutional jurisprudence dictate that a person receive fair notice not only of the conduct that will subject him to punishment, but also of the severity of the penalty that a State may impose." *BMW*, 517 U.S. at 574. To the extent an award is grossly excessive, it furthers no legitimate purpose and constitutes an arbitrary deprivation of property.

Although these awards serve the same purposes as criminal penalties, defendants subjected to punitive damages in civil cases have not been accorded the protections applicable in a criminal proceeding. This increases our concerns over the imprecise manner in which punitive damages systems are administered. We have admonished that "[p]unitive damages pose an acute danger of arbitrary deprivation of property. Jury instructions typically leave the jury with wide discretion in choosing amounts, and the presentation of evidence of a defendant's net worth creates the potential that juries will use their verdicts to express biases against big businesses, particularly those without strong local presences." Honda Motor Co. v. Oberg, 512 U.S. 415, 432 (1994). . . .

III . . .

A

"[T]he most important indicium of the reasonableness of a punitive damages award is the degree of reprehensibility of the defendant's conduct." *BMW*, 517 U.S. at 575. We have instructed courts to determine the reprehensibility of a defendant by considering whether: the harm caused was physical as opposed to economic; the tortious conduct evinced an indifference to or a reckless disregard of the health or safety of others; the target of the conduct had financial vulnerability; the conduct involved repeated actions or was an isolated incident; and the harm was the result of intentional malice, trickery, or deceit, or mere accident. . . .

Applying these factors in the instant case, we must acknowledge that State Farm's handling of the claims against the Campbells merits no praise. The trial court found that State Farm's employees altered the company's records to make Campbell appear less culpable. State Farm disregarded . . . the near-certain probability that, by taking the case to trial, a judgment in excess of the policy limits would be awarded. State Farm amplified the harm by at first assuring the Campbells their assets would be safe from any verdict and by later telling them, postjudgment, to put a for-sale sign on their house. While we do not suggest there was error in awarding punitive damages based upon State Farm's conduct toward the Campbells, a more modest punishment for this reprehensible conduct could have satisfied the State's legitimate objectives. . . .

This case, instead, was used as a platform to expose, and punish, the perceived deficiencies of State Farm's operations throughout the country. . . .

A State cannot punish a defendant for conduct that may have been lawful where it occurred. Nor, as a general rule, does a State have a legitimate concern in imposing punitive damages to punish a defendant for unlawful acts committed outside of the State's jurisdiction. Any proper adjudication of conduct that occurred outside Utah to other persons would require their inclusion, and, to those parties, the Utah courts, in the usual case, would need to apply the laws of their relevant jurisdiction. . . .

Lawful out-of-state conduct may be probative when it demonstrates the deliberateness and culpability of the defendant's action in the State where it is tortious, but that conduct must have a nexus to the specific harm suffered by the plaintiff. A jury must be instructed, furthermore, that it may not use evidence of out-of-state conduct to punish a defendant for action that was lawful in the jurisdiction where it occurred. . . .

For a more fundamental reason, however, the Utah courts erred in relying upon this and other evidence: The courts awarded punitive damages to punish and deter conduct that bore no relation to the Campbells' harm. A defendant's dissimilar acts, independent from the acts upon which liability was premised, may not serve as the basis for punitive damages. A defendant should be punished for the conduct that harmed the plaintiff, not for being an unsavory individual or business. Due process does not permit courts, in the calculation of punitive damages, to adjudicate the merits of other parties' hypothetical claims against a defendant under the guise of the reprehensibility analysis. . . . Punishment on these bases creates the possibility of multiple punitive damages awards for the same conduct; for in the usual case nonparties are not bound by the judgment some other plaintiff obtains.

The same reasons lead us to conclude the Utah Supreme Court's decision cannot be justified on the grounds that State Farm was a recidivist. . . . [C]ourts must ensure the conduct in question replicates the prior transgressions. . . .

Although evidence of other acts need not be identical to have relevance in the calculation of punitive damages, the Utah court erred here because evidence pertaining to claims that had nothing to do with a third-party lawsuit was introduced at length. . . .

B

Turning to the second *BMW* guidepost, we have been reluctant to identify concrete constitutional limits on the ratio between harm, or potential harm, to the plaintiff and the punitive damages award. We decline again to impose a bright-line ratio which a punitive damages award cannot exceed. Our jurisprudence and the principles it has now established demonstrate, however, that, in practice, few awards exceeding a single-digit ratio between punitive and compensatory damages, to a significant degree, will satisfy due process. In Pacific Mutual Life Insurance Co. v. Haslip, 499 U.S. 1 (1991), in upholding a punitive damages award, we concluded that an award of more than four times the amount of compensatory damages might be close to the line of constitutional impropriety. . . . The Court further referenced a long legislative history, dating back over 700 years and going forward to today, providing for sanctions of double, treble, or quadruple damages to deter and punish. While these ratios are not binding, they are instructive. They demonstrate what should be obvious: Single-digit multipliers are more likely to comport with due process, while still achieving the State's goals of deterrence and retribution, than awards with ratios . . . of 145 to 1.

Nonetheless, because there are no rigid benchmarks that a punitive damages award may not surpass, ratios greater than those we have previously upheld may comport with due process where "a particularly egregious act has resulted in only a small amount of economic damages." *BMW*, 517 U.S. at 582; see also *id.* (positing that a higher ratio *might* be necessary where "the injury is hard to detect or the monetary value of noneconomic harm might have been difficult to determine"). The converse is also true, however. When compensatory damages are substantial, then a lesser ratio, perhaps only equal to compensatory damages, can reach the outermost limit of the due process guarantee. . . .

In the context of this case, we have no doubt that there is a presumption against an award that has a 145-to-1 ratio. The compensatory award in this case was substantial; the Campbells were awarded $1 million for a year and a half of emotional distress. This was complete compensation. The harm arose from a transaction in the economic realm, not from some physical assault or trauma; there were no physical injuries; and State Farm paid the excess verdict before the complaint was filed, so the Campbells suffered only minor economic injuries for the 18-month period in which State Farm refused to resolve the claim against them. The compensatory damages for the injury suffered here, moreover, likely were based on a component which was duplicated in the punitive award. Much of the distress was caused by the outrage and humiliation the Campbells suffered at the actions of their insurer; and it is a major role of punitive damages to condemn such conduct. Compensatory damages, however, already contain this punitive element. See *Restatement (Second) of Torts* §908, cmt. *c* (1977) ("In many cases in which compensatory damages include an amount for emotional distress, such as humiliation or indignation aroused by the defendant's act, there is no clear line of demarcation between punishment and compensation and a verdict for a specified amount frequently includes elements of both."). . . .

[T]he argument that State Farm will be punished in only the rare case, coupled with reference to its assets (which, of course, are what other insured parties in Utah and other States must rely upon for payment of claims) had little to do with the actual harm sustained by the Campbells. The wealth of a defendant cannot justify an otherwise unconstitutional punitive damages award. . . .

C

The third guidepost in *BMW* is the disparity between the punitive damages award and the "civil penalties authorized or imposed in comparable cases." 517 U.S. at 575. We . . . have also looked to criminal penalties that could be imposed. The existence of a criminal penalty does have bearing on the seriousness with which a State views the wrongful action. When used to determine the dollar amount of the award, however, the criminal penalty has less utility. Great care must be taken to avoid use of the civil process to assess criminal penalties that can be imposed only after the heightened protections of a criminal trial have been observed, including, of course, its higher standards of proof. Punitive damages are not a substitute for the criminal process, and the remote possibility of a criminal sanction does not automatically sustain a punitive damages award.

Here, we need not dwell long on this guidepost. The most relevant civil sanction under Utah state law for the wrong done to the Campbells appears to be a $10,000 fine for an act of fraud, an amount dwarfed by the $145 million punitive damages award. The Supreme Court of Utah speculated about the loss of State Farm's business license, the disgorgement of profits, and possible imprisonment, but here again its references were to the broad fraudulent scheme drawn from evidence of out-of-state and dissimilar conduct. This analysis was insufficient to justify the award.

IV

An application of the *BMW* guideposts to the facts of this case, especially in light of the substantial compensatory damages awarded (a portion of which contained a punitive element), likely would justify a punitive damages award at or near the amount of compensatory damages. The punitive award of $145 million, therefore, was neither reasonable nor proportionate to the wrong committed, and it was an irrational and arbitrary deprivation of the property of the defendant. . . .

The judgment of the Utah Supreme Court is reversed, and the case is remanded for proceedings not inconsistent with this opinion. . . .

Justice GINSBURG, dissenting. . . .

I

The large size of the award upheld by the Utah Supreme Court in this case indicates why damage-capping legislation may be altogether fitting and proper. Neither the amount of the award nor the trial record, however, justifies this Court's substitution of its judgment for that of Utah's competent decisionmakers. . . . [O]n the key criterion "reprehensibility," there is a good deal more to the story than the Court's abbreviated account tells. [Justice Ginsburg then reviewed the evidence, in vastly greater detail than the majority had done, and found ample evidence to support the judgment.]

[Justices SCALIA and THOMAS each dissented on the ground of their persistent view that the Due Process Clause does not limit punitive damage awards. They generally reject the idea of substantive due process, and believe that any traditional procedure known to the common law in 1868 satisfies procedural due process. They also say that the Court's punitive damages cases cannot be applied in any principled way, so they feel no obligation to treat them as precedent.]

NOTES ON CONSTITUTIONAL LIMITS ON PUNITIVE DAMAGES

1. The earlier cases. The Court worked its way up to *State Farm* over a 14-year period. Here's a quick review.

a. Excessive fines. Relying on its view of original understanding, the Court held that the Excessive Fines Clause of the Eighth Amendment applies only to fines payable to the government, and not to punitive damages between private parties. Browning-Ferris Industries, Inc. v. Kelco Disposal, Inc., 492 U.S. 257 (1989). Justices O'Connor and Stevens dissented. They thought that usage was variable in the founders' time, and that "excessive punitive damages present precisely the evil of exorbitant monetary penalties that the Clause was designed to prevent." *Id.* at 287 (O'Connor, J., dissenting).

b. Procedural due process. Next the Court said that procedural due process requires meaningful jury instructions on punitive damages and meaningful appellate review of punitive verdicts, but that Alabama's procedures satisfied these criteria.

Pacific Mutual Life Insurance Co. v. Haslip, 499 U.S. 1 (1991). The Court distinguished Alabama, with a seven-factor test for reviewing punitive damages, from states that limit judicial review to whether the verdict is "grossly excessive" or "shocks the conscience." *Id.* at 21 n.10. This led many state courts to produce lists of factors for reviewing punitive damages. The Court also rejected a substantive due process attack on punishment for vicarious wrongdoing.

Justice O'Connor dissented; she thought the Alabama procedures were illusory and neither guided juries nor controlled them. Justice Scalia thought the Alabama procedures were fundamentally unfair to defendants, but he thought they were constitutional because any traditional procedure satisfies due process.

Honda Motor Co. v. Oberg, 512 U.S. 415 (1994), involved an apparently unique provision of the Oregon Constitution that entirely precluded judicial review of the amount of a damage award. The Court reviewed the power of common law judges to set aside excessive verdicts, and it held that this power was an essential component of procedural due process. Justice Ginsburg, joined by Chief Justice Rehnquist, dissented. She thought that the power to set aside excessive verdicts was rarely exercised at common law, and that, considered as a whole, Oregon exercised more control over juries than common law judges did at the time of the founding.

c. Damages defendant might have caused. In TXO Production Corp. v. Alliance Resources Corp., 509 U.S. 443 (1993), TXO tried to swindle Alliance out of valuable mineral rights, causing Alliance to incur $19,000 in attorneys' fees. In a suit for slander of title, the jury awarded Alliance these attorneys' fees plus $10 million in punitive damages. The plurality upheld the punitives on the ground that they were not disproportionate to the damage TXO *might have* caused: the loss of all future royalties from the mineral rights. A simpler example is Strenke v. Hogner, 704 N.W.2d 309 (Wis. Ct. App. 2005), where an egregiously drunk driver (.27 blood alcohol, fifth conviction) caused an accident with minor injuries. The court upheld $2,000 compensatories and $225,000 punitives in light of the death or serious injuries the driver might have caused. The Wisconsin Supreme Court had remanded the issue after splitting three to three with one justice recused. 694 N.W.2d 296 (Wis. 2005).

In *TXO*, Justices Scalia and Thomas concurred on the ground that there is no substantive due process limit on punitive damages. The Due Process Clause guarantees judicial review of verdicts (they would later join the opinion in *Honda*), but they insisted that there is no federal right to a correct result.

Justice Kennedy concurred on the ground that TXO acted with malice at the level of its senior officers, pursuant to a policy demonstrated by its having engaged in similar frauds against other victims. He insisted that the Constitution "does not concern itself with dollar amounts, ratios, or the quirks of juries in specific jurisdictions." *Id.* at 467 (Kennedy, J., concurring).

Justices O'Connor, White, and Souter dissented, principally on the ground that plaintiff's final argument to a West Virginia jury openly appealed to bias against rich companies from Texas, and that there was no other record basis for the judgment. Neither side had noted the amount of the potential royalties in the state courts.

d. The emergence of "guideposts." The Court first reversed an award of punitive damages as excessive in BMW, Inc. v. Gore, 517 U.S. 559 (1996). An Alabama jury awarded $4,000 in compensatories, and $4 million in punitives, for failure to disclose that a new BMW had been repainted. The punitives appeared to have been calculated as $4,000 per car times approximately 1,000 repainted cars that had been sold nationwide. The Alabama Supreme Court reduced the judgment to $2 million, on the ground that it was inappropriate to use out-of-state cars as a multiplier. 646 So. 2d 619 (Ala. 1994).

The U.S. Supreme Court emphasized that Alabama could not punish out-of-state conduct; some states did not even require that minor repairs be disclosed. The Court also created the three guideposts discussed in *State Farm*, and it vacated the remaining $2 million as excessive. Justice Kennedy joined the opinion as the fifth vote, without explaining why his views had changed since *TXO*.

Justice Ginsburg, joined by Chief Justice Rehnquist, dissented. She thought the out-of-state conduct was a red herring, because the Alabama courts had already corrected that error. She thought that Supreme Court review of individual punitive damages judgments was unworkable and standardless, and that state courts and legislatures were actively addressing any problem that existed. Justices Scalia and Thomas also dissented, again insisting that there is no substantive due process limit on excessive verdicts and also ridiculing the vagueness of the Court's opinion and the lack of any meaningful standard.

On remand, the Alabama court ordered a new trial unless plaintiff accepted a remittitur of all but $50,000 of the punitive damages awarded. 701 So. 2d 507 (Ala. 1997). It selected $50,000 as in the range of other Alabama verdicts in cases of repaired cars being sold as new.

2. The effects of constitutional review. A constitutional standard makes possible Supreme Court review of state tort judgments, and it allows federal courts to apply independent standards in diversity cases. The Court decided that constitutional review has a very different relationship to jury trial. On a common law argument that punitive damages are excessive, federal courts of appeals should review only the trial judge's ruling on the motion to set aside the verdict, and review that only for abuse of discretion. But on an argument that punitive damages are unconstitutionally excessive, federal judges are to review the jury verdict de novo. Cooper Industries, Inc. v. Leatherman Tool Group, Inc., 532 U.S. 424 (2001). So one clear effect of the constitutional standard is to empower judges as against jurors, and appellate judges as against trial judges, and to give defendants multiple chances for de novo review of the verdict. Courts have read de novo review as a constitutional requirement, applicable in state court as well. An example is Engle v. Liggett Group, Inc., 945 So. 2d 1246, 1263 (Fla. 2006).

Plaintiff is not entitled to a new trial if he rejects the lower amount offered by the court; the court can simply enter judgment for the lower amount. Courts have said that the constitutional maximum is not a fact to be found by a jury and that any larger verdict on retrial would again have to be rejected. Some of the cases are collected in Simon v. San Paolo U.S. Holding Co., 113 P.3d 63, 80-81 (Cal. 2005). Compare the very different constitutional rule long applied to common law decisions that a verdict is excessive (remittitur), described in Notes on Judicial Review of Jury Verdicts in section 2.G.3.

3. The verdicts in *State Farm*. A wrongful death and a permanent disability suffered by the other two drivers were worth only $185,859 to a Utah jury. The Campbells' emotional distress was worth $2.6 million, and $1 million after the trial court's remittitur. Is this disparity just the hazard of different juries hearing different cases? The difference between how juries assess damages against individual defendants and how they assess damages against corporate defendants? Or does it support the Supreme Court's suggestion that much of the compensatory award was really punitive?

4. The opinion in *State Farm*. *BMW* and *State Farm* both relied on the same three guideposts, and both invalidated enormous verdicts. But the tone of the *State Farm* opinion was very different. The review of the facts was more intrusive; the suggested ratios came closer to bright-line rules; there was a new suggestion of a one-to-one ratio when compensatories are large. *State Farm* put the *BMW* guideposts on steroids.

The majority increased from five to six (Chief Justice Rehnquist abandoned his ear-lier dissents without explanation), and there was no hint of any difficulty in holding that majority together.

5. Ratios. Many courts responded to *State Farm* by reducing punitive awards to single-digit ratios to compensatories. In *State Farm* itself, the Utah court awarded nine times compensatories, because nine is the highest single-digit number. 98 P.3d 409 (Utah 2004). Other courts have noted that what the Court actually said is that "few" awards—not none—would be upheld if the ratio exceeded single digits "to a signifi-cant degree," and that higher ratios might be justified where "a particularly egregious act has resulted in only a small amount of economic damages." And courts have found such cases.

In Mathias v. Accor Economy Lodging, Inc., 347 F.3d 672 (7th Cir. 2003), plaintiffs were guests bitten by bedbugs in defendant's Motel 6. Defendant had refused to treat the infestation more aggressively, and it had persistently misrepresented conditions. The jury awarded $5,000 in compensatories and $186,000 in punitives; the hotel had 191 rooms. The court upheld the award in an opinion by Judge Posner. "The defen-dant's behavior was outrageous but the compensable harm done was slight and at the same time difficult to quantify because a large element of it was emotional." *Id.* at 677. The small amount of damages justified a larger multiplier, in part so there would be a prospect of a sufficient judgment to attract counsel on a contingent fee basis.

In Hamlin v. Hampton Lumber Mills, Inc., 246 P.3d 1121 (Or. 2011), the court upheld $6,000 in compensatory damages and $175,000 in punitives in an employ-ment-discrimination case. The majority collected cases from around the country upholding high ratios, and concluded that ratios are "of limited assistance" when compensatories are small and do not "already serve an admonitory function." *Id.* at 1128. The dissenters thought that the Supreme Court's approval of greater-than-single-digit ratios in cases with small compensatories was confined to cases of "egre-gious misconduct." *Id.* at 1132 (Gillette, J., dissenting).

On the other hand, when compensatories are large, such as cases involving at least $1 million, many federal courts are reducing awards to a 1:1 ratio. In Lompe v. Sunridge Partners, LLC, 818 F.3d 1041 (10th Cir. 2016), plaintiff suffered carbon monoxide poisoning coming from the furnace in her apartment complex, and she sued the apartment owner and management company for negligence. The jury awarded $1.95 million in compensatory damages, including about $1 million for emotional distress, and $22.5 million in punitives against the management company, AMC. The evidence showed that AMC "knew the furnaces were nearly thirty years old despite having a useful life of about twenty years, and AMC failed to act on bids for regular safety inspections of the furnaces despite three" carbon monoxide leaks at plaintiff's apartment complex before the injury. *Id.* at 1057. Despite the repre-hensible conduct, the court concluded that a 1:1 ratio was constitutionally required, given the substantial compensatory, and especially emotional distress, damages. The dissenting judge would have reduced the punitives to a 4:1 ratio.

6. Other fines and penalties. What is the relevance of the third *BMW* guidepost? If the $10,000 civil penalty for one act of insurance fraud is a hard limit on punitive damages, that would be the end of meaningful punitive damages in most contexts. If it is not a hard limit, but some sort of indicator of how seriously the state takes the wrongdoing, it is hard to see how courts can use this guidepost in meaningful ways. In an unpublished paper written in 2008, Laycock's student Kathryn Drenning found the lower court cases in serious disarray with respect to this guidepost.

Compare Grimshaw v. Ford Motor Co., 174 Cal. Rptr. 348 (Ct. App. 1981), a case in which Ford was found to have knowingly built a car that would burst into flame in rear-end collisions at modest speeds. The court said it is "precisely because monetary penalties" on business "are so inadequate and ineffective as deterrents" that punitive damages are needed in amounts that will deter. *Id.* at 389. Legislators are elected to make public policy; jurors are not. Administrative agencies have expertise; jurors do not. But legislators and agencies are subject to capture by campaign contributors and by the industries they regulate; jurors are not. And legislators can repeal or limit punitive damages at any time. Who has the better argument over the relevance of other civil penalties?

7. Other wrongful conduct. Courts have long admitted evidence of the same or similar wrongful conduct in punitive damages trials. Similar conduct on a wide scale shows that what happened to plaintiff was deliberate corporate policy and not the unauthorized act of a rogue employee. Willingness to harm many people shows a greater need for deterrence, and a more malicious state of mind, than willingness to harm one person.

The teeth of the *State Farm* opinion was in its holding that nearly all of State Farm's other misconduct was irrelevant. This implied a very tight definition of what misconduct is sufficiently analogous to count. The Court seemed to think that refusing to pay first-party claims for property damage had nothing to do with refusing to pay liability claims, even if both refusals flowed from the same policy to arbitrarily cap payments. The Court seemed to require proof of specific Utah examples, rejecting the inference that a policy promulgated and implemented nationally must have been applied in Utah as well. The Court seemed concerned about multiple liability if the same pattern of misconduct is used to prove reprehensibility in multiple cases. The Court returned to the problem of related wrongdoing in the next case.

PHILIP MORRIS USA v. WILLIAMS
549 U.S. 346 (2007)

[Plaintiff's decedent died of lung cancer after smoking Marlboros for 40 years. The theory of the case was fraud—that Philip Morris knew for the entire 40 years that there was at least a substantial risk that smoking caused cancer, and knew for most of that time that smoking in fact caused cancer, but that it falsely and systematically sought to reassure the public and minimize the risk. When his family had tried to persuade him to quit smoking, Williams had repeated the industry's assurances that smoking was safe. The jury awarded $21,000 in "economic" damages—Williams died soon after his diagnosis, so his medical expenses were modest, and if he was retired, there may have been no lost income—$800,000 in "noneconomic" damages, and $79.5 million in punitives. The "noneconomic" damages were reduced to $500,000 in compliance with a statutory cap. In his jury argument on punitives, plaintiff's attorney emphasized all the other Oregon smokers who had been deceived by the same ads.

The Oregon court upheld the punitives, 127 P.3d 1165 (Or. 2006), after a close textual analysis of *State Farm.* It concluded that defendant's conduct was extremely reprehensible, intentionally inflicting substantial risk of serious illness or death on thousands of Oregonians. It read *State Farm* as forbidding punishment for out-of-state conduct or for conduct dissimilar to the illegal conduct directed at plaintiff, but as permitting punishment for conduct directed to others that was both in-state and similar. It concluded that what Philip Morris had done was manslaughter, a felony that the Legislature treated very seriously. It acknowledged that the punitives far exceeded a single-digit ratio to compensatories, either before or after the reduction to the statutory cap. But it said that single-digit ratios can be exceeded when the conduct is unusually reprehensible, and this was such a case.]

Justice BREYER delivered the opinion of the Court. . . .

II . . .

[T]he Constitution imposes certain limits, in respect both to procedures for awarding punitive damages and to amounts forbidden as "grossly excessive.". . . [W]e need . . . only consider the Constitution's procedural limitations.

III

In our view, the Constitution's Due Process Clause forbids a State to use a punitive damages award to punish a defendant for injury that it inflicts upon nonparties or those whom they directly represent, i.e., injury that it inflicts upon those who are, essentially, strangers to the litigation. For one thing, the Due Process Clause prohibits a State from punishing an individual without first providing that individual with "an opportunity to present every available defense." Lindsey v. Normet, 405 U.S. 56, 66 (1972). Yet a defendant threatened with punishment for injuring a nonparty victim has no opportunity to defend against the charge, by showing, for example . . . , that the other victim was not entitled to damages because he or she knew that smoking was dangerous or did not rely upon the defendant's statements to the contrary.

For another, to permit punishment for injuring a nonparty victim would add a near standardless dimension to the punitive damages equation. How many such victims are there? How seriously were they injured? Under what circumstances did injury occur? The trial will not likely answer such questions as to nonparty victims. The jury will be left to speculate. And the fundamental due process concerns to which our punitive damages cases refer—risks of arbitrariness, uncertainty and lack of notice—will be magnified.

Finally, we can find no authority supporting the use of punitive damages awards for the purpose of punishing a defendant for harming others. We have said that it may be appropriate to consider the reasonableness of a punitive damages award in light of the *potential* harm the defendant's conduct could have caused. But we have made clear that the potential harm at issue was harm potentially caused *the plaintiff.* . . .

Respondent argues that she is free to show harm to other victims because it is relevant to a different part of the punitive damages constitutional equation, namely, reprehensibility. That is to say, harm to others shows more reprehensible conduct. Philip Morris, in turn, does not deny that a plaintiff may show harm to others in order to demonstrate reprehensibility. Nor do we. Evidence of actual harm to nonparties can help to show that the conduct that harmed the plaintiff also posed a substantial risk of harm to the general public, and so was particularly reprehensible—although counsel may argue in a particular case that conduct resulting in no harm to others nonetheless posed a grave risk to the public, or the converse. Yet for the reasons given above, a jury may not go further than this and use a punitive damages verdict to punish a defendant directly on account of harms it is alleged to have visited on nonparties.

Given the risks of unfairness that we have mentioned, it is constitutionally important for a court to provide assurance that the jury will ask the right question, not the wrong one. And given the risks of arbitrariness, the concern for adequate notice, and the risk that punitive damages awards can, in practice, impose one State's (or one jury's) policies (e.g., banning cigarettes) upon other States—all of which accompany awards that, today, may be many times the size of such awards in the 18th and 19th centuries—it is particularly important that States avoid procedure that unnecessarily deprives juries of proper legal guidance. We therefore conclude that the Due Process Clause requires States to provide assurance that juries are not asking the wrong question, i.e., seeking, not simply to determine reprehensibility, but also to punish for harm caused strangers.

IV . . .

The instruction that Philip Morris said the trial court should have given distinguishes between using harm to others as part of the "reasonable relationship" equation (which it would allow) and using it directly as a basis for punishment. The instruction asked the trial court to tell the jury that "you *may* consider the extent of harm suffered by others *in determining what [the] reasonable relationship is*" between Philip Morris' punishable misconduct and harm caused to Jesse Williams, "*[but] you are not to punish the defendant for the impact of its alleged misconduct on other persons, who may bring lawsuits of their own* in which other juries can resolve their claims" (emphasis added). . . .

The court rejected that [instruction]. In doing so, it pointed out (1) that this Court in *State Farm* had held only that a jury could not base its award upon "dissimilar" acts of a defendant. 127 P.3d at 1175-1176. It added (2) that "[i]f a jury cannot punish for the conduct, then it is difficult to see why it may consider it at all." *Id.* at 1175 n.3. And it stated (3) that "[i]t is unclear to us how a jury could 'consider' harm to others, yet withhold that consideration from the punishment calculus." *Id.*

The Oregon court's first statement is correct. We did not previously hold explicitly that a jury may not punish for the harm caused others. But we do so hold now. We do not agree with the Oregon court's second statement. We have explained why we believe the Due Process Clause prohibits a State's inflicting punishment for harm caused strangers to the litigation. At the same time we recognize that conduct that risks harm to many is likely more reprehensible than conduct that risks harm to only a few. And a jury consequently may take this fact into account in determining reprehensibility. Cf., e.g., Witte v. United States, 515 U.S. 389, 400 (1995) (recidivism statutes taking into account a criminal defendant's other misconduct do not impose an "'additional penalty for the earlier crimes,' but instead . . .'a stiffened penalty for the latest crime, which is considered to be an aggravated offense because a repetitive one,'" quoting Gryger v. Burke, 334 U.S. 728, 732 (1948)).

The Oregon court's third statement raises a practical problem. How can we know whether a jury, in taking account of harm caused others under the rubric of reprehensibility, also seeks to *punish* the defendant for having caused injury to others? Our answer is that state courts cannot authorize procedures that create an unreasonable and unnecessary risk of any such confusion occurring. In particular, we believe that where the risk of that misunderstanding is a significant one—because, for instance, of the sort of evidence that was introduced at trial or the kinds of argument the plaintiff made to the jury—a court, upon request, must protect against that risk. Although the States have some flexibility to determine what *kind* of procedures they will implement, federal constitutional law obligates them to provide *some* form of protection in appropriate cases.

V . . .

We remand this case so that the Oregon Supreme Court can apply the standard we have set forth. Because the application of this standard may lead to the need for a new trial, or a change in the level of the punitive damages award, we shall not consider whether the award is constitutionally "grossly excessive." We vacate the Oregon Supreme Court's judgment and remand the case for further proceedings not inconsistent with this opinion. . . .

Justice STEVENS, dissenting. . . .

I agree with Justice Ginsburg's explanation of why no procedural error even arguably justifying reversal occurred at the trial in this case.

Of greater importance to me, however, is the Court's imposition of a novel limit on the State's power to impose punishment in civil litigation. Unlike the Court, I see no reason why an interest in punishing a wrongdoer "for harming persons who are not before the court" should not be taken into consideration when assessing the appropriate sanction for reprehensible conduct. . . .

In the case before us, evidence attesting to the possible harm the defendant's extensive deceitful conduct caused other Oregonians was properly presented to the jury. No evidence was offered to establish an appropriate measure of damages to compensate such third parties for their injuries, and no one argued that the punitive damages award would serve any such purpose. To award compensatory damages to remedy such third-party harm might well constitute a taking of property from the defendant without due process. But a punitive damages award, instead of serving a compensatory purpose, serves the entirely different purposes of retribution and deterrence that underlie every criminal sanction. This justification for punitive damages has even greater salience when, as in this case, see Ore. Rev. Stat. §31.735(1) (2003), the award is payable in whole or in part to the State rather than to the private litigant.

While apparently recognizing the novelty of its holding, the majority relies on a distinction between taking third-party harm into account in order to assess the reprehensibility of the defendant's conduct—which is permitted—from doing so in order to punish the defendant "directly"—which is forbidden. This nuance eludes me. When a jury increases a punitive damages award because injuries to third parties enhanced the reprehensibility of the defendant's conduct, the jury is by definition punishing the defendant—directly—for third-party harm.[2] A murderer who kills his victim by throwing a bomb that injures dozens of bystanders should be punished more severely than one who harms no one other than his intended victim. Similarly, there is no reason why the measure of the appropriate punishment for engaging in a

---

2. It is no answer to refer, as the majority does, to recidivism statutes. In that context, we have distinguished between taking prior crimes into account as an aggravating factor in penalizing the conduct before the court versus doing so to punish for the earlier crimes. But if enhancing a penalty for a present crime because of prior conduct that has already been punished is permissible, it is certainly proper to enhance a penalty because the conduct before the court, which has never been punished, injured multiple victims.

campaign of deceit in distributing a poisonous and addictive substance to thousands of cigarette smokers statewide should not include consideration of the harm to those "bystanders" as well as the harm to the individual plaintiff. The Court endorses a contrary conclusion without providing us with any reasoned justification. . . .

Essentially for the reasons stated in the opinion of the Supreme Court of Oregon, I would affirm its judgment. . . .

Justice GINSBURG, with whom Justices SCALIA and THOMAS join, dissenting. . . .

"[C]onduct that risks harm to many," the Court observes, "is likely more reprehensible than conduct that risks harm to only a few." The Court thus conveys that, when punitive damages are at issue, a jury is properly instructed to consider the extent of harm suffered by others as a measure of reprehensibility, but not to mete out punishment for injuries in fact sustained by nonparties. The Oregon courts did not rule otherwise. . . .

The Court's order vacating the Oregon Supreme Court's judgment is all the more inexplicable considering that Philip Morris did not preserve any objection to the charges in fact delivered to the jury, to the evidence introduced at trial, or to opposing counsel's argument. The sole objection Philip Morris preserved was to the trial court's refusal to give defendant's requested charge number 34. The proposed instruction read in pertinent part:

> . . . (1) The size of any punishment should bear a reasonable relationship to the harm caused to Jesse Williams by the defendant's punishable misconduct. Although you may consider the extent of harm suffered by others in determining what that reasonable relationship is, you are not to punish the defendant for the impact of its alleged misconduct on other persons, who may bring lawsuits of their own in which other juries can resolve their claims and award punitive damages for those harms, as such other juries see fit. . . .
>
> (2) The size of the punishment may appropriately reflect the degree of reprehensibility of the defendant's conduct—that is, how far the defendant has departed from accepted societal norms of conduct.

Under that charge, just what use could the jury properly make of "the extent of harm suffered by others"? The answer slips from my grasp. A judge seeking to enlighten rather than confuse surely would resist delivering the requested charge.

The Court ventures no opinion on the propriety of the charge proposed by Philip Morris, though Philip Morris preserved no other objection to the trial proceedings. . . .

[Justice THOMAS also dissented separately, restating his view that the Constitution has nothing to say about these issues.]

MORE NOTES ON CONSTITUTIONAL LIMITS ON PUNITIVE DAMAGES

1. The remand. The Oregon courts entered the same award on remand, holding that Philip Morris had not preserved its claim of error, because the requested instruction was erroneous on other points. 176 P.3d 1255 (Or. 2008), *cert. dis'd as improvidently granted*, 556 U.S. 178 (2009). In Professor Sharkey's view, the state court successfully resisted the federal pressure, and the U.S. Supreme Court blinked first, perhaps suggesting a lack of will for a serious fight with state courts. Catherine M. Sharkey, *Federal Incursions and State Defiance: Punitive Damages in the Wake of Philip Morris v. Williams,* 46 Williamette L. Rev. 449 (2010).

2. Other wrongful conduct. In *Philip Morris*, the other wrongdoing was not just in state and similar; it was the very same conduct. The very same ads that deceived Jesse Williams deceived other Oregon smokers. So *Philip Morris* does not distinguish the other wrongdoing. It distinguishes punishing the other wrongdoing (prohibited) from using that other wrongdoing to assess the reprehensibility of defendant's treatment of the plaintiff (permitted).

Will this distinction make a difference in results? Or will it merely require a new jury instruction? The dissenters claimed not to understand the distinction; how will juries understand it? Does *Philip Morris*'s limit on what juries can do with evidence of other wrongdoing replace or supplement *State Farm*'s stringent requirement of similarity between the wrongdoing aimed at plaintiff and any other wrongdoing considered? That is, if the jury is properly instructed not to punish other wrongdoing but simply to consider it as evidence of reprehensibility, does the other wrongdoing have to be so nearly identical?

Evaluating ten years of post-*Philip Morris* cases, Professor Jill Wieber Lens finds ongoing problems with how lower courts have handled the admission of other wrongful conduct to prove reprehensibility but not to punish. The three troublesome strategies are: exclusion of evidence of conduct related to non-parties as more prejudicial than probative, clarifying jury instructions, and close appellate review. Jill Wieber Lens, *An Undetectable Constitutional Violation*, 106 Kentucky L.J. 179 (2017-2018).

3. Ratios again. How does *Philip Morris* relate to the ratios in *State Farm*?

4. Changing justices. Of the five Justices in the *State Farm* majority, only Justice Breyer is left. Chief Justice Roberts and Justice Alito, who joined in extending the Court's precedents in *Philip Morris*, showed no interest in the Scalia-Thomas view that these cases have no basis in the Constitution. We don't know where the four newest Justices fall on these issues, which don't follow the usual liberal-conservative division. Might the Court return the policing of punitive damage amounts to the states?

5. Other approaches to the risk of multiple punishment. *State Farm* and *Philip Morris* are a new approach to a problem that courts have struggled with, the risk of multiple punishment for the same conduct. Courts had generally rejected proposals that only the first plaintiff can collect punitive damages, although several states adopted such a rule by statute, either absolutely or presumptively. Those statutes are collected in Michael P. Allen, *Of Remedy, Juries, and State Regulation of Punitive Damages: The Significance of Philip Morris v. Williams*, 63 N.Y.U. Ann. Surv. Am. L. 343, 370 n.130 (2008). The dominant approach in the lower courts had been to somehow consider the possibility of additional awards in setting or reviewing the amount, whether in common law review or constitutional review. No court ever thought it had a sufficient record to decide that a defendant had reached a legal limit on total punishment for the same course of conduct.

The asbestos cases struggling with this issue are collected in Owens-Corning Fiberglas Corp. v. Malone, 972 S.W.2d 35, 48-50 (Tex. 1998). Owens-Corning, which was telling courts that it faced confiscatory punitive damages, had told its stockholders that its future asbestos liability should have no material adverse effect on the company. That was wrong; Owens-Corning filed for bankruptcy in 2000. A tobacco example is In re Simon II Litigation, 407 F.3d 125 (2d Cir. 2005), finding no evidence in that record from which a court could determine a legal limit on total punishment of the tobacco companies.

6. Class actions. Efforts to litigate punitive damages in class actions have mostly failed, but the exceptions tend to be spectacular. *Exxon* is one example. Here are two more.

a. The Florida tobacco litigation. A Florida jury awarded $145 billion to a class of Florida smokers, but that judgment was reversed on multiple grounds—that punitives could not be determined for the class before liability had been determined to the class and that the verdict was grossly excessive. Engle v. Liggett Group, Inc., 945 So. 2d 1246 (Fla. 2006).

The Florida court also held that the jury findings about defendants' intentional wrongdoing in the class action would be binding in individual actions by class members, who would have to prove only those facts specific to individual claimants. Some 9,000 class members filed individual claims.

The Supreme Court of Florida held that the class action findings were claim preclusive, not issue preclusive, but it seems to have really meant a sort of hybrid. The issues decided in the class action went to defendants' conduct, and on those issues, all arguments that were actually litigated or that could have been litigated were barred. But each plaintiff still had to prove class membership, causation, and damages; class membership required proof that plaintiffs smoked because they were addicted. Philip Morris USA, Inc. v. Douglas, 110 So. 3d 419 (Fla. 2013).

Both the Florida court and the Eleventh Circuit rejected the argument that this use of claim preclusion violates due process. *Douglas*; Graham v. R.J. Reynolds Tobacco Co., 857 F.3d 1169 (11th Cir. 2017) (en banc), *cert. denied*, 138 S. Ct. 646 (2018). Both courts also rejected the argument that giving preclusive effect to the *Engle* findings makes it a violation of a state-law tort duty for any tobacco company to sell a cigarette in Florida, and that the *Engle*-progeny litigation is therefore preempted by the congressional decision not to ban cigarettes. *Graham*; R.J. Reynolds Tobacco Co. v. Marotta, 214 So. 3d 590 (Fla. 2017). The Supreme Court has repeatedly denied cert on the tobacco companies' due process claims, most recently in *Graham*, which also denied cert on the preemption claim. There was a global settlement of the remaining federal cases, but state judges have imposed less pressure to try the cases quickly.

A lawyer commenting on *Graham* said that plaintiffs have been winning about two-thirds of the cases, typically for seven or eight figures. But plaintiff verdicts have varied in amount from zero to billions. Lawyers for both sides agreed that the tobacco companies are reluctant to settle and that the 3,000 to 4,000 remaining cases in state court are likely to drag on. Martina Barash, *Florida Tobacco Plaintiffs, Health Advocates Breathe Easier*, 85 U.S.L.W. 1666 (June 1, 2017).

b. The West Virginia tobacco litigation. The West Virginia court tried to squeeze a little more into the class part of the case. The trial court had 1,100 consolidated tobacco cases (not a class action). It proposed a mass trial of liability, including whether punitive damages should be awarded and determination of a multiplier for assessing punitive damages. Then there would be individual trials on compensatory damages and any other individual issues, and the predetermined multiplier would be applied to each compensatory award to determine that individual plaintiff's punitives. The Supreme Court of Appeals held that this plan does not violate *State Farm*; it did not consider any other possible objections. In re Tobacco Litigation, 624 S.E.2d 738 (W. Va. 2005). Nothing came of this ambitious plan, because the jury on remand found for the tobacco companies on all but one claim, and on that claim, found that punitive damages should not be awarded. 2013 WL 8183651 (W. Va. Cir. Ct. 2013), *aff'd*, 2014 WL 5545853 (W. Va. 2014).

Defendants argued that the procedure was inconsistent with *State Farm* and *Philip Morris*, because the multiplier would have been determined without regard to the facts of individual cases. They said that plaintiffs used a variety of tobacco products, asserted a variety of legal theories, had different degrees of knowledge, and were exposed to different advertising campaigns.

7. Other obstacles to class actions. If the class is certified under Federal Rule of Civil Procedure 23(b)(3) or its state equivalents, individual plaintiffs can opt out, leaving defendants exposed to the risk of additional punitive awards after the class judgment. To avoid opt outs, courts have certified classes under Rule 23(b)(1)(B), on the theory that "adjudications with respect to individual class members" would "substantially impair or impede" the ability of other class members to protect their interests, because separate punitive damage awards might either bankrupt defendants, or accumulate to a point where further awards would violate due process, after only some of the victims had been compensated. There is no right to opt out of a Rule 23(b)(1)(B) class, but neither is there power to prevent individual plaintiffs from ignoring the class action and proceeding to judgment in another jurisdiction before any judgment in the class action.

The Supreme Court has twice rejected efforts to certify global class actions in asbestos cases. Both cases involved claims for compensatory damages that overwhelmed the defendants, and both presented proposed settlements that precluded claims for punitive damages. Amchem Products v. Windsor, 521 U.S. 591 (1997), rejected a Rule 23(b)(3) class because of conflicts of interest within the class and because the Court did not believe that common issues predominated. Ortiz v. Fibreboard Corp., 527 U.S. 815 (1999), rejected a limited-fund class certified under Rule 23(b)(1)(B). It said that the court must determine the size of the fund and not just accept the parties' agreement that the fund was limited, and that the lower courts had not sufficiently attended to conflicts of interest among the class members. *Ortiz* also said that the entire fund should be divided among the claimants, and that any other rule would create distorting incentives to substitute limited-fund class actions for bankruptcy proceedings, where the Court had just put more teeth into the much-evaded statutory rule that creditors must be paid in full before stockholders can retain anything. Bank of America v. 203 North LaSalle Street Partnership, 526 U.S. 434 (1999). But the Court left open the possibility that in limited-fund class actions, defendants might retain some of the savings accrued by avoidance of further individual litigation.

8. Sharing punitives with the state. Some state tort reform acts have made a share of punitive damages payable to the state. Do these statutes make the Excessive Fines Clause applicable? If so, should the remedy be to strike down these statutes, or to scrutinize awards more closely because the state is getting a share? Might these statutes also take plaintiff's property without compensation? Six state courts have upheld these statutes; Colorado struck one down. The cases are collected in Catherine M. Sharkey, *Punitive Damages as Societal Damages*, 113 Yale L.J. 347, 372-389, 414-440 (2003). The statutes vary considerably in their details. Some permit the state to intervene, and some do not; some give the money to the state treasury, some to special funds for various purposes. One of Professor Sharkey's six states has since rejected a renewed challenge, upholding a statute that capped punitives at three times compensatories or $50,000, whichever is greater, and awarding 75 percent of that to the state. State v. Doe, 987 N.E.2d 1066 (Ind. 2013).

The Ohio court ordered a similar division of punitive damages on its own authority. Dardinger v. Anthem Blue Cross & Blue Shield, 781 N.E.2d 121 (Ohio 2002). After upholding $30 million in punitives to the family of a brain-cancer patient who had been denied treatment, the court said:

> At the punitive-damages level, it is the societal element that is most important. The plaintiff remains a party, but the de facto party is our society, and the jury is determining whether and to what extent we as a society should punish the defendant.

> There is a philosophical void between the reasons we award punitive damages and how the damages are distributed. The community makes the statement, while the plaintiff reaps the monetary award.

Id. at 145. Noting that plaintiffs should have adequate incentive to litigate, it ordered that $10 million be paid to plaintiff, that attorneys' fees be paid out of the remainder, based on the contingent fee contract and based on the full $30 million plus postjudgment interest, and that the remainder should be used to endow a fund for cancer research at The Ohio State University.

9. The state's share in *Philip Morris*. An Oregon statute makes 60 percent of all punitive damage awards payable to the state. Philip Morris refused to pay the state's share on the ground that the state had released its claim in a 1998 global tobacco settlement of state claims for medical expenses incurred by smokers and paid by states through Medicaid benefits or employee health-insurance plans. The court rejected that defense, holding that Oregon's right to a share of the punitive award to Williams arose from the statute and the private tort judgment, and was not included in the 1998 release of claims for medical expenses. Williams v. RJ Reynolds Tobacco Co., 271 P.3d 103 (Or. 2011).

The opinion also revealed a joint litigation agreement between the Williams family and the state, in which they agreed to cooperate to ensure that Philip Morris paid the entire judgment, and to divide the judgment in different ways depending on the course of the litigation. None of the agreed splits matched the 60/40 split specified by statute. *Id.* at 107 n.7.

3. *Punitive Damages in Contract*

FORMOSA PLASTICS CORP. USA v. PRESIDIO ENGINEERS AND CONTRACTORS, INC.

960 S.W.2d 41 (Tex. 1998)

ABBOTT, Justice, delivered the opinion of the Court, in which PHILLIPS, Chief Justice, GONZALEZ, HECHT, ENOCH, OWEN, and HANKINSON, Justices, join. . . .

I

In 1989, Formosa . . . began a large construction "expansion project" at its facility in Point Comfort, Texas. Presidio . . . received an "Invitation to Bid" from Formosa on that part of the project requiring the construction of 300 concrete foundations. The invitation was accompanied by a bid package containing technical drawings, specifications, general information, and a sample contract. The bid package also contained certain representations about the foundation job. These representations included that (1) Presidio would arrange and be responsible for the scheduling, ordering, and delivery of all materials, including those paid for by Formosa; (2) work was to progress continually from commencement to completion; and (3) the job was scheduled to commence on July 16, 1990, and be completed 90 days later, on October 15, 1990.

Presidio's president, Bob Burnette, testified that he relied on these representations in preparing Presidio's bid. Because the bid package provided that the contractor would be responsible for all weather and other unknown delays, he added another 30 days to his estimate of the job's scheduled completion date. He submitted a bid on behalf of Presidio in the amount of $600,000. Because Presidio submitted the lowest bid, Formosa awarded Presidio the contract.

The job was not completed in 120 days. Rather, the job took over eight months to complete, more than twice Burnette's estimate and almost three times the scheduled time provided in the bid package. The delays caused Presidio to incur substantial additional costs that were not anticipated when Presidio submitted its bid. . . .

Presidio sued Formosa for breach of contract. . . . Presidio also brought fraudulent inducement of contract and fraudulent performance of contract claims based on representations made by Formosa that Presidio discovered were false after commencing performance of the contract. Formosa counterclaimed for breach of contract, urging that Presidio had not properly completed some of its work.

Presidio presented evidence to the jury that Formosa had an intentional, premeditated scheme to defraud the contractors working on its expansion project. Under this scheme, Formosa enticed contractors to make low bids by making misrepresentations in the bid package regarding scheduling, delivery of materials, and responsibility for delay damages. Jack Lin, the director of Formosa's civil department, admitted that Formosa acted deceptively by representing in the bid package that the contractors would have the ability to schedule the delivery of concrete when in truth Formosa had secretly decided to set up its own delivery schedule in order to save money. Formosa also scheduled multiple contractors, doing mutually exclusive work, to be in the same area at the same time. For instance, Formosa scheduled another contractor to install underground pipe in Presidio's work area at the same time that Presidio was supposed to be pouring foundations. Thomas Peña, Formosa's inspector, admitted that Formosa knew that contractors would be working right on top of each other, but this information was not passed on to the contractors. Of course, once the contractors were on the job, they would realize that, due to such unexpected delays caused by Formosa, their bids were inadequate. But when the contractors requested delay damages under the contract, Formosa would rely on its superior economic position and offer the contractors far less than the full and fair value of the delay damages. In fact, Ron Robichaux, head of Formosa's contract administration division, testified that Formosa, in an effort to lower costs, would utilize its economic superiority to string contractors along and force them to settle. Robichaux added that "if [a contractor] continued to complain then [Formosa] would take the contract from him and make sure he loses his money." Under this scheme, Formosa allegedly stood to save millions of dollars on its $1.5 billion expansion project.

The jury found that Formosa defrauded Presidio and awarded Presidio $1.5 million. . . . Based on its findings that Formosa's fraud [was] done willfully, wantonly, intentionally, or with conscious indifference to the rights of Presidio, the jury further awarded Presidio $10 million as exemplary damages. Additionally, the jury found that Formosa breached its contract with Presidio, causing $1.267 million in damages. On the other hand, the jury also concluded that Presidio did not fully comply with the contract, causing Formosa $107,000 in damages.

The trial court suggested a remittitur reducing the tort damages to $700,000 and the contract damages to $467,000 [*sic*; $461,000 was apparently intended], which Presidio accepted. Based on Presidio's election to recover tort rather than contract damages, the trial court rendered a judgment in favor of Presidio for $700,000 in actual damages, $10 million in punitive damages, prejudgment interest, attorney's fees, and costs. The damages caused by Presidio's breach of contract were offset against the judgment. . . .

[T]he court of appeals . . . affirmed. . . .

II

Formosa asserts that Presidio's fraud claim cannot be maintained because "Presidio's losses were purely economic losses related to performance and the subject matter of the contract." Formosa contends that our decision in Southwestern Bell Telephone Co. v. DeLanney, 809 S.W.2d 493 (Tex. 1991), compels us to examine the substance of Presidio's tort claim to determine whether the claim is, in reality, a re-packaged breach of contract claim. Formosa urges that, in making this determination, we should analyze the nature of the alleged injury, the source of the breached duty, and whether the loss or risk of loss is contractually contemplated by the parties. Presidio counters that a *DeLanney*-type analysis does not apply to fraud claims. For the reasons discussed below, we agree with Presidio.

A

Over the last fifty years, this Court has analyzed the distinction between torts and contracts from two different perspectives. At first, we merely analyzed the source of the duty in determining whether an action sounded in tort or contract. For instance, in International Printing Pressmen & Assistants' Union v. Smith, 198 S.W.2d 729, 735 (Tex. 1946), this Court held that "'an action in contract is for the breach of a duty arising out of a contract either express or implied, while an action in tort is for a breach of duty imposed by law.'" *Id.* (quoting 1 C.J.S. *Actions* §44).

Later, we overlaid an analysis of the nature of the remedy sought by the plaintiff. In Jim Walter Homes, Inc. v. Reed, 711 S.W.2d 617 (Tex. 1986), we recognized that, while the contractual relationship of the parties could create duties under both contract law and tort law, the "nature of the injury most often determines which duty or duties are breached. When the injury is only the economic loss to the subject of a contract itself, the action sounds in contract alone." *Id.* at 618. Because a mere breach of contract cannot support recovery of exemplary damages, and because the plaintiffs did not "prove a distinct tortious injury with actual damages," we rendered judgment that the plaintiffs take nothing on their exemplary damages claim. *Id.*

We analyzed both the source of the duty and the nature of the remedy in *DeLanney*. DeLanney asserted that Bell was negligent in failing to publish his Yellow Pages advertisement as promised. The trial court rendered judgment for DeLanney, and the court of appeals affirmed. This Court, however, held that the claim sounded in contract, not negligence, and accordingly rendered judgment in favor of Bell. We provided the following guidelines on distinguishing contract and tort causes of action:

> If the defendant's conduct—such as negligently burning down a house—would give rise to liability independent of the fact that a contract exists between the parties, the plaintiff's claim may also sound in tort. Conversely, if the defendant's conduct—such as failing to publish an advertisement—would give rise to liability only because it breaches the parties' agreement, the plaintiff's claim ordinarily sounds only in contract. In determining whether the plaintiff may recover on a tort theory, it is also instructive to examine the nature of the plaintiff's loss. When the only loss or damage is to the subject matter of the contract, the plaintiff's action is ordinarily on the contract.

DeLanney, 809 S.W.2d at 494. In applying these guidelines, we first determined that Bell's duty to publish DeLanney's advertisement arose solely from the contract. We then concluded that DeLanney's damages, lost profits, were only for the economic loss caused by Bell's failure to perform the contract. Thus, while DeLanney pleaded his action as one in negligence, he clearly sought to recover the benefit of his bargain with Bell such that Bell's failure to publish the advertisement was not a tort.

Most recently, in Crawford v. Ace Sign, Inc., 917 S.W.2d 12 (Tex. 1996), we considered the intersection of the Deceptive Trade Practices Act and contract law. Ace Sign sued Bell for omission of a yellow pages advertisement, alleging negligence, DTPA misrepresentation, and breach of contract. Bell stipulated the contract breach, and was granted summary judgment on Ace Sign's DTPA and negligence claims. The court of appeals reversed the trial court's judgment on the DTPA claim, but this Court then reversed the court of appeals. We noted that, under *DeLanney*, we were to consider "both the source of the defendant's duty to act (whether it arose solely out of the contract or from some common-law duty) and the nature of the remedy sought by the plaintiff." *Id.* at 12. We then examined the relationship of the DTPA and contract law, concluding that an allegation of mere breach of contract, without more, does not violate the DTPA. We held that, because the alleged representations of Bell were simply representations that it would fulfill its contractual duty to publish the advertisement, and a mere failure to later perform a promise does not constitute misrepresentation, Crawford could only recover in contract.

B . . .

We . . . reject the application of *DeLanney* to preclude tort damages in fraud cases. Texas law has long imposed a duty to abstain from inducing another to enter into a contract through the use of fraudulent misrepresentations. As a rule, a party is not bound by a contract procured by fraud. Moreover, it is well established that the legal duty not to fraudulently procure a contract is separate and independent from the duties established by the contract itself.

This Court has also repeatedly recognized that a fraud claim can be based on a promise made with no intention of performing, irrespective of whether the promise is later subsumed within a contract. . . .

Our prior decisions also clearly establish that tort damages are not precluded simply because a fraudulent representation causes only an economic loss. Almost 150 years ago, this Court held in Graham v. Roder, 5 Tex. 141, 149 (1849), that tort damages were recoverable based on the plaintiff's claim that he was fraudulently induced to exchange a promissory note for a tract of land. Although the damages sustained by the plaintiff were purely economic, we held that tort damages, including exemplary damages, were recoverable. Since *Graham*, this Court has continued to recognize the propriety of fraud claims sounding in tort despite the fact that the aggrieved party's losses were only economic losses. Moreover, we have held in a similar context that tort damages were not precluded for a tortious interference with contract claim, notwithstanding the fact that the damages for the tort claim compensated for the same economic losses that were recoverable under a breach of contract claim.

Accordingly, tort damages are recoverable for a fraudulent inducement claim irrespective of whether the fraudulent representations are later subsumed in a contract or whether the plaintiff only suffers an economic loss related to the subject matter of the contract. Allowing the recovery of fraud damages sounding in tort only when a plaintiff suffers an injury that is distinct from the economic losses recoverable under a breach of contract claim is inconsistent with this well-established law, and also ignores the fact that an independent legal duty, separate from the existence of the contract itself, precludes the use of fraud to induce a binding agreement. . . . We . . . conclude that, if a plaintiff presents legally sufficient evidence on each of the elements of a fraudulent inducement claim, any damages suffered as a result of the fraud sound in tort.

We thus conclude that Presidio has a viable fraud claim that it can assert against Formosa. However, this conclusion does not end our inquiry. We must also determine whether legally sufficient evidence supports the jury's fraud and damage findings.

III

A fraud cause of action requires "a material misrepresentation, which was false, and which was either known to be false when made or was asserted without knowledge of its truth, which was intended to be acted upon, which was relied upon, and which caused injury." Sears, Roebuck & Co. v. Meadows, 877 S.W.2d 281, 282 (Tex. 1994). A promise of future performance constitutes an actionable misrepresentation if the promise was made with no intention of performing at the time it was made. However, the mere failure to perform a contract is not evidence of fraud. Rather, Presidio had to present evidence that Formosa made representations with the intent to deceive and with no intention of performing as represented. Moreover, the evidence presented must be relevant to Formosa's intent at the time the representation was made.

Presidio alleges that Formosa made three representations that it never intended to keep in order to induce Presidio to enter into the contract. First, the bid package and contract represented that Presidio would "arrange the delivery schedule of [Formosa]-supplied material and be responsible for the delivery . . . of all materials (this includes material supplied by [Formosa])." Second, the bid package and the contract provided the job was scheduled to begin on July 16, 1990, and be completed on October 15, 1990, 90 days later. Third, paragraph 17 of the contract represented that Formosa would be responsible for the payment of any delay damages within its control. . . .

We conclude that Presidio presented legally sufficient evidence that Formosa made representations with no intention of performing as represented in order to induce Presidio to enter into this contract at a low bid price. In the bid package and the contract, Formosa represented that Presidio would have control of the delivery of the concrete necessary for the project. . . .

In contravention of this representation, Formosa decided, two weeks before the contract was signed, to take over the delivery of the concrete without informing Presidio. Jack Lin, Formosa's civil department director, testified that Formosa, in an effort to save money, decided to take over the concrete delivery and set up its own delivery schedule. However, Presidio was not informed of this change until after the contract was signed. Lin admitted that Formosa acted deceptively by taking over the concrete delivery and scheduling when the bid package expressly provided that the contractor would have control. He further admitted that Formosa knew that Presidio would rely on this representation in preparing its bid.

Presidio's president, Bob Burnette, testified that Presidio did in fact rely on this representation in preparing its bid. Burnette further testified that every concrete pour was delayed one-to-two days while Presidio waited for Formosa to obtain the requested concrete. Because Burnette did not calculate such delays into his bid, the actual cost of the project exceeded the contract price. . . .

Thus, legally sufficient evidence supports the jury's fraud finding. We need not consider whether any other representations Formosa allegedly made were fraudulent. . . .

NOTES ON PUNITIVE DAMAGES IN CONTRACT

1. The requirement of an independent tort. It is still the general rule that punitive damages cannot be awarded for breach of contract. But if an independent tort is committed in a contractual setting, punitive damages can be awarded for the tort. What counts as a tort in these contexts, and what makes the tort independent of the contract?

2. Distinguishing fraud from breach. In *Formosa*, the court upholds a fraud finding because defendant entered into the contract intending not to perform as promised. The court says defendant made its decision to reschedule deliveries two weeks before it signed the contract. What if it had made that decision two weeks *after* it signed the contract? Then do we have just an ordinary breach, with no punitives? Formosa's larger scheme to secure bids lower than the real cost of construction probably required fraudulent statements prior to contracting. But a scheme to shift costs to the other side by underperforming one's own obligations might be equally deliberate, might be hatched during performance, might be carried out without making any false statements to the other side, and might do just as much damage as if it had been planned and misrepresented before the contract was signed. That the breach can be accurately described with epithets—deliberate, willful, malicious, in bad faith—is not enough. There must be fraud.

3. Fraudulent performance? Note that Presidio brought claims both for fraudulent inducement and fraudulent performance. Recall S.J. Groves & Sons Co. v. Warner, reprinted in section 2.E.2. That was another case where a concrete supplier deliberately delayed deliveries, greatly delaying a bridge project. Deliberate failure to deliver is not a tort. But the court also found that Warner had "deliberately overcommitt[ed] its ability to manufacture and deliver enough concrete." 576 F.2d at 526. Was that a fraudulent representation of intent to perform when no such intent existed? After performance began, the general contractor and the state had repeated conferences with Warner, which kept promising to do better, but which in fact adhered to its policy of doing no better at all. Can an intentionally false statement during performance be fraud?

"Fraudulent performance" has long appeared as a phrase in opinions, but it seems to be little developed as a legal theory. Consider Robinson Helicopter Co. v. Dana Corp., 102 P.3d 268 (Cal. 2004), which was argued principally in terms of the economic-loss rule. Robinson manufactured helicopters. Dana supplied clutches, manufactured to precise specifications; the contract required that every delivery be accompanied by a certification that Dana had adhered to the specifications. Robinson operated under similar requirements from the Federal Aviation Administration; Robinson could not change any specification without government approval.

Dana changed the specifications on the clutches, but it continued to certify that the clutches conformed to the old specifications. The new clutches turned out to have a much higher failure rate, and the FAA eventually required a recall of all helicopters with the new clutches. No crashes or injuries resulted. The jury awarded $1.5 million in compensatory damages for the cost of the recall and $6 million in punitives. The court held that the false certificates were fraud and thus a tort independent of the breach of contract. "A decision to breach a contract and then acknowledge it has different consequences than a decision to defraud." *Id.* at 276 n.8.

Justice Werdegar dissented, fearing a flood of claims. "[R]are is the commercial contract that does not involve ongoing statements by the parties relating to their performance." *Id.* at 278. She would have required an independent tort *plus* physical damage to person or property that satisfied the economic-loss rule. Both the majority and the dissenter seemed to view the holding as novel; no one suggested that it was just an application of a settled rule about fraudulent performance.

4. The damages in *Formosa*. The *Formosa* court held the compensatory damages excessive. This is not our principal concern here, but it is significant to the claim of independent tort and a bit complicated. The essential facts were as follows: Plaintiff bid the job for $600,000, based on projected costs of $370,000 and a profit margin of $230,000. (Sixty-two percent! Maybe overhead is not in the cost figure.) The actual cost of performance was $831,000. No numbers in the opinion make any sense of the jury's damage theory.

Plaintiff's damage theory was that if defendant's plans had been disclosed, it would have accurately projected the costs and it would have bid the job for $1.3 million ($831,000 plus a 56 percent profit margin). Its actual damages were thus $700,000—the $1.3 million it would have bid but for the fraud, minus the $600,000 it actually bid because of the fraud. The court rejected this theory, over two sharp dissents. This number included the expected profit on the contract that might have been entered if defendant's plans had been disclosed in advance. But that contract had not been entered, and might never have been entered; if plaintiff had bid $1.3 million, it might not have gotten the job. The claim was in tort, not on a hypothetical contract.

Plaintiff's out-of-pocket loss from the fraud was $231,000, the difference between the cost of performance and the contract price. The court reasoned that this could be recovered in fraud as the difference between the value of what plaintiff delivered and the value of what it received.

Alternatively, Texas follows the widespread state rule that fraud plaintiffs can recover the benefit of the promised bargain—what they would have made if the false representations had been true. That would be the original expected profit of $230,000, plus the $231,000 out-of-pocket loss. The near-equality of these two numbers is coincidence. The total of $461,000 is the excess of the actual costs over the costs as originally misrepresented. Moreover, and not at all coincidentally, this total is simply plaintiff's expectancy damages for breach of the actual contract.

5. Independent damages? The court's holding on compensatory damages set up an important issue—is the tort independent of the contract if it did no damage independent of the contract damages? Requiring the tort to do some damage distinct from the damage done by breach of contract would give more significance to the independence requirement. *Formosa* rejects any such requirement, at least for fraud cases. There must be an independent tort, and there must be tort damages, but the damages need not be independent. This may turn out to be a tort-by-tort inquiry, at least in Texas. The Texas court later announced a requirement of "independent *injury*" in cases of negligent misrepresentation, for fear of converting "every contract interpretation dispute into a negligent misrepresentation claim." D.S.A., Inc. v. Hillsboro Independent School District, 973 S.W.2d 662, 663, 664 (1998). It's not clear that this was a serious risk, because mere negligence is generally well below the threshold for punitive damages even if there were an independent tort. The California court in *Robinson Helicopter* apparently did require independent tort damages: It somewhat cryptically limited its holding to misrepresentations that "expose a plaintiff to liability for personal damages independent of the plaintiff's economic loss." 102 P.3d at 276. And the Ohio court has restated its rule that punitives are available only if plaintiff "suffered a harm distinct from the breach of contract action and attributable solely to the alleged tortious conduct." Lucarell v. Nationwide Mutual Insurance Co., 97 N.E.3d 458, 468 (Ohio 2018).

6. The empirical data. Independent torts must be common. In the 2005 study by the Bureau of Justice Statistics, involving nearly 27,000 trials, punitive damages were awarded in 5.0 percent of contract cases but only 1.5 percent of tort cases. Lynn Langton & Thomas H. Cohen, *Civil Bench and Jury Trials in State Courts, 2005* at 2 table 1, 7 table 8 (NCJ 223851, Oct. 2008), available at *https://bjs.ojp.usdoj.gov/content/pub/pdf/cbjtsc05.pdf*. Claims "arising from personal injury or property damage caused by negligent or intentional acts of another" were classified as tort; cases that included an allegation of breach of contract were apparently classified as contract, although the explanation is ambiguous. *Id.* at 11. Earlier studies using somewhat different categories found similar patterns: Punitive damages are more common in financial cases than in personal injury cases.

7. Trying to explain the data. Why should this pattern persist? Commercial dishonesty and sharp dealing is more prevalent among solvent defendants than intentional personal injury; maybe it is more prevalent than serious recklessness about human safety. Or maybe commercial disputes just involve more deliberate decisions. If a party breaches a contract for strategic reasons, or adamantly stands on its own erroneous interpretation of its contract, its breach is deliberate, intentional, willful; it is easily characterized as in bad faith and malicious. If the jury rejects defendant's claim of right to do what he did, the mental state for punitives follows almost automatically. The search for an independent tort sometimes becomes a search for a technical hook to hang the verdict on.

Note that a breach motivated by a chance to sell for a higher price would be deliberate in this sense and vulnerable to jury disapproval. Consider American National Petroleum Co. v. Transcontinental Gas Pipeline, 798 S.W.2d 274 (Tex. 1990), where a pipeline company was obligated on long-term contracts to buy natural gas at prices far above market. It bought only from sellers who renegotiated their contract; it refused to pay for any gas from sellers who refused to renegotiate. It admitted that this was a breach of contract; it claimed it had no choice. This is the mirror image of the classic efficient-breach hypothetical of abandoning your contract buyers to get a higher price; the pipeline defendant was abandoning its contract sellers to get a lower price. The jury was not amused. It found an independent tort (interference with a related contract) and awarded $16 million in punitive damages, which survived an appeal. *Id.* at 275. (Note that this breach was probably not efficient; the dispute appears to have been about distribution of the gains and losses from the change in price, and plaintiffs' losses from the breach should have equaled defendant's gains.)

8. Why no punitives in contract? If juries treat intentional breach of contract like intentional tort, why does the law not embody that judgment? In part it is just doctrinal tradition; this distinction survives from the forms of action. In part it is because punitive damages are sufficiently problematic that judges have been reluctant to extend their scope. But there may be less fuzzy reasons. Recall the concern in section 2.D that even consequential damages for failure to pay money would deter reasonable opposition to claims. Certainly the deterrent effect of punitive damages would be much greater.

> [T]he breach itself[,] for whatever reason, will almost invariably be regarded by the complaining party as oppressive, if not outright fraudulent. . . .
>
> A rule that would permit an award of punitive damages upon inferences permissibly drawn from evidence of no greater persuasive value than that required to uphold a finding of the breach of contract—which may be nothing more than a refusal to pay the amount demanded and subsequently found to be owing—injects such risks into refusing and defending against questionable claims as to render them, in essence, nondisputable. The public interest cannot be served by any policy that deters resort to the courts for the determination of bona fide commercial disputes.

Travelers Indemnity Co. v. Armstrong, 442 N.E.2d 349, 363 (Ind. 1982).

9. Potentially independent torts. A wide range of arguable torts can be committed in contractual settings.

a. Bad-faith breach. The most direct assault on the traditional rule is the tort of bad-faith breach of contract. If that were generalized, it would repeal the rule. Bad faith would simply be the mental state required for punitive damages in contract, and the tort label would be no more than a label. Bad-faith breach is well established in insurance contracts but nowhere else. Some states had done something similar with employment contracts and the tort of wrongful discharge, but that trend seems to have been reversed. Plaintiffs pushed, mostly with little success, to expand the tort to any bad-faith breach of a contract where plaintiff is smaller than, or dependent on, defendant. For more on bad-faith breach, see Notes on Recovering Emotional Distress in section 2.G.3.

b. Fraud. *Formosa* illustrates one kind of fraud claim—that defendant entered into the contract consciously intending not to perform. This is a special case of fraud in the inducement; the more common fraud is to misrepresent what is being sold. Another fraud example is Pacific Mutual Life Insurance Co. v. Haslip, 499 U.S. 1 (1991), where an insurance agent took plaintiffs' premiums and bought no insurance. This was tried as a fraud case, because the agent deceived plaintiffs about what he was doing with the premiums. 553 So. 2d 537, 542 (Ala. 1989). Fraud so clearly fit that no one seems to have argued that there was also breach of a contract to provide insurance.

c. Conversion. In many breaches of contract, defendant takes or retains money or property that belongs to plaintiff. The *Haslip* plaintiffs might have pled in the alternative that the agent converted their premiums. A secured creditor who improperly forecloses on collateral is usually guilty of breach of contract, conversion, and violation of the Uniform Commercial Code, which provides statutory penalties, described in section 3.B.1, that are arguably exclusive. A good example is Texas National Bank v. Karnes, 711 S.W.2d 389, 393, 396 (Tex. Ct. App.), *rev'd on other grounds*, 717 S.W.2d 901 (Tex. 1986), where the bank repossessed a van, held it for five years, and also collected the debt in full by debiting the debtors' savings account. The jury awarded $50,000 in punitive damages for conversion and fraud, which the court of appeals reduced to $20,000. The state supreme court eliminated all the punitives, because plaintiffs had neglected to obtain a jury finding of tort damages, and without that, they had failed to prove an essential element of the independent torts.

d. Tortious interference with contract or business relations. In *American National*, first described in note 7, defendant's refusal to buy gas from plaintiff inevitably caused breaches of other contracts (called balancing agreements) allocating gas sales among plaintiff and other producers pumping from the same gas field. Breach of the sales contract interfered with the balancing agreements, and that interference was the independent tort that supported punitives.

How far does that doctrine reach? It is common that breach of one contract causes breach of another. If a buyer of custom goods breaches a contract with a manufacturer, the manufacturer may be forced to cancel orders with suppliers. Should the manufacturer's canceled supply contract be the hook on which to hang punitive damages? The Texas court apparently did not intend to include such cases. "A knowing and intentional breach of one's direct contract may also be an act tortiously interfering with a third party's contract, if it is done with a purpose and effect of preventing the third party from performing its contract with another." 798 S.W.2d at 279. A later Texas case relying on the *Restatement (Second) of Torts* says it is not enough that defendant knew his conduct would interfere with plaintiff's contract or business relations; rather, defendant must have acted with "desire" to interfere or the "intent to harm" the plaintiff. Bradford v. Vento, 48 S.W.3d 749, 757-758 (Tex. 2001).

e. Negligence. The party who must deliver goods or perform services may perform negligently. Is that just breach of contract, or can negligence be characterized as an independent tort? More precisely (because ordinary negligence will not support punitives anyway), is gross negligence in the performance of a contract an independent tort? For a negative answer, see Jim Walter Homes, Inc. v. Reed, 711 S.W.2d 617 (Tex. 1986), holding that grossly negligent construction of a house is just breach of contract. The court started from the rule that intentional breach will not support punitives for breach of contract; it then reasoned that gross negligence is less culpable than intentional wrongdoing. But if defendant intentionally built a defective house, might that have been fraud? *Jim Walter Homes* also invoked the economic harm rule: There had been no physical impact or damage to any person or thing other than the thing—the house—that was promised under the contract. See section 2.E.3.

For a holding that negligence can be an independent tort without physical injury, see Brink's Inc. v. City of New York, 717 F.2d 700, 704-706 (2d Cir. 1983). Brink's employees stole an estimated million dollars from the money they collected from New York City parking meters. Higher-level Brink's employees failed to investigate despite ample evidence of irregularities. The court upheld $5 million in punitives for Brink's negligence in hiring and supervising rank-and-file employees—*not* for the employees' conversion of the money. New York law controlled, and New York defendants are not liable for punitive damages for the torts of their rank-and-file employees. Loughry v. Lincoln First Bank, N.A., 494 N.E.2d 70, 74-75 (N.Y. 1986). The supervisory negligence was gross in *Brink's*, but it is hard to believe that either the jury or the court cleanly separated it from the evidence of theft and the parade of rank-and-file employees who took the stand and invoked their privilege against self-incrimination.

B.   OTHER PUNITIVE REMEDIES

1.   *Statutory Recoveries by Private Litigants*

Common law punitive damages are the best-known punitive remedy and perhaps the most important. But many statutes provide punitive remedies.

1. Some examples. Statutes provide for multiples of actual damages, or for recoveries based on a statutory formula, or for minimum statutory recoveries. Especially in consumer and employment cases, such provisions encourage enforcement by creating minimum recoveries that are worth suing for. One may argue that these recoveries are not really punitive, because they are essential to compensation. In many of these cases, pure compensatory damages would never be collected because the costs of litigation would exceed the recovery. Many of these statutes also authorize recovery of plaintiff's attorneys' fees.

a. Antitrust. Antitrust plaintiffs recover three times their compensatory damages. 15 U.S.C. §15(a). Many statutes provide for double recovery, either in all cases or in cases of "willful" violations. A good example is the Fair Labor Standards Act. 29 U.S.C. §216(b), recently expanded to ensure it covers restaurant servers' tips as well.

b. Secured credit. UCC §9-625 provides that if a secured party violates any of the rules governing repossession and sale of consumer collateral, the debtor may recover actual damages or all the interest plus 10 percent of the principal sum of the transaction.

c. Truth in lending. The Truth in Lending Act authorizes recovery of actual damages, plus twice the finance charge, but the recovery based on twice the finance charge cannot be less than $100 nor more than $1,000 ($400 and $4,000 for closed-end loans secured by real property or a dwelling). 15 U.S.C. §1640(a). (The statute unambiguously says something rather different from this summary, but it is equally clear that this is what Congress intended, and this is how the Court interpreted it. Koons Buick Pontiac GMC, Inc. v. Nigh, 543 U.S. 50 (2004). Justice Scalia dissented, insisting that the Court cannot correct legislative drafting errors.)

d. The Patent Act. The Patent Act provides that the court or jury "shall award the claimant damages adequate to compensate for the infringement, but in no event less than a reasonable royalty," and that "the court may increase the damages up to three times the amount found or assessed." 35 U.S.C. §284. The statutory text gives no guidance as to when damages should be increased or how much.

The Court interpreted this provision in light of a long line of decisions under similar provisions dating back to the Patent Act of 1836. Halo Electronics, Inc. v. Pulse Electronics, Inc., 136 S. Ct. 1923 (2016). Enhanced damages should be reserved for "egregious cases of culpable behavior." *Id.* at 1932. The Court put the focus on the infringer's "subjective willfulness" and on what the infringer knew and intended, and not on the "objective" unreasonableness that was the first step in the Federal Circuit's three-part test. *Id.* at 1932-1933. As administered by the Federal Circuit, objective unreasonableness meant that even egregiously willful infringers were protected if their lawyer could think of a non-frivolous argument in response to the suit for infringement. The Court heard two cases, and remanded both for application of its new approach.

e. The Copyright Act. The Copyright Act authorizes statutory damages of not less than $750 nor more than $150,000 for each willful violation. 17 U.S.C. §504(c). Is that any better notice than the common law of punitive damages? The amount is to be determined in the discretion of the finder of fact, and either side has a right to jury trial.

f. The Privacy Act. The Privacy Act provides that for certain intentional or willful violations, the United States shall be liable for "actual damages sustained by the individual as a result of the refusal or failure, but in no case shall *a person entitled to recovery* receive less than the sum of $1,000." 5 U.S.C. §552a(g)(4)(A) (emphasis added). The Court held that a plaintiff must prove some actual damages in order to collect the statutory minimum recovery. Doe v. Chao, 540 U.S. 614 (2004). The Court said that the words we have italicized require plaintiff to prove she is entitled to recovery before she can claim the $1,000. That is a plausible interpretation, but a very odd statute. As the dissenting judge below pointed out, "minimum statutory damages" are "a fairly common feature of federal legislation." But he knew of no statute where Congress had provided for "a statutory minimum to actual damages." 306 F.3d 170, 195 (4th Cir. 2002) (Michael, J., dissenting in part). Now there is one, and not just one. The Stored Communications Act, 18 U.S.C. §2707(c), which protects the privacy of e-mails, has similar language and has received the same interpretation. Van Alstyne v. Electronic Scriptorium, Ltd., 560 F.3d 199 (4th Cir. 2009).

g. No standing? The business community tried to use standing doctrine to generalize a rule that no plaintiff could recover statutory damages without first proving actual damages. The Court did not go so far, but it gave defendants part of what they wanted in Spokeo, Inc. v. Robins, 136 S. Ct. 1540 (2016). Users can search for anybody's name on Spokeo, a "people search engine," and it will search public records for that name and provide a report. *Id.* at 1543. It is not clear that it makes any effort to distinguish individuals with the same name. If it does, it certainly does not try very hard. Spokeo reported lots of false information about Robins, but it said he hadn't been harmed because the false information was positive. It reported him married, wealthy, and highly educated, when none of that was true. He said the report hurt his job searches by making him appear over-qualified. And he said it didn't matter whether he had been injured. The Fair Credit Reporting Act, 15 U.S.C. §1681 *et seq.*, authorized a recovery of $100 to $1000 for each violation, plus attorneys' fees, without proof of actual damages. He alleged not just that Spokeo had failed to use reasonable care to avoid errors, but also that it had violated several of the Act's procedural requirements. And he filed it as a class action.

The Court said that standing requires "injury in fact," which must be "concrete and particularized," and that these were two requirements, not one. Intangible injuries can be concrete. Congress can create new statutory rights, and violations of those rights can be an injury in fact, but not automatically. Robins's alleged injuries were particularized; the false information was about him, and people searching his name had not received required notices about him. But the Court was skeptical about whether all these injuries were concrete, and it remanded for further inquiry. It noted that a report of a mistaken zip code could not inflict concrete injury, so false information was not automatically enough, and it doubted that the procedural violations had inflicted concrete injury. This holding clearly undermines many applications of statutory minimum recoveries; to what extent remains to be seen.

2. Pros and cons. The advantage of statutory penalties over punitive damages is that they replace a jury's largely unguided discretion with a fixed standard. They ensure that all plaintiffs and all defendants are treated equally. In theory, they can avoid shockingly large or small verdicts, but that is not as easy to do as first appears. Inevitably there are cases in which the statutory recovery seems inappropriate. The Supreme Court in *Exxon* resisted borrowing from statutory provisions for multiple damages, because they apply to all cases arising under the statute without regard to reprehensibility, difficulty of proof, amount of compensatory damages, or other obstacles to litigation.

a. The secured-credit formula. The formula in UCC §9-625 is useless in very small transactions; on a $100 pawnshop loan at 18 percent, payable in three months, the statutory recovery would be $14.50. But on a ten-year mobile home loan of $15,000 at 12 percent, the statutory recovery would be $12,325.20. This penalty is to be imposed without discretion for any violation, whether egregious or technical.

b. Unpaid sailors. Griffin v. Oceanic Contractors, Inc., 458 U.S. 564 (1982), is an especially dramatic example of a formula not fitting the offense. The statute provided that every shipmaster or owner who failed to pay wages to a seaman "without sufficient cause shall pay to the seaman a sum equal to two days' pay for each and every day during which payment is delayed." 46 U.S.C. §596 (1976). On April 1, 1976, Oceanic withheld $412.50 of Griffin's wages, the cost of flying him home from the North Sea after he suffered an on-the-job injury. Oceanic was obligated to fly him home at its own expense. Griffin sued, joining his claim for delay in paying the $412.50 with his personal injury claim. He eventually won; Oceanic paid the judgment on September 17, 1980. Griffin earned $101.20 per day; twice his pay for four and a half years came out to $329,912. The lower courts limited the penalty period to the month Griffin was unable to work, but the Supreme Court reversed and ordered the statute enforced as written. In 1983, Congress substantially recodified Title 46 and initially reenacted the troublesome provision without substantive change.

Later it added some limitations: The provisions apply to some vessels and not others, and there is a cap on the total award in a class action, but only in cases against a vessel capable of carrying more than 500 passengers. 46 U.S.C. §§10313(g), 10504(c). That curious last provision might have been a response to Borcea v. Carnival Corp., 2007 WL 9701929 (S.D. Fla. 2007), approving a $6.25 million settlement with Carnival Cruise Lines. The settlement might have been much larger, but the court had ruled that it had discretion to toll the accrual of the statutory penalties in a class action where the employer had plausible defenses. It said that liability so vast that it would make litigation impossible would violate due process, citing suggestive precedents. Borcea v. Carnival Corp., 2006 WL 1314283 (S.D. Fla. 2006).

   c. Truth in Lending class actions. Careful drafting can increase the fit between the statutory formula and the facts of individual cases. But it requires more care than legislatures are usually able to give, and it forfeits much of the certainty that is the supposed advantage of statutory penalty formulas. Consider the Truth in Lending Act. The Truth in Lending formula produced huge liabilities in class actions, because a form with a defective disclosure would be used in thousands of transactions. Congress has repeatedly amended the statute to refine special rules for class actions. In class actions, the statute now authorizes the following penalty:

> such amount as the court may allow, except that as to each member of the class no minimum recovery shall be applicable, and the total recovery under this subparagraph in any class action or series of class actions arising out of the same failure to comply by the same creditor shall not be more than the lesser of $500,000 or 1 per centum of the net worth of the creditor.

15 U.S.C. §1640(a)(2)(B). Then the statute attempts to guide the courts' discretion:

> In determining the amount of award in any class action, the court shall consider, among other relevant factors, the amount of any actual damages awarded, the frequency and persistence of failures of compliance by the creditor, the resources of the creditor, the number of persons adversely affected, and the extent to which the creditor's failure of compliance was intentional.

15 U.S.C. §1640(a). How different is this from common law punitive damages with a statutory cap on recovery?

2. Civil Penalties Payable to the Government

In a wide range of situations, government imposes civil penalties for violations of law. They may feel just like criminal penalties to defendants who suffer them, but Congress and the Supreme Court say they are civil. And that raises some serious questions.

   1. The scope of the issue. In 1979 Professor Diver found 348 statutory civil penalties enforced by 27 federal departments and administrative agencies. Colin S. Diver, *The Assessment and Mitigation of Civil Money Penalties by Federal Administrative Agencies,* 79 Colum. L. Rev. 1435, 1438 (1979). Undoubtedly, many more have been added since he counted. He apparently counted only civil fines; many other statutes provide for civil forfeiture of property used in a crime or acquired through a crime. Civil penalties are often administratively imposed, subject to judicial review in an ordinary civil proceeding. That procedure is much cheaper and easier for the government than criminal penalties.

   2. Overview. These penalties seriously undermine the protections of criminal procedure. Substantial penalties, usually financial, are imposed without jury trial, without proof beyond a reasonable doubt, without protection against a second trial and second punishment, without a right to appointed counsel, and often by administrative agencies rather than courts. The Court generally upholds such penalties on the ground that they are remedial, not punitive. Sometimes remedial means preventive; forfeiture of unlicensed firearms prevents further violations with those firearms.

United States v. One Assortment of 89 Firearms, 465 U.S. 354 (1984). (The result (but not the rationale) in *89 Firearms* has been changed by statute. 18 U.S.C. §924(d).) Sometimes remedial means that fines are like liquidated damages, compensating the government's enforcement costs. United States v. Halper, 490 U.S. 435, 444-445 (1989). But the Court's current position seems to be that civil penalties are civil and remedial because Congress says so. Hudson v. United States, 522 U.S. 93 (1997). "'Only the clearest proof' will suffice to override legislative intent and transform what has been denominated a civil remedy into a criminal penalty." *Id.* at 100, quoting United States v. Ward, 448 U.S. 242, 249 (1980). This determination is to be made on the face of the statute; the severity of penalties in a particular case is irrelevant.

3. The dilemma. To require criminal procedure for all administrative fines would seriously hamper the regulatory process; to impose enormous punishments administratively or in summary proceedings poses obvious risks of bureaucratic abuse. The Court somehow has to distinguish punishment that requires constitutional safeguards from punishment that does not. The Court seems to have pretty much given up on the civil/criminal line, but it has imposed modest limits on the size of civil fines under the Excessive Fines Clause.

4. The Excessive Fines Clause. The Excessive Fines Clause is succinctly tucked in with two other provisions: "Excessive bail shall not be required, nor excessive fines imposed, nor cruel and unusual punishments inflicted." U.S. Const. amend. VIII. What does that mean?

a. The scope of the clause. The Excessive Fines Clause applies to both civil and criminal fines, thus avoiding any need to recharacterize civil penalties as criminal to trigger protection. Austin v. United States, 509 U.S. 602 (1993). The Clause applies to cash fines and to in rem civil forfeitures, but in either case, only if "it can only be explained as serving in part to punish." *Id.* at 610. Austin took two grams of cocaine from his mobile home to his auto body shop, where he sold the cocaine to an undercover agent; he forfeited both the mobile home and the body shop in a civil proceeding. The Court held that this forfeiture was at least partly punitive; it remanded for determination of whether the forfeiture was excessive. No further proceedings are reported.

b. Unsuccessful claims. *Austin* has not prevented enormous forfeitures. In Alexander v. United States, 509 U.S. 544 (1993), defendant was convicted of engaging in the business of selling obscene material. Only four magazines and three videotapes had been found obscene, although defendant had sold multiple copies of each through a chain of 13 stores. In a related civil forfeiture action under the Racketeer Influenced and Corrupt Organizations Act, he forfeited 10 pieces of commercial real estate, all the assets of 31 businesses, and $9 million in cash. These were the proceeds of the "racketeering enterprise" and property that had been used to facilitate or maintain control of the enterprise. The Court remanded for a determination of whether the penalty was excessive in proportion to the entire enterprise, expressly rejecting the claim that the penalty had to be proportionate to the four magazines and three videotapes. The court of appeals held that the defendant, who had been inconsistent and evasive about the property at issue, had failed to make a prima facie case of disproportion. 108 F.3d 853 (8th Cir. 1997).

Bennis v. Michigan, 516 U.S. 442 (1996), held that property used in a crime can be forfeited even if the owner is innocent, and even if the owner is a victim of the crime, at least so long as the owner voluntarily let the criminal have possession. Bennis was half owner of a car in which her husband was caught with a prostitute; the state forfeited the car as a public nuisance. The majority thought this was remedial, because it reduced neighborhood blight and deterred further violations. Because the forfeiture was wholly remedial, the Excessive Fines Clause did not apply. The Court also rejected challenges under the Takings Clause and substantive due process. Could Hilton forfeit a hotel if a prostitute were caught inside? The Court said it would deal with such cases if they ever arose.

c. A successful claim. United States v. Bajakajian, 524 U.S. 321 (1998), is the only Supreme Court case to actually invalidate an excessive fine. Federal law requires persons carrying more than $10,000 in cash out of the country to tell the government how much cash they are carrying. If the cash is properly reported, it is lawful to carry it out. Bajakajian was caught preparing to board a flight to Italy with $357,000 that he had not reported.

The Court held that forfeiture of the entire amount would be grossly disproportionate to a mere reporting offense, unrelated to any other crime. It accepted the trial court's findings that the money was lawfully acquired and intended for a lawful purpose abroad. The four dissenters plainly doubted those findings, and in any event, thought that the difficulty of disproving such stories justified full forfeiture even for bare failure to report.

5. Statutory reform. Congress provided some protections in the Civil Asset Forfeiture Reform Act of 2000, 114 Stat. 202, codified in scattered sections of Title 18. The Act requires notice, appointed counsel for certain indigents, proof by a preponderance of the evidence (that's an improvement over the previous standard), and "a substantial connection between the property and the offense." 18 U.S.C. §983(c). Section 983(g) provides a procedure for determining "proportionality" under the Excessive Fines Clause. Section 981(g) requires a stay in certain cases where the forfeiture proceeding will "burden" the privilege against self-incrimination. The Court has interpreted the underlying statute to preclude joint-and-several liability. Each member of a conspiracy can be required to forfeit the crime proceeds that he received, but he cannot be required to pay an amount equal to the crime proceeds that others received. Honeycutt v. United States, 137 S. Ct. 1626 (2017).

6. The Double Jeopardy Clause. There is also a line of double jeopardy cases that appear to have come to nothing. Here defendant's claim is that the civil penalty is a punishment for purposes of the Double Jeopardy Clause, so the government cannot impose a second punishment in a criminal prosecution. Not only does this result in two punishments (at least in ordinary English), but the government gets two chances to persuade a fact finder of defendant's guilt, and a civil proceeding prior to a criminal prosecution provides otherwise unavailable discovery and a preview of the intended defense. These consequences go to the very heart of double jeopardy protection.

In United States v. Halper, 490 U.S. 435 (1989), the Court invalidated a civil penalty of $130,000 under the False Claims Act ($2,000 for each of 65 false claims of $9 each) against a defendant who had already been criminally punished. The Court held that these penalties would be an unconstitutional second punishment if they were grossly disproportionate to the government's enforcement costs. They were grossly disproportionate to the $16,000 in enforcement costs found by the district court, but the Court remanded to give the government a second chance to prove higher enforcement costs.

After some intervening cases that went both ways, the Court "in large part disavow[ed]" *Halper*, "because of concerns about the wide variety of novel double jeopardy claims spawned in [its] wake." Hudson v. United States, 522 U.S. 93, 96, 98 (1997). Defendants were accused of misapplying bank funds; in an administrative proceeding, they paid civil fines ranging up to $16,500 and were barred from the banking business. The Court found it obvious that these penalties were civil and that the government was free to indict them for the same conduct.

7. Civil jury trial. Civil penalties assessed by administrative agencies are of course imposed with administrative procedure and without even civil juries. If the government collects a civil penalty in court, defendant is entitled to a civil jury trial on liability but not on the amount of the penalty. Tull v. United States, 481 U.S. 412 (1987). The Court avoided the constitutional requirement of civil jury trial by holding that this penalty was *punitive*—although of course not nearly so punitive as to trigger the constitutional requirements for criminal trials. Because the penalty was neither compensatory nor restitutionary, it did not depend on fact finding, so no jury was required. Congress could set the penalty in a fixed amount or delegate assessment of the penalty to judges.

Tull certainly looked punitive; the government sought $22 million, calculated at the rate of $10,000 per day of violation. The trial judge awarded only $325,000, but the Court found that part of that amount was punitive. Should the government really be able to impose a $22 million fine on a natural person without the protections of criminal procedure?

8. Limits. There are some limits. Kennedy v. Mendoza-Martinez, 372 U.S. 144 (1963), refused to allow forfeiture of citizenship as a civil penalty. *Kennedy* lists seven factors for distinguishing civil from criminal penalties, *id.* at 168-169, but the factors are amorphous and the Court has said that they are "neither exhaustive nor dispositive." United States v. Ward, 448 U.S. 242, 249 (1980).

At least formally, no cases allow imprisonment as a civil penalty. But there are cases of preventive incarceration. The Court has allowed civil proceedings to identify "sexually dangerous persons" and involuntarily commit them for treatment until they can prove they are no longer dangerous. Allen v. Illinois, 478 U.S. 364 (1986). Because the purpose was treatment, this was remedial and not punitive. The Court has upheld such commitments even when there was little prospect of successful treatment. Kansas v. Hendricks, 521 U.S. 346 (1997). The Court rejected claims that these statutes were punitive for purposes of the Self-Incrimination Clause, the Double Jeopardy Clause, or the Ex Post Facto Clause. These statutes included substantial procedural safeguards; the Court has not said whether any of these safeguards were constitutionally required.

The Court also rejected an Ex Post Facto Clause attack on an Alaska statute that required sex offenders, after their release from prison, to have their photograph, address, license plate number, and other identifying information posted on the internet. Smith v. Doe, 538 U.S. 84 (2003). The Court said this was remedial not punitive, because it was intended to warn potential victims and thus reduce the risk of further offenses. The Alaska Supreme Court later held that a similar but not identical retroactive application of the statute violated the due process clause of the Alaska Constitution. Doe v. State, 92 P.3d 398 (Alaska 2004).

CHAPTER

4

Preventing Harm: The Measure of Injunctive Relief

A. THE SCOPE OF INJUNCTIONS

1. Preventing Wrongful Acts

ALMURBATI v. BUSH

366 F. Supp. 2d 72 (D.D.C. 2005)

[Plaintiffs are six Bahraini nationals who have been classified as "enemy combatants" and held at the United States Naval Base at Guantánamo Bay. They filed a petition for habeas corpus seeking their release. Then they filed a motion, as part of the habeas case, for a preliminary injunction forbidding the government to transfer any plaintiff out of Guantánamo without 30 days' notice to the court and counsel.]

WALTON, District Judge. . . .

The petitioners allege that they "stand to suffer immeasurable and irreparable harm—from torture to possible death—at the hands of a foreign government like Pakistan, Afghanistan, Saudi Arabia or Yemen" if they are transferred to such a country. . . . [T]hey have submitted no evidence in support of [their] assertions [that they will be transferred to such a country]. Instead, the petitioners rely extensively on "a range of [allegedly] credible news reports," and statements from two of the petitioners in this case. . . . For example, the petitioners cite an article [in] the *New York Times.* This article alleges that the United States Government is "contemplating 'a plan to cut by more than half the population at its detention facility in Guantánamo Bay, Cuba, in part by transferring hundreds of suspected terrorists to prisons in Saudi Arabia, Afghanistan and Yemen.'" According to the petitioners, media reports have represented that "the U.S. Government has repeatedly transferred detainees into the custody of foreign governments that employ inhumane interrogation techniques." Moreover, one petitioner alleges that he was told by an unidentified United States official at Guantánamo Bay that "he would be sent to a prison where he would be raped." Another petitioner alleges that he was also told by an unidentified United States official at Guantánamo Bay that "he would be sent to a prison that would turn him into a woman." Notably, however, the petitioners do not allege that these statements were made by officials who will play a role in determining where they will be sent upon their release.

Despite these admittedly disturbing news reports, and the allegations of the two petitioners, . . . the respondents have submitted declarations "refut[ing] the factual scenario that [the] petitioners portray." Specifically, the respondents state that "it is the policy of the United States . . . not to repatriate or transfer individuals to other countries where it believes it is more likely than not that they will be tortured." To insure that such repatriations or transfers do not occur, the Department of Defense ("DoD") represents that it consults with other agencies and considers factors such as the particular circumstances of the proposed transfer, the country to which the transfer is being made, the individual concerned, and any concerns regarding torture or persecution that may arise. Moreover, the respondents declare that the "United States seeks humane treatment assurances whenever continued detention is foreseen after transfer and pursues more specific assurances where circumstances warrant, including assurance of access to monitor treatment after transfer.". . . Additionally, the respondents maintain that the DoD will not transfer an individual if any concerns about mistreatment of an individual in his home country or prospective destination country cannot be resolved.

With respect to the petitioners' speculation that they may be transferred to countries other than their home country of Bahrain, the DoD represents that "of the over [200] transfers, both for release and for continued detention that have occurred over the years so far, those have all been repatriations back to the home country." Thus, the likelihood that the petitioners will be sent to a country other than their home country of Bahrain seems highly improbable. And, the petitioners' counsel represented during the hearing on their motion that if the requested notices indicate that their clients would be transferred to Bahrain, "it is certainly more likely that there would be no further litigation.". . .

To obtain injunctive relief, the petitioners must show that the threatened injury is not merely "remote and speculative." Milk Industry Foundation v. Glickman, 949 F. Supp. 882, 887 (D.D.C. 1996). Here, the petitioners have failed to show that their threatened injuries are not remote and speculative. Namely, they extensively rely on news reports and articles that suggest that the government is involved in a conspiracy to ship the Guantánamo Bay detainees to countries where they will be tortured and detained indefinitely at the behest of the United States. Moreover, there is no evidence in the record that supports the petitioners' allegations that they will be transferred to any country other than Bahrain or that they will be detained by the authorities in Bahrain if and when they are released by the United States. Additionally, the petitioners have not submitted any evidence that could lead this Court to conclude that the representations made by the DoD with respect to the transfer process are not true. To the contrary, the DoD has submitted declarations of high-level officials outlining the process by which transfers are made, along with assurances that detainees will not be subjected to torture, mistreatment, or indefinite detention at the behest of the United States.

It is clear that the underlying basis for the claims advanced by the petitioners is their basic distrust of the Executive Branch. And, the predicate for their distrust is based on nothing more than speculation, innuendo and second hand media reports. This is not the stuff that should cause a court to disregard declarations of senior Executive Branch officials submitted to the Court "under the penalty of perjury.". . . Thus, because the respondents directly refute the petitioners' allegations of their potential torture, mistreatment and indefinite detention to which the United States will in some way be complicit, this Court cannot conclude, on this record, that the petitioners would suffer irreparable harm if they are transferred from the Guantánamo Bay facility. . . .

NOTES ON RIPENESS

1. Injunctions, ripeness, and the rightful position. The injunction against future violations of law seeks to maintain plaintiff in his rightful position—to ensure that he is not illegally made worse off. It seeks to prevent harm rather than compensate for harm already suffered. This is the hallmark of preventive relief, of which injunctions are by far the most important example.

An *injunction* is a court order, enforceable by sanctions for contempt of court, directing defendant to do or refrain from doing some particular thing. The injunction is a preventive remedy, because it seeks to prevent harm rather than let it happen and compensate for it, and it is a coercive remedy, because it seeks to accomplish its preventive goals by coercing defendant's behavior. The injunction against future violations of law is the simplest use of the injunction. Defendants may be ordered not to torture, not to discriminate in employment, not to fix prices, not to pollute a stream, not to build a dam, not to trespass, etc.

This chapter examines the scope of the injunction. With respect to both compensatory and preventive remedies, the goal is to restore or maintain plaintiff's rightful position. This leads to a presumption, subject to certain exceptions, that wrongdoers should compensate for all the harm they cause. But courts have never believed, even as an initial presumption, that they should prevent all the harm wrongdoers might cause. Plaintiff must first make a threshold showing that a preventive order is necessary. This is the ripeness rule: Before an injunction will issue, the threat of injury must be ripe.

2. Focusing the issue. Plaintiffs fear being sent to a third country and raped or tortured. The government does not dispute that it would be illegal to send them to a place where they would be tortured. It does not dispute that rape or torture would be irreparable injury, a requirement for injunctive relief considered in Chapter 5. Rather, the government says that it has no intention of sending them to a place where they would be raped or tortured. So why not enjoin sending them to such a place? Plaintiffs would be protected, and the government would not be restricted from doing anything it could legally do or anything it intends to do.

As the court explained the rule, in an opinion refusing to enjoin destruction of documents:

> When the party who seeks an injunction shows potential irreparable injury, he has established merely one essential condition for relief. He must demonstrate in addition that there is real danger that the acts to be enjoined will occur . . . . The proper case for an injunction must be made out by the plaintiff, and it does not suffice to say, "Issue it because it won't hurt the other party."

Humble Oil & Refining Co. v. Harang, 262 F. Supp. 39, 43-44 (E.D. La. 1966).

3. Individuation. One can imagine courts enjoining every resident of the United States from violating any rule of statutory or common law. Such an injunction would make any violation of law contempt of court. But would it have any real meaning? Would people inclined to violate the laws be any more likely to obey an injunction repeating them? One function of injunctions is to individuate the law's command, specifying its application to a particular defendant in a particular situation. A realistic probability of violation—at least a propensity to violate the law—is generally held prerequisite to such individuation. But why should that be the rule? Why isn't it enough that plaintiff make an individuated request?

Compare Tenn. Code Ann. §36-4-106(d), which provides that, from the time process is served in any divorce case, "the following temporary injunctions shall be in effect against both parties" until modified by further order. This automatic injunction is to be attached to the summons, and it must order both sides not to dissipate marital property or modify any insurance policy; to keep records of all expenditures; not to threaten, harass, abuse, or assault the other spouse; not to make disparaging remarks about the other spouse to children or employers; not to destroy any electronic evidence; and not to relocate the children outside the state or more than 50 miles from the marital home "except in the case of a removal based upon a well-founded fear of physical abuse against either the fleeing parent or the child." The ripeness rule may make less sense to legislators than to judges.

4. Prophylactic relief. The injunction requested in *Almurbati* would have done more than forbid rendition to countries that torture. It would have forbidden any transfer without 30 days' notice, giving plaintiffs an opportunity to seek to enjoin the specific transfer. This might have seemed more practical than specifying a list of countries that torture and asking the court to enjoin transfer to any of those countries. With the whole world to choose from and no one country to focus on, how would you prove which countries posed a substantial risk of torture? But the injunction actually requested would have interfered, at least somewhat, with the government's lawful discretion. The government could not have transferred plaintiffs to a prison in the United States, or to a country beyond suspicion (say, Sweden), or even to house arrest in the custody of their mothers, without 30 days' notice to court and counsel. Is that a reason to require proof of the government's bad intent? Or just a reason to fine-tune the injunction?

Compare *Almurbati* with Ahmed v. Bush, 2005 WL 1606912 (D.D.C. 2005), where the court did enjoin any transfer without 30 days' notice. The court granted this order in the course of granting the government's motion to stay the litigation (to hold the case on the docket in a dormant state) pending the resolution of other Guantánamo cases. The ripeness issue was not discussed and may not have been briefed. The court viewed the restriction on transfers as necessary to preserve the status quo and protect the plaintiff while the case was stayed. In effect it was a quid pro quo: The government could delay the litigation, but it could not retain complete freedom to transfer the plaintiff during the resulting delay.

5. The contempt power. One reason for the traditional rule may be that both sides are seeking tactical advantage in subsequent disputes. Plaintiffs want a chance to litigate any proposed transfer; the government wants to manage its prisoners without judicial supervision. But at least in *Almurbati*, any violation of the requested injunction would be unambiguous and immediately known to plaintiffs. When a violation is less clear-cut, the potential for disputes is much greater.

Consider the requested injunction against destroying documents in *Humble Oil*. Either side may be lying, and either side may be mistaken. Defendant may presently intend to destroy documents. He may not intend to now, but he may change his mind later. Someone may inadvertently destroy documents. If any documents turn up missing, plaintiff will suspect destruction. Defendant may claim the documents never existed, or that he never had them, or that they were innocently destroyed without any thought of litigation. Plaintiff may make unfounded charges, or even knowingly false charges, that defendant destroyed documents. Imagine the similar array of possible disputes in Tennessee divorce cases. The court must pass on such charges and countercharges, and an injunction affects the relevant procedure. Section 9.A will consider in detail the means of enforcing injunctions. But you have to know something about those means now to understand what is at stake if an injunction is issued and if it is not.

a. Criminal contempt. Violating an injunction is contempt of court. Contempt is a criminal offense if done willfully. Plaintiff may bring the offense to the attention of the court, and the court decides whether to ask the prosecutor to prosecute the contempt. Defendant is entitled to most of the protections of criminal procedure.

b. Compensatory civil contempt. Plaintiff may also cite defendant for civil contempt. Civil contempt is a remedial proceeding, and plaintiff prosecutes it himself. In compensatory civil contempt, the court grants compensation for any harm plaintiff suffered as a result of defendant's violation of the injunction. Compensation in contempt generally includes attorneys' fees and generally is awarded without jury trial.

c. Coercive civil contempt. Most important is coercive civil contempt, in which the court imposes conditional penalties to coerce defendant into obedience. These penalties are civil, but they may include fines, imprisonment, or both. There is no fixed limit to the penalties that can be imposed in coercive civil contempt, but the penalties must be conditional: Defendant must be able to avoid them. The court often specifies what steps defendant must take to "purge himself of contempt" and thereby avoid coercive penalties. The effect is to make the original injunction more specific, and sometimes more demanding.

d. Some examples. Thus, if the government transferred a prisoner in violation of the injunction, the court might order the prisoner returned. It might fine the relevant government agency, or individual officials, so much a day until they complied. It might even send officials to jail until the prisoner was returned. In *Humble Oil*, if the court found that defendant had destroyed some documents in violation of the injunction but that many documents remained, it might specify that the penalty for any further destruction would be a fine of $100 per page destroyed. Or it might order defendant to deliver the documents to the court for safekeeping and impose a fine of $1,000 per day until the documents were delivered. Or it might imprison defendant until he revealed the location of the remaining documents and agreed to turn them over to the court. If defendant had already destroyed all or most of the documents, the court might conclude that there was little to be gained by further coercion and impose criminal punishment for the past offense instead. Or it could order compensation if it could find a way to measure plaintiff's losses. Or it could do all three: criminal punishment for past violations, civil coercion to achieve future compliance, and compensation for past harm.

e. Ruthless or toothless? This array of enforcement devices makes contempt a potentially powerful remedy. In addition, contempt citations often go to the head of the docket. They can be adjudicated promptly and as summarily as the facts permit. This further increases the attractiveness of contempt as an enforcement device. But all of this is in the discretion of the court. The contempt power may be ruthless or toothless, depending on the individual judge and her reaction to the individual case. Contempt is especially delicate when the defendants are government officials. Fining government agencies for contempt tends to be reserved for the most egregious cases, and imprisoning government officials is extraordinarily rare even then. This judicial caution dominates even in litigation against state and local officials; still greater caution would be expected when the first named defendant is the President of the United States.

Would plaintiffs have too great a tactical advantage if they could get an injunction for the asking and file a contempt citation at the first violation? Or does the ripeness rule give defendant a free violation? It takes one violation or a serious threat to get an injunction, and it takes a second one to get any serious efforts at enforcement.

6. Alternative remedies. Contempt remedies must be compared to the remedies that are available if no injunction issues. In the ordinary case of common law tort or breach of contract, and for many statutory violations, plaintiff's remedy in the absence of an injunction would be an ordinary action for damages after the feared harm has happened.

Sometimes, damage remedies are unlikely or unavailable. In *Almurbati*, a damage claim would have to overcome a large body of immunity law and the government's claim that the cases cannot even be tried without revealing state secrets. For some constitutional and statutory rights, quite possibly including the rights in *Almurbati*, injunction remedies are available but damage remedies are not. With respect to *Humble Oil*, destruction of evidence is not a tort in most jurisdictions; courts prefer to deal with the problem in the case where the evidence was needed instead of in separate litigation.

7. Reputation. Might defendants fear that an injunction would injure their reputation by implicitly finding that they are the sort of people who would send prisoners to be tortured? Or the sort who would destroy evidence? Or is that circular? Assuming that these are legitimate fears, how do they stack up against plaintiff's fears? The ripeness rule is sufficiently settled that courts rarely give reasons for it, and concern about defendant's reputation does not seem to play much of a role in the cases.

8. Problems of proof. The rule does not require that defendant already have committed one violation before he can be enjoined from committing another. Nor does it require that defendant explicitly threaten a violation or admit his intention to violate. It is enough that there is a substantial or realistic threat of violation. But an admission, a threat, or a past violation greatly simplifies the proof. A recurring theme of these cases is that plaintiff has no real evidence of defendant's propensity to violate the law. In *Almurbati*, plaintiffs relied on press accounts; in *Humble Oil*, plaintiff's lawyer filed an affidavit that relied on anonymous hearsay.

9. Plaintiff's intentions. In addition to a real threat of wrongful conduct, plaintiff must show a real threat that she personally will be harmed by it. A dramatic example is City of Los Angeles v. Lyons, 461 U.S. 95 (1983), in which plaintiff challenged a police practice of choking arrestees until they were unconscious. Sixteen victims had died. Even though the police had already choked Lyons once, the Court held Lyons's suit to enjoin future chokings unripe, because he could not show any likelihood that he personally would be choked again. He did not allege that he was going to commit crimes or act suspiciously and then provoke the police when arrested. There were four dissenters.

10. How high a standard? *Almurbati* says only that the threatened injury cannot be "remote and speculative." Putting the point more affirmatively, the Court said in *Lyons* that plaintiff must be "realistically threatened." *Id.* at 109. We used a similar formulation without attribution in note 8: there must be "a substantial or realistic threat."

In Clapper v. Amnesty International, USA, 568 U.S. 398 (2013), the Court emphasized that the threatened injury "must be *certainly* impending." *Id.* at 401. It cited several cases for this proposition; it also acknowledged a similar number of cases saying that a "substantial risk" is sufficient. *Id.* at 414 n.5. The majority said that plaintiffs also failed to satisfy the substantial-risk test, and it characterized their threatened injury as "highly speculative" and "highly attenuated." *Id.* at 410. Supreme Court ripeness doctrine is widely viewed as inconsistent and highly manipulable, so the variety of formulations is no surprise. In Susan B. Anthony List v. Driehaus, 134 S. Ct. 2334 (2014), the Court returned to the standard of "a credible threat" of injury—in that case, of prosecution for conduct that was allegedly constitutionally protected. *Clapper*'s standard was quoted as injury "certainly impending" *or* a "substantial risk." *Driehaus* is further described in section 7.B.

11. Constitutional and remedial ripeness. Ripeness is a constitutional and jurisdictional doctrine as well as a remedial doctrine. *Almurbati* is written in terms of the law of injunctions; *Clapper* is written in terms of the law of standing to sue. The doctrines are related, and a case that is not ripe under one doctrine is unlikely to be ripe under the other. But the doctrines emphasize different purposes, and at least in theory, those purposes might occasionally suggest different results.

Constitutional ripeness emphasizes separation of powers, limiting the jurisdiction of courts, and reducing the occasions on which they interfere with judgments committed to the other two branches of government. Remedial ripeness emphasizes the competing interests of plaintiff and defendant and whether an injunction is really needed. These may just be two ways of talking about substantially the same thing, but the choice at least affects the tone of the opinions.

12. Ripeness and imminence. Ripeness is partly a matter of timing; unripe cases may ripen. It is sometimes said that the threatened harm must be imminent, or even immediate. That is true only in the sense that a threat of long-delayed harm is likely to be contingent and speculative. But where it is possible to say with substantial certainty that harm will occur eventually, and the facts are sufficiently developed for reliable decision, a suit to enjoin that harm is ripe even if the harm is not imminent. "Standing depends on the probability of harm, not its temporal proximity." 520 Michigan Avenue Associates, Ltd. v. Devine, 433 F.3d 961, 962 (7th Cir. 2006). *Devine* held a statute unconstitutional where state officials were investigating possible violations and threatening prosecution, but not, in the view of the district court, threatening *imminent* prosecution. The opinion collects similar Supreme Court cases.

13. Preliminary and permanent injunctions. The injunction requested in *Almurbati* was a preliminary injunction, to be issued before trial on the basis of a limited hearing. The important differences between preliminary and permanent injunctions are taken up in section 5.B. Those differences profoundly affect some issues, but they rarely affect ripeness. The requirement that plaintiff show defendant's propensity to violate the law applies with substantially similar effect to both permanent injunctions and preliminary injunctions.

14. The special case of destruction of evidence. *Humble Oil* refuses to enjoin destruction of evidence without a showing that defendant is likely to destroy evidence unless enjoined. Yet courts commonly order both sides to preserve evidence, usually in orders designated as discovery orders or case management orders, and often entered by mutual consent. Such an order, equally applicable to both sides, gives both sides the same tactical advantages and disadvantages and does not implicitly accuse either side of being the sort of person who would destroy evidence.

15. The merits in *Almurbati*. The Supreme Court subsequently held that courts must defer to a determination of the executive branch that a detainee is not likely to be tortured if transferred to a foreign country. Munaf v. Geren, 553 U.S. 674, 702 (2008). There are issues that remain open after *Munaf*, but this holding would pose another major obstacle to relief to any plaintiffs who succeed in showing a ripe threat of transfer.

MARSHALL v. GOODYEAR TIRE & RUBBER CO.
554 F.2d 730 (5th Cir. 1977)

Before GEWIN, RONEY and HILL, Circuit Judges.

GEWIN, Circuit Judge.

After unsuccessful informal attempts to resolve the dispute, the Secretary of Labor sued appellant Goodyear . . . alleging a violation of the Age Discrimination in Employment Act of 1967 [ADEA, now 29 U.S.C. §621 *et seq.*]. . . The allegation concerned the discharge of William G. Reed, Jr., and appellee sought to enjoin further violations and to recover Reed's lost wages. The district court found the violation alleged and granted the requested relief, including a nationwide injunction against further violations. . . .

Appellant primarily complains of the scope of the injunction. The court found a single violation—Reed's discharge—involving only the actions of the Auburndale store manager. This limited finding does not warrant such broad injunctive relief. Issuance of an injunction rests primarily in the informed discretion of the district court. Yet injunctive relief is a drastic remedy, not to be applied as a matter of course.

In determining the limitations on a district court's discretion to issue an injunction, it is appropriate to look to the ADEA, to Fair Labor Standards Act cases, since the ADEA can be enforced through FLSA provisions, and to cases involving other federal statutes regulating employment discrimination. ADEA §7(b), 29 U.S.C. §626(b), states that "[i]n any action brought to enforce this chapter the court shall have jurisdiction to grant such legal or equitable relief *as may be appropriate* to effectuate the purposes of this chapter . . ." (emphasis added). . . .

Equal Pay Act, FLSA, and ADEA cases all establish that a nationwide or company-wide injunction is appropriate only when the facts indicate a company policy or practice in violation of the statute. For example, in the leading ADEA case of Hodgson v. First Federal Savings, 455 F.2d 818, 825-826 (5th Cir. 1972), we held that the evidence entitled the Secretary to a broader injunction than that issued by the district court. The employer had a main office and five branches, all in one county. Evidence indicated that the hiring was done centrally by one personnel officer and that he had rejected several applicants for tellers' positions because of their age. The district court enjoined future violations of the ADEA "with regard to the hiring of tellers." On appeal this court concluded that the Secretary's evidence indicated the existence of a *discriminatory hiring policy* by the employer. One of the applicants, for example, was rejected for any job, not just for a teller's position. Moreover, the employer had also placed a newspaper advertisement seeking a "young man" for the position of financial advertising assistant. Inasmuch as the proof showed a *company policy* of hiring discrimination *extending beyond* the category of tellers' positions, a broad injunction against the employer's future discriminatory hiring based on age was appropriate.

This approach is also seen in Brennan v. J.M. Fields, Inc., 488 F.2d 443, 449-450 (5th Cir. 1973). There this court affirmed the district court's issuance of an injunction against the employer's entire operations, which included more than sixty retail outlets, on the basis of violations of the Equal Pay Act at three of them. The Secretary defended the injunction on the ground that the New York office's close centralized supervision of wage scales and pay policies indicated a company policy with regard to the pay differential. This court agreed with that contention. Conversely, the Second Circuit has held that "absent a showing of a policy of discrimination which extends beyond the plants at issue . . . there is no basis for a nationwide injunction." Hodgson v. Corning Glass Works, 474 F.2d 226, 236 (2d Cir. 1973) (Friendly, C.J.), *aff'd on other grounds*, 417 U.S. 188 (1974). Accordingly, the court limited the injunction's effect to the three plants in Corning, New York, where violations were shown, lifting its effect from the 26 other branch plants.[6]

The Secretary contends that in the instant case there is sufficient proof of multiple violations to warrant a nationwide injunction, relying on the proof of a discriminatory

---

6. . . . Wirtz v. Ocala Gas Co., 336 F.2d 236 (5th Cir. 1964), . . . noted the general rule that an injunction is warranted where there is a likelihood of further violations. The complementary rule is obviously that an injunction's scope should not exceed the likely scope of future violations.

job order placed by the Lakeland store. There are several difficulties in accepting this position. The principal difficulty is that the evidence as to the Lakeland incident is slight, the district court made no findings with respect to it, and the court did not rely on it in determining the scope of the injunction. The court . . . made no finding of discriminatory company policy or practice. Indeed, the district judge expressed the view that "Goodyear itself is committed to the principles of the Age Discrimination Act" and that Reed's discharge was the isolated action of Auburndale manager Coleman, who "believes that he can best run an organization if he has just got young people around."[7] . . .

In sum, the district judge relied only on the isolated fact of Reed's discriminatory discharge in enjoining appellant nationwide. . . . [R]elief should be limited to the Auburndale store. Consequently, we remand the case for the district court's further consideration of the scope of injunctive relief. . . .

NOTES ON THE SCOPE OF INJUNCTIONS TO PREVENT WRONGFUL ACTS

1. The remedies for Reed. There are two remedies in *Goodyear*. One remedy is $3,000 in back pay to Reed. This is a compensatory remedy, although the plaintiff is the Secretary of Labor rather than Reed himself. The Secretary might also have sought reinstatement for Reed but apparently did not. The measure of relief for Reed is the familiar one of restoring him to the position he would have occupied but for the wrongful discharge.

2. The injunction. The other remedy in *Goodyear* is the injunction against future violations. The Secretary is empowered by statute to seek an injunction that protects all employees, not just Reed. But the Secretary is not exempt from the ripeness requirement. Like the injunction sought in *Almurbati*, this injunction is aimed at preventing violations that have not happened and may never happen. The court holds that the scope of the past violation determines the scope of the remedy against future violations. Is that a straightforward application of the rule in *Almurbati*? Has the Secretary established a threat of age discrimination in the Auburndale store but not elsewhere?

3. The scope of defendant's wrongful policy. Suppose the court found that Reed was discharged because of a new company policy that assistant managers be under 30. Should it enjoin that policy? All age discrimination in hiring and firing? All violations of the Age Discrimination in Employment Act? All employment discrimination? What propensity would the assistant-manager policy show? Should the courts be as afraid of unnecessarily enjoining an adjudicated wrongdoer as a defendant against whom nothing has been proved?

Here is the standard doctrinal answer:

> A federal court has broad power to restrain acts which are of the same type or class as unlawful acts which the court has found to have been committed or whose commission in the future[,] unless enjoined, may fairly be anticipated from the defendant's conduct in the past. But the mere fact that a court has found that a defendant has

---

7. The district judge, in his remarks at the end of trial, faulted Goodyear for not better policing the hiring decisions of local store managers, and he apparently thought a broad injunction would encourage greater oversight. The ADEA, however, does not require centralized supervision of employment decisions. Under the Act and the authorities cited above, therefore, imposition of that burden on the Company is unwarranted absent proof, at least, of a company policy or numerous violations.

committed an act in violation of a statute does not justify an injunction broadly to obey the statute and thus subject the defendant to contempt proceedings if he shall at any time in the future commit some new violation unlike and unrelated to that with which he was originally charged.

National Labor Relations Board v. Express Publishing Co., 312 U.S. 426, 435-436 (1941). How much help is that? How great a propensity must there be? Isn't the practical content of such a rule largely in the discretion of trial courts?

4. Companywide injunctions. In Torrington Extend-A-Care Employee Assn. v. National Labor Relations Board, 17 F.3d 580 (2d Cir. 1994), the court refused to issue a nationwide injunction against a chain of nursing homes. The union emphasized that the Board had found more than 130 violations at 33 facilities. The court said that was not enough to support an injunction covering 985 nursing homes and nearly 100,000 employees. Should bigger companies be more insulated from companywide injunctions?

The Board took another shot at the same chain in Beverly California Corp. v. NLRB, 227 F.3d 817 (7th Cir. 2000). The court approved a companywide injunction, relying on the "ubiquitous" presence of regional managers at facilities engaged in unfair labor practices, the failure of the earlier order to reform the company's behavior, and evidence of violations at 15 percent of the company's facilities. But it ordered the Board to strip out of the companywide order "a laundry list" of specific provisions that were based on incidents at individual facilities; it said that these should have been included in supplemental orders directed to those facilities. *Id.* at 846-847. There is a further opinion, again ordering companywide relief, in Beverly Health & Rehabilitation Services, Inc. v. NLRB, 317 F.3d 316 (D.C. Cir. 2003). It is one thing to get a companywide injunction; it may be quite another to effectively enforce it.

5. Intellectual property examples. The well-known Gallo winery successfully sued a little-known Joseph Gallo for trademark infringement in his sales of cheese. The injunction put careful limits on defendant's use of his own name; one provision covered any "retail package of cheese or other product." The court of appeals deleted the reference to other products. The case had been about cheese, and "to enjoin the use of Joseph's name in broadcast advertisement for as-yet hypothetical other products is an abuse of discretion in the highly fact-specific area of trademark law." E. & J. Gallo Winery v. Gallo Cattle Co., 967 F.2d 1280, 1298 (9th Cir. 1992). The point is not confined to trademark law; in any context, any kind of fact that limits the scope of the violation can limit the scope of relief.

One way to think about *Gallo* is that no court had yet determined the boundaries between legal and illegal conduct if Joseph Gallo began selling some other product. Wine and cheese are often served together, and the Gallo Winery had licensed the Gallo name to a seller of cheese. There might be much less potential for misleading consumers if the Gallo Cattle Co. began selling milk or beef or leather.

More generally, the Federal Circuit holds that "an injunction that simply prohibits future infringement of a patent" is overbroad. International Rectifier Corp. v. IXYS Corp., 383 F.3d 1312, 1316 (Fed. Cir. 2004). The injunction must be limited "to devices previously admitted or adjudged to infringe, and to other devices which are no more than colorably different therefrom and which clearly are infringements of the patent." *Id.*

6. Easy cases? Where the substantive law is clear, it seems obvious that any injunction must be confined to the scope of the relevant substantive law (although even this turns out to be disputed, as we shall see). An example is Dalton v. Little Rock Family Planning Services, 516 U.S. 474 (1996), where the lower courts had enjoined enforcement of an Arkansas provision prohibiting the use of public funds to pay for abortion, except to save the mother's life. This state law violated overriding federal law, which required that Medicaid programs also pay for abortions in cases of rape and incest. The Supreme Court unanimously held that the injunction had to be confined to the Medicaid program and could not extend to all public funds. Authority to issue the injunction came from the Medicaid law; how would the court have had authority to control other public funds not subject to that law?

Because the federal law was embodied in an appropriations rider, which had to be reenacted each year and which changed from year to year, the Court also held that the injunction must be temporally limited to the continued existence of the federal law. A more common way to handle such temporal problems is the rule, considered in section 4.B, that injunctions may be modified in light of substantial changes in law and fact. We have no way to know, but it is a reasonable inference that the problem in *Dalton* was just sloppy drafting, not a runaway federal judge. The parties should have been able to fix this without litigating all the way to the Supreme Court, but they probably mistrusted each other, and anyway, they were focused on a bigger substantive issue — on which the Court denied review.

7. Harder cases and judicial discretion. The Court took a similar but somewhat different approach in Ayotte v. Planned Parenthood, 546 U.S. 320 (2006). A New Hampshire statute required parental notification before performing an abortion on a minor. The Court has upheld such statutes provided they contain certain exceptions, and the New Hampshire law contained most of the required exceptions. But it did not have an exception for cases where delay would endanger the health of the mother. The lower courts had enjoined all enforcement of the parental notification statute; the Supreme Court told the lower courts to consider enjoining enforcement of the statute only in cases where delay would endanger the mother's health. That much is entirely consistent with *Dalton*.

But the Court did not treat this as a rule derived from the rightful-position principle. Rather, it was a result derived from somewhat discretionary consideration of three factors. First, "[g]enerally speaking, when confronting a constitutional flaw in a statute, we try to limit the solution to the problem." *Id.* at 328. "[W]e try not to nullify more of a legislature's work than is necessary." *Id.* at 329.

But second, "we restrain ourselves from 'rewrit[ing]' state law to conform it to constitutional requirements' even as we strive to salvage it." *Id.* If the governing constitutional law is clearly defined, the court may be able to enter a simple and clear preventive injunction against enforcing the unconstitutional part of the statute. But if the law is not so settled, and crafting a constitutional version of the statute requires legislative judgment, it may be better to enjoin enforcement of the whole statute and leave the drafting of a replacement to the legislature.

And third, "the touchstone for any decision about remedy is legislative intent, for a court cannot 'use its remedial powers to circumvent the intent of the legislature.'" 484 U.S. at 330. This sweeping statement is surely overbroad, but the relevant point is sound: legislatures often indicate, in a severability clause or otherwise, whether they would prefer that the entire statute or only the invalid portion be invalidated if part of the statute is invalid. Usually legislatures prefer the narrower remedy, but if a legislature thinks that part of the statute without the rest would be counterproductive, a court should defer to that intention.

8. Rule 65(d)(1) and obey-the-law injunctions. Federal Rule of Civil Procedure 65(d)(1) provides an independent ground for objecting to injunctions that forbid all violations. It provides:

> **(1)** *Contents.* Every order granting an injunction and every restraining order must:
>   **(A)** state the reasons why it issued;
>   **(B)** state its terms specifically; and
>   **(C)** describe in reasonable detail—and not by referring to the complaint or other document—the act or acts restrained or required.

This rule generally precludes injunctions that merely tell defendant to "obey the law," or that are written in terms as broad as the underlying legal standard. An example is Burton v. City of Belle Glade, 178 F.3d 1175, 1201 (11th Cir. 1999), affirming the district court's refusal to issue an order "not to discriminate in future annexation decisions." And it was error to enjoin defendants "from operating a sexually-oriented business," thus incorporating an entire ordinance that covered a broad range of businesses. Jake's Ltd. v. City of Coates, 356 F.3d 896, 901 (8th Cir. 2004).

Obey-the-law injunctions do not individuate, and so very often, they fail to effectively tell the defendant what he is supposed to do. There may be many ways to violate the law, and many ways to comply; what is a violation is often at the heart of the dispute. Consider Hughey v. JMS Development Corp., 78 F.3d 1523 (11th Cir. 1996), where the trial court ordered that defendant "not discharge stormwater into the waters of the United States from its development property . . . if such discharge would be in violation of the Clean Water Act." *Id.* at 1524. The court of appeals vacated this injunction, which it characterized both as an obey-the-law injunction and as unenforceable "as an operative command." "Was JMS supposed to stop the rain from falling? Was JMS to build a retention pond to slow and control discharges? Should JMS have constructed a treatment plant to comply with the requirements of the CWA?" *Id.* at 1531-1532.

Defendants do not object to obey-the-law clauses as often as one would expect in light of these cases. Judge Posner has held that "because an injunction frequently affects third parties and consumes judicial resources, a court has an independent duty to assure that the injunctions it issues comply" with Rule 65(d)(1). Chicago Board of Education v. Substance, Inc., 354 F.3d 624, 631-632 (7th Cir. 2003). But not all judges are so concerned. It is in plaintiff's interest to have some clauses of the injunction drafted as specifically as possible, to avoid arguments about coverage and fair notice, and also to have catchall clauses worded as broadly as possible to cover any new developments and anything inadvertently omitted from the specific clauses. These preferences tend to be reflected in injunctions, both because the parties submit draft injunctions to the judge for approval, and because, by the time she has decided to issue an injunction, the judge shares the plaintiff's interest in discouraging disobedience or evasion.

9. The Securities and Exchange Commission. The SEC, and probably some other government agencies too, are great fans of obey-the-law injunctions in civil-enforcement litigation. And they often get them. But the Eleventh Circuit held that SEC cases are subject to Rule 65(d)(1), more or less like any other case. SEC v. Goble, 682 F.3d 934 (11th Cir. 2012). The court said that some provisions of some statutes are sufficiently specific that an injunction tracking the terms of such a statute complies with the Rule. The court thought it obvious that the broad anti-fraud provisions of the securities laws are not sufficiently specific to support an obey-the-law injunction. And even for two statutory sections that it viewed as more specific, the court refused to approve an injunction that simply said to obey section such and such. Instead, it required that the specific terms of the provision be set out in the injunction.

10. Equity acts in personam. If in *Goodyear* the Secretary had shown a nation-wide policy of violating the law, the geographic jurisdiction of the court would be no obstacle to a nationwide injunction. It is an ancient maxim of equity that it acts in personam—on the person of defendant. The multiple uses of this phrase are explored in section 9.A.5. One traditional use is jurisdictional: With personal juris-diction over Goodyear, the court can order Goodyear to act or refrain from acting anywhere in the world. Thus an Illinois court can order McDonald's not to cancel a franchise in Paris (Paris, France; not just Paris, Illinois) and enforce its order by holding McDonald's in contempt. Dayan v. McDonald's Corp., 382 N.E.2d 55 (Ill. App. Ct. 1978). And federal district courts can certify nationwide classes of plaintiffs and issue nationwide injunctions against government agencies. Califano v. Yamasaki, 442 U.S. 682, 702 (1979).

NOTES ON INDIVIDUAL INJUNCTIONS, CLASS INJUNCTIONS, AND NATIONWIDE INJUNCTIONS.

1. Class relief without a class action? Suppose Reed sued on his own behalf, not filing as a class representative. Then what injunction should issue? An order not to discriminate against Reed? Or an order not to discriminate against anyone at the Auburndale store? Does Reed have standing to seek an injunction protecting anyone else? Should the scope of the injunction depend on whether there was a class certi-fication? This issue can arise any time a court enjoins continuation of a policy that could be applied to others in the same way it was applied to plaintiff.

The Supreme Court has said that the class action is "an exception to the usual rule that litigation is conducted by and on behalf of the individual named parties only," and that class certification saves resources "by permitting an issue potentially affecting every [class member] to be litigated in an economical fashion under Rule 23." General Telephone Co. v. Falcon, 457 U.S. 147, 155 (1982). And the Court has questioned whether a district court had jurisdiction to enter a statewide injunction, protecting students in all school districts, when the court had certified a class that included only students from one school district and the evidence had focused on that district. Horne v. Flores, 557 U.S. 433, 469 (2009).

In Monsanto Co. v. Geertson Seed Farms, 561 U.S. 139 (2010), the Court said that "Respondents in this case do not represent a class, so they could not seek to enjoin [enforcement of] such an [administrative agency] order on the ground that it might cause harm to other parties." *Id.* at 163. This is not quite the same question as who the injunction might explicitly protect, but it is related. Justice Stevens, in a solitary dissent, responded that "although we have not squarely addressed the issue, in my view '[t]here is no general requirement that an injunction affect only the parties in the suit.'" *Id.* at 181 n.12, quoting Bresgal v. Brock, 843 F.2d 1163, 1169 (9th Cir. 1987). This was a minor point in each opinion, but definitely part of the rationale for resolving at least one issue in the case. The principal issues in *Monsanto* are described in section 5.A.1.a. Compare *Bresgal* with Los Angeles Haven Hospice, Inc. v. Sebelius, 638 F.3d 644, 664 (9th Cir. 2011), holding that "Injunctive relief generally should be limited to apply only to named plaintiffs where there is no class certification," and citing other cases to the same effect.

Parker v. Judicial Inquiry Commission, 295 F. Supp. 3d 1292 (M.D. Ala. 2018), was a rare case in which a plaintiff sought an injunction only for himself but the court broadened it to include others who were similarly situated. Parker was a state supreme court justice, running to be chief justice, who sought an injunction on First Amendment grounds barring enforcement of a state rule limiting what he could say about certain pending cases. The court granted a preliminary injunction not only for him but also for other candidates. The courts said that any relief would "necessarily affect not just Justice Parker but also his opponents and every other judge." *Id.* at 1311.

Much of the confusion in the same-sex marriage cases around the country arose from a striking neglect of this issue. These cases were nearly all filed as individual actions by one or a few couples; there were few class certifications. Yet federal district judges repeatedly issued statewide injunctions protecting all same-sex couples, and apparently only Alabama officials ever raised the issue. We repeatedly saw dozens or hundreds of couples getting married in the first days after a district court's order, often while defendants scrambled to get a stay of that order. Defendants might have done better to focus the district court's attention on the scope of the order it should issue in the first place. Couples not party to the litigation would get the protection of precedent once a judgment is affirmed on appeal, and all couples throughout the country are now protected by the precedential effect of the Supreme Court's marriage decision. Obergefell v. Hodges, 135 S. Ct. 2584 (2015). With all but the most obstreperous defendants, unambiguous precedent is good enough. But a trial court opinion has no precedential effect; only the judgment is binding. So the scope of the injunction was a critical issue that both sides neglected.

2. The rise of nationwide (or universal) injunctions as political weapons. Professor Bray views the marriage cases not as an example of neglecting a rule limiting relief to the plaintiffs, but as an example of increasingly routine acceptance of injunctions *not* limited to the plaintiffs. Samuel L. Bray, *Multiple Chancellors: Reforming the National Injunction,* 131 Harv. L. Rev. 417 (2017). He focuses on nationwide injunctions against enforcement of allegedly unconstitutional federal regulations. He argues that such injunctions reward forum shopping; conservative plaintiffs sought nationwide injunctions against Obama regulations in Texas, and liberal plaintiffs sought nationwide injunctions against Bush regulations in California (with a similar pattern emerging in litigation against Trump regulations). And when a nationwide injunction against enforcement of a federal regulation issues, the Supreme Court is more or less forced to review the first case, without waiting for a circuit split and broader and deeper exploration of the issue in the courts of appeals.

Bray can find some support in Doran v. Salem Inn, 422 U.S. 922, 931 (1975), in which the Supreme Court wrote that "neither declaratory nor injunctive relief can directly interfere with enforcement of contested statutes or ordinances except with respect to the particular federal plaintiffs, and the State is free to prosecute others who may violate the statute." *Doran* is reprinted in section 7.A.2.

The Supreme Court recently ducked a chance to weigh in more directly on the propriety of nationwide injunctions in Trump v. Hawaii, 138 S. Ct. 2392, 2423 (2018), the case concerning President Trump's third iteration of a ban on travel to the United States from eight mostly Muslim countries. The Court reversed a preliminary injunction against the ban, so it had no occasion to opine on the injunction's nationwide scope. Relying heavily on Professor Bray's argument, Justice Thomas concurred separately to express skepticism "that district courts have the authority to enter universal injunctions. These injunctions did not emerge until a century and a half after the founding. And they appear to be inconsistent with longstanding limits on equitable relief and the power of Article III courts." *Id.* at 2425 (Thomas, J., concurring in the judgment). He wrote that the term "universal injunction" was "more precise." "These injunctions are distinctive because they prohibit the Government from enforcing a policy with respect to anyone, including non-parties—not because they have geographic breadth. An injunction that was properly limited to the plaintiffs in the case would not be invalid simply because it governed the defendant's conduct nationwide." *Id.* at 2424 n.1. See note 10 in the preceding set of notes. Justice Sotomayor, who dissented on the merits, would have held that the trial court did not abuse its discretion in issuing a nationwide injunction as necessary to provide the plaintiffs with complete relief. *Id.* at 2446 n.13 (Sotomayor, J., dissenting).

The Court may have given some hints in Gill v. Whitford, 138 S. Ct. 1916 (2018), where it held that plaintiffs had not proven their standing to challenge an egregious partisan gerrymander in Wisconsin. The Court said that "A plaintiff's remedy must be tailored to redress the plaintiff's particular injury." *Id.* at 1934. And a "remedy must of course be limited to the inadequacy that produced the injury in fact that the plaintiff has established." *Id.* at 1931. All nine justices joined this opinion.

3. Defending the universal injunction. Bray's critics have responded in multiple ways, but the principal argument is that nationwide policies can inflict immediate and serious nationwide harm, which only a nationwide preliminary injunction can prevent. Spencer E. Amdur & David Hausman, *Nationwide Injunctions and Nationwide Harm,* 131 Harv. L. Rev. F. 49 (2017). Plaintiffs can plead such a case as a class action, and a preliminary injunction to protect the putative class could address the nationwide harm. That solves the conceptual or jurisdictional problem of granting relief to non-parties. But if such nationwide class injunctions became routine, the change in practice would not do anything to alleviate the practical problems that Bray identifies.

Nationwide injunctions also help assure that enforcement of federal rules is uniform and workable. A federal district court put an Obama labor rule for overtime pay on hold nationwide rather than only in states "that showed evidence of irreparable harm," because "the scope of the alleged irreparable injury extends nationwide. A nationwide injunction protects both employees and employers from being subject to different . . . exemptions based on location." State of Nevada v. U.S. Department of Labor, 218 F. Supp. 3d 520, 534 (E.D. Texas 2016). And in an earlier stage of the travel ban litigation, the Ninth Circuit said: "[E]ven if limiting the geographic scope of the injunction would be desirable, the Government has not proposed a workable alternative form of the TRO [temporary restraining order] that accounts for the nation's multiple ports of entry and interconnected transit system and that would protect the proprietary interests of the States at issue here while nevertheless applying only within the States' borders." Washington v. Trump, 847 F.3d 1151, 1167 (9th Cir. 2017), *cert. denied sub. nom.* Golden v. Washington, 138 S. Ct. 448 (2017). A Fifth Circuit case upholding a nationwide ban on an Obama immigration rule noted congressional intent that U.S. immigration laws be "enforced vigorously and *uniformly.*" Texas v. United States, 809 F.3d 134, 187-188 (5th Cir. 2015), *aff'd by an equally divided court,* 136 S. Ct. 2271 (2016) (quoting a federal immigration statute). *Texas* was filed by 24 states seeking to enjoin the regulation. Sixteen other states filed a brief defending the regulation and opposing the injunction; the injunction "protected" them anyway.

4. Reform of the universal injunction? Professor Morley argues that nationwide relief is appropriate only through class actions and only in extremely limited circumstances: where Supreme Court precedent "directly renders the challenged legal provision indisputably invalid or otherwise conclusively resolves the legal issue; the plaintiff seeks to enforce an indivisible right or contends that the challenged provision is unduly burdensome; or the entity that enacted the provision at issue would not have intended for it to continue being applied if certain people had to be exempted from it." Michael T. Morley, *Nationwide Injunctions, Rule 23(B)(2), and the Remedial Power of the Lower Courts*, 97 Boston U. L. Rev. 615, 657 (2017). By unduly burdensome, he means violations so burdensome that it would be unfair to require all the other victims to file their own lawsuits.

Is a reform that would essentially kill the nationwide injunction desirable given increased political polarization? Or would such a reform deprive those out of political power of a potent check on executive power?

Fifth Circuit Judge Gregg Costa would have Congress pass a statute requiring a plaintiff seeking a nationwide injunction to use a three-judge court, with direct mandatory appeal to the Supreme Court. To further reduce forum shopping, Judge Costa suggests that Congress could mandate random selection of the circuit to hear the case. Gregg Costa, *An Old Solution to the Nationwide Injunction Problem*, Harv. L. Rev. Blog, https://blog.harvardlawreview.org/an-old-solution-to-the-nationwide-injunction-problem/ (Jan. 25, 2018). Supreme Court justices have complained about the use of three-judge courts in redistricting cases, because mandatory appellate jurisdiction forces them to decide all these cases rather than watch circuit splits and wait for the right case. Unlike denial of a petition for certiorari, dismissal or summary affirmance of an appeal from a three-judge court counts as a ruling on the merits and a Supreme Court precedent approving the lower court result (though not necessarily the reasoning). Mandel v. Bradley, 432 U.S. 173, 176 (1977) (*per curiam*).

UNITED STATES v. W.T. GRANT CO.

345 U.S. 629 (1953)

Justice CLARK delivered the opinion of the Court.

For the first time since the enactment of the Clayton Act in 1914 the Court is called upon to consider §8's prohibitions against interlocking corporate directorates. The Government appeals from judgments dismissing civil actions brought against Hancock and three pairs of corporations which he served as a director, W.T. Grant Co. and S.H. Kress & Co., Sears Roebuck & Co. and Bond Stores, and Kroger Co. and Jewel Tea Co. Alleging that the size and competitive relationship of each set of companies brought the interlocks within the reach of §8, the complaints asked the court to order the particular interlocks terminated and to enjoin future violations of §8 by the individual and corporate defendants. Soon after the complaints were filed, Hancock resigned from the boards of Kress, Kroger and Bond. Disclosing the resignations by affidavit, all of the defendants then moved to dismiss the actions as moot. Treated as motions for summary judgment, they were granted by the District Judge. He concluded that there is not "the slightest threat that the defendants will attempt any future activity in violation of §8 (if they have violated it already)." 112 F. Supp. 336, 338 (S.D.N.Y. 1952). . . .

Both sides agree to the abstract proposition that voluntary cessation of allegedly illegal conduct does not deprive the tribunal of power to hear and determine the case, i.e., does not make the case moot. A controversy may remain to be settled in such circumstances, e.g., a dispute over the legality of the challenged practices. The defendant is free to return to his old ways. This, together with a public interest in having the legality of the practices settled, militates against a mootness conclusion. For to say that the case has become moot means that the defendant is entitled to a dismissal as a matter of right. The courts have rightly refused to grant defendants such a powerful weapon against public law enforcement.[5]

The case may nevertheless be moot if the defendant can demonstrate that "there is no reasonable expectation that the wrong will be repeated." United States v. Aluminum Co. of America, 148 F.2d 416, 448 (2d Cir. 1945). The burden is a heavy one. Here the defendants told the court that the interlocks no longer existed and disclaimed any intention to revive them. Such a profession does not suffice to make a case moot although it is one of the factors to be considered in determining the appropriateness of granting an injunction against the now-discontinued acts.

Along with its power to hear the case, the court's power to grant injunctive relief survives discontinuance of the illegal conduct. The purpose of an injunction is to prevent future violations, and, of course, it can be utilized even without a showing of past wrongs. But the moving party must satisfy the court that relief is needed. The necessary determination is that there exists some cognizable danger of recurrent violation, something more than the mere possibility which serves to keep the case alive. The chancellor's decision is based on all the circumstances; his discretion is necessarily broad and a strong showing of abuse must be made to reverse it. To be considered are the bona fides of the expressed intent to comply, the effectiveness of the discontinuance and, in some cases, the character of the past violations.

The facts relied on by the Government to show an abuse of discretion in this case are these: Hancock's three interlocking directorates viewed as three distinct violations, his failure to terminate them until after suit was filed despite five years of administrative attempts to persuade him of their illegality, his express refusal to concede that the interlocks in question were illegal under the statute and his failure to promise not to commit similar violations in the future.

Were we sitting as a trial court, this showing might be persuasive. But the Government must demonstrate that there was no reasonable basis for the District Judge's decision. In this we think it fails. An individual proclivity to violate the statute need not be inferred from the fact that three violations were charged, particularly since it is only recently that the Government has attempted systematic enforcement of §8. The District Court was not dealing with a defendant who follows one adjudicated violation with others. The only material before the District Judge on the supposed five years of administrative persuasion could easily support an inference that during that time the defendant and the Department of Justice were each trying to determine the legality of his directorships. The Government's remedy under the statute was plain. Postponement of suit indicates doubt on the prosecutor's part as much as intransigence on the defendant's. How much contrition should be expected of a defendant is hard for us to say. This surely is a question better addressed to the discretion of the trial court. The same can be said of the limited disclaimer of future intent. . . .

We conclude that, although the actions were not moot, no abuse of discretion has been demonstrated in the trial court's refusal to award injunctive relief. Moreover, the court stated its dismissals "would not be a bar to a new suit in case possible violations arise in the future." The judgments are affirmed.

Justice DOUGLAS, with whom Justice BLACK concurs, dissenting. . . .

Mr. Hancock served as a director for each of three sets of companies which, on the state of the pleadings before us, we must assume to have been competitive. The

---

5. ". . . It is the duty of the courts to beware of efforts to defeat injunctive relief by protestations of repentance and reform, especially when abandonment seems timed to anticipate suit, and there is probability of resumption." United States v. Oregon State Medical Society, 343 U.S. 326, 333 (1952).

fact that he resigned under the pressure of these proceedings should not dispose of the case. We are dealing here with professionals whose technique for controlling enterprises and building empires was fully developed and well known long before Mr. Justice Brandeis was crying out against the evils of "the money trust." Mr. Hancock is and has been for some years a partner in the investment banking firm of Lehman Bros. In 1940 he testified that when Lehman Bros. did financing for a company it was their "traditional practice" to ask for representation on the board of directors. . . .

The fact that the Lehman partner resigned to avoid a decision on the merits has little, if any, relevancy to the issue in the case, for we are here concerned with the *proclivity* of the house to indulge in the practice.

The relevant issues have never been weighed in this case. The District Court's ruling would be entitled to a presumption of validity if those various factors had been considered. But the District Court made no such considered judgment. It disposed of the case on the basis of mootness, a ruling now conceded to be erroneous. The case should go back for a consideration of the nature and extent of the web which this investment banking house has woven over industry and its effect on the "elimination of competition" within the meaning of §8 of the Clayton Act. Unless we know that much, we are in no position to judge the service an injunction against future violations may do. . . .

NOTES ON VOLUNTARY CESSATION OF WRONGFUL ACTS

1. **Jurisdiction and discretion.** Note the distinction in *Grant* between mootness sufficient to end the case or controversy and deprive the court of jurisdiction, and likelihood of repetition so low that relief should be withheld as a matter of remedial discretion. Although one doctrine is labeled "constitutional" and the other "equitable," each arises only with respect to preventive relief, and the difference between them is a murky matter of degree. These statements are equally true of ripeness: Ripeness is both a constitutional and an equitable doctrine, with little clear separation between the two versions of the rule. See note 11 following *Almurbati.*

2. **Cessation and propensity.** We might just say that defendant stopped doing what he was doing, but courts need a noun, and the common phrase for these cases is "voluntary cessation." Defendant's voluntary cessation is one common source of claims that the case is moot, or, more plausibly, that no injunction is needed. Voluntary cessation cases are really a variation on the question of propensity. Normally, the fact that he has already done it once is sufficient to cause the court to take seriously plaintiff's fear that he will do it again. But sometimes defendant says he's quit and won't do it again. That is, he says the normal inference from past conduct is not true in his case, and relief aimed at preventing future repetitions is now premature. Plaintiffs win more voluntary cessation cases than they do ripeness cases, because the past conduct hurts defendant's credibility, and because it arguably justifies inconveniencing defendant to make sure plaintiff is protected.

3. **Burden of proof.** Plaintiff has the burden of proving propensity at the beginning of a case, but defendant has the burden of proving that an injunction is no longer needed. Defendant's burden was described as "heavy" in Parents Involved in Community Schools v. Seattle School District No. 1, 551 U.S. 701, 719 (2007). Defendant must show that "subsequent events ma[ke] it absolutely clear that the allegedly wrongful behavior could not reasonably be expected to recur." *Id.*, quoting two earlier cases. Of course, the rhetorical force of "absolutely clear" is rather diluted when applied to what could "reasonably be expected."

The Eleventh Circuit uses a six-part test:

> the egregiousness of the defendant's actions, the isolated or recurrent nature of the infraction, the degree of scienter involved, the sincerity of the defendant's assurances against future violations, the defendant's recognition of the wrongful nature of the conduct, and the likelihood that the defendant's occupation will present opportunities for future violations.

U.S. Commodity Futures Trading Commission v. Southern Trust Metals, Inc., 880 F.3d 1252, 1265 (11th Cir. 2018). Is this any more informative than the Supreme Court's three factors?

4. Change of administration. The Court applied the voluntary cessation doctrine without controversy in Trinity Lutheran Church v. Comer, 137 S. Ct. 2012 (2017). The church initially qualified for a state grant to improve playground safety, but state officials then decided that it was ineligible because of a provision in the state constitution barring the expenditure of public funds in aid of any church. After the case was fully briefed in the Supreme Court, a new Governor and Attorney General, both Republicans, replaced their Democratic predecessors. Six days before oral argument, the Governor announced that he had "instructed" the relevant department to give equal treatment to future applications from religious organizations. This announcement did not fund the church's playground, because the grant application was from the 2012 funding cycle, and that money was all gone. The Attorney General's office recused itself, and the case was argued by the Solicitor General from the previous administration, who had filed the briefs.

A flurry of online commentary, mostly from opponents of funding who feared an adverse decision, insisted that the case was now moot. It seems unlikely that the new administration would voluntarily reverse its position, but it had not disabled itself from doing so. It had not even issued a regulation, but only a press release announcing an unpublished "instruct[ion]." More fundamentally, the state constitutional provision barring the funds remained in effect, and no governor could change that. Opponents of funding could sue to enforce the state constitution, and the state courts could overturn the new administration's position. The Court said that no one had "carried the 'heavy burden' of making 'absolutely clear' that [the state] could not revert" to the challenged policy. *Id.* at 2019 n.1. No one had tried to carry that burden; both sides agreed that the case was not moot.

5. Deterrence. The Court rather easily accepted a Special Master's finding that there was no "cognizable danger of recurrent violations," quoting *W.T. Grant,* in an interstate water dispute. Kansas v. Nebraska, 135 S. Ct. 1042, 1059 (2015). Nebraska had knowingly and recklessly, but not deliberately, taken more than its share of the water in the Republican River, and the Court had awarded a substantial monetary remedy, in excess of actual damages. Meanwhile, Nebraska had adopted new compliance measures that would suffice if adhered to. The Court believed that the risk of renewed monetary liability would likely keep those new measures in place. The case is more fully described in section 8.B.3.a.

6. Whose propensity? Justice Douglas is interested in the propensity of Lehman Brothers; the Court seems interested in the propensity of Hancock individually. Which is the better approach? Doesn't that depend on substantive antitrust law and the theory of the government's case?

What if Goodyear fired Coleman, the store manager who discriminated? Would that so remove the threat of future discrimination that no preventive injunction should issue? Compare Spomer v. Littleton, 414 U.S. 514 (1974), in which plaintiffs sought to enjoin racial discrimination by a county prosecutor, Berbling. Berbling was succeeded by Spomer, and Spomer was substituted as a defendant under Supreme Court Rule 35.3. This rule, modeled on Federal Rule of Civil Procedure 25(d), provides for automatic substitution of successors in suits against public officers in their official capacity. The Court did not question Spomer's substitution, but it doubted whether plaintiffs had any controversy with him. Plaintiffs had alleged that Berbling systematically discriminated; they had not alleged that Spomer would, or that the office did apart from Berbling. The Court ordered the complaint dismissed unless on remand plaintiffs could show a threat of continuing discrimination.

7. What happens when the injunction is withheld? In *W.T. Grant*, the case was dismissed without resolving the merits. That has the same effect as if the case had been held moot, or unripe. Nothing has been decided, and any renewed litigation will get a fresh start.

The situation is much more confused when the court decides the merits and holds defendant's acts illegal, but also decides that no injunction is necessary. Then we have an opinion, perhaps a momentous opinion, but no remedy or judgment to enforce that opinion. If plaintiffs do not get some relief apart from the withheld injunction, the only judgment may be to dismiss the case, even though the opinion says plaintiffs won. Yet courts sometimes withhold injunctions in such circumstances. In Hopwood v. Texas, 78 F.3d 932, 958 (5th Cir. 1996), which held affirmative action in law school admissions unconstitutional, the court declined to mandate an injunction on remand, because it was "confident that the conscientious administration at the school, as well as its attorneys, will heed the directives contained in this opinion."

There are dangers to both sides in this sometimes casual practice, especially if there is no declaratory judgment or award of damages. Ending a case with an opinion but no judgment jeopardizes defendant's claim to further appellate review and plaintiff's claim to attorneys' fees. Both these problems bedeviled the hard-fought *Hopwood* case. The Supreme Court denied certiorari, at least in part because "this Court . . . reviews judgments, not opinions." 518 U.S. 1033, 1034 (1996) (Ginsburg, J., concurring). Plaintiffs did eventually collect attorneys' fees, Hopwood v. Texas, 236 F.3d 256, 277-278 (5th Cir. 2000), a result that made practical sense but is hard to reconcile with the full import of Buckhannon Board & Care Home, Inc. v. West Virginia, 532 U.S. 598 (2001), considered in section 10.A.

8. Mootness and monetary relief. A claim for damages is never moot. See, e.g., Powell v. McCormack, 395 U.S. 486, 495-500 (1969). Similarly, a claim for restitution of defendant's unjust gains is never moot. Laskowski v. Spellings, 443 F.3d 930, 933-935 (7th Cir. 2006), *vacated on other grounds*, University of Notre Dame v. Laskowski, 551 U.S. 1160 (2007). It is always possible to grant monetary relief for past events. Similarly, claims for monetary relief rarely raise ripeness issues.

9. Nominal damages. Most courts have held or assumed that a bona fide claim for nominal damages is enough to avoid mootness. The Eleventh Circuit rejected that view in a long-running case challenging an ordinance that banned the sale of certain sex toys. The city had repealed the ordinance while the case was pending before the en banc court, and it convincingly committed not to pass any similar ordinance, leaving only a claim for nominal damages standing. The court said that some awards of nominal damages resolved live disputes or had some other practical effect, but that often, including in this case, they "would serve no purpose other than to affix a judicial seal of approval to an outcome that has already been realized." Flanigan's Enterprises, Inc. v. Davenport, 868 F.3d 1248, 1263-1264 (11th Cir. 2017) (en banc).

The majority feared that if a claim for nominal damages was enough to avoid mootness, plaintiffs could manipulate the court's jurisdiction and expand its docket. Five dissenters rejected that fear. Cases that were "otherwise moot *and* [where there were] no other possible type of damages still available" were few in number. Circuits where a claim for nominal damages keeps a case alive "seem to be weathering the storm." *Id.* at 1272.

10. Unaccepted offers of full compensation. The defendant cannot moot an alleged class action by offering to fully compensate the named plaintiff, unless the named plaintiff accepts the offer. Campbell-Ewald Co. v. Gomez, 136 S. Ct. 663 (2016). If defendants could moot class claims by offering modest sums to buy off the class representatives, then few lawyers would take these cases; both the individual claims and the class claims would wither away. That is what was at stake; what the Court said was that an unaccepted offer is a nullity, both in first-year Contracts and explicitly in Federal Rule 68 on offers of judgment. Rule 68 says that an offer not accepted within 14 days is considered withdrawn, and that the party rejecting the offer is liable for costs if she eventually obtains a judgment less favorable than the offer. The Court reserved judgment on a case in which a defendant pays the offered amount into court, or deposits it in an account in plaintiff's name, and the court enters judgment for that amount.

2. *Preventing Lawful Acts That Might Have Wrongful Consequences*

NICHOLSON v. CONNECTICUT HALF-WAY HOUSE, INC.
218 A.2d 383 (Conn. 1966)

[Plaintiffs were property owners and residents of a middle-class residential block in Hartford. Defendant purchased one of the homes in the block for use as a halfway house for parolees from the Connecticut state prison. Before the halfway house could begin operation, the trial court enjoined it as a nuisance. Defendant appealed.]

THIM, Acting Justice. . . .

A fair test of whether a proposed use constitutes a nuisance is "the reasonableness of the use of the property in the particular locality under the circumstances of the case." Wetstone v. Cantor, 127 A.2d 70, 72 (Conn. 1956). To meet this test in the instant case, the evidence must show that the defendant's proposed use of the property under the circumstances is unreasonable.

Here the proposed use of the defendant's property, in and of itself, is lawful. The only factual grounds offered to support the relief granted are the fears of the plaintiffs that the residents of the defendant's halfway house will commit criminal acts in the neighborhood and the finding that the proposed use has had a depreciative effect on land values in this area. The first of these grounds goes to the core of the plaintiffs' complaint. The real objection of the plaintiffs is to the presence in the neighborhood of persons with a demonstrated capacity for criminal activity. They fear future manifestations of such activity in their neighborhood. This present fear of what may happen in the future, although genuinely felt, rests completely on supposition. The anticipation by the plaintiffs of the possible consequences of the defendant's proposed use of the property can be characterized as a speculative and intangible fear. They have neither alleged nor offered evidence to prove any specific acts or pattern of behavior which would cause them harm so as to warrant the drastic injunctive relief granted by the court.

It is clear that the power of equity to grant injunctive relief may be exercised only under demanding circumstances.

> No court of equity should ever grant an injunction merely because of the fears or apprehensions of the party applying for it. Those fears or apprehensions may exist without any substantial reason. Indeed they may be absolutely groundless. Restraining the action of an individual or a corporation by injunction is an extraordinary power, always to be exercised with caution, never without the most satisfactory reasons.

Goodwin v. New York, New Haven & Hartford Railroad, 43 Conn. 494, 500 (1876). The fears and apprehensions of the plaintiffs in the present case, based as they are on speculation, cannot justify the granting of injunctive relief.

The plaintiffs' claim of depreciated property values is likewise ineffective as a basis for supporting the issuance of an injunction. The mere depreciation of land values, caused in this case by the subjective apprehensions of neighboring property owners and their potential buyers, cannot sustain an injunction sought on the ground of nuisance.

The plaintiffs have cited Brainard v. Town of West Hartford, 103 A.2d 135 (Conn. 1954), for the proposition that an unreasonable use of property which is merely anticipatory may be enjoined. In that case, however, the proposed use, a town dump in a residential area, was a known quantity whose attributes as a nuisance could be readily adjudged prior to the undertaking.[1] A similar factual showing has not been produced in the present case. The plaintiffs have also cited Jack v. Torrant, 71 A.2d 705 (Conn. 1950), in support of their overall position. That case involved the operation of an embalming and undertaking establishment in a residential district and is clearly distinguishable on its facts from the present situation.

Our conclusion is not intended to serve as a comment on the future operations of the defendant. We only hold that, under the present circumstances, there has been an insufficient factual showing that the defendant will make any unreasonable use of its property or that the prospective residents of its halfway house will engage in unlawful activities in the surrounding neighborhood. For the reasons already discussed, the granting of the injunction by the trial court was not justified at this time. . . .

NOTES ON RIPENESS AND UNCERTAIN CONSEQUENCES

1. The Connecticut precedents. The finding in Brainard v. Town of West Hartford, set out in footnote 1 of *Nicholson*, was based on experience at a similar dump operated by defendant. In Jack v. Torrant, also discussed in *Nicholson*, the court held that any funeral home in a residential area would be a nuisance, no matter how it was run, because it would depress the neighborhood residents by constantly reminding them of death. Does the explanation of these three cases turn on how certain the court is that the proposed use will actually be a nuisance? Would *Nicholson* have come out differently if plaintiffs had argued that the halfway house would depress them by constantly reminding them of crime? Why are feelings of depression different from feelings of fear?

---

1. The trial court in *Brainard* found that "[t]he establishment of a dump on the land purchased by the defendant would greatly depreciate the value of the plaintiffs' land, creating a noxious smoke, litter, offensive and unhealthy odors, rats, vermin, insects and fire danger."

2. Propensity but still unripe. *Nicholson* can be thought of as a ripeness case; the dispute about the effects of the halfway house is not yet ripe. But there is no issue of defendants' propensity to put the halfway house in plaintiffs' neighborhood; defendants assert their right and intention to do so. There might have been a propensity issue about details of how they intended to run it. But mostly the issue in *Nicholson* is about the uncertain consequences of defendant's conduct. Will the halfway house turn out to be a nuisance?

3. Prophylactic relief. *Nicholson* can also be thought of as a request for a prophylactic injunction, a category that will turn out to be broader and more useful. Plaintiffs want the court to prohibit the halfway house altogether to eliminate the risk that it will be harmful. This is a more extreme variation on issues suggested in *Almurbati* and in footnote 7 of Marshall v. Goodyear. The *Almurbati* plaintiffs sought an injunction ordering 30 days' notice of any transfer, to reduce the risk that they would be transferred to a country where they would be tortured; the court refused the injunction on other grounds. The trial court in *Goodyear* thought that centralized administration of personnel policy would result in fewer violations of the Age Discrimination Act. The court of appeals did not disagree with that factual premise; it simply said that the Act does not require centralized administration.

Cases such as *Goodyear* suggest that the court should not enjoin a lawful halfway house to prevent harms from violations of particular laws that apply to its operation. The court would have to enjoin the particular violations instead. But that rule is not absolute. In *Nicholson*, the substantive law of nuisance opens up the possibility of prophylactic relief. If the halfway house is sufficiently dangerous or disruptive, it will be a nuisance in this location, and if it is a nuisance, it is illegal to operate it in this location at all. There is no doubt that the court can enjoin operation of an existing nuisance. The additional question in *Nicholson* is whether and when the court can enjoin the commencement of an anticipated nuisance. That issue is examined and the cases collected in George P. Smith, *Re-Validating the Doctrine of Anticipatory Nuisance*, 29 Vt. L. Rev. 687 (2005).

4. The nuisance cases. Verbal formulations vary, but certainty is the common theme in cases where plaintiff seeks to enjoin activity that might turn out to be a nuisance. "The fact that it will be a nuisance if so used must be made clearly to appear, beyond all ground of fair questioning." Duff v. Morgantown Energy Associates, 421 S.E.2d 253, 258 (W. Va. 1992), a standard the court then paraphrased as "reasonable certainty." *Id.* at 258 n.9. The court reversed an injunction against an electrical cogeneration plant that would burn mine waste and coal, with heavy truck traffic delivering fuel and hauling away ash.

In Franklinton Coalition v. Open Shelter, 469 N.E.2d 861, 867 (Ohio Ct. App. 1983), the court held that "there was insufficient evidence to require the trial court to find that the operation of the shelter for homeless persons by defendant would necessarily constitute a nuisance at the new location merely because it did constitute a nuisance at a former location." The court relied on the hiring of a new director and operational changes in light of the earlier bad experience. Compare Citizens for a Safe Grant v. Lone Oak Sportsmen's Club, Inc., 624 N.W.2d 796 (Minn. Ct. App. 2001), where the contrast between past and predicted future went the other way. The court enjoined continued operation of a rifle range, at the request of neighbors in nearby residences, despite defendant's showing that there had never been an injury in 50 years of operation. The court made detailed findings of harm to plaintiffs short of physical injury: They were afraid, they didn't let their children play outside, and they didn't use parts of their property.

5. The purpose of the rule? What purpose does the ripeness doctrine serve in *Nicholson* and similar cases? Should socially useful enterprises that might be run lawfully and harmlessly be enjoined because they might be run unlawfully and harmfully? Should the likelihood of harmful consequences be explicitly balanced against the benefits to be created by the enterprise?

6. The uncertainty continues. The ripeness doctrine cannot solve the problem of uncertainty about the future. Development of the halfway house in *Nicholson* must proceed subject to the risk of damage liability and the risk that operation will be enjoined if the court later concludes that a nuisance has been created. This is an incentive to careful operation, but even skillful and well-intentioned defendants may not be able to prevent a nuisance. Suppose defendant alleged that it was unable to secure financing with the threat of a second lawsuit hanging over it, and it sought a declaratory judgment that operation of the halfway house would be lawful. Would that case be ripe?

Suppose that, instead of seeking to enjoin operation of the halfway house altogether, plaintiffs had sought an injunction conditioning its operation on certain safeguards, such as exclusion of sex offenders, drug addicts, alcoholics, and parolees without jobs. Would that case be ripe? Would ripeness depend on the evidence presented concerning the groups to be excluded? Suppose plaintiffs simply sought an injunction ordering defendants to prevent the inmates from harming anyone? Would that case be ripe? Would that injunction do any good?

7. Ripeness and claim and issue preclusion. Note 6 assumes that the neighbors could bring a second lawsuit later, if the halfway house turns out to be a nuisance in practice. That is probably uncontroversial if the first case is explicitly dismissed on ripeness grounds, clearly not reaching the merits. But what if the court is unclear about that? Or what if it simply says that plaintiff has made "an insufficient factual showing." Reread the last paragraph of *Nicholson*.

The Supreme Court fought over this issue in Whole Woman's Health v. Hellerstedt, 136 S. Ct. 2292 (2016). Texas passed a statute requiring every doctor performing an abortion to have admitting privileges at a local hospital and requiring all abortion clinics to meet the same standards as ambulatory surgical centers. Just "days before" the law took effect, abortion clinics and doctors filed a suit alleging that the requirement of hospital admitting privileges would force many abortion clinics to close and thus impose an undue burden on the right to abortion. Planned Parenthood v. Abbott, 748 F.3d 583, 587 (5th Cir. 2014). The district court held a hurried hearing with "a few witnesses and . . . numerous affidavits," *id.* at 588, and permanently enjoined enforcement of the requirement of admitting privileges. The court of appeals reversed on the merits, holding that the district court had applied the wrong legal standard and that under the correct standard, plaintiffs had failed to prove an undue burden on the right to choose abortion. *Id.* at 590-600. The clinics did not petition for certiorari.

Then many of the same clinics filed a new lawsuit, challenging the admitting privileges requirement for some clinics and the surgical center requirement for all clinics. They proved that many clinics had in fact closed when the admitting-privileges requirement took effect, and the clinics and the state agreed that when the surgical-center requirement was fully enforced, only seven or eight clinics would remain in the state. There had been 40 clinics before the challenged legislation, although the state offered evidence that some had closed for unrelated reasons. The district court held both requirements unconstitutional and enjoined their enforcement as to all the clinics in the state, including those who had participated in the first lawsuit.

The Supreme Court held that the second lawsuit, challenging the law after it took effect and in light of actual experience, was a different claim from the first lawsuit, challenging the law before it took effect and based on predictions of what might happen. And therefore, the first lawsuit did not preclude the second. This is important, and surely right as a general proposition. But as Justice Alito argued for three dissenters: "The Court of Appeals did not hold that the [first] challenge was premature. It held that the evidence petitioners offered was insufficient." 136 S. Ct. at 2335. Alito said that this was a ruling on the merits.

Ripeness and insufficiency of evidence can be closely related. The state had argued in the first case that the clinics' predictions that they would be forced to close did not prove that they really would close. Actual experience is far more persuasive than predictions of doom. But Justice Alito said that the actual closing of the clinics was just new evidence, and new evidence is not a basis for creating exceptions to claim or issue preclusion. He also argued that the clinics in the first case could have produced better evidence than they had.

Justice Breyer for the majority said that Alito was "simply wrong," *id.* at 2306, and Alito said the majority was "plainly wrong," *id.* at 2332. What seems to have been plainly wrong was that the district court issued a final judgment in the first case when there had not been reasonable time for preparation and full litigation. The law of preliminary injunctions, taken up in Chapter 5, is designed to avoid that problem; the court grants or refuses interim relief based on probable outcomes determined in a preliminary hearing. And it is settled that a decision granting or denying a preliminary injunction is not claim or issue preclusive in later litigation in the same case over a permanent injunction. The clinics should have vigorously opposed converting their hurried hearing into a hearing on a permanent injunction, which results in a final judgment.

The next day, Alito dissented from denial of certiorari in Stormans, Inc. v. Wiesman, 136 S. Ct. 2433 (2016). Petitioners had challenged certain regulations as unconstitutional, after a threat of enforcement but before any actual enforcement. The cert denial ended nine years of litigation, including a preliminary injunction hearing, an appeal, a 12-day trial, and a second appeal. Justice Alito ended his dissent with this footnote: "The Court's denial of certiorari does not, of course, preclude petitioners from bringing a future as-applied challenge to the Board's regulations." *Id.* at 2440 n.6. He might have cited *Whole Woman's Health* for this proposition. Or he might have explained how this footnote was consistent with his dissent in *Whole Woman's Health.* But he did neither.

8. Disguised holdings on the merits? The *Nicholson* court also held that depreciated property values, when caused by subjective apprehensions, are not grounds for an injunction. Is that a ripeness holding, or is it a holding on the merits? Will the complaint about depreciated property values ever be any riper?

PEPSICO, INC. v. REDMOND
54 F.3d 1262 (7th Cir. 1995)

Before BAUER, COFFEY, and FLAUM, Circuit Judges.
FLAUM, Circuit Judge.

Plaintiff PepsiCo, Inc., sought a preliminary injunction against defendants William Redmond and the Quaker Oats Company to prevent Redmond, a former PepsiCo employee, from divulging PepsiCo trade secrets and confidential information in his new job with Quaker and from assuming any duties with Quaker relating to beverage pricing, marketing, and distribution. The district court agreed with PepsiCo and granted the injunction. We now affirm that decision.

I.

The facts of this case lay against a backdrop of fierce beverage-industry competition between Quaker and PepsiCo, especially in "sports drinks" and "new age drinks." Quaker's sports drink, "Gatorade," is the dominant brand in its market niche. PepsiCo introduced its Gatorade rival, "All Sport," in March and April of 1994, but sales of All Sport lag far behind those of Gatorade. . . . Quaker purchased Snapple Beverage Corp., a large new-age-drink maker, in late 1994. PepsiCo's products have about half of Snapple's market share. . . .

William Redmond, Jr., worked for PepsiCo in its Pepsi-Cola North America division ("PCNA") from 1984 to 1994 [and rose to] General Manager of the business unit covering all of California. . . .

Redmond . . . signed a confidentiality agreement with PepsiCo. That agreement stated in relevant part that he

> w[ould] not disclose at any time, to anyone other than officers or employees of [PepsiCo], or make use of, confidential information relating to the business of [PepsiCo] . . . obtained while in the employ of [PepsiCo], which shall not be generally known or available to the public or recognized as standard practices.

[On November 8, 1994, Redmond accepted an offer to become Vice President-Field Operations for Gatorade. Quaker planned to integrate marketing and distribution of Gatorade and Snapple, and Redmond would be responsible for both. After he accepted the position, he told his superiors at PepsiCo that he had an offer from Quaker, somewhat misstating the exact position, and said that he was thinking about it. On November 10, he resigned at PepsiCo.]

PepsiCo filed this diversity suit on November 16, 1994, seeking . . . to enjoin Redmond from assuming his duties at Quaker and to prevent him from disclosing trade secrets or confidential information to his new employer.

[PepsiCo showed that Redmond was privy to detailed strategic and tactical plans for manufacturing, pricing, marketing, packaging, and distribution of products that competed directly with Gatorade and Snapple. As Redmond worked to market Gatorade and Snapple, he would be able to anticipate PepsiCo's every move.]

On December 15, 1994, the district court issued an order enjoining Redmond from assuming his position at Quaker through May, 1995, and permanently from using or disclosing any PCNA trade secrets or confidential information. . . .

II. . . .

A.

The Illinois Trade Secrets Act ("ITSA"), which governs the trade secret issues in this case, provides that a court may enjoin the "actual or threatened misappropriation" of a trade secret. 765 Ill. Comp. Stat. 1065/3(a). . . .

The question of threatened or inevitable misappropriation in this case lies at the heart of a basic tension in trade secret law. Trade secret law serves to protect "standards of commercial morality" and "encourage[] invention and innovation" while maintaining "the public interest in having free and open competition in the manufacture and sale of unpatented goods." 2 Melvin F. Jager, *Trade Secrets Law* §IL.03 at IL-12 (rev. ed., Clark Boardman Callaghan 1994). Yet that same law should not prevent workers from pursuing their livelihoods when they leave their current positions. . . .

This tension is particularly exacerbated when a plaintiff sues to prevent not the actual misappropriation of trade secrets but the mere threat that it will occur. While the ITSA plainly permits a court to enjoin the threat of misappropriation of trade secrets, there is little law in Illinois or in this circuit establishing what constitutes threatened or inevitable misappropriation. Indeed, there are only two cases in this circuit that address the issue. Teradyne, Inc. v. Clear Communications Corp., 707 F. Supp. 353 (N.D. Ill. 1989); AMP, Inc. v. Fleischhacker, 823 F.3d 1199 (7th Cir. 1987). [Each of those cases denied relief and permitted an employee to move to a competing position. The court in each case found the danger of wrongful disclosures insufficient to justify prohibiting the employee from taking the new job.]

[A] plaintiff may prove a claim of trade secret misappropriation by demonstrating that defendant's new employment will inevitably lead him to rely on the plaintiff's trade secrets. *See also* 1 Jager, *supra*, §7.02[2][a] at 7-20 (noting claims where "the allegation is based on the fact that the disclosure of trade secrets in the new employment is inevitable, whether . . . the former employee acts consciously or unconsciously"). . . .

The district court concluded . . . that unless Redmond possessed an uncanny ability to compartmentalize information, he would necessarily be making decisions about Gatorade and Snapple by relying on his knowledge of PCNA trade secrets. It is not the "general skills and knowledge acquired during his tenure with" PepsiCo that PepsiCo seeks to keep from falling into Quaker's hands, but rather "the particularized plans or processes developed by [PCNA] and disclosed to him while the employer-employee relationship existed, which are unknown to others in the industry and which give the employer an advantage over his competitors." *AMP*, 823 F.3d at 1202. The *Teradyne* and *AMP* plaintiffs could do nothing more than assert that skilled employees were taking their skills elsewhere; PepsiCo has done much more.

Admittedly, PepsiCo has not brought a traditional trade secret case, in which a former employee has knowledge of a special manufacturing process or customer list and can give a competitor an unfair advantage by transferring the technology or customers to that competitor. PepsiCo has not contended that Quaker has stolen the All Sport formula or its list of distributors. Rather PepsiCo has asserted that Redmond cannot help but rely on PCNA trade secrets as he helps plot Gatorade and Snapple's new course, and that these secrets will enable Quaker to achieve a substantial advantage by knowing exactly how PCNA will price, distribute, and market its sports drinks and new age drinks and being able to respond strategically. This type of trade secret problem may arise less often, but it nevertheless falls within the realm of trade secret protection under the present circumstances.[8]

Quaker and Redmond assert that they have not and do not intend to use whatever confidential information Redmond has by virtue of his former employment. They point out that Redmond has already signed an agreement with Quaker not to disclose any trade secrets or confidential information gleaned from his earlier employment. They also note with regard to distribution systems that even if Quaker wanted to steal information about PCNA's distribution plans, they would be completely useless in attempting to integrate the Gatorade and Snapple beverage lines.

The defendants' arguments fall somewhat short of the mark. Again, the danger of misappropriation in the present case is not that Quaker threatens to use PCNA's

---

8. PepsiCo does contend that Quaker may well misappropriate its new, trade-secret distribution system because Snapple has a similar system and Quaker [which only recently acquired Snapple] is not familiar with it. This argument approaches the sort of speculation we rejected in *AMP* and Judge Zagel rejected in *Teradyne*. We need not pass on its validity, however, because it is not central to PepsiCo's case.

secrets to create distribution systems or co-opt PCNA's advertising and marketing ideas. Rather, PepsiCo believes that Quaker, unfairly armed with knowledge of PCNA's plans, will be able to anticipate its distribution, packaging, pricing, and marketing moves. Redmond and Quaker even concede that Redmond might be faced with a decision that could be influenced by certain confidential information that he obtained while at PepsiCo. [They said that in such an event, Redmond would seek and follow advice from Quaker's in-house counsel.] In other words, PepsiCo finds itself in the position of a coach, one of whose players has left, playbook in hand, to join the opposing team before the big game. Quaker and Redmond's protestations that their distribution systems and plans are entirely different from PCNA's are thus not really responsive.

[Donald Uzzi, a former PepsiCo employee who left to become head of Gatorade, hired Redmond at Quaker.] The district court also concluded from the evidence that Uzzi's actions in hiring Redmond and Redmond's actions in pursuing and accepting his new job demonstrated a lack of candor on their part and proof of their willingness to misuse PCNA trade secrets, findings Quaker and Redmond vigorously challenge. The court expressly found that:

> Redmond's lack of forthrightness on some occasions, and out and out lies on others, in the period between the time he accepted the position with defendant Quaker and when he informed plaintiff that he had accepted that position leads the court to conclude that defendant Redmond could not be trusted to act with the necessary sensitivity and good faith under the circumstances in which the only practical verification that he was not using plaintiff's secrets would be defendant Redmond's word to that effect.

The facts of the case do not ineluctably dictate the district court's conclusion. Redmond's ambiguous behavior toward his PepsiCo superiors might have been nothing more than an attempt to gain leverage in employment negotiations. The discrepancy between Redmond's and Uzzi's comprehension of what Redmond's job would entail may well have been a simple misunderstanding. The court also pointed out that Quaker, through Uzzi, seemed to express an unnatural interest in hiring PCNA employees: all three of the people interviewed for the position Redmond ultimately accepted worked at PCNA. Uzzi may well have focused on recruiting PCNA employees because he knew they were good and not because of their confidential knowledge. Nonetheless, the district court, after listening to the witnesses, determined otherwise. That conclusion was not an abuse of discretion. . . .

Thus, when we couple the demonstrated inevitability that Redmond would rely on PCNA trade secrets in his new job at Quaker with the district court's reluctance to believe that Redmond would refrain from disclosing these secrets in his new position (or that Quaker would ensure Redmond did not disclose them), we conclude that the district court correctly decided that PepsiCo demonstrated a likelihood of success on its statutory claim of trade secret misappropriation. . . .

III.

For the foregoing reasons, we affirm the district court's order enjoining Redmond from assuming his responsibilities at Quaker through May, 1995, and preventing him forever from disclosing PCNA trade secrets and confidential information. . . .

NOTES ON PROPHYLACTIC INJUNCTIONS

1. The facts in *PepsiCo.* The injunction against working at Quaker continued "through May, 1995," presumably meaning May 31. The reason for that date is not disclosed in the opinion. It might have been the point at which some of Redmond's most important information expired, perhaps the last Annual Operating Plan that he had worked with. Or the choice might have been more intuitive; maybe six months, rounded up, just seemed like a reasonable waiting period. The court of appeals released its opinion in typescript on May 11. Courts sometimes have trouble moving injunction litigation as quickly as the events being litigated.

Defendants apparently did not contest the injunction never to use or disclose PepsiCo's trade secrets or confidential information. They insisted that Redmond had no intention of doing so, and that Redmond and Quaker had safeguards in place to make sure that he never did. Should the injunction against use or disclosure also have been denied, under the rule in *Almurbati*? Or was the high risk of use and disclosure at least enough to justify that injunction, whatever defendants' intentions?

2. The inevitable-disclosure theory. Courts that recognize *PepsiCo*'s inevitable-disclosure theory generally construe it narrowly and require strong evidence. Some courts reject it altogether. The conflicting cases are collected in LeJeune v. Coin Acceptors, Inc., 849 A.2d 451, 469-471 (Md. 2004). A principal argument against the theory sounds more in substantive law than in remedies. PepsiCo and Redmond could have agreed that he would not work for a competitor for a stated period of time after leaving PepsiCo. Such covenants not to compete are common in employment agreements for sensitive positions, and they are generally enforceable if they survive stringent review for reasonableness. The court in effect gave PepsiCo a six-month covenant not to compete, even though it had not contracted for one, and retroactively imposed that covenant on Redmond, even though he had not agreed to one.

Compare Mantek Division v. Share Corp., 780 F.2d 702 (7th Cir. 1986), vacating an injunction that prevented plaintiff's former employees from selling a competitor's goods anywhere in their former sales territory, because they had agreed only that they would not solicit customers they had personally served or learned about while in plaintiff's employ. The court rejected plaintiff's argument that an injunction confined to the terms of the agreement would be hard to enforce. "We do not believe that a plaintiff is entitled to an unreasonably broad preliminary injunction merely because a reasonable injunction is more difficult to enforce." *Id.* at 711.

3. The Defend Trade Secrets Act of 2016. Trade secret has always been a matter of state law, but now Congress has enacted federal remedies for misappropriation of trade secrets "related to a product or service used in, or intended for use in, interstate or foreign commerce." 18 U.S.C. §1836(b)(1). The federal Act does not authorize the *Pepsico* remedy. A federal court may grant an injunction:

> to prevent any actual or threatened misappropriation . . . on such terms as the court deems reasonable, provided the order does not—
>> (1) prevent a person from entering into an employment relationship, and that conditions placed on such employment shall be based on evidence of threatened misappropriation and not merely on the information the person knows.

18 U.S.C. §1836(b)(3)(A). Nothing in the Act appears to preempt state law; a federal court in diversity jurisdiction can still grant the *Pepsico* remedy under state law, as the Seventh Circuit did. But the new statute may have a persuasive influence.

4. The concept of prophylactic relief. *PepsiCo* is a lot like *Nicholson*, but it is not really a ripeness case. In *Nicholson*, the court will learn much more about the magnitude of the problem when the halfway house opens. But if Redmond goes to work for Quaker, it will be hard to know whether he is misusing PepsiCo's information, and the value of what he knows will steadily decline with time. If *PepsiCo* were not ripe when first presented, it probably never would be ripe. *PepsiCo* is about the scope of relief, but it is not in any meaningful sense about the timing of the litigation.

The broader question in *Nicholson* and *PepsiCo* is prophylactic relief. To what extent can the court enjoin conduct that is lawful in itself in order to prevent, or reduce the likelihood of, possible wrongful consequences? Tracy Thomas, who has written extensively about prophylactic relief, says that prophylactic injunctions enjoin the "facilitators" of wrongful conduct. Tracy A. Thomas, *The Continued Vitality of Prophylactic Relief*, 27 Rev. Litig. 99, 113 (2007). Examples turn up everywhere, some controversial and some not.

A recent example came in a lawsuit between Waymo (owned by Alphabet, the parent company of Google) and the ride-sharing company Uber over technology for self-driving cars. Both companies are developing self-driving car technology. Waymo alleged that its former employee, star engineer Anthony Levandowski, downloaded over 14,000 confidential files from company servers, started his own competing company with Uber's knowledge, and then sold the new company to Uber for $680 million while taking a position as head of Uber's self-driving car division.

The trial court determined, for purposes of considering preliminary relief, that the "purloined" files contained "at least *some* trade secrets." Waymo, LLC v. Uber Technologies, Inc., 2017 WL 2123560, *1 (N.D. Cal. May 15, 2017). Among other things, the court ordered Uber to stop Levandowski and all other employees from downloading or using any of the downloaded materials, ordered the return of all such materials to Waymo, and:

> With respect to Anthony Levandowski, defendants shall immediately (a) remove him from any role or responsibility pertaining to [self-driving technology]; (b) take all steps in their power to prevent him from having any communication on the subject . . . with any officer, director, employee, agent, supplier, consultant, or customer of defendants; and (c) prohibit him from consulting, copying, or otherwise using the downloaded materials in any way. Defendants shall instruct all their officers, directors, employees, agents, suppliers, consultants, and customers in writing of this prohibition, and further instruct them in writing to immediately report any suspected breaches thereof to the special master (or to the Court).

Id. at *13. The company fired Levandowski a few weeks later, and the case settled in February 2018 in the middle of trial, before Levandowski was called to testify. He was expected to raise his Fifth Amendment right against self-incrimination. Sarah Jeong, *Who Blinked First in Waymo v. Uber?*, The Verge, Feb. 9, 2018, https://www.theverge.com/2018/2/9/16997394/waymo-v-uber-trial-settlement-explained [https://perma.cc/W6FA-LPUU].

5. Lawful acts for an unlawful purpose. Consider Federal Trade Commission v. National Lead Co., 352 U.S. 419, 430 (1957). "Decrees often suppress a lawful device when it is used to carry out an unlawful purpose. In such instances the Court is obliged not only to suppress the unlawful practice but to take such reasonable action as is calculated to preclude the revival of the illegal practice." The commission had found a conspiracy to fix prices through the mechanism of a "zone delivered pricing system"—a system by which sellers set the same delivered price for all customers in various geographic zones. The commission's order prohibited the conspiracy; it also prohibited individual companies from using any zone delivered pricing system that resulted in prices identical to those offered by any competitor. The Court upheld the order. Individual selection of zone delivered pricing was lawful. But the practice readily lent itself to tacit or explicit price fixing; the history of its unlawful use was pervasive in the industry; there was no reason to think defendants had abandoned their purpose to fix prices if possible; and repeated proof of conspiracy on each claim of violation would be difficult.

Is this just a case where an order that precisely tracked the law would be difficult to enforce? Is it a matter of degree — of the closeness of fit between the prohibited conduct and its (previous? threatened? anticipated? feared?) use to achieve the prohibited purpose?

6. Culpability. The more egregious the violation, the greater the fears of further defiance or evasion, and the greater the desire for prophylactic injunctions that give a margin of safety to plaintiffs and the court. In Equal Employment Opportunity Commission v. Wilson Metal Casket Co., 24 F.3d 836 (6th Cir. 1994), the court enjoined Wilson, the owner of the company, from "asking any female employee to accompany him off the premises of the Company unless accompanied by at least one other employee," and from "kissing or placing his hands on any female employee in the work place." *Id.* at 842. The court did not disagree with Wilson's claim that "none of this conduct . . . is, in and of itself, unlawful." *Id.* But it held the injunction to be within the trial court's discretion to prevent recurrence of repeated incidents in which Wilson followed female employees, grabbed them, kissed them, fondled them sexually, sexually propositioned them, asked them to leave the premises with him, and in one case, forced oral sex and intercourse.

If Wilson had not been the owner, could the court have ordered the company to fire him? In fact, the owner was a corporation; Wilson owned the shares. If the injunction entered failed to work, could the court order the corporation to exclude Wilson from the premises and hire a manager?

7. Notices, monitoring, and programs to prevent violations. A common prophylactic injunction orders defendants to create programs to prevent recurring violations. A leading case is Bundy v. Jackson, 641 F.2d 934 (D.C. Cir. 1981). There, a single plaintiff suing on her own behalf proved that supervisors in a government agency were sexually harassing female employees in violation of the employment discrimination laws. The court enjoined further sexual harassment of any woman in the agency. It also ordered defendant to explain the policy against sexual harassment in posted notices and individual letters to all employees, to develop disciplinary measures for harassers, and "to develop other appropriate means of instructing employees . . . of the harmful nature of sexual harassment." *Id.* at 948 n.15. These provisions were reasonably designed to protect plaintiff from further illegal harassment, but like centralized administration in Marshall v. Goodyear, they ordered more than the statute required of its own force.

It is reasonably clear that the court in *Goodyear* would not have affirmed an injunction ordering centralized administration of personnel policies. Is that consistent with *Bundy*? Is it just that the prophylactic provisions approved in *Bundy* are much more closely related to the proven violation, and that the prophylactic provision implicitly rejected in *Marshall* would have required a larger and more structural change in defendant's operations?

Another common prophylactic provision is monitoring of defendant's compliance with the injunction. Defendant may be ordered to make periodic reports to the court or to plaintiff, or even to seek advance approval of future conduct. An example of the latter is United States v. Akers, 785 F.2d 814, 823 (9th Cir. 1986). Defendant had begun draining a swamp without getting a wetlands permit, and on at least some occasions, he had lied to the Corps of Engineers about what he was doing. The court affirmed an injunction ordering him to seek advance approval from the Corps for any dredging or filling operations, even those clearly exempt under the statute.

8. The abortion-protest cases. The Supreme Court has repeatedly reviewed constitutional challenges to prophylactic injunctions limiting protest at abortion clinics. In Madsen v. Women's Health Center, Inc., 512 U.S. 753, 768-775 (1994), the Court affirmed an injunction ordering protestors to stay off a clinic's property and to stay off public property within 36 feet of the clinic's property line; this had the effect of confining protestors to the other side of the street. It also affirmed an injunction against noise audible within the clinic during treatment hours. But it reversed a ban on signs visible from within the clinic, a ban on picketing within 300 feet of residences of clinic employees, and a provision ordering defendants not to approach, within 300 feet of the clinic, any person entering or leaving the clinic. Most of the injunction is set out in the Court's opinion.

In Schenck v. Pro-Choice Network, 519 U.S. 357, 377-385 (1997), the Court affirmed an injunction prohibiting demonstrations within 15 feet of the entrance to an abortion clinic. The injunction permitted two "sidewalk counselors" within that 15-foot zone, but it required them to cease and desist from talking to any person who asked them to leave; the Court also affirmed this cease-and-desist clause. But it reversed an injunction ordering demonstrators to stay 15 feet away from any person or vehicle seeking access to or leaving an abortion clinic. The injunction permitted one or two sidewalk counselors to approach any person in a nonthreatening way, but if the target attempted to walk away, the sidewalk counselors had to stop counseling and withdraw to a distance of at least 15 feet.

The applicable law of injunctions in these cases appears to have been state law, although no one took any notice of that. But defendants argued that the injunctions violated their freedom of speech, and that claim raised analogous issues. The Court held that the appropriate constitutional standard was that the injunction could restrict no more speech than necessary to serve the significant government interests in protecting the rights of the clinic and its patients. In *Schenck*, the Court held that the demonstrators' history of harassing patients and police officers and of obstructing entrances justified "a prophylactic measure." *Id.* at 382. It upheld the cease-and-desist clause on this basis, even though it rejected the district court's view that patients who did not wish to hear the protestors' message were entitled "to be left alone." *Id.* at 383. Justice Scalia, writing for three dissenters, argued that rejection of the district court's basis for the injunction required the Court to vacate the injunction and remand—that an appellate court could not decide whether the cease-and-desist injunction was narrowly tailored to serve the interests relied on by the majority when the district court had made no such finding.

There are intense moral commitments and deep mistrust on both sides of the controversy in these cases. Both sides are exercising constitutional rights that the court must protect. Large numbers of people are active in a small space. Conflict and misunderstanding, testing of limits and overreaching, emotional reactions, inconsistent perceptions and accounts of what happened—all these are inevitable. The judicial need for bright-line rules can be overwhelming.

In *Madsen*, the court initially enjoined defendants from blocking or interfering with public access to the clinic and from physically abusing persons entering or leaving the clinic. But when do approaching, soliciting, talking to, and trying to get the attention of a target cross over into blocking, interfering, or abusing? The two sides draw the line at very different places, sometimes at equally unreasonable places.

Any standard that requires such judgments is likely to be unworkable unless the court posts a magistrate to adjudicate all disputes immediately and at the scene. After six months' experience, finding that crowds of protestors in the street and in front of the driveway had obstructed access to the clinic despite the earlier injunction, the trial court granted a new injunction with the prophylactic provisions discussed above.

9. Meeting your friends? The California court upheld a preliminary injunction ordering 38 named and about 100 unnamed members of a street gang from "standing, sitting, walking, driving, gathering or appearing anywhere in public view with any other defendant herein, or with any other known . . . member [of the gang]." People ex rel. Gallo v. Acuna, 929 P.2d 596 (Cal. 1997). The injunction is quoted in Justice Mosk's dissent at 624-625. It also contained numerous provisions directed at specific illegal conduct. The evidence was that the gang had taken over a four-block area to such an extent that residents were afraid to leave their homes. The court held that the gang could be enjoined as a public nuisance.

The injunction also raises significant questions about how to bind the unnamed defendants, questions that go largely undiscussed in the opinion because none of the unnamed defendants appeared in court. The injunction could not be enforced against any defendants until they received actual notice of it. The power to bind absent parties to injunctions is considered in section 9.A.4.

10. File sharing. The court of appeals held it an abuse of discretion not to issue a prophylactic injunction in Capitol Records, Inc. v. Thomas-Rassett, 692 F.3d 899 (8th Cir. 2012). The district judge ordered Thomas-Rassett not to download or upload any copyrighted music. The court of appeals directed the judge to add an injunction against making any copyrighted music available for others to upload from Thomas-Rassett's computer and then download to their own. The court assumed (the legal issue was disputed) that simply making music available is not an infringement if no one uploads it. But actual uploading can be difficult to prove, and Thomas-Rassett was a willful infringer who had attempted to conceal her misconduct and thus had demonstrated "a proclivity for unlawful conduct," and these facts justified the prophylactic provision. *Id.* at 906. She did not oppose the broadening of the injunction.

11. The source of law that authorizes prophylaxis. Consider Maritrans GP Inc. v. Pepper, Hamilton & Scheetz, 602 A.2d 1277 (Pa. 1992), ordering a major Philadelphia law firm to cease representing competitors of a former client from which it had received confidential information of great value to competitors.

> A court may restrain conduct which it feels may develop into a breach of ethics; it "is not bound to sit back and wait for a probability to ripen into a certainty." United States v. RMI Co., 467 F. Supp. 915, 923 (W.D. Pa. 1979). The courts do not have to wait until the derelict attorney appears before it. . . .
>
> It might be theoretically possible to argue that Pepper and [its partners] should merely be enjoined from revealing the confidential material they have acquired from Maritrans but such an injunction would be difficult, if not impossible, to administer. As fiduciaries, Pepper and [its partners] can be fully enjoined from representing Maritrans' competitors as that would create too great a danger that Maritrans' confidential relationship with Pepper and [its partners] would be breached.

602 A.2d at 1284, 1287.

This is just *PepsiCo* applied to attorney-client relationships. But other passages suggest that the court believed that Pepper's representation of the competitors violated conflict-of-interest rules. On that theory, the substantive law created the prophylactic rule, and the court was merely enforcing the substantive rule. There is nothing controversial about that.

The remedies controversy is squarely presented when the substantive law does not create a prophylactic rule but the court issues a prophylactic injunction at the remedial stage, invoking remedial power to prohibit conduct that will not violate any substantive law. When the court enforces a common law rule, it is often unclear whether it is enforcing a prophylactic substantive rule or entering a prophylactic remedy. The controversy is greatest when the relevant substantive law was enacted by a legislature or constitutional convention and the court's prophylactic remedy clearly goes beyond what is required by the substantive law.

12. The burden of prophylaxis. The injunctions in *PepsiCo* and *Maritrans* seriously restricted defendants' economic activity; compliance was expensive. The notices and complaint procedures in *Bundy* were not free goods, but by comparison to *PepsiCo* and *Maritrans*, both the cost and the degree of interference with defendant's legitimate operations were minimal. Doesn't that have to matter? In *Akers* (note 7), the court emphasized that preclearing of exempt operations would not be onerous because the injunction required the Corps of Engineers to respond within 15 days.

The Securities and Exchange Commission commonly bars defendants who have committed fraud from acting as directors or officers of any public company. An example is SEC v. Posner, 16 F.3d 520 (2d Cir. 1994). This burdensome prophylactic remedy is now authorized by the Securities Enforcement Remedies and Penny Stock Reform Act, 15 U.S.C. §78u(d)(2), but even before that, courts justified it on the basis of "'general equitable powers' to fashion appropriate relief." 16 F.3d at 521.

There is a similar remedy, without statutory authorization, in a Federal Trade Commission case. See FTC v. Think Achievement Corp., 144 F. Supp. 2d 1013 (N.D. Ind. 2000), *aff'd without discussion of the injunction*, 312 F.3d 259 (7th Cir. 2002). The district court relied on defendants' "extensive and prolonged engagement in fraudulent, deceptive trade practices [and] the failure of prior enforcement efforts in requiring lawful activity and stopping unlawful activity" to conclude that defendants would continue to violate the law unless barred from the industry. 144 F. Supp. 2d at 1018. The opinion also collects federal cases approving prophylactic relief.

13. Prophylaxis and the rightful position. Do prophylactic remedies give plaintiff more than her rightful position, by enjoining conduct that is not wrongful? Or are they essential to achieving the rightful position in practice and not just in theory? Professor Schoenbrod, who has criticized injunctions that in his view unduly interfere with the other branches of government, also defends the necessity of prophylactic relief:

> The injunction's *aim* must be the plaintiff's rightful position, but to achieve that aim, its *terms* may impose conditions on the defendant that require actions going beyond the plaintiff's rightful position. . . . The injunction's terms . . . may have to go beyond the plaintiff's rightful position to avoid falling short of that position.

He would also require that plaintiff present "a factor not reflected in the rule's formulation that justifies departing from it." David S. Schoenbrod, *The Measure of an Injunction: A Principle to Replace Balancing the Equities and Tailoring the Remedy*, 72 Minn. L. Rev. 627, 678-679, 682 (1988). (Schoenbrod's title requires explanation. He uses "balancing the equities" to refer to remedies that do *less* than restore plaintiff to the rightful position, usually because of some countervailing hardship or other equitable consideration on defendant's side. He uses "tailoring the remedy" to refer to decisions that say the remedy should do *no more* than restore plaintiff to the rightful position. The Supreme Court sometimes says in such cases that the remedy must be tailored to the violation.)

Professor Thomas argues that prophylactic injunctions are ubiquitous and conceptually simple. Tracy A. Thomas, *The Prophylactic Remedy: Normative Principles and*

Definitional Parameters of Broad Injunctive Relief, 52 Buff. L. Rev. 301 (2004). She says prophylactic injunctions are limited by two principles: They must be aimed at the legally cognizable harm identified in the case, not at any other harm; and the factual connection between the prophylactic order and the legally relevant harm "must be sufficiently close to justify the inclusion of the conduct in the court's order," *id.* at 342-343, a requirement she analogizes to proximate cause. Does that help?

Consider three possible formulations of the principle that injunctions should be aimed at preserving plaintiff's rightful position:

a. The injunction should keep plaintiff as close as possible to the rightful position.
b. The injunction should keep plaintiff as close as possible to the rightful position, subject to the constraint that the injunction should never make plaintiff better off than the rightful position.
c. The injunction should keep plaintiff as close as possible to the rightful position, subject to the constraint that the injunction should never leave plaintiff worse off than the rightful position.

The principal difference lies in allocation of the risk of error. Formulation *a* divides that risk between the parties; formulation *b* leaves that risk entirely on plaintiff; formulation *c* leaves it entirely on defendant. Only formulation *b* would wholly preclude prophylactic relief.

There is another difference in the three formulations, derivative from the first. The constraints in formulations *b* and *c* would increase the frequency and magnitude of deviations from the rightful position. Formulation *b* might eliminate very modest provisions, like posting notices in *Bundy,* that reduce the risk of serious violations of the underlying substantive law. Formulation *c* might authorize highly expensive and intrusive remedies that only slightly reduce the risk of violations.

Formulation *a* might plausibly be modified to add the principle, familiar from the law of compensatory damages, that "the wrongdoer shall bear the risk of the uncertainty which his own wrong has created." Bigelow v. RKO Radio Pictures, reprinted in section 2.E.5. That does not mean that plaintiff always gets the highest possible estimate of damages; neither should it mean that plaintiff always gets the most expansive possible injunction. It ought to mean that if other considerations are approximately equal, doubts should be resolved in favor of plaintiff, and that it is better to give plaintiff a little too much than not enough. But none of that is very precise. Is it possible to state a more precise standard?

AN ASIDE: PREVENTIVE RELIEF AT LAW

1. Law and equity. The most common legal remedy is damages; the most common equitable remedy is the injunction. Damages compensate for harm; injunctions seek to prevent harm. An award of damages authorizes plaintiff to have the sheriff seize defendant's property; an injunction seeks to coerce defendant's behavior. It is common to speak of these differences as though they applied to all of law and equity. But in certain circumstances the law courts gave relief through specialized writs that look remarkably like injunctions. These remedies were legal, not equitable, but like injunctions, they were both preventive and coercive. Some of those remedies are still available.

2. Mandamus. Mandamus is an order to a public or corporate official, directing her to perform a ministerial duty. Mandamus can be used to require corporate officers to call a special meeting requested by the requisite number of shareholders, Auer v.

Dressel, 118 N.E.2d 590 (N.Y. 1954); to require election officials to place a candidate on the ballot, State ex rel. Stevens v. Fairfield County Board of Elections, 2018 WL 1663346 (Ohio March 29, 2018); to require a recalcitrant school board to reinstate a teacher who had not been notified of her dismissal by a statutory deadline; Victor Federation of Teachers v. Victor School District No. 7, 414 P.3d 1284 (Mont. 2018); or to compel the Secretary of State to issue a commission to a newly appointed judge, Marbury v. Madison, 5 U.S. (1 Cranch) 137, 168-173 (1803). These orders are indistinguishable from mandatory injunctions in practical effect. Often either remedy is available; sometimes, for reasons of history, local practice, or quirks in the jurisdiction and venue statutes, one is available and one is not. The federal statute grants federal jurisdiction over "any action in the nature of mandamus to compel an officer or employee of the United States or any agency thereof to perform a duty owed to the plaintiff." 28 U.S.C. §1361.

The duty to be enforced must be clear and nondiscretionary; the court cannot substitute its policy judgment for the official's. But difficult legal questions do not preclude mandamus if the official's duty is clear once the legal questions have been answered. 13th Regional Corp. v. United States Department of Interior, 654 F.2d 758, 760 (D.C. Cir. 1980).

3. Prohibition. Prohibition is an order to an inferior court or a quasi-judicial agency to prevent it from exceeding its jurisdiction or abusing its authority. It is much like an injunction against filing or prosecuting a lawsuit, but with two essential differences. First, a court with equity powers can enjoin suits in courts that are in no sense inferior to it, including courts of other jurisdictions and courts of law before the merger of law and equity. Second, and related, the equity court will never enjoin the other court or its judge; the injunction is addressed only to the plaintiff. The writ of prohibition is addressed to the inferior tribunal as well as the parties.

In modern legal systems, prohibition is a substitute for interlocutory appeal, and its availability depends on the strength of the jurisdiction's commitment to the rule that appeals should await a final judgment. In some jurisdictions, such as California, prohibition is rather freely available to review all sorts of interlocutory orders. In the federal courts, the writ is usually called mandamus instead of prohibition. Mandamus to federal district judges is supposed to be available only in extraordinary circumstances, where the judge has usurped authority or clearly abused her discretion, and where no other remedy is available. Kerr v. United States District Court, 426 U.S. 394, 402 (1976). But the appellate court often discusses the merits in deciding whether there has been a clear abuse of discretion. Thus, even when mandamus is denied, the parties may get an effective advisory opinion from the court of appeals. The practice is carefully reviewed in Robert S. Berger, *The Mandamus Power of the United States Courts of Appeals: A Complex and Confused Means of Appellate Control*, 31 Buff. L. Rev. 37 (1982).

Cheney v. United States District Court, 542 U.S. 367 (2004), in which plaintiffs sought disclosure of who advised the Vice President on energy policy, was a mandamus petition (*mandamus* as the federal label for prohibition) to limit allegedly overbroad discovery. The court of appeals said the scope of discovery is discretionary and not reviewable on mandamus; the Supreme Court said it was reviewable on mandamus here, where the Vice President claimed that excessive discovery amounted to judicial interference with the executive branch to an extent inconsistent with the separation of powers. The underlying case was a mandamus petition in the sense of note 2, to compel disclosure of certain information.

4. Certiorari. Certiorari is an order to a lower court directing it to deliver the record in the case for discretionary review by a higher court. It is well known, however mysterious the word might be, because petitions for certiorari are the principal path to review in the Supreme Court of the United States. Some state supreme courts also use certiorari, and others use similar discretionary systems for choosing their cases without using the word.

5. Habeas corpus. Habeas corpus is an order to a person holding another in custody, directing him to bring the prisoner to court and justify his further detention. If the detention is not justified, the court will order the prisoner's release. Like injunction, mandamus, and prohibition, habeas corpus takes the form of a personal command to the defendant.

Both state and federal constitutions guarantee the right to habeas corpus. Habeas corpus is a critical safeguard against arbitrary imprisonment; so long as the writ is obeyed, no one can be imprisoned without judicial review. Habeas corpus in its original and most fundamental use is illustrated in Boumediene v. Bush, 553 U.S. 723 (2008), and Hamdi v. Rumsfeld, 542 U.S. 507 (2004), both holding that even in the extraordinary conditions of the war on terror, persons held by the executive branch without charges, hearing, or counsel are entitled to some level of judicial review of their detentions. Hundreds of Guantánamo prisoners were subsequently released, some on habeas petitions and many more in anticipation of habeas petitions, and scholars credit these decisions with largely ending torture and secret American prisons in foreign countries. Jack Goldsmith, *Power and Constraint* 178-181, 188-196 (W.W. Norton 2012).

The most common use of habeas corpus today is to permit further judicial review of criminal convictions. After a criminal defendant has exhausted his appeals, he can renew constitutional and jurisdictional attacks on his conviction in a petition for habeas corpus. This use of the writ enables defendants convicted in state courts to get review of alleged federal errors in federal district courts; without the writ, the only federal review would be in the Supreme Court, where review is confined to questions of general public importance.

Habeas corpus to review criminal convictions is controversial. A person unjustly imprisoned should be released no matter when the error is discovered, but multiple rounds of judicial review are expensive, and only a tiny portion of habeas petitioners are actually released. For better or worse, both Congress and the Supreme Court have sharply restricted the scope and availability of habeas corpus review of criminal convictions. Many of these restrictions were codified in Title I of the Antiterrorism and Effective Death Penalty Act of 1996, codified in various sections of Title 28 (between §2244 and §2266).

Habeas corpus is also used in child custody cases when a person having physical control of a child refuses to release the child. For a codification of the practice, see Tex. Family Code §157.372.

3.   *Repairing the Consequences of Past Wrongful Conduct*

FORSTER v. BOSS
97 F.3d 1127 (8th Cir. 1996)

Before RICHARD S. ARNOLD, Chief Judge, WOLLMAN, Circuit Judge, and KORNMANN, District Judge.

RICHARD S. ARNOLD, Chief Judge.

This case arises out of the sale of property fronting on the Lake of the Ozarks in Missouri. The plaintiffs are the buyers of the property, James D. Forster and Joann

Forster. The defendants are the sellers, Patrick W. Boss and Janet L. Boss. The District Court awarded plaintiffs both damages, for fraud and breach of contract, and injunctive relief. Defendants appeal, arguing that plaintiffs are receiving what amounts to a double recovery: an injunction that makes them whole plus damages to compensate them for the loss of the very rights that the injunction has guaranteed. We agree with this contention in part, and accordingly affirm in part, reverse in part, and remand for further proceedings.

When defendants, the Bosses, agreed to sell the property to the Forsters, they represented that the Forsters could obtain a permit for a boat dock in front of their newly acquired property. In fact, unknown to the Forsters, the sellers had a boat-dock permit of their own that made it impossible for the Forsters to obtain the permit they had been promised. The defendants do not contest the finding made below that they were guilty of fraud in this respect. And, in fact, when the plaintiffs applied to Union Electric Company (which created the lake and has the right to grant permits) for a permit, their application was denied on the ground that the sellers, the defendants, already had a conflicting permit. To compensate the plaintiffs for this fraud, the jury awarded $12,250 in compensatory damages and $10,000 in punitive damages.

The other claim for damages on which the plaintiffs prevailed had to do with a swim dock. When the property was sold, defendants promised that they would remove their swim dock from in front of the transferred property. They did not keep this promise. The jury awarded $2,500 in compensatory damages to the plaintiffs on account of this breach of contract. . . .

The major issue on appeal arises because damages were not the only relief secured by the plaintiffs. They also got a permanent injunction ordering defendants to remove the offending swim dock. In addition, and most important, they got their boat-dock permit from Union Electric. Union was a party defendant in the District Court. It took no active part in the trial, except to enter into a stipulation agreeing that if the Court should hold plaintiffs entitled to a permit under their contract with defendants, Union would grant the permit to plaintiffs and revoke the permit previously granted to defendants. This in fact occurred, so plaintiffs now have their permit and defendants have lost theirs. No future permit may be granted to defendants that would interfere with plaintiffs' rights.

In this situation, defendants argue that the injunction has made plaintiffs whole. They have both [the swim dock removed] and their boat-dock permit. Thus, the property transferred to them has exactly the characteristics defendants agreed it would have: it has a boat-dock permit attached to it, and it is not encumbered by defendants' swim dock. If plaintiffs also receive, as damages, money to compensate them for the difference in the value of the property as promised and the value of the property as transferred, they have received a double recovery. Plaintiffs have, in effect, received not only damages for fraud and breach of contract, but also specific performance. They have both the money and the property, and are in a better position than they would have been in had there been no fraud or breach of contract in the first place.

We find this argument compelling. Plaintiffs point out that under Missouri law the measure of damages for fraud in connection with the sale of land is the difference between the value of the land on the date of sale as represented, and the value of the land on the date of sale as actually conveyed. The sale took place in 1991. At that time, according to the jury, the land as represented was worth $12,250 more than the land as conveyed. Nothing that happened thereafter, for example, an injunction guaranteeing plaintiffs their boat-dock permit, can change those facts. We understand the argument but find it too simplistic. If the argument were accepted, the entry of an injunction, or the obtaining of the boat-dock permit in some other way, would be wholly irrelevant to the recovery of damages, even though one or the other of these events occurred on the day immediately following the sale. This does not make sense. It is true, of course, that the lapse of time was greater than one day here—about three years, in fact. It is entirely possible that plaintiffs sustained some sort of damages because they had to wait for the complete fulfillment of the terms of the sale. The case, however, was not tried on that theory, and there is no evidence in this record on which damages of this interim kind could be calculated.

Plaintiffs argue that they sought redress for the violation of two separate legal rights: their right not to be defrauded and the "littoral rights" appurtenant to the purchased property. In the abstract, this proposition makes sense, but it breaks down when we consider it in the practical context of this case. The very littoral rights that plaintiffs say are protected by the injunction—the right to a boat-dock permit and the right to have defendants' swim dock moved—are the same rights for the loss of which the award of damages is designed to compensate. We cannot escape the proposition that the injunction has made plaintiffs whole in the very respects for which they sought damages. To allow them to keep both the compensatory damages and the injunction would be a double recovery.

Defendants cite Harris v. Union Electric Co., 766 S.W.2d 80 (Mo. 1989), and the citation is apt. There, plaintiffs had recovered damages on account of the inadequate description of certain redemption rights in a prospectus for bonds issued by Union Electric. They subsequently sought an injunction in a separate action to prevent Union Electric from redeeming the bonds. The Supreme Court of Missouri held that such injunctive relief was improper. The defect in the description of plaintiffs' redemption rights had already been fully remedied by the recovery of damages. They had no right to the further relief of an injunction forbidding the redemption of the bonds. Union Electric had, so to speak, bought the right to redeem the bonds, despite the prospectus's inadequate description of the redemption rights, by paying the damages awarded in the earlier action. Plaintiffs seek to distinguish the case by emphasizing their point that the injunction in this case is designed to protect their littoral rights, which, they insist, are entirely separate from their right not to be defrauded. As we have already explained, we do not agree with this contention in the circumstances of the present case. The damages award has already, in effect, paid plaintiffs in full for the deprivation of their littoral rights.

We conclude that the case must be remanded for further proceedings. On remand, it will be up to plaintiffs to elect which remedy they want—compensatory damages or the injunction. We think, however, that they should be allowed to retain the $10,000 award of punitive damages in either event. Defendants' conduct in this case was abusive, and they do not argue on appeal that the award of punitive damages was not based on sufficient evidence. Punitive damages are not designed to compensate anybody.

They are designed to punish misconduct and to deter future misconduct. The award of punitive damages, therefore, is not duplicative of the relief contained in the injunction. . . . If it is necessary under Missouri law for some compensatory damages to be awarded in order to support any award of punitive damages, the District Court is instructed to award plaintiffs compensatory damages of one dollar on their fraud claim, plus the punitive damages of $10,000.

To the extent that it holds defendants liable, the judgment is affirmed. To the extent that it allows plaintiffs to receive both compensatory damages and an injunction, the judgment is reversed. The cause is remanded for further proceedings consistent with this opinion.

KORNMANN, District Judge, concurring.

I concur. Most respectfully, I write separately only to express my opinion that plaintiffs elected a remedy. They sought and received an injunction and the fruits of it, the boat dock permit. It would be unjust for plaintiffs to receive the dock permit, as they already have, keep it, and also recover damages for the claimed loss of the dock permit. My concern is that if plaintiffs are simply allowed to "give up" the injunction, our decision may have little practical benefit for defendants who will already have lost the permit and will still owe the monetary damages. It may be that the dock permit cannot be retrieved by defendants, despite the lifting of the injunction. In the alternative, I would have the District Court determine if plaintiffs have made the election, the mandate being that plaintiffs are not to be allowed to receive and retain the dock permit as well as the $12,250.

NOTES ON REPARATIVE INJUNCTIONS

1. Injunctions after the wrong. In *Forster*, the wrongful conduct—the fraud with respect to the permit and the breach of contract with respect to the swim dock—is in the past. Those wrongful acts cannot be prevented. But it is still possible to undo their consequences, or more precisely, it is still possible to prevent the future harm those wrongful acts threaten to cause. The permit can be transferred, and the swim dock can be removed, thus averting further harm.

2. "Preventive" and "reparative" injunctions. Professor Fiss coined the label "reparative" for injunctions like the one in Forster v. Boss. He distinguished such injunctions from what he called "preventive" injunctions, like those requested in the cases from *Almurbati* to *PepsiCo*. Owen M. Fiss, *The Civil Rights Injunction* 8-12 (Indiana Univ. Press 1978). The distinction is useful, but it can be overstated, and the label "preventive" can be confusing. All injunctions are preventive in the most fundamental sense; they seek to prevent harm from wrongful conduct. The distinction between preventive and reparative injunctions is between preventing the wrongful act (transferring prisoners to a place where they will be tortured; failing to deliver a dock permit at closing), and preventing some or all of the harmful consequences of that act (retrieving transferred prisoners, thus avoiding any further torture; belatedly transferring the permit, thus avoiding further time on the lakeshore without a dock).

3. Practical differences. The distinction has no doctrinal significance, and the boundary can be fuzzy on occasion, especially with respect to a continuing course of wrongful conduct. But the distinction is helpfully descriptive. Preventive and reparative injunctions present some of the same issues, but each also presents distinctive issues that rarely arise with respect to the other.

a. Ripeness, causation, and scope. Reparative injunctions do not raise ripeness issues, because the wrongful act has already occurred. But they may raise issues of causation, or remoteness. Were all the harms plaintiff complains of actually caused by defendant's wrongful act? And how far should defendant be required to go in eliminating every vestige of the harm she caused? These issues do not arise if a preventive injunction prevents the wrongful act from being committed in the first place. Put another way, the scope of what Fiss calls a preventive injunction is based on the scope of the threatened violation; the scope of a reparative injunction is based on the scope of the harms flowing from the past violation.

b. Timing. Preventive injunctions are more likely to raise another sort of timing issue: Can the court hear the case, or enough of it, make a decision, and issue an injunction before the wrongful act occurs? Sometimes the consequences of a past wrongful act are equally imminent, but often, reparative injunction cases can be litigated on the court's regular schedule. No doubt the plaintiffs in Forster v. Boss were eager to get their boat dock, but damage plaintiffs are equally eager to get paid. No amount of delay in *Forster* would have made it impossible to transfer the permit.

c. Practicality. Reparative injunctions are more likely to raise issues of practicality. It is easy to belatedly transfer a permit, but sometimes it is difficult or impossible to reverse the consequences of a past violation of law. If defendant cut down a tree, it is impossible to restore that tree, and even if defendant plants a new tree, it may be many years before the new tree approximates the old. If defendant segregated a school system, monopolized an industry, or polluted a marsh, reparative injunctions may be possible but very difficult. See Washington v. Grace, 2012 WL 398763, *2 n.1 (M.D. Penn. 2012) ("one of the central recurring assertions in [the pro se prisoner]'s pleadings is that his genitals are shrinking and prison officials are responsible for this process. Indeed, [his] prior complaints have, *inter alia*, requested that we reverse the process and restore him to his former stature, something that is plainly beyond the power of any court to achieve.").

4. Preventive, reparative, and prophylactic injunctions. The distinction between preventive and reparative injunctions is independent of the distinction between prophylactic and nonprophylactic injunctions. Either preventive or reparative injunctions can contain prophylactic provisions. "The judicial remedy for a proven violation of law will often include commands that the law does not impose on the community at large." Chicago Teachers Union v. Hudson, 475 U.S. 292, 309 n.22 (1986).

5. The availability of reparative injunctions. Defendants occasionally argue that the court cannot order reparative relief—that it cannot attempt to undo the past violation. Such an argument is either frivolous, or, more commonly, an overly broad statement of some more serious argument, such as an argument about practicality.

a. Bell v. Southwell. This sort of litigation is illustrated by Bell v. Southwell, 376 F.2d 659 (5th Cir. 1967), ordering a new election for Justice of the Peace of Georgia's 789th Militia District. The incumbent justice had died, necessitating a special election, and the special election had been marred by racial intimidation and egregious racial discrimination at the polling places. The federal district judge enjoined any repetition at future elections (a preventive injunction aimed at future violations), but he refused to order a new election (a reparative injunction aimed at the consequences of the past violation), commenting that "the implications of such a decision would be staggering." *Id.* at 662. That may depend on the magnitude of the election—although the magnitude of the office cuts both ways. The more important the office, the greater of the wrong of a flawed or stolen election, and the greater the difficulty of attempting to rerun that election.

For the 789th Militia District, the courts could handle it. The new election provided a fairer process, and the black candidate got 200 more votes than she had gotten the first time—an increase of 62 percent. But the winning white candidate also got more votes (we infer from skimpy data that minor candidates who were on the ballot the first time had dropped out), and the white candidate's margin of victory was not much changed. Vote totals in the first election are reported *id.* at 660 n.2; totals for the second election are reported in Alan Anderson, *Local Black History Chronology*, available at *www.sumtercountyhistory.com/history/BlackHx.htm*. Thanks to James Fischer for finding this data. Other cases rerunning elections, and statutes authorizing that remedy, are collected in Steven J. Mulroy, *Right Without a Remedy? The "Butterfly Ballot"*

Case and Court-Ordered Federal Election "Revotes," 10 Geo. Mason L. Rev. 215, 226-236 (2001).

b. California v. American Stores. In California v. American Stores Co., 495 U.S. 271 (1990), the argument against reparative injunctions was based on statutory text. California sued under §16 of the Clayton Act, now 15 U.S.C. §26, for an injunction ordering American to sell the stores it had recently acquired in a merger with one of its largest competitors. Section 16 provides that any person "shall be entitled to sue for and have injunctive relief . . . against threatened loss or damage by a violation of the antitrust laws . . . when and under the same conditions and principles as injunctive relief against threatened conduct that will cause loss or damage is granted by courts of equity."

American argued that a §16 injunction against "*threatened* loss or damage" could not be issued after the merger was completed. The Court characterized this as distinguishing "prohibitory and mandatory relief," and it rejected the distinction as illusory. Although the merger was completed, harm from the merger was still threatened because the harm would persist far into the future. 495 U.S. at 282-283.

American also argued that a §16 injunction could reach only "threatened *conduct*," and could not change an existing corporate structure. The Court found that distinction illusory as well. Divestiture would be conduct, and operating the merged stores would be conduct. The Court characterized divestiture as "the most suitable remedy" and as "simple, relatively easy to administer, and sure." *Id.* at 283-284, 281.

6. Reversing last-minute violations. Perhaps the simplest example of reparative injunctions is where defendant beats plaintiff and the court to the punch, completing the unlawful act before the court can enjoin it. The court can order the transaction reversed if that is physically possible. "It has long been established that where a defendant with notice in an injunction proceeding completes the acts sought to be enjoined the court may by mandatory injunction restore the status quo." Porter v. Lee, 328 U.S. 246, 251 (1946). In *Porter*, a landlord sought to evict his tenants in violation of World War II price controls. The government sued to enjoin the eviction; while the injunction suit was pending, the landlord completed the eviction and the tenants moved out. The Court said the government was entitled to an injunction ordering the landlord to let them move back in.

NOTES ON COORDINATING MULTIPLE REMEDIES

1. The remedies in *Forster*. On the issue squarely decided in *Forster*, isn't it a no-brainer? How did the district court get it wrong? Didn't that court mechanically apply a damage rule—difference in value on the date of sale—without thinking about what that rule was trying to accomplish? The focus on the date of sale deals with changes in value, not with changes in what was conveyed. What if the seller failed to convey when scheduled? Could the buyer get specific performance, and also recover the entire value of the land in damages, because nothing that happened after the day of sale could affect the measure of damages?

2. Damages, reparative injunctions, and the rightful position. The concurring opinion emphasizes a point of general importance. The court, and to some extent the plaintiff, have a choice: The court can order delivery of a dock permit, or it can compensate for the failure to deliver one. More generally, where it is possible to prevent harm by injunction, the court can prevent it, or let it happen and compensate for it. For each element of harm, the rightful position requires that the court do one or the other, but not both. Just as there can be no double recovery in damages, there can be no double recovery in injunctions, or in a combination of damages and injunctions. This is an application of the one-satisfaction rule, briefly discussed at the end of Chapter 1. Note that it was irrelevant that the plaintiffs' offered two legal theories—fraud and littoral rights. What mattered is that both theories led to the same harm, the loss of the boat dock.

There is a similar holding in Home Pride Foods, Inc. v. Johnson, 634 N.W.2d 774, 784 (Neb. 2001), a trade secret case. Plaintiff could not recover either damages or restitution for future sales, because the court had enjoined future sales. The court collects similar cases from California and Colorado. For harm that has already happened, and for future harm that can no longer be prevented (such as permanent disability), a reparative injunction is impossible, and damages are the only option.

3. Temporary and permanent damages. The law of nuisance distinguishes permanent damages—awarded when the nuisance appears to be permanent, and often measured by the value of plaintiff's property before and after the creation of the nuisance—from temporary damages, where the future course of the nuisance is unpredictable, and damages are measured by the harm the nuisance has inflicted up to the time of trial. The distinction is reviewed at length in Schneider National Carriers, Inc. v. Bates, 147 S.W.3d 264 (Tex. 2004), which collects cases and different tests from around the country. *Forster* is not a nuisance case, but the issue is similar. The jury's award based on the value of the land with and without a dock permit is a permanent measure of damages, but the damage turned out to be only temporary, because the injunction solved the problem. As the court notes, damages for the delay—for three years without a permit—would not have been a double recovery. *Schneider* also collects Texas cases from a variety of contexts on the point at issue in *Forster*: that awarding damages for harm that an injunction prevented would be a double recovery. *Id.* at 284-285.

WINSTON RESEARCH CORP. v. MINNESOTA MINING & MANUFACTURING CO.

350 F.2d 134 (9th Cir. 1965)

Before JERTBERG and BROWNING, Circuit Judges, and FOLEY, District Judge.

BROWNING, Circuit Judge.

The Mincom Division of the Minnesota Mining and Manufacturing Company developed an improved precision tape recorder and reproducer. Somewhat later, Winston Research Corporation developed a similar machine. Mincom alleged that the Winston machine was developed by former employees of Mincom, including Johnson and Tobias, by using confidential information which they had acquired while working on the Mincom machine, and sued for damages and an injunction. The district court granted Mincom an injunction, but denied damages. Both sides appealed.

I . . .

For some uses of precision tape recorder/reproducers, the time interval between coded signals must be recorded and reproduced with great accuracy. [Mincom developed an improved solution to this problem.]

In May 1962, when Mincom had substantially completed the research phase of its program and was beginning the development of a production prototype, Johnson, who was in charge of Mincom's program, left Mincom's employment. He joined Tobias, who had previously been discharged as Mincom's sales manager, in forming Winston Research Corporation. In late 1962, Winston contracted with the government to develop a precision tape reproducer. Winston hired many of the technicians who had participated in the development of the Mincom machine to work on the design and development of the Winston machine.

In approximately fourteen months, Winston completed a machine having the same low time-displacement error as the Mincom machine.

III . . .

The district court found, and Winston concedes, that Johnson and the other former Mincom employees based Winston's development program upon the same approach to the problem of achieving a low time-displacement error as they had pursued in developing the Mincom machine. The district court further found that this general approach was not a trade secret of Mincom's. Finally, the district court found that the particular embodiment of these general concepts in the Mincom machine was Mincom's trade secret, and had been improperly utilized by the former Mincom employees in developing the Winston machine. . .

IV . . .

The district court enjoined Winston Research Corporation, Johnson, and Tobias from disclosing or using Mincom's trade secrets in any manner for a period of two years from the date of judgment—March 1, 1964. The court also required the assignment of certain patent applications to Mincom. No damages were awarded. . . .

Mincom argues that the injunction should have been permanent, or at least for a substantially longer period. Winston contends that no injunctive relief was appropriate.

Mincom was, of course, entitled to protection of its trade secrets for as long as they remained secret. The district court's decision to limit the duration of injunctive relief was necessarily premised upon a determination that Mincom's trade secrets would shortly be fully disclosed, through no fault of Winston, as a result of public announcements, demonstrations, and sales and deliveries of Mincom machines. Mincom has not seriously challenged this implicit finding, and we think the record fully supports it.

Mincom argues that notwithstanding public disclosure subsequent to its former employees' breach of faith, Mincom was entitled to a permanent injunction under the *Shellmar* rule. Winston responds that under the competing *Conmar* rule public disclosure of Mincom's trade secrets would end the obligation of Mincom's former employees to maintain the information in confidence, and that neither the employees nor their privies may be enjoined beyond the date of disclosure.[6]

Thus, Winston's argument would bar any injunction at all once there was public disclosure, and Mincom's argument would require an injunction in perpetuity without regard to public disclosure. The district court rejected both extremes and granted

---

6. The two rules take their names from Shellmar Products Co. v. Allen-Qualley Co., 87 F.2d 104 (7th Cir. 1936), and Conmar Products Corp. v. Universal Slide Fastener Co., 172 F.2d 150 (2d Cir. 1949). . . .

an injunction for the period which it concluded would be sufficient both to deny Winston unjust enrichment and to protect Mincom from injury from the wrongful disclosure and use of Mincom's trade secrets by its former employees prior to public disclosure.

We think the district court's approach was sound. A permanent injunction would subvert the public's interest in allowing technical employees to make full use of their knowledge and skill and in fostering research and development. On the other hand, denial of any injunction at all would leave the faithless employee unpunished where, as here, no damages were awarded; and he and his new employer would retain the benefit of a headstart over legitimate competitors who did not have access to the trade secrets until they were publicly disclosed. By enjoining use of the trade secrets for the approximate period it would require a legitimate Mincom competitor to develop a successful machine after public disclosure of the secret information, the district court denied the employees any advantage from their faithlessness, placed Mincom in the position it would have occupied if the breach of confidence had not occurred prior to the public disclosure, and imposed the minimum restraint consistent with the realization of these objectives upon the utilization of the employees' skills. . . .

Mincom argues that in any event a two-year injunction from March 1, 1964, was not sufficient to overcome the wrongful advantage obtained by Winston. Mincom points out that four years were required to develop its machine, whereas Winston developed its machine in fourteen months. For this reason, and because the injunction was stayed for some time, Mincom argues that injunctive relief should be granted for at least three years from the completion of appellate review.

As we have noted, the appropriate injunctive period is that which competitors would require after public disclosure to develop a competitive machine. The time (fourteen months) which Winston in fact took with the aid of the very disclosure and use complained of by Mincom would seem to be a fair measure of the proper period. The district court granted an injunction for a somewhat longer period, presumably because the Mincom machine was built in such a way as to require some time for persons unfamiliar with it to determine the details of its construction, and to compensate for delay which Mincom encountered in the final stages of its development program because Winston had hired away Mincom's key personnel. Whether extension of the injunctive period for the latter reason was proper we need not decide, for Winston has not raised that question.

We think it was proper to make the injunctive period run from the date of judgment since public disclosure occurred at about that time. . . .

Mincom argues that the district court should have awarded money damages as well as injunctive relief. We think the district court acted well within its discretion in declining to do so. Since Winston sold none of its machines, it had no past profits to disgorge. The evidence as to possible future profits was at best highly speculative. To enjoin future sales and at the same time make an award based on future profits from the prohibited sales would result in duplicating and inconsistent relief, and the choice which the district court made between these mutually exclusive alternatives was not an unreasonable one. There was evidence that Winston would probably sell its machine and realize profits after the injunction expired, but these sales and profits, as we have seen, would not be tainted by breach of confidence, since Winston could by that time have developed its machine from publicly disclosed information.

We have examined the other bases upon which Mincom sought damages and are satisfied that they were either too remote and speculative, or that the injunction made Mincom as nearly whole as possible. Mincom argues that Winston gained a wide variety of advantages from the improper use of Mincom's trade secrets—such as obtaining financing for its development program, securing a government contract, shortening its development program, and reducing its development costs. There is an obvious difficulty in assigning a dollar value to such matters. The two-year injunction deprived Winston of any benefit it might have gained from these advantages and shielded Mincom from any potential harm from Winston's competition which these advantages may have rendered unfair. Mincom suggests that by hiring away Mincom's skilled employees Winston hindered Mincom's development program and increased its cost, but, as we have noted, the district court expressly considered this delay and extended the period of the injunction for an equivalent period. . . .

[T]he judgment is affirmed.

NOTES ON REPARATIVE INJUNCTIONS AND THE RIGHTFUL POSITION

1. Comparing the damage remedy and the injunction. In *Winston*, the trial judge might have denied the injunction and awarded damages for the sales Mincom lost to Winston as a result of Winston's theft. If the court had chosen that remedy, what would the measure of damages have been? Given the substantive rule that trade secret protection ends when the secret is publicly disclosed, would Mincom have had any claim at all for damages based on sales Winston would make five or ten years after the trade secrets were disclosed? If not, is there any basis for a perpetual injunction against Winston? Is there any reason for the injunctive remedy to be more draconian or more lucrative than the damages remedy? Shouldn't both remedies be designed to put plaintiff in the position it would have occupied but for the wrong?

2. The earlier rules. The parties in *Winston* argued for competing rules based on the *Shellmar* and *Conmar* cases. In *Conmar*, Learned Hand described the perpetual injunction issued in *Shellmar* as a "penalty" for which there was no basis in principle. 172 F.2d at 156. Whether or not there is a basis for it, it is a penalty, isn't it? Some courts are still attracted to such penalties. An example is Merrill Lynch, Pierce, Fenner & Smith, Inc. v. Stidham, 658 F.2d 1098 (5th Cir. 1981), in which the court perpetually enjoined defendants from using on behalf of their new employer information acquired while they worked for Merrill Lynch. Their contract with Merrill Lynch provided only that they would not disclose such information while they were employed there. The court held that defendant's blatant breach of the temporary nondisclosure agreement justified the perpetual injunction against using the wrongfully disclosed information. The court probably would not have awarded punitive damages for breach of contract. Is that relevant to deciding whether a penalty should be built into an injunction?

Judge Hand gave no remedy at all in *Conmar*, perhaps because plaintiff didn't argue that there would be a lag between lawful disclosure and defendant's exploitation of the disclosure; the opinion does not discuss the lag-time issue.

3. Codification. The substantive rule in *Winston* has been codified, with a procedural change, in §2 of the Uniform Trade Secrets Act:

> Actual or threatened misappropriation may be enjoined. Upon application to the court, an injunction shall be terminated when the trade secret has ceased to exist, but the injunction may be continued for an additional reasonable period of time in order to eliminate commercial advantage that otherwise would be derived from the misappropriation.

14 Unif. Laws Ann. 529, 619 (2005). By 2017, the Act had been adopted by 48 states, and only New York and Massachusetts have not yet done so.

BAILEY v. PROCTOR
160 F.2d 78 (1st Cir. 1947)

[Aldred Investment Trust was a mutual fund organized before the Investment Company Act of 1940; its structure was typical of the abuses that led to the Act. Voting control of the Trust was held by the owners of $150,000 in stock; the holders of $6 million in debentures provided most of the capital. A debenture is like a bond or promissory note: It is a promise to pay a fixed sum of money, usually on a date far in the future, and to pay periodic interest until the principal is paid. Debenture holders are fixed-income investors, typically interested in a safe steady return.

The abuse in this capital structure is in its uneven and misleading distribution of risk and reward. If the Trust goes broke, the stockholders can lose no more than $150,000; the debenture holders can lose $6 million. But if the Trust does well, the debenture holders get only their interest; all the speculative profit goes to the stockholders. Their profits can be enormous as a percentage of their investment, because the $6 million invested by the debenture holders is working for the stockholders. For example, if the debenture holders are promised 6 percent interest, and the Trust earns 8 percent, that extra 2 percent of $6 million is $120,000. For the stockholders, that's an annual return of 80 percent. If the Trust invests in speculative stocks and doubles its value, the debenture holders still get only 6 percent. But that $6 million profit is a 4,000 percent return to the stockholders. Consequently, the controlling stockholders have great incentive to take risks with the debenture holders' money. The debenture holders are limited to their 6 percent return, but they don't get the safety they were seeking. On the other hand, 6 percent was considerably above market interest rates all through the 1930s and 1940s.

The Aldred Trust became insolvent, and the control group was caught in fraud and self-dealing. For these reasons, a receiver was appointed at the request of the Securities and Exchange Commission. A receiver is a court-appointed officer who takes possession and control of property and manages it under judicial supervision pending litigation. The court of appeals approved the appointment of the receiver. Aldred Investment Trust v. SEC, 151 F.2d 254 (1st Cir. 1945).

The original control group was led by a man named Hanlon. Bailey's group bought out Hanlon's group, and an enormous increase in the value of a racetrack investment made the Trust solvent again. But the district court ordered the receiver to liquidate the Trust. Bailey appealed, arguing that because the Trust was no longer insolvent and because those responsible for the fraud were no longer associated with the Trust, both reasons for the receivership had been eliminated. Bailey also argued that the court had no power to order liquidation in any event.]

Before MAGRUDER, MAHONEY, and WOODBURY, Circuit Judges.

MAHONEY, Circuit Judge. . . .

Appellants' first argument is that the district court lacked jurisdiction to liquidate the Trust. In our view the jurisdiction of the district court to act in terminating the receivership by ordering liquidation is dependent upon the jurisdiction existing at the time the receivership was commenced. At that time the Trust was insolvent and the officers-trustees were guilty of "gross abuse of trust." We then upheld the district court's decree appointing receivers, as being within the court's general equity powers. Admittedly, however, at the time of that appeal the emphasis was on the power to appoint a receiver rather than the power to order liquidation as the end of the receivership. Therefore, rather than resting our present decision on the narrower ground of the "law of the case," we now hold that a court of equity has inherent power to appoint a receiver to liquidate a corporation or investment trust where fraud, mismanagement or abuse of trust is present whether or not insolvency is likewise present. . . .

The question now presented to us is whether or not the district court has lost that power by reason of intervening solvency and the removal of the officers-trustees guilty of abuse of trust and the impossibility of their now resuming such control of the Trust due to the transfer of the controlling shares to the present appellants. In the first place we do not believe that the perhaps temporary solvency of the Trust would necessarily affect the power of the court supervising the receivership. Other grounds for the appointment of a receiver having been present, the court's jurisdiction is not defeated by the supervening solvency. Since a receivership may be inaugurated for a solvent corporation, solvency, especially where it may be of a transient nature, does not terminate jurisdiction to continue a receivership created on grounds other than insolvency. Moreover, we believe that the jurisdiction existing at the time of creation of the receivership is a continuing jurisdiction and the questions of present solvency and removal from control of the offending officers and trustees pertain not to jurisdiction but to the propriety of the exercise of such jurisdiction. Once having properly assumed jurisdiction of a corporation or trust by appointing receivers under its general equity power, a court should not terminate its supervision until or unless it becomes satisfied that equity has been done to those whose interests the court had originally been asked to protect. The court upon examination of the plans for reorganization found that none was fair and feasible, and consequently, accepted liquidation as the only other alternative. The question before us is whether we can say that the court below abused its discretion in failing to [vest] control in the present common shareholders with the terms of the Trust and the capital structure unchanged.

In considering the propriety of the order decreeing liquidation it must be remembered that reorganization of this Trust was considered, at least by the Securities and Exchange Commission, and undoubtedly by the court, a necessary prelude to any termination of the receivership other than by liquidation. Appellants at least recognized the advisability of a reorganization in their final petition before the district court.

Ordinarily, it is said that liquidation being a drastic remedy will only be decreed in an extraordinary case or where special and peculiar circumstances exist. Unfortunately the district court did not furnish us with an opinion in which it indicated the grounds for the exercise of its discretion. However, from the record we are able to garner facts which seem to us to support the manner in which such discretion was exercised.

Since 1937 the Aldred Trust assets have had a value substantially less than the principal amount of outstanding debentures. During the years 1940 to 1943 the earnings of the Trust were substantially insufficient to meet the interest charges on these debentures. Only as the result of the successful outcome of a highly speculative venture undertaken by Hanlon has the Trust been able to get its head out of water during the receivership. Temporary solvency was brought about by the sale of the Eastern Racing Association stock at a tremendous profit. Due to a post-war stock market inflation the other portfolio assets nearly doubled in value but were still less than the face amount of the outstanding debentures. The vagaries of the stock market are familiar to all of us. There seems to be doubt also as to the ability in the future of any portfolio to earn these interest requirements except by resort to speculative securities with the hope of capital appreciation.

The Securities and Exchange Commission indicated that the Aldred Trust security structure embodied the evils which led to the enactment of the Investment Company Act of 1940. The "free stock," representing only a small investment and often no equity, controlled the operations, policies and management of the almost $6,000,000 investment of the debenture holders. The inability to earn interest requirements induces the controlling shareholders to engage in capital appreciation investments or in speculative ventures to insure them a profit in one way or another, e.g., Hanlon's activities in the Eastern Racing Association stock. The present holders of the free stock, the appellants here, purchased control of Aldred, which has $5,900,000 principal amount of debentures, for $150,000. Their equity at present shows an appreciation of some $2,500,000 as a result of general market increases and the favorable sale of Eastern Racing Association stock.

The important question is not the personal honesty, integrity or ability of appellants or their proposed management, but rather the lack of balance and equality of control in the capital structure of the Trust. Specifically, the court could not feel assured that a recurrence of the events leading up to the present receivership was impossible. Insolvency was likely; lack of sufficient earnings to cover interest requirements was possible. In such event, nothing would prevent the controlling shareholders, either appellants or their successors, from embarking on new speculation to the detriment of the debenture holders. The court properly felt that the debenture holders were entitled now to the cash salvaged from what had appeared to be a doomed enterprise.

Finally, it was indicated at the argument before us that one of appellants' primary motives for the continuation of Aldred was to preserve its security structure, inasmuch as a similar trust could not now be created under the Investment Company Act. The Act itself does not require the liquidation or reorganization of existing investment companies which do not conform to the new statutory standards. But when a court of equity has exercised its jurisdiction to appoint receivers of an investment company pursuant to a complaint charging gross abuse of trust on the part of the trustees or officers, we deem it proper for the court, in determining what would be the appropriate remedy in order to afford complete relief, to take account of the fact that the capital structure is not in conformity with the standards and safeguards which Congress has now written into law. That fact, in conjunction with the other facts in the case, may well render it fair and equitable to require the liquidation of the company in the absence of an acceptable plan of reorganization.

No dissenting voice to the order of liquidation has arisen from the debenture holders who have the greater equity and whose interests the court was originally called upon to protect. It would seem that, if appellants are intent upon investing in an investment corporation or trust, they could form a new one and even solicit the present debenture holders for subscriptions. But it would be inequitable to allow them to force those with burnt fingers to remain investors in an enterprise of proven questionable value.

In view of the above considerations, we find it impossible to say that the order of liquidation was an improper exercise of equitable discretion but rather indicated a court of equity doing equity. . . .

The decision of the District Court is affirmed and the case is remanded to that court for further proceedings in accord with this opinion.

NOTES ON EQUITABLE DISCRETION

1. The measure of relief in *Bailey*. What is the measure of relief in *Bailey*? That equity should be done? What position would the debenture holders have been in if the trust had never been insolvent and Hanlon had never engaged in self-dealing? Wouldn't they have been debenture holders in a solvent trust with honest management and a risky, overleveraged financial structure that was protected by the grandfather clause in the Investment Company Act? What is the court remedying when it orders the trust liquidated?

2. Two competing traditions. The difference between *Bailey* and *Winston* is not that *Bailey* involves a receivership. We will take up receiverships in more detail in section 9.B.3; for present purposes, just treat the order to liquidate the trust as though it were an injunction.

Winston represents one tradition, which is to restore the plaintiff as near as may be to the position it would have occupied but for the violation. Call this the rightful-position approach. That still leaves some room for discretion: Whether 2 years or 18 months is the appropriate lead time to offset the effects of the violation is left to the discretion of the trial judge. Deference to the trial judge on that issue may not be much different from deference to the trial judge's application of the measure of damages.

Bailey represents a different tradition. Call it the equitable discretion approach. At its extremes, this tradition says that once there is a violation that brings a case into the equity court, the chancellor has a roving commission to do good. He should see that equity is done to all within his jurisdiction; he should liquidate the trust because that is fair, even though it is not legally required and is not necessary to restore the plaintiffs to any position they would have occupied but for the wrong. An academic formulation of this tradition claims that, at least in public law litigation, "right and remedy are pretty thoroughly disconnected." Abram Chayes, *The Role of the Judge in Public Law Litigation*, 89 Harv. L. Rev. 1281, 1293 (1976).

3. The chancellor's foot? The talk about "an equity court doing equity" is equally common in injunction and receivership cases; both are equitable remedies, developed by the English chancellors in their equity court and not in the common law courts. There is long tradition that a suit in equity is an appeal to the chancellor's conscience. The modern successor to the chancellor is the trial judge, and there is still much talk about the flexibility of equity and the discretion of trial judges in equity cases.

Such talk led to the famous complaint that relying on the chancellor's conscience as a measure of justice is like relying on the chancellor's foot as the measure of length. But this reflects a common misunderstanding of the nature of equitable discretion. Courts of last resort have frequently reiterated that equitable discretion is discretion to consider all the relevant facts, not discretion for the trial judge to do whatever he wants. The Supreme Court made the point in connection with discretionary awards of back pay to victims of employment discrimination:

> However, such discretionary choices are not left to a court's "inclination, but to its judgment; and its judgment is to be guided by sound legal principles." United States v. Burr, 25 F. Cas. 30, 35 (C.C.D. Va. 1807) (No. 14,692d) (Marshall, C.J.). The power to award backpay was bestowed by Congress, as part of a complex legislative design directed at a historic evil of national proportions. A court must exercise this power "in light of the large objectives of the Act." Hecht Co. v. Bowles, 321 U.S. 321, 331 (1944). That the court's discretion is equitable in nature hardly means that it is unfettered by meaningful standards or shielded from thorough appellate review. In Mitchell v. Robert DeMario Jewelry, 361 U.S. 288, 292 (1960), this Court held, in the face of a silent statute, that district courts enjoyed the "historic power of equity" to award lost wages to workmen unlawfully discriminated against under §17 of the Fair Labor Standards Act. The Court simultaneously noted that "the statutory purposes [leave] little room for the exercise of discretion not to order reimbursement." 361 U.S. at 296.
>
> It is true that "[e]quity eschews mechanical rules . . . [and] depends on flexibility." Holmberg v. Armbrecht, 327 U.S. 392, 396 (1946). But when Congress invokes the Chancellor's conscience to further transcendent legislative purposes, what is required is

the principled application of standards consistent with those purposes and not "equity [which] varies like the Chancellor's foot." Eldon, L.C., in Gee v. Pritchard, 36 Eng. Rep. 670, 674 (1818). Important national goals would be frustrated by a regime of discretion that "produce[d] different results for breaches of duty in situations that cannot be differentiated in policy." Moragne v. States Marine Lines, 398 U.S. 375, 405, (1970).

Albemarle Paper Co. v. Moody, 422 U.S. 405, 416-417 (1975).

4. Aristotle's conception of equity. One tradition of equity is that the judge can take account of the facts of individual cases, which may justify creating exceptions for reasons that were not considered in formulating the general rule. This idea goes back to Aristotle:

> [W]here the lawgiver has passed over some consideration and made an error through having spoken in the abstract, we should in practice correct this aberration—an aberration which even the lawgiver himself would prescribe if he were present, and for which he would have legislated if he had foreseen. . . .
>
> [T]his is the nature of what is equitable—a rectification of law on points where law is at fault owing to its universality.

Nicomachean Ethics bk. 5, ch. 14 (Walter M. Hatch trans., 1879). Aristotle was talking about a concept, not about two sets of English courts that would emerge 1,700 years later. But the English equity courts took the word from Aristotle's concept. Aristotle's theory of statutory enforcement is controversial in some circles today, but accept it for the moment and try applying it to *Bailey*.

Does the court in *Bailey* consider any fact or policy that would not have been before Congress when it enacted the grandfather clause? Do the judges distinguish their vote from the vote they might have cast if they had been senators? Do they implicitly assume that Congress sold out to the industry, and that this sellout needs to be corrected? Or might they assume that, as Lincoln said of ending the expansion of slavery, the Investment Company Act was meant to put these capital structures "in the course of ultimate extinction"?

5. Prophylactic relief? These notes have assumed that *Bailey* provides a remedy for the unfair capital structure. Another interpretation is that *Bailey* provides a prophylactic remedy to prevent the recurrence of fraud and insolvency. Was fraud and insolvency inevitable, in the way that use of trade secrets was inevitable in *PepsiCo*? Did defendants in *Bailey* have a history of fraud, like those defendants who were barred from their industries in the SEC and FTC cases? A propensity to fraud? Or merely a temptation to fraud? Was there a threat of insolvency, or merely a risk? Is the capital structure a facilitator of fraud and insolvency? Is the risk great enough to justify depriving the current defendants, who so far have done nothing illegal, of the benefits of the grandfather clause?

4. Institutional Reform Litigation (Structural Injunctions)

INTRODUCTORY NOTE: THE SCHOOL DESEGREGATION CASES

Recall Professor Fiss's vocabulary of preventive injunctions (for preventing wrongful acts), and reparative injunctions (for preventing or repairing the consequences of past wrongful acts). He further contrasted these two categories with what he called "structural" injunctions, designed to correct institutional structures operating in systematic violation of applicable law. Owen M. Fiss, *The Civil Rights Injunction* 8-12 (Indiana Univ. Press 1978).

This area of the law is now also commonly known as "institutional reform litigation." Much of the law of injunctions in the Supreme Court of the United States has been developed in these cases, in which the Court reviewed district court orders reworking the operations of schools, prisons, and many other institutions.

One way to think of structural injunctions is that they are just a collection of more specific preventive and reparative injunctions addressing a complex fact situation. On this view, factual complexity presents all kinds of practical problems, but it does not change the fundamental goal of providing a remedy for identifiable violations of law. Professor Fiss conceived of structural injunctions in grander terms; they were to reform the institutional structures that threatened legal values. These two ways of thinking about structural injunctions are related to views about the choice between restoring the rightful position and an equity court doing equity. The capital structure in *Bailey v. Proctor* could be viewed as an institutional structure that endangered legal values.

Put another way, in institutional reform litigation, courts often face a choice between sticking closely to the rightful position standard, by asking what position the plaintiffs would have been in but for the legal wrongs, and engaging in more freewheeling equitable discretion, by asking what position courts should try to put plaintiffs in given that plaintiffs faced a combination of legal and societal obstacles to fair or equal treatment and that it is hard to change the culture of an institution that has been acting illegally, often for many years. The divide often pits the Court's conservatives against the Court's liberals in highly-charged political cases.

The choice prominently played out in the Supreme Court's school desegregation cases from the 1970s through the 1990s. To understand the dispute, you may need a bit of background. In considering remedies for school desegregation, it is important to know the Court's distinction between segregation de jure (by law) and segregation de facto (in fact). De jure segregation is segregation deliberately caused by state authorities; de jure segregation violates the Constitution and must be remedied. De facto segregation is segregation from all other causes except the deliberate conduct of state authorities. The Court has always held that de facto segregation does not violate the Constitution. If school segregation results from housing segregation, and if housing segregation results from the preferences of home buyers and renters, or from discrimination by real estate brokers, landlords, and sellers, the resulting school segregation does not violate the Constitution and need not be remedied. That at least is the theory, but the theory was subjected to great stress in the remedies cases.

The early years of school desegregation proceeded cautiously, with "all deliberate speed" and with orders to admit individual students to white schools. Progress greatly accelerated after the Civil Rights Act of 1964 banned racial discrimination in any program or activity receiving federal funds, with the executive branch threatening to cut off federal funds as the enforcement mechanism. A good short history of the remedies issues is Doug Rendleman, *Brown II's "All Deliberate Speed" at Fifty: A Golden Anniversary or a Mid-Life Crisis for the Constitutional Injunction as a School Desegregation Remedy*, 41 San Diego L. Rev. 1575 (2004).

Swann v. Charlotte-Mecklenburg Board of Education, 402 U.S. 1 (1971), is one of the two poles that anchored debate for a generation. *Swann* involved desegregation of the schools in Mecklenburg County, North Carolina. The district had maintained two completely separate school systems, one for blacks and one for whites, and when necessary, it had bused students long distances to the segregated schools.

The district court drew wedge-shaped attendance zones pointed toward the central city. It also paired black and white schools not reached by the gerrymander and bused students between these schools. 311 F. Supp. 265 (W.D.N.C. 1970). The Supreme Court affirmed. The Court said that neutrally drawn attendance zones were not necessarily a sufficient remedy. New schools might have been built in locations selected to maximize segregation. School choices affect housing choices, and the segregation of schools might have contributed to the segregation of housing. Under either of these circumstances, neutrally drawn attendance zones would not achieve "truly nondiscriminatory assignments" of children to schools. 402 U.S. at 28. The Court did not seem interested in evidence on these issues. *Swann* had both rightful-position rhetoric and broad equitable-discretion rhetoric, but its result appeared to go well beyond any condition that would have existed but for de jure segregation. Professor Fiss described *Swann*—approvingly—as "the most untailored remedy imaginable." Owen M. Fiss, *Foreword: The Forms of Justice*, 93 Harv. L. Rev. 1, 46 n.94 (1979). *Swann* led to a generation of busing to desegregate large urban school systems.

The other pole of the remedies debate came in Milliken v. Bradley, 418 U.S. 717 (1974) (*Milliken I*). The district court found that state and local officials had deliberately maximized school segregation in Detroit by gerrymandering attendance zones and redrawing them in response to racial change, creating optional attendance zones in residentially changing neighborhoods, segregating feeder-school patterns, constructing new schools in locations and sizes that assured segregated student bodies, and busing students from overcrowded black schools past white schools with available space to more distant black schools. 338 F. Supp. 582, 587-589 (E.D. Mich. 1971). The district court also found that desegregation within Detroit was impossible. This finding was based on the high percentage of black students in Detroit as a whole, the likelihood of white flight to the suburbs, and distance: Many black neighborhoods were closer to white suburbs immediately north and south of the city than to white neighborhoods in the western part of Detroit. The court ordered the parties to submit proposals for a metropolitan desegregation plan and their objections to such plans. 345 F. Supp. 914 (E.D. Mich. 1972). The court of appeals affirmed, and it ordered that the suburban school districts be made parties. 484 F.2d 215 (6th Cir. 1973).

The Supreme Court reversed. It held that plaintiffs' rightful position was desegregation within Detroit, and that the courts had no power to involve the suburban districts unless the violation in Detroit had caused segregation in the suburbs. If desegregation within the neutrally drawn boundary of the Detroit district is satisfactory, why wouldn't desegregation within neutrally drawn attendance zones have been satisfactory in *Swann*? To put it the other way, if the remedy in *Swann* had to take account of the possible effects of school segregation on housing patterns, is there any reason to assume that those effects end at the school district line? Is it just that district lines define political and taxing units, and attendance-zone lines do not?

The school desegregation cases played out over decades. Over time, the Court came down more firmly on the rightful position side of the line. It wrote in Dayton Board of Education v. Brinkman, 433 U.S. 406 (1977) (*Dayton I*) that a court must "determine how much incremental segregative effect" *id.* at 420, a school system's de jure discrimination contributed to the plaintiffs' position. The Court wrote that a school desegregation remedy "must be designed to redress that difference, and only if there has been a systemwide impact may there be a systemwide remedy." *Id.*

Despite the Supreme Court's move toward narrower relief, these cases were primarily in the hands of federal district court judges, many of whom were much more willing to engage in free-wheeling equitable discretion. Some courts of appeals went along, the Supreme Court could not review all the cases, and swing votes sometimes made a Supreme Court majority for the liberals, even after *Dayton I*. The same day as

Dayton I, the Court unanimously affirmed an order for a modest program of teacher training and remedial education for students as part of the desegregation remedy in Detroit. Milliken v. Bradley, 433 U.S. 267 (1977) (*Milliken II*).

Conservatives on the Supreme Court lost patience with broader remedies, and in Missouri v. Jenkins, 515 U.S. 70 (1995) (*Jenkins III*), the Court signaled little tolerance for remedies designed to improve the often deplorable conditions in underfunded and underachieving inner city schools. The majority also noted a lack of adversity lurking in the background: many of the "defendant" school districts were quite happy when courts ordered the state to increase funds (and even raise taxes) to pay for improvements to the school system. The liberals on the Supreme Court, in contrast, believed the remedies imposed by lower courts had not yet eliminated the vestiges of discrimination; they supported broader remedies. Perhaps they had a different understanding of the plaintiffs' rightful position (as they usually claimed); perhaps they believed in more free-wheeling equitable discretion (as their critics charged).

The upshot of the desegregation cases is that the Supreme Court, at least as a matter of rhetoric, is now firmly in the rightful position camp as it reviews institutional reform litigation. But in these complex cases, the rightful position is necessarily inexact, and some Justices are much more willing than others to risk overremediation (giving plaintiffs more than the rightful position), while other Justices are much more willing to risk underremediation (giving plaintiffs less than the rightful position). Consider the divide in the next case.

BROWN v. PLATA
563 U.S. 493 (2011)

Justice KENNEDY delivered the opinion of the Court.

This case arises from serious constitutional violations in California's prison system. The violations have persisted for years. They remain uncorrected. . . .

After years of litigation, it became apparent that a remedy for the constitutional violations would not be effective absent a reduction in the prison system population. The authority to order release of prisoners as a remedy to cure a systemic violation of the Eighth Amendment is a power reserved to a three-judge district court, not a single-judge district court. 18 U.S.C. §3626(a). [Appeals from such a three-judge district court go directly to the Supreme Court.]

The appeal presents the question whether the remedial order issued by the three-judge court is consistent with requirements and procedures set forth in . . . the Prison Litigation Reform Act of 1995 (PLRA). 18 U.S.C. §3626. . . .

I

A

The degree of overcrowding in California's prisons is exceptional. California's prisons are designed to house a population just under 80,000, but at the time of the three-judge court's decision the population was [about 156,000.] The State's prisons had operated at around 200% of design capacity for at least 11 years. Prisoners are crammed into spaces neither designed nor intended to house inmates. As many as 200 prisoners may live in a gymnasium, monitored by as few as two or three correctional officers. As many as 54 prisoners may share a single toilet. . . .

Prisoners in California with serious mental illness do not receive minimal, adequate care. Because of a shortage of treatment beds, suicidal inmates may be held for prolonged periods in telephone-booth sized cages without toilets. A psychiatric expert reported observing an inmate who had been held in such a cage for nearly 24 hours, standing in a pool of his own urine, unresponsive and nearly catatonic. Prison officials explained they had "'no place to put him.'" Other inmates awaiting care may be held for months in administrative segregation, where they endure harsh and isolated conditions and receive only limited mental health services. Wait times for mental health care range as high as 12 months. In 2006, the suicide rate in California's prisons was nearly 80% higher than the national average for prison populations; and a court-appointed Special Master found that 72.1% of suicides involved "some measure of inadequate assessment, treatment, or intervention, and were therefore most probably foreseeable and/or preventable."

Prisoners suffering from physical illness also receive severely deficient care. California's prisons were designed to meet the medical needs of a population at 100% of design capacity and so have only half the clinical space needed to treat the current population. A correctional officer testified that, in one prison, up to 50 sick inmates may be held together in a 12- by 20-foot cage for up to five hours awaiting treatment. The number of staff is inadequate, and prisoners face significant delays in access to care. A prisoner with severe abdominal pain died after a 5-week delay in referral to a specialist; a prisoner with "constant and extreme" chest pain died after an 8-hour delay in evaluation by a doctor; and a prisoner died of testicular cancer after a "failure of MDs to work up for cancer in a young man with 17 months of testicular pain."[3] Doctor Ronald Shansky, former medical director of the Illinois state prison system, surveyed death reviews for California prisoners. He concluded that extreme departures from the standard of care were "widespread," and that the proportion of "possibly preventable or preventable" deaths was "extremely high."[4] . . .

B

These conditions are the subject of two federal cases. The first to commence, Coleman v. Brown, was filed in 1990. *Coleman* involves the class of seriously mentally ill persons in California prisons. . . . [A]fter a 39-day trial, the *Coleman* District Court found "overwhelming evidence of the systematic failure to deliver necessary care to mentally ill inmates" in California prisons. Coleman v. Wilson, 912 F. Supp. 1282, 1316 (E.D. Cal. 1995). . . . The court appointed a Special Master to oversee development and implementation of a remedial plan of action.

In 2007, 12 years after his appointment, the Special Master in *Coleman* filed a report stating that, after years of slow improvement, the state of mental health care in California's prisons was deteriorating. The Special Master ascribed this change to increased overcrowding. . . . [E]xisting programming space and staffing levels were

3. Because plaintiffs do not base their case on deficiencies in care provided on any one occasion, this Court has no occasion to consider whether these instances of delay—or any other particular deficiency in medical care complained of by the plaintiffs—would violate the Constitution . . . if considered in isolation. Plaintiffs rely on systemwide deficiencies in the provision of medical and mental health care that, taken as a whole, subject sick and mentally ill prisoners in California to "substantial risk of serious harm" . . . . Farmer v. Brennan, 511 U.S. 825, 834 (1994).

4. [Preventable or more-likely-than-not preventable deaths in the prison system totaled 66 in 2006, 68 in 2007, 66 in 2008, and 46 in 2009. Only data through 2007 was available to the three-judge court.] The three-judge court could not have anticipated [the apparent improvement in 2009], and it would be inappropriate for this Court to evaluate its significance for the first time on appeal. The three-judge court should, of course, consider this and any other evidence of improved conditions when considering future requests by the State for modification of its order.

inadequate to keep pace. . . . [T]he need to house the expanding population had also caused a "reduction of programming space now occupied by inmate bunks." . . . The Special Master concluded that many early "achievements have succumbed to the inexorably rising tide of population, leaving behind growing frustration and despair."

C

The second action, *Plata* v. *Brown*, involves the class of state prisoners with serious medical conditions. After this action commenced in 2001, the State conceded that deficiencies in prison medical care violated prisoners' Eighth Amendment rights. The State stipulated to a remedial injunction. The State failed to comply with that injunction, and in 2005 the court appointed a Receiver to oversee remedial efforts. The court found that "the California prison medical care system is broken beyond repair," resulting in an "unconscionable degree of suffering and death." The court found: "[I]t is an uncontested fact that, on average, an inmate in one of California's prisons needlessly dies every six to seven days due to constitutional deficiencies in the [California prisons'] medical delivery system." . . .

Prisons were unable to retain sufficient numbers of competent medical staff, and would "hire any doctor who had 'a license, a pulse and a pair of shoes.'" Medical facilities lacked "necessary medical equipment" and did "not meet basic sanitation standards." "Exam tables and counter tops, where prisoners with . . . communicable diseases are treated, [were] not routinely disinfected."

In 2008, three years after the District Court's decision, the Receiver described continuing deficiencies in the health care provided by California prisons . . . .

The Receiver explained that "overcrowding, combined with staffing shortages, has created a culture of cynicism, fear, and despair which makes hiring and retaining competent clinicians extremely difficult." "[O]vercrowding, and the resulting day to day operational chaos of the [prison system], creates regular 'crisis' situations which . . . take time [and] energy . . . away from important remedial programs." Overcrowding had increased the incidence of infectious disease, and had led to rising prison violence and greater reliance by custodial staff on lockdowns, which "inhibit the delivery of medical care and increase the staffing necessary for such care." . . .

D . . .

The three-judge court heard 14 days of testimony and issued a 184-page opinion, making extensive findings of fact. The court ordered California to reduce its prison population to 137.5% of the prisons' design capacity within two years. Assuming the State does not increase capacity through new construction, the order requires a population reduction of 38,000 to 46,000 persons. Because it appears all but certain that the State cannot complete sufficient construction to comply fully with the order, the prison population will have to be reduced to at least some extent. The court did not order the State to achieve this reduction in any particular manner. Instead, the court ordered the State to formulate a plan for compliance and submit its plan for approval by the court. . . .

II

As a consequence of their own actions, prisoners may be deprived of rights that are fundamental to liberty. Yet the law and the Constitution demand recognition of certain other rights. . . .

Just as a prisoner may starve if not fed, he or she may suffer or die if not provided adequate medical care. A prison that deprives prisoners of basic sustenance, including adequate medical care, is incompatible with the concept of human dignity and has no place in civilized society.

If government fails to fulfill this obligation, the courts have a responsibility to remedy the resulting Eighth Amendment violation. Courts must be sensitive to the State's interest in punishment, deterrence, and rehabilitation, as well as the need for deference to experienced and expert prison administrators faced with the difficult and dangerous task of housing large numbers of convicted criminals. . . . [But courts] may not allow constitutional violations to continue simply because a remedy would involve intrusion into the realm of prison administration.

Courts faced with the sensitive task of remedying unconstitutional prison conditions must consider a range of available options, including appointment of special masters or receivers . . . . When necessary to ensure compliance with a constitutional mandate, courts may enter orders placing limits on a prison's population. . . .

Before a three-judge court may be convened [to consider such an order], a district court first must have entered an order for less intrusive relief that failed to remedy the constitutional violation and must have given the defendant a reasonable time to comply with its prior orders. §3626(a)(3)(A). . . .

The three-judge court must then find by clear and convincing evidence that "crowding is the primary cause of the violation of a Federal right" and that "no other relief will remedy the violation of the Federal right." 18 U.S.C. §3626(a)(3)(E). As with any award of prospective relief under the PLRA, the relief "shall extend no further than necessary to correct the violation of the Federal right of a particular plaintiff or plaintiffs." §3626(a)(1)(A). The three-judge court must therefore find that the relief is "narrowly drawn, extends no further than necessary . . . , and is the least intrusive means necessary to correct the violation of the Federal right." *Id.* In making this determination, the three-judge court must give "substantial weight to any adverse impact on public safety or the operation of a criminal justice system caused by the relief." *Id.* Applying these standards, the three-judge court found a population limit appropriate, necessary, and authorized in this case.

This Court's review of the three-judge court's legal determinations is *de novo*, but factual findings are reviewed for clear error. . . .

A

The State contends that it was error to convene the three-judge court without affording it more time to comply with the prior orders in *Coleman* and *Plata*. . . .

2 . . .

When the three-judge court was convened, 12 years had passed since the appointment of the *Coleman* Special Master, and 5 years had passed since the approval of the *Plata* consent decree. The State does not claim that either order achieved a remedy. . . .

The State claims instead that . . . other, later remedial efforts should have been given more time to succeed. [There were new orders, or proposals, for construction of new facilities, hiring of new staff, and implementation of new procedures in each case in 2006 and later.]

[T]he failed consent decree in *Plata* had called for . . . new procedures and . . . additional staff; and the *Coleman* Special Master had issued over 70 orders directed at achieving a remedy through construction, hiring, and procedural reforms. . . .

Having engaged in remedial efforts for 5 years in *Plata* and 12 in *Coleman*, the District Courts were not required to wait to see whether their more recent efforts would yield equal disappointment. When a court attempts to remedy an entrenched constitutional violation through reform of a complex institution . . . , it may be necessary in the ordinary course to issue multiple orders directing and adjusting ongoing remedial efforts. Each new order must be given a reasonable time to succeed, but reasonableness must be assessed in light of the entire history of the court's remedial efforts. . . .

The *Coleman* and *Plata* courts had a solid basis to doubt that additional efforts to build new facilities and hire new staff would achieve a remedy. . . . A report filed by the *Coleman* Special Master in July 2009 describes ongoing violations, including an "absence of timely access to appropriate levels of care at every point in the system." A report filed by the *Plata* Receiver in October 2010 likewise describes ongoing deficiencies in the provision of medical care and concludes that there are simply "too many prisoners for the healthcare infrastructure." The *Coleman* and *Plata* courts acted reasonably when they convened a three-judge court without further delay.

B

Once a three-judge court has been convened, the court must find additional requirements satisfied before it may impose a population limit. The first of these requirements is that "crowding is the primary cause of the violation of a Federal right." 18 U.S.C. §3626(a)(3)(E)(i).

The three-judge court found the primary cause requirement satisfied by the evidence at trial. The court found that overcrowding strains inadequate medical and mental health facilities; overburdens limited clinical and custodial staff; and creates violent, unsanitary, and chaotic conditions that contribute to the constitutional violations and frustrate efforts to fashion a remedy. The three-judge court also found that "until the problem of overcrowding is overcome it will be impossible to provide constitutionally compliant care to California's prison population." . . .

The record documents the severe impact of burgeoning demand on the provision of care. At the time of trial, vacancy rates for medical and mental health staff ranged as high as 20% for surgeons, 25% for physicians, 39% for nurse practitioners, and 54.1% for psychiatrists. These percentages are based on the number of positions budgeted by the State. Dr. . . . Shansky . . . concluded that these numbers understate the severity of the crisis because the State has not budgeted sufficient staff to meet demand. . . .

Even on the assumption that vacant positions could be filled, the evidence suggested there would be insufficient space for the necessary additional staff to perform their jobs. . . . Staff operate out of converted storage rooms, closets, bathrooms, shower rooms, and visiting centers. These makeshift facilities impede the effective delivery of care and place the safety of medical professionals in jeopardy, compounding the difficulty of hiring additional staff.

This shortfall of resources relative to demand contributes to significant delays in treatment. . . . .

Prisons have backlogs of up to 700 prisoners waiting to see a doctor. A review of referrals for urgent specialty care at one prison revealed that only 105 of 316 pending referrals had a scheduled appointment, and only 2 had an appointment scheduled to occur within 14 days. Urgent specialty referrals at one prison had been pending for six months to a year.

Crowding also creates unsafe and unsanitary living conditions that hamper effective delivery of medical and mental health care. . . . Cramped conditions promote unrest and violence . . . .

Increased violence . . . requires increased reliance on lockdowns to keep order, and lockdowns further impede the effective delivery of care. In 2006, prison officials instituted 449 lockdowns. The average lockdown lasted 12 days, and 20 lockdowns lasted 60 days or longer. During lockdowns, staff must either escort prisoners to medical facilities or bring medical staff to the prisoners. Either procedure puts additional strain on already overburdened medical and custodial staff. Some programming for the mentally ill even may be canceled altogether during lockdowns, and staff may be unable to supervise the delivery of psychotropic medications.

The effects of overcrowding are particularly acute in the prisons' reception centers, intake areas that process 140,000 new or returning prisoners every year. Crowding in these areas runs as high as 300% of design capacity. . . . Inmates spend long periods of time in these areas awaiting transfer to the general population. Some prisoners are held in the reception centers for their entire period of incarceration.

Numerous experts testified that crowding is the primary cause of the constitutional violations. [The Court quoted testimony by the former warden of San Quentin and three current or former heads of prison systems in other large states.]

2

[The state's complaint that the three-judge court excluded evidence of current conditions in the prisons] lacks a factual basis. . . .

The State does not point to any significant evidence that it was unable to present and that would have changed the outcome of the proceedings. . . .

3

The three-judge court acknowledged that the violations were caused by factors in addition to overcrowding and that reducing crowding in the prisons would not entirely cure the violations. . . . [E]ven a significant reduction in the prison population would not remedy the violations absent continued efforts to train staff, improve facilities, and reform procedures. The three-judge court nevertheless found that overcrowding was the primary cause in the sense of being the foremost cause of the violation. . . .

Overcrowding need only be the foremost, chief, or principal cause of the violation. If Congress had intended to require that crowding be the only cause, it would have said so . . . .

As this case illustrates, constitutional violations in conditions of confinement are rarely susceptible of simple or straightforward solutions. In addition to overcrowding the failure of California's prisons to provide adequate medical and mental health care may be ascribed to chronic and worsening budget shortfalls, a lack of political will in favor of reform, inadequate facilities, and systemic administrative failures. . . . Only a multifaceted approach aimed at many causes, including overcrowding, will yield a solution. . . .

A reading of the PLRA that would render population limits unavailable in practice would raise serious constitutional concerns. A finding that overcrowding is the "primary cause" of a violation is therefore permissible, despite the fact that additional steps will be required to remedy the violation.

c

The three-judge court was also required to find by clear and convincing evidence that "no other relief will remedy the violation of the Federal right." §3626(a)(3)(E)(ii).

The State argues that the violation could have been remedied through a combination of new construction, transfers of prisoners out of State, hiring of medical personnel, and continued efforts by the *Plata* Receiver and *Coleman* Special Master. The order in fact permits the State to comply with the population limit by transferring prisoners to county facilities or facilities in other States, or by constructing new facilities to raise the prisons' design capacity. . . . If the State does find an adequate remedy other than a population limit, it may seek modification or termination of the three-judge court's order on that basis. . . .

Aside from asserting [that these remedies could still work], the State offers no reason to believe it is so. . . .

The common thread connecting the State's proposed remedial efforts is that they would require the State to expend large amounts of money absent a reduction in overcrowding. The Court cannot ignore the political and fiscal reality behind this case. California's Legislature has not been willing or able to allocate the resources necessary to meet this crisis absent a reduction in overcrowding. There is no reason to believe it will begin to do so now, when the State of California is facing an unprecedented budgetary shortfall. . . .

D

The PLRA states that no prospective relief shall issue with respect to prison conditions unless it is narrowly drawn, extends no further than necessary to correct the violation of a federal right, and is the least intrusive means necessary to correct the violation. 18 U.S.C. §3626(a). When determining whether these requirements are met, courts must "give substantial weight to any adverse impact on public safety or the operation of a criminal justice system." *Id.*

1

The three-judge court acknowledged that its order "is likely to affect inmates without medical conditions or serious mental illness." This is because reducing California's prison population will require reducing the number of prisoners outside the class through steps such as parole reform, sentencing reform, use of good-time credits, or other means to be determined by the State. Reducing overcrowding will also have positive effects beyond facilitating timely and adequate access to medical care, including reducing the incidence of prison violence and ameliorating unsafe living conditions. According to the State, these collateral consequences are evidence that the order sweeps more broadly than necessary.

The population limit imposed by the three-judge court does not fail narrow tailoring simply because it will have positive effects beyond the plaintiff class. Narrow tailoring requires a "fit between the [remedy's] ends and the means chosen to accomplish those ends." Board of Trustees v. Fox, 492 U.S. 469, 480 (1989). The scope of the remedy must be proportional to the scope of the violation, and the order must extend no further than necessary to remedy the violation. This Court has rejected remedial orders that unnecessarily reach out to improve prison conditions other than those that violate the Constitution. But the precedents do not suggest that a narrow and otherwise proper remedy for a constitutional violation is invalid simply because it will have collateral effects.

Nor does anything in the text of the PLRA require that result. The PLRA states that a remedy shall extend no further than necessary to remedy the violation of the rights of a "particular plaintiff or plaintiffs." 18 U.S.C. §3626(a)(1)(A). This means only that the scope of the order must be determined with reference to the constitutional violations established by the specific plaintiffs before the court.

This case is unlike cases where courts have impermissibly reached out to control the treatment of persons or institutions beyond the scope of the violation. See *Dayton*

I. Even prisoners with no present physical or mental illness may become afflicted, and all prisoners in California are at risk so long as the State continues to provide inadequate care. Prisoners in the general population will become sick, and will become members of the plaintiff classes, with routine frequency; and overcrowding may prevent the timely diagnosis and care necessary to provide effective treatment and to prevent further spread of disease. Relief targeted only at present members of the plaintiff classes may therefore fail to adequately protect future class members who will develop serious physical or mental illness. Prisoners who are not sick or mentally ill do not yet have a claim that they have been subjected to care that violates the Eighth Amendment, but in no sense are they remote bystanders in California's medical care system. They are that system's next potential victims.

A release order limited to prisoners within the plaintiff classes would, if anything, unduly limit the ability of State officials to determine which prisoners should be released. As the State acknowledges in its brief, "release of seriously mentally ill inmates [would be] likely to create special dangers because of their recidivism rates." . . .

In reaching its decision, the three-judge court gave "substantial weight" to any potential adverse impact on public safety from its order. The court devoted nearly 10 days of trial to the issue of public safety, and it gave the question extensive attention in its opinion. Ultimately, the court concluded that it would be possible to reduce the prison population "in a manner that preserves public safety and the operation of the criminal justice system."

The PLRA's requirement that a court give "substantial weight" to public safety does not require the court to certify that its order has no possible adverse impact on the public. A contrary reading would depart from the statute's text by replacing the word "substantial" with "conclusive." . . . A court is required to consider the public safety consequences of its order and to structure, and monitor, its ruling in a way that mitigates those consequences while still achieving an effective remedy of the constitutional violation.

This inquiry necessarily involves difficult predictive judgments regarding the likely effects of court orders. Although these judgments are normally made by state officials, they necessarily must be made by courts when those courts fashion injunctive relief to remedy serious constitutional violations in the prisons. These questions are difficult and sensitive, but they are factual questions and should be treated as such. Courts can, and should, rely on relevant and informed expert testimony when making factual findings. . . .

The three-judge court credited substantial evidence that prison populations can be reduced in a manner that does not increase crime to a significant degree. Some evidence indicated that reducing overcrowding in California's prisons could even improve public safety [by reducing the extent to which the prison system made criminals worse than when they entered.]

Expert witnesses produced statistical evidence that prison populations had been lowered without adversely affecting public safety in a number of jurisdictions, including certain counties in California, as well as Wisconsin, Illinois, Texas, Colorado, Montana, Michigan, Florida, and Canada.[11] . . .

---

11. Philadelphia's experience in the early 1990's with a federal court order mandating reductions in the prison population was less positive, and that history illustrates the undoubted need for caution in this area. One congressional witness testified that released prisoners committed 79 murders and multiple other offenses. See Hearing on S. 3 *et al.* before the Senate Committee on the Judiciary, 104th Cong., 1st Sess. 45 (1995) (statement of Lynne Abraham, District Attorney of Philadelphia). Lead counsel for the plaintiff class in that case responded that "[t]his inflammatory assertion has never been documented." *Id.* at 212 (statement of David Richman). . . .

The court found that various available methods of reducing overcrowding would have little or no impact on public safety. Expansion of good-time credits would allow the State to give early release to only those prisoners who pose the least risk of reoffending. Diverting low-risk offenders to community programs such as drug treatment, day reporting centers, and electronic monitoring would likewise lower the prison population without releasing violent convicts. The State now sends large numbers of persons to prison for violating a technical term or condition of their parole, and it could reduce the prison population by punishing technical parole violations through community-based programs. . . .

III

Establishing the population at which the State could begin to provide constitutionally adequate medical and mental health care, and the appropriate time frame within which to achieve the necessary reduction, requires a degree of judgment. The inquiry involves uncertain predictions regarding the effects of population reductions, as well as difficult determinations regarding the capacity of prison officials to provide adequate care at various population levels. Courts have substantial flexibility when making these judgments. "'Once invoked, "the scope of a district court's equitable powers . . . is broad, for breadth and flexibility are inherent in equitable remedies."'" Hutto v. Finney, 437 U.S. 678, 687 n.9 (1978), quoting *Milliken II*, quoting *Swann*.

Nevertheless, the PLRA requires a court to adopt a remedy that is "narrowly tailored" to the constitutional violation and that gives "substantial weight" to public safety. 18 U.S.C. §3626(a). When a court is imposing a population limit, this means the court must set the limit at the highest population consistent with an efficacious remedy. The court must also order the population reduction achieved in the shortest period of time reasonably consistent with public safety.

A

The three-judge court concluded that the population of California's prisons should be capped at 137.5% of design capacity. This conclusion is supported by the record. Indeed, some evidence supported a limit as low as 100% of design capacity. . . . Other evidence supported a limit as low as 130%. . . .

Although the three-judge court concluded that the "evidence in support of a 130% limit is strong," it found that some upward adjustment was warranted in light of "the caution and restraint required by the PLRA." . . . [T]he State's Corrections Independent Review Panel had found that 145% was the maximum "operable capacity" of California's prisons, although the relevance of that determination was undermined by the fact that the panel had not considered the need to provide constitutionally adequate medical and mental health care, as the State itself concedes. After considering, but discounting, this evidence, the three-judge court . . . imposed a limit of 137.5%.

This weighing of the evidence was not clearly erroneous. . . . The plaintiffs' evidentiary showing was intended to justify a limit of 130%, and the State made no attempt to show that any other number would allow for a remedy. . . . The three-judge court made the most precise determination it could in light of the record before it. The PLRA's narrow tailoring requirement is satisfied so long as these equitable, remedial judgments are made with the objective of releasing the fewest possible prisoners consistent with an efficacious remedy. In light of substantial evidence supporting an even more drastic remedy, the three-judge court complied with the requirement of the PLRA in this case.

B

The three-judge court ordered the State to achieve this reduction within two years. . . .

The State first had notice that it would be required to reduce its prison population in February 2009, when the three-judge court gave notice of its tentative ruling after trial. The 2-year deadline, however, will not begin to run until this Court issues its judgment. When that happens, the State will have already had over two years to begin complying with the order of the three-judge court. The State has used the time productively. At oral argument, the State indicated it had reduced its prison population by approximately 9,000 persons since the decision of the three-judge court. After oral argument, the State filed a supplemental brief indicating that it had begun to implement measures to shift "thousands" of additional prisoners to county facilities. . . .

The three-judge court, however, retains the authority, and the responsibility, to make further amendments to the existing order or any modified decree it may enter as warranted by the exercise of its sound discretion. . . . [T]he three-judge court must remain open to a showing . . . by either party that the injunction should be altered to ensure that the rights and interests of the parties are given all due and necessary protection. . . .

The State may wish to move for modification of the three-judge court's order to extend the deadline for the required reduction to five years from the entry of the judgment of this Court . . . . The three-judge court may grant such a request provided that the State satisfies necessary and appropriate preconditions designed to ensure that measures are taken to implement the plan without undue delay. . . .

If significant progress is made toward remedying the underlying constitutional violations, that progress may demonstrate that further population reductions are not necessary or are less urgent than previously believed. Were the State to make this showing, the three-judge court in the exercise of its discretion could consider whether it is appropriate to extend or modify this timeline. . . .

These observations reflect the fact that the three-judge court's order, like all continuing equitable decrees, must remain open to appropriate modification. They are not intended to cast doubt on the validity of the basic premise of the existing order. The medical and mental health care provided by California's prisons falls below the standard of decency that inheres in the Eighth Amendment. This extensive and ongoing constitutional violation requires a remedy, and a remedy will not be achieved without a reduction in overcrowding. The relief ordered by the three-judge court is required by the Constitution and was authorized by Congress in the PLRA. The State shall implement the order without further delay.

The judgment of the three-judge court is affirmed. . . .

Justice SCALIA, with whom Justice THOMAS joins, dissenting.

Today the Court affirms what is perhaps the most radical injunction issued by a court in our Nation's history . . .

There comes before us, now and then, a case whose proper outcome is so clearly indicated by tradition and common sense, that its decision ought to shape the law, rather than vice versa. One would think that, before allowing the decree of a federal district court to release 46,000 convicted felons, this Court would bend every effort to read the law in such a way as to avoid that outrageous result. . . .

The proceedings that led to this result were a judicial travesty. I dissent because the institutional reform the District Court has undertaken violates the terms of the governing statute, ignores bedrock limitations on the power of Article III judges, and takes federal courts wildly beyond their institutional capacity.

I

A. . .

What has been alleged here . . . is the running of a prison system with inadequate medical facilities. That may result in the denial of needed medical treatment to "a particular [prisoner] or [prisoners]," [paraphrasing the statutory focus on the rights of "a particular plaintiff or plaintiffs'—EDS.], thereby violating (according to our cases) his or their Eighth Amendment rights. But the mere existence of the inadequate system does not subject to cruel and unusual punishment the entire prison population in need of medical care, including those who receive it.

The Court acknowledges that the plaintiffs "do not base their case on deficiencies in care provided on any one occasion"; rather, "[p]laintiffs rely on systemwide deficiencies . . ." *Ante* n.3. But our judge-empowering "evolving standards of decency" jurisprudence (with which, by the way, I heartily disagree) does not prescribe (or at least has not until today prescribed) rules for the "decent" running of schools, prisons, and other government institutions. It forbids . . . the *denial of medical care* to those who need it. And the persons who have a constitutional claim for denial of medical care are those who are denied medical care—not all who face a "substantial risk" (whatever that is) of being denied medical care. . . .

[I]t is inconceivable that anything more than a small proportion of prisoners in the plaintiff classes have personally received sufficiently atrocious treatment that their Eighth Amendment right was violated . . . .

[W]hat procedural principle justifies certifying a class of plaintiffs so they may assert a claim of systemic unconstitutionality? I can think of two possibilities, both of which are untenable. The first is that although some or most plaintiffs in the class do not *individually* have viable Eighth Amendment claims, the class as a whole has collectively suffered an Eighth Amendment violation. That theory is contrary to the bedrock rule that the sole purpose of classwide adjudication is to aggregate claims that are individually viable. . . .

The second possibility is that every member of the plaintiff class *has* suffered an Eighth Amendment violation merely by virtue of being a patient in a poorly-run prison system, and the purpose of the class is merely to aggregate all those individually viable claims. . . . Under this theory, each and every prisoner who happens to be a patient in a system that has systemic weaknesses . . . has suffered cruel or unusual punishment, even if that person cannot make an individualized showing of mistreatment. Such a theory of the Eighth Amendment is preposterous. And we have said as much in the past:

> If . . . a healthy inmate who had suffered no deprivation of needed medical treatment were able to claim violation of his constitutional right to medical care . . . simply on the ground that the prison medical facilities were inadequate, the essential distinction between judge and executive would have disappeared: it would have become the function of the courts to assure adequate medical care in prisons.

Lewis v. Casey, 518 U.S. 343, 350 (1996). . . .

B

Even if I accepted the implausible premise that the plaintiffs have established a systemwide violation of the Eighth Amendment, I would dissent from the Court's endorsement of a decrowding order. That order is an example of what has become known as a "structural injunction." . . . [S]tructural injunctions are radically different from the injunctions traditionally issued by courts of equity . . . .

Structural injunctions depart from [the] historical practice [of limiting mandatory injunctions to requiring "a single simple act" that requires no continuing supervision. They turn] judges into long-term administrators of complex social institutions such as schools, prisons, and police departments. Indeed, they require judges to play a role essentially indistinguishable from the role ordinarily played by executive officials. Today's decision not only affirms the structural injunction but vastly expands its use, by holding that an entire system is unconstitutional because it *may produce* constitutional violations. . . .

This case illustrates one of [the] most pernicious aspects [of structural injunctions]: that they force judges to engage in a form of factfinding-as-policymaking that is outside the traditional judicial role. The factfinding judges traditionally engage in involves the determination of past or present facts based . . . upon a closed trial record. . . . In a very limited category of cases, judges have also traditionally been called upon to make some predictive judgments: which custody will best serve the interests of the child, for example, or whether a particular one-shot injunction will remedy the plaintiff's grievance. When a judge manages a structural injunction, however, he will inevitably be required to make very broad empirical predictions necessarily based in large part upon policy views—the sort of predictions regularly made by legislators and executive officials, but inappropriate for the Third Branch.

This feature of structural injunctions is superbly illustrated by the District Court's proceeding concerning the decrowding order's effect on public safety. . . . Here, the District Court [made] the "factual finding" that "the state has available methods by which it could readily reduce the prison population to 137.5% design capacity or less without an adverse impact on public safety or the operation of the criminal justice system." It found the evidence "clear" that prison overcrowding would "perpetuate a criminogenic prison system that itself threatens public safety" . . . .

The District Court cast these predictions (and the Court today accepts them) as "factual findings," made in reliance on the procession of expert witnesses that testified at trial. Because these "findings" have support in the record, it is difficult to reverse them under a plain-error standard of review. And given that the District Court devoted nearly 10 days of trial and 70 pages of its opinion to this issue, it is difficult to dispute that the District Court has discharged its statutory obligation to give "substantial weight to any adverse impact on public safety."

But the idea that the three District Judges in this case relied solely on the credibility of the testifying expert witnesses is fanciful. *Of course* they were relying largely on their own beliefs about penology and recidivism. And *of course* different district judges, of different policy views, would have "found" that rehabilitation would not work and that releasing prisoners would increase the crime rate. I am not saying that the District Judges rendered their factual findings in bad faith. I am saying that it is impossible for judges to make "factual findings" without inserting their own policy judgments, when the factual findings *are* policy judgments. . . .

[T]he dressing-up of policy judgments as factual findings is not an error peculiar to this case. It is an unavoidable concomitant of institutional-reform litigation. When a district court issues an injunction, it must make a factual assessment of the anticipated consequences of the injunction. And when the injunction undertakes to restructure a social institution, assessing the factual consequences of the injunction is necessarily the sort of predictive judgment that our system of government allocates to other government officials. . . .

The District Court also relied heavily on the views of the Receiver and Special Master, and those reports play a starring role in the Court's opinion today. . . . The use of these reports is even less consonant with the traditional judicial role than the

District Court's reliance on the expert testimony at trial. . . . Relying on the un-cross-examined findings of an investigator, sent into the field to prepare a factual report and give suggestions on how to improve the prison system, bears no resemblance to ordinary judicial decisionmaking. . . .

III

In my view, a court may not order a prisoner's release unless it determines that the prisoner is suffering from a violation of his constitutional rights, and that his release, and no other relief, will remedy that violation. Thus, if the court determines that a particular prisoner is being denied constitutionally required medical treatment, and the release of that prisoner (and no other remedy) would enable him to obtain medical treatment, then the court can order his release; but a court may not order the release of prisoners who have suffered no violations of their constitutional rights, merely to make it less likely that that will happen to them in the future. . . .

[M]y approach may invite the objection that the PLRA appears to contemplate structural injunctions in general and mass prisoner-release orders in particular. The statute requires courts to "give substantial weight to any adverse impact on public safety or the operation of a criminal justice system caused by the relief" and authorizes them to appoint Special Masters, §3626(a)(1)(A), (f), provisions that seem to presuppose the possibility of a structural remedy. It also sets forth criteria under which courts may issue orders that have "the purpose or effect of reducing or limiting the prisoner population," §3626(g)(4).

I do not believe that objection carries the day. In addition to imposing numerous limitations on the ability of district courts to order injunctive relief with respect to prison conditions, the PLRA states that "[n]othing in this section shall be construed to . . . repeal or detract from otherwise applicable limitations on the remedial powers of the courts." §3626(a)(1)(C). The PLRA is therefore best understood as an attempt to constrain the discretion of courts issuing structural injunctions—not as a mandate for their use. . . .

Justice ALITO, with whom Chief Justice ROBERTS joins, dissenting.

The decree in this case is a perfect example of what the Prison Litigation Reform Act of 1995 (PLRA) was enacted to prevent. . . .

The Eighth Amendment prohibits prison officials from depriving inmates of "the minimal civilized measure of life's necessities." Rhodes v. Chapman, 452 U.S. 337, 347 (1981). Federal courts have the responsibility to ensure that this constitutional standard is met, but undesirable prison conditions that do not violate the Constitution are beyond the federal courts' reach. . . .

I

Both the PLRA and general principles concerning injunctive relief dictate that a prisoner release order cannot properly be issued unless the relief is necessary to remedy an ongoing violation. . . .

The scope of permissible relief depends on the scope of any continuing violations, and therefore it was essential for the three-judge court to make a reliable determination of the extent of any violations as of the time its release order was issued.

Particularly in light of the radical nature of its chosen remedy, nothing less than an up-to-date assessment was tolerable.

The three-judge court, however, relied heavily on outdated information and findings and refused to permit California to introduce new evidence. . . .

[B]y the date of the trial before the three-judge court, the death rate had been trending downward for 10 quarters, and the number of likely preventable deaths fell from 18 in 2006 to 3 in 2007, a decline of 83 percent. Between 2001 and 2007, the California prison system had the 13th lowest average mortality rate of all 50 state systems. . . .

II . . .

[The PLRA's remedial limitations] largely reflect general standards for injunctive relief aimed at remedying constitutional violations by state and local governments. "The power of the federal courts to restructure the operation of local and state governmental entities is not plenary. . . . Once a constitutional violation is found, a federal court is required to tailor the scope of the remedy to fit the nature and extent of the constitutional violation." *Dayton I.*

Here, the majority and the court below maintain that no remedy short of a massive release of prisoners from the general prison population can remedy the State's failure to provide constitutionally adequate health care. This argument is implausible on its face and is not supported by the requisite clear and convincing evidence. . . .

I do not dispute that general overcrowding *contributes* to many of the California system's healthcare problems. But it by no means follows that reducing overcrowding is the only or the best or even a particularly good way to alleviate those problems. . . . The release order is not limited to prisoners needing substantial medical care but instead calls for a reduction in the system's overall population. . . . Although some class members will presumably be among those who are discharged, the decrease in the number of prisoners needing mental health treatment or other forms of extensive medical care will be much smaller than the total number of prisoners released, and thus the release will produce at best only a modest improvement in the burden on the medical care system. . . .

The State proposed several remedies other than a massive release of prisoners, but the three-judge court, seemingly intent on attacking the broader problem of general overcrowding, rejected all of the State's proposals. In doing so, the court made three critical errors.

First, the court did not assess those proposals and other remedies in light of conditions proved to exist at the time the release order was framed. . . .

Second, the court failed to distinguish between conditions that fall below the level that may be desirable as a matter of public policy and conditions that do not meet the minimum level mandated by the Constitution. . . .

Third, the court rejected alternatives that would not have provided "immediate" relief. But nothing in the PLRA suggests that public safety may be sacrificed in order to implement an immediate remedy rather than a less dangerous one that requires a more extended but reasonable period of time.

If the three-judge court had not made these errors, it is entirely possible that an adequate but less drastic remedial plan could have been crafted. Without up-to-date information, it is not possible to specify what such a plan might provide, and in any event, that is not a task that should be undertaken in the first instance by this Court. But possible components of such a plan are not hard to identify. . . .

Sanitary procedures could be improved; sufficient supplies of medicine and medical equipment could be purchased; an adequate system of records management could be implemented; and the number of medical and other staff positions could be increased. Similarly, it is hard to believe that staffing vacancies cannot be reduced or eliminated and that the qualifications of medical personnel cannot be improved by any means short of a massive prisoner release. Without specific findings backed by hard evidence, this Court should not accept the counterintuitive proposition that these problems cannot be ameliorated by increasing salaries, improving working conditions, and providing better training and monitoring of performance.

While the cost of a large-scale construction program may well exceed California's current financial capabilities, a more targeted program, involving the repair and perhaps the expansion of current medical facilities (as opposed to general prison facilities), might be manageable. After all, any remedy in this case, including the new programs associated with the prisoner release order and other proposed relief now before the three-judge court, will necessarily involve some state expenditures.

Measures such as these might be combined with targeted reductions in critical components of the State's prison population. A certain number of prisoners in the classes on whose behalf the two cases were brought might be transferred to out-of-state facilities. . . .

Finally, as a last resort, a much smaller release of prisoners in the two plaintiff classes could be considered. . . .

III

Before ordering any prisoner release, the PLRA commands a court to "give substantial weight to any adverse impact on public safety or the operation of a criminal justice system caused by the relief." §3626(a)(1)(A). This provision unmistakably reflects Congress' view that prisoner release orders are inherently risky. . . .

[T]he three-judge court in this case concluded that loosing 46,000 criminals would not produce a tally like that in Philadelphia [see note 11 of the majority's opinion] and would actually improve public safety. . . .

This is a fundamental and dangerous error. When a trial court selects between the competing views of experts on broad empirical questions such as the efficacy of preventing crime through the incapacitation of convicted criminals, the trial court's choice is very different from a classic finding of fact and is not entitled to the same degree of deference on appeal. . . .

* * *

. . . I fear that today's decision, like prior prisoner release orders, will lead to a grim roster of victims. I hope that I am wrong.

In a few years, we will see.

NOTES ON THE PRISON CASES

1. **The prison cases.** Beginning in the 1970s, the federal courts supervised the reform of prisons, jails, and mental hospitals in nearly every state. The worst of cruel and unusual conditions were greatly improved, but money, institutional inertia, and political indifference remain substantial obstacles. And inevitably, some of these decrees had unintended consequences that were counterproductive. The Supreme Court had issued narrow opinions in several prison cases, but remarkably, Brown v.

Plata is the first Supreme Court case to grapple with the central problem presented by these cases.

2. The central issue. The central problem appears to be that California's voters are not willing to spend nearly enough money to provide facilities and medical care for all the people they wish to imprison. In 2009, with the state facing a projected $42 billion budget deficit, the receiver in *Coleman* asked for $8 billion to build 7 new prison health care centers with a total of 10,000 beds. Malia Wollan, *California Asks Removal of Prison Overseer*, N.Y. Times (Jan. 29, 2009). Of course, he didn't get the money.

The courts were patient. The *Coleman* litigation was 21 years old, and the *Plata* litigation 10, by the time of the Supreme Court's decision. The state was allowed to propose its own plans for reform and compliance, and in *Plata* there is a consent decree. The evidence, and the fact finding, was massive and detailed. Justice Alito was new to the problem; he wanted to give the state more time. But from the perspective of the district judges and the prisoners, the state had already had many years.

No doubt the courts are now deeply involved in what should be an executive branch function. And releasing tens of thousands of prisoners is no doubt an extraordinary remedy. What is the alternative? Should the court order tax increases, as a lower court did in the Kansas City school desegregation case (see Missouri v. Jenkins, 495 U.S. 33 (1990) (*Jenkins II*)), and earmark the money for prisons? See the Notes on Paying for the Remedy, below. Should the court give up and let the constitutional violations continue? And if the prisons need not provide medical care, what else do they not need to provide? Would the central issue be any different if the state provided no sanitary facilities? No food? In Hutto v. Finney, 437 U.S. 678 (1978), Arkansas prisoners were fed only 1,000 calories a day, and nearly all were losing weight.

3. The Prison Litigation Reform Act. The Prison Litigation Reform Act, much discussed in *Plata*, codified remedial standards in prison cases. Its core provision, 18 U.S.C. §3626(a)(1)(A), is not confined to release orders. It requires that any prospective relief in a prison case "shall extend no further than necessary to correct the violation of the Federal right of a particular plaintiff or plaintiffs," that it be "narrowly drawn," that it extend "no further than necessary to correct the violation of the Federal right," and that it be "the least intrusive means necessary to correct the violation of the Federal right." Congress plainly thought that courts were engaged in free-wheeling equity in these cases, but it seems increasingly clear that the Court's view of appropriate injunctive remedies is not far from what Congress codified. The PLRA specifies multiple and sometimes redundant analytic steps, and the Court works its way through each of them. But do you get the sense at any point that the Court wishes it could do more than the Act permits?

The Act might be unconstitutional if it prohibited a remedy necessary to end an ongoing constitutional violation. Note the Court's brief allusion to that possibility in the fourth paragraph of part II.B.3 of the opinion. Other provisions of §3626 deter prisoner litigation in other ways, with higher filing fees, limits on attorneys' fees, and elimination of most damage claims except for physical injury.

4. Substantial risk and threatened violations. The dissents raise issues about the judicial role in these cases that are both important and serious. But in their anger at what they believe to be an outrageous result and a process run amok, they sometimes misstate what actually happened in the three-judge court. Justice Scalia thought that no prisoner's constitutional right is violated until he is denied medical care (and maybe not even then), so that there can be no such thing as a systemic violation in this context. The phrase "substantial risk" (footnote 3 of the majority's opinion) comes from earlier cases holding that the Eighth Amendment is substantively violated by holding a prisoner in unsafe conditions that pose a substantial risk of injury.

Helling v. McKinney, 509 U.S. 25 (1993). Justice Scalia dissented, and he plainly continued to reject that holding.

But even without that, injunctions are available to prevent threatened violations of law. That's the whole point of preventive injunctions. On the facts found by the district courts, doesn't California threaten to deprive every inmate of medical care every time he needs it? And given that litigation is slow, and that the need for medical care is often urgent, is there any imaginable way to effectively implement Justice Scalia's one-prisoner-at-a-time-after-he-gets-sick remedy?

5. Recent improvements. Justice Alito focuses on a decline in the death rate after the 2008 trial. Assuming these improvements are real, should we assume that less intrusive remedies are finally working after all these years? Or should we assume that the threat of a large prisoner release has finally gotten the state's attention and motivated more serious efforts?

Justice Alito also notes that California's overall prison death rate was relatively low compared to other states. The three-judge court considered that evidence, noting that it did not control for demographics, and that California's free population also had a low death rate, and concluded that this evidence of gross death rates did not overcome all the other evidence in the case. Coleman v. Schwarzenegger, 922 F. Supp. 2d 882, 941 (E.D. Cal. 2009).

6. Who would be released? The dissenters emphasized that California has been ordered to release 46,000 "convicted felons." But there is something very odd in the prison population statistics. The Court says that 140,000 prisoners enter the system every year. Yet there are only 156,000 prisoners altogether. If many of those prisoners are serving long terms, there must be tens of thousands of others who are passing through the system for less than a year at a time. Such short sentences do not suggest that California considers these people serious threats to public safety. Eliminating this enormous flow through of short-term prisoners is one potential source of substantial population reductions that may have only modest effects on public safety. The three-judge court did not say that prisoners can be released without danger to the public because rehabilitation works, as Justice Scalia seemed to assume; rather, it principally said that many prisoners in the California system are not very dangerous in the first place and can safely be released earlier or dealt with by means other than incarceration.

7. The long aftermath. The Supreme Court's opinion came down in May 2011. It took many more years and lower court orders to resolve the disputes between the parties. The much abbreviated(!) account below gives you a sense of what this type of litigation looks like in the trial court.

In 2011, the three-judge court ordered the state to reduce its prison population to 167 percent of design capacity by December, to 155 percent by June 2012, to 147 percent by December 2012, and to 137.5 percent by June 2013 (four years after the three-judge court's original order), and to file monthly progress reports. The state attempted to comply principally by authorizing the transfer of certain low-risk offenders to county jails.

In 2013, the state filed motions to vacate the court's orders and terminate the litigation. To the three-judge court, the state argued that crowding was no longer the primary cause of any deficiencies in medical care. The district court extended the deadline for reaching the 137.5-percent target to December 2013. Coleman v. Brown, 922 F. Supp. 2d 1004 (E.D. Cal. 2013) (three-judge court); Coleman v. Brown, 938 F. Supp. 2d 955 (E.D. Cal. 2013) (single judge). Plaintiffs filed repeated motions to hold defendants in contempt, but the court did not go there. "Being more interested in achieving compliance with our Order than in holding contempt hearings, this Court has exercised exceptional restraint." 922 F. Supp. 2d at 1050. California appealed again to the Supreme Court over the modified three-judge court orders. The Court dismissed for lack of an appealable order. Brown v. Plata, 570 U.S. 938 (2013). The California legislature then passed new prison legislation, and the state asked the three-judge court for more time. The state filed a motion to extend the deadline and told the three-judge court that if ordered to comply immediately, it would send thousands of prisoners to out-of-state facilities under this legislation.

In 2014, the three-judge court again extended the deadline in an unreported order. Coleman v. Brown, No. 2:90-cv-020 (E.D. Cal. Feb. 10, 2014) (ECF No. 5060 and 5061). Now the prisons were to reach 137.5 percent of capacity by February 28, 2016. The number of inmates housed out of state was not to rise above the level at the time of the order. The court again ordered changes to good-time and parole practices, and an expanded re-entry program for prisoners being released. The order created a new position, a Compliance Officer to be appointed by the court, and it set new intermediate deadlines and benchmarks for compliance.

In February 2015, the state reported to the three-judge court that it was in compliance with the court's orders, a year ahead of schedule, and that the prison population was at 136.6 percent of design capacity. A lead attorney for the prisoners said that "we went from total war . . . to where there's been a lot of cooperation and progress." Sam Stanton & Denny Walsh, *Major Progress Cited in Prison Inmate Care*, Sacramento Bee (Dec. 20, 2014). Of course it is difficult to assess the reasons for such a change from the outside, but the key appears to be the appointment of Jeffrey Beard as head of the Department of Corrections and Rehabilitation. Beard had actually testified for the plaintiffs in 2010; when he took office in December 2012, he was described as "a vocal advocate of alternative sentencing laws that move non-serious criminals into community treatment programs rather than state lockup." *Jeff Beard: The New Name in California Corrections*, Correctional News (Jan. 2, 2013), available at http://www. correctionalnews.com/articles/2013/01/2/jeff-beard-the-new-name-in-california-corrections [https://perma.cc/9ZHY-22SK].

What to make of all this? The repeated game of chicken between defendants and the court is not unusual in structural injunction cases, especially where there is political resistance to compliance. These issues are further addressed in units on modification of decrees, below in this chapter, and on enforcement of judgments in Chapter 9.

The population limit was adopted in part because it seemed more manageable and more achievable than building facilities and improving care for all the inmates. But it was not achievable until the state decided to cooperate rather than resist. In theory, the court could have just ordered a wholesale release of inmates on any one of its deadlines. Why didn't it do that? There are many possible reasons. If the court appears unreasonable, it is more likely to get reversed. It might incur even greater wrath in public opinion. It cannot be sure of the facts; what if some of the released inmates really are dangerous? What if one or a few of those released commit spectacular crimes shortly after their release? It is safer to order process, and let the state be responsible for picking individual prisoners.

And what if the court ordered the immediate release of several thousand named prisoners—an order with no wiggle room or ambiguity—and the state just said no? Then the court has to either back down or impose serious contempt sanctions. Should the warden go to jail? The governor? Both the court and the defendants know that that is the ultimate end game; neither wants to get there. Plaintiffs file contempt motions to keep the pressure on; the court denies those motions without prejudice, to let the pressure simmer.

And it may be that California officials had backed themselves into a corner. Once they told the Supreme Court, the press, and the public that the court order required them to release 46,000 dangerous felons, it might have been politically impossible to comply. Whether or not it was true, it was what they had led the public to believe. There is little reason to think that California would have dramatically improved prison health care without the litigation. But it may also be that the high-profile litigation and the orders to reduce the prison population eventually became an obstacle to reducing the prison population. Now a new leader has found ways to release significant numbers of prisoners pursuant to new programs, and without the appearance of a wholesale release of prisoners.

8. Other prison litigation. It had been widely assumed that institutional reform litigation peaked long ago and largely disappeared as the federal courts became more conservative. But a substantial survey of the cases found that widespread prison litigation continues. Margo Schlanger, *Civil Rights Injunctions Over Time: A Case Study of Jail and Prison Court Orders*, 81 N.Y.U. L. Rev. 550 (2006). Professor Schlanger found that there was little decline in prison litigation from the early 1980s to 1996, when the Prison Litigation Reform Act took effect, and that even after the PLRA, the percentage of prisons and jails under judicial supervision dropped only modestly. But the nature of this litigation changed, beginning in the 1980s, to an emphasis on more narrowly targeted complaints, tighter approaches to causation, and more rigorous proof. The PLRA thus confirmed a trend that was already well established.

A more recent study shows more substantial declines in cases filed, cases filed per prisoner, and percentage of prisoners in an institution subject to a court order. Margo Schlanger, *Trends in Prison Litigation, as the PLRA Enters Adulthood*, 5 UC Irvine L. Rev. 153 (2015). Success rates are very low, in part because 95 percent of prisoner filings are pro se. Serious institutional-reform litigation requires dedicated lawyers, and data on all cases does not tell us what is happening with the most important cases. The article does not report on cases with lawyers, but a quick and preliminary look at the data shows substantial numbers of settlements. Plaintiffs appeared to get at least some relief in a modest majority of recent cases with lawyers.

9. Other legislation. The Civil Rights of Institutionalized Persons Act authorizes the Attorney General to sue states to correct "egregious or flagrant conditions" that violate constitutional rights of persons housed in prisons, mental hospitals, and similar institutions. 42 U.S.C. §1997a(a). Attorneys General of both parties have maintained an active practice under this section, more by negotiation than by litigation. An overview, with links to complaints, briefs, settlements, litigated decisions, and reports of investigations, is available at https://www.justice.gov/crt/rights-persons-confined-jails-and-prisons [https://perma.cc/CWU9-MBQZ].

NOTES ON PAYING FOR THE REMEDY

1. Rightful position, equitable discretion, and funding. All the desegregation and institutional reform cases order remedies that require the expenditure of public funds. Some of these expenditures are very large. Are court-ordered expenditures of public funds defensible when the court orders freewheeling discretionary remedies in the tradition of Bailey v. Proctor? Are they more defensible when the courts try in good faith to restore plaintiffs to the position they would have occupied but for the wrong? Despite its indeterminacy in constitutional cases, doesn't that standard constrain discretion far more than a principle that equity courts should do equity? Isn't judicial power to order compliance with minimum constitutional standards a necessary corollary of judicial review?

2. *Jenkins II.* One stage of the Kansas City school-desegregation litigation raised the issue of paying for the remedy ordered by the trial court. *Jenkins II* was decided on a limited grant of certiorari: Assuming that the unusually expensive remedies in the case were necessary to cure the violation, could the court order the Kansas City school board to raise taxes to pay for the remedy? The Supreme Court said yes, with qualifications. Missouri v. Jenkins, 495 U.S. 33 (1990). The district court could not itself set a higher tax rate. *Id.* at 50-52. But it could order the school board to levy taxes sufficient to pay for the desegregation plan, and it could enjoin enforcement of state-law provisions that capped the property tax rate in Missouri school districts and that, even below the cap, required a voter referendum to raise taxes. The court could enjoin enforcement of these tax limits because they barred an effective remedy; once those limits were enjoined, the school board had taxing authority and could use it. *Id.* at 55-57. Four impassioned dissenters thought this a nonsense distinction; taxing authority could come only from the people of Missouri, and it had been granted only on conditions and subject to limitations that were not themselves unconstitutional. This was a judicial tax increase, taxation without representation, and a denial of due process to taxpayers who had not been parties to the litigation.

3. Separation of powers and democratic government. Is the essence of democratic government sacrificed when judges control too much of the budget? Surely legislatures should generally set priorities and spending patterns. But isn't the point of the underlying constitutional rights in these cases that there are some limits on that discretion? Doesn't the Cruel and Unusual Punishment Clause mean, for example, that states can't decide to incarcerate people under dangerous conditions—that the democratic process denied itself that option when state legislatures ratified the Eighth and Fourteenth Amendments? But if the legislature suddenly has to come up with a lot of money for some constituency that has been unconstitutionally neglected, the burden of budget balancing is more likely to fall on other relatively neglected groups than on the dominant interests that have been doing the neglecting while voting benefits for themselves.

Defendants presumably have the option to close the institution if they are unable or unwilling to run it constitutionally. See Palmer v. Thompson, 403 U.S. 217 (1971), upholding the decision of Jackson, Mississippi, to close its swimming pools rather than integrate them. How much does that option reduce separation of powers problems? Is it completely irrelevant, because shutting down is not a realistic choice for anything more important than a swimming pool? Even if shutting down is a realistic choice, does an order to "run it my way or shut it down" interfere with the very same choices as an order to "run it my way"? Or is it important that the choice to spend more money or none at all remains with the legislature, even if legislators don't find those choices very attractive? What about partial shutdowns? The California prison litigation illustrates a choice to spend the same or less money incarcerating fewer people, instead of more money incarcerating as many people as before.

4. The practical experience. In nearly all the cases, courts have been content to order program improvements. Eventually, often after some period of posturing on all sides, the political branches would find enough money to more or less comply. Plaintiffs and the court would press for further efforts and sometimes get them. Eventually, the court would accept what had been accomplished as sufficient compliance. This minuet is further explored in section 9.A.1. Court-ordered tax increases, as in *Jenkins II*, and public officials going to jail for contempt of court, are both extraordinarily rare.

NOTES ON THE FUTURE OF INSTITUTIONAL REFORM LITIGATION

1. Trusting the judges? Separation of powers was designed to restrain bad people and excessively zealous good people; the bench surely has some of each. Isn't there potential for abuse when one life-tenured judge tries to run an entire prison system, housing authority, or school district? Especially when he tries to raise taxes to achieve his goals? Are appellate review, the pressure of public opinion, and the theoretical threat of impeachment sufficient safeguards? Whatever one thinks about these things, some members of the Supreme Court do not appear to trust fellow judges with such power, which does not bode well for broad institutional reform litigation going forward.

2. The demise of the structural injunction? Jason Parkin, *Aging Injunctions and the Legacy of Institutional Reform Litigation*, 70 Vand. L. Rev. 167 (2017), notes the declining use of institutional reform litigation in federal courts and attributes the decline to three factors: "dissolution," "design," and "disuse." *Id.* at 171. Dissolution of structural injunctions has happened through government defendants seeking modifications of existing "permanent" injunctions under the eased modification standards of Horne v. Flores, the next principal case. Some structural injunctions end "by design," terminating by their own terms when a certain time period or benchmark is met. *Id.* at 170. Finally, even when structural injunctions remain "in effect on paper, they remain viable only as long as the parties and the court continue to implement and enforce them." *Id.* at 170-171. As years and decades pass by, judges, lawyers, and clients die, retire, or move away. Unless the next generation steps up, there is no one to enforce the injunction. Further, a mismatch between legal standards and the terms of the injunction is more likely as time passes. *Id.* at 171.

Is the decline of the structural injunction something to be lamented or celebrated? How much is the demise due to the Supreme Court's professed adherence to the rightful position standard and skepticism about broad remedies?

3. The rightful position standard as a tool for liberals. It is unusual for the Supreme Court to give more than the rightful position in structural injunction cases. But sometimes Court liberals can use the rightful position standard to cure underremediation. In United States v. Virginia, 518 U.S. 515 (1996), the Supreme Court struck down as unconstitutional the admissions policy of the Virginia Military Institute, a state-supported military college for men only. A severe lack of privacy and an "adversarial model" of instruction, which sounds to outsiders like severe hazing, were integral parts of the program. The state offered no comparable program for women. The court of appeals held that the male-only program was unconstitutional, 976 F.2d 890 (4th Cir. 1992), but it suggested that Virginia could remedy the violation by integrating VMI, by starting a "parallel" program for women, by privatizing VMI, or perhaps by other means. The state responded by creating the Virginia Women's Institute for Leadership at Mary Baldwin College. The leaders of VWIL concluded that lack of privacy, an adversarial model, and military drill were pedagogically inappropriate for women; they created a leadership curriculum based on cooperation. The court of appeals affirmed the adequacy of this remedy, subject to continued judicial oversight. 44 F.3d 1229 (4th Cir. 1995).

The Supreme Court affirmed the holding that the male-only program at VMI was unconstitutional but rejected VWIL as an adequate remedy. Justice Ginsburg, for a majority of the Court, wrote that:

> A remedial decree . . . must closely fit the constitutional violation; it must be shaped to place persons unconstitutionally denied an opportunity or advantage in "the

position they would have occupied in the absence of [discrimination]." See *Milliken II.* The constitutional violation in this case is the categorical exclusion of women from an extraordinary educational opportunity afforded men. A proper remedy for an unconstitutional exclusion, we have explained, aims to "eliminate [so far as possible] the discriminatory effects of the past" and to "bar like discrimination in the future." Louisiana v. United States, 390 U.S. 145, 154 (1965).

Virginia chose not to eliminate, but to leave untouched, VMI's exclusionary policy. For women only, however, Virginia proposed a separate program, different in kind from VMI and unequal in tangible and intangible facilities. Having violated the Constitution's equal protection requirement, Virginia was obliged to show that its remedial proposal "directly address[ed] and relate[d] to" the violation, see *Milliken II*, 433 U.S. at 282, i.e., the equal protection denied to women ready, willing, and able to benefit from educational opportunities of the kind VMI offers. . . . If the VWIL program could not "eliminate the discriminatory effects of the past," could it at least "bar like discrimination in the future"? See *Louisiana*, 380 U.S. at 154. A comparison of the programs said to be "parallel" informs our answer.

[There followed a lengthy showing of VMI's superiority to VWIL in terms of endowment, faculty, student qualifications, athletic facilities, science and engineering curriculum, military training, and alumni network, and of the admitted fact that for better or worse, VWIL did not offer an adversative model and lack of privacy.]

When Virginia tendered its VWIL plan, the Fourth Circuit did not inquire whether the proposed remedy, approved by the District Court, placed women denied the VMI advantage in "the position they would have occupied in the absence of [discrimination]." *Milliken II.* Instead, the Court of Appeals considered whether the State could provide, with fidelity to the equal protection principle, separate and unequal educational programs for men and women. . . .

Valuable as VWIL may prove for students who seek the program offered, Virginia's remedy affords no cure at all for the opportunities and advantages withheld from women who want a VMI education and can make the grade. In sum, Virginia's remedy does not match the constitutional violation. . . .

518 U.S. at 547-556. Chief Justice Rehnquist concurring in the judgment, agreed that inferior conditions for women violated the Constitution. On the remedy, he argued that:

> an adequate remedy might be a demonstration by Virginia that its interest in educating men in a single-sex environment is matched by its interest in educating women in a single-sex institution. To demonstrate such, the State does not need to create two institutions with the same number of faculty PhD's, similar SAT scores, or comparable athletic fields. Nor would it necessarily require that the women's institution offer the same curriculum as the men's; one could be strong in computer science, the other could be strong in liberal arts. It would be a sufficient remedy, I think, if the two institutions offered the same quality of education and were of the same overall caliber.

Id. at 565. Justice Scalia would have found no constitutional violation.

Should the rightful-position principle have equal force in both directions? That is, should the district court have any more discretion to give less than the rightful position in *Virginia* than it has to give more than the rightful position in Brown v. Plata? Note that rightful-position talk in structural injunction cases began with conservatives in the 1970s, resisting school busing decrees. In *Virginia*, Justice Ginsburg uses it to justify a complete remedy, reversing a partial and discretionary remedy from a more conservative court of appeals.

Judicial discretion is a two-edged sword: If a judge agrees with you about the value of a right, you may want him to have discretion to overenforce it. But discretion also means that if he doesn't like your right, he can underenforce it. And if he is enthusiastic about some right you abhor, he can overenforce that too. Rightful position is a pretty indeterminate standard in structural injunction cases with complex facts. But isn't it more determinate than "complete equity in the case"?

B.   MODIFYING INJUNCTIONS

INTRODUCTORY NOTES

1. Rule 60(b)(5). A permanent injunction is a final judgment. Unless vacated or modified on appeal, it is res judicata—both claim and issue preclusive—in subsequent proceedings. Federal Rule 60 and its state equivalents state the grounds on which final judgments may be modified or vacated in subsequent proceedings. Most of these grounds apply to all judgments, whether for damages or injunctions. But the third alternative in Rule 60(b)(5) applies only to remedies that operate prospectively:

> **(b) Grounds for Relief from a Final Judgment, Order, or Proceeding.** On motion and just terms, the court may relieve a party or its legal representative from a final judgment, order, or proceeding for the following reasons: . . .
> (5) . . . applying it prospectively is no longer equitable . . .

2. *Swift* and the grievous wrong standard. For 60 years, the leading case was United States v. Swift & Co., 286 U.S. 106 (1932), decided before the traditional equity practice was incorporated into Rule 60(b)(5). *Swift* was an antitrust decree, entered by consent (i.e., by settlement), designed to prevent the large meatpackers from monopolizing wholesale groceries. Justice Cardozo came down on the side of finality, with a high standard for modification:

> A continuing decree of injunction directed to events to come is subject always to adaptation as events may shape the need. The distinction is between restraints that give protection to rights fully accrued upon facts so nearly permanent as to be substantially impervious to change, and those that involve the supervision of changing conduct or conditions and thus are provisional and tentative. . . .
> The injunction, whether right or wrong, is not subject to impeachment in its application to the conditions that existed at its making. We are not at liberty to reverse under the guise of readjusting. Life is never static, and the passing of a decade has brought changes to the grocery business as it has to every other. The inquiry for us is whether the changes are so important that dangers, once substantial, have become attenuated to a shadow. . . . Nothing less than a clear showing of grievous wrong evoked by new and unforeseen conditions should lead us to change what was decreed after years of litigation with the consent of all concerned.

Id. at 114, 119.

3. *United Shoe* and modifications to achieve the original purpose. The Court held *Swift* inapplicable when a decree fails to achieve its central purpose and a party seeks modifications designed to achieve that purpose. United States v. United Shoe Machinery Corp., 391 U.S. 244 (1968). *United Shoe* was a litigated antitrust decree; the trial court refused to break up the company and instead ordered changes in its marketing practices that were expected to permit the growth of competition. When no viable competition emerged, the government moved to modify the injunction to order dissolution of the company. The Court held it an abuse of discretion to deny further relief; the opinion does not mention Rule 60.

4. Developments in the lower courts. The practice of retaining jurisdiction in structural injunction cases enabled judges to issue a series of orders, in effect modifying their earlier injunctions, without reliance on Rule 60(b)(5) and without satisfying either the *Swift* or *United Shoe* standards. Henry Friendly, one of the great circuit judges of his generation, distinguished modifications that would eliminate the central provision of a decree, or prevent achievement of its central purpose, from modifications that were more peripheral or that actually assisted achievement of the central purpose, holding that the latter were much easier to justify. New York State Association for Retarded Children, Inc. v. Carey, 706 F.2d 956, 969 (2d Cir. 1983).

5. *Rufo* and substantial change in law and fact. Rufo v. Inmates of the Suffolk County Jail, 502 U.S. 367 (1992), substantially relaxed the *Swift* standard. After losing on the merits in protracted litigation over an overcrowded jail, defendants agreed to build a new jail with one-man cells. The agreement was reached, and the decree entered, while a New York case on two-man cells was pending in the Supreme Court. Apparently, both sides chose to settle any remaining issues rather than take the risk that that case might go against them. In the event, the Court upheld two-man cells in New York City's jail. Bell v. Wolfish, 441 U.S. 520 (1979). Defendants in *Rufo* then sought permission to put two inmates in each of the new cells, alleging unexpected growth in the jail's population as a change in fact and *Bell* as a change in law. Plaintiffs responded that the order for one-man cells was a final judgment, and that even if *Bell* applied, it did not mean that defendants could put two men, awaiting trial and not yet convicted of anything, in cells designed for only one.

The Court summarized its new standard as follows: "Under the flexible standard we adopt today, a party seeking modification of a consent decree must establish that a significant change in facts or law warrants revision of the decree and that the proposed modification is suitably tailored to the changed circumstance." 502 U.S. at 393. The Court said that the significant changes relied on had to have been unforeseen, but that they need not have been unforeseeable. *Id.* at 385.

Bell did not entitle defendants to relitigate the constitutionality of two-man cells. "To hold that a clarification in the law automatically opens the door for relitigation of the merits of every affected consent decree would undermine the finality of such agreements. . . ." *Id.* at 389. Such a rule would imply that "the only legally enforceable obligation assumed by the state under the consent decree was that of ultimately achieving minimal constitutional prison standards. . . . [I]t would make necessary . . . a constitutional decision every time an effort was made either to enforce or modify the decree. . . ." *Id.* at 390.

But the Court distinguished injunctions entered in the face of uncertainty about the requirements of substantive law from injunctions entered on a firm but mistaken view of those requirements. In the latter case, a subsequent clarification could be a change in law (more precisely, a change in the parties' understanding of the law) that supported a motion to modify. 502 U.S. at 390.

6. *Agostini* and changes in law. An injunction is modifiable for significant change in law when the precedents on which it is based have been seriously undermined or eroded. Agostini v. Felton, 521 U.S. 203 (1997). But only the Supreme Court can decide that one of its own decisions has been so undermined. The Court held that the proper procedure in such cases is for the district court and court of appeals to entertain the motion to modify, because there is a claim that the law has changed, but to deny relief, because those courts cannot conclude that the law has actually changed. *Id.* at 237-238. In *Agostini*, the Supreme Court then granted certiorari, upheld the movant's claim, and ordered modification of the injunction. Note that it could have denied certiorari without explanation, no matter how much the law had changed.

7. *Frew* and "reason to modify the decree." Frew v. Hawkins, 540 U.S. 431 (2004), held unanimously that state officials cannot relitigate the minimum requirements of federal law on plaintiffs' motion to enforce a consent decree. The reasons the Fifth Circuit held otherwise were based in state sovereign immunity law, and that part of the case is explained in section 5.C.1.

The state claimed that the consent decree in *Frew* was more onerous than the federal statute it enforced. The Court said that the state's remedy, if any, was a motion to modify under Rule 60(b)(5). *Rufo*'s standard was not formally amended, but the Court had this to say in dictum:

> The federal court must exercise its equitable powers to ensure that when the objects of the decree have been attained, responsibility for discharging the State's obligations is returned promptly to the State and its officials. As public servants, the officials of the State must be presumed to have a high degree of competence in deciding how best to discharge their governmental responsibilities. A State, in the ordinary course, depends upon successor officials, both appointed and elected, to bring new insights and solutions to problems of allocating revenues and resources. The basic obligations of federal law may remain the same, but the precise manner of their discharge may not. If the State establishes reason to modify the decree, the court should make the necessary changes; where it has not done so, however, the decree should be enforced according to its terms.

540 U.S. at 442. The Court did not say what reason the state must establish — one of the *Rufo* reasons or some lesser showing. "[N]ew insights and solutions" could easily enough be described as a change in fact under *Rufo*. The idea that the injunction may be partly or entirely vacated when it achieves its purpose has been most prominently developed in the school desegregation cases.

8. Consent decrees. A consent decree is an injunction entered by agreement of the parties, subject to the approval of the court. Once entered, it is a final judgment and a permanent injunction just as much as if it had been fully litigated. The meaning of a consent decree "must be discerned within its four corners, and not by reference to what might satisfy the purposes" of either party or what the court might have ordered if plaintiffs had proved their case. Firefighters Local Union No. 1784 v. Stotts, 467 U.S. 561, 574 (1984). More recently, the Court stated the point with an implicit qualification: "[I]f a judgment is clear and unambiguous, a court must adopt, and give effect to, the plain meaning of the judgment," despite arguments that some of the parties understood it differently. Travelers Indemnity Co. v. Bailey, 557 U.S. 137, 150 (2009).

The court's authority to enter a consent decree "comes only from the statute [or other substantive law] which the decree is intended to enforce," not from the parties' consent. *Stotts*, 467 U.S. at 576 n.9, quoting System Federation v. Wright, 364 U.S. 642, 651 (1961). "The parties cannot, by giving each other consideration, purchase from a court of equity a continuing injunction." *Wright*, 364 U.S. at 651. In *Wright*, the Court used this point about the source of the decree's authority to explain why the injunction should be modified, over plaintiffs' objection, in response to a change in law.

The line between litigated decrees and consent decrees is sometimes fuzzy; parties may settle during discovery, after the court decides potentially dispositive motions, during or after trial, or after the court has ruled on liability. In *Rufo*, the parties entered into a "consent decree" after the court had entered a final judgment specifying a less detailed remedy that defendants had failed to comply with. The difference between litigated and consent decrees is more practical than doctrinal; the record will be more complete with a litigated decree, and if the case was settled early, there may be no findings of fact and little evidence of what the facts were when the decree was entered.

Frew said that federal consent decrees "must be directed to protecting federal interests," "must spring from, and serve to resolve, a dispute within the court's subject-matter jurisdiction; must come within the general scope of the case made by the pleadings; and must further the objectives of the law upon which the complaint was based." 540 U.S. at 437.

HORNE v. FLORES
557 U.S. 443 (2009)

[The Equal Educational Opportunities Act of 1974, 20 U.S.C. §1703(f), requires each state "to take appropriate action to overcome language barriers that impede equal participation by its students in its instructional programs." The Court refers to this act as "the EEOA." Students with inadequate English are referred to as English Language Learners, which the Court abbreviates ELL and often uses as an adjective. English Language Learners in Nogales, and their parents, sued various state officials in 1992, alleging that they had failed "to take appropriate action" as required by the statute.

The district court initially entered a declaratory judgment that defendants were violating the Act, because the incremental funding for English Language Learner programs was arbitrary and capricious, set at levels far below the costs required to implement the state's program for teaching English. The state provided about $150 per student, but twelve years before, it had estimated that the actual costs were $450 per student. The court expressed no view on the content of the state's program, the level of funding required, or the design of a funding mechanism. But it found grossly inadequate personnel and facilities to implement the program the state had adopted. Flores v. Arizona, 172 F. Supp. 2d 1225 (D. Ariz. 2000).

The district court subsequently issued injunctions ordering state officials to "prepare a cost study to establish the proper appropriation to effectively implement" the state's program, Flores v. Arizona, 160 F. Supp. 2d 1043, 1047 (D. Ariz. 2000), and to enact a funding scheme that "would bear a rational relationship to the actual funding needed to implement language acquisition programs in Arizona's schools so that [English Language Learners] may achieve mastery of the State's specified 'essential skills.'" 2001 WL 1028369 at *2. In this second injunction, the court extended the relief from Nogales to the entire state.

Defendants did not appeal. The state undertook a cost study, but the 2001 legislature refused to consider increased funding. Later the legislature took interim steps towards compliance, and the court extended its deadlines to the 2005 legislative session. The governor vetoed three different funding bills as inadequate. The case was assigned to a new judge (the original judge was elderly and may have been reducing his case load), who held defendants in contempt of court, exempted English Language Learners from the state's exit test for graduation until the state adequately funded its program for teaching English, and announced daily fines that would be imposed if the legislature did not fund the program within the first 15 days of its 2006 session. 405 F. Supp. 2d 1112 (D. Ariz. 2005).

The legislature eventually increased funding to $432 per student, but it limited these funds to two years per student, and it found much of the money by diverting federal funds earmarked for other purposes. The governor let this bill become law without her signature. The court held that funding was still inadequate (less in nominal dollars than the original cost estimate from nearly 20 years before), and that the two-year limit and the diversion of federal funds both violated federal law. The court of appeals vacated the contempt fines and the invalidation of the new funding statute, and remanded for consideration of defendants' motion to modify the judgments under Rule 60(b)(5). Flores v. Rzeslawski, 204 Fed. Appx. 580 (9th Cir. 2006).

After an eight-day hearing, the district court denied the motion to modify. Flores v. Arizona, 480 F. Supp. 2d 1157 (D. Ariz. 2007). The court of appeals affirmed. 516 F.3d 1140 (9th Cir. 2008).

State officials were badly divided in the later stages of these proceedings. On the motion to modify, the State Board of Education and the State of Arizona, represented by the state's Attorney General, sided with plaintiffs. This group became respondents in the Supreme Court. The Superintendent of Public Instruction (who reports to the State Board of Education), and the Speaker of the House and the President of the Senate (who had intervened as additional defendants), filed the motion to modify and became petitioners in the Supreme Court. The Court took no official notice of the fact, but all the officials supporting plaintiffs were Democrats, and all the officials opposing plaintiffs were Republicans.]

Justice ALITO delivered the opinion of the Court. . . .

III

A

Federal Rule of Civil Procedure 60(b)(5) permits a party to obtain relief from a judgment or order if, among other things, "applying [the judgment or order] prospectively is no longer equitable." Rule 60(b)(5) may not be used to challenge the legal conclusions on which a prior judgment or order rests, but the Rule provides a means by which a party can ask a court to modify or vacate a judgment or order if "a significant change either in factual conditions or in law" renders continued enforcement "detrimental to the public interest." *Rufo*, 502 U.S. at 384. The party seeking relief bears the burden of establishing that changed circumstances warrant relief, but once a party carries this burden, a court abuses its discretion "when it refuses to modify an injunction or consent decree in light of such changes." *Agostini*, 521 U.S. at 215.

Rule 60(b)(5) serves a particularly important function in what we have termed "institutional reform litigation." *Rufo*, 502 U.S. at 380. For one thing, injunctions issued in such cases often remain in force for many years, and the passage of time frequently brings about changed circumstances—changes in the nature of the underlying problem, changes in governing law or its interpretation by the courts, and new policy insights—that warrant reexamination of the original judgment.

Second, institutional reform injunctions often raise sensitive federalism concerns. Such litigation commonly involves areas of core state responsibility, such as public education.

Federalism concerns are heightened when, as in these cases, a federal court decree has the effect of dictating state or local budget priorities. States and local governments have limited funds. When a federal court orders that money be appropriated for one program, the effect is often to take funds away from other important programs.

Finally, the dynamics of institutional reform litigation differ from those of other cases. Scholars have noted that public officials sometimes consent to, or refrain from vigorously opposing, decrees that go well beyond what is required by federal law. [The core concern is that agency heads may see a federal injunction as a path to more money for their agencies.]

Injunctions of this sort bind state and local officials to the policy preferences of their predecessors. . . .

It goes without saying that federal courts must vigilantly enforce federal law and must not hesitate in awarding necessary relief. But in recognition of the features of institutional reform decrees, we have held that courts must take a "flexible approach" to Rule 60(b)(5) motions addressing such decrees. *Rufo*, 502 U.S. at 381. A flexible approach allows courts to ensure that "responsibility for discharging the State's obligations is returned promptly to the State and its officials" when the circumstances warrant. *Frew*, 540 U.S. at 442. In applying this flexible approach, courts must remain attentive to the fact that "federal-court decrees exceed appropriate limits if they are aimed at eliminating a condition that does not violate [federal law] or does not flow from such a violation." *Milliken II*, 433 U.S. at 282. "If [a federal consent decree is] not limited to reasonable and necessary implementations of federal law," it may "improperly deprive future officials of their designated legislative and executive powers." *Frew*, 540 U.S. at 441.

For these reasons, a critical question in this Rule 60(b)(5) inquiry is whether the objective of the District Court's 2000 declaratory judgment order—i.e., satisfaction of the EEOA's "appropriate action" standard—has been achieved. If a durable remedy has been implemented, continued enforcement of the order is not only unnecessary, but improper. See *Milliken II*, 433 U.S. at 282. . . .

B . . .

1

The Court of Appeals began its Rule 60(b)(5) discussion by citing the correct legal standard, but it quickly strayed. It referred to the situations in which changed circumstances warrant Rule 60(b)(5) relief as "likely rare," 540 F.3d at 1167, and explained that, to succeed on these grounds, petitioners would have to make a showing that conditions in Nogales had so changed as to "sweep away" the District Court's incremental funding determination, *id.* at 1168. . . .

Moreover, after recognizing that review of the denial of Rule 60(b)(5) relief should generally be "somewhat closer in the context of institutional injunctions against states 'due to federalism concerns,'" the Court of Appeals incorrectly reasoned that "federalism concerns are substantially lessened here, as the state of Arizona and the state Board of Education wish the injunction to remain in place." *Id.* at 1164. This statement is flatly incorrect, as even respondents acknowledge. Precisely because different state actors have taken contrary positions in this litigation, federalism concerns are elevated. And precisely because federalism concerns are heightened, a flexible approach to Rule 60(b)(5) relief is critical. "[W]hen the objects of the decree have been attained"—namely, when EEOA compliance has been achieved—"responsibility for discharging the State's obligations [must be] returned promptly to the State and its officials." *Frew*, 540 U.S. at 442.

2

In addition to applying a Rule 60(b)(5) standard that was too strict, the Court of Appeals framed a Rule 60(b)(5) inquiry that was too narrow—one that focused almost exclusively on the sufficiency of incremental funding. In large part, this was driven by the significance the Court of Appeals attributed to petitioners' failure to appeal the District Court's original order. The Court of Appeals explained that "the central idea" of that order was that without sufficient ELL incremental funds, "ELL programs would necessarily be inadequate." 516 F.3d at 1167-1168. It felt bound by this conclusion, lest it allow petitioners to "reopen matters made final when the Declaratory Judgment was not appealed." *Id.* at 1170. . . .

In attributing such significance to the defendants' failure to appeal the District Court's original order, the Court of Appeals turned the risks of institutional reform litigation into reality. By confining the scope of its analysis to that of the original order, it insulated the policies embedded in the order—specifically, its incremental funding requirement—from challenge and amendment. But those policies were supported by the very officials who could have appealed them—the state defendants—and, as a result, were never subject to true challenge.

Instead of focusing on the failure to appeal, the Court of Appeals should have conducted the type of Rule 60(b)(5) inquiry prescribed in *Rufo*. This inquiry makes no reference to the presence or absence of a timely appeal. It takes the original judgment as a given and asks only whether "a significant change either in factual conditions or in law" renders continued enforcement of the judgment "detrimental to the public interest." *Rufo*, 502 U.S. at 384. It allows a court to recognize that the longer an injunction or consent decree stays in place, the greater the risk that it will improperly interfere with a State's democratic processes.

The Court of Appeals purported to engage in a "changed circumstances" inquiry, but it asked only whether changed circumstances affected ELL funding and, more specifically, ELL incremental funding. . . .

This was a Rule 60(b)(5) "changed circumstances" inquiry in name only. In reality, it was an inquiry into whether the deficiency in ELL incremental funding that the District Court identified in 2000 had been remedied. And this, effectively, was an inquiry into whether the original order had been satisfied. Satisfaction of an earlier judgment is *one* of the enumerated bases for Rule 60(b)(5) relief—but it is not the only basis for such relief.

Rule 60(b)(5) permits relief from a judgment where "[i] the judgment has been satisfied, released or discharged; [ii] it is based on an earlier judgment that has been reversed or vacated; *or* [iii] applying it prospectively is no longer equitable." (emphasis added). . . .

To determine the merits of this claim, the Court of Appeals needed to ascertain whether ongoing enforcement of the original order was supported by an ongoing violation of federal law (here, the EEOA). See *Milliken II*, 433 U.S. at 282. It failed to do so. . . .

[T]he EEOA, while requiring a State to take "appropriate action to overcome language barriers," 20 U.S.C. §1703(f), "leave[s] state and local educational authorities a substantial amount of latitude in choosing" how this obligation is met. Castaneda v. Pickard, 648 F.2d 989, 1009 (5th Cir. 1981). Of course, any educational program, including the "appropriate action" mandated by the EEOA, requires funding, but funding is simply a means, not the end. By focusing so intensively on Arizona's incremental ELL funding, the Court of Appeals misapprehended the EEOA's mandate. And by requiring petitioners to demonstrate "appropriate action" through a particular funding mechanism, the Court of Appeals improperly substituted its own educational and budgetary policy judgments for those of the state and local officials to whom such decisions are properly entrusted. . . .

E

Because the lower courts—like the dissent—misperceived both the nature of the obligation imposed by the EEOA and the breadth of the inquiry called for under

Rule 60(b)(5), these cases must be remanded for a proper examination of at least four important factual and legal changes that may warrant the granting of relief from the judgment: the State's adoption of a new ELL instructional methodology, Congress' enactment of the No Child Left Behind Act (NCLB), 20 U.S.C. §6842 *et seq.* (2006), structural and management reforms in Nogales, and increased overall education funding.

[Arizona had switched from bilingual instruction to English-language immersion. Petitioners said that substantial academic research, and Arizona's own experience, indicated that immersion works somewhat better.

The No Child Left Behind Act required English Language Learners to "attain English proficiency," and the federal Department of Education had approved Arizona's compliance plan. The Court held that compliance with NCLB did not necessarily show compliance with EEOA, but the NCLB plan was a change in fact that must be considered on the Rule 60(b)(5) motion.

An innovative school superintendent in Nogales had "ameliorated or eliminated many of the most glaring inadequacies" in ELL instruction, 516 F.3d at 1156, and he had "achieve[d] his reforms with limited resources." *Id.* at 1157.

Overall education funding in Nogales had increased, and some of this money might be used for ELL instruction. The Court of Appeals noted that it was illegal to divert federal grants to other uses, but the Supreme Court said that was irrelevant because there was no private right of action to enforce those federal statutes. The Court of Appeals said that diverting basic education funds was not an "appropriate action," because it would hurt education in other subjects, but the Supreme Court said that choice was up to Arizona.]

These changes are critical to a proper Rule 60(b)(5) analysis, . . . as they may establish that Nogales is no longer in violation of the EEOA and, to the contrary, is taking "appropriate action" to remove language barriers in its schools. If this is the case, continued enforcement of the District Court's original order is inequitable within the meaning of Rule 60(b)(5), and relief is warranted.

IV . . .

There is no question that the goal of the EEOA—overcoming language barriers—is a vitally important one, and our decision will not in any way undermine efforts to achieve that goal. If petitioners are ultimately granted relief from the judgment, it will be because they have shown that the Nogales School District is doing exactly what this statute requires—taking "appropriate action" to teach English to students who grew up speaking another language.

***

We reverse the judgment of the Court of Appeals and remand the cases for the District Court to determine whether, in accordance with the standards set out in this opinion, petitioners should be granted relief from the judgment. . . .

Justice BREYER, with whom Justices STEVENS, SOUTER, and GINSBURG join, dissenting. . . .

II . . .

[I]t is important to keep in mind the well-known standards that ordinarily govern the evaluation of Rule 60(b)(5) motions. . . .

To show sufficient inequity to warrant Rule 60(b)(5) relief, a party must show that "a significant change either in factual conditions or in law" renders continued enforcement of the judgment or order "detrimental to the public interest." *Rufo*, 502 U.S. at 384. The party can claim that "the statutory or decisional law has changed to make legal what the decree was designed to prevent." *Id.* at 388. Or the party can claim that relevant facts have changed to the point where continued enforcement of the judgment, order, or decree as written would work, say, disproportionately serious harm.

The Court acknowledges, as do I, as did the lower courts, that *Rufo*'s "flexible standard" for relief applies. The Court also acknowledges, as do I, as did the lower courts, that this "flexible standard" does not itself define the inquiry a court passing on a Rule 60(b)(5) motion must make. To give content to this standard, the Court refers to *Milliken II*, 433 U.S. at 282, in which this Court said that a decree cannot seek to "eliminat[e] a condition that does not violate" federal law or "flow from such a violation," and to *Frew*, 540 U.S. at 441, in which this Court said that a "*consent decree*" must be "limited to reasonable and necessary implementations of federal law" (emphasis added; internal quotation marks omitted). [In a later passage, Justice Breyer noted that the passage quoted from *Milliken II* was on direct appeal, not on a motion to modify.] The Court adds that in an "institutional reform litigation" case, a court must also take account of the need not to maintain decrees in effect for too long a time, the need to take account of "sensitive federalism concerns," and the need to take care lest "consent decrees" reflect collusion between private plaintiffs and state defendants at the expense of the legislative process.

Taking these cases and considerations together, the majority says the critical question for the lower courts is "whether ongoing enforcement of the original order was supported by an ongoing violation of federal law." If not—i.e., if a current violation of federal law cannot be detected—then "'responsibility for discharging the State's obligations [must be] returned promptly to the State.'". . .

[I]nsofar as the considerations [the Court] mentions are widely accepted, the lower courts fully acknowledged and followed them. . . .

I can find no evidence, beyond the Court's speculation, showing that some state officials have "welcomed" the District Court's decision "as a means of achieving appropriations objectives that could not [otherwise] be achieved." But even were that so, why would such a fact matter here more than in any other case in which some state employees believe a litigant who sues the State is right? I concede that the State did not appeal the District Court's original order or the ensuing injunctions. But the fact that litigants refrain from appealing does not turn a litigated judgment into a "consent decree.". . .

[O]ur precedents recognize *other*, here outcome-determinative, hornbook principles that apply when a court evaluates a Rule 60(b)(5) motion. The Court omits some of them. It mentions but fails to apply others. . . .

First, a basic principle of law that the Court does not mention . . . is that, in the absence of special circumstances (e.g., plain error), a judge need not consider issues or factors that the parties themselves do not raise. . . .

Second, a hornbook Rule 60(b)(5) principle, which the Court mentions, is that the party seeking relief from a judgment or order "*bears the burden* of establishing that a significant change in circumstances warrants" that relief. *Rufo*, 502 U.S. at 383 (emphasis added). But the Court does not apply that principle.

Third, the Court ignores the well-established distinction between a Rule 60(b)(5) request to *modify* an order and a request to set an unsatisfied judgment entirely aside—a distinction that this Court has previously emphasized. Courts normally do the latter only if the "party" seeking "to have" the "decree set aside entirely" shows "that the decree has served its purpose, and there is no longer any need for the injunction." 12 James W. Moore et al., *Moore's Federal Practice* §60.47[2][c] (3d ed. 2009). . . .

Fourth, the Court says nothing about the well-established principle that a party moving under Rule 60(b)(5) for relief that amounts to having a "decree set aside entirely" must show *both* (1) that the decree's objects have been "attained," *Frew*, 540 U.S. at 442, *and* (2) that it is unlikely, in the absence of the decree, that the unlawful acts it prohibited will again occur. This Court so held in Board of Education v. Dowell, 498 U.S. 1237 (1991). [We said there] that, to show entitlement to relief, the defendants must . . . show that "it was unlikely that the [school board] would return to its former ways." *Id.* at 247. . . .

Fifth, the majority mentions, but fails to apply, the basic Rule 60(b)(5) principle that a party cannot dispute the legal conclusions of the judgment from which relief is sought. A party cannot use a Rule 60(b)(5) motion as a substitute for an appeal, say, by attacking the legal reasoning underlying the original judgment or by trying to show that the facts, as they were originally, did not then justify the order's issuance. Nor can a party require a court to retrace old legal ground, say, by re-making or rejustifying its original "constitutional decision every time an effort [is] made to enforce or modify" an order. *Rufo*, 502 U.S. at 389-390 (internal quotation marks omitted); see also *Frew*, 540 U.S. at 438 (rejecting argument that federal court lacks power to enforce an order "unless the court first identifies, at the enforcement stage, a violation of federal law").

Here, the original judgment rested upon a finding that the State had failed to provide Nogales with adequate *funding* "resources," in violation of subsection (f)'s "appropriate action" requirement. . . . When the Court criticizes the Court of Appeals for "misperceiving . . . the nature of the obligation imposed" by the Act, when it secondguesses finding after finding of the District Court, when it early and often suggests that Arizona may well comply despite lack of a rational funding plan (and without discussing how the changes it mentions could show compliance), what else is it doing but putting "the plaintiff [or] the court . . . to the unnecessary burden of re-establishing what has once been decided"? Railway Employees v. Wright, 364 U.S. 642, 647 (1961).

Sixth, the Court mentions, but fails to apply, the well-settled legal principle that appellate courts, including this Court, review district court denials of Rule 60(b) motions (of the kind before us) for abuse of discretion. A reviewing court must not substitute its judgment for that of the district court. Particularly where, as here, entitlement to relief depends heavily upon fact-related determinations, the power to review the district court's decision "ought seldom to be called into action," namely only in the rare instance where the Rule 60(b) standard "appears to have been misapprehended or grossly misapplied." *Cf.* Universal Camera Corp. v. NLRB, 340 U.S. 474, 490-491 (1951). . . .

Does the Court intend to ignore one or more of these standards or to apply them differently in cases involving what it calls "institutional reform litigation"? . . .

If the Court does not intend any such modifications of these traditional standards, then, as I shall show, it must affirm the Court of Appeals' decision. But if it does intend to modify them, as stated or in application, it now applies a new set of new rules that are *not* faithful to our cases and which will create the dangerous possibility that orders, judgments, and decrees long final or acquiesced in, will be unwarrantedly subject to perpetual challenge, offering defendants unjustifiable opportunities endlessly to relitigate underlying violations with the burden of proof imposed once again upon the plaintiffs. . . .

III . . .

[T]he Court . . . orders the lower courts . . . to conduct a "proper examination" of "four important factual and legal changes that may warrant the granting of relief from the judgment:" (1) the "adoption of a new . . . instructional methodology" for teaching English; (2) "Congress' enactment" of the No Child Left Behind Act; (3) "structural and management reforms in Nogales," and (4) "increased overall education funding."

The Court cannot accurately hold, however, that the lower courts failed to conduct a "proper examination" of these claims, for the District Court considered three of them, in detail and at length, while petitioners *no where raised* the remaining argument, which has sprung full-grown from the Court's own brow. . . .

[The shift from bilingual education to English-language immersion was still in transition, and its success was far from complete. Petitioners' witnesses claimed that the percentage of Spanish-speaking students successfully completing the English-language program had jumped from 1 percent in 2004 to 35 percent in 2006, a dramatic improvement that left much further to go. And the improvement was suspect: "the *assessment test* used in 2005 and 2006 . . . *was significantly less 'rigorous,' and consequently had been replaced.*" (emphasis by Justice Breyer). "The State's own witnesses were unable firmly to conclude that the new system had so far produced significantly improved results."

The lower courts did not relate their discussion of Arizona's policy changes to the No Child Left Behind Act because no defendant had made that argument in the lower courts.

The lower courts considered Nogales's administrative reforms at length, but "these reforms did not come close to curing the problem." Only 28 percent of Nogales's English Language Learners had passed Arizona's standardized tests for high school students. The new superintendent in Nogales testified that Nogales lacked the funds to implement the state's plan and that its implementation therefore failed, in multiple ways, to conform to the plan.

New educational funding was unlikely to be available for ELL programs, because the basic education funds were so badly needed elsewhere and because it would be flatly illegal to divert federal funds granted for other purposes. The enforcement mechanism to prevent such diversions was a cut off of the federal funds. It was irrelevant that there was no private right of action to enforce these restrictions, because this was not a suit to enforce them. The lower courts had simply assessed whether the new funding could have any actual effect on ELL instruction.

Justice Breyer concluded that the Court's claim that these changes had been insufficiently considered seemed to mean that it disagreed with the lower courts' findings and conclusions concerning these alleged changes—although very few of these findings and conclusions were explicitly held to be clearly erroneous or an abuse of discretion. Alternatively, he thought the Court's opinion could be understood as improperly putting the burden of persuasion on plaintiffs to justify the original injunction all over again.]

IV

The Court's remaining criticisms are not well founded. The Court, for example, criticizes the Court of Appeals for having referred to the "circumstances" that "warrant Rule 60(b)(5) relief as '*likely rare*'". . . . ([emphasis] added).

The Court, however, does not explain the context in which the Court of Appeals' statements appeared. That court used . . . "likely rare" . . . to refer to the *particular kind* of modification that the State sought, namely complete relief from the original judgment, even if the judgment's objective was not yet fully achieved. 516 F.3d at 1167. As far as I know it is indeed "rare" that "a prior judgment is so undermined by later circumstances as to render its continued enforcement inequitable" even though compliance with the judgment's legal determination has not occurred. *Id.* . . .

VI . . .

[The Court's new framework for reviewing motions to modify] is incomplete and lacks clear legal support or explanation. And it will be difficult for lower courts to understand and to apply that framework, particularly if it rests on a distinction between "institutional reform litigation" and other forms of litigation. Does the Court mean to say, for example, that courts must, on their own, go beyond a party's own demands and relitigate an underlying legal violation whenever that party asks for modification of an injunction? How could such a rule work in practice? Does the Court mean to suggest that there are other special, strict pro-defendant rules that govern review of district court decisions in "institutional reform cases"? What precisely are those rules? And when is a case an "institutional reform" case? . . .

[T]he Court may mean its opinion to express an attitude, cautioning judges to take care when the enforcement of federal statutes will impose significant financial burdens upon States. An attitude, however, is not a rule of law. [Anyway, the lower courts did take care.] I do not see how this Court can now require lower court judges to take yet greater care, to proceed with even greater caution, while at the same time expecting those courts to enforce the statute as Congress intended. . . .

NOTES ON MODIFICATION OF DECREES

1. The meaning of *Horne*. We have ruthlessly condensed *Horne* from 84 pages in the slip opinions. The opinion's significance is hard to assess, whether read in full or as excerpted. The majority says that it applies the existing understanding of Rule 60(b)(5), and it does not clearly state any new rules of law. Yet the tone is very different from *Rufo*; the Court seems to be pressing for easy and early modification in institutional reform cases. The real meaning of the Court's treatment of the law is inextricably entangled in its treatment of the facts, and the Justices' conflicting treatments of the facts take most of the 84 pages.

The broader significance of *Horne* remains uncertain, beyond making it significantly easier for defendants to modify or end structural injunctions. A student note by Mark Kelley points out that lower courts are divided over whether *Horne* applies equally to injunctions and consent decrees, the propriety of prophylactic institutional reform decrees after *Horne*, and the significance of the *Horne* Court's observation that "new policy insights" might "warrant reexamination of the original judgment." Mark A. Kelley, Note, *Saving 60(b)(5): The Future of Institutional Reform Litigation*, 125 Yale L.J. 272, 300 (2015). How are new policy insights different from changes in law or facts?

2. The substantive-law minimum again. The Court says that "[t]o determine the merits of this [Rule 60(b)(5)] claim, the Court of Appeals needed to ascertain whether ongoing enforcement of the original order was supported by an ongoing violation of federal law." Is that consistent with *Rufo's* holding that defendants could not relitigate the minimum requirements of substantive law on a motion to modify? Does the statement in *Horne* make sense if confined to claims that a substantial change in law or fact has eliminated the earlier violation of federal law?

3. The statewide relief. *Horne* was certified as a class action on behalf of students and parents in the Nogales Unified School District. 172 F. Supp. 2d at 1226. In 2001, without reported explanation, the court extended relief from Nogales to "Arizona's schools." 2001 WL 1028369. The attorney general had said that a Nogales-only remedy would violate the state constitution's requirement of "a general and uniform public school system." 557 U.S. at 471.

The Supreme Court pointed to obvious problems with the statewide injunction. It was "not apparent" that the plaintiff class had standing to seek statewide relief. All the evidence had focused on Nogales; no one had proved a statewide violation. "It is a question of state law, to be determined by state authorities, whether the equal funding provision of the Arizona Constitution would require a statewide funding increase to match Nogales' ELL funding, or would leave Nogales as a federally compelled exception." *Id.* No one at any point had raised any of these objections in the courts below, but petitioners suggested at oral argument that they wished to raise these objections on remand. The Court said that if petitioners objected to statewide relief, "the District Court should vacate the injunction insofar as it extends beyond Nogales unless the court concludes that Arizona is violating the EEOA on a statewide basis." *Id.*

How is this a Rule 60(b)(5) motion? What change of law or fact can there have been that affects the choice between a Nogales-only remedy and a statewide remedy? If the district court finds on remand that Arizona's changes have brought it into compliance with the Act, then presumably it will vacate the injunction as to Nogales and as to the rest of the state. But suppose it finds that Arizona is not yet in compliance. On what possible basis could it leave the injunction unmodified as to Nogales but vacate it as to the rest of the state? Wouldn't that be to reverse the statewide order on the ground that it was erroneous in the first place, eight or more years after the time for appeal had expired?

The dissenters saw no problem with the statewide relief. "A statewide program harmed Nogales' students, and the State wanted statewide relief. What in the law makes this relief erroneous?" *Id.* at 512.

4. *Horne* on remand. On remand, the trial court conducted a three-week evidentiary hearing on the state defendants' motion for 60(b)(5) relief. It also gave the plaintiffs a chance to prove a statewide EEOA violation. The trial court vacated the injunction and ordered the case dismissed. Flores v. Arizona, 2013 WL 10207656 (D. Ariz. 2013). Two years after that, the court of appeals affirmed. Flores v. Huppenthal, 789 F.3d 994 (9th Cir. 2015).

The court of appeals' opinion noted substantial change in each of the four areas highlighted by the Supreme Court. The opinion does not say how much money was available for teaching English as a second language, but total funding per pupil in the Nogales district was up 44 percent from 2000 to 2010. The state had a clear plan for teaching English language learners, Nogales was implementing that plan, students in that program who were classified as proficient for two years were performing well academically, and more than 90 percent of them were graduating. But the opinion never says what percentage of English language learners achieved proficiency for two years.

The state's new plan for teaching English gave students four hours a day of structured English immersion, and the centerpiece of the litigation on remand appeared to be the plaintiffs' objections to this four-hour model. That part of the litigation had little connection to the Supreme Court's opinion, except that it did focus on educational methods, and to some extent, educational outcomes, and not on how much money was being spent. The court of appeals held that plaintiffs lacked standing to assert a statewide violation, and in any event, implementation of the four-hour model varied from school district to school district, so that plaintiffs' objections could not be litigated on a statewide basis.

5. The motions to modify in the California prison litigation. The three-judge court in the California prison case viewed the state's 2013 motion to modify as simply an attempt to relitigate the order to reduce the prison population to 137.5 percent of design capacity. The changed circumstances to which the state pointed, at least by the court's account, were simply the passage of time, which was not a change at all; some reduction in prison population, which was wholly anticipated because it was court ordered; and some improvements in medical care, which the court found to be real but not nearly sufficient to end the constitutional violation. It also emphasized *Horne*'s reference to "a durable remedy;" nothing in California's improvements had yet been shown to be durable, and the state's recalcitrance cast serious doubt on the durability of anything that had been accomplished. Coleman v. Brown, 922 F. Supp. 2d 1004 (E.D. Cal. 2013).

6. Supplemental orders. Multiple orders, with occasional fuzziness about the status of some of them, are a function of the incremental working methods of the modern cases. A modifiable injunction is a much more powerful and effective tool than a nonmodifiable injunction. It enables a judge to make a series of orders instead of only one. She can learn by trial and error, adjust the decree in light of experience, fill loopholes in the original order, and respond more flexibly to recalcitrance. It is often understood that the first injunction is merely a start and that a long series of supplemental orders will follow. It is sometimes hard to see the difference between a modification, a supplemental decree, a "clarification" that expands the scope of the injunction, and a contempt order that directs defendants to purge their contempt by complying with new and more specific restrictions. The practice of retaining jurisdiction enabled courts to issue such supplemental orders without having to find grounds for modification under Rule 60(b)(5); recall, too, the suggestion in *United Shoe* that courts could issue orders necessary to achieve the purposes of the original decree.

7. Modifying at plaintiffs' request. Most motions to modify are filed by defendants seeking to limit or eliminate the injunction. Plaintiffs moving to modify can invoke *United Shoe*, in note 3 before *Horne*, arguing that the injunction has failed to achieve its purpose. But the D.C. Circuit has ordered the district court to consider a plaintiff's motion to modify under the substantial-change standard of *Rufo* and *Horne*. American Council of the Blind v. Mnuchin, 878 F.3d 360 (D.C. Cir. 2017). In 2008, the district court ordered the Treasury to include tactile differences in paper currency that would enable the blind to distinguish bills of different denominations. The injunction said this should be done with the next redesign of the currency, which the government did every seven to ten years. Plaintiffs did not seek any more specific deadline. But the latest redesign of the currency has been repeatedly delayed and now is not expected to happen before 2026. The court of appeals said that this long delay was a substantial change in fact that could be the basis for a motion to modify.

8. *Sua sponte* modification. A district court can modify an injunction on its own motion, so long as the parties receive proper notice. Moore v. Tangipahoa Parish School Board, 864 F.3d 401, 407 (5th Cir. 2017). *Moore* concerned a relatively minor dispute between parties to a school desegregation order in effect since 1967(!) over who should serve as the "Chief Desegregation Implementation Officer" of the school district. How could courts *not* have the power to significantly modify a court order in effect for 50 years?

9. Why injunctions and not damages? Why are injunctions more subject to modification than damage judgments? The traditional answer is that injunctions speak to the future, and justice requires some mechanism for responding to changing conditions. But many damage judgments also speak to the future, as when juries predict the duration of plaintiff's disability, the wage increases she would have received, and the interest rates she will earn on the judgment. Injustice results if the jury's predictions are inaccurate, yet the judgment cannot be modified. There is nothing inherent about that practice; the judgment could be modifiable, or it could provide for periodic payments in light of developments. Medical expenses under workers' compensation statutes are generally handled that way by administrative agencies, and courts do it with child support, which originated in ecclesiastical courts and courts of equity instead of common law.

Similarly, damage judgments cannot be reopened or modified because of a substantial change in law—not even where, shortly after a judgment becomes final, a Supreme Court decision in a different case reveals it to have been fundamentally erroneous. United States ex rel. Garibaldi v. Orleans Parish School Board, 397 F.3d 334 (5th Cir. 2005).

Modifiable judgments or periodic payments have obvious costs in terms of continued litigation. Courts are much more willing to pay those costs with respect to equitable remedies. Part of the reason may just be the separate traditions of law and equity. Is there any modern justification for the difference?

One possibility is that an injunction that becomes unduly harsh or restrictive does more harm than a damage judgment that turns out to be erroneous. The obsolete injunction may require socially wasteful conduct or forbearance, or it may harm defendant more than it helps plaintiff. The erroneous damage judgment usually causes a simple transfer payment with no net social consequences. If defendant paid too much, he has suffered his loss and gone to other things; that is not true if he is still under an overly restrictive injunction. Note 6 above describes the importance of easy modification to make injunctions more effective; part III.A of *Horne* explains the importance of modification to release public officials from judicial supervision.

NOTES ON MODIFICATION UNDER THE PRISON LITIGATION REFORM ACT

1. The modification provisions of the PLRA. The Prison Litigation Reform Act provides that any defendant or intervener is presumptively entitled to termination of any prospective relief in a prison case two years after the relief was granted or one year after the last order denying termination. 18 U.S.C. §3626(b)(1). But there is an exception:

> LIMITATION.—Prospective relief shall not terminate if the court makes written findings based on the record that prospective relief remains necessary to correct a current and ongoing violation of the Federal right, extends no further than necessary to correct the violation of the Federal right, and that the prospective relief is narrowly drawn and the least intrusive means to correct the violation.

§3626(b)(3). These provisions apply to all prison injunctions, whether entered before or after the Act. §3626(b)(1)(A)(iii). Congress has authorized defendants so inclined to annually relitigate the constitutional minimum, without any need to show a change of either law or fact. And it has provided that a generation of decrees litigated or negotiated before judges more inclined to intervene can now be relitigated before judges who are less inclined to intervene.

The single judge in the California prison litigation treated the state's motion under the modification provisions of the PLRA and made the necessary findings. And then he said that *a fortiori*, the state was not entitled to relief under Rule 60(b)(5). The three-judge court (which included the single judge as one member) said that the PLRA provision did not apply, because California had not waited two years before filing its motion. Coleman v. Brown, 922 F. Supp. 2d 1004, 1025 n.23 (E.D. Cal. 2013). This argument treated the relevant order as the timetable order issued on June 30, 2011, and not the original order to reduce the prison population issued in 2009. In the alternative, this court also made the findings necessary to keep its orders in effect. But most of the three-judge court's opinion is written in terms of *Horne* and Rule 60(b)(5).

Both opinions cite Ninth Circuit authority for the proposition that the burden of proof on a motion to modify or vacate a prison decree remains on defendants, even under the PLRA.

2. Constitutionality. Congress generally has no power to require the reopening of final judgments. Plaut v. Spendthrift Farms, Inc., 514 U.S. 211 (1995). But the application of new law to prospective relief fits the usual standards for modification under Rule 60(b)(5), and the Court has explained that the PLRA changed the law of remedies and that this change could be applied to existing decrees under *Plaut*'s exception for prospective relief. Miller v. French, 530 U.S. 327 (2000). This was technically dictum, but it is likely to become holding if necessary. What the Court actually upheld was an ancillary provision that automatically stays enforcement of most decrees unless the court rules within 30 days of the state's motion to terminate.

For examples of prospective legislation to change the outcome in a single set of cases, see Bank Markazi v. Peterson, 136 S. Ct. 1310 (2016), and Patchak v. Zinke, 138 S. Ct. 897 (2018).

3. The settlement provisions of the PLRA. The PLRA also seeks to prevent the entry of consent decrees that go beyond the constitutional minimum:

> (1) CONSENT DECREES.—In any civil action with respect to prison conditions, the court shall not enter or approve a consent decree unless it complies with the limitations on relief set forth in subsection (a) [setting conditions for litigated decrees, described in Part II of the majority opinion in Brown v. Plata].
>
> (2) PRIVATE SETTLEMENT AGREEMENTS.—
>
> (A) Nothing in this section shall preclude parties from entering into a private settlement agreement that does not comply with the limitations on relief set forth in subsection (a), if the terms of that agreement are not subject to court enforcement other than the reinstatement of the civil proceeding that the agreement settled.
>
> (B) Nothing in this section shall preclude any party claiming that a private settlement agreement has been breached from seeking in State court any remedy available under State law.

18 U.S.C. §3626(c).

This is very different from the Court's standards for entry and enforcement of consent decrees in *Frew*. See note 8 of the Introductory Notes. Could the courts function if this statute applied generally, instead of being confined to prisoner cases seeking prospective relief? Maybe so; litigators report that parties who want to settle consent to the necessary findings. Margo Schlanger, *Civil Rights Injunctions over Time: A Case Study of Jail and Prison Court Orders*, 81 N.Y.U. L. Rev. 550, 594-595 & n.144 (2006). The Act's critics feared that plaintiffs would not accept settlements that defendants could walk away from at any time, leaving plaintiffs with nothing but the right to pursue their complaint. But a consent decree is a bird in the hand, and whatever is accomplished under it may acquire the inertia of a new status quo. At any rate, the PLRA does not seem to have ended prison consent decrees.

4. Generalizing the PLRA? The Federal Consent Decree Fairness Act, S.489 and H.R.1229, 109th Congress (2005), would have provided that any state or local government or official subject to a consent decree could move to modify or vacate the decree four years after it was entered or whenever a new governor or mayor is elected. On such a motion, "the burden of proof shall be on the party who originally filed the civil action to demonstrate that the continued enforcement of a consent decree is necessary to uphold a Federal right." The decree would lapse if the court did not rule on this motion within 90 days of its filing, and the Act would apply to all consent decrees, whether entered before or after its enactment. The burden-of-proof provision went well beyond anything explicitly in the PLRA; some other provisions of the PLRA were not included.

Hearings were held in both houses in the summer of 2005, but neither bill got out of committee. The bill's academic supporters say it had substantial bipartisan support. Ross Sandler & David Schoenbrod, *From Status to Contract and Back Again: Consent Decrees in Institutional Reform Litigation*, 27 Rev. Litig. 115, 122 (2007). But it has not been reintroduced in subsequent Congresses. Sandler and Schoenbrod argue that there are all sorts of reasons why the low-level officials often tasked with negotiating consent decrees consent to far more than the law requires—not just improving their budget, but implementing what seem like good ideas at the time, freeing themselves from policy constraints imposed from above, and buying off plaintiffs with respect to demands they choose to resist or with respect to release from provisions that turn out to be unworkable. *Id.* at 117-119.

NOTES ON MODIFYING SCHOOL DESEGREGATION DECREES—AND MAYBE DECREES MORE GENERALLY

1. An alternative standard? School desegregation decrees may be modified under the *Rufo-Horne* standard, but also under what is either an alternative standard or a further specification of that standard in a particular context. *Swann*, the Supreme Court's first busing case, said there is no continuing duty to annually adjust the racial composition of student bodies in response to demographic changes, "once the affirmative duty to desegregate has been accomplished." 402 U.S. at 32. At some point, formerly segregated schools would become "unitary," *id.* at 31, and further judicial intervention would be inappropriate. *Swann* plainly suggested that busing was temporary, but it gave little clue as to how long was long enough.

The Court addressed that question in Board of Education v. Dowell, 498 U.S. 237 (1991), the Oklahoma City busing case. The school board moved to modify the busing decree; the court of appeals said no, applying the then-extant *Swift* standard. 890 F.2d 1483 (10th Cir. 1989). The Supreme Court reversed. The Court said that school desegregation decrees, "unlike the one in *Swift*, are not intended to operate in perpetuity." 498 U.S. at 248. The proper standard for modification was "whether the Board had complied in good faith with the desegregation decree since it was entered, . . . whether the vestiges of past discrimination had been eliminated to the extent practicable," *id.* at 249-250, and whether "it was unlikely that the school board would return to its former ways." *Id.* at 247.

2. Temporary remedies. There is something odd about saying that busing must be used to overcome housing segregation, but only temporarily. If a one-race school caused by residential segregation did not violate the Constitution in 1991, why should we believe that it violated the Constitution in 1971? Conversely, if it violated the Constitution in 1971, why did it not still violate the Constitution in 1991? The Court has said little to explain this oddity, but its implicit explanation seems to be that a set of presumptions approved in Dayton Board of Education v. Brinkman, 443 U.S. 526 (1979) (*Dayton II*), which attributed all segregation to proven acts of deliberate discrimination, eventually lose their evidentiary value. See Freeman v. Pitts, 503 U.S. 467, 495-496 (1992).

That was easy to understand in *Freeman*, which involved DeKalb County, Georgia, in the eastern suburbs of Atlanta, and a school district that had experienced substantial racial change. The court could examine that change and conclude that it was not caused by any unconstitutional acts of the school district. But in an urban district with long-established black neighborhoods at the core and long-established white neighborhoods at the fringe, how can the court conclude that causation has changed? Perhaps the incremental effect of past discrimination is so unknowable that the burden of proof makes all the difference, and the burden of proof has been implicitly reallocated because the costs of busing were widely perceived to exceed the benefits or simply because the judiciary became more conservative.

3. The standard in practice. Professor Parker surveyed existing school desegregation injunctions in 2003. Wendy Parker, *The Decline of Judicial Decisionmaking: School Desegregation and District Court Judges*, 81 N.C. L. Rev. 1623 (2003). Many cases appeared to be sitting dormant; incumbent school boards were content to operate under existing injunctions. School boards that sought declarations of "unitary status" (that the school district complied with the desegregation order in good faith, and that the vestiges of discrimination have been eliminated to the extent practical) usually got them, even if significant racial disparities remained. Occasionally, private citizens successfully intervened to seek declarations of unitary status over the school board's objection.

4. Generalizing the alternative standard. The idea of temporary remedies was most explicit in the school desegregation cases. But other cases, including *Frew* and *Horne*, say that responsibility for state institutions should be returned to state officials as soon as possible. A period of good-faith compliance and elimination of the vestiges of past discrimination can be understood as substantial changes in fact, or as having accomplished the purposes of the decree. This idea has begun to spread beyond the school cases, and to degenerate from a standard of eliminating the effects of the violation to the extent practical, to a standard of having tried at least a little, and perhaps implicitly, to persuade the court that it cannot overcome defendants' resistance. In Evans v. Jeff D., 2007 WL 3256620 (D. Idaho, 2007), a case about the state's treatment of emotionally and mentally disabled children in its care, the district court vacated the injunction because defendants had "made significant efforts to substantially comply." *Id.* at *5. This holding followed 27 years of resistance, delay, and broken promises, and it came only 9 months after the court held defendants in contempt of court on 21 counts. The facts of *Jeff D.* are further explored in section 10.C.

5. An additional consequence of unitary status. A declaration of unitary status now appears to make all race-conscious student assignments unconstitutional, even if they are undertaken for the purpose of preserving the benefits of a prior desegregation order. Parents Involved in Community Schools v. Seattle School District No. 1, 551 U.S. 701 (2007). Seattle was never subject to such an order, but Jefferson County, Kentucky (Louisville and its suburbs), was also at issue in *Parents Involved*. Jefferson County schools had been segregated de jure, ordered to desegregate in 1975, and declared unitary in 2000. The district adopted a voluntary plan in 2001, and the Court held much of that plan unconstitutional in *Parents Involved*. Race-based assignments could be justified only by a compelling interest in eliminating the effects of past discrimination, and the declaration of unitary status meant that there were no such effects remaining to be eliminated. *Id.* at 720-721.

C.   THE RIGHTS OF THIRD PARTIES

HILLS v. GAUTREAUX
425 U.S. 284 (1976)

[This case involved racial segregation in public housing operated by the Chicago Housing Authority. The principal violation was that, except for units reserved for the elderly, public housing was built only in African-American neighborhoods. After prolonged efforts to implement a remedy within Chicago, the court of appeals ordered consideration of a metropolitan plan. Gautreaux v. Chicago Housing Authority, 503 F.2d 930 (7th Cir. 1974). The opinion distinguished *Milliken I*, the case that reversed a metropolitan desegregation remedy for the Detroit public schools, as based on a balancing of all relevant factors, including difficulties of administration and traditions of local control, which were less pronounced in a public housing case.]

   Justice STEWART delivered the opinion of the Court. . . .

II . . .

Although the *Milliken* opinion discussed the many practical problems that would be encountered in the consolidation of numerous school districts by judicial decree, the Court's decision rejecting the metropolitan area desegregation order was actually based on fundamental limitations on the remedial powers of the federal courts to restructure the operation of local and state governmental entities. That power is not plenary. It "may be exercised 'only on the basis of a constitutional violation.'" 418 U.S. at 738, quoting *Swann*, 402 U.S. at 16. Once a constitutional violation is found, a federal court is required to tailor "the scope of the remedy" to fit "the nature and extent of the constitutional violation." *Id.* at 744. In *Milliken*, there was no finding of unconstitutional action on the part of the suburban school officials and no demonstration that the violations committed in the operation of the Detroit school system had had any significant segregative effects in the suburbs. The desegregation order in *Milliken* requiring the consolidation of local school districts in the Detroit metropolitan area thus constituted direct federal judicial interference with local governmental entities without the necessary predicate of a constitutional violation by those entities or of the identification within them of any significant segregative effects resulting from the Detroit school officials' unconstitutional conduct. Under these circumstances, the Court held that the interdistrict decree was impermissible because it was not commensurate with the constitutional violation to be repaired.

   Since the *Milliken* decision was based on basic limitations on the exercise of the equity power of the federal courts and not on a balancing of particular considerations presented by school desegregation cases, it is apparent that the Court of Appeals erred in finding *Milliken* inapplicable on that ground to this public housing case. The school desegregation context of the *Milliken* case is nonetheless important to an understanding of its discussion of the limitations on the exercise of federal judicial power. As the Court noted, school district lines cannot be "casually ignored or treated as a mere administrative convenience[,]" because they separate independent governmental entities responsible for the operation of autonomous public school systems. *Id.* at 741-743. The Court's holding that there had to be an interdistrict violation or effect before a federal court could order the crossing of district boundary lines reflected the substantive impact of a consolidation remedy on separate and independent school districts. The District Court's desegregation order in *Milliken* was held to be an impermissible remedy not because it envisioned relief against a wrongdoer extending beyond the city in which the violation occurred but because it contemplated a judicial decree restructuring the operation of local governmental entities that were not implicated in any constitutional violation.

III

The question presented in this case concerns only the authority . . . to order the Federal Department of Housing and Urban Development (HUD) to take remedial action outside the city limits of Chicago. HUD does not dispute the Court of Appeals' determination that it violated the Fifth Amendment and the Civil Rights Act of 1964 by knowingly funding CHA's racially discriminatory family public housing program, nor does it question the appropriateness of a remedial order designed to alleviate the effects of past segregative practices by requiring that public housing be developed in areas that will afford respondents an opportunity to reside in desegregated neighborhoods. But HUD contends that *Milliken* bars a remedy affecting its conduct beyond the boundaries of Chicago. First, it asserts that such a remedial order would constitute the grant of relief incommensurate with the constitutional violation to be repaired. And, second, it claims that a decree regulating HUD's conduct beyond Chicago's boundaries would inevitably have the effect of "consolidat[ing] for remedial purposes" governmental units not implicated in HUD's and CHA's violations. We address each of these arguments in turn.

A

We reject the contention that, since HUD's constitutional and statutory violations were committed in Chicago, *Milliken* precludes an order against HUD that will affect its conduct in the greater metropolitan area. The critical distinction between HUD and the suburban school districts in *Milliken* is that HUD has been found to have violated the Constitution. That violation provided the necessary predicate for the entry of a remedial order against HUD and, indeed, imposed a duty on the District Court to grant appropriate relief. Our prior decisions counsel that in the event of a constitutional violation "all reasonable methods be available to formulate an effective remedy," North Carolina State Board of Education v. Swann, 402 U.S. 43, 46 (1971), and that every effort should be made by a federal court to employ those methods "to achieve the greatest possible degree of [relief], taking into account the practicalities of the situation." Davis v. School Commissioners, 402 U.S. 33, 37 (1971). As the Court observed in Swann v. Charlotte-Mecklenburg, "Once a right and a violation have been shown, the scope of a district court's equitable powers to remedy past wrongs is broad, for breadth and flexibility are inherent in equitable remedies." 402 U.S. at 15.

Nothing in the *Milliken* decision suggests a per se rule that federal courts lack authority to order parties found to have violated the Constitution to undertake remedial efforts beyond the municipal boundaries of the city where the violation occurred. . . . [T]he District Court's proposed remedy in *Milliken* was impermissible because of the limits on the federal judicial power to interfere with the operation of state political entities that were not implicated in unconstitutional conduct. Here, unlike the desegregation remedy found erroneous in *Milliken*, a judicial order directing relief beyond the boundary lines of Chicago will not necessarily entail coercion of uninvolved governmental units, because both CHA and HUD have the authority to operate outside the Chicago city limits.

In this case, it is entirely appropriate and consistent with *Milliken* to order CHA and HUD to attempt to create housing alternatives for the respondents in the Chicago suburbs. Here the wrong committed by HUD confined the respondents to segregated public housing. The relevant geographic area for purposes of the respondents' housing options is the Chicago housing market, not the Chicago city limits. . . . To foreclose such relief solely because HUD's constitutional violation took place within the city limits of Chicago would transform *Milliken*'s principled limitation on the exercise of federal judicial authority into an arbitrary and mechanical shield for those found to have engaged in unconstitutional conduct.

B

The more substantial question under *Milliken* is whether an order against HUD affecting its conduct beyond Chicago's boundaries would impermissibly interfere with local governments and suburban housing authorities that have not been implicated in HUD's unconstitutional conduct. In examining this issue, it is important to note that the Court of Appeals' decision did not endorse or even discuss "any specific metropolitan plan" but instead left the formulation of the remedial plan to the District Court on remand. . . . HUD's contention that any remand for consideration of a metropolitan area order would be impermissible as a matter of law must necessarily be based on its claim at oral argument "that court-ordered metropolitan relief in this case, no matter how gently it's gone about, no matter how it's framed, is bound to require HUD to ignore the safeguards of local autonomy and local political processes" and therefore to violate the limitations on federal judicial power established in *Milliken*. . . .

A remedial plan designed to insure that HUD will utilize its funding and administrative powers in a manner consistent with affording relief to the respondents need not abrogate the role of local governmental units in the federal housing-assistance programs. Under the major housing programs in existence at the time the District Court entered its remedial order pertaining to HUD, local housing authorities and municipal governments had to make application for funds or approve the use of funds in the locality before HUD could make housing-assistance money available. An order directed solely to HUD would not force unwilling localities to apply for assistance under these programs but would merely reinforce the regulations guiding HUD's determination of which of the locally authorized projects to assist with federal funds.

The Housing and Community Development Act of 1974, 42 U.S.C. §1437 *et seq.*, significantly enlarged HUD's role in the creation of housing opportunities. Under the §8 Lower-Income Housing Assistance program, which has largely replaced the older federal low-income housing programs, HUD may contract directly with private owners to make leased housing units available to eligible lower income persons. As HUD has acknowledged in this case, "local governmental approval is no longer explicitly required as a condition of the program's applicability to a locality.". . . In most cases the Act grants the unit of local government in which the assistance is to be provided the right to comment on the application and, in certain specified circumstances, to preclude the Secretary of HUD from approving the application. Use of the §8 program to expand low-income housing opportunities outside areas of minority concentration would not have a coercive effect on suburban municipalities. For under the program, the local governmental units retain the right to comment on specific assistance proposals, to reject certain proposals that are inconsistent with their approved housing-assistance plans, and to require that zoning and other land-use restrictions be adhered to by builders.

In sum, . . . [t]he order would have the same effect on the suburban governments as a discretionary decision by HUD to use its statutory powers to provide the respondents with alternatives to the racially segregated Chicago public housing system created by CHA and HUD.

Since we conclude that a metropolitan area remedy in this case is not impermissible as a matter of law, we affirm the judgment of the Court of Appeals remanding the case to the District Court "for additional evidence and for further consideration of the issue of metropolitan area relief." Our determination that the District Court has the authority to direct HUD to engage in remedial efforts in the metropolitan area outside the city limits of Chicago should not be interpreted as requiring a metropolitan area order. The nature and scope of the remedial decree to be entered on remand is a matter for the District Court in the exercise of its equitable discretion, after affording the parties an opportunity to present their views.

The judgment of the Court of Appeals remanding this case to the District Court is affirmed, but further proceedings in the District Court are to be consistent with this opinion. . . .

NOTES ON RELIEF AGAINST THIRD PARTIES

1. The *Gautreaux* litigation. The lead plaintiff's name is pronounced Gŭ-tró. The court of appeals in *Gautreaux* rather clearly contemplated that the suburbs would be coerced into accepting housing if that were necessary. The Supreme Court disagreed, but it was able to affirm because the new §8 program abandoned the local consent requirement. Scattered-site housing under §8, privately built and owned but publicly subsidized, was for many years the only clear success of the *Gautreaux* litigation. By 1996, some 7,000 families, mostly headed by African-American women with low incomes, had moved to the Chicago suburbs as a result of *Gautreaux*, and HUD had made §8 its main program nationwide. The families who moved to the suburbs under *Gautreaux* reported mostly good experiences there, with better jobs for the mothers and better education for the children. Leonard S. Rubinowitz & James E. Rosenbaum, *Crossing the Class and Color Lines: From Public Housing to White Suburbia* (Univ. of Chicago Press 2000).

Meanwhile, the part of the decree ordering additional units in white neighborhoods within the City of Chicago remained largely unimplemented, mired in political resistance, and later hampered by the diversion of funds from publicly owned housing to §8 housing. In 1987, the court appointed a receiver to manage the scattered-site housing program within the city limits. By 1997, the receiver had created some 3,000 units of new public housing within the city limits.

Some of Chicago's poorest neighborhoods eventually became ripe for redevelopment, as dilapidated housing units were condemned, demolished, burned, or simply abandoned. The court had also imposed limits on building additional public housing in black neighborhoods, but it began to authorize exceptions to those limits in neighborhoods with potential for economic integration and "a longer term possibility of racial desegregation." Gautreaux v. Chicago Housing Authority, 491 F.3d 649, 657 (7th Cir. 2007). A typical such order required that half the new units be reserved for families earning less than half the area's median income and that half be reserved for families earning 50 to 80 percent of the area's median income. This produced a modest level of economic integration, reduced the risk of creating new concentrations of extreme poverty, and reduced resistance from the neighborhood. Such an order, involving 60 units of public housing, is described in Gautreaux v. Chicago Housing Authority, 475 F.3d 845, 849 (7th Cir. 2007), in an opinion decided on procedural grounds.

The suit was filed in 1966; plaintiff Dorothy Gautreaux is now deceased. The history of the case is reviewed, up to a point, in Gautreaux v. Chicago Housing Authority, 981 F. Supp. 1091 (N.D. Ill. 1997), and in Alexander Polikoff, *Gautreaux and Institutional Litigation*, 64 Chi.-Kent L. Rev. 451 (1988). The Polikoff article is part of an interesting symposium reviewing and evaluating three major structural injunctions in Chicago—the attempts to desegregate public housing, eliminate the patronage system, and ensure minority representation in the city council.

2. *Gautreaux* and the rightful position. In the Kansas City school desegregation case, the district court attempted to create a magnet school district that would attract white students from the suburbs and private schools. The Supreme Court rejected that plan in Missouri v. Jenkins, 515 U.S. 70 (1995) (*Jenkins III*). One part of the Court's reasoning was that the district court's metropolitan goals exceeded the scope of the violation, which was confined to the Kansas City school district. This violated *Milliken I*, the case that disapproved a metropolitan desegregation plan for Detroit.

The dissenters in *Jenkins III* accused the majority of implicitly overruling *Gautreaux*. The *Jenkins III* dissenters said *Gautreaux* approved metropolitan remedies so long as they did not violate the rights of third parties; the majority said *Gautreaux* depended on the geographic scope of the violation. The dissenters said:

> We held that a district court may indeed subject a governmental perpetrator of segregative practices to an order for relief with intended consequences beyond the perpetrator's own subdivision, even in the absence of effects outside that subdivision, so long as the decree does not bind the authorities of other governmental units that are free of violations and segregative effects.

Jenkins III, 515 U.S. at 170 (Souter, J, dissenting).

The majority insisted that its decision was fully consistent with *Gautreaux*: "Because the 'relevant geographic area for the purposes of the [plaintiffs'] housing options [was] the Chicago housing market, not the Chicago city limits,' we concluded that 'a metropolitan area remedy . . . [was] not impermissible as a matter of law.'" *Jenkins III*, 515 U.S. at 97, quoting *Gautreaux*, 425 U.S. at 299, 306. Who has the better of that argument?

The Court in *Milliken I* and *Jenkins III* said that if there had never been discrimination, the children of Detroit and Kansas City would have had a unitary school system within their respective city limits. If the Chicago Housing Authority had never discriminated, where would the plaintiffs have been? Wouldn't they have had a unitary public housing system within the city of Chicago? What difference does it make that the private housing market extended beyond the city limits if the violation was entirely contained within the city limits and the CHA had never shown the slightest interest in building housing in the suburbs?

3. *Gautreaux* and the rights of third parties. *Gautreaux* says that HUD, an adjudicated wrongdoer, can be ordered to take action outside the city limits to provide a remedy for discrimination inside the city limits. Does that mean the *Milliken* plaintiffs were entitled to an order directing the state of Michigan, an adjudicated wrongdoer, to provide metropolitan relief by using its powers to restructure and consolidate local school districts? The Court in *Jenkins III* emphatically denied that such an order could have issued in *Milliken*, treating the point as obvious. Why is that? Note too that the Kansas City school district, an adjudicated wrongdoer, was ordered to take action exclusively inside its geographic limits, in the hope of drawing students from outside its limits. On the geographic scope point, shouldn't *Jenkins III* have been an easier case than *Gautreaux?*

4. *Gautreaux,* federalism, and separation of powers. The majority in *Jenkins III* offered one other attempt to reconcile the cases. *Gautreaux* "involved the imposition of a remedy upon a federal agency. Thus, it did not raise the same federalism concerns that are implicated when a federal court issues a remedial order against a State." 515 U.S. at 98. The Court cited *Milliken II,* which had affirmed an order for remedial education in Detroit and had distilled a three-part test that emphasized the scope of the violation, the plaintiffs' rightful position, and "the interests of state and local authorities in managing their own affairs." 433 U.S. at 280-281. Is federalism a reason to stop short of the rightful position? Do the federal courts owe more deference to state agencies as a matter of federalism than to federal agencies as a matter of separation of powers? Deference in either context is about the balance between political control and enforcement of legal obligations.

5. The authority of *Gautreaux.* Are the three Supreme Court opinions—*Milliken I, Gautreaux,* and *Jenkins III*—ultimately irreconcilable?

6. Closely linked agencies. The metropolitan desegregation cases, whether in schools or housing, all involved central city and suburban governmental units. What if separate governmental units operate in the same territory and work together closely?

a. City and school district. Consider Bacon v. City of Richmond, 475 F.3d 633 (4th Cir. 2007), a case about handrails, wheelchair ramps, elevators, and wheelchair-accessible restrooms in the Richmond public schools. The school board needed millions of dollars to build these facilities, and the district court ordered the city to provide the money. The court of appeals reversed.

The school board and the city were separate political entities, and the school board was responsible for running the schools. The city was apparently the source of all the school board's local funding, but the school board also got state and federal money. The city owned the school buildings, but the court said it owned a bare legal title, holding the buildings in trust for the school board, which was responsible for maintaining and managing the buildings. And the disability acts were not about the owners of buildings, but about access to "services, programs or activities," and those were all run by the school board. *Id.* at 639. The court of appeals said the city was an innocent third party that could not be ordered to fund a remedy for the school board's violation. The court also emphasized that this division of responsibility was longstanding in Virginia law, and said that if governments "were to conspire to immunize themselves . . . by dividing operational control and funding authority this would, of course, be evidence of discrimination." *Id.* at 641.

b. State and local election officials. In King Lincoln Bronzeville Neighborhood Association v. Blackwell, 448 F. Supp. 2d 876 (S.D. Ohio 2006), plaintiffs alleged that there had been systematic discrimination in Ohio's administration of the 2004 general election. The ultimate relief they sought was to prevent any repetition in the next general election. But at the beginning of the case, they sought to preserve as evidence the ballots from the 2004 election. These ballots were in the possession of 88 county boards of election. State law required the boards to preserve the ballots for 22 months, but that period was about to expire. Defendant was the Secretary of State, who denied that he had authority to order the county boards to preserve the ballots.

The court said that defendant did have authority to order the ballots preserved, and it said it could order him to exercise that authority. But it didn't do that. The court said that "the most effective way" to preserve the ballots would be to order each county board to preserve them. Citing cases on the somewhat different issue of when an existing injunction can be enforced against third parties, the court said it had "inherent authority" to "enjoin a non-party" if necessary to preserve its power to adjudicate the dispute between those who were parties. This one may have been easier than the court made it; it is routine for courts to order third parties to testify or produce evidence. This case may not have been far enough along for a simple subpoena, but ordering potential witnesses to preserve evidence does not seem like much of an extension.

7. Police protection. What if a separate government agency has an independent duty to do things that would help achieve the goals of the decree? Some commentators read *Milliken I* and *Gautreaux* to mean that police could not be ordered to protect students and school officials from opponents of desegregation orders, especially where the school district is a separate political entity from the city. H.J. Escher & Lee Hyman Gudel, Comment, *Community Resistance to School Desegregation: Enjoining the Undefinable Class,* 44 U. Chi. L. Rev. 111, 154-161 (1976).

The issue of police enforcement arose In re Boung Jae Jang v. Brown, 560 N.Y.S.2d 307 (App. Div. 1990). Black demonstrators were boycotting and picketing a store owned by a Korean immigrant. Finding that the demonstrators were abusing customers, and that there had been several violent incidents, the court ordered the demonstrators to stay 50 feet from the store. It ordered the police to enforce the order. The police attempted to do so, but the demonstrators refused to comply. The police quit trying to enforce the order, and simply tried to persuade the demonstrators to moderate their behavior. Plaintiff claimed that the situation had not improved. The trial court then issued a writ of mandamus ordering the police to enforce the original order.

The police commissioner appealed. He argued that no representative of the police department had been a party to the suit, that the police had no ministerial duty to enforce court orders in civil suits between private parties, that before turning to mandamus the court should have used its contempt power against the demonstrators, that the order would anger the community and exacerbate the protest, and that how to handle such a situation was a nonjusticiable question committed to the discretion of the executive branch. The Appellate Division rejected all of these arguments. It thought the trial court had inherent authority to enforce its order, that the police had a duty to enforce the law, and that contempt proceedings would be unworkable because the demonstrators were numerous and largely anonymous. It noted that the police retained discretion as to the means of enforcing the 50-foot limit.

8. Rule 19(a). Would a strict prohibition of any relief against innocent third parties be inconsistent with the presuppositions of Federal Civil Rule 19(a), providing for the joinder of a party if "in that person's absence, the court cannot accord complete relief among existing parties"? Or is that Rule silent on the question of what such a party can be ordered to do after he is joined?

GENERAL BUILDING CONTRACTORS ASSOCIATION v. PENNSYLVANIA
458 U.S. 375 (1982)

Justice REHNQUIST delivered the opinion of the Court.

Respondents, the Commonwealth of Pennsylvania and a class of racial minorities who are skilled or seek work as operating engineers in the construction industry in Eastern Pennsylvania and Delaware, commenced this action under a variety of federal statutes protecting civil rights, including 42 U.S.C. §1981. The complaint sought to redress racial discrimination in the operation of an exclusive hiring hall established in contracts between Local 542 of the International Union of Operating Engineers and construction industry employers doing business within the Union's jurisdiction. Respondents also alleged discrimination in the operation of an apprenticeship program established by Local 542 and several construction trade associations. Named as defendants were Local 542, the trade associations, the organization charged with administering the trade's apprenticeship program, and a class of approximately 1,400 construction industry employers. Petitioners, the defendant contractors and trade associations, seek review of a judgment granting an injunction against them. . . .

I . . .

Under the terms of the [collective bargaining] agreement, the Union was to maintain lists of operating engineers, or would-be engineers, classified according to the extent of their recent construction experience. Signatory employers were contractually obligated to hire operating engineers only from among those referred by the Union from its current lists. Workers affiliated with the Union were barred from seeking work with those employers except through Union referrals. Thus, the collective bargaining agreement effectively channeled all employment opportunities through the hiring hall. . . .

Among the means of gaining access to the Union's referral lists is an apprenticeship program established in 1965 by Local 542 and the trade associations. The program, which involves classroom and field training, is administered by the Joint Apprenticeship and Training Committee (JATC), a body of trustees half of whom are appointed by the Union and half by the trade associations. . . .

The District Court . . . found that the hiring hall system established by collective bargaining was neutral on its face. But the court found that Local 542, in administering the system, "practiced a pattern of intentional discrimination and that union practices in the overall operation of a hiring hall for operating engineers created substantial racial disparities." Pennsylvania v. Local 542, Operating Engineers, 469 F. Supp. 329, 370 (E.D. Pa. 1978). The court made similar findings regarding the JATC's administration of the job training program. . . .

[T]he court found that the plaintiffs had failed to prove "that the associations or contractors viewed simply as a class were actually aware of the union discrimination," id. at 401, and had failed to show "intent to discriminate by the employers as a class," id. at 412. [Even so, the district court held that the employers and trade associations had violated the statutes and could be ordered to help provide a remedy. The court of appeals affirmed by an equally divided vote. 648 F.2d 923 (3d Cir. 1981) (en banc). The Supreme Court held that the employers and trade associations had not violated the statutes.]

IV . . .

The issue before us, therefore, is whether a party not subject to liability for violating the law may nonetheless be assessed a proportionate share of the costs of implementing a decree to assure nondiscriminatory practices on the part of another party which *was* properly enjoined.

We find respondent's arguments based on the traditional equitable authority of courts to be unpersuasive. In *Milliken II*, upon which respondents rely, and which we believe to be the case most closely in point, we expressly noted that the state petitioners had been found guilty of creating at least a portion of the constitutional violation which the order challenged in that case was designed to remedy. [The state of Michigan had been ordered to pay half the cost of the remedy in *Milliken II.*] Thus our holding there was consistent with our opinion in *Gautreaux*, where we explained the relationship between our holding in *Milliken I* and our opinion in *Swann*. We read these earlier decisions as recognizing "fundamental limitations on the remedial powers of the federal courts." 425 U.S. at 293. Those powers could be exercised only on the basis of a violation of the law and could extend no farther than required by the nature and the extent of that violation. This principle, we held, was not one limited to school desegregation cases, but was instead "premised on a controlling principle governing the permissible scope of federal judicial power, a principle not limited to a school desegregation context." *Id.* at 294 n.11.

We think that the principle enunciated in these cases, transposed to the instant factual situation, offers no support for the imposition of injunctive relief against a party found not to have violated any substantive right of respondents. This is not to say that defendants in the position of petitioners might not, upon an appropriate evidentiary showing, be retained in the lawsuit and even subjected to such minor and ancillary provisions of an injunctive order as the District Court might find necessary to grant complete relief to respondents from the discrimination they suffered at the hands of the Union. But that sort of minor and ancillary relief is not the same, and cannot be the same, as that awarded against a party found to have infringed the statutory rights of persons in the position of respondents.

The order of the District Court, insofar as it runs against petitioners, cannot be regarded as "minor" or "ancillary" in any proper sense of those terms. First, it imposes considerable burdens on the employers and associations. It directs the employers to meet detailed "minority utilization goals" in their hiring, keyed to the number of hours worked. If they are unable to do so through referrals from Local 542, they are required to hire minority operating engineers who are not affiliated with the Union. If the goals are still not satisfied, the employers must recruit and hire unskilled minority workers from the community and provide on-the-job training. The employers are also obligated to make quarterly reports detailing the extent of their compliance with these directives. Finally, the District Court imposed on the employers and the associations a share of the financial cost incidental to enforcement of the remedial decree as a whole. According to petitioners, the expense of the decree in the first year of its five-year life exceeded $200,000.

Absent a supportable finding of liability, we see no basis for requiring the employers or the associations to aid either in paying for the cost of the remedial program as a whole or in establishing and administering the training program. Nor is the imposition of minority hiring quotas directly upon petitioners the sort of remedy that may be imposed without regard to a finding of liability. If the Union and the JATC comply with the decree by training and referring minority workers, we see no reason to assume, absent supporting evidence, that the employers will not hire the minority workers referred pursuant to the collective bargaining agreement, and employ them at wages and hours commensurate with those of non-minority workers. If experience proves otherwise, the District Court will then have more than sufficient grounds for including the employers within the scope of the remedial decree.

To the extent that the remedy properly imposed upon the Union and the JATC requires any adjustment in the collective bargaining contract between petitioners and the Union, it is entirely appropriate for the District Court to fashion its injunctive remedy to so provide, and to have that remedy run against petitioners as well as the Union and the JATC. But the injunctive decree entered by the District Court as presently drawn treats petitioners as if they had been properly found liable for the Union's discrimination. A decree containing such provisions, we hold, is beyond the traditional equitable limitations upon the authority of a federal court to formulate such decrees.

Nor does the All Writs Act, 28 U.S.C. §1651(a), support the extensive liability imposed upon petitioners by the District Court. The District Court did not rely upon this Act, and we think it completely wide of the mark in justifying the relief granted by the District Court. That Act was most recently considered by this Court in United States v. New York Telephone Co., 434 U.S. 159 (1977), where we said: "This Court has repeatedly recognized the power of a federal court to issue such commands under the All Writs Act as may be necessary or appropriate to effectuate and prevent the frustration of orders it has previously issued in its exercise of jurisdiction otherwise obtained." *Id.* at 172. In *New York Telephone*, we held that the All Writs Act was available to require a third party to assist in the carrying out of a district court order pertaining to the installation of pen registers, and in doing so we noted that "[t]he order provided that the Company be fully reimbursed at prevailing rates, and compliance with it required minimal effort on the part of the Company and no disruption to its operations." *Id.* at 175.

An examination of our cases which have relied on the All Writs Act convinces us that respondents are simply barking up the wrong tree when they seek to support the injunctive order of the District Court against petitioners on the basis of the provisions of that Act. There was no need for the District Court to treat petitioners as strangers to this law suit, and therefore to rely upon some extraordinary form of process or writ to bring them before the court. Petitioners had been named as defendants by respondents in their complaint, and they litigated the injunctive liability phase of the action before the District Court. Petitioners were parties to the action in every sense of the word, and subject to the jurisdiction of the District Court both as to the imposition of liability and as to the framing of a remedial decree. The difficulty faced by respondents in supporting the decree of the District Court insofar as it grants affirmative relief and requires payment toward the cost of implementing the decree is not that petitioners would otherwise be strangers to the action. The difficulty lies instead with the fact that on the record before the District Court the petitioners could not properly be held liable to any sort of injunctive relief based on their own conduct. . . .

The judgment . . . is reversed, and the case is remanded for proceedings consistent with this opinion.

Justice O'CONNOR, with whom Justice BLACKMUN joins, concurring. . . .

II

Regarding the scope of a federal court's equitable powers to afford full relief, I agree with the Court's holding that "a party not subject to liability for violating the law [may not] be assessed a proportionate share of the costs of implementing a decree to assure nondiscriminatory practices on the part of another party which *was* properly enjoined." I also agree with the Court's ancillary holding that the District Court may not require quarterly reports from the employers detailing their compliance with the court's ill-founded injunction. Of course, since the employers are not liable for general injunctive relief, such reports are unnecessary.

Under the appropriate circumstances, however, I believe other reports properly could be required of the employers, for example, to aid the court by charting the changes resulting from the injunction imposed on the Union and the JATC. Quite recently, in Zipes v. Trans World Airlines, 455 U.S. 385 (1982), this Court held that §706(g) of Title VII authorizes a federal court to order retroactive seniority relief over the objections of a union that was not guilty of discrimination. The Court stated:

> Teamsters v. United States, 431 U.S. 324 (1977), . . . makes it clear that once there has been a finding of discrimination by the employer, an award of retroactive seniority is appropriate even if there is no finding that the union has also illegally discriminated. In *Teamsters*, the parties agreed to a decree which provided that the District Court would decide "whether any discriminatees should be awarded additional equitable relief such as retroactive seniority." *Id.* at 331 n.4. Although we held that the union had not violated Title VII by agreeing to and maintaining the seniority system, we nonetheless directed the union to remain in the litigation as a defendant so that full relief could be awarded the victims of the employer's post-Act discrimination.

455 U.S. at 400. As the Court acknowledges today, it is entirely possible that full relief cannot be granted without subjecting the petitioners to some incidental or ancillary provisions of the court's injunctive order. It is thus conceivable, for example, that quarterly reports providing employment statistics necessary for the court to ascertain whether its injunctive decree is being properly implemented could be ordered under the court's equitable powers to effectuate its decree.

[Justices MARSHALL and BRENNAN dissented on the ground that the employers and trade associations had violated the statute. They agreed with Justice O'CONNOR "that the Court's opinion does not prevent the District Court from requiring petitioners to comply with incidental or ancillary provisions contained in its injunctive order." 458 U.S. at 418 n.5. Justice STEVENS joined Part IV of the Court's opinion; his separate opinion on the meaning of the statute is omitted.]

MORE NOTES ON RELIEF AGAINST THIRD PARTIES

1. The All Writs Act. A pen register is a wiretapping device that records the numbers called but does not record the conversations. In United States v. New York Telephone, discussed in *General Building Contractors*, the United States sought an injunction ordering the telephone company to place the pen register for it. The Court found power to issue the injunction in the All Writs Act, which authorizes federal courts to "issue all writs necessary or appropriate in aid of their respective jurisdictions and agreeable to the usages and principles of law." 28 U.S.C. §1651(a).

The Court has since held that the All Writs Act does not apply to any issue addressed by a more specific federal statute. Syngenta Crop Protection, Inc. v. Henson, 537 U.S. 28 (2002). The concern in *Syngenta* was that federal courts not use the All Writs Act to evade express or implicit limitations on their authority in other legislation. This casts some doubt on the result in *New York Telephone*, but not on any ground going to the rights of third parties.

2. Affecting innocent third parties with orders directed to violators. Justice O'Connor's concurrence relies on Zipes v. Trans World Airlines and Teamsters v. United States. In those cases, the Court held that plaintiffs were entitled to be employed with seniority retroactive to the day on which they would have been hired but for the employer's discrimination. Plaintiffs would then get whatever rights the existing seniority rules provided to an employee with that much seniority. The Court held that plaintiffs were not entitled to the broader relief they sought in *Teamsters*, which would have modified the seniority rules. Even within the framework of the existing seniority rules, plaintiffs could not use retroactive seniority to displace incumbent workers. But as vacancies arose, plaintiffs could use their retroactive seniority to compete for those vacancies, jumping ahead of incumbents who had longer actual service. The effect was to freeze incumbents in the position they held at the time of the decree until plaintiffs reached their rightful position. Perhaps the implementing orders directed to the union were "minor and ancillary," but the effect on incumbent workers was substantial.

Cases ordering or prohibiting affirmative action, such as United States v. Paradise, 480 U.S. 149 (1987), or Gratz v. Bollinger, 539 U.S. 244 (2003), are another clear example of innocent third parties being substantially affected by a remedy against a wrongdoer.

3. Distilling a rule? Set aside the geographic scope issue in the desegregation cases and focus on the rights of third parties. Combining the Court's stated rules with the factual results of its cases, the law seems to be that innocent third parties can be affected (*Gautreaux*) substantially (*Teamsters, Zipes, Paradise, Gratz*), but not to the point of being restructured (*Milliken I*), by orders to defendants who violated the law. Innocent third parties may also be subjected to "minor and ancillary" orders themselves (*New York Telephone, General Building Contractors*). Is that a workable set of rules? Can you apply it to the following third parties?

a.   Statewide education officials who did not participate in local segregation but can be helpful in devising remedies. See Morgan v. Kerrigan, 509 F.2d 580, 582 n.4 (1st Cir. 1974) (refusing to dismiss as to such defendants) (pre-*Milliken*).

b.   Developers engaged in construction pursuant to an allegedly illegal permit, where wrongdoing is charged only against the officials who issued the permit. See League to Save Lake Tahoe v. Tahoe Regional Planning Agency, 558 F.2d 914 (9th Cir. 1977) (reversing dismissal as to developers, not citing *Milliken* or *Gautreaux*).

c.   A title company holding assets beneficially owned by one of the defendants. See Beverly Hills Federal Savings & Loan Association v. Webb, 406 F.2d 1275, 1279-1280 (9th Cir. 1969) (reversing dismissal as to title company).

d.   The sheriff in a suit to enjoin an eviction, where the real parties in interest are the landlord and tenant, and the sheriff is routinely executing a writ.

4. Older cases, but current law. *Gautreaux* is a 1976 case, and *General Building Contractors* is from 1982. Both are good law, and both appear to be the most recent Supreme Court cases on judicial power to enjoin parties not found to have violated the law. Perhaps the Court has not revisited the questions in any depth because the rules are clear and easy to apply. Given note 3 above and the notes below, this possibility seems doubtful. Perhaps some enterprising lawyers will get the Court interested in these questions again.

5. Bystanders who inadvertently interfere with the goals of the injunction. In Bradley v. Detroit Board of Education, 577 F.2d 1032 (6th Cir. 1978), the court vacated an injunction against locating a halfway house for state prisoners next to a magnet school designed to attract students from all over the city as part of the desegregation program. The court of appeals found the threat to desegregation speculative. The building was owned by the Salvation Army, which had agreed to sell it to the Michigan Department of Corrections; the district court joined the Salvation Army as an additional defendant and enjoined the sale of the land. Assuming that plaintiffs could show a real threat to desegregation, must they also show that the Salvation Army and Department of Corrections were each independently violating the Constitution? This isn't a "minor or ancillary" order is it? Would the court have to order the school board to buy the land? Or at least compensate the Salvation Army for the lost sale?

6. Lawful sellers selling to unlawful buyers. Compare Federal Trade Commission v. Elders Grain, Inc., 868 F.2d 901 (7th Cir. 1989), where sale of a corporate subsidiary resulted in the buyer controlling too much of the market, in violation of the anti-trust laws. The court affirmed an order to reverse the transaction, over the seller's objection that it had done nothing wrong. The seller was certainly not a monopolist, and anyway, §7 of the Clayton Act forbids only the purchase and not the sale. The Supreme Court had held this issue open in United States v. E.I. du Pont de Nemours & Co., 366 U.S. 316, 334-335 (1961). *Elders Grain* does not cite *Milliken, Gautreaux,* or *General Building Contractors.*

7. Citizens. When courts enjoin governmental units, the citizens of those units are inevitably affected. Schoolchildren are involuntarily reassigned under redrawn attendance zones or under busing plans within a single district. Justice Kennedy suggested in *Jenkins II* that the taxpayers' property was taken without due process when the court enjoined the enforcement of state limits on the local property tax. 495 U.S. at 65-70 (concurring in part). But no justice has made such an argument when courts order expensive steps toward compliance with the law, even though those steps will ultimately require taxes. These schoolchildren, taxpayers, and other affected citizens may not qualify as third parties, because the Court has also held that constituents are bound by judgments against representative governments. Washington v. Washington State Commercial Passenger Fishing Vessel Association, 443 U.S. 658, 693 n.32 (1979).

8. Procedural rights of third parties. If innocent third parties have substantive rights that limit the scope of remedies, shouldn't they also be entitled to notice and hearing so they have a chance to argue for those rights?

a. *Local 93* and the entry of injunctions. The Supreme Court has upheld a consent decree providing for racial preferences, over the objection of the union representing white workers who would be disadvantaged. Local No. 93 v. City of Cleveland, 478 U.S. 501, 528-530 (1986). The Court thought it clear that the city and its black firefighters were free to settle *their* differences in a consent decree and that white firefighters could not veto that settlement. But the Court found it equally clear that the whites would not be bound by the decree. They were free to sue the city under the Equal Protection Clause, the civil rights laws, or the collective bargaining agreement.

Does the consent decree do any good if the white firefighters are not bound? If they are to be bound, don't they have to consent?

b. Martin v. Wilks and the limited reach of claim and issue preclusion. A sharply divided Court subsequently held that white employees alleging racial discrimination in promotions are indeed free to challenge the affirmative action provisions of an earlier consent decree between their employer and black employees. Martin v. Wilks, 490 U.S. 755 (1989). The brief majority opinion says simply that no one is bound by a decree unless he was a party, that no one is obliged to intervene in a lawsuit to which he has not been made a party, and that if the black plaintiffs wanted to bind the white employees, they should have joined the white employees under Federal Rule 19. Justice Stevens filed a much longer opinion for four dissenters. He argued that compliance with the consent decree was a defense to any claim of reverse discrimination, unless the decree was "transparently invalid" or the result of fraud or collusion. *Id.* at 787. He insisted that this did not mean that the whites were "bound" by the consent decree; the majority thought that was precisely what he meant.

Congress undertook to overrule Martin v. Wilks in the Civil Rights Act of 1991, now 42 U.S.C. §2000e-2(n). The Act provides that employees are bound by an injunction if they had notice from any source that it would affect their interests, or if they were represented by a party to the action. The provision appears to have had little effect. It does not apply outside the context of employment discrimination, and even within that context, it does not bar claims under employment contracts, collective bargaining agreements, civil service laws, or state civil rights laws.

c. **Virtual representation?** More generally, the Court has rejected any notion of "virtual representation" as a basis for preclusion. Taylor v. Sturgell, 553 U.S. 880 (2008). In *Taylor*, a plaintiff requested documents under the Freedom of Information Act, 5 U.S.C. §552, sued when he didn't get them, and lost. A friend of his, represented by the same lawyer, then requested the same documents and sued in a different circuit. There was no legal relationship between the two plaintiffs and no indication that either was acting on behalf of the other. Relying on *Martin* and other cases, the Court unanimously held that the second plaintiff was not bound by the first decision, although of course defendant could cite it as a potentially persuasive precedent.

9. Other triangular disputes. The problem of binding third parties inheres in any dispute with three or more interests; it is not at all confined to discrimination cases. Consider Thomas ex rel. Baker v. General Motors Corp., 522 U.S. 222 (1998). GM had a Michigan consent decree ordering a disgruntled former employee not to testify against it in products liability cases. The Michigan court had refused to modify the decree, but numerous state and federal courts elsewhere had allowed the former employee to testify. Baker was the plaintiff in a personal injury action, based on Missouri law and pending in federal court in Missouri.

The Supreme Court thought it obvious that Baker was not bound by the Michigan decree, not having been a party there, *id.* at 237 n.11, and three Justices would have rested on that ground. *Id.* at 246-251 (Kennedy, J., concurring). But the majority went further. The Court noted that the former employee was bound, and thus forbidden to testify voluntarily, but it held that the Michigan court could not interfere with the Missouri court's order to testify in a case over which Michigan had no jurisdiction. *Id.* at 239. Justice Scalia would have held that Missouri had no duty to enforce the Michigan judgment until GM sued on the judgment in a Missouri court and got a Missouri injunction. *Id.* at 241-242 (Scalia, J., concurring). The Court took the occasion to say that it had "never placed equity decrees outside" the reach of Full Faith and Credit Clause, *id.* at 233, a point that seems obvious but that had aroused significant doubt.

Another recurring pattern is two competing interest groups and a government agency that regulates or protects one or both of them. To flesh out just one example in which the issue was not raised, consider Texas Monthly, Inc., v. Bullock, 489 U.S. 1 (1989). Texas Monthly, a commercial magazine, sued Bullock, the state tax collector, to invalidate a provision that exempted religious publications from sales tax. Should religious publishers be bound by the results of that litigation? For debate of the general issue, compare Douglas Laycock, *Consent Decrees Without Consent: The Rights of Nonconsenting Third Parties*, 1987 U. Chi. Legal F. 103, with Larry Kramer, *Consent Decrees and the Rights of Third Parties*, 87 Mich. L. Rev. 321 (1988).

10. Multiple plaintiffs with the same interest. Multiple plaintiffs with the same interest may get less protection than claimants with conflicting interests, even if no class is certified and no class representative appointed. This seems to be the implication of a wonderfully named but cryptic case, Lawyer v. Department of Justice, 521 U.S. 567 (1997).

Under the Supreme Court's redistricting doctrine, any voter in a legislative district has standing to claim that the district is unconstitutionally drawn. Lawyer and several other voters challenged Florida's District 21 as a racial gerrymander. Before any adjudication on the merits, the Attorney General and all the plaintiffs except Lawyer agreed to a settlement; Lawyer argued that he was entitled to an adjudication that the original version of District 21 was unconstitutional, and he argued that the new version of District 21, created by the proposed settlement, was also unconstitutional. Lawyer had no interest distinct from either plaintiffs or defendants; he was simply one of a large group of potential plaintiffs, differing only in their propensity to settle.

Citing *Local 93*, the Court held that Lawyer could not prevent the others from settling the dispute over the original version of District 21. *Id.* at 578-579. And it affirmed the three-judge district court's holding that the new version of District 21 was consistent with the Constitution. But that holding was based on only a "limited review," "similar to a fairness hearing." Scott v. United States Department of Justice, 920 F. Supp. 1248, 1256 & n.4 (M.D. Fla. 1996), *aff'd*, Lawyer v. Department of Justice, 521 U.S. 567 (1997). The Supreme Court appears to have assumed that this limited review was all that Lawyer was entitled to. The Court reaffirmed that "a settlement agreement subject to court approval in a nonclass action may not impose duties or obligations on an unconsenting party or 'dispose' of his claims," but it said that the agreement in *Lawyer* "did none of these things." 521 U.S. at 579. To let him insist on a judgment that the original District 21 was unconstitutional, when the settlement had eliminated that district, "would be to allow a sore winner to obscure the point of the suit." *Id.* "[T]he judicial decree is not the end but the means." *Id.* And the end of redrawing District 21 had already been achieved.

11. Enforcing the injunction. These materials address the question of who can be enjoined. Once the court enjoins a defendant who has been found to have violated the law, the injunction can be enforced against that defendant, its officers, agents, servants, employees, and attorneys, and any other persons "in active concert or participation with" any of these, but no one else. Fed. R. Civ. Proc. 65(d)(2). The rights of third parties at the enforcement stage are a separate problem, taken up in the materials on contempt, in section 9.A.4.

CHAPTER
5

Choosing Remedies

A. SUBSTITUTIONARY OR SPECIFIC RELIEF

1. *Irreplaceable Losses*

a. Injunctions

PARDEE v. CAMDEN LUMBER CO.
73 S.E. 82 (W. Va. 1911)

[Plaintiff sued to enjoin defendant from cutting timber on plaintiff's land.]

POFFENBARGER, J.

This appeal from an order dissolving an injunction awarded to prevent the cutting of timber on a tract of land . . . would necessarily and inevitably fail under a rule or principle often declared by this court, if we should adhere to it. Unless the trespass itself constitutes irreparable injury, none is shown, for there is no allegation of insolvency of the trespasser nor of any other circumstance precluding recovery of such compensation in money as the law gives for the injury done and threatened by an action.

In . . . McMillan v. Ferrell, 7 W. Va. 223 (1874), this court prescribed, as being essential and indispensable to a bill to prevent the cutting of timber, averments of good title in the plaintiff, trespass by the defendant, and the insolvency of the latter or some other circumstance, rendering an action for damages futile or unavailing, and that doctrine has been uniformly maintained ever since. However, this rule seems not to have commanded uniform approval by the public, nor by the members of the legal profession, and in later years, under conditions greatly enhancing the value of timber and altering, to a considerable extent, the method of handling it, the dissatisfaction has grown in extent and intensified in degree. . . .

Supposed adequacy of the legal remedy for the cutting of timber, regarded as a mere trespass upon land, constitutes the basis of the rule. If the legal remedy is not adequate, the whole doctrine necessarily fails. Whether it is must be determined by reference to the general policy of the law as disclosed by its application in analogous and related cases. In other words, we must see to what extent the remedies afforded by courts of law and equity protect and vindicate the right of an owner of property to keep it in such condition as he desires. If we find the general object to be the maintenance of this right, respecting all other kinds of property, we must necessarily say it ought to extend to the right of an owner of timber to allow it to stand upon his land in its natural state as long as he desires it to do so.

[¶] Timber cut down and converted into mere logs and lumber is plainly not the same thing as standing timber. It is equally manifest that the legal remedies are wholly inadequate to reconvert logs and lumber into live, standing, growing trees. Our rule permits a mere trespasser to utterly destroy the forest of his neighbor, provided he is solvent and able to respond in damages to the extent of the value thereof. It can neither restore the forest, nor prevent its destruction. It allows the property to be wholly altered in nature and character, or converts it into a mere claim for damages. After the timber has been cut, the owner may recover possession thereof by an action of detinue, or, waiving that, may recover its value, but this does not in either case restore the property to its former state, nor replace it by the return of an equivalent.

[¶] The general principles of English and American jurisprudence forbid such a result. They guarantee to the owner of property the right, not only to possession thereof and dominion over it, but also its immunity from injury, unless it be of such character that it may be substantially replaced. On the theory of adequacy of the legal remedy an injunction to prevent the sale or destruction of certain kinds of personal property will be refused, but the principles upon which this conclusion stand cannot be extended to all forms of property either real or personal, and the courts do not attempt so to extend it.

[¶] Compensation in damages is adequate in all those instances in which the property [that] is injured or destroyed may be substantially replaced with the money recovered as its value. For instance, the world is full of horses, cattle, sheep, hogs, lumber, and many other articles. Ordinarily, one of these may be replaced by another just as good. This principle is applied in a proceeding for specific performance of contracts for the sale of corporate stocks. If the stock belongs to a class found generally in the market for sale, equity refuses specific performance of the contract, because other stock of the same kind can be purchased with the money recovered as damages. If, on the other hand, the stock is limited and unobtainable in the market, specific performance will be enforced. Similarly, as no two pieces of land can be regarded as equivalent in value and character in all respects, equity will always enforce specific performance of a valid contract for the sale thereof. If personal property possesses a value peculiar to its owner, or as it is generally expressed, has a *pretium affectionis* [literally, a price of affection], equity will vindicate and uphold the right to the possession thereof and immunity from injury by the exercise of its extraordinary powers.

[¶] We observe, also, that the law gives a remedy for the possession of personal property, however trivial its value or character may be. It does not limit the owner to a claim for damages, unless the property has gone beyond the reach of its process. As equity follows the law, and, as far as possible, supplies omissions therein, so far as may be necessary to the effectuation of substantial justice, it vindicates the right of an owner to enjoy his property without injury or molestation by the exercise of its preventive powers; but, harmonizing with the great divine rule of help to those who help themselves, equity goes no further than is necessary. Therefore, if a man threatens to take away or kill his neighbor's horse, a court of equity will not interfere by injunction, because the owner may recover the value of that horse and buy another in the general market of substantially the same kind or value. For the same reason, it refuses to enforce specific performance of a contract of sale of a horse. But, if a man is about to destroy his neighbor's heirlooms, things having a peculiar value and insusceptible of replacement by purchase in the market, the legal remedy is not adequate, and a court of equity will, therefore, protect the possession and title of the owner by the exercise of its extraordinary powers. . . . Such being the general policy of the law, do we not violate it by denying to the owner of standing timber his clear and indisputable legal right to have it remain upon his land until such time as he shall see fit to convert it into a different kind of property?

[¶] Moreover, standing timber is everywhere regarded as part of the real estate upon which it grows. The cutting thereof converts it into personal property, and wholly changes its legal nature and incidents. Being a part of the land itself, it has no legal equivalent in nature or value, for no two pieces of land are alike in all respects, nor is a piece of land, stripped of its timber, with a right of action for the felled timber or for damages, the equivalent of the same land with the timber on it.

[¶] Courts universally hold that all contracts relating to real estate are subjects of equitable cognizance, because they relate to real estate. A distinction is made between contractual rights respecting real estate and liability growing out of trespasses thereon. . . . Of course, the legal remedy is adequate, if the trespass amounts to nothing more than the trampling of the grass or throwing down of the fences, acts in no way affecting the substance of the estate, but the adequacy of the remedy in such cases does not argue efficacy in those cases in which part of the real estate is actually severed and carried away, to the injury and detriment of the inheritance. In Whitehouse v. Jones, 55 S.E. 730, 734 (W. Va. 1906), Judge Brannon condemned the rule now under consideration in the following terms:

> It seems to me that this doctrine is now, always has been, unsound. Timber is of such inestimable value for building and repairing houses and fences, for fuel, and other purposes. It takes half a century or more to regrow it when once removed. A trespasser, without title, cuts it to-day, to-morrow, and on. Must you sue him in suit after suit for each day's or week's depredation? Or will you wait until he gets through, then have a long lawsuit? The timber is gone forever. The party has become insolvent. The remedy is not full and adequate.

Upon the principles and considerations here stated, we are of the opinion that the adoption of this rule was a deviation from fundamental principles of our jurisprudence. It is no doubt attributable to a lack of appreciation of the true character of timber, due to its former abundance and comparative worthlessness. In early days it was regarded as an incumbrance and burden upon lands. Having nothing but forests, the chief object or purpose of landowners everywhere was to get rid of the forests, and prepare their lands for agriculture. There was an abundance of timber, and no market for it. The soil was untillable because of the timber. . . . Timber was not regarded as anything more than an ordinary commercial article, and almost worthless because of its abundance. . . . The error, thus born, has been revealed by the great change of conditions. Timber having become scarce and of great value, the layman, lawyer, and judge has in recent years given the subject more careful, critical, and profound consideration, with the result that the error is practically admitted everywhere.

Violative of principle, as we think, the rule is also contrary to the great weight of authority. In the general struggle for relief from it, courts have in some instances based distinctions upon the relative values of the timber and the land, saying the cutting of timber, constituting the chief value of the land, will be enjoined, but we think a clear case of trespass by the cutting of timber should always be enjoined. In one sense a small quantity of timber on land is more indispensable to its enjoyment than a large quantity. . . .

For the reasons here stated, the decree complained of will be reversed, the injunction reinstated, and the cause remanded.

[Judge BRANNON's concurring opinion is omitted.]

F.W. MAITLAND, EQUITY
1-8 (1st ed., Cambridge Univ. Press 1909 (reprinted 1910))

[*Pardee* illustrates and interprets the rule that courts will not grant an equitable remedy if a legal remedy would be adequate. To understand and evaluate that rule requires a brief summary of the history of equity. The following summary is from a lecture originally delivered at Cambridge in 1906.]

What is Equity? We can only answer . . . by giving some short account of certain courts of justice which were abolished over thirty years ago. In the year 1875 we might have said "Equity is that body of rules which is administered only by those Courts which are known as Courts of Equity." The definition of course would not have been very satisfactory, but now-a-days we are cut off even from this unsatisfactory definition. We have no longer any courts which are merely courts of equity. Thus we are driven to say that Equity now is that body of rules administered by our English courts of justice which, were it not for the operation of the Judicature Acts, would be administered only by those courts which would be known as Courts of Equity.

This, you may well say, is but a poor thing to call a definition. . . . Still I fear that nothing better than this is possible. The only alternative would be to make a list of the equitable rules and say that Equity consists of those rules. . . . [I]f we were to inquire what it is that all these rules have in common and what it is that marks them off from all other rules administered by our courts, we should by way of answer find nothing but this, that these rules were until lately administered, and administered only, by our courts of equity.

Therefore for the mere purpose of understanding the present state of our law, some history becomes necessary. . . .

In Edward I's day, at the end of the thirteenth century, three great courts have come into existence, the King's Bench, the Common Bench or Court of Common Pleas, and the Exchequer. . . . The law which these courts administer is in part traditional law, in part statute law. Already in Edward I's day the phrase "common law" is current. It is a phrase that has been borrowed from the canonists—who used "*jus commune*" [literally, common law] to denote the general law of the Catholic Church; it describes that part of the law that is unenacted, non-statutory, that is common to the whole land and to all Englishmen. It is contrasted with statute, with local custom, with royal prerogative. It is not as yet contrasted with equity, for as yet there is no body of rules which bears this name.

One of the three courts, namely, the Exchequer, is more than a court of law. . . . What we should call the "civil service" of the country is transacted by two great offices or "departments"; there is the Exchequer which is the fiscal department, there is the Chancery which is the secretarial department, while above these there rises the king's permanent Council. At the head of the chancery stands the Chancellor, usually a bishop; he is we may say the king's secretary of state for all departments, he keeps the king's great seal and all the already great mass of writing that has to be done in the king's name has to be done under his supervision.

He is not as yet a judge, but already he by himself or his subordinates has a great deal of work to do which brings him into a close connexion with the administration of justice. One of the duties of that great staff of clerks over which he presides is to draw up and issue those writs whereby actions are begun in the courts of law. . . .

But by another route the Chancellor is brought into still closer contact with the administration of justice. Though these great courts of law have been established there is still a reserve of justice in the king. Those who can not get relief elsewhere present their petitions to the king and his council praying for some remedy. . . .

Very often the petitioner . . . complains that for some reason or another he can not get a remedy in the ordinary course of justice and yet he is entitled to a remedy. He is poor, he is old, he is sick, his adversary is rich and powerful, will bribe or will intimidate jurors, or has by some trick or some accident acquired an advantage of which the ordinary courts with their formal procedure will not deprive him. The petition is often couched in piteous terms, the king is asked to find a remedy for the love of God and in the way of charity. Such petitions are referred by the king to the Chancellor. Gradually in the course of the fourteenth century petitioners, instead of going to the king, will go straight to the Chancellor. . . . Now one thing that the Chancellor may do in such a case is to invent a new writ and so provide the complainant with a means of bringing an action in a court of law. But in the fourteenth century the courts of law have become very conservative and are given to quashing writs which differ in material points from those already in use. But another thing that the Chancellor can do is to send for the complainant's adversary and examine him concerning the charge that has been made against him. Gradually a procedure is established. The Chancellor having considered the petition, or "bill" as it is called, orders the adversary to come before him and answer the complaint. The writ whereby he does this is called a subpoena [literally, under penalty] — because it orders the man to appear upon pain of forfeiting a sum of money. . . . The defendant will be examined upon oath and the Chancellor will decide questions of fact as well as questions of law.

I do not think that in the fourteenth century the Chancellors considered that they had to administer any body of substantive rules that differed from the ordinary law of the land. They were administering the law but they were administering it in cases which escaped the meshes of the ordinary courts. The complaints that come before them are in general complaints of indubitable legal wrongs, assaults, batteries, imprisonments, disseisins and so forth — wrongs of which the ordinary courts take cognizance . . . . But then owing to one thing and another such wrongs are not always redressed by courts of law. In this period one of the commonest of all the reasons that complainants will give for coming to the Chancery is that they are poor while their adversaries are rich and influential — too rich, too influential to be left to the clumsy processes of the old courts and the verdicts of juries. However this sort of thing can not well be permitted. The law courts will not have it and parliament will not have it. Complaints against this extraordinary justice grow loud in the fourteenth century. In history and in principle it is closely connected with another kind of extraordinary justice which is yet more objectionable, the extraordinary justice that is done in criminal cases by the king's council. Parliament at one time would gladly be rid of both. . . . And so the Chancellor is warned off the field of common law — he is not to hear cases which might go to the ordinary courts, he is not to make himself a judge of torts and contracts, of property in lands and goods.

But then just at this time it is becoming plain that the Chancellor is doing some convenient and useful works that could not be done, or could not easily be done, by the courts of common law. He has taken to enforcing uses or trusts. [Trusts were initially called "uses" because property was conveyed to a trustee "for the use of" a beneficiary.] . . . I think we may say that had there been no Chancery, the old courts would have discovered some method of enforcing these fiduciary obligations. That method however must have been a clumsy one. A system of law which will never compel, which will never even allow, the defendant to give evidence, a system which sends every question of fact to a jury, is not competent to deal adequately with fiduciary relationships. On the other hand the Chancellor had a procedure which was very well adapted to this end. To this we may add that very possibly the ecclesiastical courts (and the Chancellor you will remember was almost always an ecclesiastic) had for a long time past been punishing breaches of trust by spiritual censures, by penance and excommunication. And so by general consent, we may say, the Chancellor was allowed to enforce uses, trusts or confidences.

Thus one great field of substantive law fell into his hand—a fruitful field, for in the course of the fifteenth century uses became extremely popular. . . . And then there were some other matters that were considered to be fairly within his jurisdiction. . . . [T]here were many frauds which the stiff old procedure of the courts of law could not adequately meet, and "accident," in particular the accidental loss of a document, was a proper occasion for the Chancellor's interference. No one could set any very strict limits to his power, but the best hint as to its extent that could be given in the sixteenth century was given by the words "fraud, accident and breach of confidence." On the other hand he was not to interfere where a court of common law offered an adequate remedy. A bill was "demurrable for want of equity" on that ground.

NOTE ON EQUITY IN THE UNITED STATES

Article III of the Constitution authorizes equity jurisdiction for the federal courts, and Congress conferred that jurisdiction in 1789. Although the same federal judges exercised both law and equity powers, these powers were still conceived of as separate. Federal district courts had a law side and an equity side, and a case had to be on one side or the other; it could not be on both.

A serious movement for merger of law and equity in the states began with the Field Code of Procedure in 1848. Only three states still have separate courts of equity today, although the merger in some other states is less than complete. The Federal Rules of Civil Procedure, adopted in 1938, completed the merger in federal courts. But equitable doctrines and especially equitable remedies are still identifiable in the merged practice, and they have become increasingly important in complex modern litigation.

Both the English and the American sides of this history are reviewed from a modern perspective, with extensive citation to sources, in Thomas O. Main, *Traditional Equity and Contemporary Procedure*, 78 Wash. L. Rev. 429, 429-476 (2003).

Talk of a federal equity power—in contrast to the Supreme Court's denial of federal authority to make common law—seems to be the principal source of confusion about whether Erie Railroad v. Tompkins applies to injunctions. In Guaranty Trust Co. v. York, 326 U.S. 99 (1945), the Court insisted in sweeping terms that *Erie* is fully applicable to diversity cases arising in equity. And then it said, in an elaborate dictum, that this did not mean that the same equitable remedies would necessarily be available in state and federal court in diversity cases. The Court did not explain in any comprehensible way how the two halves of this opinion fit together, either then or in the ensuing 70-plus years. Maybe it was the then lingering assumption that remedies were more procedural than substantive.

The choice of state or federal law in injunction cases often goes by default, in part because there are often no clearly defined differences between state and federal law. Lord & Taylor v. White Flint, reprinted below in section 5.A.2, is an unusual example of a federal court carefully attending to state precedent on whether to grant an injunction. When courts attend to the issue, they appear to generally agree that the jurisdiction that provides the substantive law controls whether there should be a permanent injunction. But there is much disagreement about what law controls preliminary injunctions. Some of the cases are collected in Jeffrey Steven Gordon, *Our Equity: Federalism and Chancery*, 72 U. Miami L. Rev. 176, 254-265 (2017).

NOTES ON THE REASONS FOR THE IRREPARABLE INJURY RULE

1. Inadequate remedy and irreparable injury. It is hornbook law that equity will not act if there is an adequate remedy at law. Inadequate remedy at law began as a rationale for the equity court's separate existence and consequently became the rationale for defining and limiting the court's jurisdiction. For if the equity court sat to correct the common law's inadequacies, it followed that there was no need for equity in cases in which the common law was satisfactory.

Another formulation of the rule is that equity will act only to prevent injury that is irreparable — i.e., irreparable at law. Despite occasional attempts to distinguish these statements, they are simply two formulations of the same rule. "Irreparable harm occurs when a party has no adequate remedy at law, typically because its injuries cannot be fully compensated through an award of damages." General Motors Corp. v. Harry Brown's, LLC, 563 F.3d 312, 319 (8th Cir. 2009). Both formulations are in common use.

The most useful attempted distinction is to use the "adequate remedy" formulation to refer to the choice of remedies at final judgment, and the "irreparable injury" formulation to refer to the requirements for interim relief pending final judgment — for preliminary injunctions and temporary restraining orders ("TROs"). Owen M. Fiss & Doug Rendleman, *Injunctions* 59 (2d ed., Foundation 1984). The rules and policy considerations at final judgment are so different from the rules and policy considerations on motions for preliminary relief that it would be a great boon if we could establish two different phrases for referring to the two different situations. But allocating "inadequate remedy" and "irreparable injury" to these two situations is almost wholly artificial; both phrases derive from the same history, and they are used interchangeably in too many cases and too many books, including Professor Fiss's *The Civil Rights Injunction*, Dan Dobbs's treatise on *Remedies* (now Dobbs and Roberts), and Laycock's own earlier work. We would do better to draw the distinction in plain English — not to artificially distinguish irreparable injury from inadequate remedy, but to say, when we mean to emphasize the real distinction, "irreparable injury before judgment" and "irreparable injury after judgment."

2. The sources of inadequacy. The defects in the common law to which equity responded were many and varied. Sometimes the problem was procedural clumsiness; sometimes harsh, antiquated, or inflexible substantive rules; sometimes the law's narrow range of remedies with its emphasis on money damages. Note the dominance of substantive issues in Maitland's account of equity. Today, the substantive primary rights created in equity have largely been absorbed into the general substantive law, but equitable remedies still seem distinctively equitable to most judges. The typical modern application of the irreparable injury rule is to a comparison between some equitable remedy that will prevent a threatened injury and money damages that will compensate for the injury after it has occurred. If money damages will be "adequate," then the injury is not irreparable and will not be prevented.

3. Modern justifications? A rule designed to preserve the jurisdictional boundaries between two courts that have long been merged should die unless it serves some modern purpose. Would any purpose be served in *Pardee* by denying the injunction and making plaintiff sue for the value of the timber?

a. Burdens on the court. It is sometimes said that injunctions impose a greater burden on the court, because they have to be enforced over time. A damage judgment results in a one-time transfer of money, after which the court's involvement is over. Burdens on the court are obvious in the structural injunction cases, although measuring and collecting damages in those cases might be even more difficult. Is there any reason to believe that it will always, or even usually, be harder to enforce an injunction than to collect a damage judgment? What about a simple preventive injunction like the one in *Pardee?* Enforcing injunctions and collecting money damages can each be very easy or excruciatingly difficult, depending on the circumstances; the contrasting methods and difficulties of each are explored in Chapter 9.

In fact, specific relief is often simpler than legal relief. Judge Friendly once wrote that injunctions are "the appropriate remedy" in class actions, and that insurmountable difficulties come from the attempt to award damages. Henry J. Friendly, *Federal Jurisdiction: A General View* 120 (Columbia Univ. Press 1973). The Supreme Court has long said that injunctions ordering divestiture are the "simple, relatively easy to administer, and sure" remedy in antitrust merger cases. California v. American Stores Co., 495 U.S. 271, 281 (1990), quoting United States v. E.I. du Pont de Nemours & Co., 366 U.S. 316, 331 (1961). More generally:

> Specific relief reduces or eliminates consequential damages, which is better for everyone: The plaintiff does not have to suffer them, the lawyers do not have to litigate them, the court does not have to measure them, and the defendant does not have to pay them.

Douglas Laycock, *The Triumph of Equity*, 56 Law & Contemp. Probs. 53, 61 (Summer 1993). As we saw in Chapter 2, measuring damages isn't always easy.

b. Defendant's liberty. It is sometimes said that the injunction is a greater intrusion on defendant's liberty. This is partly because the injunction orders him to do or refrain from specified conduct; the damage remedy leaves him free to proceed if he is willing to pay the cost. And it is partly because the injunction can be enforced by coercive or punitive measures, including imprisonment. The damage remedy is enforced only by seizing defendant's property; the court will not punish defendants who fail to pay.

Do we want to preserve the liberty to cut down other people's trees? To the extent the damage remedy preserves that liberty for defendant, doesn't it equally reduce plaintiff's liberty to grow trees? It is one thing to preserve liberty by minimizing substantive restrictions on conduct; it is another to facilitate violations of the substantive rules we find necessary. Would the liberty argument have more punch if the government were seeking the injunction?

c. Jury trial. In most jurisdictions, there is a right to jury trial at law but not in equity. Thus, it is often said that the irreparable injury rule protects the right to jury trial; plaintiff should not be able to deprive defendant of a jury by asking for an injunction instead of damages. But how often does defendant want a jury and plaintiff want a bench trial?

d. Timing. To prevent the harm, the court must resolve the liability issue before the harm has happened. There are special procedures for granting interim relief pending a full trial on the merits, but these procedures cannot fully avoid the problems of hasty decision. Compensation can be litigated at leisure, after the harm is done. The court needs to control its calendar; it needs time to reflect and decide; and defendant needs time to prepare a defense. Do these needs justify making plaintiff accept damages if damages appear to be "good enough"? Do they carry much weight with respect to reparative and structural injunctions? What about preventive injunctions where plaintiff is not in a hurry?

The timing argument as such has not been much relied on by proponents of the irreparable injury rule, but defendant's right to a full trial is a powerful reason for restricting interim relief to special situations. And timing is probably the most important practical reason why plaintiffs seek damages more often than injunctions. Many harms happen irreversibly before any court can prevent them, and victims can often get on with their lives more quickly by repairing any damage themselves and suing for reimbursement than by suing to make the wrongdoer fix the problem.

4. A system? The most ambitious argument for the continued value of the traditional distinctions is Samuel L. Bray, *A System of Equitable Remedies*, 63 UCLA L. Rev. 530 (2016). Bray includes in his system injunctions, specific performance of contracts, reformation, accounting for profits, constructive trusts, equitable liens, subrogation, and equitable rescission. He argues that these remedies are distinctive because they order litigants to act or refrain from acting. This distinctive set of remedies requires a distinctive set of managerial tools to make these remedies workable — the power to modify decrees, enforcement by contempt, masters and receivers, a looser relationship between right and remedy, and no jury trials. He might have added preliminary orders. And these distinctive remedies are subject to a distinctive set of constraints to control their costs and prevent their abuse — ripeness, no adequate remedy at law, a requirement that decrees be specific, equitable defenses (laches, unclean hands, and undue hardship are the ones he claims), maxims of equity that often suggest restraint, and residual discretion.

Professor Bray does not claim that the restrictions on equity amount to much, but he does think that they are real and worth preserving. Most importantly, he views the irreparable injury rule as relatively easy to satisfy but as a useful marker of the separateness of equity.

Professor Bray is one of the most prolific and talented remedies scholars writing today. But in our view, he has (at most) described injunctions and specific performance. The other remedies on his list do not share his essential distinguishing feature: they do not order litigants to act or refrain from acting except in occasional and incidental ways that also arise with legal remedies. They end in ordinary money judgments or simple transfers of property that present no special difficulties. We will take up these other remedies in Chapters 7 and 8, the contempt power and the specificity of decrees in Chapter 9, and the equitable defenses in section 5.A.2 and Chapter 11.

Injunctions and specific performance *do* order defendants to act or refrain from acting, but as we have already suggested, that does not necessarily make them more burdensome or complicated. Sometimes equitable remedies are more complicated than damage remedies; sometimes they are simpler. In our view, any attempt to generalize about legal or equitable remedies requires so many exceptions as to make the generalization worthless.

5. Economic analysis. Recall the economic view that profitable violations of law should sometimes be encouraged if the violator compensates his victims. If the timber is more valuable to the lumber company than to the landowner, why shouldn't the lumber company be free to take it now and pay damages when the landowner complains? Mainstream economic analysis does not argue for efficient theft. The following explanation of the economic view is based on a famous article by Guido Calabresi and A. Douglas Melamed, *Property Rules, Liability Rules, and Inalienability: One View of the Cathedral*, 85 Harv. L. Rev. 1089, 1124-1127 (1972), and on Richard A. Posner, *Economic Analysis of Law* 39-94 (9th ed., Wolters Kluwer 2014).

a. The preference for voluntary transactions. The lumber company has no reason to cut the timber without asking; it can offer to buy it from the landowner. If the landowner agrees to sell at a price the lumber company agrees to pay, we can be sure the timber has been transferred to a more valuable use. But if we ask a jury to decide the value of the timber, we introduce a risk of error. The jury will be told to award the market value of the timber; the possibility that the landowner personally values the timber at more than its market value is too speculative for the jury to consider, even if she refused to sell at the market price. If the timber is more valuable to the plaintiff than to the market, or if the jury underestimates the market value, the landowner will be undercompensated. If the timber is less valuable to plaintiff than to the market, or if the jury overestimates value, the lumber company will have to pay too much.

Economic purists do not care about the unfairness of these results. Their concern is that if lumber companies expect juries to undercompensate landowners, they will take timber even when their own use for it is not the most valuable; and if they expect juries to overcompensate, they will not take timber when they ought to. Litigation is not as reliable as voluntary transactions for directing resources to their highest and best use. And litigation, threats of litigation, and settlement negotiations are expensive. So even if it is profitable for the lumber company to steal the timber, it should be discouraged from doing so if it could negotiate directly with the landowner. An injunction against cutting forces the lumber company to buy the timber at a price acceptable to the landowner. If the landowner refuses to sell, that means she values the timber more than the lumber company does.

b. Transaction costs. Where the cost of negotiating a voluntary transaction would be high, Judge Posner would deny the injunction and leave victims to their damage remedy. There are many sources of high transaction costs, but two are both common and easy to explain. One is transactions with so many parties that it is difficult or impossible to reach agreement among them all. This includes situations where an actor's conduct puts many people at risk and there is no way to know who will get hurt.

Another common source of high transaction costs is bilateral monopoly. Bilateral monopoly exists when the parties have no alternative but to deal with each other. There is no hint of bilateral monopoly in *Pardee*. Camden Lumber could buy timber from someone else if Pardee demands too high a price, and Pardee could sell to someone else if Camden Lumber offers too low a price. If both sides want to complete the transaction, the existence of market alternatives makes it likely that they would quickly agree on something close to the market price. But if the dispute were that pollution from the lumber mill is harming Pardee's trees, their negotiations would be a bilateral monopoly. Pardee cannot buy a promise that Camden Lumber will quit polluting from anyone but Camden Lumber, and Camden Lumber cannot buy the right to poison Pardee's trees from anyone but Pardee. There would be no market alternative to guide their bargaining behavior, and they might have great difficulty reaching agreement.

To summarize the economic view: Where transaction costs are high, the usual remedy should be damages; where transaction costs are low, the usual remedy should be injunction. That is not a general preference for damages.

c. Efficient theft? Some law-and-economics literature has experimented with the idea that we should all be free to take other people's property without their consent and be liable only for damages. Strategic bargaining behavior, or even owners' "irrational" attachment to their own property, might be barriers to trade. These arguments are fundamentally inconsistent with the popular understanding of property—reflected, for example, in political resistance to the government's eminent-domain power. It would plainly be politically impossible to extend the equivalent of eminent-domain power to any private person who wants to take another's property. And any such system would savage the central economic benefit of property rights, which is that an owner has incentives to develop and invest in what he knows to be his own. This literature has not changed the law-and-economics consensus based in Calabresi and Melamed, and hostile readers may think it just shows that law and economics is impossible to parody.

Much of this literature is reviewed in Stewart E. Sterk, *Property Rules, Liability Rules, and Uncertainty About Property Rights*, 106 Mich. L. Rev. 1285 (2008). Sterk suggests, more plausibly, that some property rights and their owners can be discovered only with prohibitively expensive search costs (think about finding the owner of the copyright on a 30-year-old pamphlet), and that in such cases, remedies should be limited to damages. See also Richard L. Hasen & Richard H. McAdams, *The Surprisingly Complex Case Against Theft*, 17 Int'l Rev. L. & Econ. 367 (1997), arguing that the purely economic case against theft is uncomfortably complex, and that it ultimately depends upon demonstrating that the indirect costs of theft, such as costs of taking defensive measures to prevent it, would swamp any efficiency gains from theft.

BROOK v. JAMES A. CULLIMORE & CO.
436 P.2d 32 (Okla. 1967)

McINERNEY, Justice.

The question dispositive of this appeal is whether in a replevin action the defeated litigant in possession of property whose recovery is sought may 1) elect to retain that property as his own, against the will of the successful party; 2) impose his election by requiring the trial court to render an alternative money judgment against him; and 3) avoid delivery of the property by tendering its value as set forth in the affidavit for replevin.

Cullimore sued Brook in replevin claiming a special interest in multiple items of personal property by virtue of a chattel mortgage [a security interest in personal property] securing a note in the sum of $8,147.26 and sought possession of the personalty. As disclosed by the petition and the affidavit for replevin, the aggregate value of this property was $2,500.00. . . . Brook gave a redelivery bond. He later offered to confess judgment for the alleged value of the property. . . . Concurrently with this offer Brook attempted to satisfy the judgment he so sought to confess. . . . [H]e deposited $2,500.00 — the alleged value of the property — [with the clerk of the court]. . . . Refusing to accept this offer of confession, Cullimore moved for a hearing "to determine whether said property is available" for delivery and "if found to be available that judgment be rendered . . . [for Cullimore] for immediate possession of said property". . . .

The trial court adjudged . . . that Brook deliver to Cullimore the property whose recovery was sought. . . . No alternative money judgment was rendered against Brook. He urges on appeal that the case should be remanded with directions "to take evidence of the value of the property sought by replevin, and [to] enter a money judgment" for its value.

At common law, the right to possession of the property at the time action was commenced formed the sole issue in replevin. If the property could not be returned, there was no method by which the prevailing party could recover a judgment for the value thereof. For procurement of a money judgment in lieu of possession the successful litigant was relegated to the remedy of trover. Our statute, 12 Okla. Stat. §1580 (1961), has provided a cumulative or supplemental remedy in favor of one who succeeds in a replevin action. By the terms of this enactment, if the losing party has retained possession of the property under a redelivery bond, the successful litigant is entitled to a judgment not only for his costs and for the recovery of possession, but also, if he so chooses, to an alternative money judgment for the value of the property. In the event possession cannot be given for any reason, the prevailing party may then proceed to enforce his money judgment. . . . One on whom a new remedy is conferred may elect which course to pursue. He need not avail himself of the new remedy unless he so chooses, and if he does not, he is not barred from pursuing the old. The primary object of statutory replevin is the recovery of specific personal property and not of money. . . .

If a return of the property sought by replevin is possible, it *must* be returned. The defeated litigant is not granted an option to either relinquish possession or pay the value of the property. . . . The alternative remedy of a money judgment in replevin is extended solely for the benefit of the wronged party. . . .

Brook, against whom judgment for possession was rendered, did not have the power to retain the property and pay its value as stated in the affidavit for replevin. The property shown to be available for delivery was of substantial value. It was far from being worthless or materially deteriorated. Cullimore was willing to accept it. As prevailing party, he had a right to insist on its return. . . .

Affirmed. . . .

NOTES ON REPLEVIN AND INJUNCTIONS

1. Replevin. Why is irreplaceability critical in *Pardee* and apparently irrelevant in *Brook*? Why in *Brook* are we not even told what the property is?

The answer is historical and doctrinal. Replevin was a common law writ for possession of property. Because replevin was a legal remedy, it was never subject to the irreparable injury rule. Replevin survives in modernized form in every state. Note the statement in *Pardee* that "the law gives a remedy for the possession of personal property, however trivial its value or character may be." Ejectment provides a similar legal remedy for real property.

Replevin makes specific relief available in an important set of cases without any showing that the damage remedy is inadequate. Plaintiff's right to the property through replevin casts doubt on claims that Anglo-American law reflects a preference for substitutionary relief over specific relief—for giving plaintiff damages instead of his property. Any attempt to explain the irreparable injury rule in functional terms must explain why the rule does not apply to replevin.

2. The early common law. We now think of damages as the quintessential legal remedy, but it was not always so. Feudal society operated more in barter than in cash, and its modes of fact finding (including trials by ordeal or by wager of law) were too clumsy to determine a question of degree, such as the size or value of an injury. The Anglo-Saxons had fixed payments for various crimes and torts, but most remedies before and after the Norman conquest were specific: plaintiff was awarded possession or defendant was ordered to perform his duty. The common law had no remedy that determined the amount of damages in individual cases until the end of the twelfth century. Juries, and the later introduction of sworn witnesses, led to a rational mode of trial; newly created writs with this rational trial method displaced the older writs without it; and, perhaps because England was becoming a much more commercial society, most of these new writs provided for damages as the remedy.

Replevin and ejectment were somehow created in this period with the old specific remedies and the new mode of trial. Recall too the coercive writs we briefly examined in section 4.A.2—mandamus, prohibition, certiorari, and habeas corpus. But then the common law courts passed through a long period in which they resisted further innovations, and during that period, the equity courts took the lead in developing new substantive law and also in developing specific remedies. By the middle of the millennium, the injunction had become the dominant equitable remedy, and damages had become the dominant legal remedy, but even so, the equity courts sometimes awarded money and the law courts sometimes gave specific relief. This note is largely based on a delightful short account in 1 Edgar N. Durfee & John P. Dawson, *Cases on Remedies* 1-12 (rev. ed. 1946). A more widely available account is 2 Frederick Pollock & Frederic William Maitland, *The History of English Law Before the Time of Edward I*, at 523-526, 577-578, 595-597 (2d ed., Cambridge Univ. Press 1978 reprint).

3. The means of enforcement. One important difference between replevin and injunction has been the means of enforcement. Injunctions are enforced by the contempt power; replevin was traditionally enforced by the sheriff seizing the property and delivering it to plaintiff. A defendant unwilling to comply with an injunction may be jailed for contempt; a defendant unable to comply may be jailed if the court doesn't believe her. The risk of jail time has obvious costs, but it deters defiance and evasion. The traditional means of enforcing replevin were clumsier and more likely to fail.

The irreparable injury rule has been brought to bear on this choice. If the goods are irreplaceable, plaintiff may get an injunction ordering return of the goods; she need not rely on the riskier enforcement mechanisms of replevin. The choice is reviewed in M.T. Van Hecke, *Equitable Replevin*, 33 N.C. L. Rev. 57 (1954). This choice of enforcement methods is important, but it is not the same as the choice between returning the property or paying damages. In most cases, either replevin or injunction will restore the goods; in some cases, the goods are gone forever and neither remedy will restore them. The choice of enforcement mechanisms affects the result in only a few marginal cases.

Moreover, the difference in means of enforcement is being eliminated by modern statutes. Illinois provides that any person who conceals property subject to a court order, or refuses to deliver it to the officer executing the order, is guilty of contempt of court. 735 Ill. Comp. Stat. Ann. §5/12-301. Similar statutes and rules of court are increasingly common. These statutes make the contempt power generally available to recover goods in replevin without any showing that the legal remedy is inadequate, and thus heighten the contrast between the free availability of replevin and the traditional restrictions on injunctions. For a replevin case that illustrates all the dangers of the contempt power in doubtful cases, see Central Production Credit Association v. Kruse, 509 N.E.2d 136 (Ill. App. Ct. 1987). Defendant was jailed for two months for failing to produce a replevied tractor. He and his wife said that the tractor had been stolen, but the trial court did not believe them.

4. Scope. Replevin is of narrower scope than injunctions. Most important for present purposes, replevin lies only to *recover* goods; it does not lie to prevent a threatened destruction or dispossession. *Pardee* says that equity will not interfere "if a man threatens to take away or kill his neighbor's horse." But we doubt that a modern court would let defendant destroy plaintiff's goods for no better reason than the likelihood that they could be replaced later. Laycock found only a few cases posing the issue. But all of them after 1950, and half of them before then, enjoined the tort. Douglas Laycock, *The Death of the Irreparable Injury Rule* 60 nn.61-62 (Oxford Univ. Press 1991). An example is Thomas v. Allis, 389 S.W.2d 109 (Tex. Civ. App. 1965), enjoining sale of a disputed herd of cattle. The court said that all legal remedies were inadequate because they "would ultimately subject plaintiff to the possibility of having to accept damages in lieu of the cattle." *Id.* at 112.

5. Legislative change. No legislature has undertaken to repeal the irreparable injury rule as a general matter. But orders to turn over property are not the only context where legislatures have overridden it on particular issues. The Tennessee statute authorizing automatic injunctions in divorce cases overrides the irreparable injury rule as well as the ripeness requirement. Tenn. Code Ann. §36-4-106, further described in note 3 following Almurbati v. Bush in section 4.A.1.

CONTINENTAL AIRLINES, INC. v. INTRA BROKERS, INC.
24 F.3d 1099 (9th Cir. 1994)

Before: NOONAN, FERNANDEZ, and KLEINFELD, Circuit Judges.

KLEINFELD, Circuit Judge: . . .

Continental published discount coupons in 1991 and 1992. They were redeemable with Continental for various discounts, such as $100 off on a roundtrip airfare of $351 or more. . . . Intra acquired the coupons and sold them to travel agents, for resale to their customers. . . .

Continental wrote on the coupons and stated in a letter that they could not be sold, but assured Intra repeatedly that the condition would not be enforced. . . . Continental thought it benefitted financially from Intra's sales of the coupons in 1991 and 1992. Then in April of 1992, Continental changed its position and plainly advised Intra of the change. Intra refused to comply with the new Continental policy.

There was no evidence of harm or benefit to Continental on account of Intra's refusal to comply. . . .

Nor was there any evidence of expenses by Intra in reliance on the old policy. . . . The question, unaffected by proven injury to either side, is whether Continental was entitled to an injunction to begin enforcing its previously waived restriction on sale of the discount coupons.

The district court . . . granted summary judgment to Continental on its claims for injunctive and declaratory relief. The permanent injunction commands Intra not to sell Continental coupons:

> Defendant INTRA-BROKERS, INC., and all those acting by, through, or in concert with said defendant are hereby permanently restrained and enjoined from engaging in the barter, trade or sale of those certain CONTINENTAL AIRLINES discount travel coupons identified as either GOLD C coupons or as ENTERTAINMENT COUPONS.

. . . [F]or equitable relief to be appropriate, there must generally be no adequate legal remedy. Intra argues that Continental has an adequate legal remedy: damages for financial losses from passengers' use of the coupons Intra sold. This same argument was made in Bitterman v. Louisville & Nashville Railroad, 207 U.S. 205 (1907). There, the railroad issued non-transferable round trip discount tickets to New Orleans for the United Confederate Veterans Reunion and Mardi Gras. Brokers were buying and selling the return trip coupons. The court found the non-transferability provisions on the tickets enforceable. . . . *Bitterman* rejected the argument that the carrier had an adequate legal remedy, because the carrier would likely make many mistakes in trying to enforce the forfeiture of the non-transferable tickets, and too many lawsuits would be needed to redress the harm if an injunction were denied. . . .

It is true that Continental did not demonstrate any financial harm. That has a bearing on the appropriateness of equitable relief, because the balance of hardships may generally be considered in exercising discretion whether to grant an injunction.

The discount coupons would tend to increase Continental's volume, but decrease the average fare received. Brokering would naturally increase their use, by facilitating transfer from those who would waste them to those who would use them. Continental's revenue could be higher, lower, or the same, depending on how much the brokering affected volume by increasing the number of passengers flying, and how much it affected average price by increasing the percentage of passengers flying at a discount. There might be downward pressure on Continental's fares because of resentment of passengers paying full fare, if too many passengers were known to be flying at a discount. Continental might engender ill will among its customers if they were questioned about their coupons at the counter when they tried to check in. The effect on revenue of brokering would be hard to measure or prove, especially prospectively.

Even retrospectively, in a damages case, expert witnesses might well testify to contrary conclusions on whether revenue effects were caused by discounts, brokering, prices being too low or high, bad or good service, general market conditions, or any number of other factors. The economic analysis of the effect of brokering discount coupons is difficult and uncertain. Expensive accounting and economic analysis might be necessary.

This difficulty of establishing economic harm to Continental, lack of proof of damages, and possible immeasurability or unascertainability of harm, does not mean Continental was not harmed. In Gilder v. PGA Tour, Inc., we said, "where the threat of injury is imminent and the measure of that injury defies calculation, damages will not provide a remedy at law." 936 F.2d 417, 423 (9th Cir. 1991). . . . Continental was entitled to control whether its coupons were transferred. The difficulty and probable expense of establishing the amount of economic harm supports the proposition that damages would be an inadequate remedy, and so cuts in favor of equitable relief.

The certain harm to Continental was to its power, not its purse. Whether Continental is right or wrong about the effect of coupon brokering on its profits, it sells the transportation services and it is entitled to make its own decisions about whether to give out discount coupons, and whether to make them transferable or nontransferable. Neither Intra nor the courts are entitled to substitute their business judgment for Continental's. Nor should Continental have to spend money on accountants and economists to have to prove the amount of economic harm in order to preserve its control over its discount policies from Intra's interference. There is certain harm to Continental's control of its own business, even though the harm to its profitability is unproven or perhaps immeasurable. . . .

Continental was entitled to control its own discounting policies, including assignment of discounting coupons, and to change those policies. In the absence of evidence to support any affirmative defense, a prospective injunction enabling Continental to exercise that control was appropriate.

Affirmed.

NOTES ON THE CONTENT OF THE IRREPARABLE INJURY RULE

1. Irreplaceability. What makes a legal remedy inadequate? *Pardee* says damages are inadequate because plaintiff can't use the money to replace the trees. How broad a principle is that? Doesn't it mean that money is never adequate in itself—that money is adequate only when it can be used to replace the very thing that plaintiff lost?

a. Timber. How identical must the replacement be? Surely there were other timberlands in West Virginia that plaintiff could have bought. Why aren't they adequate? Is it because no other land will have exactly the same number, size, and species of trees? Because no other land could be brought to the same place? Does it matter how plaintiff owned and used the land? If the land were his ancestral home, or he used it only for recreation, doesn't his claim to that very land and no other look pretty strong?

What if he is a commercial timber grower? If he owns the land only to earn dollars, why aren't dollars adequate compensation? Or at least, why isn't any timberland of equal value an adequate replacement? Is it merely because the rule says all real estate is unique and the court won't look behind the rule? Is it because the unauthorized cutting interfered with his right to control and manage his own business? Or is it because, despite the contrary implications of the irreparable injury rule, it doesn't make much sense to let wrongdoers inflict harm first and pay for it later?

b. Personal property. Why is the rule said to be different for personal property? We could say that every horse is unique, just as we say that every piece of land is unique. There may not be much difference between two healthy plow horses, but there isn't much different between two units in the same condominium building either. If plaintiffs in United States v. Hatahley, reprinted in section 2.A, had found out in advance about the government's plan to round up their horses, should the court have denied an injunction because "the world is full of horses"?

What about property that is truly fungible, such as mass-produced manufactured goods, or grain commingled in an elevator?

c. Intangible rights. The principle that damages are an inadequate remedy for the loss of something irreplaceable is not limited to land and unique tangible property. The same principle applies to intangible rights that are rarely bought or sold; this is why injunctions are the standard remedy in civil rights or environmental litigation. Personal injuries can rarely be anticipated in time to prevent them by injunction, but where an injunction is possible, the irreparable injury rule is obviously satisfied. This is why there can be injunctions against domestic violence and against conduct that creates a risk of serious injury. An example of the latter is the injunction against continued operation of an unsafe firing range in Citizens for a Safe Grant v. Lone Oak Sportsmen's Club, Inc., 624 N.W.2d 796 (Minn. Ct. App. 2001). Similarly, courts have enjoined stalking, where the harm to be prevented is emotional distress. An example is Opat v. Ludeking, 666 N.W.2d 597 (Iowa 2006).

The Fifth Circuit upheld a preliminary injunction to prevent Louisiana from cutting off Medicaid reimbursement to two Planned Parenthood clinics (which offered women's health services but not abortions). "Because the Individual Plaintiffs would otherwise be denied both access to a much needed medical provider and the legal right to the qualified provider of their choice, we agree that they would almost certainly suffer irreparable harm in the absence of a preliminary injunction." Planned Parenthood of Gulf Coast, Inc. v. Gee, 862 F.3d 445, 471 (5th Cir. 2017).

d. The right to control your own business. *Continental* doesn't talk about replaceability or uniqueness, but doesn't it illustrate the same principle? Continental's right to control its own business cannot be replaced in the market. And can't we say in nearly every case of wrongdoing that defendant interferes with plaintiff's right to control his own business, or his own personal life?

Even in the case of grain stored in an elevator, a forced sale interferes with the owner's right to control his own property. A farmer may store her crop at harvest time because she expects prices to be higher in the spring. See Decatur County AG-Services v. Young, 426 N.E.2d 644 (Ind. 1981), a case where the harm had already happened (and where the timing rule for valuation limited plaintiff to the lower value at harvest time). And see Howell Pipeline Co. v. Terra Resources, Inc., 454 So. 2d 1353, 1358 (Ala. 1984), enjoining the pumping of natural gas because it would interfere with the owner's "right to determine the disposition of the natural resource he possesses."

e. Commercial losses that are difficult to measure. The "loss of customer goodwill is a prime example of intangible, irreparable harm." Southern Glaziers Distributors of Ohio, LLC v. The Great Lakes Brewing Company, 860 F.3d 844, 853 (6th Cir. 2017). Great Lakes Brewing produced a popular line of craft beers. When it ended its franchise agreement with one of its beer distributors, the distributor's president testified that he would lose not only the Great Lakes business, but also other business of customers who preferred to deal with only one or a few distributors. Any attempt to compensate all this lost business in damages would be difficult and prone to huge errors in estimating the plaintiff's losses.

f. Automatic irreparable injury for states? Chief Justice Roberts granted Maryland's request to stay an injunction preventing Maryland from collecting DNA from criminal suspects who had not yet been convicted. "[A]ny time a State is enjoined . . . from effectuating statutes enacted by representatives of its people, it suffers a form of irreparable injury." Maryland v. King, 567 U.S. 1301, 1303 (2012) (Roberts, C.J., in chambers.). When the full Court reached the merits of the DNA collection, it sided with Maryland 5-4. Maryland v. King, 569 U.S. 435 (2013).

The Chief Justice issued the stay order as the Circuit Justice (the Justice assigned to a particular circuit to handle emergency motions and applications), and he relied on an earlier single-Justice opinion of then-Justice Rehnquist. Justice Alito worked this idea into an opinion of the Court in Abbott v. Perez, 138 S. Ct. 2805, 2324 n.17 (2018), a legislative redistricting case. The Court said that "inability to enforce its duly enacted plans clearly inflicts irreparable harm on the State," citing the Chief's single-justice opinion in Maryland v. King.

The argument has gained traction in the lower courts. In Veasey v. Abbott, 870 F.3d 387, 391 (5th Cir. 2017), the Fifth Circuit stayed a district court order barring Texas from enforcing a voter identification law. Judge Graves dissented. He distinguished *King* on the ground that the Fifth Circuit had already found Texas in violation of the Voting Rights Act in an earlier stage of the litigation, and he added:

> It cannot be that the single statement from *King* has the result that a state automatically suffers an irreparable injury when a court blocks any law it has enacted—regardless of the content of the law or the circumstances of its passing. Indeed, because these laws affect—or threaten to affect—the plaintiffs' right to vote, it is the plaintiffs who have shown they will suffer an irreparable injury should the stay be implemented.

Id. at 394 (Graves, J., dissenting).

These cases involve irreparable injury to the state as defendant, and that injury must be balanced against the irreparable injury to plaintiffs if the injunction is denied. The states in these cases could probably show irreparable injury under the usual standards. DNA that is not collected while a suspect is in custody may be impossible to replace or collect later. And if anyone were really casting in-person fraudulent votes in someone else's name, it would be difficult or impossible to identify those votes and keep them from being counted later. The Roberts opinion makes it unnecessary to consider the likelihood and magnitude of these actual injuries; it substitutes an abstract injury to sovereignty that requires no proof and that may be given substantial weight in the balancing process.

2. A judicial overview. The following excerpt is from an opinion by William T. Quillen, the former Chancellor of Delaware, sitting by designation in the Superior Court. The Superior Court is Delaware's law court; its fully separate Court of Chancery decides equity matters, including many corporate-law matters involving Delaware corporations. He notes that the jurisdiction of the Court of Chancery "depends on irreparable injury or on the absence of an adequate remedy at law" and that this rule is deeply embedded in Delaware's dual-court structure.

But the truth is that we too have probably switched the burden [of persuasion] on [equitable] jurisdiction by our own definition of adequate remedy, or sufficient remedy to use the statutory term. Irreparable harm only means harm that cannot be repaired at law; it does not mean catastrophic injury. The jurisdiction in equity does not depend on the need for a remedy that is extraordinary, as that term is commonly used in the English language. To the contrary, for the remedy at law to prevail, the remedy at law must be: available as a matter of right; full, fair and complete; and as practical and efficient to the ends of justice as the equitable remedy. This is a very practical standard which favors equity in cases where the Plaintiff for good reason seeks relief other than money damage. . . . Remedies are not extraordinary or ordinary; they are choices to solve problems.

Surely we need to desert the whole idea of hierarchy between law and equity. It certainly makes no sense . . . for a modern Chancellor to describe his or her Court, perhaps the most important State Trial Court in the country, as one of limited jurisdiction because of the irreparable injury rule. On the other hand, the Superior Court should not bear any inferior status *vis-a-vis* equity because Chancellor Ellesmere triumphed over Chief Justice Coke in [1616].

USH Ventures v. Global Telesystems Group, Inc., 796 A.2d 7, 14-15 (Del. Super. Ct. 2000).

3. How the rule acquired its content. The most important thing to understand about the evolution of the irreparable injury rule is that the rule's content was litigated exclusively in the equity court. The equity court decided for itself whether to take a case on the ground that the legal remedy was inadequate. And the equity court could enjoin parties from litigating in the common law courts, a power confirmed by the king in the crisis of 1616.

> It should not be surprising that equity interpreted the irreparable injury rule in ways that expanded its jurisdiction. . . .
>
> The most important and most general rule limiting the impact of the irreparable injury rule is the definition of adequacy. A legal remedy is adequate only if it is as complete, practical, and efficient as the equitable remedy. This definition of adequacy was well established before the merger, and it is the prevailing definition today. As a defender of the traditional understanding acknowledges, the legal remedy almost never meets this standard. . . .
>
> Yet any reader of opinions knows that courts talk about irreparable injury all the time. . . . Courts talk about the irreparable injury rule when they deny specific relief for other reasons.
>
> Before we can identify those reasons, we must clear away the factor that does not guide the choice. Courts do not deny specific relief merely because they judge the legal remedy adequate. The irreparable injury rule almost never bars specific relief, because substitutionary remedies are almost never adequate. At the stage of permanent relief, any litigant with a plausible need for specific relief can satisfy the irreparable injury rule.

Laycock, *The Death of the Irreparable Injury Rule* 22-23. We will use Laycock's "complete, practical, and efficient" definition of adequacy throughout this chapter. To be clear, Laycock and the courts he is quoting used the term "efficient" here to mean "efficacious" or "effective," or perhaps "without unnecessary burdens or expense." The meaning of the phrase as a whole is clearer than the meaning of each word separately. But "efficient" here does not mean economically efficient. The phrase is much older than the law-and-economics use of the term, and there is no connection between the two usages of "efficient."

4. Other reasons for denying equitable remedies. A successful argument within the terms of the irreparable injury rule does not necessarily mean that plaintiff gets her choice of remedy. Many other conflicting considerations affect the *court's* choice of remedy. Sometimes these other considerations are stated explicitly as rules; sometimes they are dealt with indirectly in opinions that seem to be about the irreparable injury rule.

Consider City of Los Angeles v. Lyons, 461 U.S. 95 (1983), where plaintiff sought to enjoin the city's use of chokeholds that had killed 16 suspects. Or Graham v. Medical Mutual, 130 F.3d 293 (7th Cir. 1997), where plaintiff sought an injunction ordering an insurer to pay for experimental treatment for metastasizing breast cancer. The court found no irreparable injury in either case. Neither court believed that being choked to death, or dying from cancer, is an injury that can be adequately remedied by damages. In *Lyons*, the Court meant that plaintiff was at no personal risk of being choked again; it was a propensity holding. See note 9 following Almurbati v. Bush in section 4.A.1. In *Graham*, the court meant there was no evidence the experimental treatment would be more effective than what the insurer would pay for; this was a holding about causation, or about the insurer's obligations under the policy. But each court found it convenient to say that plaintiff had not proved a threat of irreparable injury.

If you take such opinions at face value, there is a steady flow of conflicting authority on the meaning of irreparable injury. Lawyers sometimes have to argue these opinions at face value, because sometimes judges do. But most of the time, lawyers will surely do better to look behind the rhetoric and identify the real considerations that seem to reconcile conflicting decisions.

5. Dead or alive. No court has explicitly repudiated the irreparable injury rule. Texas went out of its way to reaffirm the rule, in a case where it made no difference to the result. Town of Palm Valley v. Johnson, 87 S.W.3d 110 (Tex. 2001). You can't beat 500 years of precedent by citing a professor, or even two professors.

Arguing within the rule works well for plaintiffs seeking permanent injunctions or specific performance of contracts, because in almost every imaginable situation, there is well-reasoned precedent that the legal remedy is inadequate. Our claim that the rule is dead can be stated less dramatically as a claim that whenever the choice of remedy matters to plaintiff, the rule is satisfied.

What motivates judges to sometimes say that a legal remedy is adequate despite serious problems, and other times to say that a legal remedy is inadequate for reasons that seem very modest? If you entertain the possibility that the irreparable injury rule might be dead, and then ask how cases still get decided both ways, a whole new set of arguments will seem much more prominent. Once you understand these other arguments, you can argue them directly. This chapter will consider a wide range of reasons for finding legal remedies inadequate, and a wide range for reasons for withholding equitable remedies even if legal remedies *are* inadequate. We hope that this chapter will enable students to fully argue the irreparable injury rule—to argue it dead and argue it alive.

b.   Specific Performance of Contracts

CAMPBELL SOUP CO. v. WENTZ

172 F.2d 80 (3d Cir. 1948)

Before BIGGS, Chief Judge, and GOODRICH and O'CONNELL, Circuit Judges.

GOODRICH, Circuit Judge. . . .

On June 21, 1947, Campbell Soup Company . . . , a New Jersey corporation, entered into a written contract with George B. Wentz and Harry T. Wentz, who are Pennsylvania farmers, for delivery by the Wentzes to Campbell of all the Chantenay red cored carrots to be grown on fifteen acres of the Wentz farm during the 1947 season. . . . The prices specified in the contract ranged from $23 to $30 per ton according to the time of delivery. The contract price for January, 1948, was $30 a ton.

The Wentzes harvested approximately 100 tons of carrots from the fifteen acres covered by the contract. Early in January, 1948, they told a Campbell representative that they would not deliver their carrots at the contract price. The market price at that time was at least $90 per ton, and Chantenay red cored carrots were virtually unobtainable. The Wentzes then sold approximately 62 tons of their carrots to the defendant Lojeski, a neighboring farmer. Lojeski resold about 58 tons on the open market, approximately half to Campbell and the balance to other purchasers.

On January 9, 1948, Campbell, suspecting that Lojeski was selling it "contract carrots," refused to purchase any more, and instituted these suits against the Wentz brothers and Lojeski to enjoin further sale of the contract carrots to others, and to compel specific performance of the contract. The trial court denied equitable relief.[1] 75 F. Supp. 952 (E.D. Pa. 1948). . . .

A party may have specific performance of a contract for the sale of chattels if the legal remedy is inadequate. Inadequacy of the legal remedy is necessarily a matter to be determined by an examination of the facts in each particular instance.

We think that on the question of adequacy of the legal remedy the case is one appropriate for specific performance. It was expressly found that at the time of the trial it was "virtually impossible to obtain Chantenay carrots in the open market." This Chantenay carrot is one which the plaintiff uses in large quantities, furnishing the seed to the growers with whom it makes contracts. It was not claimed that in nutritive value it is any better than other types of carrots. Its blunt shape makes it easier to handle in processing. And its color and texture differ from other varieties. The color is brighter than other carrots. The trial court found that the plaintiff failed to establish what proportion of its carrots is used for the production of soup stock and what proportion is used as identifiable physical ingredients in its soups. We do not think lack of proof on that point is material. It did appear that the plaintiff uses carrots in fifteen of its twenty-one soups. It also appeared that it uses these Chantenay carrots diced in some of them and that the appearance is uniform. The preservation of uniformity in appearance in a food article marketed throughout the country and sold under the manufacturer's name is a matter of considerable commercial significance and one which is properly considered in determining whether a substitute ingredient is just as good as the original.

The trial court concluded that the plaintiff had failed to establish that the carrots, "judged by objective standards," are unique goods. This we think is not a pure fact conclusion like a finding that Chantenay carrots are of uniform color. It is either a conclusion of law or of mixed fact and law and we are bound to exercise our independent judgment upon it. That the test for specific performance is not necessarily "objective" is shown by the many cases in which equity has given it to enforce contracts for articles—family heirlooms and the like—the value of which was personal to the plaintiff.

Judged by the general standards applicable to determining the adequacy of the legal remedy we think that on this point the case is a proper one for equitable relief.

---

1. The issue is preserved on appeal by an arrangement under which Campbell received all the carrots held by the Wentzes and Lojeski, paying a stipulated market price of $90 per ton, $30 to the defendants, and the balance into the registry of the District Court pending the outcome of these appeals.

There is considerable authority, old and new, showing liberality in the granting of an equitable remedy. We see no reason why a court should be reluctant to grant specific relief when it can be given without supervision of the court or other time-consuming processes against one who has deliberately broken his agreement. Here the goods of the special type contracted for were unavailable on the open market, the plaintiff had contracted for them long ahead in anticipation of its needs, and had built up a general reputation for its products as part of which reputation uniform appearance was important. We think if this were all that was involved in the case specific performance should have been granted. [The court went on to deny specific performance on the ground that the contract was too unconscionable to be enforced in equity. That part of the opinion is discussed in section 11.A.]

NOTES ON SPECIFIC PERFORMANCE OF CONTRACTS

1. What is specific performance? A specific performance decree is a specialized form of injunction, an order to defendant to perform his contract. It typically requires affirmative conduct, but that does not make it unusual. Its availability is historically conditioned on a showing that legal remedies would be inadequate. Yet judges and lawyers sometimes argue over whether a plaintiff is seeking specific performance or an injunction. Consider Minnesota Vikings Football Stadium v. Wells Fargo Bank, 193 F. Supp. 3d 1002 (D. Minn. 2016). Wells Fargo mounted illuminated signs on office towers overlooking the stadium, in breach of a contract restricting its signage. The stadium sued to get Wells Fargo to remove the signs. The stadium said it was seeking specific performance of the contract; Wells Fargo said it was seeking an injunction against the signs. The parties apparently thought this distinction affected whether the stadium had to show irreparable injury under the Supreme Court's *eBay* decision, reprinted in section 5.A.4. But irreparable injury is a traditional prerequisite to either remedy, and anyway, Minnesota law should have applied to the stadium's contract claim. The court held that the stadium was seeking an injunction, and that the aesthetic harm from the signs was irreparable and not measurable in dollars.

Nothing was gained by this distinction between injunctions and specific performance. As another court put it when faced with the same issue, "the parties' disagreement on whether the Court should order specific performance or grant [Plaintiff's] request for a permanent injunction is legally irrelevant." Pure Wafer Inc. v. City of Prescott, 275 F. Supp. 3d 1173, 1176 (D. Ariz. 2017).

2. The facts in *Campbell*. In *Campbell*, the carrots have long since been sold and the parties are fighting over money. Normally that would make the issue moot, because the money value of a right to specific performance is expectancy damages. Contract-market damages would be $60 per ton; specific performance would give Campbell $90 carrots for $30. Actual receipt of the carrots might avoid consequential damages that would otherwise be included in a damage remedy. The choice between specific performance and damages is a choice between two ways of giving plaintiff its expectancy—between the expected carrots and the expected value of the carrots.

This equivalency broke down in *Campbell* because there was a liquidated-damage clause. The liquidated damages were $50 an acre for 15 acres; the stipulated equivalent of specific performance was $60 a ton for 62 tons. Did Campbell outsmart itself?

Consider the adequacy issue in *Campbell* as the court considered it: on the assumption that specific performance would give Campbell carrots instead of damages. But note also that the risk of mootness is great. Specific performance is often not an option because courts move too slowly; the parties must go about their business and then litigate over damages.

3. Irreplaceability again. Why does it matter whether Chantenay red-cored carrots are unique? Is it the principle of *Pardee*—that money is an adequate remedy only if it can be used to replace the very thing that plaintiff lost? If some other kind of carrot is just as good, then damages will suffice, because Campbell can use the money to buy carrots. But if no other carrots are like these carrots, money cannot replace what Campbell has lost. No other carrots are quite like these carrots, because most carrots are yellow in the middle, so that diced carrots are partly orange and partly yellow. That is not what Campbell contracted for. And if other carrots were just as good and available in the market, the price of red-cored carrots would not have tripled.

4. Other examples. *Campbell* is not a fluke. Courts frequently grant specific performance of contracts for the sale of ordinary goods if scarcity, time constraints, or the sheer size of the contract make it difficult or impossible to cover. Some examples, old and new:

a. Grapes. A federal court issued a preliminary injunction ordering what amounted to specific performance of a contract to sell defendant's grape harvest to plaintiff. The grapes were "a unique, perishable product for which Green Stripe cannot obtain a substitute on the market." Green Stripe, Inc. v. Berny's Internacionale, S.A. de C.V., 159 F. Supp. 2d 51, 57 (E.D. Pa. 2001).

b. Gravel. The Montana court granted a preliminary injunction to preserve a road contractor's access to a gravel pit that the parties owned in common. The court said without explanation that plaintiff "had no other source for gravel." Frame v. Frame, 740 P.2d 655, 657 (Mont. 1987). It is hard to believe there was a shortage of gravel in Montana, but it is easy to believe that the court did not consider the spot market an adequate substitute for owning your own supply.

c. Jet fuel. A federal court specifically enforced a contract to supply an airline's jet fuel requirements at specified airports. Fuel was in short supply because of the 1973 Arab-Israeli war and the resulting Arab embargo of oil sales to nations that supported Israel. The court did not specifically find that cover was impossible. It did say that breach would cause "chaos and irreparable damage" and that "[i]n the circumstances, a decree of specific performance becomes the ordinary and natural relief rather than the extraordinary one." Eastern Air Lines, Inc. v. Gulf Oil Corp., 415 F. Supp. 429, 443 (S.D. Fla. 1975).

d. Tomatoes. The New Jersey Chancery Court specifically enforced a contract for the sale of a tomato crop. Plaintiff had a factory and all the supplies needed to can a million cans of tomatoes in the six-week packing season. The court doubted that a reliable supply was available on the open market; it reasoned that "the very existence" of preharvest contracts for the sale of whole crops "proclaims their necessity to the economic management of the factory." Curtice Brothers Co. v. Catts, 66 A. 935 (N.J. Ch. 1907). To similar effect, also involving a tomato crop, is Campbell Soup Co. v. Diehm, 111 F. Supp. 211 (E.D. Pa. 1952).

5. A counterexample? Compare Duval & Co. v. Malcom, 214 S.E.2d 356 (Ga. 1975), a suit to specifically enforce a contract for the sale of a cotton crop. Drought had caused a shortage of cotton. Affirming a denial of cross-motions for summary judgment, the court said:

> Buyer has alleged that it "cannot go into the market and replace said cotton due to the uniqueness which now exists in the market." We note here that the mere fact that cotton prices soared after this alleged contract is not in itself adequate to show buyer entitled to specific performance.

Id. at 359. Is there a difference between the buyer's statement that cover is impossible and the court's statement that the price has soared? In economic theory, cover is never absolutely impossible; the price should rise until supply and demand are restored to balance. In practice, the market cannot reach equilibrium so quickly, especially if much of the supply is committed to long-term contracts. The market will always be in turmoil in shortage cases; how clear will it be whether cover was truly impossible? If plaintiff decides to cover at any cost, defendant may resist the damage claim on the ground that the cover price was unreasonable. How important is it that plaintiff wanted a long-term contract so he wouldn't have to scramble in the spot market? The incidental damages—the time and other resources spent arranging for cover—are hard to measure

In a case decided six weeks later, arising out of the same drought, the parties stipulated that the cotton was unique. The court specifically enforced the contracts with a *cf.* citation to *Duval.* R.L. Kimsey Cotton Co. v. Ferguson, 214 S.E.2d 360 (Ga. 1975). Do you suppose the shortage was any more severe in one case than in the other? *Duval* appears to be the deviant case; the Fifth Circuit, the supreme courts of Louisiana and Mississippi, and federal district courts in Alabama, Georgia, Louisiana, and South Carolina all specifically enforced contracts for the sale of 1973 cotton.

6. Contracts for non-market values. Irreplaceability is more obvious for promises valued for personal or non-commercial reasons. Consider Reed Foundation Inc. v. Franklin D. Roosevelt Four Freedoms Park, LLC, 964 N.Y.S.2d 152 (App. Div. 2013). Efforts to develop the Four Freedoms Park, which commemorates President Roosevelt's "Four Freedoms" speech, made little progress over many years until the Reed Foundation gave a $2.5 million grant and helped with planning and fundraising. The gift agreement required that a plaque recognizing the Foundation be placed at a specific location near a bust of the President. Years later, as the project neared completion, the Park asked permission to move the plaque. One expert witness said that the agreed location at the architectural center of the Park was like signing a donor's name across a famous painting. The court nonetheless required specific performance: "Aesthetic considerations extraneous to a contract cannot trump its terms. . . . [F]ailure to perform would deprive the Foundation of a recognition of its substantial contribution to the Park in an inscription placed in a unique location that has special significance to the Foundation." *Id.* at 156.

7. Justice Holmes. Recall Justice Holmes's famous description of contract:

> The duty to keep a contract at common law means a prediction that you must pay damages if you do not keep it,—and nothing else. If you commit a tort, you are liable to pay a compensatory sum. If you commit a contract, you are liable to pay a compensatory sum unless the promised event comes to pass, and that is all the difference.

O.W. Holmes, *The Path of the Law,* 10 Harv. L. Rev. 457, 462 (1897). He dismissed specific performance as so exceptional that it did not affect the general theory. Is that view consistent with *Campbell* and similar cases? Or is it more accurate to say that a contract entitles a promisee to the thing she was promised, and that she has to accept damages only when she can use the money to replace the thing? Was Campbell entitled to money or carrots?

8. Codification. The Uniform Commercial Code codified specific performance of sales contracts "if the goods are unique or in other proper circumstances." §2-716(1). The Official Comment states that the section "seeks to further a more liberal attitude" and that "inability to cover is strong evidence of 'other proper circumstances.'"

Once goods are identified to the contract, §2-716(3) allows the buyer to replevy the goods if he can't cover. Replevin traditionally protected property rights and not contract rights; its use in §2-716(3) is an extension. The obvious intent is to create a nondiscretionary right to the goods when the subsection's requirements are met. Most commonly, goods are identified to the contract when the seller ships them or marks specific items for delivery to the buyer. §2-501(1).

9. Plaintiff's return performance. If the court orders defendant to perform the contract, it obviously must ensure that plaintiff performs in return. Typically this can be done by requiring simultaneous performance, or if that is impractical because defendant's performance takes time, by requiring plaintiff to pay the purchase price into court or otherwise secure her obligation to pay. Many cases state an additional requirement: that plaintiff must show that she is (or in some formulations, was) "ready, able, and willing" to perform. The history and scope of this requirement is obscure; many cases ignore it or treat it as easily satisfied, and some commentators view it as vestigial.

The requirement was revived and invigorated, at least in Texas, in DiGiuseppe v. Lawler, 269 S.W.3d 588 (Tex. 2008). A deeply divided court refused specific performance, because plaintiff had not secured a jury finding that he was ready, able, and willing to perform. Defendant had not raised the issue, so the implication is that plaintiffs must prove in every case that they were ready, willing, and able. The opinion refers to plaintiff's ability to perform at the original closing and at the time of judgment; perhaps plaintiff must prove both. Four dissenters charged that the majority's rule lacks common sense, forces plaintiffs to negotiate useless loan commitments for deals tied up in litigation, and forces plaintiffs to reveal information about their financing that defendants have no right to obtain.

NOTES ON EFFICIENT BREACH OF CONTRACT

1. The basic idea. One argument against specific performance is that the spot buyers offering $90 for carrots may have a more valuable use for them, and forcing a sale to Campbell for $30 may cause the carrots to be wasted in a less valuable use. This is based on the economic view that individual willingness to pay is a good proxy for societal value. The buyer who will pay the most for carrots expects to recover his investment plus a profit, and he can do that by conferring a benefit on his customers that exceeds the price he paid for the carrots. If the spot buyer is willing to pay enough that the defendant farmers can pay Campbell's damages and still make money, then the breach of contract is said to be efficient. The spot buyers are better off, the defendant farmers are better off, Campbell is no worse off, and the carrots are put to a more valuable use, so society as a whole is better off.

2. Identifying the more valuable use. The spot buyer's higher bid proves only that the price has gone up since Campbell's contract. Campbell was also paying $90 for spot carrots. Campbell's $30 contract price shows that Chantenay carrots are worth *at least* $30 to Campbell, but it does not show that Chantenay carrots are worth *only* $30 to Campbell. The only sure way to find out who values carrots more is to sell at auction in time of shortage. The damage remedy leaves defendants free to do that.

Specific performance makes plaintiff the potential auction seller. If other buyers value carrots more than Campbell, they can offer to buy them from Campbell. But Campbell may pursue its long-term interest in the soup business instead of taking a one-time profit in carrot speculation. If it refuses to sell carrots at any price a buyer is willing to offer, that simply means that it considers its own use for the carrots more valuable than the cash alternative. There is no basis in the economic model to second-guess that judgment; an economist cannot say that some other use is more valuable even though Campbell refused to sell.

The most attractive case for efficient-breach theorists is where Campbell would have sold at a price a new buyer would have been willing to pay, but the deal is never made because Campbell and the new buyer can't find each other or can't negotiate the deal when they do. But that risk doesn't distinguish contract rights from property rights. There are owners of all sorts of things who would sell if a potential buyer could find them and offer the right price, but if those owners are not actively looking to sell, they may be difficult or impossible to find.

3. The asking-offering problem. There is another ambiguity in the economists' assumption that price is the measure of value. Campbell might refuse to sell at any price a buyer offers, even though it would have dropped out if forced to bid against that buyer in an auction. That is, its asking price is likely to be higher than its offering price. If Campbell will pay any price up to $120 but won't sell for less than $200, what is the value of carrots to Campbell? Does a buyer who would pay up to $150 have a more valuable or less valuable use of the carrots than Campbell? What if that buyer wouldn't sell for less than $225 if she owned the carrots? What if that buyer also wants the carrots for soup, but she is willing to pay more because she is richer than Campbell, or because she is trying to reduce Campbell's market share? Individual willingness to pay is a proxy for societal value, but it is a quite imperfect proxy.

4. The effect on contracts. Even if we assume that allowing the farmers to sell the carrots to the highest bidder produces some economic gains, is there any reason to believe those gains exceed the economic losses from making long-term contracts less reliable? The risk of shortage may be the most important reason Campbell wanted a long-term contract. If Campbell failed to cover because it was outbid at an auction (and if there were no liquidated-damage clause), how would it prove the damages it suffered from using nonuniform carrots?

5. The preference for voluntary transactions again. Suppose the new buyer really does have a more valuable use for the carrots. Does it follow even then that specific performance should be denied? Is a preference for efficient breach consistent with the economic preference for voluntary transactions? Why shouldn't the farmers or their new buyer have to buy Campbell's right to the carrots at a price agreeable to Campbell, instead of breaching and forcing Campbell to accept a jury's estimate of its loss?

If negotiations break down entirely, then what? If Campbell is entitled to specific performance and refuses to sell its right to the carrots, how is that different from any other owner who isn't willing to sell at the price a potential buyer is willing to pay? If Campbell is entitled only to damages and negotiations break down, the case must be tried. Someone else will get the carrots, and Campbell will get a price set by the court. That may be better, at least in a short-run and purely economic view, if we assume the carrots are really more valuable to the third party, and that Campbell's refusal to sell its rights is just a bargaining breakdown. But plainly it is not better, even in the short run, if we assume that Campbell knows its own mind and has refused to sell because it values the carrots more highly than the highest offer from the farmers or the third party.

6. Transaction costs again. Scholars on all sides of the controversy have mostly recognized that if there were no transaction costs, the parties would always transfer the carrots to the party with the most valuable use. Thus, the economic wisdom was to select the rule with the lowest transaction costs, and much of the literature turned on ever-more-detailed speculative analyses of the likely transaction costs of each remedy. Compare William Bishop, *The Choice of Remedy for Breach of Contract*, 14 J. Legal Stud. 299 (1985) (arguing that specific performance is generally more expensive), with Thomas S. Ulen, *The Efficiency of Specific Performance: Toward a Unified Theory of Contract Remedies*, 83 Mich. L. Rev. 341 (1984) (arguing that damages are far more expensive).

Transaction costs are likely to be high either way. A specific performance decree cuts out the farmers and leaves Campbell to negotiate with the new buyer. A damage remedy cuts out Campbell and leaves the farmers to negotiate with the new buyer. Either solution involves the threat of litigation between two of the parties and a voluntary transaction between two of the parties. Is there any basis for a general prediction about which will involve higher transaction costs?

Judge Posner seems to say yes. He says that a judgment ordering the farmers to perform creates a bilateral monopoly: Only the farmers can comply with the decree, and only Campbell can release them. Richard A. Posner, *Economic Analysis of Law* §4.13 at 145-146 (9th ed., Wolters Kluwer 2014). Bargaining over Campbell's damage claim is also a bilateral monopoly, but the two sides' predictions about the damage judgment may narrow the settlement range and make it easier to reach agreement.

Professor Macneil argued that any difference in transaction costs would rarely matter. There might be many possible transactions in the world "more efficient" than the existing contract, but very few of those possibilities would be sufficiently more profitable to pay the costs of unwinding the first contract, whether by negotiation or litigation. But microeconomic analysis of ordinary contract litigation imposed very high transaction costs. Ian R. Macneil, *Efficient Breach of Contract: Circles in the Sky*, 68 Va. L. Rev. 947, 954 n.28 (1982). How many opportunities for efficient breach are still profitable after paying plaintiff's losses *and* all the transaction costs. That is an empirical question, and no data are likely to become available. Economists believe that most markets function with reasonable efficiency, that in such markets most contracts will produce about the same profit, and that the margin of profit will be small. That suggests very few opportunities for unusually profitable breach.

7. The relevance of shortage. The problem of the potentially more valuable use does not arise in the absence of shortage.

> The relevance of shortage is this: if there is enough of the scarce resource to satisfy both plaintiff and defendant, or plaintiff and defendant's new customer, then neither performance nor breach will change the allocation of resources. Plaintiff will be supplied at the contract price, and all other parties will be supplied at the market price.
>
> If there is a shortage, so that one side must do without, it becomes meaningful to speak of allocating the resource to the more efficient use. But in time of shortage, damages are an inadequate remedy and the positive law allocates the resource to the party who was promised it under a valid contract. The principle of allocation is entitlement, and the entitlement is created by contract. Whatever its normative or heuristic merits, efficient breach theory does not describe the law in shortage cases.

Laycock, *The Death of the Irreparable Injury Rule* at 246-247.

More plausible opportunities for efficient breach may arise when performance turns out to be unexpectedly expensive for defendant. We will take up that possibility soon.

8. A different Posnerian view. For a Posner opinion much more sympathetic to specific performance, see Walgreen Co. v. Sara Creek Property Co., 966 F.2d 273 (7th Cir. 1992). That was not a simple sale-of-goods case but a long-term lease in which a shopping mall agreed not to rent to any competing pharmacies. Judge Posner said the injunction would be both cheaper and more accurate:

> [First, it would] substitute for the costly processes of forensic fact determination the less costly processes of private negotiation. . . . [Second, a] battle of experts is a less reliable method of determining the actual cost to Walgreen of facing new competition than negotiations between Walgreen and Sara Creek over the price at which Walgreen would feel adequately compensated for having to face that competition.

Id. at 275-276. Aren't those advantages of injunctions pretty generally applicable? In favor of damages, he argued that bargaining over the injunction is a bilateral monopoly, and he noted that injunctions are sometimes more difficult for courts to supervise. He said that trial judges should weigh these costs and benefits, and "if the balance is even the injunction should be withheld." *Id.* at 276. This is the irreparable injury rule as tiebreaker.

9. Opportunistic breach. Judge Posner now recognizes a category of "opportunistic" breach of contract that ought to be deterred:

> If a promisor breaks his promise merely to take advantage of the promisee's vulnerability in a setting (the normal contract setting) in which performance is sequential rather than simultaneous, we might as well throw the book at him. Suppose A pays B in advance for goods, and instead of delivering them B uses the money to build a swimming pool for himself. An attractive remedy in such a case is restitution. We can deter A's opportunistic behavior by making it worthless to him, which can be done by making him hand over all his profits from the breach to the promisee. No lighter sanction would deter. (Why not make his conduct criminal as well or instead? . . .)

Posner, *Economic Analysis of Law* §4.10 at 129. In an earlier edition, Posner had B using A's money "in another venture." And in explaining why this diversion was indefensible, Posner said, "The promisor broke his promise in order to make money—there can be no other reason in the case of such a breach." Richard A. Posner, *Economic Analysis of Law* §4.9 at 118-119 (6th ed., Aspen 2003).

Suppose buyer pays in advance for goods in short supply. Suppose a third party then offers seller a higher price for those goods. Suppose seller breaches his contract and sells to the third party. Is that breach opportunistic or efficient? Doesn't the promisor who breaches for a higher price always do it "in order to make money"? Can opportunistic and efficient breaches be clearly distinguished?

10. Are damages too small for breach ever to be efficient? Critics of efficient-breach theory ridicule as an absurd fiction the claim that damages leave the victim of breach unharmed. A limitation-of-remedy clause may eliminate all consequential damages. Even if there is no such clause, defendant may not have had sufficient reason to know about all the consequential damages, and thus not be liable for them, or plaintiff may not be able to prove them to the satisfaction of the court. The inconvenience and lost time of arranging a substitute contract are difficult to quantify and unlikely to be recovered. Emotional distress is sometimes suffered in contract cases, but it is never recoverable. Damages that plaintiff could have avoided are not recoverable, but they are real losses to plaintiff. Prejudgment interest may be unavailable; more commonly, both prejudgment and postjudgment interest may be simple rather than compounded and set at artificially low rates. Attorneys' fees and most other costs of litigation are generally unrecoverable. Both the costs and risks of litigation mean that most cases settle for less than the full damages plaintiff could have recovered if successful at trial. Many defendants capable of performing are nonetheless judgment proof, so that the damages can never be collected even if proved. (We seem to have lost sight of the rightful position somewhere between conception and implementation.) The neat hypotheticals that dominate the law-and-economics literature do not bear much resemblance to actual damages litigation.

"The essential purpose of a contract between commercial men is actual performance and they do not bargain merely for a promise, or for a promise plus the right to win a lawsuit." Uniform Commercial Code §2-609, Official Comment 1. This comment is not from a discussion of remedies; it explains each side's right to "adequate assurance of performance."

11. Are damages too large for breach ever to be efficient? Damages that fail to compensate plaintiff may nonetheless take all the profit away from defendants. Do contract-market damages mean that there can never be an efficient breach in a shortage case? The farmers' profits from breach are equal to the excess of the new market price ($90) over the old contract price ($30). But if there were no liquidated-damage clause, that would also be the measure of Campbell's damages. And if there are any incidentals or consequentials, the damages from breach will exceed the gains. Contrary to the implicit assumption of the efficient-breach model, Campbell's damages are not limited to the less-than-market value of its own use of the carrots. And even if that were the measure of damages, Professor Eisenberg argues that promisors almost never have information about the value of performance to the promisee—information that is essential to the theory and that the theory assumes they have. Melvin A. Eisenberg, *Actual and Virtual Specific Performance, the Theory of Efficient Breach, and the Indifference Principle in Contract Law*, 93 Cal. L. Rev. 975 (2005).

12. Thin markets. Contract-market damages may not so neatly equal the profits from breach in what are called thin markets—markets for items with no exact substitutes or for items specially built to plaintiff's specifications. But if defendant is the only supplier, replacement is impossible, and plaintiff will be presumptively entitled to specific performance. The possibility that replacement is merely difficult is taken up in the next set of notes. Where replacement is impossible or difficult, the doctrinal question will be whether defendant has encountered some problem that makes specific performance so difficult that it should be withheld despite the inadequacy of damages.

13. Business preferences. Professors Eisenberg and Miller examined contracts that were sufficiently significant to be attached to Form 8-K, on which publicly traded companies report "material events" to the Securities and Exchange Commission. Theodore Eisenberg & Geoffrey P. Miller, *Damages Versus Specific Performance: Lessons from Commercial Contracts*, 12 J. Empirical Legal Stud. 29 (2015). Thirty-one percent of these contracts provided for specific performance, including a majority of employment contracts and merger agreements. They take these provisions to indicate that sophisticated parties view specific performance as more efficient in these circumstances. Of course some of these contracting parties may also have assumed that specific performance would be available in appropriate circumstances without providing for it. And two German researchers found that experimental subjects were willing to pay more to guarantee specific performance in the event of a breach than they would pay to guarantee expectation damages, at least for some contracts. Christoph Engel & Lars Freund, *Behaviorally Efficient Remedies: An Experiment*, MPI Collective Goods Preprint No 2016/17, http://ssrn.com/abstract=2988653 (2016).

NOTES ON SPECIFIC PERFORMANCE WHERE COVER IS POSSIBLE

1. Kinda sorta replaceable. What if replacement is possible but difficult? Or what if replacement is possible with goods that are similar but different in some way that matters to plaintiff?

> There are very few . . . cases in which the goods appear entirely fungible and plaintiff seeks specific performance anyway. These cases shade into those where the goods are replaceable only with difficulty, or only with similar but not identical goods. Plaintiff argues that replacement is difficult or impossible; the court [sometimes] finds that replacement is possible and damages are adequate. Where replacement is difficult,

a majority of cases grant specific relief, but a substantial minority do not. So long as the rule persists that damages are an adequate remedy for loss of goods that are available elsewhere, some cases will fall near the line and some cases near the line will be decided each way. We can argue whether this line is worth drawing and litigating over, but for now it survives. It is the principal remnant of the irreparable injury rule.

Laycock, *The Death of the Irreparable Injury Rule* 101.

2. Why is plaintiff seeking specific performance anyway? There has been a spirited academic debate over making specific performance available even when damages could be used to cover. Professor Schwartz argues that damages are generally under-compensatory in such cases, principally because the time required to arrange for a replacement purchase is hard to monetize, and that it is wasteful to litigate over damages that specific performance could have prevented. Alan Schwartz, *The Case for Specific Performance*, 89 Yale L.J. 271, 276, 292 (1979).

Perhaps more telling, Schwartz thinks that a request for specific performance proves the inadequacy of damages. *Id.* at 277. If buyer prefers coerced performance, available only after a lawsuit, from a disgruntled promisor who has already breached at least once, to immediate cover and subsequent reimbursement, his need for specific performance must outweigh the cost of delay and the risks of further unsatisfactory performance.

3. Transaction costs again. Professor Yorio responded that damages could be made more compensatory, and that compensation isn't the only goal of remedies law anyway; the competing interests of defendants and courts must be considered. Edward Yorio, *In Defense of Money Damages for Breach of Contract*, 82 Colum. L. Rev. 1365 (1982). He argued that it is generally cheaper for disappointed buyers to cover than for breaching sellers to cover for them, so that damages will generally be a cheaper remedy to administer. Schwartz sees no reason that should be true. If replacement carrots existed in *Campbell*, probably Campbell with a network of purchasing agents was better able to find and buy them than an individual farmer. But compare Thompson v. Commonwealth, 89 S.E.2d 64 (Va. 1955), where defendant reneged on a contract to build roll-call voting machines for the Virginia legislature. Defendant was the only manufacturer of such machines, but its senior official testified that "any first class machine shop" could do it. *Id.* at 68. The court refused to force plaintiff "to assume the responsibility and risk which properly belong to defendants. If anyone is to search for a manufacturer it should be defendants." *Id.* Isn't any general assumption about comparative cover costs likely to be inaccurate in particular cases? Does the cost of case-by-case litigation justify a general rule, even if the general rule is often mistaken?

4. The effects of breach. Professor Macneil argued that all academic claims about transaction costs are far too narrowly focused and far too speculative, and that a serious inquiry into transaction costs would entail vast empirical studies. Moreover:

> If the damages rule encourages breaches without consultation, whereas the specific performance rule encourages consultation and mutually beneficial agreement, relational costs will be lower under the specific performance rule. In the real world it makes a great deal of difference whether a breach occurs, or is even threatened, or whether negotiations are viewed as leading towards mutually beneficial allocations of the increased productivity offered by the new opportunity. In the real world it makes a great deal of difference between negotiating over what is viewed as an allocation of losses, and what is viewed as the allocation of potential gains.

Macneil, *Efficient Breach of Contract*, 68 Va. L. Rev. at 959.

VAN WAGNER ADVERTISING CORP. v. S & M ENTERPRISES
492 N.E.2d 756 (N.Y. 1986)

KAYE, Judge.

Specific performance of a contract to lease "unique" billboard space is properly denied when damages are an adequate remedy to compensate the tenant and equitable relief would impose a disproportionate burden on the defaulting landlord. . . .

By agreement dated December 16, 1981, Barbara Michaels leased to plaintiff, Van Wagner Advertising, for an initial period of three years plus option periods totaling seven additional years[,] space on the eastern exterior wall of a building on East 36th Street in Manhattan. Van Wagner was in the business of erecting and leasing billboards, and the parties anticipated that Van Wagner would erect a sign on the leased space, which faced an exit ramp of the Midtown Tunnel and was therefore visible to vehicles entering Manhattan from that tunnel.

In early 1982 Van Wagner erected an illuminated sign and leased it to Asch Advertising for a three-year period commencing March 1, 1982. However, by agreement dated January 22, 1982, Michaels sold the building to defendant S & M Enterprises. . . . [O]n August 19, 1982, S & M sent Van Wagner a letter purporting to cancel the lease as of October 18. . . .

[H]aving already acquired other real estate on the block, S & M purchased the subject building in 1982 for the ultimate purpose of demolishing existing buildings and constructing a mixed residential-commercial development. The project is to begin upon expiration of a lease of the subject building in 1987, if not sooner. . . .

S & M's cancellation of Van Wagner's lease constituted a breach of contract.

Given defendant's unexcused failure to perform its contract, we next turn to a consideration of remedy for the breach: Van Wagner seeks specific performance of the contract, S & M urges that money damages are adequate but that the amount of the award was improper.[2]

Whether or not to award specific performance is a decision that rests in the sound discretion of the trial court, and here that discretion [refusing specific performance] was not abused. Considering first the nature of the transaction, specific performance has been imposed as the remedy for breach of contracts for the sale of real property, but the contract here is to lease rather than sell an interest in real property. While specific performance is available, in appropriate circumstances, for breach of a commercial or residential lease, specific performance of real property leases is not in this State awarded as a matter of course. See Gardens Nursery School v. Columbia University, 404 N.Y.S.2d 833 (N.Y. City Civ. Ct. 1978).[3]

Van Wagner argues that specific performance must be granted in light of the trial court's finding that the "demised space is unique as to location for the particular advertising purpose intended." The word "uniqueness" is not, however, a magic door

---

2. We note that the parties' contentions regarding the remedy of specific performance in general . . . mirror a scholarly debate that has persisted throughout our judicial history, reflecting fundamentally divergent views about the quality of a bargained-for promise. While the usual remedy in Anglo-American law has been damages, rather than compensation in kind, the current trend among commentators appears to favor the remedy of specific performance, but the view is not unanimous.

3. *But see* 5A Arthur L. Corbin, *Contracts* §1143 at 131 (West 1964); *id.* at 7 n.62 (Supp. 1971); 11 Samuel Williston, *Contracts* §1418A (3d ed., Baker Voorhis 1968); John N. Pomeroy & John C. Mann, *Specific Performance* §9 at 18-19 (3d ed., Banks & Co. 1926); *Restatement (Second) of Contracts* §360 cmt. *a*, illus. 2 (Am. Law Inst.1981); *id.* §360 cmt. *e*; *cf.* City Stores Co. v. Ammerman, 266 F. Supp. 766 (D.D.C. 1967), *aff'd per curiam*, 394 F.2d 950 (D.C. Cir. 1968).

to specific performance. A distinction must be drawn between physical difference and economic interchangeability. The trial court found that the leased property is physically unique, but so is every parcel of real property and so are many consumer goods. Putting aside contracts for the sale of real property, where specific performance has traditionally been the remedy for breach, uniqueness in the sense of physical difference does not itself dictate the propriety of equitable relief.

By the same token, at some level all property may be interchangeable with money. Economic theory is concerned with the degree to which consumers are willing to substitute the use of one good for another, the underlying assumption being that "every good has substitutes, even if only very poor ones," and that "all goods are ultimately commensurable." *See* Anthony T. Kronman, *Specific Performance*, 45 U. Chi. L. Rev. 351, 359 (1978). Such a view, however, could strip all meaning from uniqueness, for if all goods are ultimately exchangeable for a price, then all goods may be valued. Even a rare manuscript has an economic substitute in that there is a price for which any purchaser would likely agree to give up a right to buy it, but a court would in all probability order specific performance of such a contract on the ground that the subject matter of the contract is unique.

The point at which breach of a contract will be redressable by specific performance thus must lie not in any inherent physical uniqueness of the property but instead in the uncertainty of valuing it:

> What matters, in measuring money damages, is the volume, refinement, and reliability of the available information about substitutes for the subject matter of the breached contract. When the relevant information is thin and unreliable, there is a substantial risk that an award of money damages will either exceed or fall short of the promisee's actual loss. Of course this risk can always be reduced—but only at great cost when reliable information is difficult to obtain. Conversely, when there is a great deal of consumer behavior generating abundant and highly dependable information about substitutes, the risk of error in measuring the promisee's loss may be reduced at much smaller cost. In asserting that the subject matter of a particular contract is unique and has no established market value, a court is really saying that it cannot obtain, at reasonable cost, enough information about substitutes to permit it to calculate an award of money damages without imposing an unacceptably high risk of undercompensation on the injured promisee. Conceived in this way, the uniqueness test seems economically sound.

Id. at 362. This principle is reflected in the case law, and is essentially the position of the *Restatement (Second) of Contracts*, which lists "the difficulty of proving damages with reasonable certainty" as the first factor affecting adequacy of damages. §360(a).

Thus, the fact that the subject of the contract may be "unique as to location for the particular advertising purpose intended" by the parties does not entitle a plaintiff to the remedy of specific performance.

Here, the trial court correctly concluded that the value of the "unique qualities" of the demised space could be fixed with reasonable certainty and without imposing an unacceptably high risk of undercompensating the injured tenant. [The judgment was affirmed without opinion. 486 N.Y.S.2d 585 (App. Div. 1985).] Both parties complain: Van Wagner asserts that while lost revenues on the Asch contract may be adequate compensation, that contract expired February 28, 1985, its lease with S & M continues until 1992, and the value of the demised space cannot reasonably be fixed for the balance of the term. S & M urges that future rents and continuing damages are necessarily conjectural, both during and after the Asch contract, and that Van Wagner's damages must be limited to 60 days—the period during which Van Wagner could cancel Asch's contract without consequence in the event Van Wagner lost the demised space. . . . Both parties' contentions were properly rejected.

First, it is hardly novel in the law for damages to be projected into the future. Particularly where the value of commercial billboard space can be readily determined by comparisons with similar uses—Van Wagner itself has more than 400 leases—the value of this property between 1985 and 1992 cannot be regarded as speculative. Second, S & M having successfully resisted specific performance on the ground that there is an adequate remedy at law, cannot at the same time be heard to contend that damages beyond 60 days must be denied because they are conjectural. If damages for breach of this lease are indeed conjectural, and cannot be calculated with reasonable certainty, then S & M should be compelled to perform its contractual obligation by restoring Van Wagner to the premises. Moreover, the contingencies to which S & M points do not, as a practical matter, render the calculation of damages speculative. [S & M argued that the lease was subject to cancellation on certain contingencies, but the court said that neither contingency was likely to occur and that uncertainties must be resolved against the party who breached.] Thus, neither the need to project into the future nor the contingencies allegedly affecting the length of Van Wagner's term render inadequate the remedy of damages for S & M's breach of its lease with Van Wagner.

The trial court, additionally, correctly concluded that specific performance should be denied on the ground that such relief "would be inequitable in that its effect would be disproportionate in its harm to defendant and its assistance to plaintiff." It is well settled that the imposition of an equitable remedy must not itself work an inequity, and that specific performance should not be an undue hardship. . . . [T]he finding that specific performance would disproportionately harm S & M and benefit Van Wagner has been affirmed by the Appellate Division and has support in the proof regarding S & M's projected development of the property.

While specific performance was properly denied, the court erred in its assessment of damages. . . .

Damages should have been awarded through the expiration of Van Wagner's lease.

Accordingly, the order of the Appellate Division should be modified . . . and the case remitted to Supreme Court, New York County, for further proceedings in accordance with this opinion and, as so modified, affirmed.

WACHTLER, C.J., and MEYER, SIMONS, TITONE and HANCOCK, JJ., concur.

ALEXANDER, J., taking no part.

NOTES ON IRREPARABLE INJURY AND UNDUE HARDSHIP

1. The undue hardship defense. Do we really want to prevent redevelopment of a block of midtown Manhattan because of a billboard? There are many cases in which specific performance is burdensome to defendant. The most obvious example is where defendant is unable to perform, but the contract is not excused for impossibility or frustration of purpose. But the irreparable injury rule does not solve these cases; whether the legal remedy is adequate for plaintiff has little to do with whether the equitable remedy would be a hardship on defendant. Undue hardship to defendant is an independent reason, both of doctrine and policy, for denying specific relief.

When Judge Posner worries about bilateral monopoly in negotiations to release plaintiff's right to specific performance, his example is cases where it is impossible or very expensive for defendant to perform. These would be undue hardship cases, although he does not mention the defense of undue hardship.

Similar concerns are the centerpiece of Steven Shavell, *Specific Performance Versus Damages for Breach of Contract: An Economic Analysis*, 84 Tex. L. Rev. 831 (2006). He assumes that the parties would want to maximize the joint value they derive from the contract, and that remedies can affect this value. In general, he thinks parties to contracts to make something or do something would prefer damages, principally because of the risk that production costs might be unexpectedly high. He thinks that parties to contracts to convey property already in existence would prefer specific performance. Here there is no risk of unexpected production costs, and the greater risk is that the seller will breach inefficiently because he underestimates the property's value to the buyer.

2. The two doctrines in *Van Wagner*. The court applies both doctrines in *Van Wagner*: plaintiff's legal remedy is adequate, and specific performance would impose undue hardship. Is that a happy coincidence? Or might the court's analysis of adequate remedy be influenced by the obvious hardship of specific performance? Should the court deny specific performance on these facts if there were no hardship—if defendant simply decided to relet the advertising space to a friend, or to remove all the advertising from its buildings? What if plaintiff had conceded undue hardship but asked for specific performance up to the point at which demolition actually began?

The value of a whole block dwarfs the value of the billboard, however special the site of the billboard. But it has always seemed suspicious that S & M would not leave the billboard in place until it was time for demolition to begin. It turns out that in May 1985, ten days after the Appellate Division denied specific performance, S & M leased the billboard space on a month-to-month basis to a competitor of Van Wagner. Whatever S & M's motivation for breach, it was not merely to prepare the building for redevelopment.

3. Irreparable injury. There is much to say about the alleged adequacy of the legal remedy.

a. Irreplaceability. To say that the billboard faced an exit ramp is a serious understatement. The exit ramps curve left and right in an unbalanced Y to the north and south sides of the building. As traffic emerges from the tunnel, the driver and front-seat passenger in every car in every lane are looking directly at the billboard. And the traffic sometimes emerges in a bumper-to-bumper crawl.

The trial court found that the space facing the tunnel exit was unique for advertising purposes. The Court of Appeals responded that it is not so unique that it cannot be valued. Would the damage remedy be adequate under other cases you have read? The billboard cannot be replaced with another one facing the tunnel exit. Wouldn't that be dispositive under Pardee v. Camden Lumber? Is another billboard somewhere else more similar to what was lost than a substitute variety of carrots in *Campbell*? Is the damage remedy as complete, practical, and efficient as specific performance?

b. The rule with respect to real estate. The traditional rule is that damages are never an adequate remedy for the loss of real estate or damage to real estate. This rule is routinely applied to leases as well as to sales, and to all sorts of other claims about real estate, from encroachments to interference with easements to violation of condominium restrictions. Compare the "but see" authorities in footnote 3 of *Van Wagner* to the one trial court decision—not even a court of general jurisdiction—cited for the proposition that leases are not routinely specifically enforced; for New York cases specifically enforcing leases, see Laycock, *The Death of the Irreparable Injury Rule* at 178 n.15. A right to use the side of a building for a billboard is a very modest interest in real estate, but the location facing the tunnel exit makes it a decidedly nonfictional application of the presumption that every parcel of real estate is unique. But there is more. A lease is not merely or even mostly a contract; "its fundamental purpose remains to serve as a vehicle for the conveyance of an interest in real estate." 219 Broadway Corp. v. Alexander's, Inc., 387 N.E.2d 1205, 1207 (N.Y. 1979). Plaintiff in *Van Wagner* might have done better to assert its property rights instead of contract rights.

c. The difficulty of measuring damages. One of the most common reasons for holding legal remedies inadequate is that damages are difficult to measure, and one of the most common applications of this rule is to lost profits. As a leading nineteenth-century treatise put it, plaintiff should not be forced "to sell his possible profits at a price depending upon a mere guess." John Norton Pomeroy, *A Treatise on the Specific Performance of Contracts* §15 at 20 (Banks & Bros. 1879).

How will the court measure the damages for the last seven years of the lease, after the Asch sublease expires? Presumably it will project the rent forward, making some allowance for projected inflation. Focusing only on the loss to Van Wagner, the damage measure is not complicated. But neither is it a simple comparison of contract price to the market price of an identical replacement.

4. The aftermath. The tenant with a lease of the building that ran through 1987 was the U.S. Postal Service. When S & M refused to renew that lease, the Postal Service acquired the building by eminent domain. At that point, with the possibility of redeveloping the block eliminated, the parties settled. The post office is still there, with an enormous electronic billboard facing the tunnel exit. For a quick view of what drivers see (with traffic running free and the video running on fast forward) see *Queens Midtown Tunnel West to Queens Midtown Tunnel Exit,* available at http://vimeo.com/3002144. Constance Smith, when she was a law student at St. Mary's Law School in San Antonio, tracked down the facts in notes 3 and 4 from New York real property records and other online information.

5. Corporate acquisitions. In complex contracts, damages are likely to be hard to measure, but specific performance may also be more burdensome to the parties or the court. In Allegheny Energy v. DQE, Inc., 171 F.3d 153 (3d Cir. 1999) (applying Pennsylvania law), plaintiff sought specific performance of a merger agreement between two publicly held corporations. The district court denied relief on the ground that damages would be an adequate remedy.

The Third Circuit reversed, citing the many cases granting specific performance of contracts to acquire a business. Few of those cases involved publicly held businesses, but the court rejected plaintiff's argument that valuations by investment bankers or in the stock market made the damages measurable. The court surveyed cases from around the country, and it said that "no case that has come to our attention has found a business either not unique or not offering a unique opportunity to the buyer." *Id.* at 163. A case with much supporting precedent and no contrary precedent should have been easy, but the misleading visibility of the irreparable injury rule led the district court into error, forcing an appeal that should have been unnecessary and a delay that might have been fatal.

On remand, the court denied relief on the contractual merits, holding that DQE had a substantive right to terminate the merger agreement. 74 F. Supp. 2d 482 (W.D. Pa. 1999), *aff'd mem.*, 216 F.3d 1075 (2000). DQE's lead lawyer once told Laycock that specific performance would have been outrageously impractical. If he could prove that, that would be a defense. But it would not make the damage remedy any more adequate.

6. Replaceability and damage measurement. Difficulty of measuring damages is a corollary of difficulty of replacement.

Any case where the loss is irreplaceable on the market can also be described as a case where damages are hard to measure. The actual cost of cover is the most easily applied measure of damages. Value in an active market is nearly as easy. But value in an inactive or nonexistent market is difficult, and if plaintiff is unable to replace the item lost, there may be no actual transaction to support an assessment of value. Consequential damages can also be difficult to measure, and they arise only when plaintiff cannot immediately replace what was lost.

Laycock, *Death of the Irreparable Injury Rule* at 44-45.

Can this reasoning be applied in reverse? If the damages are reasonably measurable, does that mean the thing lost is replaceable? Or does physical uniqueness have independent significance? Appraisers can testify to the market value of art, antiques, and even rare manuscripts, and there are far more Picassos in the world than tunnels in New York. Are disappointed buyers entitled to the particular Picasso they were promised, or should it be enough that they can buy some other Picasso?

In terms of the irreparable injury rule, the underlying issue in such cases is the significance of plaintiff's desire for a particular item from a category of similar items. The trial court said that a billboard site facing the tunnel exit is unique; the Court of Appeals said that billboard sites in general are not unique. In the shortage of cars following World War II, some courts granted specific performance of contracts to sell new cars; others said that some other car would do as well. These cases are collected in Laycock, *The Death of the Irreparable Injury Rule* at 59 nn.52-55. There are a number of cases granting specific performance of contracts to sell used goods, explicitly or implicitly treating new goods of the same kind as not an adequate replacement.

And then there is Copylease Corp. v. Memorex Corp., 408 F. Supp. 758 (S.D.N.Y. 1976), in which buyer stated a claim for specific performance by alleging that seller's toner was superior to other brands. How could seller deny that? More commonly, retailers and distributors have obtained specific performance of contracts to sell prestige brands, on the ground that the brand's appeal to desirable customers cannot be replaced with a lesser brand. Examples are collected in Ross-Simons Inc. v. Baccarat, Inc., 102 F.3d 12 (1st Cir. 1996), a dispute between a discount bridal registry and a manufacturer of upscale crystal.

NOTES ON PERSONAL SERVICE CONTRACTS

1. Promises to work. Courts will not order specific performance of an employee's promise to work. Other promises in an employment contract—to preserve trade secrets or not to compete against the employer—are subject to sometimes stringent review for reasonableness, but if held reasonable, they can generally be specifically enforced.

The promise to work is different, because courts think it is impractical to force an employee to work against her will, and they think that an order to work on pain of punishment for contempt might violate the Thirteenth Amendment's ban on involuntary servitude. Most employees can be replaced at the market wage, so employers rarely have a viable damage remedy either. Even when they have such a remedy in theory, because the employee has scarce or unique skills that cannot be replaced, actual cases are rare and judges are notably reluctant to award contract damages. The cultural ethos is that employees are free to change jobs, and the law largely reflects that. Courts do not withhold specific performance because damage remedies are adequate; they withhold specific performance because they are reluctant to give any remedy at all. Both the specific performance and the damage cases are reviewed in Laycock, *The Death of the Irreparable Injury Rule* at 168-174.

2. An exception. The nearest case we know to an exception is the verdict against actor Kim Basinger for breaching a contract to act in a movie after the movie had already been widely promoted and sold with her name as the female lead. The verdict was reversed on appeal because of defective jury instructions, Main Line Pictures, Inc. v. Basinger, 1994 WL 814244 (Cal. Ct. App. 1994), but Basinger filed for bankruptcy, settled for $3.8 million, and sued her lawyers for malpractice. Ron Norton, *People Column*, St. Louis Post-Dispatch (Feb. 19, 1996). That was not exactly an employment case: Basinger was never an employee and would not have become one. The principal issue was whether her personal services corporation had ever reached agreement with the plaintiff. But certainly the alleged contract was for a specific individual to perform personal services.

3. Liquidated damages. There may be greater judicial willingness to enforce if the employee expressly agrees to a liquidated-damage clause. Examples include Ashcraft & Gerel v. Coady, 244 F.3d 948 (D.C. Cir. 2001), enforcing a liquidated-damage clause against the managing partner of a law firm, and Miami Dolphins Ltd. v. Williams, 356 F. Supp. 2d 1301 (S.D. Fla. 2005). Ricky Williams, the college hero and Heisman Trophy winner who performed erratically in the pros, abruptly quit the Dolphins on the eve of the 2004 season. His contract expressly provided for the pro rata return of his signing bonus and the return of all his incentive bonuses if he quit, refused to practice, or was "otherwise in breach of this Contract." *Id.* at 1302. An arbitrator awarded $8.6 million to the Dolphins, apparently accepting the Dolphins' argument that Florida restrictions on penalty clauses did not apply to these provisions. The federal court enforced the award, noting the federal policy of deference to arbitration under collective bargaining agreements.

4. Reinstatement. Courts will not specifically enforce an employer's promise to employ the plaintiff. But reinstatement is now the standard remedy for employees discharged in violation of the labor laws, civil service laws, employment discrimination laws, constitutions, and collective bargaining agreements. There are even employers arguing, and a few cases holding, that reinstatement should be the preferred or exclusive remedy, because juries award excessive damages. Few supervision problems have returned to court, but employees reinstated without the support of a union are at disproportionate risk of resignation or discharge.

2. Burdens on Defendant or the Court

WHITLOCK v. HILANDER FOODS, INC.
720 N.E.2d 302 (Ill. App. Ct. 1999)

[Defendant planned an addition to its grocery store that would require a retaining wall right at the property line. Plaintiff, who owned the adjoining land, gave defendant permission to place workers and equipment on his property during the construction. In September, soon after construction began, plaintiff noticed that the wall's footings were on his property. (Footings are part of the foundation and extend on either side of the wall they support.) Plaintiff met the next day with one of defendant's officers, Castrogiovanni, and said that if the footings were to stay, he would require a lease. Castrogiovanni said they would negotiate a payment for the footings. Plaintiff knew he could have insisted on immediate removal, but he "wanted to be a good neighbor," and he trusted Castrogiovanni's promise of payment. Several communications between the parties and their lawyers followed, but no agreement was reached. In mid-October, plaintiff's lawyer withdrew permission to use plaintiff's property in the construction until the issue of compensation for the footings was resolved. Defendant withdrew its workers and equipment, but continued building from its side of the line.

In November, a survey showed that the wall was three feet closer to the property line than the wall it replaced, that the wall was on defendant's property, but that the footings extended 18 inches into plaintiff's property at points below the ground. Castrogiovanni claimed that the footings for the old wall had also encroached; eventually he said he had seen them before they were torn out and they were in the same place as the new footings. Plaintiff said that if either of those things were true, he had not known about it. The lawyers exchanged written offers and counter-offers off and on through February 21, at which point defendant was offering $10,000 to settle all claims and plaintiff was demanding $30,000 for the builder's use of his property plus $2,000 a year for 20 years for the footings.

On March 11, plaintiff sued for an injunction ordering that the footings be removed from his property. The trial judge granted summary judgment for defendant, holding that the encroachment was not intentional and that plaintiff had unreasonably delayed in filing suit.]

Presiding Justice BOWMAN delivered the opinion of the court: . . .

[T]he trial court erred in concluding that, as a matter of law, the encroachment on plaintiff's property was not intentional. Whether to categorize defendant's encroachment as intentional or unintentional is potentially of crucial significance. Ordinarily, in deciding whether to order a defendant to remove an offending structure, the trial court must balance the hardship to the defendant against the benefit to the plaintiff; if the former is great and the latter slight, the court will ordinarily leave the plaintiff to his remedy at law. However, if the encroachment is deliberate, the court may issue the injunction without considering the relative hardships.

Here, the balance of hardships decisively favors defendant, as a mandatory injunction would require it to undo at least in large part a $1.5 million construction project, while the benefit to plaintiff would at most be far less clear. . . . However, we believe there is a genuine factual issue of whether defendant acted deliberately.

One who knows of a claim to land that he proposes to use as his own proceeds at his peril if he goes forward in the face of protest or warnings from the owner and places a structure on the land. Here, it is undisputed that the footings encroach on plaintiff's property and that, at some point, plaintiff told defendant that he would not simply accept the encroachment. The evidence suggests that plaintiff did not protest the encroachment until after the footings were poured. However, this proves little in itself, as the evidence suggests equally that plaintiff—and perhaps defendant—did not know in advance that defendant would encroach on plaintiff's property at all.

A fact finder could infer that, when defendant's agents started to put in the footings, they knew or could easily have learned that they were standing on plaintiff's land as they worked. In any event, a mistaken belief by defendant that it was on the right side of the line would not save it from an injunction if it could have ascertained the truth by using reasonable care. There is also a factual basis to conclude that, soon after plaintiff realized that defendant intended to make permanent use of his property, he protested and put defendant on notice that it proceeded at its peril. . . . [A]fter plaintiff made his displeasure known, defendant kept on building the new south wall even though it had not obtained . . . permission to use the property.

The record provides a basis to find that defendant knew that it was appropriating plaintiff's property and pressed ahead anyway. . . .

[Turning to the second issue, laches] will bar relief where, as a result of the plaintiff's unreasonable delay in asserting his right, the defendant has been misled or prejudiced. Whether to apply laches rests within the trial court's discretion. There are no fixed rules for when laches applies, and the court must examine all the circumstances, including the defendant's conduct. Thus, the court must ask whether the defendant has contributed to the delay of which it complains and whether the defendant knew it was violating a right and went ahead anyway in disregard of the consequences.

Given these standards, the trial court erred in holding that, as a matter of law, plaintiff's delay in bringing suit bars it from obtaining any relief. This question turns on factual and equitable issues that ought not to have been resolved at the summary judgment stage. Weighing in defendant's favor is that plaintiff did wait six months between discovering the existence of the footings and filing suit to have them removed and that, in this time, plaintiff could see that defendant continued to build its addition at a substantial cost. However, weighing in plaintiff's favor is that there is at least a factual issue of whether defendant contributed to this delay by incorrectly assuring plaintiff, perhaps in bad faith, that he would be suitably compensated for the permanent encroachment. Also, there is some issue whether the equities favor defendant, in that it was aware early on of plaintiff's protests against the encroachment yet continued apace on the construction work without obtaining plaintiff's permission to do so. The existence of such genuine factual issues casts doubt on defendant's right to invoke the equitable doctrine of laches and thus bars summary judgment on this ground.

As did the trial court, defendant emphasizes the evidence that the footings for the new wall simply occupy the same space as those for the old wall and that it is not clear how plaintiff will be harmed. However, whether the two sets of footings are equally intrusive, as well as the circumstances surrounding the existence of the old footings, are not well developed in the record before us. Moreover, if plaintiff establishes that the encroachment was deliberate or intentional, he need not show that he will suffer substantial immediate harm from the violation of his property right.

The judgment . . . is reversed, and the cause is remanded. . . .

GEIGER and GALASSO, JJ., concur.

NOTES ON UNDUE HARDSHIP

1. The remand in *Whitlock*. Injunction cases are tried without juries in Illinois (and most other states). If this case goes back to the same judge who already held that there was no genuine issue of fact, what chance does plaintiff have of now persuading that judge by a preponderance of the evidence that defendant acted intentionally and that plaintiff did not unreasonably delay? But if the trial court has a central calendar, the case is not permanently assigned to any particular judge, and plaintiff might draw a new judge at trial. Either way, how would you argue this case for plaintiff on remand? For defendant? How would you try to settle the case?

What difference does it make whether the old footings were in the same place? If defendant is trying to set up a claim of adverse possession, it will have to persuade the court that buried footings were open and notorious. A builder could look at a wall and know that footings must be under it, but plaintiff said he didn't know that. And if the wall has been moved three feet, but the new footings encroach only 18 inches, Castrogiovanni's testimony that the old footings were in the same place doesn't seem very credible.

2. *Boomer*. Perhaps the most famous undue hardship case is Boomer v. Atlantic Cement Co., 257 N.E.2d 870 (N.Y. 1970), reprinted in many torts and property books. Despite using the best available technology, defendant's cement plant was pouring dust on the homes of seven plaintiffs. The court held that the plant was a nuisance, but it refused to enjoin operation of the plant, because defendant had invested $45 million and employed over 300 workers at the plant. Instead, it gave plaintiffs damages for the reduced value of their homes.

The trial judge had awarded $185,000, but the court of appeals vacated this award and remanded for further consideration. On remand, settlements and one litigated damage judgment were apparently based not on market values before Atlantic entered the neighborhood but on the above-market prices Atlantic had paid to assemble its tract of more than five square miles. Kinley v. Atlantic Cement Co., 349 N.Y.S.2d 199 (App. Div. 1973). Payments on this basis totaled $710,000. Daniel A. Farber, *The Story of Boomer: Pollution and the Common Law*, 32 Ecology L.Q. 113, 130 (2005).

The New York court subsequently refused to apply *Boomer* in a case where the nuisance also violated a valid zoning law. Little Joseph Realty, Inc. v. Town of Babylon, 363 N.E.2d 1163 (N.Y. 1977).

3. A multifactored defense. The defense that is allowed in *Van Wagner* and *Boomer*, and remanded for trial in *Whitlock*, is called "undue hardship" or "balancing the equities." Hardship to defendant is common to all the cases, and generally the hardship must be disproportionate to any benefit plaintiff will derive from the injunction. But courts also give heavy weight to defendant's culpability and to plaintiff's diligence or acquiescence, and a wide range of factual variations can influence these assessments. The rule is a litigation doctrine and not a planning doctrine; courts worry about creating a private eminent domain power if people can cynically violate their neighbors' rights and then defend on the ground that it would be expensive to undo the harm.

There are so many factors and so many differences of degree that the cases are highly fact specific. Moreover, what some jurisdictions found culpable others did not. For example, some jurisdictions viewed polluters as deliberate wrongdoers even if they used the best possible antipollution technology; other jurisdictions disagreed. That might have been the principal source of disagreement between the majority and the dissent in *Boomer*. The breach in *Van Wagner* was intentional; the court calls it "defendant's unexcused failure to perform its contract." Yet the court balanced hardships anyway, in part because the disproportion in values was so enormous, but also because courts do not think that intentional breach of contract is as serious as intentional encroachment.

4. Defendant's culpability. Broad judicial comments about mental states cannot be taken too literally in these cases. These cases are more about good faith and blameworthiness. In the nuisance cases, courts will certainly care that defendant is (intentionally) doing less than it reasonably should to avoid the problem; they are less likely to care that it intentionally built the business that is the source of the problem. *Whitlock*'s reference to "reasonable care" suggests that negligence may be enough to refuse to consider undue hardship. But most encroachments result from somebody's negligence; in practice, the courts may have in mind some culpable degree of negligence, something like gross negligence or recklessness.

Maurice Van Hecke surveyed cases on violation of building restrictions; he found 70 cases granting the injunction and 42 refusing it, with a complex mix of factors affecting the choice. But "[m]ost frequently and significantly relied upon as an affirmative basis for injunction was the defendant's willfulness. The cases abound with such appraisals as deliberate, defiant, flagrant, intentional, premeditated, and at his peril." M.T. Van Hecke, *Injunctions to Remove or Remodel Structures Erected in Violation of Building Restrictions*, 32 Tex. L. Rev. 521, 530 (1954).

5. A split decision. An example of recklessness is Ridgway v. TTnT Development Corp., 26 S.W.3d 428, 434 (Mo. Ct. App. 2000), ordering removal of the parts of a paved road and embankment that wandered outside its easement and encroached on undeveloped land. But the court also split the difference in an unusual way. It awarded only damages for an "unreasonable use" of the easement that changed the grade and forced plaintiff to build ramps to maintain access to his land; the court did not order defendants to rebuild the whole road. 126 S.W.3d 807, 811 n.2, 816 & n.7 (Mo. Ct. App. 2004).

6. An intentional taking? One more example is Myers v. Caple, 258 N.W.2d 301 (Iowa 1977). The parties owned adjoining land in a creek bottom. Caple wanted to build a private levee that would protect 70 acres of his land. The levee would aggravate the flood problem on 29 acres of Myers' land, but only under extreme conditions. The court thought the case came down to one question: "whether Caple should be deprived of the right to reclaim and cultivate some 70 acres of his land year in and year out because in exceptional years 29 acres of Myers' land might suffer additional flooding." *Id.* at 305. The court refused an injunction and remanded for a trial on damages. It also said that Myers could renew his request for an injunction if the levee caused more problems than expected. Does *Myers* amount to private eminent domain?

7. Laches. Laches is an equitable defense, taken up in section 11.D, based on delay in filing suit with resulting prejudice to defendant. There is no indication in *Boomer* that plaintiffs objected to the cement plant until after it began operation. In *Whitlock*, plaintiff objected as soon as he saw the footings, but he did not sue until the construction was well advanced. In *Myers*, plaintiff got an injunction from the trial court before construction was completed; in *Van Wagner*, plaintiff got a decision before construction began. Suing early prevents defendant from claiming acquiescence or reliance, but it doesn't guarantee a decision for plaintiff. Suppose plaintiffs in *Boomer* had sued to prevent the cement plant from being built, before the cement company had invested much money in the site. What result then?

8. Could this conflict be avoided? In *Boomer*, *Myers*, and *Van Wagner*, the harm to plaintiff is an unavoidable side effect of an otherwise legitimate use of defendant's property. In *Whitlock*, defendant could have built its addition without encroaching at all if it had cared to do so. Should that matter?

9. The damage remedy. When the court denies the injunction because of undue hardship, plaintiff generally gets damages instead. Damages are generally inadequate in the sense that an injunction would be a better remedy; in many of these cases, plaintiff loses an interest in land that is presumed to be unique. The damages may be nominal, as in *Whitlock*, or substantial, as in *Boomer*, but either way, damages will be less than the cost of complying with an injunction.

Sometimes, especially when defendant is a government agency or plaintiff is an organization of many slightly affected individuals, it is clear that there will be no damage remedy even if the injunction is denied. For examples, compare Tennessee Valley Authority v. Hill, 437 U.S. 153, 193-195 (1978), permanently enjoining operation of a completed dam, in order to preserve an endangered species, with Weinberger v. Romero-Barcelo, 456 U.S. 305 (1982), refusing to enjoin the Navy from conducting weapons training until it got a permit authorizing it to discharge munitions into navigable waters. The Court did not doubt that the Navy needed a permit, but it exercised remedial discretion to deny an injunction.

Should defendants be allowed to plead undue hardship and also claim immunity from damages in the same case? If it is clear that there will be no damage remedy, shouldn't that count in the balance of hardships?

10. Undue hardship in damage cases. The conventional wisdom is that undue hardship is a problem only of specific relief. But similar concerns underlie rules against disproportionate measures of damage. Consider Peevyhouse v. Garland Coal & Mining Co., 382 P.2d 109 (Okla. 1962). The coal company breached a promise to restore plaintiff's land to its prior condition after exhaustion of a strip mine. On the court's (quite possibly mistaken) view of the facts, restoration would have increased the value of the land by $300 at a cost of $29,000; the court held, 5-4, that plaintiffs were not entitled to the cost of restoration. The court did not say that plaintiffs get the lesser of restoration cost or lost value. That would be the usual tort measure, but it would disregard the contract; the parties had bargained for restoration. The court denied restoration cost because that cost was "grossly disproportionate" to the lost value. *Id.* at 114. Similarly, the *Restatement (Second) of Contracts* says plaintiffs can recover the cost of completing construction contracts unless that cost is "clearly disproportionate" to benefit. §348(2)(b) (Am. Law. Inst. 1981). The *Restatement*'s standard for refusing specific performance is "unreasonable hardship or loss." §364(1)(b). *Van Wagner* and other cases use such phrases interchangeably.

Lawyers can argue either way on whether the disproportion between cost and value should matter in *Peevyhouse*. But should the answer to that question depend on whether they seek specific performance or damages for the cost of restoration?

NOTES ON THE ECONOMICS OF UNDUE HARDSHIP

1. Comparing the doctrine to the law-and-economics approach. The undue hardship rule is the law's most explicit embodiment of the economic approach. If a wrong is too expensive to correct, defendant can pay damages instead. Recall too the argument that if economics were our guide, courts would grant injunctions when the cost of bargaining between the parties is low and damages when the cost of bargaining is high. Note 2 explains how the undue hardship rule implements that insight too.

But the doctrine appears as a defense, as a limit on the pursuit of justice, and not as a first principle. It is not enough for defendant to show that the injunction costs him a little more than it saves plaintiff; the injunction must impose hardship greatly disproportionate to the benefits. The court evaluates hardship and is not confined to monetary values; defendant is not permitted to make his own decision on the basis of willingness to pay. And the defense is unavailable if defendant's conduct is too culpable. The law-and-economics scholars envision people deliberately deciding to violate rights and pay damages, at least in some contexts, but the courts allow the undue hardship defense only to defendants who acted in good faith.

2. Bilateral monopoly. Before construction began, Hilander probably could have bought the right for its footings to extend under Whitlock's property, quite possibly for a nominal sum. If Whitlock's price were too high, the company could have moved its wall back 19 inches and kept the footings on its own property. But the more it built, the more difficult the negotiations became. The longer defendant stalled and kept building, the angrier plaintiff became; recall Professor Macneil's point (in the last note before *Van Wagner*) that breach of contract produces very high transaction costs. And the more defendant built, the more bargaining leverage plaintiff acquired. Relations between the parties seem to have started out friendly and then deteriorated to a wide gap between offer and demand. This is classic bilateral monopoly. The parties can deal only with each other, and they can do a lot of bluffing before reaching a deal. If both sides are determined not to be taken advantage of, they may never reach agreement. If there are more than two parties, it is more likely that negotiations will break down. If the court had enjoined operation of the cement plant in *Boomer*, the company would have had to agree with every plaintiff on some number greater than the reduction in his property values but less than $45 million. The sheer number of transactions might preclude a deal, or a few holdouts might preclude a deal.

The bilateral monopoly is inherent in the situation; the injunction does not create it. If the court denied relief, the parties could still deal only with each other. But often a deal would be obviously impossible. Plaintiffs could not pay enough to induce defendants to tear down their wall or close their cement plant, so defendants could ignore plaintiffs' demands.

The numbers can also be the other way around. An example is Spur Industries, Inc. v. Del E. Webb Development Co., 494 P.2d 700 (Ariz. 1972) (in banc), where a new residential development and defendant's preexisting feedlot expanded toward each other until the smell of manure became a serious nuisance. The houses were worth far more than the physical plant at the feedlot. So if the court enjoined the feedlot, bargaining would be futile and it would shut down. If the court denied an injunction, the homeowners or the developer would have to pay the feedlot to shut down, and the parties would have to bargain in a condition of bilateral monopoly aggravated by multiple parties on one side.

Granting or withholding the injunction allocates the power to be unreasonable between bilateral monopolists. That is, if the court grants the injunction, plaintiff gets enormous bargaining leverage; if the court denies the injunction, defendant gets enormous bargaining leverage. A damage remedy fixes a price; equally important, the parties' predictions about a damage remedy provide a basis for bargaining. The prospect of a damage remedy thus reduces the cost of bargaining, eliminates the distributional consequences of giving one side all the bargaining leverage, and eliminates the risk of tearing down the more valuable use if the parties fail to agree. In an innovative order in *Del Webb*, the court got the same advantages by granting the injunction on condition that plaintiffs pay the cost of relocating the feedlot.

3. Do litigants bargain after judgment? The literature assumes that of course parties will buy their way out of inefficient injunctions, or inefficient refusals to enjoin. That assumption may be false. Dean Farnsworth followed up on 20 nuisance cases with reported opinions. There was no serious bargaining after judgment in any case, and none of the lawyers believed there would have been bargaining if the case had come out the other way. In a few cases, there was an initial proposal and a rejection, with no follow-up from either side; in most cases, there was not even that. The lawyers believed that acrimony from the litigation inhibited bargaining, that winners were unwilling to put a dollar value on what they had won (whether freedom from nuisance or freedom to control the use of their own property), and that losers were unwilling to pay bribes to winners. Ward Farnsworth, *Do Parties to Nuisance Cases Bargain After Judgment? A Glimpse Inside the Cathedral*, 66 U. Chi L. Rev. 373 (1999).

Professor Van Hecke asked about postjudgment negotiations in his study and got replies from one or both lawyers in 25 cases. Only two defendants had bought their way out of injunctions, and apparently not for extortionate sums. An injunction to remove a two-story apartment building was settled for $750 (in the 1920s, so about $10,000 today); the other case was settled "satisfactorily to all parties" for an undisclosed amount. Van Hecke, 32 Tex. L. Rev. at 534-537. A leading casebook has a case that was litigated to the state supreme court and then settled for $250. Jesse Dukeminier, James E. Krier, Gregory S. Alexander, Michael H. Schill, & Lior Jacob Strahilevitz, *Property* 89-93 (9th ed., Wolters Kluwer 2017) (reprinting Mannillo v. Gorski, 255 A.2d 258 (N.J. 1969)).

If postjudgment settlements in injunction cases are as scarce as these small-scale studies suggest, the Coase theorem may be mostly irrelevant after judgment. Nobel laureate Professor Ronald Coase famously argued that in a hypothetical world with zero transaction costs, the law's initial allocation of rights would be irrelevant to the ultimate allocation, because any party with a more valuable use for a right would buy it from any person who held the right. R.H. Coase, *The Problem of Social Cost*, 3 J. L. & Econ. 1 (1960). But it appears that after judgment, the initial allocation of rights is generally dispositive and parties usually do not bargain around it. Of course, parties who litigate to judgment may be a special case; these studies do not imply that people rarely buy or sell legal entitlements before they get embroiled in litigation. Nor does it necessarily imply anything about settlements after suit is filed and before an opinion is reported. But it may be that the same factors of acrimony and resistance to commodifying intangible rights inhibit settlement of injunction cases, or that they at least inhibit settlements that reverse the parties' prediction of what the court will do if the case is litigated to judgment.

4. An economic account of the relevance of good faith. There is an economic as well as a moral argument for the culpability exception to the undue hardship defense. If defendant deliberately violated plaintiff's rights, hoping to invoke undue hardship and pay assessed damages after the fact, she bypassed the market: She could have dealt directly with plaintiff. If bargaining had failed, she could have gone to court to determine her rights before spending her money; the stakes of that litigation would be much lower. But when the hardships are extremely unbalanced, it is not clear that these concerns are sufficient to justify an injunction purely in economic terms. The argument from justice and individualism has surely motivated more judges: Would-be buyers of rights should not be able to rely on a doctrine that enables them to force unwilling victims to sell their rights.

LORD & TAYLOR LLC v. WHITE FLINT, L.P.

780 F.3d 211 (4th Cir. 2015)

Before WILKINSON, AGEE, and HARRIS, Circuit Judges.
PAMELA HARRIS, Circuit Judge: . . .

I.

A.

In 1975, White Flint opened discussions with Lord & Taylor and Bloomingdale's, a nonparty to this case, about development of what would become [an indoor shopping] Mall. Ultimately, Lord & Taylor and Bloomingdale's agreed to lease land immediately adjacent to the Mall and serve as retail "anchor" tenants. In exchange, White Flint agreed that it would construct and then maintain a "first class high fashion regional [s]hopping [c]enter," on the Mall property.

The parties memorialized their understanding in a reciprocal easement agreement ("REA"), committing White Flint to continued operation of a three-story, enclosed mall on the site, and detailing the layout of the Mall and its surrounding internal roadways and parking areas. Under the REA, most of the site may be used only for retail purposes, and White Flint may build additional structures only with Lord & Taylor's consent. Any changes to the Mall, including alterations to its "architectural design or appearance," also must be approved by Lord & Taylor. All of these conditions are treated by the REA as restrictive covenants that "run with the Land," creating rights in real property. They remain operative at least through 2042, and Lord & Taylor may extend them until 2057 by exercising its final lease-renewal option.

The Mall opened in 1977 and operated smoothly for many years. More recently, however, the Mall began to experience a decline in business. . . . [I]n 2012, Bloomingdale's opted not to renew its lease at the Mall site. By 2013, 75 percent of Mall tenants, accounting for at least a third of the Mall's space, had left. Since then, the Bloomingdale's building has been demolished and the remaining businesses have closed. The Mall was shuttered permanently on January 4, 2015, and Lord & Taylor alone remains open for business.

In November 2011, White Flint released a preliminary plan to redevelop the site (the "Sketch Plan"), as part of Montgomery County's broader initiative to redevelop the surrounding area (the "Sector Plan"). The Sector Plan is a massive public-private undertaking. Once complete, it will transform the area, anchored by a station of the Washington metropolitan area subway, into a 430-acre urban center, with 14,000 new residential units and 7.5 million square feet of new mixed-use space. Execution of the Sector Plan is expected to involve $1 billion in new public works and eventually to generate $40 billion in additional tax revenue.

White Flint's Sketch Plan also is ambitious. The Sketch Plan would transform the Mall site into the sort of mixed-use development increasingly popular across the country, with a 45-acre town center including 2,400 apartment units, parks and schools, a hotel, and at least three high-rise office buildings. The Lord & Taylor store would remain, but the enclosed Mall would be demolished, along with portions of the parking lots and internal roadways surrounding Lord & Taylor. Montgomery County approved the plan in October 2012, and considers it "an essential component of the Sector Plan."

B.

Lord & Taylor objects to implementation of the Sketch Plan and the contemplated redevelopment of the Mall site. According to Lord & Taylor, what it was promised by White Flint was a "first class . . . [s]hopping [c]enter" . . . . The town center that White Flint proposes to build around its store instead, Lord & Taylor argues, violates the plain terms of the REA and will negatively affect the store's business, disrupting customer access by destroying internal roads and parking areas and denying the store the benefit of foot traffic from Mall customers. . . .

[Count II of Lord & Taylor's complaint] seeks a permanent injunction compelling White Flint to honor the terms of the REA. Specifically, Lord & Taylor asks the court to enjoin White Flint "from taking any steps to carry out or construct [the] redevelopment" in a manner inconsistent with the REA and to "require [White Flint] to abide by its obligations under the [REA] to operate a first class high fashion regional retail [s]hopping [c]enter." . . .

The district court . . . assumed . . . that the proposed redevelopment would breach the REA, and that Lord & Taylor would be entitled to damages for any harm that resulted. It concluded, however, that injunctive relief would be infeasible under the circumstances. Because of physical changes to the site (most notably the demolition of the Bloomingdale's store) and what was then a 75-percent vacancy rate, the court reasoned, an injunction requiring White Flint to operate the "first class" shopping center contemplated by the REA would require the court to supervise "rebuilding [and] bringing tenants back in" to the Mall—a task the court deemed outside its competence. "[F]or me to enter into this case and try to enjoin an ongoing development project like this is just not feasible."

II.

A. . . .

The parties agree, as do we, that Maryland substantive law applies in this diversity action, and governs Lord & Taylor's . . . claim for a permanent injunction. According to Lord & Taylor, however, the district court took a different approach, and relied instead on the federal-law standard for injunctions in denying relief.

We do not read the record that way. . . . We take the district court at its word and have no reason to doubt that it properly identified Maryland substantive law as controlling.

Lord & Taylor argues in the alternative that if the district court applied Maryland law, then it misapplied it badly, relying on factors that have no place in the analysis under Maryland precedent. Maryland law, Lord & Taylor contends, strongly favors injunctive relief for breaches of restrictive covenants—so strongly that injunctions are granted almost as a matter of course and regardless of factors like the public interest or the availability of monetary damages to compensate for a breach. If White Flint's proposed redevelopment would violate the REA—and the district court assumed as much for purposes of summary judgment—then according to Lord & Taylor, there was virtually nothing left for the court to do but enjoin the breach.

We disagree. It is true that an injunction typically is an appropriate remedy for breach of a restrictive covenant under Maryland law. But injunctive relief is not automatic, and the presumption in its favor does not displace a trial court's traditional discretion when it sits in equity, *see* Roper v. Camuso, 829 A.2d 589, 601 (Md. 2003) ("Trial courts are granted broad discretionary authority to issue equitable relief."). Indeed, the very cases cited by Lord & Taylor recognize that injunctive relief remains subject to "sound judicial discretion" even where restrictive covenants and real property rights are concerned. . . .

[O]ne thing that Maryland law makes perfectly clear is that trial courts may take account of feasibility concerns—like those relied on by the district court here—in considering injunctive relief for breach of a restrictive covenant.

In this context, as in others, trial courts retain discretion to deny specific performance or injunctive relief (Maryland case law does not distinguish between the two for these purposes) where enforcement would be "unreasonably difficult" or require "long-continued supervision" by the court. *See* Edison Realty Co. v. Bauernschub, 62 A.2d 354, 358 (Md. 1948). So, for instance, an injunction may be denied as infeasible if it would compel the parties to continue a commercial relationship, or require the court to closely monitor the caliber of their performance. *See, e.g.,* M. Leo Storch L.P. v. Erol's, Inc., 620 A.2d 408, 412-414 (Md. Ct. Spec. App. 1993) (denying injunction to enforce continuous-operation lease clause on feasibility grounds); *Edison Realty Co.,* 62 A.2d at 358 (specific performance may be denied where court would be required to issue "a multiplicity of orders . . . in its endeavor to superintend [the parties'] work"). Indeed, because such affirmative injunctions are difficult to draft clearly and even harder to enforce, Maryland courts typically will issue them only where no other relief is possible. And the inquiry into feasibility is itself wide ranging and equitable in nature, with courts instructed to consider broadly the "advantages to be gained" from injunctive relief as well as "the harm to be suffered" if an injunction is denied as infeasible. *M. Leo Storch L.P.,* 620 A.2d at 412.

Whether the district court properly exercised its discretion in determining that injunctive relief would be infeasible in this case is a separate question, which we address in turn. The point here is simply that Maryland law did not require the district court to turn a blind eye to feasibility and related equitable concerns. On the contrary: Maryland law clearly authorized the district court to go beyond the state-law presumption in favor of injunctive relief to consider the feasibility of what it was being asked to do.

B.

Even on this account of the law, Lord & Taylor argues, the district court erred, because the injunctive relief it seeks would in fact be entirely feasible. On this claim, our review of the district court's determination is highly deferential. When a district court's decision rests on evaluation of equitable considerations or other traditionally discretionary factors, we generally apply an abuse of discretion standard. That deferential approach makes perfect sense when it comes to the feasibility of equitable relief: The district court is better positioned than we are to weigh the costs and benefits of injunctive relief and, in particular, to assess the practical difficulties of enforcement of an injunction—difficulties that will fall in the first instance on the district court itself. Accordingly, we will review the district court's feasibility determination for abuse of discretion, and disturb it only if we find that the court "committed a clear error of judgment." Brown v. Nucor Corp., 576 F.3d 149, 161 (4th Cir. 2009).

Like the district court, we must take account of the practical realities of the situation. At the time of the district court's decision in December 2013, Bloomingdale's had declined to renew its lease, and the building it occupied had been demolished. Much of the Mall itself was vacant, and according to Lord & Taylor, many of the remaining tenants were on short-term leases due to expire in 2014. Restoring the Mall to its former glory, as Lord & Taylor requested in Count II of its complaint, would have required more than a negative prohibition on the site's redevelopment. It would have necessitated an affirmative injunction ordering White Flint to transform the now-fading Mall back into a "first class high fashion regional retail [s]hopping [c]enter"—the kind of order that is so hard to draft with specificity and then to enforce that Maryland courts generally will grant it only as a last resort.

In this case, affirmative injunctive relief would have been even more impractical than usual, thanks to the highly detailed provisions of the REA. An order that White Flint "abide by its obligations under the REA," as sought by Lord & Taylor, also would require judicial oversight of compliance with the myriad of REA conditions that control every facet of the Mall's operations, from the distribution of parking and interior access roads to the placement of entrances to the design of the various retail stores and restaurants that populate the Mall. And once it had ascertained that the Mall's operations were again compliant with every provision of the REA, the district court's job still would not be done: It would have to ensure that the Mall remained in compliance for the duration of the REA, at least until 2042 and potentially for over forty years. Such long-term, ongoing supervision eventually would entangle the district court in every aspect of the Mall's daily operations, with any potential violation of the REA's specifications becoming fair game in a subsequent contempt proceeding.

The cases Lord & Taylor cites to argue that all of this would be perfectly feasible suggest to us just the opposite. The scale and complexity of the Mall's operations—spread over 45 acres, and potentially involving dozens of new counter-parties as the Mall repopulates—and the duration of the proposed injunction have no parallel in the Maryland case law. The injunction sought here would be nothing like one that prohibits operation of a single nearby competitor, see Redner's Markets, Inc. v. Joppatowne G.P. L.P., 2013 WL 2903285, at *2 (D. Md. 2013) (enjoining operation of a rival grocery store in the same strip mall), or resolves a single dispute over misused office space, see City of Bowie v. MIE, Properties, Inc., 922 A.2d 509, 518, 538 (Md. 2007) (enjoining operation of a dance studio). By comparison, Maryland courts have found injunctive relief infeasible under circumstances far more streamlined and straightforward than these, involving purely bilateral commercial relations. *See M. Leo Storch L.P.*, 620 A.2d at 414 (refusing to order a tenant to reoccupy leased retail space on feasibility grounds). We can find no Maryland precedent, and Lord & Taylor provides none, even suggesting that it would be feasible for the court to craft and enforce an order directing White Flint to reboot and then maintain a "first class high fashion regional retail [s]hopping [c]enter," consistent with the REA's detailed specifications, through the year 2057.

At oral argument, Lord & Taylor refined its position, suggesting that it would be satisfied with a more limited, negative injunction that simply prohibited White Flint from moving ahead with the destruction of the Mall and its adjacent parking areas. That is essentially the same proposal Lord & Taylor offered to the district court when it moved there for a stay pending appeal. The district court rejected this version of the proposed relief as well, deeming it "unrealistic" to require White Flint to maintain the status quo of a mostly empty Mall with a demolished "anchor" store on one side. In effect, the district court held, the redevelopment had passed the point of no return.

Again, we must attend to the realities of the situation facing the district court. A negative injunction, as the court understood, would freeze in place a vacant and partially demolished Mall, tantamount to a judicially mandated blight on the area. That outcome would serve neither party to the dispute, let alone the interests of the general public. Indeed, it is so patently unworkable that Lord & Taylor defends it not on its own terms, but as a form of leverage that might encourage White Flint to resume Mall operations, consistent with the REA. But the district court cannot simply assume that best-case scenario, and must instead contend with the very real possibility that a negative injunction would produce nothing but an empty and unusable 45-acre Mall site in the heart of Montgomery County's redevelopment project.

Moreover, even if a negative injunction did send White Flint back to the drawing board and eventually to the negotiating table, feasibility concerns would remain. Should the parties dispute whether any White Flint proposal to repopulate and restore the Mall lived up to the detailed specifications of the REA or produced a sufficiently "first class" and "high fashion" shopping experience, the district court would find itself inserted once again into the thick of ongoing and complex commercial relationships. And any effort to resolve that dispute by way of injunctive relief would raise precisely the feasibility issues already described.

Taken together, these concerns are more than enough to persuade us that the district court did not commit a "clear error of judgment" in finding that injunctive relief would be infeasible. Continuous judicial supervision of commercial relationships on this scale may place a particular strain on a district court, and the decision to refuse such intervention goes to the heartland of that court's discretion to manage its own affairs. Where, as here, the district court follows applicable state law and reasonably exercises its discretion in denying injunctive relief as infeasible, we have no grounds to second guess its decision.

III. . . .

AFFIRMED.

NOTES ON PRACTICALITY AND PRIVATE LITIGATION

1. Burden on the court. Requiring White Flint to resume running its mall after the mall had essentially ceased operations, and to continue operations for more than

40 years, would impose a great hardship on White Flint. Quite possibly that burden would be enough to justify denial of specific performance to Lord & Taylor. There is also the public interest here in redevelopment, an issue we saw lurking in *Van Wagner*. As malls become less popular and sometimes abandoned, the possibility of urban blight increases. Outdoor, mixed-use developments including housing are gaining in popularity, and specific performance here would stop a major redevelopment in its tracks.

But the district court and court of appeals focused more on the burden on the court than these other factors. Courts don't want to be in the business of policing disputes over a shopping mall for decades. There is simply not enough at stake to justify use of extensive judicial resources to keep open a mall that no one but Lord & Taylor wants.

Lord & Taylor reaches a typical result in cases where private plaintiffs in long-term contracts seek specific relief that would impose great burdens on the court. Courts tend to be more willing to grant specific relief for discrete periods before trial. In Universal Health Services, Inc. v. Thompson, 24 S.W.3d 570 (Tex. Ct. App. 2000), for example, the court ordered a hospital to continue operating at a loss, pending trial of physicians' claims that they had a contractual right to use the hospital for the duration of a 15-year lease. But the trial court subsequently concluded "that it could not require the hospital to stay open" permanently; it refused specific performance. Universal Health Services, Inc. v. Renaissance Group, P.A., 121 S.W.3d 742, 743 (Tex. 2003). A judgment for $6.9 million in damages was reversed on grounds going to liability. *Id.* at 745-748. The court in Metropolitan Sports Facilities Commission v. Minnesota Twins Partnership, 638 N.W.2d 214 (Minn. Ct. App. 2002), affirmed a preliminary injunction ordering the Minnesota Twins to play their 2002 home games at the Metrodome near Minneapolis. Major League Baseball had proposed to terminate the franchise, and the Twins claimed they would lose $4 million in the season.

2. Public vs. private litigation. As we saw in Chapter 4, courts have undertaken great burdens in the structural injunction cases, some of which dragged on for decades and led judges on a path from grand constitutional principle to immersion in excruciating detail. The First Circuit had to decide an appeal from an order to fix the toilet stalls in South Boston High School. Morgan v. McDonough, 540 F.2d 527, 535 (1st Cir. 1976). Similarly in *Lord & Taylor*, there was some risk that the court would wind up reviewing the choice of tenants and the upkeep of the mall and surrounding parking lot. If White Flint accepted the basic decision to keep the mall open, court supervision might be unnecessary. If it was uncooperative, the court would have to decide everything.

A business is unlikely to have the same incentives to litigate as an elected school committee caught between a federal judge and bitterly resistant voters, and the prospect of attracting paying customers mitigates the pressure to minimize costs that plagues the prison reform cases. But White Flint had already decided this mall could not attract enough customers to make money; if it could minimize its losses by running the mall at minimum levels, its incentives might look more like those of the prison authorities.

3. More important rights. Adequacy of legal remedies is a comparative judgment, and the degree of inadequacy may vary, especially between public and private litigation. It will not be easy to calculate 40 years of damages in *Lord & Taylor*, but damages would be much worse in the school, prison, and mental health cases, where the values at stake are not dollar values at all. Shouldn't courts balance the problems with the equitable remedy against the problems with the legal remedy? More generally, courts might take the view that some rights are more important than others. School desegregation is a constitutional right belonging to the whole public; the cases in this section involve the private rights of one corporation or landowner. The Supreme Court is fond of saying that "courts of equity may, and frequently do, go much farther both to give and withhold relief in furtherance of the public interest than they are accustomed to go when only private interests are involved." Golden State Bottling Co. v. National Labor Relations Board, 414 U.S. 168, 179-180 (1973). Is that a legitimate ground for avoiding a difficult injunction? At least if the damage remedy is not grossly inadequate? The Court said it again, quoting only the portion of the sentence about going much further to give relief, in Kansas v. Nebraska, 135 S. Ct. 1042, 1053 (2015), more fully described in section 8.B.3.a.

4. Carrying on an activity and achieving a result. The *Lord & Taylor* court believed it unfeasible for the district court to assure "a sufficiently 'first class' and 'high fashion' shopping experience." Compare City Stores Co. v. Ammerman, 266 F. Supp. 766 (D.D.C. 1967), *aff'd per curiam*, 394 F.2d 950 (D.C. Cir. 1968), in which the court specifically enforced a contract to build a store for plaintiff in defendant's planned shopping mall with standards "comparable, at a minimum, to the qualities, values, approaches, and standards" of a particular mall in Los Angeles. The court assumed that everything would be "fairly simple . . . if the parties deal with each other in good faith and expeditiously." *Id.* at 778. The judge said that if the parties bothered him with details, he would appoint a master to decide how to build the store. Is that overkill? Or a necessary backstop if the court is serious about providing effective remedies?

5. The legal remedy: a $31-million verdict. How could Lord & Taylor prove the damages it would suffer from the loss of the "first class" and "high fashion" mall until 2057? The mixed-used development has not been built and may never be built. If it is built, might Lord & Taylor make more money, in the long run, with the redevelopment?

When the case went to trial after the Fourth Circuit's decision, Lord & Taylor did not try to prove damages over the 40 years remaining on the contract. Instead, it argued that it would suffer $31 million in lost profits during the time it would take for the massive redevelopment to be completed, during which time access to its store would be difficult. Second, it argued that it would cost $30 to $36 million to change the store from one with a mall entrance to a stand-alone store. And third, it argued that it was entitled to damages for lost property rights. The trial court found this third claim duplicative of the claim for lost profits, and did not allow it to go to the jury. The jury awarded $31 million, without specifying whether that went to lost profits, store reconstruction, or both. The Fourth Circuit rejected appeals from both sides. Lord & Taylor, LLC v. White Flint, L.P., 849 F.3d 567 (4th Cir. 2017).

Although White Flint had claimed that if the $31 million verdict stood, it would halt the redevelopment project, it paid the damages and said it would reevaluate its development plans given the three-and-a-half-year delay caused by the litigation. Andrew Metcalf, *White Flint Property Owners to Pay Lord & Taylor After Lengthy Legal Battle*, Bethesda Magazine (Mar. 28, 2017), http://www.bethesdamagazine.com/Bethesda-Beat/2017/White-Flint-Mall-Property-Owners-To-Pay-Lord-Taylor-after-Lengthy-Legal-Battle/ [https://perma.cc/5YM7-6N22]. A year after that statement, the minority owners of White Flint sued the majority owners, claiming they were depriving them of information about the potential sale of the property as a second headquarters for Amazon. Andrew Metcalf, *White Flint Property Draws Another Lawsuit as Amazon Decision Looms*, Bethesda Magazine (Apr. 2, 2018), http://www.bethesdamagazine.com/Bethesda-Beat/2018/White-Flint-Property-Draws-Another-Lawsuit-as-Amazon-Decision-Looms/ [https://perma.cc/J88G-393F]. Nothing had been built as of spring 2018.

3. *Other Policy Reasons*

WILLING v. MAZZOCONE
393 A.2d 1155 (Pa. 1978)

MANDERINO, Justice.

On Monday, September 29, and Wednesday, October 1, 1975, appellant, Helen Willing, demonstrated in the . . . well traveled pedestrian pathway between the two court buildings located at City Hall and at Five Penn Center Plaza. . . . [F]or several hours each day, appellant wore a "sandwich-board" sign around her neck. On the sign she had hand lettered the following:

LAW-FIRM
of
QUINN-MAZZOCONE
Stole money from me — and
Sold-me-out-to-the
INSURANCE COMPANY

As she marched back and forth, appellant also pushed a shopping cart on which she had placed an American flag. She continuously rang a cow bell and blew on a whistle to further attract attention.

Appellees in this case are . . . associated in the two member law firm of Mazzocone and Quinn. . . . When appellant refused appellees' efforts to amicably dissuade her from further activity such as that described above, appellees filed a suit in equity . . . seeking to enjoin her from further demonstration. . . .

In 1968, appellees, who have specialized in the trial of workmen's compensation matters for several years, represented appellant in such a case. . . . [A]ppellant was awarded permanent/partial disability benefits which she collected for a number of years. At the time of the initial settlement distribution with appellant, appellees deducted the sum of $150.00 as costs of the case. This sum, according to appellees' evidence, was paid in full to Robert DeSilverio, M.D., a treating psychiatrist who testified on appellant's behalf in the workmen's compensation matter. Appellees presented copies of their records covering the transaction with Dr. DeSilverio. A cancelled check for the amount of the payment, and the testimony of Dr. DeSilverio himself, confirmed appellees' account of the transaction. Appellant offered no evidence other than her testimony that the cause of her antagonism towards appellees was not any dissatisfaction with the settlement, but rather, her belief that appellees had wrongfully diverted to themselves $25.00 of the $150.00 that was supposed to have been paid to Dr. DeSilverio.

Based on this evidence, the equity court concluded that appellant was "a woman firmly on the thrall of the belief that (appellees) defrauded her, an *idee fixe* [an obsession, literally, a fixed idea] which, either by reason of eccentricity or an even more serious mental instability, refuses to be dislodged by the most convincing proof to the contrary." The Court then enjoined appellant from "further unlawful demonstration, picketing, carrying placards which contain defamatory and libelous statements and or uttering, publishing and declaring defamatory statements against the (appellees) herein." On appeal, the Superior Court modified the trial court's order to read,

Helen R. Willing . . . is permanently enjoined from further demonstrating against and/or picketing Mazzocone and Quinn, Attorneys-at-Law, by uttering or publishing statements to the effect that Mazzocone and Quinn, Attorneys-at-Law stole money from her and sold her out to the insurance company.

369 A.2d 829, 834 (Pa. Super. Ct. 1976). . . .

This case raises serious and far reaching questions regarding the exercise of the constitutional right to freely express oneself. We believe the orders issued . . . are clearly prohibited by Article I §7 of the Pennsylvania Constitution and by *Goldman Theatres v. Dana*, 173 A.2d 59 (Pa. 1961). . . .

Article I §7 . . . reads in relevant part: "The free communication of thoughts and opinions is one of the invaluable rights of man, and every citizen may freely speak, write and print on any subject, being responsible for the abuse of that liberty." As we emphasized in *Goldman Theatres*, Article I §7 . . . is designed "*to prohibit the imposition of prior restraints upon the communication of thoughts and opinions*, leaving the utterer liable only for an abuse of the privilege." 173 A.2d at 62 (emphasis added).

History supports the view that the framers of our state constitution intended to prohibit prior restraint on Pennsylvanians' right to speak.

> After the demise in 1694 of the last of the infamous English Licensing Acts, freedom of the press, at least freedom from administrative censorship, began in England, and later in the Colonies, to assume the status of a "common law or natural right." See *State v. Jackson*, 356 P.2d 495, 499 (Or. 1960). Blackstone so recognized . . . when he wrote:
>
> > The liberty of the press is indeed essential to the nature of a free state: but this consists in laying no *previous* restraints upon publications, and not in freedom from censure for criminal matter when published. Every freeman has an undoubted right to lay what sentiments he pleases before the public: to forbid this, is to destroy the freedom of the press: but if he publishes what is improper, mischievous, or illegal, he must take the consequence of his own temerity. . . .

173 A.2d at 62, quoting 4 William Blackstone, *Commentaries on the Laws of England* 151-152 (Clarendon 1769). . . .

Our conclusion that the equity court violated appellant's state constitutional right to freely speak her opinion — regardless of whether that opinion is based on fact or fantasy — regarding appellees' professional integrity obviates the need for any discussion here of federal law.

Our resolution should also render unnecessary any discussion of the Superior Court's proposed exception to the so-called traditional view that equity lacks the power to enjoin the publication of defamatory matter. We do believe, however, that the Superior Court's observation that "in the present case an action for damages would be a pointless gesture since (appellant) is indigent," requires specific comment. We cannot accept the Superior Court's conclusion that the exercise of the constitutional right to freely express one's opinion should be conditioned upon the economic status of the individual asserting that right. Conditioning the right of free speech upon the monetary worth of an individual is inconsistent not only with fundamental principles of justice . . . guaranteed by the Federal Constitution, but also violates our own Constitution's express admonitions that "[a]ll men are born equally free and independent, and have certain inherent and indefeasible rights," art. I §1, and that "[n]either the Commonwealth nor any political subdivision thereof shall deny to any person the enjoyment of any civil right, nor discriminate against any person in the exercise of any civil right," art. I §26.

In Pennsylvania the insolvency of a defendant does not create a situation where there is no adequate remedy at law. In deciding whether a remedy is adequate, it is the remedy itself, and not its possible lack of success that is the determining factor. . . .

[R]eversed. . . .

ROBERTS, Justice, concurring.

I agree with the opinion of Justice Manderino that appellant's indigency does not justify the Superior Court's radical departure from the long-standing general rule that equity will not enjoin a defamation. In Heilman v. Union Canal Co., 37 Pa. 100, 104 (1860), this Court said:

> The fact, if it be so, that this remedy may not be successful in realizing the fruits of a recovery at law, on account of the insolvency of the defendants, is not of itself a ground of equitable interference. The remedy is what is to be looked at. If it exist, and is ordinarily adequate, its possible want of success is not a consideration.

Money damages are adequate to recompense the plaintiffs for any losses they have suffered as a consequence of the defendant's defamatory publication. Thus, it was improper to grant equitable relief based on appellant's presumed inability to pay a money judgment. . . .

[T]he Superior Court conditions appellant's right to trial by jury on her economic status. One of the underlying justifications for equity's traditional refusal to enjoin defamatory speech is that in equity all questions of fact are resolved by the trial court, rather than the jury. Thus, it deprives appellant of her right to a jury trial on the issue of the truth or falsity of her speech. The right to trial by jury is more than mere form. . . .

O'BRIEN, J., joins in this concurring opinion.

EAGEN, Chief Justice, dissenting.

I dissent for the reasons articulated in my dissenting opinion in *Goldman Theatres*, 173 A.2d at 69-79. [That opinion argued that prior restraints consist only of administrative or licensing schemes that operate before the first publication of a statement, and that the prohibition even on that narrow class of prior restraints is not absolute.]

NIX and LARSEN, JJ., dissented without opinion.

[Justice POMEROY concurred on the basis of the dissenting opinion in the Superior Court.]

Addendum: The opinions below. Here is what the majority in the Superior Court had said to justify the injunction:

> First of all, the concept that equity will protect only property rights as opposed to personal rights has been expressly repudiated by our Supreme Court. In any event, the right to practice law is a property right.
>
> The second objection often advanced for refusing to enjoin defamation is that the defendant would be denied the right to have a jury pass upon the truth or falsity of the publication. This argument loses all persuasion, however, in those situations where the plaintiff has clearly established before a judicial tribunal that the matter sought to be enjoined is both defamatory and false. In the words of Dean Pound, a jury trial in such a case is a "mere form". . . . Roscoe Pound, *Equitable Relief Against Defamation and Injuries to Personality*, 29 Harv. L. Rev. 640, 657 (1916). . . . [T]he jury trial objection vanishes where there are no controverted issues of fact to submit to the jury. . . .
>
> The third argument often invoked for denying injunctive relief in defamation cases is that the plaintiff has an adequate remedy at law. This reason is premised on the theory that an award of damages will sufficiently recompense the plaintiff. . . . We . . . have difficulty accepting the idea that the payment of a sum of money is either an adequate or proper remedy in this case. In the first instance, it is obvious that a good professional and/or personal reputation is a unique and precious possession. Damage to this inestimable possession is, however, difficult to prove and measure accurately; in fact,

in most cases, more difficult than measuring property damages. More importantly, we cannot disregard the fact that in the present case an action for damages would be a pointless gesture since the defendant is indigent. In . . . Heilman v. Union Canal Co., 37 Pa. 100 (1860), . . . the Court held that "the insolvency of the defendants, is not *of itself* a ground for equitable interference." *Id.* at 104 (emphasis added). However, in the instant action not only do we have the defendant's insolvency but . . . we also have the difficulties inherent in attempting to measure in dollars the damage caused by defendant. An additional consideration militating in favor of equitable jurisdiction is the avoidance of a multiplicity of suits. In view of the defendant's unshakable conviction that plaintiffs have defrauded her, it is not unreasonable to assume that unless restrained she will persist in conducting her defamatory demonstrations secure in the knowledge that any monetary judgment would be unenforceable. To permit this would place plaintiffs in the oppressive position of resorting to ineffective actions at law whenever the defendant is inclined to denigrate them. Clearly this cannot be an "adequate remedy at law."

The final reason frequently advanced for equity's reluctance to enjoin defamation is that an injunction against the publication would be unconstitutional as a prior restraint on free expression. This is by far the most cogent of all the reasons offered in support of the traditional view. . . .

[T]he Supreme Court has never declared that all injunctions of speech do not pass constitutional muster. . . . [T]he peculiar facts of a particular case may admit of no other alternative but injunction. . . . [T]his is such a case. . . .

Furthermore, there is an inconsistency with the majority view in that it approves injunctions in trade libel cases and frowns on injunctions against defamatory publications concerning the reputation of an individual. Purchasers have been enjoined from adorning their cars with drawings of lemons and similar decorations or against advertising the identification of a vendor. Demonstrative tenants have been restrained from picketing their landlord. The owner of a hospital has been protected against the disparagement of that facility. The business interests of a real estate developer have been protected.

There is definitely a curious inversion of logic in the view that gives property rights primacy over personal rights involving reputation. There is an equal involvement of freedom of speech and expression in both categories of cases. . . .

The pivotal question and its solution depend on the presence or absence of an overriding public interest in the utterance or publication. . . . Where the public interest is minimal or non-existent then a publication which is also defamatory and unprivileged should be enjoined. . . .

[W]e perceive no public interest so substantial or significant as to permit defendant's continuing false accusations concerning plaintiff's professional conduct. On the other hand, the injury to plaintiff's reputation can be extensive and irreparable if the defendant is permitted to continue her activities. Under these circumstances, the court below properly granted the injunction.

[However,] the decree is constitutionally offensive insofar as it . . . is not sufficiently precise. It is too broad since it imposes sanctions beyond the scope of her activities which have been adjudged defamatory and false in this case. The decree must be modified [so that it enjoins only those statements already found to be false. The Superior Court's modification is quoted in the Supreme Court's opinion.]

Mazzocone v. Willing, 369 A.2d 829, 831-834 (Pa. Super. Ct. 1976), *rev'd*, 393 A.2d 1155 (Pa. 1978).

The dissent covered most of the same ground as the opinions in the Supreme Court, but it made one additional point:

While I can agree that proof of damages in a defamation case is a difficult task I am unprepared to state that because proof of damages is difficult an action for defamation at law is inadequate. If this proposition were followed to its logical conclusion, all defamation cases could initially qualify for equitable relief. This is not the law. . . .

Id. at 837 (Jacobs, J., dissenting).

NOTES ON DEFAMATION DAMAGES AND INSOLVENT DEFENDANTS

1. Irreplaceable and hard to measure? Isn't the Superior Court right that the free speech argument is the only cogent reason not to enjoin this defamation? Does the Supreme Court's attempt to explain how the legal remedy is adequate add anything? Without the free speech claim, wouldn't the rest be an embarrassment?

Is plaintiffs' reputation replaceable? Can they use damages to clear their names? They don't even know who saw the sign, let alone who gave it any credence, or who among those people might someday need a workers' compensation lawyer or have a client to refer. Defamation damages are so unmeasurable that courts traditionally allowed juries to presume damages.

2. Impossible to collect? The problem of collecting damages is independent of measuring them and replacing what was lost. Does it make any sense at all to say that a damage judgment is adequate if it can never be collected? The Pennsylvania rule is in a tiny minority; it might not even be the rule in Pennsylvania if the issue were squarely presented outside a free speech context. Cases are collected in Laycock, *The Death of the Irreparable Injury Rule* at 86-87 n.22. Recall that Pardee v. Camden Lumber treated defendant's insolvency as an uncontroversial ground for holding the damage remedy inadequate. Is there any reason to let defendant cut down plaintiff's trees if we know defendant won't be able to pay for the damage?

3. Preferring one creditor over others? But what if the trees have already been cut, and plaintiff seeks an injunction ordering defendant to turn over his few remaining assets to plaintiff in compensation? Defendant's other creditors would properly object to that. Suppose plaintiff seeks a reparative injunction ordering defendant to plant a new generation of trees. That would harm other creditors just as much as an order to pay plaintiff first. It is essential to distinguish threatened violations, which can be prevented by enjoining future harmful conduct, from past violations, the effects of which can be corrected only by requiring the insolvent defendant to spend some of her scarce remaining assets. If defendant doesn't have enough assets to go around, the legal remedy is still inadequate, but there are independent reasons not to prefer one creditor over all the others.

Bankruptcy is the equitable remedy for the case of too many creditors fighting over too few assets. In bankruptcy, the debtor's assets are distributed among her creditors under rules and priorities established in the Bankruptcy Code, with equal distributions to creditors who are similarly situated under those rules.

4. The Pennsylvania cases. Most of the Pennsylvania cases involve past injury and one creditor seeking a remedy ahead of all the others. But *Willing* is really a case where the court let defendant do harm she couldn't pay for.

Heilman v. Union Canal Co., quoted in *Willing*, is a revealing case that straddles the categories. There, the court refused to enjoin diversion of water from a stream on which plaintiff owned the water rights for a mill. For many years, the canal company had been diverting the water and paying for it, but at the time of the litigation, payments had been suspended and the canal was in the hands of trustees for the company's creditors. Each day's continued diversion of water inflicted new harm on plaintiff. But plaintiff was also one creditor and supplier of the bankrupt enterprise, seeking to elevate his own interests above the interests of all others. If he could withhold his water, he would acquire enormous bargaining leverage; he could sell the water back to the canal company on whatever terms he chose.

Today the case would be in reorganization under Chapter 11 of the Bankruptcy Code, and the problem of preserving the flow of water essential to reorganization of a canal company would be addressed under express statutory provisions. 11 U.S.C. §§363-366. The practical problem was the same in 1860. What seems to us the heart of the case appears in the following passage:

> [T]he acquiescence or assent of the [plaintiff] to the use of the water for so many years, and its use by arrangement and contract, precluded an injunction. . . .
>
> Equity would not, in such a case, destroy the defendants' works, now an important public thoroughfare, by restraining their use as a public highway, but leave the plaintiff to his remedy at law.

37 Pa. at 103-104.

The legal remedy was not adequate, but it was all the court was willing to allow. Caught between its determination not to close the canal and its recognition that plaintiff's damage remedy had limited value, and unable to see a general solution, the court hedged. First it said what is quoted in *Willing*, concluding that the remedy's "possible want of success is not a consideration." *Id.* at 104. But it immediately continued:

> It is not intended here to say that insolvency is never a consideration moving a chancellor. It frequently does, but not alone. The equitable remedy must exist independently. In balancing cases, it is a consideration that gives preponderance to the remedy.

Id.

The court is surely right that insolvency alone is not enough. But isn't the additional necessary element just that the remedy make sense in terms of insolvency policy? *Willing* presents the additional question whether the remedy makes sense in terms of free speech policy. Whether there is an additional independent ground for equitable remedies does not address either of these questions. The Superior Court in *Willing* relied on the difficulty of measuring damages to augment the impossibility of collecting them. But if none of the damages can be collected, who cares how they were measured?

5. Rich and poor alike. The Supreme Court is surely right that rich and poor should have the same rights of free speech. But enjoining the rich speaker would go as far toward that goal as not enjoining the poor speaker. Does the court really think that damage judgments have the same effect on all social classes? Those who are completely judgment proof may be undeterred, if they are sophisticated enough to understand their dubious advantage. But for those who are a little better off—who are not rich but have some nonexempt assets, or a credit rating to protect—a damage judgment can be a catastrophe. The risk of a defamation judgment may deter their speech far more than it deters the speech of a large corporation or a wealthy individual. Recall the general argument that injunctions restrict liberty more than damage judgments. Doesn't that have the most bite for the very rich and the very poor?

The devastating threat of damage judgments for defamation is a recurring theme in a leading history of the civil rights movement. See Taylor Branch, *Parting the Waters: America in the King Years 1954-63*, at 289, 295-296, 312, 370-371, 382, 391, 515, 579-582,

590, 694 (Simon & Schuster 1988). It was these cases that led the Supreme Court to impose constitutional limits in New York Times Co. v. Sullivan, 376 U.S. 254 (1964). For the use of damage actions to silence corporate critics on the internet, see Lyrissa Barnett Lidsky, *Silencing John Doe: Defamation and Discourse in Cyberspace*, 49 Duke L.J. 855 (2000).

NOTES ON PRIOR RESTRAINTS

1. The prior restraint rule. As the court's quotation from Blackstone indicates, the prior restraint rule is derived from the days when freedom of speech consisted *only* of freedom from prior restraints. In New York Times Co. v. Sullivan, the Supreme Court recognized that damage judgments for defamation can violate freedom of speech. But we are left with the notion that prior restraints are somehow special and require more justification than punishment for speech or damage judgments for speech. The special hostility to prior restraints is read into state and federal constitutions; the same policy is reflected in the nonconstitutional rule that equity will not enjoin a libel. What is the basis for this policy? Is the injunction really a greater threat to free speech?

2. Protected and unprotected speech. In the federal law of free speech, reckless or deliberate defamation is one of several categories of speech that are not constitutionally protected. Because Willing's statements were made in reckless disregard of the truth, the Supreme Court would permit a judgment against her for "compensatory" damages, which could be presumed in the absence of proof, plus punitive damages. See Gertz v. Robert Welch, Inc., 418 U.S. 323, 348-350 (1974). The Court could reach the same result, without finding recklessness, on the ground that her statements were of no public concern. Dun & Bradstreet, Inc. v. Greenmoss Builders, Inc., 472 U.S. 749, 758-761 (1985). If her statements are unprotected to that extent, why can't the courts order her not to repeat them? Conversely, if the Constitution protects her statements, why can a jury punish her for making them?

3. Prior restraints against unprotected speech. Obscenity is another category of unprotected speech. The Supreme Court has upheld injunctions against obscene expression, provided that there is an adjudication of obscenity prior to the injunction or, if later, after the "shortest fixed period compatible with sound judicial resolution." Freedman v. Maryland, 380 U.S. 51, 59 (1965). Does it follow that the injunction in *Willing* would not violate the federal Constitution, because there had been a final adjudication of reckless defamation prior to the injunction?

Similar reasoning appears in Pittsburgh Press Co. v. Pittsburgh Commission on Human Relations, 413 U.S. 376 (1973). The Court upheld an order to stop printing help-wanted ads that segregated "male" and "female" jobs. It said: "The special vice of a prior restraint is that communication will be suppressed, either directly or by inducing excessive caution in the speaker, before an adequate determination that it is unprotected by the First Amendment." *Id.* at 390. Because the speech in *Pittsburgh Press* was unprotected, it could be enjoined.

The Court has also upheld prior restraints in cases of securities fraud, Aaron v. Securities & Exchange Commission, 446 U.S. 680, 688-689 (1980); misleading advertising, Federal Trade Commission v. Colgate-Palmolive Co., 380 U.S. 374, 377, 392-395 (1965); and defendants who obtained information by promising to keep it secret, Seattle Times Co. v. Rhinehart, 467 U.S. 20, 33-34 (1984).

4. Reaffirming the traditional rule. The cases in note 3 suggest that the traditional rule against prior restraints is of declining significance. But other modern Supreme Court cases strongly relied on the rule.

a. Sexual entertainment. Vance v. Universal Amusement Co., 445 U.S. 308 (1980), invalidated a nuisance statute authorizing injunctions ordering theaters to close for a year if they had regularly shown obscene films in the past. Southeastern Promotions, Ltd. v. Conrad, 420 U.S. 546 (1975), held that a municipal auditorium could not refuse to allow a touring company to present the musical *Hair,* which included nudity, profanity, and sexual gestures. Both opinions argued that prior restraints inevitably preclude speech that would have been protected, because it is impossible to know in advance what the speaker would have said. That argument was dubious in *Southeastern,* because the company did the same show at every stop.

b. Gag orders. Nebraska Press Association v. Stuart, 427 U.S. 539 (1976), reversed an injunction ordering the press not to report confessions or other facts "strongly implicative" of the accused in a widely reported murder trial. The Court thought other remedies were adequate; its examples were remedies that do not restrain speech at all, such as changing venue or sequestering jurors. It seems unlikely that the Court would permit the press to be punished or held liable in damages for publishing truthful information about a criminal prosecution.

c. *The Pentagon Papers.* New York Times Co. v. United States, 403 U.S. 713 (1971), reversed an injunction against publishing *The Pentagon Papers,* a secret government study of the war in Vietnam. The government claimed that publication would endanger national security. A majority of the Court apparently contemplated that the *Times* could be criminally prosecuted; no such prosecution was ever filed.

5. Reconciling the two lines of cases. One line of cases affirms injunctions against speech finally determined to be unprotected; the other says injunctions against speech are especially suspect *even if* the speech is otherwise unprotected. Is there any distinction between the two lines of cases? It may be that in the second group, the speech was really protected against subsequent restraints as well, so that reliance on the rule against prior restraints was just a narrower way to write the opinion. In this view, the Court may be expected to waive the rule against prior restraints whenever it encounters a carefully drafted injunction against speech that has properly been found unprotected. *Pittsburgh Press* actually says that, but that is not how the Court writes most of the opinions. If the prediction is accurate, the federal rule is radically different from the traditional understanding invoked in *Willing.* It is no longer a rule against restraints prior to publication; it is a rule against restraints prior to adjudication.

6. Developments in the lower courts. *Willing* states the classical understanding, but a surprising number of cases have enjoined repetition of defamation. The issue is thoroughly reviewed in Balboa Island Village Inn, Inc. v. Lemen, 156 P.3d 339, 343-349 (Cal. 2007). The Inn is a restaurant and bar; Anne Lemen owns an adjacent cottage. At first she complained about noise and about drunken customers leaving the bar. Then she began circulating petitions and accosting customers. She said that the "food is shitty," that the owner's wife is "a whore," that the Inn sells drugs and sells alcohol to minors, that there is child pornography and prostitution in the Inn, and that sex videos are filmed there. *Id.* at 341-342. The trial court found these statements to be false and enjoined their repetition. The California Supreme Court vacated parts of the injunction it found to be overbroad, but it affirmed the injunction against repetition of statements adjudicated to be false, holding that an injunction after final adjudication is not a prior restraint. There were two dissents. And see Judge Posner's opinion in *McCarthy v. Fuller,* 810 F.3d 456, 462 (7th Cir. 2015), arguing that a rule that defamatory speech can never be enjoined "would make an impecunious defamer undeterrable," but noting that an injunction against defamatory statements, "if permissible at all, must not through careless drafting forbid statements not yet determined to be defamatory, for by doing so it could restrict lawful expression."

Compare Oakley, Inc. v. McWilliams, 879 F. Supp. 2d 1087, 1092 (C.D. Cal. 2012), refusing to enjoin defendant's repeated defamatory statements about the sunglass company Oakley, "even if money damages failed to deter" further repetition. As in *Willing,* the false and defamatory statements seemed to stem from defendant's mental illness. *Id.* at 1088.

Professor Ardia collected 56 cases enjoining defamation, 31 of them since 2000. David S. Ardia, *Freedom of Speech, Defamation, and Injunctions,* 55 Wm. & Mary L. Rev. 1 (2013). Nearly half of these cases involve speech on the internet, often posted by individuals with few assets from which a damage judgment might be collected. Professor Ardia argues that the law should permit these injunctions in limited circumstances; his most important proposed limitations are that the injunction be confined to statements that have been fully litigated and found to be false, and to statements that are about private matters and irrelevant to any public issue.

7. Are prior restraints special? There are many arguments for and against the prior restraint rule. But none of them track the irreparable injury rule; arguments for the prior restraint rule never claim that legal remedies are equally complete, practical, and efficient. Instead, they always claim that the injunction is in some way more effective, and that we don't want remedies against unprotected speech to be that effective.

Dean Chemerinsky, who represented the defendant in *Balboa Island,* argues that if injunctions are confined to the very statements proved at trial, they will be ineffective; defendant can make new charges or make the same charge in different words. But if they go beyond that, they necessarily enjoin speech that has never been found to be knowingly false and so they violate the First Amendment. Erwin Chemerinsky, *Injunctions in Defamation Cases,* 57 Syr. L. Rev. 157, 171-172 (2007).

Professor Siegel has made a strong originalist argument for the rule against injunctions. Stephen A. Siegel, *Injunctions for Defamation, Juries, and the Clarifying Lens of 1868,* 56 Buff. L. Rev. 655 (2008). He argues that the framers and ratifiers of the First and Fourteenth Amendments (it is the Fourteenth that applies the federal Free Speech Clause to the states) mistrusted judges in speech cases and viewed the jury as indispensable both to find the facts and, if necessary, to nullify otherwise lawful suppression of speech. Consequently, there could be no injunctions against speech, because equity courts operated without juries. Juries are often hostile to unpopular speakers, but Siegel argues that jury trial combined with judicial power to direct verdicts in favor of the speaker (but never against the speaker) provide an important double protection for speech. He collects the literature *id.* at 658 n.19.

Willing and the cases in these notes involve private figures and private disputes. A public official seeking to enjoin criticism that a judge found defamatory might be more troubling, although we allow damages in such cases, and, in theory, subsequent punishment, although actual examples are scarce.

One common argument for the traditional rule is that an injunction that forbids protected speech must be obeyed; the unconstitutionality of the injunction is not a defense to a prosecution for criminal contempt. This rule—called the collateral bar rule because it bars collateral attacks on injunctions—is not unique to speech cases. We will consider it more generally in section 9.A.3.

NOTES ON THE RIGHT TO JURY TRIAL

1. The jury trial issue in *Willing*. The court says the damage remedy preserves Willing's right to jury trial. The point is not limited to prior restraint cases; it is often offered in defense of the irreparable injury rule generally. A few states use juries in injunction cases, but in most places, injunctions are issued without juries. How important is that? Is a jury more likely to decide for Willing than a judge? Would she even get to the jury, or would she lose on a motion for summary judgment? She would at least get a jury trial on the amount of damages.

2. Who benefits from jury trial? Does it matter that jury trial is generally thought to be a bigger advantage to plaintiffs than to defendants? Most plaintiffs' lawyers prefer juries because they believe juries are more likely to act out of sympathy if liability is unclear, and because they believe that a jury's assessment of damages is likely to be bigger than a judge's. This view is especially strong in defamation cases, where judges regularly set aside or reduce jury verdicts.

No doubt there are cases where defendant may expect more sympathy from a jury than from a judge. But how general a problem is that? Is there any reason to predict that juries would favor defendant in Pardee v. Camden Lumber? What if plaintiffs' claim to the land were based on a "technicality"? What if plaintiff were a large corporate absentee landowner and defendant were a local individual?

3. Separating the choice of remedy from the mode of trial. Why must we deprive plaintiff of his preferred remedy to preserve defendant's right to jury trial? Why not try the injunction suit to a jury, submitting special issues if necessary? Professor Siegel argues that if we want injunctions against speech, we should have jury trial both on whether to issue the injunction and on any efforts to enforce it. 56 Buff. L. Rev. at 726-735. Few states have done that, but in some contexts there are ways of accomplishing the same thing. In a part of the *Pardee* opinion not reprinted in this book, the court says that a suit in ejectment was pending between the parties. Ejectment is the legal remedy to recover possession of land; it is tried to a jury, but it has no way of giving preliminary relief before final judgment. A preliminary injunction would preserve the trees until both suits were concluded; plaintiff could get specific relief, and both sides would get jury trial.

4. Jury trial where law and equity overlap. There is a large body of law on the right to jury trial in cases where plaintiff seeks some combination of legal and equitable relief or seeks an equitable remedy that has a legal equivalent. The federal rule is that all jury issues must be tried before any nonjury issues; state practice is divided. But these cases do not really turn on choice of remedy. Successful plaintiffs get the remedies they ask for, and the issue is whether the cases will be tried to juries. We will consider those cases in section 6.C.

NOTES ON AVOIDING A "MULTIPLICITY OF SUITS"

1. The risk of having to sue repeatedly. The Superior Court opinion in *Willing* mentions one other traditional ground for holding legal remedies inadequate: that the legal remedy would require "a multiplicity of suits," because plaintiff would have to sue repeatedly as defendant repeated the defamation. There is a reference to the rule in Continental Airlines v. Intra Brokers, reprinted in section 5.A.1.a, where the court paraphrases an old Supreme Court case holding that it would take "too many lawsuits" to recover the fare for all the free passes improperly transferred to persons not eligible to use them.

This rationale has been applied to all sorts of continuing courses of conduct. It can be a bit fictional where the first substantial damage award would probably resolve the dispute and deter defendant from repetitions. But predictions of deterrence are never certain, and the prospect of multiple suits is not fictional at all if defendant's conduct might be profitable even after paying plaintiff's damages, or if the likely damages are too small to pay for the litigation. Plaintiff may be deterred from suing before defendant is deterred from wrongdoing.

   2. Some examples. An example is Mutual of Omaha Life Insurance Co. v. Executive Plaza, Inc., 425 N.E.2d 503 (Ill. App. Ct. 1981), where tenants in a commercial office building sued to enjoin the landlord from setting aside some of the building's parking places for a new tenant. The trial court found that plaintiffs suffered only "inconvenience short of irreparable harm." *Id.* at 507. The appellate court reversed: "[T]he fact that no actual damages could be proved and the jury could award only nominal damages 'often furnishes the very best reason why a court of equity should interfere. . . .'" *Id.* at 508.

   In Hadley v. Department of Corrections, 840 N.E.2d 748 (Ill. App. Ct. 2005), the court ordered prison officials to stop charging indigent inmates, who were exempt by statute, a two-dollar fee for each non-emergency visit to the medical clinic. "[W]ithout an injunction, plaintiff and other indigent inmates will suffer the same small two-dollar injury over and over again." *Id.* at 756. "Irreparable injury, as used in the law of injunction, does not necessarily mean that the injury is beyond the possibility of compensation in damages, nor that it must be very great." Hogelin v. City of Columbus, 741 N.W.2d 617, 626 (Neb. 2007).

   3. Small damages are irreparable damages. These cases make an important point: A continuing small injury is irreparable *because* it is small. Judges occasionally suggest that "irreparable" means especially severe or serious, so that little injuries are not worth preventing by injunction. See, e.g., Myers v. Caple, 258 N.W.2d 301, 305 (Iowa 1977), described in note 6 following Whitlock v. Hilander Foods. But recall that *Myers* was an undue hardship case: Enjoining defendants' levee would harm defendant more than it would help plaintiff. The court's requirement of serious injury was in that context; the very next sentence invoked "the 'relative hardship' or 'balance of convenience' standard." The court conflated comparative hardship with a threshold requirement of serious injury, and that is typical of the cases that state a threshold requirement. *Mutual of Omaha* is the more common view when courts attend to the issue.

   Continental Airlines illustrates a corollary: The damage remedy is inadequate if there are no *provable* damages. Recall that in that case it was impossible to tell whether brokering the discount coupons was helping or hurting Continental financially. Damages might have been large, small, or nonexistent; it was impossible to tell.

   Should there be a threshold requirement of serious injury? There is surely something to the old maxim that the law does not take notice of trifles. But if we decide that a dispute over parking places justifies gearing up the judicial machinery, is there any reason to say the harm is great enough for damages but not for an injunction?

4.   *eBay Inc. v. MercExchange LLC: A New Federal Standard for Permanent Injunctive Relief?*

To summarize the law of injunctions so far, in order to obtain injunctive relief (as opposed to legal relief, such as damages) a plaintiff needs to prove both propensity (as discussed more fully in section 4.A) and irreparable injury (as discussed more fully in section 5.A.1). Even when a plaintiff can demonstrate propensity and irreparable injury, courts have wide equitable discretion to deny relief. An injunction may impose too great a hardship on the defendant given the benefit to the plaintiff; it may be too burdensome on the courts; or it may raise other policy concerns, such as prohibitions on involuntary servitude or interference with defendants' First Amendment rights. This is how the practice of seeking injunctive relief has been in American courts for a long time, and this still describes the practice in most American states.

But something different has happened in the federal courts. Apparently by accident, the Supreme Court changed the standard for seeking permanent injunctions. While we cannot yet say that this change has led to a great many differences in outcomes outside the patent arena, it has changed how lawyers have to litigate these cases, and it has at least incrementally increased the burden on plaintiffs to obtain such relief.

EBAY INC. v. MERCEXCHANGE, LLC

547 U.S. 388 (2006)

Justice THOMAS delivered the opinion of the Court. . . .

I

Petitioner eBay operates a popular Internet Web site that allows private sellers to list goods they wish to sell, either through an auction or at a fixed price. . . . Respondent MercExchange . . . holds a number of patents, including a business method patent for an electronic market designed to facilitate the sale of goods between private individuals by establishing a central authority to promote trust among participants. MercExchange sought to license its patent to eBay . . . , as it had previously done with other companies, but the parties failed to reach an agreement. MercExchange subsequently filed a patent infringement suit against eBay. . . . A jury found that MercExchange's patent was valid, that eBay . . . had infringed that patent, and that an award of damages was appropriate. [The trial judge refused a permanent injunction. 275 F. Supp. 2d 695, 710-715 (E.D. Va. 2003). The Federal Circuit reversed. 401 F.3d 1323, 1338-1339 (Fed. Cir. 2005).]

II

According to well-established principles of equity, a plaintiff seeking a permanent injunction must satisfy a four-factor test before a court may grant such relief. A plaintiff must demonstrate: (1) that it has suffered an irreparable injury; (2) that remedies available at law, such as monetary damages, are inadequate to compensate for that injury; (3) that, considering the balance of hardships between the plaintiff and defendant, a remedy in equity is warranted; and (4) that the public interest would not be disserved by a permanent injunction. See, e.g., Weinberger v. Romero-Barcelo, 456 U.S. 305, 311-313 (1982); Amoco Production Co. v. Village of Gambell, 480 U.S. 31, 42 (1987). The decision to grant or deny permanent injunctive relief is an act of equitable discretion by the district court, reviewable on appeal for abuse of discretion.

These familiar principles apply with equal force to disputes arising under the Patent Act. As this Court has long recognized, "a major departure from the long tradition of equity practice should not be lightly implied." *Romero-Barcelo*, 456 U.S. at 320. . . .

To be sure, the Patent Act also declares that "patents shall have the attributes of personal property," 35 U.S.C. §261, including "the right to exclude others from making, using, offering for sale, or selling the invention," §154(a)(1). According to the Court of Appeals, this statutory right to exclude alone justifies its general rule in favor of permanent injunctive relief. But the creation of a right is distinct from the provision of remedies for violations of that right. Indeed, the Patent Act itself indicates that patents shall have the attributes of personal property "[s]ubject to the provisions of this title," §261, including, presumably, the provision that injunctive relief "may" issue only "in accordance with the principles of equity," §283. . . .

Neither the District Court nor the Court of Appeals below fairly applied these traditional equitable principles in deciding respondent's motion for a permanent injunction. Although the District Court recited the traditional four-factor test . . . , it concluded that a "plaintiff's willingness to license its patents" and "its lack of commercial activity in practicing the patents" would be sufficient to establish that the patent holder would not suffer irreparable harm if an injunction did not issue. 275 F. Supp. 2d at 712. But traditional equitable principles do not permit such broad classifications. For example, some patent holders, such as university researchers or self-made inventors, might reasonably prefer to license their patents, rather than undertake efforts to secure the financing necessary to bring their works to market themselves. Such patent holders may be able to satisfy the traditional four-factor test, and we see no basis for categorically denying them the opportunity to do so. To the extent that the District Court adopted such a categorical rule, then, its analysis cannot be squared with the principles of equity adopted by Congress. . . .

In reversing the District Court, the Court of Appeals departed in the opposite direction from the four-factor test. The court articulated a "general rule," unique to patent disputes, "that a permanent injunction will issue once infringement and validity have been adjudged." 401 F.3d at 1338. The court further indicated that injunctions should be denied only in the "unusual" case, under "exceptional circumstances" and "'in rare instances . . . to protect the public interest.'" *Id.* at 1338-1339. Just as the District Court erred in its categorical denial of injunctive relief, the Court of Appeals erred in its categorical grant of such relief.

Because we conclude that neither court below correctly applied the traditional four-factor framework that governs the award of injunctive relief, we vacate the judgment of the Court of Appeals, so that the District Court may apply that framework in the first instance. In doing so, we take no position on whether permanent injunctive relief should or should not issue in this particular case, or indeed in any number of other disputes arising under the Patent Act. We hold only that the decision whether to grant or deny injunctive relief rests within the equitable discretion of the district courts, and that such discretion must be exercised consistent with traditional principles of equity, in patent disputes no less than in other cases governed by such standards. . . .

Chief Justice ROBERTS, with whom Justices SCALIA and GINSBURG join, concurring. . . .

I join the opinion of the Court. . . .

From at least the early 19th century, courts have granted injunctive relief upon a finding of infringement in the vast majority of patent cases. This "long tradition of equity practice" is not surprising, given the difficulty of protecting a right to *exclude* through monetary remedies that allow an infringer to *use* an invention against the patentee's wishes—a difficulty that often implicates the first two factors of the traditional four-factor test. This historical practice, as the Court holds, does not *entitle* a patentee to a permanent injunction or justify a *general rule* that such injunctions should issue. At the same time, there is a difference between exercising equitable discretion pursuant to the established four-factor test and writing on an entirely clean slate. "Discretion is not whim, and limiting discretion according to legal standards helps promote the basic principle of justice that like cases should be decided alike." Martin v. Franklin Capital Corp., 546 U.S. 132, 139 (2005). When it comes to discerning and applying those standards, in this area as others, "a page of history is worth a volume of logic." New York Trust Co. v. Eisner, 256 U.S. 345, 349 (1921).

Justice KENNEDY, with whom Justices STEVENS, SOUTER, and BREYER join, concurring.

The Court is correct, in my view, to hold that courts should apply the well-established, four-factor test — without resort to categorical rules — in deciding whether to grant injunctive relief in patent cases. The Chief Justice is also correct that history may be instructive in applying this test. The traditional practice of issuing injunctions against patent infringers, however, does not seem to rest on "the difficulty of protecting a right to *exclude* through monetary remedies that allow an infringer to *use* an invention against the patentee's wishes." 547 U.S. at 396 (Roberts, C.J., concurring). . . . [T]he existence of a right to exclude does not dictate the remedy for a violation of that right. To the extent earlier cases establish a pattern of granting an injunction against patent infringers almost as a matter of course, this pattern simply illustrates the result of the four-factor test in the contexts then prevalent. . . .

In . . . many instances the nature of the patent being enforced and the economic function of the patent holder present considerations quite unlike earlier cases. An industry has developed in which firms use patents not as a basis for producing and selling goods but, instead, primarily for obtaining licensing fees. For these firms, an injunction, and the potentially serious sanctions arising from its violation, can be employed as a bargaining tool to charge exorbitant fees to companies that seek to buy licenses to practice the patent. When the patented invention is but a small component of the product the companies seek to produce and the threat of an injunction is employed simply for undue leverage in negotiations, legal damages may well be sufficient to compensate for the infringement and an injunction may not serve the public interest. In addition injunctive relief may have different consequences for the burgeoning number of patents over business methods, which were not of much economic and legal significance in earlier times. The potential vagueness and suspect validity of some of these patents may affect the calculus under the four-factor test.

The equitable discretion over injunctions . . . is well suited to allow courts to adapt to the rapid technological and legal developments in the patent system. For these reasons it should be recognized that district courts must determine whether past practice fits the circumstances of the cases before them. With these observations, I join the opinion of the Court.

NOTES ON CONFUSION IN THE SUPREME COURT

1. The "traditional" test? The majority opinion has been the source of substantial mischief. Certainly the grant of a permanent injunction was never automatic on a showing of liability. But there was no "traditional" four-part test. "Remedies specialists had never heard of the four-point test." Doug Rendleman, *The Trial Judge's Equitable Discretion Following eBay v. MercExchange*, 27 Rev. Litig. 63, 76 n.71 (2007). And this test does not even include proof of ripeness or propensity, though no one doubts this is also necessary to obtain a permanent injunction. See section 4.A.1.

2. Authority? The Court cites two cases for its four-part test, *Romero-Barcelo* and *Amoco. Amoco* was a preliminary injunction case, not a permanent injunction case. Preliminary injunctions are issued before a final decision on the merits, and as we shall see in section 5.B, that is an important distinction that changes the practical content of all the rules for choosing remedies. In *Romero-Barcelo*, there had been a full trial, but that injunction would have lasted only until the completion of a permit proceeding before an administrative agency. The injunction thus had important features of both permanent and preliminary injunctions, and the Supreme Court's opinion in *Romero-Barcelo* reads as though the injunction were only preliminary. In preliminary injunction cases, there is indeed a traditional four-part test, although neither *Romero-Barcelo* nor *Amoco* actually recites any of its variations.

3. Creating four parts. In the genuinely traditional four-part test for preliminary injunctions, one element is probability of success on the merits. *Probability* of success would make no sense as applied to permanent injunctions, which are issued after success on the merits has been established. It might have been sensible to substitute *actual* success for probable success, as the Court suggested in *Amoco*, 480 U.S. at 546 n.12, and again in Winter v. Natural Resources Defense Council, Inc., 555 U.S. 7, 32 (2008), reprinted in section 5.B.1. But in *eBay*, the Court got back to four parts by separating irreparable injury from no adequate remedy.

Irreparable injury is a traditional prerequisite to injunctive relief, although as we have seen, irreparable injury is easy to show at the stage of permanent injunctions. The Court adds no adequate remedy at law as a second element of its test, putting irreparable injury in the past tense and adequate remedy at law in the present tense, perhaps to create some difference between them. To say that plaintiff must show that he "*has suffered* an irreparable injury" is inconsistent with all the cases on injunctions against *threatened* irreparable injury. That really would be "a major departure from the long tradition of equity practice [that] should not be lightly implied" from an unexplained choice of verb tense.

Undue hardship and effects on the public interest can both be reasons to withhold an injunction, but each is unusual. Certainly it makes no sense to require plaintiff to "demonstrate" all four elements of this test, implying that plaintiff must raise the issues of undue hardship and public interest and negate them in every case. Undue hardship has been a defense, with the burden on the guilty defendant to show sufficient hardship to justify excusing him from complying with the law or undoing the consequences of his past violation.

The Court appears to have mostly taken its four-part test from the district court, which took it from one earlier district court opinion; putting irreparable injury in the past tense appears to have been an innovation in the Supreme Court. Because the opinion gives no hint how any of the four parts of the test apply to the facts of the case, its abstract pronouncement has no real content. The case was litigated by an all-star cast of Supreme Court lawyers, but none of them consulted a remedies specialist.

4. Inadvertently changing the law in the direction of Justice Thomas's values? There are many ways Supreme Court justices can move the law incrementally, such as by signaling a future overruling or inviting litigants to ask for one. These methods are catalogued in Richard L. Hasen, *Anticipatory Overrulings, Invitations, Time Bombs, and Inadvertence: How Supreme Court Justices Move the Law*, 61 Emory L.J. 779 (2012). Hasen sees *eBay* as a case of inadvertence. "Inadvertence occurs when the Court changes the law without consciously attempting to do so, through attempts to restate existing law in line with the writing Justice's values." *Id.* at 792.

Before *eBay*, the common understanding was that it was up to a defendant to raise the question of the public interest as a kind of affirmative defense if the defendant believed the injunction sought by the plaintiff did not serve the public interest. Under the new test, however, the plaintiff must demonstrate that the public interest "would not be disserved" by a permanent injunction. As Professor Laycock [asked in an earlier edition of this casebook,]: "Might this mean that benefits to the public interest cannot count in favor of issuing the injunction, but that harm to the public interest is an absolute reason not to issue it? Did Justice Thomas choose that phrasing deliberately in *eBay*, or might it be inadvertent?" Whatever Justice Thomas intended, he has certainly written or signed onto a number of opinions in recent years that make it harder for plaintiffs to obtain an injunction and easier for defendants to seek modifications of injunctions that ease the burden on defendants. His inadvertence appears to line up with his values.

Id. at 794.

5. The new traditional test. There was no such test before, but there is now. The Supreme Court announcing a rule of law can make it so. By early May 2018, *eBay* had been cited in more than 3,000 federal cases and over 14,000 times overall. Before *eBay*, courts presumed irreparable injury in intellectual property cases on the ground that damages in such cases are notoriously difficult to measure. Now courts are split on whether any such presumption is permissible. Some of these cases are collected in John M. Golden, *The Supreme Court as "Prime Percolator": A Prescription for Appellate Review of Questions in Patent Law*, 56 UCLA L. Rev. 657, 697 n.242 (2009).

In the patent cases, a distinction has emerged between suits by plaintiffs who compete in the market with their defendant and those who do not; the former usually get injunctions, and the latter usually do not. Some of the cases are collected in Benjamin Petersen, Note, *Injunctive Relief in the Post-eBay World*, 23 Berkeley Tech. L.J. 193 (2008). When plaintiff and defendant compete, measuring damages requires an estimate of plaintiff's lost profits, which can depend on how much the infringement changed each side's market share and pricing. When they do not compete, damages can be measured by estimating a reasonable royalty for defendant's use of plaintiff's patent. It is not unreasonable to say that lost profits are even harder to measure than a reasonable royalty, and thus that the damage remedy is even less adequate in the cases with competition than in the cases without. But the reasonable royalty may not be easy to measure either, and neither measure allows plaintiff to replace her lost right to exclude.

Some courts are now treating *eBay* as requiring proof of all four elements as a prerequisite to injunctive relief, as opposed to looking at the four factors as a guide to equitable discretion and the balancing of costs and benefits. Professor Lemley believes this treatment is causing particular problems for trademark cases, where it is often difficult to prove either damages or future injury, raising the risk that plaintiffs who can prove liability may get no remedy at all. Mark A. Lemley, *Did eBay Irreparably Injure Trademark Law*, 92 Notre Dame L. Rev. 1795, 1796 (2017).

6. The Federal Circuit. The Federal Circuit responded to *eBay* in Robert Bosch LLC v. Pylon Manufacturing Corp., 659 F.3d 1142 (Fed. Cir. 2011). The court held that *eBay* abolishes any presumption of irreparable injury in patent cases, but that the nature of the patent holder's property right remains relevant. "While the patentee's right to exclude alone cannot justify an injunction, it should not be ignored either." *Id.* at 1149. The court treated loss of market share and pricing power as irreparable injury; such damages would be difficult to prove and measure, although the court did not say that. The court also doubted defendant's ability to pay a damage judgment. It reversed the district court's refusal to enter an injunction and ordered an injunction on remand. Judge Bryson would have remanded for further consideration.

The court returned to the issue in Nichia Corp. v. Everlight Americas, Inc., 855 F.3d 1328 (Fed. Cir. 2017). Nichia both produced products based on its patent and licensed the patent to others, but it had not given a license to Everlight. The court affirmed a finding of no irreparable injury, based on two things. First, the willingness to license the invention cut against a finding of irreparable injury but could not be dispositive. Second, plaintiff had failed to prove damages. The ambiguous opinion can be read as saying that plaintiff wasn't injured at all, so there was no issue of whether any injury was irreparable. But plaintiff offered lots of evidence on damages, which the trial judge found insufficient to carry the burden of proof. This looks more like a case in which damages weren't proved than a case in which the court could say with any confidence that there simply were no damages. Damages that are hard to prove and measure should be a reason for granting an injunction, not for withholding it. Compare Continental Airlines v. Intra Brokers in section 5.A.1.a.

Professors Holte and Seaman, examining nearly 200 patent cases in the first decade after *eBay*, found that the Federal Circuit remained much more willing overall to grant injunctions in patent cases than were district courts. "Specifically, the Federal Circuit affirmed the district court when it granted a permanent injunction nearly ninety percent of the time, but it affirmed only slightly over half the time when the district court denied an injunction." Ryan T. Holte & Christopher B. Seaman, *Patent Injunctions on Appeal: An Empirical Study of the Federal Circuit's Application of eBay*, 92 Wash. L. Rev. 145, 149 (2017).

7. A broader assessment. For a more complete analysis of *eBay*'s impact, see Mark P. Gergen, John M. Golden, & Henry E. Smith, *The Supreme Court's Accidental Revolution? The Test for Permanent Injunctions*, 112 Colum. L. Rev. 203 (2012). They describe *eBay* as having "cataclysmic effect" in the lower federal courts. *Id.* at 205. Federal courts "have now repeatedly declared the *eBay* test to have swept aside long-settled presumptions about when injunctions should issue." *Id.*

Our view is that these presumptions were generally rebuttable, but they simplified litigation and embodied the practical meaning, derived from long experience, of such concepts as irreparable injury and balance of hardships. The reasons that gave rise to the presumptions could produce the same results in individual cases, but to some judges that may seem like recreating the presumptions. The Supreme Court seems to have thought it was changing very little by invoking what it thought were "the traditional principles of equity." State courts have mostly ignored *eBay*, with a handful of exceptions.

8. Undue hardship in intellectual property. The only hint of what should have been the real issue in *eBay* comes in the penultimate paragraph of Justice Kennedy's concurring opinion. Plaintiff claimed patents on some forms of the idea of being an intermediary between buyers and sellers on the internet, although it had never developed a successful business based on those patents. After eBay's commercial success, plaintiff claimed that its patents covered important parts of eBay's operation. More generally, high-tech industries claim to have been plagued by "patent trolls" who let dormant patents lie fallow until they can be raised to assert a claim to essential parts of a substantial business developed by someone else. Patent lawyers debate how big a problem this really is, but *eBay* seemed to fit the pattern. And while *eBay* was pending in the Supreme Court, there was widespread publicity about an injunction that would shut down BlackBerry, the then-dominant predecessor to smart phones. Many of the briefs in *eBay* urged the Court to do something about this problem, but none put it in terms of the undue hardship defense.

An injunction that shut down BlackBerry or eBay would give enormous bargaining leverage to the plaintiff. These cases easily fit the pattern of classic undue hardship cases; defendant has invested much money and effort and now must pay ransom or abandon large parts of his investment. It should not matter whether that investment was in a building or a business or a technology. If defendant was not reckless with regard to plaintiff's patent rights, the undue hardship defense readily applies.

Many of the plaintiffs in cases where defendants have plausible claims of undue hardship will be plaintiffs who were not using their invention. So the emerging distinction in the district courts may address the problem, but the fit between the problem and the solution is rather poor. Courts are reaching this result in terms of irreparable injury instead of undue hardship, and it cannot be that every case without direct competition between plaintiff and defendant involves a plausible undue hardship defense. Some defendants were willful infringers; some could avoid hardship by designing around the patent. If defendant has alternatives to using plaintiff's patent, the parties can negotiate a reasonable royalty far more accurately than the court can approximate one. But if plaintiff is holding a right to shut down defendant's business, bargaining may degenerate into extortion, and if plaintiff has no right to enjoin infringement, defendant can simply ignore plaintiff's demands. Either way, a royalty set by the court may be the only way to break the deadlock.

A copyright example that explains the result in terms of undue hardship is Christopher Phelps & Associates v. Galloway, 492 F.3d 532, 544-546 (4th Cir. 2007), where the court refused to permanently enjoin sale or lease of a home built from copyrighted plans. The court found irreparable injury and no adequate remedy at law, and it awarded damages to the architects, but it refused to permanently tie up a house that had cost more than half a million dollars.

9. The outcome in *eBay*. One might assume that eBay didn't make a more explicit undue hardship argument because its lawyers didn't know the doctrine. But, quite possibly, they did know the doctrine and simply couldn't fit their client into it. The jury had found that eBay was a willful infringer, which would make it ineligible for an undue hardship defense, and eBay had claimed in the district court that it could easily design around the patent, which if true would mean that it faced no real hardship. 275 F. Supp. 2d 695, 701-702 (E.D. Va. 2003). On remand, the district court denied an injunction and awarded $30 million in damages. Mylene Mangalindan, *EBay Is Ordered to Pay $30 Million in Patent Rift*, Wall St. J. (Dec. 13, 2007). The case then settled pending appeals. *EBay Settles Patent Dispute Over "Buy It Now" Feature*, N.Y. Times (Feb. 29, 2008).

10. Fixing (or replacing) the damage remedy. Awarding lump-sum damages for all future infringement is especially unreliable. Plaintiff may lose many sales or a few; the infringement may continue for years or be quickly displaced by new technology. So instead of damages, some courts have issued injunctions ordering infringers to pay a per-unit royalty over time. A leading case is Paice LLC v. Toyota Motor Corp., 504 F.3d 1293, 1313-1316 (Fed. Cir. 2007). An ongoing royalty is an equitable remedy and not a measure of damages; *Paice* addressed the issue explicitly when the court held that there is no right to jury trial on the amount of the royalty. So this is not a decision that the royalty is an adequate remedy at law; rather, the ongoing royalty is a more appropriate equitable remedy than the injunction.

11. *Monsanto*. The Court reaffirmed "[t]he traditional four-factor test" from *eBay*, in an opinion joined by seven Justices, in Monsanto Co. v. Geertson Seed Farms, 561 U.S. 139, 157 (2010). Even more clearly than in *eBay*, the Court was troubled by specific things about this injunction; the majority thought the injunction was overbroad, premature, and insufficiently deferential to the agency, and none of these problems cast much light on the meaning of the four-part "test." And once again, the Court appeared oblivious to any difference between permanent and preliminary injunctions.

a. The facts. Monsanto manufactures Roundup, a widely-used herbicide. The company has long worked to develop Roundup-resistant crops, so that farmers can spray the crop and kill only the weeds. This case arose when Monsanto received approval from the Department of Agriculture to sell genetically modified Roundup-resistant alfalfa. Alfalfa is a major forage crop, principally harvested as hay for feeding cattle.

Plaintiffs included farmers who grow unmodified alfalfa for seed to sell to organic farmers and to farmers in countries where genetically modified crops are prohibited. The district court found that the Roundup-resistant gene could easily be transmitted to unmodified alfalfa, because alfalfa is pollinated by bees with a range of up to ten miles. This genetic contamination could destroy the business of exporting alfalfa seed or selling seed to organic farmers. And the agency had not evaluated the risk that Roundup-resistant crops would encourage overuse and accelerate the evolution of Roundup-resistant weeds that would plague all farmers.

The district court enjoined any sale, planting, or harvesting of Roundup-resistant alfalfa until the agency completed an environmental impact statement. The Supreme Court believed that this injunction went too far, erroneously precluding the agency from considering any partial deregulation in the interim, however limited and however harmless to plaintiffs. Suppose, in the Court's example, that the agency authorized the planting of Roundup-resistant alfalfa only in isolated areas far removed from any other alfalfa farm. Plaintiffs could not show a threat of irreparable injury from such a partial deregulation, because they could not show any threat of harm at all.

b. Irreparable injury. With respect to the four-part test, the Court did *not* say that environmental harm could sometimes be adequately compensated in damages or that it might not be irreparable injury. Rather, it said that the injunction forbade potential agency action that might cause no harm to plaintiffs at all. And it said that if the agency partially deregulated Roundup-resistant alfalfa in a way that threatened irreparable harm to plaintiffs, they could file a new lawsuit and seek a preliminary injunction to prevent implementation of the new agency action.

c. Permanent and preliminary injunctions again. *Monsanto* was a final judgment granting an injunction intended to last only until the agency completed its environmental impact statement. No preliminary injunction had been issued in the district court, and the litigation took two years before the permanent injunction was issued. So the permanent injunction features dominated, and the Court treated the injunction as permanent throughout its opinion. But it cited permanent and preliminary injunction cases without distinction.

12. Nothing more in the Supreme Court. In sharp contrast to its impact in the lower courts, *eBay* appears to have made little difference in the Supreme Court—which of course is consistent with the Court's view that *eBay* didn't change anything. The Court has cited *eBay* only 4 times in 12 years, and 3 of those citations were on patent issues having nothing to do with the criteria for an injunction. (There were also citations in two dissents and one concurrence.) *Monsanto* treats *eBay* as the law, but *Monsanto* clearly would have come out the same way without *eBay*; the majority had multiple reasons for reversing the injunction. The phrases "irreparable injury" and "adequate remedy at law" have appeared a combined 10 times in the 12 years since *eBay*, and 6 of those were in single-justice opinions on motions for stays of lower court orders pending further appeal. Speaking more impressionistically now, the Court affirms injunctions it approves of and *eBay* is no obstacle. It rejects injunctions it disapproves of, and only in *Monsanto* did it find it helpful to make *eBay* part of the explanation. Neither the Court nor the parties is routinely marching through the four *eBay* factors in injunction cases.

13. More supportive views. Professor Janutis reads *eBay* with great charity and finds little that is new or surprising. Courts have always had discretion to refuse injunctive relief to avoid undue hardship, and she sees little more than that going on. Rachel M. Janutis, *The Supreme Court's Unremarkable Decision in eBay Inc. v. Mercexchange, L.L.C.*, 14 Lewis & Clark L. Rev. 597 (2010). If the Court had simply said that, scholarly reaction would have been much different.

Professor Bray reviews *eBay, Monsanto,* and nine other cases, most of which appear in this chapter, and finds a strong recommitment to the separation of legal and equitable remedies. Samuel L. Bray, *The Supreme Court and the New Equity,* 68 Vand. L. Rev. 997 (2015). He notes that equitable remedies can be exceptional, in the sense of requiring some special justification, without being rare or infrequent, in the sense that that special justification is hard to show. And he thinks that something like this captures the Court's view of the matter. He offers a sympathetic description of what the Court has done rather than a sustained argument for why the Court was right to do it, but he seems to broadly approve, and to excuse acknowledged mistakes at the detail level. He concludes:

> One might look at the spectrum of the opinion writers in these cases and draw the conclusion that the tradition of equity must be hale and hearty. On the other hand, the very need to invoke a tradition can be a sign that it is losing its force. No one knows for sure which one is true here. For now, though, the Chancellor is back in the saddle, and his foot is back in the stirrup.

It seems odd to think the Chancellor is empowered by opinions that emphasize the separateness of equity and restrictions on equitable relief. One might think instead that equity is empowered when the restrictions are abandoned and equitable and legal relief are equally available.

B. PRELIMINARY OR PERMANENT RELIEF

1. The Substantive Standards for Preliminary Relief

WINTER v. NATURAL RESOURCES DEFENSE COUNCIL, INC.
555 U.S. 7 (2008)

[This case had complex facts and a complex procedural history. Active sonar, which bounces sound waves off objects in the water, is essential to the Navy's ability to detect enemy submarines. Training in the use of this sonar is therefore also essential. But active sonar sometimes injures protected marine mammals. The extent and significance of this injury was hotly disputed. The lower courts eventually entered a preliminary injunction that imposed conditions on the Navy's use of active sonar in training exercises off southern California. The impact of these conditions on the Navy's training exercises was also hotly disputed.

The President and the Secretary of Defense exempted the Navy from some environmental statutes, as they had authority to do. But the National Environmental Policy Act (NEPA), 42 U.S.C. §§4321 *et seq.* (2006), required the Navy to prepare an environmental impact statement (EIS), carefully assessing the environmental risks and any potential mitigation measures, before deciding whether to continue with the training exercises (or any other proposed action). The Navy's EIS would not be completed until the end of the training exercises. The Justices' lengthy and conflicting analyses of harm to marine mammals, harm to the Navy, and whether anyone could exempt the Navy from NEPA are omitted.]

Chief Justice ROBERTS delivered the opinion of the Court. . . .

III

A

A plaintiff seeking a preliminary injunction must establish that he is likely to succeed on the merits, that he is likely to suffer irreparable harm in the absence of preliminary relief, that the balance of equities tips in his favor, and that an injunction is in the public interest.

The District Court and the Ninth Circuit concluded that plaintiffs have shown a likelihood of success on the merits of their NEPA claim. The Navy strongly disputes this determination. . . .

The District Court and the Ninth Circuit also held that when a plaintiff demonstrates a strong likelihood of prevailing on the merits, a preliminary injunction may be entered based only on a "possibility" of irreparable harm. The lower courts held that plaintiffs had met this standard because the scientific studies, declarations, and other evidence in the record established to "a near certainty" that the Navy's training exercises would cause irreparable harm to the environment.

The Navy challenges these holdings, arguing that plaintiffs must demonstrate a likelihood of irreparable injury—not just a possibility—in order to obtain preliminary relief. On the facts of this case, the Navy contends that plaintiffs' alleged injuries are too speculative to give rise to irreparable injury, given that ever since the Navy's training program began 40 years ago, there has been no documented case of sonar-related injury to marine mammals in [southern California]. And even if . . . sonar does cause a limited number of injuries to individual *marine mammals,* the Navy asserts that plaintiffs have failed to offer evidence of species-level harm that would adversely affect *their* scientific, recreational, and ecological interests. For their part, plaintiffs assert that they would prevail under any formulation of the irreparable injury standard, because the District Court found that they had established a "near certainty" of irreparable harm.

We agree with the Navy that the Ninth Circuit's "possibility" standard is too lenient. Our frequently reiterated standard requires plaintiffs seeking preliminary relief to demonstrate that irreparable injury is *likely* in the absence of an injunction. Issuing a preliminary injunction based only on a possibility of irreparable harm is inconsistent with our characterization of injunctive relief as an extraordinary remedy that may only be awarded upon a clear showing that the plaintiff is entitled to such relief.

It is not clear that articulating the incorrect standard affected the Ninth Circuit's analysis of irreparable harm. Although the court referred to the "possibility" standard, and cited Circuit precedent along the same lines, it affirmed the District Court's conclusion that plaintiffs had established a "'near certainty'" of irreparable harm. At the same time, however, the nature of the District Court's conclusion is itself unclear. The District Court originally found irreparable harm from sonar-training exercises generally. But by the time of the District Court's final decision, the Navy challenged only two of six restrictions imposed by the court. The District Court did not reconsider the likelihood of irreparable harm in light of the four restrictions not challenged by the Navy. . . .

As explained in the next section, even if plaintiffs have shown irreparable injury from the Navy's training exercises, any such injury is outweighed by the public interest and the Navy's interest in effective, realistic training of its sailors. A proper consideration of these factors alone requires denial of the requested injunctive relief. For the same reason, we do not address the lower courts' holding that plaintiffs have also established a likelihood of success on the merits.

B

A preliminary injunction is an extraordinary remedy never awarded as of right. In each case, courts "must balance the competing claims of injury and must consider the effect on each party of the granting or withholding of the requested relief." Amoco Production Co. v. Gambell, 480 U.S. 531, 542 (1987). "In exercising their sound discretion, courts of equity should pay particular regard for the public consequences in employing the extraordinary remedy of injunction." Weinberger v. Romero-Barcelo, 456 U.S. 305, 312 (1982). In this case, the District Court and the Ninth Circuit significantly understated the burden the preliminary injunction would impose on the Navy's ability to conduct realistic training exercises, and the injunction's consequent adverse impact on the public interest in national defense. . . .

These interests must be weighed against the possible harm to the ecological, scientific, and recreational interests that are legitimately before this Court. Plaintiffs have submitted declarations asserting that they take whale watching trips, observe marine mammals underwater, conduct scientific research on marine mammals, and photograph these animals in their natural habitats. Plaintiffs contend that the Navy's use of . . . sonar will injure marine mammals or alter their behavioral patterns, impairing plaintiffs' ability to study and observe the animals.

While we do not question the seriousness of these interests, we conclude that the balance of equities and consideration of the overall public interest in this case tip strongly in favor of the Navy. For the plaintiffs, the most serious possible injury would be harm to an unknown number of the marine mammals that they study and observe. In contrast, forcing the Navy to deploy an inadequately trained antisubmarine force jeopardizes the safety of the fleet. . . .

IV . . .

[W]e do not address the underlying merits of plaintiffs' claims. While we have authority to proceed to such a decision at this point, doing so is not necessary here. . . .

At the same time, what we have said makes clear that it would be an abuse of discretion to enter a permanent injunction, after final decision on the merits, along the same lines as the preliminary injunction. An injunction is a matter of equitable discretion; it does not follow from success on the merits as a matter of course.

The factors examined above—the balance of equities and consideration of the public interest—are pertinent in assessing the propriety of any injunctive relief, preliminary or permanent. See Amoco, 480 U.S. at 546 n.12 ("The standard for a preliminary injunction is essentially the same as for a permanent injunction with the exception that the plaintiff must show a likelihood of success on the merits rather than actual success."). Given that the ultimate legal claim is that the Navy must prepare an EIS, not that it must cease sonar training, there is no basis for enjoining such training in a manner credibly alleged to pose a serious threat to national security. . . . A court concluding that the Navy is required to prepare an EIS has many remedial tools at its disposal, including declaratory relief or an injunction tailored to the preparation of an EIS rather than the Navy's training in the interim. In the meantime, we see no basis for jeopardizing national security, as the present injunction does. . . .

[O]ur analysis of the propriety of preliminary relief is applicable to any permanent injunction as well. . . .

The judgment of the Court of Appeals is reversed, and the preliminary injunction is vacated to the extent it has been challenged by the Navy. . . .

Justice GINSBURG, with whom Justice SOUTER joins, dissenting. . . .

If the Navy had completed the EIS before taking action, as NEPA instructs, the parties and the public could have benefited from the environmental analysis—and the Navy's training could have proceeded without interruption. Instead, the Navy acted first, and thus thwarted the very purpose an EIS is intended to serve. . . . I would hold that, in imposing manageable measures to mitigate harm until completion of the EIS, the District Court conscientiously balanced the equities and did not abuse its discretion. . . .

III

A

Flexibility is a hallmark of equity jurisdiction. "The essence of equity jurisdiction has been the power of the Chancellor to do equity and to mould each decree to the necessities of the particular case. Flexibility rather than rigidity has distinguished it." *Romero-Barcelo*, 456 U.S. at 312. Consistent with equity's character, courts do not insist that litigants uniformly show a particular, predetermined quantum of probable success or injury before awarding equitable relief. Instead, courts have evaluated claims for equitable relief on a "sliding scale," sometimes awarding relief based on a lower likelihood of harm when the likelihood of success is very high. This Court has never rejected that formulation, and I do not believe it does so today.

Equity's flexibility is important in the NEPA context. Because an EIS is the tool for *uncovering* environmental harm, environmental plaintiffs may often rely more heavily on their probability of success than the likelihood of harm. The Court is correct that relief is not warranted "simply to prevent the possibility of some remote future injury." 555 U.S. at 22, quoting 11A Charles Alan Wright & Arthur R. Miller, *Federal Practice & Procedure* §2948.1 at 139 (2d ed., West 1995). "However, the injury need not have been inflicted when application is made or be certain to occur; a strong threat of irreparable injury before trial is an adequate basis." Wright & Miller, §2948.1 at 155-156. . . .

B . . .

In light of the likely, substantial harm to the environment, NRDC's almost inevitable success on the merits of its claim that NEPA required the Navy to prepare an EIS, the history of this litigation, and the public interest, I cannot agree that the mitigation measures the District Court imposed signal an abuse of discretion. Cf. *Amoco*, 480 U.S. at 545 ("Environmental injury, by its nature, can seldom be adequately remedied by money damages and is often permanent or at least of long duration, i.e., irreparable. If such injury is sufficiently likely, therefore, the balance of harms will usually favor the issuance of an injunction to protect the environment.").

For the reasons stated, I would affirm the judgment of the Ninth Circuit.

[Justice BREYER, joined by Justice STEVENS, dissented in part; that opinion is omitted.]

NOTES ON PRELIMINARY RELIEF

1. Settlement. On remand in *Winter*, plaintiffs dismissed the case in exchange for the Navy's promise to do further research on how sonar affects marine mammals. *Navy Settles Lawsuit Over Whales and Its Use of Sonar*, N.Y. Times (Dec. 29, 2008).

2. The problem to be solved. A preliminary injunction is one issued before final judgment, based on a preliminary assessment of facts and law. The central problem that gives rise to the need for preliminary injunctions is the risk that plaintiff will be irreparably injured before the slow processes of litigation can reach a final decision. But the solution to this problem has its own central problem: the court is more likely to err when it acts on partial information after a preliminary hearing, and such an error may lead to an order that causes irreparable injury to defendant. The problem is how to manage these competing risks.

3. The four-part test. The opening paragraph of part III.A of the opinion recites a four-part test—the test the Court tried to transfer to permanent injunctions in *eBay*. Read literally, the Court's initial formulation treats these criteria as four separate requirements that plaintiff "must establish." But the overwhelming weight of authority in the lower courts had been that these four factors are part of a balancing test or a sliding scale. If the likelihood of success is high, plaintiff can get preliminary relief on a lesser showing of irreparable injury and balance of hardships—"a possibility of irreparable injury" in the Ninth Circuit's formulation. If the threatened irreparable injury is especially severe, plaintiff can get a preliminary injunction on a lesser showing of probability of success.

Is Justice Ginsburg right that the Court does not repudiate the sliding-scale interpretation of the four-part test? It is clear that the Court thought the Navy's interest in training dwarfed the plaintiffs' interest in whale watching. That is sufficient reason to deny a preliminary injunction under any version of the four-part test. Is all the rest dictum?

4. A mess in the lower courts. The Fourth Circuit read *Winter* as repudiating its sliding-scale understanding of the four factors. Real Truth About Obama, Inc. v. Federal Election Commission, 575 F.3d 342, 346-347 (4th Cir. 2009). The Ninth Circuit at first did the same. Stormans, Inc. v. Selecky, 586 F.3d 1109, 1126-1127 (9th Cir. 2009). On further reflection, the Ninth Circuit concluded that the sliding scale survives *Winter*, and that a party seeking a preliminary injunction must meet "one of two variants of the same standard." Under the "original" *Winter* standard, a party must show "that he is likely to succeed on the merits, that he is likely to suffer irreparable harm in the absence of preliminary relief, that the balance of equities tips in his favor, and that an injunction is in the public interest." "Under the 'sliding scale' variant of the *Winter* standard, if a plaintiff can only show that there are serious questions going to the merits—a lesser showing than likelihood of success on the merits—then a preliminary injunction may still issue if the balance of hardships tips sharply in the plaintiff's favor, and the other two *Winter* factors are satisfied." *Alliance for the Wild Rockies v. Pena*, 865 F.3d 1211, 1217 (9th Cir. 2017). How are these "variants" different? Are they consistent with the Supreme Court's opinion?

The Seventh Circuit adhered to its sliding-scale approach in a series of cases, and to its rule that plaintiff need only show a "better than negligible" chance of success on the merits (or in some formulations, "at least" a negligible chance of success) to trigger the sliding scale. D.U. v. Rhoades, 825 F.3d 331, 338 (7th Cir. 2016). But it said more recently that before getting to the sliding-scale approach, plaintiff must survive a "threshold phase" in which the plaintiff must show irreparable harm, inadequacy of legal remedies, and that the claim "has some likelihood of success on the merits." Valencia v. City of Springfield, 883 F.3d 949, 965 (7th Cir. 2018).

The D.C. Circuit found *Winter*'s implications for the sliding scale quite unclear, and has repeatedly ducked the issue, most recently in League of Women Voters v. Newby, 838 F.3d 1, 7 (2016).

A survey focused on preliminary injunctions, only in environmental cases, reported several findings. Sarah J. Morath, *A Mild Winter: The Status of Environmental Preliminary Injunctions*, 37 Seattle U.L. Rev. 155 (2013). The Second, Third, Fourth, Seventh, Eighth, Ninth, and Tenth Circuits had considered the effect of *Winter* "either implicitly or explicitly"; only the Fourth had "expressly held that *Winter* invalidates its earlier standard." Second, there had been no significant change in the rate at which preliminary injunctions were granted in environmental cases. The success rate had dropped from about 48 percent to about 46 percent, which is little change at most and may be a random blip. Third, Professor Morath found 41 such cases in the three years after *Winter*, and 33 in the three years before *Winter*, so environmentalists did not maintain their success rate by filing fewer cases. Yet she also reported that environmental lawyers who represent plaintiffs view *Winter* as a serious problem.

5. More recent Supreme Court cases. In Nken v. Holder, 556 U.S. 418 (2009), the Court addressed the standard for stays of deportation orders pending judicial review. The majority opinion invoked the traditional four-part test, relied on Hilton v. Braunskill, 481 U.S. 770 (1987), which was clearly a balancing case, and emphasized the "exercise of judicial discretion" based on "the circumstances of the particular case." 556 U.S. at 433. But it again emphasized that a "possibility" of success or of irreparable injury was not enough, quoting *Winter*. *Id.* at 434-435. The Court clearly thought that stays of removal orders should be more difficult to get than they had been in the past. Justice Kennedy, concurring for himself and Justice Scalia, seemed to more clearly reject a balancing test: "When considering success on the merits and irreparable harm, courts cannot dispense with the required showing of one simply because there is a strong likelihood of the other." *Id.* at 438. But they apparently could not persuade the Chief Justice to put such language in the opinion of the Court.

A unanimous Court quoted *Nken* for "the four traditional stay factors" in Chafin v. Chafin, 568 U.S. 165 (2013). The context was the return of children to foreign countries in international custody disputes. "[A]pplication of the traditional stay factors ensures that each case will receive the individualized treatment necessary for appropriate consideration of the child's best interests." *Id.* at 179.

In Teva Pharmaceuticals USA, Inc. v. Sandoz, Inc., 134 S. Ct. 1621 (2014), Teva asked Chief Justice Roberts, as Circuit Justice, to reinstate a preliminary injunction against patent infringement, issued by the district court and vacated by the Federal Circuit. The Supreme Court had already granted cert on the underlying issue, and the Chief said that Teva had shown a "fair prospect" of success on the merits. But Teva could recover damages for patent infringement, so it had not shown irreparable injury.

Teva said that the Federal Circuit routinely finds irreparable injury when one drug company threatens to bring out a generic version of a drug that infringes a valid patent. But Teva did not effectively explain why such harm is irreparable. The most straightforward explanation would be that such damages are difficult to calculate: How much of plaintiff's loss of market share and how much of its reduced prices were because of the infringement, and how long will those losses persist even if plaintiff eventually gets a permanent injunction for the remaining life of the patent? See *Bosch*, described in note 6 following *eBay*. Sandoz said the damages could be calculated here because the remaining life of the patent was short. This was only a single

Justice, and the conclusory opinion is only half a page, but this appears to be a case where the Court's continued belief in the irreparable injury rule actually made a difference. This would have been a preliminary injunction before Teva had fully proved its case, which should raise the standard of proof and helps explain the result, but Roberts made nothing of that.

6. The travel ban and election cases—balancing again. The Court weighed in again on these questions in one of the most contentious cases it has faced in recent years—suits to enjoin enforcement of President Donald Trump's "travel ban," which barred entry into the United States of most individuals from six predominantly Muslim countries. "Crafting a preliminary injunction is an exercise of discretion and judgment, often dependent as much on the equities of a given case as the substance of the legal issues it presents." The Court cited two pages of *Winter* for this proposition—the page where it announced the four elements to be established, and the page where it talked about balancing the equities and the hardship to the Navy. The Court continued: "The purpose of such interim equitable relief is not to conclusively determine the rights of the parties, but to balance the equities as the litigation moves forward." Trump v. International Refugee Assistance Project, 137 S. Ct. 2080, 2087 (2017). The Court did not march through all four of *Winter*'s elements.

There were two preliminary injunctions, from separate courts, in two consolidated cases, each prohibiting enforcement of the travel ban. The Court was not deciding the appeals from those preliminary injunctions; it was deciding Trump's request to stay those injunctions pending a decision on the merits. The Court left the injunctions in place with respect to persons who had a relationship with a United States person or entity, such as relatives, a job offer, or admission as a student, but it stayed enforcement of the injunctions with respect to all persons without such a relationship.

The Court did not put this in terms of *Winter*'s four elements, but the implicit rationale appeared to be that the travel ban imposed much more hardship on persons with such a relationship than on persons without. The Court later upheld a revised version of the travel ban on the merits in Trump v. Hawaii, 138 S. Ct. 2392, 2423 (2018), discussed briefly in section 4.A.1 in the notes following the *Marshall* case.

The Court weighed in again on preliminary injunction standards in an elections case involving partisan gerrymandering. In Benisek v. Lamone, 138 S. Ct. 1942 (2018), a three-judge federal district court denied a preliminary injunction which would have changed Maryland congressional district boundaries in time for the 2018 elections. One reason the district court gave for denying the injunction was that the Supreme Court was considering another gerrymandering case, from Wisconsin, which could have set the legal standard to apply. The Supreme Court affirmed the denial of a preliminary injunction in *Benisek*.

Even assuming (contrary to the district court) that the plaintiffs were likely to succeed on the merits, the district court acted well within its discretion in denying the preliminary injunction because the balance of the equities and the public interest weighed against it. The reasoning included that: plaintiffs waited years to file their lawsuit without a good excuse, courts should disfavor changes made close to the time of an election under the *Purcell* principle (described in Note 11 in the Notes on Preliminary Procedure), the underlying law was uncertain given the pending Wisconsin case, and "the 'purpose of a preliminary injunction is merely to preserve the relative positions of the parties until a trial on the merits can be held,'" University of Texas v. Camenisch, 451 U.S. 390, 395 (1981)." *Benisek*, 138 S. Ct. at 1945. *Camenisch* reappears in multiple places in section 5.B.2, and we discuss the general issue of delay as a reason to deny relief in section 11.D. *Benisek* is very much about delay but the Court did not mention laches, the main legal doctrine dealing with delay.

7. Where does that leave us? Both *Winter* and *Nken* seem to tighten the standards for granting preliminary injunctions; the tone seems hostile to plaintiffs. Each case arose on facts where there were sound substantive reasons for restricting injunctive relief: national security interests in *Winter*; congressional policy on immigration in *Nken*. As so often happens, a reason to refuse an injunction in a particular case produced opinions that seem to say that injunctions should be difficult to get generally. Each of these cases is quite explicable on its facts, but the effect of these cases may not be so confined.

Winter seems to say that plaintiff must separately prove all four factors of the traditional test, but *Nken, Chafin,* and especially *Trump* speak more of discretion and balancing interests. And in North Carolina v. Covington, 137 S. Ct. 1624 (2017), discussed in Notes on Enforcing New Rules of Law in section 5.C.2, the Court said that district courts must take account of "what is necessary, what is fair, and what is workable," and criticized the lower court because it "failed to meaningfully weigh any equitable considerations." *Id.* at 1625. That certainly sounds like balancing. But none of these opinions squarely addresses the choice between the two approaches.

8. The sliding scale. If plaintiff will die without a preliminary injunction (think stays of capital punishment), but he has only a 49 percent chance of success on the merits, should the preliminary injunction be denied because plaintiff didn't "establish" all four parts of the test?

Or consider a simple case that illustrates multiple points. Defendant moved into a suburban neighborhood with his pet bear. The poor bear was a fifth-generation captive, accustomed to humans, double caged, defanged, and declawed. His presence violated a rule of the homeowners' association, enforceable by a covenant in the deeds. Lakeshore Hills, Inc. v. Adcox, 413 N.E.2d 548 (Ill. App. Ct. 1980). The association's rule meant that plaintiff's probability of success was very nearly certain. The probability of injury appears to have been very low, but presumably there was some small chance of a death or serious injury. Is a mere possibility of devastating irreparable injury insufficient even if the probability of success is very great?

There is little reason to think the Court has laid down rules for such cases until it actually decides one. But its opening statement in *Winter* seems to say that plaintiff must separately prove all four parts of the test. So did *eBay*.

9. The Leubsdorf-Posner test. Professor Leubsdorf has offered the most precise formulation of the balancing standard: "[T]he preliminary injunction standard should aim to minimize the probable irreparable loss of rights caused by errors incident to hasty decision." John Leubsdorf, *The Standard for Preliminary Injunctions*, 91 Harv. L. Rev. 525, 540-541 (1978). He suggested as an analytic framework for implementing this standard that the irreparable injury to each side from an erroneous order be weighted by that side's probability of success on the merits. Leubsdorf's formulation is the law in Massachusetts. Packaging Industries Group, Inc. v. Cheney, 405 N.E.2d 106, 111-112 (Mass. 1980). It has not been expressly adopted elsewhere, but his core idea surely influenced the pre-*Winter* consensus about how to balance the four factors of the traditional test.

Judge Posner reduced Professor Leubsdorf's formulation to an arithmetical formula:

[G]rant the preliminary injunction if but only if

$$P \times H_p > (1 - P) \times H_d$$

or, in other words, only if the harm to the plaintiff if the injunction is denied, multiplied by the probability that the denial would be an error (that the plaintiff, in other words, will win at trial), exceeds the harm to the defendant if the injunction is granted, multiplied by the probability that granting the injunction would be an error. That probability is simply one minus the probability that the plaintiff will win at trial; for if the plaintiff has, say, a 40 percent chance of winning, the defendant must have a 60 percent chance of winning. . . . The left-hand side of the formula is simply the probability of an erroneous denial weighted by the cost of denial to the plaintiff, and the right-hand side simply the probability of an erroneous grant weighted by the cost of grant to the defendant.

This formula . . . is not offered as a new legal standard; it is intended not to force analysis into a quantitative straitjacket but to assist analysis by presenting succinctly the factors that the court must consider in making its decision and by articulating the relationship among the factors. It is actually just a distillation of the familiar four . . . factor test that courts use in deciding whether to grant a preliminary injunction.

American Hospital Supply Corp. v. Hospital Products, Ltd., 780 F.2d 589, 593 (7th Cir. 1986). Judge Posner noted that harms to third parties could be considered as part of the public interest and that "these harms can then be added to H_p or H_d as the case may be." *Id.* at 594.

10. Skipping the math. Minimizing legally unjustified irreparable injury makes sense as a goal, but the effort to reduce this inquiry to arithmetic doesn't work. There are degrees of success; plaintiff may win on some issues and lose on others or be entitled to a narrow injunction but not to a broader one. And consider again the case of the suburban bear. Posner uses the same number for probability of success and probability of harm, but the two probabilities were very different in *Lakeshore*. And there were many possible harms. What was the probability of a death, brain damage, or paralysis? Of a mangled arm? Of all the neighbors having to stay inside one morning until the bear was caught? Of the neighbors being deprived of their right not to worry about the bear? Where in Posner's formula do you put all these different probabilities? And *Lakeshore* is a very simple case.

The problem is not just that the variables cannot be quantified in fact. . . . [T]hese variables cannot be conceptualized even in theory as having discrete values that could be represented by . . . single numbers in an equation. Rather, these variables stand for ranges of possible developments, with the probabilities changing at every point in the range.

Laycock, *The Death of the Irreparable Injury Rule* at 120.

11. Comparing preliminary and permanent injunctions. Courts at the preliminary relief stage routinely find no irreparable injury in injuries they would consider irreparable after a full trial. The phrases are the same — irreparable injury or adequate remedy at law — but the meaning is very different. At the preliminary relief stage, the risk of injury must be sufficiently great and sufficiently irreparable to override the risk of error and the shortcuts with defendant's right to due process. It is not clear whether judges realize they are applying two very different standards, but comparing large numbers of cases makes clear that they are.

Balance of hardships also has a different meaning for preliminary and permanent relief. At the stage of permanent relief, defendant is an adjudicated wrongdoer and plaintiff is his victim. Plaintiff wins unless the hardship to defendant is substantially disproportionate to the benefit, and sometimes even then. At the stage of preliminary relief, no wrongdoer has been finally identified. Relative hardships must be balanced in light of the relative probability of success. Because preliminary injunctions are so much harder to get than permanent injunctions, the vast majority of all cases reciting the irreparable injury rule are preliminary relief cases.

12. The Raiders example. An especially clear example of the difference between preliminary and permanent relief is the antitrust litigation that arose when the Oakland Raiders first tried to move to Los Angeles, and the National Football League refused to approve the move. The Raiders and the Los Angeles Coliseum sued, alleging that the league's restrictions on moving franchises violated the antitrust laws. The court of appeals *reversed* a preliminary injunction ordering the league to permit the move. Los Angeles Memorial Coliseum Commission v. National Football League, 634 F.2d 1197 (9th Cir. 1980). The court found a close question on the merits, no irreparable injury, and at best an even balance of hardships.

After a lengthy trial, the district court entered a permanent injunction ordering the league to permit the move. That injunction was *affirmed*, in an opinion that discusses venue, jury instructions, and the merits of the antitrust claim, but not irreparable injury, adequate remedy, or the appropriateness of an injunction. Los Angeles Memorial Coliseum Commission v. National Football League, 726 F.2d 1381 (9th Cir. 1984). Defendants had little chance of winning on adequate remedy at the permanent injunction stage. They also had no desire to win on that ground: The NFL did not want to keep the Raiders in Oakland if that meant paying permanent damages.

If loss of the Raiders would be irreparable injury to the Coliseum after trial, why wasn't it irreparable before trial? No amount of damages would buy a pro football team for the seasons between the preliminary injunction hearing and the trial. It is not just that lost profits for a few seasons in the past were easier to measure than lost profits for the indefinite future. The court applied a higher standard at the preliminary injunction stage, because the NFL had not yet had a trial and the court didn't know whether the NFL had done anything wrong.

As it turned out, even temporary damages were hard to measure. The trial on damages took nine months. The jury awarded the Raiders $11.55 million and the Coliseum $4.86 million, each amount to be trebled under the Sherman Antitrust Act. The Coliseum's judgment was affirmed; the Raiders' judgment was remanded for trial of an offsetting benefit issue. Los Angeles Memorial Coliseum Commission v. National Football League, 791 F.2d 1356 (9th Cir. 1986). The Raiders eventually settled with the league for $18 million; in 1995, they returned to Oakland. The settlement is described in an article on a different lawsuit by the Raiders. Richard Sandomir, *Raiders Lose Lawsuit Against N.F.L.*, N.Y. Times (May 22, 2001).

13. A state-law example. In Hedlund v. River Bluff Estates, LLC, 908 N.W.2d 766 (S.D. 2018), defendant was diverting water onto plaintiffs' property, and dirt from an embankment defendant had constructed was sliding down the hill and onto plaintiffs' property. Defendant claimed that damages would be an adequate remedy, because plaintiffs could use the money to elevate a private road that ran across their property close to the property line, and this would confine the problem. The court unsurprisingly rejected that argument; defendant would still be trespassing on the portion of plaintiffs' property between the road and the property line. But "no one should be permitted to take the land of another merely because he is willing to pay the market price for it." *Id.* at 772. And defendant might eventually acquire an easement by adverse possession.

But plaintiffs were not entitled to a preliminary injunction. The violation had been ongoing for 11 years before plaintiffs filed suit, and plaintiffs did not claim that anything new was happening or threatened. The court could grant a fully effective remedy after trial, so there was no need for a preliminary injunction. Note that the court permitted the trespass to continue pending trial, a trespass that it had already decided inflicted irreparable injury. And while it did not say so explicitly, it necessarily concluded that the injury from that trespass was not irreparable at the preliminary injunction stage. Its view seemed to be that if plaintiffs could tolerate the violation for as long as they had, there was no hurry and they could tolerate it for a while longer. Another way to think about it is that a plaintiff who waited so long is in no position to demand that the court drop everything and address the issue on a preliminary basis.

14. Affirmative defenses on the merits. Occasional lower court opinions say, with no basis whatever, that consideration of affirmative defenses is irrelevant to the probability of success at the preliminary injunction stage. This claim is refuted by Gonzales v. O Centro Espirita Beneficente Uniao Do Vegetal, 546 U.S. 418 (2006), affirming a preliminary injunction under the Religious Freedom Restoration Act, 42 U.S.C. §§2000bb *et seq.* Plaintiffs showed a substantial burden on their religion; the burden of proof then shifted to the government to show that that burden was necessary to serve a compelling government interest. On the compelling interest issue, the trial court found the evidence "in equipoise." 546 U.S. at 426. It followed that the government had not carried its burden on the affirmative defense of compelling interest, and thus, that based on the evidence at the preliminary injunction hearing, plaintiffs would probably succeed on the merits. As the court summarized, "the burdens at the preliminary injunction stage track the burdens at trial." *Id.* at 429.

NOTES ON PRESERVING THE STATUS QUO

1. The status quo test. Courts commonly say that preliminary injunctions are designed to preserve the status quo. They often elaborate that they mean "the last peaceable uncontested" status quo. Clint Independent School District v. Marquez, 487 S.W.3d 538, 555 (Tex. 2016). They almost ever explain how this standard relates to the four-part test. As a descriptive matter, a peaceable and uncontested status quo is unlikely to be inflicting irreparable injury on anybody. But whenever the status quo and the four-part test point in different directions, taking the status quo test seriously leads the court to increase the risk of legally unjustified irreparable injury.

2. Manipulating or overriding the status quo. The world rarely stands still, so the status quo test is highly manipulable. What is the status quo when the parties are engaged in continuous activity? Consider Rees v. Panhandle Eastern Pipe Line Co., 377 N.E.2d 640 (Ind. Ct. App. 1978), in which the pipeline company was clearing trees and brush to widen its right-of-way on Rees's land, and Rees was objecting. The trial court thought the status quo was the company at work. The appellate court thought the status quo was that some of the trees were still standing. Both courts enjoined Rees from interfering; the appellate court thought that safety concerns justified a preliminary injunction that changed the status quo. *Id.* at 649-650. Similarly in the case of the suburban bear, the court acknowledged that it was changing the status quo because it thought the bear was dangerous. Lakeshore Hills, Inc. v. Adcox, 413 N.E.2d 548, 550 (Ill. App. Ct. 1980).

Another example is In re Providence Journal Co., 820 F.2d 1342, 1351-1352 (1st Cir. 1986). The court thought that enjoining publication of private information did not preserve the status quo of privacy, but rather disrupted the status quo of continuous publication. How convincing is that? There are more examples in notes 4 and 5.

3. Surveying the cases. Professor Lee (now Justice Lee of the Utah Supreme Court) carefully collected the federal cases and concluded that the focus on the status quo (far more intense in some circuits than in others) was doing significant harm. The status quo is in fact a lousy guide to minimizing the risk of erroneous irreparable injury, and because the concept is so manipulable, it is expensive to litigate. He found courts and litigants wasting much energy arguing over how to characterize the status quo instead of dealing with the real issues of likely success, irreparable injury, and balance of hardship. Thomas R. Lee, *Preliminary Injunctions and the Status Quo*, 58 Wash. & Lee L. Rev. 109 (2001). Judge Stephen Reinhardt, in one of the final opinions before his death, noted the scholarly and judicial criticism of the Ninth Circuit's divergent treatment of mandatory and prohibitory injunctions—it is mostly mandatory injunctions that change the status quo—but held the court bound by circuit precedent to apply "the somewhat artificial legal construct that cause so many to question the inquiry we now undertake." Hernandez v. Sessions, 872 F.3d 976, 998 (9th Cir. 2017).

4. Defending the status quo test. Consider O Centro Espirita Beneficente Uniao Do Vegetal v. Ashcroft, 389 F.3d 973 (10th Cir. 2004) (en banc), *aff'd on other grounds*, Gonzales v. O Centro Espirita Beneficente Uniao Do Vegetal, 546 U.S. 418 (2006). Seven judges reaffirmed a Tenth Circuit rule that preliminary injunctions changing the status quo are "disfavored." 389 F.3d at 977. Plaintiff "must make a strong showing both with regard to the likelihood of success on the merits and with regard to the balance of harms." *Id.* at 976. Judge Murphy, writing for all seven judges, insisted that "the underlying purpose of the preliminary injunction is to 'preserve the relative positions of the parties until a trial on the merits can be held.'" *Id.* at 977, quoting University of Texas v. Camenisch, 451 U.S. 390, 395 (1981).

Judge McConnell (now once again Professor McConnell), in a longer opinion for four of the seven, argued that preserving the status quo cannot be reduced to minimizing unjustified irreparable injury. He argued that emphasis on the status quo followed from appropriate caution in the face of uncertainty and simply from people's attachment to the status quo.

> Notwithstanding the tendency of those trained in economics to view opportunity costs as equivalent to actual expenditures, modern social science research has confirmed the reality of "loss aversion" (the tendency to attach greater value to losses than to foregone gains of equal amount), and the closely related "endowment effect" (the tendency to value already possessed goods more than prospective acquisitions). . . . Unless the district court self-consciously takes the nature of the injunction into account by applying a heightened standard, the four factors likely will lead to an overconfident approach to preliminary relief, increasing the cost and disruption from improvidently granted preliminary injunctions.

Id. at 1016-1018.

McConnell argued that injunctions reversing recent changes to the status quo were not an exception, but simply injunctions to restore the true status quo. And he accepted decisions in every circuit holding that "there are cases in which preservation of the status quo may so clearly inflict irreparable harm on the movant, with so little probability of being upheld on the merits, that a preliminary injunction may be appropriate even though it requires a departure from the status quo." *Id.* at 1013.

Judge Seymour, for six judges dissenting on the status quo issue, argued that "the very purpose of preserving the status quo by the grant of a preliminary injunction is to prevent irreparable harm pending a trial on the merits." *Id.* at 1001.

The judges also disagreed over the status quo. Plaintiff in *O Centro* was a church that uses in its worship services an herbal tea that contains a mild hallucinogenic agent. The church had been using the tea for years; for the church, the status quo was undisturbed worship. For the government, the status quo was enforcement of the drug laws. These two status quos had coexisted because the government didn't know what the church was doing. Judge Seymour found both status quos plausible and did not try to choose between them; she turned instead to the irreparable harms that would be inflicted on each side. The majority thought the last peaceable, uncontested status quo could not be a condition that existed only in secret.

COYNE-DELANY CO. v. CAPITAL DEVELOPMENT BOARD
717 F.2d 385 (7th Cir. 1983)

[The state's Capital Development Board let a contract to replace the plumbing fixtures in a state prison. Coyne-Delany got the subcontract for toilet-flush valves in the first phase of the project. Coyne-Delany's valves malfunctioned, were replaced, and again malfunctioned. When the Board announced bidding specifications for the second phase of the project, it required all bidders to use Coyne-Delany's main competitor.]

Before ESCHBACH and POSNER, Circuit Judges, and DUMBAULD, Senior District Judge. POSNER, Circuit Judge. . . .

Bids were received, but on May 7, 1979, two days before they were to be opened, Coyne-Delany sued the Board under 42 U.S.C. §1983, and on May 8 it obtained a temporary restraining order against the Board's opening the bids. The state asked that Coyne-Delany be ordered to post a $50,000 bond, pointing out that the temporary restraining order was preventing it from proceeding with the entire project and that indefinite delay could be extremely costly. But Judge Perry, the emergency motions judge, required a bond of only $5,000, in the belief that the temporary restraining order would be in effect for only a week until Judge Bua could hear the motion for a preliminary injunction. However, at the preliminary-injunction hearing Judge Bua issued the injunction but refused to increase the bond. . . .

[T]he parties stipulated that the "bond was continued for the preliminary injunction.". . .

[Coyne-Delany's premise] was that under . . . Polyvend, Inc. v. Puckorius, 377 N.E.2d 1160 (Ill. App. Ct. 1978), Coyne-Delany . . . had a property right of which it was deprived without due process of law. . . . Judge Bua said that Coyne-Delany was likely to prevail on the merits. . . . [But] *Polyvend* [was] reversed by the Illinois Supreme Court, 395 N.E.2d 1376 (Ill. 1979), after Judge Bua had granted the preliminary injunction. . . . [We therefore] held that under Illinois law a bidder . . . has no property right in being allowed to bid on a public contract and that Coyne-Delany therefore had no claim. . . . 616 F.2d 341, 343 (7th Cir. 1980).

Our decision came down on February 22, 1980, and . . . the Board at last opened the bids. . . . [The low bid was $214,000, but it was conditioned on a deadline that had expired. The Board rebid the project, and this time the low bid was $270,000.]

The Board then joined Hanover Insurance Co., the surety on the injunction bond, as an additional defendant in Coyne-Delany's civil rights suit, pursuant to Federal Rule 65.1, and moved the district court to award the Board damages of $56,000 for the wrongfully issued preliminary injunction. . . . Judge Bua refused to award . . . damages. His opinion states, ". . . It would be unreasonable to require a party to anticipate a change in the law. . . .". . .

Although the district court has unquestioned power in an appropriate case . . . not to award damages on an injunction bond even though the grant of the injunction was reversed, the district court's opinion suggests that the court may have believed it had to deny . . . damages because the lawsuit had not been brought in bad faith and was not frivolous. This would be the proper standard if the question were whether to award a prevailing defendant his attorney's fees. . . .

Rule 65(c) [requires a plaintiff who gets a preliminary injunction to post a bond] "for the payment of such costs and damages as may be incurred or suffered by any party who is found to have been wrongfully enjoined or restrained." The court is not told in so many words to order the applicant to pay the wrongfully enjoined party's damages. But it is told to require a bond or equivalent security in order to ensure that the plaintiff will be able to pay all or at least some of the damages that the defendant incurs from the preliminary injunction if it turns out to have been wrongfully issued. The draftsmen must have intended that when such damages were incurred the plaintiff or his surety . . . would normally be required to pay the damages, at least up to the limit of the bond.

Yet some courts treat the district court's discretion to award or deny damages under an injunction bond as completely open-ended unless the plaintiff acted in bad faith in seeking the preliminary injunction. . . .

[Those cases] dismiss Rule 65(c)'s requirement of a bond or other security by pointing out that the district court can require a bond of nominal amount in appropriate cases, for example if the plaintiff is indigent. But it is one thing to say that the requirement of a bond can in effect be waived when there is a good reason for doing so—a dispensation narrowly construed in this circuit—and another to say that where a substantial bond is clearly required by the equities of the case the district court nevertheless has carte blanche [unlimited power; literally, blank card] to excuse the plaintiff from paying any damages on the bond.

Most cases hold . . . that a prevailing defendant is entitled to damages on the injunction bond unless there is a good reason for not requiring the plaintiff to pay in the particular case. We agree with the majority approach. Not only is it implied by the text of Rule 65(c) but it makes the law more predictable and discourages the seeking of preliminary injunctions on flimsy (though not necessarily frivolous) grounds.

When rules prescribe a course of action as the norm but allow the district court to deviate from it, the court's discretion is more limited than it would be if the rules were nondirective. Rule . . . 65(c) establish[es] what Judge Friendly recently called "a principle of preference" guiding the exercise of the district judge's discretion. Henry J. Friendly, *Indiscretion About Discretion*, 31 Emory L.J. 747, 768 (1982). The judge must have a good reason for departing from such a principle in a particular case. It is not a sufficient reason for denying costs or damages on an injunction bond that the suit had as in this case been brought in good faith. That would be sufficient only if the presumption were against rather than in favor of awarding . . . damages on the bond. . . . The award of damages on the bond is not punitive but compensatory.

A good reason for not awarding such damages would be that the defendant had failed to mitigate damages. . . . A good reason not for denying but for awarding damages in this case . . . was that the bond covered only a small fraction of the defendant's damages. . . . Nor could $5,000 be regarded as excessive because the plaintiff was a poor person. The plaintiff is . . . a substantial corporation. . . .

The district court did allude to one factor, besides mere absence of bad faith, that supported its ruling—the change in the applicable law after the preliminary injunction was issued. . . . [I]ntermediate state appellate court . . . decisions are reversed with some frequency. We do not believe that a change in the law is always a good ground for denying costs and injunction damages to a prevailing party, but it is a legitimate consideration, perhaps especially where the prevailing party is a state agency that benefitted from a change in the law of its state. . . . In any event, a remand is necessary to allow Judge Bua to consider and weigh all the relevant factors identified in this opinion—bearing in mind the principle of preference that we have indicated should guide his equitable determination.

It remains to consider whether on remand the Board should be allowed to seek injunction damages above the limit of the bond. The surety cannot be required to pay more than the face amount of the bond, but it is a separate question whether the plaintiff can be. However, the Ninth Circuit has held in a scholarly opinion that the bond is the limit of the damages the defendant can obtain for a wrongful injunction, even from the plaintiff, provided the plaintiff was acting in good faith, which is not questioned here. Buddy Systems, Inc. v. Exer-Genie, Inc., 545 F.2d 1164, 1167-1168 (9th Cir. 1976). (Another exception might be where the plaintiff was seeking restitution rather than damages. . . .) The Supreme Court has cited *Buddy Systems* in dictum for the proposition that "a party injured by the issuance of an injunction later determined to be erroneous has no action for damages in the absence of a bond." W.R. Grace & Co. v. Local Union 759, United Rubber Workers, 461 U.S. 757, 770 n.14 (1983). . . . In asking for more [than the amount of the bond,] the Board is necessarily relying not on the bond but on some principle of equity that *Grace* says does not exist. . . .

The preliminary injunction in this case halted work on a major construction project for a year; it could easily have been two or three years, and the expenses imposed on the defendant not $56,000 but $560,000. It might be a very great boon to the legal system of this country to discourage injunction suits by putting plaintiffs at such risk, but we do not see how such an approach can be squared with the general attitude toward litigation implied by the American rule [that each side must bear its own] attorney's fees. . . . [H]aving to post a bond is . . . a deterrent just to plaintiffs. But if the plaintiff's damages are limited to the amount of the bond, at least he knows just what his exposure is when the bond is set by the district court. . . .

[A] defendant dissatisfied with the amount of bond . . . can, on appeal from the preliminary injunction, ask the court of appeals to increase the bond, which the defendant here did not do. . . .

Reversed and remanded.

NOTES ON INJUNCTION BONDS

1. Who bears the risk of error in a preliminary order? Is it plaintiff's fault that the trial court erred? Is it plaintiff's responsibility, because plaintiff asked the court to issue an order without a full trial? In considering that question, do not think only of the intervening change in law in *Coyne-Delany*. In the most common fact pattern, the judge decides at trial that he got the facts wrong at the preliminary injunction hearing. An example is Atomic Oil Co. v. Bardahl Oil Co., 419 F.2d 1097 (10th Cir. 1969). There, Atomic charged Bardahl with infringing its "Savmotor" trademark. The court issued a preliminary injunction forbidding Bardahl to sell its "Savoil" product in any of the 30 states where Atomic did business. At full trial, the court decided that consumers recognized Atomic's trademark in only 3 states, and it denied an injunction as to the other 27. The court of appeals enforced the $50,000 preliminary injunction bond. Should we hold plaintiff responsible for that sort of error more readily than for an intervening change of law? Or should defendant have to bear his own losses, just as he bears his own litigation expenses, as the cost of preserving plaintiff's access to justice?

The conventional wisdom in the federal courts, and in nearly all the states, is that plaintiff is liable, but only up to the amount of the bond. As *Coyne-Delany* suggests, there are many variations on that basic rule. There are several distinct issues.

2. The amount of the bond. The amount of the bond is in the discretion of the trial court, and is necessarily based on a very limited sketch of the potential damages. Not many opinions say anything substantial about the issue. In Axia Netmedia Corp. v. Massachusetts Technology Park Corp., 889 F.3d 1 (1st Cir. 2018), a complex dispute about contracts to provide broadband internet service in rural Massachusetts, the trial court required a $4 million bond. Defendant claimed that was inadequate because it "could plausibly expend more" than that in complying with the order. But the court of appeals said that the district court has discretion to require a bond in an amount "less than the upper bound of what the enjoined party could, in theory, expend." *Id.* at 12. And it reminded plaintiff that the bond need only cover damages up to the time of a final judgment, not all the expense that would ever be incurred if the preliminary injunction became permanent.

3. Can the court waive the bond? Federal Rule of Civil Procedure 65(c) now reads as follows: "The court may issue a preliminary injunction or a temporary restraining order only if the movant gives security in an amount that the court considers proper to pay the costs and damages sustained by any party found to have been wrongfully enjoined or restrained." *Coyne-Delany* quotes an earlier version. *Atomic Oil* says the bond is mandatory. Is it? Should it be?

a. The problem. For many plaintiffs, injunction bonds are unavailable at any price. The bond is a surety agreement, not a liability policy; plaintiff remains primarily liable for any damages imposed. Thus, insurers who write injunction bonds do not care about the risks of litigation, but only about the risk that plaintiff will not be able to pay. They will write bonds only for plaintiffs with healthy financial statements. A truly mandatory bonding rule would make preliminary relief generally unavailable in civil rights and consumer litigation, to workers in employment litigation, and, in general, to nonwealthy plaintiffs.

b. The judicial solution. The federal courts responded by making the bond requirement discretionary. The most common explanation is that the amount of the bond is discretionary, so bond could be required in a nominal amount; if that is so, waiving bond altogether is no different. City of Atlanta v. Metropolitan Atlanta Rapid Transit Authority, 636 F.2d 1084, 1094 (5th Cir. 1981).

c. The legislative history. Are you convinced? Rule 65(c) is taken from §18 of the original Clayton Antitrust Act, 38 Stat. 730, 738 (1914), enacted because Congress believed that courts were abusing TROs and preliminary injunctions against strikes by labor unions. Do you suppose Congress meant to leave the bond to the discretion of the judges it was trying to control? Doesn't the rule mean that the court has discretion only to estimate defendant's likely costs and damages, and that it must require bond in that sum? But would Congress want that rule applied to all litigants today? The courts might have made a better rule than the rule-makers. In some of the states, the rule or statute explicitly makes the bond discretionary.

d. Guiding judicial discretion. Assuming bond is discretionary, what factors should guide the court's discretion? Potential loss to defendant, financial hardship to plaintiff, and the public importance of the right being enforced are commonly cited. Crowley v. Local 82, Furniture & Piano Moving & Packers, 679 F.2d 978, 1000 (1st Cir. 1982), *rev'd on other grounds*, 467 U.S. 526 (1984). Another case notes likelihood of success on the merits and the fear that "requiring security would effectively deny access to judicial review." California ex rel. Van de Kamp v. Tahoe Regional Planning Agency, 766 F.2d 1319, 1325-1326, *modified on other grounds*, 775 F.2d 998 (9th Cir. 1985). In *City of Atlanta*, the court temporarily restrained a fare increase expected to raise $43,000 per day. The court waived bond, in part because the case was "public-interest litigation." Should that matter if plaintiff cannot show financial hardship? Is there any reason to believe the transit authority was in better financial shape than the city? Other plaintiffs in *City of Atlanta* were a union of domestic workers and a class of "paupers." Should we have a rule that encourages the city to withdraw and leave the case to plaintiffs who plainly cannot post bond?

Should preliminary relief be easier to get for plaintiffs who can post bond? Should harm to defendant that can be compensated by a bond drop out of the balancing test? If so, that might encourage financially responsible plaintiffs to stay in a case like *City of Atlanta*.

e. Inadvertent waiver. It is defendant's responsibility to ask for a bond. If the court fails to require a bond, through oversight or an erroneous decision to waive bond, the preliminary injunction is nonetheless binding. The cases are collected in Popular Bank v. Banco Popular, 180 F.R.D. 461 (S.D. Fla. 1998).

4. What triggers liability on the bond? Is there liability any time the permanent injunction is not as broad as the preliminary injunction, or must the preliminary injunction have been erroneous on the record as it then stood?

Rule 65(c) requires a bond to pay the damages of any party "wrongfully enjoined or restrained." Was the Capital Development Board "wrongfully enjoined"? Was Bardahl? Is a preliminary injunction "wrongful" if it is proper on the record compiled at the time of its issuance? If the purpose of the rule is to protect defendants from the risk of error in preliminary decisions on incomplete hearings, aren't the cases right to focus on the ultimate disposition?

University of Texas v. Camenisch, 451 U.S. 390 (1981), ratifies this approach for the federal courts. The university appealed from a preliminary injunction, but the plaintiff had graduated and the Court held that the preliminary injunction appeal was moot. Holding that liability on the preliminary injunction bond could be determined only after a trial on the merits, the Court remanded the case for trial. Liability on the bond could not be equated with whether the preliminary injunction had properly issued: "This reasoning fails . . . because it improperly equates 'likelihood of success' with 'success,' and what is more important, because it ignores the significant procedural differences between preliminary and permanent injunctions." *Id.* at 394. State cases to similar effect are collected in J.A. Preston Corp. v. Fabrication Enterprises, Inc., 502 N.E.2d 197, 203 (N.Y. 1986).

5. Can the court waive enforcement of the bond? Some courts claim discretion not to enforce the bond even if the injunction was wrongfully issued.

a. Cases claiming power to waive enforcement. The leading case for broad discretion is Page Communications Engineers, Inc. v. Froehlke, 475 F.2d 994 (D.C. Cir. 1973). The trial court preliminarily enjoined the Army from awarding a defense contract to plaintiff's competitor. The court ultimately ruled for the Army, but it declined to enforce plaintiff's $100,000 bond. The court of appeals affirmed, saying that plaintiff proceeded in good faith and "raised some solid questions," that "this was not a frivolous lawsuit," that the Army's ambiguous procedure raised "doubts as to the fairness of the procurement," and that the Army had not mentioned its comparative cost study at the preliminary injunction hearing, although the study had been completed at the time and was "significant" to the ultimate decision on the merits. *Id.* at 996.

What does this leave of the bond? If the lawsuit were frivolous and not in good faith, plaintiff would be liable for malicious prosecution quite apart from the bond. How often will plaintiff get a preliminary injunction without raising "some solid questions"? Does the case turn on the Army's failure to produce its strongest evidence? Was that the Army's "fault" or a natural consequence of holding the hearing on short notice?

b. Other cases. *Coyne-Delany* acknowledges very narrow discretion to waive enforcement; *Atomic Oil* appears to say that once the preliminary injunction is narrowed or vacated, enforcement of the bond is mandatory. A more recent Tenth Circuit case refused to enforce the bond where a TRO was proper on the merits but vacated because of a subsequently enacted statute. Kansas ex rel. Stephan v. Adams, 705 F.2d 1267 (10th Cir. 1983). The court cites the *Froehlke* line of cases; it does not cite its own decision in *Atomic Oil.*

c. The Supreme Court. Russell v. Farley, 105 U.S. 433 (1882), held that the trial court has broad discretion whether to require a bond and whether to enforce any bond that it required. But *Russell* was decided before any federal statute or rule addressed the question, and the Court has said nothing since.

6. What damages are covered by the bond? There are two main issues here.

a. Causation. The damages must be caused by the wrongful preliminary injunction; it is not enough that they were caused by the litigation. An example with a twist is Medafrica Line, S.A. v. American West African Freight Conference, 654 F. Supp. 155 (S.D.N.Y. 1987), where the court preliminarily enjoined collection of a fine from the plaintiff. By the time the preliminary injunction was vacated, plaintiff had become insolvent. The fine itself was not damage from the preliminary injunction, but inability to collect the fine was. The court enforced the bond against the insurance company.

b. Attorneys' fees. Some jurisdictions disallow all fees; some allow fees for seeking dissolution of the preliminary order. Some of the latter also allow fees for contesting the preliminary order before it was issued, and some allow fees for defending the case on the merits. The federal courts disallow fees, citing Oelrichs v. Spain, 82 U.S. (15 Wall.) 211 (1872). Like Russell v. Farley, that case has been questioned on the ground that it predates the antecedents of Rule 65(c). Dan B. Dobbs, *Should Security Be Required as a Pre-Condition to Provisional Injunctive Relief?*, 52 N.C. L. Rev. 1091, 1134-1136 (1974).

7. Does plaintiff have any liability apart from the bond? Generally no, but there are multiple exceptions. A few states impose such liability by statute. See, e.g., the Illinois Injunction Act, 735 Ill. Comp. Stat. 5/11-110. The Illinois Supreme Court has rejected constitutional attacks on strict liability for damages inflicted by an erroneous preliminary injunction. Buzz Barton & Associates, Inc. v. Giannone, 483 N.E.2d 1271 (Ill. 1985).

In extreme cases, plaintiff may be liable for malicious prosecution or abuse of process. Less rarely, plaintiff may be liable in restitution for benefits conferred by the preliminary order. For example, when a preliminary injunction allows a regulated carrier to collect higher rates than those ultimately approved, the carrier must make restitution of the surcharge, Middlewest Motor Freight Bureau v. United States, 433 F.2d 212 (8th Cir. 1970); or where an erroneous preliminary injunction allows defendant to sell a licensed product in violation of plaintiff's exclusive rights, defendant is liable for its profits when that injunction is reversed. Fleer Corp. v. Topps Chewing Gum, Inc., 539 A.2d 1060 (Del. 1988).

Finally, courts occasionally waive bond for plaintiffs who are plainly able to pay damages. These plaintiffs are held liable as though they had filed bond in an unlimited amount. Monroe Division v. DeBari, 562 F.2d 30 (10th Cir. 1977). Plaintiffs who seek a waiver on this ground save the relatively small cost of the bond at the potentially much larger cost of forgoing a cap on their liability.

2. *The Procedure for Obtaining Preliminary Relief*

CARROLL v. PRESIDENT AND COMMISSIONERS OF PRINCESS ANNE

393 U.S. 175 (1968)

Justice FORTAS delivered the opinion of the Court.

Petitioners are identified with a "white supremacist" organization called the National States Rights Party. They held a public assembly or rally near the courthouse steps in the town of Princess Anne, the county seat of Somerset County, Maryland, in the evening of August 6, 1966. The authorities did not attempt to interfere with the rally. Because of the tense atmosphere which developed as the meeting progressed, about 60 state policemen were brought in, including some from a nearby county. They were held in readiness, but for tactical reasons only a few were in evidence at the scene of the rally.

Petitioners' speeches, amplified by a public address system so that they could be heard for several blocks, were aggressively and militantly racist. Their target was primarily Negroes and, secondarily, Jews. It is sufficient to observe with the court below, that the speakers engaged in deliberately derogatory, insulting, and threatening language, scarcely disguised by protestations of peaceful purposes; and that listeners might well have construed their words as both a provocation to the Negroes in the crowd and an incitement to the whites. The rally continued for something more than an hour, concluding at about 8:25 P.M. The crowd listening to the speeches increased from about 50 at the beginning to about 150, of whom 25% were Negroes.

In the course of the proceedings it was announced that the rally would be resumed the following night, August 7.

On that day, the respondents, officials of Princess Anne and of Somerset County, applied for and obtained a restraining order from the Circuit Court for Somerset County. The proceedings were ex parte, no notice being given to petitioners and, so far as appears, no effort being made informally to communicate with them, although this is expressly contemplated under Maryland procedure. The order restrained petitioners for 10 days from holding rallies or meetings in the county "which will tend to disturb and endanger the citizens of the County." As a result, the rally scheduled for August 7 was not held. After the trial which took place 10 days later, an injunction was issued by the Circuit Court on August 30, in effect extending the restraint for 10 additional months. The court had before it, in addition to the testimony of witnesses, tape recordings made by the police of the August 6 rally.

On appeal, the Maryland Court of Appeals affirmed the 10-day order, but reversed the 10-month order on the ground that "the period of time was unreasonable and that it was arbitrary to assume that a clear and present danger of civil disturbance and riot would persist for ten months." 230 A.2d 452, 457-458 (Md. 1967). . . .

We agree with petitioners that the case is not moot. . . . [P]etitioners have sought to continue their activities, . . . and . . . the decision of the Maryland Court of Appeals continues to play a substantial role in the response of officials. . . .

In Southern Pacific Terminal Co. v. Interstate Commerce Commission, 219 U.S. 498 (1911), this Court declined to hold that the case was moot although the two-year cease-and-desist order at issue had expired. It said: "The questions involved in the orders of the . . . Commission are usually continuing . . . and their consideration ought not to be, as they might be, defeated, by short term orders, capable of repetition, yet evading review. . . ." *Id.* at 515.

These principles are applicable to the present case. The underlying question persists and is agitated by the continuing activities and program of petitioners: whether, by what processes, and to what extent the authorities of the local governments may restrict petitioners in their rallies and public meetings.

This conclusion — that the question is not moot and ought to be adjudicated by this Court — is particularly appropriate in view of this Court's decision in Walker v. City of Birmingham, 388 U.S. 307 (1967). In that case, the Court held that demonstrators who had proceeded with their protest march in face of the prohibition of an injunctive order against such a march, could not defend contempt charges by asserting the unconstitutionality of the injunction. The proper procedure, it was held, was to seek judicial review of the injunction and not to disobey it, no matter how well-founded their doubts might be as to its validity. Petitioners have here pursued the course indicated by *Walker*; and in view of the continuing vitality of petitioners' grievance, we cannot say that their case is moot. . . .

We need not decide the thorny problem of whether, on the facts of this case, an injunction against the announced rally could be justified. The 10-day order here must be set aside because of a basic infirmity in the procedure by which it was obtained. It was issued ex parte, without notice to petitioners and without any effort, however informal, to invite or permit their participation in the proceedings. There is a place in our jurisprudence for ex parte issuance, without notice, of temporary restraining orders of short duration; but there is no place within the area of basic freedoms guaranteed by the First Amendment for such orders where no showing is made that it is impossible to serve or to notify the opposing parties and to give them an opportunity to participate. . . .

The Court has emphasized that "[a] system of prior restraints of expression comes to this Court bearing a heavy presumption against its constitutional validity." Bantam Books v. Sullivan, 372 U.S. 58, 70 (1963); Freedman v. Maryland, 380 U.S. 51, 57 (1965). And even where this presumption might otherwise be overcome, the Court has insisted upon careful procedural provisions, designed to assure the fullest presentation and consideration of the matter which the circumstances permit. . . .

Measured against these standards, it is clear that the 10-day restraining order in the present case, issued ex parte, without formal or informal notice to the petitioners or any effort to advise them of the proceeding, cannot be sustained. . . .

In the present case, the record discloses no reason why petitioners were not notified of the application for injunction. They were apparently present in Princess Anne. They had held a rally there on the night preceding the application for an issuance of the injunction. They were scheduled to have another rally on the very evening of the day when the injunction was issued. And some of them were actually served with the writ of injunction at 6:10 that evening. In these circumstances, there is no justification for the ex parte character of the proceedings in the sensitive area of First Amendment rights.

The value of a judicial proceeding, as against self-help by the police, is substantially diluted where the process is ex parte, because the Court does not have available the fundamental instrument for judicial judgment: an adversary proceeding in which both parties may participate. The facts in any case involving a public demonstration are difficult to ascertain and even more difficult to evaluate. Judgment as to whether the facts justify the use of the drastic power of injunction necessarily turns on subtle and controversial considerations and upon a delicate assessment of the particular situation in light of legal standards which are inescapably imprecise. In the absence of evidence and argument offered by both sides and of their participation in the formulation of value judgments, there is insufficient assurance of the balanced analysis and careful conclusions which are essential in the area of First Amendment adjudication.

The same is true of the fashioning of the order. An order issued in the area of First Amendment rights must be couched in the narrowest terms that will accomplish the pin-pointed objective permitted by constitutional mandate and the essential needs of the public order. In this sensitive field, the . . . order must be tailored as precisely as possible to the exact needs of the case. The participation of both sides is necessary for this purpose. Certainly, the failure to invite participation of the party seeking to exercise First Amendment rights reduces the possibility of a narrowly drawn order, and substantially imperils the protection which the Amendment seeks to assure.

Finally, respondents urge that the failure to give notice and an opportunity for hearing should not be considered to invalidate the order because, under Maryland procedure, petitioners might have obtained a hearing on not more than two days' notice. But this procedural right does not overcome the infirmity in the absence of a showing of justification for the ex parte nature of the proceedings. The issuance of an injunction which aborts a scheduled rally or public meeting, even if the restraint is of short duration, is a matter of importance and consequence in view of the First Amendment's imperative. The denial of a basic procedural right in these circumstances is not excused by the availability of post-issuance procedure which could not possibly serve to rescue the August 7 meeting, but, at best, could have shortened the period in which petitioners were prevented from holding a rally.

We need not here decide that it is impossible for circumstances to arise in which the issuance of an ex parte restraining order for a minimum period could be justified because of the unavailability of the adverse parties or their counsel, or perhaps for other reasons. In the present case, it is clear that the failure to give notice, formal or informal, and to provide an opportunity for an adversary proceeding before the holding of the rally was restrained is incompatible with the First Amendment. . . .

Reversed.

Justice BLACK concurs in the result.

Justice DOUGLAS, while joining the opinion of the Court, adheres to his dissent in Kingsley Books, Inc. v. Brown, 354 U.S. 436, 446-447 (1957), and to his concurring opinion in Freedman v. Maryland, 380 U.S. 51, 61-62 (1965). [In those opinions, Justice Douglas argued that no TRO could constitutionally restrain speech, no matter how great the procedural safeguards.]

NOTES ON TEMPORARY RESTRAINING ORDERS

1. The federal rule. Temporary restraining orders are designed to prevent irreparable harm that will occur even before a preliminary injunction hearing can be held. In a sufficiently urgent case, a judge will issue a TRO from home, in the middle of the night. Federal Rule of Civil Procedure 65 puts tight restrictions on preliminary orders without notice:

> **(a) Preliminary Injunction.**
> (1) *Notice.* The court may issue a preliminary injunction only on notice to the adverse party.
>
> . . .
>
> **(b) Temporary Restraining Order.**
> (1) *Issuing Without Notice.* The court may issue a temporary restraining order without written or oral notice to the adverse party or its attorney only if:
>> **(A)** specific facts in an affidavit or verified complaint clearly show that immediate and irreparable injury, loss, or damage will result to the movant before the adverse party can be heard in opposition; and
>> **(B)** the movant's attorney certifies in writing any efforts made to give notice and the reasons why it should not be required.
>
> (2) *Contents; Expiration.* Every temporary restraining order issued without notice must state the date and hour it was issued; describe the injury and state why it is irreparable; state why the order was issued without notice; and be promptly filed in the clerk's office and entered in the record. The order expires at the time after entry—not to exceed 14 days—that the court sets, unless before that time the

court, for good cause, extends it for a like period, or the adverse party consents to a longer extension. The reasons for an extension must be entered in the record.

(3) *Expediting the Preliminary-Injunction Hearing.* If the order is issued without notice, the motion for a preliminary injunction must be set for hearing at the earliest possible time, taking precedence over all other matters except hearings on older matters of the same character. At the hearing, the party who obtained the order must proceed with the motion; if the party does not, the court must dissolve the order.

(4) *Motion to Dissolve.* On 2 days' notice to the party who obtained the order without notice — or on shorter notice set by the court — the adverse party may appear and move to dissolve or modify the order. The court must then hear and decide the motion as promptly as justice requires.

2. Legislative history. Rule 65(b) originated in §17 of the Clayton Act, 38 Stat. 730, 737 (1914). TROs without notice and of indefinite duration had effectively broken strikes without a hearing on their legality. Like the requirement of preliminary injunction bonds, what is now Rule 65(b) was part of the congressional response. The maximum duration of a TRO was ten days until the 2009 amendments to the Federal Rules of Civil Procedure, but those amendments also changed Rule 6 with respect to counting weekends and holidays in measuring short time periods, so there is little change in practical effect. We mention this detail only because all the opinions prior to late 2009 will describe the limit as ten days.

3. Constitutional limits. Does *Carroll* constitutionalize the substance of Rule 65(b)? Is there any reason to believe *Carroll* is limited to free speech cases? The essence of due process is notice and opportunity to be heard. Can those rights be denied without a showing of necessity?

4. When is notice impossible? How often will notice of a TRO hearing be impossible? Even a TRO cannot be obtained instantly; plaintiff's lawyer must prepare a complaint, a motion for TRO, one or more affidavits setting out the facts, an injunction bond, and a proposed order. And she must find defendant after the TRO is issued to tell him it exists; defendant is not bound by an order he doesn't know about. If plaintiff can find the defendant then, isn't it likely she could have found him while the papers were being prepared?

5. Deliberately withholding notice. Suppose plaintiff's lawyer knows where defendant or his lawyer is. Is it ethical to delay giving notice until after preparing all the papers and just before leaving for the courthouse? Is it sound tactics? If it becomes apparent that notice was delayed, might the court think plaintiff had reason to fear a defense? What if plaintiff fears that if she gave prompt notice, defendant could complete the threatened wrong more quickly than plaintiff's lawyer can complete the motion papers?

Sometimes plaintiffs file without notice and ask that the court proceed without notice to secure evidence that defendant could easily destroy. Some of these cases are collected in Adobe Systems, Inc. v. South Sun Products, Inc., 187 F.R.D. 636 (S.D. Cal. 1999). Plaintiff alleged that defendant was using pirated software, offering an affidavit from defendant's former network administrator. Plaintiff wanted an ex parte order for the federal marshal to search defendant's premises, seize plaintiff's software, and run an audit program that would identify every file on defendant's computer. Plaintiff alleged that this was necessary because the software could be deleted from hard drives with a few key strokes. Not enough said the court; there is always the possibility that evidence might be destroyed. Proof of propensity would be necessary to issue an injunction at all; compare Almurbati v. Bush, reprinted in section 4.A.1.

To justify proceeding ex parte, the court wanted proof that this defendant had actually destroyed evidence in a similar situation in the past.

Compare In re Vuitton et Fils S.A., 606 F.2d 1 (2d Cir. 1979), where plaintiff alleged that in dozens of prior cases, defendants selling counterfeit Vuitton leather goods had shifted infringing inventory to another entity in a network of many counterfeiters—always without records and to a person whose name they could not remember. The past behavior of the network appeared to be enough to support ex parte orders against any counterfeiter Vuitton identified.

In Running Horse, LLC v. Rodenbough Trucking & Excavation, Inc., 2016 WL 8747867 (D.N.D. 2016), a federal district court granted a TRO without notice to stop the defendant's likely sale of assets and destruction of records related to a business dispute involving allegations of fraud, theft, and breach of contract. "The court finds the threat of the Defendants' liquidation of [Defendant's company's] assets is real, imminent, and poses a significant threat of irreparable harm to" plaintiff. *Id.* at *4. The court set a further hearing with notice for the thirteenth day after issuance of the TRO to determine if the court should issue a preliminary injunction, and made the TRO effective upon plaintiff's service of the order on the defendant.

6. Legislation. The Defend Trade Secrets Act of 2016 explicitly authorizes ex parte applications to seize property "necessary to prevent the propagation or dissemination" of a trade secret. 18 U.S.C. §1836(b)(2). There are multiple procedural safeguards, including the inadequacy of remedies under Rule 65, "immediate and irreparable injury" if the seizure is not ordered, a balance of equities favoring plaintiff, likely success in proving trade secret and misappropriation, a bond (which does not limit liability for wrongful seizure), and a finding that the person against whom the order is directed "would destroy, move, hide, or otherwise make such matter inaccessible to the court, if the applicant were to proceed on notice to such person." The order is to be denied if the plaintiff publicizes the application. There is a similar provision for trademark cases. 15 U.S.C. §1116(d).

7. Capable of repetition, yet evading review. *Carroll* relied on a well-settled exception to the usual rule of refusing to decide cases that have become moot. If a dispute is capable of repetition *between the same two parties*, yet so short lived that it tends to evade judicial review, the case can still be decided on appeal because the underlying controversy between the parties continues. The rule was reaffirmed without dissent in Kingdomware Technologies, Inc. v. United States, 136 S. Ct. 1969 (2016), and in Turner v. Rogers, 564 U.S. 431 (2011).

SAMPSON v. MURRAY
415 U.S. 61 (1974)

[Plaintiff (respondent in the Supreme Court) was a probationary employee of the federal government. She was fired. Her lawyer met with a personnel officer who suggested that reports about her previous employment with a different agency might have contributed to the decision to fire her. If those reports were the reason for her discharge, she was entitled to more elaborate procedural protections, which had not been provided.

She filed this lawsuit, seeking a preliminary injunction to prevent her discharge pending an administrative appeal to the Civil Service Commission. The district judge granted a temporary restraining order forbidding her discharge for ten days. At the next hearing, he decided that he wanted to hear the testimony of W.H. Sanders, the official who had fired her. The government, which denied that the court had any jurisdiction to inquire into the facts, refused to produce Sanders. The judge extended the TRO, keeping it in effect until the government produced Sanders to testify. The government still refused to produce Sanders and appealed the order prohibiting it from firing plaintiff. The court of appeals affirmed. Murray v. Kunzig, 462 F.2d 871 (D.C. Cir. 1972).]

Justice REHNQUIST delivered the opinion of the Court.

III . . .

The District Court, exercising its equitable powers, is bound to give serious weight to the obviously disruptive effect which the grant of the temporary relief awarded here was likely to have on the administrative process. When we couple with this consideration the historical denial of all equitable relief by the federal courts in cases such as White v. Berry, 171 U.S. 366 (1898), the well-established rule that the Government has traditionally been granted the widest latitude in the "dispatch of its own internal affairs," Cafeteria Workers v. McElroy, 367 U.S. 886, 896 (1961), and the traditional unwillingness of courts of equity to enforce contracts for personal service either at the behest of the employer or of the employee, we think that the Court of Appeals was quite wrong in routinely applying to this case the traditional standards governing more orthodox "stays." Although we do not hold that Congress has wholly foreclosed the granting of preliminary injunctive relief in such cases, we do believe that respondent at the very least must make a showing of irreparable injury sufficient in kind and degree to override these factors cutting against the general availability of preliminary injunctions in Government personnel cases. . . .

IV . . .

In form the order entered by the District Court now before us is a continuation of the temporary restraining order originally issued by that court. It is clear from the Court of Appeals' opinion that that court so construed it. But since the order finally settled upon by the District Court was in no way limited in time, the provisions of Fed. Rule Civ. Proc. 65 come into play. . . .

The Court of Appeals whose judgment we are reviewing has held that a temporary restraining order continued beyond the time permissible under Rule 65 must be treated as a preliminary injunction, and must conform to the standards applicable to preliminary injunctions. We believe that this analysis is correct, at least in the type of situation presented here, and comports with general principles imposing strict limitations on the scope of temporary restraining orders. A district court, if it were able to shield its orders from appellate review merely by designating them as temporary restraining orders rather than as preliminary injunctions, would have virtually unlimited authority over the parties in an injunctive proceeding. In this case, where an adversary hearing has been held, and the court's basis for issuing the order strongly challenged, classification of the potentially unlimited order as a temporary restraining order seems particularly unjustified. Therefore we view the order at issue here as a preliminary injunction. . . .

Respondent's unverified complaint alleged that she might be deprived of her income for an indefinite period of time, that spurious and unrebutted charges against her might remain on the record, and that she would suffer the embarrassment of being wrongfully discharged in the presence of her coworkers. The Court of Appeals intimated that either loss of earnings or damage to reputation might afford a basis for a finding of irreparable injury and provide a basis for temporary injunctive relief. We disagree.[63]

Even under the traditional standards of Virginia Petroleum Jobbers Association v. Federal Power Commission, 259 F.2d 921 (D.C. Cir. 1958), it seems clear that the temporary loss of income, ultimately to be recovered, does not usually constitute irreparable injury. In that case the court stated:

> The key word in this consideration is *irreparable*. Mere injuries, however substantial, in terms of money, time and energy necessarily expended in the absence of a stay, are not enough. The possibility that adequate compensatory or other corrective relief will be available at a later date, in the ordinary course of litigation, weighs heavily against a claim of irreparable harm.

Id. at 925. This premise is fortified by the Back Pay Act, 5 U.S.C. §5596. . . . This Act not only affords monetary relief which will prevent the loss of earnings on a periodic basis from being "irreparable injury" in this type of case, but its legislative history suggests that Congress contemplated that it would be the usual, if not the exclusive, remedy for wrongful discharge. . . .

Respondent's complaint also alleges, as a basis for relief, the humiliation and damage to her reputation which may ensue. As a matter of first impression it would seem that no significant loss of reputation would be inflicted by procedural irregularities in effectuating respondent's discharge, and that whatever damage might occur would be fully corrected by an administrative determination requiring the agency to conform to the applicable regulations. . . .

Assuming for the purpose of discussion that respondent had made a satisfactory showing of loss of income and had supported the claim that her reputation would be damaged as a result of the challenged agency action, we think the showing falls far short of the type of irreparable injury which is a necessary predicate to the issuance of a temporary injunction in this type of case.[68] We therefore reverse the decision of the Court of Appeals which approved the action of the District Court. . . .

Justice DOUGLAS, dissenting. . . .

Both the District Court and the Court of Appeals were alert to the necessity to show irreparable injury before an injunction issues.

---

63. . . . We have no doubt that a district court in appropriate circumstances may be justified in resolving against a party refusing to produce a witness under his control the relevant issues upon which that witness' testimony might have touched. But it is clear from the record that the testimony of the witness Sanders was desired to test the basis upon which respondent was discharged, testimony which, of course, would go to the issue of respondent's ultimate chances for success on the merits. While the District Court may well have been entitled to resolve *that* issue against the Government at that stage of the proceeding, this conclusion in no way dispenses with the necessity for a conclusion that irreparable injury will occur, since that is a separate issue that must be proved to the satisfaction of the Court by the person seeking equitable relief.

68. We recognize that cases may arise in which the circumstances surrounding an employee's discharge, together with the resultant effect on the employee, may so far depart from the normal situation that irreparable injury might be found. Such extraordinary cases are hard to define in advance of their occurrence. We have held that an insufficiency of savings or difficulties in immediately obtaining other employment—external factors common to most discharged employees and not attributable to any unusual actions relating to the discharge itself—will not support a finding of irreparable injury, however severely they may affect a particular individual. But we do not wish to be understood as foreclosing relief in the genuinely extraordinary situation.

On that issue there is more than meets the eye.

Employability is the greatest asset most people have. Once there is a discharge from a prestigious federal agency, dismissal may be a badge that bars the employee from other federal employment. The shadow of that discharge is cast over the area where private employment may be available. And the harm is not eliminated by the possibility of reinstatement, for in many cases the ultimate absolution never catches up with the stigma of the accusation. . . . And we cannot denigrate the importance of one's social standing or the status of social stigma as legally recognized harm. . . .

Justice MARSHALL, with whom Justice BRENNAN concurs, dissenting.

In my view no appealable order has been entered in this case, and both the Court of Appeals and this Court accordingly lack jurisdiction.

The orders issued by the District Court are both temporary restraining orders. The first, issued on May 28 and captioned "Temporary Restraining Order," enjoined Mrs. Murray's dismissal until the determination of her application for an injunction. The second, issued on June 4 and also captioned "Temporary Restraining Order," provides "that the Temporary Restraining Order issued by this Court at twelve o'clock P.M., May 28, 1971, is continued until the appearance of the aforesaid W. H. Sanders.". . .

It is well settled that the grant or denial of a temporary restraining order is not appealable, except in extraordinary circumstances, not present here, where the denial of the temporary restraining order actually decides the merits of the case or is equivalent to a dismissal of the suit.

The Court holds, however, that since the temporary restraining order was extended by the District Court beyond the time limitation imposed by Fed. Rule Civ. Proc. 65(b), it became an appealable preliminary injunction. I cannot agree. Federal Rule 52(a) expressly provides that "in granting or refusing interlocutory injunctions the court shall . . . set forth the findings of fact and conclusions of law which constitute the grounds of its action." This Rule applies to preliminary injunctions, and as no findings of fact and conclusions of law have yet been filed in this case, no valid preliminary injunction was ever issued.

Nor would it make sense for this Court to review the District Court's order in this case as the grant of a preliminary injunction. Where the District Court has not entered findings of fact and conclusions of law under Rule 52(a), meaningful review is well-nigh impossible. . . .

It is suggested that if an indefinitely extended temporary restraining order remained unappealable, the District Court would have virtually unlimited authority over the parties in an injunctive action. At the outset, this cannot justify this Court's reaching the merits of Mrs. Murray's claim for a preliminary injunction. Even if the order entered by the District Court is appealable, it should be appealable only for the purposes of holding it invalid for failure to comply with Rule 52(a). . . .

In addition, the Government had other courses it could have taken in this case. In view of the District Court's error in granting a restraining order of unlimited duration without complying with the requirements for a preliminary injunction, the Government could have moved the District Court to dissolve its order indefinitely continuing the temporary restraining order. . . . Had the Government followed this course, the District Court could have corrected its error and gone on to resolve the issues presented by the application for a preliminary injunction. The end result would have been the grant or denial of a preliminary injunction, with findings of fact and conclusions of law, which we could meaningfully review.

Here, instead, we find the Supreme Court determining that although the District Court had jurisdiction to grant injunctive relief, the equities of Mrs. Murray's case did not support a preliminary injunction, when neither the District Court nor the Court of Appeals has yet confronted the latter issue. . . .

Since the majority persists in considering the merits of Mrs. Murray's claim for injunctive relief, some additional comment is in order. I agree with the majority's conclusion that Congress did not divest federal courts of their long-exercised authority to issue temporary injunctive relief pending the exhaustion of both administrative and judicial review of an employee's claim of wrongful dismissal. I cannot accept, however, the way in which the majority opinion then proceeds to take away with the left hand what it has just given with the right, by precluding injunctive relief in all but so-called "extraordinary cases," whatever they may be.

At the outset, I see no basis for applying any different standards for granting equitable relief in the context of a discharged probationary employee than the long-recognized principles of equity applied in all other situations. Indeed, it appears that the factors which the majority would have courts weigh before granting injunctive relief are all encompassed within the traditional formulations. The adequacy of backpay as a remedy, for example, is relevant in determining whether the party seeking relief has shown that "without such relief, it will be irreparably injured." *Virginia Petroleum Jobbers*, 259 F.2d at 925. Likewise, the possible disruptive effect which temporary injunctive relief might have on the office where respondent was employed or on the administrative review process itself relates to whether "the issuance of a stay [will] substantially harm other parties interested in the proceedings." *Id.*

However one articulates the standards for granting temporary injunctive relief, I take it to be well settled that a prerequisite for such relief is a demonstrated likelihood of irreparable injury for which there is no adequate legal remedy. But I cannot accept the majority's apparent holding, buried deep in a footnote, that because of the Back Pay Act, a temporary loss in income can never support a finding of irreparable injury, no matter how severely it may affect a particular individual. . . .

The availability of a backpay award several years after a dismissal is scant justice for a Government employee who may have long since been evicted from his home and found himself forced to resort to public assistance in order to support his family. And it is little solace to those who are so injured to be told that their plight is "normal" and "routine." Whether common or not, such consequences amount to irreparable injury which a court of equity has power to prevent.

Nor can I agree with the majority's analysis of Mrs. Murray's claim of damaged reputation. It is argued that Mrs. Murray can suffer no significant loss of reputation by procedural irregularities in effectuating her discharge because her claim is not that she could not as a matter of statutory or administrative right be discharged, but only that she was entitled to additional procedural safeguards in effectuating the discharge. . . .

Mrs. Murray does not seek a hearing as an end in itself, but rather to correct what she believes is a mistaken impression the agency had about her conduct in her prior job, in the hope that with the record straight, the agency would not discharge her. She seeks to save her job and to avoid the blot on her employment record that a dismissal entails. . . .

Whether the likelihood of irreparable injury to Mrs. Murray if she is not allowed to retain her job pending her administrative appeal, when balanced against the Government's interests in having her out of the office during this period, supports equitable relief in the present case is a question I would leave for the District Court. Because of Mr. Sanders' absence, the District Court cut short its hearing on the application for a preliminary injunction before either the Government or Mrs. Murray had an opportunity to present witnesses or other evidence. Mrs. Murray still has not had her day in court to present evidence supporting her allegation of irreparable injury, and what that evidence would be were she given that opportunity we can only speculate.

MORE NOTES ON IRREPARABLE INJURY

1. Bankrupting government employees. Would the majority in *Sampson* ever issue a preliminary injunction reinstating a government employee? What kind of "genuinely extraordinary situation" could there be that did not derive from "an insufficiency of savings or difficulties in obtaining other employment"? What if the mortgage company were about to foreclose on plaintiff's house? Recall the rule disallowing consequential damages for failure to pay money. (See Meinrath v. Singer Co. in section 2.D.) Doesn't that make the loss of plaintiff's house, or any other consequence you can imagine, as irreparable as injury can be? Did Justice Rehnquist really mean that the government's interest in the efficiency of the service generally outweighs plaintiff's injury even if that injury *is* irreparable?

2. Bankrupting businesses. Compare Rehnquist's opinion for the Court in Doran v. Salem Inn, Inc., reprinted in section 7.A.2. A district court preliminarily enjoined criminal prosecutions of topless dancers and the corporate owner of the bar where they danced. The owner alleged a risk of bankruptcy if the local ordinance were enforced pending trial. The Supreme Court affirmed. "Certainly [bankruptcy] meets the standards for granting interim relief, for otherwise a favorable final judgment might well be useless." *Id.* at 932. Is bankruptcy more irreparable for a business than an employee?

NOTES ON PRELIMINARY PROCEDURE

1. Classifying the order. Was the order in *Sampson* a temporary restraining order or a preliminary injunction? The Court relies on the time limit in Rule 65(b), but that limit applies only to TROs without notice. Here, the district court purports to have issued a TRO with notice. How does *that* order fit into the scheme of Rule 65? It can't be unappealable *and* of unlimited duration, can it? Does Rule 65 ever define the difference between TROs and preliminary injunctions?

2. A different answer? Two weeks after *Sampson*, the Court took another look at the problem. This time Justice Marshall wrote the opinion:

> Although by its terms Rule 65(b) . . . only limits the duration of restraining orders issued without notice, we think it applicable to the order in this case even though informal notice was given. The 1966 Amendment to Rule 65(b), requiring the party seeking a temporary restraining order to certify to the court in writing the efforts, if any, which have been made to give either written or oral notice to the adverse party or his attorney, were adopted in recognition of the fact that informal notice and a hastily arranged hearing are to be preferred to no notice or hearing at all. But this informal, same-day notice, desirable though it may be before a restraining order is issued, is no substitute for the more thorough notice requirements which must be satisfied to obtain a preliminary injunction of potentially unlimited duration. The notice required by Rule 65(a) before a preliminary injunction can issue implies a hearing in which the defendant is given a fair opportunity to oppose the application and to prepare for such opposition. The same-day notice provided in this case before the temporary restraining order was issued does not suffice.

Granny Goose Foods, Inc. v. Brotherhood of Teamsters, 415 U.S. 423, 432 n.7 (1974). In *Granny Goose*, the Court held that defendants were not in contempt of the TRO with notice, because it had expired ten days after its issuance and before they allegedly violated it.

The Illinois court reached the opposite result under a state statute substantially identical to Rule 65(b). Kable Printing Co. v. Mount Morris Bookbinders Union Local 65-B, 349 N.E.2d 36 (Ill. 1976). The Illinois court thought it quite clear that the time limit applies only to ex parte orders; it held a TRO with notice equivalent to a preliminary injunction and unlimited in duration. Even so, the Illinois appellate courts held that such an order must expire unless defendant gets a chance to present evidence and argument within a short but unspecified time. Abdulhafedh v. Secretary of State, 514 N.E.2d 563, 565 (Ill. App. Ct. 1987). It surely also matters that TROs are appealable in Illinois.

Doesn't there have to be some provision for TROs with notice to last more than 28 days? What should the court do in a case like Jurco v. Stuart, 442 N.E.2d 633, 635 (Ill. App. Ct. 1982), where there was "a six-month backlog to hear preliminary injunctions"? Is the answer that such a backlog cannot be tolerated?

3. Reconciling the cases. Are *Sampson* and *Granny Goose* consistent? *Granny Goose* says a TRO with notice, not limited by its terms to ten days' duration, is still a TRO and expires in ten days, so that violating it is not contempt. Doesn't *Sampson* say that such an order is really a preliminary injunction, appealable because of its indefinite duration? Did the defendants have an option either to appeal or defy the TRO after ten days? Note the third option suggested in the *Sampson* dissent: to move in the trial court to vacate the order.

Federal judges appear to have followed *Sampson*, at least where the judge announces that she is extending the TRO. An example is In re Criminal Contempt Proceedings Against Crawford, 133 F. Supp. 2d 249 (W.D.N.Y. 2001), an abortion-protest case with 68 defendants and vigorous litigation on both sides. The court ordered that a TRO would remain in effect until the motion for preliminary injunction was resolved, which turned out to take months. Some of the defendants violated the extended TRO and defended on the basis of *Granny Goose*. The court held them in contempt. *Granny Goose*, it said, was a case where defendant might have believed the TRO had expired because the court had not said otherwise. Here, the court expressly said it was extending the TRO; that converted it into a preliminary injunction under *Sampson*, and if the preliminary injunction existed for purposes of appeal, it also existed for purposes of contempt. *Id.* at 255-259.

The court relied on Levine v. Comcoa Ltd., 70 F.3d 1191 (11th Cir. 1995), where the trial court orally extended the TRO at the conclusion of the preliminary injunction hearing. Many cases hold that oral orders don't count as injunctions and cannot support a contempt citation. But defendant was a lawyer who heard the extension in open court; the court thought that he had no reason to doubt what the judge had meant. The extended order was enforceable, and appealable under *Sampson*.

In Tooele County v. United States, 820 F.3d 1183 (10th Cir. 2016), a trial court granted a TRO, saying that the order would remain in effect until the court decided whether or not to grant an injunction. The Tenth Circuit said that under *Sampson*, this order was a TRO for 14 days. "But on the fifteenth day, that order could be treated as a preliminary injunction, for purposes of appealability, because a temporary restraining order cannot last longer than fourteen days." *Id.* at 1187.

Do these cases mean that the 14-day limit applies only when the court overlooks it, but that courts are free to ignore it by just saying so? Or is the court free to extend the TRO beyond 14 days once it has given defendant notice and an opportunity to be heard? The judge in *Levine* extended the TRO only after hearing the evidence at a preliminary injunction hearing; the judge in *Criminal Contempt Proceedings* gave 15 days' notice of the TRO hearing, and the hearing itself lasted 3 days. Should judges have some discretion to fashion hybrid orders, where they give reasonable notice and hearing on the TRO but want to hear still more on the preliminary injunction? A TRO hearing with reasonable notice and scope gives the judge more information, but there is another problem: These summary extensions have been issued without findings of fact and conclusions of law. Findings and conclusions provide a basis for appeal; if taken seriously, the process of preparing them is also an important check on hasty decision or careless errors in the trial court.

4. Preliminary injunction hearings. The scope of the hearing on a motion for TRO or preliminary injunction depends on the complexity and urgency of the case. In Lektro-Vend Corp. v. Vendo Co., 660 F.2d 255 (7th Cir. 1981), the preliminary injunction hearing lasted 5 days; the judge heard 4 witnesses and admitted 89 exhibits. The trial on the merits lasted 23 days; the judge heard 11 witnesses and admitted 2,762 exhibits. *Id.* at 264. That proportion between the two hearings is not unusual, but if there is sufficient urgency, even complex cases can be compressed much more. The trial judge has great discretion here, but he must be evenhanded about it. Judges occasionally get impatient after the plaintiff's case and cut the defendant off without an equal chance to be heard; that is nearly always reversible. An extreme example, where the judge lost her temper and told a lawyer that making an objection for the record would be contempt of court, is Kramer Trading Corp. v. Lyons, 740 S.W.2d 522 (Tex. Ct. App. 1987). A more routine example is Visual Sciences, Inc. v. Integrated Communications Inc., 660 F.2d 56 (2d Cir. 1981).

Affidavits are commonly admitted to establish undisputed facts, and sometimes disputed facts as well. Some opinions state a strong right to a hearing when facts are disputed, Fengler v. Numismatic Americana, 832 F.2d 745, 747-748 (2d Cir. 1987), and others just as firmly say the choice between affidavits and live witnesses is discretionary, Jackson v. Fair, 846 F.2d 811, 819 (1st Cir. 1988).

5. TRO hearings. Hearings on motions for TROs tend to be much shorter. Sometimes there is a real hearing, with key witnesses explaining the key facts; sometimes there is only an informal conference with the judge, with lawyers stating their clients' version of the facts. Justice Marshall's dissent in *Sampson* implies that findings of fact and conclusions of law are not required for TROs, and that is probably the conventional wisdom, although the rule is hardly clear.

Rule 52(a), which applies to all orders "granting or refusing an interlocutory injunction," now requires the trial court to "find the facts specially and state its conclusions of law separately." An interlocutory order is an order before final judgment. It seems to be settled that TROs are *not* injunctions for purposes of Rule 52. In Nken v. Holder, 556 U.S. 418 (2009), the Court said that an injunction "is a means by which a court tells someone what to do or not to do." *Id.* at 428. That definition would include TROs, but the Court was not addressing that question; it was distinguishing injunctions from stays pending appeal.

The policy rationale for excluding TROs from Rule 52(a) is that some TROs must be issued so quickly that there is no time to prepare findings and conclusions. But a TRO must still comply with Rule 65(d)(1), which carefully provides that "[e]very order granting an injunction and every restraining order must: (A) state the reasons why it issued."

6. Consolidating the preliminary injunction hearing with the trial. Evidence admitted at a preliminary injunction hearing may be considered at the trial of the case and need not be repeated. Fed. R. Civ. P. 65(a)(2). The judge may consolidate the trial with the preliminary injunction hearing, *id.*, but only if both parties clearly understand that he has done so. University of Texas v. Camenisch, 451 U.S. 390, 395 (1981). This is a sound rule, but an emerging exception is discussed in note 13.

7. Interlocutory appeals. The usual federal rule is that no order is appealable before final judgment. But 28 U.S.C. §1292(a)(1) authorizes appeals from "interlocutory orders . . . granting, continuing, modifying, refusing or dissolving injunctions, or refusing to dissolve or modify injunctions." Most states have similar provisions. The rationale of these statutes is that interlocutory orders granting or denying injunctions may do irreparable harm before any appeal from a final judgment can be heard.

8. What counts as an injunction? For a very few cases, Congress requires that the claim be heard by a three-judge district court. The principal remaining examples are legislative redistricting cases and orders to release prisoners, illustrated in Brown v. Plata, in section 4.A.4. An order of a three-judge district court granting or denying an injunction, either permanent or preliminary, is directly appealable to the Supreme Court. 28 U.S.C. §1253. In Abbott v. Perez, 138 S. Ct 2305 (2018), the majority and dissent spent 26 pages debating what counts as an injunction under this statute.

In *Abbott,* the three-judge court held that Texas's redistricting plans violated both the Constitution and the Voting Rights Act, and that these violations "must be remedied," either by the legislature or the court, with a new redistricting plan. Perez v. Abbott, 274 F. Supp. 3d 624 (W.D. Tex. 2017). The court set prompt hearings to address remedies unless the attorney general reported within three days that the legislature would take up the issue. The court refused to stay this order, commenting that the court "has not enjoined" use of the illegal maps for the 2018 election. Texas appealed directly to the Supreme Court.

The Court held the order appealable because it had "the practical effect" of an injunction against using the illegal maps in 2018. It cited Sampson v. Murray for the proposition that district courts cannot shield their orders from appellate review by avoiding the label "injunction." Rule 65(d)(1) requires that injunctions be specific; that rule is taken up in section 9.A.6. "Where a vague injunction does not comply with Rule 65(d), the aggrieved party has a particularly strong need for appellate review. It would be odd to hold that there can be no appeal in such a circumstance." 138 S. Ct. at 2322.

Justice Sotomayor, dissenting for the four liberals, had many arguments. But the heart of it is that this was a standard case of a liability determination to be followed by further hearings on remedy. A liability determination, standing alone, is not appealable before final judgment. And in the absence of a specific injunction ordering new legislative maps, the Court could not know what it was reviewing. The political line up on a technical issue of jurisdiction suggests that each side was highly motivated to reach or avoid the merits. And on the merits, the Court decided that most of the liability determination was erroneous.

9. Appealing TROs. Section 1292 (like Rule 52) has been read *not* to authorize appeals of TROs.

a. The rule. The courts have held orders granting or denying TROs unappealable because TROs last such a short time and because the trial judge has heard so little of the merits. The trial judge can usually give relief from an erroneous order on a TRO application much more quickly than an appellate court. If that is true, why do litigants appeal orders granting and denying TROs? Sometimes appellants hope to get emergency action from the court of appeals. Sometimes they interpret the trial judge's order as reflecting hostility to their position, so that giving him more information will not change the result.

The continued vitality of the rule against appealing TROs is illustrated in McGraw-Hill Cos. v. Procter & Gamble Co., 515 U.S. 1309 (1995) (Stevens, J., as Circuit Justice).

McGraw-Hill, the publisher of *Business Week*, appealed a TRO forbidding publication of documents produced in pending litigation. The Sixth Circuit dismissed the appeal for lack of jurisdiction, and Justice Stevens refused to stay the district court's order. He doubted his own jurisdiction, and he was certain that the better course would have been a motion to dissolve the order in the district court. He noted that the TRO had been entered without the findings of fact required by Rule 65(b), and he assumed that a refusal to dissolve the TRO would have been an appealable order.

Whatever the merits of the rule against appeals from orders granting or denying TROs, its rationales do not apply when the TRO lasts longer and the trial judge refuses to dissolve it or hold the preliminary injunction hearing. In that event, shouldn't the TRO be appealable? Isn't that what *Sampson* holds? Is there any need to call it a preliminary injunction in order to make it appealable?

The rule is well settled, but it has several exceptions.

b. Exception 1: TRO with notice lasts for more than 14 days. This is the rule from *Sampson*. A TRO issued without notice, however, would presumably not be appealable because (unless extended) it would dissolve after the 14th day. This is the rule from *Granny Goose*.

c. Exception 2: TRO disposes of the entire case. There are also cases holding that orders granting or denying TROs are appealable as final judgments when they effectively dispose of the entire case. A widely cited example is United States v. Wood, 295 F.2d 772 (5th Cir. 1961). There, the United States unsuccessfully sought a TRO in federal district court against Mississippi's prosecution of a civil rights worker. The United States argued that the prosecution would discourage blacks from registering to vote, and that the prosecution would be complete before a motion for preliminary injunction could be heard. The Fifth Circuit agreed, concluding it had jurisdiction to hear the case, and reversed for the district court to reconsider the question under a proper legal standard.

d. Exception 3: TRO threatens to inflict "irretrievable" harm before TRO expires. This exception, perhaps a broader statement of the rule in Exception 2, sometimes applies in emergency election cases, such as when a court issues a TRO requiring or barring the counting of ballots in an imminent election. Northeast Ohio Coalition for Homeless v. Blackwell, 467 F.3d 999, 1005-1006 (6th Cir. 2006). The court also suggested that TROs acting as mandatory injunctions were appealable. *Id.* That would be quite a broad exception if generally applied.

e. Exception 4: TRO has the "qualities" of a preliminary injunction. This exception is perhaps the most controversial, and the Ninth Circuit applied it in one of the hotly contested Trump travel ban cases. On February 3, 2017, a federal court in Washington state issued a TRO barring enforcement of certain aspects of the travel ban. The next day, the United States appealed. The Ninth Circuit held that the appeal was permissible:

> A TRO is not ordinarily appealable. We may nonetheless review an order styled as a TRO if it "possesses the qualities of a preliminary injunction." Service Employees International Union v. National Union of Healthcare Workers, 598 F.3d 1061, 1067 (9th Cir. 2010). This rule has ordinarily required the would-be appellant to show that the TRO was strongly challenged in adversarial proceedings before the district court and that it has or will remain in force for longer than the fourteen-day period identified in Federal Rule of Civil Procedure 65(b).
>
> We are satisfied that in the extraordinary circumstances of this case, the district court's order possesses the qualities of an appealable preliminary injunction. The parties vigorously contested the legal basis for the TRO in written briefs and oral

arguments before the district court. The district court's order has no expiration date, and no hearing has been scheduled. Although the district court has recently scheduled briefing on the States' motion for a preliminary injunction, it is apparent from the district court's scheduling order that the TRO will remain in effect for longer than fourteen days. In light of the unusual circumstances of this case, in which the Government has argued that emergency relief is necessary to support its efforts to prevent terrorism, we believe that this period is long enough that the TRO should be considered to have the qualities of a reviewable preliminary injunction.

Washington v. Trump, 847 F.3d 1151, 1158 (9th Cir.), *reh'g en banc denied*, 853 F.3d 933 (9th Cir.) and *reh'g en banc denied*, 858 F.3d 1168 (9th Cir.), *cert denied sub nom.* Golden v. Washington, 138 S. Ct. 448 (2017). The district court had considered very little evidence before issuing the TRO; it contemplated a more extensive preliminary injunction hearing to come later. Might there be an emerging fifth exception to the rule against the appealability of TROs, for cases of great national or public importance?

This exception might be viewed as an application of Sampson v. Murray, because one element is that the TRO will last for more than 14 days. The apparent difference is that here, the court of appeals did not wait for the 14 days to elapse or for an explicit order extending the TRO. The government appealed the day after the TRO was issued. The court of appeals set a 2-day briefing schedule on the government's motion to stay the order, it heard oral argument over the telephone, and it issued its decision 5 days after that—still before the 14 days had elapsed.

10. Stays and injunctions pending appeal. Even with interlocutory appeals, an erroneous injunction order may do irreparable harm before the appeal can be heard. As the travel ban litigation illustrates, the procedural response to that problem is that judges at all levels of the judiciary can stay an injunction until it can be reviewed, and they can issue an injunction until an order denying it can be reviewed.

A litigant seeking a stay or injunction pending appeal must generally request it first from the trial court. Only if that is denied can he seek it from the court of appeals, and only if that is denied can he ask the Supreme Court. In an emergency, a single judge may act for an appellate court. Under Supreme Court Rule 23, application to a single Justice is the usual practice, but often the Justices consult the rest of the Court, formally or informally, before ruling on such applications. Whether to refer to the whole Court appears to be discretionary decision that depends on how difficult, controversial, and important the issue is, and maybe other factors as well; the Justices do not publicly explain these choices.

The standards for stays and injunctions pending appeal are the same as for preliminary injunctions, modified to include appropriate deference to the decision below. In the Supreme Court, probability of success depends not only on the merits but also on the probability that four Justices will consider the case important enough to review.

An injunction from an individual Justice "demands a significantly higher justification" than a stay of an injunction granted by one of the lower courts. Lux v. Rodrigues, 561 U.S. 1306, 1307 (2010) (Roberts, C.J.). This distinction was first made by the more conservative Justices, but Justice Sotomayor made essentially the same point in Hobby Lobby Stores, Inc. v. Sebelius, 568 U.S. 1401 (2012).

11. The "*Purcell* Principle:" A special rule in emergency election cases? In recent years, the Supreme Court has faced a slew of motions for stays or injunctions pending appeal in litigation about upcoming elections. Professor Baude calls these cases and other non-election-related emergency motions part of the Court's "shadow docket." William Baude, *Foreword: The Supreme Court's Shadow Docket*, 9 N.Y.U. J. of L. & Liberty 1 (2015). In the election cases, it appears that the Court has expressed a preference for lower courts not to change election rules shortly before an election, even if plaintiffs have shown likely violations of the law and irreparable harm if those violations persist. The idea seems to trace to a brief per curiam opinion in Purcell v. Gonzalez, 549 U.S. 1 (2006), a challenge to Arizona's voter identification law. The district court had denied a preliminary injunction against enforcing the law and the Ninth Circuit had granted an injunction pending appeal; neither court had made any findings of fact.

On a motion to stay the Ninth Circuit's order, the Supreme Court had this to say:

> Faced with an application to enjoin operation of voter identification procedures just weeks before an election, the Court of Appeals was required to weigh, in addition to the harms attendant upon issuance or nonissuance of an injunction, considerations specific to election cases and its own institutional procedures. Court orders affecting elections, especially conflicting orders, can themselves result in voter confusion and consequent incentive to remain away from the polls. As an election draws closer, that risk will increase.

Id. at 4-5.

Professor Hasen argues that application of this "*Purcell* Principle" might explain some of the apparent contradictions in the Supreme Court's election-law shadow docket, as when the Court in the run-up to the 2014 elections allowed Texas but not Wisconsin to enforce its strict voter ID law. Richard L. Hasen, *Reining in the* Purcell *Principle*, 43 Fla. St. U. L. Rev. 427, 428 (2016). Hasen criticizes the principle, arguing that some courts appear to consider the preference against late election changes the only important factor, even in cases where plaintiffs are likely to succeed on the merits and face irreparable harm under discriminatory voting rules. The Court recently applied the *Purcell* Principle in its unanimous per curiam opinion in Benisek v. Lamone, 138 S. Ct. 1942, 1944-1945 (2018): "a due regard for the public interest in orderly elections supported the District Court's discretionary decision to deny a preliminary injunction and to stay the proceedings."

12. Wasted appeals? One cost of interlocutory appeals is that litigants are tempted to devote their energy to the appeal of the preliminary order rather than the trial of the case. Both can proceed simultaneously, but lawyers often think there is no point to proceeding in the trial court until they hear from the appellate court. This can delay the case indefinitely, and the appellate opinion may not be worth much. It is likely to say only that the trial court did or did not abuse its discretion in assessing probabilities on a preliminary record. Unless they can get an injunction pending appeal, plaintiffs will often do better to push the case to trial than to appeal denial of a preliminary injunction.

The point is dramatically illustrated in Ashcroft v. ACLU, 542 U.S. 656 (2004), affirming a preliminary injunction against a statute regulating internet porn. The Court emphasized that preliminary injunction decisions are reviewed for abuse of discretion, and it drew the inference that if the case is close, it should affirm. The preliminary injunction was issued in 1999, affirmed by the court of appeals in 2000, vacated and remanded to the court of appeals in 2002, reaffirmed by the court of appeals in 2003, affirmed by the Supreme Court in 2004 on the ground that the case was at least close, and remanded to the district court for further fact finding. *Id.* at 664-665. It is a safe bet that the Court as it was composed in 2004 would invalidate the statute unless the government found better evidence on why filters don't work, so the parties had learned something. And the plaintiffs had gotten five years of protection from the statute. But five years of litigation had not determined whether the statute was constitutional. That ruling finally came in ACLU v. Mukasey, 534 F.3d 181 (3d Cir. 2008).

13. Appeals that suddenly turn final. In Thornburgh v. American College of Obstetricians & Gynecologists, 476 U.S. 747 (1986), the Court reviewed more than just the preliminary injunction. Plaintiffs sued to enjoin enforcement of several statutes regulating abortion. The parties stipulated the facts only for the preliminary injunction hearing, reserving the right to litigate the facts later. The district court preliminarily enjoined enforcement of one of the statutes and denied preliminary injunctions against the rest. Both sides appealed. The court of appeals entered a final judgment holding several provisions of the statutes unconstitutional. The Supreme Court affirmed!

The Court acknowledged that it was unusual to finally decide the merits on appeal from an order granting or denying a preliminary injunction. But it said that it could do so where "the facts are established or of no controlling relevance." *Id.* at 756. How can the Court know that standard is met if the parties never had a chance to litigate the facts? Two dissenters thought the holding an aberration arising from abortion politics, *id.* at 815-826 (O'Connor, J., dissenting), but the practice has spread in the lower courts. Some of the cases are collected in Office of the Commissioner of Baseball v. Markell, 579 F.3d 293, 299 (3d Cir. 2009). Where a preliminary injunction hearing might turn on a question of law, litigants need to either be prepared for a final judgment, or make a record about the kinds of additional evidence they would introduce at a trial on the merits.

ACLU v. Mukasey, in note 12, illustrates a variation on this new practice. The court of appeals said that because its 2003 opinion had reached the merits of some legal issues, instead of being confined to plaintiff's probability of success, and because no new evidence had been presented that would call those conclusions into question, the earlier opinion was law of the case—binding on subsequent appeals in the same case. 534 F.3d at 187-190. The government may have been caught by surprise. But after two trips through the court of appeals and to the Supreme Court, it may also be unlikely that either side had much new to say on the third trip to the court of appeals.

In Munaf v. Geren, 553 U.S. 674, 691-92 (2008), the Court invoked an older line of cases to similar effect. Most of these cases say that if it is clear on appeal from the preliminary injunction that plaintiff has not stated a claim on which relief can be granted, the appellate court can grant final judgment for defendant and order the complaint dismissed. But the Court also cited one famous constitutional case in which both the district court and the Supreme Court issued opinions that appear to finally resolve the legal issue against the defendant, effectively ending the litigation, even though the only order actually issued and affirmed was a preliminary injunction. Youngstown Sheet & Tube Co. v. Sawyer, 343 U.S. 579, 584-85 (1952).

14. Do we need all these procedures? Lawyers and judges sometimes blur the TRO with the preliminary injunction and the preliminary injunction with the permanent injunction. Lawyers see good reason to take interlocutory appeals that burdened courts of appeals find a waste of time. In part there is a conflict between theory and practice here; in part, an array of procedures that might be needed get in the way in cases where only some of them are needed. John Frank, who had a long and distinguished career as a practitioner in Phoenix, claimed that separate hearings on preliminary and permanent injunctions are rarely needed:

> Today the preliminary injunction commonly is determined on the basis of witnesses and there is no longer a function in most cases for the later trial proceedings. There will remain instances, of course, when, either because the court does not have time or

because the parties are not ready, the court cannot hold as full a hearing as is needed at the preliminary injunction stage to make the ultimate determination. These cases, however, are rare and should be identified in advance. In a lifetime of innumerable injunction actions, I have seen only one in which there was any real function for the third stage. The collapsing of the two procedures into one would remove the current requirement of a bond pending the permanent injunction.

John P. Frank, *The Rules of Civil Procedure—Agenda for Reform*, 137 U. Pa. L. Rev. 1883, 1897 (1989). In a similar vein, William T. Allen, then the Chancellor of Delaware and now a professor at New York University, once said to Laycock that most cases settled after he ruled on the motion for preliminary injunction, so that he rarely had to decide whether to grant a permanent injunction. But of course most damage cases settle too; it would require data rather than impressions to determine if preliminary injunction hearings make trials unnecessary.

Camenisch states the more traditional view:

   Given [its] limited purpose, and given the haste that is often necessary . . . , a preliminary injunction is customarily granted on the basis of procedures that are less formal and evidence that is less complete than in a trial on the merits. . . . In light of these considerations, it is generally inappropriate for a federal court at the preliminary-injunction stage to give a final judgment on the merits.

   Should an expedited decision on the merits be appropriate, . . . the courts have commonly required that "the parties should normally receive clear and unambiguous notice . . . either before the hearing commences or at a time which will still afford the parties a full opportunity to present their respective cases." Pughsley v. 3750 Lake Shore Drive Cooperative Building, 463 F.2d 1055, 1057 (7th Cir. 1972). . . .

   The proceedings here bear the marks of the haste characteristic of a request for a preliminary injunction: the parties have relied on a short stipulation of facts, and even the legal theories on which the University has relied have seemed to change from one level of the proceeding to another.

451 U.S. at 395, 398. We see lots of cases where the full trial matters, but then we are looking for casebook illustrations with reported opinions, and that is a highly unusual sample.

C.   PROSPECTIVE OR RETROSPECTIVE RELIEF

1.   Suits Against Officers in Their Official Capacities

EDELMAN v. JORDAN
415 U.S. 651 (1974)

[Jordan received welfare benefits under Illinois's program of Aid to the Aged, Blind, or Disabled (AABD). Illinois accepted federal matching funds for its AABD program, and agreed to run the program in compliance with the Social Security Act and its implementing regulations.

   The regulations required states to determine an applicant's eligibility and deliver the first check within 45 days of an application. Illinois routinely took up to four months to determine eligibility, and it paid benefits beginning with the month of its determination. Jordan sued Weaver, the director of the Illinois Department of Public Aid, alleging that Illinois's delays violated federal regulations and the Equal Protection Clause.

The district court entered a permanent injunction ordering the defendant officials to comply with federal regulations in the future. It also ordered the officials to pay all benefits wrongfully withheld since the effective date of the federal regulations. The court of appeals affirmed. Jordan v. Weaver, 472 F.2d 985 (7th Cir. 1973). Edelman then replaced Weaver as Public Aid Director and as the defendant in Jordan's lawsuit. Edelman's petition for certiorari challenged the validity of the regulations and the court's power to order payment of back benefits.]

Justice REHNQUIST delivered the opinion of the Court. . . .

A leading historian of the Court tells us:

> The right of the Federal Judiciary to summon a State as defendant and to adjudi-
> cate its rights and liabilities had been the subject of deep apprehension and of active
> debate at the time of the adoption of the Constitution; but the existence of any such
> right had been disclaimed by many of the most eminent advocates of the new Federal
> Government, and it was largely owing to their successful dissipation of the fear of the
> existence of such Federal power that the Constitution was finally adopted.

1 Charles Warren, *The Supreme Court in United States History* 91 (rev. ed., Little Brown 1937). . . .

The issue was squarely presented to the Court in a suit brought at the August 1792 Term by two citizens of South Carolina, executors of a British creditor, against the State of Georgia. . . . Chisholm v. Georgia, 2 U.S. (2 Dall.) 419 (1793). The decision in that case, that a State was liable to suit by a citizen of another State or of a foreign country, literally shocked the Nation. Sentiment for passage of a constitutional amendment to override the decision rapidly gained momentum, and five years after *Chisholm* the Eleventh Amendment was officially announced by President John Adams. Unchanged since then, the Amendment provides:

> The judicial power of the United States shall not be construed to extend to any suit in
> law or equity, commenced or prosecuted against one of the United States by Citizens of
> another State, or by Citizens or Subjects of any Foreign State.

While the Amendment by its terms does not bar suits against a State by its own citizens, this Court has consistently held that an unconsenting State is immune from suits brought in federal courts by her own citizens as well as by citizens of another State. Hans v. Louisiana, 134 U.S. 1 (1890). It is also well established that even though a State is not named a party to the action, the suit may nonetheless be barred by the Eleventh Amendment. In Ford Motor Co. v. Department of Treasury, 323 U.S. 459 (1945), the Court said: "[W]hen the action is in essence one for the recovery of money from the state, the state is the real, substantial party in interest and is entitled to invoke its sovereign immunity from suit even though individual officials are nominal defendants." *Id.* at 464. Thus the rule has evolved that a suit by private parties seeking to impose a liability which must be paid from public funds in the state treasury is barred by the Eleventh Amendment. . . .

Ex parte Young, 209 U.S. 123 (1908), was a watershed case in which this Court held that the Eleventh Amendment did not bar an action in the federal courts seeking to enjoin the Attorney General of Minnesota from enforcing a statute claimed to violate the Fourteenth Amendment of the United States Constitution. This holding has permitted the Civil War Amendments to the Constitution to serve as a sword, rather than merely as a shield, for those whom they were designed to protect. But the relief awarded in *Young* was prospective only; the Attorney General of Minnesota was enjoined to conform his future conduct of that office to the requirement of the Fourteenth Amendment. Such relief is analogous to that awarded by the District Court in the prospective portion of its order under review in this case.

But the retroactive portion of the District Court's order here, which requires the payment of a very substantial amount of money which that court held should have been paid, but was not, stands on quite a different footing. These funds will obviously not be paid out of the pocket of petitioner Edelman. . . .

The funds to satisfy the award in this case must inevitably come from the general revenues of the State of Illinois, and thus the award resembles far more closely the monetary award against the State itself than it does the prospective injunctive relief awarded in *Young*.

The Court of Appeals, in upholding the award in this case, held that it was permissible because it was in the form of "equitable restitution" instead of damages, and therefore capable of being tailored in such a way as to minimize disruptions of the state program of categorical assistance. . . .

We do not read *Young* or subsequent holdings of this Court to indicate that any form of relief may be awarded against a state officer, no matter how closely it may in practice resemble a money judgment payable out of the state treasury, so long as the relief may be labeled "equitable" in nature. . . . *Young* hewed to no such line. Its citation of Hagood v. Southern, 117 U.S. 52 (1886), and In re Ayers, 123 U.S. 443 (1887), which were both actions against the state officers for specific performance of a contract to which the State was a party, demonstrate that equitable relief may be barred by the Eleventh Amendment. . . .

[T]he difference between the type of relief barred by the Eleventh Amendment and that permitted under *Young* will not in many instances be that between day and night. The injunction issued in *Young* was not totally without effect on the State's revenues, since the state law which the Attorney General was enjoined from enforcing provided substantial monetary penalties against railroads which did not conform to its provisions. Later cases from this Court have authorized equitable relief which has probably had greater impact on state treasuries than did that awarded in *Young*. In Graham v. Richardson, 403 U.S. 365 (1971), Arizona and Pennsylvania welfare officials were prohibited from denying welfare benefits to otherwise qualified recipients who were aliens. In Goldberg v. Kelly, 397 U.S. 254 (1970), New York City welfare officials were enjoined from following New York State procedures which authorized the termination of benefits paid to welfare recipients without prior hearing. But the fiscal consequences to state treasuries in these cases were the necessary result of compliance with decrees which by their terms were prospective in nature. . . . Such an ancillary effect on the state treasury is a permissible and often an inevitable consequence of the principle announced in *Young*.

But that portion of the District Court's decree which petitioner challenges on Eleventh Amendment grounds goes much further than any of the cases cited. It requires payment of state funds, not as a necessary consequence of compliance in the future with a substantive federal-question determination, but as a form of compensation to those whose applications were processed on the slower time schedule at a time when petitioner was under no court-imposed obligation to conform to a different standard. While the Court of Appeals described this retroactive award of monetary relief as a form of "equitable restitution," it is in practical effect indistinguishable in many aspects from an award of damages against the State. . . . It is measured in terms of a monetary loss resulting from a past breach of a legal duty on the part of the defendant state officials.

Were we to uphold this portion of the District Court's decree, we would be obligated to overrule the Court's holding in *Ford*, 323 U.S. at 463-464. There a taxpayer, who had, under protest, paid taxes to the State of Indiana, sought a refund of those taxes from the Indiana state officials who were charged with their collection. The taxpayer claimed that the tax had been imposed in violation of the United States Constitution. The term "equitable restitution" would seem even more applicable to the relief sought in that case, since the taxpayer had at one time had the money, and paid it over to the State pursuant to an allegedly unconstitutional tax exaction. Yet this Court had no hesitation in holding that the taxpayer's action was a suit against the State, barred by the Eleventh Amendment. We reach a similar conclusion with respect to the retroactive portion of the relief awarded by the District Court in this case. . . .

The Court of Appeals held in the alternative that even if the Eleventh Amendment be deemed a bar to the retroactive relief awarded respondent in this case, . . . Illinois had "constructively consented" to this suit by participating in the federal AABD program and agreeing to administer federal and state funds in compliance with federal law. Constructive consent is not a doctrine commonly associated with the surrender of constitutional rights, and we see no place for it here. In deciding whether a State has waived its constitutional protection under the Eleventh Amendment, we will find waiver only where stated "by the most express language or by such overwhelming implications from the text as [will] leave no room for any other reasonable construction." Murray v. Wilson Distilling Co., 213 U.S. 151, 171 (1909). . . .

The mere fact that a State participates in a program through which the Federal Government provides assistance for the operation by the State of a system of public aid is not sufficient. . . .

[I]t has not heretofore been suggested that §1983 was intended to create a waiver of a State's Eleventh Amendment immunity. . . . Though a §1983 action may be instituted by public aid recipients such as respondent, a federal court's remedial power, consistent with the Eleventh Amendment, is necessarily limited to prospective injunctive relief, *Young*, and may not include a retroactive award which requires the payment of funds from the state treasury, *Ford*. . . .

The judgment of the Court of Appeals is therefore reversed and the cause remanded for further proceedings consistent with this opinion. . . .

Justice DOUGLAS, dissenting. . . .
Most welfare decisions by federal courts have a financial impact on the States. . . .
There is nothing in the Eleventh Amendment to suggest a difference between suits at law and suits in equity, for it treats the two without distinction. . . .

Justice BRENNAN, dissenting.
This suit is brought by Illinois citizens against Illinois officials. In that circumstance, Illinois may not invoke the Eleventh Amendment, since that Amendment bars only federal court suits against States by citizens of other States. Rather, the question is whether Illinois may avail itself of the nonconstitutional but ancient doctrine of sovereign immunity as a bar to respondent's claim for retroactive AABD payments. In my view Illinois may not assert sovereign immunity for the reason I expressed in dissent in Employees v. Department of Public Health & Welfare, 411 U.S. 279, 298 (1973): the States surrendered that immunity in Hamilton's words, "in the plan of the Convention," that formed the Union, at least insofar as the States granted

Congress specifically enumerated powers. . . . I remain of the opinion that "because of its surrender, no immunity exists that can be the subject of a congressional declaration or a voluntary waiver," 411 U.S. at 300 (Brennan, J., dissenting), and thus have no occasion to inquire whether . . . Congress authorized an action for AABD retroactive benefits, or whether . . . Illinois voluntarily waived the immunity. . . .

Justice MARSHALL, with whom Justice BLACKMUN joins, dissenting. . . .

[T]he Social Security Act does not impose federal standards and liability upon all who engage in certain regulated activities, including often-unwilling state agencies. Instead, the Act seeks to induce state participation in the federal welfare programs by offering federal matching funds in exchange for the State's voluntary assumption of the Act's requirements. I find this basic distinction crucial: it leads me to conclude that by participation in the programs, the States waive whatever immunity they might otherwise have from federal court orders requiring retroactive payment of welfare benefits.[4] . . .

[T]he courts' power to order retroactive payments is an essential remedy to . . . deter States from the strong temptation to cut welfare budgets by circumventing the stringent requirements of federal law. . . .

Absent any remedy which may act with retroactive effect, state welfare officials have everything to gain and nothing to lose by failing to comply with the congressional mandate. . . . Illinois officials have knowingly violated since 1968 a federal regulation on the strength of an argument as to its invalidity which even the majority deems unworthy of discussion. Without a retroactive-payment remedy, we are indeed faced with "the spectre of a state, perhaps calculatingly, defying federal law. . . ." Jordan v. Weaver, 472 F.2d at 995. . . .

NOTES ON PROSPECTIVE-ONLY REMEDIES

1. The core compromise. The law of remedies against governments and government officials is a vast and complex body of doctrine, full of technical distinctions, fictional explanations, and contested compromises. Before trying to understand the doctrinal explanations, think about *Edelman*'s central distinction as a rule for choosing remedies. Injunctions to comply with the law in the future are permitted; compensation for past violations is forbidden unless the sovereign consents to be sued. Put slightly differently, prospective remedies are generally permitted and retrospective remedies are generally forbidden. Quite similar distinctions appear in the immunity of the United States and in the law of most states' immunity from state-law claims.

If the Court is not to abandon constitutional rights altogether, it must provide some remedy for their violation, and this means it must place limits on sovereign immunity. But if it is not willing to abandon sovereign immunity altogether, it must place limits on suits against states. *Edelman* represents the core compromise. Ex parte Young explained the essence of that compromise with a transparent fiction: An officer who acts illegally is stripped of his state authority, and a suit to enjoin him is therefore not a suit against the state. That explanation, explored in detail below, doesn't make much sense. Indeed, to invoke the *Young* fiction that you are suing only the officer

---

4. In view of my conclusion on this issue, I find it unnecessary to consider whether the Court correctly treats this suit as one against the State, rather than as a suit against a state officer permissible under the rationale of Ex parte Young, 209 U.S. 123 (1908).

and not the state, you must allege that you are suing the officer in his official capacity! But however silly the explanation, the functional distinction is a straightforward rule about remedies.

More generally, the dominant theme in governmental immunity law is that injunctions are the preferred remedy, and that damages are more dangerous, more intrusive into the legitimate operations of government, and more in need of restriction. The preference for injunctions is not universal, but it is very broad. How does that fit with claims that damages are the preferred remedy because injunctions are more burdensome, or a greater threat to liberty, or generally undesirable in some other way? Whatever life may remain in the irreparable injury rule, here is a large body of law that goes the other way.

2. Sovereign immunity and irreparable injury. Harm inflicted by an immune defendant is irreparable injury; the nonexistent damage remedy is inadequate. The leading case is Toomer v. Witsell, 334 U.S. 385 (1948), in which the trial court enjoined South Carolina officials from discriminating against out-of-state shrimp fishermen. The Supreme Court affirmed:

> It is . . . clear that compliance with any but the income tax statute would have required payment of large sums of money for which South Carolina provides no means of recovery, that defiance would have carried with it the risk of heavy fines and long imprisonment, and that withdrawal from further fishing until a test case had been taken through the South Carolina courts and perhaps to this Court would have resulted in a substantial loss of business for which no compensation could be obtained.

Id. at 391-392. Plaintiffs' challenge to the state income tax was dismissed, because the state had waived its immunity to suits for tax refunds.

3. Distinguishing prospective from retrospective remedies. The line between prospective and retrospective remedies is neither self-evident nor self-executing. The Court concedes that complying with injunctions may cost money. This is obvious in *Edelman* itself; the Court affirms an order to pay timely welfare benefits in the future. The Kansas City school desegregation remedy cost $2 billion, much of it state funds paid by state officials acting under court order. See Missouri v. Jenkins, 515 U.S. 70 (1995) (*Jenkins III*), which rejected most of this remedy, but not on grounds of sovereign immunity.

The conceptual tension is greatest in reparative injunctions. In the Detroit school desegregation case, the court ordered the state to spend $6 million on remedial education. How is that different from a $6 million damage judgment, with damages measured by the cost of paying for remedial education? The Court had no doubt that the remedy was prospective relief permitted by *Edelman*: "That the programs are also 'compensatory' in nature does not change the fact that they are part of a plan that operates *prospectively* to bring about the delayed benefits of a unitary school system." Milliken v. Bradley, 433 U.S. 267, 290 (1977) (*Milliken II*).

4. Enforcing the prospective remedy. Suppose that on remand Illinois still takes four months to process welfare applications. What can the Court do about it? If it orders defendants to pay back benefits to persons whose applications were delayed after the original injunction, is that a forbidden order for the retrospective payment of money? Or an ancillary effect of securing compliance with the injunction?

"Once issued, an injunction may be enforced," and imprisonment of high state officials is not the only means. Hutto v. Finney, 437 U.S. 678, 690-691 (1978). *Hutto* upheld an award of attorneys' fees against Arkansas prison officials as a sanction for bad-faith litigation.

The Court has also held unanimously that the Eleventh Amendment does not bar the enforcement of consent decrees in which state officials agree to do more than federal law requires. Frew v. Hawkins, 540 U.S. 431 (2004). The decree was a permissible means of enforcing federal law, state officials had consented to it, and "once issued, an injunction may be enforced." *Id.* at 440, quoting *Hutto,* 437 U.S. at 690-691. Other issues in *Frew* are discussed in the Introductory Notes to section 4.B.

5. Limiting the *Young* fiction. *Edelman* is the principal limit on the fiction of Ex parte Young, but it is not the only limit.

a. No specific performance. A second limit is that the *Young* fiction cannot be used to get specific performance of a contract with the government. Only the state is party to the contract; its officers are not. So plaintiff can't prove an obligation without admitting that she is suing the state. More fundamentally, the historical origin of American disputes over sovereign immunity, symbolized by Chisholm v. Georgia, is in efforts to enforce state contracts to pay money. If immunity did not protect the states from debt collection, it would omit the central case for supporters of immunity.

Congress and most of the states have consented to suits for contract damages, usually in a specialized court such as the Court of Federal Claims. The federal consent appears in the Tucker Act, 28 U.S.C. §1491. However explained, consent to damages and immunity to specific performance reflects a preference for damage remedies in contract. That is, government reserves for itself Justice Holmes's choice between performing or paying damages. Government can choose the cheaper way out when a contract goes bad.

b. No enforcing state rights in federal court. A third limit on the *Young* fiction in federal court is that it can be used only to enforce federal rights. Pennhurst State School & Hospital v. Halderman, 465 U.S. 89 (1984). *Pennhurst* was a suit to reform Pennsylvania's institution for the mentally disabled; plaintiffs alleged both state and federal claims against state officials. The Court held the state claims barred by the Eleventh Amendment. In the Court's view, *Young* is justified only by the need to vindicate federal rights; for a federal court to tell state officials how to comply with state law would be a gross violation of state sovereignty.

Pennhurst has led to significant practical problems. It is impossible to join state and federal official-capacity claims against state officials in one action in federal court. Plaintiffs can file federal claims in federal court and abandon any state claims, or they can file all their claims in state court and abandon their federal forum. Or they can file federal claims in federal court and state claims in state court, resulting in two litigations and problems of coordination between them.

c. Congressional preemption. The Court added a fourth limit in Seminole Tribe v. Florida, 517 U.S. 44, 73-76 (1996). Where Congress has provided a detailed remedy that provides less relief than a *Young* suit against a state official, the statutory remedy preempts the *Young* remedy. This rule applied even though the statutory remedy in *Seminole Tribe* was an unconstitutional attempt to authorize suit against the state itself, and thus wholly ineffectual.

d. Limits on recovering property from the government. A fifth limit, somewhat ill defined, restricts the use of Ex parte Young suits to recover property from the government. Idaho v. Coeur d'Alene Tribe, 521 U.S. 261 (1997). The Tribe claimed Lake Coeur d'Alene and its tributaries under a federal grant setting aside the Tribe's reservation; Idaho claimed it under the equal-footing doctrine (the rule that each state is on an equal footing with every other state), as part of the state's ownership and authority over navigable waters. The court of appeals had held that the Tribe could not sue Idaho to quiet title—that would be a suit against the state—but that it could sue the relevant Idaho officials to enjoin them from regulating the Tribe's use of the land or interfering with its possession—that would be a suit under Ex parte Young. 42 F.3d 1244 (9th Cir. 1994). The Supreme Court reversed.

Each of the two opinions making up the majority suggested that the suit might be barred because it was the functional equivalent of a quiet title suit against the state. But this rationale would seem to overrule an old leading case, United States v. Lee, 106 U.S. 196 (1882), which held that a plaintiff claiming to own land could sue government officers in possession. So both opinions also emphasized that the Tribe sought not just ownership, possession, and the income from the land, but also sovereignty: If the land were part of the reservation, it would be governed by the Tribe and removed from Idaho's jurisdiction. So maybe *Coeur d'Alene* is limited to suits by Indian tribes seeking jurisdiction to govern. But plainly *Lee*'s holding is in some jeopardy. An important caveat: *Lee* at most is good law only where the government has not consented to be sued for just compensation for a taking of the disputed land. Malone v. Bowdoin, 369 U.S. 643 (1962).

The Court distinguished *Coeur d'Alene* in California v. Deep Sea Research, Inc., 523 U.S. 491 (1998). Plaintiffs there did not attempt an Ex parte Young suit; they filed an in rem admiralty action to establish their title to a sunken sailing ship they had salvaged. California responded to assert its own title, and then argued that its claim could not be adjudicated in federal court. The Court held that an in rem suit is not a suit against the state unless the state possessed the res. California was not in possession of the sunken ship; Idaho had been in possession and had exercised governing authority over the lake since statehood.

6. A bankruptcy exception to immunity? The Court relied on the in rem theory to create what appears to be a bankruptcy exception in Tennessee Student Assistance Corp. v. Hood, 541 U.S. 440 (2004), and Central Virginia Community College v. Katz, 546 U.S. 356 (2006). In *Katz*, the more far reaching of the two cases, the trustee in bankruptcy sued four state colleges to recover preferential transfers—payments, in the last 90 days before bankruptcy, of debts owed to the colleges (thus preferring the colleges over other unpaid creditors). So in the course of administering the bankrupt estate, the federal bankruptcy court was actually permitted to enter a money judgment against a state agency. The Court said that bankruptcy jurisdiction is "chiefly *in rem*—a narrow jurisdiction that does not implicate state sovereignty to nearly the same degree as other kinds of jurisdiction." 546 U.S. at 378. And this jurisdiction includes claims that may be arguably in personam but are ancillary and "necessary to effectuate the *in rem* jurisdiction of the bankruptcy courts." *Id.* Interstate conflicts over bankruptcy were a problem at the founding, the Constitution authorized a uniform federal law of bankruptcy, and adjudicating the rights of states in bankruptcy courts simply did not trigger the founding generation's concern with state sovereignty. To the extent the states had any rights of sovereign immunity in bankruptcy, those rights were surrendered "in the plan of the Convention," and the power to recover preferential transfers from states does not depend on any express congressional declaration abrogating state sovereign immunity. *Id.* at 379. Justices Roberts, Scalia, Kennedy, and Thomas dissented in a vigorous opinion by Justice Thomas.

7. Debate over Ex parte Young. *Coeur d'Alene* is most notable for the attempt of two justices to repudiate Ex parte Young. Justice Kennedy, in what was plainly written to be the opinion of the Court, said that the propriety of the *Young* fiction in any case depends on balancing plaintiff's need for relief against the state's interest in not being sued in federal court. He seemed to be working up to a holding that if there were a remedy in state court, that would often be sufficient. But only Chief Justice Rehnquist joined this part of the opinion. Justice O'Connor repudiated it, in a concurring opinion joined by Scalia and Thomas, making five votes for the result.

Ex parte Young got a vigorous reaffirmation and application in Verizon Maryland, Inc. v. Public Service Commission, 535 U.S. 635 (2002). Verizon sued the members of the commission in their official capacity, seeking an injunction against future enforcement of a commission order and a declaratory judgment that the order was ineffective both as to the present and as to the past. The Court unanimously rejected the state's immunity defense.

Justice Scalia wrote the opinion. An Ex parte Young action may proceed if the "complaint alleges an ongoing violation of federal law and seeks relief properly characterized as prospective." This was such a case. The Court noted that *Young* itself had effectively been an appeal from the decision of a state regulatory commission. The declaratory judgment as to the past would impose no monetary liability on the state; its purpose was to create a basis for imposing monetary liability on other private parties. Justice Kennedy joined the opinion, but also filed a short concurrence reasserting his view that "our Ex parte Young jurisprudence requires careful consideration of the sovereign interests of the State as well as the obligations of state officials to respect the supremacy of federal law." *Id.* at 649.

NOTES ON THE EVOLUTION OF ELEVENTH AMENDMENT DOCTRINE

1. The text of the Eleventh Amendment. The Eleventh Amendment has come a long way from its text. The three phrases struck out in the following quotation have effectively been deleted by judicial interpretation; the immunity now applies in state court, in admiralty, and in suits by citizens suing their own state.

> The judicial power ~~of the United States~~ shall not be construed to extend to any suit ~~in law or equity~~, commenced or prosecuted against one of the United States ~~by Citizens of another State, or by Citizens or Subjects of any Foreign State~~.

The explanation, as we shall see, is the Supreme Court's view that state sovereign immunity is derived from constitutional structure, and actually is completely independent of the Eleventh Amendment.

2. Ratifying the original Constitution. Article III of the Constitution authorizes federal jurisdiction over several categories of cases, including federal question cases and "Controversies between two or more states;—between a State and Citizens of another State; . . . and between a State, or the Citizens thereof, and foreign States, Citizens or Subjects."

The argument over sovereign immunity in the ratification debates focused on the provisions specifically mentioning states. Opponents of the Constitution argued that these provisions authorized suits against states. The Constitution's supporters offered several inconsistent responses. James Madison said that no state could be a defendant without its consent. Alexander Hamilton agreed, "unless . . . there is a surrender of this immunity in the plan of the convention." *The Federalist* No. 81. He found no surrender of immunity from suits to enforce debts. Other important supporters agreed that the Constitution authorized suits against states and thought this one of its strengths. These included James Wilson and Edmund Randolph, two members of the committee that drafted the jurisdictional provisions. The debates are reviewed in Clyde E. Jacobs, *The Eleventh Amendment and Sovereign Immunity* 22-40 (Greenwood Press 1972).

3. Chisholm v. Georgia and suing another state. Chisholm v. Georgia, 2 U.S. (2 Dall.) 419 (1793), upholding jurisdiction in a suit to collect a debt from a state, was decided 4-1. The majority included James Wilson; John Blair, who had been a delegate to the Convention; and John Jay, the third member of the team that wrote the *Federalist Papers.* Wilson and Jay wrote the most wide ranging of the seriatim opinions. Both seemed to think sovereign immunity inconsistent with republican government. Wilson also made the argument that shows up in Brennan's dissent nearly 200 years later: that the states had surrendered their immunity in the plan of the Convention.

> [T]he citizens of *Georgia,* when they acted upon the large scale of the *Union,* as a part of the "People of the *United States,*" did *not* surrender the Supreme or sovereign Power to that State; but, *as to the purposes of the Union,* retained it to themselves. *As to the purposes of the Union,* therefore, *Georgia is* NOT *a sovereign State.*

2 U.S. (2 Dall.) at 457.

Whatever the right answer was in theory, the states were horrified at the prospect of having to pay their debts to British creditors, debts the nation had promised they would honor in the treaty that ended the Revolutionary War. The Eleventh Amendment was promptly proposed and ratified with only token opposition.

4. Hans v. Louisiana and suing your own state. Hans v. Louisiana, 134 U.S. 1 (1890), was another suit to collect on state bonds. Hans was a citizen of Louisiana, so there was no diversity jurisdiction, and the Court could easily have said there was no federal question jurisdiction: a suit to collect on a bond "arises under" the common law of contracts. But Louisiana argued immunity, not jurisdiction. The Court said that if anyone had suggested in 1793 that citizens of Georgia could sue Georgia in federal court, the reaction would have been just as outraged as the reaction to *Chisholm.* So states must be immune from suits by their own citizens as well as immune from the suits described in the Eleventh Amendment.

Hans assumed that it was an unintended oversight that the Eleventh Amendment speaks only to diversity jurisdiction. But that assumption appears to be mistaken. The first bill introduced to overrule *Chisholm* would have explicitly barred all suits against states in federal court, including federal question cases, suits between two states, and suits by citizens of the defendant state. That draft and its background are set out in Seminole Tribe v. Florida, 517 U.S. 44, 111-112 (1996) (Souter, J., dissenting). That draft was tabled, and Congress adjourned without taking action.

In the next Congress, a new bill was introduced with the language that would become the Eleventh Amendment. So Congress did not expressly bar federal question cases; neither did it expressly permit them; but it rejected the draft that would have expressly barred them.

Professor Clark argues that the Founders were not worried about federal question cases, because they believed that Congress had no power to enact laws that could give rise to federal question cases against states, and that the federal government had no way to enforce judgments against states without provoking civil war. Bradford Clark, *The Eleventh Amendment and the Nature of the Union,* 123 Harv. L. Rev. 1819 (2010). Justice Souter says that suits to collect British debts would have been federal question cases, arising under the treaty; Professor Clark focuses on the much larger volume of debts owed to British creditors by private citizens, which could be collected without suing a state. And he thinks that the drafters preferred to closely track the language of Article III and to say that that language "shall not be construed" to authorize suits against states; in the drafting practice of the time, this signaled an explanatory amendment that restored the original meaning in response to a mistaken interpretation. Clark's theory has the virtue of making sense of the language, but it creates its own set of anomalies. For starters, how to enforce the constitutional rights against states in Article I, §10? His answer is that all those rights could be enforced in suits against individuals—including state officials as defendants. Why states would comply with judgments against their officials, but resort to war rather than comply with judgments against the state itself, is left unexplained.

5. How do you enforce the Constitution against a government with sovereign immunity? *Hans* left the Court with the anomaly first noted by Jay and Wilson: How can sovereign immunity be reconciled with republican government? The Constitution guarantees rights against states; how can those rights be enforced if the government is immune from suit? Some constitutional rights can be raised defensively if the government sues the citizen. But what if the government simply acts, without suing? What if it confiscates property, or burns books, or imprisons people without trial? What if it administers its public welfare programs in arbitrary or discriminatory ways? A government that cannot be sued can make a bill of rights meaningless. The problem had always been there, but the Civil War amendments vastly increased the number of federal rights enforceable against states, and new grants of jurisdiction brought those cases to federal court.

The traditional solution had been suits against officers. These are of two kinds. Plaintiff may sue the officer in her official capacity, to make her exercise or refrain from exercising some of the powers of her office. Or plaintiff may sue the officer in her personal capacity, to make her pay compensation out of her own pocket. There was historical precedent for both kinds of suits. Mandamus and habeas corpus are both suits against officers in their official capacity.

6. The fiction of Ex parte Young and the distinction between official-capacity suits and personal-capacity suits. Throughout the late nineteenth and early twentieth centuries, the Court experimented with suits against officers in their official capacities. These developments culminated in Ex parte Young, 209 U.S. 123 (1908). Young was the Attorney General of Minnesota. A federal court had ordered him not to enforce a railroad rate law; he violated the injunction and was committed to the custody of the federal marshal for contempt. He was not actually in jail; he had to check in with the marshal once a day. Barry Friedman, *The Story of Ex parte Young: Once Controversial, Now Canon*, in *Federal Courts Stories* (Foundation Press 2010). Young filed a habeas corpus petition arguing that a suit to enjoin him from enforcing state law was really against the state of Minnesota and thus barred by the Eleventh Amendment.

The majority explained suits against officers in their *official* capacity with a transparent fiction:

> [T]he use of the name of the State to enforce an unconstitutional act to the injury of complainants is a proceeding without the authority of, and one which does not affect, the State in its sovereign or governmental capacity. It is simply an illegal act upon the part of a state official. . . . [H]e is in that case stripped of his official or representative character and is subjected in his person to the consequences of his individual conduct.

209 U.S. at 159-160.

Justice Harlan, dissenting, thought it obvious that the only purpose of this suit was to prevent Minnesota from enforcing its rate law. If all the state's legal officers could be enjoined, it was the same as if the state had been enjoined. *Id.* at 174. If the Attorney General were really acting as an individual, there would be no violation of the Fourteenth Amendment, because his action would not be state action. The Court rejected that argument in Home Telephone & Telegraph Co. v. City of Los Angeles, 227 U.S. 278 (1913).

Similarly, if the Attorney General were really sued as an individual, the suit would continue against him when he left office. But instead his successor is automatically substituted as a defendant; that practice is now codified in Fed. R. Civ. P. 25(d). Because the real point of the suit is to test the state's policy, it makes no difference who the Attorney General is.

When the government official is sued for damages in her *personal* capacity, the suit continues against her personally after she leaves office, and plaintiff can collect from the official's personal assets. The official in her personal capacity is protected by a qualified immunity, considered in the next subsection, but not by the state's absolute immunity to retrospective relief in federal court. The distinction between official-capacity suits and personal-capacity suits is confusing on first encounter; for clear explanations in simple cases, see Hafer v. Melo, 502 U.S. 21, 25-27 (1991), and Kentucky v. Graham, 473 U.S. 159, 165-168 (1985).

The Court had to explain it again in Lewis v. Clarke, 137 S. Ct. 1285 (2017). An employee of an Indian tribe, driving on tribal business, collided with plaintiffs on I-95 in Connecticut. Plaintiffs sued the employee for damages in his personal capacity; he was not protected by the tribe's sovereign immunity. The tribe was obligated by its own rules to indemnify him, but that voluntary undertaking could not create sovereign immunity where it did not otherwise exist. The decision was unanimous.

7. An alternative explanation. Professor Harrison argues that there is nothing fictional or paradoxical about Ex parte Young. The antisuit injunction—an injunction issued at the request of *P* ordering *D* not to sue *P*—was a familiar tool of equity. *P*'s claim in *P* v. *D* would otherwise have been offered as a defense in *D* v. *P*. A defense against government prosecution does not raise issues of sovereign immunity, and such a defense is no more problematic when raised in an antisuit injunction with the citizen cast as plaintiff instead of defendant. John C. Harrison, *Ex Parte Young*, 60 Stan. L. Rev. 989 (2008). Everything he says is true, and it helps reinforce the functional explanation of Ex parte Young. But *Young* was controversial all the same, and the Court still felt the need for its fictional explanation. And as Professor Harrison recognizes, explaining *Young* as an antisuit injunction explains only the cases where government would sooner or later have had to sue the federal plaintiff to enforce state law. It does not explain *Young*'s later application to cases like *Edelman*, or the structural injunction cases, or any other case where a state has physical power to simply ignore federal law and no need to bring enforcement actions. And therefore, as he does not appear to recognize, it would not solve the problem of making constitutional rights enforceable.

8. The modern debate. However transparent the fiction, doesn't *Hans* make some such fiction essential? Would it be more honest to admit that *Hans* was a mistake? Ever since *Edelman*, and despite the appointment of 11 new Justices, the Supreme Court has been torn by a bitter and persistent 5-4 split on this issue. The majority believes that immunity from damage claims is an essential attribute of state sovereignty, that *Chisholm* was plainly wrong and *Hans* was plainly right, and that the constitutional immunity is far broader and more fundamental than the words of the Eleventh Amendment. The dissenters believe that power to enforce federal rights is an essential attribute of federal supremacy, that *Chisholm* was probably right and that *Hans* was certainly wrong, that at most *Hans* is a common law rule with no constitutional basis, and that neither *Hans* nor the Eleventh Amendment prevents Congress from authorizing damage remedies against states in federal question cases.

The fundamental issue that divides the Justices is not law and equity, or retrospective and prospective relief; it is federalism. The majority seeks to protect state autonomy and shrink the scope of federal judicial power, and it sees state immunity from damage suits as an especially important symbol of that commitment.

9. Congressional power. When it acts to enforce the Fourteenth Amendment, Congress can override state sovereign immunity and authorize retrospective relief against states. Fitzpatrick v. Bitzer, 427 U.S. 445, 456 (1976). But Congress cannot override immunity under the Commerce Clause or most of its other Article I powers. *Seminole Tribe*, 517 U.S. at 72-73. Everyone agreed in *Seminole Tribe* that Congress could not override the text of the Eleventh Amendment, so it could not authorize diversity suits against states. The majority further insisted that the Eleventh Amendment merely illustrates the states' much broader constitutional immunity, and that Congress cannot override that immunity either. The Court distinguished *Fitzpatrick* on the ground that the Fourteenth Amendment had "fundamentally altered the balance of state and federal power struck by the Constitution." *Id.* at 59. The Civil War and Reconstruction Amendments limit state immunity—but only to the extent necessary to enforce those amendments, not in all federal question cases.

Congress also has power to offer the states federal funds on condition that the funded program meet federal requirements. One of the requirements can be an express waiver of immunity; that condition must be clearly stated. The cases are collected in Cherry v. University of Wisconsin, 265 F.3d 541 (7th Cir. 2001), a suit by an English professor alleging sex discrimination in her salary. One of her claims was under Title IX of the Education Amendments of 1972, which forbids sex discrimination in federally aided education and requires schools receiving federal funds to waive their immunity from suit. The Supreme Court has not yet considered waivers coerced in this way.

10. Drawing the line. The distinction between *Fitzpatrick* and *Seminole Tribe* produced a series of cases narrowly interpreting congressional power to enforce the Fourteenth Amendment. The majority has now held that Congress lacks power to impose retrospective remedies on states that violate the patent laws, the Age Discrimination in Employment Act, or the employment provisions of the Americans with Disabilities Act. Assuming that the substance of these laws can be validly applied to states under the commerce power or the patent power, those are Article I powers that will not support a damage remedy. And the power to enforce the Fourteenth Amendment does not authorize Congress to enact the substance of the laws at issue. But Title II of the Americans with Disabilities Act, which regulates access to public services and facilities, is Fourteenth Amendment legislation (and thus will support a damage remedy against states), at least as applied to access to courthouses. The Family and Medical Leave Act is Fourteenth Amendment legislation as applied to state employees taking leave to care for a family member, because Congress thought it necessary to address a pattern of sex discrimination in employment, but not as applied to the employee's own sick leave, which is taken by both men and women. All these results were 5-4; Justice O'Connor was the usual swing vote. Most of the cases are collected in United States v. Georgia, 546 U.S. 151, 157-158 (2006); the sick-leave case is Coleman v. Court of Appeals, 566 U.S. 30 (2012).

11. The clear-statement rule. State waivers of state immunity, congressional waivers of federal immunity, and congressional overrides of state immunity all must be expressed in a clear statement in statutory text that excludes any other possible interpretation. Congressional staff have gradually come to understand the rule well enough to draft clear statements that will satisfy it; states rarely consent to suit in federal court. In Sossamon v. Texas, 563 U.S. 277 (2011), the Court held that a statute authorizing "appropriate relief against a government" was not sufficient to authorize damage suits against states. The result is hardly surprising, but Justices

Sotomayor and Breyer dissented, and the Eleventh Circuit had gone the other way. The statute at bar was the Religious Land Use and Institutionalized Persons Act, 42 U.S.C. §2000cc *et seq.*

12. State courts. Alden v. Maine, 527 U.S. 706 (1999), extended the immunity to state courts. *Alden* was a suit against the state of Maine, in a state court in Maine, by state employees seeking to recover overtime pay to which they were entitled under the Fair Labor Standards Act, now 29 U.S.C. §201 *et seq.* Congress had expressly authorized such suits, but after *Seminole Tribe*, they could not be filed in federal court. *Alden* held that they cannot be filed in state court either. The Court explicitly assumed that states will comply with federal law in good faith despite sovereign immunity; it also succinctly reviewed the multiple means by which federal law may be enforced against state officers and local governments despite sovereign immunity.

13. Sister states. States do not have federal immunity from suit in the courts of a sister state, and the forum state does not owe full faith and credit to the immunity rules of the defendant state. Nevada v. Hall, 440 U.S. 410 (1979). The full-faith-and-credit half of this proposition was unanimously reaffirmed in Franchise Tax Board v. Hyatt, 538 U.S. 488 (2003). *Hall* involved an auto accident with a state employee; *Hyatt* was a dispute over whether plaintiff was a legal resident of Nevada or California, with tax liability turning on the answer and allegations of egregious misconduct by California tax officials.

In a later round of the Hyatt litigation, the Court split 4-4 on whether Nevada v. Hall should be overruled. But it held that the Full Faith and Credit Clause required Nevada to apply the immunity law of either California or Nevada; it could not devise a special rule that treated California worse than it would have been treated under the law of either state. 136 S. Ct. 1277 (2016). The Nevada court had deprived California of the damage caps in Nevada's waiver of immunity, because "legislative control, administrative oversight, and public accountability" protected Nevada citizens from overreach by Nevada agencies, but Nevada had no such control over California agencies.

14. Admiralty. States are immune from suit in admiralty jurisdiction, despite the Eleventh Amendment's specification of suits in "law or equity." Ex parte New York, 256 U.S. 490 (1921). The reasoning is the same as in *Hans* and *Alden*: The immunity is universal and the Eleventh Amendment "is but an exemplification." *Id.* at 497.

15. Administrative proceedings. States are immune from quasi-judicial proceedings before federal administrative agencies. Federal Maritime Commission v. South Carolina State Ports Authority, 535 U.S. 743 (2002).

16. Municipalities. Municipalities are not sovereign and are not protected by the Eleventh Amendment. They can be sued in their own name in federal court, and their officials can be sued. But under the principal federal source of state and local liability, 42 U.S.C. §1983, municipalities cannot be sued for the wrongdoing of their agents or employees. They can be sued only for their official policies or customs. Monell v. New York City Department of Social Services, 436 U.S. 658 (1978). *Monell* applies to suits for injunctions or declaratory judgments as well as to suits for damages. That is, plaintiff can get an injunction against a municipality under §1983 only if a policy or custom of the municipality violates federal law. Los Angeles County v. Humphries, 562 U.S. 29 (2010).

Monell has presented many ambiguities in application. What is a policy and who is a policymaker? The city council, obviously, and formally adopted policies, but also sometimes less formal decisions by executives or senior management. A county prosecutor's impromptu instruction to "Go in and get them," ordering an unconstitutional arrest, became county policy when he said it, because he had final authority on the matter. Pembaur v. City of Cincinnati, 475 U.S. 469 (1986). But an effectively final decision to fire a city employee was not policy where that decision was subject to deferential review by the Civil Service Commission and, at least in theory, by the city council. City of St. Louis v. Praprotnik, 485 U.S. 112 (1988).

A city can be liable for failure to train its employees if that failure shows deliberate indifference to constitutional rights. City of Canton v. Harris, 489 U.S. 378 (1989). But the Court has been reluctant to find such policies, and it has required a tight connection between the failure to train and the specific misconduct that resulted. So in Connick v. Thompson, 563 U.S. 51 (2011), more fully described in section 6.A.2, plaintiff alleged that the New Orleans prosecutor's office systematically failed to train its prosecutors in their duty to disclose exculpatory evidence to criminal defendants, a policy that had resulted in plaintiff's conviction of a murder for which he had later been exonerated. Reading both the complaint and the facts narrowly, the Court refused to find such a policy, so the parish (county) had no liability. Four dissenters found in the record many other examples of evidence that should have been disclosed and a culture of deliberate indifference to the duty to disclose. They would have found a policy.

Sheriff Joe Arpaio of Maricopa County (metropolitan Phoenix), who flouted federal civil rights law for years and ran up huge liabilities in federal court, was a policymaker for the county, making the county liable for his misconduct. United States v. County of Maricopa, 898 F.3d 648 (9th Cir. 2018). This may seem obvious, but the county argued that the county commissioners could not control the independently elected sheriff, and that anyway, the sheriff is a state official, not a county official. This second argument was based on McMillian v. Monroe County, 520 U.S. 781 (1997), which held that Alabama sheriffs are state officials. That decision turned on details of Alabama law, and our impression is that few other states have succeeded in moving liability for their sheriffs from the non-immune county to the immune state.

17. Waivers of immunity. States can waive their immunity, across the board or in certain categories of claims, but they must do so expressly. College Savings Bank v. Florida Prepaid Postsecondary Education Expense Board, 527 U.S. 666 (1999). These waivers are subject to the same clear statement rule as congressional attempts to override a state's immunity.

A state can also waive or forfeit its immunity in open court, one case at a time, either explicitly or by failing to raise the issue. Lapides v. Board of Regents, 535 U.S. 613 (2002). *Lapides* also says that when a state voluntarily invokes the jurisdiction of a federal court, it waives immunity to any claim that may be asserted against it in that proceeding. So when a state is sued in state court, it cannot remove that case to federal court and then move to dismiss on grounds of sovereign immunity.

States are now arguing that although removal waives their immunity as guaranteed by the Eleventh Amendment, it does not waive their sovereign immunity as guaranteed by state law. There is a circuit split on this issue: When a state removes to federal court, does it waive its immunity in all circumstances, or only when it would not also have been immune in state court? Some circuits have added other variations. See Stroud v McIntosh, 722 F.3d 1294, 1300-01 (11th Cir. 2013).

18. Collateral consequences. Sovereign immunity can have surprising consequences even when a state has waived immunity. Any rule or decision that expands the scope of liability arguably requires a new waiver. For example, a federal statute tolling the statute of limitations, allowing state claims to be refiled in state court after they were dismissed in federal court for reasons not going to the merits, cannot be applied to states without a clear statement overriding immunity. Raygor v. Regents of University of Minnesota, 534 U.S. 533, 542-543 (2002).

The United States argued on similar reasoning that a plaintiff could not amend his complaint after the statute of limitations ran. The complaint had been timely filed, but it was missing an essential allegation. This was too much for seven justices, who analogized the case to numerous other technical errors that litigants were permitted to fix by amending. The United States had timely notice of the claim and there was no conceivable prejudice. Scarborough v. Principi, 541 U.S. 401, 421-423 (2004).

A Georgia prison guard sexually assaulted a prisoner, and the prisoner got a $200,000 judgment against the guard. The prisoner cannot attempt to collect by garnishing the guard's wages—ordering the employer to pay a portion of each paycheck to the prisoner instead of to the guard. The reason is that the motion to garnish wages is effectively a suit against Georgia, which pays the wages. Cassady v. Hall, 82 F.3d 1150 (11th Cir. 2018). There is nothing surprising here; it is one more consequence of sovereign immunity. Garnishment is explored in Section 9.B.1.

19. Indian tribes. Indian tribes are "domestic dependent nations," subject to the plenary power of Congress but sovereign as against the rest of the world. They have sovereign immunity in their own courts and in state and federal courts. This immunity extends even to commercial activities off the reservation, until and unless Congress acts to limit that immunity. Michigan v. Bay Mills Indian Community, 134 S. Ct. 2024 (2014). As the case name implies, tribes have immunity even as against states. But the Court emphasized that states can regulate tribal activity off the reservation, and enforce their laws with Ex parte Young suits, or even criminal prosecutions against tribal leaders.

Justice Kagan wrote the opinion for herself, Chief Justice Roberts, and Justices Kennedy, Breyer, and Sotomayor. Justice Thomas's dissent for himself and Justices Scalia, Ginsburg, and Alito questioned the whole concept of tribal sovereign immunity in any application. He included a section describing all the terrible things that can be done by an entity with sovereign immunity. Justice Ginsburg joined that dissent and added her view that the immunity of states is equally "beyond the pale." *Id.* at 2055.

It was Chief Justice Roberts and Justice Kennedy pointing out the dangers of sovereign immunity in Upper Skagit Indian Tribe v. Lundgren, 138 S. Ct. 1649 (2018). The dispute was over the location of the property line between a parcel owned by the Lundgrens and a parcel, off the reservation, owned by the tribe. The Lundgrens sued to quiet title to the disputed acre, and the tribe pled sovereign immunity. The Court remanded the case for consideration of whether tribes are subject to an immunity exception that allows sovereigns to be sued with respect to real property in the territory of another sovereign—in this case, the state of Washington. The Chief's concurring opinion said that if the tribe could not be sued, it could "seize property with impunity, even without a colorable claim of right." *Id.* at 1655. No one expressed any such fear about a state seizing property within its own territory in Idaho v. Coeur d'Alene Tribe, described in the previous set of notes. But the issue is the same.

20. State law. Justice Souter once reported that every state allows declaratory and injunctive relief in state court against state officials, citing cases from 49 states; he somehow missed Indiana. Idaho v. Coeur d'Alene Tribe, 521 U.S. 261, 317 n.15 (1997) (dissenting). His discussion concerned federal claims in state court, and it is conceivable that some of the cited cases are limited to that context.

Georgia held that sovereign immunity bars suits to enforce the state constitution against state officers in their official capacity. Lathrop v Deal, 801 S.E. 2d 867 (Ga. 2017). But they can still be sued for injunctions or declaratory judgments in their individual capacity—what note 6 calls personal capacity; the two phrases are interchangeable in this context. An elaborate opinion that reviews Georgia sovereign immunity law from the founding forward appears to have produced only a change to an unconventional nomenclature. The apparent reason for the opinion is that defendant officials were going for the home run. They claimed that sovereign immunity barred official-capacity suits, and that official immunity barred individual-capacity suits, so that no one could ever sue the state or any state official to enforce state law.

It remains to be seen if these individual-capacity suits in Georgia will work just like official-capacity suits elsewhere. The court noted the possibility that individual-capacity judgments would not be binding on successors in office. But without deciding that question, it also noted that any appellate decisions would be precedent binding on successors in office.

NOTES ON THE REASONS FOR SOVEREIGN IMMUNITY

1. Why sovereign immunity? Why is it so important that states not have to pay their debts or compensate for the damages they cause, whether by ordinary torts or constitutional violations? The Court rarely says; it treats sovereign immunity as obvious. In fact, most states do pay their debts, and occasional episodes of repudiation are mostly far in the past. Most states consent to be sued, with limits and exceptions, for ordinary torts and contracts. We will look at these waivers and their effects in section 6.A.1. But few states consent to pay damages for violating the Constitution or other federal law, and resistance to liability is often fierce. Professor Schauer suggests more generally that government officials may feel little obligation to obey any law they disagree with. Frederick Schauer, *When and How (If at All) Does Law Constrain Official Action?*, 45 Ga. L. Rev. 769 (2010).

Professor Young argues that states were in fiscal crisis at the time of the Eleventh Amendment, and that southern states were in fiscal crisis after the Civil War and as late as Hans v. Louisiana. And he predicts that unfunded pension and health-care obligations will put states in fiscal crisis again and vindicate the Court's expansive view of sovereign immunity. Ernest A. Young, *Its Hour Come Round at Last? State Sovereign Immunity and the Great State Debt Crisis of the Early Twenty-First Century*, 35 Harv. J.L. & Pub. Pol'y 593 (2012).

2. Quick answers. One answer is that sovereign immunity is just special privilege; governments get to make special rules for themselves. Another is that immunity defers to the consequences of fiscal irresponsibility among legislators and resistance to taxation among voters; governments have many obligations and limited revenues. Another answer is that governments can generally be trusted to do the right thing; before there were general waivers of sovereign immunity, Congress and state legislatures passed private bills to compensate people with just claims against the government. Of course this worked better for the politically well connected; it probably did not work at all for groups that were politically weak or unpopular.

3. The Appropriations Clause. Legislatures passing private bills to compensate individuals sounds strange today; legislatures are too burdened with larger matters to investigate individual claims, and perhaps too politicized to decide fairly, and we think of courts as the natural place to decide individual claims. But the argument for legislatures deciding which claims to pay is simple enough: Legislatures are responsible for the budget. The sovereign immunity of the United States is sometimes attributed to the Appropriations Clause: "No Money shall be drawn from the Treasury, but in Consequence of Appropriations made by Law." U.S. Const., art. I, §9, cl. 7. For an originalist elaboration of this argument, see Paul F. Figley and Jay Tidmarsh, *The Appropriations Power and Sovereign Immunity*, 107 Mich. L. Rev. 1207 (2009). Figley and Tidmarsh believe that legislatures in the colonial and early national period, having won control of finances from the king within recent memory, would not have surrendered part of that control to judges.

4. Is government liability really different from private liability? Recall the two basic accounts of why we have compensatory damages in the first place: economic incentives and corrective justice. We want wrongdoers to pay damages so that they will take account of the costs they impose on others, and so that victims will be compensated and justice restored. Some judges and scholars have argued that these reasons don't apply to governments. The reasons offered are diverse and complex, and we can only scratch the surface here. Most of these arguments are explored, pro and con, in Lawrence Rosenthal, *A Theory of Governmental Damages Liability: Torts, Constitutional Torts, and Takings*, 9 U. Pa. J. Const. L. 797 (2007), and Daryl J. Levinson, *Making Government Pay: Markets, Politics, and the Allocation of Constitutional Costs*, 67 U. Chi. L. Rev. 345 (2000).

a. Unbalanced incentives. One common argument is that the benefits of good government are spread widely across the society. They do not accrue to the government's coffers, and certainly not to the bank accounts of individual government employees. If damage judgments internalize the costs of government conduct, but the benefits are not internalized, incentives might be out of balance; government might be too cautious.

b. Political incentives. Governments respond more to votes than to dollars, and a monetary cost to government translates into a political cost to incumbent officials only indirectly and unpredictably. But a judgment does divert resources from whatever elected officials would otherwise have regarded as the politically optimal use of those resources, and that deterrence may be close enough.

c. Poor fit with corrective justice? Some constitutional torts cause damages not easily measured in dollars. Consider loss of the right to speak or to practice a religion, strip searches or other invasions of privacy, or racial discrimination that is humiliating but causes no financial loss. The arguments about whether to compensate pain and suffering apply here: Are these real losses that the class of potential victims should want to be "insured" against? Whatever one thinks of that argument, the government wrongdoing in *Edelman* caused indisputable financial loss, and both constitutional and ordinary torts often cause medical expenses, loss of income, and other financial loss. Think of police beatings or collisions with government vehicles. And if the whole theory of constitutional rights is that they are protected against the majoritarian political process, we can't very well let that process decide to provide no effective remedies for violations of these rights.

On the other side of the corrective justice equation, the liability may ultimately fall on taxpayers who had little to do with the wrong and little ability to control it. But that argument is easily overstated. For widespread or systemic violations, voters and taxpayers are often the source of political pressure that drives the violations. Maybe they don't want to fund education for students who don't speak English, or maybe they want the police to get tough on crime and not worry about "technicalities." And at the taxpayer level, the balance of incentives may be restored; however unevenly distributed, the benefits of good government generally accrue to some set of voters and taxpayers.

2.   *Suits Against Officers in Their Personal Capacities (and the Doctrine of Qualified Immunity)*

HARLOW v. FITZGERALD
457 U.S. 800 (1982)

Justice POWELL delivered the opinion of the Court. . . .

I

In this suit for civil damages petitioners Bryce Harlow and Alexander Butterfield are alleged to have participated in a conspiracy to violate the constitutional and statutory rights of the respondent A. Ernest Fitzgerald. Respondent avers that petitioners entered the conspiracy in their capacities as senior White House aides to former President Richard M. Nixon.

[Fitzgerald was a management analyst in the Department of the Air Force. In 1968, he testified to a congressional committee about technical problems and huge cost overruns on the C-5A cargo plane. The revelations were embarrassing to the Defense Department. At the end of the Johnson administration, a staff memo outlined three ways to get rid of Fitzgerald despite his civil service protection. One way was a reduction in force.

Nearly a year later, the Nixon administration carried out the reduction in force, eliminating Fitzgerald's job. A congressional committee investigated Fitzgerald's discharge, a reporter asked Nixon about it, and Nixon and his staff discussed the matter, but the discharge stood.

The Chief Examiner for the Civil Service Commission concluded, after 4,000 pages of testimony, that the reduction in force was motivated by "reasons purely personal to" Fitzgerald, but that there was not sufficient evidence to conclude that these reasons included his congressional testimony. Following the Civil Service decision, Fitzgerald sued Nixon and several high-ranking White House aides. After eight years of discovery, Fitzgerald had evidence that Nixon, Harlow, and Butterfield had discussed his discharge in suspicious ways, but no smoking gun. They moved for summary judgment, but the district judge held that Fitzgerald had raised an issue of fact.

Some of Fitzgerald's evidence came from secret tapes of Nixon's conversations. Those tapes were discovered in congressional hearings investigating whether the administration had covered up its connections to the burglary of the Democratic National Committee during Nixon's 1972 campaign for re-election. The witness who let slip that the tapes existed was Alexander Butterfield.

The district court] ruled that petitioners were not entitled to absolute immunity.

Independently of former President Nixon, petitioners invoked the collateral order doctrine and appealed the denial of their immunity defense.... The Court of Appeals dismissed the appeal without opinion....

II ...

[O]ur decisions consistently have held that Government officials are entitled to some form of immunity from suits for damages. As recognized at common law, public officers require this protection to shield them from undue interference with their duties and from potentially disabling threats of liability.

Our decisions have recognized immunity defenses of two kinds. For officials whose special functions or constitutional status requires complete protection from suit, we have recognized the defense of "absolute immunity." The absolute immunity of legislators, in their legislative functions, and of judges, in their judicial functions, now is well settled. Our decisions also have extended absolute immunity to certain officials of the Executive Branch. These include prosecutors and similar officials, executive officers engaged in adjudicative functions, and the President of the United States.

For executive officials in general, however, our cases make plain that qualified immunity represents the norm. In Scheuer v. Rhodes, 416 U.S. 232 (1974), we acknowledged that high officials require greater protection than those with less complex discretionary responsibilities. Nonetheless, we held that a governor and his aides could receive the requisite protection from qualified or good-faith immunity. In Butz v. Economou, 438 U.S. 478 (1978), we extended the approach of *Scheuer* to high federal officials of the Executive Branch. [Butz had been Nixon's Secretary of

Agriculture.] Discussing in detail the considerations that also had underlain our decision in *Scheuer*, we explained that the recognition of a qualified immunity defense for high executives reflected an attempt to balance competing values: not only the importance of a damages remedy to protect the rights of citizens, but also "the need to protect officials who are required to exercise their discretion and the related public interest in encouraging the vigorous exercise of official authority." 438 U.S. at 506. Without discounting the adverse consequences of denying high officials an absolute immunity from private lawsuits alleging constitutional violations . . . we emphasized our expectation that insubstantial suits need not proceed to trial:

> Insubstantial lawsuits can be quickly terminated by federal courts alert to the possibilities of artful pleading. Unless the complaint states a compensable claim for relief . . ., it should not survive a motion to dismiss. Moreover, . . . damages suits . . . can be terminated on a properly supported motion for summary judgment based on the defense of immunity. . . .

438 U.S. at 507-508.

Butz continued to acknowledge that the special functions of some officials might require absolute immunity. But the Court held that "federal officials who seek absolute exemption from personal liability for unconstitutional conduct must bear the burden of showing that public policy requires an exemption of that scope." *Id.* at 506. [The Court concluded that White House aides are not distinguishable from cabinet secretaries and are not entitled to absolute immunity.]

IV

Even if they cannot establish that their official functions require absolute immunity, petitioners assert that public policy at least mandates an application of the qualified immunity standard that would permit the defeat of insubstantial claims without resort to trial. We agree.

A

The resolution of immunity questions inherently requires a balance between the evils inevitable in any available alternative. In situations of abuse of office, an action for damages may offer the only realistic avenue for vindication of constitutional guarantees. See Bivens v. Six Unknown Named Agents, 403 U.S. 388, 410 (1971) (Harlan, J., concurring) ("For people in Bivens' shoes, it is damages or nothing"). [Defendants in *Bivens* had raided plaintiffs' house in the middle of the night, without probable cause; because plaintiff had no warning of the raid, he had no chance to sue to enjoin it.] It is this recognition that has required the denial of absolute immunity to most public officers. At the same time, however, it cannot be disputed seriously that claims frequently run against the innocent as well as the guilty—at a cost not only to the defendant officials, but to society as a whole. These social costs include the expenses of litigation, the diversion of official energy from pressing public issues, and the deterrence of able citizens from acceptance of public office. Finally, there is the danger that fear of being sued will "dampen the ardor of all but the most resolute, or the most irresponsible [public officials], in the unflinching discharge of their duties." Gregoire v. Biddle, 177 F.2d 579, 581 (2d Cir. 1949).

In identifying qualified immunity as the best attainable accommodation of competing values, . . . we relied on the assumption that this standard would permit "[i]nsubstantial lawsuits [to] be quickly terminated." *Butz*, 438 U.S. at 507-508. Yet petitioners advance persuasive arguments that the dismissal of insubstantial lawsuits without trial—a factor presupposed in the balance of competing interests struck by our prior cases—requires an adjustment of the "good faith" standard established by our decisions.

B

Qualified or "good faith" immunity is an affirmative defense that must be pleaded by a defendant official. Decisions of this Court have established that the "good faith" defense has both an "objective" and a "subjective" aspect. The objective element involves a presumptive knowledge of and respect for "basic, unquestioned constitutional rights." Wood v. Strickland, 420 U.S. 308, 322 (1975). The subjective component refers to "permissible intentions." *Id.* Characteristically the Court has defined these elements by identifying the circumstances in which qualified immunity would *not* be available. Referring both to the objective and subjective elements, we have held that qualified immunity would be defeated if an official "*knew or reasonably should have known* that the action he took within his sphere of official responsibility would violate the constitutional rights of the [plaintiff], *or* if he took the action *with the malicious intention* to cause a deprivation of constitutional rights or other injury." *Id.* (emphasis added).

The subjective element of the good-faith defense frequently has proved incompatible with our admonition in *Butz* that insubstantial claims should not proceed to trial. Rule 56 of the Federal Rules of Civil Procedure provides that disputed questions of fact ordinarily may not be decided on motions for summary judgment. And an official's subjective good faith has been considered to be a question of fact that some courts have regarded as inherently requiring resolution by a jury.

In the context of *Butz*'s attempted balancing of competing values, it now is clear that substantial costs attend the litigation of the subjective good faith of government officials. Not only are there the general costs of subjecting officials to the risks of trial—distraction of officials from their governmental duties, inhibition of discretionary action, and deterrence of able people from public service. There are special costs to "subjective" inquiries of this kind. Immunity generally is available only to officials performing discretionary functions. In contrast with the thought processes accompanying "ministerial" tasks, the judgments surrounding discretionary action almost inevitably are influenced by the decisionmaker's experiences, values, and emotions. These variables explain in part why questions of subjective intent so rarely can be decided by summary judgment. Yet they also frame a background in which there often is no clear end to the relevant evidence. Judicial inquiry into subjective motivation therefore may entail broad-ranging discovery and the deposing of numerous persons, including an official's professional colleagues. Inquiries of this kind can be peculiarly disruptive of effective government.

Consistently with the balance at which we aimed in *Butz*, we conclude today that bare allegations of malice should not suffice to subject government officials either to the costs of trial or to the burden of broad-reaching discovery. We therefore hold that government officials performing discretionary functions generally are shielded from liability for civil damages insofar as their conduct does not violate clearly established statutory or constitutional rights of which a reasonable person would have known.

Reliance on the objective reasonableness of an official's conduct, as measured by reference to clearly established law, should avoid excessive disruption of government and permit the resolution of many insubstantial claims on summary judgment. On summary judgment, the judge appropriately may determine, not only the currently applicable law, but whether that law was clearly established at the time an action occurred.[32] If the law at that time was not clearly established, an official could not reasonably be expected to anticipate subsequent legal developments, nor could he fairly be said to "know" that the law forbade conduct not previously identified as unlawful. Until this threshold immunity question is resolved, discovery should not be allowed. If the law was clearly established, the immunity defense ordinarily should fail, since a reasonably competent public official should know the law governing his conduct. Nevertheless, if the official pleading the defense claims extraordinary circumstances and can prove that he neither knew nor should have known of the relevant legal standard, the defense should be sustained. But again, the defense would turn primarily on objective factors.

By defining the limits of qualified immunity essentially in objective terms, we provide no license to lawless conduct. The public interest in deterrence of unlawful conduct and in compensation of victims remains protected by a test that focuses on the objective legal reasonableness of an official's acts. Where an official could be expected to know that certain conduct would violate statutory or constitutional rights, he should be made to hesitate; and a person who suffers injury caused by such conduct may have a cause of action. But where an official's duties legitimately require action in which clearly established rights are not implicated, the public interest may be better served by action taken "with independence and without fear of consequences." Pierson v. Ray, 386 U.S. 547, 554 (1967).[34] . . .

V

The judgment of the Court of Appeals is vacated, and the case is remanded for further action consistent with this opinion. . . .

[Opinions concurring and dissenting on the absolute immunity issue are omitted.]

NOTES ON QUALIFIED OFFICIAL IMMUNITY

1. Personal-capacity suits. *Harlow* is a suit against officers in their personal capacities. Plaintiff does not seek to control the future conduct of their office; he seeks to recover damages for past misconduct. Any damages are to be collected from the officer's personal assets, not from government funds under their control. Any attempt to collect from government funds would be barred by sovereign immunity. Governments usually indemnify employees held liable, but that is a choice for the political branches.

These distinctions create three classes of cases: suits against the sovereign, official-capacity suits under Ex parte Young, and personal-capacity suits for damages paid by the officer. Suits against the sovereign are barred unless the sovereign consents; damage remedies against officers are barred unless the law was clearly established.

---

32. As in Procunier v. Navarette, 434 U.S. 555, 565 (1978), we need not define here the circumstances under which the state of the law should be evaluated by reference to the opinions of this Court, of the Courts of Appeals, or of the local District Court.

34. We emphasize that our decision applies only to suits for civil *damages* arising from actions within the scope of an official's duties and in objective good faith. We express no view as to the conditions in which injunctive or declaratory relief might be available.

2. Qualified or absolute immunity? *Harlow* is the authoritative statement of the scope of official immunity from federal claims, not only for presidential aides, but also for most executive branch officials, whether high or low, state or federal. The immunity protects government employees; it also protects private citizens, including lawyers in private practice, who work for government as independent contractors. Filarsky v. Delia, 566 U.S. 377 (2012). It is called "official immunity" to distinguish it from the immunity of the sovereign; it is also called "qualified immunity," to distinguish it from the absolute immunity of the sovereign and a few exceptional officials: the President, legislators, judges, and prosecutors, when they act in those respective capacities. Absolute immunity for officials is taken up in section 6.A.2. State claims against state officials are governed by state law. State claims against federal officials—for example, negligent driving on government business—are largely governed by the Federal Tort Claims Act, considered in section 6.A.1.

3. Motive as an element of the violation. *Harlow* sought to make motive irrelevant to the immunity defense. But what if motive is the essence of the alleged violation? Consider the claim in *Harlow* itself. It was clearly established that public employees could not be fired for criticizing public policy. Pickering v. Board of Education, 391 U.S. 563 (1968). Doesn't that mean that Harlow and Butterfield were not immune under the Court's standard? The hard issue in the case is whether Fitzgerald was fired for criticizing the C-5A cargo plane or for some other reason. The requirement of clearly established law did not cut off discovery on that issue, or keep weak claims from going to trial if there is a little bit of evidence to support them. Motive is also the key to most equal protection claims, Washington v. Davis, 426 U.S. 229 (1976), and to some free exercise and establishment clause claims. Unless the Court makes officials absolutely immune, it cannot cut off all inquiry into motive.

In Crawford-El v. Britton, 523 U.S. 574 (1998), the Court refused to create special procedures or modify *Harlow*'s rule for motive cases. Crawford-El alleged that a prison guard took away a box of his legal materials in retaliation for his talking to the press. So the claim paralleled *Harlow*; the merits depended on defendant's motive. The Court said the law was clearly established; the dispute was over facts; and the parties would have to litigate those facts under the usual rules of civil procedure. Four dissenters proposed rules that would have made it easier to dismiss motive claims without discovery; it was unclear how stringent these proposed rules would have been.

4. Applying the clearly-established-law test. *Harlow* declined to elaborate on what it meant by "clearly established" law. Do only Supreme Court cases count? Courts of appeals? District courts? State courts? Courts in other states or circuits? Is law clearly established only when there is a case on all fours, or do officials have to make reasonable applications of clearly established principles? Can one case clearly establish anything?

Consider Wood v. Strickland, the previous leading case. Three high school girls were suspended for the rest of the semester for spiking the punch at a school event. The school board imposed this punishment at a meeting from which the girls and their parents were excluded, relying on a report that one of the girls had gotten in an unrelated fight. The girls and their parents complained that the girls had been suspended without due process.

There was an Eighth Circuit case involving two students suspended from college for two semesters. The court had said: "We do hold . . . that procedural due process must be afforded . . . by way of adequate notice, definite charge, and a hearing with opportunity to present one's own side of the case and with all necessary protective measures." Esteban v. Central Missouri State College, 415 F.2d 1077, 1089 (8th Cir.

1969). The statement was dictum in the court of appeals, but it had been holding in the district court.

Did that clearly establish the law for the Eighth Circuit? Was it clear that high schools are the same as colleges? Was it clear that three months is the same as two semesters? Did the school board have to read *Esteban* in light of decisions in other circuits involving high schools and shorter suspensions? Did it matter that the statement was dictum? What about the district court's holding? Could Arkansas school boards ignore it because it came from the Western District of Missouri? Even if the court of appeals approved the holding in dictum?

On January 11, 1972, the Eighth Circuit decided Tate v. Board of Education, 453 F.2d 975 (8th Cir. 1972), involving a high school and a three-day suspension. The Mena school board acted on February 18. Is *Tate* relevant to whether the law was clearly established in the Eighth Circuit? Could defendants show they "neither knew nor should have known" about *Tate*?

In *Tate*, plaintiffs were given a chance to ask questions when their suspensions were announced. The court held that this informal "hearing" satisfied due process because the facts were clear and the penalty was mild. Does that clearly establish that due process applies to high schools? Does it clearly establish how much of a hearing plaintiffs in Wood v. Strickland were entitled to?

On the relevance of *Tate*, see Elder v. Holloway, 510 U.S. 510 (1994), which held that whether the federal right was clearly established is a question of law, subject to de novo determination on appeal. The issue arose because the court of appeals had refused to consider a case in point, decided in the court of appeals a year before the alleged tort but not cited to the district court by either side. The Supreme Court said the case was relevant to whether the federal right had been clearly established. Is there an implicit assumption that the officer should have known about it, even though the lawyers apparently did not? Of course, a year to learn about a new case is a lot more than five weeks.

5. Keeping abreast of the law. How is an unpaid school board in Mena, Arkansas, supposed to keep informed of clearly established law? The dissenters in Wood v. Strickland thought it impossible. Can a constitutional republic be administered on the assumption that it is impossible for public officials to know the constitutional constraints that bind them? If the Court had said officials don't have to know the law, wouldn't that remove most of their incentive to find out?

School board members don't have to read the advance sheets, or know the whole Constitution. Educational associations publish newsletters summarizing legal developments affecting schools; school board lawyers subscribe to the newsletters. Well-run schools have operations manuals and in-service training for teachers. It is not so difficult to keep standard operating procedures abreast of "clearly established" law if the school board — or any other government agency — cares to do so. But there are lots of rank-and-file employees to be trained, there is deep resistance to some constitutional requirements, and there is always somebody who didn't get the word.

6. Developments since *Harlow*. Since *Harlow*, the federal courts have developed a vast body of law on the meaning of "clearly established law." The Supreme Court has taken a remarkable number of these cases in recent years, investing great effort in determining what law was clearly settled at various points in the past, often without determining what the law will be for the future. Here are a few of the more important or revealing examples.

a. Specificity.

i. In Anderson v. Creighton, 483 U.S. 635 (1987), an FBI agent searched a house without a warrant. The court of appeals denied immunity because it was clearly

established that search of a residence required either a warrant, exigent circumstances, or consent. The Supreme Court found it irrelevant whether that *principle* was
clearly established. "[T]he right the official is alleged to have violated must have been
'clearly established' in a more particularized, and hence more relevant, sense: The
contours of the right must be sufficiently clear that a reasonable official would understand that what he is doing violates that right." *Id.* at 640. The officer was entitled to
know whether the circumstances he faced were sufficiently exigent.

ii. In Ashcroft v. al-Kidd, 563 U.S. 731 (2011), the government arrested the plaintiff
as a material witness, allegedly with no intention of calling him as a witness, because
it suspected him of supporting terrorism but had no evidence sufficient to get an
arrest warrant. The Court again emphasized specificity, holding that it was not clearly
settled that pretextual use of material-witness warrants is unconstitutional, and it was
irrelevant that the Ninth Circuit thought that the unconstitutionality of the practice
could be deduced from clearly established general principles. In an opinion for the
five conservatives, Justice Scalia said: "We do not require a case directly on point, but
existing precedent must have placed the statutory or constitutional question beyond
debate." *Id.* at 741.

iii. The Court again emphasized specificity in Mullenix v. Luna, 136 S. Ct. 305
(2015). Plaintiff's decedent fled from police officers, traveling at high speeds on an
Interstate highway. Officers at three different locations deployed spike strips to punc-
ture the tires of the fleeing vehicle. An officer had to remain in position to operate
the spike strips, leaving them down for all vehicles except the suspect's, and on occasion, officers operating spike strips had been injured or killed.

Officer Mullenix thought he had a better idea. He took his rifle and stood on the
overpass where the first spike strip was deployed, planning to shoot out some essential
part of the fleeing vehicle as it approached the overpass. The officers involved had all
been trained in the operation of spike strips; none had been trained in shooting at
the engine block of a car traveling at high speeds. The officer's supervisor told him
by radio to wait and see if the spike strip worked, but he fired six shots at the fleeing
vehicle. None hit any critical part of the vehicle, but four hit the driver in the torso,
killing him.

The Fifth Circuit held that the shooting violated the clearly settled rule that officers could use deadly force against a fleeing suspect only if that suspect posed a
sufficiently "substantial and immediate threat" to the safety of others. Whether the
decedent had posed such a threat was a disputed question of fact, so the district court
had properly denied summary judgment for the officer.

The Supreme Court summarily reversed. Both spike strips and shooting carried
risks, and no case clearly settled that it was unreasonable to choose shooting over
spike strips. The Court said four times that the illegality of the officer's specific
actions had to be "beyond debate," and it said that qualified immunity protects "all
but the plainly incompetent or those who knowingly violate the law." 136 S. Ct. at 308.
Justice Sotomayor dissented.

iv. The Court summarily reversed in two other police shooting cases, finding qualified immunity without briefing or argument. Kisela v. Hughes, 138 S. Ct. 1148 (2018);
White v. Pauly, 137 S. Ct. 548 (2017). Both cases emphasize the factual details of the
encounter, holding out the possibility of a shooting so unreasonable that immunity
would be lost, but seeming generally to require a case presenting nearly identical
facts. Both cases again say that the illegality of the officer's conduct must be "beyond
debate." *Pauly* commented on the Court's frequent reversals of courts of appeals
on qualified immunity issues. These reversals had been necessary because "qualified
immunity is important to 'society as a whole,'" and because the "immunity from suit"

is "effectively lost if a case is erroneously permitted to go to trial." 137 S. Ct. at 551. *Pauly* was unanimous; Justices Sotomayor and Ginsburg dissented in *Kisela*.

b. Obvious applications. United States v. Lanier, 520 U.S. 259 (1997), was not a civil suit for damages, but a criminal prosecution under 18 U.S.C. §242, a Reconstruction-era statute that makes it a felony to deprive, under color of state law, any person "of any rights, privileges, or immunities secured or protected by the Constitution or laws of the United States." Defendant, a state judge, was convicted under this provision for 11 sexual assaults committed in his chambers. The prosecution relied on a substantive due process right to be free of sexual assault by government officials; the court of appeals reversed on the ground that Judge Lanier lacked notice that such a right existed. The court of appeals would have required a Supreme Court decision on facts "fundamentally similar" to those charged.

The Supreme Court unanimously reversed. It explicitly equated the criminal-law requirement of fair notice of what would be an offense with the qualified-immunity requirement of clearly established law. It quoted the *Creighton* standard, but it held that an official's understanding of the illegality of his conduct could come from lower court decisions and from cases that were not "fundamentally similar" but were clear enough to give reasonable notice that their principles applied. 520 U.S. at 268-270. The Court quoted with approval lower court judges who had noted that "the easiest cases don't even arise." *Id.* at 271. If a rule is too obvious ever to have been litigated, it does not follow that the first official to violate the rule gets immunity.

c. Hoped-for exceptions. What if the government hopes to create an exception to a clearly established rule? The Court has recognized only two justifications for searching a residence without a warrant: exigent circumstances and consent. Some lower courts have recognized an additional exception, which they have labeled "consent once removed," where the resident admits a visitor who then consents to the search.

In Pearson v. Callahan, 555 U.S. 223, 243-244 (2009), the defendant officers sent in an informant and burst into the residence when he signaled that he had bought drugs. The Utah Supreme Court invalidated the search and dismissed the prosecution. The Tenth Circuit held that the rule against searching residences without a warrant was clearly settled and had only the two traditional exceptions. The Supreme Court unanimously and tersely reversed; the officers were entitled to rely on cases from other circuits, and when the courts were divided, officers should not be liable in damages for choosing the wrong side. It did not appear to matter that there was no support of the consent-once-removed exception in the Tenth Circuit.

d. Division in the lower courts. Savanna Redding, a 13-year-old girl, was strip searched on the basis of a conclusory accusation that she was the source of four prescription-strength ibuprofen pills (Advil) and one over-the-counter naproxen (Aleve) found on another student. The Court held, with only Justice Thomas dissenting, that there was no constitutionally sufficient basis for searching beyond her backpack and outer clothing—no basis to suspect that pills were hidden in her underwear, and no basis to believe that any pills in circulation were especially dangerous. "[T]he combination of these deficiencies was fatal to finding the search reasonable." Safford Unified School District No. 1 v. Redding, 557 U.S. 364, 377 (2009).

But the Court also held that this rule had not been clearly settled. There were lower court opinions going both ways on strip searches of students. That would not matter "if we have been clear." *Id.* at 378. But the conflicting opinions were sufficiently numerous and well reasoned "to counsel doubt that we were sufficiently clear in the prior statement of law." *Id.* at 379. Justices Stevens and Ginsburg thought that the general principles governing student searches, announced in New Jersey

v. T.L.O., 469 U.S. 325 (1985), combined with social understandings about unconsented nudity, were ample to make the right clearly established.

Note that the Court's multifactor analysis is likely to leave a fair number of cases still not clearly settled. What if one of the two factors was present, but not both? What of novel arguments offered by school officials that were not at issue in *Redding*?

e. The Supreme Court on lower court precedent. In Wilson v. Layne, 526 U.S. 603, 617 (1999), the Court seemed to identify two ways to show that the law had been clearly established: "controlling authority in [defendant's] jurisdiction," or "a consensus of cases of persuasive authority." Unconstitutionality too obvious to have been litigated is presumably a third method. The option of showing a consensus of persuasive cases would seem to implicitly reject the rule in some circuits that cases from outside the jurisdiction are irrelevant.

But at least three times now the Court has said that it is assuming without deciding that "a controlling circuit precedent could constitute clearly established federal law in these circumstances." City and County of San Francisco v. Sheehan, 135 S. Ct. 1765, 1776 (2015); Carroll v. Carman, 135 S. Ct. 348, 350 (2014); Reichle v. Howards, 566 U.S. 658, 665-666 (2012). It is not clear what "circumstances" the Court viewed as relevant. A fourth case used a slightly different formulation, assuming that circuit precedent can clearly establish a right "despite disagreement in the courts of appeals." Taylor v. Barkes, 135 S. Ct. 2042, 2045 (2015).

Sheehan and *Taylor* appeared to go further: "to the extent that a 'robust consensus of cases of persuasive authority' could itself clearly establish the federal right," there was no such consensus in those cases. 135 S. Ct. at 2044; 135 S. Ct. at 1778. The Court seems to be edging towards a suggestion that only Supreme Court cases count. Or maybe it is drafting around disagreement on that point.

f. New decisions that unsettle settled law. In *Reichle*, plaintiff sued two Secret Service agents for arresting him while in a rope line greeting Vice President Cheney. He was charged with "harassment," but the charges were dismissed. Plaintiff offered evidence, sufficient to present a triable issue of fact, that he was arrested in retaliation for criticizing the Iraq war while in the line. But the court of appeals also found that the agents had probable cause to arrest him for making a false statement when they interviewed him.

It was clearly settled in the Tenth Circuit that law enforcement officers are liable if they make an arrest in retaliation for an exercise of the arrestee's free speech rights, even if they have probable cause for the arrest. But in Hartman v. Moore, 547 U.S. 250 (2006), the Supreme Court had held that there is no liability for a retaliatory prosecution if there was probable cause to prosecute.

The Tenth Circuit held that *Hartman*'s decision on retaliatory *prosecution* did not change the law of retaliatory *arrest* in the Tenth Circuit. The Supreme Court reversed, noting that retaliatory arrests and prosecutions had traditionally been treated similarly and that a reasonable officer might have thought *Hartman* applied, or would apply, to retaliatory arrests. So the law was no longer clearly settled when plaintiff was arrested.

Hartman was decided on April 26, 2006; plaintiff in *Reichle* was arrested on June 16, 2006. So the odds are good that the agents knew nothing about *Hartman* when they made the arrest. No matter, it was decided before they acted, so they got the benefit of it.

g. Places outside the law? The Court remanded for consideration of qualified immunity in a case where an officer shot and killed a 15-year-old boy who, allegedly, was doing nothing threatening. Hernandez v. Mesa, 137 S. Ct. 2003 (2017). The officer and the government claimed that the boy had been part of a group of boys that was throwing rocks; the complaint, taken as true on a motion to dismiss, alleged that he was not part of the rock throwing. Surely it is clearly settled that officers cannot shoot and kill without provocation. But the officer was in the United States, patrolling the border; the boy was in Mexico, and the officer and the government argued that it was not clearly settled that constitutional rights applied to the boy in Mexico or that foreign nationals outside the United States have any right not to be shot and killed without reason. That may not be how they would characterize it, but that was the bottom line of their argument, and the Court appeared to take it seriously.

On remand, the Fifth Circuit held that even if the Fourth Amendment had been violated, and even if that were clearly settled, there was no cause of action for damages. 885 F.3d 811 (5th Cir. 2018). Congress created a global cause of action for constitutional violations by state and local officials in 42 U.S.C. §1983, but there is no such statute for federal officials. When courts should judicially imply a cause of action for constitutional violations by federal officials, commonly known as *Bivens* actions, is taken up in section 6.B.

7. The sequence of decision. One problem with *Harlow* was that unclear law tended to remain unclear. If plaintiff's claim for an injunction is barred by the ripeness rule (typically because she is not at sufficient risk of having the same thing happen to her again, City of Los Angeles v. Lyons, 461 U.S. 95 (1983)), and if her damage claim is barred by qualified immunity, the court has no occasion to reach the merits, and the law may never become clearly established. The Court tried to solve this problem by holding that a court must first decide whether plaintiff has alleged a deprivation of a constitutional right. Only if plaintiff has alleged a violation should the court consider whether the law was clearly established when defendant allegedly committed the violation. Saucier v. Katz, 533 U.S. 194, 201 (2001).

Saucier engendered substantial resistance in the lower courts and in separate opinions in the Supreme Court, and it sometimes produced unexpected consequences. Sometimes the constitutional issue was hard but the issue of whether it was clearly settled was easy. Defendants who were confident of winning on immunity sometimes filed inadequate briefs on the constitutional issue. If the court said that the complaint alleged a constitutional violation but that defendant was immune, defendant had won and could not appeal, even if she or her employer had a continuing stake in the constitutionality of what she was alleged to have done. All these problems were real, but the problem of the law remaining unsettled and defendants retaining immunity for conduct of doubtful legality was also real.

The Court responded by overruling *Saucier* and leaving the sequence of issues to case-by-case discretion. Pearson v. Callahan, 555 U.S. 223 (2009). One factor in exercising that discretion may be the likelihood that the same issue will be presented in a criminal prosecution or an injunction suit, where immunity issues would not preclude its being resolved. Professor Beerman argued that the primary factor should be whether a decision on the merits is likely to create clearly settled law on an issue likely to recur. Jack Michael Beerman, *Qualified Immunity and Constitutional Avoidance*, 2009 Sup. Ct. Rev. 139. He criticized the Court for providing no guidance and feared that defendants would game the system, urging courts to reach the merits only when the plaintiff's claim is weak, and to avoid the merits when the plaintiff's claim is strong.

8. The sequence of decision in the Supreme Court. When a court of appeals holds that a defendant official has violated the law, but dismisses the claim on qualified immunity grounds because the law was not clearly established, the defendant official can seek review in the Supreme Court, and the Court can review the constitutional holding. Camreta v. Greene, 563 U.S. 692 (2011). The Court said that the official may have a continuing stake in the case if he remains in the same office and his conduct of that office is effectively restrained by a holding that what he did was illegal.

And the plaintiff may have a continuing stake if she is at risk of being subjected to the same illegal behavior again. But if the plaintiff had a continuing stake under the usual rules, she could sue for an injunction against continuing the practice, and she would generally have ample incentives to do so. For *Camreta*'s odd procedure to help solve the problem, the Court has to find that the plaintiff has a continuing stake on a much looser standard—on facts that would not support that plaintiff suing for an injunction.

In *Camreta*, the plaintiff clearly had no stake under any standard, the case was moot. The Court vacated as moot not the Ninth Circuit's judgment, but that portion of its opinion discussing the merits of the constitutional question. The usual rule is that the Court reviews judgments, not opinions, so this disposition highlights the anomalous nature of these cases.

Justices Kennedy and Thomas dissented, arguing for the normal standards of jurisdiction and justiciability in qualified immunity cases. But they hinted that perhaps the solution should be to allow plaintiffs to recover nominal damages and no attorneys' fees. There is a full argument for the nominal-damages solution in James E. Pfander, *Resolving the Qualified Immunity Dilemma: Constitutional Tort Claims for Nominal Damages*, 111 Colum. L. Rev. 1601 (2011). Why would plaintiffs' attorneys provide representation for such a claim?

In cases since *Camreta*, the Court has sometimes decided both the merits and the immunity issue, and sometimes only the immunity issue, rarely giving any explanation for its choices. Examples include Lane v. Franks, 134 S. Ct. 2369 (2014) (both issues), and Wood v. Moss, 134 S. Ct. 2056 (2014) (immunity only).

9. Empirical studies. Professors Nielson and Walker surveyed all published and unpublished court of appeals cases on Westlaw from 2009 to 2012 that cited *Pearson* and either decided a qualified immunity issue or decided the constitutional merits of a claim in which qualified immunity was offered as a defense. Aaron L. Nielson & Christopher J. Walker, *The New Qualified Immunity*, 89 S. Cal. L. Rev. 1 (2015). There were 844 cases and 1,460 separately identifiable constitutional claims. In about 45 percent of the claims, courts found the law not clearly established but went on to decide the merits of the constitutional claim. In about 28 percent, they found the law not clearly established and declined to decide the merits of the claim. And in about 27 percent of the claims, they found a violation of clearly established constitutional law. When they went on to the merits after finding the law not clearly established, they found a constitutional violation only 8 percent of the time. The article also collects and summarizes earlier empirical studies. Helpful graphs are available in the hard copy and on HeinOnline, but not on Westlaw.

10. Interlocutory appeals. The collateral order doctrine, mentioned at the end of part I of the *Harlow* opinion, permits immediate appeal of certain pretrial orders that "finally determine claims of right separable from, and collateral to, rights asserted in the action, too important to be denied review." Cohen v. Beneficial Industrial Loan Corp., 337 U.S. 541, 546 (1949). The Court has held that rejected claims of immunity fall within the doctrine, because the immunity confers a right not to be tried, not merely a defense on the merits. The Court has now applied this rule to claims of absolute immunity, qualified immunity, and Eleventh Amendment immunity. The cases are collected in Puerto Rico Aqueduct & Sewer Authority v. Metcalf & Eddy, Inc., 506 U.S. 139, 143-145 (1993).

11. The new pleading rules. The Court has tightened pleading rules across the board, and it has vigorously applied the new rules to immunity cases. Bell Atlantic Corp. v. Twombly, 550 U.S. 544 (2007), an antitrust case, held that plaintiff must plead sufficient facts to make his claim "plausible," not merely "possible." Ashcroft v. Iqbal, 556 U.S. 662 (2009), applied *Twombly* to a claim of immunity for authorizing or condoning abuse of a prisoner. Iqbal alleged widespread racial and religious discrimination and deliberate abuse of prisoners in the widespread arrests and detentions of Muslim males in late 2001. He sued defendants ranging from prison guards to former Attorney General Ashcroft. The Court held most of the allegations against high-ranking officials too conclusory to state a claim, and the remaining factual allegations insufficient to state a claim. It remanded for further consideration the abuse allegations against jail personnel.

The Second Circuit held that another set of plaintiffs had plausibly pleaded violations of clearly established law in a similar case. Turkmen v. Hasty, 789 F.3d 218 (2d Cir. 2015), *rev'd on other grounds as* Ziglar v. Abbasi, 137 S. Ct. 1843 (2017). The Supreme Court dismissed most of the complaint on the ground that there is no cause of action for damages for constitutional violations in this context; that holding is summarized in section 6.B.

One count in *Abbasi* alleged a violation of 42 U.S.C. §1985(3), which expressly authorizes damages for conspiracy to deny any person the equal protection of the laws. The Court dismissed this count on qualified immunity grounds. Plaintiffs alleged a conspiracy to imprison them, because of their race, religion, or ethnicity, beyond the point at which there was probable cause to believe they had committed an offense. The Court did not say that the law against such an imprisonment was not clearly established. Rather, it said that it is not clearly established that a conspiracy among employees of the same government department is a conspiracy. Both this case and Hernandez v. Mesa, summarized above in note 6.g, suggest that not just the primary rule governing the officer's conduct, but all collateral issues that might affect the lawsuit, must be clearly settled.

12. The new attacks on qualified immunity: originalism. Justice Thomas joined the Court's opinion in Ziglar v. Abbasi to make a majority. But he said in a concurring opinion that the whole body of law on qualified immunity is illegitimate judicial policy making, made up out of whole cloth in Harlow v. Fitzgerald. He said the legitimate basis for immunity is the common law in 1871, which Congress is presumed to have intended to apply to suits under §1983, and that the clearly-established-law standard has no basis in that common law. His argument relied in part on a draft of William Baude, *Is Qualified Immunity Unlawful?*, 106 Cal. L. Rev. 45 (2018). Baude argues that the three different justifications the Court has offered for its qualified immunity jurisprudence—that it derives from a common law good-faith defense, that it compensates for an earlier mistake in interpreting the statute, and that it is justified by a desire to give "fair warning" to elected officials—are inconsistent with a proper historical and conceptual reading of §1983. Baude further argues that just as the historical underpinnings for the Court's qualified immunity jurisprudence are being challenged, the Court is going out of its way to strengthen it.

13. The new attacks on qualified immunity: empirical evaluation. A series of empirical studies by Professor Schwartz focus on how a broad reading of qualified immunity fails to achieve the Court's goals and renders constitutional protections hollow. She found that qualified immunity is not needed to shield police officers from liability, because they almost never pay judgments or settlements; state and local governments indemnify them even when they are egregiously at fault. Joanna C. Schwartz, *Police Indemnification*, 89 N.Y.U. L. Rev. 885 (2014). She found that immunity rarely shields police officers from the burdens of discovery and trial as the Supreme Court has claimed. Joanna C. Schwartz, *How Qualified Immunity Fails*, 127 Yale L.J. 2 (2017). The

Supreme Court's emphasis on specificity, requiring detailed comparison of the facts to the precedents, may be much of the reason why discovery is necessary. Professor Schwartz also found that immunity is not needed to protect against overdeterrence, because police officers are generally not deterred by the risk of civil liability, either in the conduct of their jobs or in the decision to become police officers in the first place. Joanna C. Schwartz, *The Case Against Qualified Immunity*, 93 Notre Dame L. Rev. 1797 (2018).

This lack of benefits comes with a significant cost: "the Court's qualified immunity decisions have . . . made it increasingly difficult for plaintiffs to show that defendants have violated clearly established law, and increasingly easy for courts to avoid defining the contours of constitutional rights." *Id.* at 1814. Qualified immunity protects many government employees other than police officers, but claims of police misconduct are a large percentage of qualified immunity cases. And while Professor Schwartz is careful to make no claims that go beyond her data, it seems likely that her findings would apply to many other government employees as well.

14. Another rationale for immunity rules. For a masterful overview and critique of the Court's body of immunity rules, see John C. Jeffries, Jr., *The Liability Rule for Constitutional Torts*, 99 Va. L. Rev. 207 (2013). He offers a different argument for a (reformed) version of qualified immunity: Strict liability for damages for all constitutional violations would severely inhibit the development of constitutional law. If every extension of constitutional doctrine led to damage liability, even for violations that occurred before the extension was announced, courts would be reluctant to expand constitutional rights or adapt them to new situations. It therefore makes sense to limit damage liability to cases where defendants had reasonable notice of the constitutional rule they violated. But he thinks that the current emphasis on a factually similar precedent goes far beyond what is required for reasonable notice.

15. The merits of *Harlow*'s claim. One other point, to avoid misleading you. Fitzgerald's constitutional claim would now be barred by Bush v. Lucas, 462 U.S. 367 (1983). *Bush* held that a discharged federal employee's remedy before the Civil Service Commission is exclusive and precludes constitutional litigation. A similar claim against a state official could proceed under the Free Speech Clause and 42 U.S.C. §1983. Not all state employees have a civil service remedy, and even if they do, they can file federal claims under §1983 without exhausting state remedies. Patsy v. Board of Regents, 457 U.S. 496 (1982).

16. State law. Most states have adopted some version of qualified immunity for state-law claims against state officials, but Maryland and Montana have expressly rejected it as inconsistent with judicially enforceable constitutional rights. Dorwart v. Caraway, 58 P.3d 128, 138-140 (Mont. 2002); Clea v. City Council, 541 A.2d 1303, 1311-1314 (Md. 1988).

NOTES ON ENFORCING NEW RULES OF LAW

1. A broader perspective on qualified immunity. One way to think about qualified immunity is that it is a rule about enforcing new rules of law. A new rule must be clearly established before government officials can be held liable in damages for violating it. The problem of newly announced rules arises in other contexts as well, and not all the cases go the same way.

2. The law before the 1990s. At one time, the Court claimed broad discretion to balance the interest in reliance on the old rule against the interest in immediate enforcement of the new rule. The leading case was Chevron Oil Co. v. Huson, 404 U.S. 97, 105-109 (1971), refusing to apply a decision that shortened a statute of limitations to actions that were timely filed under prior law.

In equity cases, this power to protect reliance on earlier law was sometimes explained as equitable discretion to refuse a reparative injunction and order a remedy that would be purely prospective. Thus in City of Los Angeles v. Manhart, 435 U.S. 702, 718-723 (1978), the Court held that defendant's pension plan violated the employment discrimination laws, because it segregated actuarial tables by sex and thus paid smaller monthly benefits to women than to men. The Court ordered the City to use unified tables in future calculations, but it refused to order any adjustment for benefits already accrued. The Equal Pay Act, 29 U.S.C. §206(d)(1), precluded the remedy of reducing benefits to men, and the Court feared that ordering increased benefits for women would jeopardize the solvency of the fund.

Sometimes the Court finds even prospective relief too intrusive if ordered immediately. Structural injunctions inevitably take effect in stages; Brown v. Board of Education famously ordered schools to desegregate "with all deliberate speed." 349 U.S. 294, 301 (1955) (*Brown II*). Prison reform cases tend to proceed very slowly, in part because it is so difficult to find money to implement a remedy. Northern Pipeline Construction Co. v. Marathon Pipe Line Co., 458 U.S. 50, 87-88 (1982), allowed unconstitutionally appointed bankruptcy judges to serve for six months while Congress tried to fix the problem.

Equitable-discretion talk is not available when plaintiff seeks damages for violation of a rule of law announced after the violation, but *Chevron* was. If the new rule did not apply retroactively, there could be no remedy for past violations. Marino v. Bowers, 657 F.2d 1363, 1365-1370 (3d Cir. 1981). And as we have seen, in suits against government officials, the Court limits damages with qualified-immunity rules.

3. Equity and new rules in election cases. The Court's reapportionment and voting rights cases have never invalidated prior laws enacted under unconstitutional voting rules, see Cipriano v. City of Houma, 395 U.S. 701, 706 (1969), and even when the old legislature has most of its term yet to serve, the Court does not always, or even usually, require immediate reapportionment and special elections. Connor v. Williams, 404 U.S. 549, 550-551 (1972).

The Court returned to the issue in North Carolina v. Covington, where a three-judge district court found that North Carolina's state legislative districts were racially gerrymandered. There was an appeal to the Supreme Court within the Court's mandatory jurisdiction, and the Court summarily affirmed with no opinion. 137 S. Ct. 2211 (2017).

The district court also ordered that the terms of all incumbent legislators be shortened from two years to one, and that special elections be held to fill the vacancies for the second year. The Supreme Court summarily vacated that order, in a brief per curiam opinion, because the district court "failed to meaningfully weigh any equitable considerations." 137 S. Ct. 1624, 1625 (2017). A court must take account of "what is necessary, what is fair, and what is workable," *id.*, and when deciding whether to order a special election, "there is much for a court to weigh." Ordering a special election in every racial gerrymandering case would be "clearly at odds with our demand for careful case-specific analysis." *Id.* at 1626.

On remand, the three-judge court determined that "the widespread, serious, and longstanding nature of the constitutional violation—among the largest racial gerrymanders ever encountered by a federal court—counsels in favor of granting Plaintiffs' request." Covington v. North Carolina, 270 F. Supp. 3d 881, 884 (M.D.N.C. 2017). It further found that any intrusion on the state's sovereignty is more than justified by the severity and scope of that violation and its adverse impact on North Carolina voters' right to choose—and hold accountable—their representatives, especially since the legislature took no action toward remedying the constitutional violation for many weeks after affirmance of this Court's order, and the Legislative Defendants have otherwise acted in ways that indicate they are more interested in delay than they are in correcting this serious constitutional violation.

Id. But the court also determined that special elections could no longer be held: "The compressed and overlapping schedule such an election would entail is likely to confuse voters, raise barriers to participation, and depress turnout, and therefore would not offer the vigorously contested election needed to return to the people of North Carolina their sovereignty." *Id.*

4. Nonretroactivity is forbidden? Federal nonretroactivity law came under sharp attack in the Supreme Court in the 1990s. Harper v. Virginia Department of Taxation, 509 U.S. 86 (1993), held that there can be no selective nonretroactivity—i.e., that any decision applied retroactively to the parties must be applied retroactively to all other persons whose claims are not barred by statutes of limitation, claim preclusion, and the like. *Id.* at 94-97. *Harper* illustrates a recurring fact pattern in this series of cases: new decisions holding state taxes unconstitutional.

Another recurring pattern is variations on *Chevron*—decisions retroactively shortening a statute of limitations. An example is Reynoldsville Casket Co. v. Hyde, 514 U.S. 749 (1995), which treated *Chevron* as overruled. *Reynoldsville* says that retroactive application of a new decision requires a retrospective remedy, unless there is some other legal rule, based on something more than mere reliance on the old law, that independently precludes a remedy. For example, taxpayers who paid a tax without protest might be barred by a rule that only those who paid under protest could sue for a refund. The Court said the qualified-immunity rules are such an independent rule, based not only on reliance but also on the financial burden on the public and the fear of deterring public officials from doing their duty. Are those independent reasons or merely the consequences of not protecting reliance?

5. Except when it's required? Compare Reich v. Collins, 513 U.S. 106 (1994). Georgia statutes provided that taxpayers could challenge illegal taxes either before payment, by posting a bond and refusing to pay, or after payment, by suing for a refund. But the Georgia Supreme Court held that the refund remedy did not apply to unconstitutional taxes. The Supreme Court of the United States unanimously reversed. A remedy either before or after payment would suffice, but Georgia could not retroactively eliminate what had appeared on the face of the statute to be a "clear and certain" refund remedy. This appears to be a holding that retroactive application of new decisions is sometimes unconstitutional. No justice in *Reich* bothered to reconcile the holding with any of the earlier opinions.

Reich also reaffirms a long line of cases holding that states must provide some remedy for taxpayers subjected to unconstitutional taxes. *Id.* at 109-110. The state has a choice. It may permit taxpayers to challenge the tax without paying it, by suing to prevent collection (a procedure analogous to Ex parte Young), or even by raising the issue on a tax return and waiting for the state to start enforcement proceedings. Or the state may collect the taxes and permit suits for refunds. This rule survived Alden v. Maine, 527 U.S. 706 (1999), which held that the Eleventh Amendment protects states from federal claims for money in state court. The explanation is that the state has a choice, and in this context, most states prefer to require the taxpayer to pay the tax under protest and then sue for a refund. See *id.* at 740. That way, the state has the money pending the litigation. Even better, only well-informed taxpayers will know to file a protest, especially with respect to new theories for challenging the tax, and only reasonably determined taxpayers will pay and then sue for a refund.

6. De facto officers. In Ryder v. United States, 515 U.S. 177 (1995), defendant's conviction in a court-martial was affirmed by a military court that included two judges who had been unconstitutionally appointed by an unauthorized appointing officer. The next higher court also affirmed, invoking the "de facto officer doctrine" to validate official acts taken before the improper appointment was discovered. The Supreme Court reversed, holding that the party who first raises an Appointments Clause issue is entitled to relief; otherwise, there would be no incentive to raise such issues. That certainly makes sense. But isn't it inconsistent with the *Harper-Reynoldsville* ban on selective nonretroactivity?

There is a similar decision in Nguyen v. United States, 539 U.S. 69 (2003), involving an Article I judge without life tenure, sitting by designation in the court of appeals. The Court rejected arguments that there had been a quorum of validly appointed judges and that petitioner had not complained of the defect when there was time to fix it.

7. Legislation. The Court's sometime insistence on retroactive application of new court decisions was accompanied by a renewed presumption *against* retroactive application of new statutes. Landgraf v. USI Film Products, 511 U.S. 244, 265-273 (1994). The distinction is almost entirely formal; legislatures make new law, but courts find old law—even when they overrule precedent and find this "old law" for the first time.

In the statutory cases, the Court understands retroactive application principally in terms of upsetting vested rights or imposing damage liability for acts that were not illegal when committed. It is not a retroactive application to base prospective relief on a new statute enacted after the events that first led to litigation. *Id.* at 273. Thus, injunctions are available to secure compliance with the new statute in the future, even if the dispute arose prior to enactment, and as we saw in section 4.B, existing injunctions may be modified because of a significant change in law, including changes enacted by statute.

8. State courts. The Supreme Court has rejected constitutional attacks on prospective application of new decisions by state courts. Great Northern Railway v. Sunburst Oil & Refining Co., 287 U.S. 358 (1932). State courts have taken a range of positions on the question: Some follow *Chevron*; some proclaim a firm rule of no selective retroactivity; some say it depends on the circumstances. Overlapping sets of cases are collected in Lunsford v. Saberhagen Holdings, 208 P.3d 1092, 1098-1099 (Wash. 2009), DiCenzo v. A-Best Products Co., 897 N.E.2d 132, 139 (Ohio 2008), and Findley v. Findley, 629 S.E.2d 222, 226-227 (Ga. 2006). Each court puts a somewhat different spin on the trend in state courts.

9. The big picture. This flurry of cases seems to have come to an end, and the results do not fit together very well. Considering the range of prospective-only remedies surveyed in these notes, we doubt that the Court is willing to live with a fixed rule of universal retroactivity. Whatever the limits of the new rule, it is clear that this battle was fought over theories of jurisprudence and judicial discretion, and that the Supreme Court's preference for retroactivity does not represent a preference for damage remedies.

The cases that insist on retroactivity have the effect of limiting the scope of any preference for prospective remedies, but at their furthest reach, they do not reverse it. Nothing in these cases limits the right to an injunction to force compliance with the new rule of law in the future. What they hold is that retrospective remedies are available even in contexts where retrospective remedies might have been thought especially problematic. The principle of these cases is that retrospective and prospective remedies are equally available in actions to enforce new rules of law. That principle is subject to exceptions that are not very well defined, but the tenor of each exception is to sometimes make retrospective remedies unavailable—to prefer prospective relief within the scope of the exception.

NOTES ON THE FEAR OF DAMAGE REMEDIES

1. A preference for injunctions. The law of governmental immunity, and, at least until recently, the law of nonretroactivity, are two substantial bodies of law that generally prefer prospective to retrospective relief. Changes in the federal law of nonretroactivity limit this preference in cases outside the scope of governmental immunities, but these changes have not reversed or eliminated the preference.

The preference for injunctions in government litigation has two important exceptions. One is the governmental preference for collecting taxes and making taxpayers sue for refunds. The other is that with respect to contracts, Congress and most states have consented to be sued for damages but assert sovereign immunity to specific performance, allowing government to choose the cheaper course with respect to each contract.

Not all prospective relief is equitable, and not all retrospective relief is legal. Recall that the Court in Edelman v. Jordan rejected plaintiff's attempt to distinguish equitable restitution from legal damages. Thus, a preference for prospective relief is not a mirror image of the irreparable injury rule's asserted preference for legal relief. But it is a substantial reversal in practice, because the most important prospective remedy is the injunction, and the most important retrospective remedy is damages.

2. Other limits on damages. The fear of damage remedies also appears in other doctrines and practices:

> For systemic violations of the Constitution, damages are unthinkable and the injunction is de facto the exclusive remedy. For example, I know of no case in which any plaintiff has recovered damages for an unconstitutionally segregated education, and I am confident that judges faced with a class action claiming such damages would find a way to deny it. . . .
>
> Some conservative justices dissented bitterly from the Court's decision to imply *damage* remedies to enforce the Constitution. But Chief Justice Rehnquist has acknowledged that courts can imply *equitable* remedies to enforce the Constitution. The new conservative majority has allowed Congress to sharply limit constitutional remedies, and the most common statutory limitation is to provide remedies without damages or with sharply limited compensation.
>
> In the related area of implied rights to enforce federal statutes, . . . the governmental defendants, supported by the United States as amicus curiae, argued that the implied right of action should be limited to prospective relief and backpay, and that damages should be precluded.

Douglas Laycock, *The Triumph of Equity*, 56 L. & Contemp. Probs. 53, 64, 75 (Summer 1993).

There are few rules in private law that so overtly prefer injunctions to damages. But there is the same widespread view that damages are a dangerous remedy, and there are as many rules restricting damages as there are rules restricting injunctions:

> Damage remedies are also limited or precluded by rules that make certain elements of damage noncompensable even when clearly suffered. Examples include the rule

against recovery of economic losses in tort in the absence of physical impact, the rules against consequential damages for delay in payment of money or in eminent domain, and the rule against recovery of emotional distress caused by breach of contract. Statutes often limit tort damages to amounts that may be substantially less than the fact-finder's valuation of damages actually suffered. . . .

The entire tort reform movement is aimed at common law damage actions and the discretionary power of juries. . . .

The class of repeat defendants is saying loud and clear that it fears excessive damages far more than it fears excessive injunctions or excessive contempt sanctions.

Id. at 63, 75, 80.

3. Final thoughts on choosing remedies. Is it still a reasonable summary to say that Anglo-American law prefers legal remedies to equitable remedies? Or is it more accurate to say that there is no general preference, but rather a set of rules and factors for choosing among remedies based on their costs and benefits in particular situations? Is the irreparable injury rule dead or alive? If it is still alive, should we kill it or revive it?

CHAPTER

6

Remedies and Separation of Powers

A. MORE ON GOVERNMENTAL IMMUNITIES

We examined the core principles of sovereign immunity law in section 5.C.1. But sovereigns often waive their immunity, usually with many exceptions and conditions. Immunity and its exceptions have given rise to a vast body of law. Different sources of law interact in complex ways; what seems to be given in one rule may be taken away in another. In this chapter, we will examine immunity issues that do not go so directly to the choice between damages and injunctions. Once immunity is waived, new issues emerge.

1. Consented Suits Against the Government

STONE v. NORTH CAROLINA DEPARTMENT OF LABOR
495 S.E.2d 711 (N.C. 1998)

WHICHARD, Justice.

Plaintiffs commenced this negligence action against . . . the North Carolina Department of Labor . . . pursuant to the Tort Claims Act, N.C. Gen. Stat. §§143-291 to 143-300.1 (1993) (amended 1994). . . . Defendants moved . . . to dismiss. . . . Deputy Commissioner . . . Alston denied the motions. The full [Industrial] Commission affirmed. . . .

The Court of Appeals affirmed. . . . 480 S.E.2d 410 (N.C. Ct. App. 1997). . . .

Because these claims arise upon defendants' motions to dismiss, we treat plaintiffs' factual allegations . . . as true. On 3 September 1991 a fire started in a hydraulic line near a deep fat fryer in the Imperial Foods Products chicken plant. . . . The fire . . . spread rapidly through the interior of the plant. Plaintiffs are either former employees of Imperial Foods who suffered injury in the fire or personal representatives of the estates of employees who died in the fire. . . . [Employees] could not easily escape . . . because the exits in the plant were unmarked, blocked, and inaccessible. After the fire . . . defendants . . . conducted their first and only inspection in the plant's eleven-year history of operation. . . . [D]efendants discovered numerous violations of the Occupational Safety and Health Act of North Carolina (OSHANC), including the plant's inadequate and blocked exits and inadequate fire suppression system. Defendants issued eighty-three citations . . . for violations of OSHANC standards. Plaintiffs alleged . . . that defendants had a duty under OSHANC to inspect the plant, defendants breached that duty by failing to inspect until after the fire, defendants' breach caused plaintiffs' injuries or deaths, and plaintiffs' injuries or deaths entitle them to damages in tort. . . .

The Tort Claims Act provides that the State is liable "under circumstances where [it], if a private person, would be liable to the claimant in accordance with the laws of North Carolina." N.C. Gen. Stat. §143-291. Defendants . . . contend . . . that they are not liable to plaintiffs because under the public duty doctrine, they owe no legal duty to the individual plaintiffs. Defendants assert that their obligation . . . to inspect workplaces in North Carolina serves the public at large, not individual employees. Plaintiffs assert . . . that the public duty doctrine does not . . . bar plaintiffs' claims because it does not apply to the liability of a private person, and under the Tort Claims Act, the State is liable if a private person would be. We disagree, and we reverse. . . .

Private persons do not possess public duties. Only governmental entities possess authority to enact and enforce laws for the protection of the public. . . . If the State were held liable for performing or failing to perform an obligation to the public at large, the State would have liability when a private person could *not*. The public duty doctrine, by barring negligence actions against a governmental entity absent a "special relationship" or a "special duty" to a particular individual, serves the legislature's express intention to permit liability against the State only when a private person could be liable. . . .

Our determination of legislative intent is also "guided by . . . certain canons of statutory construction." Electric Supply Co. v. Swain Electric Co., 403 S.E.2d 291, 294 (N.C. 1991). Acts . . . in derogation of sovereign immunity should be strictly construed. . . .

In passing the Tort Claims Act, the legislature incorporated the common law of negligence. The public duty doctrine forms an integral part of that common law. . . . Until the legislature clearly expresses that immunity is to be waived even in situations in which the common law public duty doctrine would otherwise apply to bar a negligence claim, we construe the Tort Claims Act as incorporating the existing common law rules of negligence, including that doctrine. . . .

Plaintiffs argue that even if the public duty doctrine applies . . . under the Tort Claims Act, . . . it applies only to claims against *local governments* for failure to *prevent crimes*.

When this Court first recognized the public duty doctrine, it discussed the doctrine in terms of the facts before it. In the context of a claim against a sheriff, we explained that, under the doctrine, "a *municipality* and its agents act for the benefit of the public, and therefore, there is no liability for the failure to furnish *police protection* to specific individuals." Braswell v. Braswell, 410 S.E.2d 897, 901 (N.C. 1991) (emphasis added).

Once this Court recognized the doctrine, however, our Court of Appeals applied it to a variety of local governmental operations [and] to a state agency. While this Court has not heretofore applied the doctrine to a state agency or to a governmental function other than law enforcement, we do so now.

The policies underlying recognition of the public duty doctrine in *Braswell* support its application here. . . . [W]e explained that the doctrine was necessary to prevent "an overwhelming burden of liability" on governmental agencies with "limited resources." *Id.* at 901. We stated:

> The amount of protection that may be provided is limited by the resources of the community and by a considered legislative-executive decision as to how those resources may

be deployed. For the courts to proclaim a new and general duty of protection in the law of tort . . . would inevitably determine how the limited police resources . . . should be allocated and without predictable limits.

Id., quoting *Riss v. City of New York*, 240 N.E.2d 860, 860-861 (N.Y. 1968). . . .

[A] government ought to be free to enact laws for the *public protection* without thereby exposing its supporting taxpayers . . . to liability for failures of omission in its attempt to enforce them. It is better to have such laws, even haphazardly enforced, than not to have them at all.

Grogan v. Commonwealth, 577 S.W.2d 4, 6 (Ky. 1979) (emphasis added).

Further, we do not believe the legislature . . . intended to impose a duty upon this agency to each *individual* worker in North Carolina. . . . [T]he most the legislature intended was that the Division prescribe safety standards and secure some reasonable compliance through spot-check inspections made "as often as practicable." N.C. Gen. Stat. §95-4(5) (1996). . . .

Because the governmental entity owes no particular duty to any individual claimant, it cannot be held liable for negligence . . . . Absent a duty, there can be no liability.

In *Braswell* this Court recognized two exceptions to the public duty doctrine "to prevent inevitable inequities to certain individuals." 410 S.E.2d at 902. It explained that exceptions to the doctrine exist: (1) where there is a special relationship between the injured party and the governmental entity; and (2) when the governmental entity creates a special duty by promising protection to an individual, the protection is not forthcoming, and the individual's reliance on the promise of protection is causally related to the injury suffered. These exceptions are narrowly construed and applied. . . .

N.C. Gen. Stat. §95-4(5) . . . provides that the Commissioner of Labor is "charged with the duty" to visit and inspect "at reasonable hours, as often as practicable," all of the "factories, mercantile establishments, mills, workshops, public eating places, and commercial institutions in the State." It also imposes on the Commissioner a duty to enforce these inspection laws and request prosecution of any violations found. It creates no private cause of action for individual claimants for violations of OSHANC.

Although §95-4 imposes a duty upon defendants, that duty is for the benefit of the public, not individual claimants as here. Plaintiffs' claims thus fall within the public duty doctrine, and to state claims for actionable negligence, plaintiffs must allege facts placing the claims within one of the exceptions to the doctrine. They make no such "special relationship" or "special duty" allegations. The claims therefore must fail.

The dissent asserts that we have eviscerated the Tort Claims Act, nullified it, rendered it obsolete, left it purposeless, absolved the State of all liability, and barred all negligence claims against the State. These assertions are hyperbolic and overwrought. A myriad of reported and unreported cases, covering a great variety of fact situations, have allowed recovery against the State under the Tort Claims Act. Nothing in this opinion even hints at the overruling of those cases. Absent legislative change, the Act functions and will continue to function as it has for almost half a century. We simply hold, with sound reason and substantial grounding in the law of both this and other jurisdictions, that in this limited new context, not heretofore confronted by this Court, the Act was not intended to and does not apply absent a special relation-ship or special duty. . . .

Reversed and remanded.

ORR, Justice, dissenting.

The majority opinion erroneously takes a limited and obscure common law con-cept, the public duty doctrine, which has traditionally applied only to municipalities and their law enforcement responsibilities, and expands the doctrine's application to effectively eviscerate the Tort Claims Act. . . .

The recognition of the public duty doctrine in this country is traced to . . . South v. Maryland, 59 U.S. (18 How.) 396 (1855). The case involved a negligence suit brought by plaintiffs to recover against a sheriff . . . for failure to keep the peace and protect the plaintiffs. The Court stated:

> Actions against the sheriff for a breach of his ministerial duties in the execution of process are to be found in almost every book of reports. But no instance can be found where a civil action has been sustained against him for his default or misbehavior as conservator of the peace, by those who have suffered injury to their property or persons through the violence of mobs, riots, or insurrections.

Id. at 403. The Court went on to examine several earlier British decisions and con-cluded that because no special right was alleged, the cause of action failed.

In reviewing this seminal decision and other authorities, I can find no common law basis for the majority taking the public duty doctrine beyond the original bounds of local law enforcement. . . . [T]o the extent that other . . . jurisdictions have bent and skewed the common law to expand the doctrine, we . . . should not . . . follow such an ill-advised course. . . .

The public duty doctrine, moreover, should not be applied here because, unlike in *Braswell*, this suit was brought under the Tort Claims Act. The public duty doctrine should not be used to *grant the State immunity* when the express intent of the Tort Claims Act was to *remove immunity* and make the State liable for its wrongs. . . .

[I]t is patently unreasonable to interpret the Act's requirement that the State be treated like a private person as absolving the State of all liability. The very reason for this language is to eliminate the common law doctrine of sovereign immunity. . . .

The majority's second argument, that the Act incorporates the public duty doctrine because it incorporates the common law, is also erroneous. [After its origin in 1855], "the public duty doctrine was widely accepted by most state courts." Ezell v. Cockrell, 902 S.W.2d 394, 397 (Tenn. 1995). When most states abolished sovereign immunity by statute, the doctrine came under attack. Some state courts abolished the doctrine, arguing that it was simply sovereign immunity under another guise and to apply it was inconsistent with statutes that eliminated immunity. Other states . . . limited the applica-tion of the public duty doctrine to apply only in situations involving police protection.

In North Carolina, the common law tradition of the public duty doctrine was never extended by this Court beyond its limited application to municipalities and law enforcement. . . . [T]his Court only recognized the doctrine for the first time in 1991 . . . . To argue, as the majority does, that by enacting the Tort Claims Act in 1951, the Legislature somehow incorporated the expansive public duty doctrine enunciated by the majority is at best, simply wrong.

In its third argument, the majority asserts that the *Braswell* rationale of preventing enormous liability on agencies with limited resources applies here as well. . . . [D]amages are capped under the Tort Claims Act . . . ". . . at $150,000 for causes arising on or after 1 October 1994." Parham v. Iredell County, 489 S.E.2d 610, 613 (N.C. Ct. App. 1997). Thus, the majority's fear of an "overwhelming burden of liability" has already been directly addressed by the General Assembly. . . .

In *Braswell*, there was a potential for overwhelming and unlimited liability because the plaintiff was claiming that the police failed to protect her from an unpredictable criminal act. . . . In this case, we are dealing with inspections which are required to be carried out on a regular, predictable basis. Here, the duty to perform is clearly set out and can be accomplished. It is feasible. . . . [T]his case does not involve determining how "limited police resources should be allocated," as was the issue in *Braswell*. Instead, this case is more similar to what we differentiated in *Braswell*, where we stated that dealing with police resources was "quite different from the predictable allocation of resources and liabilities when public hospitals, rapid transit systems, or even highways are provided." 410 S.E.2d at 901-902. . . .

FRYE, J., joins in this dissenting opinion.

NOTES ON THE PUBLIC DUTY DOCTRINE

1. **Government consent to suit.** Legislatures have steadily eroded immunity by consenting to more and more classes of lawsuits. These waivers have gone much further in some states than in others, but they rarely include constitutional claims, many of which are politically unpopular. In other contexts, especially for routine torts and contracts, broad immunity has politically unacceptable consequences. So legislatures began to waive immunity, often with limits and restrictions.

2. **The argument for waiver.** Is there any reason to distinguish a pedestrian run over by a Greyhound bus from a pedestrian run over by a school bus? The victim's injuries are a real cost; immunity doesn't make that cost go away. Is it fair, or even rational, to impose all those costs on the victim instead of distributing them among all the taxpayers?

Suppose the state supported 99 percent of the cost of government through general taxation fairly apportioned, and 1 percent through a negative lottery. If your name were drawn in the lottery, you would be liable for an additional tax, in a random amount, ranging from $10 to $10 million. Wouldn't such a scheme violate the Equal Protection Clause? How is it different to impose the cost of government accidents on victims? Or to refuse payment to an occasional creditor? Even if governments respond badly to economic incentives (see Notes on the Reasons for Sovereign Immunity in section 5.C.1), can that justify such an arbitrary distribution of the costs of government?

3. **The range of potential government liabilities.** Government injures people in a vast variety of ways, and liability for some of these injuries is troubling even to diehard opponents of immunity. One of the exclusions in the Federal Tort Claims Act is that the United States shall not be liable for "any claim for damages caused by the fiscal operations of the Treasury or by the regulation of the monetary system." 28 U.S.C. §2680(i). Probably the courts would not have imposed such liability anyway, but it's hard to blame Congress for being cautious. Investors gain and lose millions every time the Federal Reserve Board meets, and surely some of its decisions are negligent or worse. Justice Jackson once said that "it is not a tort for government to govern." Dalehite v. United States, 346 U.S. 15, 57 (1953) (dissenting). But how can courts or legislatures reliably draw the line between tortfeasing and governing?

4. **No tort duty to the public?** The public duty doctrine is one attempt to draw the line. It has a long history with respect to municipal governments, which never had

full sovereign immunity. In the twentieth century, the doctrine acquired more prominence at the state level as legislatures waived immunity. The doctrine purports to distinguish duties owed to particular individuals from duties owed to the whole public;
for liability purposes, a duty owed to all is a duty owed to no one. But that is at most
a crude approximation of the real distinction.

Each of us owes a duty to everyone around us to exercise reasonable care to avoid
inflicting physical injury. This duty does not depend on any relationship between
the negligent actor and the person injured. For a large corporation—say, Federal
Express—with trucks all over the country, this duty looks a lot like a duty to the whole
public. Why isn't that a duty owed to no one because it is owed to everyone? Because
that is not what courts mean by a duty to the whole public. Drivers in state vehicles
owe the same duty of care to each member of the whole public as drivers in FedEx
trucks, and if the state has waived sovereign immunity for auto accidents, the public
duty doctrine is no defense.

5. No duty to prevent harm caused by others? A better first approximation of the
apparent working rule is that government has no liability for failing to prevent harm
inflicted by someone else, unless it undertook a duty to specially protect a particular
person or group. Another recurring theme is judicial deference to decisions committed to the political branches, and especially to decisions about the allocation of
scarce resources.

When Massachusetts prospectively abolished the public duty doctrine, Jean W. v.
Commonwealth, 610 N.E.2d 305 (Mass. 1993), the legislature responded by codifying
the doctrine's principal applications. Mass. Ann. L. ch. 258 §10. There is no liability
for omitted or negligent inspections, for release or escape of prisoners unless gross
negligence is shown, for failures of police or fire protection unless the victim relied
on "explicit and specific assurances of safety or assistance," or for failure to diminish
the harmful consequences of conditions or situations not originally caused by the
government or its employees.

This last category, failure to diminish harm caused by others, is subject to four
exceptions in which immunity *is* waived: reliance on explicit and specific assurances,
intervention that "causes injury to the victim or places the victim in a worse position
than he was in before the intervention," any claim based on negligent maintenance
of public property, and medical malpractice by government employees. Is that a workable set of rules? Do the distinctions make policy sense? Are the no-liability categories
mostly variations on failing to prevent harm caused by others?

6. Narrowing, eliminating, or reinstating the public duty doctrine. In the aftermath
of *Stone* and other public duty cases, North Carolina codified the public duty doctrine.
N.C. Gen. Stat. §143-299.1A. The state supreme court construed the legislature's
understanding of the doctrine "to be a more limited one than the common law might
have led us to understand." Ray v. North Carolina Department of Transportation, 727
S.E.2d 675, 680 (N.C. 2012).

> By the plain language of the statute, the public duty doctrine is a defense only if the
> injury alleged is the result of (1) a law enforcement officer's negligent failure to protect
> the plaintiff from actions of others or an act of God, or (2) a . . . failure to perform
> a health or safety inspection required by statute. In all other cases the public duty
> doctrine is unavailable to the State as a defense.

Id. at 680-681.

Some states have eliminated the public duty doctrine. An example is Coleman v.
East Joliet Fire Protection District, 46 N.E.3d 741 (Ill. 2016). Among other reasons,

the court cited the doctrine's "muddled and inconsistent" application in the courts. *Id.* at 756. The court counted six other states (Kansas, Missouri, Nebraska, New Mexico, Oregon, and Wisconsin) rejecting the doctrine either by judicial decision or statute. It noted that after courts in some other states had abolished the doctrine, state legislatures had reinstated it.

The Iowa Supreme Court continued to apply the doctrine in a case barring a lawsuit for the death of a ten-year-old child in a speedboat that hit a dredge pipe on a state lake. The child's mother argued that the state had not required the dredge operator to adequately mark the location of the pipe. Estate of McFarlin v. State 881 N.W. 2d 51 (Iowa 2016). The dissent said the doctrine should be abolished, calling it "an anachronistic common law framework that we often avoid." *Id.* at 67.

7. Government inspections in North Carolina. In all inspection cases, someone else creates the dangerous condition; the government merely fails to prevent it. In *Stone,* there were no assurances specific to the workers in the Imperial plant. The government's error was not that a negligent or corrupt inspector overlooked the violations but that the plant had never been inspected at all. This is almost certainly a resource allocation problem; the legislature has not provided sufficient funding. In the 2015-2016 fiscal year, the state had 219,897 establishments with employees; it conducted 2,635 inspections. *North Carolina Occupational Safety and Health Annual Comparison Report October 2015-September 2016,* at 2, 5, available at https://www.labor.nc.gov/documents/osh-annual-comparison-report-program-statistics-2015-2016 [https://perma.cc/JBA3-UPML]. Would the dissenters' position in *Stone* make the labor department a defendant in every case of a workplace injury arising out of a hazardous condition that could have been corrected pursuant to a proper inspection?

8. The police-protection cases. New York had a long series of police-protection cases:

a. Threatened informants. Willie Sutton was the gangster famous for his answer to the question, "Why do you rob banks?" "Because that's where the money is." He should also be famous for a different aftermath of his arrest. Arnold Schuster memorized Sutton's face on a wanted poster and provided information leading to Sutton's arrest. Schuster's role in the capture was widely publicized, and Schuster began to receive threats, which the police discounted. Three weeks later, Schuster was murdered. Schuster v. City of New York, 154 N.E.2d 534 (N.Y. 1958). *Schuster* has come to stand for the proposition that "a municipality possesses a special duty to provide police protection to an informer who collaborates with the police in the arrest and prosecution of a criminal." Florence v. Goldberg, 375 N.E.2d 763, 766 (N.Y. 1978).

b. Attacks after explicit warnings. Linda Riss left her boyfriend, attorney Martin Pugach, and became engaged to another man. Pugach repeatedly made specific threats of death or serious injury; she repeatedly asked the police for help, and they did nothing. On the day after her engagement party, a thug hired by Pugach threw acid in her face, blinding one eye, damaging the other, and leaving permanent scars. The court found no liability. The duty to protect persons from violence was owed to the whole public, and the city had never promised Riss any individual protection. Riss v. City of New York, 240 N.E.2d 860 (N.Y. 1968).

Riss had a long and strange aftermath. In 1974, eight months after Pugach's release from prison, he married Linda Riss. She has said the marriage is probably better than most. Richard Haitch, *Love Story: Part II,* N.Y. Times (Feb. 22, 1987). Pugach was later acquitted of multiple counts of abusing and threatening to kill his mistress after she ended a five-year affair; he was convicted of one minor violation. Riss said the prosecution was "a waste of taxpayers' money." Norimitsu Onishi, *Jury Clears Man, 70, of Abuse Charges,* N.Y. Times (May 1, 1997). He said, "[T]here aren't any more women and there won't be"; she said, "We are now like an old married couple." Joseph P. Fried, *No More Public Dramas for a "Dull" Mr. and Mrs.*, N.Y. Times (Dec. 10, 2000). A documentary movie, *Crazy Love*, triggered a new round of news coverage, including a long feature story. Paul Schwartzman, *Blind to His Faults: She Spurned Him, He Maimed Her, and They Lived Happily Ever After, Sort Of*, Wash. Post (June 6, 2007). The story finally ended when Linda Riss died in 2013. Margalit Fox, *Linda Riss Pugach, Whose Life Was Ripped from Headlines, Dies at 75*, N.Y. Times (Jan. 23, 2013).

Braswell, the North Carolina case discussed in *Stone*, was a more typical case of domestic abuse: a husband repeatedly threatened to kill his wife, the police refused any special protection, and he killed her. Contrast Christmas v. Cabarrus County, 664 S.E.2d 649 (N.C. Ct. App. 2008), where the state's intermediate court (before the enactment of the North Carolina statute limiting the public duty doctrine) held that the public duty doctrine did not protect a county department of social services that failed to properly investigate reports of child abuse received over a period of six weeks before the child was killed. The court said that this case was about social services, not law enforcement. *Braswell* and *Christmas* are both about a failure to prevent domestic violence. Is the difference just in which local agency failed to respond? Is the social service agency's duty to investigate child abuse more specific than the police department's duty to protect citizens? (*Christmas* was decided as a matter of state tort law. The more famous federal case holds that there is no liability under the federal Constitution for failing to prevent child abuse, however egregious the failure. DeShaney v. Winnebago County, 489 U.S. 189 (1989).)

c. Crossing guards. A six-year-old boy was hit by a car while crossing a busy street on the way home from school. His mother had relied on a crossing guard, who had called in sick. Police regulations required the police to notify the school principal if they had to leave a crossing unprotected; they didn't notify the principal. The court held that the police had voluntarily assumed a duty to "children crossing designated intersections while traveling to and from school at scheduled times"—a special class much narrower than the general public—and plaintiff had relied on that duty. Florence v. Goldberg, 375 N.E.2d 763, 767 (N.Y. 1978).

Suppose the city withdrew selected crossing guards because of a budget crisis. Would that be a nonreviewable decision about how to allocate public services? Would the city have to notify people who had relied on crossing guards? Would notice to school principals suffice? What about media coverage of the city's budget problems?

d. Bungled 911 calls. A woman was killed by an intruder long after she called 911. The county had advised people not to call their local police, but to call 911 instead. That advice went to the whole public. "In addition, and most significantly," when the victim did call 911, she was assured that help would be there "right away." De Long v. County of Erie, 457 N.E.2d 717, 721 (N.Y. 1983). The court said the county had created a special relationship sufficient to support a duty of care.

e. Promises to help. In Sorichetti v. City of New York, 482 N.E.2d 70 (N.Y. 1985), there were specific promises of help and a complete failure to actually help. But there was no reliance; the court said that the victim's mother, "in her helpless and distraught state, had no alternative but to seek the assistance of the police." *Id.* at 76. The court found liability anyway. It emphasized that the police had promised help, whereas they had clearly told Linda Riss that they would not help.

In Cuffy v. City of New York, 505 N.E.2d 937 (N.Y. 1987), one of the plaintiffs told the police he would move his family out of their apartment unless the police arrested the neighbors who had repeatedly threatened them. The police promised an arrest the next morning, so the family stayed put. The police never came, and the next night, the neighbors attacked with knives and baseball bats, severely injuring the three plaintiffs. The court said the police had specifically promised protection, but by noon of the second day, it was clear they were not keeping that promise. So it was no longer reasonable to rely on it by staying in the house, and therefore, no recovery. *Sorichetti* is extensively discussed on other issues, but it gets only a "see also" citation on reliance.

f. A test? The New York court found a duty when a husband stabbed his wife to death eight minutes after two police officers left the house. Mastroianni v. County of Suffolk, 691 N.E.2d 613 (N.Y. 1997). By this time, the court had distilled a four-part test: assumption of an affirmative duty to act through promises or actions, knowledge that inaction could lead to harm, direct contact between the municipal employees and the victim, and justifiable reliance.

9. The United States. The Federal Tort Claims Act provides, subject to many exceptions, that the United States is liable for negligence if a private person would be liable under state law for the same conduct. 28 U.S.C. §1346(b)(1). In United States v. Olson, 546 U.S. 43 (2005), two miners were permanently disabled when a nine-ton slab of earth fell from the ceiling of the mine where they were working. The government had failed to inspect the site despite multiple grounds for finding a duty to do so. There are no private mine inspectors in Arizona, but Court said that the "circumstances" under which a private person would be liable need only be similar, not identical. So private safety inspectors of any kind provided a relevant analogy; if they would be liable, the government should be liable. The Court rejected any analogy to state or municipal inspectors. *Olson* and the cases on which it relies in effect hold that there is no public duty doctrine in the Tort Claims Act, although that language is not used.

It does not follow that the United States had a duty in *Stone.* Federal inspectors from the Department of Agriculture were in the Imperial chicken plant almost daily. They approved Imperial's plan to lock the doors as a means of controlling flies. But they were responsible only for food safety; they had no training, and no authority, with respect to worker safety, and they did not voluntarily undertake to examine worker safety. The court held that no private person similarly situated would have a duty under North Carolina to interfere with the company's responsibility for worker safety. Dawkins v. United States, 226 F. Supp. 2d 750 (M.D.N.C. 2002).

The federal Occupational Safety and Health Administration is responsible for worker safety. It, too, is underfunded and cannot inspect everyone. Either it, too, had never gotten around to this plant, or else it had an agreement with North Carolina under which the state would do the inspections.

NOTES ON THE GOVERNMENTAL/PROPRIETARY DISTINCTION

1. The distinction's intuitive appeal. Another attempt to draw the line between immunity and liability is the governmental/proprietary distinction. States and cities do many things that could be done by private enterprise. New York sold bottled mineral water by mail order. New York v. United States, 326 U.S. 572 (1946). Alabama ran a railroad. Parden v. Terminal Railway, 377 U.S. 184 (1964), *overruled on other grounds,* College Savings Bank v. Florida Prepaid Postsecondary Education Expense Board, 527 U.S. 666 (1999). South Dakota owned a cement plant. Reeves, Inc. v. Stake, 447 U.S. 429 (1980). It is often tempting to distinguish such activities from core governmental activities, such as police and fire protection.

2. And its unworkability. Unfortunately, no court has ever generated a coherent set of precedents applying the distinction. Many government activities defy classification;

efforts to draw lines in the vast middle sometimes lead to madness. One example will suffice: In Texas, sanitary sewers are governmental, but storm sewers are proprietary. That's not a very plausible distinction in itself. But what happens if both kinds of sewer are in the same ditch, and the ditch caves in and kills a worker? It depends on which pipe he was working on at the moment of the cave-in. City of Houston v. Bush, 566 S.W.2d 33 (Tex. Civ. App. 1978).

3. Is everything governmental? Justice Douglas said that whatever government does is governmental—that whenever a governmental unit undertakes a nontraditional activity, it does so to accomplish some public purpose thought sufficient by its legislature. New York v. United States, 326 U.S. at 591 (Douglas, J., dissenting). If South Dakota elected a socialist government and took over all the means of production, wouldn't all the factories be serving governmental functions?

4. The distinction in disguise? New York abolished the governmental/proprietary distinction when it repealed governmental immunity. But consider the court's description of the public duty doctrine in *Riss*:

> It is necessary immediately to distinguish those liabilities attendant upon government activities which have displaced or supplemented traditionally private enterprises, such as are involved in the operation of rapid transit systems, hospitals, and places of public assembly. . . . To be equally distinguished are certain activities of government which provide services and facilities for the use of the public, such as highways, public buildings and the like, in the performance of which the municipality or the State may be liable under ordinary principles of tort law. The ground for liability is the provision of the services or facilities for the direct use by members of the public.
>
> In contrast, this case involves the provision of a governmental service to protect the public generally from external hazards and particularly to control the activities of criminal wrongdoers.

240 N.E.2d at 860. Doesn't that version of the public duty contain a lot of the governmental/proprietary distinction in disguise?

NOTES ON THE DISCRETIONARY FUNCTION EXCEPTION

1. The statutory text. The principal federal attempt to formulate a limit on government tort liability appears in the Federal Tort Claims Act, which excludes any claim "based upon the exercise or performance or the failure to exercise or perform a discretionary function or duty on the part of a federal agency or an employee of the Government, whether or not the discretion involved be abused." 28 U.S.C. §2680(a). Similar provisions appear in many state tort claims acts.

2. The first interpretation. For much of the Act's history, the leading case was Dalehite v. United States, 346 U.S. 15 (1953). *Dalehite* involved the worst industrial disaster in American history, and the Court may have stretched the exception to avoid enormous liability. After World War II, the United States tried to feed the populations of Germany, Japan, and Korea, all suffering from shortages of food and fertilizer. Surplus explosives factories were converted to production of chemically similar fertilizers, and a shipload of this fertilizer exploded in the harbor at Texas City, Texas, destroying the entire dock area and killing 560 people. For a full account, see Hugh W. Stephens, *The Texas City Disaster, 1947* (Univ. of Texas Press 1997).

The trial court found that the fertilizer was bagged and loaded in a negligent manner and that this negligence caused the explosion. But those who bagged and loaded followed specifications laid down in Washington. Because the fatal decisions were "all responsibly made at a planning rather than operational level and involved considerations more or less important to the practicability of the Government's fertilizer program," they were all within the discretionary function exception. *Id.* at 42. There were three dissents:

> The common sense of this matter is that a policy adopted in the exercise of an immune discretion was carried out carelessly by those in charge of detail. We cannot agree that all the way down the line there is immunity for every balancing of care against cost, of safety against production, of warning against silence.

Id. at 58 (Jackson, J., dissenting). Justice Jackson didn't think decisions about how to bag and load fertilizer had been made at cabinet level. But if they had been, he thought the cabinet should be more careful.

3. Asking the right question? The discretionary function exception has generated its share of conflicting decisions. *Dalehite* surely got it off to a bad start. But does it at least focus on the right question? Isn't separation of powers the core concern? If policy choices are committed to the political branches and may be taken for political reasons, should courts review those decisions for negligence?

Deciding how much to expand the money supply is a discretionary function. What about deciding that New York City needs, or can afford, 30,000 police officers? Should that decision be immune if some crime victim finds an expert to testify that anything fewer than 35,000 was negligent? But recent discretionary-function cases go far beyond this sort of policy choice.

4. The current interpretation. The Court eventually repudiated the distinction between the operational level and the planning level, insisting that that language in *Dalehite* was "merely description" and not part of a legal standard. United States v. Gaubert, 499 U.S. 315, 326 (1991).

Gaubert was the largest shareholder in a failed savings and loan. (Savings and loans were financial institutions similar to banks, but they operated under a different regulatory regime and specialized in housing loans). Gaubert alleged that the Federal Home Loan Bank Board had threatened to take over his S&L unless new management were installed, that it had recommended the new managers, that it had given them detailed operational advice, and that this interference and advice had been negligent and had caused the S&L to fail. The Fifth Circuit held that installing new management was an immune discretionary function, but that the operational advice was not.

The Supreme Court unanimously reversed on the government's appeal. It said that a "discretionary act is one that involves choice or judgment," *id.* at 325, and that this could occur at any level of government. Discretionary functions included day-to-day business judgment in pursuit of the policy of minimizing S&L losses and preserving the government insurance fund. In a sentence that has had large and possibly unintended consequences, the Court said that "the focus of the inquiry is not on the agent's subjective intent in exercising the discretion conferred by statute or regulation, but on the nature of the actions taken and on whether they are susceptible to policy analysis." *Id.* at 325.

5. Safety inspections. Are safety inspections a discretionary function? The Federal Aviation Administration licenses new aircraft after spot-checking their components; the agency does not have nearly enough resources to check everything. In United States v. S.A. Empresa de Viacao Aerea Rio Grandense, 467 U.S. 797 (1984), commonly cited as *Varig Airlines,* plaintiffs sued for damages arising out of a crash caused by a component that the government had not inspected. Not surprisingly, the Court held that the design of the spot-check policy was a discretionary function, so that the government was not liable for components it deliberately decided not to inspect.

In Berkovitz v. United States, 486 U.S. 531 (1988), the government approved a private manufacturer's distribution of a polio vaccine that caused permanent paralysis in plaintiff. Plaintiff alleged that government officials approved the vaccine without receiving the safety data or making the safety determinations required by government regulations, and in the alternative, that they approved its release knowing that it failed to comply with government safety standards. The Court held that none of these claims was barred by the discretionary function exception.

Plaintiff also alleged in the alternative that the government officials erroneously found that the vaccine complied with government standards. The Court said that application of the discretionary function exception to this claim depended on the facts. Plaintiff argued that compliance was a matter of "objective scientific standards"; if so, the Court said, a mistake in applying these standards was not a discretionary function. The government argued that compliance depended in part on policy judgments that balanced risk against benefit; if so, the Court said, such judgments were a discretionary function and courts could not review the balance in a tort suit.

6. Hurricane Katrina. In the wake of Hurricane Katrina in 2005, government emergency services failed on a massive basis, many people died, and some of their survivors filed lawsuits. An example is Freeman v. United States, 556 F.3d 326 (5th Cir. 2009). Two of the decedents died at the New Orleans Convention Center, where evacuees were housed in terrible conditions; the other died after being stranded on a highway interchange for three days. All three were chronically ill to begin with, and they suffered from heat exhaustion and lack of food, water, and medical care. The National Response Plan set out many duties that federal agencies failed to perform. But these alleged duties were stated in "generalized, precatory, or aspirational language that is too general to prescribe a specific course of action for an agency or employee to follow." *Id.* at 338. The court seemed to think the plan imposed no enforceable duties at all; it might also have said that the plan left ample discretion about how any duties were to be performed.

Other plaintiffs sued the Army Corps of Engineers for negligence that caused or aggravated the flooding. The district court held that the Corps negligently maintained the Mississippi River Gulf Outlet, an artificial channel that once connected the river to the gulf, and that this negligence caused the flooding of the Lower Ninth Ward and St. Bernard Parish. The discretionary function exception did not apply, because the Corps had violated objective engineering principles. In re Katrina Canal Breaches Consolidated Litigation, 647 F. Supp. 2d 644 (E.D. La. 2009).

The court of appeals initially affirmed on all claims. 673 F.3d 381 (5th Cir. 2012). With respect to the discretionary function exception, the court accepted the district court's view that the Corps had not made a public-policy judgment, but rather, had misapplied "objective scientific principles." *Id.* at 391. The decision was unanimous.

On petition for rehearing, the same panel unanimously changed its mind. 696 F.3d 436 (5th Cir. 2012). The court on rehearing said that the government "need not have actually considered any policy implications; instead, the decision must only be 'susceptible to policy analysis,'" *id.* at 451, citing the most recent in a line of decisions that traced back to *Gaubert*'s mention of "susceptible to policy analysis."

7. Nashville. The Sixth Circuit applied the discretionary function exception in a case arising out of a disastrous flood in Nashville. A.O. Smith Corp. v. United States,

774 F.3d 359 (6th Cir. 2014). Plaintiffs alleged that the reservoir above Nashville was nearly full, and that the Corps of Engineers had three-days warning from the Weather Service, which forecast more than six inches of rain. Plaintiffs alleged that the Corps failed to release water before the storm and failed to warn people downstream when it was forced to release vast quantities of water after the reservoir completely filled. They alleged that the Corps's Water Manager left the office for six hours early in the crisis, and again overnight, and that employees seeking authority to release water could not get answers. The court held that all these alleged decisions were "susceptible to policy analysis." *Id.* at 365, 366, 370.

8. Bernard Madoff. Bernard Madoff ran the largest Ponzi scheme ever, inflicting some $65 billion in losses. Some of his victims sued the United States, alleging that the scheme would have been exposed much sooner if the Securities and Exchange Commission had exercised even a minimal level of competence. Baer v. United States, 722 F.3d 168 (3d Cir. 2013); Molchatsky v. United States, 713 F.3d 159 (2d Cir. 2013). But both courts said that how to go about investigating fraud is a discretionary function.

9. Supervising employees. An FBI agent used FBI surveillance and recording equipment to monitor his wife. After the divorce, she sued the agency for failing to have policies that would have prevented such personal misuse of the equipment. The FBI was protected by the discretionary function exception. Gordio-González v. United States, 873 F.3d 32 (1st Cir. 2017). "Inherent in the performance of supervisory tasks are considerations of policy, a balancing of competing interests, and careful decisionmaking regarding the level of micro-management of one's subordinates." *Id.* at 37.

10. What is *not* a discretionary function these days? Are courts using the discretionary function exception to give de facto sovereign immunity for any activity more complex than a government driver running someone over? Consider Thacker v. Tennessee Valley Authority, 868 F.3d 979 (11th Cir. 2017). A power line had fallen into the Tennessee River, and TVA employees were trying to lift it out. Two boaters came into contact with the line; one was killed and the other seriously injured.

The Eleventh Circuit held that removing the line from the water was a discretionary function. "[T]he challenged actions plainly involved public-policy considerations. The challenged actions and decisions in this case could require TVA to consider, among other things, its allocation of resources (such as personnel and time), public safety, cost concerns, benefits, and environmental impact." *Id.* at 983. Balancing cost against the benefit to safety is the essence of the economic definition of negligence. Is negligence itself now a discretionary function?

Plaintiff filed a cert. petition, No. 17-1201:

> Such wholly functional work—of just the sort that would attract a cogent tort claim if done negligently by a private actor—is exactly where the FTCA meant to extend governmental liability. If the TVA's challenged work in this case does fall into the discretionary-function exception, moreover, then it is hard to imagine what falls outside it.

2018 WL 1419882, at *26.

NOTES ON FEDERAL WAIVERS OF IMMUNITY

1. The general pattern. The federal statutory waivers are important because suits against the federal government are so important. They are also as good an example as any of statutes waiving immunity. One waiver for contract cases, with a specialized court to hear them, and a separate waiver for tort cases, with a lot of exceptions, is a common pattern. Another common pattern, not illustrated in the federal waivers, is a waiver with a liability limit stated in dollars, like the $150,000 limit in *Stone*. That limit is per injured person per occurrence, and it has since been raised to $1 million. N.C. Gen. Stat. §143-299.2. Some states have per occurrence limits, which can produce nominal recoveries in cases with multiple victims.

2. The Federal Tort Claims Act. The Tort Claims Act consents to suit

> for injury or loss of property, or personal injury or death caused by the negligent or wrongful act or omission of any employee of the Government while acting within the scope of his office or employment, under circumstances where the United States, if a private person, would be liable to the claimant in accordance with the law of the place where the act or omission occurred.

28 U.S.C. §1346(b)(1).

There are a number of exceptions; the most important is the discretionary function exception, discussed above. The United States is not liable for prejudgment interest or punitive damages. 28 U.S.C. §2674. The requirement of a "wrongful" act means the United States is not liable under any state rule imposing strict liability. Laird v. Nelms, 406 U.S. 797 (1972). There is no liability for enforcing unconstitutional statutes, for losing letters in the post office, for actions of the military in time of war, for damages caused by fiscal operations of the Treasury or regulation of the monetary system, for claims arising in a foreign country, for most intentional torts by employees other than law enforcement officers, or for several other miscellaneous kinds of claims. 28 U.S.C. §2680. There is a judicially created exception for any injuries incident to military service, whether or not they fall within the express exception for combat operations. Feres v. United States, 340 U.S. 135 (1950).

The Tort Claims Act incorporates "the law of the place where the act or omission occurred," and this "place" is understood to be a state. The United States is liable "under circumstances" in which a private person would be liable under this state's law, and a federal employee's official duties may help define the "circumstances," but the tort duty must be imposed by state law. Thus, there is no liability for breach of a duty imposed solely by federal law. Some of the cases are collected in Federal Deposit Insurance Corp. v. Meyer, 510 U.S. 471, 478 (1994).

The many exceptions, and arguments about the proper analogy to liabilities of private persons under state law, give rise to much litigation. For example: The United States is not liable for "any claim arising out of the loss, miscarriage, or negligent transmission of letters or postal matter." 28 U.S.C. §2680(b). The Supreme Court held that this language does not exclude liability for personal injuries allegedly suffered when plaintiff tripped over mail that a letter carrier negligently placed on her porch instead of in the mailbox. Dolan v. United States Postal Service, 546 U.S. 481 (2006). The Postal Service argued that leaving the mail for the recipient is the final step in "transmission," and thus that plaintiff had alleged "negligent transmission." The Court noted that, on this theory, negligently driving a mail truck would also be negligent transmission of the mails, and that this would defeat a central purpose of the Tort Claims Act; Congress certainly thought the government should be liable for its motor vehicle accidents.

3. The intentional-tort exception. The Tort Claims Act:

shall not apply to . . . (h) Any claim arising out of assault, battery, false imprisonment, false arrest, malicious prosecution, abuse of process, libel, slander, misrepresentation, deceit, or interference with contract rights: *Provided,* That, with regard to acts or omissions of investigative or law enforcement officers of the United States Government, the [Tort Claims Act] **shall apply** to any claim arising . . . out of assault, battery, false imprisonment, false arrest, abuse of process, or malicious prosecution.

28 U.S.C. §2680(h) (boldface emphasis added). The law-enforcement proviso was enacted in response to Bivens v. Six Unknown Agents, reprinted in section 6.B, which implied a cause of action for damages for an unconstitutional search by federal agents. *Bivens* claims run against the employees; the proviso lets victims within its scope sue the United States instead. Some of the lower courts read additional requirements into the proviso, limiting the waiver of immunity to specific contexts, usually involving investigation or arrest.

The Court unanimously rejected all those cases in Milbrook v. United States, 569 U.S. 50 (2013), where a prisoner alleged that he was sexually assaulted by a guard. The Court said that these rules narrowing the waiver of immunity had no basis in the statutory text. In fact, they had so little basis that the Solicitor General confessed error and agreed that immunity had been waived. But the government's usual approach to sovereign immunity is to litigate tenaciously and aggressively; its argument in the mail delivery case in note 2 is much more typical.

4. "Shall not apply." Section 2680, which lists the exceptions to the Tort Claims Act, begins by saying, "The provisions of this chapter and of section 1346(b) of this title shall not apply to—" and then lists all the exceptions. The Court has held that this means not merely that the waiver of immunity shall not apply, but that nothing in the chapter (§§2671 to 2680) applies to claims within the exceptions. Simmons v. Himmelreich, 136 S. Ct. 1843 (2016).

Himmelreich sued the United States, alleging that the negligence of its employees caused him to be severely beaten by a fellow prisoner. The case was dismissed under the discretionary function exception. Himmelreich separately filed a constitutional tort suit against individual employees. Normally, a judgment in an action under the Tort Claims Act "shall constitute a complete bar to any action by the claimant, by reason of the same subject matter, against the employee of the government whose act or omission gave rise to the claim." 28 U.S.C. §2676. But that provision "shall not apply" to any case falling within one of the exceptions. So a judgment dismissing the claim against the United States because the claim falls within one of the exceptions does not bar a subsequent action against the employees.

5. The Westfall Act. If a plaintiff sues a federal employee under state law, the Attorney General may certify that the employee was acting in the course and scope of his federal employment. The result of such a certification is that the case is removed to federal court, the claim against the employee is dismissed, the United States is substituted as the defendant, and the case proceeds under the Tort Claims Act. This provision appears in 28 U.S.C. §2679(b) to (d), commonly known as the Westfall Act for the case it responded to, Westfall v. Erwin, 484 U.S. 292 (1988). *Westfall* held that federal employees are immune from state tort suits only for their discretionary acts, not for ministerial acts. The Act makes federal employees absolutely immune for acts within the course and scope of their employment; the United States as the substituted defendant has the benefit of all the exceptions to the Tort Claims Act, including the discretionary function exception, but it absorbs the liability for torts not within any exception.

The Westfall Act has generated surprising complexities. The Attorney General may be tempted to protect federal employees by certifying freely, or he may be deterred by the prospect of the liability falling on the United States. Those conflicting incentives disappear when the United States is immune but the employee would not be. In Gutierrez de Martinez v. Lamagno, 515 U.S. 417 (1995), the Attorney General certified that a federal employee in Colombia, driving drunk with an unidentified woman after midnight, was acting within the scope of his employment. Maybe so. The Act said that the Attorney General's certification "shall conclusively establish scope of office or employment for purposes of removal." 28 U.S.C. §2679(d)(2). But the Court held that this certification is subject to (highly deferential) judicial review for purposes of substituting defendants. If the court finds that the employee's action was not within the course and scope of his employment, the case can proceed against the employee.

On remand, the court of appeals upheld the scope-of-employment certification. The unidentified woman turned out to be another federal agent; the male agent was returning her to her hotel, allegedly from a dinner meeting where government business was discussed; and the court concluded that although he had been drinking, he was not drunk. Gutierrez de Martinez v. Drug Enforcement Administration, 111 F.3d 1148 (4th Cir. 1997).

The Attorney General can certify that the federal-employee defendant acted within the scope of his employment, and then, after the case is removed, deny that the alleged conduct ever happened. Osborn v. Haley, 549 U.S. 225 (2007). The Court thought that it would make no sense if the Act protected guilty federal employees but failed to protect innocent federal employees.

6. The Tucker Act. The Tucker Act consents to suit on any claim "founded either upon the Constitution, or any Act of Congress or any regulation of an executive department, or upon any express or implied contract with the United States, or for liquidated or unliquidated damages in cases not sounding in tort." 28 U.S.C. §1491(a)(1).

a. Claims based on federal law. The statutory reference to the Constitution, statutes, and regulations is misleading. The Tucker Act consents to suit on such claims, but it does not create a private right to sue. A law can be enforced via the Tucker Act only if the substantive law expressly or by strong implication creates a cause of action for damages. United States v. Testan, 424 U.S. 392 (1976). In *Testan,* plaintiffs were civil servants who had been paid less than they would have been paid if their positions had been properly classified. The Classification Act created a substantive right to proper classification, but it did not create any right to damages for improper classification. The Back Pay Act created a right to back pay for unlawful discharge, but not for improper classification. So even though the claim was founded on a federal statute, it was not a statute that created liability for damages, and the Tucker Act was no help. "The other source of law need not *explicitly* provide" for damages, but it must "fairly be interpreted as mandating compensation by the Federal Government." United States v. Navajo Nation, 556 U.S. 287, 290 (2009).

In United States v. Bormes, 568 U.S. 6 (2012), the Court unanimously reaffirmed a line of cases holding that "[w]here a specific statutory scheme provides the accoutrements of a judicial action, the metes and bounds of the liability Congress intended to create can only be divined from the text of the statute itself." *Id.* at 14. And therefore, the substantive statute must waive sovereign immunity; the waiver in the Tucker Act is irrelevant.

There is an obvious potential for a Catch-22 here. If the substantive statute does not create a cause of action, the Tucker Act is no help, because it does not create a cause of action either. And if the substantive statute does create a cause of action—at least if it creates it in any detail—the Tucker Act is no help, because it cannot supplement or expand the substantive statute. In *Bormes*, the Fair Credit Reporting Act created a cause of action for damages against "any person" who violated its terms, and defined "person" to include "any . . . government or governmental subdivision or agency." 15 U.S.C. §1681a(b). The Court remanded for consideration of whether this language was sufficient to waive sovereign immunity.

b. Contract claims. The most important function of the Court of Federal Claims is to adjudicate disputes over government contracts. But it cannot grant specific performance. The Tucker Act has long been construed to authorize only damages and certain kinds of incidental equitable relief that fall short of specific performance. United States v. Jones, 131 U.S. 1, 18-19 (1889). For modern acknowledgment of the rule, see Goist v. United States, 85 Fed. Cl. 726, 738 (2009).

Much government contract litigation involves routine procurement and construction disputes, but sometimes government breaches for political or policy reasons that touch on separation of powers. One dramatic example is the vast body of litigation arising out of United States v. Winstar Corp., 518 U.S. 839 (1996). Attempting to manage the savings-and-loan crisis of the 1980s, the executive branch induced strong financial institutions to buy insolvent ones, in part by promising special regulatory treatment. These were quite specific written contracts, with much money invested in reliance. Fearing that these deals merely prolonged the life of weak financial institutions, Congress then imposed much less favorable regulatory treatment by statute, instantly rendering some of the merged institutions insolvent for purposes of banking regulation. It is not a tort for government to govern, but it may be a breach of contract. Congress could change the regulation, but the government was liable for the resulting damages.

7. The Administrative Procedure Act. Sovereign immunity is a barrier to ordinary judicial review of administrative action, usually overridden by provisions for judicial review in the statute creating each agency. For statutes that neglected this detail, mandamus or some other suit against officers in their official capacity could usually be made to work, but there was litigation about boundaries and exceptions. In 1976, Congress waived immunity in any "action in a court of the United States seeking relief other than money damages and stating a claim that an agency or an officer or employee thereof acted or failed to act in an official capacity or under color of legal authority." 5 U.S.C. §702.

An explicit exception provides that nothing in §702 "confers authority to grant relief if any other statute that grants consent to suit expressly or impliedly forbids the relief which is sought." So, for example, §702 can't be used to get around the implicit disallowance of specific performance in the Tucker Act.

There has also been litigation over the phrase "relief other than money damages." In Bowen v. Massachusetts, 487 U.S. 879 (1988), the Court held that federal district courts could review administrative decisions disallowing state expenditures that would be reimbursed by the United States if allowed. This review ended in an order to federal officials to pay money from the Treasury, but the Court said this was specific relief ordering payment of the very money due, and that "money damages" meant substitutionary relief, money that compensated for some loss already suffered. *Bowen* should mean that the United States is liable in restitution, because that, too, is "relief other than money damages," but that does not appear to have been squarely decided.

Three circuits have now held that a judgment for the specific amount of money the government originally owed the plaintiff is not specific relief unless it can be paid from the original appropriation for that purpose. If that appropriation has lapsed, or been fully expended, the plaintiff is seeking different money as a substitute for the original money. That is money damages and the government is immune. Modoc Lassen Indian Housing Authority v. United States Department of Housing and Urban Development, 881 F.3d 1181, 1195-1199 (10th Cir. 2017), *petition for cert. filed*, No. 17-1353 (Mar. 27, 2018). This renders *Bowen* pretty much useless, because the original appropriation will almost surely be gone by the time the litigation is concluded; Judge Matheson dissented in *Modoc*.

8. Sue-and-be-sued clauses. Statutes creating government corporations and independent agencies often say that the entity can "sue and be sued." These clauses are a general waiver of sovereign immunity for suits against that entity. Franchise Tax Board v. United States Postal Service, 467 U.S. 512 (1984). This waiver includes claims that could not be brought under the Tort Claims Act. Federal Deposit Insurance Corp. v. Meyer, 510 U.S. 471, 480-483 (1994). That at least is federal law. A remarkable series of Texas cases hold that sue-and-be-sued clauses do not waive immunity. "All [such a clause] *clearly* says is that the City can be sued and impleaded in court *when* suit is permitted, not that immunity is waived for all suits." Tooke v. City of Mexia, 197 S.W.3d 325, 344 (Tex. 2006).

9. Other waivers. There are many more specific waivers scattered through the United States Code; waivers are often required to solve the simplest problems. For example, it is impossible to garnish the wages of government employees unless the government consents to the garnishment suit. In 42 U.S.C. §659(a), Congress consented to garnishment suits seeking to collect alimony and child support.

2.   *Suits Against Officers — Absolute Immunity*

VAN DE KAMP v. GOLDSTEIN
555 U.S. 335 (2009)

Justice BREYER delivered the opinion of the Court.

We here consider the scope of a prosecutor's absolute immunity from claims asserted under 42 U.S.C. §1983. . . . We ask whether that immunity extends to claims that the prosecution failed to disclose impeachment material due to: (1) a failure properly to train prosecutors, (2) a failure properly to supervise prosecutors, or (3) a failure to establish an information system containing potential impeachment material about informants. We conclude that a prosecutor's absolute immunity extends to all these claims.

I

In 1998, respondent Thomas Goldstein (then a prisoner) filed a habeas corpus action in the Federal District Court for the Central District of California. He claimed that in 1980 he was convicted of murder; that his conviction depended in critical part upon the testimony of Edward Floyd Fink, a jailhouse informant; that Fink's testimony was unreliable, indeed false; that Fink had previously received reduced sentences for providing prosecutors with favorable testimony in other cases; that at least some prosecutors in the Los Angeles County District Attorney's Office knew about the favorable treatment; that the office had not provided Goldstein's attorney with that information; and that, among other things, the prosecution's failure to provide Goldstein's attorney with this potential impeachment information had led to his erroneous conviction. Goldstein v. City of Long Beach, 481 F.3d 1170, 1171-1172 (9th Cir. 2007).

After an evidentiary hearing the District Court agreed with Goldstein that Fink had not been truthful and that if the prosecution had told Goldstein's lawyer that Fink had received prior rewards in return for favorable testimony it might have made a difference. The court ordered the State either to grant Goldstein a new trial or to release him. The Court of Appeals affirmed the District Court's determination. And the State decided that, rather than retry Goldstein (who had already served 24 years of his sentence), it would release him.

Upon his release Goldstein filed this §1983 action against petitioners, the former Los Angeles County district attorney and chief deputy district attorney. Goldstein's complaint (which for present purposes we take as accurate) asserts in relevant part that the prosecution's failure to communicate to his attorney the facts about Fink's earlier testimony-related rewards violated the prosecution's constitutional duty to "insure communication of all relevant information on each case [including agreements made with informants] to every lawyer who deals with it." Giglio v. United States, 405 U.S. 150, 154 (1972). Moreover, it alleges that this failure resulted from the failure of petitioners (the office's chief supervisory attorneys) adequately to train and to supervise the prosecutors who worked for them as well as their failure to establish an information system about informants. And it asks for damages based upon these training, supervision, and information-system related failings.

Petitioners, claiming absolute immunity from such a §1983 action, asked the District Court to dismiss the complaint. The District Court denied the motion to dismiss on the ground that the conduct asserted amounted to "administrative," not "prosecutorial," conduct; hence it fell outside the scope of the prosecutor's absolute immunity to §1983 claims. The Ninth Circuit, considering petitioners' claim on an interlocutory appeal, affirmed the District Court's "no immunity" determination. We now . . . reverse. . . .

II

A half-century ago Chief Judge Learned Hand explained that a prosecutor's absolute immunity reflects "a balance" of "evils." Gregoire v. Biddle, 177 F.2d 579, 581 (2d Cir. 1949). "[I]t has been thought in the end better," he said, "to leave unredressed the wrongs done by dishonest officers than to subject those who try to do their duty to the constant dread of retaliation." *Id.* In Imbler v. Pachtman, 424 U.S. 409 (1976), this Court considered prosecutorial actions that are "intimately associated with the judicial phase of the criminal process." *Id.* at 430. And, referring to Chief Judge Hand's views, it held that prosecutors are absolutely immune from liability in §1983 lawsuits brought under such circumstances. *Id.* at 428.

The §1983 action at issue was that of a prisoner freed on a writ of habeas corpus who subsequently sought damages from his former prosecutor. His action, like the action now before us, tracked the claims that a federal court had found valid when granting his habeas corpus petition. In particular, the prisoner claimed that the trial prosecutor had permitted a fingerprint expert to give false testimony, that the prosecutor was responsible for the expert's having suppressed important evidence, and that the prosecutor had introduced a misleading artist's sketch into evidence.

In concluding that the prosecutor was absolutely immune, the Court pointed out that legislators have long "enjoyed absolute immunity for their official actions," *id.* at 417; that the common law granted immunity to "judges and . . . jurors acting within the scope of their duties," *id.* at 423, and that the law had also granted prosecutors absolute immunity from common-law tort actions, say, those underlying a "decision to initiate a prosecution," *id.* at 421. The Court then held that the "same considerations of public policy that underlie" a prosecutor's common-law immunity "countenance absolute immunity under §1983." *Id.* at 424. Those considerations, the Court said, arise out of the general common-law "concern that harassment by unfounded litigation" could both "cause a deflection of the prosecutor's energies from his public duties" and also lead the prosecutor to "shade his decisions instead of exercising the independence of judgment required by his public trust." *Id.* at 423.

Where §1983 actions are at issue, the Court said, both sets of concerns are present and serious. The "public trust of the prosecutor's office would suffer" were the prosecutor to have in mind his "own potential" damages "liability" when making prosecutorial decisions—as he might well were he subject to §1983 liability. *Id.* at 424. This is no small concern, given the frequency with which criminal defendants bring such suits, *id.* at 425 ("[A] defendant often will transform his resentment at being prosecuted into the ascription of improper and malicious actions to the State's advocate"), and the "substantial danger of liability even to the honest prosecutor" that such suits pose when they survive pretrial dismissal; see also *id.* (complex, close, fair-trial questions "often would require a virtual retrial of the criminal offense in a new forum, and the resolution of some technical issues by the lay jury"). A "prosecutor," the Court noted, "inevitably makes many decisions that could engender colorable claims of constitutional deprivation. Defending these decisions, often years after they were made, could impose unique and intolerable burdens upon a prosecutor responsible annually for hundreds of indictments and trials." *Id.* at 425-426. The Court thus rejected the idea of applying the less-than-absolute "qualified immunity" that the law accords to other "executive or administrative officials," noting that the "honest prosecutor would face greater difficulty" than would those officials "in meeting the standards of qualified immunity." *Id.* at 425. Accordingly, the immunity that the law grants prosecutors is "absolute." *Id.* at 424.

The Court made clear that absolute immunity may not apply when a prosecutor is not acting as "an officer of the court," but is instead engaged in other tasks, say, investigative or administrative tasks. *Id.* at 431 n.33. To decide whether absolute immunity attaches to a particular kind of prosecutorial activity, one must take account of the "functional" considerations discussed above. In *Imbler*, the Court concluded that the "reasons for absolute immunity appl[ied] with full force" to the conduct at issue because it was "intimately associated with the judicial phase of the criminal process." *Id.* at 430. The fact that one constitutional duty at issue was a positive duty (the duty to supply "information relevant to the defense") rather than a negative duty (the duty not to "use . . . perjured testimony") made no difference. After all, a plaintiff can often transform a positive into a negative duty simply by reframing the pleadings; in either case, a constitutional violation is at issue.

Finally, the Court specifically reserved the question whether or when "similar reasons require immunity for those aspects of the prosecutor's responsibility that cast him in the role of an administrator . . . rather than that of advocate." *Id.* at 430-431. It said that "[d]rawing a proper line between these functions may present difficult questions, but this case does not require us to anticipate them." *Id.* at 431 n.33.

In the years since *Imbler*, we have held that absolute immunity applies when a prosecutor prepares to initiate a judicial proceeding, or appears in court to present evidence in support of a search warrant application. We have held that absolute immunity does not apply when a prosecutor gives advice to police during a criminal investigation, when the prosecutor makes statements to the press, or when a prosecutor acts as a complaining witness in support of a warrant application. This case, unlike these earlier cases, requires us to consider how immunity applies where a prosecutor is engaged in certain administrative activities.

III

Goldstein claims that the district attorney and his chief assistant violated their constitutional obligation to provide his attorney with impeachment-related information, because, as the Court of Appeals wrote, they failed "to adequately train and supervise deputy district attorneys on that subject," 481 F.3d at 1176, and because, as Goldstein's complaint adds, they "failed to create any system for the Deputy District Attorneys handling criminal cases to access information pertaining to the benefits provided to jailhouse informants and other impeachment information." We agree with Goldstein that, in making these claims, he attacks the office's administrative procedures. We are also willing to assume with Goldstein, but purely for argument's sake, that *Giglio* imposes certain obligations as to training, supervision, or information-system management.

Even so, we conclude that prosecutors involved in such supervision or training or information-system management enjoy absolute immunity from the kind of legal claims at issue here. Those claims focus upon a certain kind of administrative obligation—a kind that itself is directly connected with the conduct of a trial. Here, unlike with other claims related to administrative decisions, an individual prosecutor's error in the plaintiff's specific criminal trial constitutes an essential element of the plaintiff's claim. The administrative obligations at issue here are thus unlike administrative duties concerning, for example, workplace hiring, payroll administration, the maintenance of physical facilities, and the like. Moreover, the types of activities on which Goldstein's claims focus necessarily require legal knowledge and the exercise of related discretion, e.g., in determining what information should be included in the training or the supervision or the information-system management. And in that sense also Goldstein's claims are unlike claims of, say, unlawful discrimination in hiring employees. Given these features of the case before us, we believe absolute immunity must follow.

A

We reach this conclusion by initially considering a hypothetical case that involves supervisory or other office prosecutors but does not involve administration. Suppose that Goldstein had brought such a case, seeking damages not only from the trial prosecutor but also from a supervisory prosecutor or from the trial prosecutor's colleagues—all on the ground that they should have found and turned over the impeachment material about Fink. *Imbler* makes clear that all these prosecutors would enjoy absolute immunity from such a suit. The prosecutors' behavior, taken individually or separately, would involve "[p]reparation . . . for . . . trial," 424 U.S. at 431 n.33, and would be "intimately associated with the judicial phase of the criminal process" because it concerned the evidence presented at trial. *Id.* at 430. And all of the considerations that this Court found to militate in favor of absolute immunity in *Imbler* would militate in favor of immunity in such a case.

The only difference we can find between *Imbler* and our hypothetical case lies in the fact that, in our hypothetical case, a prosecutorial supervisor or colleague might himself be liable for damages *instead of* the trial prosecutor. But we cannot find that difference (in the pattern of liability among prosecutors within a single office) to be critical. Decisions about indictment or trial prosecution will often involve more than one prosecutor within an office. We do not see how such differences in the pattern of liability among a group of prosecutors in a single office could alleviate *Imbler*'s basic fear, namely, that the threat of damages liability would affect the way in which prosecutors carried out their basic court-related tasks. Moreover, this Court has pointed out that "it is the interest in protecting the proper functioning of the office, rather than the interest in protecting its occupant, that is of primary importance." Kalina v. Fletcher, 522 U.S. 118, 125 (1997). Thus, we must assume that the prosecutors in our hypothetical suit would enjoy absolute immunity.

B

Once we determine that supervisory prosecutors are immune in a suit directly attacking their actions related to an individual trial, we must find they are similarly immune in the case before us. We agree with the Court of Appeals that the office's *general* methods of supervision and training are at issue here, but we do not agree that that difference is critical for present purposes. That difference does not preclude an intimate connection between prosecutorial activity and the trial process. The management tasks at issue, insofar as they are relevant, concern how and when to make impeachment information available at a trial. They are thereby directly connected with the prosecutor's basic trial advocacy duties. And, in terms of *Imbler*'s functional concerns, a suit charging that a supervisor made a mistake directly related to a particular trial, on the one hand, and a suit charging that a supervisor trained and supervised inadequately, on the other, would seem very much alike.

That is true, in part, for the practical reason that it will often prove difficult to draw a line between *general* office supervision or office training (say, related to *Giglio*) and *specific* supervision or training related to a particular case. To permit claims based upon the former is almost inevitably to permit the bringing of claims that include the latter. It is also true because one cannot easily distinguish, for immunity purposes, between claims based upon training or supervisory failures related to *Giglio* and similar claims related to other constitutional matters . . . . And that being so, every consideration that *Imbler* mentions militates in favor of immunity.

As we have said, the type of "faulty training" claim at issue here rests in necessary part upon a consequent error by an individual prosecutor in the midst of trial, namely, the plaintiff's trial. If, as *Imbler* says, the threat of damages liability for such an error could lead a trial prosecutor to take account of that risk when making trial-related decisions, so, too, could the threat of more widespread liability throughout the office (ultimately traceable to that trial error) lead both that prosecutor and other office prosecutors as well to take account of such a risk. Indeed, members of a large prosecutorial office, when making prosecutorial decisions, could have in mind the "consequences in terms of" damages liability whether they are making general decisions about supervising or training or whether they are making individual trial-related decisions. *Imbler*, 424 U.S. at 424.

Moreover, because better training or supervision might prevent most, if not all, prosecutorial errors at trial, permission to bring such a suit here would grant permission to criminal defendants to bring claims in other similar instances, in effect claiming damages for (trial-related) training or supervisory failings. Further, given the complexity of the constitutional issues, inadequate training and supervision suits could, as in *Imbler*, "pose substantial danger of liability even to the honest prosecutor." *Id.* at 425. Finally, as *Imbler* pointed out, defending prosecutorial decisions, often years after they were made, could impose "unique and intolerable burdens upon a prosecutor responsible annually for hundreds of indictments and trials." *Id.* at 425-426.

At the same time, to permit this suit to go forward would create practical anomalies. A trial prosecutor would remain immune, even for *intentionally* failing to turn over, say *Giglio* material; but her supervisor might be liable for *negligent* training or supervision. Small prosecution offices where supervisors can personally participate in all of the cases would likewise remain immune from prosecution; but large offices, making use of more general office-wide supervision and training, would not. Most important, the ease with which a plaintiff could restyle a complaint charging a trial failure so that it becomes a complaint charging a failure of training or supervision would eviscerate *Imbler.*

We conclude that the very reasons that led this Court in *Imbler* to find absolute immunity require a similar finding in this case. We recognize, as Chief Judge Hand pointed out, that sometimes such immunity deprives a plaintiff of compensation that he undoubtedly merits; but the impediments to the fair, efficient functioning of a prosecutorial office that liability could create lead us to find that *Imbler* must apply here.

C

We treat separately Goldstein's claim that the Los Angeles County District Attorney's Office should have established a system that would have permitted prosecutors "handling criminal cases to access information pertaining to the benefits provided to jailhouse informants and other impeachment information." We do so because Goldstein argues that the creation of an information management system is a more purely administrative task, less closely related to the "judicial phase of the criminal process," *Imbler,* 424 U.S. at 430, than are supervisory or training tasks. He adds that technically qualified individuals other than prosecutors could create such a system and that they could do so prior to the initiation of criminal proceedings.

In our view, however, these differences do not require a different outcome. The critical element of any information system is the information it contains. Deciding what to include and what not to include in an information system is little different from making similar decisions in respect to training. Again, determining the criteria for inclusion or exclusion requires knowledge of the law.

Moreover, the absence of an information system is relevant here if, and only if, a proper system would have included information about the informant Fink. Thus, were this claim allowed, a court would have to review the office's legal judgments, not simply about *whether* to have an information system but also about *what kind* of system is appropriate, and whether an appropriate system would have included *Giglio*-related information *about one particular kind of trial informant.* Such decisions—whether made prior to or during a particular trial—are "intimately associated with the judicial phase of the criminal process." *Imbler,* 424 U.S. at 430. And, for the reasons set out above, all *Imbler*'s functional considerations . . . apply here as well.

We recognize that sometimes it would be easy for a court to determine that an office's decision about an information system was inadequate. Suppose, for example, the office had no system at all. But the same could be said of a prosecutor's trial error. Immunity does not exist to help prosecutors in the easy case; it exists because the easy cases bring difficult cases in their wake. And, as *Imbler* pointed out, the likely presence of too many difficult cases threatens, not prosecutors, but the public, for the reason that it threatens to undermine the necessary independence and integrity of the prosecutorial decision-making process. Such is true of the kinds of claims before us, to all of which *Imbler*'s functional considerations apply. Consequently, where a §1983 plaintiff claims that a prosecutor's management of a trial-related information system is responsible for a constitutional error at his or her particular trial, the prosecutor responsible for the system enjoys absolute immunity just as would the prosecutor who handled the particular trial itself.

***

For these reasons we conclude that petitioners are entitled to absolute immunity in respect to Goldstein's claims that their supervision, training, or information-system management was constitutionally inadequate. Accordingly, the judgment of the Court of Appeals is reversed, and the case is remanded for further proceedings consistent with this opinion. . . .

NOTES ON PROSECUTORIAL IMMUNITY

1. The policy of absolute immunity. Most government employees have only qualified immunity, considered in section 5.C.2. But a few get absolute immunity. Why are prosecutors so special? One answer is that they would be sued more often than other officials. They prosecute hundreds or thousands of criminal defendants, most of whom are guilty; they are subject to many constitutional rules that they frequently violate; and many convicted criminals are notoriously chronic litigants. For every valid claim, there might be many marginal and unmeritorious claims. Other rules would eliminate many of the weak claims. As a general rule, no one can file a federal suit for damages arising out of a criminal conviction until that conviction has been set aside by appeal, habeas corpus, or executive clemency. Heck v. Humphrey, 512 U.S. 477 (1994). Possible exceptions are debated in Spencer v. Kemna, 523 U.S. 1 (1998). Even with such rules in place, the Court has feared that the costs of abolishing absolute immunity might be very high.

The costs of retaining absolute immunity are also high. Goldstein spent 24 years of his life in prison, on the basis of probable perjury from an informant who apparently made a career of selling his perjured testimony to Los Angeles prosecutors in exchange for more lenient treatment of his other crimes. Justice Breyer states the facts at a high level of generality; here is a more forthcoming account:

> In 1979 Goldstein was an engineering student and Marine Corps veteran with no criminal history. He became a murder suspect after an eyewitness to an unrelated shooting saw the gunman enter Goldstein's apartment building. No witness or forensic evidence connected Goldstein with the murder victim, but Long Beach police detectives showed Goldstein's photograph, among others, to Loran Campbell, an eyewitness to the homicide. Campbell did not recognize anyone in the photo lineup, and Goldstein did not match Campbell's description of the suspect. However, a detective asked if Goldstein could have been the person Campbell saw running from the scene. Campbell said it was possible, though he was not certain.
>
> Goldstein was arrested and placed in a jail cell with Edward Floyd Fink, a heroin addict and convicted felon. At Goldstein's trial, Fink testified that Goldstein said he was in jail because he shot a man in a dispute over money. Fink claimed he received no benefit as a result of his testimony. Goldstein was convicted of murder in 1980.

Goldstein v. Superior Court, 195 P.3d 588, 590 (Cal. 2008). Absolute immunity means that the seriousness of the wrongdoing, and the seriousness of the consequences, are irrelevant.

2. Investigative activities. Prosecutors have only qualified immunity when they act as investigators, and this has not been an empty category. Thus, a prosecutor was not absolutely immune for erroneously advising police officers that they could question a suspect under hypnosis. Burns v. Reed, 500 U.S. 478 (1991). That advice was part of the prosecutor's investigation function, and it required only the qualified immunity illustrated by Harlow v. Fitzgerald, 457 U.S. 800 (1982). The Court emphasized that absolute immunity should be narrowly confined, in part because qualified immunity is now "ample" to protect "all but the plainly incompetent or those who knowingly violate the law." *Burns*, 500 U.S. at 495.

The Court applied *Burns* to the prosecutor's own investigative conduct in Buckley v. Fitzsimmons, 509 U.S. 259 (1993). The case was decided on motion to dismiss, so all the alleged facts come from the complaint. The prosecutor, Fitzsimmons, was investigating a highly publicized rape-murder of a child, and the only identification evidence was a single bootprint. After three experts had been unable to link Buckley's boots to the print, Fitzsimmons allegedly conspired with an expert "well known for her willingness to fabricate unreliable expert testimony." *Id.* at 262. Even with this expert's testimony, the grand jury failed to indict. Two months later, with no additional evidence—and 12 days before a hotly contested primary in which Fitzsimmons was defeated for reelection—Fitzsimmons procured an indictment and held a press conference at which he falsely claimed that numerous pieces of evidence linked Buckley to the crime. Buckley's trial ended in a hung jury; his retrial was abandoned when the allegedly dishonest expert died, and another person eventually confessed to the crime. Buckley spent more than two years in jail awaiting trial.

The Court unanimously agreed that the press conference was not part of the prosecutorial function and was protected only by qualified immunity. A majority of five held that Fitzsimmons's early meetings with the expert witness were more in the nature of investigation than of advocacy, in part because the advocacy function did not begin until there was probable cause to charge a particular suspect. So prosecutors appear to be immune for knowingly introducing false evidence at trial, but not for knowingly helping to create the false evidence. Justice Scalia argued that the false evidence probably did no damage until introduced at trial.

3. Dumping the liability on subordinates. In *Fitzsimmons*, where the prosecutor gave bad advice to police officers, the Court thought it would be incongruous to hold that the prosecutor was absolutely immune for giving the advice but that the police officers were not absolutely immune for following it. The Court had not minded this incongruity in Malley v. Briggs, 475 U.S. 335 (1986), where a police officer was held liable for executing a warrant that he should have known was invalid; the judge who issued the warrant would have had absolute immunity. A later decision emphasized that an officer in Malley's situation will usually be protected by qualified immunity, and that it is the rare case where a reasonable officer should recognize the invalidity of a judicially approved warrant. Messerschmidt v. Millender, 565 U.S. 535 (2012). The dissenters in *Messerschmidt* thought the officer had used a report of a specific assault, committed with a specific weapon, to authorize a general search of the suspect's residence for any evidence of gang affiliation or other weapons violations. The majority spun a theory of how a reasonable officer might have thought it was all related; without holding the warrant valid, they concluded that a reasonable officer might have thought it valid.

The Eighth Circuit imposed liability only on the police officer in Snider v. City of Cape Girardeau, 752 F.3d 1149 (8th Cir. 2014). Plaintiff cut up an American flag and threw the pieces in the street as an act of political protest. The officer sought an arrest warrant for a violation of Missouri's flag-desecration statute, the prosecutor submitted the request to a judge, and the judge issued the warrant. A reporter called the prosecutor to ask if he had ever heard of Texas v. Johnson, 491 U.S. 397 (1989), which upheld the right to burn a flag. The prosecutor read the case and dismissed the prosecution; plaintiff was released after eight hours in jail.

The officer had never heard of Texas v. Johnson either, but the law had been clearly established for 20 years, so there was no qualified immunity. The city was not liable because the arrest did not result from any city policy; see note 6 below. Plaintiff did not seek damages from the judge or prosecutor, each of whom presumably had absolute immunity. The court awarded $7,000 in compensatory damages against the officer. Probably the city indemnified him, but we don't know that. The court also awarded $61,000 in attorneys' fees jointly and severally against the officer and Missouri, which had intervened in a futile effort to defend the constitutionality of its statute. States are not immune from awards of attorneys' fees.

4. The prosecutor's own perjury. Prosecutors are not immune for their own false statements of fact in an affidavit, even if the affidavit is an integral part of pleadings and other documents charging a defendant with an offense. Kalina v. Fletcher, 522 U.S. 118 (1997). The Court unanimously held that in the affidavit, the prosecutor was acting as the complaining witness and was subject to the same rules as any other complaining witness. Courtroom witnesses have immunity, but out-of-court complaining witnesses can be liable for malicious prosecution.

5. Misconduct before grand juries. The Court unanimously held that an investigator in the prosecutor's office has absolute immunity for his allegedly perjured testimony to the grand jury. Rehberg v. Paulk, 566 U.S. 356 (2012). He was the only witness before the grand jury, so plaintiff argued that he was the complaining witness and within the rule of *Kalina.* The Court held him immune, and within the rule of witnesses at trial. Unlike the prosecutor in *Kalina,* and unlike the complaining witness at common law, defendant here was just a witness, without the power to decide whether to initiate a prosecution. The opinion offers a succinct overview of absolute immunity in general and of witness immunity in particular.

But the Second Circuit has held prosecutors liable for presenting false evidence to a grand jury. Morse v. Fusto, 804 F.3d 538 (2d Cir. 2015). The prosecutors presented a spreadsheet said to summarize a dentist's fraudulent billings to Medicaid; the chart was riddled with errors and exaggerations and the jury found that the prosecutors knew that. The dentist was indicted, and later acquitted, but his practice was destroyed. The court said that the prosecutors' work before the grand jury was investigative, and that it was clearly established that prosecutors cannot present false evidence.

The jury awarded $6.7 million compensatory and $1 million punitive, which the trial judge reduced to $4.6 million and $100,000. The compensatory reduction was in the award for emotional distress and pain and suffering; $4.2 million for lost earnings was not reduced. 2013 WL 4647603 (E.D.N.Y. 2013). These are huge sums for an Assistant United States Attorney; presumably they were paid by the United States. Eliminating or reducing immunity would leave prosecutors at risk of such huge judgments. But that would be because prosecutorial misconduct inflicts huge losses. Those losses are real, whether or not a factfinder ever puts a number on them or anyone ever has to compensate them.

6. Other remedies for prosecutorial misconduct. Unjustified convictions may be reversed on appeal, and habeas corpus provides an unusual means for further judicial review when evidence of prosecutorial misconduct is uncovered. Goldstein was eventually released on habeas corpus. But prosecutorial misconduct is hard to discover and prove, and the perception that most habeas petitions lack merit has led courts and legislatures to create many obstacles to habeas relief—obstacles that almost certainly block a significant fraction of the meritorious petitions along with the frivolous ones.

Prosecutors may be disciplined by the court or by the bar; staff prosecutors may be disciplined by their supervisors or even discharged. In theory, rogue prosecutors may be prosecuted criminally. It is generally thought that these mechanisms are less likely to chill prosecutorial independence, because an aggrieved litigant cannot invoke them at will. The problem is the opposite: Any form of discipline appears to be quite rare. It seems to take a combination of egregious misconduct and public scandal to get action against a misbehaving prosecutor. The violation in *Van de Kamp* was revealed when a courageous lawyer in the prosecutor's office pursued a grand jury investigation into the use of jailhouse informants:

> In 1990, [the grand jury] issued a public report concluding that misuse of jailhouse informants had been pervasive over the preceding 10 years. The grand jury found that the Los Angeles County District Attorney's office had demonstrated a "deliberate and informed declination to take the action necessary to curtail the misuse of jailhouse informant testimony." Among other deficiencies, it had failed to create a centralized index of potential impeachment information about informants, including any benefit they received for their testimony and their history of cooperation with law enforcement.

Goldstein v. Superior Court, 195 P.3d 588, 590 (Cal. 2008).

Goldstein sued the jurisdictions that prosecuted him, and his claim against Los Angeles County survived a motion to dismiss. Goldstein v. City of Long Beach, 2006 WL 3206148 (9th Cir. 2006). The Supreme Court of California held that it could not, or would not, order release of the grand jury transcripts. 195 P.3d at 592-599. The federal district court ordered that Goldstein be given at least some access to those transcripts. Goldstein v. City of Long Beach, 603 F. Supp. 2d 1242 (C.D. Cal. 2009).

Cities and counties have no immunity, but they are liable only for their *policies*, not for the misconduct of their employees. See note 16 following Edelman v. Jordan in section 5.C.1). Of course, no jurisdiction will have a stated policy of introducing perjured evidence, or of refusing to disclose exculpatory information—even if its prosecutors do these things with some frequency. *Goldstein* may be the rare case where plaintiff can show a de facto policy.

In 2010, the City of Long Beach settled with Goldstein for "nearly $8 million." Andrew Blankstein, *Long Beach to Pay Man $8 Million*, L.A. Times (Aug. 12, 2010). And his claim against Los Angeles County appears to have settled for an undisclosed sum. The docket shows settlement conferences followed by an unexplained dismissal with prejudice on plaintiff's motion. Goldstein v. City of Long Beach, No. 2:04-cv-09692 (C.D. Cal. 2014).

7. Another egregious example. In Connick v. Thompson, 563 U.S. 51 (2011), Thompson served 18 years, 14 of them on death row, for an armed robbery and murder he did not commit. The case focused primarily—exclusively in the majority's view of the case—on the prosecutor's failure to turn over a blood sample that exonerated Thompson of the armed robbery. When that misconduct was revealed, the state courts vacated the murder conviction, because the armed robbery conviction had made it impossible, as a strategic matter, for Thompson to testify in his own defense at the murder trial. On a new trial, the jury acquitted him of murder in 35 minutes.

Thompson then sued for damages, and a jury awarded $14 million. Thompson's theory was that the prosecutor's office, as a governmental agency, was liable for a policy of failing to train prosecutors about their obligation to disclose exculpatory evidence. So the applicable rules were not the prosecutor's absolute immunity in his personal capacity, but the rules on municipal liability. Earlier cases established that a municipality could be liable for a policy of deliberate indifference to constitutional rights, including a policy of failure to train. Proof of such a policy usually requires a pattern of similar violations, but the Court has left open the possibility that such a policy could be proved by one violation that was sufficiently obvious or egregious.

The Supreme Court reversed the damage award. It found no unconstitutional policy of inadequate training, because it said that Thompson had not relied on a pattern of failing to disclose, and because the one violation involving the blood sample did not by itself show such a policy. Justice Ginsburg, dissenting for herself and Justices Breyer, Sotomayor, and Kagan, found many other examples of evidence that should have been disclosed, and a culture of deliberate indifference to the obligation to disclose such evidence.

8. More on municipal liability. The Court has unanimously held that *Monell* applies to suits for injunctions or declaratory judgments as well as to suits for damages. That is, plaintiff can get an injunction against a municipality under §1983 only if a policy or custom of the municipality violates federal law. Los Angeles County v. Humphries, 562 U.S. 29 (2010).

In Lozman v. City of Riviera Beach, 138 S. Ct. 1945 (2018), plaintiff had been sharply at odds with the city's policy of taking waterfront properties by eminent domain, and he presented substantial evidence that the city council had adopted an unwritten policy to silence him, culminating in his arrest as he attempted to address a meeting of the council. The Court held that if his arrest were pursuant to such a policy, then it was unconstitutional even if there had been probable cause for the arrest. It distinguished the far more common cases of alleged retaliatory arrests by individual police officers, where there is an unresolved circuit split on whether the existence of probable cause is a complete defense.

9. Injunctive and declaratory relief. Prosecutors are not immune from injunctive and declaratory suits against them in their official capacity. Prosecutors are the typical defendants in Ex parte Young suits to enjoin enforcement of laws alleged to be unconstitutional. More on this in section 5.C.1.

NOTES ON OTHER ABSOLUTE IMMUNITIES

1. Absolutely immune functions. Judges, legislators, and the President of the United States have absolute immunity similar to that of prosecutors. All these immunities depend not on the office held, but on the function performed. That is, acts are not immune if they are not prosecutorial, not judicial, not part of the legislative process, or not in the President's official capacity. Similarly, an official who performs a judicial, prosecutorial, or legislative function acquires absolute immunity even if he does not hold a corresponding title.

In Supreme Court v. Consumers Union, 446 U.S. 719 (1980), the Court held that the Virginia Supreme Court acted legislatively when it promulgated disciplinary rules for the state's lawyers, and that it acted as a prosecutor when it initiated proceedings to enforce those rules. It was entitled to legislative and prosecutorial immunity, respectively, but not to judicial immunity. In a sense this was an academic exercise; all three of these immunities are absolute. Classification mattered more in Butz v. Economou, 438 U.S. 478 (1978), where the Court analyzed the functions of federal agency officials. Hearing officers get judicial immunity for adjudicative functions, even if they are in the executive branch. Agency attorneys who prosecute violations in front of such hearing officers get prosecutorial immunity.

2. Judicial immunity. Judges are the second large class of defendants with absolute immunity.

a. Reasons. The reasons for absolute judicial immunity are similar to those for prosecutors. Every judgment produces at least one loser. Many losers will be angry; many will find it hard to believe that any honest judge could have ruled against them. It is easy to allege that the judge was biased, or took a corrupt and malicious dislike to the plaintiff or his lawyer, or took a bribe from the other side. It might be harder to get past a motion for summary judgment, but plaintiff is entitled to discovery before the court rules on such a motion. The fear has been that the costs of such lawsuits would far outweigh the benefits.

Justice Powell emphasized another reason: Judicial errors are corrected by appeal, not by suing the judge. Stump v. Sparkman, 435 U.S. 349, 369-370 (1978) (Powell, J., dissenting). Indeed, judicial immunity and the right of appeal arose at the same time. The writ of error, under which a higher court reviews the record for errors of law, replaced the writs of false judgment and attaint. The writ of false judgment was a suit against the judge; attaint was a similar procedure against jurors. In neither was the reviewing court limited to the record of the original proceeding, and either could end with an amercement, or money fine, against the judge or juror found to have given false judgment. The amount of amercements was discretionary, and generally small. The development is reviewed in J. Randolph Block, *Stump v. Sparkman and the History of Judicial Immunity*, 1980 Duke L.J. 879, 881-885.

b. Jurisdiction. The traditional formulation of the rule is that a judge is absolutely immune for judicial acts within her jurisdiction. If a judge acts without jurisdiction, she's no longer a judge, but a usurper. But that formalism provides inadequate protection when a judge errs on debatable questions of jurisdiction. So the Court added that she must act in clear excess of jurisdiction, offering the example of a probate judge hearing a criminal case. Bradley v. Fischer, 80 U.S. (13 Wall.) 335, 351-352 (1871).

The Second Circuit found a clear absence of jurisdiction in Maestri v. Jutkofsky, 860 F.2d 50 (2d Cir. 1988). A town justice issued an arrest warrant on a private citizen's complaint; the complaint showed on its face that the incident occurred in another town over which the judge had no jurisdiction. The court said the judge was not immune, because he acted in clear absence of geographic jurisdiction.

The references to jurisdiction apparently mean jurisdiction over the subject matter. In Stump v. Sparkman, Judge Stump had approved a document titled "Petition to Have Tubal Ligation Performed on Minor and Indemnity Agreement," authorizing the sterilization of a 15-year-old girl, with no notice or hearing of any kind. 435 U.S. at 351 n.1. The girl's mother alleged that her daughter was "somewhat retarded," and that she feared "unfortunate circumstances." *Id.* The mother indemnified the doctor and the hospital. The daughter was told she has having an appendectomy; she did not learn what had happened until years later, when she and her husband sought fertility treatment. The daughter resided within the court's jurisdiction, but there was no service of process or any other step to acquire jurisdiction over her person. The Court treated this as merely a procedural error and held the judge immune. Justice Powell dissented; he thought the judge had forfeited his immunity by precluding any possibility of appeal.

Does geography, or the limits on probate judges, help explain what makes us unhappy about Judge Stump? Isn't there something fundamentally wrong with the jurisdiction test?

c. Judicial act. Justice Stewart wrote for three justices who dissented on the ground that what Judge Stump did was not a judicial act. The act had none of the attributes that supported judicial immunity: there was no case, no litigants, no possibility of appeal, and not even a pretext of principled decision making. The mother's illusions about the judge's power, or the judge's own say-so, could not make it a judicial act.

The boundaries were extended further in Mireles v. Waco, 502 U.S. 9 (1991). Waco, a public defender, failed to appear before Judge Mireles at the day's initial call of cases, because he was in another judge's courtroom for a matter pending there. Judge Mireles ordered two police officers to bring Waco in, and he allegedly ordered them to use excessive force in the process. They did. The Court held the judge immune; getting lawyers to appear was a judicial act, and excessive force was just a mistake in the means.

Compare Zarcone v. Perry, 572 F.2d 52 (2d Cir. 1978), where a deputy sheriff brought Judge Perry a bad cup of coffee. On Perry's orders, the deputy handcuffed the coffee vendor and marched him through the courthouse in full view of dozens of people. Judge Perry then conducted a sort of hearing, in which he threatened the vendor with loss of his livelihood and offered to "drop the charges" if the vendor would admit he did something wrong.

The vendor sued the judge, and a jury awarded $140,000 in compensatory and punitive damages. The judge apparently never argued immunity. Was his lawyer guilty of malpractice? No doubt Judge Perry "violated . . . procedural requirements regarding contempt citations," *Stump*, 435 U.S. at 361, but procedural error is irrelevant. A contempt hearing is a judicial act. *Stump* says that the lack of a docket number and a case filing in the clerk's office doesn't matter. Did Judge Perry act in clear excess of all jurisdiction? The court said no, on analogous facts, in Adams v. McIlhany, 764 F.2d 294 (5th Cir. 1985). Judge McIlhany summarily jailed the plaintiff for criminal contempt—for writing letters to the judge complaining about his conduct. The Fifth Circuit acknowledged settled state and federal law prohibiting judges from summarily punishing out-of-court conduct, but it said it would construe jurisdiction "broadly when immunity is the issue." *Id.* at 299.

It gets worse. In Malina v. Gonzales, 994 F.2d 1121 (5th Cir. 1993), Malina honked his horn and motioned to a slow-moving driver. The driver, who turned out to be Judge Gonzales, put a red light on his dashboard and pulled Malina over. Three hours later, a police officer came to Malina's home and told him to be in Judge Gonzales's courtroom the next morning. In a courtroom closed to the public, the judge charged Malina with six offenses and set a hearing date, saying that this would teach Malina to pull over when summoned. Malina said that he had been uncomfortable pulling over because the judge's car had been unmarked and anyone could buy a flashing light. At that point, the judge cited Malina for contempt and sentenced him to five hours in jail. The court held that pulling him over on the highway, informally summoning him to court, and charging him with criminal offenses were all nonjudicial acts. But holding him in contempt and sending him to jail was judicial, and immune.

A municipal judge in Niagara Falls jailed 46 people who happened to be in his courtroom when someone's cell phone rang. He said he would jail them all if the owner of the cell phone did not confess, and he did. In re Restaino, 890 N.E.2d 224 (N.Y. 2008). The opinion upholds his removal from office; there are no reported damage actions. Wouldn't he be immune under *McIlhany* and *Malina*?

d. Stealing from funds under judicial supervision. A woman physically and mentally disabled by medical malpractice obtained a $3 million settlement. Her mother was appointed as conservator to manage the money under the supervision of the Mississippi Chancery Court. The chancellor, Judge Joe Dale Walker, rejected the mother's petition to spend $145,000 to buy a house for her daughter, instead ordering that a special-needs house be custom built. Bids were solicited, and Judge Walker's nephew's construction company bid $250,000. The judge told the nephew to raise his bid because the other bids were higher. After some additional shenanigans, the nephew was eventually paid $326,000 to build the house. Applying both Mississippi and federal law, the court held that he was absolutely immune from civil liability. Newsome v. Shoemake, 234 So. 3d 1215 (Miss. 2017). We assume that the nephew is liable; the mother also named other defendants who played collateral roles.

We took these facts from the complaint, but the allegations appear to be at least substantially true. Both the Mississippi Commission on Judicial Performance and the United States Attorney investigated. Judge Walker pled guilty to witness tampering in the federal investigation and was removed from office. Mississippi Commission on Judicial Performance v. Walker, 172 So. 3d 1165 (Miss. 2015).

e. Conspiring with the prosecutor. If a judge and a prosecutor meet to plot strategy or rig the result of a pending case, they both have absolute immunity. The leading case is Ashelman v. Pope, 793 F.2d 1072 (9th Cir. 1986) (en banc).

f. Bribery. A judge does not forfeit his immunity by taking a bribe. But the private citizens who bribe him, or conspire with him in any other way, have no immunity and can be liable under §1983. One who acts jointly with a government official acts under color of law, and the judge's "[i]mmunity does not change the character of the judge's action or that of his co-conspirators." Dennis v. Sparks, 449 U.S. 24, 28 (1980).

g. Administrative functions. Absolute immunity does not extend to judges' administrative functions. Forrester v. White, 484 U.S. 219 (1988). The judge in that case fired his probation officer; the probation officer sued for employment discrimination. Judges are presumably entitled to qualified immunity in their administrative functions, but the Court left that issue open on remand. Cases drawing the line between judicial and administrative functions are collected in another case of a discharged employee, Meek v. County of Riverside, 183 F.3d 962, 967 n.2 (9th Cir. 1999).

h. Quasi-judicial immunity. The Court has said that judicial immunity extends to "all persons—governmental or otherwise—who were integral parts of the judicial process." Briscoe v. LaHue, 460 U.S. 325, 335 (1983). That turns out to be an overstatement, but only a little bit. *Briscoe* held that police officers who testify in criminal trials are absolutely immune from suit for damages caused by their alleged perjury; nongovernmental witnesses have the same immunity. *Briscoe* has been extended to a wide range of judicial adjuncts, often under the label "quasi-judicial immunity." Examples include mediators, arbitrators, case evaluators, court-appointed monitoring committees, law clerks, probation officers, a psychiatrist who interviewed a criminal defendant, and law enforcement officials who execute a facially valid court order. Some of the cases are collected in Hester v. Dickerson, 576 F. Supp. 2d 60, 62-63 (D.D.C. 2008), and in Webb v. Greene County Sheriff's Office, 494 F. Supp. 2d 779, 788-789 (S.D. Ohio 2007).

The bribers in *Dennis* were not immune, presumably because their conduct was not in the normal course of the judicial process. And in Antoine v. Byers & Anderson, Inc., 508 U.S. 429 (1993), the Court held that a court reporter is not absolutely immune for failing to produce a transcript, thus hampering a criminal appeal. The Court said it is not enough that the court reporter's task is important and difficult; it does not get absolute immunity because it entails no discretion.

i. Other remedies. As with prosecutors, judges are subject to disciplinary proceedings, impeachment, and criminal prosecution; most state judges are subject to

552   6. Remedies and Separation of Powers

periodic election or reappointments. If there is publicity about an egregious case, these remedies can work. Judges Jutkofsky, Perry, Retsaino, and Walker were removed from office. But often they don't work; Judge Stump was reelected.

Judges can also be sued in their judicial capacity for injunctive relief under Ex parte Young. Pulliam v. Allen, 466 U.S. 522 (1984). Such suits are rare; they are often barred by abstention doctrines (if plaintiff is party to a pending case), ripeness problems (if no case is pending), or claim preclusion (if the case is over). Plaintiff in *Pulliam* somehow got an injunction against Judge Allen's practice of requiring criminal defendants to post bond even when they were charged with offenses for which they could not be imprisoned. Without deciding whether the particular injunction was proper, the Supreme Court held that judges are not immune to official capacity suits. Congress has since amended the principal statute on attorneys' fees to immunize judges (and their judicial budgets) from fees and costs, unless a judge is held liable for an act "clearly in excess of such officer's jurisdiction." 42 U.S.C. §1988(b).

3. Legislative immunity. Legislators are absolutely immune from any kind of suit, including criminal prosecutions and suits for damages, injunctions, and declaratory judgments. The origin of this sweeping immunity is in the speech or debate clauses of state and federal constitutions. The federal version says that "for any Speech or Debate in either House, they shall not be questioned in any other Place." U.S. Const. art. I, §6. The federal clause does not protect state legislators, and state clauses can't bind the federal courts. But the Supreme Court read a similar immunity into §1983, concluding that Congress surely did not intend to disturb the immunities of state legislators. Tenney v. Brandhove, 341 U.S. 367 (1951). Absolute legislative immunity also protects local legislators, such as members of a city council. Bogan v. Scott-Harris, 523 U.S. 44 (1998).

Why is legislative immunity so much more sweeping than judicial and prosecutorial immunity? The Court has said that any kind of suit would distract legislators from their duties, but the Court could have said the same thing about judges and prosecutors. In rejecting even injunctions against allegedly abusive congressional investigations, the Court relied on the constitutional provision that legislators shall not even be "questioned" in any other place. Eastland v. United States Serviceman's Fund, 421 U.S. 491, 501-503 (1975). It may also matter that legislators inherently have the broadest discretion of any government officials, and that they are most directly accountable to the electorate. In addition, most legislative acts have to be implemented by the executive branch and by judges, and the constitutionality of legislation can be decided in suits to enforce it or to enjoin its implementation.

The immunity extends to any act that is part of the legislature's deliberative process; it is not limited to speeches and debates. The leading case is Gravel v. United States, 408 U.S. 606 (1972). Senator Gravel convened a midnight meeting of the Subcommittee on Buildings and Grounds of the Senate Committee on Public Works and read the *Pentagon Papers* into the record. The *Pentagon Papers* were a secret history of the war in Vietnam. Gravel's aides then arranged to have the *Pentagon Papers* published by Beacon Press. The Court rejected the government's argument that Gravel was not immune because the committee meeting was a pretense. But the Court held that arranging for private publication was not immune legislative business.

Gravel held that the senator's immunity extended to his aides. This point was much debated in Harlow v. Fitzgerald, reprinted in section 5.C.2, where the Court held that the President's immunity does *not* extend to his aides.

Legislative immunity does not preclude criminal prosecution of legislators who take bribes. United States v. Brewster, 408 U.S. 501 (1972). The Speech or Debate

Clause precludes proof that defendant took any legislative steps on behalf of those who paid the bribe, but proof of such steps is not necessary to conviction. The offense is complete when the legislator takes the bribe, whether or not he delivers what he promised.

A prominent example involved United States Senator Robert Menendez of New Jersey, who was charged with multiple counts of official corruption. A friend of the Senator gave him large campaign contributions, personal gifts, and free trips, and the Senator lobbied the executive branch on the friend's behalf. The Third Circuit rejected the Senator's attempt to exclude evidence of his lobbying efforts. United States v. Menendez, 831 F.3d 155 (3d Cir. 2016), *cert. denied*, 137 S. Ct. 1332 (2017). Menendez argued the meetings were about policy and other protected legislative activity and therefore inadmissible, but the Third Circuit disagreed, holding that "the predominant purpose of the challenged acts was to pursue a political resolution to Dr. Melgen's disputes and not to discuss broader issues of policy, vet a presidential nominee, or engage in informal information gathering for legislation. It was not to engage in true legislative oversight . . . ." *Id.* at 173. And the Supreme Court held long ago that legislative lobbying on behalf of constituents is not immune legislative business. United States v. Johnson, 383 U.S. 169 (1966).

Menendez's trial resulted in a hung jury, and the government declined to prosecute him again. Nick Corasintini and Kate Zernike, *After Years of Investigation, A Sudden Folding of the Case Against Menendez*, N.Y. Times (Feb. 4, 2018). A Senate ethics panel then "severely admonished" him for accepting gifts from Dr. Melgen as the senator prepared to run for reelection. Maggie Astor, *Menendez Is "Severely Admonished" by Senate Panel for Accepting Gifts*, N.Y. Times (Apr. 26, 2018).

4. Presidential immunity. The President of the United States is absolutely immune from suits for damages for any action taken in his official capacity. Nixon v. Fitzgerald, 457 U.S. 731 (1982). The Court distinguished the President from governors, cabinet officers, and presidential aides. No other official is as indispensable as the President; no other official is as visible. He would be an obvious target for suits, but he should not be distracted by the need to defend them or deterred in his exercise of office by fear of liability.

Even the President can be sued for acts that are *not* performed in his official capacity. Clinton v. Jones, 520 U.S. 681 (1997). The Court said that the "principal rationale" for official immunity "is inapplicable to unofficial conduct." *Id.* at 692-693. The Court expressly did not decide whether the President could be sued in state court or "whether a court may compel the attendance of the President at any specific time or place." *Id.* at 691. The "unofficial" conduct was alleged to have been committed under color of state law—in the President's former capacity as governor of Arkansas. But as governor, he was entitled only to qualified immunity. Scheuer v. Rhodes, 416 U.S. 232 (1974).

The Court's prediction that such private litigation would not significantly interfere with the President's public duties turned out to be incredibly naive. The country became preoccupied with President Bill Clinton's sex life and whether he had perjured himself. The House impeached him, but the Senate acquitted.

The President is not wholly immune from judicial process even in his official capacity. In United States v. Nixon, 418 U.S. 683 (1974), the Court unanimously enforced a subpoena against the President. The subpoena was issued in a criminal prosecution of some of the President's aides, to obtain tapes of the President's conversations. Congressional reaction to the evidence disclosed pursuant to the subpoena forced the President to resign.

The Court has also enjoined presidential acts in litigation against his subordinates. The best-known example is Youngstown Sheet & Tube Co. v. Sawyer, 343 U.S. 579 (1952). Secretary of Commerce Sawyer seized the nation's steel mills to continue war production despite a strike against the private owners. He acted pursuant to President Truman's orders, but the Court enjoined the seizure.

In Knight First Amendment Institute v. Trump, 302 F. Supp. 3d 541 (S.D.N.Y. 2018), a federal court issued a declaratory judgment that President Trump violated the First Amendment rights of people he "blocked" from reading and responding to his tweets on Twitter. The court declined to issue an injunction, but added: "A declaratory judgment should be sufficient, as no government official—including the President—is above the law, and all government officials are presumed to follow the law as has been declared." *Id.* at 549.

5. An overview. John Jeffries finds the Court's immunity doctrines in constitutional cases incoherent:

> There is no liability rule for constitutional torts. There are, rather, several different liability rules, ranging from absolute immunity at one extreme to absolute liability at the other. . . . Most defendants—including federal, state, and local officers—are neither absolutely immune nor strictly liable. Instead, they are protected by qualified immunity, a fault-based standard approximating negligence as to illegality.
>
> This fracturing of constitutional torts into disparate liability rules does not reflect any plausible conception of policy. Although the Court occasionally makes functional arguments about one or another corner of this landscape, it has never attempted to justify the overall structure in those terms. Nor could it. The proliferation of inconsistent policies and arbitrary distinctions renders constitutional tort law functionally unintelligible. Blame may be cast on the shadow (though certainly not the terms) of the Eleventh Amendment, on the incorporation into constitutional tort doctrine of bits and pieces of the common law, and on accidents of timing and personnel: when and under what circumstances did particular issues come to the Court? However sympathetic one may be [to the difficulties caused by such factors], the fact remains that constitutional tort doctrine is incoherent. It is so shot through with inconsistency and contradiction as to obscure almost beyond recognition the underlying stratum of good sense.

John C. Jeffries, Jr., *The Liability Rule for Constitutional Torts*, 99 Va. L. Rev. 207, 207-208 (2013).

He would sharply limit absolute immunity to the bounds of its core justifications. Simplifying somewhat, those bounds would be legislative work on generally applicable legislation that can be challenged in litigation with the executive branch, prosecutorial misconduct in the courtroom and constrained by the adversary process, and judicial decisions subject in fact to correction on appeal. He would eliminate any distinction between state and local government, preferably by interpreting §1983 to override sovereign immunity in constitutional cases. He would reform and generalize qualified immunity: Governments and government officials should be liable in damages when they reasonably should have known that their conduct was unconstitutional. He collects cases of obvious unconstitutionality where defendants were held immune because there was no case with sufficient factual similarity to satisfy current judicial understandings of the clearly-established-law test; he would impose liability in such cases.

He does not discuss *Goldstein* or *Thompson*, but he does discuss the lack of deterrence for violations of the duty to disclose exculpatory evidence. And he collects studies finding rampant violations of that duty. *Id.* at 227 n.68.

B.   CREATING CAUSES OF ACTION

BIVENS v. SIX UNKNOWN NAMED AGENTS
403 U.S. 388 (1971)

Justice BRENNAN delivered the opinion of the Court. . . .

Petitioner's complaint alleged that . . . respondents, agents of the Federal Bureau of Narcotics acting under claim of federal authority, entered his apartment and arrested him for alleged narcotics violations. The agents manacled petitioner in front of his wife and children, and threatened to arrest the entire family. They searched the apartment from stem to stern. Thereafter petitioner was taken to the federal courthouse in Brooklyn, where he was interrogated, booked, and subjected to a visual strip search.

On July 7, 1967, petitioner brought suit in Federal District Court. . . . [H]is complaint asserted that the arrest and search were effected without a warrant, and that unreasonable force was employed in making the arrest; [and] that the arrest was made without probable cause [in violation of the Fourth Amendment]. Petitioner claimed to have suffered great humiliation, embarrassment, and mental suffering as a result of the agents' unlawful conduct, and sought $15,000 damages from each of them. The District Court . . . dismissed . . . . 276 F. Supp. 12 (E.D.N.Y. 1967). The Court of Appeals . . . affirmed . . . . 409 F.2d 718 (2d Cir. 1969). . . . We reverse.

I

Respondents do not argue that petitioner should be entirely without remedy. . . . In respondents' view, however, the rights that petitioner asserts . . . are creations of state and not of federal law. Accordingly, they argue, petitioner may obtain money damages to redress invasion of these rights only by an action in tort, under state law, in the state courts. In this scheme the Fourth Amendment would serve merely to limit the extent to which the agents could defend the state law tort suit by asserting that their actions were a valid exercise of federal power: if the agents were shown to have violated the Fourth Amendment, such a defense would be lost to them and they would stand before the state law merely as private individuals. Candidly admitting that it is the policy of the Department of Justice to remove all such suits from the state to the federal courts for decision, respondents nevertheless urge that we uphold dismissal of petitioner's complaint in federal court, and remit him to filing an action in the state courts in order that the case may properly be removed to the federal court for decision on the basis of state law. . . .

[R]espondents' thesis rests upon an unduly restrictive view of the Fourth Amendment's protection against unreasonable searches and seizures by federal agents. . . . Respondents seek to treat the relationship between a citizen and a federal agent unconstitutionally exercising his authority as no different from the relationship between two private citizens. . . . [T]hey ignore the fact that power, once granted, does not disappear like a magic gift when it is wrongfully used. An agent acting—albeit unconstitutionally—in the name of the United States possesses a far greater capacity for harm than an individual trespasser exercising no authority other than his own. Accordingly, as our cases make clear, the Fourth Amendment operates as a limitation upon the exercise of federal power regardless of whether the State in whose jurisdiction that power is exercised would prohibit or penalize the identical act if engaged in by a private citizen. . . . And "where federally protected rights have been invaded, it has been the rule from the beginning that courts will be alert to adjust their remedies so as to grant the necessary relief." Bell v. Hood, 327 U.S. 678, 684 (1946). . . .

That damages may be obtained for injuries consequent upon a violation of the Fourth Amendment by federal officials should hardly seem a surprising proposition. Historically, damages have been regarded as the ordinary remedy for an invasion of personal interests in liberty. . . . "[I]t is . . . well settled that where legal rights have been invaded, and a federal statute provides for a general right to sue for such invasion, federal courts may use any available remedy to make good the wrong done." *Id.* The present case involves no special factors counseling hesitation in the absence of affirmative action by Congress. We are not dealing with a question of "federal fiscal policy," as in United States v. Standard Oil Co., 332 U.S. 301, 311 (1947). In that case we refused to infer . . . that the United States could recover damages from one who negligently injured a soldier and thereby caused the Government to pay his medical expenses and lose his services. . . . [W]e pointed out that "the United States . . . has power at any time to create the liability." *Id.* at 316. . . .

[¶] Finally, we cannot accept respondents' formulation of the question as whether the availability of money damages is necessary to enforce the Fourth Amendment. For we have here no explicit congressional declaration that persons injured by a federal officer's violation of the Fourth Amendment may not recover money damages from the agents, but must instead be remitted to another remedy, equally effective in the view of Congress. The question is merely whether petitioner, if he can demonstrate an injury consequent upon the violation by federal agents of his Fourth Amendment rights, is entitled to redress his injury through a particular remedial mechanism normally available in the federal courts. "The very essence of civil liberty certainly consists in the right of every individual to claim the protection of the laws, whenever he receives an injury." Marbury v. Madison, 5 U.S. (1 Cranch) 137, 163 (1803). Having concluded that petitioner's complaint states a cause of action under the Fourth Amendment, we hold that petitioner is entitled to recover money damages for any injuries he has suffered as a result of the agents' violation of the Amendment. . . .

II

The judgment . . . is reversed and the case is remanded for further proceedings consistent with this opinion. . . .

Justice HARLAN, concurring. . . .

II

The contention that the federal courts are powerless to accord a litigant damages for a claimed invasion of his federal constitutional rights until Congress explicitly authorizes the remedy cannot rest on the notion that the decision to grant compensatory relief involves a resolution of policy considerations not susceptible of judicial discernment. Thus, in suits for damages based on violations of federal statutes lacking any express authorization of a damage remedy, this Court has authorized such relief where, in its view, damages are necessary to effectuate the congressional policy underpinning the substantive provisions of the statute.

If it is not the nature of the remedy which is thought to render a judgment as to the appropriateness of damages inherently "legislative," then it must be the nature of the legal interest offered as an occasion for invoking otherwise appropriate judicial relief. But I do not think that the fact that the interest is protected by the Constitution rather than statute or common law justifies the assertion that federal courts are powerless to grant damages in the absence of explicit congressional action authorizing the remedy. . . .

[T]he presumed availability of federal equitable relief against threatened invasions of constitutional interests appears entirely to negate the contention that the status of an interest as constitutionally protected divests federal courts of the power to grant damages absent express congressional authorization. . . .

If explicit congressional authorization is an absolute prerequisite to the power of a federal court to accord compensatory relief regardless of the necessity or appropriateness of damages as a remedy simply because of the status of a legal interest as constitutionally protected, then it seems to me that explicit congressional authorization is similarly prerequisite to the exercise of equitable remedial discretion in favor of constitutionally protected interests. Conversely, if a general grant of jurisdiction to the federal courts by Congress is thought adequate to empower a federal court to grant equitable relief for all areas of subject-matter jurisdiction enumerated therein, then it seems to me that the same statute is sufficient to empower a federal court to grant a traditional remedy at law. Of course, the special historical traditions governing the federal equity system might still bear on the comparative appropriateness of granting equitable relief as opposed to money damages. That possibility, however, relates, not to whether the federal courts have the power to afford one type of remedy as opposed to the other, but rather to the criteria which should govern the exercise of our power. To that question, I now pass.

III

The major thrust of the Government's position is that, where Congress has not expressly authorized a particular remedy, a federal court should exercise its power to accord a traditional form of judicial relief . . . only where the remedy is "essential," or "indispensable for vindicating constitutional rights." While this "essentiality" test is most clearly articulated with respect to damage remedies, apparently the Government believes the same test explains the exercise of equitable remedial powers. . . .

These arguments for a more stringent test to govern the grant of damages in constitutional cases seem to be adequately answered by the point that the judiciary has a particular responsibility to assure the vindication of constitutional interests such as those embraced by the Fourth Amendment. . . . [T]he Bill of Rights is particularly intended to vindicate the interests of the individual in the face of the popular will as expressed in legislative majorities. . . .

The question then, is . . . whether compensatory relief is "necessary" or "appropriate" to the vindication of the interest asserted. In resolving that question, it seems to me that the range of policy considerations we may take into account is at least as broad as the range of [those] a legislature would consider with respect to an express statutory authorization of a traditional remedy. . . .

I think it is clear that Bivens advances a claim of the sort that, if proved, would be properly compensable in damages. . . .

[T]he limitations on state remedies for violation of common-law rights by private citizens argue in favor of a federal damages remedy. The injuries inflicted by officials acting under color of law, while no less compensable in damages than those inflicted by private parties, are substantially different in kind . . . . It seems to me entirely proper that these injuries be compensable according to uniform rules of federal law, especially in light of the very large element of federal law which must in any event control the scope of official defenses to liability. . . .

It will be a rare case indeed in which an individual in Bivens' position will be able to obviate the harm by securing injunctive relief from any court. However desirable a direct remedy against the Government might be as a substitute for individual official liability, the sovereign still remains immune to suit. Finally, assuming Bivens' innocence of the crime charged, the "exclusionary rule" is simply irrelevant. For people in Bivens' shoes, it is damages or nothing. . . .

Chief Justice BURGER, dissenting.

I dissent from today's holding which judicially creates a damage remedy not provided for by the Constitution and not enacted by Congress. We would more surely preserve the important values of the doctrine of separation of powers—and perhaps get a better result—by recommending a solution to the Congress as the branch of government in which the Constitution has vested the legislative power. [The Chief Justice wrote at length about the Court's effort to enforce the Fourth Amendment with the exclusionary rule, which he thought was ineffective at deterring violations and too costly in terms of lost convictions; it also provided no remedy at all for the innocent. He thought the *Bivens* damage remedy would be ineffective because jurors would sympathize with police officers and because individual officers would have few assets from which to collect judgments. He thought that Congress should create a damage remedy enforced by an administrative agency, and that if Congress created an effective remedy, the exclusionary rule should be overruled.]

Justice BLACK, dissenting. . . .

There can be no doubt that Congress could create a federal cause of action for damages for an unreasonable search in violation of the Fourth Amendment. Although Congress has created such a federal cause of action against *state* officials acting under color of state law, it has never created such a cause of action against federal officials. . . . For us to do so is, in my judgment, an exercise of power that the Constitution does not give us.

Even if we had the legislative power to create a remedy, there are many reasons why we should decline to create a cause of action where none has existed since the formation of our government. The courts of the United States as well as those of the States are choked with lawsuits. . . .

Cases could be cited to support the legal proposition which I assert, but it seems to me to be a matter of common understanding that the business of the judiciary is to interpret the laws and not to make them. . . .

[Justice BLACKMUN's dissenting opinion is omitted.]

NOTES ON IMPLIED REMEDIES FOR CONSTITUTIONAL VIOLATIONS

1. The scope of *Bivens*. Some courts thought that *Bivens* announced a rule about the Fourth Amendment and not a rule about constitutional rights generally. The Supreme Court first rejected that view, then changed its mind.

a. *Bivens* as a general constitutional rule. The Supreme Court rejected the claim-by-claim approach in Davis v. Passman, 442 U.S. 228 (1979), a sex-discrimination suit against a congressman who fired a member of his staff. Congress had exempted itself from the employment discrimination statute, so she sued under the equal protection component of the Fifth Amendment's Due Process Clause. The Court found an implied cause of action under *Bivens*.

In Carlson v. Green, 446 U.S. 14 (1980), the Court implied a right to sue for damages from unconstitutional prison conditions. The Court said broadly that "*Bivens* established that the victims of a constitutional violation by a federal agent have a right to recover damages." This right could be defeated if there were "special factors counseling hesitation," or if Congress had "provided an alternative remedy which it explicitly declared to be a *substitute* for recovery directly under the Constitution and viewed as equally effective." *Id.* at 18-19.

b. *Bivens* as a claim-by-claim possibility. There followed a period in which the Court often found "special factors counseling hesitation" and recognized no new claims under *Bivens*. Eventually, and without acknowledging the change, the Court appeared to reinstate the claim-by-claim approach that it had rejected in *Davis* and *Carlson*:

> The first question is whether to devise a new *Bivens* damages action. . . . *Bivens* held that the victim of a Fourth Amendment violation by federal officers had a claim for damages, and in the years following we have recognized two more nonstatutory damages remedies . . . *Davis* . . . *Carlson*. But we have also held that any freestanding damages remedy for a claimed constitutional violation has to represent a judgment about the best way to implement a constitutional guarantee; it is not an automatic entitlement no matter what other means there may be to vindicate a protected interest, and in most instances we have found a *Bivens* remedy unjustified. We have accordingly held against applying the *Bivens* model to claims of First Amendment violations by federal employers, Bush v. Lucas, 462 U.S. 367 (1983), harm to military personnel through activity incident to service, United States v. Stanley, 483 U.S. 669 (1987), and wrongful denials of Social Security disability benefits, Schweiker v. Chilicky, 487 U.S. 412 (1988). We have seen no case for extending *Bivens* to claims against federal agencies, Federal Deposit Insurance Corp. v. Meyer, 510 U.S. 471 (1994), or against private prisons, Correctional Services Corp. v. Malesko, 534 U.S. 61 (2001).

Wilkie v. Robbins, 551 U.S. 537, 549-550 (2007). This passage seems to require plaintiff to show why a new remedy should be "devise[d]," although the next paragraph again speaks of "special factors counseling hesitation" and of the existence of alternative remedies that amount "to a convincing reason for the Judicial Branch to refrain from creating a new and freestanding remedy in damages." *Wilkie* was an unusual case; government agents had allegedly harassed plaintiff for years to extort him into conveying an easement over his land without compensation. The majority saw no way to draw the line between hard bargaining and illegal harassment, and it saw this vagueness in the claim as a special factor counseling hesitation.

Justices Thomas and Scalia wrote separately to say that *Bivens* and its progeny were relics of another era and should be "limited 'to the precise circumstances that they involved.'" *Id.* at 568. Justices Ginsburg and Stevens dissented.

2. "Special factors counseling hesitation." The cases listed in *Wilkie* have a variety of rationales. *Bush* and *Schweiker* hold that when Congress creates a statutory remedy, the statutory remedy preempts any *Bivens* remedy. The statutory remedies typically provide back pay for government employees or back benefits for beneficiaries of social welfare programs, but no consequential damages, emotional distress, punitive damages, attorneys' fees, or jury trial.

Stanley is based on deference to the military even in extreme circumstances; plaintiffs had been used as unwitting experimental subjects in a study of the effects of

LSD. The Court also refused to create a *Bivens* remedy for black sailors alleging racial discrimination. Chappell v. Wallace, 462 U.S. 296 (1983).

FDIC v. Meyer reasons that a *Bivens* suit against a government agency would be too much like suing the government itself; the defendant in *Bivens* actions is the individual officer or employee who violated the law. *Malesko* refused a *Bivens* action against a private corporation acting under color of federal law — a firm managing a halfway house for federal prisoners — because such a corporation is more like a government agency than like an individual employee.

3. The controversy over *Bivens*. If constitutional rights are supposed to protect minorities and isolated individuals from oppressive majorities, how can Congress have power to decide whether and to what extent these rights ought to be enforced? Could Congress effectively repeal the Bill of Rights by refusing to create remedies?

No one has ever suggested that lack of express statutory authorization is relevant to injunctions ordering federal officials to obey the Constitution. Such injunctions against *state* officials long predate the statutory authorization in §1983; in Osborn v. President of the Bank of the United States, 22 U.S. (9 Wheat.) 738 (1824), the Court enjoined the Treasurer of Ohio from collecting an unconstitutional tax from the bank. Justice Black joined the unanimous opinion in Bolling v. Sharpe, 347 U.S. 497 (1954), ordering the District of Columbia to desegregate its schools. That was an implied cause of action under the Fifth Amendment Due Process Clause. Surely Black didn't mean to repudiate it in his *Bivens* dissent. How is authorizing a damage remedy any more an inherently legislative function than authorizing an equitable remedy? But if damages are no different, why did so many lawyers file injunction cases before anyone filed a damage case? Justice Rehnquist's dissent in *Carlson* said simply that the history was different.

4. The Takings Clause. Justice Rehnquist also conceded that damage actions have long been available for violations of the Takings Clause. But he said that Clause is unique because it specifically requires "just compensation."

5. The congressional response. Congress responded to *Bivens* by waiving sovereign immunity and making the United States liable for "assault, battery, false imprisonment, false arrest, abuse of process, or malicious prosecution" by "investigative or law enforcement officers of the United States." 28 U.S.C. §2680(h).

6. The bigger picture of a plaintiff's claim. Plaintiffs seeking a federal remedy against a state or the federal government must identify a substantive right, a grant of jurisdiction, a private right of action, and an override or waiver of immunity. The Court treats the four hurdles as almost entirely independent; that Congress attended to three of them implies nothing about congressional intent with respect to the one it neglected. In *Bivens*, the Fourth Amendment created the substantive right. Jurisdiction was conferred by 28 U.S.C. §1331. The Court subsequently decided that the agents have only qualified immunity. Harlow v. Fitzgerald, reprinted in section 5.C.2. That left the question whether Congress said anything about a private remedy or left the courts wholly on their own.

7. State law. State courts are divided on implied damage remedies to enforce state constitutions. For example, compare Brown v. State, 674 N.E.2d 1129 (N.Y. 1996) (yes), with Lewis v. State, 629 N.W.2d 868 (Mich. 2001) (generally no). Some courts consider the question one clause at a time. Binette v. Sabo, 710 A.2d 688 (Conn. 1998). In many states, the law is unclear or the issue has not arisen. The cases are collected in 1 Jennifer Friesen, *State Constitutional Law: Litigating Individual Rights, Claims, and Defenses* §7.07 at 7-20 to 7-66 (4th ed., LexisNexis 2006 & Supp.), and Annotation, 75 A.L.R. 5th 619 (2000 & Supp.).

8. Is *Bivens* worth the trouble? *Bivens* litigation has been widely criticized on the basis of anecdotal claims that *Bivens* suits are almost uniformly unsuccessful. The first systematic study found that that is apparently not true. Alexander A. Reinert, *Measuring the Success of Bivens Litigation and Its Consequences for the Individual Liability Model*, 62 Stan. L. Rev. 809 (2010). Classifying and counting real cases poses definitional problems with respect to both the numerator and the denominator, so these numbers should be viewed as approximate.

Professor Reinert found 252 *Bivens* filings in 2001, 2002, and 2003 in 5 federal districts—the districts centered on New York, Brooklyn, Philadelphia, Chicago, and Houston. Nearly half of these were prisoner claims, and more than three-quarters were filed pro se. (No attorneys' fees statute applies to *Bivens* claims.) Even so, 16 percent appeared to end in a settlement or judgment for plaintiff. The apparent success rate was 9.5 percent for the pro se claims and 38.9 percent for the claims with counsel. He counted a claim as successful if it ended in a judgment for plaintiff, a settlement, or a voluntary dismissal. This is a common methodology in empirical research on litigation, because voluntary dismissals often indicate settlement. But some unknowable number of voluntary dismissals are for other reasons. Reinert examined the individual docket sheets to try to detect such dismissals, but he cannot be sure that he found them all. The ambiguity matters, because dismissals accounted for 30 of his 39 successful claims. On the other hand, 8 cases in his sample were still pending in 2009, with extensive discovery and motion practice; some of these eventually increased the number of successes.

Ross J. Corbett and James E. Pfander looked specifically at *Bivens* cases involving the war on terror. *Appendix: An Empirical Assessment of Bivens Claims*, in James E. Pfander, *Constitutional Torts and the War on Terror* 167-180 (Oxford University Press 2017). In their sample of 41 cases, they coded 9 as a success (8 settlements and 1 voluntary dismissal). They excluded claims by military personnel, military contractors, and domestic prisoners. Although this 22 percent success rate was similar to the results in the Reinert study, they found that "none of the *Bivens* claims involving the military, intelligence services, or extraordinary rendition yielded a successful outcome." *Id.* at 167. Also, "claims based on foreign conduct were uniformly unsuccessful." *Id.* at 168. And "defendants were successful in the cases they appealed 100 percent of the time." The findings were consistent with Pfander's thesis that *Bivens* claims have been wholly unsuccessful in reining in government overreach in the war on terror cases.

9. Creeping ever closer to repudiation? Much in line with these findings from Corbett and Pfander, the Court held that there is no *Bivens* remedy for well-pleaded claims that in the wake of the September 11 attacks, Arabs and Muslims were imprisoned in harsh conditions on the basis of their religion or ethnicity, even after they had been cleared of any connection to terrorism. Ziglar v. Abbasi, 137 S. Ct. 1843 (2017). The Court said that any claim that differs in any significant way from the claims in *Bivens, Carlson,* or *Green* has to be assessed for any special factor that might counsel hesitation. And this assessment has to begin from the premise that expanding *Bivens* is disfavored. The cases refusing to allow *Bivens* claims are not a series of cases with special factors counseling hesitation; they are now the general rule.

There was also a well-pleaded claim that the guards abused these prisoners, and that the warden knew about it and allowed it to continue. The Court remanded that claim to the Second Circuit to decide in the first instance whether there were special factors counseling hesitation. Justice Thomas concurred in the result to make a majority to dispose of the case, but he would have preferred outright reversal and an opinion confining *Bivens* to the precise circumstances of *Bivens, Carlson,* or *Green.*

Justice Breyer, joined by Justice Ginsburg, dissented on all issues. (Justices Kagan and Sotomayor were recused). Breyer said that this was not a new context; *Green* had also been a suit about prison conditions. Congress had not created any other remedy, and it was far too late for an injunction. And the national security context was not a sufficient factor counseling hesitation. The alleged violations had continued long after the immediate aftermath of September 11, and there were ample other safeguards protecting defendant officials — stringent pleading requirements, qualified immunity, the courts' power to limit discovery, and the substantive law, which recognizes that measures that would be unconstitutional in normal times might be constitutional in emergencies. And he thought it would be indefensible for state officials to be liable for their constitutional torts but federal officials not.

The Court appeared to reaffirm *Bivens* in its original Fourth Amendment context. It reaffirmed judicial power to order compliance with the Constitution in the future. And it did not formally say that there could never be another *Bivens* cause of action beyond those recognized in *Bivens*, *Carlson*, and *Green*. But lower court judges may draw that inference.

10. Does *Abbasi* signal a broader deterioration of remedies for constitutional violations? Professor Vladeck sees *Abbasi* as "all but shut[ting] the door on *Bivens* remedies." Stephen I. Vladeck, *Implied Constitutional Remedies After Abbasi*, 1 ACS Sup. Ct. Rev. 179 (2018). He says it "may be only the first step toward a far deeper and more troubling retrenchment by the federal courts from inferring constitutional rights more generally." *Id.* at 180.

Professor Leah Litman also puts *Abbasi* in a larger context. *Remedial Convergence and Collapse*, 106 Cal. L. Rev. (forthcoming), http://ssrn.com/abstract=3157777 (2018 draft). Professor Litman looks at the Supreme Court's narrowing of remedies, especially in the context of claims of unconstitutional police conduct, from habeas corpus, to the exclusionary rule, to immunities to *Bivens* claims.

The convergence that she describes is partly a matter of applying similar restrictions to all the remedies, and partly a kind of shell game, where the Court limits or denies each remedy based in part on an unjustified assumption that some other remedy will be available.

> For example, in criminal cases, the Court will hold that an application of the exclusionary rule is unwarranted and point to the possibility of civil damages as an alternative remedy, while in civil cases where damages are sought, the Court will hold that an officer is immune from damages and point to the exclusionary rule as an alternative remedy. But when the same standard dictates the availability of different remedies that are supposed to substitute for one another, courts will be foreclosing all of the remedies when they rely on that standard to deny one of the remedies.

SSRN Draft at 6. Professor Litman says that *Abbasi* "made the convergence between the *Bivens* standard and the qualified immunity, habeas, and exclusionary-rule standards more explicit." *Id.* at 23.

To echo a point made at this book's Introduction, what good is a constitutional right without an effective remedy?

NOTES ON IMPLIED REMEDIES FOR STATUTORY VIOLATIONS

1. Clashing views of causes of action. Is a private cause of action to enforce a statute a matter of remedy, traditionally left to courts? Or part of the primary substantive right and exclusively entrusted to Congress? The traditional view was that the intended beneficiaries of a statute could sue for damages caused by a violation unless the statute implied that such claims should not be allowed. Justice Harlan took that as a given in his concurring opinion in *Bivens*.

The Court's conservatives now absolutely reject that view with respect to both statutes and the Constitution. With respect to statutes, they think that federal courts have no power whatever to create causes of action for damages, that Congress should do so explicitly, and that only in the most extraordinarily clear cases should the courts decide that Congress did so implicitly. Although defended in terms of congressional intent, these cases apply a rule that Congress must affirmatively overcome judicial antipathy to private rights of action. For a defense of such presumptions in favor of particular outcomes as a form of soft judicial review, see Ernest A. Young, *Constitutional Avoidance, Resistance Norms, and the Preservation of Judicial Review*, 78 Tex. L. Rev. 1549 (2000). The Court's hostility to implied causes of action has generally prevailed since 1979.

The Court's liberals don't want to return to the traditional presumption in favor of damage actions. Justice Stevens, writing for the Court in Merrill Lynch, Pierce, Fenner & Smith, Inc. v. Curran, 456 U.S. 353 (1982), suggested that the increasing quantity and complexity of legislation required a change from the old approach. He wanted only an honest inquiry into probable congressional intent, considering all the evidence, including legislative history and background presumptions at the time the statute was enacted.

Certainly Congress could enact a code of federal remedies if it wanted to, or include exclusive remedies provisions in every statute. If it took that route, courts would clearly be bound. But it has not taken that route. Anglo-American law has a rich inventory of common law and equitable remedies, created by the courts and largely left to the courts. Why can't Congress rely on general remedial principles as part of the legal background against which it legislates? Why shouldn't the Court at least honor congressional reliance on those principles before 1979, when that was the Court's rule too?

2. The turnaround. The Court's turnaround is conventionally but erroneously dated from Cort v. Ash, 422 U.S. 66 (1975). *Cort* identified four "factors" that had been discussed in earlier implied cause of action cases:

> First, is the plaintiff "one of the class for whose *especial* benefit the statute was enacted," Texas & Pacific Ry. v. Rigsby, 241 U.S. 33, 39 (1916) — that is, does the statute create a federal right in favor of the plaintiff? Second, is there any indication of legislative intent, explicit or implicit, either to create such a remedy or to deny one? Third, is it consistent with the underlying purposes of the legislative scheme to imply such a remedy for the plaintiff? And finally, is the cause of action one traditionally relegated to state law, in an area basically the concern of the States, so that it would be inappropriate to infer a cause of action based solely on federal law?

Id. at 78. The Court noted that where the first factor was clearly established, "it is not necessary to show an intention to *create* a private cause of action, although an explicit purpose to *deny* such a cause of action would be controlling." *Id.* at 82. This formulation did not significantly change earlier law; Justice Brennan wrote it for a unanimous Court.

The big shift came in Touche Ross & Co. v. Redington, 442 U.S. 560 (1979). Without acknowledging any change, the Court demoted the first *Cort* factor and made the second dispositive. "[O]ur task is limited solely to determining whether Congress intended to create the private right of action." *Id.* at 568. "It could not be plainer that we effectively overruled the Cort v. Ash analysis in *Touche Ross*." Thompson v. Thompson, 484 U.S. 174, 189 (1988) (O'Connor, J., concurring). For a time thereafter, the majority read legislative history with a strong predisposition to find no intent to create a private remedy. More recently, the Court has generally said that legislative history is irrelevant to this question and that congressional intent to create a cause of action must be set forth in the statutory text.

3. Lingering effects of the transition. The Court has continued to enforce implied rights of action that it recognized before the change. In Morse v. Republican Party, 517 U.S. 186 (1996), the Court even recognized an implied right of action under §10 of the Voting Rights Act of 1965, 52 U.S.C. §10306, relying on previous decisions under other sections of the same act and apparent congressional ratification of those decisions. But the norm has been to narrowly construe earlier cases implying rights of action and to slice the implied-right-of-action question finer and finer. In Stoneridge Investment Partners, LLC v. Scientific-Atlanta, Inc., 552 U.S. 148 (2008), the Court said that the implied right of action for securities fraud (under SEC Rule 10b-5) is grandfathered in, but that it "should not be extended beyond its present boundaries." *Id.* at 165. Expansion is for Congress, not the Court.

4. Section 1983. When plaintiff sues a state official for violating federal law, 42 U.S.C. §1983 creates the cause of action. But the Court increasingly treats §1983 claims like implied causes of action. The key move came in Gonzaga University v. Doe, 536 U.S. 273 (2002). Gonzaga is a private institution, but the state court held that it had acted under color of law when it released confidential student information to state officials. This dubious holding was not at issue in the Supreme Court. Just assume that Gonzaga was public.

Gonzaga was a suit under §1983 for violating the Family Educational Rights and Privacy Act, 20 U.S.C. §1232g (FERPA). The statute protects the privacy of student records. The Court acknowledged that §1983 creates a private remedy, but it said that that remedy applies only to private rights, and private rights cannot be implied; Congress must create them. "A court's role in discerning whether personal rights exist in the §1983 context should therefore not differ from its role in discerning whether personal rights exist in the implied right of action context." Finding no express rights-creating language, the Court held that FERPA creates no private rights and cannot be enforced in a §1983 suit.

Other cases hold that the §1983 remedy is implicitly repealed with respect to statutes that create their own detailed enforcement mechanism. A claim under the general provisions of §1983 should not be allowed to bypass statutory limits in the more specific remedy. The leading case is Middlesex County Sewerage Authority v. National Sea Clammers Assn., 453 U.S. 1 (1981). More generally, the Court will confine plaintiffs to a cause of action and remedy created by Congress if it believes that Congress meant the statutory remedy to be exclusive; and if the statutory remedy is specified in reasonable detail, the Court will generally infer that it is meant to be exclusive.

5. The reach of *Gonzaga*. The reach of *Gonzaga* is unclear. If §1983 actions are available only where Congress separately creates a private cause of action, then §1983 is effectively repealed. The Court plainly did not go that far. The Court sometimes says that statutory language expressly stating rights for potential plaintiffs is more likely to suffice than language stating what the regulated entity cannot do. Few constitutional provisions would create private rights under that approach ("Congress shall make no law . . ." focuses on what government can and cannot do, not mentioning the rights of any individual), but it is surely inconceivable for the Court to now hold that the Bill of Rights creates no private rights. And probably the Court will not undo private enforcement of statutes that have long been held to create private rights. But it may not find many more such rights-creating statutes. FERPA itself repeatedly referred to "the rights" of students and their parents, but that was not enough.

6. Narrowing express rights of action. The European Union and 26 of its member states sued RJR Nabisco, alleging violations of RICO, the Racketeer Influenced and Corrupt Organizations Act. RJR allegedly laundered drug money as part of the means to smuggle untaxed cigarettes into EU countries, and gave material aid to terrorism by selling cigarettes to Iraq in violation of international sanctions. Of course, RJR denied the allegations.

The Court presumes that federal statutes do not apply outside the United States unless Congress says so. But it unanimously agreed that Congress had said so with respect to money laundering and aid to terrorism, each of which is a predicate offense for RICO liability. RJR Nabisco, Inc. v. European Community, 136 S. Ct. 2090 (2016). And RICO expressly creates a private right of action for "any person injured in his business or property by reason of a violation of" the section with extraterritorial application. 18 U.S.C. §1964(c). But the Court held, 4-3, that Congress has to separately indicate its intention that the private cause of action be available extraterritorially. Because Congress had not separately so indicated, the case must be dismissed. "Any person" was not clear enough to mean persons suffering injury abroad. Congress may need to sprinkle clear statements through statutes, one for every element of the cause of action.

7. Equitable claims. Recall that in *Bivens*, no one questioned the long tradition of enforcing the Constitution with injunctions. Congress had not created a cause of action for injunctions against federal officials either, but the fight was over causes of action for damages. The same distinction ran through the cases on implied causes of action to enforce statutes. Equitable remedies got little explicit attention, but the fight was over damage actions.

That appeared to change in Alexander v. Sandoval, 532 U.S. 275 (2001). *Alexander* was a suit under Title VI of the Civil Rights Act of 1964, 42 U.S.C. §2000d, and its implementing regulations, to require Alabama to administer its driver's license exam in foreign languages. Congress had explicitly codified a private cause of action to sue for racial discrimination in violation of Title VI. But Alabama argued that this cause of action reached only deliberate discrimination, and that Congress had not created a private cause of action to challenge facially neutral policies that disadvantaged racial minorities.

The parties argued it out under the Court's implied cause of action cases. Plaintiffs made nothing of the fact that they sought only an injunction, and neither the majority nor the dissenters mentioned that fact. *Alexander* appeared to silently extend the whole body of implied-cause-of-action law to equity.

8. Back from the brink. But consider the case that follows, Armstrong v. Exceptional Child Center. It is not your typical implied cause of action case. The statute does not prohibit fraud, discrimination, or some other harmful act; it imposes a vague affirmative duty to pay reasonable fees for medical care. And it is not an ideal teaching case; the opinion assumes the law summarized in this set of notes without explaining it. But it is the Court's latest word on the subject. And it at least partially rescues private suits for injunctions, without ever acknowledging that *Alexander* pointed the other way.

ARMSTRONG v. EXCEPTIONAL CHILD CENTER, INC.

135 S. Ct. 1378 (2015)

Justice SCALIA delivered the opinion of the Court, except as to Part IV.

We consider whether Medicaid providers can sue to enforce §(30)(A) of the Medicaid Act, codified as amended at 42 U.S.C. §1396a(a)(30)(a).

I

Medicaid is a federal program that subsidizes the States' provision of medical services to [certain categories of the needy.] Like other Spending Clause legislation, Medicaid offers the States a bargain: Congress provides federal funds in exchange for the States' agreement to spend them in accordance with congressionally imposed conditions.

In order to qualify for Medicaid funding, . . . Idaho adopted, and the Federal Government approved, a Medicaid "plan" . . . . Idaho's plan includes . . . in-home care for individuals who [would otherwise require hospital or skilled nursing care].

Section 30(A) of the Medicaid Act requires Idaho's plan to:

> provide such methods and procedures relating to the utilization of, and the payment for, care and services available under the plan . . . as may be necessary to safeguard against unnecessary utilization of such care and services and to assure that payments are consistent with efficiency, economy, and quality of care and are sufficient to enlist enough providers so that care and services are available under the plan at least to the extent that such care and services are available to the general population in the geographic area . . . .

[Respondents provide covered in-home care to Medicaid beneficiaries.] They sued petitioners—two [Idaho] officials[,] . . . claiming that Idaho violates §30(A) by reimbursing providers of [in-home care] at rates lower than §30(A) permits. They asked the court to enjoin petitioners to increase these rates. [The lower courts granted summary judgment to the providers. Inclusion, Inc. v. Armstrong, 835 F. Supp. 2d 960 (D. Idaho 2011), *aff'd*, 567 F. App'x 496 (9th Cir. 2014).]

II

The Supremacy Clause, U.S. Const. art. VI, cl. 2 [makes federal law supreme over contrary state law.]

[T]his Clause creates a rule of decision: Courts "shall" regard the "Constitution," and all laws "made in Pursuance thereof," as "the supreme Law of the Land." They must not give effect to state laws that conflict with federal laws. It is equally apparent that the Supremacy Clause is not the "source of any federal rights," Golden State Transit Corp. v. City of Los Angeles, 493 U.S. 103, 107 (1989), and certainly does not create a cause of action. It instructs courts what to do when state and federal law clash, but is silent regarding who may enforce federal laws in court . . . .

It is unlikely that the Constitution gave Congress . . . broad discretion with regard to the enactment of laws, while simultaneously limiting Congress's power over the manner of their implementation . . . . If the Supremacy Clause includes a private right of action, then the Constitution *requires* Congress to permit the enforcement of its laws by private actors, significantly curtailing its ability to guide the implementation of federal law. . . .

It is true enough that we have long held that federal courts may in some circumstances grant injunctive relief against state officers who are violating, or planning to violate, federal law. See, *e.g.,* Ex parte Young. But that has been true not only with respect to violations of federal law by state officials, but also with respect to violations of federal law by federal officials. Thus, the Supremacy Clause need not be (and in light of our textual analysis above, cannot be) the explanation. . . .

The ability to sue to enjoin unconstitutional actions by state and federal officers is the creation of courts of equity, and reflects a long history of judicial review of illegal executive action, tracing back to England. It is a judge-made remedy, and we have never held or even suggested that, in its application to state officers, it rests upon an implied right of action contained in the Supremacy Clause. . . .

III

A

We turn next to respondents' contention that, quite apart from any cause of action conferred by the Supremacy Clause, this suit can proceed against Idaho in equity.

The power of federal courts of equity to enjoin unlawful executive action is subject to express and implied statutory limitations. See, *e.g.,* Seminole Tribe v. Florida, 517 U.S. 44 (1996). . . . [T]he Medicaid Act implicitly precludes private enforcement of §30(A), and respondents cannot, by invoking our equitable powers, circumvent Congress's exclusion of private enforcement.

Two aspects of §30(A) establish Congress's "intent to foreclose" equitable relief. Verizon Maryland, Inc. v. Public Service Commission, 535 U.S. 635, 647 (2002). First, the sole remedy Congress provided for a State's failure to comply with Medicaid's requirements . . . is the withholding of Medicaid funds by the Secretary of Health and Human Services. §1396c. As we have elsewhere explained, the "express provision of one method of enforcing a substantive rule suggests that Congress intended to preclude others." Alexander v. Sandoval, 532 U.S. 275, 290 (2001).

The provision for the Secretary's enforcement by withholding funds might not, *by itself,* preclude the availability of equitable relief. But it does so when combined with the judicially unadministrable nature of §30(A)'s text. It is difficult to imagine a requirement broader and less specific than §30(A)'s mandate . . . . The sheer complexity associated with enforcing §30(A), coupled with the express provision of an administrative remedy, shows that the Medicaid Act precludes private enforcement of § 30(A) in the courts.

B

The dissent agrees with us that the Supremacy Clause does not provide an implied right of action, and that Congress may displace the equitable relief that is traditionally available to enforce federal law. It disagrees only with our conclusion that such displacement has occurred here.

The dissent insists that, "because Congress is undoubtedly aware of the federal courts' long-established practice of enjoining preempted state action, it should generally be presumed to contemplate such enforcement unless it *affirmatively* manifests a contrary intent." (emphasis added). But a "long-established practice" does not justify a rule that denies statutory text its fairest reading. . . . We have no warrant to revise Congress's scheme simply because it did not "affirmatively" preclude the availability of a judge-made action at equity. . . .

Finally, the dissent speaks as though we leave these plaintiffs with no resort. That is not the case. Their relief must be sought initially through the Secretary rather than through the courts. The dissent's complaint that the sanction available to the Secretary (the cut-off of funding) is too massive to be a realistic source of relief seems to us mistaken. We doubt that the Secretary's notice to a State that its compensation scheme is inadequate will be ignored.

IV

The last possible source of a cause of action for respondents is the Medicaid Act itself. They do not claim that, and rightly so. Section 30(A) lacks the sort of rights-creating language needed to imply a private right of action. It is phrased as a directive to the federal agency charged with approving state Medicaid plans, not as a conferral of the right to sue upon the beneficiaries of the State's decision to participate in Medicaid. The Act says that the "Secretary shall approve any plan which fulfills the conditions specified in subsection (a)," the subsection that includes §30(A). We have held that such language "reveals no congressional intent to create a private right of action." *Alexander*, 532 U.S. at 289. And again, the explicitly conferred means of enforcing compliance with §30(A) by the Secretary's withholding funding, suggests that other means of enforcement are precluded. . . .

The judgment of the Ninth Circuit Court of Appeals is reversed. . . .

Justice BREYER, concurring in part and concurring in the judgment.

I join Parts I, II, and III of the Court's opinion.

Like all other Members of the Court, I would not characterize the question before us in terms of a Supremacy Clause "cause of action." Rather, I would ask whether "federal courts may in [these] circumstances grant injunctive relief against state officers who are violating, or planning to violate, federal law." I believe the answer to this question is no.

That answer does not follow from the application of a simple, fixed legal formula . . . . Rather, I believe that several characteristics of the federal statute before us, when taken together, make clear that Congress intended to foreclose respondents from bringing this particular action for injunctive relief.

For one thing, as the majority points out, §30(A) of the Medicaid Act sets forth a federal mandate that is broad and nonspecific. But, more than that, §30(A) applies its broad standards to the setting of rates. The history of ratemaking demonstrates that administrative agencies are far better suited to this task than judges. . . .

At the same time, §30(A) applies broadly, covering reimbursements provided to approximately 1.36 million doctors, serving over 69 million patients across the Nation. . . .

For another thing . . . I would ask why . . . other forms of relief are inadequate. . . . [T]he Secretary can withhold federal funds. If withholding funds does not work, the federal agency may be able to sue a State to compel compliance with federal rules.

Moreover, why could respondents not ask the federal agency to interpret its rules to respondents' satisfaction, to modify those rules, to promulgate new rules or to enforce old ones? Normally, when such requests are denied, an injured party can seek judicial review of the agency's refusal . . .

[T]he law may give the federal agency broad discretionary authority to decide when and how to exercise or to enforce statutes and rules. As a result, it may be difficult for respondents to prevail on an Administrative Procedure Act claim unless it stems from an agency's particularly egregious failure to act. But, if that is so, it is because Congress decided to vest broad discretion in the agency to interpret and to enforce §30(A). I see no reason for this Court to circumvent that congressional determination by allowing this action to proceed.

Justice SOTOMAYOR, with whom Justices KENNEDY, GINSBURG, and KAGAN join, dissenting.

Suits in federal court to restrain state officials from executing laws that assertedly conflict with the Constitution or with a federal statute are not novel. To the contrary, this Court has adjudicated such requests for equitable relief since the early days of the Republic. . . .

I

A

That parties may call upon the federal courts to enjoin unconstitutional government action is not subject to serious dispute. Perhaps the most famous exposition of this principle is our decision in Ex parte Young . . . .

A suit, like this one, that seeks relief against state officials acting pursuant to a state law allegedly preempted by a federal statute falls comfortably within this doctrine. . . . We have thus long entertained suits in which a party seeks prospective equitable protection from an injurious and preempted state law without regard to whether the federal statute at issue itself provided a right to bring an action. Indeed, for this reason, we have characterized "the availability of prospective relief of the sort awarded in Ex parte Young" as giving "life to the Supremacy Clause." Green v. Mansour, 474 U.S. 64, 68 (1985).

Thus, even though the Court is correct that it is somewhat misleading to speak of "an implied right of action contained in the Supremacy Clause," that does not mean that parties may not enforce the Supremacy Clause by bringing suit to enjoin preempted state action. . . .

B

Most important for purposes of this case is not the mere existence of this equitable authority, but the fact that it is exceedingly well established—supported, as the Court puts it, by a "long history." Congress may . . . either expressly or implicitly preclude Ex parte Young enforcement actions with respect to a particular statute or category of lawsuit. But because Congress is undoubtedly aware of the federal courts' long-established practice of enjoining preempted state action, it should generally be presumed to contemplate such enforcement unless it affirmatively manifests a contrary intent. . . .

In this respect, equitable preemption actions differ from suits brought by plaintiffs invoking 42 U.S.C. §1983 or an implied right of action to enforce a federal statute. Suits for "redress designed to halt or prevent the constitutional violation rather than the award of money damages" seek "traditional forms of relief." United States v. Stanley, 483 U.S. 669, 683 (1987). By contrast, a plaintiff invoking §1983 or an implied statutory cause of action may seek a variety of remedies—including damages—from a potentially broad range of parties. Rather than simply pointing to background equitable principles authorizing the action that Congress presumably has not overridden, such a plaintiff must demonstrate specific congressional intent to *create* a statutory right to these remedies. For these reasons, the principles that we have developed to determine whether a statute creates an implied right of action, or is enforceable through §1983, are not transferable to the Ex parte Young context.

II

In concluding that Congress has "implicitly preclude[d] private enforcement of §30(A)," the Court ignores this critical distinction and threatens the vitality of our Ex parte Young jurisprudence. The Court identifies only a single prior decision—*Seminole Tribe*—in which we have ever discerned such congressional intent to foreclose equitable enforcement of a statutory mandate. . . .

In *Seminole Tribe*, the plaintiff Indian Tribe had invoked Ex parte Young in seeking to compel the State of Florida to "negotiate in good faith with [the] tribe toward the formation of a compact" governing certain gaming activities, as required by a provision of the Indian Gaming Regulatory Act, 25 U.S.C. §2710(d)(3), 517 U.S. at 47. [But in §2710(d)(7), Congress had detailed a statutory right to sue with multiple steps, limited remedies, and limited means of enforcement for the remedies that were available.] As we explained: "If §2710(d)(3) could be enforced in a suit under Ex parte Young, §2710(d)(7) would have been superfluous; it is difficult to see why an Indian tribe would suffer through the intricate scheme of §2710(d)(7) when more complete and more immediate relief would be available under Ex parte Young." 517 U.S. at 75.

What is the equivalent "carefully crafted and intricate remedial scheme" for enforcement of §30(A)? The Court relies on two aspects of the Medicaid Act, but, whether considered separately or in combination, neither suffices.

First, the Court cites §1396c, which authorizes the Secretary . . . to withhold federal Medicaid payments to a State . . . . But in striking contrast to the remedial provision set out in the Indian Gaming Regulatory Act, §1396c provides no specific procedure that parties actually affected by a State's violation of its statutory obligations may invoke in lieu of Ex parte Young—leaving them without any other avenue for seeking relief from the State. [And if the problem is that the State is not spending enough money on Medicaid,] agency action resulting in a reduced flow of federal funds to that State will often be self-defeating. Far from rendering §1396c "superfluous," then, Ex parte Young actions would seem to be an anticipated and possibly necessary supplement to this limited agency-enforcement mechanism. . . .

Second, . . . the Court focuses on the particular language of §30(A), contending that this provision, at least, is so "judicially unadministrable" that Congress must have intended to preclude its enforcement in private suits. . . .

Of course, the broad scope of §30(A)'s language is not irrelevant. But rather than compelling the conclusion that the provision is wholly unenforceable by private parties, its breadth counsels in favor of interpreting §30(A) to provide substantial leeway to States, so that only in rare and extreme circumstances could a State actually be held to violate its mandate. The provision's scope may also often require a court to rely on [the Department of Health and Human Services], which is "comparatively expert in the statute's subject matter." Douglas v. Independent Living Center, 565

U.S. 606, 614 (2012). . . . Finally, because the authority invoked for enforcing §30(A) is equitable in nature, a plaintiff is not entitled to relief as of right, but only in the sound discretion of the court. . . .

The Court's error today has very real consequences. Previously, a State that set reimbursement rates so low that providers were unwilling to furnish a covered service for those who need it could be compelled by those affected to respect the obligation imposed by §30(A). Now, it must suffice that a federal agency, with many programs to oversee, has authority to address such violations through the drastic and often counterproductive measure of withholding the funds that pay for such services. Because a faithful application of our precedents would have led to a contrary result, I respectfully dissent.

NOTES ON ENFORCING FEDERAL STATUTES WITH INJUNCTIONS

1. The federal equity power. All nine Justices appear to agree that there is a long-standing, judge-made right to sue to enjoin violations of federal law, and that Congress does not have to create this cause of action. That seems to rescue injunction suits from the implied-cause-of-action jurisprudence applied to the injunction in Alexander v. Sandoval. Both the majority and the dissent cite *Alexander* for various points, but neither opinion makes any effort to overrule it, limit it, or explain what was going on there. It appears that if a plaintiff makes the mistake of asking for an implied cause of action, she gets *Alexander*. If she asks for an injunction under the federal equity power, she gets *Armstrong*.

2. Congressional power to preclude the injunctive remedy. Congress need not create the right to sue for an injunction, but Congress can eliminate it, explicitly or implicitly. The injunctive remedy is not secure if the Court too freely finds that Congress has implicitly rejected it. How far in that direction does *Armstrong* go?

The substantive standard in §30(A) of the Medicaid Act was not only vague; its elements tended to conflict. Reimbursement rates must be high enough to ensure access equal to what is available for paying patients, but low enough to achieve efficiency and economy and to avoid unnecessary use of the covered services. A holding that Congress would not have wanted that standard judicially enforced does not threaten to undermine the injunctive remedy more generally. Even the dissenters seemed to envision judicial review so deferential that it would rarely make a difference.

3. The remedy of cutting off federal financial aid. But the Court also says that Congress provided a different remedy; the Secretary can cut off Idaho's Medicaid. And this remedy implies that Congress wanted no other. That is a much more sweeping rationale; it threatens to eliminate enforcement by injunction in all Spending Clause legislation—all statutes that offer states money on condition that they comply with federal law.

The Court rejected the argument that the funds-cutoff remedy precludes a private cause of action as late as Cannon v. University of Chicago, 441 U.S. 677 (1979). But the conservative justices have generally accepted that argument; they invoked it in both *Alexander* and *Armstrong*. And in general, the Court has been especially reluctant to imply causes of action to enforce Spending Clause statutes.

4. Other alternative remedies. In Elgin v. Department of the Treasury, 567 U.S. 1 (2012), plaintiffs sought to enjoin enforcement of a law that bars from government employment any male who failed to register for the stand-by draft. The Court held that the administrative remedies under the Civil Service Reform Act, 5 U.S.C. §1101 *et seq.*, were exclusive—even though the agency could not consider the constitutional claim. The Federal Circuit would be able to consider the constitutional claim when it reviewed the agency's action.

There is a similar holding in Sandoz Inc. v. Amgen Inc., 137 S. Ct. 1664 (2017), interpreting a specialized patent statute for drugs derived from living organisms and far too complex to be worth summarizing here. The point for our purposes is that a complex federal statute authorized a declaratory judgment for the violation plaintiff alleged, but did not mention injunctions. The Court held that the declaratory judgment was the exclusive federal remedy.

Is the injunctive remedy rescued from the fire but only as far as the frying pan? Congress does not have to create it, but it may be very easy for Congress to preclude it, either intentionally or inadvertently.

5. Switching sides on clear statement rules. The conservative Justices have frequently invoked clear statement rules, requiring Congress to express itself clearly and affirmatively in statutory text to create a cause of action for damages or to waive or override sovereign immunity. See notes 1 and 6 preceding *Armstrong*. But in *Armstrong*, it is Justice Sotomayor who says Congress should not be read to eliminate the equitable remedy unless it "affirmatively manifests a contrary intent." And it was Justice Scalia for the majority arguing without apparent embarrassment that the Court must give the "statutory text its fairest reading," and "[w]e have no warrant to revise Congress's scheme simply because it did not 'affirmatively' preclude the availability of a judge-made action at equity."

6. Defining the remedies for implied causes of action. When the Court implies a cause of action, or when Congress creates a cause of action without specifying remedies, what remedies should the courts provide? Franklin v. Gwinnett County Public Schools, 503 U.S. 60 (1992), was a suit for damages for sexual harassment, under Title IX of the Education Amendments of 1972, 20 U.S.C. §1681 *et seq.* Congress had expressly created a cause of action but legislated no details. Defendants argued that the remedy for this cause of action should be confined to injunctions, and possibly back pay in employment cases, and should not include damages. Compare this defense preference for injunctions to the presumptions of the irreparable injury rule.

The Court said that Congress must create causes of action, and a cause of action is not to be implied from a substantive right. But the retrenchment on private rights of action had not changed the longstanding rule about remedy: "if a right of action exists . . . and Congress is silent on the question of remedies, a federal court may order any appropriate relief." *Id.* at 69. "That a statute does not authorize the remedy at issue 'in so many words is no more significant than the fact that it does not in terms authorize execution to issue on a judgment.'" *Id.* at 68.

Barnes v. Gorman, 536 U.S. 181 (2002), held that even where a court may order "any appropriate relief" under *Franklin*, punitive damages are not appropriate relief for violating a civil rights statute that applies to programs receiving federal financial assistance. Where civil rights compliance is a condition on the receipt of federal funds, violating the condition is a breach of contract, and punitive damages are not an appropriate remedy for breach of contract.

7. The elements and defenses of implied causes of action. In general, the elements of an implied cause of action are stated in the substantive statute that the cause of action is designed to enforce. Under a Spending Clause statute such as Title VI or Title IX, defendant must have clear notice of what conduct will give rise to liability, so that it has the option of turning down the federal money and avoiding the associated liability. Any private right of action must be confined to the scope of this notice. Davis v. Monroe County Board of Education, 526 U.S. 629 (1999).

Even so, Congress may not have specified answers to all the questions that arise in the course of adjudicating claims to enforce the statute. Any answer that favors the plaintiff can be attacked as illicitly expanding the cause of action. In Jackson v. Birmingham Board of Education, 544 U.S. 167 (2005), a girls' basketball coach complained that the school discriminated against the girls' team, and he was fired. Employment discrimination statutes commonly prohibit retaliation, but there is no retaliation provision in Title IX, which prohibits discrimination "on the basis of sex."

Justice O'Connor for the majority held that "when a funding recipient retaliates against a person *because* he complains of sex discrimination, this constitutes intentional 'discrimination' 'on the basis of sex,'" in violation of the statutory text. 544 U.S. at 174. Title IX would be unenforceable if schools were free to fire or expel anyone who complained of sex discrimination. Justice Thomas, dissenting for four, said that "the majority returns this Court to the days in which it created remedies out of whole cloth to effectuate its vision of congressional purpose," substituting "its policy judgment for the bargains struck by Congress, as reflected in the statute's text." *Id.* at 195. The Court also implied retaliation protection in 42 U.S.C. §1981, a Reconstruction-era statute, expanded by statutory amendment in 1989, that prohibits racial discrimination in making, administering, or enforcing contracts. CBOCS West, Inc. v. Humphries, 553 U.S. 442 (2008). This time, only Justice Scalia joined the Thomas dissent.

Compare Gebser v. Lago Vista Independent School District, 524 U.S. 274 (1998), where a conservative majority implied substantive elements that limited the cause of action. The dissenters did not claim that this was illegitimate, but only that the elements implied were mistaken.

8. Other remedies. Lack of a private cause of action does not inevitably make a statute a dead letter. There may be criminal penalties for its violation, and there is often an administrative agency to enforce it. But there is a problem of resources: The agency can typically investigate only a handful of cases. Recall the limited number of inspections of North Carolina workplaces, in section 6.A.1. The federal government once told the Supreme Court that every year it can inspect fewer than 4 percent of the employers subject to the Fair Labor Standards Act. Employees v. Department of Public Health & Welfare, 411 U.S. 279, 287 (1973). A damage action for victims creates a vast army of potential enforcers. Private enforcers will demand compensation for victims; public enforcers sometimes won't or can't. But judges also fear that private enforcers will be too aggressive and bring too many cases, or too many dubious cases.

The most commonly provided remedy in Spending Clause statutes is that federal officials can cut off federal funds. But that is like a nuclear weapon, good only for deterrence. The Secretary can threaten it, but he can't really do it. And if a presidential administration doesn't like the statutory requirement, or sympathizes with the fund recipients who are violating it, the Secretary won't even threaten.

9. *Bivens* again. The *Bivens* remedy for constitutional violations initially survived the repudiation of implied rights of action, on the theory that statutory rights are created by Congress, and "it is entirely appropriate" for Congress to decide "who may enforce them and in what manner." Davis v. Passman, 442 U.S. 228, 241 (1979). But constitutional rights must be enforced through courts "unless such rights are to become merely precatory." *Id.* at 242. There were four dissents, and those dissenters now have the additional votes to keep *Bivens* narrowly confined.

C.   THE RIGHT TO JURY TRIAL

CHAUFFEURS LOCAL NO. 391 v. TERRY
494 U.S. 558 (1990)

[Plaintiffs were truck drivers transferred to their employer's terminal in Winston-Salem, North Carolina. Plaintiffs soon became embroiled in a persistent dispute with other drivers, previously laid off from that terminal, over the interpretation of seniority rules in the collective bargaining agreement. Both groups of drivers were members of defendant's union, and in a series of grievance proceedings to enforce the contract, the union took the side of the original Winston-Salem drivers. As a result of this interpretation of the rules, plaintiffs were repeatedly laid off.

Plaintiffs sued their employer under §301 of the National Labor Relations Act, 29 U.S.C. §185, for breach of the collective bargaining agreement. They sued the union for breach of its duty to fairly represent them in the grievance proceedings. They sought an injunction ordering the employer to follow their interpretation of the seniority rules, reinstatement with full seniority, and compensatory damages for lost wages and health benefits. They dropped the demand for an injunction and reinstatement when the employer filed for bankruptcy.

The district court held that plaintiffs were entitled to jury trial. On an interlocutory appeal, the court of appeals affirmed. 863 F.2d 334 (4th Cir. 1988).]

Justice MARSHALL delivered the opinion of the Court, except as to Part III-A. . . .

II

The duty of fair representation . . . requires a union "to serve the interests of all members without hostility or discrimination toward any, to exercise its discretion with complete good faith and honesty, and to avoid arbitrary conduct." Vaca v. Sipes, 386 U.S. 171, 177 (1967). . . .

Because most collective-bargaining agreements accord finality to grievance or arbitration procedures . . . , an employee normally cannot bring a §301 action against an employer unless he can show that the union breached its duty of fair representation in its handling of his grievance. Whether the employee sues both the labor union and the employer or only one of those entities, he must prove the same two facts to recover money damages: that the employer's action violated the terms of the collective-bargaining agreement and that the union breached its duty of fair representation.

III . . .

The Seventh Amendment provides that "[i]n Suits at common law, where the value in controversy shall exceed twenty dollars, the right of trial by jury shall be preserved." . . .

To determine whether a particular action will resolve legal rights, we examine both the nature of the issues involved and the remedy sought. "First, we compare the statutory action to 18th-century actions brought in the courts of England prior to the merger of the courts of law and equity. Second, we examine the remedy sought and determine whether it is legal or equitable in nature." Tull v. United States, 481 U.S. 412, 417-418 (1987). The second inquiry is the more important in our analysis.[4]

A . . .

The Union contends that this duty of fair representation action resembles a suit brought to vacate an arbitration award because respondents seek to set aside the result of the grievance process. In the 18th century, an action to set aside an arbitration award was considered equitable. . . .

The arbitration analogy is inapposite. . . . No grievance committee has considered respondents' claim that the Union violated its duty of fair representation; the grievance process was concerned only with the employer's alleged breach of the collective-bargaining agreement. . . .

The Union next argues that respondents' duty of fair representation action is comparable to an action by a trust beneficiary against a trustee for breach of fiduciary duty. Such actions were within the exclusive jurisdiction of courts of equity. This analogy is far more persuasive than the arbitration analogy. Just as a trustee must act in the best interests of the beneficiaries, a union . . . must exercise its power to act on behalf of the employees in good faith. Moreover, just as a beneficiary does not directly control the actions of a trustee, an individual employee lacks direct control over a union's actions taken on his behalf.

The trust analogy extends to a union's handling of grievances. In most cases, a trustee has the exclusive authority to sue third parties who injure the beneficiaries' interest in the trust, including any legal claim the trustee holds in trust for the beneficiaries. The trustee then has the sole responsibility for determining whether to settle, arbitrate, or otherwise dispose of the claim. Similarly, the union typically has broad discretion in its decision whether and how to pursue an employee's grievance against an employer. . . .

Respondents contend that their duty of fair representation suit is less like a trust action than an attorney malpractice action, which was historically an action at law. . . .

Unlike employees represented by a union, a client controls the significant decisions concerning his representation. Moreover, a client can fire his attorney if he is dissatisfied with his attorney's performance. This option is not available to an individual employee who is unhappy with a union's representation, unless a majority of the members of the bargaining unit share his dissatisfaction. Thus, we find the malpractice analogy less convincing than the trust analogy.

Nevertheless, the trust analogy does not persuade us to characterize respondents' claim as wholly equitable. The Union's argument mischaracterizes the nature of our comparison of the action before us to 18th-century forms of action. As we observed in Ross v. Bernhard, 396 U.S. 531 (1970), "The Seventh Amendment question depends on the nature of the *issue* to be tried rather than the character of the overall action." *Id.* at 538 (emphasis added). . . .[6] When viewed in isolation, the duty of fair representation

---

4. Justice Stevens' analysis emphasizes a third consideration, namely whether "the issues [presented by the claim] are typical grist for the jury's judgment." This Court, however, has never relied on this consideration "as an independent basis for extending the right to a jury trial under the Seventh Amendment." *Tull,* 481 U.S. at 418 n.4. . . .

6. The dissent characterizes this opinion as "pars[ing] legal elements out of equitable claims." The question whether the Seventh Amendment analysis requires an examination of the nature of each element of a typical claim is not presented by this case. The claim we confront here is not typical; instead, it is a claim consisting of discrete issues that would normally be brought as two claims, one against the employer and one against the union. . . . Consideration of the nature of the two issues in this hybrid action is therefore warranted.

issue is analogous to a claim against a trustee for breach of fiduciary duty. The §301 issue, however, is comparable to a breach of contract claim—a legal issue.

Respondents' action against the Union thus encompasses both equitable and legal issues. The first part of our Seventh Amendment inquiry, then, leaves us in equipoise as to whether respondents are entitled to a jury trial.

B

Our determination under the first part of the Seventh Amendment analysis is only preliminary. In this case, the only remedy sought is a request for compensatory damages representing backpay and benefits. Generally, an action for money damages was "the traditional form of relief offered in the courts of law." Curtis v. Loether, 415 U.S. 189, 196 (1974). This Court has not, however, held that "any award of monetary relief must *necessarily* be 'legal' relief." *Id.* (emphasis added). Nonetheless, because we conclude that the remedy respondents seek has none of the attributes that must be present before we will find an exception to the general rule and characterize damages as equitable, we find that the remedy sought by respondents is legal.

First, we have characterized damages as equitable where they are restitutionary, such as in "action[s] for disgorgement of improper profits," *Tull*, 481 U.S. at 424. The backpay sought by respondents is not money wrongfully held by the Union, but wages and benefits they would have received from [their employer] had the Union processed the employees' grievances properly. Such relief is not restitutionary.

Second, a monetary award "incidental to or intertwined with injunctive relief" may be equitable. *Id.* at 424. Because respondents seek only money damages, this characteristic is clearly absent from the case.[8]

The Union argues that the backpay relief sought here must nonetheless be considered equitable because this Court has labeled backpay awarded under Title VII of the Civil Rights Act of 1964 as equitable. . . . We are not convinced.

The Court has never held that a plaintiff seeking backpay under Title VII has a right to a jury trial. Assuming, without deciding, that such a Title VII plaintiff has no right to a jury trial, the Union's argument does not persuade us that respondents are not entitled to a jury trial here. Congress specifically characterized backpay under Title VII as a form of "equitable relief." 42 U.S.C. §2000e-5(g) (1982). Congress made no similar pronouncement regarding the duty of fair representation. Furthermore, the Court has noted that backpay sought from an employer under Title VII would generally be restitutionary in nature, in contrast to the damages sought here from the Union. . . .

We hold, then, that the remedy of backpay sought in this duty of fair representation action is legal in nature. Considering both parts of the Seventh Amendment inquiry, we find that respondents are entitled to a jury trial on all issues presented in their suit.

---

8. Both the Union and the dissent argue that the backpay award sought here is equitable because it is closely analogous to damages awarded to beneficiaries for a trustee's breach of trust. Such damages were available only in courts of equity because those courts had exclusive jurisdiction over actions involving a trustee's breach of his fiduciary duties. The Union's argument, however, conflates the two parts of our Seventh Amendment inquiry. Under the dissent's approach, if the action at issue were analogous to an 18th-century action within the exclusive jurisdiction of the courts of equity, we would necessarily conclude that the remedy sought was also equitable because it would have been unavailable in a court of law. This view would, in effect, make the first part of our inquiry dispositive. We have clearly held, however, that the second part of the inquiry—the nature of the relief—is more important to the Seventh Amendment determination. The second part of the analysis, therefore, should not replicate the "abstruse historical" inquiry of the first part, Ross v. Bernhard, 396 U.S. at 538 n.10, but requires consideration of the general types of relief provided by courts of law and equity.

IV . . .

[W]e therefore affirm. . . .

Justice BRENNAN, concurring in part. . . .

I agree with the Court that respondents seek a remedy that is legal in nature and that the Seventh Amendment entitles respondents to a jury trial on their duty of fair representation claims. I therefore join Parts I, II, III-B, and IV of the Court's opinion. I do not join [any of Part III except for III-B], because I believe the historical test can and should be simplified.

The current test . . . requires a court . . . to determine whether the historically analogous right was vindicated in an action at law or in equity, and to examine whether the remedy sought is legal or equitable. . . . However, this Court . . . has repeatedly discounted the significance of the analogous form of action. . . . I think it is time we dispense with it altogether. I would decide Seventh Amendment questions on the basis of the relief sought. . . .

Requiring judges, with neither the training nor time necessary for reputable historical scholarship, to root through the tangle of primary and secondary sources to determine which of a hundred or so writs is analogous to the right at issue has embroiled courts in recondite controversies better left to legal historians. . . .

Furthermore, inquiries into the appropriate historical analogs for the rights at issue are not necessarily susceptible of sound resolution under the best of circumstances. . . . "[T]he line between law and equity . . . was not a fixed and static one. . . . The borrowing by each jurisdiction from the other was not accompanied by an equivalent sloughing off of functions. This led to a very large overlap between law and equity." Fleming James, Jr., *Right to a Jury Trial in Civil Actions*, 72 Yale L.J. 655, 658-659 (1963). . . .

[T]he rule I propose would remain true to the Seventh Amendment, as it is undisputed that, historically, "[j]urisdictional lines [between law and equity] were primarily a matter of remedy." John C. McCoid, II, *Procedural Reform and the Right to Jury Trial: A Study of Beacon Theatres, Inc. v. Westover*, 116 U. Pa. L. Rev. 1 (1967).[7] . . .

Justice STEVENS, concurring in part.

[T]he duty of fair representation action resembles a common-law action against an attorney for malpractice more closely than it does any other form of action. . . .

[T]he Court surely overstates this action's similarity to an action against a trustee. Collective bargaining involves no settlor, no trust corpus, and no trust instrument executed to convey property to beneficiaries chosen at the settlor's pleasure. . . . Union members, as a group, . . . have the power to hire, fire, and direct the actions of their representatives—prerogatives anathema to the paternalistic forms of the equitable trust. . . .

[T]he commonsense understanding of the jury . . . is appropriately invoked when disputes in the factory, the warehouse, and the garage must be resolved. In most duty of fair representation cases, the issues, which require an understanding of the realities of employment relationships, are typical grist for the jury's judgment. Indeed, the law defining the union's duty of fair representation has developed in cases tried to juries. . . .

---

7. . . . Where Justice Kennedy and I differ is in our evaluations of which historical test provides the more reliable results. . . . [A]ll too often the first prong of the current test requires courts to measure modern statutory actions against 18th-century English actions so remote in form and concept that there is no firm basis for comparison. In such cases, the result is less the discovery of a historical analog than the manufacture of a historical fiction. By contrast, the nature of relief available today corresponds more directly to the nature of relief available in Georgian England. . . .

Duty of fair representation suits are for the most part ordinary civil actions involving the stuff of contract and malpractice disputes. There is accordingly no ground for excluding these actions from the jury right. . . .

I therefore join [the Court's] judgment and all of its opinion except for Part III-A.

Justice KENNEDY, with whom Justices O'CONNOR and SCALIA join, dissenting. . . .

I . . .

Justice Marshall . . . states an important and correct reason for finding the trust model better than the malpractice analogy. . . . [T]he client of an attorney, unlike a union member or beneficiary, controls the significant decisions concerning his litigation and can fire the attorney if not satisfied. . . .

Further considerations fortify the conclusion. . . .

Although the union is charged with the responsibility of reconciling the positions of its members, the lawyer's duty of loyalty long has precluded the representation of conflicting interests. A lawyer, at least absent knowing waiver by the parties, could not represent both the respondents and the senior laidoff workers as the Union has done in this case.

The relief available in a duty of fair representation action also makes the trust action the better model. To remedy a breach of the duty of fair representation, a court must issue an award "fashioned to make the injured employee whole." Electrical Workers v. Foust, 442 U.S. 42, 49 (1979). The court may order an injunction compelling the union, if it is still able, to pursue the employee's claim, and may require monetary compensation, but it cannot award exemplary or punitive damages. This relief parallels the remedies prevailing in the courts of equity in actions against trustees for failing to pursue claims. . . .

These remedies differ somewhat from those available in attorney malpractice actions. . . . No one maintains that clients could obtain from [common law] courts the injunctive relief offered in duty of fair representation actions. . . . [C]ompensatory damages in malpractice cases resembled the monetary relief now awarded in duty of fair representation actions. Yet . . . juries did have the authority to award exemplary damages in at least some tort actions. Although the parties have not cited any punitive damage award in an attorney malpractice action prior to 1791, courts have awarded such damages since the 19th century. . . .

When all rights and remedies are considered, [plaintiff's] action resembles a suit heard by the courts of equity more than a case heard by the courts of law. From this alone it follows that the respondents have no jury trial right on their duty of fair representation claims against the Union.

II . . .

A

In three cases we have found a right to trial by jury where there are legal claims that, for procedural reasons, a plaintiff could have or must have raised in the courts of equity before the systems merged. In Beacon Theatres, Inc. v. Westover, 359 U.S. 500 (1959), Fox, a potential defendant threatened with legal antitrust claims, brought an action for declaratory and injunctive relief against Beacon, the likely plaintiff. Because only the courts of equity had offered such relief prior to the merger of the two court systems, Fox had thought that it could deprive Beacon of a jury trial. Beacon, however, raised the antitrust issues as counterclaims and sought a jury. We ruled that, because Beacon would have had a right to a jury trial on its antitrust claims, Fox could not deprive it of a jury merely by taking advantage of modern declaratory procedures to sue first. . . .

In Dairy Queen, Inc. v. Wood, 369 U.S. 469 (1962), we held, in a similar manner, that a plaintiff, by asking in his complaint for an equitable accounting for trademark infringement, could not deprive the defendant of a jury trial on contract claims subsumed within the accounting. Although a court of equity would have heard the contract claims as part of the accounting suit, we found them severable under modern procedure.

In Ross v. Bernhard, 396 U.S. 531 (1970), a shareholder-plaintiff demanded a jury trial in a derivative action asserting a legal claim on behalf of his corporation. . . . [W]e recognized that only the courts of equity had procedural devices allowing shareholders to raise a corporation's claims. We nonetheless again ruled that modern procedure allowed trial of the legal claim to a jury.

These three cases responded to the difficulties created by a merged court system. They stand for the proposition that, because distinct courts of equity no longer exist, the possibility or necessity of using former equitable procedures to press a legal claim no longer will determine the right to a jury. Justice Marshall reads these cases to require a jury trial whenever a cause of action contains legal issues and would require a jury trial in this case because the respondents must prove a breach of the collective-bargaining agreement as one element of their claim.

I disagree. The respondents, as shown above, are asserting an equitable claim. Having reached this conclusion, . . . *Beacon, Dairy Queen,* and *Ross* . . . are inapplicable. Although we have divided self-standing legal claims from equitable declaratory, accounting, and derivative procedures, we have never parsed legal elements out of equitable claims absent specific procedural justifications. Actions which, beyond all question, are equitable in nature may involve some predicate inquiry that would be submitted to a jury in other contexts. For example, . . . in an action against a trustee for failing to pursue a claim the beneficiary must show that the claim had some merit. But the question of the claim's validity, even if the claim raises contract issues, would not bring the jury right into play in a suit against a trustee. . . .

We have characterized the breach of contract and duty issues as "inextricably interdependent". . . . DelCostello v. Teamsters, 462 U.S. 151, 164-165 (1983). The absence of distinct equitable courts provides no procedural reason for wresting one of these elements from the other.

B

The Court also rules that . . . respondents have a right to a jury trial because they seek money damages. . . . [W]e have not adopted a rule that a statutory action permitting damages is by definition more analogous to a legal action than to any equitable suit. In each case, we look to the remedy to determine whether, taken with other factors, it places an action within the definition of "Suits at common law.". . .

In *Curtis,* . . . we ruled that the availability of actual and punitive damages made a statutory antidiscrimination action resemble a legal tort action more than any equitable action. We made explicit that we did not "go so far as to say that any award of monetary relief must necessarily be 'legal' relief." 415 U.S. at 196. Although monetary damages might cause some statutory actions to resemble tort suits, the presence of monetary damages in this duty of fair representation action does not make it more analogous to a legal action than to an equitable action. Indeed, as shown above, the injunctive and monetary remedies available make the duty of fair representation suit less analogous to a malpractice action than to a suit against a trustee.

In *Tull*, the availability of damages again played a critical role in determining the right to a jury trial. In an environmental suit by the Government for injunctive relief and a civil penalty, both an equitable public nuisance action and a legal action in debt seemed appropriate historical models. We decided between them by noting that only the courts of law could award civil penalties. In the present case, however, one cannot characterize both the trust analogy and the legal malpractice comparisons as appropriate; the considerations discussed above, including the remedy available, all make the trust model superior. As we stated in *Tull*, "[o]ur search is for a single historical analog, taking into consideration the nature of the cause of action and the remedy as two important factors." 481 U.S. at 422 n.6. . . .

In Granfinanciera, S.A. v. Nordberg, 492 U.S. 33 (1989), . . . [w]e held that, despite some evidence that both the courts of law and equity had jurisdiction over fraudulent conveyances, only a court of law could entertain an action to recover an alleged fraudulent transfer of a determinate sum of money. As in *Curtis* and *Tull*, however, the particular importance of monetary damages in *Granfinanciera* does not carry forward into this case. The courts of equity could and did award the kind of damages sought by the respondents here. The respondents' mere request for backpay in no way entitles them to a jury under the Seventh Amendment.

III . . .

The Seventh Amendment "preserves" the right to jury trial in civil cases. We cannot preserve a right existing in 1791 unless we look to history to identify it. . . . If we abandon the plain language of the Constitution to expand the jury right, we may expect Courts with opposing views to curtail it in the future. It is true that a historical inquiry into the distinction between law and equity may require us to enter into a domain becoming less familiar with time. . . . The historical test, nonetheless, has received more criticism than it deserves. Although our application of the analysis in some cases may seem biased in favor of jury trials, the test has not become a nullity. We do not require juries in all statutory actions.

I would hesitate to abandon or curtail the historical test out of concern for the competence of the Court to understand legal history. . . .

IV

Because of the employer's bankruptcy, the respondents are proceeding only against the Union in the suit before us. In a typical duty of fair representation action, however, union members may sue both their union and their employer. . . . In this case, we do not have to . . . decide whether *Beacon, Dairy Queen,* or *Ross* would require a jury trial in a suit against an employer. I would deny a jury trial to the respondents here, but would leave these other questions for a later time. . . .

NOTES ON THE EVOLUTION OF THE FEDERAL RIGHT TO JURY TRIAL

1. *Beacon Theatres.* Justice Kennedy accurately summarizes the Court's cases, but some of those cases raised larger issues that you need to know more about. By far the most important is Beacon Theatres v. Westover. *Beacon* is best explained on the narrow ground offered by Justice Kennedy: A potential defendant cannot deprive a potential plaintiff of jury trial by suing to enjoin the potential plaintiff's damage action or for a declaratory judgment that there is no liability. But the opinion also announced much broader principles.

Beacon said that the merger of law and equity changed the scope of the Seventh Amendment, because it was now possible to provide in suits at law remedies that previously could be provided only in equity. Any suit that could be filed at law must be, and if legal and equitable issues or proceedings were joined in a single case, the legal issues must be tried first, and to a jury. As the scope of legal remedies expanded, so did the constitutional right to jury trial. The irreparable injury rule safeguarded the right to jury trial, and injuries that might have been irreparable in a dual court system would often not be irreparable under merged procedure.

2. Equitable cleanup jurisdiction. *Beacon* inverted longstanding practice and presumptions. Historically, equity courts asserted "cleanup jurisdiction" to decide all issues in a case, including damage issues, if the case was properly filed in equity. And they would retain a jurisdiction once asserted, even if a legal remedy subsequently became available. This practice was not limited to cases where the legal remedy might not provide a fair and orderly adjudication. For example, in American Life Insurance Co. v. Stewart, 300 U.S. 203 (1937), the insurer sued to cancel a life insurance policy for fraud. Then the insured died and the beneficiary sued on the policy. Fraud was a defense to the policy, and there was no risk the beneficiary's suit would be abandoned or fail to resolve the controversy. The beneficiary's suit was for breach of contract, plainly a suit at law and triable to a jury. But the Court unanimously affirmed the trial court's decision to first decide the insurer's equitable claim for cancellation. That decision is implicitly overruled in *Beacon*; the court would now be required to hold the cancellation claim and try the contract claim to a jury.

State courts interpreting state rights to jury trial rejected *Beacon*'s broader principles and adhered to the traditional practice by a ratio of about three to one. Gregory Gelfand, *Smith v. University of Detroit: Is There a Viable Alternative to Beacon Theatres?*, 45 Wash. & Lee L. Rev. 159, 168-172 (1988).

3. Separating the question of relief from the question of jury trial. The Court reaffirmed *Beacon*'s broad principles in *Dairy Queen*. But the facts involved a national chain's rather transparent effort to avoid jury trial in a suit against one of its franchisees. The Court held that plaintiff's contract claims must be tried to a jury, and that plaintiff could not avoid jury trial by demanding an accounting for the sums due under the contract.

Despite the Court's emphasis on the irreparable injury rule as a protection for jury trial, neither *Beacon* nor *Dairy Queen* limits the relief to which plaintiff is entitled. Both plaintiffs were entitled to preliminary injunctions if needed pending the jury trial and to permanent injunctions if needed after the jury trial. These cases were aimed at procedural maneuvers that "while granting Fox no additional protection unless the avoidance of jury trial be considered as such, would compel Beacon to split his antitrust case, trying part to a judge and part to a jury." 359 U.S. at 508.

That's why the jury trial issue is here, in a chapter on separation of powers, and not in Chapter 5, on choosing remedies. The division of authority between judge and jury, and the boundary between law and equity, are all in the judicial branch; they are not what we usually think of as separation of powers. But this is a sort of allocation of power, and there is no better place to put the issue. The right to jury trial is emphatically not about choosing remedies; plaintiff gets the remedy he is entitled to under other rules. Plaintiff's choice of remedy partly controls the right to jury trial, and the right to jury trial partly controls the sequence in which issues are decided, but the right to jury trial does not control or limit the choice between two remedies that are meaningfully different from each other.

4. Legal claims in equitable procedures. The most clearly settled application of *Beacon* and *Dairy Queen* is Ross v. Bernhard, 396 U.S. 531 (1970). A substantive legal claim, brought in an equitable procedure, such as a class action, a shareholder's derivative suit, or interpleader, is triable to a jury. This is a consequence of the merger and is utterly contrary to the practice of 1791.

The dissenters in *Beacon, Dairy Queen,* and *Ross* said that there is no limit to the process of breaking lawsuits down into issues. A specific performance suit raises contract issues that could be tried to a jury. The plurality in *Terry* says in footnote 6 that it doesn't intend to go that far. Can you define the difference between a legal claim joined with an equitable claim, a legal claim in an equitable procedure, and a legal element in an equitable claim?

5. Factual issues and legal issues. However that messy set of questions works out, do not confuse it with a different set: Even in legal claims triable to juries, factual issues are for the jury and legal issues are for the judge. The interpretation of a legal document is generally a legal issue, even if parole evidence is admitted to explain it. Thus, the interpretation of patent claims is for the judge, even in an infringement action triable to a jury. Markman v. Westview Instruments, 517 U.S. 370 (1996). On this issue too, the Court looked to analogous practice in 1791.

6. Issue preclusion. All the cases assume that the decision of the judge or jury, whichever comes first, will bind the other decision maker. The Court finally so held in Parklane Hosiery Co. v. Shore, 439 U.S. 322 (1979). But the rule is different if judicial error causes the equitable claim to be tried first. Trying the equitable claim first is not harmless error, and the only effective remedy is to vacate the judgment on both claims, try the legal claim to a jury, and then redetermine the equitable claim in light of the verdict. Lytle v. Household Manufacturing, Inc., 494 U.S. 545 (1990). *Lytle* was an employment discrimination claim filed in two counts, one for a legal remedy and one for an equitable remedy.

7. An exception for the government? Waivers of sovereign immunity almost never allow jury trial in consented suits against the government, and the Seventh Amendment does not apply. That is settled law, reaffirmed in Osborn v. Haley, 549 U.S. 225, 252 (2007). It is more speculative to suggest that the government also gets special treatment as plaintiff. But it might. Several cases have let the government avoid jury trial with arguments that probably would not have been available to a private litigant. The majority in *Terry* says that monetary relief "incidental to or intertwined with injunctive relief" may be equitable, citing dictum in Tull v. United States, 481 U.S. 412 (1987), and holding in Mitchell v. Robert DeMario Jewelry, 361 U.S. 288 (1960). *Mitchell* relied squarely on the equitable cleanup doctrine, repudiated the year before in *Beacon*. It also relied on rhetoric about the power of equity to enforce congressional policy. Both *Mitchell* and *Tull* were government enforcement actions, and nonjury monetary relief incidental to equitable relief may be limited to that context, although *Terry* quotes *Tull* in a case with two private litigants.

In *Tull*, the government sued to collect a civil penalty for filling in wetlands and for an injunction requiring Tull to restore the wetlands he had unlawfully filled in. The Court found the penalty claim most analogous to the common law action of debt, which was used to collect penalties in eighteenth-century England. It rejected the government's analogies to various equitable actions, and it rejected the claim that the penalty was incidental to the injunction. But the Court limited the jury trial to liability; it held that the jury need not fix the amount of the penalty. The Court noted that fixing the amount of the penalty required "highly discretionary calculations that take into account multiple factors," and such calculations were "traditionally performed by judges." 481 U.S. at 427.

8. Flirting with doctrinal disaster. *Tull*'s broader ground of decision was truly mind boggling: that the Seventh Amendment does not apply "to the remedy phase of a civil trial." *Id.* at 426 n.9. If the Court were serious, judges could determine damages in federal personal injury cases as long as juries determine liability, and there would be no constitutional limit on remittitur and additur.

The Court quietly buried the *Tull* dictum in Feltner v. Columbia Pictures Television, 523 U.S. 340 (1998). *Feltner* holds that the Seventh Amendment entitles either party to jury trial on the amount of statutory "in-lieu" damages under the Copyright Act, 17 U.S.C. §504(c). The current version of this provision authorizes plaintiff to recover, "instead of actual damages and profits, an award of statutory damages . . . in a sum of not less than $750 or more than $30,000 as the court considers just." The Court found it dispositive that similar discretionary damage provisions were tried to juries in the eighteenth century.

The Court did not mention *Tull*'s dictum that the Seventh Amendment does not apply to the remedy phase. But one substantial paragraph emphasized that damages have always been for the jury. 523 U.S. at 353-354. And the Court suggested some doubt about *Tull*'s holding on statutory penalties. *Id.* at 354 n.8, 355 n.9. For criticism of *Feltner* and defense of *Tull* (and of more aggressive review of jury verdicts), see Colleen P. Murphy, *Judicial Assessment of Legal Remedies*, 94 Nw. U. L. Rev. 153 (1999).

9. Practicality? Does it matter that jury trial is slower and more expensive, and that many federal judges consider civil juries a nuisance? The Seventh Amendment applies to all cases where the amount in controversy is over $20; it costs far more than that to empanel a jury. Is it legitimate to ignore or undermine the Seventh Amendment if we no longer think it's worth the trouble it causes? Do constitutional rights do any good if courts can pick and choose which ones to enforce?

Plaintiffs generally demand juries even in complex securities and antitrust cases where there is a substantial risk the jury will never understand the claim. Lawyers believe that juries are more likely to be influenced by sympathy for victims, and more likely to measure damages generously. In a few kinds of cases, it is defendants who prefer jury trial. Examples are individuals sued by large institutions, and police officers sued by suspected criminals. Litigators aren't always right about who will benefit from jury trial, but their generalizations have substantial basis in experience and at least some basis in empirical research. Aren't these expected advantages the substance of the constitutional right to jury trial? Is trial efficiency a sufficient reason to construe such a right narrowly? It's not much of a safeguard that judges trust themselves to be fair.

10. Juries in equity. One way to avoid the whole problem would be to try equity cases to juries. Several states have experimented with the practice; a few have declared it unconstitutional. The history is reviewed state by state in M.T. Van Hecke, *Trial by Jury in Equity Cases*, 31 N.C. L. Rev. 157 (1953). Equity cases are submitted on special verdicts or interrogatories, preserving issues of equitable discretion for the court. The line between fact and discretion is thin. In Texas, for example, whether there is a sufficient threat of future violations to justify an injunction is for the judge. State v. Texas Pet Foods, 591 S.W.2d 800 (Tex. 1979). The undue hardship defense—whether the cost of the injunction so far outweighs its benefits that relief should be denied—is also for the judge. Merrick v. Evergreen Helicopters, 649 S.W.2d 807 (Tex. Ct. App. 1983).

An alternative is to try equity cases to advisory juries. But this does not eliminate the need to characterize the case. If the verdict is advisory, the judge must enter her own findings of fact and conclusions of law. Fed. R. Civ. P. 52(a), and similar state rules. See Abner A. Wolf, Inc. v. Walch, 188 N.W.2d 544 (Mich. 1971), remanding for such findings. If a legal claim is mischaracterized as equitable and tried to an advisory jury, there is authority that the case must be retried; it is not a sufficient remedy to simply treat the advisory verdict as binding. Fischer Imaging Corp. v. General Electric Co., 187 F.3d 1165 (10th Cir. 1999).

NOTES ON CHARACTERIZING CLAIMS AS LEGAL OR EQUITABLE

1. The ERISA cases. The jurisdictional boundaries of 1791 do not track anyone's conception of sound policy about the scope of jury trial in the twenty-first century. The result has been a good bit of manipulation of the law-equity boundary, some of it result oriented, some of it just puzzling. Perhaps the most striking comparison is between *Terry* and a line of cases under the Employee Retirement Income Security Act, 29 U.S.C. §1132(a)(3), which authorizes "appropriate equitable relief."

a. *Mertens* and *Great West*. Mertens v. Hewitt Associates, 508 U.S. 248 (1993), was a suit against pension plan actuaries for causing the plan to be underfunded, and thus depriving retirees of their benefits. It was undisputed that a pension plan is a trust, that ERISA is modeled on trust law, and that premerger equity courts awarded compensation to trust beneficiaries from trustees and third parties who participated in a breach of trust. So plaintiffs and the United States argued that compensation from the actuaries was "appropriate equitable relief," just as Justice Kennedy argued in *Terry* that compensation from the union was equitable by analogy to trust law. Defendants in *Mertens* argued that plaintiffs were seeking damages, and whatever the practice in 1791, everyone knows that damages are a legal remedy. This was Justice Marshall's argument in *Terry*. The consequence of this argument in *Mertens* was that plaintiffs had no claim, because the statute does not authorize legal relief.

The majority in *Mertens*, like the majority in *Terry*, held that the trust context was irrelevant and that plaintiffs were really seeking damages. But four justices switched sides, two in each direction. A cynic might say that Scalia and Kennedy voted for no jury trial in *Terry* and no remedy at all in *Mertens*. But the same cynic would not say that Rehnquist and White had the opposite preferences, even though they cast the opposite votes.

Elsewhere in *Mertens*, the Court accepted the trust analogy to the extent of recognizing that plan members could recover illicit profits earned by plan fiduciaries at the expense of the plan, and that this would be "appropriate equitable relief." *Id.* at 260. This language became holding in Harris Trust & Savings Bank v. Salomon Smith Barney Inc., 530 U.S. 238 (2000). And the courts of appeals are in agreement that when a beneficiary sues "to recover benefits due to him under the terms of his plan," 29 U.S.C. §1132(a)(1)(B), he does not get a jury trial, because the plan is basically a trust and a suit to recover trust benefits is equitable. The cases are collected in Thomas v. Oregon Fruit Products Co., 228 F.3d 991, 996-997 (9th Cir. 2000). The trust analogy appears to be sometimes dispositive and sometimes irrelevant.

It gets stranger. Justice Scalia's opinion in *Mertens* said that lawyers were no longer familiar with the 1791 line between law and equity, so when Congress said "equitable relief," it probably did not use the phrase precisely. It probably meant "those categories of relief that were *typically* available in equity (such as injunction, mandamus, and restitution, but not compensatory damages)." This dictum came back to haunt him in Great-West Life & Annuity Insurance Co. v. Knudson, 534 U.S. 204 (2002), where a medical insurer sued the insured to recover its share of her personal injury recovery. Defendant did not actually have the money; it had been paid to her attorney and to a trust to pay for her future medical care. The requested relief was in restitution, but even so, the Court held that it was legal, not equitable, for plausible reasons that will not make much sense until you are introduced to restitution in section 8.A.1. Some restitutionary remedies were created in the law courts, and others in the equity courts. Again Justice Scalia wrote for the Court, explaining that this restitution claim was more like assumpsit (legal) than constructive trust (equitable). He explained that *Mertens* had not involved restitution at all, and so it had not required him to attend to "this fine distinction" within restitution.

The dissenters thought he was right the first time; it should be enough that restitution is often equitable, and Congress did not have the faintest idea of the difference between assumpsit and constructive trust. They would have read the limitation to "appropriate equitable relief" simply to exclude consequential and punitive damages. They belittled Scalia's "rarefied" distinction, but Justice Marshall had made a quite similar point in part III.B of *Terry*, when he distinguished the claim for lost wages (damages) from a claim for "money wrongfully held" by defendant or for "disgorgement of improper profits" (both restitutionary). At least in *Great-West* we can recognize the lineup. Justices Stevens, Souter, Ginsburg, and Breyer voted for the corporate plaintiff, and Justices Rehnquist, O'Connor, Scalia, Kennedy, and Thomas voted for the injured employee-spouse defendant. This may superficially run counter to the justices' presumed sympathies, but not when you see that they had turned it into another ideological battle about the scope of federal equity.

b. Reconsidering *Great-West*. Relying on dictum in Sereboff v. Mid Atlantic Medical Services, Inc., 547 U.S. 356 (2006), six of eight circuits to consider the issue had allowed claims to general assets, claims apparently barred by *Great-West*. But the Court reaffirmed *Great-West* in Board of Trustees of the National Elevator Industry Health Benefit Plan v. Montanile, 136 S. Ct. 651 (2016), more fully described in section 2.E.2.

c. *CIGNA*. There is another elaborate discussion of ERISA remedies in CIGNA Corp. v. Amara, 563 U.S. 421 (2011). For any change in retirement plans, the plan administrator is required to disclose the changes to the employees in comprehensible form in a plan summary. When CIGNA made substantial changes to its plan, its disclosures assured the employees that CIGNA was saving no money from these changes and that no employee would be worse off because of them. In fact, the company was saving $10 million a year, and most employees were made worse off in multiple ways. The company could have imposed these changes without consent after full disclosure, but that might have caused employee unrest.

The lower courts held that they could enforce the retirement plan as it would have been if it had conformed to the disclosures, and that they could do this under 29 U.S.C. §1132(a)(1)(B), which authorizes suits by beneficiaries to enforce plans. But the Supreme Court held that this section authorized enforcement only of the plan as written, and that the disclosures were not part of the plan. The district court had also noted the possibility of "other appropriate equitable relief" under §1132(a)(3). The Supreme Court remanded for further consideration of this theory, with a substantial analysis suggesting that what the district court had done "closely resembles three other traditional equitable remedies." *Id.* at 440.

First, it might be reformation of the plan. Reformation, taken up in section 7.C, judicially amends documents to conform to the parties' mutual understanding of what the documents said or to what one side fraudulently represented that they said.

Second, it might be estoppel, which prevents a party from denying now what he earlier represented as true. This book treats estoppel as a remedial defense in section 11.C; the Court also, and plausibly, treated it as an equitable remedy.

And third, the district court's order of back benefits to employees who had already retired might be a "surcharge" of the trustee of the retirement plan, the traditional equitable label for actions to recover money or property due under a trust. Here, the trust analogy again appeared to be dispositive.

And while detrimental reliance was an element of estoppel, it was not an element of reformation or surcharge. So the plan could be reformed, and the trustee surcharged under the plan as reformed, without a showing that the employees could have done anything different if they had received proper disclosures. Whether those remedies were appropriate on the facts of the case was left for the district court on remand, but the Supreme Court's view seemed pretty clear. Justices Scalia and Thomas thought the entire analysis of §1132(a)(3) was an advisory opinion that should not have been issued.

d. Implementing *CIGNA*. On remand in *CIGNA*, the lower courts reformed the plan for fraud and mistake, and ordered benefits paid under the plan as reformed. Amara v. CIGNA Corp., 775 F.3d 510 (2d Cir. 2014). At least eight circuits have recognized estoppel claims in the wake of *CIGNA*, often in cases involving individual claimants who were promised benefits they never got. These cases are collected in Guerra-Delgado v. Popular, Inc., 774 F.3d 776 (1st Cir. 2014). The First Circuit did not follow the trend. It will recognize an estoppel claim, if ever, only when the written plan is ambiguous, and so far, it has not found an ambiguous plan. The Ninth Circuit has also limited *CIGNA* to narrow circumstances.

2. Back pay in Title VII. The previously unexamined view that restitution is equitable has been decisive in employment discrimination suits under Title VII of the Civil Rights Act of 1964. Title VII authorizes injunctions against discrimination, and such "affirmative action as may be appropriate, which may include . . . reinstatement . . . with or without back pay" and any "other equitable relief" the court "deems appropriate." 42 U.S.C. §2000e-5(g). The lower courts have uniformly concluded that back pay under this provision is a form of equitable restitution. But the essential element of a restitution claim is missing: Plaintiff performed no work, so the employer got no benefit and is not unjustly enriched by not paying plaintiff any wages. And if we strong-arm our way past that obstacle and declare back pay to be restitutionary, this claim would more plausibly be legal restitution than equitable restitution.

But Congress feared, and the courts have feared, that jury trials would nullify the statute. That might not be true today, but it would have been true in much of the country in 1964. The statutory talk of equitable relief was a deliberate attempt to avoid jury trial, recognized as such at the time; one of the arguments against the statute was that it eroded the right to jury trial. The Supreme Court has never decided whether this effort to avoid jury trial succeeded, but after more than 50 years and repeated explanations of the lower court practice in Supreme Court dicta, it is reasonable to consider the matter settled.

Is it legitimate to let Congress evade the Seventh Amendment in this way? The Amendment was aimed as much at Congress as at the judiciary; its supporters feared that Congress would entrust the enforcement of unpopular laws to courts without juries. Charles W. Wolfram, *The Constitutional History of the Seventh Amendment*, 57 Minn. L. Rev. 639, 664-665, 706-707 (1973). Isn't that exactly what Congress did, and consciously so, in the Civil Rights Act of 1964? Is there implied authorization for such evasion in the enforcement provisions of the Thirteenth, Fourteenth, and Fifteenth Amendments? If constitutional rights in a democracy are intended to protect minorities from oppressive majorities, how can juries be expected to enforce constitutional rights? Can the Seventh Amendment be reconciled with the others by the power to enforce constitutional rights by injunction and the power to set aside jury verdicts that are unsupported by the evidence?

3. Damages in employment discrimination cases. Civil rights plaintiffs paid a price for avoiding jury trial: Back pay was the only monetary remedy available under Title VII. Because the statute didn't authorize damages, plaintiffs couldn't recover consequential damages, punitive damages, or damages for emotional distress. Does that make the provision constitutional, by proving that it isn't really a damage remedy in disguise?

There is a long-standing alternative remedy for the full range of damages in race cases under the Civil Rights Act of 1866, 42 U.S.C. §1981, and cases under this provision have always been tried to juries. In the Civil Rights Act of 1991, Congress authorized damages for intentional discrimination in nonrace cases brought under Title VII, and it authorized jury trials if plaintiff claims damages. 42 U.S.C. §1981a. But these Title VII damages are capped at amounts ranging from $50,000 to $300,000, depending on the size of the employer. Congress in 1964 feared jury nullification; Congress in 1991 feared excessive verdicts. The presumed bias has been reversed, but mistrust of juries is a constant.

The damage cap in §1981a applies only to money that could not be recovered under the original provisions of Title VII. The Court has now confirmed that what has come to be known as "front pay"—pay for the period after judgment and before reinstatement, or before plaintiff finds another job if reinstatement is not ordered—is available under Title VII and thus not subject to the cap in §1981a. Pollard v. E.I. du Pont de Nemours & Co., 532 U.S. 843 (2001). This holding was based on reasonably clear statutory language and not on any distinction between law and equity. But the implication would seem to be, and the lower courts have held, that front pay is equitable relief in lieu of reinstatement.

4. Section 1983 cases. The Court has held, unsurprisingly, that suits under 42 U.S.C. §1983, for damages caused by violations of federal rights under color of state law, are tort suits triable to a jury. City of Monterey v. Del Monte Dunes, 526 U.S. 687 (1999). That had been the universal practice. The Supreme Court took up the issue because of a novel application—a suit against a city for damages caused by land use regulation that violated the Takings Clause. Four dissenters would have analogized the claim not to tort, but to condemnation and inverse condemnation (the usual procedure by which a landowner sues for compensation in the courts of the government that took his land). They thought that these were unusual actions at law not triable to juries. The plurality thought that they were not analogous, because the §1983 claim lies only if the state refuses a remedy in inverse condemnation. Justice Scalia concurred on the ground that the Court should make one rule for all §1983 cases and make no analogies to the underlying constitutional violation.

5. *Dairy Queen* and the profits of infringing intellectual property. There is a lively debate about the right to jury trial when plaintiff sues to recover defendant's profits from an infringement of copyrights, trademarks, or trade secrets. It will be much easier to understand the arguments after you know more about restitution; we will briefly consider that debate in section 8.B.1.

NOTES ON SPECIALIZED TRIBUNALS

1. Administrative agencies. Congress also has broad power to commit claims to administrative agencies without juries. The rationale has varied somewhat over the

years. But the leading case rests on the recurring view that actions before administrative agencies are not suits at common law, so the Seventh Amendment is simply
irrelevant. Atlas Roofing Co. v. Occupational Safety & Health Review Commission,
430 U.S. 442 (1977). On that rationale, can't Congress avoid jury trial at will by committing everything to agencies instead of courts? No, the Court said:

> Our prior cases support administrative factfinding in only those situations involving
> "public rights," e.g., where the Government is involved in its sovereign capacity under
> an otherwise valid statute creating enforceable public rights. Wholly private tort, con-
> tract, and property cases, as well as a vast range of other cases, are not at all implicated.

Id. at 458.

Even so, it has been hard to find any limit to the concept of public rights. Back
pay to individual workers under the National Labor Relations Act is a public right,
presumably because the Board brings suit on the worker's behalf. NLRB v. Jones
& Laughlin Steel Corp., 301 U.S. 1, 48-49 (1937). Can Congress make any private
right public by providing that the action be brought in the name of the agency?
Compensation of injured workers is often entrusted to administrative agencies; how is
that different from "wholly private tort" cases? And *Atlas Roofing* repeats the dictum of
Pernell v. Southall Realty, 416 U.S. 363, 383 (1974): "We may assume that the Seventh
Amendment would not be a bar to a congressional effort to entrust landlord-tenant
disputes, including those over the right to possession, to an administrative agency."
Laycock's colleagues in administrative law—at Texas, Michigan, and Virginia—view
Atlas Roofing's "public rights" dictum as wholly inconsistent with modern administra-
tive law.

2. Compulsory arbitration. The Court upheld a statute requiring arbitration of
compensation claims arising when one manufacturer of pesticides forces another to
share proprietary data on health, safety, and environmental effects. Thomas v. Union
Carbide Agricultural Products Co., 473 U.S. 568 (1985). The Court held that disputes
between private litigants on federal claims do not require Article III courts, at least
if the matter could have been decided by an agency. The whole opinion took a dim
view of the public rights doctrine. There was no jury trial claim in the case, but that
presumably doesn't matter. Having held that the case is subject to compulsory arbitration, the Court would surely say the arbitration proceeding is not a suit at common
law and thus not subject to the Seventh Amendment.

3. Bankruptcy courts. The bankruptcy courts have presented recurring jury trial
issues. The Court seems to view them as more than an administrative agency but
less than a court. Bankruptcy judges serve without life tenure, and technically they
are "adjuncts" to district courts, with resulting limits on their jurisdiction. 28 U.S.C.
§§151, 157. The nearest historical equivalents to bankruptcy were equitable. Most
claims against the debtor or his trustee, most disputes among creditors who file
claims, and most counterclaims against creditors who file claims may be adjudicated
in the bankruptcy proceeding, without an Article III judge and without a jury.

But claims cannot be resolved in this way if they are not part of the equitable process of determining claims against the bankrupt estate.

4. Claims against parties who did not file in the bankruptcy case. Granfinanciera
S.A. v. Nordberg, 492 U.S. 33 (1989), involved claims on behalf of the debtor's estate
against defendants who had not filed a claim in the bankruptcy proceeding. The
trustee in bankruptcy sued Granfinanciera to recover a fraudulent transfer of the
debtor's property. The Court said the fraudulent transfer claim was a right long known
to the common law, and Congress could not make it public merely by assigning it to

another tribunal. At one point the Court said the test is whether a claim is "so closely integrated into a public regulatory scheme as to be a matter appropriate for agency resolution," citing *Thomas*, described in note 2. At another point, the Court said that Congress can create new public rights that are closely analogous to common law rights, but it implied that Congress could do so only where "traditional rights and remedies were inadequate to cope with a manifest public problem." This was not such a case. All of this would seem to imply that the fraudulent transfer claim could not be heard in the bankruptcy court at all, even if the bankruptcy judge empanels a jury. But the Court said it was not deciding that issue.

5. Greater content for public rights? The restriction to public rights got some new life in Stern v. Marshall, 564 U.S. 462 (2011). This was part of the long-running litigation by and on behalf of Anna Nicole Smith to recover her share of the estate of the fabulously wealthy husband she married when she was 26 and he was 89.

She filed for bankruptcy, and her deceased husband's son filed a defamation claim against her in the bankruptcy court. That was clearly part of the bankruptcy case, because it was a claim against the bankrupt estate. Smith filed a counterclaim for tortious interfering with the gift her husband had allegedly intended to make to her. The question in the Supreme Court was whether her counterclaim could be adjudicated in the bankruptcy court. The Court said no.

Earlier cases were explained as cases of a counterclaim that was based on bankruptcy law and that could be adjudicated in the course of adjudicating the creditor's claim. Smith's state-law tort claim was not based on bankruptcy law. And although it was sufficiently related to her stepson's claim that the lower courts had held it to be a compulsory counterclaim, it presented significant issues of law and fact not presented by the stepson's claim. (Try not to be confused by the fact that the stepson was nearly 30 years older than his stepmother).

Recognizing that its discussions of "the public rights exception" had "not been entirely consistent," the Court held that Smith's common law tort claim was not a claim of public right. "[W]hat makes a right 'public' rather than private is that the right is integrally related to particular federal government action." *Id.* at 490-91. The Court considered several other factors mentioned in earlier public-right cases, and said that Smith's claim did not satisfy any of them. It also emphasized that bankruptcy courts are courts (although not Article III courts), and that they decide a broad range of issues, so they are unlike administrative agencies with special expertise. So the administrative-agency cases might be different from the bankruptcy cases.

Justice Scalia, concurring, thought the long list of factors from earlier cases was wholly unworkable. He would have held, quoting his concurring opinion in *Granfianciera*, that "a matter of public rights . . . must at a minimum arise between the government and others." *Id.* at 503.

Justice Breyer, dissenting for himself and Justices Ginsburg, Sotomayor, and Kagan, thought the majority's opinion was entirely too formalistic, and that it relied too much on older cases and gave little weight to more recent cases. He would have held that even private disputes can be committed to non-Article-III tribunals sitting without juries if there is no threat to the independence of the judiciary. Letting bankruptcy courts adjudicate counterclaims was constitutional, even as applied to common law tort claims like the one at issue here, because of a list of practical considerations that bore little resemblance to the majority's list of factors.

6. Patent validity. Patents are granted in a non-adversary administrative process. Under longstanding law, a party challenging the validity of a patent had to sue in court and overcome a strong presumption of validity. In 2012, under the curious label "inter partes review" (literally, among-the-parties review), Congress provided that some of the basic grounds for challenging patents could be asserted in an administrative adversary proceeding before the Patent and Trademark Appeal Board. 35 U.S.C. §311. The Court upheld this procedure in an opinion by Justice Thomas. Oil States Energy Services, LLC v. Greene's Energy Group, LLC, 138 S. Ct. 1365 (2018). The Court said that a patent is clearly a public right, granted by the government and revocable by the government in an administrative proceeding outside the Article III courts. And because the revocation proceeding didn't have to be in court, it did not require a jury trial. Justice Gorsuch dissented, joined by Chief Justice Roberts. They argued that a patent once granted is a property right, which for some purposes it clearly is, and that it deserved the protection of adjudication by judges independent of the executive branch.

CHAPTER

7

Preventing Harm Without Coercion: Declaratory Remedies

A.   DECLARATORY JUDGMENTS

1.   *The General Case*

NASHVILLE, CHATTANOOGA, & ST. LOUIS RAILWAY v. WALLACE
288 U.S. 249 (1933)

Justice STONE delivered the opinion of the Court.

Appellant brought suit in the Chancery Court of Davidson County, Tennessee, under the Uniform Declaratory Judgments Act of that state, to secure a judicial declaration that a state excise tax levied on the storage of gasoline is, as applied to appellant, invalid under the Commerce Clause and the Fourteenth Amendment of the federal Constitution. A decree for appellees was affirmed by the Supreme Court of the State, and the case comes here on appeal. . . .

[T]his Court . . . invited the attention of counsel to the question "whether a case or controversy is presented in view of the nature of the proceedings in the state court.". . . [T]he judicial power with which this Court is invested by article III §1 of the Constitution, extends by article III §2, only to "cases" and "controversies"; if no "case" or "controversy" is presented for decision, we are without power to review the decree of the court below.

In determining whether this litigation presents a case within the appellate jurisdiction of this Court, we are concerned, not with form, but with substance. Hence, we look not to the label which the legislature has attached to the procedure followed in the state courts, or to the description of the judgment which is brought here for review, in popular parlance, as "declaratory," but to the nature of the proceeding which the statute authorizes, and the effect of the judgment rendered upon the rights which the appellant asserts.

Section 1 of the Tennessee Declaratory Judgments Act confers jurisdiction on courts of record "to declare rights . . . whether or not further relief is or could be claimed" and provides that "no action or proceeding shall be open to objection on the ground that a declaratory judgment or decree is prayed for. The declaration may be either affirmative or negative in form and effect and such declaration shall have the force and effect of a final judgment or decree." By §2 it is provided that "any person . . . whose rights, status or other legal relations are affected by a statute . . . may have determined any question of construction or validity arising under the . . . statute . . . and obtain a declaration of rights . . . thereunder."

Under §6, the Court may refuse to render a declaratory judgment where, if rendered, it "would not terminate the uncertainty or controversy giving rise to the proceeding." Declaratory judgments may, in accordance with §7, be reviewed as are other orders, judgments or decrees, and under §8 "further relief based on a declaratory judgment or decree may be granted whenever necessary or proper." Section 11 requires that "when declaratory relief is sought all persons shall be made parties who have or claim any interest which would be affected by the declaration, and no declaration shall prejudice the rights of persons not parties to the proceeding."

This statute has often been considered by the highest court of Tennessee, which has consistently held that its provisions may only be invoked when the complainant asserts rights which are challenged by the defendant, and presents for decision an actual controversy to which he is a party, capable of final adjudication by the judgment or decree to be rendered. . . .

Proceeding in accordance with this statute, appellant filed its bill of complaint in the state Chancery Court, joining as defendants . . . the Attorney General and the state officials charged with the duty of collecting the gasoline privilege tax imposed by the Tennessee statute. [The state taxed gasoline stored in Tennessee; the railroad alleged that this tax burdened interstate commerce, because the gasoline was used both within and without the state.] The relief prayed was that the taxing act be declared unconstitutional as applied to appellant. [The state courts upheld the tax on the merits.]

That the issues thus raised and judicially determined would constitute a case or controversy if raised and decided in a suit brought by the taxpayer to enjoin collection of the tax cannot be questioned. The proceeding terminating in the decree below was between adverse parties, seeking a determination of their legal rights upon the facts alleged in the bill and admitted by the demurrer. . . . [V]aluable legal rights[,] asserted by the complainant and threatened with imminent invasion by appellees, will be directly affected to a specific and substantial degree by the decision of the question of law; the question lends itself to judicial determination and is of the kind which this Court traditionally decides. The relief sought is a definitive adjudication of the disputed constitutional right of the appellant, in the circumstances alleged, to be free from the tax, and that adjudication is not subject to revision by some other and more authoritative agency. Obviously the appellant, whose duty to pay the tax will be determined by the decision of this case, is not attempting to secure an abstract determination by the Court of the validity of a statute or a decision advising what the law would be on an uncertain or hypothetical state of facts. Thus the narrow question presented for determination is whether the controversy before us, which would be justiciable in this Court if presented in a suit for injunction, is any the less so because through a modified procedure appellant has been permitted to present it in the state courts, without praying for an injunction or alleging that irreparable injury will result from the collection of the tax.

While the ordinary course of judicial procedure results in a judgment requiring an award of process or execution to carry it into effect, such relief is not an indispensable adjunct to the exercise of the judicial function. This Court has often exerted its judicial power to adjudicate boundaries between states, although it gave no injunction or other relief beyond the determination of the legal rights which were the subject of controversy between the parties, and to review judgments of the Court of

Claims, although no process issues against the Government. As we said in Fidelity National Bank v. Swope, 274 U.S. 123, 132 (1927),

> Naturalization proceedings, suits to determine a matrimonial or other status, suits for instruction to a trustee or for the construction of a will, bills of interpleader, so far as the stakeholder is concerned, bills to quiet title where the plaintiff rests his claim on adverse possession, are familiar examples of judicial proceedings which result in an adjudication of the rights of litigants, although execution is not necessary to carry the judgment into effect, in the sense that no damages are required to be paid or acts to be performed by the parties.

The issues raised here are the same as those which under old forms of procedure could be raised only in a suit for an injunction or one to recover the tax after its payment. But the Constitution does not require that the case or controversy should be presented by traditional forms of procedure, invoking only traditional remedies. The judiciary clause of the Constitution defined and limited judicial power, not the particular method by which that power might be invoked. It did not crystallize into changeless form the procedure of 1789 as the only possible means for presenting a case or controversy otherwise cognizable by the federal courts. Whenever the judicial power is invoked to review a judgment of a state court, the ultimate constitutional purpose is the protection, by the exercise of the judicial function, of rights arising under the Constitution and laws of the United States. The states are left free to regulate their own judicial procedure. Hence, changes merely in the form or method of procedure by which federal rights are brought to final adjudication in the state courts are not enough to preclude review of the adjudication by this Court, so long as the case retains the essentials of an adversary proceeding, involving a real, not a hypothetical controversy, which is finally determined by the judgment below. As the prayer for relief by injunction is not a necessary prerequisite to the exercise of judicial power, allegations of threatened irreparable injury which are material only if an injunction is asked, may likewise be dispensed with if, in other respects, the controversy presented is, as in this case real, and substantial. . . . Accordingly, we must consider the constitutional questions raised by the appeal. [On the merits, the Court upheld the tax.]
    Affirmed.

NOTES ON DECLARATORY JUDGMENTS AND RIPENESS

1. The federal act. The Uniform Act has been very widely adopted in the states. Congress responded to *Wallace* by enacting the federal Declaratory Judgment Act in 1934, loosely based on §§1 and 8 of the Uniform Act (both quoted in *Wallace*). 28 U.S.C. §§2201-2202. The federal act explicitly requires an "actual controversy" and does not authorize declarations of status. *Id.* at §2201(a). It was upheld against constitutional attack in Aetna Life Insurance Co. v. Haworth, 300 U.S. 227 (1937), in which the insurer sought a declaration that four policies had lapsed for nonpayment. The insured had claimed benefits under a clause that waived premiums if he became disabled, but he had not sued on the policies, and the insurer denied that he was disabled. The Court said that the statute and the Constitution used "controversy" in the same sense, and that "actual" was in the statute for emphasis only, so that the statute enacted the constitutional ripeness requirement.

2. An unripe complaint. Public Service Commission v. Wycoff Co., 344 U.S. 237 (1952), contains the classic description of an unripe declaratory judgment action.

Wycoff sought a declaration that its hauling business was interstate commerce. The Court said:

> The complainant in this case does not request an adjudication that it has a right to do, or to have, anything in particular. It does not ask a judgment that the Commission is without power to enter any specific order or take any concrete regulatory step. It seeks simply to establish that, as presently conducted, respondent's carriage of goods between points within as well as without Utah is all interstate commerce. One naturally asks, "So what?"

Id. at 244. This appears to more accurately describe plaintiff's inept pleadings than the underlying dispute. Wycoff argued that its role in interstate commerce exempted it from the authority of the commission. The commission disagreed, and it had threatened to shut Wycoff down for lack of an intrastate hauling license, which it had refused to grant. The majority found no evidence that the commission was about to act on its threat. And it thought that if the commission ever did act, the facts might have changed so that any declaration the Court issued would have become obsolete without resolving the dispute. Justices Douglas and Reed both found a clear controversy.

3. Drawing the line. Are you convinced that there is a difference of constitutional significance between *Wycoff* and *Wallace*? Section 12 of the Uniform Act says that the Act's purpose is "to settle and to afford relief from uncertainty and insecurity with respect to rights, status and other legal relations." Unif. Declaratory Judgment Act, §12, 12A Unif. Laws Ann. 752 (2008). Isn't the declaratory judgment plaintiff most in need of relief from uncertainty when the party who would normally initiate the litigation delays doing so? Even so, courts shouldn't grant declaratory judgments to resolve law professors' hypotheticals. A line must be drawn, but it should not surprise you to learn that the line has never been consistent. Especially when ripeness turns on the likelihood that defendant will assert the rights that plaintiff is challenging, or on the political considerations that underlie the case or controversy requirement, the ripeness doctrine is amorphous and unpredictable. For further analysis and examples, see Steffel v. Thompson and the notes following it in section 7.A.2.

4. Revisiting earlier examples. Reconsider the ripeness cases in Chapter 4. Would it have mattered to those cases if plaintiffs had sought declaratory judgments instead of injunctions? Could the prisoners in Guantánamo have gotten a declaratory judgment that the government was not entitled to transfer them to countries where they might be tortured? Was there an actual controversy if the court didn't believe the government intended any such transfers? What about Nicholson v. Connecticut Half-Way House? Could the court have declared anything useful?

5. Terminating the uncertainty. Section 6 of the Uniform Act says the declaratory judgment may be denied if it "would not terminate the uncertainty or controversy giving rise to the proceeding." Is that a functional test that gives some content to the ripeness requirement?

A good example of a §6 case is Dodson v. Maroney, 447 N.E.2d 1256 (Mass. App. Ct. 1983). Plaintiff sought a declaratory judgment that Mae Askling's will was invalid for undue influence and lack of testamentary capacity. Mae Askling was still alive. The court said the controversy could not be resolved, because she could revoke the will and write another at any time. It also said that no "exceptional circumstance" justified litigation before the usual opportunity for a will contest following Askling's death.

What if Askling sued for a declaratory judgment that her will was valid? What if she alleged that she would not be around to testify and let the judge observe her sound mind when the time for a will contest arrived? Arkansas, Ohio, and North Dakota authorize such suits by express statute, but the statutes are controversial and apparently little used. The statutes and the controversy are briefly described in Thomas P. Gallanis, *Family Property Law: Cases and Materials on Wills, Trusts and Estates* 213 (6th ed., Foundation 2014). Probate lawyers and scholars apparently assume that a general declaratory judgment act does not override a lack of authorization for such a suit in the probate code.

NOTES ON DECLARATORY JUDGMENTS, IRREPARABLE INJURY, AND SUPPLEMENTAL RELIEF

1. Comparing declaratory judgments and simple preventive injunctions. Is there any practical difference between a declaratory judgment that the tax is unconstitutional and an injunction ordering the state authorities not to collect the tax? Both remedies are designed to protect plaintiff from having to pay the tax. The injunction would include a personal command; the declaratory judgment would not. How significant is that?

2. Negating the irreparable injury rule. As *Wallace* notes, plaintiff need not show irreparable injury to get a declaratory judgment. The only reference to other remedies in the Uniform Act is §1, which says courts can declare rights "whether or not further relief is or could be claimed." 12 Unif. Laws Ann. 336 (2008). The Federal Rules are more explicit: "The existence of another adequate remedy does not preclude a declaratory judgment that is otherwise appropriate." Fed. R. Civ. P. 57. There are occasional decisions applying an irreparable injury rule anyway, but *Wallace* states the overwhelmingly dominant view.

If declaratory relief serves the same preventive functions as coercive relief, should the same irreparable injury rule apply to both kinds of remedy? Do the declaratory judgment acts indirectly repeal the irreparable injury rule, at least for simple preventive injunctions, by providing a functionally equivalent remedy to which the rule does not apply? Are there any surviving reasons for the irreparable injury rule that apply to preventive injunctions but not to declaratory judgments?

3. Supplemental relief. Suppose the railroad had won on the merits in *Wallace*, that defendants had ignored the declaratory judgment, and that the railroad had sought an injunction under §8, which says that "further relief based on a declaratory judgment or decree may be granted whenever necessary or proper." Should the railroad have to show irreparable injury then? Should it be enough that defendants' defiance of the declaratory judgment threatened a multiplicity of suits?

Supplemental relief can also be compensation for damages caused by failure to comply with the declaratory judgment. An example is Horn & Hardart Co. v. National Rail Passenger Corp., 843 F.2d 546 (D.C. Cir. 1988), where a tenant refused to vacate leased space despite a declaratory judgment that the landlord had validly terminated the lease.

4. When is a declaratory judgment "appropriate"? Even without an irreparable injury rule, the existence of other remedies is not wholly irrelevant. When is a declaratory judgment "appropriate" under Rule 57? Doesn't plaintiff have to show some need to have her uncertainty relieved? How different is that from irreparable injury, properly understood? Whatever the answer to that question, there is at least a psychological difference. "Irreparable injury" has a more formidable ring than "uncertainty." The proponents of declaratory judgment acts argued that declaratory judgments would be available where injunctions were not.

5. Claim and issue preclusion. A declaratory judgment has "the force and effect of a final judgment or decree." 28 U.S.C. §2201(a); Unif. Act §1. A declaratory judgment is therefore issue preclusive in subsequent litigation with respect to all issues actually decided. The cases are collected in Annotation, 10 A.L.R.2d 782 (1950 & Supp.).

Claim preclusion is a bit different, because of the statutory provisions for supplemental relief. A request for such further relief is not barred because it was not included in the original request for declaratory judgment. But this rule has limits. If the initial action sought more than just a declaratory judgment, most courts hold that all related relief should have been sought at the same time. An example is Mycogen Corp. v. Monsanto Co., 51 P.3d 297 (Cal. 2002), where, in the first case, plaintiff got a declaratory judgment that it had validly exercised an option and a decree ordering specific performance of the resulting contract. It could not thereafter file a second suit for damages for breach of the same contract. *Mycogen* also collects some cases going the other way.

An original claim that included more than declaratory relief should not bar supplemental relief that becomes necessary only because the loser refuses to comply with the declaratory judgment. The issue is noted but not decided in *Horn & Hardart* in note 3.

CARDINAL CHEMICAL CO. v. MORTON INTERNATIONAL, INC.

508 U.S. 83 (1993)

Justice STEVENS delivered the opinion of the Court. . . .

Morton International . . . is the owner of two patents on chemical compounds used in polyvinyl chloride. . . . In 1983 Morton filed this action in the United States District Court for the District of South Carolina alleging that petitioners, Cardinal Chemical Co. and its affiliates . . . , had infringed those patents. Cardinal filed an answer denying infringement and a counterclaim for a declaratory judgment that the patents are invalid. While this case was pending in the District Court, Morton filed two other actions against other alleged infringers of the same patents. . . . The defendants in both cases, like Cardinal, filed counterclaims for declaratory judgments that the patents were invalid. . . . [T]he Louisiana case was tried first and, in 1988, resulted in a judgment for the defendant finding no infringement and declaring the patents invalid. On appeal, the Federal Circuit affirmed the finding of no infringement but vacated the judgment of invalidity [without deciding the merits]. The Delaware case is still pending. . . .

The South Carolina District Court concluded, as had the Louisiana District Court, that the patentee had failed to prove infringement and that the defendant-counterclaimant had proved by clear and convincing evidence that both patents were invalid [because the patent failed to describe the chemical structure with sufficient precision for others in the industry either to use it or to avoid infringing it]. Accordingly, the Court mandated two separate judgments: one dismissing the action for infringement with prejudice, and another on the counterclaim, declaring the patents invalid.

Again, Morton appealed to the Federal Circuit, challenging both the dismissal of its infringement claim and the judgment of invalidity. Cardinal filed a cross-appeal contending that it was entitled to an award of fees . . . and that Morton should be sanctioned for prosecuting a frivolous appeal. . . . Again, however, after affirming the dismissal of the infringement claim, the Federal Circuit vacated the declaratory judgment. 959 F.2d 948 (Fed. Cir. 1992). . . .

Cardinal filed a petition for certiorari asserting that the Federal Circuit errs in applying a per se rule to what should be a discretionary matter. Morton did not oppose the grant of certiorari, but instead pointed out that it also had an interest in having the validity issue adjudicated.[9] It explained that, after the Federal Circuit had twice refused substantive review of findings that its two patents were invalid, the patents have been effectively stripped of any power in the marketplace.

> If Morton were to proceed against another infringer, the district court, in all like-lihood, would accept the twice-vacated invalidity holdings, just as the district court below adopted wholesale the [Louisiana] district court's invalidity holdings, without any independent evaluation as to whether those holdings were correct. Further, any future accused infringer would, in all likelihood, argue for an award of attorney's fees as Cardinal has done here, on the ground that Morton should have known better than [to] sue on an "invalid patent". . . .
>
> The value of Morton's patents is therefore essentially zero. . . . [Morton] has lost valu-able property rights . . . without due process of law.

Morton's Brief 16-17. . . .

II

In Electrical Fittings Corp. v. Thomas & Betts Co., 307 U.S. 241 (1939), the District Court held one claim of a patent valid but not infringed. . . . [T]he successful defen-dant appealed. . . . We . . . held that although the defendant could not compel the appellate court to revisit the finding of validity (which had become immaterial to the disposition of the case), it could demand that the finding of validity be vacated.

[This holding is similar to the Federal Circuit practice, but it is also] critically dif-ferent. The issue of invalidity in *Electrical Fittings* was raised only as an affirmative defense to the charge that a presumptively valid patent had been infringed, not (. . . as here) as a basis for a counterclaim seeking a declaratory judgment of patent invalidity. An unnecessary ruling on an affirmative defense is not the same as the nec-essary resolution of a counterclaim for a declaratory judgment.

In Altvater v. Freeman, 319 U.S. 359 (1943), as here, the defendant *did* file a coun-terclaim seeking a declaratory judgment that the patent was invalid. The District Court found no infringement, but also granted the declaratory judgment requested by the defendant. . . . Distinguishing our holding in *Electrical Fittings*, we wrote:

> To hold a patent valid if it is not infringed is to decide a hypothetical case. But . . . [w]e have here not only bill and answer but a counterclaim. Though the decision of non-infringement disposes of the bill and answer, it does not dispose of the counter-claim which raises the question of validity. . . . The requirements of a case or contro-versy are of course no less strict under the Declaratory Judgments Act than in case of other suits. But we are of the view that the issues raised by the present counterclaim were justiciable and that the controversy between the parties did not come to an end on the dismissal of the bill for non-infringement, since their dispute went beyond the single claim and the particular accused devices involved in that suit.

Id. at 363-364.

---

9. . . . Although both Morton and Cardinal do agree on the correct answer to the question presented, they do so only so that they can reach their true dispute: the validity of Morton's two patents, a subject on which they are in absolute disagreement. Further, it is clear that no collusion between the parties has brought them here. . . . The Federal Circuit's improper finding of mootness cannot itself moot this case.

Presumably because we emphasized . . . the ongoing nature of the *Altvater* parties' dispute, the Federal Circuit has assumed that a defendant's counterclaim under the Declaratory Judgment Act should always be vacated unless the parties' dispute extends beyond the terms of the patentee's charge of infringement. . . .

III

Under its current practice, the Federal Circuit uniformly declares that the issue of patent validity is "moot" if it affirms the District Court's finding of noninfringement and if, as in the usual case, the dispute between the parties does not extend beyond the patentee's particular claim of infringement. . . . In the trial court, of course, a party seeking a declaratory judgment has the burden of establishing the existence of an actual case or controversy.[17]

In patent litigation, a party may satisfy that burden, and seek a declaratory judgment, even if the patentee has not filed an infringement action. Judge Markey has described

> the sad and saddening scenario that led to enactment of the Declaratory Judgment Act. In the patent version of that scenario, a patent owner engages in a danse macabre, brandishing a Damoclean threat with a sheathed sword. . . . Before the Act, competitors victimized by that tactic were rendered helpless and immobile so long as the patent owner refused to grasp the nettle and sue. After the Act, those competitors were no longer restricted to an in terrorem choice between the incurrence of a growing potential liability for patent infringement and abandonment of their enterprises; they could clear the air by suing for a judgment that would settle the conflict of interests. The sole requirement for jurisdiction under the Act is that the conflict be real and immediate, i.e., that there be a true, actual "controversy" required by the Act.[*]

Arrowhead Industrial Water, Inc. v. Ecolochem, Inc., 846 F.2d 731, 734-735 (Fed. Cir. 1988). Merely the desire to avoid the threat of a "scarecrow" patent, in Learned Hand's phrase, Bresnick v. United States Vitamin Corp., 139 F.2d 239, 242 (2d Cir. 1943), may therefore be sufficient to establish jurisdiction under the Declaratory Judgment Act. If, in addition to that desire, a party has actually been charged with infringement of the patent, there is, *necessarily*, a case or controversy adequate to support jurisdiction of a complaint, or a counterclaim, under the Act. In this case, therefore, it is perfectly clear that the District Court had jurisdiction to entertain Cardinal's counterclaim for a declaratory judgment of invalidity.

It is equally clear that the Federal Circuit, even after affirming the finding of noninfringement, had *jurisdiction* to consider Morton's appeal from the declaratory judgment of invalidity. A party seeking a declaratory judgment of invalidity presents a claim independent of the patentee's charge of infringement. If the District Court has jurisdiction (established independently from its jurisdiction over the patentee's charge of infringement) to consider that claim, so does (barring any intervening events) the Federal Circuit.

---

17. . . . [T]he Declaratory Judgment Act affords the district court some discretion in determining whether or not to exercise that jurisdiction, even when it has been established.

* [A *danse macabre*, literally a macabre dance, is a dance in which a skeleton leads people to their graves. The Damoclean sword was suspended over Damocles by a hair. Perhaps the skeleton must put the sword back on its hair so his hands will be free to grasp the nettle. *In terrorem*, literally, in terror, refers to something done for deterrence or intimidation.]

There are two independent bases for this conclusion. First, the Federal Circuit is not a court of last resort. . . . The Federal Circuit's determination that the patents were not infringed is subject to review in this Court, and if we reverse that determination, we are not prevented from considering the question of validity merely because a lower court thought it superfluous. . . .

Second, while the initial burden of establishing the trial court's jurisdiction rests on the party invoking that jurisdiction, once that burden has been met courts are entitled to presume, absent further information, that jurisdiction continues. If a party to an appeal suggests that the controversy has, since the rendering of judgment below, become moot, that party bears the burden of coming forward with the subsequent events that have produced that alleged result. See United States v. W.T. Grant Co., 345 U.S. 629, 633 (1953). . . . [T]here was no such change in this case. . . .

IV

The Federal Circuit's practice is therefore neither compelled by our cases nor supported by the "case or controversy" requirement of Article III. Of course, its practice might nevertheless be supported on other grounds. . . . If, for example, the validity issues were generally more difficult and time-consuming to resolve, the interest in the efficient management of the Court's docket might support such a rule. . . .

[T]here are even more important countervailing concerns. Perhaps the most important is the interest of the successful litigant in preserving the value of a declaratory judgment that, as Chief Judge Nies noted, "it obtained on a valid counterclaim at great effort and expense." 967 F.2d 1571, 1577 (Fed. Cir. 1992) (dissenting from denial of rehearing en banc). A company once charged with infringement must remain concerned about the risk of similar charges if it develops and markets similar products in the future. Given that the burden of demonstrating that changed circumstances provide a basis for vacating the judgment of patent invalidity rests on the party that seeks such action, there is no reason why a successful litigant should have any duty to disclose its future plans to justify retention of the value of the judgment that it has obtained.

Moreover, our prior cases have identified a strong public interest in the finality of judgments in patent litigation. . . .

We . . . emphasized the importance to the public at large of resolving questions of patent validity in Blonder-Tongue Laboratories, Inc. v. University of Illinois Foundation, 402 U.S. 313 (1971). In that case we overruled Triplett v. Lowell, 297 U.S. 638 (1936), which had held that a determination of patent invalidity does not estop the patentee from relitigating the issue in a later case brought against another alleged infringer. We also commented at length on the wasteful consequences of relitigating the validity of a patent after it has once been held invalid in a fair trial, and we noted the danger that the opportunity to relitigate might, as a practical matter, grant monopoly privileges to the holders of invalid patents. As this case demonstrates, the Federal Circuit's practice of routinely vacating judgments of validity after finding noninfringement creates a similar potential for relitigation and imposes ongoing burdens on competitors who are convinced that a patent has been correctly found invalid.

Indeed, as Morton's current predicament illustrates, the Federal Circuit's practice injures not only the alleged infringer, and the public; it also may unfairly deprive the patentee itself of the appellate review that is a component of the one full and fair opportunity to have the validity issue adjudicated correctly. . . . The Federal Circuit's practice denies the patentee such appellate review, prolongs the life of invalid patents, encourages endless litigation (or at least uncertainty) over the validity of outstanding patents, and thereby vitiates the rule announced in *Blonder-Tongue.*

In rejecting the Federal Circuit's practice we acknowledge that factors in an unusual case might justify that Court's refusal to reach the merits of a validity determination—a determination which it might therefore be appropriate to vacate. A finding of noninfringement alone, however, does not justify such a result. Nor does anything else in the record of this case. The two patents at issue here have been the subject of three separate lawsuits, and both parties have urged the Federal Circuit to resolve their ongoing dispute over the issue of validity; it would be an abuse of discretion not to decide that question in this case. Accordingly, the judgment of the Court of Appeals is vacated, and the case is remanded to that Court for further proceedings consistent with this opinion. . . .

[Justice SCALIA's concurring opinion is omitted.]

NOTES ON THE YOUNG DILEMMA

1. The risk of ever-expanding liability. Declaratory-judgment plaintiffs often sue because they face a threat of ever-expanding liability if the litigation is delayed.

a. *Cardinal Chemical.* The problem of the scarecrow patent is a special case of the problem of potential plaintiffs who assert claims without filing suit. Such a potential plaintiff may seek a monetary settlement, or he may seek to control the potential defendant's behavior. In the patent context, the alleged infringer might negotiate a license and pay royalties, or she might stop selling the allegedly infringing product. She can sell the product only at the risk of liability; every sale increases the potential judgment if the patent holder eventually sues and prevails. If the alleged infringer pays royalties or quits selling the product, the patent holder gets the benefit of a successful lawsuit without the risk of losing the lawsuit. If the infringement claim is weak but the alleged infringer has no way to bring the issue to court, a continuing threat of suing for infringement may be more valuable than actually suing for infringement.

b. *Wallace.* A similar problem arises with respect to allegedly unconstitutional statutes. Why do you suppose the railroad in *Wallace* sued for a declaratory judgment that the taxes were unconstitutional, instead of simply not paying the taxes and waiting for the state to try to collect them? Perhaps in part it was to show good faith and avoid appearing as a scofflaw. But it is also likely that there were penalties for nonpayment of the tax, and that the penalties would cumulate over time if litigation were delayed. The declaratory judgment enabled the railroad to find out what its rights were without incurring the risk of additional penalties.

2. The injunction remedy. With or without declaratory judgment acts, potential defendants in such situations generally have an injunction remedy. A potential civil defendant can sue to enjoin the potential plaintiff from filing suit. An example that became famous for other reasons is Beacon Theatres, Inc. v. Westover, 359 U.S. 500, 502-503, 508 (1959), discussed in note 1 following Chauffeurs Local v. Terry, reprinted in section 6.D. Beacon claimed that Fox Theatres was violating the antitrust laws; Fox sued Beacon to enjoin it from suing or threatening to sue Fox and for a declaratory judgment that Fox was not violating the antitrust laws.

Similarly, one who believes that a criminal or regulatory law is unconstitutional can sue the prosecutor to enjoin enforcement of the law. Note that the *Wallace* opinion assumed throughout that the railroad's claim could have been presented in a suit to enjoin collection of the tax. The Court treated suits to enjoin enforcement of unconstitutional state laws as an uncontroversial remedy, and it reasoned from that premise as it considered the declaratory judgment.

3. Ex parte Young again. The leading case on the availability of injunctions is Ex parte Young, 209 U.S. 123 (1908), which we first encountered in connection with state sovereign immunity in section 5.C.1. Recall that a railroad sued the Attorney General of Minnesota to enjoin enforcement of a railroad rate law. The Court held that the suit was not barred by the state's immunity. *Young* reappears in this chapter because the Court also held that the injunction was necessary to avoid irreparable injury.

If the railroad complied with the rate law, it would forfeit its asserted constitutional rights. Loss of constitutional rights is nearly always irreparable injury, because constitutional rights are usually hard to value, and because even if they can be valued, defendants are often immune from suits for damages. It is inconceivable that the railroad could recover lost freight charges from Minnesota or from any state officer.

The railroad could avoid this irreparable harm by violating the rate law. But the rate law might be constitutional; the railroad could violate the law only by risking criminal penalties for the railroad and its agents. Criminal penalties also inflict irreparable injury. That is their point, and usually the injury is deserved. But if the railroad thought the statute was unconstitutional, the risk of criminal penalties becomes the price of a court ruling.

The choice between forfeiting asserted constitutional rights and risking penalties is the *Young* dilemma. A suit to enjoin enforcement of the law avoids the dilemma; it allows the railroad to obtain a ruling on the law's constitutionality without risking penalties.

4. Reviewing administrative agencies. The Administrative Procedure Act provides that courts can review final actions of administrative agencies, but only when "there is no other adequate remedy in a court." 5 U.S.C. §704. This is an obvious analogue of the irreparable injury rule, and the *Young* dilemma applies. The Court held that excavating wetlands without an environmental permit, waiting for an enforcement action, and then defending on the ground that no permit was required because the wetlands at issue are not "waters of the United States," is not an adequate remedy where draconian penalties would apply if the court decided that a permit was required. U.S. Army Corps of Engineers v. Hawkes Co., 136 S. Ct. 1807 (2016). The puzzle is why the government even tried to argue otherwise.

5. Creating federal jurisdiction. The *Young* remedy has been controversial at times, principally because it has the large side effect of allowing litigation to be brought in federal court. This is because, as a general matter, a federal question in a well-pleaded complaint confers federal jurisdiction but a federal defense does not. So if the state sues to enforce its law, and the railroad defends on the ground that the law is unconstitutional, the case cannot be removed to federal court. But if the railroad files its own suit alleging that its constitutional rights are about to be violated by enforcement of the state law, that case can be filed in either state or federal court as the railroad chooses.

6. Don't be distracted by jurisdiction. The *Young* dilemma is real and requires a remedy, whether or not anyone is trying to manipulate jurisdiction. Note that the railroad in *Wallace* sued in state court, where the state would have sued to collect the taxes, and the alleged infringer in *Cardinal Chemical* counterclaimed in the very same court where the patent holder sued for infringement.

The citizen's need for relief from the *Young* dilemma has remained constant, but the advantages of federal jurisdiction have changed dramatically. During most of the first century and a quarter after the Civil War, plaintiffs with civil rights or civil liberties claims preferred federal court; state officials preferred state court. That preference has reversed in many states; it is now common for plaintiffs to file their constitutional claims in state court and for defendant state officials to remove such cases to federal court. Plaintiffs may prevent removal, but only by abandoning their federal claims and pleading only state claims in state court. If they plead state and federal claims together, defendants may remove the entire case to federal court. 28 U.S.C. §1441.

7. Previewing the *Younger* rules. Plaintiff's ability to sue in federal court when seeking relief from the *Young* dilemma produced much litigation and many complexities in the years when plaintiffs preferred federal court and state officials preferred state court. This body of law is explored in greater depth in the next section, but the basic rules can be summarized here.

If a state enforcement action is pending, the defendant must present his federal defense in state court; he cannot sue in federal court to enjoin either the pending prosecution or any threatened future prosecutions, or to declare the state law unconstitutional. If no state prosecution is pending, a potential state defendant can sue in federal court to have the law declared unconstitutional, because otherwise he would face the dilemma of forfeiting his rights or risking further penalties. The federal plaintiff may seek a preliminary injunction to prevent enforcement of the state law during the pendency of the declaratory judgment action, and the dilemma of forfeiting rights or risking penalties shows the necessary irreparable injury. Through all the twists and turns of litigation over federalism, the *Young* dilemma has remained good law.

8. Remedies for all. Do not let your assessment of the *Young* dilemma be biased by your reaction to the railroads' claims in *Young* and *Wallace*. Congress has largely repealed federal court jurisdiction to interfere with state rate laws and state tax laws, confining those cases to state court. Apart from such special legislation, a generally applicable remedial theory is available to the whole economic and political spectrum. Harris and Steffel were prosecuted or threatened with prosecution for distributing political leaflets. The Salem Inn and its employees were threatened with prosecution for topless dancing. In Cameron v. Johnson, 390 U.S. 611 (1968), plaintiffs relying on the *Young* dilemma were civil rights workers trying to register black voters in Mississippi; in Allee v. Medrano, 416 U.S. 802 (1974), they were migrant farm workers trying to organize a union; in Toomer v. Witsell, 334 U.S. 385 (1948), they were out-of-state shrimpers fighting local protectionism. *Beacon Theatres* and *Cardinal Chemical* were ordinary business litigation.

9. Why do we need declaratory judgments? If the *Young* dilemma is irreparable injury, why did we need declaratory judgment acts for cases like *Wallace* and *Cardinal Chemical*? Maybe we didn't. But there was a perception that the traditional restrictions on equitable relief made the injunction against suing on a threatened claim unavailable in some cases where it was needed. When that belief became entrenched in some substantive law specialty, it could be self-fulfilling. The Federal Circuit has said that there is no record of an alleged patent infringer ever suing to enjoin the patent holder from suing on the patent. In re Lockwood, 50 F.3d 966, 973-974, 979 (Fed. Cir.), *vacated on other grounds*, 515 U.S. 1182 (1995). That may be overstated; some cases that were at least near equivalents are collected in Joseph Rossman, *Declaratory Judgments*, 17 J. Pat. Off. Soc'y 3, 8-10 (1935). The antisuit injunction was a familiar tool of equity, but for whatever reasons of policy, formalism, or lack of imagination, it was apparently not much used to enjoin suits for patent infringement.

Of course there were sound reasons for sometimes denying antisuit injunctions. When *A* sued *B* to enjoin *B* from suing for damages, *B* traditionally lost her right to jury trial and her ability to choose the forum. Either of these concerns might be a reason to say that *A* was not entitled to an injunction, and either might be "explained" in terms of adequate remedy at law. Not all declaratory judgment claims involve an escalating risk of penalties; in some cases the claim of irreparable injury is considerably more attenuated. And it is likely that the traditional restrictions on equity had more teeth a century ago, although even then injunctions were freely available in many contexts.

We are left with a tradition that the uncertainty and actual controversy necessary to sustain a declaratory judgment may be a little bit less than the propensity and irreparable injury necessary to sustain an injunction. No one can clearly articulate the difference, and it is hard to find or imagine examples where a declaratory judgment should be granted but an injunction should not. But it is routine that a declaratory judgment should suffice and that the express coercive threat of an injunction appears unnecessary.

10. Ripeness. The usual ripeness requirement for a suit to prevent the declaratory defendant from suing the declaratory plaintiff is that the declaratory plaintiff have a reasonable fear of liability. An example is Rhoades v. Avon Products, Inc., 504 F.3d 1151 (9th Cir. 2007). This depends partly on his intent to do something the declaratory defendant objects to, and partly on the declaratory defendant's intent to do something about it. But if the declaratory remedy is to solve the problem of those who make threats without actually suing, the required intent to enforce cannot be set too high.

11. Continued resistance in the Federal Circuit. The Federal Circuit, which has jurisdiction of all patent appeals, has a history of resisting declaratory relief. Consider MedImmune, Inc. v. Genentech, Inc., 549 U.S. 118 (2007). Genentech claimed that one of its patents covers MedImmune's principal product. MedImmune could not afford the risk of liability, so it signed a licensing agreement with Genentech. It promised to pay royalties until or unless the patent was held invalid, stating that it was doing so under protest and reserving all its rights. It paid the royalties due under the agreement, and sued for a declaratory judgment that the Genentech patent was invalid.

The Federal Circuit held that there was no case or controversy. 427 F.3d 958 (Fed. Cir. 2005). MedImmune faced no risk of suit, because it was in full compliance with the licensing agreement. In effect, the court said that a litigant seeking to use a declaratory judgment to resolve its *Young* dilemma must leave itself exposed to the risk of liability in order to preserve its standing to file the declaratory judgment claim. The Supreme Court reversed. It was settled that a citizen facing a coercive threat from the government need not expose himself to penalties in order to create a case or controversy. The Court saw no reason why coercive threats from private entities were any different, and it found the *Altvater* case (discussed in *Cardinal Chemical*) to have decided the issue.

MedImmune requires plaintiff to show under "all the circumstances" a controversy "of sufficient immediacy and reality to warrant the issuance of a declaratory judgment." 549 U.S. at 127, quoting a phrase that goes back to the earliest days of the federal Declaratory Judgment Act. But if "immediacy" were taken literally, it would make the ripeness requirement more stringent for declaratory judgments than for injunctions. See note 12 following Almburbati v. Bush in section 4.A.1, on threatened harms that are ripe but not imminent.

In Sandoz, Inc. v. Amgen, Inc., 773 F.3d 1274 (Fed. Cir. 2014), the Federal Circuit applied *MedImmune*'s "immediacy and reality" test to deny declaratory relief. The pharmaceutical manufacturer Sandoz sought a declaration that a competitor's patent on a product to treat rheumatoid arthritis was invalid and that if Sandoz offered, sold, or imported a drug "biosimilar" to that product, it would not be infringing.

In denying declaratory relief, the court wrote that "[t]he immediacy requirement is concerned with whether there is an immediate impact on the plaintiff and whether the lapse of time creates uncertainty." *Sandoz*, 773 F.3d at 1277. "We have assessed 'reality' by examining any uncertainties about whether the plaintiff will take an action that will expose it to potential infringement liability and, if so, exactly what action." *Id.* at 1278. The court held that Sandoz did not present a case or controversy under the "immediacy and reality" test because the company was still involved in clinical trials and had not yet filed an application with the FDA for approval of its product. But clinical trials and the FDA approval process are very expensive, and the court's decision required Sandoz to invest that money without knowing the reach or validity of Amgen's competing patents. Sandoz had not sued out of idle curiosity.

The Federal Circuit applied *Sandoz* in AIDS Healthcare Foundation, Inc. v. Gilead Sciences, Inc. 890 F.3d 986 (Fed. Cir. 2018). Plaintiff alleged that the patents on several drugs were invalid, but it conceded that they were protected for five years by a separate statute. Plaintiff wanted to buy generic versions of these drugs, but it said that all generic drug manufacturers rejected its orders for fear of patent infringement. So it sued for a declaratory judgment that the patents were invalid. The Federal Circuit said that plaintiff's interest in buying the drugs was not enough, and that there was no case or controversy unless a plaintiff was prepared to make the generic versions. And it said the controversy was not "immediate," given the five years of concededly valid protection, and that it was irrelevant that litigation over patent validity might easily take five years.

12. Burden of proof. The declaratory judgment action reverses the usual party alignment. The potential plaintiff in a suit for damages becomes the defendant in the declaratory judgment action; the declaratory plaintiff fears becoming the defendant in a damages suit. Plaintiffs usually bear the burden of proof. But the declaratory judgment action could not achieve its purpose if the declaratory plaintiff bore the burden of disproving the feared damage claim that the damages plaintiff would normally have to prove.

The Supreme Court unanimously held that an alleged patent infringer, who sues for a declaratory judgment that he is not infringing, does not bear the burden of proving non-infringement. The burden of proving infringement remains on the patent holder, where it would be if the patent holder had sued the alleged infringer for infringement. Medtronic, Inc. v. Mirowski Family Ventures, LLC, 571 U.S. 191 (2014). The Court emphasized that the Declaratory Judgment Act is procedural, but the burden of proof is substantive. The point is not confined to patent cases; it should apply to declaratory judgments generally.

13. Mootness. A declaratory judgment claim can become moot in the same ways that an injunction claim can become moot. In Already, LLC v. Nike, Inc., 568 U.S. 85 (2013), Nike accused Already of trademark infringement, Already counterclaimed for a declaratory judgment that the trademark was invalid, and Nike sought to moot the case by filing with the court a covenant not to sue. Already argued that the case was not moot, in part because investors were refusing to invest additional funds because of fear of further trademark litigation with Nike. Applying the voluntary cessation doctrine, the Court held that there was no reasonable prospect of Nike resuming its trademark litigation. And then it said that irrational fears by potential investors were not enough to keep a moot case alive. Compare the allegedly irrational fears of potential homebuyers in Nicholson v. Connecticut Halfway House in section 4.A.2.

NOTES ON DECLARATORY JUDGMENTS, JUDICIAL DISCRETION, AND TACTICAL ADVANTAGE

1. Judicial discretion. Disputes over the propriety of declaratory judgment actions are generally disputes over tactical litigation advantage. Defendant may resist declaratory relief if she benefits from prolonged uncertainty, as in the scarecrow patent cases. Or the parties may be fighting over some tactical advantage unrelated to the purposes of declaratory judgment law.

Such concerns underlie the frequent statement that courts have broad discretion to decide whether to entertain a declaratory action. Wilton v. Seven Falls Co., 515 U.S. 277, 288 (1995). The language in *Wilton* was general, but the context was forum shopping. Plaintiff was an insurance company that had denied coverage and refused to defend in a case that ended in a $100 million judgment against its insured. The insurer sued in federal court for a declaratory judgment that there was no coverage; the insured sued on the policy in state court, joining additional claims and nondiverse defendants to prevent removal. Even though the federal claim had been filed first, the federal court stayed proceedings in deference to the state court action. It found that the coverage issue could be fairly resolved in the state court action, and that this would avoid piecemeal litigation and prevent forum shopping. The Supreme Court affirmed, deferring to the discretion of the trial court.

In Stevens v. Osuna, 877 F.3d 1293 (11th Cir. 2017), a professor who studies immigration sought a declaratory judgment to require immigration judges and officials to let her observe future immigration hearings unless there was a good reason, stated on the record, to close the hearing. The courts declined relief. Plaintiff had repeatedly modified her request to make it more workable, and her "failure to state definitely and consistently the declaratory relief sought is in itself a sufficient basis to deny such discretionary relief as a declaratory judgement." *Id.* at 1312. Further, having a federal court "instruct immigration tribunals in how to discharge their duties" would raise "a sensitive point for separation of powers[,] among other things." *Id.* at 1313.

The D.C. Circuit has set out these non-exhaustive factors for exercising discretion:

> Whether it would finally settle the controversy between the parties; whether other remedies are available or other proceedings pending; the convenience of the parties; the equity of the conduct of the declaratory judgment plaintiff; prevention of procedural fencing; the state of the record; the degree of adverseness between the parties; and the public importance of the question to be decided.

Morgan Drexen, Inc. v. Consumer Financial Protection Bureau, 785 F.3d 684, 696-697 (D.C. Cir. 2015).

2. The limits of federal jurisdiction. Maneuvering to put a case in state or federal court is common. Sometimes the party who files a declaratory action is able to hold the case in federal court. Sometimes, as in *Wilton*, there is federal jurisdiction but the court makes a discretionary decision not to exercise it. And sometimes the declaratory judgment action does not confer federal jurisdiction at all.

A leading case is Skelly Oil Co. v. Phillips Petroleum Co., 339 U.S. 667, 670-674 (1950). Phillips sought a declaratory judgment that Skelly's alleged federal defense to a state-law claim for breach of contract was not a valid defense. The Court treated that as a disguised suit for breach of contract, and it dismissed. In Textron Lycoming Reciprocating Engine Division v. United Automobile Workers, 523 U.S. 653 (1998), the declaratory plaintiff asserted a state-law defense to an anticipated federal claim. That too was dismissed. The Court noted that in suits by patent infringers to declare patents invalid, the infringers assert a federal claim—the point being that the claim of invalidity depends squarely on federal law. *Id.* at 660 n.4. The same reasoning presumably applies to suits challenging the constitutionality of laws the federal plaintiff intends to violate; the federal plaintiff's claim arises under the U.S. Constitution. The lesson seems to be that a litigant who would use a declaratory action to assert federal jurisdiction must himself be asserting a primary federal right; it is not enough to challenge a federal right that will be asserted by the other side.

3. Declarations of nonliability. Tactical advantage is usually the motive when a potential defendant sues for a declaration that he has no liability arising out of some completed event. There is no bright-line rule, but the point of declaratory judgments is not to relieve anxiety about past events; their principal purpose is to resolve uncertainty that future conduct might depend on. There is an especially strong presumption that personal injury plaintiffs are entitled to choose their forum. An example that collects many others is BASF Corp. v. Symington, 50 F.3d 555 (8th Cir. 1995). Symington sued for personal injuries in New Jersey; BASF promptly sued in North Dakota for a declaratory judgment that Symington's claim was barred by the North Dakota statute of limitations. The court dismissed the declaratory action, effectively leaving the choice of limitations law to the New Jersey court.

BASF also collects cases seemingly going the other way—permitting potential defendants to sue for a declaratory judgment that an affirmative defense precluded liability—where the declaratory action served some purpose the court viewed as legitimate. Consider Ditzler v. Spee, 180 N.W.2d 178 (Minn. 1970). Mother and child were injured in the same car, but only the mother sued. Under Minnesota's one-way issue-preclusion rules, defendant would be bound in a subsequent suit by the child if the mother won, but the child would not be bound if the mother lost. To avoid giving the child two chances on the same issue, the court let defendant sue the child for a declaratory judgment of nonliability and consolidate that case with the mother's in a single trial.

4. Insurance disputes. Disputes about insurance coverage, which can arise in a multitude of variations, often present strong competing interests that have divided courts.

a. An example. Consider Nationwide Insurance v. Zavalis, 52 F.3d 689 (7th Cir. 1995). Aleck Zavalis and other Big Ten undergraduates undertook to burn "F-O-O" in the artificial turf of their university's football field. The fire got out of control and did $600,000 damage; the university sued. Zavalis was covered for negligence on his parents' homeowners' policy; the university claimed that he performed his prank negligently and did damage he never intended. The insurer sued Zavalis for a declaratory judgment that his tort was intentional and outside the scope of the policy. After a remand, the court held that Zavalis acted intentionally and that the insurer had no obligation to defend him. Nationwide Insurance v. Board of Trustees, 116 F.3d 1154 (7th Cir. 1997). It was also revealed that F-O-O was short for "Foofur," a blue hound dog from a cartoon show in the 1980s, and—no surprise—that Zavalis and his friends had been seriously drunk.

This case arose partly from a genuine ambiguity about what Zavalis did, and partly from deliberate underpleading by the plaintiff in an attempt to stay within the insurance policy. In a remarkably frequent example of such underpleading, the insured pleads guilty or is convicted of a criminal offense, and the victim or his family sues for negligence resulting in personal injury. An example is Love v. Chartis Property Casualty Co., 734 F. App'x 184 (4th Cir. 2018), where defendant was convicted of second-degree murder but the victim's mother alleged in her civil suit that the killing was merely negligent. That policy excluded "criminal" acts as well as intentional acts, so the court easily concluded that the insurer had no liability.

b. The problem. There is no happy solution in such cases. Refusing the declaratory judgment generally means that the insurer has to defend the claim. The insured gets a defense under the policy, and the tort plaintiff gets to postpone the coverage issue. When plaintiff pleads only negligence, the insurer can't defend on the ground that the tort was really intentional; the insurance-provided lawyer owes professional duties to the insured. The insurer can defend under a reservation of rights and then refuse to pay the judgment. The insured, or more likely the tort plaintiff with an assignment of the insured's rights, will then sue the insurer on the policy. The plaintiff will say the judgment is for negligence; the insurer will defend on the ground that the first jury was wrong and the tort was really intentional.

Uncertainty about coverage also causes problems for the insured and the tort plaintiff, but they would sometimes rather delay resolution, require the insurer to defend the case, and then take a clean shot at the insurer after a judgment or settlement.

c. Inability to terminate the controversy. Suppose the declaratory action is allowed to proceed. If the facts are unclear, the parties still may not get an unambiguous declaration that there is or is not coverage. Consider Horace Mann Insurance Co. v. Barbara B., 846 P.2d 792 (Cal. 1993), where a seventh-grade teacher had pleaded guilty to sexually molesting one of his students. The teacher's insurer sued for a declaratory judgment that there was no coverage; the state supreme court decided that there was no coverage for molesting but that there might be coverage for some of the teacher's less egregious misconduct.

Eventually, a divided court held the teacher's conduct to be outside the policy. 71 Cal. Rptr. 2d 350 (Ct. App. 1998). The trial appears to have been a farce, in which the student alleged only negligence and sought damages only for aggressive public flirtation, not for the daily sexual contact that had gone on in private and continued for an entire school year. Plaintiff and her witnesses said the public conduct did as much damage as the far more egregious private conduct; the jury awarded $500,000. The defense appears to have been that the public and private misconduct were inseparable, and thus not compensable in negligence. When litigation incentives are sufficiently distorted, no creative use of remedies is likely to sort out the mess.

5. The big picture. The policy of the declaratory judgment acts is generally to reduce the risk of legal uncertainty. But insurance policies are all about allocating risk. The insurance cases require a judgment about the goals of insurance law and whether the risk of prolonged uncertainty should fall on the insurer or the insured; a careful analysis of the declaratory judgment act is not much help. The proposed *Restatement of Liability Insurance* mostly ducks. It says that the insurer may seek a declaratory judgment "subject to any applicable rules of the jurisdiction regarding the scope and timing of declaratory-judgment actions." §18 cmt. *j* (Am. Law Inst., Proposed Final Draft 2, 2018). The *Restatement* is clear that the insurer must defend the tort suit if any allegation of the complaint would be covered by the policy, until and unless it gets a final adjudication that the claim is not covered.

2.   *The Special Case of Interfering with State Enforcement Proceedings*

STEFFEL v. THOMPSON
415 U.S. 452 (1974)

[Steffel and his friend Becker were passing out antiwar leaflets in a shopping center. They were threatened with arrest and prosecution for trespassing if they persisted. Steffel quit passing out leaflets; Becker continued and was prosecuted. Both then filed this action seeking an injunction against enforcing the criminal trespass statute against them and a declaratory judgment that the statute was being applied in violation of their First Amendment rights. The state court voluntarily stayed Becker's prosecution pending the federal case. The lower courts denied all relief. 334 F. Supp. 1386 (N.D. Ga. 1971), *aff'd*, 459 F.2d 919 (5th Cir. 1972). Only Steffel petitioned for certiorari, and only with respect to the declaratory judgment.]

Justice BRENNAN delivered the opinion of the Court. . . .

I

At the threshold we must consider whether petitioner presents an "actual controversy," a requirement imposed by Article III of the Constitution and the express terms of the Federal Declaratory Judgment Act, 28 U.S.C. §2201. . . .

[P]etitioner has alleged threats of prosecution that cannot be characterized as "imaginary or speculative," Younger v. Harris, 401 U.S. 37, 42 (1971). He has been twice warned to stop handbilling that he claims is constitutionally protected and has been told by the police that if he again handbills at the shopping center and disobeys a warning to stop he will likely be prosecuted. The prosecution of petitioner's handbilling companion is ample demonstration that petitioner's concern with arrest has not been "chimerical." Poe v. Ullman, 367 U.S. 497, 508 (1961). In these circumstances, it is not necessary that petitioner first expose himself to actual arrest or prosecution to be entitled to challenge a statute that he claims deters the exercise of his constitutional rights. . . .

Nonetheless, there remains a question as to the continuing existence of a live and acute controversy that must be resolved on the remand we order today. . . . Since we cannot ignore the recent developments reducing the Nation's involvement in [Vietnam], it will be for the District Court on remand to determine if subsequent events have so altered petitioner's desire to engage in handbilling at the shopping center that it can no longer be said that this case presents "a substantial controversy, between parties having adverse legal interests, of sufficient immediacy and reality to warrant the issuance of a declaratory judgment." Maryland Casualty Co. v. Pacific Coal & Oil Co., 312 U.S. 270, 273 (1941).

II . . .

Sensitive to principles of equity, comity, and federalism, we recognized in *Younger* that federal courts should ordinarily refrain from enjoining ongoing state criminal prosecutions. We were cognizant that a pending state proceeding, in all but unusual cases, would provide the federal plaintiff with the necessary vehicle for vindicating his constitutional rights, and, in that circumstance, the restraining of an ongoing prosecution would entail an unseemly failure to give effect to the principle that state courts have the solemn responsibility, equally with the federal courts "to guard, enforce, and protect every right granted or secured by the constitution of the United States." Robb v. Connolly, 111 U.S. 624, 637 (1884). In Samuels v. Mackell, 401 U.S. 66 (1971), the Court also found that the same principles ordinarily would be flouted by issuance of a federal declaratory judgment when a state proceeding was pending, since the intrusive effect of declaratory relief "will result in precisely the same interference with and disruption of state proceedings that the long-standing policy limiting injunctions was designed to avoid." *Id.* at 72.[11] We therefore held in *Samuels* that, "in cases where the

---

11. The Court noted that under 28 U.S.C. §2202 a declaratory judgment might serve as the basis for issuance of a later injunction to give effect to the declaratory judgment, and that a declaratory judgment might have a res judicata effect on the pending state proceeding. 401 U.S. at 72.

state criminal prosecution was begun prior to the federal suit, the same equitable principles relevant to the propriety of an injunction must be taken into consideration by federal district courts in determining whether to issue a declaratory judgment." *Id.* at 73.

Neither *Younger* nor *Samuels*, however, decided the question whether federal intervention might be permissible in the absence of a pending state prosecution. . . .

[T]he relevant principles of equity, comity, and federalism "have little force in the absence of a pending state proceeding." Lake Carriers' Association v. MacMullan, 406 U.S. 498, 509 (1972). When no state criminal proceeding is pending at the time the federal complaint is filed, federal intervention does not result in duplicative legal proceedings or disruption of the state criminal justice system; nor can federal intervention, in that circumstance, be interpreted as reflecting negatively upon the state court's ability to enforce constitutional principles. In addition, while a pending state prosecution provides the federal plaintiff with a concrete opportunity to vindicate his constitutional rights, a refusal on the part of the federal courts to intervene when no state proceeding is pending may place the hapless plaintiff between the Scylla of intentionally flouting state law and the Charybdis of forgoing what he believes to be constitutionally protected activity in order to avoid becoming enmeshed in a criminal proceeding.

When no state proceeding is pending and thus considerations of equity, comity, and federalism have little vitality, the propriety of granting federal declaratory relief may properly be considered independently of a request for injunctive relief. Here, the Court of Appeals held that, because injunctive relief would not be appropriate since petitioner failed to demonstrate irreparable injury . . . it followed that declaratory relief was also inappropriate. Even if the Court of Appeals correctly viewed injunctive relief as inappropriate—a question we need not reach today since petitioner has abandoned his request for that remedy[12]—the court erred in treating the requests for injunctive and declaratory relief as a single issue. "[W]hen no state prosecution is pending and the only question is whether declaratory relief is appropriate[,] . . . the congressional scheme that makes the federal courts the primary guardians of constitutional rights, and the express congressional authorization of declaratory relief, afforded because it is a less harsh and abrasive remedy than the injunction, become the factors of primary significance." Perez v. Ledesma, 401 U.S. 82, 104 (1971) (Brennan, J., concurring).

The subject matter jurisdiction of the lower federal courts was greatly expanded in the wake of the Civil War. A pervasive sense of nationalism led to enactment of the Civil Rights Act of 1871, empowering the lower federal courts to determine the constitutionality of actions, taken by persons under color of state law, allegedly depriving other individuals of rights guaranteed by the Constitution and federal law. See 42 U.S.C. §1983; 28 U.S.C. §1343(3). Four years later, in the Judiciary Act of March 3, 1875, Congress conferred upon the lower federal courts, for but the second time in their nearly century-old history, general federal-question jurisdiction subject only to a jurisdictional-amount requirement. See 28 U.S.C. §1331. With this latter enactment, the lower federal courts "ceased to be restricted tribunals of fair dealing between citizens of different states and became the *primary* and powerful reliances for vindicating

---

12. We note that, in those cases where injunctive relief has been sought to restrain an imminent, but not yet pending, prosecution for past conduct, sufficient injury has not been found to warrant injunctive relief. There is some question, however, whether a showing of irreparable injury might be made in a case where, although no prosecution is pending or impending, an individual demonstrates that he will be required to *forgo* constitutionally protected activity in order to avoid arrest.

every right given by the Constitution, the laws, and treaties of the United States." Felix Frankfurter & James M. Landis, *The Business of the Supreme Court* 65 (Macmillan 1928) (emphasis added). These two statutes, together with the Court's decision in Ex parte Young, 209 U.S. 123 (1908) — holding that state officials who threaten to enforce an unconstitutional state statute may be enjoined by a federal court of equity and that a federal court may, in appropriate circumstances, enjoin future state criminal prosecutions under the unconstitutional Act — have "established the modern framework for federal protection of constitutional rights from state interference." *Perez*, 401 U.S. at 107 (Brennan, J., concurring). . . .

Congress in 1934 enacted the Declaratory Judgment Act. That Congress plainly intended declaratory relief to act as an alternative to the strong medicine of the injunction and to be utilized to test the constitutionality of state criminal statutes in cases where injunctive relief would be unavailable is amply evidenced by the legislative history of the Act, traced in full detail in *Perez*, 401 U.S. at 111-115 (Brennan, J., concurring). . . .

The "different considerations" entering into a decision whether to grant declaratory relief have their origins in the preceding historical summary. First, as Congress recognized in 1934, a declaratory judgment will have a less intrusive effect on the administration of state criminal laws. As was observed in *Perez*, 401 U.S. at 124-126 (Brennan, J., concurring):

> Of course, a favorable declaratory judgment may nevertheless be valuable to the plaintiff though it cannot make even an unconstitutional statute disappear. A state statute may be declared unconstitutional in toto — that is, incapable of having constitutional applications; or it may be declared unconstitutionally vague or overbroad — that is, incapable of being constitutionally applied to the full extent of its purport. In either case, a federal declaration of unconstitutionality reflects the opinion of the federal court that the statute cannot be fully enforced. . . . Even where a declaration of unconstitutionality is not reviewed by this Court, the declaration may still be able to cut down the deterrent effect of an unconstitutional state statute. The persuasive force of the court's opinion and judgment may lead state prosecutors, courts, and legislators to reconsider their respective responsibilities toward the statute. Enforcement policies or judicial construction may be changed, or the legislature may repeal the statute and start anew. Finally, the federal court judgment may have some res judicata effect, though this point is not free from difficulty and the governing rules remain to be developed with a view to the proper workings of a federal system. What is clear, however, is that even though a declaratory judgment has "the force and effect of a final judgment," 28 U.S.C. §2201, it is a much milder form of relief than an injunction. Though it may be persuasive, it is not ultimately coercive; noncompliance with it may be inappropriate, but is not contempt.

Second, engrafting upon the Declaratory Judgment Act a requirement that all of the traditional equitable prerequisites to the issuance of an injunction be satisfied before the issuance of a declaratory judgment is considered would defy Congress' intent to make declaratory relief available in cases where an injunction would be inappropriate. . . . Thus, the Court of Appeals was in error when it ruled that a failure to demonstrate irreparable injury — a traditional prerequisite to injunctive relief, having no equivalent in the law of declaratory judgments, *Aetna; Wallace* — precluded the granting of declaratory relief. [*Wallace* is reprinted in section 7.A.1; *Aetna* is described in note 1 following *Wallace*.]

The only occasions where this Court has disregarded these "different considerations" and found that a preclusion of injunctive relief inevitably led to a denial of declaratory relief have been cases in which principles of federalism militated altogether against federal intervention in a class of adjudications. See Great Lakes Dredge & Dock Co. v. Huffman, 319 U.S. 293 (1943) (federal policy against interfering with the enforcement of state tax laws); *Samuels.* In the instant case, principles of federalism not only do not preclude federal intervention, they compel it. Requiring the federal courts totally to step aside when no state criminal prosecution is pending against the federal plaintiff would turn federalism on its head. When federal claims are premised on 42 U.S.C. §1983 . . . we have not required exhaustion of state judicial or administrative remedies, recognizing the paramount role Congress has assigned to the federal courts to protect constitutional rights. But exhaustion of state remedies is precisely what would be required if both federal injunctive and declaratory relief were unavailable in a case where no state prosecution had been commenced. . . .

We therefore hold that, regardless of whether injunctive relief may be appropriate, federal declaratory relief is not precluded when no state prosecution is pending and a federal plaintiff demonstrates a genuine threat of enforcement of a disputed state criminal statute, whether an attack is made on the constitutionality of the statute on its face or as applied. The judgment . . . is reversed, and the case is remanded for further proceedings consistent with this opinion. . . .

Justice STEWART, with whom Chief Justice BURGER joins, concurring.

While joining the opinion of the Court, I add a word by way of emphasis.

Our decision today must not be understood as authorizing the invocation of federal declaratory judgment jurisdiction by a person who thinks a state criminal law is unconstitutional, even if he genuinely feels "chilled" in his freedom of action by the law's existence, and even if he honestly entertains the subjective belief that he may now or in the future be prosecuted under it. . . .

The petitioner in this case has succeeded in objectively showing that the threat of imminent arrest, corroborated by the actual arrest of his companion, has created an actual concrete controversy between himself and agents of the State. . . . Cases where such a "genuine threat" can be demonstrated will, I think, be exceedingly rare.

[Concurring opinions by Justices WHITE and REHNQUIST are omitted.]

MORE NOTES ON THE YOUNG *DILEMMA*

1. Irreparable injury? Ex parte Young, 209 U.S. 123 (1908), described in note 3 following *Cardinal Chemical,* held that the choice between forfeiting asserted constitutional rights or risking penalties is irreparable injury. Justice Brennan's Scylla and Charybdis (mythical sea monsters from Greek mythology often referenced to mean choosing between two evils) is just a restatement of the *Young* dilemma. Is that dilemma no longer irreparable injury? Does it matter whether the Court calls the injury irreparable, as long as it provides a remedy?

2. Preserving the preventive remedy. *Steffel* was the key decision in extricating the Court from a major fight over federal suits to enjoin enforcement of unconstitutional state laws:

> From 1971 to 1977 the Supreme Court decided at least thirty-four cases on federal interference with state law enforcement. These cases relied on the irreparable injury rule to reinforce the majority's view of federalism, and the irreparable injury argument was most prominent in the early cases in the series, when the law was most unsettled. . . . The rules became settled again, litigants learned to play by the new rules, and the flood of litigation slowed. The more recent cases deal with marginal issues and details of implementation.

Douglas Laycock, *The Death of the Irreparable Injury Rule* 134-135 (Oxford Univ. Press 1991).

3. The *Younger* doctrine. Younger v. Harris, 401 U.S. 37 (1971), has given its name to this large body of modern cases. The *Younger* doctrine bars most federal relief that would directly or indirectly interfere with a pending state proceeding to enforce state law. More specifically, *Younger* applies in three circumstances: (1) where the federal claim would interfere with "ongoing state criminal prosecutions;" (2) where the federal claim would interfere with "civil enforcement proceedings" (meaning proceedings to enforce state law with civil penalties); and (3) where the federal claim would interfere with orders "uniquely in furtherance of the state courts' ability to perform their judicial functions" (principally meaning proceedings to enforce civil judgments between private parties). Sprint Communications, Inc. v. Jacobs, 571 U.S. 69, 73 (2013).

Sprint involved a complicated dispute between Sprint and a local Iowa phone company. The Iowa Utilities Board resolved Sprint's state and federal claims, on the merits and against Sprint, and over the objection that the Federal Communications Commission had exclusive jurisdiction of the federal claim. Sprint then filed suit in federal court to enjoin enforcement of the Board's order. Sprint also filed a petition for review of the Board's order in state court, presenting its state-law claims and also, in an "abundance of caution," in case its federal lawsuit was dismissed, presenting its federal claim to the state court.

The Board argued that it was seeking to enforce its order, and that the federal suit interfered both with its administrative proceedings and with the state court's review of those proceedings. But the Supreme Court treated this as ordinary parallel civil litigation. It emphasized that the civil-enforcement proceedings to which it had applied *Younger* were generally initiated by the state, that they involved alleged misconduct by the private litigant, and that they were often quasi-criminal. This case involved none of those things. The administrative proceeding and both the state and federal lawsuits were civil proceedings initiated by Sprint, complaining about activities of the local phone company.

As this reasoning suggests, *Younger* does not preclude parallel state and federal litigation in ordinary civil cases. Such parallel litigation is fairly common, and while one court often stays its proceedings in deference to the other, that is not required or universal. The leading case permitting both actions to proceed simultaneously still appears to be Kline v. Burke Construction Co., 260 U.S. 226 (1922).

4. *Younger* extensions and exceptions. *Younger* has been extended to enforcement of state judgments even between private parties, Pennzoil Co. v. Texaco, Inc., 481 U.S. 1 (1987), and to state administrative proceedings, Ohio Civil Rights Commission v. Dayton Christian Schools, Inc., 477 U.S. 619 (1986).

There is a very narrow exception for collateral issues, such as pretrial detention, that can be decided without interfering with the state proceeding and cannot be raised within it. Gerstein v. Pugh, 420 U.S. 103, 108 n.9 (1975). There is an equally narrow exception for proceedings before tribunals biased by prejudgment and monetary interest. The only example in the Supreme Court is Gibson v. Berryhill, 411 U.S. 564, 578-579 (1973), where the state required optometrists employed by a corporation to present their claims to a board made up of independent optometrists. In theory there is an exception for bad-faith prosecutions, but it has never been successfully invoked in the Supreme Court.

There is a partial exception for damage claims. "[F]ederal courts have the power to dismiss or remand cases based on abstention principles only where the relief being sought is equitable or otherwise discretionary." Quackenbush v. Allstate Insurance Co., 517 U.S. 706, 731 (1996). But most circuits have taken this to mean only that abstention should be implemented by staying the federal damage action rather than dismissing it. The cases are collected in Gilbertson v. Albright, 381 F.3d 965, 978 n.13, 980 n.15 (9th Cir. 2004). Gilbertson was a land surveyor whose license had been revoked by a state agency. He was appealing the loss of his license in the state courts, and he sued the members of the agency for damages in federal court. Damages would not be available in the state court proceeding to review the agency action, but if he succeeded in state court, he could return to federal court to pursue his damage claim. If he lost in state court, that decision would presumably be preclusive in the federal case.

5. The relevance of a pending prosecution. Does a pending prosecution eliminate the *Young* dilemma?

a. Past violations. If the federal plaintiff has already violated the statute, he has already incurred the risk of penalties. If the statute is constitutional, he can be punished for that violation; if not, he can't be. Whether or not there is a pending prosecution, there is no *Young* dilemma with respect to the past violation. In terms of the *Young* dilemma, it doesn't matter whether the constitutional issue is decided in a criminal case or a separate injunction case.

b. Continuing courses of conduct. But what if the federal plaintiff wants to pass out leaflets again? Even if he is the target of a pending prosecution — *especially* if he is the target of a pending prosecution — he still faces the choice between risking additional penalties or forfeiting his asserted constitutional rights. There has been no ruling on his constitutional claim, and the prosecutor's attention is focused on him. Isn't that exactly the *Young* dilemma?

That issue was raised in Roe v. Wade, 410 U.S. 113 (1973). One of the plaintiffs, Dr. Hallford, had been indicted for performing abortions. He conceded that the federal court could not enjoin his pending prosecution, but he sought an injunction against any additional prosecutions for future violations. Every day patients came to his clinic. Every day he had to decide whether to risk additional felony prosecutions or turn those patients away, knowing that long before his criminal case was decided, it would be too late for those patients to abort. Without analysis, the Court found "no merit" in the distinction between past and future violations. *Id.* at 126-127.

How did the pending prosecution help Dr. Hallford? Wasn't the prosecution for past violations irrelevant to his *Young* dilemma with respect to future violations? Didn't he really need a preliminary injunction?

c. Constitutional claims in the pending prosecution. Was it enough for Dr. Hallford that the pending prosecution promised an eventual end to his *Young* dilemma? Relief may not be as quick as a preliminary injunction, and he and some patients might suffer irreparable injury pending final judgment. But that might be only temporary. The Court has assumed that the criminal case will resolve the constitutional challenge "in all but unusual cases," as Justice Brennan put it in *Steffel*. Once there was a final judgment in the state prosecution, Dr. Hallford would know his constitutional rights.

There is something to that argument, but not as much as first appears. This temporary irreparable injury may last a long time. Just as the infringement suit in *Cardinal Chemical* failed to determine the validity of the patent, so a criminal prosecution may fail to determine the validity of the statute. Most obviously, defendant may be acquitted on the facts; more generally, the court is obligated to decide on nonconstitutional grounds if it can. Consider the case of Sanford Zwickler, who made two trips to the Supreme Court of the United States and a separate trip to the New York Court of Appeals without getting a ruling on his constitutional claim, which finally became moot. See People v. Zwickler, 213 N.E.2d 467 (N.Y. 1965); Zwickler v. Koota, 389 U.S. 241 (1967); Golden v. Zwickler, 394 U.S. 103 (1969).

NOTES ON THE STEFFEL *SOLUTION*

1. The equivalence of injunctions and declaratory judgments. In Samuels v. Mackell, 401 U.S. 66 (1971), the Court said that a pending prosecution bars a declaratory judgment that the statute is unconstitutional, because the declaratory judgment would stop the prosecution as effectively as an injunction. Is that consistent with *Steffel's* elaborate explanation of the differences between the two remedies? In practice, declaratory judgments that statutes are unconstitutional have been as effective as injunctions against enforcement. Such declaratory judgments have once again become routine, and sometimes the Court affirms injunctions against enforcing state laws without noting any distinction. A prominent example is Planned Parenthood v. Casey, 505 U.S. 833, 845, 901 (1992), enjoining enforcement of certain restrictions on abortion. In Roark v. South Iron R-1 School District, 573 F.3d 556 (8th Cir. 2009), the court vacated a declaratory judgment as unnecessary where the district court had also granted a permanent injunction. The injunction fully protected plaintiffs and was more precisely drafted.

2. The myth of mildness. *Steffel* says that the declaratory judgment is "a much milder form of relief than an injunction," and Professor Bray thinks that claim is worth refuting, because a fair number of people have taken that statement seriously. Samuel L. Bray, *The Myth of the Mild Declaratory Judgment*, 63 Duke L.J. 1091 (2014). He demolishes the idea that declaratory judgments are any less effective, any less likely to be obeyed, or any less binding than an injunction. In Knight First Amendment Institute v. Trump, 302 F. Supp. 3d 541 (S.D.N.Y. 2018), described more fully in the note on presidential immunities in section 6.A.2, President Trump started "unblocking" plaintiffs whom he had blocked on Twitter after a federal court issued a declaratory judgment that the blocking violated plaintiffs' First Amendment rights. The judge declined to issue an injunction, finding it unnecessarily intrusive. Charlie Savage, *White House Unblocks Twitter Users Who Sued Trump, But Appeals Ruling*, N.Y. Times (June 5, 2018). Why didn't Trump wait to unblock plaintiffs until after the appeal?

Bray argues that the real difference between the two remedies is that the injunction gives the court far more "managerial" capacity. The declaratory judgment gives a binding answer to a legal question and leaves implementation of that answer to the parties. The injunction tells defendant what she must do; those instructions must be specific and if necessary they can be very specific; this specification can be modified in response to changed circumstances; and the contempt power is available if needed. He also argues, less successfully in our view, that there is a difference in the ripeness requirement, and that declaratory judgments really are available in situations where an injunction would not be.

3. The reverse removal power. In Hicks v. Miranda, 422 U.S. 332 (1975), the Court held that the federal proceeding must be dismissed if a prosecution is commenced "before any proceedings of substance on the merits." *Id.* at 349. Any other rule would "trivialize the principles of Younger v. Harris." *Id.* at 350. Four dissenters thought the majority trivialized *Steffel. Id.* at 353 (Stewart, J., dissenting).

In *Hicks*, the trial court had denied a temporary restraining order, in part because plaintiffs had failed to show probability of success on the merits. Each side had filed substantial written submissions on the motion for the TRO, and the court had held that motion under advisement for nearly a month. Presumably these were not "substantial proceedings on the merits," but the majority did not explain why not or how much more was required.

Professor Fiss has described *Hicks* as creating a "reverse removal power." Owen M. Fiss, *Dombrowski*, 86 Yale L.J. 1103, 1134-1136 (1977). The reference is to federal statutes authorizing state-court defendants to remove certain cases to federal court. 28 U.S.C. §1441 *et seq.* There is nothing in *Hicks* to prevent the prosecutor from routinely prosecuting anyone who files a suit challenging the constitutionality of a state statute. But the federal plaintiff has a countermove, which is explored in the next principal case.

4. Ripeness again. *Steffel* requires the federal plaintiff to beat the prosecutor to the courthouse, and *Hicks* requires him to win the race by a wide margin. But the ripeness requirement prevents him from getting there too early; he must show a real threat of prosecution. These rules have a potential for squeezing litigants out of federal court altogether, with half the cases being dismissed as unripe and the rest being dismissed because there is a pending prosecution.

Whether this happens depends mostly on the administration of the ripeness requirement. Most of the Court's cases hold or assume that a suit to enjoin enforcement is ripe when the statute is on the books and plaintiff wants to violate it. But Justice Stewart's concurrence in *Steffel,* and some opinions of the Court, suggest that plaintiff must receive something like a personal threat from the prosecutor before he can sue. Is there any justification for such a stringent ripeness requirement? Doesn't plaintiff have to assume that if he publicly violates the law, the state will sooner or later take notice and prosecute him?

5. Reconciling the ripeness cases? Justice Powell explained the variations in the ripeness requirement in a dissenting opinion in Ellis v. Dyson, 421 U.S. 426 (1975) Justice Stewart and Chief Justice Burger, who had said in *Steffel* that ripe cases would be "exceedingly rare," joined in this opinion.

> In several cases we have found constitutional challenges to state and federal statutes justiciable despite the absence of actual threats of enforcement directed personally to the plaintiff. In each such case, however, the challenged statute applied particularly and unambiguously to activities in which the plaintiff regularly engaged or sought to engage. . . . The plaintiffs, therefore, were put to a choice. Unless declaratory relief was available, they were compelled to choose between a genuine risk of criminal prosecution and conformity to the challenged statute, a conformity that would require them to incur substantial deprivation either in tangible form or in forgoing the exercise of asserted constitutional rights. In such circumstances we have recognized that the challenged statute causes the plaintiff present harm, and that the "controversy is both immediate and real." Lake Carriers' Association v. MacMullan, 406 U.S. 498, 508 (1972).
>
> *Steffel* does not depart from this general analysis. The difference . . . lies in the nature of the statute involved. *Steffel* concerned a general trespass ordinance that did not, on its face, apply particularly to activities in which Steffel engaged or sought to engage. The statute was susceptible of a multitude of applications that would not even arguably exceed constitutional limitations on state power. But the threatened prosecution of Steffel, following the arrest and prosecution of his companion, demonstrated that the state officials construed the statute to apply to the precise activities in which Steffel had engaged and proposed to engage in the future. There was, therefore, no question that Steffel was confronted with a choice identical in principle and practical consequence to that faced by plaintiffs in the above cases. . . . Whichever choice he made, the harm to Steffel was real and immediate.
>
> The pleadings in this case reveal no like circumstances. They merely aver that the Dallas [loitering] ordinance has a "chilling" effect on First Amendment rights of speech and association. This averment, moreover, is related not to petitioners specifically, but rather to the "citizens of Dallas." . . . The complaint nowhere alleges that the

ordinance has been applied to particular activities, assertedly within the scope of First Amendment protection, in which *petitioners* regularly engage or in which they would engage but do not because of fear of prosecution.

421 U.S. at 447-449. The majority vacated *Ellis* for reconsideration in light of *Steffel* without reaching the ripeness issue or any other issue.

If we take the Powell dissent in *Ellis* as the hard-liners' position on ripeness, ripeness doesn't appear to be much of a problem. Doesn't any plaintiff who clearly faces the *Young* dilemma have a ripe controversy? Isn't that the way it should be? Is it unreasonable to require the state to assert improbable applications of a statute before deciding the constitutionality of such applications?

6. The latest word on ripeness. The Court devoted a full opinion to ripeness in Susan B. Anthony List v. Driehaus, 134 S. Ct. 2334 (2014). The bottom line is that plaintiff has standing to challenge the constitutionality of a statute if he faces "a credible threat" of future prosecution. *Id.* at 2342. And the Court took a realistic view of the risk to plaintiffs, despite several unusual steps between them and prosecution. Plaintiffs sought both declaratory and injunctive relief, and nothing in the Court's opinion suggests any distinction between the two.

An Ohio statute prohibited false statements in political campaigns, if the false statement was made knowingly, or in some cases, with reckless disregard of the truth. Any person could file an administrative complaint with the Ohio Elections Commission. If a complaint were filed in the last 90 days before a general election, the Commission was required to proceed on a stringent accelerated schedule. If the Commission found a violation by clear and convincing evidence, it was required to refer the case to a county prosecutor for criminal prosecution as a first-degree misdemeanor; the potential penalty for a first offense was six months in jail and a $5,000 fine. The Commission was handling 30 or 40 cases a year; the Court did not say how many criminal prosecutions followed, if any.

One plaintiff had issued press releases claiming that Congressman Driehaus had voted for government-funded abortions; Driehaus said this statement was false. The dispute turned on whether the Affordable Care Act (better known as Obamacare), for which Driehaus had voted, provided government funds for abortions. Driehaus filed a complaint; the Commission found probable cause; and the parties agreed to postpone the merits hearing until after the election. Driehaus lost the election and withdrew his complaint. Plaintiffs said they desired to make the same charge against other incumbents in future election cycles, but they feared renewed prosecution. One plaintiff also said that a billboard company had cancelled an advertising contract after receiving a threat of prosecution from Driehaus.

The court of appeals found no ripe threat of future prosecution. 525 F. App'x 415 (6th Cir. 2013). Plaintiffs did not allege that they intended to knowingly or recklessly make false statements, and Driehaus had joined the Peace Corps and gone to Africa; he would not be running again.

The Supreme Court unanimously reversed. Plaintiffs had alleged that they intended to "engage in a course of conduct arguably affected with a constitutional interest." 134 S. Ct. at 2343. This somewhat vague formulation appears to mean only that plaintiffs claimed constitutional protection for their intended conduct. Plaintiff's course of conduct was arguably prohibited by the challenged statute. It mattered not that plaintiffs believed their statements to be true; the Commission had already found probable cause to believe that they were false. Plaintiffs wanted to talk about the Affordable Care Act, not just about Driehaus.

And there was a credible threat of future prosecution, as illustrated most obviously by the history of past enforcement, by the finding of probable cause, and by the fact that any person could file a complaint. Even the administrative process before the Commission could seriously disrupt a campaign, but the Court did not have to decide whether that threat alone was sufficient to support a ripeness finding. That threat combined with the more attenuated threat of criminal prosecution was certainly sufficient.

On remand, the Sixth Circuit held the Ohio statute unconstitutional. Susan B. Anthony List v. Driehaus, 814 F.3d 466 (6th Cir. 2016). The Commission was also a defendant, so there was someone to defend the statute.

7. Suits to declare the meaning of a criminal statute. Consider a possible corollary of Justice Powell's explanation of ripeness. Suits to declare criminal statutes unconstitutional are common. Suits to declare that proposed conduct is not within the criminal statute are rare, and courts are more reluctant to entertain them. An example is Adult Video Association v. United States Department of Justice, 71 F.3d 563 (6th Cir. 1995), refusing to declare whether the movie *After Midnight* was obscene under community standards in the Western District of Tennessee.

How is this case different from *Steffel?* Both plaintiffs said the legal uncertainty made them afraid to exercise their rights. But in *Adult Video*, there was no evidence that the government considered the movie obscene or contemplated prosecution of those who showed it. Without a fairly specific ripeness requirement, one might ask for a declaration that *The Wizard of Oz* is not obscene. There may also be some sense that the *Adult Video* declaration would duplicate the heart of the criminal trial in a way that the constitutional challenge does not. But ripeness is the point the court emphasized.

Compare New Hampshire Hemp Council, Inc. v. Marshall, 203 F.3d 1 (1st Cir. 2000), where the court declared that growing industrial hemp for rope production is a violation of the marijuana laws. There the government's position was clear, and the threat of prosecution was real. The issue was "an abstract one of statutory interpretation." The court thought there would be no "untoward" "flood" of cases, because "most issues in criminal cases turn on multiple facts that cannot be taken in isolation or definitively known in advance." *Id.* at 5.

DORAN v. SALEM INN, INC.

422 U.S. 922 (1975)

[Plaintiffs Salem Inn, Tim-Rob Bar, and M & L Restaurant all featured topless dancers. The Town of North Hempstead passed a new ordinance forbidding such entertainment. All three plaintiffs initially complied. On August 9, 1973, they filed this suit in federal court seeking a declaratory judgment that the ordinance was unconstitutional and a temporary restraining order and preliminary injunction against its enforcement. On August 10, M & L resumed topless dancing. M & L and its dancers were served with criminal summonses on August 10, 11, 12, and 13. On September 6, the federal court preliminarily enjoined enforcement of the ordinance. The court recognized that M & L's complaint was barred by *Younger*, but it thought it would be anomalous to grant relief to two plaintiffs without granting relief to the third. Salem Inn, Inc. v. Frank, 364 F. Supp. 478 (E.D.N.Y. 1973). The court of appeals affirmed, noting that it was much more efficient to resolve all three claims in one case instead of two. 501 F.2d 18 (2d Cir. 1974).]

Justice REHNQUIST delivered the opinion of the Court. . . .

[W]e are faced with the necessity of determining whether the holdings of *Younger,* *Steffel,* and *Samuels* must give way before such interests in efficient judicial administration as were relied upon by the Court of Appeals. We think that the interest of avoiding conflicting outcomes in the litigation of similar issues, while entitled to substantial deference in a unitary system, must of necessity be subordinated to the claims of federalism in this . . . area of the law. The classic example is the petitioner in *Steffel* and his companion. Both were warned that failure to cease pamphleteering would result in their arrest, but while the petitioner in *Steffel* ceased and brought an action in the federal court, his companion did not cease and was prosecuted on a charge of criminal trespass in the state court. The same may be said of the interest in conservation of judicial manpower. As worthy a value as this is in a unitary system, the very existence of one system of federal courts and fifty systems of state courts, all charged with the responsibility for interpreting the United States Constitution, suggests that on occasion there will be duplicating and overlapping adjudication. . . .

We do not agree with the Court of Appeals, therefore, that all three plaintiffs should automatically be thrown into the same hopper for *Younger* purposes, and should thereby each be entitled to injunctive relief. We cannot accept that view, any more than we can accept petitioner's equally Procrustean view that because M & L would have been barred from injunctive relief had it been the sole plaintiff, Salem and Tim-Rob should likewise be barred not only from injunctive relief but from declaratory relief as well. While there plainly may be some circumstances in which legally distinct parties are so closely related that they should all be subject to the *Younger* considerations which govern any one of them, this is not such a case — while respondents are represented by common counsel, and have similar business activities and problems, they are apparently unrelated in terms of ownership, control, and management. We thus think that each of the respondents should be placed in the position required by our cases as if that respondent stood alone.

Respondent M & L could have pursued the course taken by the other respondents after the denial of their request for a temporary restraining order. Had it done so, it would not have subjected itself to prosecution for violation of the ordinance in the state court. When the criminal summonses issued against M & L on the day immediately following the filing of the federal complaint, the federal litigation was in an embryonic stage and no contested matter had been decided. In this posture, M & L's prayer for injunction is squarely governed by *Younger.*

We likewise believe that for the same reasons *Samuels* bars M & L from obtaining declaratory relief, absent a showing of *Younger*'s special circumstances, even though the state prosecution was commenced the day following the filing of the federal complaint. Having violated the ordinance, rather than awaiting the normal development of its federal lawsuit, M & L cannot now be heard to complain that its constitutional contentions are being resolved in a state court. Thus M & L's prayers for both injunctive and declaratory relief are subject to *Younger*'s restrictions.

The rule with regard to the co-plaintiffs, Salem and Tim-Rob, is equally clear, insofar as they seek declaratory relief. Salem and Tim-Rob were not subject to state criminal prosecution at any time prior to the issuance of a preliminary injunction by the District Court. Under *Steffel* they thus could at least have obtained a declaratory judgment upon an ordinary showing of entitlement to that relief. . . .

[S]ince we have previously recognized that "[o]rdinarily . . . the practical effect of [injunctive and declaratory] relief will be virtually identical," *Samuels,* 401 U.S. at 73, we think that Salem and Tim-Rob were entitled to have their claims for preliminary injunctive relief considered without regard to *Younger*'s restrictions. At the conclusion of a successful federal challenge to a state statute or local ordinance, a district court can generally protect the interests of a federal plaintiff by entering a declaratory judgment, and therefore the stronger injunctive medicine will be unnecessary. But prior to final judgment there is no established declaratory remedy comparable to a preliminary injunction; unless preliminary relief is available upon a proper showing, plaintiffs in some situations may suffer unnecessary and substantial irreparable harm. Moreover, neither declaratory nor injunctive relief can directly interfere with enforcement of contested statutes or ordinances except with respect to the particular federal plaintiffs, and the State is free to prosecute others who may violate the statute. . . .

While we regard the question as a close one, we believe that the issuance of a preliminary injunction in behalf of respondents Salem and Tim-Rob was not an abuse of the District Court's discretion. As required to support such relief, these respondents alleged (and petitioner did not deny) that absent preliminary relief they would suffer a substantial loss of business and perhaps even bankruptcy. Certainly the latter type of injury sufficiently meets the standards for granting interim relief, for otherwise a favorable final judgment might well be useless.

The other inquiry relevant to preliminary relief is whether respondents made a sufficient showing of the likelihood of ultimate success on the merits. Both the District Court and the Court of Appeals found such a likelihood. . . .

Although the customary "barroom" type of nude dancing may involve only the barest minimum of protected expression, . . . this form of entertainment might be entitled to First and Fourteenth Amendment protection under some circumstances. . . .

[W]e cannot conclude that the District Court abused its discretion by granting preliminary injunctive relief. . . . The judgment of the Court of Appeals is reversed as to respondent M & L, and affirmed as to respondents Salem and Tim-Rob. . . .

[An opinion of Justice DOUGLAS, dissenting from the denial of relief to M & L, is omitted.]

NOTES ON PRELIMINARY INJUNCTIONS AGAINST PROSECUTION

1. Justifying the *Younger* rules. If Salem Inn might go bankrupt without a preliminary injunction, doesn't M & L face the same risk? Isn't M & L even more likely to go bankrupt if its competitors continue to offer topless entertainment while it is deterred by repeated prosecutions? The *Younger* rules must be justified, if at all, by federalism concerns; they cannot be justified by the view that defense of the criminal prosecution is generally an adequate remedy. Differences between the defensive and injunctive remedies are elaborated in Douglas Laycock, *Federal Interference with State Prosecutions: The Need for Prospective Relief*, 1977 Sup. Ct. Rev. 193.

2. Litigating under *Doran*. If you're representing a client who believes a statute is unconstitutional, how should you advise him after *Doran*? How should you proceed if you're the prosecutor?

3. The limits of preliminary relief. What happens if the ordinance is eventually upheld? The preliminary injunction would then be vacated, and there would be no permanent injunction and no declaratory judgment that the ordinance is unconstitutional. Could Salem Inn and its dancers then be prosecuted for violations committed under the protection of the preliminary injunction? If a preliminary injunction doesn't confer permanent immunity, doesn't it leave plaintiffs in the *Young* dilemma?

Justices Stevens, Marshall, and Brennan debated these issues in Edgar v. MITE Corp., 457 U.S. 624 (1982). The majority did not reach the issue, holding that it

b. Illinois. Edgar v. MITE arose in Illinois, where the Model Penal Code provision had been limited to reliance on appellate decisions "later overruled or reversed." 720 Ill. Comp. Stat. 5/4-8(b)(3). The Illinois courts have accordingly held that reliance on a trial-court judgment dismissing a criminal prosecution on the merits is not a defense to a subsequent prosecution for an identical offense. People v. Knop, 557 N.E.2d 970, 974-975 (Ill. App. Ct. 1990). What does that say about the Court's basic assumption in *Younger*—that defense of a criminal prosecution will authoritatively resolve the constitutional issue?

c. Precedent. There are older cases going both ways on whether reliance on a preliminary injunction is a defense when the statute is silent. Such a defense was allowed in United States v. Mancuso, 139 F.2d 90 (3d Cir. 1943), and in several cases collected in City of Marysville v. Cities Service Oil Co., 3 P.2d 1060 (Kan. 1931). It was disallowed in State v. Wadhams Oil Co., 134 N.W. 1121 (Wis. 1912), and State v. Keller, 70 P. 1051 (Idaho 1902).

The en banc D.C. Circuit has assumed that *Mancuso* is still good law. Clarke v. United States, 915 F.2d 699, 702 (D.C. Cir. 1990). *Clarke* involved not a preliminary injunction but a final declaratory judgment that the law was unconstitutional. That declaratory judgment had been affirmed on appeal, and a petition for rehearing had been denied on the merits, but the case was set for argument to consider whether it had become moot. The government sought to have the declaratory judgment vacated as moot, because the law at issue was an appropriations rider that had been allowed to lapse. Plaintiffs argued that the case was not moot, because they might be prosecuted if the declaratory judgment were vacated. The government conceded at oral argument that the declaratory judgment would be a complete defense to any prosecution for violations committed under its protection. The court accepted that concession; it also said that federal judicial power to prevent federal prosecutions presents a much clearer and simpler question than Edgar v. MITE, which involved federal judicial power to prevent state prosecutions. Seeing no risk of prosecution, the court vacated the declaratory judgment as moot.

NOTES ON FEDERAL LITIGATION AFTER STATE-COURT JUDGMENTS

1. *Younger* after judgment. The usual rules for protecting finality of judgments and preventing repeated litigation of the same issues are the rules of claim preclusion and issue preclusion, which are part of the first-year civil procedure course. But occasionally the Supreme Court has addressed these issues with variations on Younger v. Harris. In Huffman v. Pursue, Ltd., 420 U.S. 592 (1975), the Court held that *Younger* barred a suit to enjoin enforcement of a state-court injunction, at least until state appeals had been exhausted. It is almost unimaginable that the Court would entertain such a suit *after* state appeals had been exhausted; issue preclusion would have been a more straightforward ground for decision. Interjurisdictional claim and issue preclusion is codified in the Full Faith and Credit Act, which requires that state judgments be given "the same full faith and credit in every court within the United States . . . as they have by law or usage in the courts of such State . . . from which they are taken." 28 U.S.C. §1738.

2. *Rooker-Feldman*. Another variation is the *Rooker-Feldman* doctrine, derived from Rooker v. Fidelity Trust Co., 263 U.S. 413 (1923), and District of Columbia Court of Appeals v. Feldman, 460 U.S. 462 (1983). *Rooker-Feldman* bars a federal trial court from reviewing a state-court judgment, and lower courts had broadly construed it to apply to a variety of claims that might in any way be construed as interfering with

a state-court judgment. But the Supreme Court has unanimously confined the doctrine to its original facts. *Rooker-Feldman* now applies only to litigants who lose in state
court and then file a new federal claim directed squarely at reviewing or relitigating
the state-court judgment. Exxon Mobil Corp. v. Saudi Basic Industries Corp., 544 U.S.
280 (2005).

The Court viewed *Exxon Mobil* as a legitimate example of parallel state and federal litigation. Saudi Basic sued Exxon Mobil in state court; Exxon Mobil counterclaimed. Exxon Mobil also filed its claim in a separate action in federal court "to
protect itself in the event it lost in state court on grounds (such as the state statute of
limitations) that might not preclude relief in the federal venue." 544 U.S. at 293-294.
When Exxon Mobil eventually got a judgment on its counterclaim in the state trial
court, the federal court dismissed its federal suit on *Rooker-Feldman* grounds, even
though state appeals were pending. The Supreme Court reversed: Exxon Mobil filed
its federal claim before the judgment in state court, and Exxon Mobil had not lost in
state court; under the new formulation of the rule, either of these grounds is enough.

The Court repeated its narrow understanding of *Rooker-Feldman* in Skinner v.
Switzer, 562 U.S. 521 (2011), a case in which a convicted criminal defendant sued to
force DNA testing of key evidence in the case, noting that it had applied the *Rooker-
Feldman* doctrine only twice.

B.   QUIET TITLE AND THE LIKE

NEWMAN MACHINE CO. v. NEWMAN
166 S.E.2d 63 (N.C. 1969)

The hearing below was on demurrer. The . . . allegations may be summarized as follows: . . .

3. George F. Newman, Jr. [the defendant], owned 64.77% of all the issued and
outstanding shares of capital stock of plaintiff corporation. In March 1950 he made a
gift of certain of his shares to himself as trustee for his children. Thereafter and until
February 6, 1959, he owned individually 53.299% of the capital stock and owned *as
trustee for his children* 11.477% of said shares. In addition, he also owned individually
65% of the outstanding shares of capital stock of three affiliated corporations. . . .

5. On February 6, 1959, . . . Newman . . . sold to the plaintiff corporation at $135.25
per share all [the] shares of [its] stock which he owned. This included both the
53.299% he owned individually and the 11.477% he owned as trustee. The total purchase price was $785,802.50. . . .

8. On February 5, 1965, defendant notified plaintiff by letter that defendant's attorneys were investigating the transaction involving the sale of the stock. On August 27,
1965, defendant requested copies of plaintiff's audit report for the years 1957, 1958,
1959 and 1960; and on November 17, 1965, defendant's attorneys examined copies
of said audit reports at plaintiff's offices. . . . [O]n March 24, 1966, defendant's attorneys wrote plaintiff [that the audit reports showed that Newman had been defrauded
and that the price paid for his shares had been "grossly inadequate." The attorneys
said that they had advised Newman that he was entitled to rescind the transaction or
sue for damages, and that he was legally obligated to sue with respect to the shares
he owned as trustee. They said that Newman had requested them to file suit, but that
they would be willing to discuss settlement first.]

9. Defendant, through his attorneys, continued to make demands on plaintiff and to threaten legal action against plaintiff, including threat of receivership. These threats have seriously jeopardized plaintiff's corporate existence, hampered long-range planning, and seriously affected plaintiff in the conduct of its business affairs.

10. William M. York, Sr., President of plaintiff corporation, is 70 years of age and will be a material witness in any litigation. His evidence should be preserved.

11. A real controversy exists between plaintiff and defendant. The threats constitute a cloud on the title to the shares of stock purchased by plaintiff from . . . Newman [as] Trustee, and this action is brought for the purpose of settling the controversy and removing the cloud on plaintiff's title to the stock in question. . . .

12. Plaintiff prays the court for judgment declaring that it has good title to the 11.477% of its shares of stock purchased from defendant trustee. . . .

Defendant's demurrer was overruled by the trial judge. . . . [T]he Court of Appeals reversed, 163 S.E.2d 279 (N.C. Ct. App. 1968). . . .

HUSKINS, Justice.

A demurrer tests the sufficiency of a pleading, admitting, for that purpose, the truth of factual averments well stated and such relevant inferences of fact as may be deduced therefrom. . . . Demurrers in declaratory judgment actions are controlled by the same principles applicable in other cases. Even so, it is rarely an appropriate pleading to a petition for declaratory judgment. If the complaint sets forth a genuine controversy justiciable under the Declaratory Judgment Act, it is not demurrable even though plaintiff may not be entitled to prevail on the facts alleged in the complaint. This is so because [on the demurrer] the Court is not concerned with whether plaintiff's position is right or wrong but with whether he is entitled to a declaration of rights with respect to the matters alleged.

The complaint and demurrer present these questions:

(1) Does the complaint state a cause of action justiciable under the Declaratory Judgment Act?
(2) Does the complaint state a cause of action in equity to quiet title to personal property?

Plaintiff contends for an affirmative answer to both questions, while defendant argues that an action to quiet title to personalty cannot be maintained in this jurisdiction because there is statutory provision for such suits only with respect to real property. N.C. Gen. Stat. §41-10. Defendant further contends that the type of dispute pictured by the complaint does not qualify for consideration under the Declaratory Judgment Act because (a) a genuine controversy does not exist, (b) the action does not include all necessary parties, (c) the action involves primarily issues of fact rather than questions of law, and (d) the object of the action is "to bag" in advance an impending lawsuit by becoming plaintiff now so as to avoid becoming defendant later.

The excellent briefs of the parties are largely devoted to discussions of whether the complaint states a cause of action justiciable under the Declaratory Judgment Act. We find it unnecessary to decide the first question, however, in view of the conclusion we have reached on the second.

We hold that the complaint states a cause of action to remove cloud and quiet title to personalty and that such action may be maintained in this State. Since the courts generally apply the same principles when title to personalty is involved as they do when title to land is clouded, brief reference to some of the requirements in equity suits to remove cloud and quiet title to realty prior to enactment of N.C. Gen. Stat. §41-10 is helpful to an understanding of the question before us.

Under the old equity practice,

> A bill quia timet [literally, because he fears] was intended to prevent future litigation, by removing existing causes which might affect the plaintiff's title. If one in possession of land under a legal title knew that another was claiming an interest in the land under a title adverse to him, there was no adequate remedy at law for such occupant to test the validity of such claim. Being in possession, he could not sue at law, and the adverse claimant would not sue, so that the adverse claim might be asserted at some future time when the evidence to rebut it might be lost, or at any rate the existence of such claim cast a cloud upon his title which would affect its value. His remedy was a bill in equity against the adverse claimant to have the cloud removed by a decree of the court and thereby quiet his title.

Atwell Campbell McIntosh, *North Carolina Practice and Procedure in Civil Cases* §986 (West 1929). . . .

Prior to 1893, in equity suits to remove cloud or quiet title to realty plaintiff was required to allege and show: (1) that he had no adequate remedy at law; (2) that he was in rightful possession of the land in question; and (3) that the defendant's adverse claim was such as to affect plaintiff's title injuriously. . . . In Busbee v. Lewis, 85 N.C. 332 (1881), plaintiff sought to remove a cloud upon his title and was denied equitable relief because a valid legal objection was apparent on the face of the record.

> [A] court of equity will not . . . remove a . . . cloud . . . based upon a deed alleged in the complaint to be void upon its face, since, if it really be so, the party has always at hand a certain defense against the deed, whenever it may be urged against him.

Id. at 335.

Because the General Assembly considered . . . *Busbee* . . . an inconvenient or unjust application of the equitable doctrines involved, it enacted N.C. Gen. Stat. §41-10, providing . . . that "[a]n action may be brought by any person against another who claims an estate or interest in real property adverse to him for the purpose of determining such adverse claims. . . ." That enactment was designed to avoid some of the limitations imposed upon the remedies formerly embraced by a bill of peace or a bill *quia timet*, and to establish an easy method of quieting titles of land against adverse claims.

Since we have no statute regarding suits in equity to remove cloud or quiet title to personalty, we apply to such suits the same principles which obtained prior to enactment of N.C. Gen. Stat. §41-10 when title to land was involved.

Although such suits were usually brought only in cases involving real property, "the generally accepted view is that a bill to quiet the title or to remove a cloud on the title to personal property may be maintained in equity, in the absence of statutory authorization, where, by reason of exceptional circumstances, there is no adequate remedy at law." Annotation, 105 A.L.R. 291 (1936). In Loggie v. Chandler, 49 A. 1059 (Me. 1901), it was held that a cloud upon the title to personal property in the form of a recorded chattel mortgage could not be removed; but Pomeroy says "there seems no good reason for thus restricting the jurisdiction, and the instances are not infrequent where it has been exercised, in cases of void recorded chattel mortgages, spurious issues of shares of stock, etc." 5 John Norton Pomeroy, *Equity Jurisprudence* §2151 (4th ed., Bancroft-Whitney 1919). . . .

Even though there is no statute in North Carolina authorizing suits to quiet title to personalty, we adhere to the general rule that such suits may be maintained in equity where, due to exceptional circumstances, there is no adequate remedy at law. Here, plaintiff is in possession of the stock it purchased from defendant trustee, and defendant is claiming an interest in it adverse to plaintiff. Being in possession plaintiff cannot sue at law, and defendant will not sue — at least he has not done so during almost two years of threats and demands. His adverse claim may be asserted in court at some future time when plaintiff's evidence to rebut it may be lost. The existence of such a claim casts a cloud upon plaintiff's title to the stock and may adversely affect its value. Under these circumstances plaintiff is entitled to invoke the equitable assistance of the court to remove this cloud and quiet the title to ownership of said stock when defendant, for whatever reasons of his own, continues to threaten but refuses to act. With the ever increasing importance of personal property in the business world of today, especially stocks, bonds, and other intangibles, there is no sound reason why this equitable remedy should not be available to quiet title to personalty as well as realty. . . .

Reversed and remanded.

NOTES ON BILLS TO QUIET TITLE AND RELATED ACTIONS

1. The choice of remedy in *Newman*. Wouldn't a declaratory judgment have worked just as well in *Newman*? Is there any difference between a judgment quieting title in plaintiff and a judgment declaring plaintiff to be the owner? Why is the court still bogged down in the defects of the common law actions to try title?

2. The common law remedies. The most important common law actions in disputes over real property were ejectment and trespass. Neither was available unless defendant had interfered with plaintiff's possession. Trespass was a damage action. Ejectment was essentially a restitutionary action; its aim was to restore plaintiff to possession. Its availability was expanded by elaborate fictional pleadings, but the plea that defendant was in possession could not be fictional. Either ejectment or trespass might resolve title if both sides agreed to use a single action as a test case, but neither worked for a party in possession with an uncooperative antagonist. An owner who lost a chance to sell his property because a third party falsely cast doubt on his title could recover damages in slander of title. But that action would not lie against a defendant who claimed title in himself. There were no reasons for these restrictions that would be persuasive to modern lawyers; all these actions were artificially encumbered for reasons having much more to do with history than with logic or policy, and it rarely occurred to the common law to question such limitations.

A claimant in disputed possession of personal property faced similar obstacles. If he were out of possession, he could sue in replevin, detinue, trover, or conversion, and recover damages, possession, or both. But as long as he remained in possession, the common law provided no remedy. Ejectment, replevin, and similar actions to recover possession were introduced in Brook v. Cullimore, reprinted in section 5.A.1.a; they are considered further in section 8.E.

3. The equitable remedies. The equity court responded to the defects in the legal remedies with the bill to remove cloud on title. A cloud on title is any document tending to prove title, or a lien, in someone other than the plaintiff. A plaintiff in possession could sue to remove such a cloud. The bill to remove cloud traditionally raised only the validity of the document, not the general question of who owned the property. If plaintiff prevailed, the court would order the document rescinded, cancelled, or reformed. In *Newman*, the bill is used to determine adverse claims not supported by any document.

4. The statutory remedies. The bill to quiet title is generally a statutory action that improves on the bill to remove cloud on title. The judgment usually determines ownership, not merely the validity of a single claim. The statutory actions can usually be brought by a plaintiff in or out of possession. But in some states, whether the plaintiff is in possession determines the right to jury trial. If defendant is in possession, the action is still called ejectment, or analogized to ejectment, and either party can demand a jury; if not, the action is analogized to removing a cloud on title and said to be equitable. Thomson v. Thomson, 62 P.2d 358 (Cal. 1936). *Thomson* is still good law; it is cited to deny jury trial on a somewhat analogous claim in Corder v. Corder, 161 P.3d 172, 180 (Cal. 2007). What some states call a bill to remove cloud may be called bill to quiet title in other states. Some states call it a bill to determine adverse claims.

5. Some examples. When quiet title is operating smoothly, the remedy is entirely straightforward and the litigation is about who owns the property. This is as it should be, but it produces few interesting discussions of how the remedy works. A memorable application is Maine v. Adams, 672 S.E.2d 862 (Va. 2009), rejecting Maine's claim to a 1776 print of the Declaration of Independence, and quieting title in a private citizen from Virginia. Another is Black Hills Institute v. South Dakota School of Mines, 12 F.3d 737 (8th Cir. 1993), a suit to quiet title to "Sue, the most complete and valuable *Tyrannosaurus rex* skeleton known to man." Both *Adams* and *Black Hills* illustrate that the court in a quiet title action can declare the defendant to be the owner. *Black Hills* also shows that if necessary to complete relief, the court in a quiet title action can order the loser to turn the property over to the winner—a remedy more restitutionary than declaratory. When the party already in possession is held to be the owner, no such order is necessary; the judgment simply declares who is the owner.

6. Cancellation. Cancellation is an equitable remedy closely related to the bill to remove a cloud on title, and sometimes indistinguishable from it. An example is Northwest Carpets, Inc. v. First National Bank, 630 S.E.2d 407 (Ga. 2006), cancelling a deed that had been given to secure a debt. The debt had been paid, but the lender refused to surrender the deed, apparently hoping to use it to claim the property pursuant to a later debt that was unsecured. Two simpler examples are Eagle National Bank v. Burks, 502 So. 2d 69 (Fla. Dist. Ct. App. 1987), cancelling a note and mortgage on which the statute of limitations had run, and Novak v. Schellenberg, 718 S.W.2d 822 (Tex. Ct. App. 1986), cancelling a deed obtained from feeble parents by fraud and undue influence.

7. Cancellation and irreparable injury. Some jurisdictions took the view that cancellation was not available if it would be an adequate remedy to wait to be sued on the instrument and then defend that lawsuit. A leading example is Johnson v. Swanke, 107 N.W. 481 (Wis. 1906). Johnson paid for a horse with a nonnegotiable promissory note for $3,000. The horse was worthless; sellers had fraudulently misrepresented its value. The court denied cancellation, holding that plaintiff could wait to be sued on the note. The court noted the defect in the legal remedy:

> He would necessarily suffer embarrassment and anxiety by having [the note] outstanding against him, till the holder might see fit to enable him to show its true character and obtain a judicial decree in respect thereto by way of defense. Most men would so tire of such a situation as to be constrained to buy their peace, rather than to have it postponed till such time as their adversary might see fit to attack.

Id. at 482. But the Wisconsin precedents held that this defect was outweighed by the note holder's right to jury trial.

The English rule made cancellation routinely available in fraud cases; the American cases were divided. Even the *Johnson* court implied that it would cancel a *negotiable* note in otherwise identical circumstances. A negotiable note could have been sold to a holder in due course, who would take the note free of Johnson's fraud defense unless he had notice of it. That would eliminate Johnson's defensive legal remedy, although he could sue the sellers for reimbursement if he were required to pay the note.

We suspect that few courts would follow *Johnson* today; courts that care about jury trial could arrange for it by letting defendant counterclaim on the note and trying the counterclaim first. But note another problem: How is worry about an outstanding note different from worry about potential liability for damages to a personal injury victim? Ownership of the horse was not at issue; there was no need to decide whether to invest more money in an asset that might be reclaimed by another. Should it matter that there is a piece of paper that could be physically cancelled? Are the personal injury cases just a special protection for plaintiffs with physical injuries?

8. Vocabulary. "Cancellation" is sometimes used interchangeably with "rescission," especially with respect to contracts, and it is hard to see any practical difference. So far as we can tell, there is no consensus on vocabulary. There is some tendency to speak of rescinding contracts and cancelling other instruments.

9. Before or after performance. It is useful to distinguish "rescission" or "cancellation" in purely executory examples from "rescission and restitution" or "cancellation and restitution" where value has been transferred and must be returned. If a contract is wholly executory, a party can simply announce that she is rescinding and wait to see if the other side does anything. If she sues for cancellation or rescission before either side has begun to perform, she is in effect seeking a declaratory judgment that she is entitled to rescind. But rescission more commonly refers to the remedy available when the contract has been wholly or partly performed. At that point, the contract can be rescinded, or cancelled, only if each party returns all that she has received under the contract and pays for anything that cannot be physically returned. In these circumstances, rescission is a restitutionary remedy; we will consider it in section 8.B.3.b.

Similarly, if plaintiff seeks to cancel a note or deed after she has already transferred cash or tangible property pursuant to the note or deed, she may obtain restitution or damages along with the order of cancellation. An example is Memphis Hardwood Flooring Co. v. Daniel, 771 So. 2d 924 (Miss. 2000), where defendant had obtained timberlands by fraud and undue influence. The court cancelled the deed and awarded double damages under a Mississippi statute for the timber already cut.

10. Re-execution. The opposite of cancellation is also available. Equity will order re-execution of a lost instrument if there is clear proof of its original execution and terms. An example is Smith v. Lujan, 588 F.2d 1304 (9th Cir. 1979). This remedy can also be understood as declaratory: It anticipates the dispute that would arise when something came to turn on whether the instrument had ever existed.

11. Classifying these remedies. All these nonpossessory remedies represent early efforts to provide declaratory relief in situations where such relief is especially needed. Sometimes these remedies were coercive in form; for example, defendant would be ordered to physically cancel his deed and, if necessary, imprisoned until he did so. But these remedies were always declaratory in purpose and effect. They resolved questions of ownership before there was a trespass or ouster, or even a threat of either, and before a suit for damages or a conventional injunction or an order at law for possession would lie. In short, they removed uncertainty by declaring rights. Increasingly, these actions are declaratory in form. It is no longer necessary to coerce the losing litigant into physically giving effect to the court's determination. Under Federal Rule 70 and similar state provisions, the court can make the decree self-executing or order a court official to execute legal documents on defendant's behalf.

These remedies can also be thought of as restitutionary: Defendant would be unjustly enriched if he could benefit from a legal document that should be cancelled. The restitutionary function is dominant when defendant has the property and is ordered to give it back. The declaratory function is more prominent when plaintiff is still in possession. As always, the point is to understand the remedies, not to worry about their classification.

12. Why not declaratory judgments? The general declaratory judgment act is a twentieth-century invention. It is not limited to specific subjects or contexts, and it seems capable of replacing all the more specialized declaratory remedies discussed in this section. But there does not seem to be much prospect of its actually doing so. This is largely because a system based on precedent is backward looking: The cases describe the earlier forms, older lawyers who have already learned about them have no incentive to change the system, and younger lawyers forced to learn about them have no power to change the system. It is partly because the earlier forms seem to grant more relief, although it is hard to think of any practical difference between, for example, an order to surrender an instrument for cancellation and a declaratory judgment that the instrument is without effect and creates neither rights nor duties.

In Toledo Museum of Art v. Ullin, 477 F. Supp. 2d 802 (N.D. Ohio 2006), the court entertained a declaratory judgment to determine title to works of art stolen by the Nazis in 1938. Plaintiff sued for a declaratory judgment, apparently hoping to avoid the statute of limitations that would apply to a claim in quiet title, conversion, or restitution. The court had no trouble with the idea of determining title in a declaratory judgment action, but it still held the claim barred by limitations.

The Texas court had an actual reason not to allow declaratory judgments to be used in place of that state's statutory action of trespass to try title. The Texas declaratory judgment act has a provision for attorneys' fees; the trespass-to-try-title act does not. Martin v. Amerman, 133 S.W.3d 262 (Tex. 2004). Texas courts remain divided over precisely when it is appropriate to bring a declaratory judgment action rather than a trespass-to-try-title claim. One appeals court recently held that "[i]f a dispute involves a claim of superior title and the determination of possessory interests in property, it must be brought as a trespass-to-try-title action." Jinkins v. Jinkins, 522 S.W.3d 771, 786 (Tex. Ct. App. 2017). Meanwhile, in 2007, the legislature had amended the declaratory judgment act to permit declaratory judgments to determine boundary disputes. Tex. Civ. Prac. & Remedies Code §37.004(c). Does this patchwork of laws concerning declarations over property rights make any sense?

13. Arguments about the scope of these remedies. Even if the older remedies persist, the availability of the declaratory judgment to fill any gaps should lead to less and less litigation of the *Newman* sort, in which the parties argue over the precise scope of the older remedies. But things that should happen do not necessarily happen; there is a surprising amount of litigation over the scope of the older remedies. Some examples:

a. Boundary disputes. Some courts distinguish mere boundary disputes from true title disputes; ejectment is the remedy for the one and quiet title for the other. Huffman v. Peterson, 718 N.W.2d 522 (Neb. 2006).

b. Claims void on their face. Demura v. County of Volusia, 618 So. 2d 754 (Fla. Dist. Ct. App. 1993), held that quiet title would not lie to remove a judgment lien from plaintiff's homestead, because the homestead exemption made the lien wholly ineffectual and there was no dispute to resolve. This is the argument that North Carolina rejected in the statute described in *Newman*. The court did say that plaintiffs could file for a declaratory judgment that the property was their homestead, if there were a real dispute about that.

For a squarely contrary case, see Tarrant Bank v. Miller, 833 S.W.2d 666 (Tex. Ct. App. 1992), removing the cloud of a judgment lien on a homestead. Plaintiff in *Tarrant Bank* had a contract to sell the property, but contrary to the Florida court's wishful thinking, the title company had refused to issue a title insurance policy and the buyer had backed out of the deal. Plaintiff also recovered $17,000 in compensatory and punitive damages.

Tarrant Bank is the typical case; *Demura* is the outlier. The usual rule is that a bill to remove cloud can be used against anything "that has a tendency, even in a slight degree, to cast doubt upon the owner's title," and that "the density of the cloud can make no difference in the right to have it removed." Robinson v. Khan, 948 P.2d 1347, 1349 (Wash. Ct. App. 1998).

c. Plaintiff out of possession. Friedman v. Monaco & Brown Corp., 610 A.2d 885 (N.J. Super. Ct. App. Div. 1992), says that quiet title will not lie if plaintiff is out of possession, but it goes on to emphasize that this plaintiff had been out of possession for 50 years and had no colorable claim of title since a 1939 judgment foreclosing his mother's interest. His proper remedy was a motion to vacate that judgment; treating the bill as such a motion, the court rejected his claim on the merits and also as untimely.

d. Plaintiff not claiming an interest in the property. The Supreme Court has held that a suit seeking to divest the United States of title to land is not a quiet title suit if the plaintiff does not himself claim an interest in the land. Match-E-Be-Nash-She-Wish Band of Pottawatomi Indians v. Patchak, 567 U.S. 209 (2012). This odd question arose when a neighbor sued to stop construction and operation of an Indian casino by alleging that the Indians didn't own the land.

14. The declaratory judgment claim in *Newman*. Consider defendant's four objections to maintenance of a declaratory judgment action in *Newman*. We are not told who the allegedly necessary party is, so we can't evaluate that. (Just guessing, the allegedly necessary parties were the Newman children, who were fully represented by their father as trustee.) Is there anything to the other three? Do you have any doubt about the existence of an actual controversy? Don't most declaratory judgment actions involve potential defendants as plaintiffs? Is there anything wrong with that? Finally, why should issues of fact be a barrier to declaratory relief? The objection that factual issues should not be decided is often made, and occasionally made successfully, in declaratory litigation. The argument was summarily rejected in the very first case under the federal act. Aetna Life Insurance Co. v. Haworth, 300 U.S. 227, 242 (1937).

C. REFORMATION

HAND v. DAYTON-HUDSON
775 F.2d 757 (6th Cir. 1985)

Before LIVELY, Chief Judge, and CONTIE and WELLFORD, Circuit Judges.

CONTIE, Circuit Judge.

Plaintiff John Hand appeals from the entry of summary judgment . . . in favor of defendant Dayton-Hudson Corporation in a diversity action alleging breach of an employment contract and age discrimination. The district court found that Hand had fraudulently altered a release which both parties subsequently signed. The court reformed the release to conform to its original meaning. For the reasons set forth below, we affirm.

I.

The historical facts are undisputed. Appellant Hand is an attorney and had been employed by appellee Dayton-Hudson Corp. from 1967 to 1982. In February of 1982, appellant lost his job with Dayton-Hudson allegedly as a result of a major restructuring by Dayton-Hudson.

Upon firing Hand, Dayton-Hudson made an offer to pay him $38,000 if Hand agreed to release Dayton-Hudson of any claims he might have against it. Hand refused this offer, asserting that he was already entitled to this sum under his employment contract. A release was nonetheless drafted according to the terms originally offered by Dayton-Hudson, and was given to Hand for consideration. He was told he must accept or reject Dayton-Hudson's offer by March 20, 1982. . . . [O]n March 19th . . . Hand met with Dayton-Hudson's agent . . . and the parties signed the document Hand brought with him.

Prior to the signing, Hand had prepared another release which provided that he was releasing all claims "except as to claims of age discrimination and breach of contract." Except for the changes made by Hand to limit the terms of the release, Hand's release was identical to the original prepared by Dayton-Hudson. The typewriter on which it was written was of the same type and model; the number and structure of paragraphs were identical; all other language and punctuation was identical; and the headings were also identical. . . . Hand attached the outline of termination benefits to this release in the same manner that it had been attached to the original release. Despite the changes made, the documents appeared superficially identical.

On December 7, 1983, Hand filed a complaint in district court alleging age discrimination and breach of contract claims against Dayton-Hudson. Dayton-Hudson answered that Hand had fraudulently procured its agent's signature on the modified release and requested reformation of the release to conform to the original offer made by Dayton-Hudson. . . . After a hearing, the court granted summary judgment on the issue of fraud, reformed the release, and held that summary judgment was appropriate [on the contract and discrimination claims] since Hand's claims were precluded by the reformed release.

II.

Upon review of a district court's grant of summary judgment, this court must determine whether there was any genuine issue of material fact when the evidence is viewed in the light most favorable to the party opposing the motion. . . . Hand asserts that the district court erred in finding on a summary judgment motion that Hand had committed fraud. Hand also asserts that summary judgment was inappropriate because reformation is not a proper remedy when there is not a mutual mistake of fact, even in the presence of fraud.

A . . .

Hand, in his affidavit, [stated that] he "prepared the release knowingly and deliberately" and that he intended to "turn the tables" on Dayton-Hudson. . . . Hand committed fraud by not informing Dayton-Hudson of the changes he made in the release.

The defendant was excused from not having read the new document because the general rule of being held responsible for contracts one signs, even if one has not read them, "is not applicable when the neglect to read is not due to carelessness alone, but was induced by some stratagem, trick, or artifice on the part of the one seeking to enforce the contract." Komraus Plumbing & Heating, Inc. v. Cadillac Sands Motel, Inc., 195 N.W.2d 865, 868 (Mich. 1972). . . . The failure to read most definitely resulted from Hand's clever scheme, and, accordingly, does not bar Dayton-Hudson from challenging the validity of the fraudulent release. . . .

B.

Appellant Hand further contends that reformation is not a proper remedy in this case. Under Michigan law, reformation generally requires a mutual mistake of fact. To grant reformation when there is merely a unilateral mistake would be harming one party while benefiting another without regard to what the parties actually intended. This would be equivalent to drafting a new contract between the parties[,] which courts are reluctant to do. However, there is an exception to the requirement for mutual mistake under Michigan law. "[W]here there is mistake on one side and fraud or inequitable conduct on the other reformation may be decreed." DeGood v. Gillard, 231 N.W. 102, 103 (Mich. 1930).

To use this exception, the finding that one person knew the writing did not reflect the other party's intent must be supported by clear and convincing evidence. This exception is consistent with the *Restatement (Second) of Contracts* §166[,] which provides that if a party's "assent is induced by the other party's fraudulent misrepresentation as to the contents or effect of a writing . . . the court . . . may reform the writing to express the terms of the agreement as asserted."

The appellant asserts that this exception can only be invoked when there has been a meeting of the minds regarding the terms of the release; and since appellant never intended to release his asserted claims against Dayton-Hudson, he argues there was no meeting of the minds. This interpretation of the law is too narrow. Although some Michigan cases involve "meeting of the minds" fact patterns, other cases suggest that the exception to the mutual mistake requirement is designed primarily to combat the inequities which naturally result from the fraudulent inducement of an innocent party to sign a contract the guilty party knew did not reflect the other party's intent. . . .

Hand's conduct falls squarely within the exception established by the Michigan case law. Hand was aware of Dayton-Hudson's position and he intentionally modeled a new release after its offer. His obvious goal was for Dayton-Hudson to believe that it was signing the original document it had given Hand—that Hand was accepting Dayton-Hudson's offer rather than [making] a counteroffer. Therefore, since there was a mistake by Dayton-Hudson which was induced by Hand's fraud, the district court correctly applied Michigan law by reforming the release to conform to the defrauded party's understanding.

Accordingly, the judgment of the district court is AFFIRMED.

WELLFORD, Circuit Judge, concurring:

I fully concur in the rationale . . . in Part I and Part II-A . . . that Dayton-Hudson . . . is not precluded from challenging the validity of the release, and further, that it would not be precluded from setting the release aside and recouping the $38,000 it paid over to Hand on false pretenses and/or concealment of a material fact. The difficulty with Part II-B . . . is my reservation and uncertainty that Michigan law permits a reformation binding Hand to Dayton-Hudson's version of the termination arrangement particularly since Hand contends that his pre-existing rights would entitle him to as much as $38,000 in the event of his discharge. I refrain from dissent, however, because Hand's unconscionable conduct as an attorney upon whom Dayton-Hudson had a reasonable right to rely as a former client should not be the basis to give him a "second bite at the apple," and to relitigate his age discrimination claim.

Under the circumstances, since Hand has never offered to return the $38,000 improperly obtained by him . . . , I am satisfied that justice is served by the affirmance. . . . I therefore concur in the result. . . .

NOTES ON REFORMATION

1. *Hand* and the standard case. The standard explanation of reformation is that the parties had an actual agreement, and that the writing does not reflect that agreement. When there is such a mutual mistake in the writing that records the agreement, the writing is reformed to reflect the actual agreement. Was there ever an actual agreement in *Hand*? Should it be enough that Hand led Dayton-Hudson to believe there was an actual agreement? Won't the defendant who fraudulently changes a writing always be able to say he never agreed to the other side's terms? The explanation varies, but unilateral mistake induced by fraud is also a settled ground for reformation.

Moreover, many cases say it is enough to reform a contract that one side knew about the other's unilateral mistake and said nothing. An example is Scion Breckenridge Managing Member, LLC v. ASB Allegiance Real Estate Fund, 68 A.3d 665, 678-679 (Del. 2013), overruling earlier contrary Delaware precedent. And the *Restatement (Second) of Contracts* §(20)(2)(a) (Am. Law Inst. 1981) states an analogous rule, providing that when the parties have different understandings of the terms, one party knows of the other's different understanding, and the other party does not, a contract is formed in accordance with the understanding of the innocent party.

2. Reformation or rescission? Reformation was not the only remedy available in *Hand*. The release could also have been rescinded for fraud. Be sure you understand the difference.

Reformation leaves the release in effect as reformed. Hand gets to keep the $38,000; Dayton-Hudson is still released; Hand cannot sue for breach of contract or age discrimination.

Rescission would reverse the transaction. Dayton-Hudson would get its $38,000 back, Hand would get the release back, and Hand *could* sue for breach of contract and age discrimination.

The court has a choice of remedies in *Hand* because it is willing to hold Hand to his false representations. In cases of mutual mistake, which do not involve fraud, there is no choice between reformation and rescission. Sometimes one is appropriate and sometimes the other, but not both. If the parties had an actual agreement, the writing should be reformed to reflect that agreement. The mistake was in the writing.

If the parties made a mistake about the premises of their agreement—a mistake about some fact in the world outside their word-processing machines—reformation is not a solution. The court cannot reform the contract because it cannot know what the parties would have agreed to but for the mistake.

3. An example. To make the distinction concrete, consider Castle v. Daniels, 475 N.E.2d 149 (Ohio Ct. App. 1984). Plaintiffs sold part of their land to defendants. Before they closed the deal, they walked the boundaries together; both sides understood that defendants were not buying the barn and hayfield. But the deed's description of the land included the barn and hayfield. Three years later, plaintiffs successfully sued to reform the deed.

Suppose instead the parties had agreed to buy and sell plaintiffs' entire tract and the deed had accurately described the tract. Suppose also the problem was that both sides had been absentee owners, and they both thought the tract was a barn and hayfield, when in fact it was wetlands with no commercial value and development precluded by environmental laws. But for the mistake, would they have agreed to a sale at all? At what price? The court can rescind the whole transaction, or it can refuse relief if it thinks they assumed the risk of what they didn't know, but it can't reform the writing to make a new contract for the parties.

4. Other law bearing on *Hand*. Judge Wellford relies on Hand's failure to tender back the $38,000. A later Michigan decision holds that a plaintiff who signs a release and then sues anyway must tender any consideration received for the release, and must do so not later than when he files the complaint. Stefanac v. Cranbrook Educational Community, 458 N.W.2d 56 (1990). Such requirements are limited by the Older Workers' Benefit Protection Act, 29 U.S.C. §626(f)(1), which imposes protective procedural requirements on agreements releasing claims under the Age Discrimination in Employment Act. Releases that do not comply with these requirements are voidable at the election of the employee. The Supreme Court has held that workers may rescind a voidable release and sue for age discrimination without tendering back any severance pay or other consideration they received in exchange for the release. Oubre v. Entergy Operations, Inc., 522 U.S. 422 (1998).

5. Evidentiary problems. If the parties agree that the written contract does not reflect their actual agreement, they can reform it themselves. *Hand* is unusual in having a defendant who admits that he unilaterally changed the writing and litigates anyway. If litigation is required, plaintiff must prove by clear and convincing evidence (beyond a reasonable doubt in a few states) that both sides originally intended something that defendant denies ever having intended and that is inconsistent with what they wrote down. Plaintiff is likely to lose unless he has some sort of evidence to resolve the swearing match. The prior draft was probably critical in *Hand*; what might Hand have testified to otherwise? The course of dealing was critical in *Castle*; plaintiffs had harvested the hay for three years before defendants objected. Testimony of third parties, such as lawyers and brokers, may resolve the dispute, but attorney-client privilege and duties of confidentiality sometimes prevent that for the lawyers. In Drake v. Hance, 673 S.E.2d 411 (N.C. Ct. App. 2009), where the deed conveyed lots 11 and 15, the key piece of evidence was the earlier contract, which provided only for the sale of lot 11. And in In re Platt, 413 P.3d 818 (Mont. 2018), there was an earlier draft of the contract and also an e-mail, written when the parties were still on friendly terms, instructing the attorney who was drafting the documents, which led the court to conclude that contract reformation was appropriate to reflect the parties' original intentions.

Defendant's employees may be willing to testify that the original understanding was different from what their employer now claims, but that cannot always be expected. The problem is not so much deliberate perjury, although there is some of that. Perhaps more important, it is easy for a witness to convince himself that he has always believed what it is now in his interest to believe. And of course, plaintiffs often think defense witnesses must be lying when the problem is that the parties failed to agree in the first place: Plaintiff thought one thing and defendant another, and there was no agreement inconsistent with the writing. It is not enough for plaintiff to prove that there was a mistake or that the writing is inaccurate; plaintiff must prove what the actual agreement was. Neither the statute of frauds nor the parol evidence rule prohibits testimony on these issues.

6. Unspoken agreements. What if both parties intended the same thing, but they never expressed that intent to each other and it is not reflected in the writing? Board of Trustees v. Insurance Corp., 969 F.2d 329 (7th Cir. 1992), was a dispute over the policy limits of an insurance policy. There was a $5 million limit per year; the question was whether there was a separate $5 million limit for a four-month rider issued to adjust the policy's anniversary date. Representatives of the insured, the insurance broker, and the insurer all testified that they intended a separate $5 million limit for the rider, although none of them had ever discussed that intention and the rider was unclear. The court reformed the rider to reflect their shared intention.

7. The rights of third parties. A similar insurance case also raised the question of third-party rights. Here reformation in accordance with the parties' intent reduced the coverage stated in the policy by $1 million. American Employers Insurance Co. v. St. Paul Fire & Marine Insurance Co., 594 F.2d 973 (4th Cir. 1979). The resulting $1 million liability fell on an excess insurer, American. American was not party to the mistake and didn't know about it. Should that be enough to prevent reformation? What if American didn't know the relevant terms of the underlying policy either, or didn't rely on them? In that case, wouldn't American be seeking a million-dollar windfall from the mistake? The standard for protecting third parties is formulated in varying ways, but reliance is usually the essential element.

Sometimes third parties benefit from reformation. Consider Patton v. Ditmyer, 2006 WL 3896780 (Ohio Ct. App. 2006). The Pattons bought a house and four lots from the Arnolds; the deed misdescribed the Arnolds' property and included the Ditmyers' house. The court reformed the deed and quieted title in the Ditmyers.

8. Classifying the remedy. Like quiet title, reformation can be classified in more than one way. Restitution scholars commonly claim it as restitutionary, because it deprives defendant of unjust enrichment from the mistake. The comments to *Restatement (Third) of Restitution and Unjust Enrichment* §12 (Am. Law Inst. 2011) carefully distinguish the remedy, reformation, from the substantive law of restitution and contract that governs "mistake in expression" in operative legal documents.

We have treated reformation as declaratory, because it can be brought to resolve the potential claims created by the mistaken writing before those claims give rise to any other justiciable dispute. Castle v. Daniels in note 3 is a pure suit to reform the deed. Plaintiffs had not been dispossessed, so nothing was restored to them; there was no suit for any other relief between the parties. Reforming the deed was the functional equivalent of a bill to quiet title. The remedy looks more restitutionary when the property has changed hands and must be returned. And as always, classification is only an aid to understanding; nothing turns on debates at the margin.

9. Ripeness and irreparable injury. Reformation is an equitable remedy. There does not seem to be any ripeness or irreparable injury requirement, although not many cases are filed in which these issues could plausibly be raised. Usually, the mistake is not discovered, or no one is motivated to do anything about it, until some other dispute has arisen. Thus, it is quite common to see suits for reformation and breach of the contract as reformed, suits for reformation and counterclaims for breach of the contract as written, suits for breach of the contract as written and counterclaims for reformation, or suits for reformation of a deed and to quiet title in the intended owner.

10. A Supreme Court example or two. The Court appeared to authorize reformation of a retirement plan on the basis of deceptive disclosures about the plan in plan summaries issued to employees in CIGNA v. Amara, 563 U.S. 421 (2011). The case is further described in Section 6.C.

Kansas v. Nebraska, 135 S. Ct. 1042 (2015), more fully described in Section 8.B.3.a, involved a dispute over the waters of the Republican River. There was an interstate compact from 1943, a Supreme Court interpretation of the compact in 2000, and a settlement agreement in 2002. The settlement agreement had a technical appendix specifying how Nebraska's water usage would be calculated. It turned out that in dry years, the calculation method did not work as intended, and the error was large. The Supreme Court modified the calculation method to correct the error.

The Court used forms of the word "modify" ten times, and forms of the word "reform" four times, to describe what it was doing. The Court relied on its power to equitably apportion the water even as it interpreted and enforced the states' agreement. It talked more as though it were modifying the earlier judgment than reforming a contract. And it emphasized that it was making a technical correction to achieve the principal goals of the agreement.

The four dissenters argued that the rules for reformation were not satisfied. The problems with the calculation method resulted from neglecting an important fact about the world, not from any error in drafting. The Court could not reform the contract to make it fair and equitable, or even to make the technical detail better conform to the larger purpose set out in in the agreement. And in this seemingly technical dispute, the four dissenters were Justices Roberts, Scalia, Thomas, and Alito.

D.   DECLARATORY RELIEF AT LAW

NOTES ON NOMINAL DAMAGES

1. Nominal damages as a way to reach the merits. Recall part III of Carey v. Piphus, reprinted in section 2.G.3. The Court said that violations of the Due Process Clause were so important that plaintiff could recover one dollar even if he had not been injured. Why would anyone sue for nominal damages? And why would the courts allow such suits? The most obvious purpose was to obtain a form of declaratory relief in a legal system with no general declaratory judgment act. When a landowner sued his neighbor for nominal damages in trespass, he presumably was not interested in the dollar, but in the court's determination that the neighbor was trespassing. The suit for nominal damages might resolve an underlying dispute about the location of a boundary, or about an easement entitling the neighbor to cross the land. The common law courts would not declare such matters directly, but the suit for nominal damages allowed them to do so indirectly. Suits for nominal damages can still be used in this way today, although it is rarely necessary to do so.

In Carey v. Piphus, nominal damages were the consolation prize in an action for actual damages that plaintiff failed to prove. Here too they can be said to serve a declaratory function. The court might have been reluctant to issue a declaratory judgment that the school board had once violated plaintiff's right to due process; if no other charges were pending against plaintiff, the question could easily be considered moot. Awarding one dollar allows the court to decide that the school board violated the Due Process Clause and embody that decision in a judgment. But it is easy to overstate the importance of this. An opinion saying that the school board violated the Due Process Clause but plaintiff proved no actual damages would guide the school board's future behavior as effectively as a judgment for nominal damages. And the unavailability of formal declaratory relief is least troubling where there is formally no continuing controversy; if either side could show a need for a declaratory judgment to eliminate uncertainty, the court would probably issue it.

Professor McConnell argued, when he was a judge, that courts should not decide a claim for nominal damages unless there is an actual controversy that would support a claim for a declaratory judgment. Utah Animal Rights Coalition v. Salt Lake City Corp., 371 F.3d 1248 (10th Cir. 2004). He recognized that this is not the law. But as noted in section 4.A.1 in the notes following United States v. W.T. Grant Co., the Eleventh Circuit has now held that a claim of nominal damages alone is not enough to save a case that is otherwise moot. Flanigan's Enterprises, Inc. v. Davenport, 868 F.3d 1248 (11th Cir. 2017) (en banc).

2. Attorneys' fees. An award of nominal damages under a federal statute that provides for attorneys' fees makes plaintiff a prevailing party and thus eligible to recover fees from defendant. But the Court has decided that the appropriate fee for such a plaintiff should "usually" be zero. Farrar v. Hobby, 506 U.S. 103, 115 (1992). Justice O'Connor, concurring, thought that a fee award might be reasonable if plaintiff had prevailed on an important legal issue. But plainly a plaintiff in such a case should seek a declaratory judgment or injunction, and not merely nominal damages for violation of the principle established in the judgment.

3. Class actions. The Ninth Circuit has held that when nominal damages are awarded in a class action, the award must run to each class member, not just to the class representatives. Cummings v. Connell, 402 F.3d 936 (9th Cir. 2005). The difference is significant; the court awarded one dollar to each of 37,000 class members. The district court had considered awarding one cent to each class member; it rejected that alternative on the grounds that it "would more trivialize plaintiffs' constitutional rights than vindicate them" and that defendant would still bear the cost of cutting 37,000 checks. Id. at 942 n.4. Instead, it awarded one dollar each to the seven class representatives. Cases elsewhere, collected in the Ninth Circuit opinion, appear to be split.

The district court also awarded substantial attorneys' fees in *Cummings*. The Ninth Circuit appeared to approve, but it remanded the fee issue so the district court could consider whether a judgment for $37,000 instead of $7.00 justified a larger fee.

NOTES ON QUO WARRANTO

1. The writ. Quo warranto (literally, by what authority) is a specialized writ for determining the right to hold a public office or corporate franchise. Like mandamus, prohibition, and habeas corpus, quo warranto is a relic of the writ system that has survived to the present. The action is typically brought in the name of the state, or the attorney general, but in most states there are procedural devices that allow a competing claimant to the office to initiate and control the action.

2. And its varied uses. Quo warranto can be used to raise almost any ground that renders an incumbent ineligible for his office. Examples include a county commissioner with a burglary conviction in his past, Reed v. State ex rel. Davis, 961 So. 2d 89 (Ala. 2006); a village clerk who was not a resident of the village, State ex rel. Myers v. Brown, 721 N.E.2d 1053 (Ohio 2000); an elected candidate who got on the ballot with defective nominating petitions, Burns v. Kurtenbach, 327 N.W.2d 636 (S.D. 1982); and corporate directors elected only by a group of minority shareholders, Hale v. Liljeberg, 895 So. 2d 28 (La. Ct. App. 2005). The writ can also be used to test whether an office holder is exceeding his powers and usurping the authority of another office. Halverson v. Hardcastle, 163 P.3d 428 (Nev. 2007).

The writ can be used to question whether the office itself exists, Gwinn v. Kane, 339 A.2d 838 (Pa. Commw. Ct.), *aff'd*, 348 A.2d 900 (Pa. 1975) (using quo warranto to test the creation of an office of special prosecutor), or whether a school board or municipality exists, People ex rel. Lerch v. Sandman, 170 N.E. 211 (Ill. 1930). Some states use the writ to test municipal annexations, presumably on the theory that the question is whether the municipal corporation is authorized to govern in the annexed area. O'Shields v. City of Memphis, 2017 WL 715151 (Tenn. Ct. App., Feb. 23, 2017).

Some states use quo warranto to challenge irregularities in election procedures. Delgado v. Sunderland, 767 N.E.2d 662 (N.Y. 2002). Quo warranto was one of the many claims asserted in the Florida Supreme Court in the litigation over the 2000 presidential election. Palm Beach County Canvassing Board v. Harris, 772 So. 2d 1220 (Fla.), *vacated as* Bush v. Palm Beach County Canvassing Board, 531 U.S. 70 (2000). The quo warranto claim appears to have been a hedge against jurisdictional uncertainties; the Florida court relied on the much more specific and developed provisions of the Florida statutes on election contests.

3. Classifying the remedy. This is another remedy that is hard to classify. Its form is ambiguous, but its basic effect is clear enough. The entry of a judgment against defendant immediately and of its own force ousts defendant from the office. There is no order to defendant to vacate, and no writ of execution directing the sheriff to remove her; this is what makes it seem declaratory. But it has immediate operative effect: An individual defendant is immediately out of office, Foster v. Kansas ex rel. Johnston, 112 U.S. 201, 204-205 (1884); a municipal defendant immediately ceases to exist, *Lerch*. The cases and statutes call it a judgment of ouster. 735 Ill. Comp. Stat. 5/18-108.

Moreover, fines or damages can be imposed on defendant, although this is apparently rare, and the writ can be used to forfeit corporate charters as a penalty for illegal conduct. An example is Attorney General v. Diamond Mortgage Co., 327 N.W.2d 805 (Mich. 1982), in which the attorney general sought to revoke Diamond's corporate charter for repeated violations of the usury and consumer protection laws. In these applications, the writ seems principally punitive.

NOTE ON CORAM NOBIS

A far more obscure survivor of the writ system is coram nobis (literally, in our presence), a writ by which a court could correct clerical errors in the entry of a judgment after the usual time for appeal or corrective motions had expired. In the United States, the writ was expanded to reach fundamental errors deemed too important to leave uncorrected. The writ has been abolished in federal civil cases, Fed. R. Civ. P. 60(e), because Rule 60 codifies the grounds and procedures for modifying judgments. But it survives in federal criminal cases, and the Supreme Court has held that military courts have coram nobis jurisdiction. United States v. Denedo, 556 U.S. 904 (2009).

The writ looks declaratory because it is needed only when the defendant is no longer in custody, so that habeas corpus is unavailable. Denedo sought to vacate a 1998 court-martial conviction on the ground of ineffective assistance of counsel; the conviction mattered because the government was using it to deport him. The writ was available to present his claim. Considering the merits on remand, the U.S. Navy-Marine Corps Court of Criminal Appeals rejected his ineffective assistance of counsel claim. 2010 WL 996432 (N.M. Ct. Crim. App. 2010).

More famously, coram nobis was used to vacate, for prosecutorial misconduct, the convictions of those criminal defendants who tested the internment of Japanese-Americans during World War II. See, e.g., Korematsu v. United States, 584 F. Supp. 1406 (N.D. Cal. 1984). The government did not appeal, and we are told that it did not defend very vigorously.

CHAPTER
8

Benefit to Defendant as the Measure of Relief: Restitution

<hr>

A. RESTITUTION FROM INNOCENT DEFENDANTS—AND SOME WHO ARE TREATED AS INNOCENT

1. *Introducing Restitution—Mistake*

BLUE CROSS HEALTH SERVICES, INC. v. SAUER
800 S.W.2d 72 (Mo. Ct. App. 1990)

CARL R. GAERTNER, Presiding Judge.

Blue Cross Health Services, Inc. . . . appeals from the order granting defendants R.T. Sauer Agency, Ltd., and Robert Sauer a new trial. We reverse and remand . . . with directions to reinstate the judgment.

William R. Sauer's medical, drug and alcohol problems since childhood left him "physically and mentally incapacitated." On June 6, 1984, William R. Sauer, upon admission to Missouri Baptist Hospital, informed the admission clerk he carried Blue Cross Health Insurance but did not have his Blue Cross card with him. [In fact, his coverage had recently been terminated for nonpayment of premiums. His father, Robert T. Sauer, had been paying the premiums.] At the time of admission, William R. Sauer gave his address as P.O. Box 176, Chesterfield, Missouri. [This was the address of his father's wholly owned business, the R.T. Sauer Agency.]

In 1984, Missouri Baptist Hospital Patient Accounts' Department had an on-line computer [link] with Blue Cross. Although William had provided his middle initial on admission, a hospital employee . . . failed to transmit his middle initial. The computer noted coverage for a William J. Sauer of Milwaukee, Wisconsin. The clerk, apparently assuming a change of address for . . . William J. Sauer, entered the address William R. Sauer had provided.

From July 27, 1984 through February 22, 1985, Blue Cross mistakenly mailed sixty-six checks [totaling more than $22,000] to William Sauer at P.O. Box 176, Chesterfield, Missouri[,] which were intended to cover medical services for William J. Sauer's child in Milwaukee . . . . Each check was [accompanied by] a form entitled "Explanation of Benefits." [The checks were variously endorsed by the son, the father, and the father's business. Some were deposited to the father's personal account and some to his business account; the court is not clear, but apparently, some were cashed by the son or deposited to his account.]

In March, 1985, Blue Cross discovered the mistake. A demand letter was sent to William R. Sauer on March 29, 1985. . . .

Blue Cross filed suit in equity against William R. Sauer and the R.T. Sauer Agency on May 14, 1985, praying that the court impose a constructive trust upon the funds of the defendants for the use and benefit of the plaintiff based on unjust enrichment and mistake. An interlocutory default judgment was entered against defendant William R. Sauer. . . . Robert T. Sauer was added as a defendant in 1988. Defendants twice moved for a transfer of the case from an equity division to a law division and for a jury trial. Both motions were denied. After a non-jury trial the court ordered that Blue Cross recover $22,023.29 from defendant William R. Sauer of which $6,773.01 should be allocated as a joint and several obligation of defendants William R. Sauer and Robert T. Sauer, and $5,141.92 should be allocated as a joint and several obligation of defendants William R. Sauer and the R.T. Sauer Agency. . . .

[The trial court granted a new trial to the father and his business, and transferred the case to the law division,] "for the reason that defendants were entitled to a trial by jury." [Blue Cross appealed the grant of a new trial.]

[T]he theory alleged by Blue Cross . . . is that the defendants were unjustly enriched by the retention of money paid to them inadvertently or by mistake. The petition prayed "that the court impose a constructive trust upon the funds of defendants for the use and benefit of plaintiff." It is axiomatic that an action seeking a form of relief obtainable only through a court of equity does not fall within the purview of the right to a trial by jury. . . . It is equally axiomatic that one who pleads and proves a cause of action cognizable at law . . . may not convert the matter into a non-jury proceeding in equity merely by seeking an equitable remedy to which the pleaded facts show no entitlement.

The remedy for unjust enrichment is restitution. A person who pays money to another by mistake is entitled to restitution from the payee or other beneficiary of the payment. This is true even though the mistake is due solely to the payor's "lack of care," *Restatement of Restitution* §59 at 232 (1937), or "inadvertence," as well as where the payee shares in payor's mistake. *Id.* §22 cmt. *a* at 98. A person entitled to restitution can find a remedy in equity or at law depending upon the circumstances of the particular case. . . .

[T]he very essence of the remedy of constructive trust is the identification of specific property or fund as the res [literally, the thing; the property subject to the trust] upon which the trust may be attached. Blue Cross did not allege and the evidence did not establish any such identifiable property or fund. . . .

The appropriate action when one party has been unjustly enriched through the mistaken payment of money by the other party is an action at law for money had and received. Nothing in the record shows Blue Cross is entitled to anything more than a simple money judgment. . . . Notwithstanding the fact [that] Blue Cross prayed for the equitable remedy of a constructive trust, in the absence of any allegation of the existence of specific property or fund constituting the res upon which the trust might be imposed, its petition failed to invoke equity jurisdiction. It follows that the pre-trial motions seeking a jury trial were erroneously denied.

However, . . . it does not follow that defendants are entitled to a new trial. . . . Had the case been tried to the jury Blue Cross would have been entitled to a directed verdict at the close of the evidence.

Generally, restitution will be ordered when a payment is made under a mistake of fact. The payment by Blue Cross to defendants, rather than to William J. Sauer, was such a mistake of fact and no circumstances disclosed by the evidence would make it inequitable to require return of the payment. "It has long been accepted that a payor's lack of care will not diminish his right to recover, or somehow justify retention of the windfall by an unintended beneficiary." Western Casualty & Surety Co. v. Kohn, 638 S.W.2d 798, 801 (Mo. Ct. App. 1982). Thus, the affirmative defenses of contributory negligence or comparative fault alleged in a conclusory manner by defendants do not constitute a defense. . . .

As an additional affirmative defense, defendants allege . . . that they have so changed their position that it would be unjust to require restitution. The burden of proving a change in position warranting denial of restitution is upon the defendant. The record is utterly devoid of any evidence tending to show a change of circumstances or position. . . . Robert T. Sauer asserts . . . that because he was not joined as a party defendant in this action until three years after its commencement, the mere passage of time is enough to infer a change of position. However, as the owner, director, and president of R.T. Sauer Agency, which was served with process in this action less than three months after the last of the erroneously mailed checks was received, he can hardly claim to have acted to his detriment in ignorance of Blue Cross' demand for restitution or any good-faith belief of entitlement to the windfall. . . .

The number and amounts of the checks are not disputed. Having thoroughly reviewed the record we find no disputed issue of fact which could be submitted to a jury for determination. . . .

Accordingly, the order granting a new trial is reversed and the cause is remanded with direction to reinstate the judgment.

STEPHAN and SIMEONE, JJ., concur.

INTRODUCTORY NOTES ON RESTITUTION

1. The source of liability. Why are the Sauers liable? They did not breach a contract; they no longer have any contract with Blue Cross. Blue Cross did not allege or prove any tort. The source of liability, and the cause of action, is unjust enrichment: Blue Cross sent the checks by mistake, and it would be unjust for the Sauers to keep the money. The fault could be entirely on Blue Cross, and the Sauers could be absolutely innocent, but they would be liable in unjust enrichment.

2. Innocent and not so innocent. The Sauers might have committed torts that Blue Cross did not allege, but probably not. Cashing the check might once have been a conversion, but no more. Uniform Commercial Code §3-420(a) repeals Blue Cross's right to sue for conversion, on the theory that Blue Cross has an adequate remedy against its bank, which paid the checks on what turned out to be forged endorsements. But that remedy is lost if Blue Cross's own negligence substantially contributed to the making of the forged signature. UCC §3-406(a). That negligence defense would present a jury question as between Blue Cross and its bank. Whoever wound up bearing the loss, whether Blue Cross or the bank, would have the restitution remedy against the Sauers. Here Blue Cross apparently chose to go after the Sauers, some of whom appeared to be solvent, rather than pick a dubious fight with its bank. Assuming that the part of the judgment awarded only against the younger Sauer turned out to be uncollectible, and if the statute of limitations had not run out, Blue Cross could still try to pursue its bank for that part of the loss.

With conversion off the table, what tort is left? The son misrepresented his insurance status to the hospital. Innocently? Negligently? Fraudulently? How would Blue Cross prove that? That misrepresentation set in motion a chain of events that (foreseeably?) caused Blue Cross to mail checks to the wrong William Sauer. The only solvent defendants, the father and his company, misrepresented nothing. There was no point in pursuing a misrepresentation claim.

A claim against the father or his company for negligent failure to disclose the mistaken payments would depend upon convincing a court that the father or company had a common law duty to disclose mistaken payments, and we are unaware of tort cases so holding.

In most cases of money paid by mistake, the recipient does nothing to cause the mistake. Up to the point at which he learned enough about the checks to wonder why they were coming, the father and his company were completely innocent. After he receives money that is obviously not his and refuses to give it back, he no longer looks so innocent. But he did not contribute to the mistake.

3. Primary rights and duties arising from unjust enrichment. The law of restitution and unjust enrichment is partly about remedies and partly about primary rights and duties. Just as there are rules that impose liability in tort and contract, there are rules that impose liability in unjust enrichment. But this substantive law of unjust enrichment largely dropped out of the curriculum when the modern Remedies course was created. Restitutionary remedies were absorbed into the new Remedies course; the old courses in Restitution were abandoned, and no one picked up the restitutionary causes of action based on unjust enrichment. There is not room to fix that mistake here; our focus will necessarily be on remedies. But we will take a quick look at the restitutionary causes of action, because they're important and because the restitutionary remedy varies with defendant's culpability, so that different causes of action in unjust enrichment lead to different measures of restitution.

4. The first *Restatement*. The modern law of restitution and unjust enrichment has ancient roots, but it was not united as a field and given the name "restitution" until the American Law Institute's *Restatement of Restitution* (1937). Restitution developed through a number of more specific remedies and causes of action: constructive trust, equitable lien, accounting for profits, subrogation, rescission, indemnity, contribution, various forms of quasi-contract, and more. Each had a separate origin and its own set of historical limitations. Some originated in equity, some at common law. The *Restatement*'s great contribution was to identify a general principle uniting these disparate claims and remedies. A *Restatement (Second)* was started and abandoned in the 1980s.

5. The *Restatement (Third)*. The *Restatement (Third) of Restitution and Unjust Enrichment* (2011) is a twenty-first century restatement of the law in modern terms, using the old vocabulary only where essential. We cite it heavily here, partly because it usually offers the clearest and most current explanation available, and partly because the reporter's notes collect the cases and scholarly literature on every issue. Laycock was an active adviser to this *Restatement*, but the credit goes to the reporter, Andrew Kull of the University of Texas. He has greatly clarified the law and made it much more accessible to modern lawyers. The *Restatement (Third)* addresses general principles in §§1-4, causes of action in §§5-48, remedies in §§49-61, and defenses in §§62-70. Unless otherwise noted, references to "the *Restatement*" refer to the *Restatement (Third)*.

6. Vocabulary. Vocabulary remains slippery even when obsolete terms are eliminated. "Unjust enrichment" generally describes the benefits that defendant has received and also the cause of action to recover those benefits. "Restitution" may mean either the cause of action or the remedy. Restitutionary remedies are generally based on unjust enrichment, but "restitution" is also applied to some older contract remedies that predate the modern usage and the association with unjust enrichment. Literally, "restitution" is just a synonym for restoration: Nonlegal dictionaries define it as restoration of property to its true owner, and despite the modern association with unjust enrichment, judges sometimes think of restitution as a way of making plaintiff whole or restoring a previous status quo. Convicted criminals are often required to pay "restitution" to their victims, a practice briefly examined in section 9.B.2, in Notes on Coercing the Payment of Money in Other Contexts. But restitution in that context means compensation for harm; it is akin to damages and wholly irrelevant to the restitution in this chapter.

7. Restitution and damages. Some cases speak of restitution as an alternative measure of damages, but that is confusing. It is better to think of restitution as an alternative measure of monetary recovery, entirely distinct from damages. Damages are based on plaintiff's loss; restitution is based on defendant's gain.

The distinction appears in simple form in *Sauer*. The damages to Blue Cross are the whole $22,000 plus interest. But the unjust enrichment to each defendant is just what that defendant gained. The son was enriched by the whole $22,000, because the checks were cashed in his name, and if he gave some of the money to his dad, that's his problem and not Blue Cross's (unless giving the money to Dad was a change of position, an affirmative defense discussed in note 10). The dad, and the dad's business, are each liable only for the amount they actually received. Their liability is based on what they gained, not on what Blue Cross lost. And although the court talks about joint and several liability, it does not mean that each defendant is liable for all the unjust enrichment. It means only that some of the money enriched more than one defendant.

8. Measuring restitution. The measure of restitution seems obvious here; it is the amount of cash that each defendant received, presumably with interest, although the court does not mention that. The *Restatement (Third)* says that interest should run against an innocent recipient from the date she had notice of plaintiff's rights. §53(4)(c).

It also says that where an innocent defendant is enriched by a money payment, the measure of restitution is the amount of the payment or "the resulting increase in the defendant's net assets," whichever is less. §49(2). Normally, a $1,000 payment will increase the recipient's net assets by $1,000. A few odd cases account for the odd formulation.

Suppose that plaintiff somehow pays defendant's debt to a third party. An example that arises with some frequency is that City mistakenly assesses Neighbor for the taxes on Owner's property. Neighbor pays $5,000 to City. But when the mistake is discovered, Owner proves that the property has been assessed for more than it is worth and the taxes he actually owed were only $4,000. Neighbor has a restitution claim against City for $5,000. See *Restatement (Third)* §19, on recovery of mistaken, excessive, or illegal taxes. But states often make it difficult to assert that claim. Neighbor also has a restitution claim against Owner. See *id.* §7, on mistaken payment of another's obligation. But Owner's enrichment is only $4,000. Neighbor paid $5,000, but he reduced Owner's actual liability by only $4,000, because that is all that Owner owed.

An example is Buckett v. Jante, 767 N.W.2d 376 (Wis. Ct. App. 2009), where Neighbor paid the taxes for 25 years and Owner defended on the ground that he had *also* paid the taxes because City had double billed, and that the land had been overassessed. On the double-billing theory, only the City is unjustly enriched; Owner has no enrichment at all. On remand, Owner failed to prove that he had also paid the taxes on the property. Neighbor's liability for restitution was limited to 12 years, on the theory that he might have figured out what was happening if he had investigated a mysterious extra tax bill that he received in 1993. This extra tax bill was in fact wholly unrelated to the property at issue; this part of the holding looks suspiciously like an attempt to split the difference. The court awarded Neighbor an equitable lien on the property to secure the judgment. Buckett v. Jante, 787 N.W.2d 60 (Wis. Ct. App. 2010). Equitable liens are taken up in section 8.C.3 below.

9. Law and equity. Many courts are confused or misinformed about the legal or equitable origins of restitution, but the *Sauer* court got the jury-trial issue exactly right.

a. A red herring. There are important restitutionary remedies that originated in equity, including constructive trust. Plaintiff needs a constructive trust when she seeks to recover a specific asset or from a specific fund. But Blue Cross sought no such thing. It sought a simple money judgment in restitution, to be collected from defendants' general assets in the same way a damage judgment would be collected. On these facts, that is a legal remedy. What Blue Cross sought and got can simply be described as a judgment in restitution, or a judgment in unjust enrichment.

b. Money had and received. The court describes the claim in *Sauer* as one for "money had and received," which was a form of quasi-contract. We could probably do without these two phrases at this point, but they still appear in the cases, and they are useful as reminders of history and of the legal origins of much of restitution. For money paid by mistake, and for most other forms of unjust enrichment, a plaintiff could recover a simple money judgment in the common law courts, in a contractual form of action that became known as quasi-contract. Money had and received was one form of a common law writ called *indebitatus assumpsit*, which means "being already indebted, he undertook" (to pay). This phrase is certainly no longer needed, but it is still in use in some states, notably California. It makes a cameo appearance in United States v. California, 507 U.S. 746, 751 (1993).

c. Moses v. Macferlan. The classic early citation is Lord Mansfield's opinion in Moses v. Macferlan, 97 Eng. Rep. 676 (K.B. 1760). Moses had endorsed four promissory notes to Macferlan, with an agreement that Macferlan would collect from the original maker of the notes and would not sue Moses on the endorsements. But Macferlan did sue Moses on the endorsements, and he got a judgment in a court of limited jurisdiction that had no authority to consider the side agreement. Moses paid the judgment and sued to recover the money. He sued not on the written agreement but rather in what we would now call restitution. The court and the parties used all the old labels: action "*quasi ex contractu,*" or quasi-contract, *indebitatus assumpsit,* and money had and received. In trying to get a handle on these strange phrases, it may help to arrange them in order of generality: money had and received was one form of *indebitatus assumpsit,* which was roughly equivalent to quasi-contract, which is still today one form of restitution.

Describing money had and received, the court said:

> [I]t lies for money paid by mistake; or upon a consideration which happens to fail; or for money got through imposition, (express, or implied;) or extortion; or oppression; or an undue advantage taken of the plaintiff's situation, contrary to laws made for the protection of persons under those circumstances.
>
> In one word, the gist of this kind of action is, that the defendant, upon the circumstances of the case, is obliged by the ties of natural justice and equity to refund the money.

Id. at 682. Today, a court would probably say that Moses must sue on his actual contract with Macferlan and could not sue in restitution instead. Subject to that, the quoted description of money had and received is a little loose but still essentially accurate today.

   d. Jury trial. Because Blue Cross's restitution claim could have been brought at common law, either party would have a right to jury trial in federal court and in most states. The legal and equitable origins of restitution are reviewed in *Restatement (Third)* §4.

   10. Change of position. Defendants' knowledge is not an element of Blue Cross's claim to recover money paid by mistake. But defendants' lack of knowledge—more precisely, lack of notice—is an element of their claimed defense of change of position. All three defendants in *Sauer* had notice that someone else had a claim to the checks. Notice requires only knowledge of facts sufficient to make it prudent to conduct a further inquiry that would have revealed the truth. *Restatement (Third)* §69. The father's knowledge that he had stopped paying premiums was enough for him. The Explanation of Benefits that came with every check, listing services from unknown medical providers in Milwaukee, should have been enough for everybody, although these can be hard to read and are often ignored.

   Sometimes a person can receive money by mistake and not realize it's a mistake. It may look like money he was expecting. If a large business owes an uncertain amount of money to an individual, the individual is likely to assume the business calculated correctly. He may not even have a reasonable way to verify the amount. In Home Insurance Co. v. Honaker, 480 A.2d 652 (Del. 1984), a driver's insurer mistakenly paid $25,000 in personal injury benefits to a passenger injured in her car; the policy limits were $10,000. The passenger had no reason to question these payments; there is no indication in the opinion that he had ever seen the policy.

   One who receives an unusual amount of money in addition to her regular income may make some unusual expenditure that she would not have made if she had not received the extra money. This is the change of position. In *Honaker*, the passenger had spent the money on ordinary living expenses, which normally don't count as a change of position. But the insurer was focused on other issues there, and the passenger might have economized much more aggressively during his period of disability if he had not had the insurance money coming in. Change of position is addressed in *Restatement (Third)* §65.

NOTES ON THE GROUNDS FOR RESTITUTION

   1. Mistake. To err is human, and mistake is a large source of restitution litigation. The *Restatement (Third)* states a general right to recover benefits conferred by mistake in §5, and works through various kinds of mistake in §§6-12.

   a. Some examples. People mistakenly pay money they don't owe, or pay more than they owe, or pay it to the wrong person. In Wachovia Bank, N.A. v. Thomasko, 529 S.E.2d 554 (S.C. Ct. App. 2000), the bank's teller mistook "old pesos" for "new pesos" issued after a devaluation, and paid $21,000 for Mexican pesos worth only $500. The bank was entitled to the amount of the overpayment.

   There are many cases where businesses pay the same invoice twice, or banks wire the same funds twice. The right to restitution is clear in such cases, so reported cases with sophisticated defendants generally turn on defenses. An example we will see again later is In re Dow Corning Corp., 192 B.R. 428 (Bankr. E.D. Mich. 1996), where one clerk paid the fax copy of an invoice and another clerk paid the mail copy of the same invoice. In In re JD Services, Inc., 284 B.R. 292 (Bankr. D. Utah 2002), a check for $7,250 was coded as $725,000, and the larger amount was credited to the payee's account. The payee was bankrupt, and this cash infusion did not save it.

A slightly more complex example involved the American Psychological Association. In re APA Assessment Fee Litigation, 766 F.3d 39 (D.C. Cir. 2014). Members of the association alleged that the APA sent out misleading dues statements to make it appear that voluntary fees which went to APA's sister lobbying organization were mandatory fees. The court held this was a claim for a mistaken payment of money not due, quoting *Restatement (Third)* §6 cmt. *c*: "Payments resulting from a misunderstanding of the extent of . . . a contractual obligation present a characteristic issue of restitution." 766 F.3d at 47. The cases later settled as a class action. 311 F.R.D. 8 (D.D.C. 2015).

b. Mistakes and uncertainties. The kind of mistake that counts is where the person making the mistake has no idea he's making a mistake. For a restitution plaintiff claiming mistake, it is best to have been totally clueless. When Blue Cross mailed the insurance checks to Missouri, it did not occur to anyone to doubt the address in its computer. If a person is aware of some uncertainty and pays anyway, she's not making a mistake; she is knowingly taking a risk or settling a dispute. If two parties settle their dispute without perfect knowledge of all the facts (the typical situation in most settlements), neither side can later claim mistake when some new fact is discovered. Similarly, a party making expenditures knowing its rights are at risk in litigation cannot claim unjust enrichment if the gamble proves wrong. See Dowling Family Partnership v. Midland Farm, 865 N.W.2d 854 (S.D. 2015) (citing *Restatement (Third)* §5) where plaintiff planted wheat on disputed acreage that he lost before harvest.

The rule that one cannot recover payments made in the face of uncertainty is somewhat misleadingly called the voluntary payment rule. The *Restatement (Third)* §6 cmt. *e* tries to clarify what this phrase really means. The key to the rule is not that plaintiff paid voluntarily, but that she paid despite notice or awareness that she might not owe some of the money.

2. Equity and good conscience. One still sees unjust enrichment defined in the broad terms suggested by the second paragraph of the quotation from Lord Mansfield. Justice Cardozo said the defendant must return any benefit "received in such circumstances that the possessor will give offense to equity and good conscience if permitted to retain it." Atlantic Coast Line Railroad v. Florida, 295 U.S. 301, 309 (1935). Such formulations have the obvious problems that they give little guidance and they invite juries to second-guess the fairness of transactions covered by other rules of law. They have the great advantage that they give courts flexibility to deal with unjust enrichment that falls between the cracks of existing rules, whether from changing social norms, the cleverness of subtle wrongdoers, or the human tendency to neglect legal requirements in conducting personal relationships.

For a defense of something like the equity-and-good-conscience standard, see Peter Linzer, *Rough Justice: A Theory of Restitution and Reliance, Contracts and Torts*, 2001 Wis. L. Rev. 695. His lead examples are cases of long-term unmarried couples, whose finances may be as entangled as those of married couples, but who are not protected by family law and who rarely have a contract. Courts might deny any recovery as a way of encouraging marriage, but once that policy is abandoned (whether as futile, unduly harsh, or inconsistent with a new policy of freedom to choose marital status), unjust enrichment is a more honest and workable explanation of recovery than straining to find oral or implied contracts.

3. Specific grounds. The other approach to defining unjust enrichment is illustrated by the first paragraph quoted from Lord Mansfield: listing specific grounds for restitution. Sections 5 to 48 of the *Restatement (Third)* state rules for establishing a prima facie liability in unjust enrichment. Most of these rules are reasonably objective; some leave a fair amount of judicial discretion. Section 28 states a rule, with support in decided cases, for the breakup of unmarried couples, a rule that would not have existed a generation ago. The *Restatement (Third)* is plainly resistant to claims that cannot be stated as rules, but it leaves room for doctrinal growth and it inevitably leaves some room at the margins for equity and good conscience.

4. A general definition with more content? The *Restatement (Third)* also offers a general definition, one that is more specific than equity and good conscience. Unjust enrichment is legally unjustified enrichment: "Unjustified enrichment is enrichment that lacks an adequate legal basis; it results from a transfer that the law treats as ineffective to work a conclusive alteration in ownership rights." §1 cmt. *b*. Thus, a transfer of money or property pursuant to a valid contract, or in payment of a valid obligation, or as a valid gift, is justified; a transfer by mistake, or a transfer accomplished by tort, is not justified, and the resulting enrichment is unjust.

5. The preference for contract. A second large and defining principle is that restitution is generally unavailable to a claimant who should have made a contract with the recipient but failed to do so. *Restatement (Third)* §2(3). Would-be plaintiffs cannot deliver unrequested goods or services and then demand payment for the benefit. In the older cases, such plaintiffs are called "volunteers" or "officious intermeddlers." A corollary is that one who *does* have an enforceable contract is bound by the contract's terms; subject to one controversial exception, she cannot sue for restitution of the value of benefits conferred and thus ask the court to redetermine the price or any other terms of the contract. §2(2).

An example is Toulson v. Continental Casualty Co., 877 F.3d 725 (11th Cir. 2017), where an insured filed a class action against her long-term care insurer. She alleged a claim in unjust enrichment, but the insurance policy controlled. "A claim for unjust enrichment is based on an implied contract; where there is a specific contract that governs the relationship of the parties, the doctrine has no application." *Id.* at 742. On this point, Moses v. Macferlan is no longer good law. Lord Mansfield gave plaintiff a choice of suing on his contract or suing in restitution, but today's courts would require him to sue on his contract.

6. No forced exchanges. Closely related to the preference for contract is a strong presumption against forcing an innocent defendant to pay for benefits she never requested and might not want. *Restatement (Third)* §2(4). This is not an issue with benefits received in cash, but it is a serious problem when plaintiff demands cash payment for a noncash benefit. Such forced exchanges would present problems of valuation, liquidity, and autonomy. That an item has a market value of $1,000 is no evidence that it is worth that much to the recipient (valuation), that she has the resources to buy it (liquidity), or that she has any desire to buy it (autonomy). This principle has a very broad reach, but as we will see, it has some exceptions.

SOMERVILLE v. JACOBS
170 S.E.2d 805 (W. Va. 1969)

HAYMOND, President:

The plaintiffs, W.J. Somerville and Hazel M. Somerville, . . . the owners of Lots 44, 45 and 46 in the Homeland Addition to the city of Parkersburg, . . . believing that they were erecting a warehouse building on Lot 46 . . . , mistakenly constructed the building on Lot 47 owned by the defendants, William L. Jacobs and Marjorie S. Jacobs. . . . Construction . . . was completed in January 1967 and by deed dated January 14, 1967 the Somervilles conveyed Lots 44, 45 and 46 to the plaintiffs Fred C. Engle and Jimmy C. Pappas who subsequently leased the building to the Parkersburg

Coca-Cola Bottling Company. . . . Soon after the building was completed but not until then, the defendants learned that the building was on their property and claimed ownership of the building and its fixtures on the theory of annexation. The plaintiffs then instituted this proceeding for equitable relief . . . and in their complaint prayed, among other things, for judgment in favor of the Somervilles for $20,500.00 as the value of the improvements made on Lot 47, or, in the alternative, that the defendants be ordered to convey their interest in Lot 47 to the Somervilles for a fair consideration. . . .

[T]he circuit court required the defendants within 60 days to elect whether they would (1) retain the building and pay W.J. Somerville $17,500.00 or suffer judgment . . . in that amount, or (2) convey . . . Lot 47 . . . to W.J. Somerville for . . . $2,000.00 cash. [Defendants appealed.]

[The parties stipulated that the Somervilles had relied on a survey, that Lot 47 had been worth $2,000 before the construction, and that it was worth $19,500 with the warehouse. Engle and Pappas had paid $19,500 for Lots 44, 45, and 46, and the warehouse; the court does not explain why the parties thought the warehouse and one lot had the same value as the warehouse and three lots.]

The statute dealing with allowance for improvements to real estate, W. Va. Code art. 5, ch. 55 (1931), provides for allowance for improvements only to a defendant against whom a . . . judgment shall be rendered for land where no assessment of damages has been made and permits such defendant . . . to . . . petition . . . that he may be allowed the fair and reasonable value of such improvements. That statute has no application to . . . this case. . . .

[The court reviewed cases from many jurisdictions.] From the foregoing authorities it is manifest that equity . . . will . . . grant relief to one who, through a reasonable mistake of fact and in good faith, places permanent improvements upon land of another, with reason to believe that the land so improved is that of the one who makes the improvements, and that the plaintiffs are entitled to the relief . . . they seek in this proceeding. . . .

[T]he narrow issue here is between two innocent parties and the solution of the question requires the application of principles of equity and fair dealing between them. . . .

[D]efendants claim the ownership of the building. Under the common law doctrine of annexation, the improvements passed to them as part of the land. . . . The record does not disclose any express request by the plaintiffs for permission to remove the building from the premises if that could be done without its destruction, which is extremely doubtful as the building was constructed of solid concrete blocks on a concrete slab, and . . . defendants will not consent to . . . removal of the building even if that could be done. . . .

[I]f the defendants retain the building and refuse to pay any sum as compensation . . . they will be unjustly enriched in the amount of $17,500.00, . . . and . . . Somerville will suffer a total loss of . . . the value of the building. If, however, the defendants are unable or unwilling to pay for the building . . . but, in the alternative, would convey the lot upon which the building is constructed to the plaintiff W.J. Somerville upon payment of . . . $2,000.00, . . . the plaintiffs would not lose the building and the defendants would suffer no financial loss because they would obtain payment for the agreed full value of the lot and the only hardship imposed upon the defendants, if this were required, would be to order them to do something which they are unwilling to do voluntarily. . . . [T]o use the language of the Supreme Court of Michigan in Hardy v. Burroughs, 232 N.W. 200, 201 (Mich. 1930), "It is not equitable . . . that defendants profit by plaintiffs' innocent mistake, that defendants take all and plaintiffs nothing."

To prevent such unjust enrichment of the defendants, and to do equity between the parties, this Court holds that an improver of land owned by another, who through a reasonable mistake of fact and in good faith erects a building entirely upon the land of the owner, with reasonable belief that such land was owned by the improver, is entitled to recover the value of the improvements from the landowner and to a lien upon such property which may be sold to enforce the payment of such lien, or, in the alternative, to purchase the land so improved upon payment to the landowner of the value of the land less the improvements and such landowner, even though free from any inequitable conduct in connection with the construction of the building upon his land, . . . must, within a reasonable time, either pay the improver the amount by which the value of his land has been improved or convey such land to the improver upon . . . payment by the improver to the landowner of the value of the land without the improvements. . . .

[The court then distinguished many cases, mostly on the ground that plaintiffs in those cases had been more careless and more responsible for their own mistake.] In Cautley v. Morgan, 41 S.E. 201 (W. Va. 1902), [the parties agreed that plaintiff could build a party wall extending 10 inches into defendants' property. Six years later, defendants discovered that plaintiff had built the wall 16 inches into their property. The court ordered the extra six inches removed.] [T]he court said: ". . . [T]hat party, upon whom a duty devolves and by whom the mistake was made, should suffer the hardship rather than he who had no duty to perform and was no party to the mistake." *Id.* at 204. It appears, however, . . . that the plaintiff . . . had sufficient data to enable her to avoid the mistake if she had used the data with proper care. . . . Accordingly she was not entitled to equitable relief and the case is distinguishable . . . for those reasons and for the additional reason that the loss of a portion of the wall of the width of only six inches would be a relatively insignificant hardship compared to the complete loss here . . . of an entire building of the admitted value of $17,500.00. . . .

[In *Cautley*, discussing one of the cases granting a buy-sell remedy,] the court, by way of dictum, said: "The exercise of such a judicial power, unless based upon some actual or implied culpability on the part of the party subjected to it, is a violation of constitutional right." *Id.* at 203. The same . . . dictum . . . appears in Kirchner v. Miller, 39 N.J. Eq. 355, 358 (Ch. 1885), [and in] Olin v. Reineccke, 168 N.E. 676, 678 (Ill. 1929). [The court distinguished *Kirchner* as a case where the court found no hardship because the encroachment could be removed for $75.00.] In no other of the many cases that have been considered does any such statement appear. . . . Of course, in an ordinary situation, no court could or would undertake to require a person to convey his land to another who might desire it, but such conveyance may properly be required in litigation in which the rights of the parties . . . are involved and which are subject to determination upon principles of equity. . . .

Affirmed.

CAPLAN, Judge, dissenting: . . .

Although the majority expresses a view which it says would result in equitable treatment for both parties, I am of the opinion that such view is clearly contrary to law and to the principles of equity and that such holding . . . will establish a dangerous precedent. . . .

Cautley v. Morgan, 41 S.E. 201 (W. Va. 1902), . . . cannot realistically be distinguished. . . . The opinion reasoned that the plaintiff had the duty to see that the wall was properly located and that she had sufficient data to enable her to avoid the mistake if she had used the data with proper care. Certainly, in the instant case the plaintiff, had he caused to be made a proper survey and had exercised proper care, would have constructed the . . . building on his own property rather than on that of the defendant. . . . [F]ailure to use proper care is more evident in this case than it was in *Cautley*. . . .

[T]he language which says that such taking of property violates a constitutional right is not mere dictum. . . .

What of the property owner's right? The solution offered by the majority is designed to favor the plaintiff, the only party who had a duty to determine which lot was the proper one and who made a mistake. The defendants in this case . . . had no duty to perform and were not parties to the mistake. Does equity protect only the errant and ignore the faultless? Certainly not.

It is not unusual for a property owner to have long range plans for his property. . . . He should be permitted to feel secure in his future plans. . . . It is very likely that a property owner in the circumstances of the instant case either cannot readily afford the building mistakenly built on his land or that such building does not suit his purpose. Having been entirely without fault, he should not be forced to purchase the building. . . .

[F]or the court to permit the plaintiff to force the defendants to sell their property . . . is unthinkable and unpardonable. This is . . . condemnation of private property by private parties for private use. . . . Under no theory of law or equity should an individual be permitted to acquire property by condemnation. . . .

I am aware of the doctrine that equity frowns on unjust enrichment. However, . . . the circumstances of this case do not warrant the application of such doctrine. . . . [A]s between two parties in the circumstances of this case he who made the mistake must suffer the hardship rather than he who was without fault.

I would reverse . . . and remand . . . with directions that the trial court give the defendant, . . . the party without fault, the election of purchasing the building, of selling the property, or of requiring the plaintiff to remove the building from defendant's property. . . .

Judge Berry concurs in the views expressed in this dissenting opinion.

NOTES ON MISTAKEN IMPROVERS

1. The historic debate. *Somerville* illustrates one of the great substantive debates about restitution: Is one who mistakenly improves the property of another entitled to restitution for the benefit conferred? Many courts initially took the dissent's view of the matter. One who built on the land of another had no remedy, except where the landowner knew what was happening and stood by silently while the improver built. There were many mistaken improvements in the early period; surveys and land records were sketchy on the frontier. The rule was politically unpopular; general policy at the time encouraged development, and this would seem to require favoring the improver who built something over the passive landowner. Besides, the passive landowner was often that most unpopular figure, the Eastern speculator.

Most states enacted statutes to protect the good-faith improver. Some state courts declared these statutes unconstitutional; others rendered them nearly useless through narrow construction; many gave them reasonable scope. Many of the statutes were narrowly drafted in any event, focused on the problems arising from frontier development; they do not apply to many of the modern cases. Most modern courts have held, as in *Somerville*, that the statutes do not preclude a common law or equitable claim in restitution in cases outside the scope of the statute, and most courts are now willing to grant such a remedy.

2. How it happens. The problem did not end with the closing of the frontier; there are a surprising number of ways to build your house on someone else's land. *Somerville* was a surveying error. Another common problem is attempted transactions that are later reversed. An example is Manning v. Wingo, 577 So. 2d 865 (Ala. 1991), where plaintiffs bought a house from the estate of a divorced man. The ex-wife still owned a half interest in the house, but the heirs told her that the bank had foreclosed on the house, and several years passed before she learned the truth and sued to recover her interest in the house. Meanwhile, the buyers had paid the mortgage, current taxes, and back taxes, and made substantial improvements to the house. The ex-wife got the house—the court does not explain why the whole house instead of a half interest—subject to the buyers' claim for restitution. Restitution was implemented with the buy-sell remedy illustrated in *Somerville*: The ex-wife could sell the house or pay for the improvements. The dissenters thought the state of the title had been clear and that the buyers had been too careless to deserve restitution.

3. Distinguishing improvements from encroachments. Some courts speak of mistaken improvements as a form of encroachment, and there is no bright line between the two. But there is a practical distinction: In the encroachment cases, there is no unjust enrichment. If the footings of a building extend a few inches over the property line, as in *Hilander Foods* in section 5.A.2, there is no benefit to the neighboring landowner, and the only issue is whether the encroacher must remove the footings or pay for the right to keep them where they are. In Heartwood Forestland Fund IV, LP v. Hoosier, 781 S.E.2d 391 (W. Va. 2015), Hoosier erected a modular home on Heartwood's land. Contrasting the situation in *Somerville*, the court found no enrichment: "[N]o evidence shows Hoosier's modular home to be an improvement or benefit to Heartwood's 5.6 acres. To the contrary, Heartwood has shown that the presence of the home is harming its timber hauling business by obstructing its sole access to the public road." *Id.* at 396. And in Amkco, Ltd. v. Welborn, 21 P.3d 24 (N.M. 2001), where Amkco's truck stop encroached 58 feet into Welborn's land, and the diesel island was over the line, Welborn wanted the island removed, perhaps because it had no value without the rest of the truck stop. A claim to unjust enrichment arises when the mistaken improver builds something with value independent of whatever is on the mistaken improver's side of the line—something that would enrich the landowner if she were able to keep it without compensation.

4. Forced exchanges. Many mistakes can be corrected by returning the benefit; no one has to pay for anything. When a building can be removed, as with the modular home in *Heartwood*, that greatly simplifies the problem; the mistaken improver can remove it at his own expense.

But most buildings attached to the land cannot be moved at reasonable cost. When removal is not feasible, the general principle against forced exchanges comes under great pressure. The mistaken improver is not an aggressive seller sending unwanted goods but an innocent victim of his own mistake. The defendant can keep a valuable property for free or demand an unreasonable price to settle, as in the undue hardship cases in section 5.A.2. The loss to plaintiff and the corresponding benefit to defendant are often so large that it has seemed intolerable to refuse any remedy. But as the amount in controversy increases, so do the problems of valuation, liquidity, and autonomy inherent in forced exchanges. The *Somerville* defendants may not want a concrete-block warehouse on their property; they might have had more ambitious plans. Either granting or denying relief can be harsh.

5. The buy-sell remedy. The judicially imposed buy-sell remedy is a unique response to these difficulties, unlike any other remedy in Anglo-American law. It is reminiscent of dividing the last piece of cake with "I'll cut, you choose." The court sets the values on the land and the building, and then the innocent landowner gets to choose whether to buy the building or sell the land. He gets a choice of which forced exchange to accept, but there is no disguising that this is a forced exchange.

6. Gaps between cost and value. Often in these cases, the improvements are not worth what it cost to build them. With a building designed for plaintiff's purposes on defendant's property, there is likely to be some loss of value when the building is transferred to defendant. This might not have been a problem in *Somerville*, with a brand-new building that was built to be sold or rented at the market price. The court says that plaintiffs alleged that the value of the improvements was $20,500. That allegation was wholly implausible, because they had already sold the improvements and three lots for $19,500. A later West Virginia opinion says that $20,500 was the cost of construction. Realmark Developments, Inc. v. Ranson, 588 S.E.2d 150, 155 (W. Va. 2003). But it is not characterized that way in *Somerville* itself.

Loss of value was undoubtedly a problem in *Manning*. Improvements to an existing house never add as much value as they cost. And that's before we consider subjective factors: Mrs. Manning may not like the Wingos' taste, or may not want or need the things they added. This is one of many contexts where, with an innocent defendant, the benefits will be valued at what they cost or what they are worth, whichever is less.

Realmark states the opposite rule: cost or value, whichever is greater. That was the right rule on the facts of that case, because the defendant was not innocent. His tenants had an option to purchase the property at the end of their lease. Relying on an unenforceable oral agreement that he would finance the purchase, they invested substantial sums in improvements. The landlord reneged on the financing deal and sold the property to someone else, making a large profit off the tenants' improvements. Rules that adjust the measure of restitution in response to defendant's culpability are taken up in section 8.B.

The West Virginia court again committed to the greater of cost or value, in another case with a culpable defendant, in Ward v. Ward, 783 S.E.2d 873, 880 n.7 (W. Va. 2016). Neither *Realmark* nor *Ward* suggests any distinction between innocent and wrongdoing defendants.

In *Ward*, a mother allowed her son and daughter-in-law to build a log cabin on the mother's property. The son and daughter-in-law lived on the property and paid the property taxes for that portion of the land. They also apparently did some property management and household services in lieu of rent. After 15 years, the son died and the mother sought to evict the daughter-in-law and the grandchildren. The daughter-in-law testified that the mother had said that the son would inherit the land, and that she had orally given them the acre around the long cabin. But there was no deed, and the acre had not been subdivided, because the cabin did not comply with the building code. These facts are a near cousin of the mistaken improver cases; the son and his wife knew that they did not own the land, but relied on a reasonable expectation that they eventually would own it.

The court held that the mother could evict the family but that the daughter-in-law could recover in unjust enrichment. The trial court had awarded $50,000, the cost of the log cabin building kit, but the supreme court remanded for further hearings on the amount of the enrichment.

> [N]o record has been made as to the current value of the improvement to [the mother]'s property, i.e., the log cabin home; how much [the daughter-in-law], and her late husband, have expended in building and maintaining the same through ordinary household repairs and upkeep; the amount of property taxes [the daughter-in-law] and her family have paid for this portion of [the mother]'s lot; the costs that [the daughter-in-law] and her late husband have incurred in caring for the property upon which the log home is situate; or any other factors that are indicative of the log cabin's valuation.

Id. at 881. The court also awarded the daughter-in-law an equitable lien (taken up in section 8.C.3) to secure payment of the amount found to be due, and it said that she could live in the cabin until the judgment was paid.

What about the value of the household services done by the daughter-in-law? If she has stopped doing those services in lieu of rent, shouldn't there be an offset to the mother for the value of rent?

7. Comparative fault. There is a wide range of possible fault in these cases, from innocence through negligence and recklessness to reneging on unenforceable deals and outright fraud.

a. The improver. If negligence barred recovery, there could be no law of mistake. *Sauer* says that Blue Cross's carelessness in making the mistaken payments is irrelevant. But in *Sauer*, the remedy was simply to return the money. In the mistaken-improver cases, where the remedy requires a forced exchange, courts are more interested in just how careless the mistaken improver was. Distinguishing reasonable and unreasonable mistakes, or innocent and culpable mistakes, may be a matter of knowing it when you see it. In *Somerville*, the majority thought plaintiffs were innocent because they relied on the surveyor; we don't get the details of what went wrong. In *Manning*, the majority seemed to think plaintiffs were innocent because they had *not* consulted a lawyer or title company. Plaintiffs were clueless about the process of buying a house and relied only on the seller. The cases are fact intensive, but in general, a plaintiff who builds despite actual notice that she might be making a mistake will not recover; a plaintiff who has only constructive notice—such as a filing in land records that she neglected to check—will not be barred on the ground that the mistake is her own fault.

b. The owner. The defendants in *Somerville* were a good deal more innocent than the Sauers. They did nothing to induce the building of the warehouse. They did nothing analogous to cashing checks. They just stopped by their property one day and found a brand new warehouse. No doubt they tried to take advantage of the situation after they discovered it. Hard bargaining and insisting on their property rights may not be admirable, but it is not a legal wrong. And it is sometimes hard to tell whether the owner is cynically taking advantage or genuinely attached to the property.

The ex-wife in *Manning* seems to have been guilty only of gullibility and naivete. Both sides in *Manning* were innocent victims of a more sophisticated bad guy. That is a very common source of hard legal problems.

c. Knowing misconduct. The mistaken-improver cases become much easier if one side is clearly in the wrong. The improver who knows he is building on someone else's land will get no remedy. And an innocent improver will get a much more generous remedy against an owner who knows what is happening and says nothing, hoping to get a free warehouse.

8. Relative hardship. The hardships at issue are not just a matter of money. The uses of the land and the parties' attachment to it can also matter. A forced exchange of defendant's home would be much more intrusive than a forced exchange of raw land held for investment. Fortunately, most of these cases involve empty land. Owners have to be uninvolved with their property, or at least away on a long trip, for these mistakes to happen without their noticing.

9. The *Restatement*. The *Restatement (Third)* endorses the buy-sell remedy. §10 cmt. *b*. It also endorses balancing the equities in light of the parties' relative fault and relative hardships, *id.* cmt. *e*, and it says that any remedy "that subjects the owner to a forced exchange will be qualified or limited to avoid undue prejudice to the owner." §10. The cases of disappointed expectations, as in *Ward*, are just enough different that they get their own treatment in §27.

NOTES ON OTHER GROUNDS FOR RESTITUTION

1. Emergencies. One who reasonably provides essential goods or services in an emergency is excused from not securing a promise to pay in advance, and so may sue for unjust enrichment. This is the least controversial exception to the rule against forced exchanges: The law presumes that defendant would have wanted emergency assistance if it had been possible to ask him (and if he had been in his right mind).

a. Saving life. The classic example is the doctor or hospital that treats an unconscious patient. In re Crisan's Estate, 107 N.W.2d 907 (Mich. 1961). An opinion that collects others is Credit Bureau Enterprises, Inc. v. Pelo, 608 N.W.2d 20 (Iowa 2000), where a suicidal man was involuntarily committed. He had to pay for the frustration of his suicidal intentions.

The benefit in these cases is measured by the market value of the treatment, whether or not successful, and not by the value of the life saved or the pain and suffering avoided. If contract had been possible, the patient would have paid for medical care even if unsuccessful, and he would have paid no more if his life were saved. These cases are reviewed in *Restatement (Third)* §20.

b. Saving property. But if one intervenes in an emergency to protect property, the value of the benefit is the value of the services or the value of the property damage avoided, whichever is less. The benefit to a property owner of saving his property cannot be more than the value of the property. If it had been possible to ask the owner whether the restitution plaintiff should spend more than the property was worth to save the property, most owners would have said no. These cases are reviewed in *id.* §21.

2. Performing another's duty to a third party. Closely related are cases where the restitution plaintiff performs someone else's duty to a third party. *Id.* §22. These cases also arise from emergency intervention, or at least situations of some urgency, when the person who owes the duty is unavailable, incapacitated, or for some reason refusing to perform. People who use their own money to pay a family member's bills during that person's final illness, or who pay the funeral expenses, sometimes have to sue ungrateful representatives of the estate in restitution to get reimbursed. An example is In re Estate of Boyd, 972 P.2d 1075 (Colo. Ct. App. 1998). In a recurring situation, medical providers treat prisoners without securing a contract with the jurisdiction operating the prison. See Emergency Physicians Integrated Care v. Salt Lake County, 167 P.3d 1080 (Utah 2007), upholding a claim in restitution.

In an Indiana case, a pregnant woman became seriously ill, but she and her husband belonged to a faith-healing sect and refused to seek medical treatment. An anonymous tipster called the sheriff, who took the woman to the hospital. Her husband emphatically told the hospital that the family rejected medical care, had no insurance, and would not pay. The court held that his wife could refuse treatment for herself, but that the parents could not refuse treatment for the baby, and were obligated to pay. Given the emphatic refusals to agree to pay for treatment, there could be no real contract, either express or implied. The liability was in restitution for the reasonable value of the services. Schmidt v. Mutual Hospital Services, Inc., 832 N.E.2d 977 (Ind. Ct. App. 2005).

3. Joint ownership of property. One owner of an interest in property may make necessary expenditures—paying taxes, insurance, and the mortgage, and making necessary repairs—even if her co-owners are insolvent, unavailable, or uncooperative. The owner who pays has a claim in unjust enrichment for the others' proportionate share. See *Restatement (Third)* §26. An example is Storms v. Bergsieker, 835 P.2d 738 (Mont. 1992), where two unrelated owners shared an easement over an access road and a bridge. Plaintiff paid for necessary repairs to the bridge, and defendant was liable for his share of the costs. But such co-owners have no similar claim for discretionary improvements to the property. This is the principle of no forced exchanges; the other owners might not have wanted the improvements.

4. But not neighbors. There is no such claim when work on plaintiff's own property confers benefits on a neighbor. Usually this is obvious. If someone buys a rundown house and repaints it, repairs it, and landscapes it, everyone in the neighborhood may benefit, but no one expects them to pay.

The rule can be more striking when the project is one where cooperation would be the norm, but it can be hard to distinguish free riding from lack of interest or from reasonable objections. In Dailing v. Hall, 1 S.W.3d 490 (Mo. Ct. App. 1999), plaintiff approached his neighbor about rebuilding the mile-long fence between their ranches. The neighbor didn't seem interested. Plaintiff rebuilt the fence and sued the neighbor for half the cost. The neighbor got a better fence too, but he didn't have to help pay for it.

Or consider Birchwood Land Co. v. Krizan, 115 A.3d 1009 (Vt. 2015), where plaintiff built a road and water, sewer, and electrical connections so that it could develop a piece of raw land. All this infrastructure made defendant's neighboring parcel developable too; its value jumped from $11,000 to $117,000. But the court found no unjust enrichment. The benefit to defendant was an incidental effect of plaintiff's own improvements. Requiring plaintiff to pay for improvements that they might not want would be a forced exchange, even though the odds are very high that defendant wanted these improvements. There is a similar result in Dinosaur Development, Inc. v. White, 265 Cal. Rptr. 525 (Ct. App. 1989), where defendant apparently asked the city to require that the road be built in such a way that it would benefit defendant's parcel too.

Protecting against forced exchanges sometimes leaves this sort of collective action problem. These cases were bilateral monopoly; the neighboring landowners could deal only with each other, and in *Birchwood* and *Dinosaur*, whoever developed first would have to build the infrastructure. Restitution would have led to sensible cost sharing; these might have been cases where restitution was superior to contract. But such cases are scarce between neighbors, and the courts were not willing to depart from the general rule.

5. Court orders later reversed. Here is one more settled ground for restitution: Money paid or collected pursuant to the order of a court or administrative agency, subsequently vacated or reversed, must be refunded. The simplest case is a money judgment later reversed. Cases of overturned court orders are restated and collected in *Restatement (Third)* §18.

For example, in Miga v. Jensen, 299 S.W.3d 98 (Tex. 2009), the judgment debtor initially posted a supersedeas bond, which prevents the creditor from collecting on the judgment pending appeal. The bond guarantees the judgment will be paid if the appeal is unsuccessful. After the court of appeals affirmed the judgment, the only remaining appeal was discretionary review in the state supreme court, a time-consuming long shot. Meanwhile, a $23 million judgment was accruing interest at rates far above market. So the judgment debtor withdrew the supersedeas bond and paid the judgment in full. After the state supreme court granted review and reduced the judgment to about $1 million, the judgment creditor resisted restitution of the $22-million difference on the ground that there had been no compulsion—the supersedeas bond had fully protected the judgment debtor against any seizure of property. The court awarded restitution, finding compulsion in the high interest rate, which was true enough. More fundamentally, the court said that "any payment made in response to a judgment is treated as a payment made under compulsion" for this purpose. *Id.* at 104, quoting *Restatement (Third)* §18 cmt. *c* (Tent. Draft 1, 2001).

2.   *Measuring Restitution from the Innocent—and More Restitutionary Causes of Action*

BONINA v. SHEPPARD

78 N.E.3d 128 (Mass. App. Ct. 2017)

KAFKER, C.J. . . .

The issue presented in this case is whether a substantial, uncompensated contribution by one unmarried cohabitant to improve the home owned by the other is recoverable in restitution. The plaintiff, Stephen Bonina, and the defendant, Jane A. Sheppard, were involved in a long-term nonmarital relationship. The plaintiff, a contractor, expended significant funds and labor to improve the home in which the couple lived for sixteen years, which was owned by the defendant. When the relationship ended, the plaintiff brought this action against the defendant claiming, inter alia, that she had been unjustly enriched by his contributions to the home. . . .

BACKGROUND . . . .

The plaintiff and the defendant met on New Year's Eve, 1989, and began dating shortly thereafter. Three years later, the parties became interested in purchasing a home in Bolton that had been vacant for two years. The home was owned by Concord Co–Operative Bank . . . . During negotiations with the bank, the parties coauthored a letter declaring their serious interest in the home, and explaining that the cost to bring the home to livable condition was $43,500, based on estimations by the plaintiff and another contractor. In May, 1993, the defendant purchased the home for $131,500 in her name only, becoming the sole obligor on the mortgage.

As it turned out, the entire home had to be gutted, and the necessary repairs cost much more than anticipated. The parties moved into the home in September, 1993. The plaintiff thereafter paid half of the mortgage payments, taxes, and living expenses during the cohabitation. He used various places in the home as his office for his contracting business.

In 1994, the parties constructed an addition to the living room. Between 1993 and 1998, the plaintiff spent $74,068.94 on improvements and maintenance of the home, which included the addition, as well as a new furnace, windows, a gas stove, and a new basement floor. The plaintiff spent "countless hours" performing the "overwhelming majority" of the work. The defendant spent $35,544.17 on improvements and maintenance during this period.

The parties were engaged on Christmas Eve, 1999. Around this time, the parties extended the kitchen to make a better passageway to a room that the plaintiff planned to use as his office. While this work was being performed, the parties decided to build a second floor above the office. From 1999 to 2004, the plaintiff spent approximately $98,352.02 on improvements to the home, most of which went toward materials to construct the addition and the second floor, such as roofing, siding, flooring, and electrical and plumbing work. The defendant spent $46,532.99.

In 2005, the plaintiff contributed approximately $17,967.32 for a new septic system. From 2006 to 2008, the plaintiff contributed an additional $3,572.24 for repairs and maintenance. The defendant's contributions during this time were minimal.

Shortly thereafter, the relationship deteriorated, and the plaintiff moved out in February, 2009. By this time, the plaintiff had contributed $93,744.94 towards the monthly mortgage payments, which represented approximately one-half of the payments due during the sixteen years that he lived in the home. The plaintiff then brought this action seeking restitution for his contributions to the home under an unjust enrichment theory. The trial judge found that the "majority" of the plaintiff's costs reflected materials to construct the three additions, including lumber, cement, insulation, piping, and flooring, as well as other items that became permanent fixtures of the home, including windows, doors, appliances, the septic system, and the furnace. The judge deducted the plaintiff's costs for maintenance of the home, such as fence painting and lawn mowing, as well as those related to "short-term benefits," such as extension cords, light bulbs, and log splitting; the judge found that the plaintiff had received the benefit of those items. After deducting those latter amounts, the judge awarded the plaintiff $156,913.07 in restitution, which represented his costs to purchase the materials and the fixtures to improve the home.

DISCUSSION.

1. UNMARRIED COHABITANTS AND UNJUST ENRICHMENT.

"Cohabitation in Massachusetts does not create the relationship of husband and wife in the absence of a formal solemnization of marriage, . . . [and] the incidents of the marital relationship [do not] attach to an arrangement of cohabitation." Sutton v. Valois, 846 N.E.2d 1171 (Mass. App. Ct. 2006). Unmarried cohabitants, however, "may lawfully contract concerning property, financial, and other matters relevant to their relationship." *Id.* Equitable relief is also available, including restitution for unjust enrichment. . . .

Unjust enrichment occurs when a party retains the property of another "against the fundamental principles of justice or equity and good conscience." Santagate v. Tower, 833 N.E.2d 171. 176 (Mass. App. Ct. 1994). The plaintiff must establish "not only that the defendant received a benefit, but also that such a benefit was unjust." Metropolitan Life Insurance Co. v. Cotter, 984 N.E.2d 835 (Mass. 2013). Whether the benefit was unjust "turns on the reasonable expectations of the parties." *Id.*

The defendant claims that the trial judge erred in determining that she was unjustly enriched because the parties were in a romantic relationship when the plaintiff made his contributions to the home. We disagree. The parties' romantic relationship does not prevent the plaintiff from recovering from the defendant under an unjust enrichment theory. In Massachusetts, there is no presumption that a claimant's contributions during a romantic relationship are gratuitous. The judge's factual findings demonstrate that the substantial contributions made by the plaintiff to improve the home were not meant to be gifts to the defendant. The trial judge found, for example, that the plaintiff "believed that [the parties] were to jointly purchase the home, make improvements, increase its value, and eventually buy a bigger home."

The *Restatement (Third) of Restitution and Unjust Enrichment* §28(1) (2011) specifically provides for a remedy in these circumstances, stating,

> If two persons have formerly lived together in a relationship resembling marriage, and if one of them owns a specific asset to which the other has made substantial, uncompensated contributions in the form of property or services, the person making such contributions has a claim in restitution against the owner as necessary to prevent unjust enrichment upon the dissolution of the relationship.

Unjust enrichment in this context is based on the "claimant's frustrated expectations." *Id.* cmt. *c.* Recovery is allowed because the claimant would not have conferred the benefit, "except in the expectation that the parties' subsequent relationship would be something other than it proved to be." *Id.*

In the present case, in accordance with §28(1), the plaintiff's contributions to improve the defendant's home were substantial. The trial judge found that his compensable contributions totaled $156,913.07, which allowed three additions to be built and to remain permanent fixtures of the home. These contributions were also uncompensated because the defendant did not reimburse him and, although the plaintiff lived in the home for sixteen years, he paid $93,744.94 toward the mortgage. The judge found that the mortgage payments were "more than adequate for [the plaintiff's] use and occupancy [of] the residence." As such, the plaintiff could seek restitution for his contributions to the defendant's home under an unjust enrichment theory.

2. PROPER MEASURE OF RESTITUTION.

The defendant next claims that the trial judge erred by measuring the plaintiff's restitution as the costs he incurred in improving the home, rather than the increased value of the home with the improvements. We disagree, and conclude that, in the particular circumstances of this case, the judge did not abuse his discretion in determining that the plaintiff's costs in improving the home constituted a proper measure of unjust enrichment and restitution.

We begin by recognizing that measuring restitution for unjust enrichment poses special difficulties and, as such, trial judges need "considerable discretion" to fashion appropriate remedies. *Restatement (Second) of Contracts* §371 cmt. *a* (1981). See 1 Dan B. Dobbs, *Law of Remedies* §4.1(4), at 566 (2d ed. 1993) ("The chief remedial problem of restitution is perhaps its measurement"). "[R]esolution of these problems varies greatly depending on the circumstances." *Restatement (Second) of Contracts* §371 cmt. *a.* Thus, "[t]o the extent that the benefit may reasonably be measured in different ways, the choice is within the discretion of the court." *Id.* These problems are particularly pronounced in the context of unmarried cohabitants. The parties often have built a life together over many years, and the trial judge must "untangl[e]" complicated property interests that arose during the relationship. *Restatement (Third) of Restitution and Unjust Enrichment* §28 reporter's note *a.*

That being said, we recognize that "[r]estitution cannot be measured by the plaintiff's losses, only by the defendant's gains." 1 Dobbs, §4.5(4), at 651. Restitution is distinct from damages, "which measures compensation for loss rather than disgorgement of the defendant's gain." 3 *id.* §12.1(1), at 9. The plaintiff's costs to confer the benefit, however, may be evidence of, and relevant to, determining the value of the benefit received by the defendant. *Restatement (Third)* §49 cmt. *d.* Indeed, §49(3)(b) of the *Restatement (Third)* specifically lists "cost to the claimant of conferring the benefit" as a possible measure of restitution for unjust enrichment claims for nonreturnable benefits.[3] The *Restatement* further provides, "Cases in which the cost to the claimant is the only plausible measure of benefit conferred are in fact very numerous. Obvious illustrations include cases in which the claimant recovers out-of-pocket costs in maintaining or repairing property for which the defendant is solely or jointly responsible." *Id.* reporter's note *e.* The *Restatement* explains,

> [I]n many cases a reasonable way to value the benefit conferred on the defendant is to value the services and materials provided by the plaintiff. This is because the cost of the services and materials provided is roughly equivalent to the value of the benefit conferred, and the cost . . . is susceptible to proof at trial, whereas the value conferred is not.

Id.

In the context of unmarried cohabitants, there are numerous reasons why a plaintiff's actual costs may be a prudent and reliable measure of the benefit conferred on a defendant. In these relationships, the parties often have made substantial, uncompensated contributions to property over many years without a business-like or market-based approach to their financial arrangements. Instead, the contributions reflect their romantic relationship, shared expenses, and expectation of continuing to live together as a couple. See *Restatement (Third)* §28 cmt. *c.* The correlation of costs with benefits is especially valid where, as here, the costs that the plaintiff incurred were for construction materials and fixtures for the defendant's home. In these circumstances, there is a direct dollar-for-dollar correlation between the costs incurred by the plaintiff and the benefit conferred on the defendant. Moreover, in the present case, neither the plaintiff nor the defendant presented evidence regarding other possible measures of unjust enrichment, such as the increased value of the home resulting from the materials and the services. As such, the trial judge had no other reliable, measurable basis on which to calculate the award.[6]

We further note that the benefit conferred on the defendant might actually have been greater than the recovery that the plaintiff sought based on his costs. As a contractor, the plaintiff contributed significant skills, labor, and expertise to the renovations, for which he did not charge the defendant. The trial judge found that the plaintiff performed the "lion's share" of the labor needed to improve the property, and spent "countless hours" doing the "overwhelming majority" of the work. There was obvious value to these services, but the plaintiff did not seek at trial to recover or

---

3. The other possible measures of enrichment are "the value of the benefit in advancing the purposes of the defendant," "the market value of the benefit," and "a price the defendant has expressed a willingness to pay." *Restatement (Third)* §49(3).

6. The defendant also claims that the judge undervalued her own contributions to the home and the various benefits that the plaintiff himself enjoyed from the home in crafting the award. We disagree. The judge recognized that the defendant contributed more financially to the initial renovation than the plaintiff, credited her for other funds she expended, and noted that she "offered minimal assistance" in terms of "physical labor." Regardless, the defendant retained the home. The trial judge also acknowledged that the plaintiff enjoyed various benefits of his contributions while he lived in the home, including having an office there. The judge noted that the plaintiff's mortgage and tax payments were "more than adequate for [his] use and occupancy [of] the residence" and, thus, did not reduce the plaintiff's recovery on this basis.

to present evidence of the fair market value of his services. See 3 Dobbs, §12.20(2), at 461 (benefit can be measured by "the market value of the labor and materials package—what it would cost the owner to purchase such services and materials in the market"). Rather, he only sought reimbursement for his costs in purchasing the materials and the fixtures. The defendant therefore undoubtedly received a substantial discount in improving her home, which the trial judge aptly noted and took into consideration in measuring her unjust enrichment.

We therefore hold that in this case, where the costs incurred by the plaintiff directly relate to the benefit conferred on the defendant, and neither party presented reliable evidence of other possible measures of unjust enrichment, the trial judge did not abuse his discretion in valuing the plaintiff's restitution as his costs in improving the home. "This was a sound weighing of the equities based on the specific facts of this case."[10] Bakwin v. Mardirosian, 6 N.E.3d 1078 (Mass. App. Ct. 2014).

Judgment Affirmed.

NOTES ON MEASURING RESTITUTION FROM INNOCENT DEFENDANTS

1. Further appeal. The Supreme Judicial Court denied review. 477 Mass. 1109 (2017).

2. Innocent, but not mistaken? Cases of unmarried cohabitants seeking restitution are common, but they do not fall into the mistake category. After Bonina spent over $150,000 on improvements to Sheppard's house, what did he think would happen if the couple split up? Courts could say that unmarried cohabitants are conferring gifts in the relationship or that they assume the risk of loss by conferring goods or services without entering into a marriage or domestic partnership. But they typically do not. The *Restatement (Third)* §28 cmt. *b*, notes that "Cases involving former cohabitants repeatedly allow restitution to claimants who—had they been dealing with someone else—might have been found either to have acted gratuitously or to have assumed the risk that the expenditures in question would ultimately be of primary benefit to someone other than themselves."

Compare Estate of Henry v. Woods, 77 N.E.3d 1200 (Ind. Ct. App. 2017), where a personal assistant moved in with the decedent and provided unpaid housekeeping and nursing services to him for 14 years. When the decedent passed away, the assistant sued the estate to be paid for those services. The majority held that she could recover $125,000 in unjust enrichment. Indiana presumes that family members providing such services do so gratuitously, but that presumption did not apply here. A concurring judge believed that the presumption should apply, but that the assistant had rebutted it. In the concurring judge's view, the assistant had proven an implied-in-fact contract between the parties that the decedent would pay her after his death. This is not a restitution theory, but a contract theory: that the parties by their actions

---

10. The defendant also claims that the trial judge erred by not barring or reducing the plaintiff's recovery based on his unclean hands. The doctrine of unclean hands denies equitable relief "to one tainted with the inequitableness or bad faith relative to the matter in which [he] seeks relief." Murphy v. Wachovia Bank, N.A., 36 N.E.3d 48 (Mass. App. Ct. 2015). The judge's over-all factual findings regarding the relationship, however, provide no support for such a finding. Neither party behaved dishonorably. Rather, the relationship did not work out as the parties expected. "We are in no position to substitute our judgment for that of the judge on credibility questions." Commonwealth v. Werner, 967 N.E.2d 159 (Mass. App. Ct. 2012). In these circumstances, the trial judge did not err by not barring or reducing the plaintiff's recovery.

entered into an agreement that she would take care of him in exchange for (uncertain) benefits.

3. The *Restatement (Third)* view on the substantive right. The *Restatement* provision applies only to persons who "formerly lived together in a relationship resembling marriage." §28. The live-in housekeeper/nurse in *Estate of Henry* probably was not in such a relationship, although the Indiana court relied on the cases of unmarried cohabitants. Should it matter whether a relationship was sexual?

Cases of unpaid care for the elderly have been around forever. Here the relationship looks more like personal services, and the parties generally anticipate that the relationship will end with the death of the older person, so they are more likely to talk about what will happen then. Even without an express promise, it is easier to find an implied contract. Couples in sexual relationships almost never make contracts, and talk of implied contracts is generally a fiction. It is the unmarried cohabitant cases, all from the 1970s and later, that have led to the growth of the unjust enrichment theory.

The *Restatement (Third)* groups the case of unmarried cohabitants (§28) into a broader topic on "self-interested intervention," which also includes the cases where plaintiff spends money to protect jointly owned or leased property (§26), the cases where plaintiff spends money on property that she reasonably expects to own someday (§27), and cases where a lawyer or litigant recovers a common fund that benefits others similarly situated (§29). The first two rules were briefly encountered in section 8.A.1; the common fund cases are the subject of section 10.B. There is also a narrow residual category for other cases presenting sufficiently similar issues and no risk of a forced exchange (§30).

4. Cost or value again. In *Bonina*, the defendant argued that the trial court should have used the increased value of the property rather than cost of improvements to measure the restitutionary recovery. She might have assumed that this would be a smaller number, or she might have been hoping to escape liability altogether because the plaintiff had not offered evidence of the increased value. The court rejected the argument, because she had not offered any evidence of the increased value either, and also because it thought that in cases involving unmarried cohabitants, cost was a "prudent and reliable" measure given that "the contributions reflect their romantic relationship, shared expenses, and expectation of continuing to live together as a couple," "without a business-like or market-based approach to their financial arrangements."

This plaintiff, a professional contractor, apparently kept unusually precise cost information for improvements. Most cohabitants would have a harder time proving the costs of improvements to property made over a 16-year period. On the flip side, real estate appraisers should be able to give opinions on how much the improvements increased the value of the property. But depending on the circumstances, those opinions might not be very precise. And not all the cases are about improvements to real estate, although that is a fertile source of litigation.

Suppose real estate experts agree that the improvements increased the property's value by $300,000 (or $100,000), compared to the costs of just under $157,000. How to choose between the two? See footnote 10 of the court's opinion, noting that "[n]either party behaved dishonorably." Culpability cannot be a tiebreaker here. *Bonina* didn't face the choice. Cost was the only measure proved, and the court said that measure sufficed.

Why is cost to plaintiff a measure of enrichment to defendant? Cost to plaintiff sounds like plaintiff's damages, not defendant's gain. But often, "the cost of the services and materials provided is roughly equivalent to the value of the benefit conferred, and the cost of the services and materials provided is susceptible to proof at trial, whereas the value conferred is not." Midcoast Aviation, Inc. v. General Electric Credit Corp, 907 F.2d 732, 744 (7th Cir. 1990). Or, as the *Bonina* court put it, "In these circumstances, there is a direct dollar-for-dollar correlation between the costs incurred by the plaintiff and the benefit conferred on the defendant." That is true in terms of what defendant would have had to pay for the materials. It is probably not true in terms of the effect on the value of the house.

5. The *Restatement* take on cost or value. The *Bonina* court notes (in footnote 3) that the *Restatement (Third)* lays out alternative rules for measuring benefit in the case of innocent recipients, but it doesn't give much detail.

a. Section 49 — measures of enrichment. Section 49 lists five potential measures of restitution for benefits conferred in a form other than money. One is reserved for conscious wrongdoers; hold that for later. Four apply to innocent defendants: the cost to plaintiff, the market value, an agreed price, or the value "in advancing the purposes of the defendant." §49(3). Very often, one of these measures is far more readily provable than the others, and very often, every measure that is provable yields a similar number. But sometimes these measures can differ substantially.

Cost and change in market value were the choices at issue in *Bonina*, and they are usually straightforward enough conceptually, even if evidence is sometimes disputed or hard to find. Value in advancing the purposes of the recipient is sometimes described as subjective value, but subjective value is speculative and generally unprovable; that is not what this phrase means. The *Restatement*'s comment further describes this measure as "demonstrable value to the recipient, given what we know about the recipient's situation." §49 cmt. *d*. Sometimes it is clear that a benefit with substantial market value is worth little or nothing to the recipient. If plaintiff builds a warehouse on land where defendant is preparing to build a large office tower, there may be nothing to do but tear down the warehouse. In that case, defendant has no benefit; he has suffered damages equal to the cost of demolition.

b. Section 50 — innocent recipients. Section 49 gives no guidance on choosing among its four measures. That is left to §50, which offers several rules for choosing a measure of restitution where the recipient is innocent. If the benefits were conferred at the recipient's request, the presumptive measure is the market value or an agreed price. §50(2)(b). A valid agreed price would be preferred if there is one. Market value also applies to the cases of emergency intervention to save life or health, where we presume that the services would have been wanted and treat them as though they had been requested.

If nonemergency benefits were conferred without any request, then often plaintiff cannot recover at all. Restitution may result in a forced exchange, and probably plaintiff should have sought defendant's agreement. Where plaintiff can recover, the benefits are to be valued by the measure that yields the smallest recovery. §50(2)(a). This rule is often summarized in the cases as the lesser of cost or value.

If the benefits were unrequested, there won't be an agreed price, and there is usually no finding of a separate value to the recipient, so lesser of cost or value is usually the same as the smallest measure of restitution. Somewhat redundantly, but for clarity and emphasis, §50(4) adds that the restitution plaintiff can never recover more than her cost from an innocent recipient. And §50(3) adds that an innocent recipient can never be liable in restitution for an amount that would make him worse off (net of litigation costs) than if the transaction giving rise to liability had not occurred.

FARASH v. SYKES DATATRONICS, INC.
452 N.E.2d 1245 (N.Y. 1983)

COOKE, Chief Judge.

Plaintiff claims that he and defendant entered an agreement whereby defendant would lease a building owned by plaintiff, who was to complete its renovation and make certain modifications on an expedited basis. Defendant, however, never signed any contract and never occupied the building. Plaintiff commenced this litigation, and defendant unsuccessfully moved to dismiss for failure to state a cause of action. . . . [T]he Appellate Division reversed. . . . 456 N.Y.S.2d 556 (App. Div. 1982). . . .

Plaintiff pleaded three causes of action in his complaint. The first was to enforce an oral lease for a term longer than one year. This is clearly barred by the Statute of Frauds, Gen. Oblig. Law, §5-703(2). The third cause of action is premised on the theory that the parties contracted by exchanging promises that plaintiff would perform certain work in his building and defendant would enter into a lease for a term longer than one year. This is nothing more than a contract to enter into a lease; it is also subject to the Statute of Frauds. . . .

Plaintiff's second cause of action, however, is not barred by the Statute of Frauds. It merely seeks to recover for the value of the work performed by plaintiff in reliance on statements by and at the request of defendant. This is not an attempt to enforce an oral lease or an oral agreement to enter a lease, but is in disaffirmance of the void contract and so may be maintained. That defendant did not benefit from plaintiff's efforts does not require dismissal; plaintiff may recover for those efforts that were to his detriment and that thereby placed him in a worse position. "The contract being void and incapable of enforcement in a court of law, the party . . . rendering the services in pursuance thereof, may treat it as a nullity, and recover . . . the value of the services." Erben v. Lorillard, 19 N.Y. 299, 302 (1859).

The dissent's primary argument is that the second cause of action is equivalent to the third, and so is also barred by the Statute of Frauds. It is true that plaintiff attempts to take the contract outside the statute's scope and render it enforceable by arguing that the work done was unequivocally referable to the oral agreement. This should not operate to prevent recovery under a theory of quasi contract as a contract implied by law, which "is not a contract at all but an obligation imposed by law to do justice even though it is clear that no promise was ever made or intended." John D. Calamari & Joseph M. Perillo, *The Law of Contracts* §1-12 at 19 (2d ed., West 1977). . . . [P]laintiff's attempt to make his acts directly referable to the unenforceable contract simply is irrelevant. . . .

The *Restatement* provides that an injured party who has not conferred a benefit may not obtain restitution, but he or she may "have an action for damages, including one for recovery based on . . . reliance." *Restatement (Second) of Contracts* §370 cmt. *a* (1981).

> [T]he injured party has a right to damages based on his reliance interest, including expenditures made in preparation for performance or in performance, less any loss that the party in breach can prove with reasonable certainty the injured party would have suffered had the contract been performed.

Id. §349. The *Restatement* recognizes an action such as is involved here. *Id.* §139. . . .

A lesson in this area can be taken from Professors Calamari and Perillo:

> The basic aim of restitution is to place the plaintiff in the same economic position as he enjoyed prior to contracting. Thus, unless specific restitution is obtained in Equity,

the plaintiff's recovery is for the reasonable value of services rendered, goods delivered, or property conveyed less the reasonable value of any counter-performance received by him. The plaintiff recovers the reasonable value of his performance whether or not the defendant in any economic sense benefitted from the performance. The quasi-contractual concept of benefit continues to be recognized by the rule that the defendant must have received the plaintiff's performance; acts merely preparatory to performance will not justify an action for restitution. "Receipt," however, is a legal concept rather than a description of physical fact. If what the plaintiff has done is part of the agreed exchange, it is deemed to be "received" by the defendant.

Calamari and Perillo §15-4 at 574.

We should not be distracted by the manner in which a theory of recovery is titled. On careful consideration, it becomes clear that the commentators do not disagree in result, but only in nomenclature. Whether denominated "acting in reliance" or "restitution," all concur that a promisee who partially performs (e.g., by doing work in a building or at an accelerated pace) at a promisor's request should be allowed to recover the fair and reasonable value of the performance rendered, regardless of the enforceability of the original agreement.

Accordingly, the order of the Appellate Division should be modified . . . by reinstating plaintiff's second cause of action. . . .

JASEN, Judge (dissenting). . . .

[P]laintiff . . . is merely engaging in a blatant attempt to circumvent the . . . Statute of Frauds. . . .

The majority fails to specify the theory of recovery upon which it bases its conclusion that "plaintiff may recover for those efforts that were to his detriment and that thereby placed him in a worse position." Insofar as this conclusion is based upon quasi contract, it is incorrect for the well-established rule in this State is that in order for a plaintiff to recover under such a cause of action, he must demonstrate that the defendant was unjustly enriched by his efforts. The rule has been clearly set forth by this court and consistently followed:

> [a] *quasi* or constructive contract rests upon the equitable principle that a person shall not be allowed to enrich himself unjustly at the expense of another. In truth it is not a contract or promise at all. It is an obligation which the law creates, in the absence of any agreement, when and because the acts of the parties or others have placed in the possession of one person money, or its equivalent, under such circumstances that in equity and good conscience he ought not to retain it. . . .

Bradkin v. Leverton, 257 N.E.2d 643, 645 (N.Y. 1970). Since, as the majority correctly points out, defendant did not benefit from plaintiff's efforts, no recovery under quasi contract may be had.

The "lesson" provided by Professors Calamari and Perillo . . . is inapposite . . . because §15-4 of their text deals exclusively with actions based on breach. . . . [I]nsofar as this statement would allow recovery by the plaintiff under a theory of restitution, even though the defendant has not been benefited by any of plaintiff's efforts, such is not the law in New York. . . . Moreover, assuming *arguendo* the accuracy of the legal principle stated by Calamari and Perillo, this principle does not accord relief to the plaintiff in the instant appeal. . . . [P]laintiff's acts in renovating his building were "merely preparatory to performance" of the alleged oral contract whereby plaintiff and defendant agreed to enter into a two-year lease. Thus, even if §15-4 were applicable, plaintiff would not be entitled to the relief which the majority is offering. . . .

Similarly, the *Restatement (Second) of Contracts* lends no support to the majority's view. While it is true that §370 would allow a party to maintain "an action for damages, including one for recovery based on . . . reliance," a reading of the entire section, including its cite to §349 as the sole authority for this proposition, makes clear that such an action is based strictly on a theory of promissory estoppel, a theory which . . . has never been asserted by the parties and which this court has heretofore declined to adopt.

The majority also mistakenly relies on a quote from §349—

> [T]he injured party has a right to damages based on his reliance interest, including expenditures made in preparation for performance or in performance, less any loss that the party in *breach* can prove with reasonable certainty the injured party would have suffered had the *contract* been performed.

(Emphasis supplied). This passage, by its very terms, deals solely with remedies available where a party has breached an existing contract. . . .

It appears that the majority . . . is recognizing a cause of action sounding in promissory estoppel. This is implicit in its reference to *Restatement* §139. . . . Section 139 is quite simply one of the estoppel sections of the *Restatement*. . . .

While the doctrine of promissory estoppel has been recognized and applied in certain cases, to do so here, where the issue has not been pleaded or addressed in the parties' affidavits and has neither been argued nor briefed, is ill-advised. . . . [W]e are not presented here with an inexperienced or unsophisticated plaintiff who is unable to protect his own financial interests. To the contrary, Max Farash is a "prominent and successful . . . developer," see Farash v. Smith, 453 N.E.2d 537, 539 (N.Y. 1983), who owns thousands of residential housing units . . . and at least eight commercial buildings in downtown Rochester. . . . Surely a sophisticated businessman such as Max Farash knew that he could have easily insured that defendant would pay for the extensive renovation work plaintiff performed on his own building merely by obtaining defendant's promise to that effect. Plaintiff's failure to obtain such a promise leads inevitably to the conclusion that defendant never intended to pay for such renovation and, thus, never agreed to do so. Nevertheless, the majority unnecessarily provides plaintiff with an opportunity to go before a jury and request that the defendant, who received nothing from the plaintiff, be ordered to pay for the improvements made on plaintiff's own building. Nothing in logic or existing law supports such a result.

In the absence of either a contract requiring defendant to pay for plaintiff's renovation or some evidence that defendant was unjustly enriched, thus allowing plaintiff to recover under a cause of action sounding in quasi contract, defendant should not be held potentially liable to plaintiff for such renovation costs. . . .

Jones, Wachtler, and Meyer, JJ., concur with Cooke, C.J. . . . Simons, J., concurs with Jasen, J. . . .

NOTES ON THE BENEFIT REQUIREMENT

1. Restitution for unenforceable contracts. Performance of a supposed contract that turns out to be unenforceable for some reason is a commercially important source of restitution claims, often involving innocent recipients of benefits. A contract may be unenforceable under the statute of frauds or for indefiniteness, or discharged for impossibility or frustration. The contract may be illegal. One of the parties to the contract might have lacked legal capacity. Rules for these varied situations are elaborated in *Restatement (Third)* §§31-34. In most of these cases, the party who partly performed can recover the cost or value of the benefits she conferred.

2. Quantum meruit. Cases of unenforceable contracts are often encountered in the first-year contracts course under the heading quantum meruit. The phrase means "as much as he has deserved," and that amount is typically measured by market value. Quantum meruit was one of the common law claims in quasi-contract, roughly parallel to money had and received.

3. Where's the benefit? In all the other cases we have read, there was clearly a benefit to defendant, whatever the difficulties of valuing it. But sometimes that is not clear at all. Did defendant benefit from plaintiff's renovations? Should that matter? The real difficulty is that the expenditures were probably wasted: To the extent that they were tailored to defendant's special needs, they produced no benefit to anybody. If plaintiff is to recover, doesn't it have to be explained as reliance damages?

4. A doctrinal mess. The majority's quotations from the *Restatement (Second) of Contracts* and from Calamari and Perillo are from sections about breach of enforceable contracts; the dissenter is right that these quotations do not apply to *Farash*. But both sources stated (both then and now) the same rule for contracts that are unenforceable under the statute of frauds. Joseph M. Perillo, *Calamari and Perillo on Contracts* §19.44 at 729 (7th ed., West 2014); *Restatement (Second) of Contracts* §§139(1), 375 (Am. Law Inst. 1981). The dissenter is also right that §139 is a promissory estoppel provision. He doesn't cite the cases, but the New York court has unanimously held, both before and after *Farash*, that "the doctrine of promissory estoppel may not be used to preclude the raising of the Statute of Frauds." Cohen v. Brown, Harris, Stevens, Inc., 475 N.E.2d 116, 118 (N.Y. 1984); *accord*, Scheuer v. Scheuer, 126 N.E.2d 555, 557-558 (N.Y. 1955).

Courts applying New York law continue to view *Farash* as allowing plaintiff's reliance to substitute for proof of defendant's benefit in quantum meruit. Learning Annex Holdings, LLC v. Cashflow Technologies, Inc., 652 Fed. Appx. 67, 70-71 (2d Cir. 2016). And the latest edition of Perillo states:

> In quasi-contract cases it is usually stated that the plaintiff's recovery is the value of "benefits conferred" on the defendant. . . [T]he concept of "benefit" is so flexible as to be misleading. Indeed, the weight of decided cases supports a rule to the effect that the measure of recovery is the injury incurred by the plaintiff in reliance on the contract.

Perillo §19.44 at 729 (citing *Farash*). *Farash* does not appear to have been well argued, and the court is confused about details, but the result is not unusual and the court is right about the big picture: Explanations vary more than results.

5. Explaining *Farash*. Plaintiff could concede that there was no contract and sue in restitution for the benefits conferred. In the somewhat old-fashioned vocabulary of *Farash*, plaintiff may "disaffirm" the "void contract" and sue in quasi-contract. The court will imply a promise to pay for the benefit. But that leaves the difficulty of finding any benefit.

The *Farash* majority is clear that it wants to compensate reliance and it says the explanation doesn't matter. That may be a rule that New York lawyers can live with in the run of cases. The remaining difficulty is conceptual: How are the hard cases to be explained? Consider the possibilities in Table 8-1.

Table 8-1

	Is there an enforceable contract?	
	Yes	*No*
Is there a nonfictional benefit?		
Yes	Plaintiff may sue on the contract	Plaintiff may sue in restitution
No	Plaintiff may sue on the contract	*Farash*

The problem is how to explain the recovery in the lower-right cell. If the recovery is on the contract, the court must reconcile that with the statute of frauds, and it must openly state a rule of recovery on the contract limited to reliance. But it has seemed important to many courts not to be enforcing the unenforceable contract, especially when it is a statute that makes it unenforceable, and restitution (if it can be made to fit) is a source of liability off the contract. Moreover, a theory that leads to specific performance or expectancy damages looks like enforcing the contract by another name; limiting recovery to the benefit or reliance gives practical consequences to the claim that the court is not enforcing the contract. If the recovery in the lower-right cell is in restitution, the requirement of a benefit must be either fictionalized or abandoned. Both routes have been used.

6. Fictional benefits. Some courts would say that the remodeling expenses are a benefit to defendant because it asked for the remodeling. That defendant never moved in—that it never took possession of its benefit—is irrelevant. Fictional benefits create confusion among those who read the rule and do not read that it's a fiction. More important, they create litigation over the limits of the fiction. Mere preparation can be reliance damages, but most courts remain unwilling to say that mere preparation is a benefit. Was the remodeling in *Farash* bargained-for performance, because defendant specifically asked for it? Or was it mere preparation for the performance of leasing the remodeled space? Should anything turn on such a question? Cases of mere preparation have not yet forced the New York court to choose between reliance explanations and benefit explanations.

7. Abandoning the benefit requirement. If a court can imply a fictional promise to pay for a benefit, why not imply a fictional promise to pay for reliance? Professor Dawson, one of the great twentieth-century restitution scholars, would have eliminated the benefit requirement altogether in cases of restitution after part performance of an unenforceable contract. He thought that the point of restitution in these cases is to reverse the transaction, not to avoid unjust enrichment, and that the language of "enrichment" and "benefit" had come to be misleading. John P. Dawson, *Restitution Without Enrichment*, 61 B.U. L. Rev. 563 (1981); John P. Dawson, *Restitution or Damages?*, 20 Ohio St. L.J. 175, 190-192 (1959). In effect, he would equate restitution with reliance.

Professor Kull has convincingly shown that the word "restitution" has an older usage in contract law that is closely related to reliance and sometimes indistinguishable from it. Restitution often had its literal meaning of restoration, and restoration sometimes meant restoring to plaintiff what he had transferred to defendant, *or* restoring plaintiff to the precontractual status quo. Either form of "restitution" could be a remedy on the contract, distinct from the word's occasional use in the early law of quasi-contract. The *Restatement of Contracts* (1932) used "restitution" in this way, and Professor Corbin's famous contracts treatise repeatedly used "restitution" to include what we would now call reliance. Quotations are collected in Andrew

Kull, *Disgorgement for Breach, the "Restitution Interest," and the Restatement of Contracts*, 79 Tex. L. Rev. 2021, 2031-2038 (2001). With restitution and reliance not clearly distinguished in the law of contract, it is hardly surprising that they were not clearly distinguished in the law of quasi-contract.

Fuller and Perdue undertook to clearly distinguish "reliance" and "restitution" in their famous article in 1936. L.L. Fuller & William R. Perdue, Jr., *The Reliance Interest in Contract Damages*, 46 Yale L.J. 52 (1936). Then, in 1937, the *Restatement of Restitution* firmly linked restitution to unjust enrichment and to remedies off the contract. The older usage faded from legal memory, but the resulting confusion is on display in *Farash*. The *Restatement (Second) of Contracts* (1981) added to the confusion when it tried to reconcile the restitutionary remedies on the contract from the first *Restatement of Contracts* with the newer usage in the first *Restatement of Restitution*.

Inevitably, we will have problems communicating if we use the same word to mean two different things and don't even realize we're doing it. If courts think it just to allow recovery in the lower-right cell of Table 8-1, and if they want to explain it in terms of restitution or quasi-contract, maybe it would be best to say explicitly that plaintiff can recover either benefits or reliance in quasi-contract. That solution is proposed in Aaron R. Petty, *The Reliance Interest in Restitution*, 32 S. Ill. U. L.J. 365 (2008).

8. The *Restatement (Third)*. The *Restatement (Third)* emphatically rejects the explanation in *Farash* and similar cases. §31 cmt. *c*. In the *Restatement*'s view, a coherent account of restitution requires that restitution be based on unjust enrichment, and that account necessarily requires that there actually be enrichment. On that view, *Farash* can only be understood as a recovery of reliance based on promissory estoppel or on the otherwise unenforceable contract. That explanation has the great advantage of making conceptual sense. Professor Dawson in the previous note proposed to surrender to the conceptual confusion in the cases; the *Restatement (Third)* proposes to clarify it.

9. Denying recovery. Courts occasionally say that the implied promise in restitution is to pay for the benefit to defendant, there is no benefit here, and plaintiff cannot recover. Courts are more likely to reach this result when the plaintiff seems undeserving on some other ground. An example is W.F. Magann Corp. v. Diamond Manufacturing Co., 775 F.2d 1202, 1206-1208 (4th Cir. 1985), where plaintiff recovered for a partially completed construction job. Plaintiff had spent $120,000 to rent a pump that was never used; the court said defendant got no benefit from the pump. True enough, but the court could also have said that the expenditure was a waste and that the waste was plaintiff's fault.

10. Other solutions. There are other possible solutions to performance under an unenforceable contract.

a. The part-performance doctrine. There has long been a doctrine in equity, applied mostly to real estate cases, that part performance takes the case out of the statute of frauds and makes the contract specifically enforceable. The doctrine is reviewed in Messner Vetere Berger McNamee Schmetterer Euro RSCG Inc. v. Aegis Group PLC, 711 N.E.2d 953 (N.Y. 1999). Arguably the merger of law and equity ought to mean that plaintiff can recover expectancy damages on such a contract, and at least one court has so held. Miller v. McCamish, 479 P.2d 919 (Wash. 1971). Part performance shows detrimental reliance, but it also serves an evidentiary function: The performance must be unambiguously referable to the contract. To be convincing as evidence, the part performance must generally have been accepted by the party invoking the statute of frauds. Courts often say possession must have changed hands. It is hard to see how Farash's work on his own building proves the existence of a contract with a defendant who neither signed a lease nor took possession.

b. Promissory estoppel. Promissory estoppel is a modern doctrine for enforcing otherwise unenforceable promises if there has been detrimental reliance. It originated in cases of promises without consideration, but it can plausibly be applied to promises that are unenforceable for any other reason. The *Restatement (Second) of Contracts* applies promissory estoppel to the statute of frauds, with recovery limited to reliance damages. §139. It fits cleanly into existing conceptual categories and could largely solve the problem. Most states have applied promissory estoppel in statute-of-frauds cases, but New York and a few others have refused. Some of the cases are collected in Perillo, §19.48 at 733-736.

Note too that if promissory estoppel is available in the lower-right cell of Table 8-1, there is no reason for it not to be available in the upper-right cell, giving plaintiff a choice between benefit or reliance. There is much to be said for the view that all four cells of the table present problems of contract and that contract doctrine ought to solve its own problems.

11. The continued force of the unenforceable contract. Farash tried to "make his acts directly referable to the unenforceable contract," but the majority says that "simply is irrelevant." Can that possibly be right? Could plaintiff sue defendant for the cost of improvements to some other building that defendant never promised to lease? It is only because of the unenforceable contract that plaintiff's claim is even plausible. As Professor Perillo noted in making a broader point about litigating restitution where the parties tried and failed to make a contract, "[A]t every step and turn questions of fact and questions of law are definitively or partially resolved by reference to the contract." Joseph M. Perillo, *Restitution in a Contractual Context*, 73 Colum. L. Rev. 1208, 1216 (1973).

MORE NOTES ON THE MURKY BORDERS OF CONTRACT AND RESTITUTION

1. Implied contracts. A contract implied in fact is a real contract, inferred from the parties' words and actions, but often lacking a price term any more specific than a reasonable price or the market price. Courts and commentators have repeatedly explained the conceptual difference between these contracts implied in fact and the restitution claim in quasi-contract, which is sometimes called a "contract implied in law." The phrase is misleading because a contract implied in law is a fiction, not a real contract.

But very often, it is impossible to tell whether the court found a real implied contract on the facts or awarded restitution because justice requires that the court impose an obligation to pay. It rarely matters, because either way, the measure of recovery is likely to be the market value or (what is usually the same thing) the reasonable value of the performance. *Estate of Henry*, in note 2 following Bonina v. Sheppard, illustrates the point: The majority awarded restitution and the concurring opinion implied a contract, but both agreed on the bottom line.

2. Quantum meruit again. Quantum meruit is a measure of contract damages when there is an enforceable contract without a specific price term; it is a measure of restitution when there is no enforceable contract. These multiple applications of the same concept are the consequence of our legal ancestors using contract writs to create rights to restitution. Quantum meruit is a measure of recovery; it is also a cause of action.

3. No agreement at all. Consider a variation on the theme in Anderson v. Schwegel, 796 P.2d 1035 (Idaho Ct. App. 1990). Schwegel, who owned an auto-body shop, orally agreed to restore Anderson's 1935 Plymouth for $6,000. Anderson thought that price included everything except upholstery; Schwegel thought it included only the body work, which was the only work he did himself. Neither was aware of the other's understanding. After a further conversation, and with Anderson's approval, Schwegel subcontracted the engine work to another shop. Schwegel sent an itemized statement that exceeded $6,000, and Anderson did not object. Then Anderson said he wanted to make the car roadworthy, and again with his approval, repairs to safety items were subcontracted to a third shop. The final bill totaled $9,800. Anderson had paid $5,000 as the work proceeded and he insisted that only $1,000 remained due. The court found that the total amount billed by Schwegel, including a 20 percent mark-up from cost, represented the reasonable value of the benefit received by Anderson, and awarded that amount in restitution.

In *Anderson*, the attempt to make a real contract failed, and no real contract can be implied in fact, because there was no agreement on the price, either express or implied. So the claim cannot be in contract, express or implied; it can only be in restitution. There was no agreement that turned out to be unenforceable; with respect to price, there was no agreement at all. The parties acted in the mistaken belief that they had an enforceable contract. The *Restatement (Third)* categorizes such cases as mistaken belief in a contract, §9 cmt. *f*, rather than as unenforceable contracts. Not much turns on this categorization as such. But the categories may reflect something more important: Did Anderson ever indicate in any way his view that restoration of the car was worth $9,800 to him?

4. The *Restatement (Third)* applied to *Anderson*. Recall the four measures in *Restatement (Third)* §§49 and 50: the cost to plaintiff, the market value, an agreed price, or the value in advancing defendant's purposes. Liability for market value or an agreed price if the recipient requested the goods or services does not apply when the recipient's request or apparent agreement on price is the result of fraud or mistake. §50 cmt. *d*. In *Anderson*, both parties' understanding of the price was invalid because of mistake in the initial negotiation. Anderson argued for the lesser of cost or value; the increase in the car's value was likely less than the cost of restoration, and quite possibly a lot less. But the court awarded the market value of the restoration—all the body shop's reasonable charges, including its profit.

The key to *Anderson* has to be that Anderson saw an invoice for more than $6,000, didn't object, and requested more work after that. He was put on notice of his mistake and carried on without seeking clarification. At that point, it is reasonable to treat him as having implicitly agreed to pay the market value. The court used that market value as the measure of restitution. It might also have said that at that point, a contract implied in fact was finally formed.

5. Unenforceable contracts for contingent fees. A Dallas law firm had four written fee agreements with its client Albert Hill, each covering a specific litigation. But Hill was involved in more than 20 interrelated cases, and the firm gradually got involved in more and more of them and eventually did much of the work of negotiating a global settlement. There was allegedly an oral agreement for a contingent fee for this additional work, but Hill refused to sign a written version of that agreement. The law firm kept working, even though Texas, like many states, requires that contingent-fee contracts for legal services be in writing. The oral fee agreement was unenforceable.

The state supreme court held that the firm could recover for its extra services in quantum meruit, but that the unenforceable oral agreement could play no role in determining the reasonable value of those services. Hill v. Shamouon & Norman, LLP, 544 S.W.3d 724 (Tex. 2018). The court remanded for a new trial in which all evidence based on the oral fee agreement would be excluded.

The law firm's expert witness at the first trial had testified that the services above and beyond what were covered by the four written fee agreements were worth more than $15 million. But that testimony was based squarely on the unenforceable oral agreement. The jury at the first trial award $7.25 million, a number that was unsupported by any evidence once the expert testimony was excluded from consideration. The firm's highest estimate of the hours its lead lawyer had spent on the extra cases was 400 hours; the highest hourly rate it had ever charged Hill was $650. Those hours at that rate would come to $260,000, not $7.25 million. No doubt associates and younger partners also spent some hours on the cases, but the quantum meruit award on remand or settlement looks to be a small fraction of what the alleged oral agreement would have provided.

6. Enforceable contracts. Enforceable contracts can also give rise to restitution issues that cannot be resolved by contract liability alone. A plaintiff who is compelled to do more than the contract requires can recover for the extra work if she performs under protest. *Restatement (Third)* §35. And a plaintiff who partly performs and then breaches is generally entitled to credit for what he paid or for the value of work performed, including a claim in restitution if the value of what he has done without pay exceeds the damages he has caused by his breach. Here there is an enforceable contract, but the party in breach has no claim on that contract. Her claim in restitution is examined in *Restatement* §36.

Under either of these sections, plaintiff is using the restitutionary remedy to help enforce the terms of the contract. What makes defendant's enrichment unjust is that it is not authorized by the contract. These are not cases of plaintiffs seeking to substitute his or the court's sense of what is unjust for the terms of the contract.

B.   RECOVERING MORE THAN PLAINTIFF LOST

1.   *Disgorging the Profits of Conscious Wrongdoers*

OLWELL v. NYE & NISSEN CO.
173 P.2d 652 (Wash. 1946)

MALLERY, Justice.

On May 6, 1940, plaintiff, E.L. Olwell, sold and transferred to the defendant corporation his one-half interest in Puget Sound Egg Packers. . . . By the terms of the agreement, the plaintiff was to retain full ownership in an "Eggsact" egg-washing machine, formerly used by Puget Sound Egg Packers. The defendant promised to make it available for delivery to the plaintiff on or before June 15, 1940. It appears that the plaintiff arranged for and had the machine stored in a space adjacent to the premises occupied by the defendant but not covered by its lease. Due to the scarcity of labor immediately after the outbreak of the war, defendant's treasurer, without the knowledge or consent of the plaintiff, ordered the egg washer taken out of storage. The machine was put into operation by defendant on May 31, 1941, and thereafter for a period of three years was used approximately one day a week in the regular course of the defendant's business. Plaintiff first discovered this use in January or February of 1945 when he happened to be at the plant on business and heard the machine operating. Thereupon plaintiff offered to sell the machine to defendant for $600 or half of its original cost in 1929. A counter offer of $50 was refused and approximately one month later this action was commenced to recover the reasonable value of defendant's use of the machine. . . . The court entered judgment for plaintiff in the amount of $10 per week for the period of 156 weeks covered by the statute of limitations, or $1,560. . . .

The theory of the respondent was that the tort of conversion could be "waived" and suit brought in quasi-contract, upon a contract implied in law, to recover, as restitution, the profits which inured to appellant as a result of its wrongful use of the machine. With this the trial court agreed and in its findings of facts found that the use of the machine

> resulted in a benefit to the users, in that said use saves the users approximately $1.43 per hour of use as against the expense which would be incurred were eggs to be washed by hand; that said machine was used by Puget Sound Egg Packers and defendant, on an average of one day per week from May of 1941, until February of 1945 at an average savings of $10.00 per each day of use.

In substance, the argument . . . is that the principle of unjust enrichment, or quasi-contract, is not of universal application, but is imposed only in exceptional cases because of special facts and circumstances and in favor of particular persons; that respondent had an adequate remedy in an action at law for replevin or claim and delivery; that any damages awarded to the plaintiff should be based upon the use or rental value of the machine and should bear some reasonable relation to its market value. . . .

It is uniformly held that in cases where the defendant tort feasor has benefited by his wrong, the plaintiff may elect to "waive the tort" and bring an action in assumpsit for restitution. Such an action arises out of a duty imposed by law devolving upon the defendant to repay an unjust and unmerited enrichment.

It is clear that the saving in labor cost which appellant derived from its use of respondent's machine constituted a benefit.

According to the *Restatement of Restitution* §1 cmt. *b* (1937), "A person . . . *confers a benefit not only where he adds to the property of another, but also where he* saves the other from expense or loss. The word 'benefit,' therefore denotes any form of advantage." (Italics ours).

It is also necessary to show that while appellant benefited from its use of the egg-washing machine, respondent thereby incurred a loss. It is argued by appellant that since the machine was put into storage by respondent, who had no present use for it, and for a period of almost three years did not know that appellant was operating it and since it was not injured by its operation and the appellant never adversely claimed any title to it, nor contested respondent's right of repossession upon the latter's discovery of the wrongful operation, that the respondent was not damaged because he is as well off as if the machine had not been used by appellant.

The very essence of the nature of property is the right to its exclusive use. Without it, no beneficial right remains. However plausible, the appellant cannot be heard to say that his wrongful invasion of the respondent's property right to exclusive use is not a loss compensable in law. To hold otherwise would be subversive of all property rights since his use was admittedly wrongful and without claim of right. The theory of unjust enrichment is applicable in such a case.

We agree with appellant that respondent could have elected a "common garden variety of action," as he calls it, for the recovery of damages. . . . If, then, respondent had been *limited* to redress *in tort* for damages, . . . the court below would be in error in refusing to . . . find . . . the value of the machine. In such a case the award of damages must bear a reasonable relation to the value of the property.

But respondent here had an election. He chose rather to waive his right of action *in tort* and to sue *in assumpsit* on the implied contract. Having so elected, he is entitled to the measure of restoration which accompanies the remedy.

> . . . If the value of what was received and what was lost were always equal, there would be no substantial problem as to the amount of recovery, since actions of restitution are not punitive. In fact, however, the plaintiff frequently had lost more than the defendant has gained, and sometimes the defendant has gained more than the plaintiff has lost.
>
> In such cases the measure of restitution is determined with reference to the tortiousness of the defendant's conduct or the negligence or other fault of one or both of the parties in creating the situation giving rise to the right to restitution. If the defendant was tortious in his acquisition of the benefit he is required to pay for what the other has lost although that is more than the recipient benefited. *If he was consciously tortious in acquiring the benefit, he is also deprived of any profit derived from his subsequent dealing with it.* If he was no more at fault than the claimant, he is not required to pay for losses in excess of benefit received by him and he is permitted to retain gains which result from his dealing with the property.

Restatement of Restitution, Introductory Note to ch. 8, topic 2, Measure of Recovery, at 596 (italics ours).

Respondent may recover the profit derived by the appellant from the use of the machine. . . .

NOTES ON RECOVERING MORE THAN PLAINTIFF LOST

1. *Olwell* in modern vocabulary. Restating *Olwell* in modern vocabulary, defendant was unjustly enriched by his unauthorized use of the machine, and plaintiff can recover restitution of the amount of the unjust enrichment. And because defendant was a conscious wrongdoer—because it took without asking something that it knew belonged to another—restitution is measured by the largest measure of restitution rather than the smallest, recovering all the profits defendant earned by using the machine. It is irrelevant that this number is far more than plaintiff's damages, or that on one view of the case—not the law's view—plaintiff has no damages at all.

2. Rightful position? Is the remedy consistent with the goal of restoring plaintiff to his rightful position? Isn't it a $1,500 windfall for him? Does the remedy restore *defendant* to the position *it* would have occupied but for the wrong?

3. Sorting the cases. Many wrongful acts do not benefit the wrongdoer. A reckless driver may inflict great damage, but he does not profit by his wrong, and his victim can sue only for damages. In another large group of cases, plaintiff's loss is exactly equal to defendant's gain. The checks in Blue Cross v. Sauer were no more valuable in defendants' hands than in plaintiff's. Where unjust enrichment is less than or equal to damages, the significance of restitution is that it creates a cause of action that otherwise would not exist, or might not exist, or would at least be more complicated to prove. But in *Olwell* there is plainly a cause of action in tort, for conversion. The significance of restitution is that defendant's gain exceeds plaintiff's loss, so that suing in restitution increases the size of the judgment.

4. Another example. A similar classic case is Edwards v. Lee's Administrator, 96 S.W.2d 1028 (Ky. 1936). Edwards discovered the entrance to a cave on his land and developed it as a tourist attraction. This was the Great Onyx Cave, now part of Mammoth Cave National Park. One-third of the cave was under Lee's land. Lee's part of the cave was completely inaccessible to him, but it belonged to him under Kentucky law. The court granted restitution of the profits Edwards earned from showing Lee's part of the cave. It noted other kinds of cases in which plaintiff suffered no losses, nominal losses, unprovable losses, or losses less than defendant's profits, including the commercially important unfair competition cases. "The law, in seeking an adequate remedy for the wrong, has been forced to adopt profits received, rather than damages sustained, as a basis of recovery. . . . The philosophy of all these decisions is that a wrongdoer shall not be permitted to make a profit from his own wrong." *Id.* at 1032. That is the traditional rationale for making defendant repay profits in excess of plaintiff's loss. Is that a moral judgment?

5. Law and economics? Is *Olwell* consistent with the economic explanation of law? Isn't it more productive for Nye & Nissen to use the egg washer every day than for Olwell to let it sit idle? Why shouldn't Nye & Nissen be encouraged to use the egg washer? Even if Olwell were harmed, wouldn't the economic theory limit him to compensatory damages? If the law followed the economic theory, why would it ever allow recovery based on defendant's profits?

The economic preference for voluntary transactions helps explain restitution in economic terms. Judge Posner encountered restitution of profits in a copyright case, Taylor v. Meirick, 712 F.2d 1112 (7th Cir. 1983). His response was that defendant should have negotiated a license, and that he should be deterred from infringing:

> It is true that if the infringer makes greater profits than the copyright owner lost, . . . the owner is allowed to capture the additional profit even though it does not represent a loss to him. It may seem wrong to penalize the infringer for his superior efficiency and give the owner a windfall. But it discourages infringement. By preventing infringers from obtaining any net profit it makes any would-be infringer negotiate directly with the owner of a copyright that he wants to use, rather than bypass the market by stealing the copyright and forcing the owner to seek compensation from the courts for his loss. Since the infringer's gain might exceed the owner's loss, especially as loss is measured by a court, limiting damages to that loss would not effectively deter this kind of forced exchange.

Id. at 1120.

Judge Posner later generalized this analysis to "any intentional-tort case." Williams Electronic Games, Inc. v. Garrity, 366 F.3d 569, 576 (7th Cir. 2004). Intentional torts "involve not a conflict between legitimate (productive) activities but a coerced transfer of wealth to the defendant in a setting of low transaction costs." Richard A. Posner, *Economic Analysis of Law* §6.15 at 240 (9th ed., Aspen 2014). Where transaction costs are low, he of course believes that people should bargain with each other. See Notes on the Reasons for the Irreparable Injury Rule, in section 5.A.1.a; see also his views on efficient breach of contract in section 5.A.1.b.

6. Bilateral monopoly? The lines between high and low transaction costs, and between legitimate productive activity and coerced transfers of wealth, are not always clean. Nye & Nissen's egg business was a legitimate productive enterprise; so was Edwards's development of the cave. But both businesses overreached. Nye & Nissen might have assumed that Olwell would not object to its "borrowing" the machine that, for whatever reason, it had been unable or unwilling to buy. That assumption was not a defense. Edwards knew where his cave extended; the court found that "the trespasses were willful, and not innocent." 96 S.W.2d at 1030.

One source of high transaction costs is bilateral monopoly—the situation where plaintiff and defendant have no one to deal with but each other. Plainly there was bilateral monopoly in *Edwards*; Lee had a large part of the only cave, and Edwards had the only entrance. There probably wasn't a true bilateral monopoly in *Olwell*, but certainly there were constraints on the parties' options. We don't know whether anyone else would have wanted plaintiff's used egg washer or what they would have paid for it; plaintiff does not appear to have been looking for buyers. Probably defendant had other sources of supply, although it is possible that egg washers were already scarce because factories were converting to war production. Certainly any other egg washer was less convenient, and more expensive, than the one stored in the back room. If the parties were effectively in a bilateral monopoly, they might have had great difficulty agreeing on a price for sale or lease of the egg washer.

Their inability to agree on a price after Olwell discovered the conversion is some evidence that bilateral monopoly actually existed, but it is not much evidence. Olwell's anger at being wronged and Nye & Nissen's anger at being accused might have caused those negotiations to break down so quickly. As Professor Macneil once suggested, committing profitable violations of law is itself a source of high transaction costs. Ian R. Macneil, *Efficient Breach of Contract: Circles in the Sky*, 68 Va. L. Rev. 947, 968-969 (1982).

It seems likely that a sale of the egg washer from Olwell to Nye & Nissen would have been profitable for both sides. Yet the parties could not complete the sale. That is the greatest risk in situations with high transaction costs — that deals will fall through even though both sides would have benefited. If the law were really committed to making sure resources are moved to their most valuable use, wouldn't it deny restitution in cases like *Olwell* and *Edwards*? Don't these cases treat the prevention of wrongful profits as a more important goal? Where transaction costs are truly low, theories of corrective justice and theories of economic efficiency can both explain a wide range of restitution cases.

7. Rental value. So far we have considered *Olwell* on the assumption that but for the wrong, the egg washer would have sat idle. Why isn't it equally plausible to assume that if defendant had not converted it, defendant would have bought it or rented it from plaintiff, or bought or rented a similar machine from someone else? Suppose the fair market rental were $10 per month. On that assumption, defendant has saved $1,560 in labor costs by converting plaintiff's egg washer, but it could have made the same savings honestly by paying $360 in rent. How much has it been enriched? How much of the enrichment is unjust? Why does the court so casually reject rental value as the measure of recovery?

On the assumption of $10 per month, $360 is the value of the egg washer as such for three years; $1,200 is the surplus value created by putting it to use in defendant's business. Restitution of $360 would be restitution of the market value, an option that would be available if the conversion were found to be innocent. Market value would of course also be the measure of plaintiff's damages, but in conversion, plaintiff generally has a choice of damage measures. He could take the egg washer back and sue for the rental value, or treat the conversion as permanent and sue for the sales value.

8. Profits. However one considers the $360, the bigger argument is over what to do with the $1,200 created by putting the egg washer to a new use. Is this value created by defendant's wrongful conversion or by its industry? Isn't it created by both? Does the propriety of awarding the whole $1,560 depend on causation, or on the perceived need for deterrence and how strongly we disapprove of the conversion? What incentives would we create if the liability for taking the machine without consent were capped at the price that would have been paid in a consensual transaction?

9. Vocabulary for the measures of restitution. The choice between fair rental value and the $1,560 in profits as measured by the court is fundamental to the law of restitution. But the vocabulary for expressing that distinction is not very clear.

a. The courts and the first *Restatement*. The $1,560 is often called "profits," as in *Olwell*. This usage may be derived from the equitable remedy of accounting for profits, illustrated in the next principal case.

The whole theory of restitution is that we are measuring defendant's enrichment; courts also talk about his gains and his benefit. "Enrichment," "gains," and "profits" have sufficiently similar meanings in ordinary English that it is potentially confusing for them to have fundamentally distinct meanings in the law of restitution. But so they do. "Enrichment" and "benefit" are generic words for the benefit to defendant however measured; "gains" may be used the same way. "Profits" usually means an amount greater than the market value of what defendant initially took from plaintiff. This is relatively clear in the first *Restatement*, which talks about "any profit derived from [a wrongdoer's] subsequent dealing with" the property. *Restatement of Restitution*, Introductory Note to ch. 8, topic 2, at 596.

When using the word "profits," it is critical to distinguish the profits plaintiff lost, an element of damages, from the profits defendant made, an element of restitution. Note too that plaintiff's lost profits are profits he would have earned but for the wrong but did not earn in fact. Defendant's profits are profits earned in fact that would not have been earned but for the wrong.

b. The *Restatement (Third)*. The *Restatement (Third)* offers a series of guiding principles and more specific definitions. Conscious wrongdoers are liable for "the net profit attributable to the underlying wrong." §51(4). "The object of restitution in such cases is to eliminate profit from wrongdoing while avoiding, so far as possible, the imposition of a penalty." *Id.* "Profit" is defined to include use value of the property taken (typically interest or rental value), proceeds from the sale or exchange of the property taken, and "consequential gains." §51(5)(a). "Consequential gains" means "profits realized through the defendant's subsequent dealings with" an asset taken in violation of plaintiff's rights. §53(3).

"Consequential gains" is not a phrase that courts have used, but it explains much. It appeared in earlier editions of this casebook, and Professors Dobbs and Roberts devote a section of their treatise to "consequential benefits." Dan B. Dobbs & Caprice L. Roberts, *Law of Remedies* §4.4(3) at 439-452 (3d ed., West 2018). As with direct and consequential damages, the market value of the egg washer measures the initial impact of the wrong; the saved labor costs is what defendant gained as a consequence, after the initial taking.

c. "Disgorgement." There is another word in common use to express the distinction between market value and larger measures of profit: "disgorgement." This seems to us an unfortunate choice, but we need some word for this purpose, and this is the word the legal system appears to have chosen. The word appears in a fair number of cases, often without explanation, but nearly always referring to an award of profits that exceeds the market value of what was taken from plaintiff. The *Restatement (Third)* recognizes the word for this purpose, §3 cmt. *a*, §51(4), but doesn't actually use it in its own explanations of how to measure recovery. The reporter prefers to speak simply of "restitution," and to keep always in mind that the measure of restitution will depend, in substantial part, on defendant's culpability. We will use the word "disgorgement" when it is important to focus attention on the difference between restitution of market value and restitution of some more inclusive measure of defendant's profits.

The Securities and Exchange Commission enforces "disgorgement" remedies in fraud cases, but it has persuaded courts of appeals to require much more than disgorgement of profits. Defendants are sometimes denied credit for their expenses, and co-conspirators can be required to disgorge money they never received but that some other conspirator did. The Court said that this remedy imposes a penalty, a characterization that mattered for statute of limitations purposes. Kokesh v. Securities and Exchange Commission, 137 S. Ct. 1635 (2017). But the Court reserved judgment on whether the courts of appeals had correctly interpreted disgorgement in this context, and it repeatedly quoted the *Restatement*, including a comment that disgorgement becomes punitive when defendant is denied appropriate deductions for marginal costs. *Restatement (Third)* §51 cmt. *h*. So the holding that disgorgement is punitive appears to be confined to the SEC cases, and to invite renewed challenges to what the SEC calls "disgorgement."

10. An example on the other side of the line. Compare *Olwell* and especially *Edwards* with Beck v. Northern Natural Gas Co., 170 F.3d 1018 (10th Cir. 1999), where the gas company leased the right to store natural gas in an underground formation under land owned by plaintiffs. The gas leaked into a second formation, also owned by plaintiffs but not included in the lease, and eventually this was discovered. The leak had enabled the gas company to store more gas, and thus to sell more gas in periods of peak demand. Plaintiffs sued in restitution and recovered $100 an acre, the rental value of the second formation. The court rejected their claims to the gas company's profits from the extra gas sales.

Why rental value in *Beck* but disgorgement of operating profits in *Olwell* and *Edwards*? The *Beck* court said that "in this case, there is no indication that, but for Northern's actions of storing gas in the [second] formation, profits gained as a result would have gone to the landowners." *Id.* at 1024. Isn't that equally true in *Olwell* and *Edwards*?

Defendant's enrichment must be at plaintiff's expense—without that requirement, any human on the planet could sue for defendant's enrichment. In *Olwell* and *Edwards*, plaintiffs satisfied this requirement by showing that defendant used plaintiff's property to earn profits. That was also true in *Beck*. The *Beck* requirement—that plaintiff would have earned the same profits—is far more stringent.

The more conventional explanation for *Beck* is that defendant was an innocent recipient, not a conscious wrongdoer. It didn't know that its gas was in the second formation, and as soon as that appeared to be a possibility, it investigated thoroughly. *Olwell* relied squarely on this distinction; reread the quotation at the end of the opinion. If disgorgement of profits is reserved for conscious wrongdoing, and if Judge Posner concedes that disgorgement is appropriate in cases of intentional tort, then the tension between restitution and economic analysis of law largely disappears.

NOTES ON THE RESTITUTIONARY CAUSES OF ACTION AGAINST WRONGDOERS

1. Who are these wrongdoers you keep talking about? The previous set of notes talk a lot about wrongdoers, and conscious wrongdoers, without pointing to any very precise line. Intentional torts is a good first approximation. But wrongdoing is a broader category than what most lawyers mean by tort. Statutory and equitable violations are included, and fiduciaries are held to a higher standard.

Definitions in the *Restatement (Third)* start with "misconduct," a defined term that is not in common legal use. "Misconduct" means "an actionable interference . . . with the claimant's legally protected interests for which the defendant is liable under §§13-15 or §§39-46 of this *Restatement*." §51(1). These sections state rules for fraud (§13), duress (§14), undue influence (§15), opportunistic breach of contract (but not ordinary breaches) (§39), trespass and conversion (§40), misappropriation of financial assets (§41), infringement of intellectual property (§42), breach of fiduciary duty (§43), homicide (§45), intentional and wrongful interference with a donative transfer (§46), and any other "conscious interference with another's legally protected interests . . . , unless competing legal objectives" make disgorgement inappropriate (§44(1)).

Homicide leads to unjust enrichment when the killer would inherit from the victim. An example that collects all the statutes and some of the cases is Cook v. Grierson, 845 A.2d 1231 (Md. 2004). But *Cook* reaches a distinctly minority result, disinheriting the murderer's innocent children and not just the murderer. Interference with a donative transfer means the use of wrongful means to prevent a person—usually a person near death—from disposing of her property as she intends. If the property goes instead to the person who interfered, that person is unjustly enriched. Many of these are fraud or undue influence cases, but in others, the heirs have done such diverse things as defame their siblings to their dying parents or, sometimes by stealth and sometimes by force, prevent the signing of a new will. A clear example of the latter, where defendant created a physical disruption at the dying woman's bedside, is Pope v. Garrett, 211 S.W.2d 559 (Tex. 1948).

Section 44 is obviously a catch-all provision, making disgorgement presumptively available for intentional wrongs defined elsewhere in the law and not the subject of a specific section in the *Restatement (Third)*. A principal application is tortious interference with contract, but courts are divided on whether competing legal objectives make disgorgement inappropriate there. Cases are collected in Trugreen Cos. v. Mower Brothers, Inc., 199 P.3d 929 (Utah 2008). The corporate defendant hired away many of plaintiff's key employees and put them to work in violation of their covenants not to compete. The court refused disgorgement but said that defendant's profits were evidence of plaintiff's damages. Courts tend to protect employees' freedom to move on (see Notes on Personal Service Contracts in section 5.A.1.b), but this opinion is also a clear judicial endorsement of efficient breach.

2. Conscious wrongdoers and defaulting fiduciaries. Conscious wrongdoing means "knowledge of the underlying wrong" or "a known risk that the conduct in question violates the rights of the claimant." §51(3). Disgorgement of net profits is available against "a conscious wrongdoer" and against "a defaulting fiduciary without regard to notice or fault." §51(4).

3. Other forms of fault. There is an intermediate category for recipients who did not breach one of the legal duties in sections 13-15 or 39-46, but who are nonetheless substantially responsible for their own enrichment. Such a recipient is at fault if she was negligent, if she breached an enforceable or unenforceable contract, if she misrepresented something either innocently or tortiously, if she unreasonably failed to avoid or rectify the unjust enrichment despite notice and opportunity, or if she acted reprehensibly or in bad faith, *and* this fault is "a significant cause" of her unjust enrichment. §52(1). An example of breach of an unenforceable contract is Realmark Developments, Inc. v. Ranson, 588 S.E.2d 150 (W. Va. 2003), described in note 6 following Somerville v. Jacobs, in section 8.A.1.

Most of these categories are probably self-explanatory, but what is unreasonable failure to avoid unjust enrichment? Suppose Laycock knows that a builder is mistakenly building a house on his vacant lot, but he says nothing and lets the construction go on to completion. Laycock would not be a wrongdoer within the meaning of §51—he would not have breached any of the listed legal duties—but he would be failing to avoid unjust enrichment, and no doubt also acting in bad faith. His silence would be a principal cause of the builder continuing to invest money and labor in Laycock's property, and thus a principal cause of Laycock's unjust enrichment. The

Sauers were responsible for much of their own unjust enrichment, because they failed to speak up after the first few checks came from Blue Cross. They failed to "avoid" further enrichment in the form of the checks that arrived later, and refused to "rectify" their enrichment by returning the money. But as far as we know, they had done nothing profitable with the money, so nothing turned on the degree of their responsibility.

In all these cases under §52, the measure of restitution can be flexibly adjusted to account for relative fault, to ensure that the recipient bears costs attributable to her own fault, and to avoid or mitigate any loss to the restitution plaintiff. §52(2). The recipient loses the protections stated in §50 for innocent recipients, §52(2)(a), and in the case of bad faith or reprehensible conduct, restitution "may be measured as if the recipient were a conscious wrongdoer." §52(2)(c). If the recipient is more responsible for her enrichment than the claimant, change of position is not a defense. §52(3).

4. Wrongdoers without notice. Conversion and trespass are strict liability torts; infringement of intellectual property is often strict liability. A recipient who commits such a wrong without fault—typically, without being on notice that he is doing anything wrong—is not liable for consequential gains. §53(3). You might call these people unconscious wrongdoers, but that could be misunderstood. They do not have to pass out; they just have to be unaware that they are doing anything wrong. Copyright infringement is a statutory exception; even innocent infringers are liable for their profits.

5. Quasi-contract again. When we first encountered the idea of quasi-contract, our focus was on the distinction between law and equity. Now focus on the distinction between tort and contract.

a. Waive the tort and sue in assumpsit. Plaintiff in *Olwell* had a choice; he could sue for damages or for restitution. The court describes that not just as a choice between two remedies, but as a choice between two causes of action. The court says that plaintiff can waive the tort and sue in assumpsit.

Under the forms of action, the damage action was under some writ sounding in tort, such as trespass, case, or (for conversion of goods) trover. The restitution action was in assumpsit, a writ sounding in contract. The writ in trover would allege that defendant had wrongfully taken the egg washer and that plaintiff had suffered damages; the writ in assumpsit would allege that defendant, being enriched by use of the egg washer, had implicitly promised to pay for it.

b. Vocabulary. For most of the twentieth century, it was more common to speak of quasi-contract than assumpsit, and increasingly, it is more common to speak of restitution than of quasi-contract. But the older terms have not entirely disappeared. And calling the claim assumpsit or quasi-contract has had one lasting consequence.

c. The statute of limitations. Even though the underlying wrong is breach of a duty imposed by law, plaintiff generally gets the statute of limitations applicable to suits in contract. Why? Because of the old explanation that he waived the tort and sued in assumpsit, or quasi-contract. An example with a good opinion is Federal Deposit Insurance Corp. v. Bank One, Waukesha, 881 F.2d 390 (7th Cir. 1989), permitting a fraud claim to be brought in quasi-contract under the contract statute of limitations. The statute of limitations for contract is usually longer, so this is sometimes an independent reason for choosing the restitution remedy instead of the tort remedy.

d. Two caveats. It is essential to understand two things. First, a quasi-contract is not a contract and often has nothing to do with enforcing agreements. In these cases of conscious wrongdoers, defendant never *promised* to pay; if he had, the suit would be on the actual contract. Defendant rarely *intended* to pay, and it does not matter if he explicitly intended not to. The duty to pay is imposed by the court; any talk of implied promise is a fiction.

Second, talk of waiving the tort is quite misleading. If plaintiff really waived the tort, she would have nothing left to sue for; it is the tort that makes defendant's enrichment unjust. As Judge Easterbrook said in *Bank One*, a case of restitution of the profits of fraud, "No tort, no unjust enrichment." 881 F.2d at 392.

e. Two explanations. Probably the simplest way to explain these cases is to say that compensation of plaintiff's damages and disgorgement of defendant's profits are alternative remedies for the underlying tort. That is effectively the modern law, whatever the tangled history of the writ system. See Douglas Laycock, *The Scope and Significance of Restitution*, 67 Tex. L. Rev. 1277, 1286 (1989).

Professor Kull, the reporter for the *Restatement (Third)*, thinks it is easier to explain these cases by saying that there is a cause of action in tort for damages, and there is a cause of action in unjust enrichment for restitution, including disgorgement. Andrew Kull, *Rationalizing Restitution*, 83 Cal. L. Rev. 1191 (1995). But "nothing practical turns on this disagreement," except the statute of limitations, because on Professor Kull's view, the claim for unjust enrichment "incorporates as its predicate the substantive elements" of the claim for the underlying wrong. *Restatement (Third)* §1 cmt. *e(3)*. Apart from the measure of recovery, the unjust enrichment claim must be identical to the tort claim. This identity follows from the basic premise that unjust enrichment is legally unjustified enrichment; calling the cause of action "unjust enrichment" or "assumpsit " instead of tort or conversion does not change what plaintiff has to prove to show that the enrichment is unjustified.

6. No restitution when damages are adequate? Chris Kyle, a decorated Navy SEAL whose best-selling autobiography *American Sniper* was later made into a film, wrote in his book about punching and knocking down a person he called "Scruff Face" after that person allegedly made offensive remarks about the SEALS following the funeral of a SEAL killed in combat. In a later television interview, Kyle confirmed that Scruff Face was former professional wrestler and Minnesota governor Jesse Ventura.

Ventura sued for defamation, saying the incident never happened. He sought both damages for defamation and disgorgement of profits based on the idea that the false story helped sell the book. A divided jury found that Kyle defamed Ventura, awarded $500,000 in damages, and recommended $1.25 million for unjust enrichment, which the trial court then awarded. (The court treated the unjust enrichment claim as equitable and the jury as advisory.) The Eighth Circuit reversed the damages because Ventura's lawyers had repeatedly referred to Kyle's insurance coverage, both in cross-examination and closing argument. It reversed the award for unjust enrichment as impermissible under Minnesota law. Ventura v. Kyle, 825 F.3d 876, 886-888 (8th Cir. 2016).

The court said that Minnesota did not allow a claim for unjust enrichment if legal remedies were adequate, and that no reported case had allowed an unjust enrichment remedy for defamation. The court also relied on a Minnesota decision that seemed to require, on very different facts, a pre-existing relationship between the parties for an unjust enrichment claim. The case later settled. CBS Minnesota, *Ventura Rails Against "American Liar" After End of Defamation Case* (Dec. 4, 2017), http://minnesota.cbslocal.com/2017/12/04/jesse-ventura-amerian-liar-amiercan-sniper/ [sic] [https://perma.cc/K68N-6M2A].

Multiple things seem to be going on here. First, recall defendant's argument in *Olwell* that unjust enrichment is available "only in exceptional cases because of special facts and circumstances." *Olwell* rejected that argument, as do the *Restatements* and the many cases on which they rely; they treat unjust enrichment as a general principle, presumptively available whenever a defendant profits from his wrong. But a fair number of cases go the other way, treating the unjust enrichment remedy as exceptional, discretionary, or available in some contexts and not in others.

Second, the lack of unjust enrichment precedent in defamation cases is real, and the explanation cannot entirely be that no one ever thought to try it before. Most defamation lawyers who thought of it must have had the sense that it is unavailable, and so did the occasional judge confronted with a claim for it. There are constitutional limits on punitive damages for defamation, and maybe there is constitutional resistance to any remedy that awards more than compensation for actual damages. And maybe there is a sense that even if restitution of profits has been generalized, it has not reached everywhere.

Third, accounting for profits (in the next principal case) is an equitable remedy to recover a wrongdoer's profits. It communicates in plain English much better than quasi-contract or waiving the tort and suing in assumpsit. So it is increasingly common to treat recovery of defendant's profits as simply equitable, forgetting or dismissing the traditional ability to do the same thing at law. And that makes the irreparable injury rule available to help "explain" results denying relief. Damages in *Kyle* were not as complete, practical, and efficient—certainly not as complete—as the larger number the jury awarded for unjust enrichment. And defamation damages are so difficult to measure that it may be meaningless to speak of adequate remedies. But the court said that full compensation for the jury's assessment of the harm to Ventura was an adequate remedy.

This does not appear to be an isolated example. A student note sees a larger trend to deny restitutionary remedies using the irreparable injury rule, especially in Minnesota, but the idea has been picked up elsewhere. Eric J. Kopopka, Note, *Hey, That's Cheating: The Misuse of the Irreparable Injury Rule as a Shortcut to Preclude Unjust Enrichment Claims*, 114 Colum. L. Rev. 2045 (2014). He also cites cases squarely rejecting the argument.

Fourth, quite apart from pleading in more modern terms, Ventura didn't want to waive the tort and sue in assumpsit. He wanted both. The profits from the book do not duplicate or measure the same thing as the harm to Ventura's emotions or reputation. Apart from concerns about protecting free speech, why couldn't he recover both?

A more sensible way to have resolved this case might have been to say that the anecdote was such a small part of the book, and the problem of apportioning profits between this anecdote and the rest of the book would be so difficult, and the risk of error so high, that it was better to confine the plaintiff to damages. Or that as a matter of law, Ventura could not prove that *any* of the book's profits were attributable to the anecdote. But suppose the facts were different—suppose that more extensive defamatory claims were the central point of the book and used to advertise the book. Should a person who deliberately defames for profit be allowed to profit by that wrong?

MAIER BREWING CO. v. FLEISCHMANN DISTILLING CORP.

390 F.2d 117 (9th Cir. 1968)

[Plaintiffs distilled and distributed Black and White scotch whisky. The Black and White trademark was registered and well established with consumers. Defendant Maier began brewing a cheap beer under the Black and White label. Maier distributed the beer exclusively through defendant Ralph's Grocery Co. The court found that defendants deliberately infringed the trademark, that there was no competition between the two products, but that consumers might think that the beer and the scotch were produced by the same company.]

Before BROWNING and DUNIWAY, Circuit Judges, and BYRNE, District Judge.

BYRNE, District Judge. . . .

The present appeal is from the awarding by the District Court of an accounting by the defendants of their profits ($34,912 from Maier Brewing and $29,849 from Ralph's Grocery Co.) accrued from the sale of beer under the name Black & White. . . .

[A]ppellants . . . contend that even if the District Court had jurisdiction to enter an order for an accounting of profits, the making of such an order in this case was not merited by the facts. Appellants allege that . . . the District Court granted an accounting of profits as a matter of right upon the finding of an infringement and the granting of an injunction. This must be so, they argue, since the appellees have shown no injury to themselves, no diversion of sales from them to the appellants, no direct competition from which injury may be inferable, and no palming off or fraudulent conduct. The equitable limitation upon the granting of monetary awards under the Lanham Act, 15 U.S.C. §1117, would seem to make it clear that such a remedy should not be granted as a matter of right. It therefore becomes appropriate for us to examine the remedy of an accounting of profits as provided by §1117 and to determine its applicability to the facts in this case.

Section 1117 provides that a trademark registrant shall be entitled, upon the finding of an infringement and "subject to the principles of equity,"

> to recover (1) defendant's profits, (2) any damages sustained by the plaintiff, and (3) the costs of the action. . . . In assessing profits the plaintiff shall be required to prove defendant's sales only; defendant must prove all elements of cost or deduction claimed. In assessing damages the court may enter judgment, according to the circumstances of the case, for any sum above the amount found as actual damages, not exceeding three times such amount. If the court shall find that the amount of the recovery based on profits is either inadequate or excessive the court may in its discretion enter judgment for such sum as the court shall find to be just, according to the circumstances of the case. Such sum, in either of the above circumstances shall constitute compensation and not a penalty.

This language . . . apparently confers a wide scope of discretion upon the district judge. . . .

There appear to be two distinct views as to the basis for awarding an accounting of profits. The majority of cases seem to view an accounting of profits by the defendant as a method of shifting the burden of proof as to damages for lost or potentially lost sales from the plaintiff to the defendant. The minority view, which is apparently the more recent trend, bases the accounting of profits on the equitable concepts of restitution and unjust enrichment. The rationale behind this view, as expressed in Monsanto Chemical Co. v. Perfect Fit Products Manufacturing Co., 349 F.2d 389 (2d Cir. 1965), the leading case in this trend, is that the infringer has taken the plaintiff's property as represented by his trade-mark and has utilized this property in making a profit, and that if permitted to retain the profit, the infringer would be unjustly enriched.

Those courts which utilize an accounting of profits as a means of compensating the plaintiff for sales which he has lost as a result of his customers being diverted to the infringer, have, as a result of this premise, required that there be competition between the parties before this recovery can be granted. Clearly, if there is no competition, there can be no diversion of customers. It does not necessarily follow, however, that just because there is no direct competition an accounting of profits can serve no reasonable end.

The legislative history of the Lanham Act expressly states the purpose of the Act:

> This bill . . . has as its object the protection of trade-marks, securing to the owner the good will of his business and protecting the public against spurious and falsely marked goods. The matter has been approached with the view of protecting trademarks and *making infringement and piracy unprofitable.*

S. Rep. No. 79-1333, 79th Cong., 2d Sess. 1-2 (1946) (emphasis added).

It is unnecessary for this court to determine whether all of the decisions under the Lanham Act which have viewed an accounting of profits as merely a method of compensating the trade-mark registrant for his lost or diverted sales have fulfilled these goals. The question which we must answer is whether such a restrictive approach to an accounting of profits fulfills these goals today. We think it does not. . . .

Earlier in our country's history it may have been necessary to copy both the trade-mark and the product of another in order to obtain a free ride on the good reputation of that product and its maker. In such an instance requiring direct competition between the parties as a prerequisite to the granting of an accounting of profits would have been both just and logical. This, however, is the age of television and mass communications. Fortunes are spent in publicizing a name, often with only slight reference to the real utility of the product. The theory behind this modern advertising is that once the name or trade-mark of a product is firmly associated in the mind of the buying public with some desired characteristic—quality, social status, etc.—the public will buy that product. . . .

Although courts will protect this psychological value of the trade-mark by means of an injunction against infringement, even where the products are of different descriptive qualities and are, therefore, not in competition, those courts which treat an accounting solely as a method of compensating for the diversion of customers fail to fully effectuate the policies of the Act. . . .

These courts are protecting the trademark owner from only the most obvious form of damages—the diversion of sales, and are not in fact providing protection to the value of the good will built up in the trade-mark itself. No recognition is given to the possibility that customers who believe that they are buying a product manufactured by the plaintiff—whether such product is competitive or non-competitive—may be so unhappy with that product that they will never again want to buy that product or any other product produced by the same manufacturer, who they believe to be the plaintiff. Nor do these opinions recognize that, even if the infringing product is of higher quality than that bearing the registered trade-mark, the trade-mark registrant has been deprived of his right to the exclusive use and control of the reputation of his product. . . .

[A]lthough the granting of an injunction, upon the finding that a confusion of source may exist between the trade-marked product and the infringing product, protects the public from buying this particular falsely marked product from this particular infringer in the future, it does not necessarily protect them from similar future acts of commercial piracy by the same party. To accomplish this, the courts must, as was recognized in the legislative history of the Act quoted above, make acts of trade-mark infringement, or at the very least acts of deliberate trademark piracy, unprofitable. As the court in *Monsanto* recognized, it is possible for a party to adopt a deliberate business pattern of trade piracy—selling his product under the trade-mark of one reputable company until enjoined and then merely adopting the trade-mark of another company and continuing his fraudulent activities. . . .

Thus, it must be determined if the concept of unjust enrichment, utilized "subject to the principles of equity," will properly serve to effectuate the policies of the Lanham Act. It would. . . . [T]his concept will not of course make an accounting of profits automatic. Situations will exist where it would be unduly harsh to grant such recovery. Cases exist where the infringement is entirely innocent; where rather than attempting to gain the value of an established name of another, the infringer has developed what he imagined to be a proper trade name only to find out later that his name caused confusion as to the source of, and therefore infringed, a product with a registered trade-mark. In such a case an injunction fully satisfies both the policy of the Act and the equities of the case. . . .

[T]he purposes of the Lanham Act can be accomplished by making acts of deliberate trade-mark infringement unprofitable. In the case where there is direct competition between the parties, this can be accomplished by an accounting of profits based on the rationale of a returning of diverted profits. In those cases where there is infringement, but no direct competition, this can be accomplished by the use of an accounting of profits based on unjust enrichment rationale. Such an approach to the granting of accountings of profits would, by removing the motive for infringements, have the effect of deterring future infringements. The courts would therefore be able to protect the intangible value associated with trade-marks and at the same time be protecting the buying public from some of the more unscrupulous members of our economic community. . . .

We conclude that the District Court reached the correct and proper conclusion when, upon finding that the appellants "knowingly, wilfully and deliberately infringed the said trade-mark 'Black & White,'" it granted the appellees an accounting of the appellants' profits.

The appellants make . . . further arguments to the effect that . . . the award was of the profits of both Maier Brewing and Ralph's Grocery Co. and hence constitutes more than a single full satisfaction. . . .

[T]his contention is based upon the assumption that the accounting of profits in this action was utilized as a method of compensating the appellees for diversion of sales. [But] this was not the basis for the accounting in this action. The dollar amount of the recovery in an accounting for profits under the unjust enrichment rationale has no relation to the damages, if any, sustained by the plaintiff in the action.

The decision of the District Court is affirmed.

MORE NOTES ON RECOVERING MORE THAN PLAINTIFF LOST

1. Accounting for profits. Accounting for profits is the equitable remedy for recovering the profits of wrongdoing. Like quasi-contract, it has disparate roots and a tangled history. There was a remedy of equitable accounting, available to resolve disputes over commercial accounts with many transactions and an uncertain balance. Closer to what we are interested in, and probably older, equity would order a trustee to account for his management of the trust, and this naturally included accounting for any profits the trustee had wrongfully taken for himself. The trustee's obligations to account were extended to other fiduciaries. Later, with respect to nonfiduciaries, courts began to say that if the equity court enjoined wrongdoing, it could also grant an accounting of the profits from that wrongdoing. Here the accounting remedy was viewed as ancillary to the injunction. Intentional wrongdoing will usually be enjoined, so this move made the equitable remedy, accounting for profits, generally available across the whole range of cases in which defendants must disgorge their profits.

Accounting for profits is a label that makes sense in ordinary English and to lawyers who don't know this history. The phrase communicates much better than assumpsit, quasi-contract, or even disgorgement. The phrase is sometimes shortened to a word—an accounting—but that may risk confusion with the equitable accounting in commercial disputes. The *Restatement (Third)* rather noncommittally says that remedies that pursue the object of eliminating all profit from wrongdoing "are often called 'disgorgement' or 'accounting.'" §51(4).

2. Law and equity again. Historically, defendant's profits could be recovered at law in quasi-contract, as in *Olwell*, or in equity in an accounting for profits. The Supreme Court has generally treated recovery of defendant's profits in intellectual property cases as equitable, without much modern attention to the question. Faced with a case where the characterization mattered, the Court had this to say:

> Like other restitutional remedies, recovery of profits "is not easily characterized as legal or equitable," for it is an "amalgamation of rights and remedies drawn from both systems." *Restatement (Third)* §4, cmt. *b*. Given the "protean character" of the profits-recovery remedy, see *id.*, cmt. *c*, we regard as appropriate its treatment as "equitable" in this case.

Petrella v. Metro-Goldwyn-Mayer, Inc., 134 S. Ct. 1962, 1967 n.1 (2014). This avoids arguments about history and may be as sensible a solution as any. The issue was the availability of laches, an equitable defense based on plaintiff's unreasonable delay in filing suit. *Petrella* is more fully described in section 11.D.

This is the first time either of your editors has encountered the word "restitutional." "Restitutionary" outnumbers "restitutional" more than 13 to 1 in state and federal cases and law review articles on Westlaw. Adding even more vocabulary to the law of restitution is unhelpful.

3. Accounting for the profits of trademark infringement. Here is a commercially significant set of cases where defendants may have large profits and plaintiffs may have no provable damages. The older cases that awarded defendant's profits only when they bore some relationship to plaintiff's losses did not worry much about the closeness of the relationship. The only extension of liability in *Maier* and *Monsanto* (discussed in *Maier*) is to award profits where there is no competition at all between the two products. Is that a good rule? Isn't it required by the statutory text and by congressional intent to make trademark infringement "unprofitable"?

In *Monsanto*, the court found that defendant Perfect Fit had carried out four separate promotions involving deliberate mislabeling with a popular brand name. "Perfect Fit has, it appears, taken up trademark infringement as its principal line of business." 349 F.2d at 396. The court thought an accounting for profits was essential because injunctions against each violation were insufficient to deter new violations. There can be no claim that Perfect Fit's profitable violations were efficient: Perfect Fit earned its profits by deceiving its customers, and there is no economic presumption that involuntary or misunderstood transactions are value maximizing. Deceiving a customer bypasses the market as much as stealing from her.

4. Damages in *Maier*? Certainly no customers who bought the beer in *Maier* thought they were getting scotch. At worst, some consumers would think the distillers of Black and White scotch brewed Black and White beer. If they were disappointed with the beer, they might think less of the scotch. More significant, putting the label on a cheap beer would undermine Fleischmann's efforts to position Black and White as a premium brand. Whatever the value of that damage, defendants' profits don't measure it very well. Could a jury put a number on the harm to plaintiffs' reputation?

Or is the damage too uncertain and speculative to be recoverable? No recoverable damage is not necessarily the same as no damage. We saw in the irreparable injury cases that the law will provide a remedy for damage it can't measure.

There is no violation of the trademark laws if there is no possibility of confusion. Thus, the court noted that a Black and White Dry Cleaners would not have to account to Fleischmann for its profits. That substantive rule ensures at least the possibility that plaintiff will have been damaged. But it doesn't create any relationship between defendant's profits and plaintiff's loss.

5. Remedies for infringement of intellectual property. It is a bit of a puzzle why federal courts were uncertain about disgorgement of defendant's profits in trademark cases as late as the 1960s. They had been awarding disgorgement of defendant's profits in copyright and patent cases since the nineteenth century. A copyright example is Callaghan v. Myers, 128 U.S. 617, 663-667 (1888); a patent example is Rubber Co. v. Goodyear, 76 U.S. (9 Wall.) 788, 801-804 (1869). Each of these opinions treated the remedy as routine and went directly to calculation issues.

Congress and state legislatures have since imposed statutory variations on the remedies for infringement of intellectual property, including the novel remedy of discretionary awards not measured by plaintiff's damages *or* by defendant's profits.

a. Trademark. The trademark statute is quoted in *Maier*; infringers are liable for all their profits, but the court has discretion to award more or less than that. This discretion was entirely unguided by the statute until a 1984 amendment mandated treble plaintiff's damages or treble defendant's profits, "unless the court finds extenuating circumstances," for intentional use of a "counterfeit mark." 15 U.S.C. §1117(b). More recent amendments added an option to claim statutory damages of not less than $1,000 or more than $200,000 for use of a counterfeit mark, or not more than $2 million if the violation was "willful." §1117(c). A counterfeit mark is one that is "identical with, or substantially indistinguishable from," plaintiff's registered mark. §1127.

b. Copyright. Copyright infringers are liable for all damages plus all profits "not taken into account in computing the actual damages." 17 U.S.C. §504(b). But plaintiff may waive actual damages and actual profits, and elect "statutory damages" in an amount between $750 and $30,000 per violation "as the court considers just." §504(c)(1). The maximum goes up to $150,000 for infringements "committed willfully"; the minimum is reduced to $200 for innocent infringements and to zero for certain good-faith infringements by not-for-profit defendants. §504(c)(2).

Juries often calculate monetary remedies in ways that are hard to reconstruct, and they may have special trouble with the overlap between plaintiff's damages and defendant's profits. In Williams v. Bridgeport Music, Inc., 2015 WL 4479500 (C.D. Cal. 2015), a jury found that the song "Blurred Lines," the world's best-selling single in 2013, infringed the copyright in Marvin Gaye's 1977 hit song "Got to Give It Up." Plaintiffs' damage theory argued that defendants should have paid a royalty for using the infringing elements of the song, and that a reasonable royalty would have been 50 percent of defendant's revenues. Plaintiffs had lost the amount of that hypothetical royalty, and that loss was damages to plaintiffs, even though the number was largely based on defendant's revenue.

Plaintiffs also sought to recover defendants' profits. The judge instructed the jury that "You may not include in an award of profits any amount that you took into account in determining actual damages." After some argument, the parties agreed that plaintiffs' damage claim was based on $8 million in publishing revenue received by the writers among the defendants; the amount of that revenue had been stipulated. The judge told the jury to consider that $8 million in awarding damages and not to consider it again in awarding profits. The jury awarded $4 million in damages. The defense lawyers later realized that they had misremembered; the stipulated publishing revenue was not $8 million, but about $6.4 million. The judge ordered a remittitur to 50 percent of the correct amount of publishing revenue. *Id.* at *26.

The jury also awarded the profits earned by a different set of defendants, the artists and producer who recorded the infringing song. The gross recording revenue was stipulated; now the issue was how much of that revenue was attributable to the infringing elements of the song. The jury awarded about 40 percent of the artist's revenue but 187 percent of the producer's revenue. *Id.* at *27. The court upheld the award of profits against the artist, but remitted the award of the producer's profits to the same 40 percent of his revenue. *Id.* at *29. The trial court also ordered the defendants to pay a 50 percent royalty on future sales. *Id.* at *44-45.

The Ninth Circuit affirmed these portions of the judgment. Williams v. Gaye, 895 F.3d 1106, 1128-1130 (9th Cir. 2018, as amended). There was a dissent, but it went to the infringement issues, not the remedies issues. The case was Williams v. Gaye, not Gaye v. Williams, because the side we have referred to as "defendants" filed the first lawsuit, seeking a declaratory judgment that their song was not infringing. The declaratory judgment defendants counterclaimed for damages and profits.

c. Patent. Patent infringers are liable only for damages, "in no event less than a reasonable royalty." 35 U.S.C. §284. But the court may award up to three times actual damages. *Id.* Liability for the infringer's profits was repealed in 1946, apparently on the ground that these profits had been too burdensome to litigate, especially where the patented invention was simply one component in a larger product. But sometimes—most clearly where there are only two competitors in the market and no close substitutes for the patented product—plaintiff can prove the infringer's sales and profits as evidence of sales and profits plaintiff would have made but for the infringement. A clear example is Kori Corp. v. Wilco Marsh Buggies and Draglines, Inc., 761 F.2d 649, 653-655 (Fed. Cir. 1985).

In WesternGeco LLC v. Ion Geophysical Corp., 138 S. Ct. 2129 (2018), defendant manufactured components in the United States and sold them to customers abroad, who assembled them into a finished product indistinguishable from plaintiff's patented product. The Court rejected defendant's argument that plaintiff could not recover damages for lost foreign sales. The Court presumes that U.S. laws do not have extraterritorial effect, but here, the statutory "focus" was on infringement, which occurred in the United States. In addition, although the Court did not emphasize the point beyond quoting the statute, the Patent Act specifically provided for liability for infringing products sold abroad. 35 U.S.C. §271.

d. Design patents. Disgorgement of defendant's profits survives with respect to design patents, which cover "ornamental" features of a product. 35 U.S.C. §171. One who infringes a design patent "shall be liable to the owner to the extent of his total profit." 35 U.S.C. §289. The lower courts interpreted "total profit" to mean total profit from the product, and not total profit attributable to the patented design. This interpretation was not textually compelled; the next sentence, which preserves other remedies, says that plaintiff "shall not twice recover the profit *made from the infringement.*" The italicized language implies causation, and the two sentences could be read together. But the refusal to apportion between the infringing design and the rest of the product gets ambiguous support from legislative history from 1887. That legislation was inspired by a case about a carpet pattern, where the design appears to have been the product's only distinctive feature.

The Supreme Court tried to solve the problem in Samsung Electronics Co. v. Apple Inc., 137 S. Ct. 429 (2016). The Court did not address causation or apportionment;

for whatever reason, Samsung had abandoned that argument. But Samsung argued, and the Court held, that the statute authorized an award of the total profit from the "article of manufacture" to which the design was applied, and that the relevant article of manufacture could be either the final product sold to consumers or a component of that final product. And such a component need not be sold separately.

The Court's proposed solution may not have helped. When the case was retried, the jury awarded $533 million in profits attributable to infringement of design patents—more than the $399 million the first jury had awarded before the Supreme Court's attempt to clarify. Soon after the jury verdict, the case settled on undislosed terms. Maria Armental, *Apple and Samsung Settle Seven-Year-Old iPhone Patent Dispute*, Wall St. J. (June 27, 2018).

e. Trade secrets. The Uniform Trade Secrets Act, enacted in 47 states as of 2018 (http://www.uniformlaws.org/Act.aspx?title=Trade%20Secrets%20Act [https://perma.cc/T5WC-NCFR]), allows "both the actual loss caused by misappropriation and the unjust enrichment caused by misappropriation that is not taken into account in computing actual loss." §3(a), 14 Unif. Laws Ann. 633 (2005). The Act refers to both of these as measures of "damages." The Act also authorizes "a reasonable royalty" "[i]n lieu of damages measured by any other methods," *id.*, and if the violation was "willful and malicious," punitive damages not to exceed twice the amount awarded as damages, unjust enrichment, or a reasonable royalty. §3(b). There is now a federal remedy for misappropriation of trade secrets, in addition to existing state remedies. The monetary remedies precisely track those in the Uniform Act, including the misuse of the word "damages" to describe recovery for unjust enrichment. 18 U.S.C. §1836(b)(3)(B).

6. Reasonable royalty and other measures of market value. The reasonable royalty mentioned in the patent and trade secret statutes is the market value of a license to use intellectual property. This is like the rental value measure that was rejected in *Olwell.*

a. The *Restatement (Third)*. Generalizing the point, the *Restatement (Third)* says that a wrongdoer must pay not less than the market value of benefits obtained through wrongdoing. §51(2). This ensures that wrongdoers must pay the value of what they took even if they earn no profits with it. For similar reasons, a wrongdoer is liable for interest, rental value, or use value, whether or not he actually earned interest, rent, or any other form of income. §53 cmt. *b.*

b. Some examples. Market value may be the only available measure either because there are no damages and no profits to recover, or because any other measure is too hard to prove. In Linkco, Inc. v. Fujitsu Ltd., 232 F. Supp. 2d 182 (S.D.N.Y. 2002), defendant hired one of plaintiff's former directors and copied plaintiff's software for monitoring Japanese securities filings. But plaintiff had no lost sales or lost profits, because it never got its product to market and it went out of business before its software was copied. And there were no profits to disgorge, because defendant never made any money selling the infringing product. (During the internet bubble of the 1990s, lots of companies with big dreams never made any money.) But if defendant had come to plaintiff seeking permission to use the software, the two companies would have negotiated a deal: maybe an outright sale, maybe some sort of license, maybe a lump sum payment, maybe a percentage of future sales. It is hard to know what the price might have been, but experts in the industry can testify to that. Plaintiff is entitled to that price, whether or not defendant would have made any money after paying it.

The issue frequently arises when plaintiff's copyrighted art or photography is used without permission in advertising or sales brochures. Plainly there is a market value for a license to use the image, but it is impossible to say whether or how much that image increased sales. An example with a substantial discussion of this issue is Davis v. The Gap, Inc., 246 F.3d 152, 161-172 (2d Cir. 2001). The Gap argued that reasonable royalty was unavailable, because it is not mentioned in the Copyright Act; the court disagreed.

c. Damages, restitution, or something else? *Davis* treated the reasonable royalty as damages—as the amount plaintiff lost by not being paid for a license. This is how the Patent Act treats it. Other courts have treated a reasonable royalty as restitution of the amount defendant saved by not paying. University Computing Co. v. Lykes-Youngstown Corp. 504 F.2d 518, 536-538 (5th Cir. 1974). *Linkco*, a trade secret case, treated reasonable royalty as an independent third measure, which is how the Uniform Trade Secrets Act seems to treat it. The unpaid royalty would seem to measure both damages to plaintiff and benefit to defendant, but the *Restatement (Third)* has the simplest explanation: Defendant was enriched by what he took, and whatever that was, market value is a standard measure of its value.

When defendant takes tangible property from plaintiff, as in *Olwell*, it is clear that plaintiff has lost something, and courts usually think of the market value as damages. But it can be explained either way. Consider Cross v. Berg Lumber Co., 7 P.3d 922 (Wyo. 2000), where defendant borrowed plaintiff's road grader, initially with permission, but then kept it for years, refused to return it, claimed that some unknown person had hauled it away, and hid it far from the road; plaintiff found it only with an aerial search. There was no evidence of what defendant had done with the grader or any profits he had earned with it, but there was evidence of market value. The court awarded $2,500 per month as the market rental value—for 27 months, or a total of $67,500—plus $11,300 in repair costs and $4,600 in search costs, plus return of the grader in replevin. The grader had cost $19,700 new. The trial court described the rental value as damages for loss of use; the state supreme court described it as restitution of unjust enrichment. The opinion says some confused things about the relationships among restitution, enrichment, damages, law, and equity, but it helpfully collects a number of cases.

d. Reasonable royalty in *Maier*. Suppose that Fleischmann had been unable to prove defendants' profits in *Maier*. What would be a reasonable royalty? Fleischmann is likely to say that it would not have licensed its upscale trademark for a cheap beer at any price, and certainly not at any price defendants would have been willing to pay. But there are occasional deals licensing upscale marks to downscale products, and experts could testify to a range of possible market prices. "The question is not what the owner would have charged, but rather what is the fair market value." *Davis*, 246 F.3d at 166.

e. The Federal Circuit. There is a good explanation of the Federal Circuit's approach to reasonable royalty in Aqua Shield v. Inter Pool Cover Team, 774 F.3d 766, 770-773 (Fed. Cir. 2014). It is based on a "hypothetical negotiation" to reconstruct what royalty the parties would have agreed to. A key input into that negotiation would have been the infringer's anticipated profits from use of the invention, based on what was known at the time. The infringer's actual profits "may be relevant, but only in an indirect and limited way—as some evidence bearing on a directly relevant inquiry into anticipated profits."

This hypothetical negotiation simply adapts to the patent context the law's general definition of value as what a willing buyer would pay and a willing seller would accept, each having reasonable knowledge of the facts and neither under any compulsion to buy or sell. See the penultimate paragraph of the *September 11* opinion in section 2.B. In the patent context, the seller had the monopoly conferred by the patent, and depending on how badly the infringer needed to use that invention, the infringer might have been under some compulsion to buy. In patents as elsewhere, the court's task is to estimate what the parties would have agreed to. But the lack of market alternatives often makes this difficult, and many patent lawyers seem to think the process of litigating reasonable royalty is in disarray.

Of course the evidence must take account of exactly what defendant took and what he did with it. The Fifth Circuit overturned a reasonable royalty award because the expert who testified to the likely price in a hypothetical negotiation "did not discuss what portion of [the infringer]'s profits were attributable to its infringement" and there was other evidence that the infringer earned zero profits through its infringement. Streamline Production Systems v. Streamline Manufacturing, 851 F.3d 440, 461 (5th Cir. 2017). It rejected an unjust enrichment claim on similar grounds. In Williams v. Gaye, the copyright case in note 5 above, the court used the idea of a hypothetical transaction both to set the amount of damages for past sales and a future royalty rate.

7. Culpability. As *Maier* suggests, trademark law reserves accounting for profits for intentional infringers. This follows the general distinction in the law of restitution. The rule has come under some pressure from a 1999 amendment to §1117, which now authorizes recovery of plaintiff's damages or defendant's profits for "a violation under section 1125(a) or (d) . . . or a willful violation under section 1125(c)." 15 U.S.C. §1117(a). The implication is that violations under §1125(a), which is the primary section on trademark infringement, need not be willful. Courts seem to be saying that willfulness remains a factor in deciding whether to award defendant's profits, although it can no longer be a prerequisite. The debate is well illustrated in Banjo Buddies, Inc. v. Renosky, 399 F.3d 168 (3d Cir. 2005).

The Copyright Act has been interpreted to create a right to recover defendant's profits without regard to culpability. An example is Three Boys Music Corp. v. Bolton, 212 F.3d 477 (9th Cir. 2000), awarding $5.4 million against infringers who appear to have unconsciously borrowed from a song they heard as teenagers a quarter-century before.

8. Jury trial. Accounting for profits was an equitable remedy, suggesting the possibility that there might be no right to jury trial in states that follow the historic division between law and equity. On the other hand, accounting for profits ends in an ordinary money judgment, and historically, disgorgement in quasi-contract provided the same relief; either of these two reasons should be enough to give a right to jury trial in federal court and in states that follow the federal rule. Plaintiff should not be able to evade defendant's right to jury trial by labeling the relief as an accounting for profits. See Chauffeurs v. Terry and Dairy Queen v. Wood in section 6.C. The Supreme Court viewed *Dairy Queen* as a breach of contract claim pled as an accounting for profits.

But the Federal Circuit, distinguishing *Dairy Queen* and relying in part on the Supreme Court's recent opinion in *Petrella* (which characterized disgorgement as an equitable remedy), held that there is no right to a jury trial when plaintiff seeks disgorgement of profits as a remedy for misappropriating trade secrets. Texas Advanced Optoelectronics Solutions, Inc. v. Renesas Electronics America, Inc., 895 F.3d 1304 (Fed. Cir. 2018, as amended). The Ninth Circuit has reached the same conclusion in a trademark case. Fifty-Six Hope Road Music, Ltd. v. A.V.E.L.A., 778 F.3d 1059, 1067 (9th Cir. 2015).

A district court in Illinois found three competing approaches in the cases:

> The first category generally interprets *Dairy Queen* to hold that, where a plaintiff demands an infringer's profits, a right to a jury trial exists regardless of the theory behind profits. A second line of cases suggests that a jury right may exist depending on the theory of profits; where profits are a proxy for damages, a jury right exists, but where profits are premised on unjust enrichment, a jury right does not exist. The third group continues to characterize disgorgement as equitable, and some of these cases distinguish *Dairy Queen* on the ground that it involved contract damages.

Black and Decker Corp. v. Positec USA, Inc., 118 F. Supp. 3d 1056, 1062-1063 (E.D. Ill. 2015). This issue had long been under the radar for a long time, but it is now becoming a hot topic for litigation.

9. The source of profits. How much of defendants' profit is derived from the trademark violation? Is it all the profits from the beer, as the court apparently assumed? Or is it defendants' profits from the beer less what they would have earned if they had sold the same beer under a different label? Did the Black and White label enable them to raise the price? Did it enable them to sell more six packs? Doesn't it seem likely that they would have earned most of the same profits anyway—that most of their profits came from the beer and not from the label?

2.   *Measuring the Profits*

SHELDON v. METRO-GOLDWYN PICTURES CORP.
309 U.S. 390 (1940)

Chief Justice HUGHES delivered the opinion of the Court. . . .

Petitioners' complaint charged infringement of their play "Dishonored Lady" by respondents' motion picture "Letty Lynton," and sought an injunction and an accounting of profits. The . . . Court of Appeals . . . found and enjoined the infringement and directed an accounting. 81 F.2d 49 (2d Cir. 1936). Thereupon the District Court . . . awarded to petitioners all the net profits made by respondents from their exhibitions of the motion picture, amounting to $587,604.37. 26 F. Supp. 134 (S.D.N.Y. 1938). The . . . Court of Appeals reversed, holding that there should be an apportionment and fixing petitioners' share of the net profits at one-fifth. 106 F.2d 45, 51 (2d Cir. 1939). . . .

Petitioners' play "Dishonored Lady" was based upon the trial in Scotland, in 1857, of Madeleine Smith for the murder of her lover,—a *cause celebre* [a celebrated legal case] included in the series of "Notable British Trials" which was published in 1927. The play was copyrighted as an unpublished work in 1930, and was produced here and abroad. . . . There had been negotiations for the motion picture rights in petitioners' play, and the price had been fixed at $30,000, but these negotiations fell through.

As the Court of Appeals found, respondents in producing the motion picture in question worked over old material; "the general skeleton was already in the public demesne [a law-French spelling of domain]. A wanton girl kills her lover to free herself for a better match; she is brought to trial for the murder and escapes." But not content with the mere use of that basic plot, respondents resorted to petitioners' copyrighted play. They were not innocent offenders. From comparison and analysis, the Court of Appeals concluded that they had "deliberately lifted the play"; their "borrowing was a deliberate plagiarism." It is from that standpoint that we approach the questions now raised. . . .

The District Court thought it "punitive and unjust" to award all the net profits to petitioners. The court said that, if that were done, petitioners would receive the profits that the "motion picture stars" had made for the picture "by their dramatic talent and the drawing power of their reputations." "The directors who supervised the production of the picture and the experts who filmed it also contributed in piling up these tremendous net profits." The court thought an allowance to petitioners of 25 percent of these profits "could be justly fixed as a limit beyond which complainants would be receiving profits in no way attributable to the use of their play in the production of the picture." But, though holding these views, the District Court awarded all the net profits to petitioners, feeling bound by . . . Dam v. Kirk La Shelle Co., 175 F. 902, 903 (2d Cir. 1910), a decision which the Court of Appeals has now overruled. . . .

First. Petitioners insist fundamentally that there can be no apportionment of profits in a suit for a copyright infringement; that it is forbidden both by the statute and the decisions of this Court. We find this basic argument to be untenable.

The Copyright Act in §25(b) provides that an infringer shall be liable

(b) To pay to the copyright proprietor such damages as the copyright proprietor may have suffered due to the infringement, as well as all the profits which the infringer shall have made from such infringement, . . . or in lieu of actual damages and profits, such damages as to the court shall appear to be just. . . .

We agree with petitioners that the "in lieu" clause is not applicable here, as the profits have been proved and the only question is as to their apportionment.

Petitioners stress the provision for recovery of "all" the profits, but this is plainly qualified by the words "which the infringer shall have made from such infringement." This provision in purpose is cognate to that for the recovery of "such damages as the copyright proprietor may have suffered due to the infringement." The purpose is thus to provide just compensation for the wrong, not to impose a penalty by giving to the copyright proprietor profits which are not attributable to the infringement.

Prior to the Copyright Act of 1909, there had been no statutory provision for the recovery of profits, but that recovery had been allowed in equity both in copyright and patent cases as appropriate equitable relief incident to a decree for an injunction. That relief had been given in accordance with the principles governing equity jurisdiction, not to inflict punishment but to prevent an unjust enrichment by allowing injured complainants to claim "that which, *ex aequo et bono*, is theirs, and nothing beyond this." Livingston v. Woodworth, 56 U.S. (15 How.) 546, 560 (1853).* Statutory provision for the recovery of profits in patent cases was enacted in 1870. . . .

In passing the Copyright Act, the apparent intention of Congress was to assimilate the remedy with respect to the recovery of profits to that already recognized in patent cases. . . .

Petitioners invoke the cases of Callaghan v. Myers, 128 U.S. 617 (1888), and Belford, Clark & Co. v. Scribner, 144 U.S. 488 (1892). In . . . *Callaghan* . . . , the copyright of a reporter of judicial decisions was sustained with respect to the portions of the books of which he was the author, although he had no exclusive right in the judicial opinions. On an accounting for the profits made by an infringer, the Court allowed the

* [This phrase, "*ex aequo et bono*," appears in many older restitution cases, starting at least as early as Lord Mansfield's 1760 opinion in Moses v. Macferlan. It is translated as "according to what is just and good," or more loosely but more commonly as "according to equity and good conscience."]

deduction from the selling price of the actual and legitimate manufacturing cost. With reference to the published matter to which the copyright did not extend, the Court found it impossible to separate the profits on that from the profits on the other. And in view of that impossibility, the defendant, being responsible for the blending of the lawful with the unlawful, had to abide the consequences, as in the case of one who has wrongfully produced a confusion of goods. A similar impossibility was encountered in *Belford,* a case of a copyright of a book containing recipes for the household. The infringing books were largely compilations of these recipes, "the matter and language" being "the same as the complainant's in every substantial sense," but so distributed through the defendants' books that it was "almost impossible to separate the one from the other." The Court ruled that when the copyrighted portions are so intermingled with the rest of the piratical work "that they cannot well be distinguished from it," the entire profits realized by the defendants will be given to the plaintiff. . . .

[T]hese cases do not decide that no apportionment of profits can be had where it is clear that all the profits are not due to the use of the copyrighted material, and the evidence is sufficient to provide a fair basis of division so as to give to the copyright proprietor all the profits that can be deemed to have resulted from the use of what belonged to him. Both the Copyright Act and our decisions leave the matter to the appropriate exercise of the equity jurisdiction upon an accounting to determine the profits "which the infringer shall have made from such infringement."

Second. The analogy found in cases of patent infringement is persuasive. There are many cases in which the plaintiff's patent covers only a part of a machine and creates only a part of the profits. The patented invention may have been used in combination with additions or valuable improvements made by the infringer and each may have contributed to the profits. . . .

In . . . Dowagiac Manufacturing Co. v. Minnesota Moline Plow Co., 235 U.S. 641 (1915), . . . we . . . referred to the difficulty of making an exact apportionment and . . . observed that mathematical exactness was not possible. What was required was only "reasonable approximation" which usually may be attained "through the testimony of experts and persons informed by observation and experience." Testimony of this character was said to be "generally helpful and at times indispensable in the solution of such problems." The result to be accomplished "is a rational separation of the net profits so that neither party may have what rightfully belongs to the other." *Id.* at 647.

We see no reason why these principles should not be applied in copyright cases. . . .

Petitioners stress the point that respondents have been found guilty of deliberate plagiarism, but we perceive no ground for saying that in awarding profits to the copyright proprietor as a means of compensation, the court may make an award of profits which have been shown not to be due to the infringement. That would be not to do equity but to inflict an unauthorized penalty. To call the infringer a trustee *ex maleficio* [trustee by virtue of wrongdoing] merely indicates "a mode of approach and an imperfect analogy by which the wrongdoer will be made to hand over the proceeds of his wrong." L.P. Larson, Jr., Co. v. Wm. Wrigley, Jr., Co., 277 U.S. 97, 99-100 (1928). . . . Where there is a commingling of gains, he must abide the consequences, unless he can make a separation of the profits so as to assure to the injured party all that justly belongs to him. When such an apportionment has been fairly made, the copyright proprietor receives all the profits which have been gained through the use of the infringing material and that is all that the statute authorizes and equity sanctions. . . .

Third. The controlling fact in the determination of the apportionment was that the profits had been derived, not from the mere performance of a copyrighted play, but from the exhibition of a motion picture which had its distinctive profit-making features, apart from the use of any infringing material, by reason of the expert and creative operations involved in its production and direction. . . . And, in this instance, it plainly appeared that what respondents had contributed accounted for by far the larger part of their gains.

Respondents had stressed the fact that, although the negotiations had not ripened into a purchase, the price which had been set for the motion picture rights in "Dishonored Lady" had been but $30,000. And respondents' witnesses cited numerous instances where the value, according to sales, of motion picture rights had been put at relatively small sums. But the court below rejected as a criterion the price put upon the motion picture rights, as a bargain had not been concluded and the inferences were too doubtful. The court also ruled that respondents could not count the effect of "their standing and reputation in the industry." The court permitted respondents to be credited "only with such factors as they bought and paid for; the actors, the scenery, the producers, the directors and the general overhead."

The testimony showed quite clearly that in the creation of profits from the exhibition of a motion picture, the talent and popularity of the "motion picture stars" generally constitutes the main drawing power of the picture, and that this is especially true where the title of the picture is not identified with any well-known play or novel. Here, it appeared that the picture did not bear the title of the copyrighted play and that it was not presented or advertised as having any connection whatever with the play. It was also shown that the picture had been "sold," that is, licensed to almost all the exhibitors as identified simply with the name of a popular motion picture actress before even the title "Letty Lynton" was used. In addition to the drawing power of the "motion picture stars," other factors in creating the profits were found in the artistic conceptions and in the expert supervision and direction of the various processes which made possible the composite result with its attractiveness to the public.

Upon these various considerations, with elaboration of detail, respondents' expert witnesses gave their views as to the extent to which the use of the copyrighted material had contributed to the profits in question. The underlying facts as to the factors in successful production and exhibition of motion pictures were abundantly proved, but, as the court below recognized, the ultimate estimates of the expert witnesses were only the expression "of their very decided opinions." These witnesses were in complete agreement that the portion of the profits attributable to the use of the copyrighted play in the circumstances here disclosed was very small. Their estimates given in percentages of receipts ran from five to twelve percent; the estimate apparently most favored was ten percent as the limit. One finally expressed the view that the play contributed nothing. There was no rebuttal. But the court below was not willing to accept the experts' testimony "at its face value." The court felt that it must make an award "which by no possibility shall be too small." Desiring to give petitioners the benefit of every doubt, the court allowed for the contribution of the play twenty percent of the net profits.

Petitioners are not in a position to complain that the amount thus allowed by the court was greater than the expert evidence warranted. . . . Nor can we say that the testimony afforded no basis for a finding. What we said in . . . *Dowagiac* . . . is equally true here, — that what is required is not mathematical exactness but only a reasonable approximation. That, after all, is a matter of judgment; and the testimony of those who are informed by observation and experience may be not only helpful but, as we have said, may be indispensable. Equity is concerned with making a fair apportionment so that neither party will have what justly belongs to the other. Confronted with the manifest injustice of giving to petitioners all the profits made by the motion picture, the court in making an apportionment was entitled to avail itself of the experience of those best qualified to form a judgment in the particular field of inquiry and come to its conclusion aided by their testimony. We see no greater difficulty in the admission and use of expert testimony in such a case than in the countless cases involving values of property rights in which such testimony often forms the sole basis for decision. . . .

The judgment of the . . . Court of Appeals is affirmed. . . .

Justice MCREYNOLDS took no part in the decision of this case.

NOTES ON APPORTIONING PROFITS

1. The movie. The movie starred Joan Crawford and Robert Montgomery. Both, but especially Crawford, were major figures in their time. MGM sold the movie to theaters as "Production No. 208, Joan Crawford No. 2." The district court also enjoined further distribution of the movie. MGM did not buy its way out of this injunction; *Letty Lynton* is known in film circles as the lost Crawford movie. The profits at issue were earned between the movie's release in 1932 and the injunction in 1936. In 1947, United Artists released *Dishonored Lady*, starring Hedy Lamarr and based on authorized use of plaintiffs' play. Information about both movies is available at the Internet Movie Database, *www.imdb.com.*

The trial court considered the sums paid other authors as evidence of the value of plaintiff's contribution. Novelist Margaret Mitchell got $50,000 for the movie rights to *Gone with the Wind.* But the author of *Peter Pan* got 7 percent of the movie's gross receipts, which would be much more than 7 percent of the profits.

2. The problem of apportionment. There are multiple calculation issues in these cases. The $587,000 figure for profits from the movie was also litigated, but hold that question for now. The issue in the Supreme Court was how to apportion those profits between the stolen script and everything that MGM legitimately contributed to the movie. There is more than one way to apportion, and the method used often depends on what evidence is available.

3. Production inputs and ballpark estimates. *Sheldon* apportioned profits to the various inputs required to make the movie, and the method of apportionment in *Sheldon* was simply to estimate the importance of the misappropriated input. Is *Sheldon* consistent with the decisions it distinguishes? If a ballpark estimate is sufficient, why would it ever be impossible to apportion profits between infringing and noninfringing components? Why not just count the proportion of stolen recipes in Belford v. Scribner and prorate the profits? That would be analogous to the solution in Edwards v. Lee's Administrator, in the notes following *Olwell,* where the Kentucky court prorated profits on the basis of linear feet in the cave. And surely the uncopyrighted court decisions were more important than the copyrighted headnotes in Callaghan v. Myers. Why not have an expert testify to that effect and give an opinion that the headnotes contributed no more than 10 or 20 percent of the profits?

Defendants did not offer such evidence in the earlier cases, and perhaps the Court was unwilling to make estimates without expert guidance. For a modern decision refusing to apportion, see Business Trends Analysts, Inc. v. Freedonia Group, Inc., 887 F.2d 399, 407 (2d Cir. 1989), where infringing and noninfringing portions of a report were identified but defendants offered almost no evidence about the relative importance of each.

4. Songs. *Sheldon*'s methodology is commonly used in music cases to allocate profits between the infringing song and others on the same album or CD, and between the music and the lyrics of the infringing song. An example is Three Boys Music Corp. v. Bolton, 212 F.3d 477 (9th Cir. 2000). The case involved two somewhat similar songs named "Love Is a Wonderful Thing," a minor hit by the Isley Brothers in 1964 and a major hit by Michael Bolton in 1991. The jury found that Bolton's song accounted for 28 percent of the profits from his CD, and that the infringing elements accounted for 66 percent of the profits from the song. *Id.* at 487. Sixty-six percent of 28 percent of the profits from the CD came to $5.4 million. Relying on *Three Boys Music Corp.*, the Ninth Circuit in Williams v. Gaye, 895 F.3d 1106 (9th Cir. 2018, as amended), affirmed the trial court's determination that 40 percent of the profits of the song "Blurred Lines" came from elements of the infringed Marvin Gaye song, "Got to Give It Up." Defendants unsuccessfully argued that the evidence supported at most a 5 percent allocation. *Id.* at 1129.

5. Apportionment by sales. Two years after *Sheldon,* the Supreme Court took a different approach to apportionment in a trademark case. Mishawaka Rubber & Woolen Manufacturing Co. v. S.S. Kresge Co., 316 U.S. 203 (1942). *Mishawaka* allocated profits to sales. The Court held that defendant need not account for profits from sales to consumers who were not confused by the mislabeling. But defendant bore the burden of proving how many such consumers there were. The Court recognized that this burden is "as often as not impossible to sustain." *Id.* at 206.

Could defendant meet its burden with a marketing survey showing how many customers in a random sample were confused by the label? Defendant tried that in Truck Equipment Service Co. v. Fruehauf Corp., 536 F.2d 1210, 1221-1223 (8th Cir. 1976). The survey showed that only 20 percent of defendant's customers purchased for reasons having anything to do with plaintiff's infringed product. The court rejected the survey's relevance without passing on its evidentiary sufficiency. It thought that allowing an infringer to keep 80 percent of its profits from sales of infringing items was "clearly inadequate" to deter infringement. The case appears to squarely conflict with *Mishawaka.* Is it just wrong? Or does apportionment on the basis of sales look more attractive in theory when it is impossible in fact?

In Starbucks Corp. v. Wolfe's Borough Coffee, Inc., 588 F.3d 97 (2007), Starbucks sued a competitor for trademark infringement for selling coffee products called "Charbucks Blend" and "Mister Charbucks."

> The only evidence as to actual confusion submitted by Starbucks was a telephone survey where 3.1% of 600 respondents named Starbucks as a possible source of a "Charbucks" product; 30.5% of 600 respondents "immediately thought of "Starbucks" upon hearing "Charbucks"; and 9% of consumers "immediately thought of coffee . . . after hearing "Charbucks." . . . Starbucks' own witness, a Director of Brand Management, testified that Starbucks had no knowledge that any consumer had ever actually become confused that Charbucks was a Starbucks product.

Id. at 117. The court found no evidence of confusion, and thus no infringement, so it never got to apportioning profits based on sales. If it did, how helpful would such evidence be to Starbucks' claim that a significant part of the competitor's sales came from confused consumers? Maybe this case further confirms *Mishawaka*'s comment about the great difficulty of proof.

6. *Maier Brewing.* Could the court have apportioned profits in *Maier Brewing?* Presumably, experts could testify about how much brewers or distributors would pay for a well-known label. Or they could testify to the relative importance of the label and other inputs. Would either kind of testimony be enough under *Sheldon?*

7. Calculating the profits from the movie. The $587,000 figure for profits from the movie was determined in the lower courts. By statute in the trademark and copyright cases, and often in judge-made law as well, plaintiffs need prove only gross receipts; defendant has the burden of proving its expenses. Receipts and most expenses could mostly be found in real numbers in MGM's records, although there were issues about which expenses counted and how to treat overhead. There were no real numbers for the value of the play, because it was neither bought nor sold separately from the rest of the movie.

8. The bought-and-paid-for standard. Defendants in *Sheldon* were given credit only for things they "bought and paid for," with no allowance for the contribution of their "standing and reputation" in the industry. Perhaps more important, the "bought and paid for" standard excludes the value of defendants' labor. In *Callaghan*, the case of the law reports discussed in *Sheldon*, the Court reasoned that plaintiff should not have to pay for the time defendants spent infringing his copyright. Corporate infringers like MGM pay for labor and get to deduct salaries under the bought-and-paid-for standard. Thus, that standard is in tension with the rationale that plaintiff should not have to pay for work done by infringers.

The *Restatement (Third)* elaborates and perhaps tweaks the bought-and-paid-for rule:

> A conscious wrongdoer or a defaulting fiduciary may be allowed a credit for money expended in acquiring or preserving the property or carrying on the business that is the source of the profit subject to disgorgement. By contrast, such a defendant will ordinarily be denied any credit for direct contributions in the form of services, or for expenditures incurred directly in the commission of a wrong to the claimant.

§51(5)(c). This rule is presumptive; it can be "modified to meet the circumstances of a particular case." §51(5). Brooks v. Conston, 72 A.2d 75 (Pa. 1950), shows why the rule is sometimes modified. Defendant by fraud and undue influence acquired a chain of millinery stores at a grossly inadequate price. He operated the stores for four years, increased the number of stores, and greatly increased the chain's value, before plaintiff sued for rescission. The delay in suing was excused by defendant's continued undue influence. The court required defendant to disgorge all the profits of all the stores, including the newly acquired ones, but it allowed credit for the salaries he paid himself and his wife. "The wrong that Conston committed was in his original acquisition of the stores, not in his operation of them," *id.* at 79; his operation of them inured to the great benefit of plaintiff, and working without salary for four years would be a serious hardship even for a conscious wrongdoer.

9. *Olwell* again. Whenever you see profits far in excess of the market value of the thing taken, it is prudent to ask whether profits from some other input have been included. Professor Palmer thought some of the profits in *Olwell* must have been fairly attributable to the rest of the business. 1 George E. Palmer, *Law of Restitution* §2.12 at 160-161 (Little Brown 1978). Certainly the egg washer was much more valuable with the addition of an egg business, just as the play in *Sheldon* was much more valuable with the addition of Joan Crawford and MGM. Could the *Sheldon* approach be used to apportion profits between the egg washer and the other components of Nye & Nissen's business? Or did the court have a more direct measure in *Olwell?* The labor savings presumably went straight to the bottom line; the court could figure exactly what Nye & Nissen's profits would have been without the egg washer. When that is true, is any other basis for apportionment defensible?

HAMIL AMERICA, INC. v. GFI
193 F.3d 92 (2d Cir. 1999)

Before OAKES, JACOBS, and POOLER, Circuit Judges.
  OAKES, Senior Circuit Judge:

I. INTRODUCTION

Hamil America, Inc. sued GFI . . . SGS Studio, Inc. and J.C. Penney Company, Inc. for copyright infringement. According to Hamil America, GFI copied one of Hamil America's floral fabric patterns, SGS manufactured garments using the infringing GFI fabric and sold the garments to J.C. Penney, and J.C. Penney sold the garments in its retail stores. Hamil America prevailed at trial and was awarded damages against all three defendants. [The court affirmed findings that GFI Pattern No. 330 was a deliberate copy of the more expensive Hamil America Pattern No. 96.]

III. DISCUSSION . . .

C. DAMAGES . . .

Under the current Copyright Act, a copyright owner can elect to recover either "actual damages and profits" under 17 U.S.C. §504(b), or "statutory damages" under 17 U.S.C. §504(c). At Hamil America's request, the district court awarded damages under 17 U.S.C. §504(b). Hamil America could recover "the actual damages suffered by [it] as a result of the infringement, *and* any profits of the infringer that are attributable to the infringement and are not taken into account in computing the actual damages." 17 U.S.C. §504(b) (emphasis added). . . .

1. Calculation of the Infringers' Profits

Section 504(b) of the Copyright Act authorizes a copyright owner to recover the infringer's profits. That section expressly provides that "[i]n establishing the infringer's profits, the copyright owner is required to present proof only of the infringer's gross revenue, and the infringer is required to prove his or her deductible expenses and the elements of profit attributable to factors other than the copyrighted work." 17 U.S.C. §504(b). Put another way, the infringer's profits are calculated as the gross sales of infringing goods minus the costs that the infringer proves are attributable to the production and sale of those goods.

In compliance with this statutory procedure, Hamil America submitted proof of GFI's gross revenue from the sale of the infringing dress patterns, and GFI submitted a schedule of its deductible expenses that included both the actual costs of production of the infringing pattern as well as its general, or "fixed," overhead expenses. The district court rejected GFI's submission to the extent that it sought deductions for overhead expenses, stating that GFI "would have had general administrative expenses of 'X' amount whether [it] sold [the infringing] goods or not." The court also rejected certain specific expenses, such as country club dues, on the ground that they were not "incremental costs of producing [the infringing] fabric." The court asked GFI to adduce the "actual cost of the goods, what it actually cost [GFI] to manufacture [the] specific items." The district court accepted GFI's amended cost schedule, which showed only the variable costs of producing and selling the infringing pattern, and which excluded general overhead items such as rent, insurance, and depreciation.

GFI argues that the district court erred in excluding an allocation of general overhead expenses in its calculation of GFI's profits and that we must remand for recalculation of damages. We agree.

Our analysis begins with *Sheldon v. Metro-Goldwyn Pictures Corp.,* 106 F.2d 45 (2d Cir. 1939) (L. Hand, J.), in which a motion picture studio infringed the copyright on a certain play. The district court allowed a deduction for overhead expenses based on the ratio that the cost of producing the infringing movie bore to the total costs of the movie studio. On appeal, the copyright holder argued that the infringers should not have been permitted any deduction for overhead expenses absent a showing that the overhead had been increased by the production of the infringing movie. . . . This court affirmed, noting generally that, "'[o]verhead' which does not assist in the production of the infringement should not be credited to the infringer; that which does, should be; it is a question of fact in all cases." *Id.* at 54.

Turning to the specific facts of the *Sheldon* case, the court applied its general rule as follows:

> In the case at bar the infringing picture was one of over forty made by the defendants, using the same supervising staff and organization, which had to be maintained if the business was to go on at all. Without them no picture could have been produced; they were as much a condition upon the production of the infringing picture as the scenery, or the plaintiffs' play itself.

Id. The court thus concluded that certain categories of general overhead expenses—in this case, those relating to creating and maintaining a "supervising staff and organization"—were appropriately deducted from gross revenue. The court then considered various methods of allocating those overhead expenses to the production of the infringing movie, and selected the method that was most fair, accurate, and practical in light of the infringing company's structure and products. Given the impossibility of determining the overhead costs that were directly related to the production of the infringing motion picture, the court permitted a deduction of a portion of overhead expenses based on the cost of production of the motion picture:

> [T]o make a perfect allocation one would have to examine what part of the time of all the employees whose pay went into the "overhead", was given to each picture; and so of the other expenses. That was obviously impossible. It is on the whole more likely that a given picture required that proportion of the general services represented by its cost of production, than that each picture shared those services equally. . . . The [cost of production] solution appears to us as nearly right as was practically possible.

Id. at 52-53. . . .

Sheldon thus contemplates a two-step procedure for deducting overhead expenses from an infringer's profits. The first step is to determine what overhead expense categories (such as rent, business, entertainment, personnel and public relations) are actually implicated by the production of the infringing product. Once a sufficient nexus is shown between a category of overhead and the production or sale of the infringing product, a court need not scrutinize for inclusion or exclusion particular items within the overhead category. For example, if "entertainment expenses" is a category of overhead implicated in the line of business that produced or sold the infringing product, then country club dues included within that category should not be singled out for exclusion, as they were by the district court here. Rather, the court should limit its inquiry to the sufficiency of the nexus between the expense category and production of the infringing product.

The second step is to arrive at a fair, accurate, and practical method of allocating the implicated overhead to the infringement. The infringer has the burden of "offering a fair and acceptable formula for allocating a given portion of overhead to the particular infringing items in issue." 4 Melville B. Nimmer & David Nimmer, *Nimmer on Copyright* §14.03[B] at 14-39 (Matthew Bender 1996). The reasonableness of the proffered overhead allocation formula is a question of fact in all cases.[5]

Sheldon's approach has been consistently applied by this Court. In subsequent cases, we have assumed that general overhead expenses were deductible and reviewed only the sufficiency of the nexus between the expense and the infringing product and/or the adequacy of the adduced formula for allocating overhead costs to the production of the infringing product. . . .

[W]e rejected an infringer's allocation of company overhead, which was based on the percentage of the company's net sales to the infringing line of goods, on the ground that the proffered allocation was not the most reliable method available to the infringer. See Manhattan Industries, Inc. v. Sweater Bee by Banff, Ltd., 885 F.2d 1, 7-8 (2d Cir. 1989). We reasoned that although an infringer "need not prove its overhead expenses and their relationship to the production of the contemptuous goods in 'minute detail,' it must still carry its burden of demonstrating a *sufficient nexus* between each expense claimed and the sales of the unlawful goods." *Id.* (emphasis added). See also Gaste v. Kaiserman, 863 F.2d 1061, 1071 (2d Cir. 1988) (rejecting a 90 percent allocation of overhead to an infringing song that represented 90 percent of the infringer's sales); Wilkie v. Santly Bros., 139 F.2d 264, 265 (2d Cir. 1943) (holding that general allocation formula should allocate overhead equally to each song produced by the infringer because there was no evidence that the infringing song contributed more to the overhead costs than the publisher's other 47 songs).

Despite the clear precedent on the deduction of overhead expenses established by *Sheldon* and its progeny, the district court here prohibited GFI from deducting any overhead whatsoever unless GFI could show that its overhead was actually increased by its production of Pattern No. 330. *See* Hamil America, Inc. v. SGS Studio, Inc., 1998 WL 19991 at *3 (S.D.N.Y. 1998) ("[T]he Court must examine the facts to determine those incremental cost[s] of the infringer that were increased as a direct result of the production and sale of the infringing goods . . . and to separate them from those fixed costs that would have been incurred in any event."). The court appears to have based its holding at least in part on the fact that the infringement by GFI was willful, relying on cases from other jurisdictions suggesting that willful or deliberate infringers may not deduct overhead when calculating the profit the plaintiff is entitled to recover.

Unlike the district court, we are not prepared to abandon the teachings of *Sheldon* in favor of a hard and fast rule denying all overhead deductions to willful infringers. But we share the district court's concern that willful infringers should not be permitted to subsidize the sale of legitimate goods with the sale of infringing goods by "passing part of its fixed cost on to the copyright holder." *See id.* at *2. We also recognize that "a rule of liability which merely takes away profits from an infringement would offer little discouragement to infringers." F.W. Woolworth Co. v. Contemporary Arts, 344

---

5. Some methods of allocating overhead to the infringement proffered in previous cases include: the production cost of the infringing product as a percentage of the total production costs, the number of infringing products as a percentage of total products, and the dollar sales from the infringing product as a percentage of total dollar sales.

U.S. 228, 233 (1952). We therefore conclude that *Sheldon*'s two-step approach must be applied with particular rigor in the case of willful infringement.

Every infringer shoulders the burden of demonstrating a "sufficient nexus between each expense claimed and the sales of the unlawful goods," *Manhattan Industries*, 885 F.2d at 8, before it may deduct any overhead expenses from its profits. When infringement is found to be willful, the district court should give extra scrutiny to the categories of overhead expenses claimed by the infringer to insure that each category is directly and validly connected to the sale and production of the infringing product. Unless a strong nexus is established, the court should not permit a deduction for the overhead category.

An infringer also bears the burden of proposing a fair and acceptable formula for allocating a portion of overhead expenses to the infringing items at issue. The district court must determine that the particular allocation formula is optimal and sound, and all presumptions are drawn against the infringer. See 4 Nimmer & Nimmer §14.03[B] at 14-40 ("[If] the computation of profits and costs is uncertain due to the failure of the [infringer] to keep adequate records of costs, any doubt in the evidence will be resolved in favor of the plaintiff."). The allocation formula of a willful infringer should be held to a particularly high standard of fairness, and the court should not hesitate to reject a formula which allows the willful infringer to deduct more of its overhead than was directly implicated in the manufacture of the infringing product.

Because the district court erred under *Sheldon* in applying a blanket prohibition of all overhead deductions, we reverse on this issue and remand for a recalculation of GFI's profits. In that proceeding, GFI, as a willful infringer, must demonstrate a direct and valid nexus between each claimed overhead expense category and the production of GFI Pattern No. 330 and propose a fair and acceptable formula for allocating a portion of overhead to the pattern's production. The district court, applying the heightened scrutiny appropriate in cases of willful infringement, will have the latitude to adopt or reject certain categories of overhead, and to accept, reject, or amend GFI's overhead allocation formula. Of course, if the resulting calculation causes the district court to reconsider its finding that Hamil America "will be fully compensated on its claims," see 1998 WL 19991 at *3, the court could award Hamil America its "actual damages" in lieu of, or in addition to, GFI's recalculated profits. See 17 U.S.C. §504(b).

2. Hamil America's Lost Profits

Hamil America raises one issue on cross-appeal: whether the district court erred when it determined that Hamil America could not recover for lost profits that it might have earned from sales to those of its customers who purchased GFI's infringing design. It relies on three facts: (1) Hamil America and GFI had several shared customers; (2) the shared customers bought samples of Hamil America Pattern No. 96 with the probable intention to purchase more Hamil America fabric; and (3) the shared customers did not purchase the fabric from Hamil America after the less expensive version offered by GFI appeared on the market. Hamil America reasons that it is entitled to damages for lost profits, as it would have sold Pattern No. 96 to the shared customers had GFI not made the infringing pattern. It argues that it is entitled to a total judgment against GFI in the amount of $240,782, rather than the $201,049 that was awarded by the district court.

GFI argued below that Hamil America should not recover lost profits, because the shared customers would not have purchased the fabric at Hamil America's above-market prices. GFI also pointed out that those customers purchased GFI's fabric several months after they had purchased Hamil America's samples, and concluded that the commercial failure of Hamil America's pattern "had nothing to do with the availability of [GFI's] pattern."

The district court agreed that the shared customers may well have declined to purchase Hamil America's fabric, due to its higher price, and held that Hamil America could not recover the alleged lost profits. The court further noted that Hamil America could not recover both for its hypothetical sales to the shared customers and for GFI's actual sales to those same customers.[7] The court elected to measure GFI's actual profits from sales to the shared customers, rather than speculate as to what Hamil America might have earned had it sold Pattern No. 96 to the shared customers.

As Nimmer states, "[i]n the absence of convincing evidence as to the volume of sales that plaintiff would have obtained but for the infringement, the measure of lost profits may be rejected as too speculative." 4 Nimmer & Nimmer §14.02[A] at 14-11. The district court rejected Hamil America's request for lost profits as too speculative. In our view, this conclusion was not clearly erroneous. In the absence of more reliable evidence of Hamil America's lost profits, the district court was entitled to rely on the less abstract calculation of damages from GFI's sales to the shared customers. We therefore affirm on this issue.

IV. CONCLUSION

Because the district court erroneously prohibited GFI from deducting any overhead expenses in the calculation of its profits, we reverse in part and remand for recalculation of damages. . . .

NOTES ON CALCULATING PROFITS

1. Vocabulary again. The court carefully and repeatedly distinguishes restitution of defendant's profits from recovery of plaintiff's lost profits. Yet it repeatedly uses the word "damages" to refer to both measures of recovery. The court is not confused, but readers might be. It would surely be better to confine the word "damages" to measures of plaintiff's loss, and to settled usage concerning punitive damages, and to use "restitution," "disgorgement," or "accounting for profits" to describe recovery of defendant's profits.

2. Two methods of calculating. The accounting in *Hamil* looks rather different from the Supreme Court's apportionment in *Sheldon.* The play generated few numbers to work with; the Court had to calculate profits at the level of the movie, estimate the relative importance of the play, and apportion profits pro rata based on that estimate. Call that the pro rata method. With a component not sold separately, that is sometimes the best the court can do. *Hamil* contemplates apportioning overhead pro

---

7. . . . A copyright plaintiff may recover its own lost profits, which are part of the plaintiff's "actual damages," as well as the defendant's profits. But a "plaintiff may not recover damages that have already been taken into account in computing its actual damages." 4 Nimmer & Nimmer §14.03 at 14-29. Thus, "[a] plaintiff may not recover its full lost profits plus all of the defendant's profits, for this would constitute a forbidden double recovery." *Id.* §14.02[A] at 14-10. Thus, if Hamil America were in fact entitled to recover lost profits, it would have had to set off its recovery for GFI's profits by those profits already taken into account to determine Hamil America's lost profits, because Hamil America could not recover twice. Hamil America properly performed this analysis below, when Hamil America contended that it had lost profits of $149,823, and that GFI's profits not taken in account in computing Hamil America's lost profits were $90,959, for a total judgment against GFI in the amount of $240,782.

rata, although based on proportions found in defendants' books rather than impressionistic judgment.

Hamil calculates profits more directly, considering all the revenues and expenses attributable to the infringing product. There is no plausible claim that GFI added any substantial value to what it copied, so there is no need to apportion profits from the pattern to infringing and noninfringing inputs. But it is still necessary to separate profits from that pattern from profits on other patterns and other products. Call this the incremental-change method. Courts do not distinguish these methods doctrinally; this is largely a matter of what evidence is available. When sufficient data are available, courts usually try to calculate directly how much profit came from the infringing product. Note too that this choice is either-or. If the court can actually account for an item of income or expense, then it would be double counting to take account of that same item in any further apportionment that is done pro rata.

The *Restatement (Third)* distinguishes issues of causation and remoteness, apportionment, and deductions and credits. §51 cmts. *f-h.*

3. Overhead. Courts have partly divided, and partly hedged, on overhead. The Second Circuit is squarely committed to including an allocated portion of overhead. The Ninth Circuit, after a long evolution, now more or less agrees; the Ninth Circuit cases are reviewed in Oracle America, Inc. v. Google Inc., 131 F. Supp. 3d 946 (N.D. Cal. 2015).

The *Restatement (Third)* would apparently deny credit for most overhead. "[D]efendant will not be allowed to deduct expenses (such as ordinary overhead) that would have been incurred in any event, if the result would be that defendant's wrongful activities—by defraying a portion of overall expenses—yield an increased profit from defendant's operations as a whole." §51 cmt. *h.*

So who's right? Consider *Sheldon.* MGM made more than 40 movies in 1932, including *Letty Lynton.* Say 40 as a round number. The Second Circuit allowed MGM to count (roughly) 1/40 of its overhead as a cost of making *Letty Lynton* (subject to proof that *Letty Lynton* was more or less expensive to make than the average MGM movie that year, or that some of the overhead did not contribute to *Letty Lynton*). If 1/40 of overhead is allocated to *Letty Lynton,* the overhead allocable to the other 39 movies declines by 1/40, and the profit on each of those movies goes up.

Quite apart from how the court accounts for costs, the underlying economic point is simply that MGM increased its sales by $1.7 million (the gross receipts of *Letty Lynton*) without any (proven) increase in overhead. As the infringing part of the business grows in proportion to the total business, the profitable effect of absorbing part of the overhead will increase proportionately. But this effect can reach only so far; at some point, the growth of the infringing part of the business will force an increase in overhead, and everyone agrees the court should take account of that.

4. Taxes. Income taxes have also generated substantial debate. The federal rule is that conscious wrongdoers cannot deduct the taxes paid on the profits they disgorge. L.P. Larson, Jr., Co. v. Wm. Wrigley, Jr., Co., 277 U.S. 97, 100 (1928). Justice Holmes offered the irrelevant reason that plaintiff would have to pay taxes on the judgment. The Sixth Circuit offered the more sensible reason that defendant will get a tax deduction when it pays the judgment; a deduction in calculating the judgment would be double counting for taxes. Schnadig Corp. v. Gaines Manufacturing Co., 620 F.2d 1166, 1169-1171 (6th Cir. 1980).

The Alabama Supreme Court got it right in Scrushy v. Tucker, 955 So. 2d 988 (Ala. 2006). It held that former HealthSouth CEO Richard Scrushy, who committed accounting fraud, had to return the full amount of his bonuses without a deduction for taxes. "Scrushy was credited with the gross amount, and HealthSouth was concomitantly deprived of the amount paid to Scrushy in bonuses, regardless of whether Scrushy paid a certain percentage of those funds in taxes. Whether Scrushy can obtain a refund of the taxes paid upon his restitution of the bonuses is a matter between Scrushy and the taxing authorities." *Id.* at 1012.

The Alabama and Sixth Circuit explanations have nothing to do with willfulness, but the federal courts of appeals appear to be divided on the treatment of income taxes when the infringement is not willful. The cases are collected in Three Boys Music Corp. v. Bolton, 212 F.3d 477, 487-488 (9th Cir. 2000). And the district judge in *Oracle America* (in the preceding note) thought that the tax issue is open in the Ninth Circuit even with respect to willful infringers, but predicted that the court would eventually follow *Larson.*

5. Distinctions in culpability. If the goal is to calculate profits, does it make sense to vary the calculation rules on the basis of defendant's culpability? Is this emphasis on culpability a corollary of the underlying rule that only conscious wrongdoers have to disgorge at all? (Remember that the statute has changed that underlying rule in copyright.) Do variations in what costs are subtracted from revenues allow for variations in culpability? Or do they reflect a lack of confidence in the methods for calculating profits?

6. Burden of proof. Recall that defendant has the burden of proving its costs. Should defendant be liable for gross receipts if it has no records sufficient to support an allocation of expenses? The court said yes in Blackman v. Hustler Magazine, Inc., 800 F.2d 1160 (D.C. Cir. 1986), although there the court plainly suspected that defendant had "lost" its records deliberately. In Gaste v. Kaiserman, 863 F.2d 1061, 1071 (2d Cir. 1988), the court let the jury estimate "the minimum amount that [defendants] in all likelihood spent."

Plaintiff at least has the burden of showing gross receipts from the infringing product, not gross receipts from the whole enterprise. Judge Posner once said that "if General Motors were to steal your copyright and put it in a sales brochure, you could not just put a copy of General Motors' corporate income tax return in the record and rest your case for an award of infringer's profits." Taylor v. Meirick, 712 F.2d 1112, 1122 (7th Cir. 1983). The *Restatement (Third)* says that plaintiff must prove "at least a reasonable approximation of the amount of the wrongful gain. Residual risk of uncertainty in calculating net profit is assigned to the defendant." §51(5)(d).

7. Indirect profits. Plaintiffs sometimes claim that the thing taken contributed to profits in remote parts of defendants' operation. A leading example is Frank Music Corp. v. Metro Goldwyn Mayer, Inc. 772 F.3d 505 (9th Cir. 1985), where defendants used parts of plaintiffs' musical in the stage show at their Las Vegas hotel. Defendants reported to their stockholders that their "hotel and gaming operations . . . continue to be materially enhanced by the popularity of the hotel's entertainment[, including] 'Hallelujah Hollywood,' the spectacularly successful production revue" that included the infringing material. 772 F.2d at 517, quoting MGM's annual report. The court ultimately affirmed findings that ten percent of the profits from the show were attributable to the infringing material, and that the profits from the show consisted of all the profits from ticket sales to the show ("direct profits") plus two percent of profits of the hotel and casino ("indirect profits"). 886 F.2d 1545, 1548-1550 (9th Cir. 1989). Other examples are collected in Mackie v. Rieser, 296 F.3d 909 (9th Cir. 2002), which holds that plaintiff there failed to prove any of the indirect profits he sought to recover.

Applying *Frank* and *Mackie,* a federal district court rejected a claim for indirect profits against Apple when the company used a photograph of the band "She & Him" in a television commercial selling iPhones. The photograph appeared in five seconds of a 30-second advertisement entitled "Concert." The photographer presented no evidence that either the photograph or the "Concert" commercial caused any iPhone sales. Thale v. Apple Inc., 2013 WL 3245170, *8 (N.D. Cal. 2013). The court added that "nothing prevented Plaintiff from presenting some form of expert analysis that could explain . . . the method upon which it would be possible to establish a *causal link* between use of the Photo and iPhone 3GS sales based on the evidence accumulated by" plaintiff. *Id.* at *8 n.20. Maybe not, but she surely would have done better to ask for a reasonable royalty.

8. The *Restatement (Third).* The *Restatement (Third)* declines to state precise rules for calculating profits. There is sophisticated analysis in the comments, but the black letter says: "[T]he court may apply such tests of causation and remoteness, may make such apportionments, may recognize such credits or deductions, and may assign such evidentiary burdens, as reason and fairness dictate, consistent with the object of restitution as specified in subsection (4)." §51(5). Subsection 4 says the object is to recover all net profits without imposing a penalty.

9. Similar problems in damages. The difficulties of allocating costs and expenses in the calculation of profits are not peculiar to restitution. They also arise in calculating plaintiff's lost profits as damages. Lost profits from breach of contract, damage to business property, antitrust violations, or common-law business torts can all raise these issues. Lost profits as damages can actually be more difficult to measure, because the counterfactual element is more dominant; the court is trying to measure the profits that would have been earned from sales that never happened. On the other hand, the intellectual property torts that make up many of the most important restitution cases tend to present peculiarly difficult questions of impressionistic apportionment among intangible factors.

3.   *Breach of Contract*

a.   Disgorging the Profits from Opportunistic Breach

MAY v. MUROFF
483 So. 2d 772 (Fla. Dist. Ct. App. 1986)

LETTS, Judge.

In the interim between entering into a contract to sell his land and the final closing thereof, the seller improperly sold fill from the land in question to a third party for $240,000. The purchaser claims that $240,000. We agree he should be entitled to it.

The trial court . . . concluded that the purchaser had been damaged by the illegal sale of the fill, but computed those damages on a per acre removed cost, vis-a-vis the total acreage being sold, resulting in a purchase price reduction of $122,067. As the seller and the trial court saw it, when land is permanently damaged, the proper assessment of damages is the difference between the value of the land before and after the injury. Thus, since the purchaser here lost 25 acres, that is what he should be compensated for. We disagree.

The seller's breach here was deliberate and he should not be permitted to profit by his own wrong and enjoy a windfall profit of $117,933. The purchaser, under the facts and circumstances of this case, is entitled to the fruits of this wrongfully received windfall. The purchaser should be entitled to the value of the materials removed which is readily determined from the record at $240,000.[1] . . .

---

1. Both parties agree that the cost of restoration of the land would be an inappropriate remedy since the cost of the restoration would greatly exceed the diminution in the value of the property.

Accordingly, this cause is affirmed in part and reversed in part and remanded for the entry of final judgment in favor of the purchaser in conformance herewith. . . .

HURLEY, J., and LEVY, DAVID L., Associate Judge, concur.

NOTES ON DISGORGING THE PROFITS FROM BREACH OF CONTRACT

1. The holding in *May*. "Fill" is dirt, rock, or a mixture of the two used to fill in low-lying land. The 25 lost acres were apparently under water after the fill was removed.

No statement of substance has been omitted from this very short opinion. The court did cite a Massachusetts case with analogous facts (removing trees instead of fill) and a similar result but somewhat different reasoning. Laurin v. DeCarolis Construction Co., 363 N.E.2d 675 (Mass. 1977). Defendant breached the contract, and the ordinary remedy would be contract damages. What, if anything, makes this breach special?

2. Efficient breach? Was this an efficient breach? Plaintiff was promised land with an agreed price of *X*. That land is now worth *X* minus $122,000, so defendant, and the trial court, offered plaintiff the land plus $122,000. They say that makes him whole; it gives him all the value he was promised. Does the court of appeals disagree? Why does it reverse?

The economic justification for disgorgement of profits is that it forces defendants to buy what they want in voluntary transactions. Why shouldn't they have to buy releases from contracts in voluntary transactions as well? Recall that we asked this same question when we considered the economic analysis of specific performance.

3. The assumption of no disgorgement. Disgorgement is a generalized remedy for conscious wrongdoing, but there has been a tendency to assume that it is generally unavailable in contract. Neither the first nor second *Restatement of Contracts* mentions disgorgement. The reporter for the *Restatement (Second)* argued against disgorgement, with some exceptions to account for cases that he felt obliged to recognize. E. Allan Farnsworth, *Your Loss or My Gain? The Dilemma of the Disgorgement Principle in Breach of Contract*, 94 Yale L.J. 1339 (1985).

Profitable breaches of contract are scarce in the real world, so disgorgement will be scarce no matter what the rule is. The fad for efficient breach viewed profits from breach of contract as a good thing, but even Judge Posner now recognizes a vaguely defined set of "opportunistic" breaches that ought to be deterred by disgorgement of profits. "If a promisor breaks his promise merely to take advantage of the promisee's vulnerability in a setting (the normal contract setting) in which performance is sequential rather than simultaneous, we might as well throw the book at him." Richard A. Posner, *Economic Analysis of Law* §4.10 at 129 (9th ed., Wolters Kluwer 2014). See note 9 in Notes on Efficient Breach of Contract in section 5.A.1.b.

Fuller and Perdue focused attention on the restitution interest. See Notes on Expectancy and Reliance in section 2.C, and note 7 following *Farash* in section 8.A.2. But disgorgement was not part of Fuller and Perdue's restitution interest, because they were thinking more about restoration than about unjust enrichment, and with that focus, the profits of breach do not seem to be conferred by plaintiff. Seller's profits in *May* seem to come from the purchaser of the fill. But the profits also came from violating the rights of plaintiff. Weren't these profits "at the expense of" plaintiff in the same sense as the profits in *Olwell* or *Maier Brewing*?

If disgorgement is to be available in contract, we will have to distinguish consciously wrongful breaches from breaches that were unintentional, unavoidable, negligent, arguably justified, and so on. Contract doctrine is uncomfortable with such distinctions, but courts are not immune to their influence.

4. Enforcing the contract. Recall the broad principle that there can be no claim for unjust enrichment when there is an enforceable contract between the parties. Disgorgement for deliberate or opportunistic breach is consistent with that principle. A plaintiff seeking disgorgement in such a case "is not attempting to use the vehicle of restitution to rewrite the terms of an agreement the parties allegedly made." Enslin v. The Coca-Cola Co., 136 F. Supp. 3d 654, 678 (E.D. Pa. 2015). Rather, plaintiff is suing on the contract, alleging breach, and seeking a restitutionary remedy for that breach.

5. The cases. Whatever scholars and even judges might have assumed, courts were awarding defendant's profits from intentional breach of contract when the facts were right. Sometimes courts explain the judgment as disgorgement of profits, sometimes as an indirect way of measuring plaintiff's damages. Sometimes the damage explanation is plausible, sometimes not. The opinions are often short, as in *May*; they are sometimes confused or ambiguous about their legal theory. But whatever the explanation, courts have awarded a money judgment measured by defendant's profits from the breach of contract in a wide range of cases. Cases are collected in Melvin A. Eisenberg, *The Disgorgement Interest in Contract Law*, 105 Mich. L. Rev. 559 (2006), and Gareth Jones, *The Recovery of Benefits Gained from a Breach of Contract*, 99 L.Q. Rev. 443 (1983).

6. The specific-performance explanation. *May* is arguably special because it was a real estate contract. A buyer of real estate is entitled to specific performance. If he had filed suit in time, buyer could have compelled a conveyance before seller could remove the fill. Then, if he wanted, buyer could have sold the fill for $240,000. This was Professor Farnsworth's explanation for the real estate cases.

The same reasoning applies when the seller conveys the whole parcel in breach of contract. In Coppola Enterprises, Inc. v. Alfone, 531 So. 2d 334 (Fla. 1988), there was a contract to sell a house for $106,000. After construction delays and a dispute between the parties, seller sold the house to someone else for $170,000. The court awarded seller's profits to the buyer without determining whether the seller had acted in bad faith. The court treated the case as obvious, but a reader might reasonably speculate that the right to specific performance was enough to dispense with the usual requirement of conscious wrongdoing.

Coppola unambiguously awarded restitution of defendant's profits, not plaintiff's damages. If courts would consistently say that market value cannot be lower than $170,000 on *Coppola*'s facts, plaintiff's contract-market damages would be $64,000, and the disgorgement remedy would be no more lucrative than damages. But some courts may find that the market value is less than $170,000, treating the high offer as aberrational. One way to view disgorgement in these cases is that it avoids litigation over market value. Still, if we take seriously the notion that market value might be only $160,000, so that plaintiff has suffered only $54,000 in damages, disgorgement deters a profitable breach by taking all the profit out of it.

The specific-performance explanation is not limited to real estate. If a buyer of grapes is entitled to specific performance because his business depends on a reliable supply of a perishable product, Green Stripe, Inc. v. Berny's Internacionale, S.A. de C.V., 159 F. Supp. 2d 51 (E.D. Pa. 2001), and the seller sells all his grapes to a third party at a higher price, should the contract buyer get the seller's profits from the wrongful sale? Is that any different from *Coppola*?

7. Other examples. Courts have awarded disgorgement for breach of covenants not to compete. A sale-of-business example is Y.J.D. Restaurant Supply Co. v. Dib,

413 N.Y.S.2d 835 (Sup. Ct. 1979); a competing customer example—a client bidding against his investment adviser—is Eden Hannon & Co. v. Sumitomo Trust & Banking Co., 914 F.2d 556, 563-564 (4th Cir. 1990). A faithless-employee example is National Merchandising Corp. v. Leyden, 348 N.E.2d 771, 774-776 (Mass. 1976), but more cases say no when defendant is a former employee. Those cases are collected in Trugreen Cos. v. Mower Brothers, Inc., 199 P.3d 929 (Utah 2008).

Disgorgement is an attractive remedy where plaintiff withholds some portion of what he promised under the contract but does so without inflicting significant damage. An example is American Standard, Inc. v. Schectman, 439 N.Y.S.2d 529 (App. Div. 1981). Schectman bargained for restoration of his land after a demolition project, although the land would have little value whether restored or not.

In Watson v. Cal-Three, LLC, 254 P.3d 1189 (Colo. Ct. App. 2011), one party to a condominium project made bad faith allegations against another, to the title company and elsewhere, making it impossible for the victim to sell any units and allowing the wrongdoer to regain control of the property and sell the units for his own account at a profit. The trial court characterized his actions as deliberate, willful, and wanton. The court of appeals held that disgorgement of his profits was an appropriate remedy.

8. A general rule? The *Restatement (Third)* has undertaken to state a rule: "If a deliberate breach of contract results in profit to the defaulting promisor and the available damage remedy affords inadequate protection to the promisee's contractual entitlement, the promisee has a claim to restitution of the profit realized by the promisor as a result of the breach." §39(1). This set of breaches is labeled "opportunistic."

a. Profitable. A breach has to be profitable or the question of disgorgement does not arise. Profitable breach is defined straightforwardly as a breach leading to gains, net of potential liability in contract damages, greater than the breaching party could have earned by performance. §39(3).

b. Deliberate. This is a rule for intentional breach of contract, typically motivated by the potential for extra profit. These deliberate breachers are treated as conscious wrongdoers, just like those who commit intentional torts or breaches of fiduciary duty. The requirement of "deliberate" breach excludes "cases in which breach results from defendant's inadvertence, negligence, or unsuccessful attempt at performance." But for believers in "efficient breach," most efficient breaches are deliberate in this sense. What about them?

Professor Roberts argues that in "contractual contexts, the wrong being committed must be something more than simple breach of a promise. Rather, in determining whether disgorgement is appropriate, a court must also look to the method of the breach — the how and the why." Caprice L. Roberts, *Supreme Disgorgement*, 68 Fla. L. Rev. 1413, 1431 (2016). She supports disgorgement to prevent unjust enrichment and deter "conscious advantage taking," while recognizing that the "rationale for disgorgement is in tension with some of the principles behind conventional contract doctrine, such as the compensation norm, strict liability, the choice principle and efficient breach of contract." *Id.* at 1440. She also supports treating knowing or reckless breaches as deliberate for this purpose. *Id.* at 1431.

c. Inadequate remedy? In many of the cases in which disgorgement is most attractive, the damage remedy is strikingly inadequate. These are the cases in which deliberate breach most clearly looks like "conscious advantage taking." Consider breaches of contracts to protect confidential information, where no amount of damages will restore secrecy once the information is revealed. Enslin v. Coca-Cola in note 4 is such a case.

Similarly, damages measured by market value were minimal in *Schectman*. Where plaintiff bargained for a specific result without regard to its market value, and then is deprived of the promised result, market-based compensation is largely useless. The *Restatement (Third)*'s view is that breach is attractive in such cases precisely because the measure of damages fails to protect the contractual entitlement that plaintiff bargained for.

But the inadequacy of the legal remedy need not be so extreme. In *May*, 25 acres of land had a market value. But awarding that value would not enable plaintiff to restore the 25 acres, and the court awarded disgorgement of profits. In the *Restatement (Third)* formulation, damages are "ordinarily" inadequate for this purpose when "damages will not permit the promisee to acquire a full equivalent to the promised performance in a substitute transaction." §39(2).

We saw that in injunction and specific performance cases (section 5.A), judges often use the adequate-remedy-at-law rule as a proxy for concerns about the costs of implementing injunctions and specific performance. But many of those costs are irrelevant to disgorgement, which is a monetary remedy requiring no judicial supervision. Probably the most common reason for not seeking specific performance is timing; the courts move so much more slowly than the operation of plaintiff's business. But that is also irrelevant to disgorgement, because the remedy can be administered after the fact, just like the damage remedy. A court that accepts §39 can focus precisely on the question of whether damages would enable plaintiff to obtain a full equivalent of what she bargained for.

d. Undue hardship and the like. Suppose the court would refuse specific performance because of undue hardship — because performance would cost far more than anyone anticipated and far more than it would be worth. Would it make any sense to award disgorgement of all the money defendant saved by not performing? Maybe such a breach should be treated as excused rather than "deliberate" in the sense of §39. The comment explicitly recognizes that disgorgement should not be awarded in such a case. §39 cmt. *i.*

9. Did the Supreme Court adopt §39 of the *Restatement (Third)*? Kansas v. Nebraska, 135 S. Ct. 1042 (2015), awarded partial disgorgement for a reckless breach of contract. A settlement agreement divided the waters of the Republican River between the two states. Nebraska was the upstream state, with physical power to take more than its share of the water. And it did. The Court's Special Master did not find that Nebraska deliberately took more than its share, but he found that Nebraska was reckless, regulating water use in a way that it knew created a substantial risk that it would take more than its share.

And it turned out that this irrigation water was substantially more valuable in Nebraska than in Kansas. (The Nebraska portion of the river is further west, where the climate is more arid.) The Special Master found that Kansas's damages were $3.7 million and that Nebraska's gains were likely several times that. He recommended awarding Kansas's damages plus partial disgorgement of $1.8 million. It is not clear how he arrived at the $1.8 million figure, but the Court approved it.

Relying on the *Restatement* as well as other sources, the Court held that Nebraska had been sufficiently culpable to justify disgorgement, that its breach had been profitable, and that if it were liable only for compensatory damages, it would have incentives to deliberately breach. But it rejected Kansas's demand for disgorgement of all Nebraska's profits, emphasizing its equitable discretion and Nebraska's diligent compliance in recent years. Partial disgorgement had been sufficient to achieve the purpose of obtaining Nebraska's compliance.

Over the last generation, the Court has tended to the view that equitable remedies should be tied to the position the parties would have occupied but for the wrong. But this opinion clearly comes down on the side of equitable discretion. In part, the Court emphasized that disputes between two sovereign states are special and that its obligation to be fair and equitable predominated. And of course this was a case in which the Court exercised discretion to award *less* than full relief, not more. Compare United States v. Virginia, 518 U.S. 515 (1996), described in the final set of notes in section 4.A.4, where the Court relied on the rightful-position principle to insist that plaintiff get a complete remedy, not a partial remedy.

Justices Scalia, Thomas, and Alito dissented in *Kansas*. They thought disgorgement was inappropriate in contract cases, but that if it were to be awarded, it should be based on a calculation of defendant's profits and not a discretionary compromise with no visible rationale for the number selected. Justice Thomas cited a comment by the Special Master suggesting that the disgorgement award might have been a disguised award of attorneys' fees, which would not otherwise be authorized.

10. Developments elsewhere. Professor Roberts welcomes §39 and Kansas v. Nebraska, but worries that the decision may have limited influence, given the "quasi-public nature of the contract" and the Supreme Court's "tortured history with restitution and with several lines of remedies cases more broadly." 68 Fla. L. Rev. at 1420. The Fifth Circuit predicted that Texas would not recognize disgorgement as an alternative remedy for opportunistic breach, notwithstanding §39 and Kansas v. Nebraska. Hoffman v. L & M Arts, 838 F.3d 568, 585-586 (5th Cir. 2016). But Enslin v. Coca-Cola in note 4, and Watson v. Cal-Tree in note 7, each relied in part on §39.

b. Rescission

MOBIL OIL EXPLORATION & PRODUCING SOUTHEAST, INC. v. UNITED STATES

530 U.S. 604 (2000)

Justice BREYER delivered the opinion of the Court.

Two oil companies, petitioners here, seek restitution of $156 million they paid the Government in return for lease contracts giving them rights to explore for and develop oil off the North Carolina coast. The rights were not absolute, but were conditioned on the companies' obtaining a set of further governmental permissions. The companies claim that the Government repudiated the contracts when it denied them certain elements of the permission-seeking opportunities that the contracts had promised. We agree that the Government broke its promise; it repudiated the contracts; and it must give the companies their money back.

[The facts were complex, but the essence is that the leases incorporated as contractual terms the Outer Continental Shelf Lands Act (OCSLA), 43 U.S.C. §1331 *et seq.* That Act specified environmental standards and time limits for the government to approve or disapprove development of the leases. Congress subsequently enacted the Outer Banks Protection Act (OBPA), Pub. L. No. 101-380, §6003, 104 Stat. 555 (1990) (repealed 1996), which added additional environmental reviews and prohibited approvals within the OCSLA time limits. The government withheld approval in compliance with the new act, and the Court held that this was a substantial breach of contract. But the court of appeals had held that this breach caused no damages, because the OCSLA standards gave North Carolina an effective power to veto the project, and North Carolina would have done so.]

I

A . . .

"When the United States enters into contract relations, its rights and duties therein are governed generally by the law applicable to contracts between private individuals." United States v. Winstar Corp., 518 U.S. 839, 895 (1996) (plurality opinion). . . . [W]hen one party to a contract repudiates that contract, the other party "is entitled to restitution for any benefit that he has conferred on" the repudiating party "by way of part performance or reliance." *Restatement (Second) of Contracts* §373 (1979). The *Restatement* explains that "repudiation" is a "statement by the obligor to the obligee indicating that the obligor will commit a breach that would of itself give the obligee a claim for damages for total breach." *Id.* §250. And "total breach" is a breach that "so substantially impairs the value of the contract to the injured party at the time of the breach that it is just in the circumstances to allow him to recover damages based on all his remaining rights to performance." *Id.* §243.

As applied to this action, these principles amount to the following: If the Government said it would break, or did break, an important contractual promise, thereby "substantially impair[ing] the value of the contract[s]" to the companies, *id.*, then (unless the companies waived their rights to restitution) the Government must give the companies their money back. And it must do so whether the contracts would, or would not, ultimately have proved financially beneficial to the companies. The *Restatement* illustrates this point as follows:

> A contracts to sell a tract of land to B for $100,000. After B has made a part payment of $20,000, A wrongfully refuses to transfer title. B can recover the $20,000 in restitution. The result is the same even if the market price of the land is only $70,000, so that performance would have been disadvantageous to B.

Id. §373 cmt. *a*, illustration 1. . . .

II . . .

D

Finally, the Government argues that repudiation could not have hurt the companies. Since the companies could not have met the [OCSLA] requirements, they could not have explored (or ultimately drilled) for oil in any event. Hence, OBPA caused them no damage. . . . This argument, however, misses the basic legal point. The oil companies do not seek damages for breach of contract. They seek restitution of their initial payments. Because the Government repudiated the lease contracts, the law entitles the companies to that restitution whether the contracts would, or would not, ultimately have produced a financial gain or led them to obtain a definite right to explore. If a lottery operator fails to deliver a purchased ticket, the purchaser can get his money back—whether or not he eventually would have won the lottery. And if one party to a contract, whether oil company or ordinary citizen, advances the other party money, principles of restitution normally require the latter, upon repudiation, to refund that money.

III

Contract law expresses no view about the wisdom of OBPA. We have examined only that statute's consistency with the promises that the earlier contracts contained. We find that the oil companies gave the United States $156 million in return for a contractual promise to follow the terms of pre-existing statutes and regulations. The new statute prevented the Government from keeping that promise. The breach "substantially impair[ed] the value of the contract[s]." *Restatement (Second) of Contracts* §243. And therefore the Government must give the companies their money back. . . .

[T]he judgment . . . is reversed. We remand the cases for further proceedings consistent with this opinion. . . .

[Justice STEVENS dissented on the ground that the government's breach should not be treated as total.]

NOTES ON RESCISSION FOR BREACH OF CONTRACT

1. Rescission. The Court cancels the transaction and reverses all benefits that have been exchanged pursuant to the transaction. The government gets its mineral rights back, released from any further obligation to Mobil, and Mobil gets its money back, released from any further obligation to the government. The remedy is called rescission, although the Court does not use that word. It is sometimes called rescission and restitution, to emphasize the fact that neither side can rescind without restoring what it received from the other side.

2. Rightful position? What positions would the parties occupy but for the government's breach? Assuming that the government would have rightfully rejected Mobil's drilling application under the preexisting law, Mobil's expectancy was to pay $156 million and finish with nothing.

Rescission conceives the rightful position differently. Not having gotten the rights it paid for, Mobil was entitled to its money back. Instead of speculating about what might have been, simply undo the transaction and restore everyone to their original position. If no relevant values have changed between the time of the original transaction and the time of rescission, rescission is no more lucrative than damages, and often less, because plaintiff gets none of its expected profit. But here, values have changed dramatically. There was always a risk that drilling would not be approved, but that risk has increased to near certainty. Rescission gets Mobil out of a bad bargain.

3. An example with tangible property. In Cherry v. Crispin, 190 N.E.2d 93 (Mass. 1963), sellers fraudulently concealed the fact that their house was infested with termites. Buyers attempted to rescind when they discovered the termites a few days after moving in. Damages were measurable as the cost of extermination and repair plus any residual reduction in the value of the house. With rescission, plaintiffs got all their money back and defendants got the house back. Each side had to pay in cash for incidental benefits that could not be returned: rent for the time plaintiffs lived in the house and the cost of paint and other minor improvements plaintiffs added to the house.

Rescission eliminates the risk of error in measuring damages. Instead of estimating the value of the house with and without termites and paying the difference in cash, rescission in kind restores the values exactly. But as in *Mobil*, restoration in kind equals restoration to the original precontract values only if the values have not changed except for the discovery of the termites. If the value of real estate has generally declined since the contract, the discovery of termites gives plaintiffs a chance to get out of a bad bargain.

4. A classic example. In Bush v. Canfield, 2 Conn. 485 (1818), the contract was for 2,000 barrels of flour to be delivered in New Orleans at $7 a barrel. The price of flour in New Orleans had declined to $5.50, but it was seller who breached, failing to deliver any flour. Buyer promptly sought restitution of his $5,000 down payment. Seller argued that buyer would have lost $3,000 if the contract had been performed, and that buyer should be limited to this negative expectancy. That is, seller should be able to keep $3,000 even though he had delivered nothing. The court rejected that argument. Buyer was entitled to a refund, and the doctrinal explanation is that he could rescind the contract and recover restitution of his down payment. The rule is codified in UCC §2-711(1), which provides that an aggrieved buyer "in addition to recovering so much of the price as has been paid" may recover damages for non-delivery.

5. Plaintiff's choice. Plaintiff gets to choose whether to rescind or sue for damages. Plaintiff may choose rescission because of its simplicity (no need to litigate the value of anything), because of personal preferences not reflected in market values (she's more troubled by termites than the average buyer is), or because she has lost confidence in defendant and the transaction (if he lied about this, what else might he have lied about?). These reasons make sense if there has been no substantial change, adverse to plaintiff, in the value of what was exchanged. Where values have changed, rescission is a one-way option: Plaintiff can choose rescission if she would lose money from performance or choose expectancy damages if she would make money from performance.

This section emphasizes rescission's potential to get plaintiff out of a bad bargain, yielding a recovery in excess of expectancy damages, because that is the most dramatic application of rescission. But it is not the typical application. When a change in values makes the contract a loser for one side, that same change often makes the contract unexpectedly profitable for the other side. It makes no sense for the party with the unexpected profits to breach. So cases where rescission is the easiest way to unwind a failed transaction greatly outnumber the cases where rescission is especially lucrative for plaintiff.

6. Distinguishing reliance. If plaintiff with a losing contract sues for reliance damages, he recovers nothing; his reliance recovery is limited by his negative expectancy. See Notes on Expectancy and Reliance in section 2.C. Whatever the basis for this rule, the important point here is that it has never been applied to rescission. If expectancy were a cap on rescission, losing contracts could never be rescinded; Bush could not even recover his down payment on the undelivered flour.

7. What kind of breach justifies rescission? The grounds must be substantial to justify giving plaintiff this option to enforce or undo the contract. Courts resist plaintiffs using a minor dispute or technicality to get out of a bad deal.

The Court in *Mobil* uses the unfortunate phrase "total breach," which is found in both *Restatements of Contracts*. But "total" breach never meant that defendant had done absolutely nothing toward performance of his contract. "Total" meant only a breach sufficiently important that it justified plaintiff in stopping her own performance and treating the contract as at an end. The *Restatement (Third) of Restitution and Unjust Enrichment* avoids the phrase "total breach," because it is so easily misunderstood, using instead "material" breach. §37(1). Another adjective often used in the cases is "substantial."

Whatever the phrase, the important thing is to focus on the question we are trying to answer: Is the breach important enough to justify giving plaintiff the option of either suing for damages or rescinding the whole contract? For contrasting answers to that question, compare Eliker v. Chief Industries, Inc., 498 N.W.2d 564 (Neb. 1993), where buyers rescinded their purchase of a newly constructed house because of serious foundation problems, with Smith v. Continental Bank, 636 P.2d 98, 100 (Ariz. 1981), where the court held that defects that could be repaired for $2,235 "were not substantial enough to merit rescission of a $33,000 house sale." *Smith* also appeared to be influenced by the fact that the seller was a bank that had foreclosed on the builder; the bank was not in the construction business and had given no implied warranties.

Restatement (Third) §54(4) provides that plaintiffs cannot get rescission even in cases where defendants commit a material breach when rescission would result in "injustice." Injustice may occur when it is impossible to fully undo the transaction, and defendant cannot be fairly compensated in some other way or defendant is not enough at fault to justify the unfairness of a partial undoing of the contract. *Id.* §54(3).

8. Limits on rescission for plaintiffs owed only money. With tightly limited exceptions, one who lends money or sells on credit cannot rescind and reclaim the property when the debtor fails to pay. See *Restatement (Third)* §37(2), flatly rejecting rescission in this context.

The reason has nothing to do with the logic of rescission, but it is essential to the law of secured and unsecured credit. With secured credit, the lender gets a mortgage or security interest in specific property, called collateral; if the loan is not repaid, the lender can take the collateral. With unsecured credit, the lender has only the right to sue the borrower for the amount due and try to collect out of the borrower's general assets. Borrowers and lenders can bargain over this choice. A borrower who gives collateral usually gets a lower interest rate but has less freedom to manage his own property, because the lender now also has an interest in that property. A lender who takes collateral must give notice to other potential lenders, and potential purchasers of the collateral, by filing a record of the transaction in the real estate records or Uniform Commercial Code records.

A sale on credit is just a specialized form of lending. If an unpaid seller could reclaim the property sold just by suing for rescission, the distinction between secured and unsecured credit would be obliterated in the sales context. It would be as though every credit sale were on secured credit. So unpaid sellers generally cannot rescind. Neither can unpaid lenders or any other contract plaintiff who is owed only money. But the UCC recognizes a narrow right of rescission for sellers who move quickly after discovering that their buyer was insolvent when he received the goods. UCC §2-702(2). And this right is generally good in bankruptcy if the buyer files for bankruptcy within 45 days after delivery. 11 U.S.C. §546(c).

9. Partial rescission. Plaintiff cannot affirm the profitable parts of a contract and rescind the losing parts. He must rescind the entire contract, or the entirety of some identifiably separate exchange within the contract. A simple example is Philip Carey Manufacturing Co. v. General Products Co., 151 A.2d 487, 494-495 (R.I. 1959), where plaintiff paid for 19,000 medicine cabinets to be delivered on request, and defendant could not deliver the final 3,271 cabinets. Because there was a stated price per cabinet, it was easy to decide that plaintiff could rescind with respect to the undelivered cabinets, without having to rescind with respect to the cabinets already delivered.

10. Irreparable injury? Decisions granting rescission almost never discuss the irreparable injury rule; they treat plaintiff as having a free choice of damages or rescission if sufficient grounds are shown. But courts that deny rescission because the breach is not sufficiently important sometimes also say that damages for the breach would be an adequate remedy. An example is Helm Brothers, Inc. v. Trauger, 389 N.W.2d 600 (N.D. 1986), refusing to forfeit a long-term mineral lease for minor breaches of a collateral obligation.

Think about the termite-infested house in Cherry v. Crispin. Is it reasonable for plaintiffs to decide they no longer want this house, even if it is repaired at defendants' expense? Is this the flip side of specific performance and injunctions? If injunction plaintiffs are entitled to the very thing they lost, should these plaintiffs be able to get rid of the very thing they no longer want? Should they have to buy a house for a jury's estimate of value?

11. Law and equity. The modern tendency is to treat rescission as equitable, but this is historically inaccurate. If plaintiff had paid money or delivered goods, he could rescind by tendering whatever he had received from defendant and suing at law to recover his money or replevy his goods. But if he had delivered a promissory note or securities, or conveyed real estate, rescission required the court to cancel the instruments or compel defendant to reconvey. This relief was available only in equity.

However obsolete it may be, the distinction creates the possibility of demanding jury trial or avoiding discussion of irreparable injury on the ground that a particular case involves legal rather than equitable rescission. Versions of the distinction are codified in some states. An example is Barker v. Ness, 587 N.W.2d 183 (N.D. 1998), granting rescission of the purchase of a house where the seller had concealed a problem with water in the basement. The court rejected defendant's demand for jury trial, on the ground that plaintiff (whether by accident or design is not clear) had sued in equity. Often rescission is simply assumed to be equitable. In Jackowski v. Borchelt, 209 P.3d 514, 523 (Wash. Ct. App. 2009), the court held there was no right to a jury trial when home buyers sought to rescind the sales contract after landslide damage to the home. "One of the main issues is whether the Jackowskis are entitled to rescind the contract, which is clearly equitable."

NOTES ON ELECTION OF REMEDIES

1. The necessity of choice. There is a fundamental difference between reversing the transaction and going back to the beginning (seller gets her property back and buyer gets his money back), or enforcing the transaction with specific performance or expectancy damages (seller keeps the money, buyer keeps the property, and buyer gets compensation for any damages). It is no technicality to say that plaintiff must choose.

2. The technical doctrine. Unfortunately, the resulting doctrine became enmeshed in technicalities. "At best this doctrine of election of remedies is a harsh, and now largely obsolete rule." And that was a century ago. Friederichsen v. Renard, 247 U.S. 207, 213 (1918).

The theory was that plaintiff could either affirm or rescind the contract. An affirmance was generally held to be irrevocable. Thus, if the plaintiff sued on the contract, orally affirmed its existence, or even delayed in claiming rescission, rescission became unavailable. Curiously, a decision to rescind did not necessarily preclude a subsequent suit on the contract. A decision to rescind could generally be revoked until defendant relied on it, until plaintiff recovered what he had given up under the contract, or until a judgment was entered. And most courts allowed plaintiff to plead in the alternative. Some jurisdictions required him to elect before trial, and some before submission to the jury. Some would submit the case to the jury in the alternative.

The doctrine led to harsh results when the damage action turned out to be a loser for some technical reason, or when the damage recovery turned out to be much smaller than the restitutionary recovery. Some of our greatest judges refused to hold plaintiffs to an apparent election of a remedy on which no recovery could be had, saying that "[t]here would be no sense or principle in such a rule." Schenck v. State Line Telephone Co., 144 N.E. 592, 593 (N.Y. 1924) (Cardozo, J.), quoting Snow v. Alley, 30 N.E. 691, 692 (Mass. 1892) (Holmes, J.).

3. The modern doctrine. Increasingly, the cases hold plaintiff to an initial election only when defendant would be prejudiced by a change in theories. The *Restatement* formulation requires that more than one remedy be available in fact, that the two remedies be inconsistent, and that defendant "materially changes his position in reliance on" plaintiff's initial choice. *Restatement (Second) of Contracts* §378 (Am. Law Inst. 1981).

In *Mobil*, the Court said that a party does not waive its right to rescind by continuing to perform for a time after defendant's breach or repudiation, or by continuing to urge defendant to perform. At least on the facts before it, the Court said that Mobil would have waived the right to rescind only by accepting "significant postrepudiation performance." 530 U.S. at 623. That is, if plaintiff successfully urges the breaching party to resume performance, plaintiff cannot thereafter rescind. Presumably, other forms of detrimental reliance on an apparent election would also count. But the Federal Circuit found *Mobil* ambiguous on whether detrimental reliance is essential to an election of remedies. Old Stone Corp. v. United States, 450 F.3d 1360, 1372 (Fed. Cir. 2006), and the issue does not appear to have been resolved in the Federal Circuit as of 2018.

4. Speculating at defendant's expense. There is a closely related rule that plaintiff cannot knowingly speculate at defendant's expense. A defrauded buyer of stock cannot wait until the statute of limitations is about to expire, and then sue for damages if the stock has gone up and rescission if it has gone down. At least if the property is of a kind that fluctuates in value, plaintiffs who want rescission must demand it promptly after learning of their grounds. A good example is Baumel v. Rosen, 412 F.2d 571 (4th Cir. 1969), where plaintiffs were fraudulently induced to sell stock too cheap, suspected fraud almost immediately, but waited through three years of dramatic price increases to seek rescission. This rule is sometimes viewed as an application of election of remedies and sometimes as an application of laches or estoppel.

But compare Petrella v. Metro Goldwyn Mayer, Inc., 134 S. Ct. 1962 (2014), where plaintiff filed her copyright suit only after MGM had invested in a remake of the claimed movie, and the remake turned out to be profitable. The Court said that "there is nothing untoward about waiting to see whether . . . litigation is worth the candle." *Id.* at 1976. *Petrella* is further discussed in section 11.C on estoppel and 11.D on laches.

5. Other delay. The more time has gone by, the more difficult rescission is to implement, and the more resistant courts may be. It turns out that the most important variable in allowing rescission for mutual mistake is whether plaintiff tried to rescind before or after the contract was performed. Andrew Kull, *Mistake, Frustration, and the Windfall Principle of Contract Remedies*, 43 Hastings L.J. 1 (1991). Grant Gilmore said the same thing to Laycock's first-year Contracts class in 1970.

6. Rescission and damages? A plaintiff claiming restitution may have incidental or consequential damages that are not compensated by recovery of what he gave to defendant. For example, a buyer may have paid shipping costs in addition to the price. When the sale is rescinded and the purchase price returned, he still has lost the shipping costs. Or he may have spent money trying to repair the goods before rescinding, or the defective goods may have damaged his other property. Sellers and parties to other kinds of contracts may suffer similar losses. Finally, the party who rescinds loses his expected profit from the contract. Courts have generally allowed recovery of non-duplicative damages, but they have split on lost profits. The cases are reviewed in 1 Palmer, *Restitution* §3.9. With respect to contracts for the sale of goods, UCC §2-721 provides that rescission does not bar recovery of damages; there is no exception for lost profits

Professors Brooks and Stremitzer argue on economic grounds that it should not be difficult to rescind, but that any recovery following rescission should be limited to restitution of what plaintiff transferred to defendant. Richard R.W. Brooks & Alexander Stremitzer, *Remedies On and Off Contract*, 120 Yale L.J. 690 (2011). They think that the right to rescind provides inexpensive and efficient incentives to higher-quality performance. They are ambivalent about whether rescission plus reliance damages erodes those benefits, but emphatic that rescission plus expectancy damages undoes them.

NOTES ON LOSING CONTRACTS WHERE THE BENEFIT CANNOT BE RETURNED

1. "Rescission" where rescission is impossible. When a contract is rescinded and some of the benefits received cannot be returned in kind, the recipient must pay for them. This obligation to pay for benefits necessarily requires judicial valuation of the benefit. Valuing an incidental benefit, like a new coat of paint, is usually not a problem. But when the unreturnable benefit is the bargained-for performance under the contract, judicial valuations have raised a large controversy.

Consider Boomer v. Muir, 24 P.2d 570 (Cal. Ct. App. 1933), the most famous case in this line. Muir was the general contractor, and Boomer a subcontractor, on a contract to build a hydroelectric plant. Boomer was to build one dam for the project, and Muir was to supply Boomer with materials and equipment. There were delays and cost overruns from the beginning, which each side blamed on the other. Finally, with Boomer's dam 95 percent complete, he abandoned the work. A jury found that Boomer's withdrawal was justified by Muir's breach in failing to deliver materials.

The court doesn't give all the relevant numbers in *Boomer*; the numbers here include some reasonable assumptions consistent with the numbers the court does give. The contract price was $333,000. Boomer had received $313,000 in progress payments, and would have been entitled to another $20,000 if he finished the job. Boomer had spent $571,000 building as much as he did, not counting any waste that was his own fault. It would have cost another $29,000 to finish the job, making a total construction cost of $600,000.

How much should Boomer recover? His expectancy was negative; if the contract had been fully performed he would have lost $267,000. But the court said he could rescind the contract and sue for the value of the benefit he had conferred on Muir—the value of a nearly finished dam, measured by the reasonable cost of building it. He recovered $258,000, the difference between what he had spent and what he had already been paid.

Boomer appears to state the majority rule, but most of the cases involve less spectacular disparities between the contract price and other measures of value. For a more recent example with a big disparity, see United States ex rel. CJC, Inc. v. Western States Mechanical Contractors, Inc., 834 F.2d 1533, 1537-1541 (10th Cir. 1987), where plaintiff "grossly underbid" the job and the work was valued at more than 60 percent above the contract price.

2. Changing the price term. Why should Muir have to pay $571,000 for a benefit he was promised for less than $333,000? If the contract allocated to Boomer the risk that the work might cost more than expected, and if the court would not set the contract aside for unconscionability or mutual mistake, why does Muir's breach justify reallocating the risk? Why is the court redetermining an agreed value and making a new contract for the parties?

Boomer says that a plaintiff seeking restitution rescinds the contract and sues in quantum meruit. Muir can't rely on the contract price because the contract has been rescinded. How helpful is that? Is rescinding the contract here like waiving the tort in *Olwell?*

If there were really no contract, Boomer would have no claim. He can't demand payment for an unwanted dam; he is entitled to restitution only to the extent that the dam complies with the specifications in the contract. If Muir can rely on the contract specifications, why can't he rely on the contract price?

In the standard rescission case, where each side returns what it received from the other, none of these problems arise. Plaintiffs get out of losing contracts, but not because they ask the court to revalue their performance. The court does not have to determine the value of anything. In Bush v. Canfield, where seller tried to keep part of buyer's down payment to reflect the drop in the price of flour, it was defendant who sought to overturn the contract price with new information about value. Defendant was not permitted to do that in *Bush;* why should plaintiff be permitted to do it in *Boomer?*

Most courts hold that the contract price is admissible evidence on the value of the benefit. A court unhappy with *Boomer* can avoid it without rejecting it by finding that the value of the benefit is equal to the contract price; an example is Constantino v. American S/T Achilles, 580 F.2d 121 (4th Cir. 1978).

3. Fictional rescission. Talk of rescission in cases like *Boomer* is clearly fictional. If the court were really reversing the transaction, Muir would get all his money back, and Boomer would get the dam. Of course that would make no economic sense; Boomer has no use for the dam, Muir's customer does, and the dam is permanently affixed to the customer's land. So the contract goes forward. Both sides mostly but not entirely perform, and the court changes the price.

The more modern cases and commentators have abandoned the fiction of rescission. The *Restatement (Second) of Contracts* (1981) acknowledges restitution of the value of part performance as an alternative remedy on the contract. §§344(c), 345(c)-(d), 371, 373. But this new explanatory theory does not appear to have changed the measure of recovery. The black letter is studiously ambiguous, but comment *d* to §373 appears to approve the result in *Boomer.*

4. Raising the stakes. The *Boomer* rule greatly increases the stakes of litigation on facts that are often highly uncertain. Both parties may complain about the other's performance, exchanging escalating charges and countercharges until one side accuses the other of substantial breach and terminates the contract. Who breached first? That becomes a jury question. But instead of being a dispute about the last $20,000 due under the contract and the last 5 percent of the work, *Boomer* became a dispute about $258,000 in quantum meruit and the cost or value of the first 95 percent of the work.

5. A limit. The *Boomer* rule has an exception: If plaintiff has fully performed and defendant owes only money, plaintiff is limited to the contract price and cannot recover restitution. *Restatement (Second) of Contracts* §373(2). This appears to be an application of the general rule against rescission for plaintiffs who are owed only money, although the reason for that rule does not apply here, because Boomer will not be taking the dam back in any event.

6. A different explanation. Distinguish two plausible explanations for the huge cost overrun in *Boomer*. One, plaintiff misbid the job, either by mistake or because of some unexpected difficulty in performance. Or two, defendant's persistent failure to deliver promised supplies and equipment drove up the cost. Under the first set explanation, plaintiff made a disastrous contract and was rescued by defendant's breach. Under the second, defendant's breach caused the disaster. A *Boomer*-style remedy in the first set of cases is a windfall to plaintiff. But a *Boomer*-style remedy in the second set may be rough justice; it puts the burden of the cost overrun on the party who caused it. Professor Gergen reports that a majority of cases applying the *Boomer* rule are in this second category. Mark P. Gergen, *Restitution as a Bridge over Troubled Contractual Waters*, 71 Fordham L. Rev. 709 (2002).

In this second set of cases, plaintiff has a damage remedy for the contract price of the finished work plus the consequential damages caused by defendant's breach. But that would require proof of causation, which may be complex or difficult. And there may be limitation-of-remedy clauses that preclude such a damage claim. The restitution claim avoids those difficulties. But avoiding the difficulties means that the restitution theory is available even when defendant did not cause the cost overrun, or when the court in a damage action would have upheld the limitation-of-remedy clause. *Boomer* may do rough justice in a range of cases, but it is seriously overinclusive.

Another way to simplify proof of causation is with presumptions. If plaintiff proves that defendant's breach was extensive and caused much expense in proportion to the scope of the work, some courts will presume that the entire cost overrun is attributable to defendant. This is a damage theory, and it seems to me to provide a much better allocation of risk than the restitution theory in *Boomer*.

7. The *Restatement (Third)*. The *Restatement (Third)* squarely rejects *Boomer* and adopts Professor Gergen's solution. It states a right to "performance-based damages," measured either by reliance damages (subject to expectancy as a limit), §38(2)(a), or by the value of the uncompensated contractual performance, subject to the allocable portion of the contract price as limit, §38(2)(b). Consequential damages for loss caused by the breach may be added to either measure. §38(3). Comment *f* urges jurisdictions that adopt the proposed rule not to require unrealistic precision in proof of consequential damages. The remedies of §38 are plainly damage remedies for breach, not restitution remedies. They are included in a *Restatement of Restitution and Unjust Enrichment* because the problem has traditionally been discussed in terms of restitution and lawyers will expect to find the answer there.

A California court relied on §38 and other sources to conclude that "plaintiff bears the burden to establish the amount he or she expended in reliance on the contract," but that defendant bears the burden of proving "the amount of plaintiff's expenses that were unnecessary and/or (2) how much the plaintiff would have lost had the defendant fully performed (i.e., absent the breach)," and that reliance damages must be reduced by these two amounts. Agam v. Gavra, 186 Cal. Rptr. 3d 295, 308 (Ct. App. 2015). The Court of Federal Claims, also relying on the *Restatement (Third)*, reached a similar conclusion in a dispute between Chevron and the government. Chevron U.S.A., Inc. v. United States, 116 Fed. Cl. 202, 208 (2014). Chevron proved over $17 million in reliance damages in a dispute over oil and gas rights. The government also paid over $900,000 in sanctions for bad faith claims of privilege during discovery.

NOTES ON OTHER GROUNDS FOR RESCISSION

1. Other contexts and other grounds. Rescission and restitution is the quintessential restitutionary remedy. Restatement sections on mistake, fraud, duress, undue influence, lack of capacity, and lack of authority all say simply that a "transfer" of property under such circumstances is "subject to rescission and restitution." *Restatement (Third)* §§5, 13-17. It doesn't matter whether the property is transferred by contract, by deed, or by check; if the transfer is reversible, the simplest remedy is rescission. Lawyers and judges sometimes speak of the court cancelling instead of the plaintiff rescinding, but the idea is the same in each case.

2. Fraud. Cherry v. Crispin, in note 3 following *Mobil*, illustrates rescission for fraud. Mutual Benefit Life Insurance Co. v. JMR Electronics Corp., 848 F.2d 30 (2d Cir. 1988), applying New York law, says that even innocent misrepresentation is enough in the insurance context if the misrepresentation is material. In *Mutual*, the insured lied about his smoking habit on the insurance application; after he died, the insurer rescinded the policy for fraud. An example of deeds cancelled for fraud is Memphis Hardwood Flooring Co. v. Daniel, 771 So. 2d 924 (Miss. 2000), where dealers bought an elderly victim's timber for less than half its value.

3. Undue influence. An example of a deed cancelled for fraud and undue influence is Perez v. Lomeli, 2008 WL 2514463 (Cal. Ct. App. 2008), where a 90-year-old who could not read or write signed a deed giving his house to his neighbors rather than to the children who took care of him. He liked the neighbors because they gave them certain foods that his children had told the neighbors he was not allowed to eat because of health restrictions.

Here, there was no contract at all; a gift was rescinded. In undue influence cases, defendant takes advantage of some vulnerability—physical or economic dependence, limited mental capacity, illiteracy in English—to overcome the victim's will. The cases often arise within families and the victims are often elderly, but neither of those tendencies in the cases is necessary to a claim.

4. Mutual mistake of fact. As with breach, mistake must go to basic assumptions and defeat the purpose of the contract. Thus in O'Connor v. Harger Construction, Inc., 188 P.3d 846 (Idaho 2008), buyer successfully rescinded a purchase of land and a home where both buyer and builder believed they would be able to obtain an easement for access to the property, and the cost to build the home and driveway without an easement was considerably higher.

5. Unilateral mistake, not relied on. In Florida Insurance Guaranty Association, Inc. v. Love, 732 So. 2d 456 (Fla. Dist. Ct. App. 1999), the Loves' attorney offered to settle a personal injury claim for $210,000. The insurer rejected that demand, and offered to settle for $215,000. The Loves promptly accepted. The insurer replied that it had meant to offer $115,000; the larger offer was a typo. Probably there was no enforceable settlement contract here; the insurer's "counteroffer" was so obviously a mistake that the Loves had no power to accept it. But assuming that offer and acceptance had completed a settlement contract, the court allowed the insurer to rescind. Detrimental reliance by the Loves would have barred the claim, but reliance was also impossible, because they were on notice of the insurer's mistake. Reformation was not an option, because the parties had not agreed on any number different from the one in the writing.

Compare Stavrinides v. Vin di Bona, 2018 WL 317821 (N.D. Cal. Jan. 8, 2018), where a wife submitted two videos to the television show "America's Funniest Home Videos." She signed an agreement allowing the company to use the videos, but then she tried to rescind it, claiming mistake. The television show posted one of the videos on Facebook and the couple sued. The court held the two mistakes she claimed—that she didn't understand the contract terms and that her husband did not want the videos submitted—were not enough to justify rescission under California law. *Id.* at *3.

6. Duress. An example of duress is Soneet R. Kapila, P.A. v. Guiseppe America, Inc., 817 So. 2d 866 (Fla. Dist. Ct. App. 2002). On the eve of trial, an expert witness refused to testify unless his client made an additional payment. The court allowed recovery of the payment on grounds of duress.

C. RESTITUTIONARY RIGHTS IN SPECIFIC PROPERTY

1. *Constructive Trusts*

PAOLONI v. GOLDSTEIN

331 F. Supp. 2d 1310 (D. Colo. 2004)

KANE, Senior District Judge. . . .

This matter is before me on Plaintiffs' Motion for Summary Judgment Against . . . the Iglesias Family Trust. . . .

DISCUSSION . . .

A. FACTS

Viewed in the light most favorable to the Trust, the evidence presented by the Plaintiffs establishes the following:

On or about January, 1997, [Richard] Doggett and others created . . . the American Benefits Group Program ("ABG Program"). . . .

Mr. Doggett . . . received substantial sums of money derived from the fraudulent sale of viatical settlement contracts in the ABG Program, including from sales to investors whose claims against ABG are at issue in this action. In an effort to hide and dissipate these fraudulently obtained assets, Mr. Doggett established foreign and domestic corporations and trusts. . . .

One of the entities involved in this shell game . . . was the Iglesias Family Trust, a trust settled by Doggett for the purpose of purchasing a condominium. Specifically, in December, 1998, Mr. Doggett caused Chambley Corporation, a corporation formed and controlled by him, to disburse $137,000 derived from the fraudulent sale of viatical settlement contracts . . . to Joseph Ieracitano as Trustee for the Iglesias Family Trust. The Trust then used these funds to purchase a condominium unit located at 1500 Ocean Blvd., Unit 404, Pompano Beach, Florida. Mr. Doggett resides in the condominium unit.

B. ANALYSIS

A constructive trust is an equitable device used to compel one who unfairly holds a property interest to convey that interest to another to whom it justly belongs. This equitable remedy may be imposed when property has been acquired in such circumstances that the holder of legal title may not in equity and good conscience retain the beneficial interest. The beneficiary of a constructive trust may obtain, through tracing, not merely what was lost but also other property or profits traceable to that lost property. The party holding the subject property need not have performed a wrongful act for a constructive trust to be imposed, and such trusts have been imposed in a wide variety of cases in which equity dictated this remedy. The purpose of the constructive trust is to prevent the defendant from being unjustly enriched at the plaintiff's expense. . . .

Under the undisputed facts stated above, the Trust purchased the referenced condominium unit with funds it received from Chambley Corp. . . . It is undisputed that these funds were profits received by Mr. Doggett as a result of his participation in the scheme to defraud. . . . There is no evidence in the record that the Trust was a bona fide purchaser of the condominium unit.

There is also no evidence in the current record that any other specific property or asset held by the Trust is derived from or traceable to Mr. Doggett's fraud on Plaintiffs and subject to a constructive trust or equitable lien on this basis. Given the circumstances of the Trust's formation and its utilization of funds fraudulently obtained from investors in the ABG Program, however, Plaintiffs are entitled in equity to an accounting from the Trust to enable them to determine if the Trust holds any other property or assets derived from or traceable to the ABG Program and to a permanent injunction barring the Trust and related persons from disposing of any property or assets derived from or traceable to this source.

CONCLUSION

For the reasons stated above, I ORDER . . . :

A. The condominium unit . . . is subject to a constructive trust of which the Iglesias Family Trust is the trustee and Plaintiffs . . . are the beneficiaries.

B. As trustee of the constructive trust . . . , the Iglesias Family Trust shall execute a Quit Claim Deed conveying the referenced condominium unit to Viatical Administrators, Inc. for the benefit of the Plaintiffs. . . . [There were many plaintiffs, and Viatical Administrators, Inc., appears to be an entity created to collect defendants' assets and distribute them to plaintiffs.] The Quit Claim deed shall be executed and delivered to the Clerk of this Court within thirty days. . . .

C. Plaintiffs shall have an equitable lien on the referenced condominium unit, which lien shall relate back to the date on which the Iglesias Family Trust acquired the unit.

D. The Iglesias Family Trust shall provide to Plaintiffs within thirty days . . . a complete . . . accounting of all income, receipts, disbursements, expenditures, assets, and liabilities, including the whereabouts of any asset of the Iglesias Family Trust, from January 1, 1997 to the present.

E. The Iglesias Family Trust, its trustees, officers, agents, servants, employees, attorneys, and those persons in active concert or participation with it who receive actual notice of this Order by personal service or otherwise, are hereby permanently enjoined from directly or indirectly transferring, selling, encumbering, impairing, or otherwise disposing of in any manner assets and property derived from or traceable to the sale of viatical settlement contracts in the American Benefits Group. . . .

NOTES ON CONSTRUCTIVE TRUSTS

1. Express trusts. A trust is a device for separating the legal ownership and control of property from its beneficial enjoyment. An owner conveys property to a trustee for the benefit of one or more named beneficiaries; the trustee agrees to hold the property subject to the trust. Before the merger of law and equity, law courts would not enforce the trust. The equity courts would acknowledge the trustee as the legal owner, but they would order him to manage and distribute the property in accordance with the directions in the trust instrument. Both sets of rights can now be adjudicated in the single merged court in most states, but the substantive law is still that the trustee is the legal owner and the beneficiary is the equitable owner.

Owners of property create express trusts for many reasons. Trusts can be used to provide professional money management, to consolidate control of a business, to divide the beneficial interest among multiple beneficiaries, to avoid taxes, probate, or creditors, and for many other purposes. The beneficial interest can be divided over time, as in the common trust that pays the income to a surviving spouse for life and then the principal to the adult children. Everything that was once done with legal future interests is now done more simply and flexibly with trusts.

A trustee is constantly subject to the temptation to use trust assets for his own benefit. To combat that temptation, the equity courts developed strict rules of fiduciary duty. Trustees can collect fees for their services in amounts authorized by the trust instrument or approved by the court, but they are not permitted to profit from the trust in any other way. The trustee must account to the beneficiary for her management of the trust and for any profits earned with trust assets. Except for charitable trusts, which are permitted to last forever, the trustee must eventually turn the assets over to the beneficiary entitled to become the legal owner at the termination of the trust.

2. The origins of constructive trusts. The trust provides an obvious analogy for courts faced with a defendant who has acquired the legal ownership of assets in a way that the court considers unjust. Declare him a trustee for the plaintiff and apply the whole body of trust law, including the duty to account for profits and the duty to turn trust assets over to the beneficiary. This is the basic technique of the constructive trust. In the earliest cases, constructive trusts were used to plug loopholes in express trusts: If a trustee transferred trust assets into his own name, the court would say that he still held them in trust, this time a constructive trust. If he sold trust assets to a buyer who knew that the sale was a breach of trust, the equity courts would hold that the buyer took title as a constructive trustee. Then they imposed constructive trusts on other kinds of fiduciaries, such as attorneys, agents, and employees. In all these cases, there was a real fiduciary relationship, voluntarily assumed by the defendant.

3. The facts in *Paoloni*. We don't get the details of the fraud in *Paoloni*, but the court does not suggest that Doggett was a fiduciary. He appears to have just been an investment promoter who lied to his customers. The underlying fraud need not concern us, but strange words still deserve explanation. A viatical settlement is a euphemistically named transaction (from a Latin adjective that means of or relating to a road or a journey) in which a person sells his life insurance policy to an investor at a discount to face value. Often, but not necessarily, the seller is seriously ill. If premiums are still required to keep the policy in effect, the investor must pay them. The insured gets to use the cash while he is still alive, and he is relieved of the burden of paying premiums. The investor gets a good return if the insured dies as soon as expected, but loses money if the insured lives too long, or worse (from an investment perspective), recovers. A middleman is needed to bring insureds together with investors, and there is an obvious potential for that middleman to misrepresent the risks of the investment or the life expectancy of the insured. Doggett apparently did just that.

4. Constructive trust in *Paoloni*. The constructive trust in *Paoloni* is not being used to reinforce the borders of fiduciary relationships. Certainly Doggett's accomplices never intended to be trustees for the plaintiffs. The court can impose all the features of an express trust, but fundamentally, the constructive trust is a remedy for unjust enrichment.

Doggett acquired money by fraud; some of that money was used to buy the condo. Plaintiffs could sue for damages, or for disgorgement of the profits of the fraud, and they could try to collect their judgment by having the sheriff "execute" on any of Doggett's property, including the condo. Execution is examined in section 9.B.1; the short version is that the sheriff seizes the property and sells it at auction to raise money to pay the judgment. Legal title to the condo is held by Ieracitano as trustee of the Iglesias Family Trust, but on the court's account of the facts, Doggett's transfer of money to the trust was a fraudulent transfer and thus reversible. Plaintiffs could execute on the condo even though the trust now appears to own it.

So what does the constructive trust add? Doggett may have many unpaid creditors, any one of whom could ask the sheriff to execute on the condo. The constructive trust treats the fraud plaintiffs not as creditors, but as the equitable owners of the condo. Doggett's other creditors can't levy on the condo, because it doesn't belong to Doggett. He (or his nominee, Ieracitano as trustee) holds it as trustee for the plaintiffs. That's the standard case of constructive trust.

In this case, there may be more. Doggett is living in the condo, and the condo is in Florida, so it may be his homestead, entirely exempt from the claims of his creditors. But even if the condo is Doggett's homestead, it is not exempt from the claims of its rightful owner, and the court says the plaintiffs are the rightful owners.

(The homestead exemption may also explain why Doggett is now living in Florida even though his fraud was apparently centered in Colorado. On the other hand, it may not even be his homestead. We don't know who is named as beneficiary of the Iglesias Family Trust. Presumably Doggett is one of the beneficiaries, but if not, he may not be able to claim the condo as his homestead. Or if he has another home elsewhere, only one can be his exempt homestead.)

5. The identification requirement. Why do plaintiffs get this special status? Because the money acquired by fraud—money that rightfully belongs to plaintiffs—was used to buy the condo. The condo equitably belongs to plaintiffs because the purchase money equitably belonged to plaintiffs. But plaintiffs have to prove that connection. They have to show that Doggett bought the condo with money from the fraudulent sales, and not with some other money. We take up the details of how they prove this in section 8.C.2.

For now, just be clear on the difference between a simple disgorgement claim and a constructive trust claim. A disgorgement plaintiff must show that defendant earned profits from the fraud. She must show causation—that the profits were derived from the fraud—and she must quantify the profits. But she need not show what happened to the money. She can collect the judgment out of any of defendant's nonexempt assets. The constructive trust plaintiff must trace the money from herself to the fraudster to the property she wants to claim in constructive trust. That's an extra burden, but successfully carrying that burden yields substantial advantages.

In a case like *Paoloni*, with many plaintiffs who were victims of the same fraudulent scheme, plaintiffs can trace collectively. It is enough to show that the money came from one or more of the plaintiffs; they need not show which plaintiff.

6. Fractional constructive trusts. What if Doggett had bought the condo partly with the profits from the fraud and partly with money from legitimate sources? Then he and the plaintiffs could each be given ownership interests in proportion to their contribution. An example is Provencher v. Berman, 699 F.2d 568 (1st Cir. 1983) (Breyer, J.), where the court awarded plaintiff a 47.9% interest in a house owned by defendants. The proportions are based on contributions to equity, not the total cost of the house. To simplify the numbers, if defendants buy a house with $10,000 of stolen money, $20,000 of their own money, and $170,000 of borrowed money, plaintiff can claim one-third of the house. Plaintiff's interest, like defendant's interest, will be subject to the lender's mortgage.

Provencher is also a good citation for another point that is essential to these cases but often left implicit. The plaintiff who traces her money into an identifiable asset is entitled to an ownership interest in the asset, and not just to a judgment for her share of the value of that asset.

7. Implementing the constructive trust. Appellate opinions usually say only that defendant does or does not hold the property as constructive trustee; they often leave the consequences of that holding implicit. The trial court in *Paoloni* spells it out: Defendant must convey the condo to plaintiffs (or in this case, plaintiffs' nominee). Defendant must also account for anything else it might have received from the proceeds of the fraud.

8. Constructive trust and accounting for profits. Defendant must also account for any profits it earned with the trust property. *Paoloni* doesn't mention that accounting, probably because nothing suggests any cash profits from the condo. Doggett should have to pay rent for the time he lived in the condo, but Doggett was in bankruptcy and any claims against him had to be filed in the bankruptcy court.

The constructive trustee's duty to account is illustrated, with lots of detail, in Anderson v. Bellino, 658 N.W.2d 645 (Neb. 2003). The parties were joint owners of LaVista Lottery, Inc., which held a license to run a legal gambling establishment in one town. Defendant formed another corporation, LaVista Keno, Inc., to acquire another license to run a similar establishment in another town. The court held that defendant had breached his fiduciary duty to LaVista Lottery when he took this opportunity for his own newly created company. So defendant held LaVista Keno in constructive trust for LaVista Lottery.

But as the litigation dragged on, LaVista Keno had been operating, with income and expenses. Some of the expenses were the necessary expenses of running the business, comparable to the legitimate expenses of making the movie in Sheldon v. MGM or the infringing fabric in Hamil America v. GFI, the cases in section 8.B.2. But defendant had also taken salary and management fees from LaVista Keno, and used corporate funds to pay personal expenses. The court treated these as profits defendant had earned from the trust property. The actual money paid out was probably no longer identifiable, but the court entered a money judgment against defendant for the amount of these profits.

9. Constructive trust and equitable lien. A constructive trust treats the plaintiff as owner; an equitable lien treats defendant as the owner but gives plaintiff a lien. We will take up the grounds for an equitable lien in section 8.C.3, but one point matters here. Any plaintiff entitled to a constructive trust can choose to have—in addition or instead—an equitable lien. *Provencher* in note 6 collects authorities for this "virtually universal rule." 699 F.2d at 570. Plaintiffs get both in *Paoloni*, without explanation. What is the point of that? Plaintiffs traced $137,000 of their money into the condo. What happens if the condo is now worth $160,000? What happens if it is now worth $100,000?

RUFFIN v. RUFFIN

2000 WL 198078 (Va. Ct. App. 2000)

Present Judges BENTON, COLEMAN, and WILLIS . . .
  PER CURIAM. . . .

BACKGROUND . . .

The wife filed . . . for divorce on August 19, 1996. Based upon evidence presented at a hearing held on September 19, 1996, the trial court entered a *pendente lite* [pending litigation] order . . . directing husband to pay $120 a week in child support and $80 a week in spousal support, beginning September 20, 1996. Husband did not make any support payments until January 1997. On September 28, 1996, husband won $4.9 million in a lottery, with a gross payout for twenty years exceeding $243,000 per annum. . . .

CONSTRUCTIVE TRUST

Wife contends that the trial court erred by failing to find that husband's lottery winnings were subject to a constructive trust for her benefit and that of the parties' children. Wife argues that husband used his last available funds to purchase the lottery tickets instead of paying his court-ordered child and spousal support. The commissioner found no evidence of fraud or unjust enrichment warranting the imposition of a constructive trust on husband's winnings. The trial court agreed with that finding.
  We find no error in the trial court's determination.

> Constructive trusts arise, independently of the intention of the parties, by construction of law; being fastened upon the conscience of him who has the legal estate, in order to prevent what otherwise would be a fraud. They occur not only where property has been acquired by fraud or improper means, but also where it has been fairly and properly acquired, but it is contrary to the principles of equity that it should be retained, at least for the acquirer's own benefit.

Rash v. Hilb, Rogal & Hamilton Co., 467 S.E.2d 791, 795 (Va. 1996) (emphasis omitted). "[T]he burden of establishing the grounds for the imposition of a constructive trust [is] by clear and convincing evidence." Hill v. Brooks, 482 S.E.2d 816, 820 (Va. 1997). "Moreover, in order to be entitled to the benefit of a constructive trust, a claimant's money must be 'distinctly traced' into the chose in action, fund, or other property which is to be made the subject of the trust." Crestar Bank v. Williams, 462 S.E.2d 333, 335 (Va. 1995).
  Wife contends that the $2 husband used to purchase the winning lottery ticket on September 28, 1996 were already owed to her and their children pursuant to the *pendente lite* order of the trial court at the September 19, 1996 hearing. She argues that a constructive trust arose as of September 20, 1996, the date when his first support payments were due. However, no fund existed on that date upon which to impose a constructive trust, as husband did not win the lottery until eight days later. It is true that husband's first and second weekly payments were outstanding on the day husband purchased the winning lottery ticket. However, as acknowledged by wife, husband had limited funds on September 20 due in part to the fact he recently had

purchased a car. Although husband's car payments were undoubtedly a greater drain on his ability to pay support than the $2 he used to purchase the lottery tickets, wife argued that the money husband used to purchase the tickets was traceable solely to funds obligated for support.

While husband's failure to pay his court-ordered support was reprehensible, wife failed to present sufficient evidence of fraud or unjust enrichment to warrant the imposition of a constructive trust on his lottery winnings. Husband purchased the lottery tickets pursuant to his habit established throughout the marriage. As a result of his winnings, he was capable of providing greater financial support to his children than at any time during the marriage. We cannot say that husband's good fortune so reeked of injustice as to require the imposition of a constructive trust on his lottery winnings. . . .

Affirmed.

MORE NOTES ON CONSTRUCTIVE TRUSTS

1. How is *Ruffin* different from *Paoloni*? Is *Ruffin* just a discretionary matter of degree? If the husband's good fortune "reeked" more strongly of injustice, should we get a different result? Or is there a difference in kind?

2. The wife's claim. On September 28, the husband owed two weeks of support payments, or $400. Assume that on that date, considering everything he owned in the world, he had less than $400 in cash or in assets readily convertible to cash. In that case, he owed it all to his wife and kids. If he had paid them on time, he would have had no cash for lottery tickets. That means his failure to pay is a but-for cause of his winning the lottery. But does it mean that his cash was really their cash? Did he acquire the lottery ticket with their property?

What if he had other overdue debts on September 28? Then whose cash did he use to buy the lottery ticket? What if he had other payments due on October 1, with no prospect of being able to pay them on time?

3. Unjust enrichment and unpaid debt. Constructive trust is a remedy for unjust enrichment. The enrichment must be acquired from plaintiff, or at least acquired at the expense of plaintiff, as in cases of conscious wrongdoers who enrich themselves by violating plaintiff's rights. And the enrichment must be traceable to particular property in defendant's hands. But a creditor with an unsecured claim—even for child support—has no property right in any specific asset of the debtor.

So what if husband had borrowed two dollars from his estranged wife and used that two dollars to buy the winning lottery ticket? And suppose he bought the ticket the day after he was supposed to pay her back. Now does she get a constructive trust? Well, no. While he has the two dollars, they are his dollars; he can do what he wants to with him. She has a claim to be paid, not a claim to any particular two dollars—even if she loaned him a two-dollar bill and she can still identify it. "[B]efore judgment (or its equivalent) an unsecured creditor has no rights at law or in equity in the property of his debtor." Grupo Mexicano de Desarrollo, S.A. v. Alliance Bond Fund, Inc., 527 U.S. 308, 330 (1999).

Remember the general rule that there can be no unjust enrichment claim where there is an enforceable contract. See Notes on Other Grounds for Restitution in section 8.A.1. A promise to repay a debt is a valid contract. Failure to repay is addressed by the contract, not by the law of restitution. This is another way to explain why failure to repay cannot give rise to a constructive trust.

4. Preferring property rights. The whole point of constructive trust is to prefer property rights over lesser rights arising from contract and other sources of obligations to pay. By the time you finish this chapter, you may wonder whether the law has drawn the line at the right place. But if a constructive trust could be imposed on money that should have been used to pay debts, vastly more claims would qualify, and the goal of returning property to its rightful owner before paying the recipient's debts would be wholly lost. On the other hand, any claim that arises in unjust enrichment can support a constructive trust if the enrichment is received and retained in the form of identifiable property or its proceeds.

5. Family property disputes. Mrs. Ruffin did not have sufficient grounds, but other family members often do. Constructive trusts are commonly used to restore ownership of property in disputes within families. Families put property in one relative's name instead of another's for all sorts of reasons, often subject to informal understandings that are breached when the family has a falling out. Family members acquire property from each other through mistake, undue influence, fraud, or even by murdering the person from whom they will inherit. Constructive trust is an obvious device for restoring such property to the rightful owner. Some of these cases grow out of divorce, but most are disputes among blood relatives.

A revealing example is Herston v. Austin, 603 So. 2d 976 (Ala. 1992). Plaintiff put a savings account, a certificate of deposit, and her house in her son's name. When he didn't care for her as promised, she sued to get them back. The court "set aside" the deed to the house, and imposed a constructive trust on the savings account and CD. This nicely illustrates the functional equivalence of declaratory and restitutionary forms in this context. Presumably, she might also have sued to quiet title.

A multiparty example is Baizley v. Baizley, 734 A.2d 1117 (Me. 1999), where a grandmother gave land to her oldest grandson, on the understanding that he would share equally with his two younger siblings when they matured. He refused to share; fortunately, grandma was still alive and able to testify. The court imposed a constructive trust to divide the land, awarding one-third to each of the two plaintiffs and leaving one-third to defendant.

6. The *Restatement (Third)*. The *Restatement (Third)* addresses constructive trusts in §55. It makes constructive trust available in any case in which defendant "is unjustly enriched by the acquisition of title to identifiable property at the expense of the claimant or in violation of the claimant's rights." §55(1). If defendant has acquired possession but not title, the remedy is replevin or ejectment and not constructive trust.

7. Irreparable injury. The irreparable injury rule is commonly ignored in constructive trust cases. The damage remedy is usually inadequate anyway, because the damages are unmeasurable or uncollectible. In the United States, the tracing feature of constructive trusts is not available in any legal remedy. But where plaintiff seeks restitution from a solvent defendant, quasi-contract will often yield the same recovery as constructive trust, and where there are no profits other than the value of the thing taken, damages will work as well. The irreparable injury rule may be invoked in such cases to protect defendant's right to jury trial, but such cases appear to be scarce and getting scarcer. Professor Palmer reviews the older cases in 1 George E. Palmer, *The Law of Restitution* §§1.6, 2.19 (Little Brown 1978).

IN RE LEITNER
236 B.R. 420 (Bankr. D. Kan. 1999)

JOHN T. FLANNAGAN, Bankruptcy Judge.

This case is about constructive trusts in bankruptcy. In 1986, Leo G. Wetherill hired Gary D. Leitner to perform legal and accounting services for L.G.W. Energy

Resources, Inc., Wetherill's closely held company. Between 1986 and 1992, Leitner embezzled a large sum of money from L.G.W. Energy Resources, Inc.[2] Leitner put some of the purloined funds into a new home for himself and his wife. When Wetherill discovered the fraud in 1992, he (and his company) sued the Leitners, alleging [that] Leitner's fraud created a constructive trust. . . . Leitner filed Chapter 7 bankruptcy and the trustee, Carl Clark, brought this adversary proceeding contesting the existence of a constructive trust. . . . The Court denies Mr. Clark's motion for summary judgment because Wetherill and L.G.W. are the beneficiaries of a constructive trust on the home, which prevents the home from becoming property of the estate.

BACKGROUND

Wetherill sued Leitner in the District Court of Johnson County, Kansas. . . . The amended petition sought a constructive trust on a home at 15623 Acuff Lane in Olathe, Johnson County, Kansas, that Leitner had allegedly purchased with the embezzled funds. Wetherill also asked for a prejudgment attachment of the home, which he received by order dated March 5, 1993. He recorded the attachment order with the Register of Deeds of Johnson County, Kansas, on March 8, 1993.

Although at first Leitner resisted Wetherill's suit, he later admitted his fraud in his answer and filed an affidavit confessing his wrongdoing. Hoping for entry of a prompt judgment, Wetherill's counsel prepared a journal entry and delivered it to the state court judge, the Honorable Lawrence E. Sheppard. Before Judge Sheppard could sign the journal entry, however, Leitner filed this Chapter 7 bankruptcy case on April 15, 1993. . . .

[O]n October 28, 1993, the Court ordered the automatic stay lifted to allow Wetherill and L.G.W. to proceed in state court . . .

Mr. Clark did not appeal the Court's order, nor did he defend Wetherill's state court action against Leitner. Rather, he agreed with Wetherill and other interested parties to sell the residence, pay off the mortgages against it, and hold the remaining sale proceeds pending further litigation. The residence ultimately sold for $410,000. From the sale proceeds, Clark disbursed $272,627.42 to Farm & Home Savings to discharge its first mortgage and $75,000.00 to Mark Twain Kansas Bank to discharge its second mortgage. Clark is currently holding the balance of the proceeds of $67,285.44 plus accrued interest. [These three numbers add to nearly $415,000. Probably the court neglected to mention interest earned before the disbursements.]

On April 16, 1996, before this Court could address Mr. Clark's summary judgment motion, Judge Sheppard, freed from the automatic stay, signed the journal entry confessing judgment that Wetherill's counsel had previously submitted. The journal entry of judgment declared that Leitner held the residence in constructive trust for Leo G. Wetherill and L.G.W. Energy Resources, Inc.

Mr. Clark has stipulated in the pretrial order that Leitner purchased the home . . . with money stolen from L.G.W. Energy Resources, Inc.

DISCUSSION

One solution to this problem is that the constructive trust issue has been decided. . . .

The prejudgment attachment was sufficient judicial action to recognize Wetherill's equitable interest in the home, which Leitner held in constructive trust. . . . This

---

2. In the transcript of Leitner's criminal case, the prosecutor alleged the amount to be nearly $1,000,000.00.

prebankruptcy activity was sufficient to establish the constructive trust. The state court, freed from the stay, has decided the trust question in Wetherill's favor postbankruptcy.

Another solution considers whether a bankruptcy court should ever impose a constructive trust based on state law when a state court has not done so before a debtor has filed a bankruptcy. In 1994, the Sixth Circuit answered this question negatively in In re Omegas Group, Inc. The Court observed: "[A] constructive trust is fundamentally at odds with the general goals of the Bankruptcy Code."[7] The decision held that a constructive trust is an equitable remedy that is effective only from the entry of a final judgment. Hence, if a debtor files bankruptcy before a state court imposes a constructive trust on specific property, no constructive trust exists to prevent that property from becoming property of the bankruptcy estate.

The *Omegas* view has not been universally accepted, however. In a recent article, Andrew Kull criticized the *Omegas Group* decision as misunderstanding the historical roots of constructive trust law as a branch of restitution law.[8] A bankruptcy court in Maine concluded: "Properly applied, constructive trust theory does not conflict with the Code's distribution scheme."[9] And a Virginia bankruptcy judge announced:

> *Omegas* notwithstanding, I can only conclude that the concept of constructive trust is not inherently incompatible with the fair treatment of creditors in bankruptcy. I further find that it is within the discretion of the bankruptcy court to allow a constructive trust claim that is otherwise compatible with applicable state property law.[10]

Under state constructive trust law generally, if a wrongdoer obtains property by fraud or other improper means, a court can impose a constructive trust to protect the injured party. The constructive trust is a legal fiction that adopts the analogy of a trust and declares that a beneficiary owns an equitable interest in property. The constructive trust imposes a duty on the trustee to hold the equitable property interest in trust for its owner, the beneficiary.

When a debtor has been declared a constructive trustee before filing a petition in bankruptcy, there is no problem. The beneficiary's equitable interest in the property does not enter the bankruptcy estate. This is so because the equitable interest held in constructive trust for the beneficiary is not property of the debtor. Under 11 U.S.C. §541(a), the commencement of a bankruptcy case creates an estate that includes all legal and equitable interests of the debtor in property wherever located as of the date the case is commenced. And under section §541(d), property in which the debtor holds no equitable interest, because he holds it in trust for the beneficiary, does not enter the bankruptcy estate. Only the bare legal title to the property held by the debtor enters the bankruptcy estate, and the debtor/constructive trustee holds that legal title subject to a duty to convey it to the beneficiary of the constructive trust. The beneficiary's equitable interest does not become property of the estate.

But when a debtor has not been declared a constructive trustee before filing a petition in bankruptcy, there is a problem. The problem involves the status of state law on when a constructive trust becomes effective. The majority rule on this question is announced by the Pennsylvania bankruptcy court . . . :

---

7. 16 F.3d 1443, 1451 (6th Cir. 1994), quoting In re Stotler & Co., 144 B.R. 385, 388 (Bankr. N.D. Ill. 1992).

8. Andrew Kull, *Restitution in Bankruptcy: Reclamation and Constructive Trust*, 72 Am. Bankr. L.J. 265 (1998).

9. In re Reider, 177 B.R. 412, 415 (Bankr. D. Me. 1994).

10. In re Dameron, 206 B.R. 394, 400 (Bankr. E.D. Va. 1997), *aff'd on other grounds*, 155 F.3d 718 (4th Cir. 1998).

> Although a constructive trust may not be judicially decreed until many years subsequent to the transaction giving rise to the trust, the accepted theory is that the constructive trust is in existence at the inception of the transaction, . . . and the beneficiary is possessed with an equitable interest in the trust property prior to the declaration of the constructive trust.[11]

Thus, under the majority state law rule, a constructive trust arises at the time of the occurrence of the events giving rise to the duty to reconvey the property, not at the date of final judgment declaring the trust as *Omegas* held.

When bankruptcy intervenes before a constructive trust is imposed by a state court and the bankruptcy court finds a constructive trust by applying state law, the bankruptcy court's judgment is effective back to the date of the wrongful conduct. The injured party is deemed the equitable owner of the property and his equitable interest does not pass into the bankruptcy estate. The majority rule as it operates in bankruptcy is premised on an idea expressed by Justice Black in a case under the 1898 Bankruptcy Act: "The Bankruptcy Act simply does not authorize a trustee to distribute other people's property among a bankrupt's creditors."[13]

So far as this Court's research has shown, no Kansas case has ruled on whether a constructive trust is effective from the "inception of the transaction" rather than from the date of entry of a final judgment declaring the trust. . . .

[T]his Court predicts that Kansas would follow the majority rule if faced with circumstances that would otherwise result in fraud being successfully perpetrated on an innocent party. Kansas, of course, has long recognized fraud as grounds for imposing a constructive trust. Here, Leitner has admitted his fraud. And Carl Clark's stipulation in the pretrial order satisfies the requirement that the misappropriated money be traceable to the home. The facts of this case leave no doubt that a constructive trust is equitably justified under Kansas law. The only doubt is whether the highest court of the state would adopt the "relation back" rule to prevent the fraud. The Court has found nothing in the Kansas cases to indicate that the Kansas Supreme Court would do other than apply the majority rule to do justice.

The Court therefore holds that Wetherill owned the equitable interest in the residence on the date Leitner filed bankruptcy. Leitner held only bare legal title to the property, which he was obligated to convey to Wetherill and his company. This being the case, the equitable interest in the home was owned by Wetherill, and that interest was not Leitner's property when he filed bankruptcy. Consequently, it did not become property of the estate, *a fortiori* the home's proceeds are likewise not property of the estate. . . .

Mr. Clark has also argued that §547(b) operates to avoid the constructive trust and the attachment lien as preferential transfers. These arguments lack merit because neither the trust nor the attachment were a "transfer of an interest of the debtor in property." Section 547(b) requires a transfer by the debtor before it can operate. The constructive trust was not a transfer by the debtor. The debtor did not own any equitable interest in the home that he could transfer. Although the prejudgment attachment is normally viewed as creating a lien, in this instance it was merely an enforcement tool to protect Wetherill's already existing equitable ownership in the home. It did not transfer any equitable interest from the debtor because Wetherill already held the equitable ownership of the home.

---

11. In re Aultman, 223 B.R. 481, 482 (Bankr. W.D. Pa. 1998), quoting Grubbs v. Dembec, 418 A.2d 447, 451 n.1 (Pa. Super. Ct. 1980).

13. Pearlman v. Reliance Insurance Co., 371 U.S. 132, 135-136 (1962).

The trustee's motion for summary judgment is denied. The trustee is ordered to convey the bare legal title to Wetherill forthwith. . . .

NOTES ON CONSTRUCTIVE TRUSTS IN BANKRUPTCY

1. Equality in bankruptcy. A trustee in bankruptcy is appointed to represent the unsecured creditors of a bankrupt debtor. In liquidation, the simplest and most common type of bankruptcy, the trustee's job is to gather all the assets of the bankrupt, convert them to cash, and divide the proceeds among the creditors. Secured creditors generally get to keep their collateral. In addition, Congress has conferred special priority on some unsecured claims, such as unpaid taxes and wages. Each remaining creditor gets a pro rata share of the assets that are left after secured creditors and priority creditors have been paid. The basic principle of bankruptcy is that all unsecured nonpriority creditors should share equally.

2. Creditors and owners. It doesn't follow that owners of property should share equally with unsecured nonpriority creditors. The real debate in *Leitner* is whether the victim of embezzlement should be treated as an owner or as just another creditor. *Leitner* illustrates the traditional answer. Plaintiffs who have restitution claims and can still identify their property in defendant's hands can reclaim their property. The effect is that these plaintiffs recover in full, and fewer assets remain for creditors to share pro rata.

Note that there are two requirements. Plaintiffs with restitution claims get no preference if they cannot identify their property or its proceeds. And ordinary creditors get no preference even if they can identify the proceeds of their loan. Plaintiff must have a claim to restitution in kind; his substantive claim must be one that lets him claim to be a dispossessed owner and not a mere creditor. The typical claims involve fraud, misappropriation, or mistake.

If both requirements are met, the court says that plaintiff's property never belonged to the bankrupt defendant, so it does not belong to the trustee in bankruptcy. Moreover, successful plaintiffs can reclaim not just their original property but also new assets shown to have been purchased with their property. Wetherill recovers the money from the sale of the house that Leitner bought with the money he stole from Wetherill.

3. Why return identifiable property? The explanation has a fictional component and a substantive component. The constructive trust is fictional; Leitner obviously had no intention of holding the stolen money as trustee. The substantive point is strongest in just such a case; Leitner's creditors had no right to be paid with stolen money. Fraud is less egregious; mistake is not even wrongful. But the rule is not based on wrongdoing as such. So long as we can identify the property as belonging to plaintiff, Justice Black's point applies: Leitner's creditors cannot be paid with "other people's property."

The requirement that the property be identifiable rests on the idea that if a victim can find the very thing he lost, it's still his. Consider the clearest case. A thief picks your pocket on the steps of the courthouse and walks through the door to the bankruptcy court. He has your wallet with your cash and ten pieces of identification bearing your name. You are in hot pursuit, but he files for bankruptcy just before you catch up to him. Should your wallet and its cash be part of the bankrupt estate, so that you share with all his other creditors? Or should the law honor your claim that "that is *my* wallet!"?

One of Laycock's Texas colleagues who teaches bankruptcy said that you should share pro rata. How are you any different from hundreds of other victims whose pockets he picked but who can't identify their cash? "It is the merest fortuity that you can identify the property that you lost, and that fortuity should have no legal significance."

Is the law recognizing a fortuity, or is it recognizing widely shared intuitions about ownership? If the latter, can the law successfully ignore such intuitions in a democratic society? Assuming those intuitions are dispositive in the case of the stolen wallet, are they equally forceful when identification becomes more attenuated?

4. The nature of the claim. Even if the pickpocket victim in hot pursuit is no different from other pickpocket victims, are pickpocket victims different from the bank that issued the pickpocket's credit card? The requirement that there be a claim for constructive trust serves to separate victims of fraud, misappropriation, and mistake from ordinary creditors. Restitution plaintiffs are pursuing property rights. Ordinary creditors have only contract rights, and no legitimate expectation of being repaid with the proceeds of crime or tort.

Courts also say that other creditors accepted the risk of insolvency when they extended credit, but that victims of fraud did not. An example is In re Teltronics, Ltd., 649 F.2d 1236, 1240-1242 (7th Cir. 1981). How persuasive is that? The pickpocket's victim never agreed to transfer his wallet at all; he plainly did not assume the risk that the pickpocket would go broke and be unable to return it. Similarly, Wetherill never agreed to lend money to Leitner. But what about the investors in *Paoloni*? They did not extend credit to the promoter who defrauded them. But they did part with their money voluntarily. Maybe they assumed the risks of the investment but not the risks of fraud. Or maybe the other explanation is more fundamental: Fraud is a tort, and the other creditors have no right to be paid with the proceeds of tort.

5. Fraud in the extension of credit. Consider the defrauded consumers in *Teltronics*. They paid cash in advance for watches to be delivered later. It turned out there were no watches; there was only a newspaper ad offering cheap watches and a post office box to receive the checks. Those who ordered watches might not have thought of themselves as lenders, but they were; they assumed the risk that Teltronics would go broke and not be able to deliver the watches. That could have happened without fraud; it happens whenever a merchant goes bankrupt. There are always customers who put down deposits for goods on order, or paid in advance for warranties or service contracts. How are the victims in *Teltronics* different from these customer creditors? The doctrinal answer is that fraud makes the transaction subject to rescission; failure to pay does not. Victims of fraud have a restitution claim; unpaid lenders who were not defrauded have only a contract claim.

It is also settled that failing to disclose your desperate financial condition (as distinguished from affirmatively misrepresenting it) is not fraud. An unusually clear example is In re North American Coin & Currency, Ltd., 767 F.2d 1573, *modified on other grounds*, 774 F.2d 1390 (9th Cir. 1985). If the rule were otherwise, there would be fraud litigation about any bad loan made in the run-up to bankruptcy.

What about concealing from creditors a fraud on someone else? No bank or supplier would have given credit to Teltronics if it had known the company was engaged in a massive fraud on its customers. The simple-minded fraud in *Teltronics* was certain to be disclosed, and the disclosure was certain to destroy the business. Realistically, weren't all the creditors victims of the fraud? Maybe so, but the court saw a bright-line distinction between defrauded consumers and ordinary creditors.

6. Why two requirements? If fraud victims are simply more deserving, why not give them a priority claim to all the assets? Why distinguish between fraud victims who can identify what they lost and fraud victims who can't? The identification requirement is a rough-and-ready compromise between the interests of fraud victims and the interests of other creditors. In bankruptcy, the question is not whether the bankrupt fraudster is unjustly enriched but whether his creditors would be unjustly enriched if they were paid with the fraud victim's property. If the victim can no longer identify his property, we cannot say with any confidence that the victim's property is being used to pay the creditors. Maybe the fraud victim's money has already been spent. The identification requirement is a serious limit on claims of constructive trust.

7. The backlash. Constructive trusts are controversial among bankruptcy lawyers. Plaintiffs frequently claim constructive trusts on flimsy or nonexistent grounds, and as *Leitner* illustrates, trustees in bankruptcy instinctively oppose them with equal disregard for the merits. The *Omegas* opinion, quoted in *Leitner*, said that constructive trusts would no longer be recognized in Sixth Circuit bankruptcies, with the possible exception of constructive trusts created by statute or imposed by judicial decree prior to the bankruptcy petition. 16 F.3d at 1450-1451. This sweeping dictum was quite unnecessary to the result and quite uninformed by the kinds of facts that generate more plausible claims for constructive trust. The constructive trust claimant in *Omegas* was an ordinary contract creditor; the alleged fraud consisted merely of not disclosing the debtor's precarious financial condition; and there was apparently no attempt whatever to identify the proceeds of the payment, which was commingled in the bankrupt's general cash. Thus, there were multiple grounds on which to hold that there was no plausible claim to a constructive trust.

Omegas has been followed, criticized, and distinguished. Its potential for harsh results is illustrated in In Re Dow Corning Corp., 192 B.R. 428 (Bankr. E.D. Mich. 1996), where Dow Corning sent a $300,000 invoice by fax and by mail. One clerk paid the fax copy, a different clerk paid the mailed copy, and Dow Corning filed for bankruptcy before anyone noticed the mistake. The bankruptcy judge criticized *Omegas* as lacking any basis either in bankruptcy law or state law, but followed it as controlling authority; the second $300,000 stayed with the bankrupt to be divided among Dow Corning's creditors. No appeal is reported.

8. *Omegas* in other circuits. *Omegas* has been the subject of much litigation in bankruptcy courts, but so far has not been adopted in any other circuit. The Seventh Circuit rejected *Omegas* in In re Mississippi Livestock, Inc., 745 F.3d 299 (7th Cir. 2014). The court agreed with the Sixth Circuit that the constructive trust should be used "sparingly" in bankruptcy, but that did not mean never:

> [I]n our opinion, the Sixth Circuit's view draws too sharp a line between constructive trusts and ordinary trusts. We are confident that state law is up to the task of policing any possible abuses of the constructive trust. . . . Moreover, to the extent that the Sixth Circuit relied on the idea that a constructive trust cannot exist until a court has expressly imposed that remedy, we understand that issue to be controlled by state law.

Id. at 306. The court also noted that *Omegas* had been "sharply criticized" in an earlier edition of this casebook. *Id.*

Without resolving the dispute between the Sixth and Seventh Circuits, the Eighth Circuit cited both *Omegas* and *Mississippi Livestock* for the proposition that constructive trusts should be used sparingly in bankruptcy. In re WEB2B Payment Solutions, Inc., 815 F.3d 400, 408 (8th Cir. 2016).

9. A deeper dive. The holding in *Omegas* depends on the argument that when Congress recodified the law of bankruptcy in 1978, it implicitly repealed the then-existing law of constructive trusts in bankruptcy by failing to explicitly codify it. Supporting and opposing this premise leads to a series of detailed arguments about the meaning of various sections of the Bankruptcy Code and their relationship to underlying principles of law and equity. Detailed notes on these arguments appear on this casebook's website and in the Fourth Edition of the book. The best analysis of the whole issue is Andrew Kull, *Restitution in Bankruptcy: Reclamation and Constructive Trust*, 72 Am. Bankr. L.J. 265 (1998); he rejects the *Omegas* argument. The short version is that each of these statutory arguments depends on the claim that the constructive trust somehow transfers the debtor's interest in the property. But as *Leitner* holds, the whole theory of the constructive trust is that the constructive trust claimant is the true owner, so that the debtor had no interest in the property.

10. The *Restatement (Third)*. By long tradition, *Restatements* generally restate the common law and rarely claim to interpret statutes. So the *Restatement (Third)* addresses this issue only in part. It says that the right to restitution from identifiable property is superior to the claims of creditors, including claims of creditors who have acquired a lien by any form of involuntary process. §60(1). The comments and Reporter's Notes say that this rule is very long settled, and obviously could not have developed if it had not been recognized in bankruptcy. They explain that *Omegas* has no basis in statutory text or legislative history and would be a revolutionary change. But, for the record, the comment also says that the meaning of the Bankruptcy Code "is ultimately outside the scope of this Restatement." §60 cmt. *f.*

2. *Tracing the Property*

IN RE ERIE TRUST CO.
191 A. 613 (Pa. 1937)

Argued before KEPHART, C.J., and SCHAFFER, MAXEY, DREW, LINN, STERN, and BARNES, JJ. . . .

STERN, Justice.

In the estate of W.W. Gingrich, deceased, the orphans' court of Erie County filed an adjudication surcharging Erie Trust Co., the executor, in the sum . . . of $25,819.80, representing cash taken from the estate by the company as commissions, to which, as the court held, it was not entitled. Erie Trust Co. having become insolvent, and the Secretary of Banking having taken possession as receiver, the beneficiaries of the Gingrich estate sought priority in distribution for the amount of this surcharge. The court of common pleas denied their right to a preference over general creditors. . . .

Where improperly converted assets of a trust estate are traced into the fund for distribution, a preference has always been allowed on the theory that such assets never have become a part of those of the trustee but at all times have remained, whether in their original or substituted form, the property of the cestui que trust [the trust beneficiary], and therefore the trustee's general creditors are not entitled to any share in their distribution. The claim of the trust beneficiary in such a case is not really for a preference, or to establish an equitable lien, but rather for the reclamation of his own property. . . . An illustration of a claim on an *unpreferred* surcharge would be one based upon an act of negligence or mismanagement on the part of the trustee, as, for example, a failure to dispose of nonlegal securities in the trust, or allowing trust funds to remain uninvested for an undue period of time. But in the present case the claim of appellants is to recover, as their own property either in its original or changed form, cash actually taken from their estate by the trustee. . . .

We thus come to the principal question involved: Have appellants been able to trace the converted cash of the estate into the assets in the hands of the receiver for distribution? The court below held that this requirement had not been met. The $25,819.80 taken by Erie Trust Co. from the Gingrich estate was placed in the general cash funds of the company. The lowest amount of actual cash in those funds from the time when the money was taken from the estate until the receiver was appointed was $2,865.40, together with "cash items" of $1,937.63. The lowest amount of the company's deposits in other banks was $6,373.23. During this period the company deposited a large amount of cash in another bank, and also invested some general cash funds in various securities (Church of the Covenant bonds and the "Leichner" mortgage). The bonds were in the possession of the company at the time the receiver took possession; the mortgage had been foreclosed and the mortgaged premises purchased by the company. No trust funds of other claimants have been transferred without authority to the company's general cash funds, and no other claim for a preference based upon any such transfer is involved in the present liquidation proceedings. It is the contention of appellants that in tracing the cash taken from the Gingrich estate and mingled by Erie Trust Co. with its own general cash funds, the commingled fund is to be considered as being coextensive with all of the cash on hand, cash items and cash on deposit with other banks, and therefore the balance on hand of all such items is impressed with the trust and subject to recapture as representing appellants' property; moreover, that the securities purchased from any such funds after the conversion of appellants' money, and now before the court for distribution, are likewise so subject as constituting a substituted form of the cash originally converted by the trustee.

The principles underlying the tracing of trust funds have been the subject of so much confusion in the law, and their formulation has had such a checkered history, that it is frequently impossible to reconcile decisions in the same jurisdiction, much less to harmonize those in the courts of different states. Although it may be said in general that the tendency has been toward a gradual liberalization of the requirements of identification of the trust res, the progress in that regard has been far from continuous. While from early times equity allowed a cestui que trust to follow the trust property through any change in form or species into which it may have been transmuted, this privilege originally was not extended to the case of money unless the beneficiary could identify the particular bills or coin which had constituted the trust res. But in the famous case of Knatchbull v. Hallett, [1879] 13 Ch. 696, Sir George Jessel, M.R., . . . established the principle that not only could a cestui que trust trace a cash asset of the trust into a fund in which it had become commingled with moneys of the trustee, but that, where the latter made withdrawals from the mixed account, the presumption was that the money thus withdrawn was his own, and the cestui que trust could claim that the balance represented the trust property. There evolved the generally accepted doctrine that the beneficiary was entitled to the lowest balance to which the commingled fund at any time became depleted, such minimal residue being considered sufficiently identified as constituting the trust fund.

[¶] The variance in later decisions arose from differences in viewpoint as to the boundaries properly to be ascribed to the "commingled fund." If a defaulting trustee mingled trust assets with his own, did the mixed fund embrace his general assets, or consist only of the specific assets with which the trust res had been mingled? More particularly, in the case of a bank which had improperly transferred to its own funds cash from an estate of which it was trustee, could the cestui que trust reclaim his property from the general assets of the bank, or only from its general cash funds, or, adopting a still more rigid requirement, only from the exact cash fund or particular bank deposit in which the cash of the estate was placed or deposited? There are some jurisdictions which hold that the trust property, even without any special identification, and even though the beneficiary cannot show that it came in some form or other into the hands of the receiver, can be reclaimed out of the general assets of the bank; the theory being that those assets were augmented and the bank unjustly enriched by its appropriation of the trust property, and its general creditors should have no right to profit thereby. This doctrine, however, has been discarded in several of the states which originally adopted it, and the view which presently prevails in most jurisdictions is that the cestui que trust must identify the trust res by tracing it into some *specific* funds or assets of the bank; the problem remaining to determine *how* specifically the commingled fund must be differentiated from the general assets. . . .

[I]n Pennsylvania, . . . it is not sufficient for a cestui que trust merely to show that the general assets of the trustee have been increased by an unauthorized appropriation of trust property, but he must also identify the trust res by tracing it into some specific property, funds, or assets. We have no hesitation in holding in the present case that the deposits of the trustee company in other banks are to be considered, together with the cash on hand and the cash items, as constituting a single fund, sufficiently differentiated from the company's general assets to meet the requirements of the law in regard to the tracing of trust property. We are led to this conclusion by the fact that banks and individuals alike generally regard cash on hand and deposits in banks as a unit of cash resources distinct from assets consisting of securities and other forms of personal property. To insist upon a separate tracing of cash funds and credit balances in banks would be to dissociate legal principles from practicalities. The intricacies of bookkeeping and accounting systems, the complexities of banking usage, the difficulty of identifying cash through a series of transactions, the frequency with which balances are shifted from one bank to another and indiscriminate withdrawals made therefrom, are such that ordinarily it would be virtually impossible to distinguish between cash, cash items, and deposits in other banks. Indeed, as a legal proposition, there is as little reason to attempt such a differentiation as there would be to establish one between moneys kept in different vaults of the same bank, compartments of a cash register, or pockets of a purse. Therefore, even though appellants have not in this case traced the money from their estate into any particular fund or bank deposit, they are, in our opinion, entitled to the lowest level of the cash and cash items, and funds of Erie Trust Co. on deposit in other banks, reached between the time when the conversion occurred and when the secretary of banking took possession of the assets of the company.

It follows as a necessary corollary from this ruling that investments made by the trust company, after the time of the conversion, from funds on deposit in other banks, are also subject to the claim of appellants in this proceeding. If the deposits themselves are to be considered part of the fund into which the trust res has been sufficiently traced, any securities into which such deposits were transmuted must be regarded as merely substituted forms of the trust property. As early as In re Oatway, [1903] 2 Ch. 356, it was held that where a trustee commingled trust moneys with his own, from the mixed account purchased an investment in his own name, and subsequently dissipated the balance of the fund, the beneficiary could impress the trust upon such investment. The fictional presumption that the money withdrawn from a commingled fund is the trustee's own should not be applied to defeat the cestui que trust's rights where the balance left is insufficient to meet the trust obligation. . . .

[¶] The application of this rule to the present case entitles appellants, in addition to their rights in the general cash funds already stated, to pursue the balance of their claim of $25,819.80 into the Church of the Covenant bonds and the "Leichner" mortgage (subsequently foreclosed and now held in the form of real estate) purchased by Erie Trust Co. out of its general cash funds after the conversion by it of the trust money.

The decree of the court below is reversed, and the record remitted, with directions to enter a decree in accordance with this opinion. . . .

NOTES ON TRACING

1. Tracing through exchanges. In In re Leitner, in section 8.C.1, tracing was so simple that it never became an issue—and we don't get many details. Leitner embezzled about $1 million, and the trustee stipulated that he used part of that money to buy a house. Probably this meant that he used the embezzled money for the down payment, because there were also substantial mortgages on the house. The stipulation should also mean that stolen money was used to make the mortgage payments. But the portion going to principal in the early years of a mortgage is so small that the trustee in bankruptcy might have let that issue go.

Tracing the money into the house was step one. Then the house was sold under court supervision, the mortgages paid off, and the remaining money placed in an account maintained by the trustee. This is step two—tracing the house into the cash proceeds of the house. There was no difficulty identifying the cash at this step, because the trustee, not Leitner, sold the house and received the cash.

Each step illustrates the essential concept of the tracing rules: Courts trace through physical exchanges. It is not enough that Leitner stole the money and that he bought a house. Wetherill must show that Leitner used the stolen money, and not some other money, to buy the house. This proof was apparently easy in *Leitner*; the trustee conceded the point. But often, this proof is difficult; claims can fail for lack of proof.

2. Commingled funds. In *Erie Trust*, the law treated depositors as ordinary creditors, but trust beneficiaries as the owners of their property. The bank had no right to fees from that property in amounts greater than the amount approved by the court.

The misappropriation victims in *Erie Trust* cannot identify their property in the obvious way that Wetherill could identify his. The money wrongfully taken from the Gingrich estate was promptly commingled with the bank's own money. Yet the court invokes tracing rules that enable the victims to identify particular dollars or assets as the ones they lost. *Erie Trust* conveniently illustrates in one opinion all the major tracing rules, which have not changed much in the intervening decades.

Wrongfully acquired money can be commingled with the wrongdoer's own money in many ways and places, but by far the most common way is in a simple bank account. We speak of money being "deposited" and thereafter resting "in" a bank account, but even this is a fiction. Legally, a bank account is a debt that the bank owes to the depositor, and practically, the bank uses the deposited money for its own purposes or lends it to other customers. All rules for tracing cash through bank accounts start with the fiction that the victim's dollars are "in" the account. Courts could reach the same results by noting that the victim's dollars were exchanged for the bank's obligation to repay, but the conventional fiction is less cumbersome.

3. The lowest intermediate balance rule. If the bank takes the tracing plaintiffs' money and puts it in the bank's own account, along with other money lawfully belonging to the bank, and doesn't spend anything from the account, it is fairly easy to say that the plaintiffs' money is in the account.

a. The presumption that the wrongdoer spends his own money first. But what happens when the bank spends something from that account? Courts irrebuttably presume that the bank, being conscious of its fiduciary duties, intended to spend its own money first. Thus, as long as the amount in the account exceeds the amount of misappropriated funds that were deposited there, all the plaintiffs' money is still in the account.

This presumption continues to apply if the balance in the account falls below the amount of misappropriated funds that were deposited there. Because the wrongdoer withdrew his own money first, whatever is left in the account belongs to the plaintiffs. The presumption is contrary to fact; the bank thought it had lawfully collected its fees and was not aware of any fiduciary duty whatever with respect to this account. The presumption has even been applied when the wrongdoer said explicitly that he was withdrawing the money to keep the plaintiff from getting it. Universal C.I.T. Credit Corp. v. Farmers Bank, 358 F. Supp. 317 (E.D. Mo. 1973). It is best to dispense with talk of intent and simply say the rule is that defendant is irrebuttably presumed to spend his own money first.

New money lawfully acquired by the bank and deposited in the account is not treated as replacing earlier withdrawals of the tracing plaintiffs' money, unless the wrongdoer actually so intended. That is, deposits are treated factually and not fictionally.

b. Simplifying. The resulting rule is the lowest intermediate balance rule: If the balance in the account ever drops below the amount of plaintiffs' money deposited in the account, the lowest balance the account ever reaches is a limit on the plaintiffs' claim to the account. That is, if at some point the balance drops to $10, plaintiffs had at most $10 in the account, and subsequent deposits of the bank's own money cannot change that. Instead of applying the presumption step by step to every transaction in the account, it is usually enough to look for the lowest intermediate balance.

"Intermediate" in the lowest intermediate balance rule can refer to two pairs of events: between the last deposit of plaintiffs' money and the adjudication, or between two deposits of plaintiffs' money. If the balance drops to $10, and then $100 stolen from plaintiff is added to the account, plaintiff can claim to have $110 in the account.

Cases invoking the lowest intermediate balance rule are collected in State ex rel. Insurance Commissioner v. Blue Cross & Blue Shield, 638 S.E.2d 144, 157-158 (W. Va. 2006), and in Meyer v. Norwest Bank Iowa, N.A., 112 F.3d 946, 950-951 (8th Cir. 1997), a quarter-million dollar dispute where the lowest intermediate balance was $6,008.18.

4. The presumption that the wrongdoer invests the plaintiffs' money first. The presumption in note 3 benefits tracing plaintiffs when the money withdrawn from the account is dissipated. But it works against plaintiffs when the money withdrawn is invested in a valuable asset. Plaintiffs might prefer to claim the asset instead of the lowest intermediate balance left in the account. The tracing fictions let them do so. The bank bought Church of the Covenant bonds and the Leichner mortgage with money from the commingled accounts, so plaintiffs get to claim the bonds and the mortgage as "their" property. The bank's other creditors cannot claim a share, because these investments "never belonged to the bank."

Again, the presumption is allowed to defy the wrongdoer's probable intention, but it is not allowed to defy chronological possibilities. Thus, tracing plaintiffs cannot claim investments that were purchased before their funds were deposited in the account. And if the balance in the account falls below the sum taken from the plaintiffs and is subsequently replenished with the wrongdoer's own funds, the lowest intermediate balance rule limits plaintiffs' claim to any subsequent investments. Plaintiffs can claim a share of the investment equal to the fraction that could have been purchased with the lowest intermediate balance. If $1,000 of plaintiffs' money remained in the account under the lowest intermediate balance rule, and the investment cost $3,000, plaintiffs can claim one-third of the investment.

5. Combining the two presumptions. The combined effect of these two tracing fictions is that the wrongdoer is presumed to dissipate his own money and preserve the tracing plaintiffs' money. Commingled assets that can still be found, in or out of the commingled account, belong to plaintiffs; assets that have disappeared belonged to the wrongdoer. But for any property to belong to plaintiffs, it must be possible for it to have been purchased with plaintiffs' money. Once plaintiffs trace their money into a commingled account, anything that was possible is presumed in their favor, but the impossible is not presumed.

6. Simple exchanges again. By using the fiction that plaintiffs' money was withdrawn from the commingled account to make investments, the court identifies the Leichner mortgage as plaintiffs' property. But the Leichner mortgage has been foreclosed; now the bank has the Leichner real estate instead. It is easy enough to say that the real estate belongs to plaintiffs too, and the court so holds. Tracing through such a direct exchange does not even require an additional fiction.

7. Theory and practice. In theory, plaintiffs can trace through as many such exchanges as have occurred, so long as they can identify the property at each step. Thus, if the Leichner real estate were sold and the money invested in Microsoft stock, the victims could claim the stock. If the Microsoft stock were sold and the money deposited in a commingled account, and then money from the account were used to buy IBM stock, plaintiffs could use the tracing fictions for commingled accounts again to reach the IBM stock.

In practice, every additional step increases the difficulty of identifying the property and the court's skepticism at efforts to do so. And in practice, bad guys tend to spend their money rather than invest it, and they tend to get caught when they no longer have enough cash to cover up what they're doing. So cases tracing into profitable investments are rather scarce. In most tracing cases, the lowest intermediate balance rule is enough to resolve the issues.

8. Defining a commingled account. In *Erie Trust*, plaintiffs did not trace their money into any particular account. The most they can say is that the bank misappropriated cash, so the bank must have put their cash into one of the places where it kept cash. Unfortunately for plaintiffs, the bank kept cash in several places, and plaintiffs did not prove which account received their funds. Probably they couldn't find out, but perhaps they found out and didn't like the answer. If their cash went into an account that had been entirely dissipated, tracing through that account would produce no recovery. For whatever reason, tracing seems to fail at the very first step in *Erie Trust*.

The court avoids these problems by treating all the bank's cash accounts as one. The court says that it would be unrealistic to treat each cash account as separate. Undoubtedly that is true, but if we were being realistic, we would have to change the tracing fictions much more substantially than that. There is a contrary holding in In re MJK Clearing, Inc., 371 F.3d 397 (8th Cir. 2004). In *MJK*, money allegedly acquired by fraud was deposited in an identified account, and by the end of the day, that account was overdrawn. Tracing ended at that point; the lowest intermediate balance was zero. We have not found any cases explicitly choosing between *Erie Trust* and *MJK* on this issue.

9. Swelling of assets. Some courts went even further than *Erie Trust* during the Great Depression, when there were many bank failures. Under the swelling-of-assets theory, all the wrongdoer's assets were treated as a single account, and the lowest intermediate balance rule was applied to the wrongdoer's gross assets. This nearly eliminated the tracing requirement altogether. Unless gross assets were at some point less than the amount misappropriated, claims of fraud and misappropriation were paid before other claims. That straightforward preference has generally been repudiated; other creditors have successfully insisted on the tracing requirement as a limit on the special treatment of fraud and misappropriation victims.

Just because defendant at some point took $10,000 of plaintiff's money does not mean that defendant now has $10,000 more than he would have had but for the misappropriation. It is possible—indeed, likely—that because defendant had more money, he spent more money. The tracing presumptions may be crude, but they attempt to distinguish cases where plaintiff's money can still be found from cases where it cannot be found and might have been entirely dissipated.

10. Do these rules make sense? Even without the swelling-of-assets theory, identification has come a long way from the victim in hot pursuit of the pickpocket. How sensible are the tracing rules as a means of balancing the interests of misappropriation victims against the interests of other creditors? It can be said in their favor that the tracing rules are fictions only with respect to withdrawals; for the most part, the victim must actually identify deposits in the ordinary English sense of "identify." But elasticity in the definition of accounts allows some slippage even from that requirement; the Gingrich heirs never did identify exactly what happened to their money in *Erie Trust*.

11. The *Restatement (Third)*. The *Restatement (Third)* addresses tracing through simple exchanges in §58, and tracing through commingled funds in §59. It concisely summarizes the rules examined here. Section 58 says that "a claimant entitled to restitution from property may obtain restitution from any traceable product of that property, without regard to subsequent changes of form." §58(1). Section 59 says that plaintiff may trace into "the balance of the commingled fund or a portion thereof," or into "property acquired with withdrawals from the commingled fund, or a portion thereof," or into "a combination of the foregoing." §59(1). As against wrongdoers and persons responsible for their own unjust enrichment, withdrawals "are marshaled so far as possible in favor of the claimant." §59(2)(a). "Subsequent contributions by the recipient do not restore property previously misappropriated" unless defendant "affirmatively" so intends. §59(2)(b). The traceable product of the plaintiff's property after a withdrawal "may not exceed the fund's lowest intermediate balance." §59(2)(c). Tracing against an innocent defendant is limited by the rules for measuring disgorgement, so that tracing cannot increase plaintiff's recovery beyond the limits set out in §50 and summarized in note 5 of the Notes on Measuring Restitution from Innocent Defendants in section 8.A.2.

IN RE JD SERVICES, INC.

284 B.R. 292 (Bankr. D. Utah 2002)

[JD Services, Debtor, filed a petition for reorganization in bankruptcy on August 24, 2000. On August 28, one of its subsidiaries deposited a check for $7,250.00 into an account at Bank of America. The Bank improperly coded the check as $725,000.00 instead of $7,250.00, and it gave immediate credit for the check.

On August 30, the Debtor wire transferred $800,000 from this account to a new account at First Security Bank. The parties agreed that the extra $717,750 was included in this transfer. This tracing step is unexplained; maybe only a nominal balance was left at Bank of America.

Bank of America noticed the error and notified Debtor on September 5. On September 13, Debtor and First Security agreed to put a hold on the First Security account in the amount of $717,750. No one claimed that Debtor had acted in bad faith. The court held that Debtor was unjustly enriched by the mistake, and that the funds mistakenly deposited were held in constructive trust for Bank of America for so long as they could be identified.

Debtor continued to operate as a going concern, and between August 28 and September 13, some $6.5 million passed through the First Security account, all in the ordinary course of business. Some of the initial deposits to the account bounced, and beginning September 1, First Security put lengthy holds on deposits before making funds available.

When the court refers to "the Bank," it means Bank of America, not First Security.]
GLEN E. CLARK, Chief Judge. . . .

UNDISPUTED FACTS . . .

20. The parties stipulated to information contained in a report prepared by or at the direction of [First Security's branch manager] reflecting the activity with regard to the Account. . . .

22. Given the information contained in the Report, the Debtor's account balance can be analyzed from two different approaches. One approach is to analyze the amounts on deposit as the "Collected Balance," which is the total funds on deposit . . . regardless of whether or not the funds are available for withdrawal or use by the Debtor. The other approach is to analyze the amounts on deposit as the "Available Balance," which is the total funds available to the Debtor for withdrawal at any given time. The available balance approach takes into account only local deposits that have been on deposit for at least seven business days and non-local checks that have been on deposit for at least eleven business days.

23. If the Account balance is analyzed using the Collected Balance approach, the lowest intermediate balance for the time period between August 30, 2000, and September 13, 2000, would be no less than $717,750.00 at the end of any given day.

24. If the Account balance is analyzed using the Available Balance approach, the lowest intermediate balance for the time period between August 30, 2000, and September 13, 2000, would be no less than $394,460.47 at the end of any given day.

25. Page 4 of the Report shows that on September 6, 2000, the Account balance using the Available Balance approach may have dropped to as low as $162,524.28. However, the Trustee and First Security agree that the Report does not necessarily reflect the order that individual items were received by First Security or processed during the day. It is undisputed that at the end of the day on September 6, 2000, the Available Balance was $394,460.47.

DISCUSSION

TRACING OF FUNDS . . .

If funds held in constructive trust have been commingled, the beneficiary of the constructive trust must trace the funds using the lowest intermediate balance rule. . . .

A constructive trust, like any other trust, must have a trust res at all times. A trust is created in property and exists only so long as there is an identified and ascertainable interest in property to be the trust res. In circumstances where a constructive trust is declared postpetition, the beneficiary of the constructive trust must trace the funds to identify the trust res in the same manner as if there were no bankruptcy. "Property interests are created and defined by state law. Unless some federal interest requires a different result, there is no reason why such interests should be analyzed differently simply because an interested party is involved in a bankruptcy proceeding." Butner v. United States, 440 U.S. 48, 55 (1979). Bankruptcy Courts are directed to apply "reasonable assumptions" to govern the tracing of trust funds. Begier v. Internal Revenue Service, 496 U.S. 53, 67 (1990). To impose the same tracing requirements as are required under state law is reasonable and will cause no greater hardship on the Bank than it would experience outside a bankruptcy setting. Furthermore, a tracing requirement is reasonable when weighed against bankruptcy policy which demands equality of distribution among creditors of equal rank. If the Bank successfully traces its funds, return of the trust res to the Bank will not violate bankruptcy policy because the Bank will be receiving its own money and not property of the estate. If the Bank cannot trace the funds, the Bank becomes a creditor to the extent of its loss, and must be treated on an equal basis with other postpetition creditors. . . .

For the above reasons, the Bank must trace its funds held in constructive trust utilizing the lowest intermediate balance rule.

COLLECTED BALANCE VS. AVAILABLE BALANCE

Under the lowest intermediate balance rule, any funds removed from a commingled account are presumed to be the Debtor's funds to the extent the funds exceed the beneficiary's equitable interest. If the Trustee deposits other funds into the commingled account, it is generally held that the Trustee is not replenishing trust funds. New deposits are not subject to the equitable claim of the trust beneficiary and subsequent withdrawals are presumed to draw first upon the new funds. Applying the rule, a constructive trust beneficiary may retrieve the lowest balance recorded after the funds were commingled. In this case, the Court is provided with two approaches by which it may trace the constructive trust funds placed in the Account: Collected Balance and Available Balance. The Collected Balance approach focuses only on the dates of deposit and withdrawal of funds and ignores the hold imposed upon new deposits to the Account. The Available Balance approach takes into account the hold imposed by First Security on new deposits to the Account. By taking into consideration the hold imposed upon new deposits, the Available Balance approach partially rebuts the presumption that subsequent withdrawals following a new deposit were drawn first on the new deposits. The additional information utilized by the Available Balance approach adds precision to the tracing process and minimizes the commingling of constructive trust funds with new deposits.

Of the two approaches, the Available Balance approach most accurately traces the actual funds that were placed into the Account and will be used by this Court for purposes of computing the lowest intermediate balance of funds held in constructive trust. Use of the Available Balance approach to compute the lowest intermediate balance of the constructive trust funds entitles the Bank [to] the return of constructive trust funds totaling $394,460.47. [The Bank has an unsecured claim for the remaining $323,289.53. Because the claim arose after the bankruptcy petition, it will get a priority in bankruptcy—under the Bankruptcy Code, not from anything having to do with restitution.]

INTEREST

The Bank, in its motion for summary judgment, seeks entitlement to the interest actually earned on the funds held in constructive trust. Because the funds held in

constructive trust have always belonged to the Bank, it is entitled to the interest actually earned by the $394,460.53 in constructive trust funds held from August 28, 2000,
until paid. . . .

NOTES ON THE MECHANICS OF TRACING

1. Constructive trust for mistake. Hold the tracing issues for a minute and assume
that the money was equally (and indisputably) identifiable in all the cases we have
read. What about the grounds for constructive trust?

a. *JD Services.* Is Bank of America's claim to constructive trust for mistake just as
good as the Gingrich heirs' claim to recover money taken in breach of fiduciary duty,
as Wetherill's claim to recover embezzled money, and as the Paoloni plaintiffs' claim
to recover money taken from them by fraud? Should it matter that no wrongdoing
was alleged or proved in *JD Services,* and that Bank of America's blunder was its own
fault? Note that there is no wrongdoing *by the creditors* in the fraud, embezzlement, or
fiduciary duty cases either. Should JD Service's creditors have a right to be paid with
Bank of America's money if it was taken "only" by mistake?

b. Other examples. American cases on constructive trust for mistake are collected in Chase Manhattan Bank N.A. v. Israel-British Bank (London), [1981] Ch.
105, where Chase paid $2 million to Israel-British and, later the same day, paid it
again. Israel-British failed before the mistake was discovered. Chase could recover the
money via constructive trust, but only if it could identify the payment or its proceeds
in defendant's hands.

In In re Unicom Computer Corp., 13 F.3d 321 (9th Cir. 1994), the court granted a
constructive trust of the last two month's rent on an equipment lease, some $64,000,
paid by mistake to the broker who arranged the deal instead of to the owner of the
equipment. The court quite possibly gave insufficient attention to whether the payment was identifiable.

And in Brown v. Brown, 152 S.W.3d 911 (Mo. Ct. App. 2005), two deeds were
recorded in the wrong order, so that the last deed conveyed the family home back
to the elderly mother instead of, as she had intended, to mother and daughter as
joint tenants with right of survivorship. When the mother died without a will, the
property passed to all her children in equal shares. The court imposed a constructive trust on behalf of the daughter, who should have taken the property under the
joint tenancy. The court relied mostly on the testimony of the lawyer who drafted
the deeds.

2. Arbitrary results? Now go back to the mechanics of tracing. One argument
against the tracing fictions is that they tend to produce arbitrary results in all but the
simplest cases. How much Bank of America recovers depends on the history of the
account subsequent to the mistake—on $6.5 million in deposits and withdrawals
that have nothing to do with the wrong. If a large check clears the day before a large
deposit is made available, the lowest intermediate balance may be close to zero; if
the check arrives the day after the deposit, the lowest intermediate balance may still
exceed the full amount of the loss.

3. End of day or intraday? The result also depends on whether the court considers
only the balance at the end of each day or also considers fluctuations during a single
day. Historically, most cases relied on closing daily balances, holding out the possibility that this could be rebutted by a showing of the actual order in which items were
paid. The cases are collected in 1 George E. Palmer, *The Law of Restitution* §2.16(a) at
200-201 (Little Brown 1978).

In the older cases, such evidence was rarely available; today, with pervasive computerization, banks know the exact order in which items were posted to an account. Laycock's banker told him that except for items presented face to face at the teller window, banks post all of a day's checks in a batch at the end of the day, and each bank has a formula for deciding the order in which a day's items are posted. Within these batches, nearly all banks post deposits before withdrawals. This order for posting may be arbitrary, and is rarely chronological; checks are often posted in order of size. But if an account is overdrawn, the items posted last are the ones that bounce. First Security might have done things differently, or maybe its branch manager just focused on the arbitrariness of the formula rather than the consequences for bouncing checks. Did the trustee in bankruptcy give up too easily on the intraday balance?

4. Collected balance or available balance? It is no accident that the lowest intermediate available balance is much lower than the lowest intermediate collected balance. With the available balance, checks were subtracted immediately but deposits were not added for a week or more. Did the court make an arbitrary choice between the two means of calculating? Or did it hold that the debtor could not withdraw its own money first when there was a hold on that money?

5. The lowest intermediate balance is usually low. Cash tends to disappear rapidly when companies are going broke or bad guys are getting caught. Large balances are scarce, and continuous large balances scarcer still. Statisticians have shown that if the cash flow through the account is large in proportion to the closing daily balances, the probability is very high that the balance will approach zero over any period of a few days or more. Michael O. Finkelstein & Herbert Robbins, *A Probabilistic Approach to Tracing Presumptions in the Law of Restitution*, 24 Jurimetrics J. 65 (1983).

6. Inexorable logic? The arbitrariness in complex cases is the direct consequence of rules that seem fairer in simple cases. If 100 stolen dollars are added to an account with 50 legitimately earned dollars, it is easy to say the stolen dollars are in the account. It seems harsh to say the stolen dollars are already unidentifiable and gone forever. If $50 is spent, it is easy to say the remaining $100 is stolen. Once you say that, all the money in the account is stolen, and it logically follows that if another $10 is spent, the remaining $90 is still stolen money. This is the essential leap in the tracing fictions; if you don't like the fictions, you have to say that the $90 is unidentifiable. But if you say that, what sense does it make to say the $100 was identifiable the day before? Or at any point after it was deposited?

If you say the $90 is identifiable as stolen money, and if 60 more legitimately earned dollars are then deposited, it is not even fictional to say the $60 was earned and is not the money that was stolen. Once you say that, you have the whole lowest intermediate balance rule with all its sometime arbitrariness.

7. Problems of proof. *Ruffin* says that plaintiff must prove her right to constructive trust by clear and convincing evidence. Such statements are common, and sometimes true. As the court explains in Hopwood v. Pickett, 761 A.2d 436 (N.H. 2000), this rule is necessary when plaintiff is claiming property that defendant appears to own under recorded deeds or other written instruments. This is the same rule we saw in reformation, in section 7.C; a litigant who seeks to overcome written records with oral testimony is held to a high burden of proof. In *Hopwood*, the court required only a preponderance of the evidence for plaintiff's claim that her surviving brother had murdered their deceased brother, and thus could not inherit.

The tracing cases reflect two very different standards of proof, and they sometimes talk about it explicitly. When the dispute is between the victim and the wrongdoer, uncertainties are resolved against the wrongdoer, and plaintiff can sometimes fill gaps in the record with inference or circumstantial evidence. But when the real dispute is between the victim and other innocent creditors of the wrongdoer, the restitution plaintiff is held to a higher standard of proof. These two standards are labeled "strict" and "liberal" tracing in In re Goldberg, 168 B.R. 382, 385 (B.A.P. 9th Cir. 1994). Goldberg got a $17,000 check by mistake, cashed it, and shortly thereafter made a $15,000 down payment on a house. The victim of the mistake couldn't trace the funds; the debtor at one point seemed to admit that he had used those funds, then tried to withdraw that admission. He gave no other account of how he had made the down payment without using those funds. 158 B.R. 188 (Bankr. E.D. Cal. 1993). Both the Bankruptcy Court and the Bankruptcy Appellate Panel held that the funds were sufficiently traced under liberal tracing standards. Those standards applied because the homestead was exempt from the claims of other creditors, so the real contest was between the victim and the beneficiary of the mistake.

There are cases where large sums of money disappear for a while and then reappear in the hands of a defendant with no other apparent source for such a sum of money. In Ayers v. Fay, 102 P.2d 156 (Okla. 1940), the ne'er-do-well administrator of an estate withdrew the estate's assets in cash and disappeared, reappearing shortly thereafter in Oklahoma with large sums of cash. He lived beyond his apparent means, had a heart attack, married his nurse, and left his money to her when he died. The heirs of the Vermont estate sued his Oklahoma widow in restitution. Emphasizing that the defendant was not a creditor, the court held the money sufficiently traced.

NOTES ON ADVANCED TRACING ISSUES

1. Tracing into assets worth more than plaintiff lost. We have seen that restitution awards the profits of conscious wrongdoers to their victims, even when those profits exceed the victims' losses. Tracing is one way to do this; defendant may use misappropriated property to acquire more valuable property. Recall the attempt to trace into the winning lottery ticket in Ruffin v. Ruffin in section 8.C.1.

Suppose that in *Erie Trust* the Leichner property were suddenly worth $50,000 because of an oil strike on adjacent land. If the Gingrich heirs are the true owners of the land, shouldn't the whole $50,000 belong to them? Even though they lost only $25,000? That is the logical conclusion of a constructive trust, and most courts would probably reach that result if the wrongdoer were solvent. Otherwise defendant would profit from his own wrong. Such windfall gains are rare, and solvent defendants nearly as rare, so the issue has not been widely litigated.

2. But what if defendant is insolvent? In *Erie Trust*, the wrongdoer was bankrupt. Should the heirs still recover $50,000 through a constructive trust? Professor Palmer reported that "although the issue is seldom noted in the cases, . . . almost as a matter of course" the courts award no more than the victim's actual losses when other creditors remain unpaid. 1 George E. Palmer, *The Law of Restitution* §2.14(c) at 183-184 (Little Brown 1978). This can be explained as an equitable lien rather than a constructive trust: Victims get a judgment for the amount of their loss and a lien on the traced asset to secure the judgment. Or it can be explained as subordination, as in the *Restatement (Third)*.

3. The *Restatement (Third)*. The *Restatement (Third)* says that the portion of any restitution claim "exceeding the claimant's loss is subordinated to the claims of the recipient's creditors." §61(a). This limitation applies to disgorgement of cash as well as to tracing claims to identifiable property. So plaintiff gets all the profits from a conscious wrongdoer, but only plaintiff's loss if other creditors are unpaid, plus whatever can be paid of the restitution claim with amounts remaining after the other creditors are paid.

A similar provision says that restitution "from assets that would otherwise go to innocent dependents of a deceased recipient is limited to the amount of the claimant's loss." §61(b). The target here is life insurance. If defendant uses stolen money to buy a life insurance policy and promptly dies, the investment can be extraordinarily profitable. There are a fair number of these cases, but in most of them, the deceased also stole lots of other money that could not be traced, so that the policy proceeds do not exceed the victim's losses.

A bankruptcy court followed this rule in In re Dreier LLP, 452 B.R. 391, 439-440 (S.D.N.Y. 2011):

> Based on a theory of equity, "if a supracompensatory award to the restitution claimant would come at the expense of a third party who is innocent of the underlying wrong: typically, an unpaid creditor or a surviving dependent of the wrongdoing recipient," a court may exercise its discretion in declining to award a recovery to the restitution claimant.

Id. at 440, quoting *Restatement (Third)* §61, cmt. *a.*

4. Disproportion. Think again about Ruffin v. Ruffin. Suppose the husband *had* bought the winning lottery ticket with the wife's money. Suppose he stopped by to see the kids, pocketed two dollars sitting on the counter, and used those bills to buy the lottery ticket—and his wife can prove it because he gleefully told the story to a friend. The $4.9 million in lottery winnings is the traceable product of the stolen two dollars. Does Mrs. Ruffin get a constructive trust over the whole $4.9 million?

Maybe not under the *Restatement (Third)*. Tracing "may be limited" where the property traced "is grossly disproportionate to any loss on which the claimant's right to restitution is based." §58(3)(c). Note that it doesn't say "must be"; culpability may matter to the choice. The illustration of this provision is based on a hypothetical. A life insurance case might provide a real example, but those cases are treated separately (see note 3). Tracing into the winning lottery ticket is a beloved classroom hypothetical, and someday it may happen, but in the real world, nothing like it appears to have happened in a restitution case.

But there are at least two cases of drug dealers using their illegal drug income to buy a winning lottery ticket. People v. $35,315.00 United States Currency, 64 N.E.3d 854 (Ill. App. Ct. 2016); United States v. Betancourt, 422 F.3d 240 (5th Cir. 2005). The lottery winnings in *Betancourt* were $5.4 million! Identifiable proceeds of crime are generally returned to the rightful owner or forfeited to the prosecuting jurisdiction, and with drug dealer defendants, neither court was troubled by any argument about disproportionality.

5. Multiple claimants. What if there are many victims of a fraud? The fraudster is presumed to withdraw his own money first, but it is impossible for each plaintiff to insist that the fraudster withdrew the other victims' money before touching the plaintiff's money. Money that is unambiguously identifiable, without resort to presumption or fiction, generally goes back to its owner (although some cases now dissent from that). Money that can be identified only with the help of presumptions is shared pro rata by all victims of the fraud.

a. The original Ponzi scheme. The classic case is Cunningham v. Brown, 265 U.S. 1 (1924). In December 1919, Charles Ponzi advertised that he would borrow money from anyone willing to lend; he promised a 50 percent return in 90 days. He claimed that he could pay such returns by exploiting distortions in exchange rates resulting from World War I. To boost the confidence of potential victims, he also offered to refund principal on demand before the 90 days were up. By July of 1920, Ponzi was taking in a million dollars a week from small investors.

He accumulated the money in checking accounts. He used the money received from later victims to pay the promised 50 percent return to earlier victims. This feature—using principal from new victims to pay the promised income to earlier victims—is the essence of what are now known as Ponzi schemes. Such a scheme can work for as long as the pool of victims continues to expand; sooner or later it must collapse when there is not enough new money to pay off older obligations.

On August 2, a Boston newspaper reported that Ponzi was hopelessly insolvent. Thousands of victims demanded refunds and Ponzi honored their claims until his funds were exhausted on August 9. Thousands of others were left unpaid. Ponzi's trustee in bankruptcy successfully claimed that the refunds were voidable preferences—payments that must be returned because they had preferred some creditors over others in the last days before bankruptcy. Those who had received the preferences said they had rescinded for fraud and reclaimed their own property, but no victim before the Court could identify his property without the aid of presumptions, and the Court refused to let plaintiffs invoke the tracing presumptions against other fraud victims. The Court treated all the fraud victims as a group, with an equal right to priority over any other creditors. Those who had gotten their money out had to put it back in, and then all the proceeds of the fraud were divided among all the victims.

The rule of Cunningham v. Brown is applied, and explained in a short and simple opinion, in In re Foster, 275 F.3d 924 (10th Cir. 2001). You get tracing, a clear explanation of lowest intermediate balance, and no tracing fictions as between multiple victims, all in just over two pages.

b. Bernard Madoff. Cunningham v. Brown is of obvious relevance to the notorious Ponzi scheme perpetrated by Bernard Madoff. In re Bernard L. Madoff Investment Securities LLC, 424 B.R. 122 (Bankr. S.D.N.Y. 2010). Madoff offered private investment management with fabulous profits for many years; in fact, there were no investments and all the profits were fictitious. Investors who withdrew money were paid with the money from new investors. The court held that the trustee in bankruptcy can recover "profits" paid out to withdrawing investors—all amounts withdrawn minus all amounts invested—within the statute of limitations. *Id.* at 135-136 & n.29.

Because Madoff's scheme was structured as equity investments rather than as loans, these payments are recoverable as fraudulent transfers rather than as preferences. Distributions of "profits" are fraudulent transfers because the investors gave nothing of value in exchange for these fictitious profits. For an opinion more extensively devoted to explaining that rule, see Donell v. Kowell, 533 F.3d 762, 770-778 (9th Cir. 2008). After the distributed "profits" are returned to the trustee, each investor gets a pro rata distribution of the available funds, calculated on the basis of his net investment—money put in less money taken out, with no credit for the fictitious profits shown on his monthly statements.

The court of appeals affirmed on the essential disputed point—that the rights and liability of Madoff's customers should be based on their cash investment net of withdrawals, and not on the last fictitious statement of their supposed holdings. 654 F.3d 229 (2d Cir. 2011).

c. What if some victims' money was segregated? In *Cunningham* and *Madoff*, no victim could identify her money without the aid of presumptions. Compare Securities & Exchange Commission v. Credit Bancorp, Ltd., 290 F.3d 80 (2d Cir. 2002), where one victim was induced to transfer 8 million shares of Vintage Petroleum to the company operating the Ponzi scheme. When the case was decided, the shares were sitting in the fraudster's account, unchanged in form and easily identifiable without regard to any presumption. This is as close as the real world gets to the pickpocket on the courthouse steps. Even so, the court included the shares in the pool of assets to be distributed pro rata to all the victims. And it cited several recent cases to similar effect.

Professor Andrew Kull, the reporter for the *Restatement (Third)*, condemns these cases as the unexplained "product of error and inattention," distributing one victim's property to other victims. §59, reporter's note *g*. Kull seems clearly right under traditional rules, but when several circuits have done it, this may be a new trend rather than an error. What Cunningham v. Brown actually says is that victims could reclaim their own money if they could identify it, 265 U.S. at 11, but that they could not use fictional presumptions in their attempt to identify it, *id.* at 12-13. The *Restatement (Third)* states the same rule. §59(4).

Professor Kull has expanded on his criticism in Andrew Kull, *Ponzi, Property, and Luck,* 100 Iowa L. Rev. 291 (2014). He says that "[n]ew decisions in Ponzi cases start from a simple premise: that it would be inequitable that victims' recoveries (and hence losses) 'be skewed based on fortuity even though everyone was defrauded in the same manner.'" *Id.* at 319, quoting Commodity Futures Trading Commission v. Rolando, 2008 WL 5225851, *4 (D. Conn. 2008). Kull writes that "judges in the recent Ponzi cases see themselves not as returning property to its owners, but as allocating losses. . . . What was once a problem in property has become a problem in tort." Kull, 100 Iowa L. Rev. at 319.

An English example with great facts is Commerzbank AG v. IMB Morgan PLC, [2005] 1 Lloyd's Rep. 298 (Ch. 2004), involving proceeds of a Nigerian e-mail scam. Yes, some people answer those e-mails, and some people send thousands of dollars to cover the "expenses" of transferring millions of dollars back to the victim. Of course the return transfer never comes. The fraudster had two accounts, one in U.S. dollars and one in British pounds, each containing the money of victims who had paid in that currency. The court treated the two accounts as completely separate and identifiable to the pool of victims who had paid in that currency, but it treated the money within each account as not further identifiable to individual victims. Dollar victims got 9 percent of their money back; pound victims got 46 percent, because the fraudsters had spent less money from the pound account.

6. Tracing through replacements. There is a separate line of cases—a handful of cases—that appears to trace through replacements rather than exchanges.

a. Life insurance and divorce. Most of these arise out of divorce decrees that require one spouse to maintain life insurance for the benefit of the other. To simplify the prose, assume that Husband is to maintain life insurance for Wife 1. Husband may change the beneficiary on an existing policy, or the existing insurance policy may lapse for some reason, usually a change of employment. Then Husband gets a new policy and names Wife 2 as beneficiary. Then he dies, leaving an insolvent estate. Wife 1 could sue for breach of contract, or sue for violation of the divorce decree, but there are no assets from which to collect a judgment. She gets nothing unless she gets a constructive trust in the insurance policy.

It is clear that no money from Policy 1 was used to acquire Policy 2. Policy 2 is not traceable under the usual rules, and some courts have ruled for Wife 2 on that basis. Other courts have granted Wife 1 a constructive trust in Policy 2, on the ground that Policy 2 was a replacement for Policy 1 and therefore subject to the requirements of the divorce decree. The leading case is Rogers v. Rogers, 473 N.E.2d 226 (N.Y. 1984). In Foster v. Hurley, 826 N.E.2d 719 (Mass. 2005), where it was the wife's life insurance at issue, the court granted Husband 1 a constructive trust in the policy that had existed at the time of divorce (she had changed the beneficiary), but not in a second policy acquired later, even though the first policy was not large enough to satisfy the divorce decree. *Rogers* talks about relaxing the usual tracing rules, but the *Restatement (Third)* wisely views *Rogers* as simply applying a different rule. §48, reporter's note *d(4)*, §58, reporter's note *e.*

These cases, and similar state statutes (some protecting the first spouse, some the second), are often preempted by federal law. Preemption can arise when federal benefits are at issue; more generally, ERISA (the Employee Retirement Income Security Act) can preempt with respect to insurance with private employers. An example that cites some of the others is Hillman v. Maretta, 569 U.S. 483 (2013).

In Egelhoff v. Egelhoff, 532 U.S. 141, 152 (2001), the Court reserved judgment on whether ERISA preempts state-law rules that bar killers from inheriting from their victim. The Court hinted that these rules might be so old and well established that they could survive. And the Seventh Circuit subsequently held that ERISA does not preempt the Illinois slayer statute. The effect on ERISA was too attenuated, and Congress surely did not intend to preempt the slayer rule and reward killers. So a wife who murdered her husband but was acquitted on grounds of insanity could not collect his pension. The pension went to their child, who was the alternative beneficiary. Laborers' Pension Fund v. Miscevic, 880 F.3d 927 (7th Cir. 2018), *cert. denied*, 138 S. Ct. 2633 (2018).

b. Time zones. Consider Agip (Africa) Ltd. v. Jackson, [1991] Chancery 547 (Ct. App.), where the Banque de Sud in Tunis telexed Lloyd's Bank in London to credit an account of defendants' company with $518,000, and telexed Citibank in New York to debit the Banque de Sud's account and credit Lloyd's account with the same sum. It turned out that the Banque de Sud was acting on a forged payment order. Citibank and Lloyd's both executed their instructions at the opening of business on January 7, which meant that Lloyd's paid out in London five hours before it collected in New York. Defendants argued that the money credited to their company's account could not possibly have been the money that Citibank received from the Banque de Sud, and thus tracing failed. The court of appeal disagreed.

Citibank was neither insolvent nor a wrongdoer; why not cover the five-hour gap by tracing through Citibank's obligation to reimburse Lloyd's? Isn't that asset just as real as a credit to Lloyd's account in New York? The *Restatement (Third)* argues that physical exchanges are irrelevant here; it is enough that the funds from Citibank were the replacement for the funds from Lloyd's.

TRACING PROBLEMS

This problem set consists of three separate problems. Each involves the same characters and the same starting position.

Scum manages a trust fund for his aged mother. At the beginning, the trust contains the following assets:

- 100 shares of Microsoft worth $30 per share
- 100 shares of Exxon Mobil worth $50 per share
- 100 shares of Walmart worth $60 per share

Scum has $10,000 of his own cash in a separate checking account.

Scum encounters financial difficulties and begins to embezzle from his mother's account. He eventually files for bankruptcy. There are many creditors, so a damage judgment for the amount embezzled will not be worth much. In each problem, each transaction occurs on a separate day in the order listed. Identify the assets on which his mother can impose a constructive trust. Disregard brokerage commissions.

Problem 8-1

1. Scum sells 100 shares of Walmart from his mother's account, receiving $6,000 in cash.
2. He takes the cash to another broker and buys 300 shares of General Electric at $20.
3. General Electric drops to $10, so the shares are now worth $3,000.
4. There is still $10,000 in Scum's personal checking account.

Problem 8-2

1. Scum sells 100 shares of Microsoft from his mother's account, receiving $3,000 in cash. He deposits the money in his checking account, raising the balance to $13,000.
2. He withdraws $12,000 from the checking account and flies to Las Vegas. He loses the entire $12,000 gambling. This leaves $1,000 in the account.
3. He receives a $4,000 legal fee and deposits that money in the checking account, raising the balance to $5,000.
4. He sells 100 shares of Exxon Mobil from his mother's account, receiving $5,000 in cash. He deposits the money in the checking account, raising the balance to $10,000.
5. He writes an $8,000 check on the checking account, buying 1,000 shares of Casino Co. at $8. This leaves $2,000 in the account.
6. He loses the remaining $2,000 in the account in a poker game.
7. Casino Co. rises to $12, so the 1,000 shares are now worth $12,000.

Problem 8-3

1. Scum sells 100 shares of Walmart from this mother's account, receiving $6,000 in cash. He deposits the money in his checking account, raising the balance to $16,000.
2. He writes a $6,000 check on his own account, buying 300 shares of General Electric at $20. This leaves $10,000 in the account.
3. He loses $8,000 in a poker game and pays with money from his checking account. This leaves $2,000 in the account.
4. General Electric drops to $10, so the 100 shares are now worth $3,000.

3.   Equitable Liens and Subrogation

IN RE MESA

232 B.R. 508 (Bankr. S.D. Fla. 1999)

RAYMOND B. RAY, Bankruptcy Judge.

   This matter came before the Court for evidentiary hearing on March 2, 1999 upon the Objection of Travelers Indemnity Company . . . to Debtor's Claimed Homestead Exemption. . . .

FINDINGS OF FACT

In June 1996, the Debtor, Alberto V. Mesa, and Keith S. McKay purchased a residence located at 2749 N.E. 28th Street in Fort Lauderdale, Florida. . . . The Debtor scheduled his one-half interest in this home as exempt property under the home-stead exemption provided in art. X, §4(a) of the Florida Constitution.

The Debtor and McKay acquired the home as tenants in common and resided together in the home, sharing living expenses. The Debtor testified that the home was purchased for $215,000.00, but that the present market value of the home is $250,000.00. Schedule D to the Voluntary Petition lists first and second mortgages held by NationsBank in the respective amounts of $157,000.00 and $67,649.55. The Debtor testified that the second mortgage was to secure a home improvement loan, but that the money was actually used to finance a new business started by McKay after he lost his job with Travelers. Assuming the Debtor's estimate of present fair market value to be correct, and that the mortgage loans have not been paid down, there is approximately $25,000.00 of equity in the home.[3]

At the time the Debtor and McKay purchased the home, McKay was a claims adjuster for Travelers. Upon acquiring the home, the Debtor and McKay commenced an extensive home renovation project. New electrical work, plumbing, and air conditioning were installed throughout the house. Three bathrooms were completely remodeled and new fixtures were installed. The kitchen and garage were completely remodeled, all of the windows and flooring were replaced, and an addition to the master bedroom was built. In the Debtor's words, "It was redone almost completely."

To fund the project, McKay fraudulently caused checks, payable by Travelers, to be issued to the Debtor (17 checks totaling $147,977.70), the Debtor's mother, Rogelia Tarifa, (4 checks totaling $35,528.15) and to construction contractors and suppliers (checks totaling $194,909.76).

The Debtor testified that these amounts were used to pay for the home remodeling project, and that he was told by McKay that the checks were drawn on McKay's retirement account. . . .

Based upon the overall facts and circumstances, and in view of the many contradictions and gaps in the Debtor's explanation for what transpired, and also in consideration of the Debtor's demeanor on the witness stand, the Court disbelieves the Debtor's testimony that he lacked knowledge of the fraudulent diversion of Travelers' funds. The Court finds that the Debtor knew that some or all of the funds were obtained fraudulently by McKay. The Court further finds that the Debtor knowingly assisted and participated in the fraud by accepting payments made to him, by assisting in the use of his mother's account, and by actively participating in the use of the fraudulently obtained funds to pay for the home renovations and improvements.

CONCLUSIONS OF LAW

The Debtor seeks an exemption for his one-half interest in the home in reliance upon art. X, §4(a), which provides an exemption for homestead property.[5] Travelers objects to the homestead exemption on two grounds: (1) that the Debtor knowingly assisted McKay in fraudulently obtaining funds from Travelers and using such funds to pay for improvements to the homestead; and (2) that the Debtor would be unjustly

---

3. However, based on the purchase price of $215,000.00 and the amounts invested in renovating the home, . . . it is possible that the present market value exceeds the $250,000.00 amount estimated by the Debtor. The parties did not introduce any appraisals or other independent evidence of the value of the home as improved.

5. 11 U.S.C. §522(b)(2)(A) provides that a debtor may exempt property which is exempt under state law. . . . Thus, but for the objection interposed by Travelers, the Debtor's interest in his homestead would be exempt.

enriched at the expense of Travelers should the Court not impose an equitable lien on the home. . . .

[T]he Court has found, based on substantial evidence, that the Debtor was not innocent of wrongdoing, but knowingly assisted in and benefitted from the fraudulent scheme. Under the facts presented, there is ample authority for the imposition of an equitable lien in favor of Travelers.

Art. X, §4(a) . . . grants an exemption from forced sale of a homestead subject to certain stated exceptions. The homestead exemption, however, is subject to equitable liens "beyond the literal language. . . ." Palm Beach Savings & Loan Association v. Fishbein, 619 So. 2d 267, 270 (Fla. 1993).

In Jones v. Carpenter, 106 So. 127 (Fla. 1925), . . . the defendant, the president of an insolvent corporation, tortiously converted corporate funds to pay for labor and improvements to a recently acquired home. The creditors of the corporation elected a bankruptcy trustee who filed an action against the defendant to impose a lien on the homestead. The defendant asserted the homestead exemption as a defense. The Florida Supreme Court concluded that it could not let the defendant enjoy "tortiously acquired property" and granted an equitable lien in favor of the corporation's creditors. *Id.* at 130.

The rule stated in *Jones* that a homestead cannot be employed as an instrumentality of fraud has been restated in numerous Florida cases. It has been relied on in bankruptcy cases to disallow a homestead exemption or to impose a lien on homestead property. . . .

The funds at issue in this case were stolen from Travelers and invested in improvements to the Debtor's homestead. . . . *See also* In re Popek, 188 B.R. 701 (Bankr. S.D. Fla. 1995) (denying objection to homestead exemption where creditor did not allege that debtor purchased homestead with fraudulently obtained funds "traceable to the objecting creditor"). . . .

Thus, this case can be decided squarely within the holding of *Jones v. Carpenter* which remains the law in Florida.

As an additional argument, Travelers relies on the exception in art. X, §4(a) for "obligations contracted for the purchase, improvement or repair" of a homestead. McKay and the Debtor contracted with various construction contractors and suppliers to improve the homestead. These creditors were paid at least $194,909.76 with funds which were fraudulently obtained from Travelers. Therefore, Travelers argues, it should be equitably subrogated to the position of the contractors and suppliers, and should be granted an equitable lien for this amount. The Court agrees. . . . However, in view of the Court's conclusion . . . that Travelers is entitled to an equitable lien for the total amount invested in the home remodeling project, it is not necessary to impose an equitable lien for a lesser amount based on a subrogation theory.

CONCLUSION AND ORDER

The Debtor knew about and assisted in the fraudulent obtaining of funds from Travelers. The imposition of an equitable lien in favor of Travelers is necessary to prevent the Debtor from using the homestead exemption as an instrument of fraud and to prevent the Debtor's unjust enrichment at Travelers' expense. An equitable lien may provide a means for Travelers to recover at least a portion of the funds which were misappropriated.

The amount of the equitable lien must be based on the amount of funds obtained from Travelers which were invested in the remodeling of the home and related expenses. Checks totaling $194,909.76 were paid to various contractors and suppliers involved in the home remodeling project. The Debtor testified that the amounts deposited in and withdrawn from his mother's account (totaling $35,528.15) also were used for the remodeling project. The Debtor also testified that the seventeen checks payable to him (totaling $147,977.70) were used to pay for expenses associated with the home remodeling project, except, perhaps, for portions of two checks which the Debtor claims to have received in partial repayment of his down payment on the purchase of the home.

The total of these amounts, $378,415.61, dwarfs the present equity in the house, which, according to the Debtor's testimony, may not be more than $25,000. Nevertheless, the Court will impose an equitable lien for the full amount of $378,415.61. If, contrary to the Debtor's testimony, a smaller amount was invested in the home improvements, there is no prejudice to the Debtor since the total amount paid to contractors and suppliers alone far exceeds the probable equity in the home.

Based on the foregoing, it is hereby

ORDERED AND ADJUDGED as follows:

1. Travelers' objection to homestead exemption is sustained.

2. Travelers is granted an equitable lien in the amount of $378,415.61 which shall bear interest at the Federal rate of interest applicable to Federal judgments.

3. The Debtor's homestead exemption shall not be a defense to any action by Travelers to enforce its equitable lien by foreclosure or otherwise. . . .

NOTES ON EQUITABLE LIENS

1. The basic idea. The equitable lien is a money judgment secured by a lien on specific property; occasionally, it is just a lien for a specific amount, with no judgment collectible out of defendant's other assets. It is not fictional; once created, it is a real lien. But like the quasi-contract and the constructive trust, it is a lien created by the court, without regard to the intentions of the parties. Like the constructive trust, it is enforceable in bankruptcy (subject to the objections of those who think *Omegas* is a great opinion), and so it protects against the risk of defendant's insolvency.

And it is a tracing remedy; Travelers must prove that its money was used to remodel the house. The lien attaches to specific property into which the victim's money can be traced. If Mesa and McKay had used their home improvement loan for the home improvements, and used the stolen money to start McKay's business, Travelers would have to trace its money into the business instead of into the house.

2. Equitable lien and constructive trust. In *Paoloni* and *Leitner*, in section 8.C.1, the victims of fraud and embezzlement got the house (or its proceeds) in constructive trust. Travelers gets only an equitable lien on the house. What is the difference?

There will be no difference at the bottom line for Travelers, because the value of its equitable lien is much greater than the equity in the house. Travelers will foreclose its lien, get all the cash proceeds from the house, and have an unsecured judgment for the rest of the embezzled money. But suppose that only $10,000 of Travelers' money could be traced into the house. How does the court know whether to give an equitable lien for $10,000 instead of a constructive trust over a fractional portion of the house?

In *Paoloni* and *Leitner*, the wrongfully acquired money was used to buy the house. Plaintiffs who can trace their money into the purchase price are treated as purchasers, or as fractional co-purchasers if defendant used some of the victims' money and some of his own. In *Mesa*, defendant already owned the house. Travelers' money was not used to buy it, but only to improve it. Equitable lien is the standard remedy when plaintiff's money is traced into improvements to defendant's property. For a substantial discussion of that rule, see Campbell v. Superior Court, 34 Cal. Rptr. 3d 68, 79-81 (Ct. App. 2005).

3. Why does it matter? The difference matters when the property changes in value. An owner gets the benefit of any appreciation and bears the risk of any depreciation. A lien holder has a secured claim for her fixed amount, whatever happens to the value of the property.

Consider Robinson v. Robinson, 429 N.E.2d 183 (Ill. App. Ct. 1981), where, in 1969-1970, a young couple built their house on his parents' land. They reasonably expected to eventually own the land, but that never happened; when they divorced sometime in the late 1970s, his parents still owned the land and everything attached to the land, including the new house. The 1970s and early 1980s were a period of very high inflation. The house appears to have cost about $27,000 plus the labor of family and friends; when the case was tried, it was worth $56,000; and after remand from the appellate court, it was probably worth more. It made a big difference whether the ex-wife was given half the cost in 1969 (treating the house as an improvement to the parents' land) or half the value of the house in 1981 (treating her as a half owner of the house). The Illinois courts did not really attend to this choice, and they awarded something of a hybrid remedy. They called the remedy equitable lien, but they awarded half the value of the house at the time of trial, secured by a lien on the house.

The categories should not be so rigid as to prevent that choice. Treating her as a half-owner responded to the equities of the situation. But setting a fixed dollar value on her claim at the time of trial might have enabled defendants to buy her half without having to sell the house. If the house had to be sold after all, it might have made sense to give her half the proceeds instead of an amount fixed at trial. Whatever the choice, it is important to make the choice on a reasoned basis and not by default or failure to consider the alternatives.

4. An aside: the substantive theory in *Robinson*. *Robinson* was a variation on mistaken improvers. The young couple was not mistaken in the necessary sense of wholly oblivious to the possibility that the land was not theirs. They knew it was not theirs, but they had a reasonable expectation that it would become theirs. There are enough such cases that the *Restatement (Third)* treats them separately in §27. Another case like this is Ward v. Ward, discussed in the Notes on Mistaken Improvers in section 8.A.1, involving the son and daughter-in-law who build the $50,000 cabin on the mother's land. The court said the daughter-in-law would be entitled to an equitable lien in an amount to be determined on remand, and that she could stay on the property in the meantime.

5. Heads, I win; tails, you lose. The strongest remedy courts can give a plaintiff is a choice between constructive trust and equitable lien. If plaintiff can trace into property worth more than she lost, she will elect the constructive trust. If the traceable property is worth less than she lost, she will seek a money judgment for the full amount of the loss and an equitable lien on the traceable property to secure the judgment. Then she can claim the property under the equitable lien and still have a personal judgment for the rest of her loss. In effect, gains go to the victims, and losses fall on the wrongdoer. This choice is generally available to victims of a conscious wrongdoer or misappropriating fiduciary. See note 9 following *Paoloni*, in section 8.C.1.

6. Why so many house cases? It is not entirely coincidence that three cases in the tracing materials involve tracing into houses. We haven't been looking for house cases, and the rules on tracing into houses are no different than the rules on tracing into other assets. But most bad guys steal for consumption, not for investment, and most consumption quickly disappears. A house is a consumption item that neither disappears nor quickly depreciates, and it is not surprising that successful tracing plaintiffs often trace their money into houses.

7. What did Mesa know and why do we care? The court finds that Mesa knew his partner had stolen the money used to remodel the house. But why should that matter? Mesa paid nothing for his share of the improvements paid for with the embezzled money; even if he completely believed the claim that all the money came from his partner's retirement account, Mesa did nothing in reliance on that belief. We take up the rights of third parties in section 8.D.

8. Innocent defendants. Many equitable lien defendants are innocent recipients of benefits that improve or preserve their property. Plaintiffs who work on the wrong property by mistake, or save property in an emergency, or pay more than their share of the necessary expenses on jointly owned property, typically get an equitable lien on the property they benefited. The lien is for the value of the benefit or the cost of producing it, whichever is less.

9. A limited remedy to protect defendants. Sometimes courts award equitable liens subject to conditions, creating a limited remedy to protect innocent defendants. Where a money judgment would impose a forced exchange, the court may award a nonrecourse equitable lien—a lien enforceable only against the traced property, with no judgment collectible from any other asset. If a forced sale of the property would also impose a hardship, the court can prohibit plaintiff from enforcing the lien until defendant dies or voluntarily sells the property.

An example is Jones v. Sacramento Savings & Loan Association, 56 Cal. Rptr. 741 (Ct. App. 1967). Here the defendant is sleazy but technically innocent; the court viewed him as not having done anything wrong. An unidentified lender loaned a builder money to buy lots in a subdivision. The lender recorded a first mortgage, but that mortgage had a clause providing that it would be subordinated to a construction mortgage under certain conditions. Sacramento Savings loaned substantially more money to build houses on the lots. It filed its mortgage second, relying on the first mortgage's subordination clause. The builder completed the houses and then defaulted on both loans.

At this point, Jones bought the first mortgage from the first lender for a fraction of its face value. Both Jones and Sacramento foreclosed and bought the houses at their own foreclosure sale. The court held that Sacramento had failed to satisfy the conditions of the subordination clause, so that Jones had first priority and his foreclosure sale cut off Sacramento's junior interest. The effect was that Jones had bought finished houses for a fraction of the cost of the undeveloped lots. The court held that this was unjust enrichment and awarded Sacramento an equitable lien. But it severely restricted Sacramento's right to enforce the lien:

> Equity imposes a lien here not to vindicate a wrong but to prevent unjust enrichment. The objective may be accomplished by a decree impressing the lien but without demanding an immediate sale. Equitable liens in favor of Sacramento Savings should be paid off at such times and under such circumstances as will avoid undue hardship on Jones. . . . Framing of an appropriate decree to protect the parties' respective interests should await further inquiry and consideration by the trial court.
>
> The circumstances do not call for an award of interest as part of the lien, either before or after judgment. . . . The judgment imposing the lien will not be a money judgment, will simply establish a charge on property and will not bear interest in favor of the equitable lienholder. We leave open the question whether interest would run in

the event the landowner failed to pay off the equitable liens in compliance with such conditions as the trial court might embody in the judgment.

Id. at 747.

10. Bungled voluntary liens. *Jones* also illustrates the use of equitable liens to save bungled transactions that were intended to create voluntary liens. There are lots of simpler cases in which a borrower promises to give a mortgage but the parties forget to sign the mortgage documents or the lender forgets to record the mortgage. As between the borrower and lender, it is easy to say the borrower is unjustly enriched. By mistake, he has gotten the loan without giving the mortgage. The temptation to give the lender a mortgage anyway has been almost irresistible.

But the costs of creating an equitable lien typically fall on other creditors. A simple example is In re Destro, 675 F.2d 1037 (9th Cir. 1982), enforcing an equitable lien in bankruptcy even though the mortgage documents had never been signed. A more complicated example is In re Howard's Appliance Corp., 874 F.2d 88 (2d Cir. 1989), where a Long Island retailer bought air conditioners on secured credit. The seller-lender filed in the New York UCC records, which was ineffective after the buyer-debtor began storing the air conditioners at a warehouse in New Jersey. The New Jersey location was a breach of contract, but seller's shipping department knew all about it and shipped direct to New Jersey. No one told the credit manager. The court gave the seller a constructive trust in the air conditioners; the choice between constructive trust and equitable lien didn't matter, because the debt greatly exceeded the value of the air conditioners.

Other creditors could have been paid out of the proceeds of these air conditioners, or out of the property that Destro intended to mortgage but didn't. Why prefer a lender who wanted collateral but bungled the deal over other creditors who deliberately loaned unsecured? At one level, these are cases of restitution for mistake. But this is a special category of mistake; to recognize such claims undermines the integrity of the filing system, which is designed to give other potential creditors notice of all outstanding liens. No lender relies on his debtor receiving two payments for the same invoice, but lenders do rely on the financial information available in the filing system, and the Bankruptcy Code presumes such reliance in every case. Note too that the consequences of filing mistakes tend to last much longer than the consequences of cash mistakes. If you pay the same bill twice, you are protected in bankruptcy only so long as you can identify your cash; even with the help of the tracing fictions, that protection is likely to be short lived. If you forget to file a mortgage, your potential claim to be relieved of that mistake would last as long as the mortgage lasts.

Jones is a less controversial example, because Jones had full notice of Sacramento's claim, no one else appears to have been affected, and there seems to be little doubt that Jones will get back all the money he loaned and more. But those who want to maximize the reliability of the rules relating to mortgages and security interests would object even to *Jones*.

11. The *Restatement (Third)*. The *Restatement (Third)* addresses equitable liens in §56. The remedy is said to be available when "the claimant's assets or services are applied to enhance or preserve the value of particular property to which the recipient has legal title," §56(1)(a), or whenever "the connection between unjust enrichment and the recipient's ownership of particular property makes it equitable that the claimant have recourse to that property for the satisfaction of the recipient's liability in restitution," §56(1)(b). This second provision fails in the *Restatement*'s ambition to reduce the law of restitution to specific rules.

The section explains that an equitable lien "secures the obligation of the recipient to pay the claimant the amount of the recipient's unjust enrichment as separately determined," and that foreclosure "is subject to such conditions as the court may direct." §56(2). Any claimant entitled to constructive trust "may elect to obtain an equitable lien on the property instead," §56(3), so the powerful choice of remedy described in note 5 is made available to all plaintiffs who can establish a claim to constructive trust. Finally, "equitable lien may also be used to restrict the claimant's recovery, in cases where restitution via personal liability or constructive trust would exceed the limits" established to protect innocent defendants or third parties. §56(4). There is no suggestion of any limit to protect the recording statutes; Illustration 15 to §56 is based on Jones v. Sacramento Savings.

12. Capping recovery against innocents. Here's an example of using equitable liens to limit recovery. In Rotary Club v. Chaprales Ramos de Peña, 773 P.2d 467 (Ariz. Ct. App. 1989), a wealthy Mexican citizen left her Tucson residence to the Rotary Club for charitable purposes. She later sold the Tucson house for a series of payments to be made over five years; under Arizona law, these payments became the bequest to the Rotary Club. She died during the five years, and a Mexican probate court struck the Rotary Club from the list of legatees for failure to appear and prove its legal capacity to inherit under the will. But the Arizona court found that there had been no effective notice or service of process, and so it refused to enforce the Mexican judgment against the Rotary Club. Meanwhile, decedent's daughter had used the stream of payments to buy another property in Tucson.

The court held that the daughter was unjustly enriched, but also that she had innocently relied on an apparently valid judgment of the Mexican court. The Rotary Club could trace its money into the purchase price of the new house, which would normally result in a constructive trust. And the new house had appreciated in value. Following the first *Restatement*'s provision equivalent to §50 of the *Restatement (Third)*, the court held that the Rotary Club could not recover more than it had lost from an innocent defendant. And the way to accomplish that was to award an equitable lien for the amount of the original stream of payments, not a constructive trust for a fractional interest in the house.

MORT v. UNITED STATES
86 F.3d 890 (9th Cir. 1996)

Before BEEZER and HAWKINS, Circuit Judges, and ZILLY District Judge.*. . .
    ZILLY, District Judge: . . .

BACKGROUND

[This case arose out of a series of loan transactions secured by real property in Nevada. Simplifying slightly:

Dec. 12, 1990:   DeLee Trust borrows $30,000 from the Kerns; gives mortgage on property.

---

* The Honorable Thomas S. Zilly, United States District Judge for the Western District of Washington, sitting by designation.

Aug. 24, 1992:   IRS files tax lien on the property for $33,000 in income tax
                       due from the Trust.
Nov. 13, 1992:   Trust borrows $38,000 from the Belmonts; gives mortgage on
                       property. Uses loan proceeds to pay off Kerns and to pay off a
                       state tax lien.
                          Fidelity National Title fails to discover federal tax lien and
                       insures title for the Belmonts' interest in the property
Dec. 21, 1992:   Belmonts sell their note, mortgage, and rights under the title
                       policy to the Morts for $38,000.
Aug. 12, 1993:   IRS seizes the property pursuant to its tax lien.

So to summarize, the four liens on the property were filed in this order:
Kern
IRS
Belmont
Mort]

The Morts then filed a complaint in the United States District Court for the District
of Nevada seeking injunctive relief and a declaratory judgment that their trust deed
interest was superior to the federal tax lien [because they were subrogated to the
Kern mortgage, which had priority over the IRS tax lien.] The district court dismissed
the Morts' complaint without prejudice, concluding that the Morts could not bring
their claim for equitable subrogation without first pursuing their legal remedies
against the title insurer. 874 F. Supp. 283 (D. Nev. 1994). . . .

DISCUSSION

I

The district court offered no authority in support of its decision not to exercise equity
jurisdiction in this case, and we are unable to find any. . . . Equitable relief should not
be denied . . . unless the available legal remedy is against the same person from whom
equitable relief is sought.

The Morts have no legal remedy against the IRS. Their only potential legal remedy
is against Fidelity, which is not a party to this action in equity. Because the availability
of a legal remedy against a third party does not bar equitable relief, the district court
abused its discretion in refusing to exercise its equitable jurisdiction.

II . . .
A. Applicable Law

Equitable subrogation is a state-law doctrine. . . . The Internal Revenue Code recognizes that [tax liens are subject to subrogation rights.] 26 U.S.C. §6323(i)(2) (1994).

There is limited Nevada authority on the doctrine of equitable subrogation. The
Nevada Supreme Court first applied the doctrine in Laffranchini v. Clark, 153 P. 250
(Nev. 1915), where it held that the holder of an invalid mortgage was entitled to be
equitably subrogated to the priority position of the lender whose loan she had paid.
Though the Nevada courts have applied equitable subrogation in other contexts,
they have not addressed the equitable subrogation of mortgage or trust deed interests since *Laffranchini*. Where Nevada law is lacking, its courts have looked to the law
of other jurisdictions, particularly California, for guidance. . . .

B. Equitable Subrogation

The doctrine of equitable subrogation allows a person who pays off an encumbrance to assume the same priority position as the holder of the previous encumbrance. Equitable subrogation is generally appropriate where (1) the subrogee made the payment to protect his or her own interest, (2) the subrogee did not act as a volunteer, (3) the subrogee was not primarily liable for the debt paid, (4) the subrogee paid off the entire encumbrance, and (5) subrogation would not work any injustice to the rights of the junior lienholder. Equitable subrogation is a broad equitable remedy, and therefore it applies not only when these five factors are met, but also "whenever 'one person, not acting as a mere volunteer or intruder, pays a debt for which another is primarily liable, and which in equity and good conscience should have been discharged by the latter.'" Han v. United States, 944 F.2d 526, 529 (9th Cir. 1991). . . .

1. Volunteer Status

A volunteer, stranger, or intermeddler is "one who thrusts himself into a situation on his own initiative, and not one who becomes a party to a transaction upon the urgent petition of a person who is vitally interested, and whose rights would be sacrificed did he not respond to the importunate appeal." *Laffranchini*, 153 P. at 252. Parties may be considered volunteers if, in making a payment, they have no interest of their own to protect, they act without any obligation, legal or moral, and they act without being requested to do so by the person liable on the original obligation. A person who lends money to pay off an encumbrance on property and secures the loan with a deed of trust on that property is not a volunteer for purposes of equitable subrogation. In contrast, a person who purchases property at a foreclosure sale is a volunteer and therefore not entitled to subrogation over a tax lien.[3]

The government's argument that the Morts are mere volunteers is based in large part on the Morts' status as assignees of the Belmonts. The government emphasizes that the Belmonts, not the Morts, paid off the Kern note, and the Morts did not acquire the Belmonts' interest in the note and trust deed until after the senior encumbrances had been paid off. We reject the government's argument that the Morts are mere volunteers as a result of their assignee status.

Although Nevada courts have not considered whether an assignee assumes the assignor's equitable subrogation rights, the general rule in most states is that where a valid assignment of a mortgage has been consummated with proper consideration, the assignee is vested with all the powers and rights of the assignor. In this case, the Morts purchased the note and deed of trust, with assignment of rights, from the Belmonts. The Belmonts made a loan to the DeLee Trust to pay off the senior Kern note, and thus, had the Belmonts retained their interest, they would have been entitled to be equitably subrogated to the Kerns' priority position.[4] The Morts, as assignees of the Belmonts, assumed all the rights the Belmonts had in the DeLee note and deed of trust including the Belmonts' right to equitable subrogation of their interest. Thus, the Morts have the same rights to equitable subrogation as the Belmonts.

---

3. . . . In forced sale cases, the purchasers are not paying off existing debts but rather extinguishing all liens by paying any purchase price. Purchasers at forced sales do not pay money in order to satisfy the debt of another, and therefore equitable subrogation does not apply. . . .

4. Government counsel conceded at oral argument that the Belmonts would have been entitled to equitable subrogation had they retained their interest in the note and deed of trust. It is undisputed that the Belmonts were not volunteers and acted to protect their own interests.

2. Injustice to the IRS

The IRS argues that even if the Morts may assert the Belmonts' rights to equitable subrogation, the doctrine should still not be applied because it would work an injustice to the rights of the government. We reject that argument, finding it to be wholly without merit.

At the time the IRS filed its tax lien, the tax lien was subordinate to the Kern mortgage. If the Morts are equitably subrogated to the priority position of the Kern mortgage, the IRS will be in the same position it was in at the time the tax lien was filed. If equitable subrogation is denied, however, the government will receive a windfall, moving up to a better position than it originally had. Under these circumstances, there is no basis for the government's argument that it will suffer harm from equitably subrogating the Morts' interest.

We are equally unpersuaded by the government's argument that the Morts and their title insurer would be unjustly enriched if appellants are equitably subrogated.[5] The Morts are innocent parties. Though they may have had . . . constructive notice of the federal tax lien at the time they acquired their interest from the Belmonts, constructive knowledge does not by itself bar equitable subrogation. As to the unjust enrichment of the title insurance company, the appellee has cited several cases where the title insurance company's negligence has barred the application of equitable subrogation, but in each case the title insurance company itself was seeking equitable subrogation. The equities in those cases are substantially different and for that reason, the cases are inapposite.

CONCLUSION

We hold that the district court abused its discretion in ruling that the appellants must first seek relief from their title insurer before bringing an action for equitable subrogation against the IRS. We further hold that the Morts are entitled to be equitably subrogated to the priority position of the lender whose loan was paid off by the Belmonts. We reverse and remand for entry of judgment in favor of the Morts. . . .

NOTES ON SUBROGATION

1. Vocabulary. "Subrogation" is an old synonym for "substitution"; one claimant is substituted for the other. The subrogee is the person asserting someone else's claim by subrogation; the subrogor is the person to whom the subrogee is subrogated and the person whose claim the subrogee seeks to assert. We will mostly avoid these words, because they are hard to keep straight. But they appear in the cases, and occasionally, to reduce wordiness, they will appear here.

2. Insurance subrogation. We first encountered subrogation as a potential solution, increasingly adopted by law or by contract, to the debate over the collateral-source rule. See note 1 following *Oden v. Chemung County*, in section 2.E.2. The collateral-source rule potentially allowed a personal injury victim to recover from his insurer and also from the tortfeasor. One way to avoid that double recovery is to require the injury victim to reimburse his insurer. Subrogation attacks the problem directly, by giving the injury victim's cause of action to his insurer. The insurer, who

---

5. The IRS's argument that the title insurer is the real party of interest in this case is also without merit. There is no evidence of collusion between the Morts and Fidelity.

pays the victim's medical bills, is substituted for the victim and allowed to assert her claim against the tortfeasor.

Subrogation avoids the need to choose between double recovery for the injury victim or exoneration of the tortfeasor. Both double recovery and exoneration can be characterized as unjust enrichment. The personal injury victim would be unjustly enriched if he collected twice for the same injury; the tortfeasor would be unjustly enriched if the victim's insurer paid for damages the tortfeasor caused.

3. Subrogation to a claim in other contexts. Subrogation in this sense is not limited to insurers. Subrogation claims can arise any time an obligation owed by one person is paid by another person who is, or might be, independently or secondarily liable. If the party secondarily liable pays the claim, he is subrogated to the claim against the party primarily liable. An example with a detailed opinion is State ex rel. Palmer v. Unisys Corp., 637 N.W.2d 142 (Iowa 2001). Unisys administered the state's Medicaid program, which provides medical care to the poor. The state contracted directly with health maintenance organizations; Unisys processed the claims and made the payments. By mistake, it paid excessive rates to the HMOs. The state sued Unisys to recover the excess payments; Unisys sued the HMOs for reimbursement. Unisys was subrogated to the claim the state could have filed directly against the HMOs.

More often, the subrogee pays the claim for some business reason of its own and without waiting to be sued. Consider American National Bank & Trust Co. v. Weyerhaeuser Co., 692 F.2d 455 (7th Cir. 1982). The bank managed investments for the state of Illinois. Somebody mishandled the state's response to a tender offer for Weyerhaeuser shares; the mistake cost about $70,000. The bank might have made the mistake, or Weyerhaeuser might have made the mistake, but plainly, the state did not make the mistake. The bank reimbursed its customer, protecting its business relationship and protecting the one clearly innocent party. Then the bank sued Weyerhaeuser, asserting its right to be subrogated to the state's claim for breach of contract. The court upheld the bank's right to subrogation; on remand, the bank still had to prove the state's claim on the merits.

For similar holdings in cases where one potential defendant took care of its customers and then sued in subrogation, see In re Air Crash Disaster, 86 F.3d 498, 549-552 (6th Cir. 1996), where the plane's manufacturer paid the families of the passengers and then asserted their claims against the airline, and Mattingly, Inc. v. Beatrice Foods Co., 835 F.2d 1547, 1560-1563 (10th Cir. 1987), where a swimming-pool installer reimbursed its customers and then sued the manufacturer of the material used to coat the pools. That case settled pending a petition for rehearing, so the opinion was vacated. 852 F.2d 516 (10th Cir. 1988). But the vacated opinion usefully collects cases holding that a moral obligation is sufficient to take the paying party out of the volunteer category.

4. The effect of substitution. In every application of subrogation, the person asserting subrogation gets exactly the rights — neither more nor less — of the person to whom he is subrogated. The point is illustrated by United States v. California, 507 U.S. 746, 756-759 (1993). The United States sought to recover sales and use tax paid by a federal contractor and then billed to the United States under a cost-plus contract. The Court held that the United States could be subrogated to the contractor's claims for a tax refund. But the contractor had already sued unsuccessfully, and moreover, the elapsed time from the disputed tax payment to the filing of the government's suit exceeded the statute of limitations. Because a suit by the contractor at that point would be barred by statutes of limitation and also by claim preclusion, the suit by the United States was also barred.

An important clarification generally goes unstated: The subrogation plaintiff gets the subrogor's rights as they existed just before the subrogor was paid. Weyerhaeuser cannot defend on the ground that Illinois no longer has a claim after the bank reimbursed it, and the IRS in *Mort* cannot argue that the Kerns no longer have a lien because they have already been paid.

5. Subrogation to a lien. The subrogation claim in *Mort* bears a sufficient family resemblance to the claims in notes 2 and 3 that we can see why the same name is used. The Morts are subrogated to the Kerns' lien just as Unisys was subrogated to Iowa's claim and American Bank was subrogated to Illinois's. But the two contexts are sufficiently different that the *Restatement (Third)* treats them in separate sections: subrogation as a claim in §24, and subrogation as a remedy in §57.

Subrogation to an unsecured claim, as in notes 2 and 3, gives the subrogation plaintiff an unsecured claim. And it arises in the specific context of two parties who are, or may be, separately liable for the same debt. Subrogation as a remedy can arise in a wide range of contexts; two parties liable for the same debt is only one example, and not the most common. The focus is nearly always on preserving a lien, or some other right to preferred treatment in insolvency, for the benefit of the subrogation plaintiff.

The Delaware court refused to allow subrogation on facts similar to *Mort* in Eastern Savings Bank, FSB v. CACH, LLC, 124 A.3d 585 (Del. 2015). Eastern refinanced mortgages on the home of a couple named Johnson; CACH filed a judgment lien on the same home. Eastern made its loan on December 19; CACH recorded its lien in the real estate records on December 21; Eastern's mortgage was recorded on December 29. So CACH had priority unless Eastern was subrogated to the mortgages it refinanced, which had been recorded long before.

The court said that Eastern had an adequate legal remedy in suing the title company, which should have found the CACH lien before it disbursed Eastern's funds. The court's opinion shows limited familiarity with the law of subrogation; preserving an equity court mostly for purposes of corporate law does not necessarily preserve knowledge of the rest of equity. Justice Seitz, dissenting, explained how subrogation is supposed to work.

6. Why not contract? Is subrogation consistent with the rule that a litigant cannot claim unjust enrichment if she could have made a contract? Consider the two refinancing transactions in *Mort*. The Belmont loan refinanced the Kern loan; the Mort loan refinanced the Belmont loan. The two refinancings appear to be economically identical. But the Morts took an assignment from the Belmonts; the Belmonts did not take an assignment from the Kerns. If they had, the Morts could rely on the chain of assignments instead of the equitable doctrine of subrogation.

Why wouldn't the Belmonts get an assignment? And why should the law rescue them if they didn't? Part of the explanation is that subrogation is probably older than the rule against restitution claims where there could have been a contract. But there is more to be said. The party that would be unjustly enriched without subrogation is the IRS. Was there any prospect of making a contract with it? And the IRS is not being asked to pay for something it might not have wanted; the IRS is being left right where it started, with a second lien that is junior to the Kern lien. When a borrower wants to refinance with a new lender, the original lender may or may not be willing to cooperate with an assignment. When the parties did not contract for subrogation or an assignment of rights, equitable subrogation fills the gap, and the courts never talk about whether the parties should have made a contract.

7. Subrogation for "volunteers." The defense that the subrogation plaintiff was a volunteer has had a long and occasionally perverse history in subrogation cases. "Volunteer" has been a dysfunctional label; the argument has not often been linked to the preference for contract over restitution or to the risk of forced exchanges. Subrogation plaintiffs confer benefits in money, and no one is prejudiced by allowing subrogation.

True "volunteers" basically do not exist in these cases. There may be a very occasional troublemaker who buys up claims against his enemies—and who can take express assignments instead of relying on subrogation. Except for him, people simply do not go around paying other people's debts for no good reason. Volunteer cases nearly always involve either a refinancing or some sort of mistake or disputed liability. The "volunteer" had a reason for paying, and the primary obligor tries to escape responsibility by arguing that the volunteer's reason was not good enough.

Mostly courts understand this. *Mort* rejects the IRS's volunteer argument, and the courts rejected the claims in note 3 that subrogation plaintiffs who made their customers whole were mere volunteers. But occasionally a court gets this wrong. Consider Inland Real Estate Corp. v. Tower Construction Co., 528 N.E.2d 421 (Ill. App. Ct. 1988), where a syndicator of real estate partnerships spent nearly $700,000 repairing structural damage to a building that it managed and had sold to investors. The court said that the syndicator was a mere volunteer and could not be subrogated to the investors' claims against the architects who designed the building.

A near miss with more egregious facts is American Nursing Resources, Inc. v. Forrest T. Jones & Co., 812 S.W.2d 790 (Mo. Ct. App. 1991). A nursing home patient assigned her medical insurance benefits to the nursing home. Jones, who processed and paid claims for the insurer, paid the patient directly by mistake. The patient's lawyer son cashed the checks, invested the proceeds in commodities futures, and lost all the money. When the mistake was discovered, Jones paid the nursing home and cross-claimed against the patient and her son in subrogation. The trial court directed a verdict for the lawyer son! The court said that Jones was a mere volunteer. The court of appeals reversed. Don't we need to restate the volunteer rule in terms that make clear what's really at stake?

On facts that were a simpler version of *Mort*, a federal court applying Michigan law refused subrogation. Bednarowski & Michaels Development, LLC v. Wallace, 293 F. Supp. 2d 728 (E.D. Mich. 2003). A taxpayer's property was subject to a mortgage when the IRS filed a tax lien. Plaintiff paid off the mortgage as part of a transaction to buy two-thirds of the property; plaintiff financed the deal with his own mortgage lender. The court said that plaintiff and his lender were both volunteers and took subject to the tax lien. The result is that the IRS gets paid without regard to the mortgage that was ahead of it, and (depending on the size of the tax lien) plaintiff and his lender may lose their entire investment. Isn't the IRS unjustly enriched at the expense of plaintiff and his lender? The volunteer rule strikes again.

8. Subrogation to other rights. Subrogation as a remedy is most commonly used to acquire a lien that will be paid ahead of other creditors. But that is not the only application.

a. Liens on exempt property. A person who pays off a valid lien on property that is generally exempt from liens can be subrogated to the valid lien. Most of these cases involve loans that are unsecured (often by mistake rather than design), where the loan proceeds are used to pay off liens on a homestead. An example is LaSalle Bank N.A. v. White, 246 S.W.3d 616 (Tex. 2007). It is illegal, and unenforceable, to take a home equity lien on an agricultural homestead in Texas. During the real estate bubble of the early 2000s, LaSalle did it anyway. Of course, the borrower failed to pay. Of the loan proceeds, $185,000 went to pay off a valid purchase-money mortgage, $9,000 to pay back taxes secured by a valid tax lien, and $57,000 in cash to the borrower. LaSalle was subrogated to the purchase-money mortgage and the tax lien, but it was an unsecured creditor with respect to the $57,000 cash-out loan.

b. Nondischargeable claims. The Bankruptcy Code lists 19 classes of debts that are nondischargeable, including unpaid taxes, claims for injuries inflicted by drunk drivers, debts incurred through fraud, embezzlement, or larceny, and claims for "defalcation" by a fiduciary. 11 U.S.C. §523(a). A lender whose funds are used to pay off such a nondischargeable claim is subrogated, so he also gets a nondischargeable claim. Some of the cases are collected in In re Barnes, 317 B.R. 187, 193-194 (Bankr. M.D. Ga. 2004). The debtors in *Barnes* invested their minor daughter's personal injury settlement in a hardware store, which failed when Walmart came to town. They were replaced as guardians of the daughter's estate, and the insurance company that had issued their guardianship bond made good the daughter's losses. The insurer was subrogated to the daughter's claim that this investment had been a defalcation and that the liability to the daughter's estate was nondischargeable. Of course, the disabled daughter did not actually claim anything; the insurer asserted the claim the daughter could have made if she had been willing and able to sue her parents.

c. Priorities in bankruptcy. Some unsecured claims get priority in bankruptcy, paid after the secured creditors but before the other unsecured creditors. Consider In re Missionary Baptist Foundation, 667 F.2d 1244 (5th Cir. 1982). A supermarket cashed payroll checks for employees of the foundation; the checks bounced and the foundation filed for bankruptcy. Unpaid wages are a priority claim. Before 1978, the supermarket could be subrogated to the employees' priority, but 11 U.S.C. §507(d) expressly repeals that subrogation right. The court held that the employees' endorsement of the checks also made the supermarket an assignee, and §507(d) does not apply to express assignments. So an express assignment can get you a priority in bankruptcy when subrogation cannot.

Section 507(d) is unambiguous but mysterious. There are ten categories of priority claims; §507(d) repeals subrogation with respect to seven of them. No commentator has been able to identify any rationale either for repealing subrogation or for distinguishing three kinds of claims from the other seven. The legislative history is completely silent.

9. Subrogation as a remedy for wrongdoing. Subrogation can be a remedy for wrongdoing when the wrongfully acquired funds are used to pay off a secured debt. So in In re Mesa, some of the checks were made payable directly to contractors and suppliers who had construction liens on the house. The court says that Travelers, the embezzlement victim, could be subrogated to those construction liens. Instead, the court proceeded more directly, giving Travelers an equitable lien on the property for all the embezzled money spent to remodel it.

Another example is Banton v. Hackney, 557 So. 2d 807, 825 (Ala. 1989). Defendant sold his company for more than $1 million; buyers sought to rescind the sale for fraud. In the meantime, $550,000 of this money had been used to pay off two mortgages, one on his house and one on a condominium. The trial court held that plaintiff was subrogated to the rights of the two mortgage lenders. The state supreme court left the resulting liens in place pending a remand for further proceedings on the fraud claim.

10. Subrogation and equitable lien. Cases like *Mesa* and *Banton* illustrate the large overlap between subrogation and equitable lien. In each case, the court awarded an equitable lien because the wrongfully acquired money was used to improve the property or reduce the mortgage on the property. And in each case, the court said that the money was paid to a person who had a lien (the contractors in *Mesa*, the mortgage lenders in *Banton*), so subrogation was also appropriate. Sometimes the choice doesn't matter; sometimes subrogation specifies more precisely how the funds are traced. The choice matters most in cases like *Mort*, where the priority of multiple liens is at issue. A plaintiff who is subrogated to the rights of a senior lien holder gets the benefit of that lien holder's senior position.

NOTES ON INDEMNITY AND CONTRIBUTION

1. The distinction. Contribution, indemnity, and subrogation as a claim all involve the three-cornered relationship between a person with an underlying substantive claim (call her *P*) and two persons who have potential liability on that claim (call them D_1 and D_2). D_1 pays the claim and then asserts that D_2 had primary responsibility. In the succinct formulation of the *Restatement (Third)*: If D_1 and D_2 are jointly and severally liable, the remedy is indemnity or contribution. If they are not jointly and severally liable (either they are independently liable, or one of them is not liable at all), the remedy is in subrogation. §§23-24.

Common cases of joint and several liability are principal and agent, contractor and subcontractor, borrowers and guarantors on promissory notes, partners, and of course, joint tortfeasors. Cases of independent liability generally involve two people who each have some independent relationship with *P*. The most common examples are *P*'s insurers and medical providers, who have no relationship with the tortfeasor who injured *P*. American Bank (note 3 of the preceding set of notes) provided financial services to Illinois, and Illinois was a shareholder in Weyerhaeuser, but there was no relationship between Weyerhaeuser and the bank.

2. Why it matters. The only practical consequence of this distinction is the statute of limitations. The subrogation plaintiff gets exactly the rights of the person he is subrogated to, so the statute is running even before the subrogation plaintiff pays the earlier claim. United States v. California in note 4 of the previous set of notes is an example. But in indemnity and contribution, by long tradition, limitations runs from when the plaintiff pays the claim.

The distinction is illustrated in Great American Insurance Co. v. United States, 575 F.2d 1031 (2d Cir. 1978). Great American insured a house that was rented to federal witnesses under the protection of United States marshals. When the witnesses moved out of the house, they allegedly took the fixtures with them, doing $19,000 worth of damage. The owner (*P*) filed a claim with Great American (D_1), and Great American denied coverage. The owner sued on the policy and recovered a judgment two years later. Great American then sued the United States (D_2) for reimbursement.

Great American first claimed to be subrogated to the rights of the owner, but that suit was barred by the statute of limitations. So Great American also sued for indemnity. But indemnity was unavailable, because the insurer and the United States had completely separate liabilities, not joint and several liabilities. Great American had no relationship with the United States; it was in the case only because of its insurance contract with the owner. The court did not put it in these terms, but Great American and the owner had no power to make a contract that deprived the United States of the protections of the statute of limitations.

3. Distinguishing indemnity from contribution. An indemnity plaintiff claims a right to be completely reimbursed—like the unsuccessful insurer in *Great American*. Had the insurer filed its claim in time, it would have argued that the United States was entirely responsible for the loss.

Contribution can be thought of as partial indemnification. If two or more parties are jointly liable for the same obligation, and one pays more than her share, she is entitled to contribution from the others, so that each pays her share. Her "share" may be fixed by agreement in the original obligation, by comparative fault, or by a presumption of equal responsibility. If one party's share (as between the joint obligors) is 100 percent, the other party will claim indemnity for any payment she has to make.

Contribution and indemnity are universally available when two or more parties are jointly liable on a contract. The traditional rule was that there could be no contribution or indemnity between joint tortfeasors. But that rule has generally been repudiated, because it makes little sense in a regime of comparative fault.

4. Claims under federal statutes. The Supreme Court has been reluctant to allow contribution between parties who jointly violate statutes. In Northwest Airlines, Inc. v. Transport Workers Union, 451 U.S. 77 (1981), the airline unsuccessfully sought contribution from its unions for Equal Pay Act violations; in Texas Industries, Inc. v. Radcliff Materials, Inc., 451 U.S. 630 (1981), one party to a price-fixing conspiracy unsuccessfully sought contribution from the others.

But the Court permitted contribution in suits for securities fraud under Securities and Exchange Commission Rule 10b-5. Musick, Peeler & Garrett v. Employers Insurance, 508 U.S. 286 (1993). *Musick* held that a corporation and its officers, directors, and securities underwriters could sue for contribution from attorneys and accountants who had also participated in the fraud. Moreover, the insurer who paid most of the claim on behalf of the contribution plaintiffs could be subrogated to their claim for contribution.

There has been a vigorous and inconclusive debate over the wisdom of contribution in antitrust cases, but the Court did not join in the debate in any of these cases. Rather, each opinion focuses on the text and history of the particular statute, an approach that grows out of the Court's recent view (examined in section 6.B) that Congress must specify the remedies for statutory violations.

5. A novel context. In Paroline v. United States, 134 S. Ct. 1710 (2014), defendant had images of a victim's childhood sexual abuse on his computer; so did many thousands of others who collected child pornography. The issue was how much he had to pay in compensation to the victim under 18 U.S.C. §2259. This compensation is ordered as part of sentencing under the confusing label "restitution." The Court rejected the victim's argument that each individual who possessed the photographs would have to pay for all of her damages. She could not prove that any identifiable amount of her emotional distress was attributable to the particular defendant before the Court.

Of greater relevance here, the Court rejected the argument that it would be "fair and practical" to make each possessor of the photographs jointly and severally liable for the entire amount of the victim's losses, with a right to contribution from defendants who had paid less than their share. *Id.* at 1725. "[T]here is scant authority for her contention that offenders convicted in different proceedings in different jurisdictions and ordered to pay restitution to the same victim may seek contribution from one another. There is no general federal right to contribution." *Id.* The statute did not create a right to contribution, and the Court declined to imply a cause of action. *Id.* The Court held that sentencing judges should award a "reasonable" amount of restitution against each defendant separately, more than "token," but not "severe" in the case of defendants who had made only a modest contribution to the total problem.

D.   DEFENSES AND THE RIGHTS OF THIRD PARTIES

1.   *Bona Fide Purchasers*

NEWTON v. PORTER
69 N.Y. 133 (1877)

ANDREWS, J.

This is an equitable action brought to establish the right of the plaintiff to certain securities, the proceeds of stolen bonds, and to compel the defendants to account therefor.

In March, 1869, the plaintiff was the owner of $13,000 of government bonds, . . . negotiable by delivery, which . . . were stolen from her, and soon afterwards . . . the bonds were sold by the thief and his confederates, and the proceeds divided between them. William Warner loaned a part of his share in separate loans and took the promissory notes of the borrower therefor. George Warner invested $2,000 of his share in the purchase of a bond and mortgage, which was assigned to his wife Cordelia without consideration.

In January, 1870, [the three Warners] were arrested [and indicted] upon the charge of stealing the bonds, or as accessories to the larceny. . . . The Warners employed the defendants, who are attorneys, to defend them in the criminal proceedings, and in any civil suits which might be instituted against them in respect to the bonds[. To] secure them for their services and expenses, . . . William Warner transferred to the defendants Miner and Warren promissory notes taken on loans made by him out of the proceeds of the stolen bonds, amounting to $2,250 . . . , and Cordelia Warner, for the same purpose, assigned to the defendant Porter the bond and mortgage above mentioned.

The learned judge at Special Term found that the defendants had notice at the time they received the . . . securities, that they were the avails and proceeds of the stolen bonds, and directed judgment against them for the value of the securities, it appearing on the trial that they had collected or disposed of them and received the proceeds.

The doctrine upon which . . . this case proceeded . . . : that the owner of negotiable securities stolen and afterwards sold by the thief may pursue the proceeds of the sale in the hands of the felonious taker or his assignee with notice, through whatever changes the proceeds may have gone, so long as the proceeds or the substitute therefor can be distinguished and identified, and have the proceeds or the property in which they were invested subjected . . . to a lien and trust in his favor . . . , is founded upon the plainest principles of justice and morality, and is consistent with the rule in analogous cases . . . in courts of law and equity. It is a general principle of the law of personal property that the title of the owner cannot be divested without his consent. The purchaser from a thief, however honest and *bona fide* [literally, good faith] the purchase may have been, cannot hold the stolen chattel against the true proprietor, but the latter may follow and reclaim it wherever or in whosoever hands it may be found. The right of pursuit and reclamation only ceases when its identity is lost and further pursuit is hopeless; but the law still protects the interest of the true owner by giving him an action . . . for . . . conversion of the chattel against any one who has interfered with his dominion over it, although such interference may have been innocent . . . and under a claim of right, and in reliance upon the title of the felonious taker. The extent to which the common law goes to protect the title of the true owner has a striking illustration in those cases in which it is held that where a willful trespasser converts a chattel into a different species, as for example, timber into shingles, wood into coal, or corn into whiskey, the product in its improved and changed condition belongs to the owner of the original material.

[¶] The rule that a thief cannot convey a good title to stolen property has an exception in case of money or negotiable securities transferable by delivery, which have been put into circulation and have come to the hands of *bona fide* holders. The right of the owner to pursue and reclaim the money and securities there ends, and the holder is protected in his title. The plaintiff was in this position. The bonds . . . had . . . been sold to *bona fide* purchasers, and she was precluded from following and reclaiming them.

The right of the plaintiff in equity to have the notes and mortgage[,] while they remained in the possession of the felons or of their assignees with notice, subjected to a lien and trust in her favor, and to compel their transfer to her as the equitable owner, does not, we think, admit of serious doubt. . . . She could maintain an action

. . . for a conversion of the property against the felons. But . . . they are wholly insolvent. Unless she can elect to regard the securities in which the bonds were invested as a substitute . . . for the bonds, she has no effectual remedy. The thieves certainly have no claim to the securities in which the proceeds of the bonds were invested as against the plaintiff. . . . If the avails remained in their hands, in money, the direct proceeds of the sale, can it be doubted that she could reach it[?]. . . And this equitable right to follow the proceeds would continue and attach to any securities or property in which the proceeds were invested, so long as they could be traced and identified, and the rights of *bona fide* purchasers had not intervened. . . .

The doctrine is . . . applied most frequently in cases of trusts, where trust moneys have been . . . diverted from the purposes of the trust and converted into other property. In such case a court of equity will follow the trust fund into the property into which it has been converted, and appropriate it for the indemnity of the beneficiary. It is immaterial in what way the change has been made, whether money has been laid out in land, or land has been turned into money, or how the legal title to the converted property may be placed. Equity only stops the pursuit when the means of ascertainment fails, or the rights of *bona fide* purchasers for value, without notice of the trust, have intervened. The relief will be moulded and adapted to the circumstances of the case, so as to protect the interests and rights of the true owner.

It is insisted by the counsel for the defendants that the doctrine . . . has no application to a case where money or property acquired by felony has been converted into other property. There is, it is said, . . . no trust relation between the owner of the stolen property and the thief, and the law will not imply one for the purpose of subjecting the avails of the stolen property to the claim of the owner. It would seem to be an anomaly in the law, if the owner who has been deprived of his property by a larceny should be less favorably situated in a court of equity . . . than one who . . . has been injured by the wrongful act of a trustee to whom the possession of trust property has been confided. The law in such a case will raise a trust . . . out of the transaction, for the very purpose of subjecting the substituted property to the purposes of indemnity and recompense. . . .

It is, however, strenuously insisted that the defendants had no notice when they received the securities that they were the . . . proceeds of the bonds. That if they had notice they would stand in the position of their assignors, and that the property in their hands would be affected by the same equities as if no transfer had been made, is not denied. The learned judge, at Special Term, found . . . that the defendants had notice of the larceny of the bonds, and the use made of the money arising from their sale, at the time they received the notes and mortgage. . . .

The testimony was conflicting. The circumstances under which the defendants took the transfer of the securities were certainly unusual, and the facts then known by the defendants were calculated to create a strong presumption that the notes and mortgage came from investments of the stolen property. It was for the trial court to weigh the testimony. . . . [W]e content ourselves with stating our conclusion, that the finding was warranted by the evidence. . . .

The judgment should be affirmed. . . .

NOTES ON TRACING INTO THE HANDS OF THIRD PARTIES

1. The facts of Newton v. Porter. Newton v. Porter is one of the famous leading cases of the American law of tracing. The rules it applies are still good law today. Be sure you understand what happened at each step in the series of transactions.

a. The claim against the thieves. Could Newton recover the bonds from the thieves? Why? The claim to the bonds in the hands of the thieves does not even require a constructive trust. Because the thieves do not get title to the bonds, the bonds could be recovered in replevin or simply seized by the police and returned to the owner.

The thieves sold the bonds for cash. If that cash could be found, we would be talking about constructive trust in identifiable proceeds. They used the cash to buy a different bond, a mortgage, and promissory notes. Are these securities still identifiable proceeds? How might Newton prove that?

b. The claim against the purchaser of the bonds. Somebody bought the stolen bonds. That person does not appear in the litigation. Was there a claim against him? Why not?

c. The claim against the wife. The thief who bought the new bond and the mortgage gave those securities to his wife. Was there a claim against her? Why? What if she had not been an accessory to the theft?

d. The claim against the attorneys. The promissory notes, the new bond, and the mortgage, were used to pay the defense attorneys. Why is there a claim against them? Are they situated any differently from the wife?

Exactly what is the claim against the attorneys? They no longer have the notes, the new bond, or the mortgage. The court does not talk about tracing or identifying the cash proceeds. Rather, the court suggests that the attorneys have to "account" for the proceeds. Recall that accounting for profits ends in an ordinary money judgment, not a constructive trust.

e. The claim against the investor who bought from the attorneys. We don't hear anything about the person who bought from the attorneys. Is there a claim against him? Why not?

2. Tracing into the hands of third parties. When a plaintiff with a right to restitution of specific property learns that defendant has transferred the property to a third person, plaintiff has two potential remedies. He can pursue the proceeds of the original property in the hands of the original defendant, *Restatement (Third)* §58(1), and he can pursue the original property in the hands of the third party—or a fourth, fifth, or *n*th party. §58(2). Prima facie, the original plaintiff is entitled to recover his property from whoever now holds it, but some of those parties will have a defense. The defense depends mostly on how they acquired the property, and partly on what kind of property it was. The rules for cash and negotiable securities are a little different from the rules for other kinds of property, but the core rule, for any kind of property, is that bona fide purchasers for value take free of unrecorded equitable interests such as rights to restitution.

In the restitution context, we speak of these cases as tracing cases, because the property must at least be transferred from the original defendant to a third party before the rights of third parties can be at issue. But tracing need not be involved in the claim against the original defendant. A simple claim for rescission, in which plaintiff and defendant must each return what she received from the other, becomes a third-party tracing case when defendant transfers the property to a third party.

3. The conflict between owners and third parties. The bad guy who dishonestly acquires property from one victim and sells it to another victim is a recurring problem for the law. The bad guy is typically insolvent, unidentified, disappeared, beyond the seas, or in many of the older cases, hanged. Both victims are innocent, but one of them must bear the loss. The bona fide purchaser for value in the common law, and the Uniform Commercial Code's various permutations of the idea—the good-faith purchaser for value in the law of sales, the holder in due course in the law of negotiable instruments, the protected purchaser in the law of securities transfers, and the buyer in ordinary course of business in the law of secured transactions—are all variations on the basic rules for addressing this problem. The defense of bona fide purchaser for value in the context of restitution is addressed in *Restatement (Third)* §66.

4. Purchase. To be a bona fide purchaser for value, one must first be a purchaser. But "purchaser" here does not have its ordinary English meaning. In the UCC definition, "'[p]urchase' includes taking by sale, lease, discount, negotiation, mortgage, pledge, lien, security interest, issue or reissue, gift or any other voluntary transaction creating an interest in property." §1-201(b)(29). So one who buys the property is a purchaser, but so is one who lends money in exchange for a mortgage or security interest. One who cashes a check is a purchaser of the check. One who receives property as a gift is a purchaser; that won't do the donee any good, but it helps explain protection for others who buy from the donee. One who acquires a part interest in property is a purchaser of that interest. This UCC definition codifies the common law understanding.

The only people excluded by this sweeping definition are people who acquire their interest without consent of the person they acquire it from. A thief is not a purchaser. More important, a creditor who acquires a judicial lien, or has the sheriff sell the property at an execution sale, is not a purchaser. Moreover, the statutes creating such liens generally make the lien applicable only to the actual interest of the judgment debtor. Both the definition of purchaser and the limited reach of the judicial lien statutes are ways of saying that an owner, including a restitution plaintiff with a claim to specific property, prevails over unsecured creditors—and over the trustee in bankruptcy, who largely represents unsecured creditors.

5. "Bona fide," or notice. "Bona fide" literally means good faith, but the law is both simpler and more complicated than that.

a. Common law and equity. In this context, good faith has traditionally meant something more specific than a subjective inquiry into good faith. It meant simply that the purchaser acquired his interest without notice of plaintiff's competing claim. Notice, in this context, means information sufficient to cause a reasonable person to conduct a further inquiry that would reveal the claim. *Restatement (Third)* §69(2)(c).

Were the attorneys on notice in Newton v. Porter? Is every criminal defense attorney always on notice that the client might be paying with the fruits of the crime? Or the fruits of some other crime? Was there more specific information, perhaps creating more specific notice, in Newton v. Porter? A similar modern case is In re Bell & Beckwith, 838 F.2d 844 (6th Cir. 1988). The attorney in *Bell* should have suspected that he was being paid with proceeds of the fraud, and therefore had a duty to inquire and could not qualify as a good-faith purchaser.

There is a similar holding in Federal Trade Commission v. Network Services Depot, Inc., 617 F.3d 1127 (9th Cir. 2010). The court emphasized that once an attorney is on notice that the money used to pay his fees might be proceeds of wrongdoing, it is not enough to merely ask the client and take his word for it.

b. The Uniform Commercial Code. Amendments to the UCC redefined good faith to require "honesty in fact and the observance of reasonable commercial standards of fair dealing." §1-201(b)(20). This matters to restitution cases, because many applications of the defense of bona fide purchaser for value are codified at various places in the UCC. One who acquires goods by fraud can give good title to a "good faith purchaser for value" under §2-403(1); one must acquire a negotiable instrument "in good faith" to be a holder in due course under §3-302(a)(2). One place where this has mattered is in the art market. There are cases holding that art dealers now have a greater duty than before to inquire into the provenance of a work of art if it is offered at an unusually low price or if anything else about the transaction should arouse suspicion. Some of the cases are collected in Overton v. Art Finance Partners, LLC, 166 F. Supp. 3d 388 (S.D.N.Y. 2016).

And consider Maine Family Federal Credit Union v. Sun Life Assurance Co., 727 A.2d 335 (Me. 1999). An insurance agent personally delivered checks for $120,000 to the beneficiaries of a life insurance policy. And he persuaded the beneficiaries to endorse the checks to himself and a confederate for investment. The confederate deposited the checks in his account at the credit union. The beneficiaries began to have doubts and asked Sun to stop payment on the checks, which it did. But the confederate had already withdrawn the money.

Under the old standard of notice, it was settled that banks did not have to put holds on deposits that were valid on their face. Giving immediate credit for a large deposit might be foolish, but it was not bad faith. But now good faith requires "reasonable commercial standards of fair dealing." What does that mean with respect to large out-of-state checks with third-party endorsements? Under that standard, a jury found that the credit union had not acted in good faith. It therefore was not a holder in due course and it took the checks subject to the beneficiary's fraud claim. The Maine court affirmed, in an opinion that collects preamendment cases and discusses the apparent significance of the statutory change.

Because the credit union was not a holder in due course, it could not collect the checks from Sun. That may not sound like a restitution case, even if the issues are the same. But because it didn't have to pay the old checks, Sun could issue new checks and the beneficiaries could get their money back. In effect, they rescinded their endorsements because the endorsements were induced by fraud. In the end, this was in fact a restitution case.

6. Value. A bona fide purchaser without notice of plaintiff's claim is still not protected unless she gave value. Fundamentally, this means she had to pay for what she received. One who receives property as a gift is a purchaser, but she is not a purchaser for value. The *Restatement (Third)* explores value in §68.

a. Promises. Statutory definitions of "value," including in the UCC, have modest variations in response to context. In general, value includes cash or other property. It includes services or other performance under a contract to the extent that performance is completed. A mere promise of future performance is consideration at common law, and it is value under UCC §1-204(4). But it is not value under the *Restatement (Third)*, because the court can release such a promise. §68(b). An unperformed promise that has become irrevocable counts as value by any standard.

To unpack that distinction, suppose that Bad Guy obtains goods from Victim 1 by fraud, and sells the property to Victim 2 in exchange for a promissory note. The court can order the property returned to Victim 1 and cancel the note to Bad Guy. Both victims are protected. But if Bad Guy has sold the note to Bank for cash, and if Bank took the note without notice of the underlying fraud, the Bank takes free of Victim 2's defenses. Because it is too late to cancel the note, Victim 2 is treated as having given value, and if he took without notice of the fraud, he gets to keep the property.

b. Past consideration. Past consideration generally does not count as value, because the person receiving the disputed property did not rely on that property when she delivered the past consideration. An example is Groza-Vance v. Vance, 834 N.E.2d 15, 28-30 (Ohio Ct. App. 2005), where a divorce decree entitled ex-wife to certain property at ex-husband's death. The ex-husband left that instead to his adult daughter by a previous marriage, because she had taken care of him in his declining years. That did not count as value; the ex-wife got the property via constructive trust. But a controversial exception largely swallows the rule: Antecedent debt generally counts as value. We take up this exception in the next principal case.

c. Spouses. Transfers to spouses are generally gifts, but transfers in divorces are generally in exchange for release of marital rights. In Notes on Advanced Tracing Issues, in section 8.C.2, we saw cases where Wife 1 gets a constructive trust over a life insurance policy naming Wife 2 as beneficiary. Those cases have said that Wife 2 is a donee, not a bona fide purchaser for value. That is a little troubling for something as basic as life insurance, and perhaps more troubling because there is no traditional tracing in those cases. It may be more straightforward to say that the courts must protect Wife 1 and her children because the ex-husband will not. But the holding that Wife 2 is a donee applies a rule that is clearly right in more basic applications. It cannot be that fraudsters can launder their fraudulent acquisitions by simply giving them to a spouse.

7. Void and voidable. All of this law is applied against a background distinction between void and voidable title. As between the parties to a defective transaction, the distinction between void and voidable title has no consequences. But it looms large as soon as one of these original parties transfers what he received to a third party. With respect to third parties, the difference is this: A void title is no title at all; one who holds void title cannot convey any property right to a third party, not even a bona fide purchaser for value. One who holds voidable title can give good title to a bona fide purchaser for value. So how to know which your bad guy has?

a. The rule for everything other than cash and certain near equivalents. In general, a voluntary transaction, however defective, passes a voidable title. This is why "purchaser" is defined as anyone who acquires the property in a voluntary transaction. When title is passed voluntarily, one side may be entitled to rescind and reclaim his property, but until he does so, the other side has a voidable title and the power to sell the property to a bona fide purchaser.

An outright theft conveys no title, or what is the same thing, it conveys a void title. Anyone who buys from a thief has to give the property back, and if he has resold the property in the meantime, he is strictly liable for the conversion. Consider Regent Alliance Ltd. v. Rabidzadeh, 180 Cal. Rptr. 3d 610 (Ct. App. 2014). Regent, a manufacturer of children's clothing, stored clothing in YHK's warehouse. YHK sold some of the clothing, with no colorable claim of authority, to the defendants. The defendants had no idea the goods were stolen; they sold the clothing to customers in their clothing store. The court found it entirely settled that defendants were liable for conversion even though they were innocent bona fide purchasers for value. But this time there was a dissenter, complaining of the majority's "rigid and formalistic application of the law of conversion." *Id.* at 619.

There are also some curious common law rules that put certain extreme cases of apparently voluntary transactions into the void category. Most victims of fraud confer voidable title on the fraudster, but if the victim has no opportunity to learn what he is signing, the transaction is void. So where a supervisor asked his illiterate employee to sign a "character reference," and the document turned out to be a guarantee of the supervisor's bank loan, the document was void (not just voidable) and unenforceable by the bank. Schaeffer v. United Bank & Trust Co., 370 A.2d 1138 (Md. 1977).

b. The rule for cash and certain near equivalents. There are special rules for cash and for securities payable to bearer, which are designed to be transferred like cash, by simple delivery with no endorsement required. Even a thief can give good title to stolen cash to a bona fide purchaser for value. A "purchaser" of cash is typically a person who sells something to the thief; if she takes the cash in good faith and without notice of the underlying theft, she is a bona fide purchaser for value.

c. Putting it all together. A bona fide purchaser for value can get good title to cash, superior to the claims of a restitution plaintiff, without exception. A bona fide purchaser for value can get good title to other property, superior to the claims of a restitution plaintiff, unless that property was stolen or acquired in a transaction so tainted by wrongdoing that the law treats it as equivalent to theft. A recipient is not a bona fide purchaser for value if she took with notice of the restitution claim or if she did not give value.

Here's one other way to think about how this all fits together. A bona fide purchaser for value is generally protected. That rule has an exception: Even a bona fide purchaser for value is not protected if her title derives from a thief. But that rule also has an exception: Even one whose title derives from a thief is protected if she is a bona fide purchaser of cash.

8. Improvements by willful trespassers. The opinion in Newton v. Porter notes the rule that when a willful trespasser converts a raw material into a more valuable product, the owner of the raw material can recover the more valuable product. These cases are a harsh application of the bought-and-paid-for rule in section 8.B.2; the owner does not have to pay for the trespasser's labor in improving the materials. For a real example of recovering corn converted into whiskey, see Silsbury v. McCoon, 3 N.Y. 379 (1850).

2.   *Payment for Value*

BANQUE WORMS v. BANKAMERICA INTERNATIONAL
570 N.E.2d 189 (N.Y. 1991)

ALEXANDER, Judge.

On April 10, 1989, [the New York office of] Security Pacific International Bank . . . mistakenly wired $1,974,267.97 on behalf of Spedley Securities . . . , an Australian corporation, into the account of Banque Worms, a French Bank, maintained with BankAmerica International [in New York]. Initially intending to make payment on its debt to Banque Worms under a revolving credit agreement, Spedley instructed Security Pacific, which routinely effected wire transfers for Spedley, to electronically transfer funds from Security Pacific to Banque Worms' account at BankAmerica.

A few hours after directing this wire transfer, Spedley, by a second telex, directed Security Pacific to stop payment to Banque Worms and to make payment instead to National Westminster Bank USA (Natwest USA) for the same amount. At the time Security Pacific received the telexes, Spedley had a credit balance of only $84,500 in its account at Security Pacific, but later that morning, Security Pacific received additional funds sufficient to cover the transaction and then began to execute the transaction. However, in mistaken disregard of Spedley's second telex canceling the wire transfer to Banque Worms, Security Pacific transferred the funds into Banque Worms' account at BankAmerica. . . . That afternoon, Security Pacific executed Spedley's second payment order and transferred $1,974,267.97 to Natwest USA. Spedley's account at Security Pacific was debited twice to record both wire transfers thus producing an overdraft. . . .

Security Pacific's attempt to obtain funds from Spedley . . . was unavailing because by that time, Spedley had entered into involuntary liquidation.

[All the banks sued each other in federal court. Security Pacific settled with BankAmerica, leaving the real dispute between Security Pacific and Banque Worms.]

[T]he District Court, applying the "discharge for value" rule, granted judgment for Banque Worms. Security Pacific appealed to the . . . Second Circuit, arguing that

New York neither recognized nor applied the "discharge for value" rule in situations such as this; that the controlling rule under New York law was the "mistake of fact" rule pursuant to which, in order to be entitled to retain the mistakenly transferred funds, Banque Worms was required to demonstrate detrimental reliance. The case is before us upon a certified question from the Second Circuit inquiring "[w]hether in this case, where a concededly mistaken wire transfer by [Security Pacific] was made to [Banque Worms], a creditor of Spedley, New York would apply the 'Discharge for Value' rule as set forth at §14 of the *Restatement of Restitution* or, in the alternative, whether in this case New York would apply the rule that holds that money paid under a mistake may be recovered, unless the payment has caused such a change in the position of the receiving party that it would be unjust to require the party to refund.". . .

[U]nder the circumstances of this case, the "discharge for value" rule should be applied, thus entitling Banque Worms to retain the funds mistakenly transferred without the necessity of demonstrating detrimental reliance.

I

A

In the area of restitution, New York has long recognized the rule that "if A pays money to B upon the erroneous assumption of the former that he is indebted to the latter, an action may be maintained for its recovery. . . ." Ball v. Shepard, 95 N.E. 719, 721 (N.Y. 1911). This rule has been applied where the cause of action has been denominated as one for money had and received, for unjust enrichment or restitution, or upon a theory of quasi contract. Where, however, the receiving party has changed its position to its detriment in reliance upon the mistake so that requiring that it refund the money paid would be "unfair," recovery has been denied.

This rule has evolved into the "mistake of fact" doctrine, in which detrimental reliance is a requisite factor, and which provides that "money paid under a mistake of fact may be recovered back, however negligent the party paying may have been in making the mistake, unless the payment has caused such a change in the position of the other party that it would be unjust to require him to refund." National Bank of Commerce v. National Mechanics' Banking Association, 55 N.Y. 211, 213 (1873).

The *Restatement of Restitution*, on the other hand, has established the "discharge for value" rule which provides that "[a] creditor of another or one having a lien on another's property who has received from a third person any benefit in discharge of the debt or lien, is under no duty to make restitution therefor, although the discharge was given by mistake of the transferor as to his interests or duties, if the transferee made no misrepresentation and did not have notice of the transferor's mistake." §14(1) (1937).

The question as to which of these divergent rules New York will apply to electronic fund transfers divides the parties and prompts the certified question from the Second Circuit. Security Pacific argues that New York has rejected the "discharge for value" rule and has required that detrimental reliance under the "mistake of fact" rule be demonstrated in all cases other than where the mistake was induced by fraud. Banque Worms, on the other hand, invokes the "discharge for value" rule, arguing that because it is a creditor of Spedley and had no knowledge that the wire transfer was erroneous, it is entitled to keep the funds. It points out, as indicated by the official comment to §14(1) of the *Restatement of Restitution*, that the "discharge for value" rule is simply a "specific application of the underlying principle of bona fide purchase" set forth in §13 of the *Restatement. Id.* §14 cmt. *a.* . . .

[O]ne may find . . . language in a myriad of cases that arguably lends support to the proposition that New York, long ago, embraced the "discharge for value" rule.

On the other hand, cases can also be cited where the language employed supports the contrary view—that New York not only eschews the "discharge for value" rule, as Security Pacific argues, but also embraces exclusively the detrimental reliance rule. . . . These cases for the most part, however, present issues involving more traditional aspects of mistake and restitution, and do not satisfactorily address the unique problems presented by electronic funds transfer technology. . . .

B

Electronic funds transfers have become the preferred method utilized by businesses and financial institutions to effect payments and transfers of a substantial volume of funds. . . . Funds are moved faster and more efficiently than by traditional payment instruments, such as checks. . . . Most transfers are completed within one day and can cost as little as $10 to carry out a multimillion dollar transaction. . . . [N]early $1 trillion in transactions occur each day, averaging $5 million per transfer and on peak days, this figure often approaches $2 trillion. . . .

The [Clearing House Interbank Payment System] network [CHIPS] handles 95% of the international transfers made in dollars. . . . These funds are transferred through participating banks located in New York because all of the banks belonging to the CHIPS network must maintain a regulated presence in New York. As a result, this State is considered the national and international center for wholesale wire transfers.

The low cost of electronic funds transfers is an important factor in the system's popularity and this is so even though banks executing wire transfers often risk significant liability as a result of losses occasioned by mistakes and errors, the most common of which involve the payment of funds to the wrong beneficiary or in an incorrect amount. [Because earlier statutes on paper payment systems did not adequately respond to issues raised by wire transfers, the American Law Institute and the National Conference of Commissioners on Uniform State Laws proposed a new Article 4A of the Uniform Commercial Code. A] major policy issue facing the drafters of UCC article 4A was determining how the risk of loss might best be allocated, while preserving a unique price structure. In order to prevent or minimize losses, the industry had adopted and employed various security procedures designed to prevent losses such as the use of codes, identifying words or numbers, call-back procedures and limits on payment amounts or beneficiaries that may be paid. . . .

In 1990, the New York State Legislature adopted the new article 4A. . . . Although the new statute . . . may not be applied retroactively to resolve the issues presented by this litigation, the statute's . . . history . . . can . . . serve as persuasive authority. . . .

II . . .

Establishing finality in electronic fund wire transactions was considered a singularly important policy goal. Payments made by electronic funds transfers in compliance with . . . article 4A are to be the equivalent of cash payments, irrevocable except to the extent provided for in article 4A.

This concern for finality in business transactions has long been a significant policy consideration in this State. In a different but pertinent context, we observed in Hatch v. Fourth National Bank, 41 N.E. 403, 404 (N.Y. 1895), that "to permit in every case of the payment of a debt an inquiry as to the source from which the debtor derived the money, and a recovery if shown to have been dishonestly acquired, would disorganize all business operations and entail an amount of risk and uncertainty which no enterprise could bear."

A consequence of this concern has been the adoption of a rule which precludes recovery from a third person, who as the result of the mistake of one or both of the parties to an original transaction receives payment by one of them in good faith in the ordinary course of business and for a valuable consideration. . . . We have previously held that from these considerations, "[t]he law wisely . . . adjudges that the possession of money vests the title in the holder as to third persons dealing with him and receiving it in due course of business and in good faith upon a valid consideration." Stephens v. Board of Education, 79 N.Y. 183, 187-188 (1879).

The "discharge for value" rule is consistent with and furthers the policy goal of finality in business transactions and may appropriately be applied in respect to electronic funds transfers. When a beneficiary receives money to which it is entitled and has no knowledge that the money was erroneously wired, the beneficiary should not have to wonder whether it may retain the funds; rather, such a beneficiary should be able to consider the transfer of funds as a final and complete transaction, not subject to revocation.

We believe such an application accords with the legislative intent and furthers the policy considerations underlying article 4A. . . . Although no provision of article 4A calls, in express terms, for the application of the "discharge for value" rule, the statutory scheme and the language of various pertinent sections, as amplified by the Official Comments to the UCC, support our conclusion that the "discharge for value" rule should be applied in the circumstances here presented. . . .

Where a duplicate payment order is erroneously executed or the payment order is issued to a beneficiary different from the beneficiary intended by the sender, the receiving bank in either case is entitled to recover the erroneously paid amount from the beneficiary "to the extent allowed by the law governing mistake and restitution." *See* UCC §4A-303(a), (c). ["Receiving bank" here refers to the bank that received the payment order, not the bank that received the money.]

Although it seems clear . . . that the drafters of UCC article 4A contemplated that the "discharge for value" rule could appropriately be applied in respect to electronic fund transfers, Security Pacific argues that to do so would undermine the low cost structure of wholesale electronic fund transfers and impose extraordinary risks upon banks implementing these enormously large transactions. This argument is unpersuasive. Article 4A contemplates, in the first instance, that a mistake such as occurred here can be effectively held to a minimum through the utilization of "commercially reasonable" security procedures in effecting wire transfers. These security procedures are for the purpose of verifying the authenticity of the order or detecting error in the transmission or content of the payment order or other communication. . . .

[U]nder UCC 4A-202(b), . . . [i]f the bank accepts an unauthorized payment order without verifying it in compliance with a security procedure [previously agreed to], the loss will fall on the bank. . . .

Application of the "discharge for value" rule to the circumstances presented here is particularly appropriate. The undisputed facts demonstrate that Security Pacific executed Spedley's initial order directing payment to Banque Worms notwithstanding having already received a cancellation of that order. . . . [T]he second transfer to Natwest USA was executed despite the fact that Spedley's account did not have sufficient funds to cover this second transfer. Moreover, it appears that, as a creditor of Spedley, Banque Worms was a beneficiary entitled to the funds who made no "misrepresentation and did not have notice of the transferor's mistake."

Accordingly, we conclude, in answer to the certified question, that the "discharge for value" rule[,] as set forth at §14 of the *Restatement of Restitution*, should be applied in the circumstances in this case. . . .

NOTES ON PAYING DEBTS WITH OTHER PEOPLE'S PROPERTY

1. Pronunciation. A Paris lawyer tells us that the bank's name should be pronounced Bonk Vŏrms, with the "r" sounded but barely perceptible. We're not sure many speakers of midwestern American English can actually make the sound she made.

2. Antecedent debt. Antecedent debt — debt that dates from before the transaction at issue — generally counts as value, although the definition of "value" in *Restatement (Third)* §68 declines to state a rule and leaves the question to "local law." Antecedent debt counts as value in many commercial contexts under UCC §1-204(2). In such a context, or in a jurisdiction that recognizes antecedent debt as value more generally, a creditor who receives a mistaken payment and applies it to the antecedent debt is a purchaser for value under *Restatement (Third)* §66. But this rule also gets more explicit separate treatment in §67, which says that "a payee without notice takes payment free of a restitution claim" to the extent that the payment reduces the amount of any preexisting claim of the payee. §67(1). Sections 66 and 67 in the *Restatement (Third)* correspond to §§13 and 14 in the original *Restatement of Restitution*, which the court cites in *Banque Worms*. Whatever the justification for §14 of the first *Restatement*, the *Restatement (Third)* had little choice but to follow. We find it hard to see much justification for this rule, but our complaint is with the judicial and legislative trend, not with the *Restatement (Third)*.

3. What's the difference between §66 and §67? Section 67 deals with payments in cash; §66 deals with transfers of other kinds of property. Cash is sufficiently important to deserve separate treatment, and as we have seen, the bona fide purchase rules for cash are different from the rules for other property. A related difference is that there is no "purchaser" requirement in §67. And §67 covers the payment of antecedent debt without regard to whether such debt counts as value in any other context. A creditor can retain payments collected involuntarily from any cash in the hands of its debtor, even if that cash actually belonged to someone else.

Note that a thief could not pay his debts with stolen goods under §66, because a thief cannot give good title to anything but cash and cash equivalents. But a thief can pay his debts with stolen cash under §67. In Transamerica Insurance Co. v. Long, 318 F. Supp. 156 (W.D. Pa. 1970), a surprisingly conscientious bank robber used the proceeds of the robbery to pay his back taxes. The government got to keep the stolen money, because the robber had paid an antecedent debt. The *bankruptcy court* cannot distribute other people's property to creditors. But it turns out that *the debtor* can indeed pay his debts with other people's property.

4. Reliance? The rationale for §67, and for counting antecedent debt as value, is very different from the rest of the bona fide purchaser rule. In general, one who pays money by mistake can recover that money until and unless someone without notice relies on the payment. A purchaser who gives present value has relied on the apparent validity of the transaction; he will be made worse off if he has to return the property to its true owner and cannot recover the value he gave to the intermediary who has now gone broke or gone missing.

But how would Banque Worms be worse off if it had to return the $1.97 million? Before the mistaken transfer, it had a large claim against a debtor (Spedley) who was about to go bankrupt. If it returns the mistaken transfer, it will still have a large claim against Spedley. Banque Worms agreed to loan all that money to Spedley; Security Pacific did not. Banque Worms consciously took the risk of Spedley's insolvency. Security Pacific did not voluntarily extend credit to Spedley; it insisted on funds being deposited before it did anything. Security Pacific was careless, but lack of care does not bar recovery in mistake cases.

5. Change of position? At the very beginning of this chapter, in Blue Cross v. Sauer, we briefly examined the defense of change of position. A defendant who receives money by mistake and innocently spends it may not have to repay the money. Bona fide purchase and payment for value are sometimes explained as special cases of change of position. *Restatement (Third)* §66 cmt. *a.* But change of position has a reliance requirement; defendant is protected only if she spends money she would not have spent if she had not received the mistaken payment. It is easy to see the analogy with respect to bona fide purchase for present value; the purchaser spends money in reliance on his apparent acquisition of whatever he thinks he is purchasing. But the analogy breaks down with payment for antecedent value. Why no reliance requirement there?

6. Finality of payments? Are you persuaded that creditors simply can't be exposed to the risk that they were paid with funds to which the payor was not entitled? A contrary rule would not require them to worry about every payment received, or segregate every payment until the statute of limitations ran out. Every bank and every substantial business maintains a reserve for bad debts. The risk of a debt being paid with money that doesn't belong to the debtor is trivial compared to all the other ways in which debts can go bad. The effect of requiring reliance might be a tiny increase to the bad debt reserve; more likely, the incremental risk is so small that it would not get separate attention. Very occasionally, a payment would have to be refunded. That would be one more risk of doing business. Why does that risk loom so much larger to courts, legislators, and lobbyists than the risk of loss to the true owners of the money?

Banque Worms says the New York cases had gone both ways. Just the year before, in a case involving duplicate transmission of a $223,000 wire transfer, the Appellate Division had had no doubt that New York law required reliance before the recipient could keep the money. Manufacturers Hanover Trust Co. v Chemical Bank, 559 N.Y.S.2d 704 (App. Div. 1990). The Court of Appeals denied an appeal in that case on the same day that it decided *Banque Worms.* 569 N.E.2d 874 (N.Y. 1991). Whether the law was uncertain or whether it was settled in favor of a reliance requirement, the inability of New York banks to confidently retain stolen or mistaken payments does not appear to have hampered New York's status as a financial center, a status the court recognizes in part I.B of the opinion.

7. Presuming reliance? The comments to the *Restatement (Third)* suggest that anyone who receives a payment will soon rely on it. §67 cmt. *b.* On that view, the payment rule simplifies litigation by presuming the reliance that otherwise would have to be proved. Some reliance is clear and easily proved. If the creditor releases the collateral, or stamps a promissory note paid and returns it to the debtor, or extends new credit because the old debt has been paid down, that is reliance. And each of those examples could easily be assimilated to a requirement of giving present value. If a creditor who is short of cash receives a substantial payment, he may rely by making expenditures he otherwise would not have made. That might be harder to prove, but that is the typical defense of change of position, restated in *Restatement (Third)* §65.

Banque Worms did none of those things. The mistake was promptly discovered; Banque Worms had released none of its rights against Spedley. The amount in controversy was enough to be worth suing over, but not enough to make a significant difference to the bank's cash position unless Banque Worms was also on the brink of failure—which it wasn't. It is very hard to see how a large international bank could rely on a payment of $1.97 million in any way other than releasing rights against the debtor.

8. A settled rule. Despite the skeptical tone of these comments, the rule of §67 is well established. New York law was either unsettled or contrary, but *Banque Worms* ended that. Most cases in most jurisdictions appear to support the rule, and codifications (as in the UCC definition of "value") have become more expansive over the years. The commercial supporters of finality of payments have sold their case to decision makers.

And the rule has very early roots. Suppose that Embezzler forges Employer's signature on a check payable to Merchant. Suppose further that Merchant deposits the check and Bank, not noticing the forged signature, pays the check. It is settled that Bank cannot get its money bank. UCC §3-418. This rule originated in Price v. Neal, 97 Eng. Rep. 871 (K.B. 1762), an opinion by Lord Mansfield, who also wrote the foundational restitution opinion in Moses v. McFerlan in 1760. The rule of Price v. Neal is equally foundational to the law of negotiable instruments.

But it is hard to draw a line between Price v. Neal and *Banque Worms*. In each case, the bank paid by mistake. In each case, the recipient of the payment did nothing in reliance on the bank's payment. If the payment were reversed, Banque Worms would still have its claim against Spedley, and Merchant in our hypothetical would still have its claim on the check against Embezzler. Those claims may not be very attractive, but the losing quality of those claims arose when Banque Worms made the bad loan and when Merchant took the bad check. Refunding the mistaken payment would leave them no worse off than before they received the mistaken payment. But reliance has never been required in the forged check cases, and it is generally not required in the antecedent debt cases.

9. The minority rule. There is a minority rule, vigorously reaffirmed in Wilson v. Newman, 617 N.W.2d 318 (Mich. 2000). *Wilson* is a lot like Blue Cross v. Sauer, the case that opened this chapter. Wilson got a judgment against Newman, and tried to collect the judgment from Newman's life insurance policies. The insurer, Allmerica Financial, had policies on Robert L. Newman with a cash value of $43,000, and it paid that sum to Wilson. Then it discovered that its insured was a different Robert L. Newman; it held no assets that belonged to Wilson's judgment debtor. But Wilson refused to return the money.

The court granted judgment to the insurer for restitution of the $43,000. It emphatically rejected §14 of the first *Restatement*, the section relied on in *Banque Worms*. Among other things, the court said:

> Courts often say that when one of two innocent parties must suffer a loss, it should be borne by the one whose conduct made the loss possible. However, such analysis does not apply in this case. Under the result reached by the lower courts, Allmerica Financial will unquestionably suffer a loss. It will have paid more than $43,000 to the plaintiffs, and will also continue to owe that amount to its Colorado policyholder, whom it mistakenly believed to be defendant Newman. By contrast, absent some showing of specific prejudice, . . . the plaintiffs will not suffer loss as a result of restitution. The plaintiffs had a judgment against defendant Newman, which they were entitled to collect by whatever means the law permits. After restitution of the mistaken payment by Allmerica, they would be left in exactly the same position, possessed of the same judgment, which they may proceed to attempt to collect.

617 N.W.2d at 322 n.4. Wilson said he had in fact relied, by "forgoing other collection efforts that may not now be available." *Id.* at 322. The court said that would be reliance and would make out a valid defense if proved, but no such evidence had been offered. The court decided the case summarily; two dissenters would have granted

full argument. No court in another state has cited *Wilson* favorably; its holding is rejected in The National Bank v. FCC Equipment Financing, Inc., 801 N.W.2d 17 (Iowa Ct. App. 2011).

10. Subrogation. Note that Security Pacific can now be subrogated to Banque Worms's claim against Spedley. That is apparently useless here, or at least does not seem likely to lead to a full recovery. If Banque Worms had sufficient collateral, Security Pacific would be protected. But in that case, Banque Worms would have been protected even if it had to return the mistaken payment.

E.   REPLEVIN, EJECTMENT, AND THE LIKE

1. Restitutionary in form and function but historically unrelated. Replevin and ejectment are ancient writs for the recovery of property: replevin for personal property and ejectment for real estate. They were common law writs, with no historic connection to quasi-contract or constructive trust, so they are not usually included in treatments of restitution. They work in cases where defendant has possession but not title, so a constructive trust is not required. Yet clearly they are restitutionary remedies in the most literal sense; they restore to plaintiff, in kind, the very property that she lost.

2. Why we need them. These writs perform a function that is too basic for any legal system to do without. Think about the ways in which someone else may be holding your personal property. If he simply stole it, you call the police. If the police find the stolen goods and the facts are sufficiently clear, the police will return the goods to you without any legal proceedings.

The facts may not be so clear. If the thief plausibly claims to be entitled to possession, the police cannot adjudicate such disputes. And the party in possession may not be a thief at all. Maybe he bought them from the thief, innocently or otherwise. Maybe the goods have been stored, and there is a dispute about the storage charges; maybe the goods have been loaned, and the borrower refuses to return them; maybe there is a genuine dispute about ownership; or maybe both parties own a divided interest in the goods and there is a dispute about who is entitled to possession.

Secured credit is an especially important case of divided interests. Suppose a lender loans money secured by an interest in the borrower's goods. In the language of the UCC, the lender becomes the secured party, the borrower becomes the debtor, and the goods become the collateral. If the debtor fails to pay, the secured party can repossess without going to court, but only if she is physically able to do so without a breach of peace. UCC §9-609(b). Cars parked on the street are repossessed this way all the time. If the debtor claims that the repossession was wrongful, he can (among other remedies) sue to replevy the car.

Far more commonly, it is the secured party who sues to replevy the collateral. If collateral is inside the debtor's house, office, or factory, and the debtor is unwilling to turn it over, the secured party cannot seize the collateral without a breach of peace. Of course the secured party may sue on the debt; she may also sue to replevy her collateral. Whatever the context, replevin is enforced by sending the sheriff to seize the goods and deliver them to the successful plaintiff.

3. Brook v. Cullimore. We read a replevin case back in section 5.A.1, Brook v. James A. Cullimore & Co. That was a secured party recovering his collateral. The case illustrated both replevin's most common modern use and its traditional mechanics. Plaintiff alleged that he was entitled to the collateral and posted a bond for its value; if a judge finds these allegations sufficient and credible, that is normally enough to entitle plaintiff to possession pending trial. But in *Brook*, defendant filed a "redelivery bond," which entitled him to retain possession pending trial. At that point, the normal course would be for the parties to try the merits, which in a secured credit context, turn on whether the debtor is in default and the secured party is entitled to repossess.

What actually happened in *Brook* was a little different. Defendant confessed judgment for the alleged value of the collateral and tried to pay the judgment in cash. Plaintiff successfully insisted on his right to the collateral, thus producing a casebook illustration of plaintiff's entitlement to specific relief in replevin. The first time we read the case, it was to compare this routine specific relief with the allegedly extraordinary nature of specific relief by injunction. Defendant was willing to pay the alleged value to keep the goods, and plaintiff was unwilling to let them go for that price, so plaintiff must have deliberately underestimated the value to avoid posting a larger bond. This maneuver wound up costing him a lot more than he saved; he had to take an appeal to get the goods.

4. Damages in replevin. The replevin plaintiff has a choice; she can sue for the goods or for their value. She will usually plead a claim for the value of the goods as damages for conversion. But as *Brook* illustrates, many modern replevin statutes let her recover damages in the replevin action. This simplifies the litigation in cases where plaintiff initially sues for the goods and then discovers that the goods have been lost, destroyed, damaged, or sold to a bona fide purchaser.

Plaintiff can also recover damages for the time during which she was dispossessed. An example of that is Welch v. Kosasky, 509 N.E.2d 919 (Mass. App. Ct. 1987), involving a dispute over antique silver. The silver was stolen from plaintiffs in 1974; defendant bought it from a dealer a month later and sold it to another dealer in 1981. The plaintiffs recognized some of the silver in the dealer's window; follow-up investigation found the rest. In addition to recovering the silver, they got a judgment for $10,000 for loss of use of the silver during the time it was missing and $22,000 for damage to two pieces that defendant had altered. The trial court found that defendant knew or should have known that the silver was stolen, but that fact should not have been necessary to the result. Recall that even a bona fide purchaser cannot get good title from or through a thief.

Welch is substantially parallel to *Olwell* and the "borrowed" egg washer. In each case, the tort was conversion of a chattel; in each case, plaintiff waived the tort and sued in assumpsit. (Yes, they still said that in Massachusetts in 1987.) But the measure of benefit was different, principally because the egg washer was steadily depreciating but the silver, if it had not been damaged, would have appreciated substantially.

The usual rule is that damages are measured as of the time of the tort; courts have struggled to compensate lost appreciation in cases of converted art and collectibles. *Welch* used a restitution theory that didn't actually work very well. In a case of stolen art recovered many years after the theft, the New York court focused simply on the position plaintiff would have been in but for the wrong, disregarding conventional rules about the time for measuring damages. Menzel v. List, 246 N.E.2d 742 (N.Y. 1969). And in a famous case where the executors of an artist's estate sold his paintings at less than fair market value in a transaction tainted by conflict of interest, the court relied on trust law to award the lost appreciation. In re Estate of Rothko, 372 N.E.2d 291 (N.Y. 1977).

5. Ejectment. Ejectment was the principal writ for recovery of land. Like replevin, it ended in a judgment for possession, and the sheriff would evict defendant if he did not leave voluntarily. Plaintiff could also recover damages for the use of the land during the period of dispossession (sometimes called mesne profits, which is pronounced mean profits). The elaborate fictional pleadings required at common law have been abolished by modern statutory remedies, more often called quiet title than ejectment. These remedies are reviewed in section 7.B.

6. Forcible entry and detainer. There was no form of preliminary relief in ejectment. In merged procedure, plaintiff might seek a preliminary injunction on appropriate facts. But there is also a separate summary remedy for possession in simple cases, usually known as forcible detainer or sometimes as unlawful detainer. The remedy is statutory, and the statutes usually define two wrongs and two remedies.

Forcible entry is a damage action for forcibly entering land and dispossessing the occupant. Even the true owner can be liable for forcible entry, because the emphasis is on the use of private force and the associated risk of violence.

Forcible detainer is the summary action for possession. In most states, it can be used only against defendants who have no colorable claim of title. In Texas, for example, the remedy is available only against holdover tenants, tenants at will, and tenants of persons who acquired possession by forcible entry. Tex. Prop. Code Ann. §24.002.

The action is typically heard in a court of very limited jurisdiction, such as a justice-of-the-peace court, without authority to determine title. If there is a title dispute, plaintiff must sue in ejectment or quiet title to get it resolved.

7. Constitutional limits. Replevin was traditionally administered through the preliminary steps of bond and counterbond to determine who was entitled to possession pending trial. Instead of a preliminary hearing to determine each side's probability of success on the merits, as in preliminary injunctions, preliminary relief was based on willingness and ability to post a bond.

This procedure worked well for secured creditors, and some states streamlined it even further. Plaintiff could get possession merely by filing a bond and filling out a form that alleged in conclusory fashion that he was entitled to the property; a clerk would issue the writ. In theory defendant could file a redelivery bond and demand a hearing. But often the clerk's automatic issuance of the writ ended the matter. Defendants did not respond, often because they had no defense, but also because they did not know they could still assert a defense, did not know how to assert a defense, or could not post a bond. Even if defendant eventually recovered his property, he had been deprived of it in the meantime. And in many states, there was no guarantee that the hearing would be promptly scheduled.

These procedures have been modernized in light of Fuentes v. Shevin, 407 U.S. 67 (1972), and Mitchell v. W.T. Grant Co., 416 U.S. 600 (1974). *Fuentes* held that due process required some kind of hearing before seizure of property. *Mitchell* held that it was sufficient for plaintiff to state the details of his claim in an affidavit or verified complaint and for a judge to review the affidavit and sign the writ, provided that defendant could demand a prompt hearing at which the burden of proof would be on the plaintiff. The process of conforming procedures in each state to the minimum standard approved in *Mitchell* has led to a general rewriting and modernization of replevin statutes. For a detailed modern statute, with helpful commentary on the historical practice and the reasons for change, see N.Y. C.P.L.R. §7101 *et seq.* It is not clear that all courts adhere to the new rules; it is clear that consumer debtors are no more likely than before to invoke their right to a hearing.

Forcible detainer procedures came under similar constitutional attack in Lindsey v. Normet, 405 U.S. 56 (1972). All forcible detainer statutes guarantee the tenant some sort of hearing before eviction, but the hearing is often quite limited. Under the Oregon statute at issue in *Lindsey*, the hearing could be held on as little as two days' notice to the tenant. The tenant could get an additional two-day continuance; he could get a longer continuance only by filing a bond to cover rent as it accrued. The tenant could not raise any affirmative defenses, although he could sue for breach of the lease in a separate action. The Supreme Court upheld all of these provisions.

The Oregon statute also provided that the tenant could not appeal unless he filed a bond for double the amount of the rent that would accrue between commencement of the action and final judgment. If the tenant lost the appeal, he forfeited the entire bond whether or not the landlord had suffered any damage. The Court struck down this provision as a discriminatory burden on the right to appeal.

CHAPTER
9

Ancillary Remedies: Enforcing the Judgment

Ancillary remedies help implement some other remedy. This chapter examines the ancillary remedies used to enforce judgments. We need a course in remedies because litigation does not end with the liability determination. Neither does it end with the award of a remedy. A wealthy defendant with liquid assets may write a check for the judgment, but many defendants are unable or unwilling to pay. A cooperative defendant may immediately set about fully complying with an injunction, but many are recalcitrant. One of Laycock's Texas colleagues is fond of saying that a money judgment is nothing but a handsome piece of paper suitable for framing. He could say the same thing about an injunction. But he would be exaggerating. Judgments come in ordinary typescript on ordinary paper; they are not even suitable for framing. A judgment is an important step toward what plaintiff wants, but it is not what she wants. The judgment must be enforced.

A. ENFORCING COERCIVE ORDERS: THE CONTEMPT POWER

1. The Three Kinds of Contempt

INTERNATIONAL UNION, UNITED MINE WORKERS v. BAGWELL

512 U.S. 821 (1994)

Justice BLACKMUN delivered the opinion of the Court. . . .

I . . .

[T]he union engaged in a protracted labor dispute with . . . the companies over alleged unfair labor practices. In April 1989, the companies filed suit in the Circuit Court of Russell County, Virginia, to enjoin the union from conducting unlawful strike-related activities. The trial court entered an injunction which . . . prohibited the union and its members from . . . obstructing ingress and egress to company facilities, throwing objects at and physically threatening company employees, placing tire-damaging "jackrocks" on roads used by company vehicles, and picketing with more than a specified number of people at designated sites. [A jackrock is a piece of wood with nails driven through in multiple directions, so that when it is thrown on a road, a nail will be sticking up no matter how it lands.]

On May 16, 1989, the trial court held a contempt hearing and found that petitioners had committed 72 violations of the injunction. After fining the union $642,000 for its disobedience, the court announced that it would fine the union $100,000 for any future violent breach of the injunction and $20,000 for any future nonviolent infraction . . . .

In seven subsequent contempt hearings held between June and December 1989, the court found the union in contempt for more than four hundred separate violations of the injunction, many of them violent. . . . [E]ach contempt hearing was conducted as a civil proceeding before the trial judge, in which the parties conducted discovery, introduced evidence, and called and cross-examined witnesses. The trial court required that contumacious acts be proved beyond a reasonable doubt, but did not afford the union a right to jury trial.

As a result of these contempt proceedings, the court levied over $64,000,000 in fines against the union, approximately $12,000,000 of which was ordered payable to the companies. . . . [T]he court ordered that the remaining roughly $52,000,000 in fines be paid to the Commonwealth of Virginia and Russell and Dickenson Counties . . . .

While appeals from the contempt orders were pending, the union and the companies settled the underlying labor dispute, agreed to vacate the contempt fines, and jointly moved to dismiss the case. A special mediator representing the Secretary of Labor, and the governments of Russell and Dickenson Counties, supported the parties' motion to vacate the outstanding fines. The trial court granted the motion to dismiss, dissolved the injunction, and vacated the $12,000,000 in fines payable to the companies. After reiterating its belief that the remaining $52,000,000 owed to the counties and the Commonwealth were coercive, civil fines, the trial court refused to vacate these fines . . . .

[T]he court appointed respondent John L. Bagwell to act as Special Commissioner to collect the unpaid contempt fines on behalf of the counties and the Commonwealth.

The Court of Appeals of Virginia reversed and ordered that the contempt fines be vacated pursuant to the settlement agreement. 402 S.E.2d 899 (Va. Ct. App. 1991). . . .

[T]he Supreme Court of Virginia reversed. . . . Because the trial court's prospective fine schedule was intended to coerce compliance with the injunction and the union could avoid the fines through obedience, the court reasoned, the fines were civil and coercive and properly imposed in civil proceedings. 423 S.E.2d 349 (Va. 1992). . . .

II

A

"Criminal contempt is a crime in the ordinary sense," Bloom v. Illinois, 391 U.S. 194, 201 (1968), and "criminal penalties may not be imposed on someone who has not been afforded the protections that the Constitution requires of such criminal proceedings." Hicks v. Feiock, 485 U.S. 624, 632 (1988). . . . In contrast, civil contempt sanctions, or those penalties designed to compel future compliance with a court order, are considered to be coercive and avoidable through obedience, and thus may be imposed in an ordinary civil proceeding upon notice and an opportunity to be heard. Neither a jury trial nor proof beyond a reasonable doubt is required.

Although the procedural contours of the two forms of contempt are well established, the distinguishing characteristics of civil versus criminal contempts are somewhat less clear. In the leading early case addressing this issue in the context of imprisonment, the Court emphasized that whether a contempt is civil or criminal turns on the "character and purpose" of the sanction involved. Gompers v. Bucks Stove & Range Co., 221 U.S. 418, 441 (1911). Thus, a contempt sanction is considered civil if it "is remedial, and for the benefit of the complainant. But if it is for criminal contempt the sentence is punitive, to vindicate the authority of the court." *Id.*

As *Gompers* recognized, however, the stated purposes of a contempt sanction alone cannot be determinative. . . . Most contempt sanctions . . . to some extent punish a prior offense as well as coerce an offender's future obedience. The *Hicks* Court accordingly held that conclusions about the civil or criminal nature of a contempt sanction are properly drawn, not from "the subjective intent of a State's laws and its courts," 485 U.S. at 635, but "from an examination of the character of the relief itself," *id.* at 636.

The paradigmatic coercive, civil contempt sanction . . . involves confining a contemnor indefinitely until he complies with an affirmative command such as an order "to pay alimony, or to surrender property ordered to be turned over to a receiver, or to make a conveyance." 221 U.S. at 442. Imprisonment for a fixed term similarly is coercive when the contemnor is given the option of earlier release if he complies. In these circumstances, the contemnor is able to purge the contempt and obtain his release by committing an affirmative act, and thus "carries the keys of his prison in his own pocket." *Id.*

By contrast, a fixed sentence of imprisonment is punitive and criminal if it is imposed retrospectively for a "completed act of disobedience," 221 U.S. at 443, such that the contemnor cannot avoid or abbreviate the confinement through later compliance. . . . "[T]he defendant is furnished no key, and he cannot shorten the term by promising not to repeat the offense." *Id.* at 442.

This dichotomy between coercive and punitive imprisonment has been extended to the fine context. A contempt fine accordingly is considered civil and remedial if it either "coerce[s] the defendant into compliance with the court's order, [or] . . . compensate[s] the complainant for losses sustained." United States v. United Mine Workers, 330 U.S. 258, 303-304 (1947). Where a fine is not compensatory, it is civil only if the contemnor is afforded an opportunity to purge. Thus, a "flat, unconditional fine" totaling even as little as $50 . . . is criminal if the contemnor has no subsequent opportunity to reduce or avoid the fine through compliance.

A close analogy to coercive imprisonment is a per diem fine imposed for each day a contemnor fails to comply with an affirmative court order. Like civil imprisonment, such fines exert a constant coercive pressure, and once the jural command is obeyed, the future, indefinite, daily fines are purged. Less comfortable is the analogy between coercive imprisonment and suspended, determinate fines. *Mine Workers* involved a $3,500,000 fine imposed against the union for nationwide . . . strike activities. Finding that the determinate fine was both criminal and excessive, the Court reduced the sanction to a flat criminal fine of $700,000. The Court then imposed and suspended the remaining $2,800,000 as a coercive civil fine, conditioned on the union's ability to purge the fine through full, timely compliance with the trial court's order.[4] The Court concluded, in light of this purge clause, that the civil fine operated as "a coercive imposition upon the defendant union to compel obedience with the court's outstanding order." 330 U.S. at 307.

---

4. Although the size of the fine was substantial, the conduct required of the union to purge the suspended fine was relatively discrete. [The union was required to issue certain notices concerning the validity of a disputed labor contract.]

This Court has not revisited the issue of coercive civil contempt fines addressed in *Mine Workers*. Since that decision, the Court has erected substantial procedural protections in other areas of contempt law, such as criminal contempts and summary contempts. Lower . . . courts . . . nevertheless have relied on *Mine Workers* to authorize a relatively unlimited judicial power to impose noncompensatory civil contempt fines.

B . . .

The traditional justification for the relative breadth of the contempt power has been necessity: Courts independently must be vested with "power to impose silence, respect, and decorum, in their presence, and submission to their lawful mandates, and . . . to preserve themselves and their officers from the approach and insults of pollution." Anderson v. Dunn, 19 U.S. (6 Wheat.) 204, 227 (1821). Courts thus have embraced an inherent contempt authority, as a power "necessary to the exercise of all others." United States v. Hudson, 11 U.S. (7 Cranch) 32, 34 (1812).

But the contempt power also uniquely is "liable to abuse." *Bloom*, 391 U.S. at 202. Unlike most areas of law, where a legislature defines both the sanctionable conduct and the penalty to be imposed, civil contempt proceedings leave the offended judge solely responsible for identifying, prosecuting, adjudicating, and sanctioning the contumacious conduct. Contumacy "often strikes at the most vulnerable and human qualities of a judge's temperament," *Bloom*, 391 U.S. at 202, and its fusion of legislative, executive, and judicial powers "summons forth . . . the prospect of 'the most tyrannical licentiousness.'" Young v. United States ex rel. Vuitton et Fils, S.A., 481 U. S. 787, 822 (1987) (Scalia, J., concurring in judgment), quoting *Anderson*, 19 U.S. at 228. . . .

Our jurisprudence in the contempt area has attempted to balance the competing concerns of necessity and potential arbitrariness by allowing a relatively unencumbered contempt power when its exercise is most essential, and requiring progressively greater procedural protections when other considerations come into play. The necessity justification for the contempt authority is at its pinnacle, of course, where contumacious conduct threatens a court's immediate ability to conduct its proceedings, such as where a witness refuses to testify, or a party disrupts the court. . . . In light of the court's substantial interest in rapidly coercing compliance and restoring order, and because the contempt's occurrence before the court reduces the need for extensive factfinding and the likelihood of an erroneous deprivation, summary proceedings have been tolerated. . . .

If a court delays punishing a direct contempt [one committed in the presence of the court] until the completion of trial . . . due process requires that the contemnor's rights to notice and a hearing be respected. There "it is much more difficult to argue that action without notice or hearing of any kind is necessary to preserve order and enable [the court] to proceed with its business," Taylor v. Hayes, 418 U.S. 488, 498 (1974). . . . Direct contempts also cannot be punished with serious criminal penalties absent the full protections of a criminal jury trial.

Still further procedural protections are afforded for contempts occurring out of court. . . . Summary adjudication of indirect contempts is prohibited, and criminal contempt sanctions are entitled to full criminal process. Certain indirect contempts nevertheless are appropriate for imposition through civil proceedings. Contempts such as failure to comply with document discovery, for example, while occurring outside the court's presence, impede the court's ability to adjudicate the proceedings before it and thus touch upon the core justification for the contempt power. Courts traditionally have broad authority through means other than contempt—such as by striking pleadings, assessing costs, excluding evidence, and entering default judgment—to penalize a party's failure to comply with the rules of conduct governing the litigation process. Such judicial sanctions never have been considered criminal, and the imposition of civil, coercive fines to police the litigation process appears consistent with this authority. Similarly, indirect contempts involving discrete, readily ascertainable acts, such as turning over a key or payment of a judgment, properly may be adjudicated through civil proceedings since the need for extensive, impartial factfinding is less pressing.

For a discrete category of indirect contempts, however, civil procedural protections may be insufficient. Contempts involving out-of-court disobedience to complex injunctions often require elaborate and reliable factfinding. Such contempts do not obstruct the court's ability to adjudicate the proceedings before it, and the risk of erroneous deprivation from the lack of a neutral factfinder may be substantial. Under these circumstances, criminal procedural protections such as the rights to counsel and proof beyond a reasonable doubt are both necessary and appropriate to protect the due process rights of parties and prevent the arbitrary exercise of judicial power.

C

In the instant case, neither any party nor any court of the Commonwealth has suggested that the challenged fines are compensatory. At no point did the trial court attempt to calibrate the fines to damages caused by the union's contumacious activities . . . . The issue . . . is . . . whether these fines . . . are coercive civil or criminal sanctions. . . .

Petitioners argue that because the injunction primarily prohibited certain conduct rather than mandated affirmative acts, the sanctions are criminal. Respondent . . . urges that because the trial court established a prospective fine schedule that the union could avoid through compliance, the fines are civil . . . .

Neither theory satisfactorily identifies those contempt fines that are criminal and thus must be imposed through the criminal process. . . .

[T]he distinction between coercion of affirmative acts and punishment of prohibited conduct is difficult to apply when conduct that can recur is involved, or when an injunction contains both mandatory and prohibitory provisions. Moreover, in borderline cases injunctive provisions containing essentially the same command can be phrased either in mandatory or prohibitory terms. Under a literal application of petitioners' theory, an injunction ordering the union: "Do not strike," would appear to be prohibitory and criminal, while an injunction ordering the union: "Continue working," would be mandatory and civil. In enforcing the present injunction, the trial court imposed fines without regard to the mandatory or prohibitory nature of the clause violated. . . . In a case like this involving an injunction that prescribes a detailed code of conduct, it is more appropriate to identify the character of the entire decree. Cf. *Hicks*, 485 U.S. at 639 n.10 (internal quotations omitted) (Where both civil and criminal relief is imposed "the criminal feature of the order is dominant and fixes its character for purposes of review"). . . .

Had the trial court simply levied the fines after finding the union guilty of contempt, the resulting "determinate and unconditional" fines would be considered "solely and exclusively punitive." *Hicks*, 485 U.S. at 632-633. Respondent nevertheless contends that the trial court's announcement of a prospective fine schedule allowed the union to "avoid paying the fine[s] simply by performing the . . . act required by the court's order," *Hicks*, 485 U.S. at 632, and thus transformed these fines into coercive, civil ones. . . .

[T]he fact that the trial court announced the fines before the contumacy, rather than after the fact, does not in itself justify respondent's conclusion that the fines are civil or meaningfully distinguish these penalties from the ordinary criminal law. Due process traditionally requires that criminal laws provide prior notice both of the conduct to be prohibited and of the sanction to be imposed. The trial court here simply announced the penalty—determinate fines of $20,000 or $100,000 per violation—that would be imposed for future contempts. The union's ability to avoid the contempt fines was indistinguishable from the ability of any ordinary citizen to avoid a criminal sanction by conforming his behavior to the law. The fines are not coercive day fines, or even suspended fines, but are more closely analogous to fixed, determinate, retrospective criminal fines which petitioners had no opportunity to purge once imposed. We therefore decline to conclude that the mere fact that the sanctions were announced in advance rendered them coercive and civil as a matter of constitutional law.

Other considerations convince us that the fines challenged here are criminal. The union's sanctionable conduct did not occur in the court's presence or otherwise implicate the court's ability to maintain order and adjudicate the proceedings before it. Nor did the union's contumacy involve simple, affirmative acts, such as the paradigmatic civil contempts examined in *Gompers* [publishing statements forbidden by the injunction]. Instead, the Virginia trial court levied contempt fines for widespread, ongoing, out-of-court violations of a complex injunction. In so doing, the court effectively policed petitioners' compliance with an entire code of conduct that the court itself had imposed. The union's contumacy lasted many months and spanned a substantial portion of the State. The fines assessed were serious, totaling over $52,000,000. Under such circumstances, disinterested factfinding and even-handed adjudication were essential, and petitioners were entitled to a criminal jury trial. . . .

III

The judgment of the Supreme Court of Virginia is reversed. . . .

Justice SCALIA, concurring. . . .

That one and the same person should be able to make the rule, to adjudicate its violation, and to assess its penalty is out of accord with our usual notions of fairness and separation of powers. And it is worse still for that person to conduct the adjudication without affording the protections usually given in criminal trials. . . .

Incarceration until compliance was a distinctive sanction, and sheds light upon the nature of the decrees enforced by civil contempt. That sanction makes sense only if the order requires performance of an identifiable act (or perhaps cessation of continuing performance of an identifiable act). A general prohibition for the future does not lend itself to enforcement through conditional incarceration, since no single act (or the cessation of no single act) can demonstrate compliance and justify release. . . .

[In traditional equity practice, the] mandatory injunctions issued upon termination of litigation usually required "a single simple act." Henry McClintock, *Principles of Equity* §15 at 32-33 (2d ed., West 1948). Indeed, there was a "historical prejudice of the court of chancery against rendering decrees which called for more than a single affirmative act." *Id.* §61 at 160. And where specific performance of contracts was sought, it was the categorical rule that no decree would issue that required ongoing supervision. . . .

Even equitable decrees that were prohibitory rather than mandatory were, in earlier times, much less sweeping than their modern counterparts. Prior to the labor injunctions of the late 1800's, injunctions were issued primarily in relatively narrow disputes over property.

Contemporary courts have abandoned these earlier limitations upon the scope of their mandatory and injunctive decrees. They routinely issue complex decrees which involve them in extended disputes and place them in continuing supervisory roles over parties and institutions. . . .

When an order governs many aspects of a litigant's activities, rather than just a discrete act, determining compliance becomes much more difficult. Credibility issues arise, for which the factfinding protections of the criminal law (including jury trial) become much more important. And when continuing prohibitions or obligations are imposed, the order cannot be complied with (and the contempt "purged") in a single act; it continues to govern the party's behavior, on pain of punishment—not unlike the criminal law. . . .

***

The use of a civil process for contempt sanctions "makes no sense except as a consequence of historical practice." Weiss v. United States, 510 U.S. 163, 198 (1994) (Scalia, J., concurring in part). As the scope of injunctions has expanded, they have lost some of the distinctive features that made enforcement through civil process acceptable. It is not that the times, or our perceptions of fairness, have changed (that is in my view no basis for either tightening or relaxing the traditional demands of due process); but rather that the modern judicial order is in its relevant essentials not the same device that in former times could always be enforced by civil contempt. So adjustments will have to be made. We will have to decide at some point which modern injunctions sufficiently resemble their historical namesakes to warrant the same extraordinary means of enforcement. We need not draw that line in the present case, and so I am content to join the opinion of the Court.

Justice GINSBURG, with whom Chief Justice REHNQUIST joins, concurring in part . . . .

II . . .

Two considerations persuade me that the contempt proceedings in this case should be classified as "criminal" rather than "civil." First, were we to accept the logic of Bagwell's argument that the fines here were civil, because "conditional" and "coercive," no fine would elude that categorization. The fines in this case were "conditional," Bagwell says, because they would not have been imposed if the unions had complied with the injunction. The fines would have been "conditional" in this sense, however, even if the court had not supplemented the injunction with its fines schedule; indeed, any fine is "conditional" upon compliance or noncompliance before its imposition. Furthermore, while the fines were "coercive," in the sense that one of their purposes was to encourage union compliance with the injunction, criminal contempt sanctions may also "coerce" in this same sense, for they, too, "ten[d] to prevent a repetition of the disobedience." Gompers, 221 U.S. at 443. . . .

Second, the Virginia courts' refusal to vacate the fines, despite the parties' settlement and joint motion, is characteristic of criminal, not civil proceedings. . . . [W]ith the private complainant gone from the scene, and an official appointed by the Commonwealth to collect the fines for the Commonwealth's coffers, it is implausible to invoke the justification of benefiting the civil complainant. The Commonwealth here pursues the fines on its own account, not as the agent of a private party, and without tying the exactions exclusively to a claim for compensation. If, as the trial court declared, the proceedings were indeed civil from the outset, then the court should have granted the parties' motions to vacate the fines.

***

. . . I join the Court's judgment and all but Part II-B of its opinion.

NOTES ON THE THREE KINDS OF CONTEMPT

1. The basic distinctions. *Bagwell*'s explanation of the traditional differences among criminal contempt, coercive civil contempt, and compensatory civil contempt was settled law in the federal courts and in most states. Even so, the reports are full of cases in which trial judges confused criminal contempt with coercive civil contempt. The most common error has been to impose unconditional penalties in civil proceedings, as in the first contempt hearing in *Bagwell*. The fines payable to the companies in *Bagwell* also suggest confusion: If they were coercive, they should have been payable to the government; if they were compensatory, the court should have required evidence of damages. In re Chase & Sanborn Corp., 872 F.2d 397 (11th Cir. 1989). The Supreme Court has emphasized that the distinctions depend entirely on the form of the sanctions, and not on the judge's purposes or motivations. Hicks v. Feiock, 485 U.S. 624, 631-637 (1988).

There is also a tendency to think that the distinction has to do with the nature of defendant's act—that some contempts are criminal and others civil. But the distinction is in the proceeding, not in the contempt. Any contempt can be the subject of civil or criminal proceedings or both, just like any battery. The only difference that relates to defendant's act is the required state of mind: Even inadvertent violations of the injunction are civil contempt, but only willful violations are criminal contempt. Food Lion, Inc. v. United Food & Commercial Workers, 103 F.3d 1007, 1016-1017 (D.C. Cir. 1997). But courts have some discretion: While willfulness is not required for civil contempt, "technical and/or inadvertent violations are factors to be considered in deciding a motion for contempt." Grubbs v. Safir, 2018 WL 1225262, *9 (S.D.N.Y. Feb. 26, 2018). An appeal has been filed in the Second Circuit, No. 18-670.

2. Criminal contempt. Criminal contempt is criminal punishment for a past offense; the punishment is not conditional on future compliance. Criminal contempt is prosecuted in the name of the sovereign; the civil plaintiff is in the position of a complaining witness. He can report the contempt, but he cannot require the court or prosecutor to proceed criminally, or stop them from continuing if he settles the case. Any fines are payable to the government.

a. Procedural protections. The prosecution may begin with notice rather than indictment, but at trial, defendant gets substantially all the protections of criminal procedure, including proof beyond a reasonable doubt. The Double Jeopardy Clause protects against separate prosecutions for criminal contempt and for an underlying criminal offense subsumed in the injunction, such as assault or jackrocking in *Bagwell*. United States v. Dixon, 509 U.S. 688 (1993).

b. Jury trial. Defendant cannot constitutionally be sentenced to more than six months in jail without a jury trial. Bloom v. Illinois, 391 U.S. 194 (1968). Substantial criminal fines can be imposed without jury trial, and the upper limit is undefined. Muniz v. Hoffman, 422 U.S. 454 (1975), held that a $10,000 fine imposed on a local union with 13,000 members did not trigger the right to jury trial; *Bagwell* says that $52 million does require a jury trial, at least if the facts are complex, even for an international union. A New York court has held that a fine of $2.5 million does not require jury trial when imposed on a union with 33,000 members and with $3.6 million in its treasury. New York City Transit Authority v. Transit Workers Union, 822 N.Y.S.2d 579 (App. Div. 2006). The judge can avoid jury trial by announcing in advance that she will not impose a sentence that would require a jury trial. United States v. Linney, 134 F.3d 274 (4th Cir. 1998). The whole debate grows out of the doctrine that the right to jury trial does not apply to "petty offenses."

c. The collateral bar rule. The offense is complete when defendant willfully violates an injunction, even if the injunction is later held erroneous. Thus, defendant cannot challenge the validity of the injunction in a prosecution for criminal contempt. Walker v. City of Birmingham, 388 U.S. 307 (1967), reprinted in section 9.A.3. This controversial rule is called the collateral bar rule, because it bars certain collateral attacks on the validity of injunctions.

3. Civil contempt. Civil contempt is prosecuted in the name of the plaintiff and largely controlled by the plaintiff. He initiates it with a motion, and up to a point he can abandon it or settle it; *Bagwell* turns in part on whether he eventually loses control. The collateral bar rule does not apply, because the civil plaintiff is not entitled to benefit from an erroneous injunction. United States v. United Mine Workers, 330 U.S. 258, 295 (1947). Civil contempt may be either coercive or compensatory. "A large body of case law holds that civil contempt must be proven by clear and convincing evidence, though it is in tension with the Supreme Court's insistence on a presumption in favor of the less onerous standard of preponderance of the evidence in federal civil cases." Securities and Exchange Commission v. First Choice Management Services, Inc., 678 F.3d 538, 544 (7th Cir. 2012) (Posner, J.). But once a violation is proved, the amount of damages in compensatory civil contempt need be proved only by a preponderance of the evidence. Federal Trade Commission v. Kuykendall, 371 F.3d 745, 754 (10th Cir. 2004). The Ninth Circuit has held that civil contempt proceedings are exempt from the automatic stay of other court proceedings that issues in every bankruptcy case. Dingley v. Yellow Logistics, LLC, 852 F.3d 1143 (9th Cir. 2017).

4. Compensatory civil contempt. Compensatory civil contempt is like an action for damages or restitution. Before it issues an injunction, the court decides that damages would be an inadequate remedy. Now that the injunction is violated, it awards compensation after all. Damages are inadequate, but they are not useless; recall that adequacy is relative. In any event, damages are now the best the court can do.

a. Measuring the damages. Defendant forced the case into this posture by violating the injunction, which may be a reason to more aggressively resolve uncertainties against defendant, but the contempt context does not change the measure of damages. An example is United States v. City of Miami, 195 F.3d 1292 (11th Cir. 1999), where two promotions were awarded in violation of a consent decree in an employment discrimination case. It was impossible to tell who, among a class of 35 candidates, would have gotten the promotions if the decree had been followed. The district court in compensatory contempt awarded full back pay and other benefits to all 35 candidates. The court of appeals reversed, holding that the back pay for two positions should be divided pro rata among the candidates.

b. Disgorgement. Despite the compensatory label, plaintiff can recover defendant's profits, at least if disgorgement of profits would be an appropriate measure of recovery for the underlying wrong. The leading case is Leman v. Krentler-Arnold Hinge Last Co., 284 U.S. 448 (1932); a modern example is Marshak v. Treadwell, 595 F.3d 478 (3d Cir. 2009). Both cases involve contempt of an injunction against infringing intellectual property. The Seventh Circuit held that a trial court can choose a measure for compensatory contempt based on plaintiff's losses or defendant's gains, but it "must explain why it chose the calculation method it did and how the record supports its calculations." Federal Trade Commission v. Trudeau, 579 F.3d 754, 773 (7th Cir. 2009).

c. Jury trial. Because compensatory contempt is ancillary to the injunction suit, there is no jury trial in most jurisdictions. Partly for that reason, about ten states reject compensatory contempt, including California, Illinois, and Texas. Doug Rendleman, *Compensatory Contempt: Plaintiff's Remedy When a Defendant Violates an Injunction*, 1980 U. Ill. L.F. 971, 982-983 n.49. In those states, plaintiff must file an ordinary action for damages.

d. *Bagwell* and compensatory contempt. Does *Bagwell* require any greater procedural protections in compensatory contempt proceedings involving complex facts and large liabilities? A panel of the Tenth Circuit said yes, but the en banc court said no. Federal Trade Commission v. Kuykendall, 312 F.3d 1329 (10th Cir. 2002), *vacated*, 371 F.3d 745 (10th Cir. 2004). The district court entered a consent decree enjoining certain fraudulent telemarketing practices; those practices continued unabated for five more years after the decree. The district court found defendants in contempt, found that the violations had cost consumers $39 million, and ordered that amount to be paid into a fund from which to compensate the victims.

The panel held that due process required greater procedural protection than the trial court's conclusory finding of damages. The panel affirmed the finding of contempt, but remanded for a jury trial on the amount of consumer losses. The opinion separated the due process inquiry from the categories of civil and criminal contempt. It should not be necessary to label a proceeding criminal in order to hold that more process is due.

But that is precisely the point that the en banc court rejected. The en banc court held that *Bagwell* recognizes only two kinds of contempt and two sets of procedures—criminal contempt with criminal procedure and civil contempt with the special civil procedure traditionally used in civil contempt. Greater procedural protections are required only if the court reclassifies the contempt proceeding as criminal. There is no sliding scale, at least in the Tenth Circuit.

5. The order to show cause. In most courts, contempt is still enforced with an odd procedure, the order to show cause. Plaintiff alleges the contempt in a motion, and if the court is satisfied that the motion deserves a hearing, it orders defendant to appear and show cause why he should not be held in contempt. The procedure is clearly described in Wyatt v. Rogers, 92 F.3d 1074, 1078 n.8 (11th Cir. 1996).

6. Special prosecutors. In *Bagwell*, a special commissioner was appointed to collect the fines. This is necessary in civil contempt only when the civil plaintiff attempts to settle the case over the court's objection, and perhaps it is always illegitimate, as Justice Ginsburg implies. It is more common in criminal contempt. The court may ask the prosecutor to prosecute the contempt, or it may appoint any member of the bar as special prosecutor. Federal courts may appoint a special prosecutor only if the United States Attorney declines to prosecute. Young v. United States ex rel. Vuitton et Fils S.A., 481 U.S. 787 (1987). *Young* and many states reject the practice of appointing plaintiff's attorney as special prosecutor; her duties to her client may conflict with the proper exercise of prosecutorial discretion.

7. A high-profile example with twists: Sheriff Joe Arpaio. In long-running litigation against Maricopa County, Arizona (metropolitan Phoenix) and its long-time sheriff, Joe Arpaio, the federal district court ordered defendants not to detain persons they believed to be in the country without authorization but whom they had no basis to detain for violations of state law. The court later found, on a civil standard of proof, that Sheriff Arpaio made no effort to comply with the injunction and that his officers, acting under pre-existing policy, routinely violated it. Plaintiffs and the county agreed to a $500,000 fund to be administered in compensatory civil contempt to compensate persons who were detained in violation of the injunction. Melendres v. Arpaio, 2016 WL 3996453 (D. Ariz. 2016). Section 5.C.1, in note 16 of Notes on the Evolution of Eleventh Amendment Doctrine, discusses the county's liability for Arpaio's actions.

The court also referred Arpaio to the United States Attorney for criminal contempt. 2016 WL 4414755 (D. Ariz. 2016). The United States, which had intervened in the case as an additional plaintiff, filed criminal contempt charges in October 2016. After a five-day bench trial before a different judge, the court found Arpaio guilty of criminal contempt. United States v. Arpaio, 2017 WL 3268180 (D. Ariz. July 31, 2017). Arpaio claimed that he was held in contempt for doing what the Trump Administration now demands that all local governments do, and on August 25, President Trump pardoned him. The trial judge cancelled the sentencing hearing and dismissed the prosecution with prejudice, but after a further hearing, she denied Arpaio's motion to vacate all orders in the case, including the finding of guilt. The pardon spared him any punishment, but it did not "revise the historical facts" of the case. 2017 WL 4839072 (D. Ariz. Oct. 19, 2017).

Arpaio appealed the trial court's refusal to vacate its orders in the criminal contempt case, and the government indicated that it would support his appeal. The court of appeals has ordered the appointment of a special prosecutor to defend the district court's judgment. United States v. Arpaio, 887 F.3d 979 (9th Cir. 2018). Judge Tallman, dissenting, argued that the government was still defending the interests of the United States as it perceived them, and that amici seeking the appointment of a special prosecutor were really seeking a backdoor way to litigate their claim that the pardon was unconstitutional. All three judges appeared to agree that amici had missed the deadline for appealing the district court's decision to dismiss the prosecution.

The Supreme Court upheld a presidential pardon of criminal contempt in Ex parte Grossman, 267 U.S. 87 (1925). The amici argue that *Arpaio* is different, because the injunction was issued to protect the constitutional rights of private parties. There are few if any limits on the pardon power, so this argument seems unlikely to go anywhere even if they get past their apparent procedural default.

NOTES ON COERCIVE CONTEMPT

1. When does coercive contempt move from civil to criminal? Coercive contempt depends on a conditional penalty; defendant is coerced to comply because the penalty will be bigger if he doesn't. Go to jail until you comply, or pay a fine for each day of noncompliance, or pay a fine for each violation. Defendant can avoid the penalty by complying.

In *Bagwell*, the court specified conditional fines before the violations, and tried to collect them after the violations. In Hicks v. Feiock, the Court said that such "[a] conditional penalty . . . is civil, because it is specifically designed to compel the doing of some act," and one threatened with a conditional penalty can avoid the penalty by complying with the injunction. 485 U.S. 624, 633 (1988). Does collection of such fines now require criminal procedure in all cases? Only where the facts are complex? Only where the fines are large? Can you state the constitutional rule in *Bagwell*?

The Second Circuit has held that "the fact that the sanctions were issued after [defendant] has ceased violating the Injunction does not transform them into retrospective, punitive penalties because [defendant] had the opportunity to purge its contemptuous conduct" after the fines were threatened and before they were imposed.

CBS Broadcasting, Inc. v. Filmon.com, Inc., 814 F.3d 91, 103 (2d Cir. 2016). "To hold otherwise would negate the coercive purpose of prospective fee schedules, and 'compliance with laws and orders could never be brought about by fines in civil contempt proceedings.'" *Id.* at 102, citing similar cases from the Ninth and D.C. Circuits. The Second Circuit said that unlike *Bagwell,* its case did not involve "widespread, ongoing . . . violations of a complex injunction," and the fine—$90,000—was "a relatively minor amount" for a technology company operating nationwide. *Id.* at 103. Defendant had retransmitted copyrighted television shows with a technology that it claimed was outside the scope of the Copyright Act; once the legal issue was resolved, the injunction was simply to stop operating.

The Eighth Circuit also relied on both complexity and the size of the fines in a case going the other way. Jakes, Ltd. v. City of Coates, 356 F.3d 896 (8th Cir. 2004). The injunction ordered defendants not to run "a sexually-oriented business at their current location," and later threatened a fine of $1,000 per day of violation. *Id.* at 898. Defendant quit offering live nude dancing and began offering lap dances from women in bikinis. The district court found a violation and imposed $68,000 in fines for 68 days of violation. The court of appeals found the fine "substantial," "unconditional," and "essentially punitive." *Id.* at 903. The injunction was also complex, because it covered a broad range of activities and it required a determination of what happened in those lap dances. The injunction effectively incorporated an entire ordinance that punished violations as misdemeanors; defendants should not get fewer procedural protections than if they had been charged directly under the ordinance. But the court said its "conclusion would likely be different if Jake's had continued to offer live nude dancing after the district court entered the first contempt order," because "[i]n that case, the second contempt proceeding would involve conduct that was previously adjudged to be contumacious and was continued in defiance of a coercive prospective fine." *Id.* at 903 n.5. Does the court mean that those facts would not be complex enough to trigger *Bagwell?*

In Goodyear Tire & Rubber Co. v. Haeger, 137 S. Ct. 1178, 1186 (2017) the Supreme Court, citing *Bagwell,* held that "a sanction, when imposed pursuant to civil procedures, must be compensatory rather than punitive in nature." When a court seeks to impose an additional penalty for a litigant's misbehavior, "a court would need to provide procedural guarantees applicable in criminal cases, such as a 'beyond a reasonable doubt' standard of proof." *Id.* Does this help? The misconduct in *Goodyear* was failure to produce documents requested in discovery, and the sanction was compensatory rather than coercive; the Court held in essence that compensation in excess of the rightful position is punitive.

2. Three-step contempt. When conditional fines are used for coercive contempt, the process often breaks into three distinct steps. First, the court issues the injunction. Second, it adjudicates the first violations and threatens specific fines for further violations. Third, it adjudicates further violations and collects the fines. The third step is not easily pigeonholed. When the court threatened to fine the union $100,000 for each violent violation, the threat was remedial and prospective. After the threats had failed, enforcing the fines looks punitive and retrospective. The fines are no longer conditional, because the condition has been fulfilled. But the law must keep its promises, or coercive contempt will no longer coerce. Coercive fines must be collected, but must they be collected with civil procedure?

3. The purpose of the steps. What is the purpose of the second step of coercive contempt? When the court issues an injunction, defendant knows he can be fined or imprisoned for violating it. When the court finds defendant in contempt and announces a coercive sanction, it specifies the future penalty. What does that add to the injunction? If telling defendant what the penalty is going to be makes injunctions more effective, why not tell him when the injunction is issued? Is there any need to wait for a violation before specifying the penalty?

The three steps of coercive contempt are even more puzzling if the court is not bound to impose the penalty it threatened. In *Bagwell*, the judge had threatened to double the fines every day. He appears to have imposed more than $100,000 per violation, but only a tiny fraction of that amount doubled daily. Why threaten a particular penalty if the threat itself can be unlimited for all practical purposes, and if the actual penalty has no necessary relation to the threatened penalty? One court has said that a judge at the third step of coercive contempt "should not feel bound in any way by the specific amount" threatened at the second step. Labor Relations Commission v. Fall River Education Association, 416 N.E.2d 1340, 1350 (Mass. 1981). Does the second step serve any purpose in that scenario?

4. How much to threaten. Defendant's wealth is relevant to the size of coercive fines; the court must ask how much it takes to deter *this* defendant. Fines per day or per violation increase the difficulty of assessing ability to pay. When the trial court in *Bagwell* said $100,000 per violent violation, it did not anticipate 400 violations. If it set smaller fines, so the union could reasonably afford 400 violations, would it be inviting 400 violations? Isn't plaintiff entitled to a fine that will deter immediately? Does it defeat the purpose if defendant is entitled to have that fine reduced if it accumulates to unduly burdensome levels? Of course, once the fine accumulates beyond the amount of defendant's net worth plus foreseeable income, further accumulations are meaningless.

5. Waiving accumulated fines. Coercive fines are payable to the government, not to the civil plaintiff. The point was actually litigated in Cadle Co. v. Lobingier, 50 S.W.3d 662, 668-670 (Tex. Ct. App. 2001). It is therefore common for settlement agreements to attempt to waive the fines; plaintiff gives up nothing, and if the settlement is honored, defendant is relieved of a large obligation. The court is not bound by such settlements, but the court is relieved to have the case off its docket and a bitter conflict resolved, so often the court will acquiesce. Is it troubling for contempt fines to serve just as a free bargaining chip for plaintiff? Or is that simply one of the ways that fines coerce compliance?

6. Imprisonment. The original and simplest form of coercive contempt is to imprison the contemnor until he complies. This avoids the conundrums of three-step coercive contempt. There are only two steps: First the injunction is issued, and then defendant is found in contempt and sent to jail. Conditional penalties do not accumulate to be collected later, because imprisonment is continuous: every instant he refuses to comply, and every instant he remains in prison for that refusal.

But imprisonment has disadvantages. Some injunctions can be obeyed only if defendant is at large. Consider National Labor Relations Board v. Blevins Popcorn, 659 F.2d 1173 (D.C. Cir. 1981), where the court was trying to force an employer to bargain with its employees' union. It can't very well bargain if its officers are in prison. At best the court can imprison them until they promise to bargain, and then let them out and see if the fear of returning to prison induces them to keep their promise. Imprisonment is expensive to the state, especially if there are many contemnors.

Imprisoning a few leaders may create martyrs; few judges have been willing to imprison the rank and file. A rare exception is the Middletown, New Jersey, teachers' strike, where three judges summoned the teachers in alphabetical order and gave them a choice of returning to work or going to jail. More than 200 went to jail, some for as long as four days, before the union and the school board agreed to nonbinding mediation. Candy J. Cooper, *Mediation Agreement Frees Jailed Teachers; Middletown Schools to Reopen Monday*, Bergen County Record (Dec. 8, 2001).

7. Gamesmanship. There is psychology and gamesmanship in coercive contempt; moderate threats may be more effective than harsher threats. A threat should not be so great that the contemnor doubts the court's will to carry it out, or so great that there is no room for further escalation. In strike cases, and other cases where the litigants have a continuing relationship, harsh sanctions may end the contempt but ruin the relationship.

Such tactical considerations help explain the three steps of coercive fines. Some judges have stretched the contempt process out into an indefinite number of steps, especially in structural injunctions against government defendants. Early contempt proceedings may result not in a finding of contempt, but in a clarification of the order, making it more specific. Or the court may find defendants in contempt and indicate that they may purge themselves of contempt by doing A, B, and C, which turn out to be more detailed specifications of the obligations of the original injunction. The court can continue this process indefinitely, slowly tightening the screws.

8. Prosecution for offenses other than contempt. The principal alternative to the injunction in *Bagwell* would have been criminal prosecution for each act of violence. That would have required identifying individual perpetrators, who were presumably unknown in many cases. It would have required full criminal trials; the court could not have adjudicated more than 400 violations in eight hearings lasting only one or two days each. The pool of potential jurors was presumably divided over the strike; the risk of hung juries might have been substantial.

Conceivably, the union as an organization could have been criminally prosecuted for conspiracy, and then found guilty of substantive offenses pursuant to the conspiracy without identifying individual perpetrators. Such a prosecution would be at the frontiers of conspiracy law, and it would have required full criminal jury trial. Human offenders could be imprisoned, but fines are the only criminal penalty that could be applied to the union as an entity.

9. Necessity or abuse of power? Were the contempt fines in *Bagwell* necessary because the criminal process was wholly inadequate to protect the rights of the companies and their replacement workers, including their right to life and physical safety? Or were these fines a massive circumvention of hard-won procedural protections against excessive penalties and judicial abuse? Might they be both? "Government by injunction"—the use of injunctions to bypass juries, increase penalties, and sometimes create new substantive prohibitions, especially in the context of labor strife—was a major and recurring political issue from 1896 to 1932. Most of the story is told in Felix Frankfurter and Nathan Greene, *The Labor Injunction* (Macmillan 1930). In 1932, Congress enacted the Norris-LaGuardia Act, 29 U.S.C. §101 *et seq.*, which, with narrow exceptions, deprives federal courts of jurisdiction to enjoin strikes. The Act would not prevent federal injunctions against the unlawful tactics at issue in *Bagwell*.

10. The irreparable injury rule. If you think the fines in *Bagwell* are abusively large, is that an argument for retaining the irreparable injury rule? Is there any chance whatever that the trial judge would have found no irreparable injury in *Bagwell*? Don't we have to address any abuses directly, and not with an easily rebutted presumption against issuing injunctions in the first place?

11. Contempt against federal government agencies. The use of contempt against state and local governments and government officials is rare but not unheard of, as the next set of notes dramatically illustrates. Professor Parillo took an exhaustive look at the use of civil and criminal contempt against *federal* government agencies and officials, and he reached four conclusions:

First, the federal judiciary is willing to issue contempt findings against federal agencies and officials. Second, while several individual federal judges believe they can (and have tried to) attach sanctions to these findings, the judiciary as an institution — particularly the higher courts — has exhibited a virtually complete unwillingness to allow sanctions, at times intervening dramatically to block imprisonment or budget-straining fines at the eleventh hour. Third, the higher courts, even as they unfailingly halt sanctions in all but a few minor instances, have bent over backward to avoid making authoritative pronouncements that sanctions are categorically unavailable, thus keeping the sanctions issue in a state of low salience and at least nominal legal uncertainty. Fourth, even though contempt findings are practically devoid of sanctions, they nonetheless have a shaming effect that gives them substantial if imperfect deterrent power. The efficacy of judicial review of agency action rests primarily on a strong norm, shared in the overlapping communities that agency officials inhabit, that officials comply with court orders. Shame-inducing contempt findings by judges are the means to weaponize that norm.

Nicholas R. Parillo, *The Endgame of Administrative Law: Governmental Disobedience and the Judicial Contempt Power*, 113 Harv. L. Rev. 685, 697 (2018).

NOTES ON THE YONKERS CONFRONTATION

1. Liability. The Yonkers public housing case, while now somewhat dated, provides a dramatic and unusually detailed illustration of coercive contempt. At the trial on the merits, the court found that the City of Yonkers had built all its public housing in black neighborhoods, and that it had done so for the purpose of maintaining residential segregation. United States v. Yonkers Board of Education, 624 F. Supp. 1276 (S.D.N.Y. 1985), *aff'd*, 837 F.2d 1181 (2d Cir. 1987). The school board was a defendant because the deliberate housing segregation was linked to deliberate school segregation.

2. The remedy. The court's first remedial order directed the city to designate sites for 200 units of public housing in white neighborhoods, and to begin planning for additional units. United States v. City of Yonkers Board of Education, 635 F. Supp. 1577 (S.D.N.Y. 1986). The city refused to comply. Plaintiffs sought a contempt citation, but the court sought voluntary compliance. Fruitless negotiations consumed all of 1987. After the judgment on the merits had been affirmed, the city agreed to build the 200 units and to enact specific legislation creating zoning, tax, and other incentives to developers to build 800 more units. The city council formally approved a consent decree, and the court entered that decree as a judgment.

The city immediately came under intense political pressure to repudiate the consent decree. It offered to return $30 million of federal housing funds if it could be relieved of its obligation to build the 200 units. The court refused the offer.

3. The contempt. The principal confrontation came on the promise to enact incentives to build the 800 units. Several months of maneuvering produced no result. But during this time, a consultant for the city drafted an ordinance to implement the consent decree. On July 26, 1988, the judge ordered the city council to enact the consultant's draft by August 1. He scheduled a contempt hearing for August 2. And he specified the coercive sanctions for civil contempt: $500 per day for each council member who voted against the ordinance, and imprisonment beginning on August 11. Imprisoned council members would be released to attend meetings to vote on the ordinance. Against the city, he threated fines of $100 the first day, doubling each day thereafter until the ordinance was enacted. Probably the court did not do the math, but the fines would total $12,700 the first week, $1.6 million the second, $209 million the third, and $26.8 billion at the end of four weeks. The fine for each additional day would slightly exceed the total of all the earlier fines. The city's annual budget was $337 million.

On August 1, and again on August 15, the council rejected the ordinance by a vote of four to three. On August 2, the court found the city and the four recalcitrant councilmen in civil contempt.

4. The appeal. Fines accrued until August 9, when the court of appeals stayed the contempt sanctions and ordered an expedited appeal. The appeal was argued on August 17 and decided on August 26. The court of appeals affirmed the district court in all respects, except that it capped the fines at $1 million a day.

The court of appeals stayed its mandate for seven days to permit emergency motions in the Supreme Court. It ordered that when its mandate issued, contempt sanctions would resume running as though it were still August 9. That is, individual contemnors would be two days away from jail, and the fines against the city would resume at the eighth day of the trial court's original schedule. On September 1, the Supreme Court stayed the contempt sanctions against the individual defendants, but it refused a further stay against the city. Spallone v. United States, 487 U.S. 1251 (1988).

5. Increasing the pressure. The trial judge maximized the pressure on the city by insisting that the fines be paid as they accrued. The city council met regularly to transfer funds from other accounts to pay the fines. (Why would they defy the court on enacting the ordinances but not defy the court on paying the fines?) The Emergency Financial Control Board, a state agency that supervised Yonkers' finances, adopted a "doomsday plan" to progressively lay off most city workers and preserve emergency services for as long as possible. Political pressures in the city shifted toward compliance. In the wee hours of the morning on September 10, when one more day of defiance would cost $819,200, two council members changed their votes and the ordinance was enacted. These developments were chronicled in the nation's daily newspapers; we relied on judicial opinions and the New York Times.

6. Coercing the legislature instead of the executive. Yonkers apparently had no independent executive branch. But it did have a city manager and an administrative bureaucracy that was prepared to implement the ordinance. All defendants argued that the court should simply order the ordinance into effect without the formality of a council vote. No one appears to have argued that the court lacked power to do that. Why not take that way out?

The trial court said that Yonkers had to face up to its responsibilities, and "that is not going to be accomplished by this court adopting the ordinance." Quoted in 856 F.2d at 451. The court of appeals said the choice between ordering the ordinance into effect and ordering the council to adopt it was a discretionary choice between two remedies, unassailable here because the city had agreed to adopt the ordinance. *Id.* at 453-454. What was at stake in this fight over coercing the council instead of the more pliant bureaucracy?

Compare Clarke v. United States, 886 F.2d 404 (D.C. Cir. 1989), *vacated as moot,* 915 F.2d 699 (D.C. Cir. 1990), invalidating an act of Congress withholding the appropriation for the District of Columbia unless the D.C. city council exempted religious schools from its gay-rights ordinance. The court said that Congress could have enacted the exemption directly, but the attempt to coerce the city council's vote violated the free speech rights of its members. The court of appeals in *Yonkers* summarily rejected a similar First Amendment argument. 856 F.2d at 457. What about legislative immunity modeled on the Speech or Debate Clause? Should a court have power to punish legislators for voting wrong? Is it coherent to say that some legislative votes are illegal? Unconstitutional?

7. The cert petition. The Supreme Court denied the city's petition for certiorari, 489 U.S. 1065 (1989), but it eventually reversed the contempt sanctions against the council members. Spallone v. United States, 493 U.S. 265 (1990). The Court said that sanctions for refusing to enact the ordinance should have run only against the city. Those sanctions were likely to be sufficient, and only if they failed after a reasonable time should the trial court have considered personal sanctions against individual council members. The Court said that personal sanctions are a "much greater perversion of the normal legislative process" than sanctions against the city. 493 U.S. at 280. Council members should not be induced to consider their personal interests in avoiding fine or imprisonment. Should this reasoning also apply to the executive branch officials who are the usual defendants in suits against public entities? Surely the Court couldn't say that the state is immune and injunctions must run against state officials, but that the state officials can't be coerced to comply because coercion is better directed to the state itself. Local governments are not immune in federal court; with municipal defendants, the Court has a choice.

8. Passive resistance. *Bagwell* and *Yonkers* test the limits of coercive contempt. Most defendants are less defiant, and most judges are more tempered. Yonkers soon reverted to the more traditional method of dragging its feet instead of openly defying the court. The district court entered at least three supplemental injunctions, and there were at least two more appeals. These developments are reviewed in United States v. Secretary of Housing & Urban Development, 239 F.3d 211 (2d Cir. 2001). Why is foot dragging so much more successful than defiance? Consider the following analysis of the contempt power in institutional reform cases.

COLIN DIVER, THE JUDGE AS POLITICAL POWERBROKER: SUPERINTENDING STRUCTURAL CHANGE IN PUBLIC INSTITUTIONS

65 Va. L. Rev. 43, 99-103 (1979)

The utility of sanctions depends upon their severity and credibility. Certainly, all but the most desperate or defiant of defendants perceive citation for contempt or displacement of personal authority as painful enough to overcome their strongest resistance.[278] If a judge could use these sanctions costlessly, he certainly would possess adequate power as a political actor. Nevertheless, much to the consternation of some plaintiffs' advocates, judges seldom threaten and almost never impose sanctions, even in the face of protracted noncompliance. In fact, the only sanction used with any frequency in reported cases is the relatively mild and largely compensatory action of awarding plaintiffs their attorney's fees. Analysis of three other possible penalties—contempt, transfer of authority, and closure of the institution—indicates why these approaches often are not feasible in politicized litigation.

In practice, courts seldom exercise their contempt power against governmental defendants. This reluctance probably reflects a fear of polarizing the dispute by creating a martyr around whom disaffected groups can rally. The imputation of personal guilt inherent in the contempt citation clashes with the perception that nonpersonal and largely systemic factors cause institutional failure. Furthermore, a court often

---

278. Outright defiance of court orders in institutional reform cases is extremely rare. Even in the celebrated case of school desegregation in Boston, the school committee skirted a direct confrontation. Those who do defy judicial commands, such as leaders of illegally striking labor unions, typically are assured of overwhelming support among their major constituencies.

finds as the appropriate object of a potential contempt order a person whose continuing cooperation is indispensable to the implementation process.

Similar concerns explain the reluctance of trial judges to displace the authority of a recalcitrant official by means such as appointing a receiver, transferring operating authority, or removing him outright. Displacement of a central figure not only alienates other political allies, but it also exacerbates the dislocation that reform unavoidably occasions. Some judges, moreover, may entertain doubts that a successor would behave differently, for he will be subject to the same conflicting pressures as his predecessor. . . .

Judged by the frequency with which they threaten to close institutions, courts seem to regard this device as an effective inducement. Closure would inflict on most defendants the inconvenience of having to make alternative arrangements for residents as well as the personal discomfort attendant to adverse publicity or diminution of authority and responsibility. It also redresses directly the violations alleged—closing the institution releases the plaintiffs from the illegal conditions of their confinement. This remedial quality gives the threat of closure further credibility. In practice, however, closing an institution would cause such serious dislocations that it is not a realistic option, and courts virtually never have ordered it. Selective closure, involving particular facilities or buildings or enjoining further admissions, is a more realistic threat, but the prospect that officials simply will reassign residents to other equally deplorable settings diminishes its utility.

In considering what sanctions to use, a judge faces a classic strategic dilemma in bargaining games: whether and how to use a threat of mutually disadvantageous action as an inducement to action. . . . A madman's threat is convincing precisely because his opponent can not be sure that he will not pursue a mutually damaging course of action. [But] we expect, instinctively, that judges will not act like madmen. . . . The historical failure of judges to impose harsh sanctions even in the face of protracted noncompliance stands as convincing evidence that they will not do so in the future.

2.   How Much Risk of Abuse to Overcome How Much Defiance?

a.   Perpetual Coercion?

ANYANWU v. ANYANWU

771 A.2d 672 (N.J. Super. Ct. App. Div. 2001)

Before Judges STERN, COLLESTER and FALL.

The opinion of the court was delivered by COLLESTER, J.A.D. . . .

[P]laintiff Edith Anyanwu appeals from an order of the Family Part, Morris County, on February 9, 2001. The order released the defendant, Longy Anyanwu, from custody in the Morris County Correctional Facility, to which he was confined on August 14, 1997. The parties are citizens of Nigeria who have resided in the United States for over twenty years. Defendant was a professor at Montclair State University prior to his incarceration.

The parties were married in Baltimore, Maryland, on August 25, 1984. Defendant claims an earlier marriage in Nigeria on May 26, 1984, but plaintiff maintains this was only a customary ceremony to announce their engagement and that defendant was not even present. Their two children were born in the United States: Uchechi, born June 1, 1985; Ogechi, born October 19, 1986, and now deceased. The children had dual citizenship with Nigeria.

By 1996 there were significant marital problems. Plaintiff . . . obtained a Final Restraining Order [against domestic violence] which she later voluntarily dismissed. Defendant filed for a divorce in Nigeria in August 1996, although plaintiff contends that she was never served.

In June of 1997 the parties and their children traveled to Nigeria where they have over 100 family members. Plaintiff avers that while in Nigeria defendant told her that the marriage was over, confiscated her passport and denied her access to the children. Claiming that she was in fear for her physical safety, she returned alone to the United States in July 1997. Later that month defendant also returned. The children remained in Nigeria.

[In August 1997, defendant was jailed for contempt of an order directing him to produce the children in open court. On appeal, the Appellate Division directed a trial on his claim that it was impossible to retrieve the children. At that trial, he testified that his father refused to return the children, and he introduced a letter from the chairman of a Nigerian court stating that that court had assumed jurisdiction of the children and that "as long as Nigeria remains independent I shall not honor any document signed by Longy because as long as he is [in] prison and in Chains . . . *any document he signs cannot be free of duress.*" Defendant refused to submit any documents to Nigerian authorities requesting return of the children. The trial court held that he had not carried his burden of proving inability to comply.

On a second appeal, the Appellate Division interpreted the order as requiring only defendant's best efforts to secure the return of his children. It directed the trial court to specify more concretely what defendant must do to comply. In January 1998, the trial court ordered seven specific actions, including specific requests to defendant's father, to the Nigerian court, to the Nigerian President, and to the American embassy in Nigeria. The Appellate Division affirmed in a third appeal. Meanwhile, the parties made inconsistent claims about the actions of various Nigerian courts, and they and the court learned that Ogechi had died, reportedly from malnutrition.

In 1999, another motion for release was denied, on the ground that defendant had made no effort to comply with the order, and that denial was affirmed in a fourth appeal.

In 2001, defendant again moved for release, offering two new documents in evidence. One was a letter from a vice-consul in the American embassy, reporting the failure of all the efforts of Edith's lawyers and of the embassy on her behalf (or perhaps on behalf of the American court), reporting that the recent detention of the children's Nigerian guardian on account of Ogechi's death "has not helped matters," reporting that Uchechi could not be found, and suggesting that plaintiff return to Nigeria and negotiate directly with defendant's family. The second document was a letter from a lawyer at the African Legal and Civil Rights Center in Washington, arguing that defendant was helplessly caught between two stubborn governments, and claiming that child custody litigation was unknown in Nigeria and that the two extended families were responsible for children in case of divorce.]

The review hearing on defendant's motion was conducted on February 9, 2001. Although both parties were present, neither testified. . . . The defendant submitted a 128 page *pro se* brief setting forth his factual allegations in support of his argument that he was unable to comply with the prior orders and should therefore be released. . . .

The review hearing conducted fell short of the requirements set forth in prior case law. Catena v. Seidl, 327 A.2d 658 (N.J. 1974), held that the contemnor had the burden of proving that continued confinement had no coercive effect and had become punitive. The case required that the burden be satisfied by competent proofs as opposed to *ex parte* affidavits and reports. Factual issues were to be resolved only through live testimony and cross-examination. . . .

[T]here was no live testimony presented at the review hearing, and the only new submissions were two unauthenticated letters containing hearsay statements and opinions of uncertain reliability and credibility. The hearing was therefore inadequate . . . .

We further hold that the trial judge misapplied the standard for discharge from confinement pursuant to an order of commitment directing compliance with an earlier court order. The trial court's reliance only on the duration of confinement and the perceived refusal of defendant to comply was insufficient to carry the requisite burden of proof and persuasion. . . .

Since the legal justification for incarceration for civil contempt is to force compliance, commitment for that purpose cannot continue if it does not have or has lost its coercive power and thereby has become punitive.

Incarceration obviously loses its coercive power where the party committed is unable to comply with the court order he is charged with violating. In the instant case . . . defendant is not held in the Morris County Correctional Facility for failure to perform the feat of producing his living child in a New Jersey courthouse. Since 1997 he has been required only to make good faith efforts to comply with orders toward effectuating that result. . . .

The standard for review . . . is whether there is a substantial likelihood that continued incarceration would accomplish the purpose of causing the person confined to comply with the order on which confinement is based. . . .

No hard and fast rule or fixed period of time defines when coercive commitment becomes punitive, but refusal to comply is in itself insufficient for a finding that the commitment has lost its coercive power. Otherwise the same willful defiance of a lawful order that precipitated the commitment would justify its dissolution and mock rather than vindicate the remedial power of the court. . . .

The trilogy of *Catena* cases is instructive. . . . Gerardo Catena refused to answer questions relating to organized crime before the State Commission of Investigation despite receipt of testimonial immunity. He was cited for contempt and committed to jail until he purged himself by testifying. Catena's intransigence was to the point that he claimed that rather than testify "they'd have to carry me out of there feet first." In three opinions over the ensuing five years the Supreme Court rejected Catena's argument that his continued incarceration had lost its coercive force until the seventy-three year old defendant's health had significantly deteriorated. Even then the Court underscored that refusal of the contemnor to comply over time does not transform the initial commitment into punitive incarceration.

> [W]e want to make it perfectly clear that in similar circumstances a person's insistence that he will never talk, or confinement for a particular length of time[,] does not automatically satisfy the requirement of showing "no substantial likelihood." Each case must be decided on an independent evaluation of all of the particular facts. Age, state of health and length of confinement are all factors to be weighed, but the critical question is whether or not further confinement will serve any coercive purpose.

Catena v. Seidl, 343 A.2d 744, 747 (N.J. 1975). . . .

In King v. Department of Social and Health Service, 756 P.2d 1303 (Wash. 1988), a children's welfare agency obtained an order directing parents to bring their child to court after receipt of abuse allegations. The child was not produced, and the parents were incarcerated. The mother was released after a finding that she had no information as to the child's whereabouts, but the father remained confined for over a year because of his refusal to disclose the child's location. The Court of Appeals held that the coercive aspect of the order had become secondary to the punitive nature of the father's confinement and ordered his release. The Supreme Court of Washington reversed, holding that the mere passage of time did not convert coercive restraint to punitive contempt and further stated: "In deciding whether a contemnor's incarceration should continue, the trial court should also consider the significance of the ends to be achieved. It is appropriate for the court to balance its interests in enforcing compliance with a particular order [and] a contemnor's liberty." 756 P.2d at 1310. See also Sanders v. Shephard, 645 N.E.2d 900 (Ill. 1994) (affirming denial of motion to vacate order of contempt based on defendant's failure to produce his daughter or disclose her whereabouts and including as factor to be considered the significance of the ends to be achieved by the underlying order); but see Morgan v. Foretich, 564 A.2d 1, 5 n.2 (D.C. 1989) (holding that the significance of order to be enforced should not be considered).

Almost four years have passed since these parties first presented themselves in a New Jersey courtroom. Even a casual observer can see that their lives have gotten much worse and that they have each suffered deeply. One of their children is dead. The other [is] somewhere far away. Their assets are depleted. The defendant lost his job and his liberty. The hostility between them remains unabated. To continue this stalemate solves nothing. . . . It would be naive to assume that defendant would remain within the reach of the court if released. Based on the history of this case, it appears certain that he will go to Nigeria and forever frustrate the plaintiff's search for her child.

Many legal and factual issues remain unresolved. The authenticity and effect of Nigerian court orders are disputed, including whether a valid Nigerian marriage predated the ceremony in the United States. The impact, if any, of Nigerian law and customs has not been explored to any significant extent. And of course the best interest of the child remains unknown. . . .

We suggest . . . that the judge give consideration to appointment of a guardian *ad litem* [for the litigation] to represent the interests of the child.

The guardian can proceed under the authority of the court and act impartially to report to the court on applicable issues including Nigerian law and customs. The guardian can seek out the assistance of relatives of both parties in the United States and Nigeria to assist in breaking this sad impasse. The guardian would be able to communicate with officials in Nigeria and the United States as a neutral party endeavoring to locate the child and assure the court of her status and well-being. If possible, the guardian could mediate some of the differences between the parties consistent with the best interest of the child. Furthermore, the particularized directive to defendant contained in the January 4, 1998 order must be examined and reformulated to specifically describe the action or actions required of defendant to effectuate compliance and obtain his release. The guardian would be able to assist the court in this respect as well. . . .

[T]here should be periodic progress conferences and hearings in order to resolve this difficult matter as expeditiously as possible.

Reversed and remanded. . . .

NOTES ON PERPETUAL COERCION

1. The aftermath. On remand, the trial court appointed a Nigerian-born lawyer as special master. He found Uchechi at a boarding school, and arranged for a phone conference with the judge and a videotaped message to the parents. Uchechi said she wanted to finish school in Nigeria and apply to college in the United States, and she wanted her dad out of jail. After a final round of emergency appeals in March 2002, her father was released on modest bail and subject to travel restrictions. Uchechi returned to the United States in the fall of 2002. Margaret McHugh, *Mom Embraces Her Daughter After Long Global Custody Battle*, Newark Star-Ledger (Nov. 2, 2002). The *Star-Ledger* story reports that Ogechi, the daughter who died of malnutrition, suffered from a congenital intestinal disorder.

2. The problem. The theory of coercive imprisonment is that defendant must stay in jail until he complies. But courts have resisted the corollary that if he never complies, he never gets out. Distinguish two closely related issues in *Anyanwu*. First, defendant cannot be imprisoned for failing to do the impossible. That is uncontroversial, but it is often difficult to discern what is possible. Second, many modern cases say that coercive imprisonment must end, even though compliance is possible, if there is no reasonable prospect of coercing defendant to comply. Discerning who is so stubborn is even more difficult than discerning what is impossible.

3. Impossibility. The impossibility defense is often plausible in child custody cases; the imprisoned parent may lose control of the child and even knowledge of where the child is. Those with custody of the child may honor the imprisoned parent's every request, but if not, there may be little he can do from a jail cell. The court suspects that the imprisoned parent can retrieve the child with a phone call, but it has no good way to be sure.

The impossibility defense arises most often in the context of injunctions to pay money, or to turn over specific assets to plaintiff. If defendant no longer has the money or the property, he can't turn it over. How is the court to know whether compliance is really impossible? We will see in section 9.B.2 that orders to pay money out of defendant's general assets and enforced by the contempt power are rarely available except in family law cases. But contempt is used to enforce orders to turn over specific funds or assets known to have recently been in defendant's possession.

Defendant bears the burden of proving present inability to comply. United States v. Rylander, 460 U.S. 752, 757 (1983). Thus, everything turns on whether the court believes defendant's tale of how he lost or dissipated the property. In Commodity Futures Trading Commission v. Wellington Precious Metals, 950 F.2d 1525 (11th Cir. 1992), the court did not believe that defendant had lost $2.8 million through bad investments with friends and relatives. In one of the leading turnover cases, the Supreme Court suggested that if defendant still denies having the property despite long imprisonment, the trial judge should eventually believe him even though she did not believe him originally. "His denial of possession is given credit after demonstration that a period in prison does not produce the goods." Maggio v. Zeitz, 333 U.S. 56, 76 (1948). Compare Drake v. National Bank of Commerce, 190 S.E. 302 (Va. 1937), where the court did not believe that Drake had lost $18,000 from his jacket pocket while bird hunting. Eight months later, in an unpublished order, the court believed him and released him. Professor Rendleman dug up the files. Owen M. Fiss and Doug Rendleman, *Injunctions* 1091 (2d ed. 1984).

A contemnor claiming impossibility needs to specifically explain why compliance is impossible; he cannot rely on general assertions. In Securities and Exchange Commission v. Louks, 2016 WL 5868597 (D. Minn. 2016), the court jailed a defendant who had defrauded investors of $4.3 million until he either returned the money or submitted an affidavit explaining in detail why that was impossible. The court rejected defendant's affidavit: "Vague statements about 'all reasonable efforts' and 'working my tail off' do not come close to providing the information required by the . . . order." He gave defendant another chance to prove impossibility.

4. Self-imposed impossibility. Some defendants deliberately make themselves incapable of complying. It is tempting to reject their impossibility defense on the ground that the impossibility is of their own making. The Supreme Court denounced the strategy in *Maggio*, 333 U.S. at 64. But courts do it anyway; for cases from four circuits that are said to reject self-imposed impossibility as a defense, see Chicago Truck Drivers Union Pension Fund v. Brotherhood Labor Leasing, 207 F.3d 500, 506 (8th Cir. 2000). But in each of these cases, there appears to have been reason to doubt whether compliance was really impossible.

5. Ordering defendant to try. In *Anyanwu*, the court ordered only that defendant try to bring his daughter home. How much was at stake in his refusal to make good-faith requests to his family and to Nigerian officials? Could the court assess the prospects that such requests would do any good? Were the courts and the parties diverted from the merits to a contest of wills?

Compare United States v. Joyce, 498 F.2d 592 (7th Cir. 1974). Joyce was an American, and a corporate officer of a British insurance company that did business in the United States. The court ordered Joyce to use "his best offices" to produce the corporation's records for inspection by the Internal Revenue Service. The court of appeals held that injunction too vague to support a conviction for criminal contempt. In the alternative, it held that he was not guilty because it was impossible for him to get the documents.

Should *Joyce* come out the other way if the injunction specified the steps Joyce should take to try to get the documents? If he were charged with civil contempt and coerced to try harder? If the court were trying to retrieve a child instead of corporate records? Or is *Joyce* inconsistent with *Anyanwu*?

6. Too stubborn to be coerced. A remarkable number of defiant defendants sit in jail for months or years rather than obey an injunction. The longest running such case in the United States appears to be that of Beatty Chadwick, who transferred $2.5 million in marital assets into offshore accounts, beyond reach of a Pennsylvania divorce court. The court ordered the money returned and held Chadwick in civil contempt when he refused. Chadwick attempted to flee the jurisdiction, but was arrested on April 5, 1995 and remained in jail in coercive contempt until July 10, 2009. He spent these 14 years in continuous state and federal litigation seeking his release. A trial judge finally released him on the ground that imprisonment was having no coercive effect. The opinion is unreported, but it is described in United States v. Harris, 582 F.3d 512, 518 n.7 (3d Cir. 2009); *id.* at 512 n.13 (DeBois, J., concurring).

Another example involves treasure-hunter Tommy G. Thompson. Avi Selk, *A Treasure Hunter Found 3 Tons of Sunken Gold—and Can't Leave His Jail Cell Until He Says Where It Is*, Washington Post (Dec. 14, 2016). Thompson led an expedition in the 1980s to find the S.S. Central America, a steamer that went down in a hurricane in 1857, causing the loss of 425 people and three tons of gold; the resulting contraction of the money supply contributed to the Panic of 1857 and an economic depression. Thompson's expedition found the ship and recovered the gold from deep at sea, with investors backing the voyage.

The investors later accused Thompson of selling off much of the recovered gold himself and keeping the profits. Authorities issued an arrest warrant, followed by a two-year manhunt. They eventually found Thompson, but not 500 gold coins, some of which could be worth $1 million each. In April 2015, Thompson said the coins were in Belize and promised to reveal the exact location, but then he claimed he had forgotten where he left them. He has been held in jail ever since, with the court saying that he was faking his memory problems. Meanwhile, $50 million of the recovered gold that Thomson did not hide has gone on sale, and those investors who lived long enough may finally get some of their promised return. Beth Burger, *Justice Insider: Another Hearing, Another Excuse for Tommy Thompson*, Columbus Dispatch (Jan. 2, 2018); Associated Press, *Over $50M of Treasure Once Lost at Sea Set to Go On Display*, New York Post (Jan, 30, 2018); Williamson v. Recovery Limited Partnership, 2017 WL 117601, *1 (S.D. Ohio Mar. 30, 2017).

7. A dissenting view. Judge Alito, before he became Justice Alito, rejected one of Beatty Chadwick's petitions for habeas corpus. Chadwick v. Janecka, 312 F.3d 597 (3d Cir. 2002). Federal review on habeas is limited to deciding whether the state court's decision was "contrary to, or involved an unreasonable application of, clearly established Federal law, as determined by the Supreme Court of the United States." 28 U.S.C. §2254(d). In context, this can only mean federal *constitutional* law; the federal law of civil contempt would not be binding on Pennsylvania, although the opinion did not seem to make that distinction. Judge Alito relied on a sentence in *Bagwell* stating that the "paradigmatic" civil contempt sanction "involves confining a contemnor indefinitely until he complies." The Supreme Court was certainly not thinking about the *Anyanwu* issue when it said "indefinitely until he complies," but Judge Alito relied on that phrase at least for the limited proposition that there was no "established" law in the Supreme Court that required release when imprisonment lost its coercive effect. The more recent Third Circuit opinion in *Harris* reads that same dictum in *Bagwell* to control the federal law of contempt and to reject any right to be released when coercion fails. 582 F.3d at 518-519.

8. Recalcitrant witnesses. A federal witness who refuses to testify can be held no more than 18 months, even in coercive contempt, and even if the testimony is still needed. 28 U.S.C. §1826. The other circuits do not share the Third Circuit's reading of *Bagwell*, and it has become common to move for release before the 18 months has expired, on the ground that imprisonment has lost its coercive effect. An example is In re Grand Jury Proceedings, 347 F.3d 197 (7th Cir. 2003), involving a witness who had been held in civil contempt for refusing to testify in a different jurisdiction five years before. In the earlier case, he went on a hunger strike and was force fed for 180 days before the court released him on the ground that coercion had failed. The witness argued that that experience showed that he could not be coerced and that he should be released in the new case. The Seventh Circuit disagreed. This investigation was different, his stated reasons for not testifying were different, he was older, and, the implication was, perhaps he was weaker or less determined.

9. Fact finding. How can a court know whether a contemnor is incurably recalcitrant? Any contemnor can beat his chest and swear he'll never give in. Wally Klump spent 13 months in jail for refusing to remove his cattle from federal land. The judge brought him from the jail to the courthouse and he once again said he would not obey. That same week, he told a reporter that he would die in jail. Charlie LeDuff, *For 28 Cows and Precious Water, a Man's Got to Sit in Jail*, N.Y. Times (May 9, 2004). The next week, he agreed to obey. Charlie LeDuff, *Rancher Has Change of Heart*, N.Y. Times (May 13, 2004). How can a judge decide whether the defiant contemnor before him is about to crack, or will crack eventually? In contrast to the New Jersey courts, which insist on live testimony in these cases, and a dissenter in *Catena* who wanted a psychiatric evaluation, the Second Circuit has said it is enough to take defendant's affidavit and let his lawyer argue. Simkin v. United States, 715 F.2d 34 (2d Cir. 1983).

Contemnors who make these motions generally try to offer a convincing reason for their recalcitrance. Does the court have anything to go on other than the convincing power of the proffered reason and the length of imprisonment already imposed without effect? The most common reasons in witness cases are fear of retaliation and loyalty to some claim of privilege that the court has rejected. Thus, reporters have refused to reveal their sources. In re Grand Jury Subpoena, 201 Fed. Appx. 430 (9th Cir. 2006). The reporter in that case was released after more than seven months, when he agreed to turn over the original of video footage that he had already posted on his blog and the government agreed not to call him as a witness. The deal was reached through court-supervised mediation. Bob Egelko & Jim Herron Zamora, *The Josh Wolf Case: Blogger Freed After Giving Video to Feds*, San Francisco Chronicle (April 4, 2007).

10. Costs, benefits, and incentives. Think about how the prospect of possible release changes the dynamic of coercive contempt. The imprisoned contemnor can focus his energies on a series of motions seeking release. He never has to give up hope. The longer he stays in jail, the stronger the evidence that his will is unbreakable and the closer he is to possible release. A firm resolve to leave him there forever if necessary would surely be more effective.

But what are the costs of such a firm resolve in the case of someone who is truly unbreakable? There are humanitarian reasons to end imprisonment, and economic ones too. While a contemnor is in prison, society loses his production and supports him in expensive quarters. If violation of the injunction were treated as a completed criminal offense, the maximum sentence would surely be much less than life in prison. How much should it matter that the contemnor is seeking release before his offense is completed—that he continues to defy the court even as he seeks its mercy?

11. Other solutions. Reported opinions releasing contemnors from civil coercion on the ground that coercion is ineffective are a fairly recent phenomenon. But we have found no American case where the contemnor died in prison. Maybe the traditional rhetoric caused most contemnors to eventually obey, or maybe courts found ways to quietly release the most stubborn. *Maggio* and *Drake* in note 3 show one way out; the court can eventually find that compliance is impossible. Some cases become moot; recalcitrant witnesses are freed when their testimony is no longer needed.

Investment advisor Martin A. Armstrong served seven years for civil contempt of an order to turn over a missing $15 million. Armstrong v. Guccione, 470 F.3d 89 (2d Cir. 2006). He spent part of the seven years in solitary confinement as punishment for damaging a prison air vent. Gretchen Morgenson, *Adviser Jailed Since 2000 Pleads Guilty in Securities Fraud Case*, N.Y. Times (Aug. 18, 2006). Solitary was not imposed to increase the coercive effect of the contempt sentence. But why not? Might tightening the conditions of confinement be a better solution than prolonging these standoffs for years? Armstrong pled guilty to investment fraud and got no sentencing credit for the time he was held for contempt. He was released after 11 years, seven of it in coercive contempt. Dealbook, *Ex-Adviser Out of Jail after 11 Years, Including 7 for Contempt*, N.Y. Times (Mar. 15, 2011).

Would fines be better, or worse? When Toni Locy, a reporter for USA Today, refused to disclose her sources, a judge imposed graduated fines that soon rose to $5,000 per day. He also ordered that she pay from personal assets with no contributions from her employer or anyone else. Hatfill v. Mukasey, 539 F. Supp. 2d 96 (D.D.C. 2008). An appeal was pending when the underlying case settled and the plaintiff told the court of appeals that he no longer needed her testimony. Charlie Savage, *A Onetime "Person of Interest" Moves a Step Closer to Public Exoneration*, N.Y. Times (Aug. 2, 2008). The threat of financial destruction may have greater coercive power because from the beginning it appears more permanent. But it may also quickly become meaningless, once it exceeds the contemnor's total wealth.

Statutory limits on coercive contempt, like the 18-month rule in the recalcitrant witness statute, are a simple solution. They no doubt reduce the coercive effect of imprisonment, but except for hardened criminals accustomed to prison, the loss of deterrence is probably small.

12. Criminal contempt instead? Judge Posner urged heavier use of criminal contempt, with the right to jury trial, and careful restriction of coercive contempt to cases where coercion might work. In re Crededio, 759 F.2d 589 (7th Cir. 1985) (dissenting). Would it be appropriate to give Longy Anyanwu four more years for criminal contempt if four years of coercion has failed? Or if some shorter period of coercion had failed? If prosecutors did that on a regular basis, it might reduce the attractiveness of trying to convince the judge that coercion has failed. But there would be a fixed maximum sentence, and there would be more procedural safeguards. Criminal sentences over six months would require jury trial.

The jury can matter where there is a genuine factual dispute, and it may serve as a check on prosecutorial discretion even where the fact of contempt is clear. Susan McDougal, a defiant witness who refused to testify in Kenneth Starr's special-prosecutor investigation of President Bill Clinton, served the full 18 months in coercive contempt. Then she was charged with criminal contempt and obstruction of justice; the jury acquitted on obstruction and hung on contempt. Neil A. Lewis, *Federal Jury Acquits McDougal On One Charge and Is Split on 2*, N.Y. Times (Apr. 13, 1999).

Ordinary prosecutors sometimes use this tactic too. But the government has little interest in bringing criminal contempt prosecutions to help private litigants like Edith Anyanwu. And many states have very short maximum sentences for criminal contempt; substituting criminal for coercive contempt in those states would be nearly equivalent to a get-out-of-jail-free card.

13. A foreign example. Israeli divorce law is religious law administered by orthodox rabbis. Jewish law requires both spouses to consent to divorce, but if the grounds are serious enough, consent will be coerced. In 1962, Yahiya Avraham was imprisoned for refusing to give his wife a divorce. Over the years, he refused repeated pleas and offers of rewards from teams of rabbis. He died in prison 32 years later, at the age of 81. Los Angeles Times (Dec. 6, 1994).

Avraham seems odd, because in most legal systems, the court would grant the divorce without consent. But Anglo-American law long engaged in similar persistent efforts to coerce defendants into doing things that the court or marshal could do just as well. Federal Rule 70 and similar state rules are designed to eliminate unnecessary standoffs by authorizing the court to appoint agents to sign documents or perform other actions on behalf of recalcitrant defendants. But when a recalcitrant defendant has hidden property, or information, or a child, or anything else unavailable to the court or to other parties in the case, coercion is the only solution.

14. Sanctions other than fine and imprisonment? In City of Quincy v. Weinberg, 844 N.E.2d 59 (Ill. App. Ct. 2006), the city complained that defendant's house and yard were filled with junk. The city alleged zoning violations, fire code violations, and a nuisance. The court entered a series of injunctions ordering the place cleaned up, a series of contempt orders for noncompliance, and a series of modest sanctions. A psychiatrist testified that defendant's violations resulted from "severe obsessive-compulsive disorder."

After five years of unsuccessful enforcement efforts, the trial ordered defendant "to divest himself of title to the property." The appellate court reversed. Forced sale of defendant's residence was not "the least possible power adequate to the end proposed," quoting Spallone v. United States, 493 U.S. 265, 276 (1990). Such a sanction was "subject to grave abuses," and it was unnecessary because the court could authorize the city to remove "defendant's 'illegal' property" itself. *Id.* at 70-71. Those quotation marks around "illegal" may suggest that the court also thought the city was overreaching on the merits, but that issue was not presented.

In West Virginia, family law courts can order home confinement as an alternative to incarceration for civil contempt. W. Va. Code §51-2A-9. Consider B.L. v. A.D., 2018 WL 300574, *3 (W. Va. Jan. 5, 2018). Plaintiff had obtained a $500,000 judgment against the contemnor for infecting plaintiff with H.I.V. The contemnor received a distribution of nearly $375,000 from his mother's estate but refused to pay, claiming without any proof he had distributed the money in small, anonymous donations to various charities. It was undisputed that he had transferred $11,000 to his business.

The trial court ordered the contemnor to remain in home confinement until he paid $363,000 toward the judgment. West Virginia's high court affirmed a trial court's denial of a contemnor's fifth attempt to dissolve a contempt order of home confinement.

> The findings . . . describe petitioner's seeking leave of the court to travel outside the state for medical treatment as "a ruse to secure a vacation in Florida over the Christmas holiday." The appendix record on appeal reveals that petitioner initially denied the existence of the asset distribution and eventually began moving money among accounts and making large cash withdrawals in aid of concealing his wealth.

Id. at *3 n.3. Wouldn't jail be a better option for this contemnor?

b. Anticipatory Contempt

GRIFFIN v. COUNTY SCHOOL BOARD

363 F.2d 206 (4th Cir. 1966)

[Prince Edward County, Virginia, was one of the four school districts in Brown v. Board of Education, 347 U.S. 483 (1954), the original school desegregation decision. The county responded by closing its public schools for five years. During that time, the county made tuition grants to parents of children attending private schools organized for white children.

In 1961, the federal district court ordered the school board to quit paying tuition grants until it reopened the public schools. 198 F. Supp. 497 (E.D. Va. 1961). In 1964, the Supreme Court authorized the district court to order the county to reopen its public schools. 377 U.S. 218 (1964). The district court issued such an order on June 25, and the county appropriated funds to reopen the schools at the beginning of the fall semester. With the public schools now legally open, the county moved to pay tuition grants for the previous school year, 1963-1964. The district court enjoined those payments on July 9, but it refused to enjoin tuition grants for 1964-1965 and later. Resuming tuition grants would lead to an all-black public school and an all-white tax-supported "private" school. Plaintiffs appealed on July 17, and on July 28, plaintiffs moved to accelerate the appeal.]

Before HAYNESWORTH, Chief Judge, and SOBELOFF, BOREMAN, BRYAN, and BELL, Circuit Judges, sitting en banc.

BRYAN, Circuit Judge. . . .

As we were not then in session, the Chief Judge requested the Clerk to ask the Board of Supervisors to stipulate that no tuition grants would be paid pending the appeal. . . . [T]he Clerk was told "during the late evening of August 4" that the Board would not make the stipulation. . . .

Meanwhile, during the night of August 4 and early morning of August 5, 1964, the Board met and decided to enlarge substantially the tuition grants for the session

1964-65. . . . That night white parents were notified of the Board's action. Checks totaling about $180,000 were distributed before 9 o'clock A.M. and most of them cashed at that hour, August 5 . . . .

[T]he District Judge made the following undisputed findings . . . :

> . . . The Commonwealth Attorney and [four] members of the Board of Supervisors . . . agreed that if the Board of Supervisors would . . . authorize . . . immediate payment . . . , this could be done before the Court of Appeals could do anything about it. . . .
>
> Some twenty or thirty volunteers assisted the secretary of the Board in processing the applications and making out the necessary checks. County bonds were sold in Richmond the next morning to raise the money necessary for the payment of these checks.
>
> Twelve hundred seventeen tuition grant applications were filed during the night of August 4-5. . . . Each applicant was paid [for the fall semester 1964.] . . .

That these acts of the Board of Supervisors constituted a contempt of this court is beyond cavil. The Board undertook to put the money then available for tuition grants—and then wholly subject to its orders—beyond its control as well as that of the court. In doing so the Board took upon itself to decide its right to exercise, in favor of the private school, the Board's general power to appropriate public funds. This use of power was, as the Board was acutely aware, an arrogation of this court's responsibility. Obviously, the aim was to thwart the impact of any adverse decree which might ultimately be forthcoming on the appeal. In effect it was a "resistance to its [this court's] lawful writ, process, order, rule, decree, or command." 18 U.S.C. §401(3). . . .

Although this court had not issued an injunction against the appropriation of the moneys to tuition grants, the Board knew that if the plaintiffs succeeded this would be its ultimate decree, as in fact it became. 339 F.2d 486 (4th Cir. 1964). That potential decree was thus then within the statute. Furthermore, the appeal was itself a "process" which was alive at the time of the disbursement and was resisted by the disbursement.

In Merrimack River Savings Bank v. Clay Center, 219 U.S. 527 (1911), a temporary injunction had been issued by a Federal District Court to prevent the destruction by a municipality of a public utility's poles and wires. . . . The suit was dismissed on jurisdictional grounds. However, for and during an appeal to the Supreme Court, the injunction was continued in force. On this review the dismissal was upheld. But before the mandate of dismissal had been issued or could issue, and in the period allowed for presenting an application for a rehearing, the city cut down the poles, destroyed a large section of the wires and thus put the utility out of business. This conduct was declared to be contempt of the Supreme Court:

> It does not necessarily follow that disobedience of such an injunction, intended only to preserve the status quo pending an appeal, may not be regarded as a contempt of the appellate jurisdiction of this court, which might be rendered nugatory by conduct calculated to remove the subject matter of the appeal beyond its control, or by its destruction. This we need not decide, since *irrespective of any such injunction actually issued the wilful removal beyond the reach of the court of the subject-matter of the litigation . . . [on] appeal . . . is, in and of itself, a contempt of the appellate jurisdiction of this court.* . . . Unless this be so, a reversal of the decree would be but a barren victory, since the very result would have been brought about by the lawless act of the defendants which it was the object of the suit to prevent.

Id. at 535-536 (accent added.) . . .

The contempt power declared in . . . *Merrimack* . . . was not suggested to be rooted in the inherent power of the Supreme Court rather than in the statute now embodied in 18 U.S.C. §401(3). . . .

That inferior courts have the same contempt power as the Supreme Court exerted in *Merrimack*, and that similar conduct is contempt of the lower courts, were unequivocally enunciated in Lamb v. Cramer, 285 U.S. 217, 219 (1932). There, as in the case now on review, no injunction or order had been issued restraining disposition of the property in suit. Nevertheless, receipt and possession of a part of the res [the property], pendente lite [pending litigation], by a transferee of the defendant-owner was adjudged a contempt of the trial court. The Court had no difficulty in concluding that there was contempt despite the absence of a current restraining order.

While *Lamb* did not specifically mention the statute, the Court obviously did not think it barred prosecution of the transferee for contempt. . . . The anticipated final judgment was not considered to be presently beyond the contemplation of the statute. Indeed, the contrary is implicit in the opinion. The diversion of the res was held to be contumacious because it "tended to defeat any *decree* which the court *might ultimately* make in the cause." (Accent added.)

Civil and not criminal contempt was the gravamen of *Lamb* and is here too. This was a predominant consideration of the Supreme Court and probably accounts for no advertence to the contempt statute, which seems worded more appropriately for criminal contempt. The omission means nothing, for the primary reasoning of the Court was that the res was in gremio legis [literally, in the lap of the law] and the conveyance of it in part was a disturbance of the constructive possession of the trial court. Whether the decision in *Lamb* was founded on this conception of judicial custody or on the statute, of which the Court was hardly unaware, is immaterial. Either ground supports our holding that the Board of Supervisors was in contempt. . . .

We find the Board of Supervisors and its members guilty of civil contempt. Accordingly, the Board and its constituent individuals, . . . personally and in their own right, will be ordered jointly and severally to restore to the County Treasurer of Prince Edward County, through recapture or otherwise, an amount equal to the disbursements authorized and made by their resolutions of August 4-5, 1964. . . .

HAYNESWORTH, Chief Judge, with whom BOREMAN Circuit Judge, joins (dissenting). . . .

It is clear that this Court has an inherent power to punish contempts. It was originally defined by the seventeenth section of the Judiciary Act of 1789 as the power to punish by fine or imprisonment all contempts of authority in any cause or hearing before the Court. But the power has since been limited and redefined by the Act of Congress of March 2, 1831, now 18 U.S.C. §401. The statute prescribes:

> A court of the United States shall have power to punish by fine or imprisonment, at its discretion, such contempt of its authority, and none other as
>> (1) Misbehavior of any person in its presence or so near thereto as to obstruct the administration of justice;
>> (2) Misbehavior of any of its officers in their official transactions;
>> (3) Disobedience or resistance to its lawful writ, process, order, rule, decree, or command.

Considerable doubt was expressed in Ex parte Robinson, 86 U.S. (19 Wall.) 505 (1873), as to whether this statute could limit the contempt power of the Supreme Court, which derives its existence and powers from the Constitution, and it is obvious from *Merrimack* that the Court has since gone beyond the statute. But *Robinson* made it clear that there can be no question about the limiting effect the statute has upon the courts of appeals and the district courts. As courts created, not by the Constitution, but, through the power that document vested in Congress, exercise of their inherent contempt powers must be confined to the bounds that Congress has fixed. . . .

Phrases (1) and (2) of the statute are not applicable here. The majority finds, under phrase (3), that there was disobedience or resistance to a lawful writ, process, order, rule, decree, or command of this Court. Yet none in fact existed to be disobeyed or resisted. The plaintiffs sought no temporary restraining order or injunction, and none was issued . . . . The stipulation requested of the defendants by this court cannot be expanded to fit into any of the things specified in §401(3).

The word "process," as used in the statute in its context of writs, orders and decrees, obviously means more than the pendency of an appeal or of some other relevant judicial proceeding. It has been traditionally used to encompass such things as a summons, a subpoena, an attachment, a warrant, a mandate, a levy and, generically, other writs and orders. In the context of other orders and writs, "process" can reasonably be understood to mean no more than the sum of more explicit terms, such as "original process," "summary process," "mesne [interlocutory] process" and "final process," all of which clearly refer to papers issuing from the court and embodying its commands or judgments, or notice of them. Construed so expansively as the majority's suggestion of equivalence with the pendency of any relevant judicial proceeding, it would entirely contravene the clearly limiting purpose of the congressional act. . . .

This court declared itself in Ex parte Buskirk, 72 F. 14 (4th Cir. 1896). . . .

Buskirk was a party in a judicial proceeding in a district court for a determination of the ownership of a tract of timber. In open court, he entered into a stipulation that none of the timber would be cut until the court had decided the question of ownership. Nevertheless, pending the court's decision, he began cutting the timber and intentionally removed it beyond the reach of the court. This court held because of the statute, "[h]owever reprehensible such conduct . . . may have been . . . it nevertheless did not constitute a contempt to the court or its orders."

My brothers now overrule Buskirk without deigning to mention it. . . .

Four of our sister circuits have embraced the same construction of the statute . . . . No court of appeals, until now, has toyed with any other reading. . . .

The holding in Lamb v. Cramer, 285 U.S. 217 (1932), is of some comfort to the majority, but [not much].

Lamb was a lawyer, who, assertedly in payment of accrued legal fees, accepted a transfer of some of the property in litigation, upon which the adverse parties had specific liens. Concurrently, a supplemental bill in equity to require his restoration of the property to the custody of the court was filed and a rule issued against Lamb to show cause why he should not return the property to the custody of the court or be held in contempt. . . . [T]he Court of Appeals [held] that the supplemental bill in equity and the citation were each appropriate means to require restoration of the property to the control of the court . . . . [T]he Supreme Court . . . affirmed . . . .

Clearly, the only purpose of the citation in Lamb was the procurement of the return of property in the actual possession and under the control of the attorney, an officer of the court. It was not to punish him or to compel him to replace out of his own funds dissipated assets or money. The most significant thing about the Lamb cases, however, is that attention in both the Court of Appeals . . . and the Supreme Court was focused upon a very different problem. In neither court was there a citation of the statute with which we are concerned or of the cases which had established a uniform interpretation of it. The Supreme Court wrote in Lamb as if the affront had been to itself. One can only suppose that it did so because the statute had not been called to its attention[6] for the Supreme Court had made it perfectly clear in *Robinson* that the subordinate, statutory federal courts are subject to the statute, and that their powers to punish contempts are effectively limited by it.

If the holding in *Lamb* may be regarded as an interpretation of the unmentioned statute, one may more reasonably conclude that it was an application of §401(2) rather than §401(3) . . . .[8]

The large issue in this case was the constitutionality of a continuing program of disbursement of tuition grants allegedly for the purpose of continued maintenance of segregated school systems. The payment of such tuition grants for one-half year did not abort the appeal or frustrate adjudication of the large issue. It was an unwarranted disbursement of public funds, but the Supervisors, themselves, are not now in possession of any part of those moneys. They are not officers of this court punishable under §401(2) for official transgressions. What is attempted here is far from what was accomplished in *Lamb*, and, to me, is inconsistent with an appropriate deference to an explicit congressional command of unquestioned constitutionality which limits our jurisdiction and authority. . . .

[T]he conduct of the Supervisors was contemptible, but I . . . dissent from [the] conclusion that it was contemptuous and punishable as such, when the conclusion is dependent upon a reading of the statute which relegates it to meaninglessness. Such an unsympathetic construction is particularly inappropriate when the statute was clearly intended to inhibit our authority . . . .

NOTES ON CONTEMPT OF ANTICIPATED INJUNCTIONS

1. Is preliminary relief irrelevant? If *Griffin* is rightly decided, what purpose is served by the rules for injunctions pending appeal? If plaintiffs had sought an injunction pending appeal, the court would have had to balance probability of success and risk of irreparable injury before granting it. Does *Griffin* mean that defendants must always act as though there were an injunction pending appeal, even when there isn't? And doesn't the logic of *Griffin* apply equally to the trial court? Does every defendant in an injunction suit have to act as though a temporary restraining order had been issued? Is he in contempt if he does something plaintiff seeks to have enjoined, even though plaintiff made no motion for a TRO or preliminary injunction? Or does the vast body of law on preliminary relief imply that *Griffin* is wrongly decided?

2. The requirement of an order in other contexts. *Griffin* also appears to be inconsistent with cases holding that it is not contempt to violate a judicial decision that does not contain an explicit command. Thus, violation of a declaratory judgment is not contempt. Steffel v. Thompson, 415 U.S. 452, 471 (1974), reprinted in section 7.A.2; for a state example, see South Euclid Fraternal Order of Police v. D'Amico, 505 N.E.2d 268 (Ohio 1987).

Less obviously, an order approving and implementing a settlement agreement, without more, does not order the parties to comply with terms of the agreement not expressly set out in the order. Kokkonen v. Guardian Life Insurance Co., 511 U.S. 375

6. It was of little moment in any event, for clearly the court had the power to compel the attorney to restore the property which he had taken with notice . . . of the specific liens held by the adverse parties.

8. . . . Twenty-four years after *Lamb* . . . , the Supreme Court held that an enrolled attorney was not an officer of the court within the meaning of §401(2), but that was not the prevailing notion when Lamb sought to retain the fruits of his malfeasance. If the explanation of Lamb's failure, and that of the courts which decided his case, to deal with the statute does not lie in an absence of awareness of it, speculation about the reason for ignoring it must be against a background of the law as it was understood at the time.

(1994). Litigants often bargain over whether to embody their settlement in a contract or a consent decree; defendants who successfully insist on contract avoid exposure to the contempt power. The Prison Litigation Reform Act takes advantage of this rule to provide that no consent decree can be entered in federal prison litigation without findings sufficient to support a litigated decree. But the Act notes that the parties can enter into "a private settlement agreement" enforceable in a state law contract action.

Many courts hold that injunctions must be in writing and that it is not contempt to violate an oral order; other courts disagree if the oral order is sufficiently clear. Compare Ex parte Price, 741 S.W.2d 366 (Tex. 1987) (no contempt), with Stella Sales, Inc. v. Johnson, 985 P.2d 391, 399 (Wash. Ct. App. 1999) (contempt). In jurisdictions where an unwritten order is not enough, how can an order that is neither written nor spoken be enough?

3. Inconsistent precedents. Both sides in *Griffin* accurately report the precedents they rely on. Most cases say that defendant is not in contempt unless she knows about a clear order and disobeys it. But every once in a while, when a court gets mad enough, it holds someone in contempt for violating an order that hasn't been made yet. *Merrimack* and *Lamb* are still the most relevant opinions from the Supreme Court; there is a similar holding in Toledo Scale Co. v. Computing Scale Co., 261 U.S. 399, 426-428 (1923).

In Ashcraft v. Conoco, Inc., 218 F.3d 288 (4th Cir. 2000), the clerk of the court gave a reporter a stack of documents, including an unsealed envelope marked on the outside as follows: "CONFIDENTIAL SETTLEMENT AGREEMENT FILED UNDER SEAL TO BE OPENED ONLY BY THE COURT." A paralegal had placed this notice pursuant to the judge's instructions, but no judge had signed the notice and nothing on the envelope indicated the authority for the notice. The reporter read the documents in the envelope, and the court of appeals reversed the resulting contempt conviction: "The threshold requirement . . . is that there in fact be a 'decree' of the court," *id.* at 295, and this unsigned sentence was not a decree. A dissenter argued that the warning was a decree. He did not argue that no decree was needed, and neither opinion cited *Griffin*. Are the cases distinguishable?

4. An exception for *Griffin*? Having said all that, isn't *Griffin* appealing on the facts? Didn't defendants show contempt for the court—in the nonlegal sense of "contempt"—as clearly as if they had violated a direct order?

5. Limits to *Griffin*? If *Griffin* were accepted as good law, what should be its limits? Should it matter how likely the court is to issue the injunction? In *Merrimack*, defendants had already won their case in the Supreme Court of the United States. They were held in contempt because they didn't wait to see if there would be a petition for rehearing. Should it matter that rehearings in the Supreme Court are extraordinarily rare?

Is it more important that if the Supreme Court entered an injunction at all, it would certainly be to preserve the poles? Compare In re Sixth & Wisconsin Tower, 108 F.2d 538 (7th Cir. 1939). One bondholder sent a letter to other bondholders, urging them to reject a reorganization plan. The trial court held the letter writer in civil contempt on the ground that the plan and his objections were then before the court for decision. The court of appeals reversed on the ground that there had been no order not to send the letter. Did defendant have any way to predict that the court might, if asked, forbid him to send letters to other bondholders?

6. Punishing the anticipatory contemnor. *Griffin* and the cases it relies on involve compensatory contempt; they impose what amount to damage remedies. Other cases impose punishment for violating orders that had not yet been issued.

a. Sanctions for bad-faith litigation tactics. In Chambers v. NASCO, Inc., 501 U.S. 32 (1991), plaintiff notified defendant that he would file suit for specific performance and move for a TRO to prevent encumbrance or alienation of the property subject to the contract. Before the court could rule on the TRO, defendant conveyed the property to his sister as trustee and recorded the deeds. All nine Justices appeared to assume that this was litigation misconduct that could be punished with an award of attorneys' fees against defendant and disciplinary sanctions against his lawyers. No one either questioned or defended that assumption, and the contempt power was not invoked. The issue before the Court was inherent power to punish bad-faith litigation tactics, and evading the TRO was just one of many examples. The case is described more fully in Notes on Exceptions to the American Rule, in section 10.A.

b. Class action management orders? Inherent power? Kleiner v. First National Bank, 751 F.2d 1193 (11th Cir. 1985), was a class action on behalf of persons who had borrowed money from the bank. While the judge had under advisement a motion to forbid communications between the bank and the class, the bank persuaded 2,800 borrowers to opt out of the class. One hundred seventy-five loan officers were assigned to the task so that they could finish before they could be stopped. The bank's counsel had advised that the calls were legal but that the judge would be furious and might undo the opt outs.

The judge did more than that. She voided the opt outs, assessed the bank $58,000 in costs and attorneys' fees, fined the lawyers $50,000, and disqualified them on the eve of trial. The court of appeals affirmed. "The decision to take the question of informal contacts with class members under advisement acted as an order." *Id.* at 1200. The order did not have to comply with Rule 65, because it was not an injunction; it was a class action management order under Rule 23(d). But it was punishable by contempt and subject to the collateral bar rule. The attorneys in *Kleiner* had not received the procedural protections required for a $50,000 fine in criminal contempt, but that was okay: "A trial judge possesses the inherent power to discipline counsel for misconduct." *Id.* at 1209. Compare International Longshoremen's Association v. Philadelphia Marine Trade Association, 389 U.S. 64, 75 (1967), defining an injunction "within the meaning of Rule 65(d)" as any "equitable decree compelling obedience under the threat of the contempt power."

The Massachusetts court threw out an award of $240,000 in attorneys' fees, imposed as a sanction against a lawyer who derailed a settlement by sending letters to 106 creditors who were not yet parties, claiming that he could get full recoveries for them. Wong v. Luu, 34 N.E.3d 35 (Mass. 2015). The lawyer had violated no order, statute, rule, or contractual obligation; he had not been held in contempt. Massachusetts judges have inherent power to impose sanctions on conduct that interferes with the "fair administration of justice," but the court said that settlements are not necessary to the fair administration of justice.

c. The effect of *Bagwell*? The $50,000 fine in *Kleiner* and the disbarment in *Chambers* take these cases well beyond *Griffin*. Granted that lawyers and clients both behaved badly in each case, should serious punishment be imposed without procedural protections and without clear notice of what is prohibited? Can these cases survive *Bagwell*?

Maybe not. Consider F.J. Hanshaw Enterprises, Inc. v. Emerald River Development, Inc., 244 F.3d 1128 (9th Cir. 2001). Near the end of a bitter proceeding to divide partnership assets, one of the partners tried to bribe the court-appointed receiver. After substantial hearings to confirm the facts, the trial judge imposed sanctions of $500,000 payable to the government and $200,000 payable to the other side for litigation expenses. Relying on *Bagwell*, the court of appeals held that "when a court uses its inherent powers to impose sanctions that are criminal in nature, it must provide the same due process protections that would be available in a criminal contempt proceeding." *Id.* at 1139. The $500,000 payable to the government was criminal; the $200,000 payable to the other side was civil.

7. The Sixth Circuit. The *Griffin* issue has arisen at least twice in the Sixth Circuit.

a. Taking advantage of a gap in orders. In Brown v. City of Upper Arlington, 637 F.3d 668 (6th Cir. 2011), plaintiff got a temporary restraining order in state court to prevent the city from cutting down a large tree, located on city property but in front of plaintiff's home. The city removed the case to federal court. When the TRO expired at the end of its allotted time, the federal judge said: "I would expect that between now and the time the Court issues its decision," if the City decides to take action it will notify the court and plaintiff's counsel immediately. *Id.* at 670. "The City agreed." *Id.* And the City literally kept its word.

On October 29, the court rejected plaintiff's federal claims on the merits and dismissed the case with leave to refile the state-law claims in state court. Plaintiff's lawyer immediately notified the City's lawyer that he would refile in state court no later than October 31. On the morning of October 30, the City cut down the tree. The trial judge held the City in contempt and ordered it to replace the tree and pay plaintiff's attorneys' fees.

The court of appeals reversed. The court treated it as obvious that no order had been violated, and plaintiff seemed to concede that "none of these conventional grounds" for contempt applied. *Id.* at 672. Plaintiff relied principally on Chambers v. NASCO in note 6.a, which the court distinguished on the ground that if the City had interfered with the jurisdiction of any court, it was that of the state courts, not the federal district court.

Neither *Griffin* nor §401 was cited, and of all the cases debated in *Griffin*, only *Merrimack* was cited. The court distinguished *Merrimack* on the ground that the Supreme Court had punished contempt of the lower court's injunction, which was still in effect and not vacated by a mere opinion before the issuance of the mandate. But that is not what the Supreme Court had said.

b. Sloppy drafting. In Gascho v. Global Fitness Holdings, LLC, 875 F.3d 795 (6th Cir. 2017), a corporate defendant running a gym business settled a class action, agreeing to pay $1.3 million plus attorneys' fees and claims administrators' fees. The $1.3 million was put in escrow but not the money for the fees. The settlement agreement was embodied in a court order, but by its terms the order did not take effect until all appeals ended. By the time the Supreme Court declined to hear appeals of class members objecting to the settlement, the defendant had ended its business and paid its managers over $10 million in sketchy "tax distributions." There was no money left for the fees. The district court found the defendant in contempt, but the Sixth Circuit reversed, noting that the settlement agreement did not obligate the parties to do anything until the end of the appeals process. The court said that the parties could have required escrow for the fees as it had for the class member payment. "When a class-action settlement calls for payment from a company with shaky finances, self-help is indispensable." *Id.* at 802.

8. The Ninth Circuit. A federal district court, in a long-running dispute over land rights between ranchers and the government, held two federal employees in contempt for allegedly violating the ranchers' water rights. The Ninth Circuit reversed. The two employees had violated no order, and their actions came "nowhere near meeting the correct legal standard for contempt." United States v. Estate of Hage, 632 Fed. Appx. 338 (9th Cir. 2016). The court "acknowledge[d] that extreme circumstances may warrant the use of contempt for out-of-court conduct unrelated to a court order," citing *Lamb* and *Merrimak*, and calling them "cases at least 80 years old that we have never had occasion to apply." *Id.* at 339.

9. The aftermath of *Griffin*. The 50th anniversary of Brown v. Board of Education brought a long retrospective on the school closing in Prince Edward County. June Kronholz, *Education Gap—After 45 Years, A School Lockout Still Reverberates*, Wall St. J. (May 17, 2004). The county was rural and somewhat poor when the schools closed in 1959, and it is rural and somewhat poor today; it has lost substantial ground as compared to neighboring Cumberland County. Prince Edward has a whole set of middle-aged adults—mostly black, but also some whites whose parents could not afford the private school—who still suffer from losing so much education. Some of the older kids did not return when the schools reopened; younger kids were skipped over several grades, and some of them can barely read or write.

In 2004, the county had one elementary school, one middle school, and one high school, and they were all integrated. The population was 62 percent white, but the elected sheriff was black and there were blacks on the city council and county board.

NOTES ON CONTEMPT STATUTES

1. The federal contempt statute. The contempt statute at issue in *Griffin*, 18 U.S.C. §401, dates from 1831. It was enacted in response to Judge James Peck in St. Louis, who punished as contempt a letter to the editor sharply criticizing one of his decisions. The House of Representatives impeached Judge Peck. The Senate acquitted, but Congress promptly enacted the statute in substantially its present language. The story is retold in George Cochran, *The Reality of "A Last Victim" and Abuse of the Sanctioning Power*, 37 Loy. L.A. L. Rev. 691, 695-700 (2004).

The statute remains a mystery. It is not even settled whether it applies to civil contempt. It is codified in the title on crimes, and it limits the power to punish. It does not mention the power to coerce or compensate. Judge Peck's scandal involved criminal contempt, but surely Congress would have been just as offended if he had jailed his critic until he promised to quit criticizing. The better view is that the statute applies to both civil and criminal contempt; the argument is well developed in Armstrong v. Guccione, 470 F.3d 89, 105-108 (2d Cir. 2006).

2. State contempt statutes. Many state statutes sharply limit the penalties for criminal contempt. Courts generally abide by such statutes but sometimes strike them down for infringing the court's "inherent" contempt power. The Kentucky court and legislature fought over this for a generation. Those cases are reviewed in Norton v. Commonwealth, 37 S.W.3d 750, 754-755 (Ky. 2001); the battle continued in A.W. v. Commonwealth, 163 S.W.3d 4 (Ky. 2005), and seems to have stopped there.

3. Coordinating contempt with the rest of the criminal law. Statutes also address some of the problems that arise when the same act violates an injunction and a criminal statute. Federal statutes require jury trials in such cases, 18 U.S.C. §3691, and limit punishment for the contempt to six months in jail and a $1,000 fine, 18 U.S.C. §402. This limits the court's ability to increase the punishment by issuing an injunction. Presumably, the statutes do not apply to coercive contempt. More important, they do not apply to cases in which the United States is the plaintiff. Aren't those the cases where they're most likely to be needed?

3. The Collateral Bar Rule

WALKER v. CITY OF BIRMINGHAM
388 U.S. 307 (1967)

Justice STEWART delivered the opinion of the Court.

On Wednesday, April 10, 1963, officials of Birmingham, Alabama, filed a bill of complaint in a state circuit court asking for injunctive relief against 139 individuals and two organizations. . . .

The circuit judge granted a temporary injunction as prayed in the bill, enjoining the petitioners from, among other things, participating in or encouraging mass street parades or mass processions without a permit as required by a Birmingham ordinance.

Five of the eight petitioners were served with copies of the writ early the next morning. Several hours later four of them held a press conference. There a statement was distributed, declaring their intention to disobey the injunction because it was "raw tyranny under the guise of maintaining law and order." At this press conference one of the petitioners stated: "That they had respect for the Federal Courts, or Federal Injunctions, but in the past the State Courts had favored local law enforcement, and if the police couldn't handle it, the mob would." [Petitioners led marches on April 12, Good Friday, and April 14, Easter Sunday.]

The next day the city officials who had requested the injunction applied to the state circuit court for an order to show cause why the petitioners should not be held in contempt for violating it. At the ensuing hearing the petitioners sought to attack the constitutionality of the injunction on the ground that it was vague and overbroad, and restrained free speech. They also sought to attack the Birmingham parade ordinance upon similar grounds, and upon the further ground that the ordinance had previously been administered in an arbitrary and discriminatory manner.

The circuit judge refused to consider any of these contentions, pointing out that there had been neither a motion to dissolve the injunction, nor an effort to comply with it by applying for a permit from the city commission before engaging in the Good Friday and Easter Sunday parades. Consequently, the court held that the only issues before it were whether it had jurisdiction to issue the temporary injunction, and whether thereafter the petitioners had knowingly violated it. Upon these issues the court found against the petitioners, and imposed upon each of them a sentence of five days in jail and a $50 fine, in accord with an Alabama statute.[3]

The Supreme Court of Alabama affirmed.[4] That court, too, declined to consider the petitioners' constitutional attacks upon the injunction and the underlying Birmingham parade ordinance. . . .

Howat v. Kansas, 258 U.S. 181 (1922), was decided by this Court almost 50 years ago. That was a case in which people had been punished by a Kansas trial court for refusing to obey an antistrike injunction issued under the state industrial relations act. They had claimed a right to disobey the court's order upon the ground that the state statute and the injunction based upon it were invalid under the Federal Constitution. The Supreme Court of Kansas had affirmed the judgment, holding that the trial court

> had general power to issue injunctions in equity and that, even if its exercise of the power was erroneous, the injunction was not void, and the defendants were precluded from attacking it in this collateral proceeding . . . that, if the injunction was erroneous, jurisdiction was not thereby forfeited, that the error was subject to correction only by the ordinary method of appeal, and disobedience to the order constituted contempt.

258 U.S. at 189.

---

3. . . . The circuit court dismissed the contempt proceedings against several individuals on grounds of insufficient evidence. . . .

4. The Alabama Supreme Court quashed the conviction of one defendant because of insufficient proof that he knew of the injunction before violating it, and the convictions of two others because there was no showing that they had disobeyed the order. . . .

This Court, in dismissing the writ of error, not only unanimously accepted but fully approved the validity of the rule of state law upon which the judgment of the Kansas court was grounded:

> An injunction duly issuing out of a court of general jurisdiction with equity powers upon pleadings properly invoking its action, and served upon persons made parties therein and within the jurisdiction, must be obeyed by them however erroneous the action of the court may be, even if the error be in the assumption of the validity of a seeming but void law going to the merits of the case. It is for the court of first instance to determine the question of the validity of the law, and until its decision is reversed for error by orderly review, either by itself or by a higher court, its orders based on its decision are to be respected, and disobedience of them is contempt of its lawful authority, to be punished.

258 U.S. at 189-190.

The rule of state law accepted and approved in Howat v. Kansas is consistent with the rule of law followed by the federal courts. United States v. United Mine Workers, 330 U.S. 258 (1947).

In the present case, however, we are asked to hold that this rule of law, upon which the Alabama courts relied, was constitutionally impermissible. . . . Whatever the limits of Howat v. Kansas,[6] we cannot accept the petitioners' contentions in the circumstances of this case.

Without question the state court that issued the injunction had, as a court of equity, jurisdiction over the petitioners and over the subject matter of the controversy. And this is not a case where the injunction was transparently invalid or had only a frivolous pretense to validity. We have consistently recognized the strong interest of state and local governments in regulating the use of their streets and other public places. When protest takes the form of mass demonstrations, parades, or picketing on public streets and sidewalks, the free passage of traffic and the prevention of public disorder and violence become important objects of legitimate state concern. . . .

The generality of the language contained in the Birmingham parade ordinance upon which the injunction was based would unquestionably raise substantial constitutional issues concerning some of its provisions. The petitioners, however, did not even attempt to apply to the Alabama courts for an authoritative construction of the ordinance. Had they done so, those courts might have given the licensing authority granted in the ordinance a narrow and precise scope . . . . [I]t could not be assumed that this ordinance was void on its face.

The breadth and vagueness of the injunction itself would also unquestionably be subject to substantial constitutional question. But the way to raise that question was to apply to the Alabama courts to have the injunction modified or dissolved. The injunction in all events clearly prohibited mass parading without a permit, and the evidence shows that the petitioners fully understood that prohibition when they violated it.

---

6. In In re Green, 369 U.S. 689 (1962), the petitioner was convicted of criminal contempt for violating a labor injunction issued by an Ohio court. Relying on the pre-emptive command of the federal labor law, the Court held that the state courts were required to hear Green's claim that the state court was *without jurisdiction* to issue the injunction. The petitioner in *Green*, unlike the petitioners here, had attempted to challenge the validity of the injunction *before* violating it by promptly applying to the issuing court for an order vacating the injunction. The petitioner in *Green* had further offered to prove that the court issuing the injunction had agreed to its violation as an appropriate means of testing its validity.

The petitioners also claim that they were free to disobey the injunction because the parade ordinance on which it was based had been administered in the past in an arbitrary and discriminatory fashion. In support of this claim they sought to introduce evidence that, a few days before the injunction issued, requests for permits to picket had been made to a member of the city commission. One request had been rudely rebuffed, and this same official had later made clear that he was without power to grant the permit alone, since the issuance of such permits was the responsibility of the entire city commission. Assuming the truth of this proffered evidence, it does not follow that the parade ordinance was void on its face. The petitioners, moreover, did not apply for a permit either to the commission itself or to any commissioner after the injunction issued. Had they done so, and had the permit been refused, it is clear that their claim of arbitrary or discriminatory administration of the ordinance would have been considered by the state circuit court upon a motion to dissolve the injunction.

This case would arise in quite a different constitutional posture if the petitioners, before disobeying the injunction, had challenged it in the Alabama courts, and had been met with delay or frustration of their constitutional claims. But there is no showing that such would have been the fate of a timely motion to modify or dissolve the injunction. There was an interim of two days between the issuance of the injunction and the Good Friday march. The petitioners give absolutely no explanation of why they did not make some application to the state court during that period. The injunction had issued ex parte; if the court had been presented with the petitioners' contentions, it might well have dissolved or at least modified its order in some respects. If it had not done so, Alabama procedure would have provided for an expedited process of appellate review. It cannot be presumed that the Alabama courts would have ignored the petitioners' constitutional claims. Indeed, these contentions were accepted in another case by an Alabama appellate court that struck down on direct review the conviction under this very ordinance of one of these same petitioners. Shuttlesworth v. City of Birmingham, 180 So. 2d 114 (Ala. Ct. App. 1965), further appeal pending.

The rule of law upon which the Alabama courts relied in this case was one firmly established by previous precedents. . . . This is not a case where a procedural requirement has been sprung upon an unwary litigant when prior practice did not give him fair notice of its existence.

The Alabama Supreme Court has apparently never in any criminal contempt case entertained a claim of nonjurisdictional error. In Fields v. City of Fairfield, 143 So. 2d 177 (Ala. 1962), *rev'd on other grounds*, 375 U.S. 248 (1963), decided just three years before the present case, the defendants, members of a "White Supremacy" organization who had disobeyed an injunction, sought to challenge the constitutional validity of a permit ordinance upon which the injunction was based. The Supreme Court of Alabama, finding that the trial court had jurisdiction, applied the same rule of law which was followed here . . . .

The rule of law that Alabama followed in this case reflects a belief that in the fair administration of justice no man can be judge in his own case, however exalted his station, however righteous his motives, and irrespective of his race, color, politics, or religion. This Court cannot hold that the petitioners were constitutionally free to ignore all the procedures of the law and carry their battle to the streets. One may sympathize with the petitioners' impatient commitment to their cause. But respect for judicial process is a small price to pay for the civilizing hand of law, which alone can give abiding meaning to constitutional freedom.

Affirmed.

Chief Justice WARREN, whom Justices BRENNAN and FORTAS join, dissenting.

Petitioners in this case contend that they were convicted under an ordinance that is unconstitutional on its face because it submits their First and Fourteenth Amendment rights to free speech and peaceful assembly to the unfettered discretion of local officials. They further contend that the ordinance was unconstitutionally applied to them because the local officials used their discretion to prohibit peaceful demonstrations by a group whose political viewpoint the officials opposed. The Court does not dispute these contentions, but holds that petitioners may nonetheless be convicted and sent to jail because the patently unconstitutional ordinance was copied into an injunction—issued ex parte without prior notice or hearing on the request of the Commissioner of Public Safety—forbidding all persons having notice of the injunction to violate the ordinance without any limitation of time. . . . I do not believe that the fundamental protections of the Constitution were meant to be so easily evaded, or that "the civilizing hand of law" would be hampered in the slightest by enforcing the First Amendment in this case. . . .

Petitioners are Negro ministers who sought to express their concern about racial discrimination in Birmingham . . . by holding peaceful protest demonstrations in that city on Good Friday and Easter Sunday 1963. For obvious reasons, it was important for the significance of the demonstrations that they be held on those particular dates. A representative of petitioners' organization went to the City Hall and asked "to see the person or persons in charge to issue permits, permits for parading, picketing, and demonstrating." She was directed to Public Safety Commissioner Connor, who denied her request for a permit in terms that left no doubt that petitioners were not going to be issued a permit under any circumstances. "He said, 'No, you will not get a permit in Birmingham, Alabama to picket. I will picket you over to the City Jail,' and he repeated that twice." A second, telegraphic request was also summarily denied, in a telegram signed by "Eugene 'Bull' Connor," with the added information that permits could be issued only by the full City Commission, a three-man body consisting of Commissioner Connor and two others.[1] According to petitioners' offer of proof, the truth of which is assumed for purposes of this case, parade permits had uniformly been issued for all other groups by the city clerk on the request of the traffic bureau of the police department, which was under Commissioner Connor's direction. The requirement that the approval of the full Commission be obtained was applied only to this one group.

Understandably convinced that the City of Birmingham was not going to authorize their demonstrations under any circumstances, petitioners proceeded with their plans despite Commissioner Connor's orders. On Wednesday, April 10, at 9 in the evening, the city filed in a state circuit court a bill of complaint seeking an ex parte injunction. The complaint recited that petitioners were engaging in a series of demonstrations as "part of a massive effort . . . to forcibly integrate all business establishments, churches, and other institutions" in the city, with the result that the police department was strained in its resources and the safety, peace, and tranquility were threatened. It was alleged as particularly menacing that petitioners were planning to

---

1. . . . The attitude of the city administration in general and of its Public Safety Commissioner in particular are a matter of public record, of course, and are familiar to this Court from previous litigation. The United States Commission on Civil Rights found continuing abuse of civil rights protesters by the Birmingham police, including use of dogs, clubs, and firehoses. Commissioner Eugene "Bull" Connor, a self-proclaimed white supremacist, made no secret of his personal attitude toward the rights of Negroes and the decisions of this Court. He vowed that racial integration would never come to Birmingham, and wore a button inscribed "Never" to advertise that vow. . . .

conduct "kneel-in" demonstrations at churches where their presence was not wanted. The city's police dogs were said to be in danger of their lives. Faced with these recitals, the Circuit Court issued the injunction in the form requested, and in effect ordered petitioners and all other persons having notice of the order to refrain for an unlimited time from carrying on any demonstrations without a permit. A permit, of course, was clearly unobtainable; the city would not have sought this injunction if it had any intention of issuing one.

Petitioners were served with copies of the injunction at various times on Thursday and on Good Friday. Unable to believe that such a blatant and broadly drawn prior restraint on their First Amendment rights could be valid, they announced their intention to defy it and went ahead with the planned peaceful demonstrations on Easter weekend. On the following Monday, when they promptly filed a motion to dissolve the injunction, the court found them in contempt, holding that they had waived all their First Amendment rights by disobeying the court order.

These facts lend no support to the Court's charges that petitioners were presuming to act as judges in their own case, or that they had a disregard for the judicial process. They did not flee the jurisdiction or refuse to appear in the Alabama courts. Having violated the injunction, they promptly submitted themselves to the courts to test the constitutionality of the injunction and the ordinance it parroted. They were in essentially the same position as persons who challenge the constitutionality of a statute by violating it, and then defend the ensuing criminal prosecution on constitutional grounds. It has never been thought that violation of a statute indicated such a disrespect for the legislature that the violator always must be punished even if the statute was unconstitutional. . . .

The . . . ordinance upon which the injunction was based . . . is patently unconstitutional on its face. Our decisions have consistently held that picketing and parading are means of expression protected by the First Amendment, and that the right to picket or parade may not be subjected to the unfettered discretion of local officials. . . . The only circumstance that the court can find to justify anything other than a per curiam reversal is that Commissioner Connor had the foresight to have the unconstitutional ordinance included in an ex parte injunction, issued without notice or hearing or any showing that it was impossible to have notice or a hearing, forbidding the world at large (insofar as it knew of the order) to conduct demonstrations in Birmingham without the consent of the city officials. This injunction was such potent magic that it transformed the command of an unconstitutional statute into an impregnable barrier, challengeable only in what likely would have been protracted legal proceedings and entirely superior in the meantime even to the United States Constitution.

I do not believe that giving this Court's seal of approval to such a gross misuse of the judicial process is likely to lead to greater respect for the law any more than it is likely to lead to greater protection for First Amendment freedoms. The ex parte temporary injunction has a long and odious history in this country, and its susceptibility to misuse is all too apparent from the facts of the case. As a weapon against strikes, it proved so effective in the hands of judges friendly to employers that Congress was forced to take the drastic step of removing from federal district courts the jurisdiction to issue injunctions in labor disputes. The Norris-LaGuardia Act, 29 U.S.C. §101-115. The labor injunction fell into disrepute largely because it was abused in precisely the same way that the injunctive power was abused in this case. Judges who were not sympathetic to the union cause commonly issued, without notice or hearing, broad restraining orders addressed to large numbers of persons and forbidding them to engage in acts that were either legally permissible or, if illegal, that could better have been left to the regular course of criminal prosecution. The injunctions might later be dissolved, but in the meantime strikes would be crippled because the occasion on which concerted activity might have been effective had passed. Such injunctions, so long discredited as weapons against concerted labor activities, have now been given new life by this Court as weapons against the exercise of First Amendment freedoms. Respect for the courts and for judicial process was not increased by the history of the labor injunction.[8]

Nothing in our prior decisions, or in the doctrine that a party subject to a temporary injunction issued by a court of competent jurisdiction with power to decide a dispute properly before it must normally challenge the injunction in the courts rather than by violating it, requires that we affirm the convictions in this case. The majority opinion in this case rests essentially on a single precedent, and that a case the authority of which has clearly been undermined by subsequent decisions. *Howat* was decided in the days when the labor injunction was in fashion. . . .

Insofar as *Howat* might be interpreted to approve an absolute rule that any violation of a void court order is punishable as contempt, it has been greatly modified by later decisions. In In re Green, we reversed a conviction for contempt of a state injunction forbidding labor picketing because the petitioner was not allowed to present evidence that the labor dispute was arguably subject to the jurisdiction of the National Labor Relations Board and hence not subject to state regulation. If an injunction can be challenged on the ground that it deals with a matter arguably subject to the jurisdiction of the National Labor Relations Board, then a fortiori it can be challenged on First Amendment grounds.[9]

It is not necessary to question the continuing validity of the holding in *Howat*, however, to demonstrate that neither it nor *Mine Workers* supports the holding of the majority in this case. In *Howat* the subpoena and injunction were issued to enable the Kansas Court of Industrial Relations to determine an underlying labor dispute. In *Mine Workers*, the District Court issued a temporary antistrike injunction to preserve existing conditions during the time it took to decide whether it had authority to grant the Government relief in a complex and difficult action of enormous importance to the national economy. In both cases the orders were of questionable legality, but in both cases they were reasonably necessary to enable the court or administrative tribunal to decide an underlying controversy of considerable importance before it

---

8.

> The history of the labor injunction in action puts some matters beyond question. In large part, dissatisfaction and resentment are caused, first, by the refusal of courts to recognize that breaches of the peace may be redressed through criminal prosecution and civil action for damages, and, second, by the expansion of a simple, judicial device to an enveloping code of prohibited conduct, absorbing, en masse, executive and police functions and affecting the livelihood, and even lives, of multitudes. Especially those zealous for the unimpaired prestige of our courts have observed how the administration of law by decrees which through vast and vague phrases surmount law, undermines the esteem of courts upon which our reign of law depends. Not government, but "government by injunction," characterized by the consequences of a criminal prosecution without its safeguards, has been challenged.

Felix Frankfurter & Nathan Greene, *The Labor Injunction* 200 (Macmillan 1930).

9. The attempt in footnote 6 of the majority opinion to distinguish *Green* is nothing but an attempt to alter the holding of that case. The opinion of the Court states flatly that "a state court is without power to hold one in contempt for violating an injunction that the state court had no power to enter by reason of federal pre-emption." 369 U.S. at 692. The alleged circumstance that the court issuing the injunction had agreed to its violation as an appropriate means of testing its validity was considered only in a concurring opinion. Although the petitioner in *Green* had attempted to challenge the order in court before violating it, we did not rely on that fact in holding that the order was void. Nor is it clear to me why the Court regards this fact as important, unless it means to imply that the petitioners in this case would have been free to violate the court order if they had first made a motion to dissolve in the trial court.

at the time. This case involves an entirely different situation. The Alabama Circuit Court did not issue this temporary injunction to preserve existing conditions while it proceeded to decide some underlying dispute. There was no underlying dispute before it, and the court in practical effect merely added a judicial signature to a pre-existing criminal ordinance. . . .

It is not necessary in this case to decide precisely what limits should be set to the *Mine Workers* doctrine in cases involving violations of the First Amendment. Whatever the scope of that doctrine, it plainly was not intended to give a State the power to nul-lify the United States Constitution by the simple process of incorporating its uncon-stitutional criminal statutes into judicial decrees. I respectfully dissent.

Justice DOUGLAS, with whom Justices WARREN, BRENNAN, and FORTAS concur, dissenting. . . .

The right to defy an unconstitutional statute is basic in our scheme. Even when an ordinance requires a permit to make a speech, to deliver a sermon, to picket, to parade, or to assemble, it need not be honored when it is invalid on its face.

By like reason, where a permit has been arbitrarily denied, one need not pursue the long and expensive route to this Court to obtain a remedy. The reason is the same in both cases. For if a person must pursue his judicial remedy before he may speak, parade, or assemble, the occasion when protest is desired or needed will have become history and any later speech, parade, or assembly will be futile or pointless.

Howat states the general rule that court injunctions are to be obeyed until error is found by normal and orderly review procedures. See *Mine Workers*, 330 U.S. at 293-294. But there is an exception where "the question of jurisdiction" is "frivolous and not substantial." *Id.* at 293. Moreover, a state court injunction is not per se sacred where federal constitutional questions are involved. *Green* held that contempt could not be imposed without a hearing where the state decree bordered the fed-eral domain in labor relations and only a hearing could determine whether there was federal pre-emption. In the present case the collision between this state court decree and the First Amendment is so obvious that no hearing is needed to deter-mine the issue. . . .

A court does not have *jurisdiction* to do what a city or other agency of a State lacks *jurisdiction* to do. . . . An ordinance—unconstitutional on its face or patently uncon-stitutional as applied—is not made sacred by an unconstitutional injunction that enforces it. It can and should be flouted in the manner of the ordinance itself. Courts as well as citizens are not free "to ignore all the procedures of the law," to use the Court's language. The "constitutional freedom" of which the Court speaks can be won only if judges honor the Constitution.

Justice BRENNAN, with whom Justices WARREN, DOUGLAS, and FORTAS join, dissenting.

Under cover of exhortation that the Negro exercise "respect for judicial process," the Court empties the Supremacy Clause of its primacy by elevating a state rule of judicial administration above the right of free expression guaranteed by the Federal Constitution. . . .

II

The Court's religious deference to the state court's application of the *Mine Workers'* rule in the present case is in stark contrast to the Court's approach in *Green*. . . . One must wonder what an odd inversion of values it is to afford greater respect to an "arguable" collision with federal labor policy than an assumedly patent interference with constitutional rights. . . .

Constitutional restrictions against abridgments of First Amendment freedoms limit judicial equally with legislative and executive power. Convictions for contempt of court orders which invalidly abridge First Amendment freedoms must be condemned equally with convictions for violation of statutes which do the same thing. I respectfully dissent.

NOTES ON THE DUTY TO OBEY ERRONEOUS INJUNCTIONS

1. The historical context. Bull Connor won this battle, but he had long since lost the war. These marches in Birmingham, and similar protests elsewhere across the South, were aimed at a system of rigid racial segregation in almost every aspect of social life. The system was not limited to segregated schools, housing, and employment; it extended to segregated restaurants, lunch counters, hotels, restrooms, water fountains, elevators, bus stations, buses, parks, churches, movie theaters, stadiums, jails, hospitals, cemeteries, and more. To Americans born in the 1960s and later, the extent and rigor of racial segregation in the South in the first two-thirds of the twentieth century is almost unimaginable.

Dr. Martin Luther King led the marches in Birmingham and was one of the defendants whose conviction was affirmed in *Walker.* His "Letter from Birmingham Jail," the classic statement of the civil rights movement and its commitment to nonviolent resistance, was written during his incarceration for contempt of this injunction. Birmingham was in the national news all through the spring of 1963, and "Bull Connor's police dogs and fire hoses" became a metaphor for bitter resistance to desegregation. News coverage of Birmingham contributed to a massive shift in public opinion that made possible the Civil Rights Act of 1964. Those who peacefully stood up to the dogs and fire hoses were heroes and heroines, but their story is fading from collective memory as the population ages and the nation struggles with its current racial problems.

For the full story, see Taylor Branch, *Parting the Waters: America in the King Years 1954-63* (Simon & Schuster 1988). For articles focused on Birmingham and *Walker,* see David Luban, *Difference Made Legal: The Court and Dr. King,* 87 Mich. L. Rev. 2152 (1989); David Benjamin Oppenheimer, *Martin Luther King, Walker v. City of Birmingham, and the Letter from Birmingham Jail,* 26 U.C. Davis L. Rev. 791 (1993). *Letter from Birmingham Jail* is reprinted at 26 U.C. Davis L. Rev. 835 (1993).

2. The ordinance. Some defendants were prosecuted directly under the parade ordinance. The Supreme Court unanimously held the ordinance unconstitutional in Shuttlesworth v. City of Birmingham, 394 U.S. 147 (1969). *Shuttlesworth* lets us consider *Walker* without being distracted by lingering doubts about whether the ordinance and injunction were really unconstitutional. The injunction was even broader than the ordinance, and thus even more clearly unconstitutional.

3. The collateral bar rule. Once it is clear that the injunction was unconstitutional, *Walker* depends wholly on the rule that an injunction cannot be attacked in a prosecution for criminal contempt. The criminal offense is complete when defendant defies the court. It does not matter whether the court was right or wrong, and the offense is not undone if the injunction is later reversed. This rule is often called the collateral bar rule. Several states reject the rule; state cases pro and con are collected in People v. Gonzales, 910 P.2d 1366, 1374 n.4 (Cal. 1996).

The collateral bar rule does not apply in civil contempt. Plaintiff is not entitled to benefit from an erroneous injunction, either by recovering compensation or coercing compliance. The Court was very clear about this in United States v. United Mine Workers, 330 U.S. 258, 295 (1947); a more recent example is Ashcraft v. Conoco, Inc., 218 F.3d 288, 302-303 (4th Cir. 2000), where the court vacated a judgment in compensatory civil contempt (for contempt of a real decree that had been entered, but erroneously). Yet courts get confused on this point too. See Mid-American Waste Systems, Inc. v. City of Gary, 49 F.3d 286 (7th Cir. 1995), where the court applied the collateral bar rule to civil contempt, without noticing the distinction or referring to *Mine Workers.*

4. Distinguishing claim and issue preclusion. The collateral bar rule is relevant only when ordinary rules of claim and issue preclusion do not apply, which is to say, the rule is relevant to preliminary injunctions and temporary restraining orders, and it makes those preliminary orders preclusive in criminal contempt. A *final* judgment is preclusive in subsequent litigation, and this rule applies to proceedings to enforce a permanent injunction, including in civil contempt as well as criminal. This explanation fits the Supreme Court's cases, although the Court has never clearly explained the distinction.

The issue arose in Travelers Indemnity Co. v. Bailey, 557 U.S. 137 (2009). Travelers was the principal liability insurer for Johns Mansville, the bankrupt supplier of asbestos. In 1986, the bankruptcy court enjoined further litigation against Mansville and its insurers. A dispute subsequently arose about the scope of this injunction. Plaintiffs argued that the injunction did not apply to certain claims, and that if it did, the bankruptcy court had exceeded its jurisdiction. The Supreme Court held that the injunction did apply to those claims, and that the bankruptcy court's jurisdiction was now res judicata and could not be relitigated in proceedings to enforce the injunction.

There are earlier cases holding permanent injunctions to be res judicata in subsequent contempt proceedings, although *Travelers* does not cite them. Local 28 of Sheet Metal Workers v. Equal Employment Opportunity Commission, 478 U.S. 421, 441 n.21 (1986), is such a case, and it cites others. But it also cites *Walker*, and fails to distinguish its res judicata holding from the collateral bar rule.

The res judicata issue came up again in Salazar v. Buono, 559 U.S. 700 (2010). The district court issued a permanent injunction that was affirmed in the court of appeals. The parties promptly filed motions in the trial court to enforce or modify the injunction, and on the government's appeal from rulings on those motions, it tried to renew one of its arguments from the first appeal. It argued that the first appeal was interlocutory for all practical purposes. Just about the only thing a splintered Court agreed on was that the first judgment was preclusive. *Id.* at 712 (plurality); *id.* at 730 (Scalia, J., concurring in the judgment); *id.* at 736 (Stevens, J., dissenting); *id.* at 760 (Breyer, J., dissenting). A final judgment is a final judgment, no matter how quickly the second round of litigation begins.

5. The jurisdiction exception. The traditional formulation of the collateral bar rule is that defendant must obey if the court that issued the injunction had jurisdiction. If the court lacked jurisdiction, the injunction can be ignored. What's so special about jurisdiction? The dissenters in *Walker* argued that surely the First Amendment is more important than some technical rule allocating jurisdiction between state courts and the National Labor Relations Board. Would the majority disagree? Does anyone think that jurisdiction is the only value *important* enough to justify disobedience?

The jurisdiction exception has a different source. If a drunk claiming to be Chief Justice John Roberts starts issuing orders, no one is bound to obey. The drunk lacks authority to issue the orders. Similarly, the idea is that a court without jurisdiction lacks authority to enjoin. But unlike a drunk, a court gets the benefit of the doubt. "Only when a court is so obviously traveling outside its orbit as to be merely usurping judicial forms and facilities, may an order issued by a court be disobeyed and treated as though it were a letter to a newspaper." *Mine Workers*, 330 U.S. at 310 (Frankfurter, J., concurring).

6. Jurisdiction to consider jurisdiction. Who decides whether the court has jurisdiction? In the first instance, the trial court decides for itself.

a. *Mine Workers*. *Mine Workers* carried the collateral bar rule further than *Walker*. The case arose when a period of persistent labor strife disrupted production in the nation's coal mines. The United States seized the mines, negotiated a new labor agreement, and ran the mines as government properties, accounting to the owners for any profits. When the union went on strike against the government, the government got a TRO to stop the strike. But the Norris-LaGuardia Act deprives federal courts of jurisdiction to enjoin strikes. 29 U.S.C. §101 *et seq.*. There are some express exceptions, but none that applied to the case. Even so, the United States argued that the Act does not apply when the sovereign is the employer. Five justices agreed. It followed that the trial court did have jurisdiction, and that the injunction was proper on the merits. 330 U.S. at 269-289.

A different majority subscribed to an alternative holding based on the collateral bar rule. Frankfurter and Jackson believed, and Vinson, Burton, and Reed assumed arguendo, that the Norris-LaGuardia Act applied. On that view, the trial court ultimately lacked jurisdiction to enjoin the strike. Still, they said, whether the Act applied to the United States was a close question, and the trial court had jurisdiction to decide that question. That is, it had jurisdiction to determine the scope of its own jurisdiction, even if it lacked jurisdiction to determine the merits. And, this majority said, the trial court had power to preserve the status quo while it exercised its power to determine jurisdiction. So it had jurisdiction to issue a TRO against the strike while it decided whether the Norris-LaGuardia Act applied, even if it ultimately turned out that the Act did apply and the court lacked jurisdiction to enjoin the strike. 330 U.S. at 289-295.

Justices Rutledge and Murphy rejected that theory, largely on the ground that the plain language of the Norris-LaGuardia Act permitted no such exception. The majority conceded that Rutledge and Murphy would be right if the claim of an exception for the United States were frivolous. A judge has jurisdiction to consider jurisdiction, but only if there is a nonfrivolous claim of jurisdiction over the merits. Justices Black and Douglas found this whole debate unnecessary to the decision and expressed no views. So the vote on the collateral bar holding was 5 to 2.

b. In re Green. In re Green, 369 U.S. 689 (1962), is much debated in *Walker* and somewhat distorted by both sides. *Green* is easy to reconcile with *Walker* but harder to reconcile with *Mine Workers*. The brief majority opinion rests squarely on the ground that the state court appeared to lack jurisdiction because of federal preemption. And assuming that the state court might have had jurisdiction, the Court said that due process required a hearing where defendant could contest jurisdiction before he was punished for contempt. Justice Harlan concurred on other grounds. He found the majority approach irreconcilable with *Mine Workers*. The state court's claim of jurisdiction was not frivolous, so its orders were binding until jurisdiction was finally determined.

The majority's answer to Harlan was apparently the single sentence about due process. Another answer might be that Harlan overstated the *Mine Workers* rule. If the state court in *Green* went straight to the merits without ever considering jurisdiction, was it exercising its jurisdiction to consider jurisdiction? Or was it exercising nonexistent jurisdiction over the merits? The concept of jurisdiction to consider jurisdiction is central to *Mine Workers*, and arguably requires explicit attention to the jurisdictional issue. Of course, if the court decides that it has jurisdiction, that determination becomes law of the case until reversed, and may be binding under the collateral bar rule. Thus, an erroneous determination of jurisdiction probably confers jurisdiction over the merits, at least for a while.

c. *Catholic Conference.* The requirement that the court actually consider its jurisdiction was made explicit, in a related context, in United States Catholic Conference v. Abortion Rights Mobilization, 487 U.S. 72 (1988). The Catholic Conference was a nonparty witness in a suit between Abortion Rights Mobilization and the government. The Catholic Conference refused to comply with a subpoena and was held in *civil* contempt. A civil contempt order against a nonparty witness is immediately appealable. On appeal, the Catholic Conference argued that the subpoena was void because the trial court lacked jurisdiction over the underlying action. The Supreme Court agreed that a nonparty witness could raise that issue. It noted that the trial court could subpoena evidence necessary to determine whether it had jurisdiction. But because the documents demanded here were plainly relevant to the merits rather than to jurisdiction, and because the trial court had already decided that it had jurisdiction before it issued this subpoena, the court could not enforce the subpoena unless it had jurisdiction over the merits.

7. **Personal jurisdiction.** The Court says the Alabama trial court "without question" had jurisdiction over defendants. Is that true? How did it acquire jurisdiction? Formal service of process, or notice pursuant to a valid long-arm act, is usually required to obtain jurisdiction over the person of defendants. Murphy Brothers, Inc. v. Michetti Pipe Stringing, Inc., 526 U.S. 344, 350 (1999). Formal service is not required before a TRO, but a year after *Walker*, the Court decided Carroll v. President and Commissioners of Princess Anne, reprinted in section 5.B.2. *Carroll* requires efforts at informal notice before applying for a TRO; this informal notice obviously substitutes for formal service. Does informal notice perform only the notice function of formal service, or does it also perform the jurisdictional function? Doesn't something have to substitute for the jurisdictional function of service? Should defendants have argued that the Alabama court lacked personal jurisdiction, because they were not served and there was no effort to notify them or explain why they could not be notified?

8. **Jurisdictional limits and constitutional limits.** Is the traditional emphasis on jurisdiction convincing, even on its own terms? If a court that clearly exceeds jurisdictional limits is a pretender, why isn't a court that clearly exceeds constitutional limits a pretender? Don't constitutional limits deprive the whole government of power, just as jurisdictional limits deprive particular courts or agencies of power? If a court has no power to exceed its jurisdiction, why does it have power to violate the Constitution?

9. **Other exceptions?** *Walker* holds open the possibility of two exceptions other than lack of jurisdiction. The majority says that "this is not a case where the injunction was transparently invalid or had only a frivolous pretense to validity." It also says that "this case would arise in quite a different constitutional posture if the petitioners, before disobeying the injunction, had challenged it in the Alabama courts, and had been met with delay or frustration of their constitutional claims." Might either of those disclaimers produce an exception with real content? How "transparently invalid" does the injunction have to be, if the *Walker* injunction wasn't transparent enough? How much delay or frustration would you put up with before advising a client to defy an injunction?

The First Circuit allowed collateral attack on an injunction it found transparently invalid. In re Providence Journal Co., 820 F.2d 1342 (1st Cir. 1986), *modified,* 820 F.2d 1354 (1st Cir. 1987) (en banc), *cert. dis'd,* 485 U.S. 693 (1988). The *Journal* had lawfully obtained from the FBI information about the late Raymond Patriarca, an alleged organized crime leader. Patriarca's son obtained a TRO forbidding the *Journal* to publish anything from the FBI's files, and the *Journal* defied the TRO. The *Journal* and its editor were held in criminal contempt. The *Journal* was fined $100,000; the editor was sentenced to 18 months in jail, suspended on condition of 200 hours of public service.

Judge Wisdom, sitting by designation, found the order transparently invalid. He distinguished *Walker* on the ground that pure speech was more protected than marching in the streets, and on the ground that the law of gag orders against newspapers was especially clear after Nebraska Press Association v. Stuart, 427 U.S. 539 (1976), described in Notes on Prior Restraints in section 5.A.3. The en banc court added a requirement that the targets of such orders seek emergency relief from an appellate court before defying the order. But it implied that publication need not be delayed pending such a request. Other cases interpreting the exceptions for transparently invalid orders, none of them finding the exception satisfied, are collected in State v. Wright, 870 A.2d 1039 (Conn. 2005).

10. A real exception. The collateral bar rule is designed to discourage defiance. A countervailing rule is applied to cases where it is thought important to discourage appeals. Subpoenas and discovery orders to parties are unappealable. A party who receives such an order may move to quash in the trial court, but a denial of the motion to quash is also unappealable. To appeal, the witness or litigant must defy the order and be convicted of criminal contempt. The conviction is appealable, and the validity of the underlying order can be raised on appeal. If the appeal is unsuccessful, appellant faces punishment for contempt. The purpose and effect is to deter appeals by putting a price on failure. The Supreme Court has explained that *Walker* does not apply to such cases. United States v. Ryan, 402 U.S. 530, 532 n.4 (1971).

11. Relief from the federal courts? Rightly or wrongly, defendants in *Walker* feared delay and frustration in the state courts. What's wrong with a rule that says they have to obey the injunction until it is set aside, but that they can go to the federal district court for a counter injunction granting permission to march? The federal court could enjoin Bull Connor from enforcing the state injunction. Whatever the appeal of that solution, the Supreme Court has precluded it in a series of cases beginning with Younger v. Harris, 401 U.S. 37 (1971). The *Younger* doctrine is considered in section 7.A.2.

12. Jurisdiction to consider jurisdiction again. One other case you should know about is United States v. Shipp, 203 U.S. 563 (1906). Shipp was the sheriff of Hamilton County, Tennessee. He had custody of a black prisoner, Johnson, sentenced to death for rape of a white woman. Johnson filed a writ of habeas corpus alleging racial discrimination in jury selection and mob domination of his trial. The federal trial court denied the writ, but stayed execution for ten days to permit an appeal to the Supreme Court. Johnson appealed, and on the ninth day, the Court issued a further stay of execution. The order was telegraphed to Shipp and reported in the Chattanooga papers. That night, Johnson was lynched by a mob, and Shipp was charged with aiding the mob instead of protecting his prisoner. Only Tennessee could prosecute him for murder, but the United States prosecuted him for contempt of the Supreme Court's stay order.

Shipp defended on the ground that both federal courts lacked jurisdiction. The federal courts had jurisdiction only if Johnson presented a substantial federal question. Shipp argued that Johnson's federal claims were "absolutely frivolous" and created a mere pretense of federal jurisdiction. The Court rejected the argument:

> It has been held, it is true, that orders made by a court having no jurisdiction to make them may be disregarded without liability or process for contempt. But even if the

Circuit Court had no jurisdiction to entertain Johnson's petition, and if this court had no jurisdiction of the appeal, this court, and this court alone, could decide that such was the law. It and it alone necessarily had jurisdiction to decide whether the case was properly before it. . . . Until its judgment declining jurisdiction should be announced, it had authority from the necessity of the case to make orders to preserve the existing conditions and the subject of the petition. . . . [T]he law contemplates the possibility of a decision either way, and therefore must provide for it.

Id. at 573. The story of Johnson's trial for rape, and of Shipp's trial before the Supreme Court for contempt of that Court, is fully told in Mark Curriden and Leroy Phillips, Jr., *Contempt of Court* (Anchor Books 2001).

Should Shipp go unpunished if the Court would have upheld Johnson's conviction? Should he go unpunished if the Court would have concluded that Johnson's claims were so frivolous they conferred only a pretense of jurisdiction? Can the law afford any exception that authorizes litigants to decide for themselves whether to obey court orders? Should defendants be tempted to convince themselves that the court's claim to jurisdiction is frivolous?

13. Distinguishing *Shipp* and *Walker*. If Shipp should be punished even if Johnson's claims were frivolous, how is *Walker* different? *Shipp* at least differs in degree; death is the ultimate irreparable injury. But any time there is an injunction, some court has decided that defendant will suffer irreparable injury if the injunction is violated.

Is it that Walker was exercising a constitutional right but Shipp wasn't? Many conservative judges would say that Tennessee's right to enforce the death penalty is as much a constitutional right as Walker's right to speak — that the Constitution guarantees state rights as well as individual rights. They wouldn't defend a lynch mob, but they would reject the idea that *Shipp* and *Walker* can be distinguished on that basis.

Is it that *Shipp* involves a confusion between jurisdiction and the merits? The Supreme Court has always said that frivolous federal questions do not confer federal jurisdiction. The cases are collected in Hagans v. Lavine, 415 U.S. 528, 537-538 (1974). But when a litigant presents a frivolous federal question to a federal court, that court must pronounce it frivolous. That is not a decision that some other court should answer the question — the usual meaning of jurisdiction. It is an answer to the question, a decision on the merits, although labeled jurisdictional. If we accept that reformulation, then the Court unquestionably had jurisdiction in *Shipp*. And there was no error even on the merits in its stay order. It was proper to keep Johnson alive pending final decision, even if the final decision would be adverse. We think this is what Justice Rutledge means in an extraordinarily cryptic passage in his *Mine Workers* dissent. It is a good argument. But it is not what the Court said in *Shipp*, and it is not consistent with the Court's adherence to the fiction that it lacks jurisdiction over frivolous questions. And if the federal courts had jurisdiction to preserve the status quo in *Shipp* and *Mine Workers*, why didn't the state court have jurisdiction to preserve the status quo in *Walker*? And do any of these jurisdictional niceties have anything to do with the reasons that almost everyone would punish Sheriff Shipp but many people would exonerate Reverend Walker?

14. The policy choice. Does the wisdom of the collateral bar rule ultimately come down to predictions about the frequency of cases like *Walker* and cases like *Shipp*? In all cases in which judges issue injunctions that defendants are tempted to violate, will the judges be right more often than the defendants, or will the defendants be right more often than the judges? What will be the relative costs of each set of errors? And would there really be more defiance without the collateral bar rule? How much more?

15. *Walker* in retrospect. In a retrospective look at *Walker*, Professor Kennedy says that Dr. King's lawyers let him down by not seeking direct review. "Whatever lay behind the omission, the absence of a filing of some sort manifested a lapse of capacity or judgment. It would have been prudent to have filed a petition for review immediately contesting the injunction and requesting expedited review." Randall Kennedy, *Walker v. City of Birmingham Revisited*, 2018 Sup. Ct. Rev. 313, 324-325. Kennedy quotes conflicting recollections from the lawyers, including one who said there had been a deliberate decision not to file in state court before the march. In their petition for rehearing, defendants had told the Supreme Court that there were few lawyers, hundreds of illegal arrests, and no time to deliberate on legal strategy in response to the injunction. They also said that even with expedited review, it had been taking up to nine months to get appellate review of preliminary injunctions in Alabama.

Professor Kennedy directs most of his criticism at the Supreme Court:

> Still, the mistake on the part of King's camp does not justify *Walker*. Avenues for an alternative holding were available. One would have entailed abandoning the collateral bar rule at least with respect to certain categories of dispute. . . . Another alternative was posited by the office of the Solicitor General. . . . They contended that disobedience to an injunction should not preclude a testing of its validity when the order "broadly suppresses the exercise of First Amendment rights, in a context that permits no effective alternative means of expression and no timely opportunity to obtain relief from the ban.". . . .
>
> Justice Stewart's opinion also hints at an alternative outcome. *Walker*, he insisted, was "not a case where the injunction was transparently invalid or had only a frivolous pretense to validity," implying that the presence of those features would have led to a different conclusion. But there was good reason to believe that the order was "transparently invalid." . . .
>
> *Walker v City of Birmingham* should prompt sober reflection. That people were compelled to resort to political protest to challenge widespread and blatant racial discrimination in mid-twentieth century America was disgraceful. That they were arrested and jailed by local authorities intent upon suppressing their message is outrageous. That this persecution was then blessed by the United States Supreme Court was tragic—with a bit of absurdity thrown in for good measure. Of all the places to proclaim the civilizing hand of law, the Supreme Court chose a case that absolved judicial white supremacists and relegated to jail Martin Luther King, Jr.

Id. at 325-330.

16. The penalty. The maximum penalty for criminal contempt in Alabama was five days. What if it had been five years?

JOHN LEUBSDORF, CONSTITUTIONAL CIVIL PROCEDURE

63 Tex. L. Rev. 579, 624-627 (1984)

Contempt proceedings furnish the most egregious instance of institutionalized partiality. Six sets of rules combine to leave the alleged contemner subject to a judge's arbitrary power. First, the judge can punish the contemner for violating the judge's own order—and in institutional reform cases and others, the judge may have a considerable stake in enforcing that order. Two constitutional rules limit this power: that a sentence of more than six months in prison can be given only by a jury and that a new judge must replace any judge who becomes personally embroiled with the contemner and who waits until the end of the trial to hold him in contempt. Even these limits exist, probably, because the Court could avoid its usual reluctance to disturb civil procedure by classifying the proceedings to which the limits apply as "criminal contempt."

Second, the judge can punish summarily and without hearing contempt occurring in his presence, a procedure without parallel in our jurisprudence. Third, many states do not allow the defendant in a criminal contempt proceeding to contest the legality or even the constitutionality of the order he is charged with violating. A judge can thus punish someone for violating an order that the judge had no right to issue. That order may have been issued without any chance for the alleged contemner to be heard if the order was a temporary restraining order issued without a hearing, or if the contemner was not a party.

Fourth, the judge can choose from an extraordinary bouquet of sanctions. For civil contempt, he can require payment of damages and attorney fees and also can imprison the contemner or make him pay daily fines until he complies; for criminal contempt, the judge can inflict fines and imprisonment that even compliance will not terminate. . . .

Fifth, a contemner might not be able to obtain adequate appellate review of the charge. If found guilty of criminal contempt, he may appeal at once, but he may not be able to challenge the validity of the order he violated. If he is found in civil contempt, he may challenge the validity of the violated order, but if he is a party to the suit in which the contempt occurred, he probably will have to wait until the suit reaches an appealable final judgment. In practice, therefore, the judge's decision may be unreviewable.

Sixth, the judge can control the procedures within which the contemner must defend himself by deciding whether the proceedings shall be for civil or criminal contempt or both. This decision determines whether a private party or the government will prosecute, what safeguards the defendant will receive, and when the defendant will be able to appeal.

Although something can be said for most of these rules individually, together they are insupportable. Ironically, defenders of these rules invoke the supremacy of law to justify the shoddy treatment of those who defy judicial authority, yet it is that very supremacy that a judge's arbitrary power offends. Courts would not lose their ability to enforce their judgments if contempt proceedings were always assigned to a new judge, if summary contempt proceedings without hearings were abolished, if contemners not offered a hearing before an order was entered were allowed to challenge its legality, or if all those found guilty of contempt were allowed to appeal immediately.

These reforms have been delayed not because the rule of law requires arbitrary judicial power or even because the oppressive contempt rules are unexamined relics of the past. The rules survive because judges are reluctant to restrict their own power.

4.   *The Rights of Third Parties*

PLANNED PARENTHOOD GOLDEN GATE v. GARIBALDI
132 Cal. Rptr. 2d 46 (Ct. App. 2003)

Haerle, J.

I. Introduction

In 1995 Planned Parenthood Association of San Mateo County obtained a permanent injunction limiting demonstration activity outside its clinic in San Mateo (the

1995 injunction). [The injunction was affirmed in part in Planned Parenthood Association v. Operation Rescue, 57 Cal. Rptr. 2d 736 (Ct. App. 1996) (*Parenthood I*).] In February 2001, Planned Parenthood Golden Gate (PPGG) [a successor organization created by merging the original plaintiff with other entities] filed the instant action seeking a declaration that the 1995 injunction applies to appellants, Rossi Foti . . . and Jeannette and Louie Garibaldi . . . .

II. Factual and Procedural Background

A. the 1995 injunction. . .[2]

The 1995 injunction was entered against two named defendants, Operation Rescue of California (ORC) and Robert Cochran (Cochran). According to its terms, the 1995 injunction applies to: "Defendants and their agents, employees, representatives and all persons acting in concert or participation with them, or either of them, and all persons with actual notice of this judgment.". . .

The 1995 injunction . . . restrain[s] and enjoin[s] individuals subject to the 1995 injunction from directly or indirectly: (1) "Entering or blocking or obstructing the free and direct passage of any other person into or out of" the clinic; (2) "Demonstrating, picketing, distributing literature, or counseling" on clinic property "or within fifteen (15) feet of such private property"; (3) "Entering or blocking or obstructing the ingress or egress of any vehicle to or from any parking area" in front of or behind the clinic; (4) "Obstructing or impeding the movement of any person" who is moving between a vehicle and the clinic or using a walkway leading to the clinic; (5) "Shouting, screaming or otherwise producing loud noises which can be heard" in the clinic; (6) "Physically touching[,] threatening to physically touch, or shouting" at people entering or exiting the clinic. . . .

III. Discussion

A. summary judgment
1. Standard of Review and Issues Presented . . .

[T]he trial court granted PPGG summary judgment because it found that Foti and the Garibaldis are bound by the 1995 injunction as a matter of law. By its terms, the 1995 injunction applies to ORC and Cochran, the named defendants in *Parenthood I*, and to two additional categories of individuals: (1) ORC's and/or Cochran's "agents, employees representatives and all persons acting in concert or participation with

---

2. [From 1988 to 1995, Robert Cochran and Operation Rescue of California] organized and coordinated regular protests at the clinic. Those protests included "several 'very large . . . blockades' of more than 100 protestors [that] resulted in the clinic's temporary closure. Typically, 'rows of people block[ed] all the doors' to the clinic. On at least one occasion police arrested protestors inside the clinic. . . . Patients found the protests threatening, and some did not come into the clinic for appointments. Noise from the protests could be heard in the patient waiting room, which abuts the sidewalk. The protests caused the clinic to shift its entrance doors and to hire and train staff for an 'escort program' to bring patients through the protestors." *Parenthood I*, 57 Cal. Rptr. at 739. Patients were angered, upset and frightened by these protestors who tried to prevent people from driving into the clinic parking lot and demonstrated so loudly they could be heard inside the clinic. There was evidence that the patients' heightened stress levels complicated their medical procedures. Some required additional counseling or medication. Others canceled or delayed appointments in order to avoid protestors. The evidence showed that delaying an abortion procedure increased the likelihood patients would experience complications.

them or either of them" (the in concert provision) and (2) "all persons with actual notice of this judgment" (the actual notice provision). PPGG maintains that both of these provisions apply to Foti and the Garibaldis as a matter of law. Appellants maintain that the actual notice provision of the 1995 injunction is unconstitutional and invalid, and that there are disputed issues of material fact as to whether the in concert provision of the injunction applies to them. . . .

2. The Injunction's "Actual Notice" Provision Is Invalid

"An injunction is obviously a personal decree. It operates on the person of the defendant by commanding him to do or desist from certain action." People ex rel. Gwinn v. Kothari, 100 Cal. Rptr. 2d 29 (Ct. App. 2000). Indeed it may "deprive the enjoined parties of rights others enjoy precisely because the enjoined parties have abused those rights in the past." People v. Conrad, 64 Cal. Rptr. 2d 248 (Ct. App. 1997). Thus, it is well established that "injunctions are not effective against the world at large." *Kothari*, 100 Cal. Rptr. 2d at 35. On the other hand, the law recognizes that enjoined parties "may not nullify an injunctive decree by carrying out prohibited acts with or through nonparties to the original proceeding." *Conrad*, 64 Cal. Rptr. 2d at 251. Thus, an injunction can properly run to classes of persons with or through whom the enjoined party may act. However, "a theory of disobedience of the injunction cannot be predicated on the act of a person not in any way included in its terms or acting in concert with the enjoined party and in support of his claims." Berger v. Superior Court, 167 P. 143, 144 (Cal. 1917).

These legal principles establish that the actual notice provision in the 1995 injunction is not enforceable.

> [P]ersonal jurisdiction and notice are not enough to subject a person to the restraint of an injunction. The *order* must be directed against that person, either by naming that person as an individual or by designating a class of persons to which that person belongs.
>
> If the person charged with violation was neither named in the injunction individually or as a member of a class, nor as aiding or abetting a person so included, he cannot be brought within the prohibition merely by being served with a copy of the writ.

6 B.E. Witkin, *California Procedure* §391 at 318 (4th ed., West 1997). . . .

PPGG contends the "actual notice provision is an indispensable tool to effectuate the court's power to grant equitable relief among all parties affected by the intense emotions surrounding the abortion debate." In fact, the actual notice provision is inconsistent with the very nature and purpose of injunctive relief because it purports to extend a remedy beyond the context of the specific dispute which justifies that remedy.

> An injunction, by its very nature, applies only to a particular group (or individuals) and regulates the activities, and perhaps the speech, of that group. It does so, however, because of the group's past actions in the context of a specific dispute between real parties. The parties seeking the injunction assert a violation of their rights; the court hearing the action is charged with fashioning a remedy for a specific deprivation, not with the drafting of a statute addressed to the general public.

Madsen v. Women's Health Center, Inc., 512 U.S. 753, 762 (1994).

The intensity of the "abortion debate" does not somehow entitle PPGG to broader relief than parties seeking equitable relief in other contexts. If anything, the opposite is true.

> As a general matter, . . . protestors enjoy full constitutional protection for the expression and communication of their views concerning the public issue of abortion. This is particularly true when these protected activities occur on the public streets and sidewalks, traditionally viewed as the quintessential public forum. An injunction curtailing protected expression will be upheld only if the challenged provisions of the injunction burden no more speech than necessary to serve a significant government interest.

Parenthood I, 57 Cal. Rptr. 2d at 741. The actual notice provision cannot satisfy this requirement; because it purports to enjoin all demonstrators in addition to the enjoined parties, the restriction is overbroad on its face.

PPGG argues that, without the actual notice provision, one anti-choice protestor can simply be replaced with another and avoid the reach of the injunction. But anti-choice protestors are not fungible. A "'mutuality of purpose' is not enough" to bind non-parties to an injunction restricting demonstration activity at an abortion clinic; "it must be [their] actual relationship to an enjoined party, and not their convictions about abortion, that make them contemners." *Conrad*, 64 Cal. Rptr. at 251. Put another way, if we permit PPGG to utilize an actual notice provision to obtain injunctive relief against all anti-abortion protestors, the injunction would be content-based and virtually impossible to justify under current First Amendment jurisprudence.

PPGG's legitimate concern that an enjoined party might attempt to undermine the effect of an injunction by enlisting the aid of a nonparty can be adequately addressed by a provision extending the reach of the injunction to agents, employees and those who act in concert with an enjoined party. The 1995 injunction contains such a provision. That in concert provision ensures that "a nonparty to an injunction is subject to the contempt power of the court when, with knowledge of the injunction, the nonparty violates its terms with or for those who are restrained." *Id.*

PPGG argues the actual notice provision should be approved as a time-saving device. According to PPGG, requiring it to litigate with appellants in order to obtain injunctive relief against them would be a waste of time because: (1) the restrictions imposed by the 1995 injunction were expressly approved in *Parenthood I*; (2) "the behavior of each, individual protestor is not determinative of the ultimate remedy" to which PPGG is entitled; and (3) a separate trial "will not produce different injunctive relief." Virtually every prong of this argument is erroneous.

First, the *Parenthood I* court affirmed in part *and reversed in part* the judgment imposing the 1995 injunction against ORC and Cochran. The court upheld a restriction which precluded appellants from demonstrating within 15 feet of the San Mateo clinic (the 15 foot exclusion zone provision). However it found that other provisions of the 1995 injunction were overbroad and unconstitutional because they burdened more of the defendants' speech than was justified by the evidence. [*Parenthood I* reversed an injunction against "approaching" any staff member, patient, or companion who "has made it unmistakably clear that he or she does not wish to be approached," and an injunction against coming within 250 feet of a named physician's residence.]

Second, although the *Parenthood I* court upheld the 15-foot exclusion zone provision, it did not, as PPGG intimates, approve that provision against all protestors who demonstrate at the San Mateo clinic. In reaching its decision, the court expressly acknowledged this restriction affected the constitutionally protected speech rights of appellants in that case; its practical effect was that those appellants had to stay off the public sidewalk at the front of the clinic and to move either to the sides or across the street. Nevertheless, the court found the restriction was justified as to those appellants because there was evidence that (1) they actually obstructed access to the clinic and intimidated patients; (2) they had violated a less restrictive exclusion provision imposed by a prior injunction; and (3) they could easily be seen and heard from across the street. Thus, "inclusion of all the sidewalk fronting the clinic property within the 15-foot exclusion zone" did not burden "more speech than was necessary to prevent intimidation and permit access." *Parenthood I*, 57 Cal. Rptr. 2d at 742.

As the appellate decision in *Parenthood I* illustrates, the behavior of the individual protestors and/or the specific groups against whom an injunction is sought clearly is determinative of the ultimate remedy. In that case, evidence regarding the defendants' actual protest activities at that clinic *and* the adverse effect those activities had on legitimate state interests justified the 15-foot exclusion zone provision as a restriction that burdened no less of the *defendants'* speech than was necessary. This evidence was necessary to affirm the judgment against Cochran and ORC.

Third, PPGG's conclusion that a separate trial "will not produce different injunctive relief" is apparently based on the mistaken notion that the state's interests in regulating anti-abortion protest activity are so strong that restrictions like the 15-foot exclusion zone imposed by the 1995 injunction can and should be applied to all anti-abortion protestors as a matter of course.

Clearly, "[t]he state has strong concerns in: (1) protecting the freedom of women to seek lawful services in connection with pregnancy, (2) the delivery of those services with appropriate privacy, (3) preserving public safety and order by ensuring the free flow of vehicular and pedestrian traffic, and (4) preserving property rights." *Id.* at 741. However, simply articulating these interests, as PPGG has done here, does not answer whether a particular restriction violates a particular individual's First Amendment rights. To answer that question, the court must engage in a fact-specific inquiry in order to ensure that the challenged restriction does not burden more speech than necessary to serve a significant government interest. The outcome of that inquiry certainly does depend on the specific behavior of the individual(s) against whom the restriction is imposed.[7]

[¶] PPGG argues that the actual notice provision in the 1995 injunction is analogous to the restriction approved by the United States Supreme Court in Hill v. Colorado, 530 U.S. 703 (2000). *Hill* involved a First Amendment challenge to a provision in a Colorado statute that regulates speech-related conduct within 100 feet of the entrance to any health care facility. The 1995 injunction is not analogous to the Colorado statute at issue in *Hill*. As noted above, injunctions are not effective against the world at large. "This is not just because the world at large is not fairly deemed

---

7. People ex rel. Gallo v. Acuna, 929 P.2d 596 (Cal. 1997), does not support PPGG's argument to the contrary. The *Acuna* court rejected various challenges to provisions in a *preliminary* injunction that was entered against individual members of an alleged street gang who were sued for violating the state's public nuisance statutes. That preliminary injunction, which precluded named individuals from engaging in specific activities in a designated neighborhood did not contain a provision extending its scope to any person with notice.

Moreover, the *Acuna* court's analysis is fundamentally inconsistent with PPGG's arguments in this case. For example, the court found the preliminary injunction at issue in that case was not overbroad within the meaning of the First Amendment because "[t]he only individuals subject to the trial court's interlocutory decree . . . are *named parties* to this action." *Id.* at 611. The court also found that the injunction did not infringe the defendants' constitutionally protected associational interests because the evidence of the gang members' activities established that the restrictions burdened no more speech than necessary to serve a significant governmental interest. Finally, the *Acuna* court found the preliminary injunction could properly have been entered against the gang as a group or against the 38 individual defendants who were members of that gang. As the court explained, "there was sufficient evidence . . . that the gang and its members . . . were responsible for the public nuisance, that each of the individual defendants either admitted gang membership or was identified as a gang member, and that each was observed by police officials in the . . . neighborhood" where the challenged activities had occurred. *Id.* at 618. . . .

likely to abuse constitutional rights; it is also because injunctions are fashioned and enforced without the safeguards that attend the passage and govern the enforcement of more general prohibitions." *Conrad,* 64 Cal. Rptr. 2d at 250. Injunctions "carry greater risks of censorship and discriminatory application than do general ordinances." *Madsen,* 512 U.S. at 764. Furthermore, an injunction is a "judicial remed[y] tailored to specific circumstances rather than 'a legislative choice regarding the promotion of particular societal interests.'" Planned Parenthood Shasta-Diablo, Inc. v. Williams, 898 P.2d 402, 407 (Cal. 1995), quoting *Madsen,* 512 U.S. at 764. In light of these fundamental distinctions between legislation and injunctions, PPGG's reliance on *Hill* is misplaced.

PPGG's final contention is that this court should enforce the actual notice provision because it effectuates one of the basic policies underlying injunctive relief—to prevent a multiplicity of judicial proceedings. The policy against multiplicity of judicial proceedings is intended to prevent conflicting or vexatious litigation. This policy is not effectuated by the actual notice provision which purports to bind a nonparty to a judgment which abridges the free exercise of speech in a public forum solely on the basis that the nonparty has notice of the judgment. Absent evidence that Foti and the Garibaldis act together with or on behalf of parties enjoined by the 1995 injunction, the controversy between these appellants and PPGG does not involve the same parties, subject matter, or facts which supported the judgment pursuant to which the 1995 injunction was entered.

For all of these reasons, we hold the actual notice provision does not bind Foti and the Garibaldis to the 1995 injunction. Actual notice of an injunction is a requirement but cannot be an independent ground upon which to apply an injunction to a nonparty. Therefore, the 1995 injunction applies to the defendants against whom it was entered (ORC and Cochran) and their agents, employees, representatives and all persons acting in concert or participation with them, or either of them who have actual notice of the judgment.

3. There Are Triable Issues Regarding Application of the "In Concert" Provision . . .

[This part of the opinion is unpublished.]

IV. DISPOSITION

The . . . summary judgment in favor of PPGG is reversed. . . .

We Concur: KLINE, P.J., and RUVOLO, J.

NOTES ON CONTEMPT PROCEEDINGS AGAINST THIRD PARTIES

1. Distinguishing two issues. In section 4.C, we considered whether third parties could be made parties to injunctive litigation and ordered to help provide a remedy. *Parenthood* raises a different question: Can an injunction bind persons who have not been made parties? Can plaintiff and the court skip the step of getting an injunction against Foti and the Garibaldis, and just cite them for contempt of the injunction issued against Cochran and ORC?

2. Rule 65(d)(2). Federal Rule 65(d)(2) and similar state provisions address the core of the problem. The Rule has been subdivided into two subparts, so all the older cases refer simply to Rule 65(d). The relevant subpart provides:

(2) *Persons Bound.* The order binds only the following who receive actual notice of it by personal service or otherwise:

(A) the parties;

(B) the parties' officers, agents, servants, employees, and attorneys; and

(C) other persons who are in active concert or participation with anyone described in Rule 65(d)(2)(A) or (B).

Fed R. Civ. P. 65(d)(2). The 1995 injunction in *Parenthood* put similar language into the injunction itself, apparently as a matter of California case law. Any person, including Roti and the Garibaldis, would be bound by the injunction and subject to contempt proceedings if they actively cooperated with Cochran or ORC in demonstrating at the San Mateo clinic. The court remanded the case for fact finding on that issue.

Rule 65(d)(2) originated in §19 of the Clayton Act, 38 Stat. 730, 738 (1914), and as with other provisions of that Act incorporated into Rule 65, the primary target was the antistrike injunction. Even more than in the abortion-protest cases, the strike cases involved large groups of people bitterly resisting federal courts; in the strike cases, the courts were backed up by federal troops when things got really rough. The courts felt the need to control everyone who might interfere with strike breakers, just as the trial court in *Parenthood* felt the need to control everyone who might interfere with the abortion clinic.

3. All persons with notice. Courts have frequently chafed at the restrictions of Rule 65(d)(2). Faced with difficult situations involving large groups of potentially disruptive people, they issue injunctions "against all persons with actual notice of this judgment." That is the language in *Parenthood*; there was a similar provision in the Alabama injunction in *Walker*. The Supreme Court unanimously reversed such a clause in Chase National Bank v. City of Norwalk, 291 U.S. 431, 436-438 (1934). The opinion by Justice Brandeis said that such a clause is "clearly erroneous" and "violates established principles of equity jurisdiction and procedure." But courts inclined to ignore Rule 65 have been just as willing to ignore *Chase*.

4. Prophylactic injunctions. The appellate court in *Parenthood* emphasized clause 2 of the 1995 injunction, which prohibits picketing or distributing literature on the public sidewalk within 15 feet of the clinic's property. There is nothing illegal about picketing on the public sidewalk. The public sidewalks are a public forum under free speech law; every citizen is entitled to use them to express opinions. The court had found, after a full trial and appeal, that Cochran and ORC have forfeited this right by misusing it to harass patients at the clinic. How do we know that Roti and the Garibaldis have forfeited this right?

5. Injunctions against illegal acts. The appellate court doesn't say much about the rest of the injunction. Clauses 1, 3, and 4 prohibit obstructing the movement of any person approaching the clinic. Is there any defense to an injunction against that? Can the court know whether there's a defense before Roti and the Garibaldis have a chance to present any defenses they may have? How do we know that Roti and the Garibaldis have a propensity to obstruct the movement of persons approaching the clinic?

6. A leading counterexample. A leading case going beyond the limits of Rule 65 is United States v. Hall, 472 F.2d 261 (5th Cir. 1972). At least three things enhance its authority: The opinion was written by John Minor Wisdom, a great judge and one of the heroes of the desegregation era; it has been favorably cited by the Supreme Court; and it helps judges justify orders that they feel the need to make.

a. The facts. *Hall* arose out of court-ordered desegregation of the public schools in Duval County, Florida. It is one of many cases in which desegregation plans were hampered by protestors, sometimes white and sometimes black. The trial judge issued a supplemental injunction directed to "[a]nyone having notice of this order," sharply restricting access to the campus of Ribault High School in Jacksonville. The persons at whom this order was directed were not made parties to the case and were not notified of the hearing at which the order was issued. But the court did direct that the order be personally served on seven named persons, including Eric Hall. Hall promptly violated the order and was convicted of criminal contempt. No one claimed that Hall was acting in concert with a party; it was the defendant school board that sought to have him enjoined. In affirming Hall's conviction, Judge Wisdom said some remarkable things.

b. Protecting the adjudication of rights between the parties. First Judge Wisdom had to distinguish *Chase National Bank*, introduced in note 3. The bank successfully sued the city for an injunction against destroying utility wires and poles that were subject to the bank's mortgage. The state was also seeking to destroy the wires and poles, and the state seems to have been the target of the all-persons-with-notice clause. The state also appears to have been in active concert with the city, but the all-persons-with-notice clause would have made it unnecessary to prove that.

Judge Wisdom said that the *Chase* injunction established the bank's rights against the city, and it was no interference with those rights if someone else destroyed the wires and poles. But the school desegregation injunction established plaintiffs' right to a desegregated education, and established the school board's duty to provide such an education, and Hall's protests were interfering with the school board's efforts to comply with the injunction against the school board. "In short, the activities of persons contributing to racial disorder at Ribault imperiled the court's fundamental power to make a binding adjudication between the parties properly before it." *Id.* at 265.

The bank's adjudicated right in *Chase National Bank* was good only against its named defendant. Do the school desegregation plaintiffs have a right good against the whole world? Is there more to the point about interfering with performance of the school board's adjudicated duties? In *Parenthood*, were Roti and the Garibaldis interfering with performance of Cochran's and ORC's obligation not to disrupt the clinic?

c. Rule 65(d)(2). Judge Wisdom said that the purpose of Rule 65(d)(2) was not to limit judicial authority, but to codify the historical practice. The historical practice included those courts that had issued injunctions against all persons having notice of the injunction, so despite its language, Rule 65(d)(2) does not prohibit such injunctions. This account is simply impossible to reconcile with the origins of Rule 65(d)(2) in congressional efforts to control what it viewed as judicial abuses in the antistrike injunctions.

d. The lack of notice and hearing. Judge Wisdom said it was permissible to issue the injunction against protesting at Ribault High without notice or hearing for its targets, because Eric Hall had violated the injunction within ten days of its issuance. It could thus be understood as a temporary restraining order without notice, which used to be limited to ten days in duration (it is now 14 days). This might have been an afterthought; there is no clear indication that the trial judge considered this order a TRO, or that any further steps were taken to make Hall a party and give him his day in court, or that anyone thought that something further would have to be done to keep the injunction in effect for more than ten days. Less ambiguously, there is no mention of any effort to notify Hall before the TRO issued, or to explain why he could not be notified; considered as a TRO, the order appears to be invalid under Carroll v. President and Commissioners of Princess Anne, reprinted in section 5.B.2. *Carroll* had been decided nearly four years before the trial court acted in *Hall*, and *Hall* was a free-speech case: Hall was engaged in political protest at a government facility. The parties found Hall to serve him with the injunction; why couldn't they find him to give notice of the motion?

The TRO theory doesn't help much, but at most it could help for 10 days. The cleanest way to separate the two questions is to ask what would have happened if Hall had violated the injunction on the 11th day. Can the court issue an order addressed to the entire population and enforce it with criminal contempt?

e. *Hall* and *Parenthood*. The court in *Parenthood* declined to discuss *Hall*, apparently because plaintiff had simply put it in a string cite without discussing it. The court said only that none of the cases in the string cite "affirmed a provision which extended the scope of a permanent injunction to any person with notice of it." 132 Cal. Rptr. 2d at 52 n.5. That is true in a sense, because *Hall* treated the order as a TRO. For purposes of the policy embodied in Rule 65(d)(2), should the difference between a TRO and a permanent injunction matter?

NOTES ON THE ARRAY OF THEORIES FOR BINDING THIRD PARTIES

1. Parties, officers, agents, servants, employees, and attorneys. Respondeat superior is enough to tell you that the party is in contempt if his agents violate the injunction. But Rule 65(d)(2) allows the courts to go further. The agents themselves are in contempt, even though they did not have a chance to litigate. The leading case involves a particularly troubling application. In Ex parte Lennon, 166 U.S. 548 (1897), a nonunion railroad got an injunction ordering union railroads to handle its cars. Lennon was a union engineer. He refused to haul a nonunion car and was prosecuted for criminal contempt of the injunction against his employer. Should agents be bound by injunctions against their employers? Or should the court coerce the defendant, and let her worry about how to control her employees?

Lennon shows that contempt can run against rank-and-file employees. But it cannot run against randomly selected employees; the employee charged with contempt must have had some responsibility for compliance with the injunction. Some of the cases are collected in United States v. Voss, 82 F.3d 1521-1526 (10th Cir. 1996).

The requirement of job responsibility is clearest when the injunction ordered a corporation to do something, and nobody did it. Consider Central States Pension Funds v. Transcon Lines, 1995 WL 472705 (N.D. Ill. 1995). In a suit over past-due contributions to a pension fund, a consent decree ordered Transcon to make specific payments on specific dates. After those dates passed with no payments, Transcon filed for bankruptcy. The pension funds then sought to recover $360,000 from David Hellhake, a corporate vice president, in compensatory contempt. This makes sense if Hellhake was responsible for making the payments, or even if he was in position to instruct the person who was responsible for making the payments. It would make no sense at all if he were a truck driver. Even if he were independently wealthy (so the judgment would be collectible), a truck driver would have no ability, and thus no obligation, to make large payments of corporate funds. *Transcon* went off on other issues, but the court did not seem to doubt that Hellhake could be held in contempt if he had notice of the injunction.

2. Persons in active concert. An injunction binds all "persons in active concert or participation with" any of the parties described in note 1. This is a check on subterfuge; defendant cannot get his friends and relatives to violate the injunction for him. Persons in active concert did not get a chance to litigate either, but at least they have deliberately allied themselves with someone who did. Coconspirator doctrine suggests a rationale for binding people in active concert with a party. Most persons in active concert will also be agents, but that is not required.

An example that highlights the line is Additive Controls & Measurement Systems, Inc. v. Flowdata, Inc., 154 F.3d 1345 (Fed. Cir. 1998). The court enjoined Additive Controls (Adcon) from infringing Flowdata's patent. Galen Cotton, the president and controlling shareholder of Adcon, started a new company, Truflo, and produced a similar infringing product. They hired an engineer, Harshman, to do some of the work. The court held that Cotton and Truflo were in contempt, because Cotton was "legally identified" with Adcon, and because Truflo was his creation and merely a continuation of Adcon. But Harshman was not in contempt until he learned enough about the injunction to know that he would be violating it if he continued in active concert with Cotton and Truflo. Another example of a new corporate entity formed for the purpose of evading an injunction, and thus bound because in active concert with the defendant, is Marshak v. Treadwell, 595 F.3d 478 (3d Cir. 2009).

There are two well-known intellectual-property cases involving brothers as defendants. In the first, John Staff had employed his brother Joseph to sell the infringing goods that gave rise to the original suit. The court enjoined John and "his agents, employees, associates and confederates" from infringing or "aiding or abetting or in any way contributing to the infringement." Alemite Manufacturing Corp. v. Staff, 42 F.2d 832, 832 (2d Cir. 1930). Joseph then left John's employ and started his own business, manufacturing the same infringing product.

Joseph clearly would have been in contempt had he continued to infringe as John's employee, or if his new business were conducted "in active concert" with John. The brothers could not avoid the injunction merely by creating a new entity or rearranging their hierarchy. But at Joseph's contempt hearing, the court found that John had nothing to do with Joseph's business. On those facts, Learned Hand held that there was no more power to punish Joseph "than a third party who had never heard of the suit." Id. at 833. G.&C. Merriam Co. v. Webster Dictionary Co., 639 F.2d 29 (1st Cir. 1980), is astonishingly similar to Alemite and reaches the same result.

Just as persons in active concert with parties can be liable for violating an injunction, so too the party is in contempt if it assists or facilitates the non-party's violation. "[A] party may be held in contempt for giving a non-party the means to violate an injunction." Institute of Cetacean Research v. Sea Shepherd Conservation Society, 774 F.3d 935, 950 (9th Cir. 2014). In Sea Shepherd, the courts had enjoined an antiwhaling organization and its leaders from interfering with a Japanese institute that captured and killed whales. After the court issued the injunction, the organization adopted a "separation strategy" to transfer substantial assets to allied foreign organizations, and some of the organization's leaders worked with the foreign allies to try to stop the institute's whale hunt. The foreign organizations repeatedly engaged in activities that would have violated the injunction if performed by the defendants. The court held that a party subject to an injunction who gives a non-party the means to violate the court's order "need not affirmatively desire to cause a violation of the injunction; it is enough that the party know a violation is highly likely to occur." Id.

3. Successors in interest. Suppose that in Alemite, John Staff sold his infringing business to a stranger. Does the stranger take the business subject to the injunction? Is he personally bound? There is no mention of successors or assigns in Rule 65.

The issue has arisen repeatedly under the National Labor Relations Act, and the Supreme Court has been troubled by it. In Regal Knitwear Co. v. National Labor Relations Board, 324 U.S. 9, 14 (1945), the Court suggested that successors were bound only if they were in active concert with the original employer, as when the successor was "merely a disguised continuance of the old employer." But in Golden State Bottling Co. v. NLRB, 414 U.S. 168 (1973), the Court held that a bona fide purchaser who bought with knowledge that a Labor Act violation remained unremedied was bound by the order to remedy it. There was some hint that this was a special rule for labor cases; there was also a *cf.* citation to *Hall.* And there was a broader statement that Rule 65(d) was intended to bind defendants and "those identified with them in interest, in 'privity' with them, represented by them or subject to their control." *Id.* at 179, quoting *Regal Knitware,* 324 U.S. at 14. Successors were in privity, and "[p]ersons acquiring an interest in property that is a subject of litigation are bound by, or entitled to the benefit of, a subsequent judgment, despite a lack of knowledge." 414 U.S. at 179. The reference to "lack of knowledge" was plainly dictum. But doesn't the symmetry of acquiring both the burdens and benefits of past judgments make sense? Recall that the plaintiff in *Parenthood* was a successor to the original plaintiff.

The Federal Circuit applied *Golden State* in a patent case and explored the scope of *Golden State*'s "legally identified" category for binding others to injunctions in Asetek Danamark A/S v. CMI USA, Inc., 842 F.3d 1350, 1364-1369 (Fed. Cir. 2016). The court explained that the inquiry is fact specific and requires "particular caution" to protect the principle that each person should have "his own day in court." *Id.* at 1364. It remanded the case to the district court for additional detailed fact-finding about the relationship of the original party and its affiliate, "both in their businesses and in this litigation." *Id.* at 1367. The Eleventh Circuit has held in an unfair competition case that successors are bound only if they knew about the injunction when they acquired the enjoined company or its assets. ADT LLC v. Northstar Alarm Services, LLC, 853 F.3d 1348, 1355 (11th Cir. 2017).

4. Successors in public office. Federal Rule of Civil Procedure 25(d) provides that when a litigant who is a public officer leaves office, his successor is automatically substituted as a party. It follows under Rule 65(d)(2) that the successor is automatically bound by injunctions issued against his predecessor, and the cases so hold. A rare example where this had to be litigated is Lucy v. Adams, 224 F. Supp. 79 (N.D. Ala. 1963), *aff'd mem.,* 328 F.2d 892 (5th Cir. 1964), involving an injunction ordering the registrar of the University of Alabama to admit black applicants.

This is not quite the same as saying the successor can be ordered to discontinue illegal practices of the predecessor that have not yet been enjoined. That depends on whether there is a likelihood that the successor will continue the illegal practices. In Spomer v. Littleton, 414 U.S. 514 (1974), plaintiffs alleged "willful and malicious racial discrimination" by a prosecutor. When a new prosecutor was elected and substituted as a defendant, the Court found no allegation that discrimination was "the policy of the office" or "that Spomer intends to continue the asserted practices of" his predecessor. *Id.* at 521. The Court ordered the complaint dismissed unless on remand plaintiffs could show a threat of continuing discrimination. The distinction is between policies of the office and personal misconduct of the former incumbent; examples are collected in Williams v. Wilkinson, 132 F. Supp. 2d 601, 609 (S.D. Ohio 2001).

5. In rem injunctions. An in rem injunction is an injunction ordering the whole world not to interfere with some property that is in the custody of the court or under supervision by the court. Judge Wisdom relied heavily on these in rem injunctions in *Hall.*

a. Orders consolidating litigation. The most common in rem injunction is the automatic stay triggered by the filing of every bankruptcy petition. All the world is enjoined from pursuing claims against the debtor anywhere but in the bankruptcy court. The automatic stay is explicitly authorized by statute, 11 U.S.C. §362, and that overrides Rule 65(d)(2). But §362 was not enacted until 1978; bankruptcy courts issued similar stays for decades without statutory authorization. And similar injunctions are issued in analogous nonstatutory contexts. When receivers are appointed to manage disputed assets, all the world is enjoined from interfering with the receivership. An example is United States v. Acorn Technology Fund LP, 429 F.3d 438 (3d Cir. 2005). A party that wants to file or continue a lawsuit elsewhere must file a motion in the receivership court to lift the stay. Huntington National Bank v. Saint Catharine College, Inc., 2017 WL 6347971, *6-8 (W.D. Ky. Dec. 12, 2017). The automatic stay and its analogs are relatively uncontroversial, perhaps because they are viewed as a means of consolidating litigation in a single court that will continue to honor the substantive rights of the parties.

b. Enjoining public nuisances. Another form of in rem injunction is much more controversial and much less necessary. Where a building has been used for illegal purposes—as a brothel, a pornographic movie theater, a gambling hall, a drug den, or most commonly, an illegal bar—courts have enjoined any person with notice from using the building for those purposes. Professor Rendleman, in the most substantial academic treatment of the whole third-party issue, calls the in rem injunction "the prohibition movement's gift to equity." Doug Rendleman, *Beyond Contempt: Obligors to Injunctions*, 53 Tex. L. Rev. 873, 911 (1975).

The talk about any person with notice in these injunctions was probably unnecessary; the targets were successors. But in rem injunctions were used to bind successors who were not in active concert with the original defendant and who were not shown to have had notice of the injunction when they bought the property. This was often before the adoption of Rule 65(d)(2) or its equivalent in the relevant state. And some states rejected the concept. A Texas statute authorizing such injunctions was struck down as a prior restraint in Vance v. Universal Amusement Co., 445 U.S. 308 (1980). But *Vance* did not turn on the third-party issue and does not affect in rem injunctions in nonspeech contexts.

6. Political representation. An injunction against a state binds its citizens, at least with respect to "public rights." An example is the Washington fishing litigation, in which the Supreme Court also relied on other theories in the alternative.

In the 1850s, the United States entered into treaties guaranteeing fishing rights to Indian tribes in the Pacific Northwest. The main subject of the treaties was salmon and similar fish that migrate in predictable runs up coastal rivers. In a series of cases culminating in 1979, the Supreme Court interpreted the treaties as promising the Indians approximately half the catch unless their needs were fully satisfied by a smaller share.

To enforce that right, the trial court had to control all fishing in the watersheds. There were 800 Indian commercial fishers, 6,600 non-Indian commercial fishers, and 280,000 licensed sport fishers; there was also widespread defiance of the court's orders. The court's solution was to monitor the catch from each run and to close fishing areas to non-Indians whenever non-Indians collectively were about to exceed their share of a run. The court ordered the state of Washington to set up a telephone hotline that would tell callers what waters were open. Then it issued an injunction against all non-Indians with Washington fishing licenses, ordering them not to fish without first checking the hotline and obeying its directions. This part of the injunction went far beyond Rule 65(d)(2), and commercial fishing associations challenged it on that ground. The Supreme Court rejected the argument in a long footnote. It never actually mentioned Rule 65(d)(2):

> In our view, the commercial fishing associations and their members are probably subject to injunction under either the rule that nonparties who interfere with the

implementation of court orders establishing public rights may be enjoined, e.g., *Hall*, cited approvingly in *Golden State*, 414 U.S. at 180, or the rule that a court possessed of the res in a proceeding in rem, such as one to apportion a fishery, may enjoin those who would interfere with that custody. But in any case, these individuals and groups are citizens of the State of Washington, which was a party to the relevant proceedings, and "they, in their public rights as citizens of the State, were represented by the State in those proceedings, and, like it, were bound by the judgment." Tacoma v. Taxpayers, 357 U.S. 320, 340-341 (1958). Moreover, a court clearly may order them to obey that judgment. See *Golden State* at 179-180.

Washington v. Washington State Commercial Passenger Fishing Vessel Association, 443 U.S. 658, 693 n.32, *modified on other grounds*, 444 U.S. 816 (1979).

Does the array of theories in the Washington fishing case leave much of Rule 65(d)(2)? Should citizens be bound by the injunction against the state if the state had not vigorously opposed the injunction? Does it follow that all the citizens of a school district are bound by the school district's participation in school desegregation litigation? That would be another way to write *Hall*. Should political representation work for private associations too? What about citizens of Oregon and British Columbia who fish in Washington waters? Aliens residing in Washington?

What about the citation to *Hall*? Has the Supreme Court decided that *Hall* is good law? That it is "probably" good law?

7. Political representation on steroids? Consider Nevada v. United States Department of Labor, 2018 WL 1383236 (E.D. Tex. March 19, 2018). During the Obama Administration, the Department of Labor issued regulations expanding the class of employees protected by the maximum-hour and overtime-pay provisions of the Fair Labor Standards Act. A federal judge in Texas held the regulations invalid and issued an injunction ordering defendants not to enforce them. The opinion said that the injunction was nationwide; the injunction itself did not explicitly say that, but nothing in the injunction limited its geographic scope. Here is the injunction:

> Therefore, the Department's Final Rule described at 81 Fed. Reg. 32,391 is enjoined. Specifically, Defendants are enjoined from implementing and enforcing the following regulations as amended by 81 Fed. Reg. 32,391; [listing ten specific sections of 29 C.F.R.] pending further order of this Court.

We can see what the judge thought he was doing in the first sentence, but the sentence is actually incoherent. Injunctions order parties to act or refrain from acting; they cannot order the regulation to do anything, and the sentence does not specify what the regulation is supposed to do. The second sentence is the operative order. It is addressed to "defendants," and the only defendants were the Department of Labor and some of its subdivisions and officials. The government appealed, but the Trump Administration later suspended that appeal while it considered repealing the regulation.

Meanwhile, in New Jersey, an employee sued Chipotle Mexican Grill for overtime pay under the regulation. Chipotle responded by filing a contempt citation against the employee and her attorneys in Texas. The trial judge held them in civil contempt, ordered them to dismiss their New Jersey lawsuit, and awarded Chipotle its attorneys' fees. The court said the employee was bound by the injunction because the government had represented her interests, and the lawyers were bound because they were her attorneys. The court did not discuss the fact that the government had stopped representing the employee's interests when it suspended the appeal.

Neither the employee, nor so far as appears, the lawyers, had minimum contacts with Texas. The district court's injunction had no precedential effect, because it was not from an appellate court; the New Jersey court was free to decide the validity of the regulations for itself. The Texas court's only source of authority is its judgment, the injunction against the Labor Department defendants. All the employee and her attorneys had done was to present to a federal court her claim that she was not bound by the injunction and that the regulations were valid and still in effect until rescinded. But that was an attempt to "enforce" the regulations, and so a violation of the injunction — *if* the employee were bound by it. Good faith was not a defense to civil contempt, which is true. The court has stayed enforcement of the contempt order pending an appeal; the appeal is No. 18-40246 in the Fifth Circuit.

8. Defendant class actions. Another possible solution in the Washington fishing case would be for plaintiffs to sue some non-Indian fishers as representatives of a class of all non-Indian fishers, and for the court to enjoin the class. Is that any better? If you were a defendant, would you want the plaintiffs to pick your representative? Defendant class actions work fairly well when the class is tightly knit and there is an entity to organize the defense. Examples are suits against union members as a class, or stockholders as a class, or local officials as a class, where the union, the corporation, or the state can organize the defense.

Suits against a more amorphous defendant class are much more troublesome. Their most common use is against patent infringers to adjudicate the validity of the patent. That issue is absolutely identical with respect to every alleged infringer, and the named defendant cannot possibly defend himself without defending all the others as well. The case is typically broken into separate actions to decide whether each class member's product infringes the patent and to assess damages. The cases and problems are sympathetically reviewed in Note, *Defendant Class Actions*, 91 Harv. L. Rev. 630 (1978).

9. Supplemental injunctions. The tried and true solution is to join additional violators as additional defendants and enjoin them after proper notice and hearing. Plainly Planned Parenthood could sue Roti and the Garibaldis and litigate the need for an injunction against them. If dozens of new demonstrators suddenly show up, they are likely to be in active concert with each other, although that has to be proved.

What if they are not in active concert? Is it practical to enforce the fishing treaties by joining non-Indian fishers as defendants, one by one as they are caught fishing in closed areas? Finding them in closed areas would establish a ripe controversy and justify an injunction; if they were caught again they would be in contempt. Is that too cumbersome to be effective? Does it achieve any real benefits? Every non-Indian fisher would get one or more free violations, but would he get any more procedural protection? The meaning of the treaties was settled by precedent; it is hard to think of any individual defenses they might present.

10. Compare damage claims. The need to bind third parties can also arise in damage actions, when plaintiff fears that the defendants actually named may not be able to pay the judgment. In Nelson v. Adams USA, 529 U.S. 460 (2000), defendant got a large award of attorneys' fees against the corporate plaintiff. Defendant then moved to amend its pleading to seek fees against the individual who owned all the shares of the corporate plaintiff, and simultaneously to amend the judgment to make the fee award binding on the individual owner. The Supreme Court unanimously reversed, citing the individual defendant's due process right to be heard on whether the judgment should bind him. There is a substantially identical holding in Zenith Radio v. Hazeltine Research, 395 U.S. 100, 108-112 (1969). *Zenith* invalidated both a damage judgment and an injunction against a corporate parent who had not been named in the pleadings; the case is curiously not cited in *Nelson*.

The Court compared the proceedings in *Nelson* to those in *Alice in Wonderland*. Is it any less *Alice in Wonderland* when additional defendants are added to an injunction without notice or hearing?

NOTES ON THE NOTICE REQUIREMENT

1. The basic requirement. No one can be in contempt of an injunction she hasn't been told about. Cases are collected in United States v. Voss, 82 F.3d 1521, 1525 (10th Cir. 1996). Rule 5 and Rule 65(a)(1) require actual notice of the court's order to parties, and Rule 65(d)(2) requires actual notice to parties and anyone else subject to the injunction. And the Due Process Clause requires at least constructive notice—notice sufficient to cause a reasonable person to inquire further—to anyone who is to be bound. Central States Pension Funds v. Transcon Lines, 1995 WL 472705 (N.D. Ill. 1995). The due process holding was required because a drafting glitch in the old Rule 65(d) resulted in the notice requirement of the rule not applying to officers, agents, servants, employees, or attorneys.

2. How much notice? Most cases are about whether defendant had notice, not whether notice is an element of contempt. Personal service is not required; "it is a matter of no consequence how the . . . injunction is brought to the knowledge or notice of the defendant." State v. Mernar, 786 A.2d 141, 142 (N.J. Super. Ct. App. Div. 2001). But in *Mernar*, the court suggested that it might be a defense that defendant was too drunk to understand the order when he received it.

One who knows an order has been entered is responsible for finding out what it said, and a client may be in contempt if her counsel knew about an order and failed to inform her. Perfect Fit Industries, Inc. v. Acme Quilting Co., 646 F.2d 800 (2d Cir. 1981). In King v. Allied Vision, Ltd., 65 F.3d 1051, 1058 (2d Cir. 1995), the court said it was enough that notice had been published in the *New York Law Journal*. This constructive notice can be justified, if at all, only on the ground that defendant and its counsel knew they were in a lawsuit and had a duty to monitor the proceedings for the orders that would be issued sooner or later. It might have also mattered that defendant was a persistent contemnor; the court might not have believed its claim that it had not known about the injunction.

3. Notice to large numbers of people. Notice was a recurring problem in the Washington fishing litigation. There were hundreds of prosecutions for criminal contempt, and in every one, the government had to prove beyond a reasonable doubt that defendant had timely notice of the injunction. Some defendants were personally served; some were sent copies of the injunction by certified mail; some admitted to having heard about it.

The government argued that individual fishers weren't entitled to notice, because they were in privity with the state of Washington. The court of appeals rejected that argument on due process grounds. United States v. Baker, 641 F.2d 1311 (9th Cir. 1981). It also refused to take judicial notice that there had been such widespread publicity that everyone must have heard about it, and it rejected the argument that commercial fishers had a duty of inquiry because their industry was so heavily regulated. Compare In re Jersey City Education Association, 278 A.2d 206 (N.J. Super. Ct. App. Div. 1971), in which the court inferred that all members of a teachers' union knew of an antistrike injunction. In that case, plaintiff put in detailed evidence of massive local news coverage.

It has been held sufficient for sheriffs to read injunctions to demonstrators over bullhorns. United States v. Gedraitis, 690 F.2d 351 (3d Cir. 1982). In a similar case involving demonstrators at the Seabrook nuclear plant in New Hampshire, some defendants argued that they had been distracted during the announcement and didn't know what had been said. But the court concluded that a posted sign, evidence of discussions of the injunction among the demonstrators, two bullhorn announcements, and a chorus of "no" to the second bullhorn announcement, were sufficient evidence to support a conviction of everyone there.

4. Notifying the other side. In the bullhorn cases, defendants learn about the injunction from the other side. In *Mernar* in note 2, plaintiff handed the injunction to defendant; in Ex parte Jackman, 663 S.W.2d 520 (Tex. Ct. App. 1983), plaintiff's attorney orally explained the contents of the injunction to defendant. Should it matter if defendant is represented by counsel and plaintiff communicates directly with defendant? It is unethical for an attorney to communicate directly with an adversary party who is represented by counsel. ABA Model Rule of Professional Conduct 4.2. Should defendant have a defense to contempt if plaintiff's attorney violated that rule when he gave notice of the injunction? Shouldn't there be an implied exception to the ethical rule if defendant is about to inflict irreparable harm and his attorney can't be found?

5. The credibility of notice. Consider this war story. In 1972, Laycock was a poll watcher in a working-class precinct in Chicago. Charges of vote fraud were rampant. During the morning, volunteers delivered photocopies of a TRO to nearly 5,000 precincts in Cook County. In his precinct, one of the election judges looked at the TRO and said: "This isn't from a court. Things from courts come with seals." She ignored the TRO for the rest of the day.

Was she in contempt? Does that depend on whether the trier of fact believes she was in good faith in rejecting the TRO's authenticity? If she gets off, is it because she didn't have notice or because her violation wasn't willful? If the latter, she's still liable in compensatory contempt; recall that willfulness is required only for criminal contempt.

5.   The Maxim That Equity Acts in Personam

The "maxims of equity" were pithy sayings framed at grand levels of generality, frequently quoted and generally not much help in deciding real cases. One of these maxims that deserves examination is that "equity acts in personam."

1. A maxim with five meanings. What is distinctive about contempt is the attempt to coerce the plaintiff into personally obeying the court's order. This is in sharp contrast to the traditional methods of enforcing money judgments, which we consider in section 9.B. The law courts traditionally relied on the sheriff to collect judgments; they did not expect defendants to cooperate. This difference is commonly described in the maxim that equity acts in personam; by contrast, the law is said to act in rem. This statement may be more misleading than helpful; certainly it requires substantial clarification.

There are at least five different uses of the distinction between in rem and in personam. The maxim that equity acts in personam is invoked in most of these senses, and courts and commentators often fail to distinguish them.

2. Plaintiff's substantive right. The distinction may refer to the theory of the plaintiff's substantive right. She may have a personal claim against the defendant, based on defendant's own conduct — the defendant's tort, or breach of contract, or breach of fiduciary duty. Or she may have a property right, good against anyone in the world, without regard to the individual conduct of most of the world's population. The common law has always created both in personam and in rem rights. Equity for a long time claimed to create only in personam rights.

Equity used the distinction in this sense to explain the law of trusts. The trustee owned the assets; he had a property right good against the world. The beneficiary was said to have only a personal right good against the trustee. This personal right was eventually surrounded by so many remedies that it came to be nearly as good as a property right. But the fiction is sometimes useful, so it has not been abandoned.

3. Jurisdiction. A second usage refers to the basis of a court's territorial jurisdiction. A suit is in personam if jurisdiction is based on authority over the defendant's person, and in rem if jurisdiction is based on authority over a particular piece of property. This is the sense in which in rem and in personam is encountered in the first-year civil procedure course. In rem jurisdiction is of limited significance after Shaffer v. Heitner, 433 U.S. 186 (1977). *Shaffer* held that all claims of territorial jurisdiction must be based on authority over persons, and cannot be based solely on authority over their property.

Before *Shaffer* the common law courts asserted jurisdiction both in rem and in personam. Equity claimed to act only in personam. Acting in personam is very helpful when a court has jurisdiction over a defendant and wants to affect property or conduct abroad. But the notion that equity acted *only* in personam broke down. Thus, the court where the property is located has jurisdiction to foreclose mortgages, even though mortgage foreclosure is equitable. *Shaffer* changed only the language and not the results of these cases. See 433 U.S. at 207-208.

4. Defendant's liability. A third usage refers to the nature of the liability to be imposed by a lawsuit. A suit is in personam if plaintiff seeks a judgment against defendant personally. Such a judgment imposes a personal liability or duty on defendant. A personal liability may be collected out of any of defendant's property; a personal duty may be enforced through contempt proceedings. A suit is in rem if plaintiff seeks to recover or directly affect particular property and no other, and not to impose a personal liability or duty on defendant. Actions at law may be either in rem or in personam in this sense. Suits in equity were traditionally said to be only in personam, but again this was abandoned when it became too inconvenient. Thus, Judge Wisdom in *Hall* relied on in rem injunctions, a phrase that would be an oxymoron if we took seriously the notion that equity acts only in personam. What is questionable about in rem injunctions is not that they are in rem, but that they are sometimes directed at people who have not been given their day in court.

5. The judgment. A fourth usage of in rem and in personam refers to the form of the court's final order. Judgments at law are written as declarations of rights, and this is called in rem. Decrees in equity were historically written as direct orders to defendant, and this is called in personam. Thus, the law court would say, "Ordered, adjudged, and decreed that plaintiff have judgment for $10," or "that plaintiff shall have title to Blackacre and possession thereof." The equity court would say to defendant, "You pay plaintiff $10," or "You convey and deliver Blackacre to plaintiff."

Equity used the in personam idea in this sense to explain how it could enjoin suits in other courts without being disrespectful. The equity decree never addressed the law court. It never said, "The judgment at law is void." Instead, it said to defendant, "You stop enforcing your judgment at law."

6. The means of enforcement. The final usage is the one we started with, referring to the traditional means of enforcing judgments and decrees. Common law judgments were enforced by sheriffs and similar officials. They would seize defendant's property and sell it to pay the judgment, or forcibly evict defendant from Blackacre. Equity decrees were traditionally enforced through the contempt power. This difference in means of enforcement is closely related to the difference in the form of judgments; a personal command in the judgment is a prerequisite to personal coercion as a means of enforcement.

Neither law nor equity used either method of enforcement exclusively. See Walter Wheeler Cook, *The Powers of Courts of Equity*, 15 Colum. L. Rev. 106 (1915). When a defendant refused to obey decrees and stubbornly resisted coercion, equity sent officials called sequestrators to "sequester" his property, sell it, and pay the proceeds to plaintiff. Similarly, common law plaintiffs could often have defendants arrested and imprisoned, a rather obvious effort to coerce payment. Common law imprisonment for debt is now much restricted and little used, but not quite eliminated. And as mentioned in note 13 following *Anyanwu*, under Federal Rule 70 and its state equivalents, the court can appoint agents to do things in defendant's name, thus awarding specific equitable relief without the need to coerce defendant.

7. Surviving uses of the maxim. The conceptualisms of in rem and in personam are largely in the past. The merger of law and equity makes much of the traditional distinction irrelevant. Today, the notion pops up only occasionally, often to explain results that could be better explained some other way. But it is still one way to highlight a basic choice about the means of enforcing judgments. It remains true that we coerce defendants to obey injunctions, but we usually do not coerce them to pay money judgments. Even so, there is much more use of coercion in the collection of money judgments than the traditional maxim would lead you to expect. Section 9.B explores the means of collecting money judgments and asks why we don't use the contempt power more generally.

6. *Drafting Decrees*

One key to effective enforcement is a well-drafted judgment. A simple damage judgment on a general verdict for a single plaintiff is relatively easy to draft, although a careless lawyer can mess it up. Other judgments are more complex. Injunctions, declaratory judgments, and class action judgments always require very careful drafting. The judge generally asks the parties to draft a decree for her approval. If necessary, a good judge will throw out both parties' drafts and do her own, but she prefers not to. A successful plaintiff's lawyer can usually write the decree if he does it competently and doesn't overreach. That is an important tactical opportunity; you shouldn't forfeit it with sloppy drafting.

NOTES ON THE REQUIREMENT THAT INJUNCTIONS BE SPECIFIC

1. Rule 65(d)(1). In this section you will get to draft an injunction. There are several things to keep in mind as you draft. Perhaps most important is Federal Rule 65(d)(1), and corresponding state rules:

> **(1) Contents.** Every order granting an injunction and every restraining order must:
>   (A) state the reasons why it issued;
>   (B) state its terms specifically; and
>   (C) describe in reasonable detail—and not by referring to the complaint or other document—the act or acts restrained or required.

In addition, there is the rule that the injunction should not forbid wrongful acts unlike those already committed or threatened, considered in section 4.A.1.

2. Tactical considerations. There are tactical considerations as well as formal rules. Plaintiff wants an injunction to leave no loopholes for future evasion. He wants it sufficiently precise that contempt sanctions are a meaningful possibility. The problem is highlighted by the Boston School Committee's announcement that it would obey "nothing but direct orders." Morgan v. McDonough, 540 F.2d 527, 534 (1st Cir. 1976). Sometimes defendants will observe the spirit of the decree, but you can't count on that.

3. Two opportunities for defendants. Defendants get two chances to attack the specificity of an injunction. They can appeal the order entering the injunction on the ground that it violates Rule 65(d)(1). Or they can defend against the contempt citation on the ground that the injunction failed to specify what they were supposed to do or refrain from doing. In criminal contempt, the collateral bar rule prevents defendants from raising errors in the injunction at the contempt stage. See Walker v. City of Birmingham, reprinted in section 9.A.3. But they can still raise specificity claims, on the ground that the violation could not have been willful if defendant could not understand the injunction. Cases are collected in Harris v. City of Philadelphia, 47 F.3d 1342, 1349 (3d Cir. 1995), a case enforcing a jail-reform consent decree.

Defendants can raise specificity issues on direct appeal following a default judgment. City of New York v. Mickalis Pawn Shop LLC, 645 F.3d 114, 143 (2d Cir. 2011), citing cases from the Second and Seventh Circuits. The opinion is also a nice review of how not to draft an injunction. "An injunction is overbroad when it seeks to restrain the defendants from engaging in legal conduct, or from engaging in illegal conduct that was not fairly the subject of litigation." *Id.* at 145. In addition to violating these restrictions, the injunction ordered defendants to "adopt those practices that in the opinion of the Special Master serve to prevent" various harms the injunction sought to prevent, and it enjoined "failure to cooperate with the Special Master." *Id.* The court held that these delegations of authority violated Rule 65(d). The City defended the injunction principally on the ground that twenty other defendants had agreed to substantially identical injunctions in settlements.

4. Some obvious examples. Here are two injunctions that fail any test of specificity.

a. No order. A clear case of an unintelligible decree is International Longshoreman's Assn. v. Philadelphia Marine Trade Assn., 389 U.S. 64 (1967), refusing to enforce an order "to comply with and to abide by" a certain arbitration award. The award had resolved a particular dispute, but contained no command for the future. The employer and union disagreed over the precedential value of the award.

b. A garbled and overbroad order. In Chicago Board of Education v. Substance, Inc., 354 F.3d 624, 632 (7th Cir. 2003), where a disgruntled teacher was publishing the school board's standardized tests, defendants were enjoined from "copying distribution of copies, making derivative copies, displaying copies an performing copies of the Board's examinations, including but not limited to the CASE examinations, whenever created by the Board." Judge Posner commented that "[t]his is an *appallingly* bad injunction." The missing comma or conjunction in the first clause, and the typo before "performing," turned the injunction into gibberish. The ban on display and performance had no basis in what the parties had litigated. The protection of all exams, whether or not copyrighted, and whether or not secure, from the founding of the school district to the end of time, was overbroad. The court directed that the injunction be modified to enjoin the defendants "just from copying or publishing or otherwise distributing copies of secure Chicago public school tests, in whole or substantial part, in which the school board has valid and subsisting copyright, without the board's authorization." "No evidentiary basis has been laid for a broader injunction."

5. Some less obvious examples. Here are some more plausible injunctions that defendant successfully claimed were ambiguous or not specific.

a. "A trade name which includes the word FALCON." Vertex Distributing owned a trademark on the phrase "Falcon Foam," and it sued Falcon Foam Plastics for infringing that mark. The case settled and the court entered a consent decree ordering Falcon Foam not to use its corporate name "or any colorable imitation" for promotional purposes. The dispute at the contempt hearing turned on the following exception in the original decree:

> [D]efendants may do business using a trade name which includes the word FALCON providing, however, that when defendants use a trade name incorporating FALCON therein, defendants shall include a falcon bird perched on the "F" of FALCON wherever possible and practical and, in particular, on signs, delivery vehicle markings, letterheads, packaging, product markings, advertising materials, business cards, and Telephone Directory Yellow pages listings.

Defendants thereafter used the name Falcon. They generally included the bird perched on the F. They included the bird logo in large Yellow Pages ads, but omitted it from small Yellow Pages ads. At the contempt hearing, defendants argued that it was not "possible and practical" to include the bird logo in small ads. Plaintiff disagreed. Plaintiff also argued that defendants could not use the name Falcon alone, but only as part of a longer trade name that "includes" the word Falcon.

The court found no contempt. It held that the "possible and practical" language was ambiguous, and that defendants' interpretation was not unreasonable. It issued a clarifying order requiring the bird logo in all Yellow Pages ads henceforth. It held that defendants could use the name Falcon alone, because the decree did not require them to make it part of a longer name. The court was obviously impressed by defendant's efforts to comply with the decree. Vertex Distributing v. Falcon Foam Plastics, 689 F.2d 885 (9th Cir. 1982).

Did plaintiff get all that it bargained for? Didn't the consent decree already say that it was feasible to include the bird logo in all Yellow Pages ads? What about the other issue? Is "Falcon" "a trade name that includes the word Falcon"? If the parties meant to require that some other word always be used with Falcon, what should they have said?

b. "Best efforts." United States v. Joyce, 498 F.2d 592 (7th Cir. 1974), discussed in note 5 following *Anyanwu*, reversed a criminal contempt conviction for failure to use "best offices" to secure corporate records from abroad. "Best efforts" was too vague for criminal contempt.

c. "Bona fide offer of settlement." Hess v. New Jersey Transit Rail Operations, 846 F.2d 114 (2d Cir. 1988), reversed a fine for contempt of an order to make a "bonafide offer of settlement" in a personal injury case, citing *Joyce* and commenting that "bonafide" is as vague as "best offices." It also seems doubtful that the court had authority to command a settlement offer no matter how specific the order was.

The National Labor Relations Act expressly requires employers and unions to "bargain collectively" and "in good faith," but it does not require either party "to agree to a proposal," and it does not require "the making of a concession." 29 U.S.C. §§158(a)(5), 158(b)(3), and 158(d). The National Labor Relations Board issues orders to comply with these duties; these orders are enforced by orders of courts of appeals that are in turn enforceable by the contempt power. There are vast numbers of cases, and the NLRB and the courts struggle to make any sense of it.

d. "Appropriate psychiatric treatment . . . as medically indicated." A consent decree in a California prison case required defendants to "provide appropriate psychiatric treatment for all inmates . . . as medically indicated." A mediator was appointed to help resolve disputes about implementation of the decree. One appellate panel enforced the decree, finding "a sufficiently specific standard with which to judge defendants' compliance." Gates v. Gomez, 60 F.3d 525, 530 (9th Cir. 1995). A later panel refused to enforce the decree, finding no evidence that "appropriate treatment" or "medically indicated" had "any specific meaning . . . in the prison psychiatric context." Gates v. Shinn, 98 F.3d 463, 471 (9th Cir. 1996). *Shinn* distinguished *Gomez* on the ground that the dispute in *Gomez* was about shooting agitated inmates with rubber bullets, a procedure "so clearly inappropriate" that it clearly violated the consent decree. *Id.* at 472. But in *Shinn*, the dispute was over 13 standards recommended by the mediator; the prison's psychiatric expert disagreed with those standards, and the language of the decree was too vague to resolve the dispute. Nor could the defendants be held in contempt for disobeying the mediator; the mediator had no power to go beyond the decree.

6. But courts sometimes approve overly broad injunctions. United Construction Products brought a patent infringement and unfair competition claim against Tile Tech, Inc. Tile Tech gave late, deficient responses to discovery, and the trial court sanctioned it for its conduct. The trial court later granted a default judgment for United, which included entering a preliminary injunction against Tile Tech infringing on United's patent. In part, the injunction prohibited Tile Tech from "any and all acts of infringement of the [patent], including making, using, importing, selling, offering for sale, advertising, marketing or promoting the sale of any adjustable building surface support product incorporating the [patent], or any substantially similar adjustable building support product sold, advertised, marketed or promoted in the United States."

Tile Tech appealed to the Federal Circuit arguing, among other things that the injunction was overly broad in covering "substantially similar" products. The Federal Circuit disagreed, and said that Tile Tech could figure out when it was infringing by applying the "two-step test that this court set out" in an earlier case. United Construction Products, Inc. v. Tile Tech, Inc., 843 F.3d 1363, 1372 (Fed. Cir. 2016). Even if the Federal Circuit's two-step test was sufficiently clear, note the use of the word "including" in the order. What other act of infringements might be covered by the injunction?

7. Ask for exactly what you want. In Waste Management v. Kattler, 776 F.3d 336, 343 (5th Cir. 2015), the Fifth Circuit reversed an order holding an attorney in contempt for failing to turn over an iPad tablet when the court's order called only for turning over "images"—the files that were on the tablet and not the tablet itself.

8. A suggested standard? The First Circuit, quoting a selection of earlier cases, says that the specificity requirements "are designed to prevent uncertainty and confusion and to avoid basing a contempt citation on a decree too vague to be understood." An "injunction must simply be framed so that those enjoined will know what conduct the court has prohibited." "[E]laborate detail is unnecessary." But "any ambiguities and omissions . . . redound to the benefit of the person charged with contempt." Axia Netmedia Corp. v. Massachusetts Technology Park Corp., 889 F.3d 1, 12-13 (1st Cir. 2018).

An order to defendant to "continue to provide, through its affiliates . . . the same level of [internet] service that those affiliates are currently providing" was good enough. Defendant knew, or could "readily discern, the precise level of services its affiliates had been providing," and the affiliates' responsibilities were spelled out in a 32-page Transitional Services Agreement. *Id.* at 6. Think about this reasoning as you read the next set of notes, on the rule against incorporating other documents. But if the court had tried to fully specify the level of required service, in legal language within the four corners of the injunction, might the result have been less clear than what the court actually did?

The court also offered this example of a bad injunction: "an order that 'judgment . . . is entered in accordance with' an opinion that merely states that the plaintiff is 'entitled to . . . injunctive relief,' without more." *Id.* at 12, citing Massachusetts Association of Older Americans v. Commissioner of Public Welfare, 803 F.2d 35 (1st Cir. 1986).

9. A looser standard for civil contempt? In civil contempt, courts occasionally say that defendant should have asked for clarification if he thought the injunction ambiguous. An example is Glover v. Johnson, 934 F.2d 703 (6th Cir. 1991), a prison case about educational programs in a women's prison. "[W]e find the language unambiguous and, even if it were ambiguous, defendants' failure to request the court to clarify, explain, or modify the language in the decade since the order was served precludes raising an ambiguity argument at this time." *Id.* at 708-709.

The leading case in this line is McComb v. Jacksonville Paper Co., 336 U.S. 187 (1949). The injunction in *McComb* ordered defendant to comply with the minimum-wage, overtime-pay, and record-keeping provisions of the Fair Labor Standards Act, 29 U.S.C. §201 *et seq.* Defendant evaded the injunction in imaginative ways; the district court found that defendant used a "false and fictitious" method of computing compensation. But it refused to hold defendant in contempt. Because nothing in the injunction specifically forbade those computations, the trial court thought the violations were not willful. Instead, it amended the injunction to forbid such computations in the future.

The Supreme Court reversed, saying that defendant should have asked for clarification if it were unsure how to comply. The government won in *McComb* partly because it had the advantage of an injunction as broad as the statute (and a pattern of past violations broad enough to support such an injunction). Broad language tends to wipe out errors of underinclusiveness; vagueness or ambiguity in a narrow injunction is much more dangerous to plaintiffs.

Moreover, the Court did not view this as a case in which defendant might plausibly have thought its conduct was not forbidden, and the injunction might have been as clear as possible under the circumstances. The government and trial court could not imagine all the possible ways of violating the Act and specifically enjoin each one. The Court feared an endless succession of evasive schemes, none of which would be contempt in the view of the lower courts. That concern has little force in cases where the ambiguity could have been avoided.

Justices Frankfurter and Rutledge dissented. They thought injunctions should be strictly enforced, but that "to be both strict and indefinite is a kind of judicial tyranny." *Id.* at 501. They thought that general language was always dangerous, because it could be plausibly interpreted after the fact to apply to conduct not contemplated when the injunction was issued.

10. An impossible standard in Texas? Some jurisdictions require extraordinary specificity in injunctions. Consider In re Lakeside Realty, Inc., 2004 WL 212580 (Tex. Ct. App. 2004), where the court ordered defendant to "remove such covered parking structures" as plaintiffs had objected to, "remove the concrete poured over the objection of plaintiffs, and restore the area to an [*sic*] grass lawn area with sprinklers that are attached to the existing system within 90 days of the signing of this decree." The court of appeals threw out a conviction for contempt. "[T]he order does not specifically identify which covered parking structures are to be removed, the location of the concrete that is to be removed, what area of the property is to be restored and how, or any specifications for the installation of the additional sprinklers." *Id.* at *3. Does the injunction have to incorporate the architectural drawings for the sprinklers? Does it make any sense to have to work out those details before an injunction can be issued?

In Ex parte Acker, 949 S.W.2d 314, 316 (Tex. 1997), the injunction ordered defendant to pay for health insurance "beginning on the 1st day of June and . . . each and every month thereafter." The court vacated a finding of contempt because the order did not say which year the payments were to begin. Such cases follow the Texas rule, in which "the focus is on the wording of the judgment itself." Ex parte Reese, 701 S.W.2d 840, 841 (Tex. 1986). But the injunction need not be "full of superfluous terms and specifications adequate to counter any flight of fancy a contemnor may imagine." Ex parte Blasingame, 748 S.W.2d 444, 446 (Tex. 1988). Do the procedural shortcuts of a contempt citation justify this level of strict construction, remitting plaintiff to an independent suit or a motion to clarify if the injunction is not perfectly clear? Or do cases like *Lakeside* and *Acker* allow defendants to defy injunctions and defend their contempt with word games?

Compare *Acker* to King v. Allied Vision, Ltd., 65 F.3d 1051 (2d Cir. 1995), where the injunction ordered defendant to take "immediate steps" to send a notice to all its retail distributors. Defendant waited three weeks to send the notice, and argued that there was no firm deadline. The court was untroubled. "Whatever constitutes 'immediate,' it is certainly less than three weeks." *Id.* at 1058.

11. Enjoining police harassment. Here is part of what Chief Justice Burger called the "remarkable injunction" in Allee v. Medrano, 416 U.S. 802, 846 (1974) (dissenting). The injunction was entered to prevent the Texas Rangers and other law enforcement officials from abusing and intimidating organizers for a union, the United Farm Workers:

> 16. It is further ordered, adjudged and decreed by the Court that Defendants, their successors, agents and employees, and persons acting in concert with them, are permanently enjoined and restrained from any of the following acts or conduct directed toward or applied to Plaintiffs and the persons they represent, to-wit:
>
> A. Using in any manner Defendants' authority as peace officers for the purpose of preventing or discouraging peaceful organizational activities without adequate cause.
>
> B. Interfering by stopping, dispersing, arresting, or imprisoning any person, or by any other means, with picketing, assembling, solicitation, or organizational effort without adequate cause.
>
> C. Arresting any person without warrant or without probable cause which probable cause is accompanied by intention to present appropriate written complaint to a court of competent jurisdiction.
>
> D. Stopping, dispersing, arresting or imprisoning any person without adequate cause because of the arrest of some other person.
>
> E. As used in this Paragraph 16, Subparagraphs A, B, and D above, the term "adequate cause" shall mean (1) actual obstruction of a public or private passway, road, street, or entrance which actually causes unreasonable interference with ingress, egress, or flow of traffic; or (2) force or violence, or the threat of force or violence, actually committed by any person by his own conduct or by actually aiding, abetting, or participating in such conduct by another person; or (3) probable cause which may cause a Defendant to believe in good faith that one or more particular persons did violate a criminal law of the State of Texas other than those specific laws herein declared unconstitutional, or a municipal ordinance.

Id. at 811-812 n.7.

The Chief Justice had many objections to this injunction. Most important, he thought it would not "provide meaningful relief," because contempt proceedings "would be far too cumbersome and heavy-handed to deal effectively with large numbers of violations." *Id.* at 858 n.20, quoting Comment, *The Federal Injunction as a Remedy for Unconstitutional Police Conduct,* 78 Yale L.J. 143, 147 (1968). The majority focused on whether plaintiffs were entitled to any injunction at all, and seemed untroubled by the form and drafting of the injunction.

Are "peaceful organizational activities," "adequate cause," "probable cause," and "good faith" any more specific than the terms that caused trouble in note 5 — "possible and practical," "best offices," "bona fide," and "appropriate"? Does the definition of "adequate cause" solve the problem? It at least helps, and defining terms is often a useful drafting technique.

Is there any way to make this injunction more specific? Is there any way of controlling the enjoined conduct that is less "cumbersome and heavy-handed" than contempt citations?

12. The costs of bad drafting. Even when plaintiff prevails on the contempt citation, lack of specificity always creates a litigable issue that might have been avoided. Extra litigation is expensive, and clients don't like to pay you to litigate the meaning of something you should have written more clearly. Litigable issues create risk; you are likely to wind up settling for less than you could have achieved if you had drafted the order more clearly. Consent decrees are sometimes ambiguous because the parties reached agreement by fudging some issues; that may be unavoidable. Ambiguities inevitably arise, even in litigated decrees, because humans lack the capacity to see the future and there are limits to the power of language. But certainly when you win on the merits, it is well worth the time to draft the injunction as carefully as possible. Your victory will be embedded in, and largely reduced to, the specific language in the injunction. The injunction is not a postscript to the lawsuit; the lawsuit is prologue to the injunction.

13. The Supreme Court muffs or avoids the details. In Trump v. International Refugee Assistance Project, 137 S. Ct. 2080 (2017), more fully described in section 5.B.1, the Supreme Court stayed in part the injunctions entered by two district courts against enforcement of President Trump's executive order barring immigration from six predominantly Muslim countries. The Court's opinion concluded:

> The Government's application to stay the injunction with respect to §§6(a) and (b) is accordingly granted in part. Section 6(a) may not be enforced against an individual seeking admission as a refugee who can credibly claim a bona fide relationship with a person or entity in the United States. Nor may §6(b); that is, such a person may not be excluded pursuant to §6(b), even if the 50,000–person cap has been reached or exceeded. As applied to all other individuals, the provisions may take effect.
>
> **3**
>
> Accordingly, the petitions for certiorari are granted, and the stay applications are granted in part.
> *It is so ordered.*

Probably the Court thought this was clear enough, or maybe there was not consensus to be more specific. It gave some discursive examples of the kinds of relationships it had in mind. But it did not actually draft a revised injunction to be entered on remand, or edit the language of the district courts' injunctions to show what remained in effect and what was stayed. And of course it did not enter an injunction of its own; that would have posed the risk of contempt hearings in the Supreme Court. So there was no order anywhere that complied with Rule 65 and also with the Court's opinion.

Predictably, a dispute broke out immediately. The government interpreted "relationship" very narrowly, claiming for example that grandparents have no relevant relationship with grandchildren in the United States, and instructing rank and file officials that doubts should be resolved against persons seeking admission—despite the "credibly claim" language in the opinion. After some procedural sparring, the District Court in Hawaii issued a modified injunction protecting a broader set of relatives and also refugees with "a formal assurance" of reception and placement services. Hawaii v. Trump, 263 F. Supp. 3d 1049 (D. Hawaii 2017), *aff'd*, 871 F.3d 646 (9th Cir. 2017). The Supreme Court stayed enforcement of the order with respect to refugees with formal assurances but no other U.S. relationship after the district court's decision, Trump v. International Refugee Assistance Project, 137 S. Ct. 2080 (2017), and again after the court of appeals' decision, Trump v. Hawaii, 138 S. Ct. 1 (2017).

14. Money judgments. Money judgments are generally simpler to draft; most of the time, all they really need to say is who wins and how much. But judges can bungle them, usually through simple inattention. An example is Cooke v. Jackson National Life Insurance Co., 882 F.3d 630 (7th Cir. 2018), where the trial court entered two orders indicating that plaintiff won and was entitled to attorneys fees, but neither of which specified how much money plaintiff was entitled to. Neither was an appealable final judgment without an amount. The court said that a judgment "should be a self-contained document, saying who won and what relief has been awarded, but omitting the reasons for this disposition, which should appear in the court's opinion." *Id.* at 631.

NOTES ON THE RULE AGAINST INCORPORATING OTHER DOCUMENTS

1. Rule 65(d)(1) again. Reread Rule 65(d)(1), reprinted in note 1 of the previous set of notes. This time, focus on the requirement that the injunction describe the acts to be enjoined, but "not by reference to the complaint or other document." This is the rule against incorporating other documents. The principal abuse the rule aims at is referring to the allegations of the complaint or the findings of a judicial opinion in the case. The injunction is to be a self-contained document. But it is hard to avoid relying on information outside its four corners.

Rule 54(a), which applies to all judgments—injunctions, money judgments, and judgments for defendants—says that a judgment "should not include recitals of pleadings, a master's report, or a record of proceedings."

2. The Washington fishing case again. The court in the Washington fishing litigation tried to allocate the fish harvest between thousands of Indian and non-Indian fishers; we first encountered it when we considered how to bind third parties to obey decrees. The injunction also raised difficult drafting problems. Here is the key part of that ingenious injunction:

> 1. All Puget Sound and other marine waters easterly of Donilla Point-Tatoosh line and their watersheds, all Olympic Peninsula watersheds, and all Grays Harbor and its watersheds are hereby closed to all net salmon fishing except during such times and such specific waters as are opened by State or tribal regulations or regulations of the United States conforming to the orders of this Court in this case.
>
> 2. All reef net, gill net and purse seine fishermen licensed by the State of Washington, all other persons who attempt to net or assist in netting salmon in the waters described in paragraph 1, the Puget Sound Gillnetters Association, the Purse Seine Vessel Owners Association, the Grays Harbor Gillnetters Association and all persons in active concert or participation with them are hereby enjoined and prohibited from engaging in taking, possessing, or selling salmon of any species taken from such waters, unless such person has first ascertained from the Washington Department of Fisheries telephone "hot-line," 1-800-562-5672 or 1-800-562-5673, that the area to be fished is open for fishing by non-treaty fishermen at the time the individual intends to fish, *provided*, that this

provision shall not apply to persons exercising treaty fishing rights in accordance with the orders of this Court.

3. The defendant State of Washington is directed to maintain a continuous telephone hot-line service free of charge to any caller from within the State of Washington to provide information on areas within the waters described in paragraph 1 of this order that are open to net salmon fishing by non-treaty fishermen in conformity with the orders of this Court. The defendant shall furnish to this Court and to the United States Attorney a transcript of the daily hot-line messages.

The court of appeals approved the injunction in Puget Sound Gillnetters Association v. United States District Court, 573 F.2d 1123 (9th Cir. 1978), *vacated on other grounds as* Washington v. Washington State Commercial Passenger Fishing Vessel Association, 443 U.S. 658 (1979). Subsequently, individual defendants in contempt citations attacked the validity of the injunction. Here is the court of appeals' response:

All that the injunction requires a fisherman to do is to call the hot-line before going fishing, and then to refrain from fishing in any area which the hot-line tells him is closed. We find paragraph 2 clear, concise, and comprehensible. That is the only paragraph that Dolman was required to obey. We find nothing in paragraph 1 that conflicts with paragraph 2. Paragraph 1 does not purport to authorize fishing in waters declared open by state or tribal or United States regulations. It merely declares that all relevant waters are closed except those opened by such regulations. But it does not do what counsel says it does, that is, require fishermen to know those regulations and follow them. Instead, all it requires is, in paragraph 2, that the fisherman comply with what the hot-line tells him about open or closed waters. If the hot-line tells him that an area is closed, he is not to fish there; if it tells him that an area is open, he may fish there.

The injunction is as specific as the nature of the subject matter—regulation of fishing in Puget Sound—permits.

United States v. Olander, 584 F.2d 876, 880-881 (9th Cir. 1978), *vacated on other grounds as* Dolman v. United States, 443 U.S. 914 (1979).

The court is persuasive that the state regulations weren't improperly incorporated into the injunction. But was the hotline recording improperly incorporated?

Certainly the injunction is not guilty of the abuses the incorporation rule aims at. It does not say, "Don't do any of the things described in the complaint," and it does not do anything that raises comparable problems of having to know the contents of documents that may not be readily accessible. It is hard to see how this injunction could work without the hotline. Yet inescapably, the conduct forbidden is described by reference to something outside the injunction. Might Rule 65(d)(1) mean that hotline recordings are simply not an available option? Or is it dispositive that the court did the best it could under the circumstances? Does it help to say the telephone recording is not a "document"? Reread Rule 65(d)(1).

3. Obey-the-law injunctions. Do injunctions to obey the law raise incorporation problems as well as specificity problems? Don't they incorporate the statute and related regulations, and require defendants to know the contents of those external documents? Is that all right because defendants are presumed to know the law anyway? That wasn't the view of the court of appeals in the Washington fishing cases.

One of the contempt charges in *McComb* was that defendants had classified employees as executives in disregard of the relevant regulations. Was there any way to avoid construing the injunction in light of the underlying law? Should the court copy the regulations into every injunction? Classify defendant's employees and specifically list those that are exempt? Classifying all the employees may be burdensome, but isn't the injunction supposed to individuate the law's command? Still, isn't it illusory to think that any injunction can be understood without knowledge of some additional information from somewhere?

Consider Mitchell v. Seaboard System Railroad, 883 F.2d 451, 454 (6th Cir. 1989), vacating an injunction against "engaging in any further employment practices violative of Title VII with respect to the plaintiff and in keeping with the opinions expressed herein." The court said that both the reference to "the opinions expressed herein" and "the reference to Title VII" violated the rule against incorporation. Compare Gulf King Shrimp Co. v. Wirtz, 407 F.2d 508, 517 (5th Cir. 1969), affirming an injunction against "violating the provisions of sections 15(a)(4) and 15(a)(5) of the Fair Labor Standards Act of 1938, as amended, in any of the following manners." There followed a detailed decree. The court of appeals found it "significant that the injunction does not . . . rely on the statute for clarification of what is otherwise unclear in the decree itself. . . . The statutory material is . . . given as a parenthetical reference, not as a substantive command."

4. Carrying a good idea too far. Consider the injunction in Allee v. Medrano, discussed in note 11 of the preceding set of notes. That injunction ordered the Texas Rangers not to arrest union members without "probable cause." "Probable cause" is a phrase from the Fourth Amendment, defined in thousands of precedents interpreting it. That doesn't mean the precedents are improperly incorporated, does it?

Every injunction is written in English and makes no sense unless one knows the meaning of the English words that appear there. That surely doesn't mean the dictionary is improperly incorporated. The rule requires some implicit baseline of general knowledge, and that surely includes general legal background as well as the English language. What cannot be incorporated is facts and law specific to the case and to the disagreement between the parties. The court's resolution of those disagreements must be spelled out.

5. Incorporating defendant's own policies. Civil rights organizations brought suit against the Louisiana Secretary of State alleging that the Secretary was violating voter registration procedures mandated by the National Voter Registration Act of 1993, 52 U.S.C. §20501 *et seq.* The district court agreed, but found that the Secretary had made substantial strides towards complying with the NVRA during the litigation. The court issued an injunction which, among other things, required the Secretary to "maintain in force" his "policies, procedures, and directives" related to the coordination and enforcement of the NVRA.

The Fifth Circuit reversed. It held the order was too vague because it "refers generally to the defendant's policies without defining what those polices are or how they can be identified." Scott v. Schedler, 826 F.3d 207, 212 (5th Cir. 2016). Further, the order violated the rule against incorporating other documents by ordering the Secretary "to maintain in place certain undefined policies, procedures, and directives." *Id.* at 213.

On remand, the district court ordered the Secretary "to adopt and maintain in force and effect rules, that by virtue of this Order shall be binding and enforceable, governing NVRA compliance by the Louisiana Department of Health and Hospitals and Department of Children and Family Services for in person transactions at agency offices with respect to each application for service or assistance, each recertification, renewal or change of address form relating to such service or assistance, unless the service or benefit applicant declines voter registration services in writing by returning a voter declination/declaration form to the agency at the time of the subject transactions." Scott v. Schedler, No. 2:11-CV-00926. Doc. 566, at 2 (E.D. La., Aug. 11, 2016).

The court also ordered "that such rules shall include provisions for periodic NVRA training, monitoring of agency compliance, and enforcement of compliance for in person transactions at agency offices." *Id.*

DRAFTING YOUR OWN INJUNCTION

Before drafting your own injunction, you should read the rest of this section and consider the examples of how other drafters responded to difficult situations. You should also reread the notes on the scope of preventive injunctions in section 4.A.1.

Try drafting an injunction for Equal Employment Opportunity Commission v. Boh Brothers Construction Company, LLC, 731 F.3d 444 (5th Cir. 2013) (en banc). *Boh Brothers* is an employment discrimination case. Assume that under applicable law, a suit by the EEOC allows a court to grant firmwide relief.

And don't worry about the details of employment discrimination law. It is enough to know that the statute reads as follows:

> It shall be . . . unlawful . . . for an employer . . . to discriminate against any individual . . . because of such individual's . . . sex . . . .

42 U.S.C. §2000e-2(a).

Assume that the statute has been interpreted to bar "hostile work environments" and applies specifically to same-sex harassment. Oncale v. Sundowner Offshore Services, Inc., 523 U.S. 75 (1998). Thus, there is no dispute that the conduct described below violates the statute. Your goal is to forbid discrimination of the sort experienced by Kerry Woods, without giving employees more protection than the statute requires. Try to describe as precisely as possible what it is you are forbidding. You don't need to include a separate statement of facts and conclusions of law. Here are the facts:

> This Title VII case arises out of alleged sexual harassment by Chuck Wolfe, the superintendent of an all-male crew on a construction site operated by Boh Bros. Construction Company ("Boh Brothers"). During a three-day jury trial, the Equal Employment Opportunity Commission ("EEOC") presented evidence that Wolfe subjected Kerry Woods, an iron worker on Wolfe's crew, to almost-daily verbal and physical harassment because Woods did not conform to Wolfe's view of how a man should act. The jury found in favor of the EEOC on its hostile-environment claim, awarding compensatory and punitive damages.
>
> Woods is an iron worker and structural welder. Boh Brothers hired Woods on November 3, 2005, to work on crews repairing the Twin Spans bridges between New Orleans and Slidell after Hurricane Katrina. In January 2006, the company transferred Woods to a bridge-maintenance crew. Wolfe was the crew superintendent, with about five employees under his supervision.
>
> The worksite was an undeniably vulgar place. Wolfe and the crew regularly used "very foul language" and "locker room talk." According to other crew members, Wolfe was a primary offender: he was "rough" and "mouthy" with his co-workers and often teased and "ribbed on" them.
>
> By April 2006, Woods had become a specific and frequent target of Wolfe's abuse. Wolfe referred to Woods as "pussy," "princess," and "faggot," often "two to three times a day." About two to three times per week—while Woods was bent over to perform a task—Wolfe approached him from behind and simulated anal intercourse with him. Woods felt "embarrassed and humiliated" by the name-calling and began to look over his shoulder before bending down. . . .

According to Wolfe, some of his teasing originated from Woods's use of Wet Ones instead of toilet paper, which Wolfe viewed as "kind of gay" and "feminine." . . .

Woods complained about Wolfe's treatment to his foreman, Tim Carpenter, "two or three times." . . .

[Another supervisor] subsequently investigated Woods's complaint, although he did not document any aspect of his investigation. He spoke with both Wolfe and a crew foreman for about ten minutes each and determined that Wolfe's behavior, though unprofessional, did not constitute sexual harassment. [The supervisor] did not notify the company's general counsel about Woods's harassment allegations. . . .

In February 2007, Boh Brothers laid Woods off for lack of work. That March, Woods filed an EEOC charge of discrimination, alleging sexual harassment . . .

The EEOC brought this enforcement action on Woods's behalf in September 2009, claiming sexual harassment . . . under Title VII. Following a three-day trial, the jury returned a verdict in favor of Woods on the harassment claim . . . . The jury awarded Woods $201,000 in compensatory damages and $250,000 in punitive damages. The district court reduced the compensatory damages award to $50,000 to comply with the $300,000 statutory damages cap. 42 U.S.C. § 1981a(b)(3)(D).

[The court is now considering the injunction to be issued.]

B. COLLECTING MONEY JUDGMENTS

1. *Execution, Garnishment, and the Like*

CREDIT BUREAU, INC. v. MONINGER
284 N.W.2d 855 (Neb. 1979)

Heard before KRISHOVA, C.J., and BOSLAUGH, MCCOWN, CLINTON, BRODKEY, WHITE and HASTINGS, JJ.

BRODKEY, Justice.

This is an appeal from an order of the District Court for Custer County . . . awarding the proceeds from a sheriff's sale of a 1975 Ford pickup truck to the Broken Bow State Bank . . . . We reverse and remand.

The facts . . . are not in dispute. The Credit Bureau of Broken Bow . . . obtained a default judgment against John Moninger . . . in the amount of $1,518.27 on October 20, 1977. . . . On May 16, 1978, Moninger renewed his prior note to the Bank in the amount of $2,144.74. The renewed note was to be secured by a security agreement on feeder pigs and a 1975 Ford pickup owned by Moninger, but no security agreement was entered into at that time. On June 27, 1978, at the request of the Bureau, a writ of execution was issued on its judgment in the amount of $1,338.50, the balance remaining due on the judgment.

The deputy county sheriff who received the writ examined the motor vehicle title records on July 7, 1978, to determine if a lien existed as of that date on the pickup owned by Moninger. Finding no encumbrance of record, the deputy sheriff proceeded to Moninger's place of employment to levy on the vehicle. The deputy sheriff found Moninger, served him with a copy of the writ, and informed Moninger that he was executing on the pickup. Moninger testified he informed the officer that there was money borrowed from the Bank against the pickup, and that the Bank had title to the vehicle. Following this conversation, the officer proceeded to the vehicle, "grabbed ahold of the pickup," and stated: "I execute on the pickup for the County of Custer." The officer did not take possession of the vehicle at that time, nor did he ask for the keys to the vehicle.

On July 10, 1978, after being informed of the events which occurred on the 7th, the Bank and Moninger executed a security agreement on the vehicle which was then filed. Notation of the security interest was made on the title to the pickup truck that same day. The vehicle was seized by deputy sheriffs on July 13, 1978, and sold at sheriff's sale on August 14, 1978, for $2,050.

The sheriff filed a motion in the county court for a determination of the division of the proceeds from the sheriff's sale. The Bank joined the action by application for the proceeds of the sheriff's sale, basing its claim on its alleged status as a secured creditor. Prior to a hearing on these matters, a stipulation was entered into by all parties whereby this dispute was limited to the distribution of the proceeds of the sheriff's sale, the pickup having previously been sold. . . .

The Bureau first assigns as error the ruling of the trial court which found the Bank's security interest in the vehicle to be superior to the execution lien of the Bureau. Specifically, the Bureau contends that the actions of the deputy sheriff on July 7, 1978, amounted to a valid levy which bound the vehicle for the satisfaction of the Bureau's judgment against Moninger. Neb. Rev. Stat. §25-1504. On that date, the Bank held only an unperfected security interest in the vehicle. [Actually, the Bank held no interest on that date, because the debtor had not signed a security agreement. See UCC §9-203.]. . . .

The correctness of the Bureau's position turns on . . . [w]hether the Bureau was in fact a lien creditor on July 7, 1978 . . . .

Section 9-301 defines a lien creditor as "a creditor who has acquired a lien on the property involved by attachment, levy or the like. . . ." A lien on personal property is acquired in this state at the time it is "seized in execution." §25-1504. Therefore, the Bureau became a lien creditor within the meaning of §9-301 when the sheriff levied on the vehicle.

The rule by which to test the validity of a levy has been earlier set out by this court. "'A manual interference with chattels is not essential to a valid levy thereon. It is sufficient if the property is present and subject for the time to the control of the officer holding the writ, and that he in express terms asserts his dominion over it by virtue of such writ.'" Battle Creek Valley Bank v. First National Bank, 88 N.W. 145 (Neb. 1901). We believe a review of the record makes it clear that a valid levy did occur before the Bank had perfected its security interest in the chattel.

The deputy sheriff expressly asserted his dominion over the vehicle by virtue of the writ. He likewise exerted control over the vehicle as against all others at the time of levy. At that time the deputy sheriff informed Moninger that he was sorry that he had to execute on the vehicle but that it was his job. He further stated that he hoped Moninger would straighten the problem out with the Bureau. It should be noted that the officer's report, as well as the return on the writ, clearly indicated that the officer "executed" on the vehicle on July 7, 1978. On the basis of this evidence, we conclude that a valid levy took place at that time.

The Bank would have us hold that the pickup should have been physically seized to make the levy valid. We do not believe that failure to take physical possession in this case goes to the validity of the levy. . . . Whether . . . the officer took physical possession after he levied relates to the ability of the officer to produce the property levied on, and to his possible civil liability for failure to do so, not to the validity of the levy. It is, of course, possible that the failure of a levying officer to protect and preserve the property levied upon might give rise to an action between the officer, or his bonding company, and the judgment creditor. . . .

We therefore hold that the Bureau was a lien creditor . . . . The Bureau attained this status on July 7, 1978. The record discloses that the Bank did not perfect its security interest in the vehicle until July 10, 1978, when it filed a security agreement entered into on that date. . . . The Bureau thus has prior rights to the proceeds of the sheriff's sale. . . .

If the Bank had timely complied with the statute in the instant matter, this dispute would not have arisen. . . .

The judgment of the District Court is . . . reversed and the cause remanded for further proceedings not inconsistent with this opinion.

NOTES ON EXECUTION

1. The mechanics of execution. *Credit Bureau* gives you a good look at the mechanics of execution. The basic steps are the same everywhere: The court issues a writ, the writ is delivered to the sheriff or constable, she levies on the debtor's property, and she eventually sells the property on which she levied. But the case illustrates the minority rule on one important point; most states require the sheriff to assert effective control over the property, which the Nebraska sheriff did not initially do in *Credit Bureau.* The writ is called a writ of execution in most states, but a few states still use the common law term, writ of fieri facias, or its nickname, fi fa. As the *Credit Bureau* opinion illustrates, "levy" and "execute" are often used interchangeably.

The proceeds of the sheriff's sale go first to the sheriff to pay the costs of execution, then to pay off liens on the property. The judgment creditor has an execution lien by virtue of the levy, but he may not have the only lien. There may be a security interest, as in *Credit Bureau,* or a mortgage. There may be mechanic's liens, a landlord's lien, or a variety of other common law or statutory liens. There may be a tax lien. There may be other judgment creditors with execution liens. A trustee in bankruptcy or some other representative of general creditors may claim the property. Someone may claim to be the true owner of the property or claim a right to restitution of the property. All these claims must be ranked from first priority to last priority. Then they will be paid in order until the money runs out. Any money left over is returned to the debtor, but that doesn't happen very often. If a debtor can't pay your client, he probably can't pay a lot of other people either; it is important to be at the head of the line. If you are at the end of the line, you might do better in bankruptcy, where liens acquired in the last 90 days are undone and unsecured creditors share pro rata.

2. The UCC priority rules. The priority contest in *Credit Bureau* is governed in part by the Uniform Commercial Code. Under §9-301 at the time of the opinion (now §9-317(a)), the Credit Bureau wins if it got its execution lien before the bank perfected its security interest. The Code also tells us that the bank perfected its interest on July 10, when it noted its interest on the pickup's certificate of title. §9-302(3) then, §9-311 now. In Nebraska, the county treasurer (at the time of *Credit Bureau,* the county clerk) keeps a copy of the certificate of title, Neb. Rev. Stat. Ann. §60-152, and it is apparently these files that the deputy sheriff checked. The Code does not tell us (then or now) when the Credit Bureau got its execution lien. That is left to common law or nonuniform statutes. And the states do not agree on the answer.

3. Nonuniform priority rules. In most states the priority of an execution lien on personal property is based on when the sheriff levies on the property. Nebraska is typical in this respect. But in some states, the lien has priority from the time the writ is delivered to the sheriff, at least if a valid levy is made thereafter, from issuance of the writ, from docketing of the judgment, or even from the entry of the judgment.

In a handful of states, a judgment creditor can establish priority in personal property by filing a statement for public record; that option is described in note 9. The rules for real estate are generally different: Docketing the judgment in a county where the debtor owns real estate creates a judgment lien on all the debtor's real estate in the county. A judgment docket is generally indexed by the judgment debtor's name, and real estate title searchers must examine the judgment docket as well as the deed records.

All of these statements are somewhat oversimplified. The basic priority rule is first in time, first in right, but there are exceptions, and much depends on the identity of the competing claimant. In most states it is possible to have priority over other execution liens without having priority over bona fide purchasers for value. The complexities are examined in David Gray Carlson and Paul M. Shupack, *Judicial Lien Priorities under Article 9 of the Uniform Commercial Code: Part I*, 5 Cardozo L. Rev. 287 (1984), and *Part II—Creditor Representatives, Bank Receivers, Fixtures, Crops, and Accessions*, 5 Cardozo L. Rev. 823 (1984). Article 9 has been revised since that article was written, but few states have undertaken any systematic revision of the law of execution.

4. Special priorities for the government. Governments are often creditors, and they often make special priority rules for their own benefit. Sometimes they defer to competing interests; sometimes not. The Tax Lien Act, 26 U.S.C. §6321 *et seq.*, enacted in 1966, generally makes federal tax liens subject to earlier liens. There are some commercially significant exceptions, but the basic rule is first-in-time, first-in-right.

Unfortunately, there is a separate statute, dating back to 1797, that simply says that when a person is insolvent and not in bankruptcy court, "the United States Government shall be paid first." 31 U.S.C. §3713. Taken literally, this statute entirely wipes out the careful balancing of interests in the Tax Lien Act. And some cases had taken it literally. The Supreme Court finally solved the problem by holding that the 1797 Act merely establishes priorities among unsecured claims; it does not apply to mortgages, liens, or security interests. United States v. Estate of Romani, 523 U.S. 517 (1998).

5. Effecting a valid levy. States that require a levy to establish priority disagree on what constitutes a levy. In Nebraska and several other states, levy is a ceremonial procedure, much like early explorers claiming land for European kings. It is hard to see what purpose is served by announcing the levy in the presence of the pickup. Most states require the sheriff to physically take possession if that is possible. If the goods are unmanageable, the seizure may be somewhat symbolic, but the sheriff must exercise as much actual control as the nature of the goods permits. For example, he may disable a large machine or attach signs to it with chains and padlocks. Many of the cases are conflicting, and many define levy in vague terms that make it hard to know just how much actual control the sheriff has to exercise.

6. Secret liens. The UCC enacts a strong policy against secret liens. That is why the bank's security interest in *Credit Bureau* was not perfected until it noted its interest on the certificate of title. That policy can be traced at least to Twyne's Case, 76 Eng. Rep. 809 (Star Chamber 1601). Are execution liens in Nebraska consistent with that policy? What should happen if Moninger sold the pickup to an innocent purchaser after the formal levy and before the actual seizure? Does that purchaser have any way to know about the Credit Bureau's execution lien? Should he be bound by it if he can't know about it? Some states protect good-faith purchasers of property subject to secret judicial liens, and some do not. If a good-faith purchaser after the levy gets good title, should the sheriff be liable to the Credit Bureau for loss of the pickup?

7. Working with the sheriff. Sheriff's offices are often overworked and understaffed. Equally important, it is not their money they are trying to collect, and they don't know anything about the debtor. The creditor and his attorney have more time and more incentive to find assets, and more knowledge about where to look. Sheriffs and their deputies will often be quite cooperative about coming to a particular place at a particular time to serve a hard-to-find defendant, or to levy on an asset that is about to disappear. But the creditor or his attorney must tell the sheriff when and where to go.

8. Search warrants? Goods subject to execution are often inside buildings, including homes. A few courts have said that the sheriff needs a warrant based on probable cause to believe that specific leviable goods will be found within the building. Cases are collected in Dorwart v. Caraway, 966 P.2d 1121, 1129-1138 (Mont. 1998). Writs of execution, which generally issue ministerially at the request of judgment creditors, are not enough in this view.

If Fourth Amendment standards are fully applicable to execution, nearly every writ of execution will also require a warrant, and execution will become even more cumbersome, expensive, and ineffectual than it already is. But if we don't permit warrantless general searches to enforce the criminal law, why should we permit them to enforce a civil judgment?

Moreover, the sheriff looking for leviable goods may also find evidence of crime. He might even use the writ of execution as an excuse to search for evidence of crime. In State v. Griess, 651 N.W.2d 859 (Neb. Ct. App. 2002), the sheriff levied on a motor home, inventoried the contents, and found drugs. The court suppressed the evidence found in the search, relying principally on State v. Hinchey, 374 N.W.2d 14 (Neb. 1985), one of the cases holding that a writ of execution does not authorize entry into a home, and relying also on the Nebraska rule that the sheriff could have executed on the motor home without entering it or seizing control of it.

9. Judgment liens by filing. A judgment creditor in California can file a statement in the filing system for security interests under the UCC. Cal. Civ. Proc. Code §697.510 *et seq.* Such a filing creates a statewide judgment lien on most categories of personal property used in business, anywhere in the state, including property acquired later, with priorities integrated with the UCC priority system for secured credit. To enforce the lien and actually get money from a persistently uncooperative defendant, it will still be necessary to eventually seize and sell the property subject to the lien. But the statute enables judgment creditors to establish their priority without much of the waste and gamesmanship of execution. The California statute, and similar statutes in Maine and Connecticut, are described in William J. Woodward, Jr., *New Judgment Liens on Personal Property: Does "Efficient" Mean "Better"?*, 27 Harv. J. Legis. 1 (1990). The Maine provision reaches consumer goods as well.

There are hardly any reported cases under these statutes. It may be that creditors use the statutes and they work smoothly, but the lack of cases suggests a lack of use. It seems unlikely that a new form of lien could be widely enforced without triggering resistance and litigation.

10. Supersedeas. Execution can follow quickly after entry of judgment. If the judgment debtor wants to delay execution pending appeal, he has to file a supersedeas bond. The bond must generally be in the full amount of the judgment, plus some margin to allow for interest. Judgment debtors who lack sufficient assets to pay the judgment also lack sufficient assets to post a bond. They can still appeal, but they cannot prevent execution on nonexempt assets pending appeal unless they file for bankruptcy. If the judgment is reversed, the judgment creditor is liable in restitution and in some states, for consequential damages. The risks to both sides and the resulting opportunities for bargains are explored, in the context of Texaco, Inc. v. Pennzoil Co. (reprinted in section 2.D), in Douglas Laycock, *The Remedies Issues:*

Compensatory Damages, Specific Performance, Punitive Damages, Supersedeas Bonds, and Abstention, 9 Rev. Litig. 473, 500-516 (1990).

The problem in *Pennzoil* was that no one could post an $11 billion bond, even though Texaco had $23 billion in mostly illiquid assets from which the judgment could eventually be collected—assuming Texaco didn't fraudulently convey the assets while the appeal was pending. Texas responded by amending its rules to provide for a waiver or reduction of the bond in certain cases. The required bond cannot exceed the lesser of half the judgment debtor's net worth or $25 million, and "shall" be reduced further to the extent necessary to avoid "substantial economic harm" to the judgment debtor. But the court may enjoin "dissipating or transferring assets" other than in the normal course of business. Tex. Civ. Prac. & Remedies Code §52.006.

NOTES ON EXEMPTIONS

1. The Nebraska exemptions. Judgment debtors can keep their exempt property even if the judgment remains unpaid. All states exempt some property from execution, but there is enormous variation in the generosity of state exemptions. The Nebraska exemptions will illustrate as well as any. In many states, the pickup in *Credit Bureau* would have been exempt, but not in Nebraska before a 1997 amendment.

Nebraska now exempts "the immediate personal possessions of the debtor and his or her family"; all "necessary" clothing; $3,000 worth of household goods; $5,000 worth of tools, equipment, books, or supplies used in the debtor's principal trade or business; the debtor's interest, up to $5,000, in a motor vehicle; and professionally prescribed health aids for the debtor or his dependents, Neb. Rev. Stat. §25-1556 (beginning in 2018, these limitations are adjusted for inflation every five years); $5,000 in other personal property, §25-1552; $60,000 equity in a homestead, §40-101; burial plots used exclusively for burial purposes and not held for profit, §§12-517, 12-605; any tax refund from the earned income credit, §25-1553; interests in a tax-qualified pension or profit sharing plan "to the extent reasonably necessary for the support of the debtor and any dependent," unless the plan was established or amended to increase contributions within two years of the judgment, §25-1563.01; all retirement and deferred compensation funds, without limit, from state and local governmental entities, §14-2111(1), §16-1038(1), §23-2322, §24-710.02, §48-1401(10), §79-948, §79-9,104(1), §84-1324, §84-1505(3); all pensions payable to persons who became disabled in the service of the United States as soldiers, sailors, or marines, §25-1559; all proceeds, including interest, of any settlement for personal injuries or death, §25-1563.02; $100,000 in cash value of life, health, and accident insurance (with an exception for those convicted of some crimes), §§44-371, 44-1089(2); all workers' compensation benefits, §48-149; all unemployment benefits, §48-647(1); all public assistance payments, §68-1013; and any charity or relief from a private society, §44-1089(1). Finally, 75 percent of current wages for a person without dependents, 85 percent for a person with dependents, and 100 percent if the weekly wages do not exceed 30 hours' pay at the minimum wage, are exempt from garnishment or any form of seizure within 60 days of their receipt. §§25-1558, 25-1560. Some of these exemptions are unavailable with respect to specially treated claims, mostly child support and taxes.

2. The Texas exemptions. In states with very generous exemptions, execution is largely ineffective against ordinary citizens. The Texas exemptions contain modern provisions and also provisions retained from the nineteenth century. Texas exempts home furnishings; "provisions for consumption"; farming or ranching vehicles and implements, tools, equipment, books, and apparatus (including boats and motor vehicles used in a trade or profession); clothing; jewelry; two firearms; athletic and sporting equipment (including bicycles); one motor vehicle for each driver in the family; 2 horses, mules, or donkeys and a saddle, blanket, and bridle for each; 12 head of cattle; 60 head of other livestock; 120 fowl; forage on hand for the consumption of this livestock; and any number of household pets, all subject to an aggregate limit of $50,000 for a single adult or $100,000 for a family. Tex. Prop. Code §§42.001(a), 42.002. In addition, not subject to any limit, Texas exempts all current wages, professionally prescribed health aids, alimony and child support, and a bible or book of sacred writings of any other religion, §42.001(b); a homestead of unlimited value surrounded by 10 urban acres or 200 rural acres (100 rural acres for a single adult), §41.001, §41.002; burial plots, §41.001; and unlimited amounts accumulated in any tax-qualified pension or profit sharing plan or individual retirement account, §42.0021. Jewelry cannot exceed $12,500 for a single adult or $25,000 for a family. §42.002(a)(6). Debtors cannot be ordered to turn over the proceeds of exempt property. Tex. Civ. Prac. & Rem. Code §31.002(f). This provision was enacted when creditors started going after cash and paychecks right after wages were paid.

For the average family, these exemptions leave only their cash in the bank and any investments not in a tax-qualified plan. The average family doesn't have much of either, and what it does have is likely to be proceeds of exempt wages. A determined creditor can keep after them, picking up a few dollars here and there, but it's usually more trouble than it's worth. For more on exemptions, see In re Marriage of Logston, reprinted in section 9.B.2.

3. What is the policy here? The original rationale of exemptions was to ensure that debt collection did not leave debtors without the means of subsistence. What could be the rationale of the Texas exemptions? It is not quite that no debtor should have to pay involuntarily. But might it be that debt collection should not cause any debtor to suffer a loss of social status or a decline in his standard of living?

Economic theory predicts that creditors should be reluctant to lend in high exemption states, and that debtors should be reluctant to pay: Savvy Texas debtors should file for bankruptcy, stiff their creditors, and keep their fancy house, large retirement plan, and $100,000 worth of luxury goods. But they don't. There are individual abuses, but empirical studies have found no effects from variations in state exemptions. There are no statistically significant differences in ratios of debt to income among debtors in bankruptcy in Texas, Illinois, and Pennsylvania, even though exemptions differ sharply. Teresa A. Sullivan, Elizabeth Warren, and Jay Lawrence Westbrook, *As We Forgive Our Debtors* 241 (Oxford Univ. Press 1989).

4. The special problem of retirement accounts. Retirement accounts accumulate money intended for subsistence in old age. Amounts of money that are very large considered as a lump sum will finance only modest retirement when spread over 20, 30, or 40 years. Employer-sponsored plans qualified under ERISA (the Employee Retirement Income Security Act) are protected from creditors and are not part of the employee's bankruptcy estate so long as the employer retains control. 29 U.S.C. §1056(d)(1); Patterson v. Shumate, 504 U.S. 753 (1992). This is a form of exemption, although it is typically thought of somewhat differently: The beneficiary doesn't own the property.

Texas exempts retirement accounts without limit; Nebraska exempts them "to the extent reasonably necessary for the support of the debtor or any dependent," with a check on abuses and with special treatment for most governmental pensions. Such exemptions are relevant to distributions from retirement plans and to non-ERISA plans, mostly individual retirement arrangements (IRAs). The resulting issues have mostly been litigated in bankruptcy cases.

The federal Bankruptcy Code contains a set of federal exemptions, 11 U.S.C. §522, that apply in bankruptcy court unless the debtor's state has opted out, in which case that state's exemptions apply. This federal provision exempts any "*payment under* a stock bonus, pension, profit-sharing, annuity, or similar plan or contract on account of illness, disability, death, age, or length of service, to the extent reasonably necessary for the support of the debtor and any dependent" (our emphasis), with a narrow exception aimed at abuses by corporate insiders. 11 U.S.C. §522(d)(10)(E). Resolving a persistent circuit split, the Supreme Court held that IRAs are within this exemption. Rousey v. Jacoway, 544 U.S. 320 (2005).

In 2005, Congress added a separate exemption for *accumulations* in retirement plans. This exemption is available whether the debtor elects the state or federal exemptions; it appears in §522(b)(3)(C) and again in §522(d)(12). Rather than require a judge to decide how big a retirement accumulation is "reasonably necessary," Congress set a presumptive number, rebuttable on a showing of special circumstances such as disability or unusual medical bills. The exemption for IRAs is presumptively capped at $1,283,025, indexed for inflation. §522(n). It may sound absurd to let a person keep over $1 million while discharging all his debts; certainly most Americans do not retire with $1 million stashed away. But the mandatory distribution at age 70 from a million-dollar IRA is only a little over $36,000 per year, which is less than the median income.

5. Inherited IRAs. If the owner of an IRA dies with money left in the IRA, she can leave it to her heirs as an inherited IRA. The heirs (the rules are different for a surviving spouse) are free to withdraw all the money immediately if they choose; they owe tax on the withdrawal but no tax penalty. They are required to begin taking mandatory minimum withdrawals, whatever their age. The Supreme Court unanimously held that these rules show that funds in an inherited IRA are not held for anyone's retirement, and thus are not "retirement funds" and not exempt from creditors in bankruptcy. Clark v. Rameker, 134 S. Ct. 2242 (2014).

The case involved a joint bankruptcy for a married couple. The wife had inherited a $450,000 IRA from her mother, and the account still held about $300,000 at the time of bankruptcy. That money is now available to the creditors. The effect of the decision may just be that well-advised middle-class debtors spend all the money in an inherited IRA before they file for bankruptcy.

6. Spendthrift trusts. Families can shelter wealth in spendthrift trusts, in which one person gives or bequeaths assets in trust for the benefit of another, and the trust instrument provides that neither the beneficiary nor her creditors can reach the principal. This is basically how the protection for ERISA-qualified retirement plans works, but it is also available for inheritances. Such clauses are generally enforceable against all creditors except those entitled to child or spousal support. A few states make an exception for intentional torts, but most apparently do not. A good example is Young v. McCoy, 54 Cal. Rptr. 3d 847 (Ct. App. 2007), refusing to invade a spendthrift trust to collect an award of criminal restitution on behalf of a shooting victim. Cases that illustrate the minority rule of invading spendthrift trusts to collect judgments for intentional torts are collected in Duvall v. McGee, 826 A.2d 416 (Md. 2003); *Duvall* itself rejects those cases.

7. Forfeiture? In Sommer v. Maharaj, 888 N.E.2d 891 (Mass. 2008), the court allowed plaintiff to collect his judgment out of exempt IRA assets and refused to let defendant argue her claim for exemption. This was imposed as a penalty for extreme litigation misconduct over a period of years, which consisted of concealing assets, including the IRA accounts, and defying the court's efforts to enforce its judgment.

The Supreme Court has held that bankruptcy courts have no power to override exemptions in this way. Law v. Siegel, 134 S. Ct. 1188 (2014). The reasoning was straightforward; the Bankruptcy Code spells out exemptions, and grounds for forfeiting exemptions, in great detail, and courts have no inherent power to add to the list.

The facts of Law v. Siegel were spectacular. The bankrupt debtor filed documents in his own bankruptcy, in the name of a fictitious Lili Lin, claiming a mortgage on his homestead. Had the scheme succeeded, the debtor would have retrieved all the money payable to Lili Lin—$147,000 according to the phony filings.

The trustee in bankruptcy spent more than $500,000 in attorneys' fees combatting the nonexistent Lili Lin. The debtor's only asset was $75,000 of the equity in his house, the amount that was exempt under California law. The Court said the trustee could not recover from that exempt equity. But it said the bankruptcy court could sanction the debtor for litigation misconduct, and because the misconduct occurred after the bankruptcy petition, the sanctions would not be dischargeable in the bankruptcy. Whether it is worthwhile for the trustee to spend more money pursuing that remedy, in hopes of collecting out of the debtor's post-bankruptcy income, is a very different question.

DIXIE NATIONAL BANK v. CHASE

485 So. 2d 1353 (Fla. Dist. Ct. App. 1986)

Before BARKDULL, HUBBART, and NESBITT, JJ.
    HUBBART, Judge. . . .

I . . .

On July 14, 1983, Stephen W. Chase II . . . filed a motion for a writ of garnishment against Jim Gore . . . . The motion requested that the clerk of the circuit court issue a writ of garnishment directed to the Dixie National Bank . . . and stated that: (1) on June 2, 1983, the garnishor creditor Chase received a final judgment against the defendant debtor Gore in the amount of $48,473.50, and (2) the said defendant has visible property on which levy could be made to satisfy the above judgment.

[T]he clerk of the circuit court issued a writ of garnishment directing the garnishee Dixie Bank to file and serve an answer within twenty days [stating whether the Bank was indebted to Gore at the time the writ was served, at the time the Bank answered, or at any time in between, and whether the Bank knew any other person who was indebted to Gore or in possession of Gore's property. The Bank answered on July 20:] . . .

> Garnishee is indebted to the defendant, JIM GORE, in the amount of $32.86 and it was so indebted to said [d]efendant at the time of service of this writ, at the time of this [a]nswer and between such period and it knows of no person indebted to said defendant, or who may have any of the effects of said defendant in their hands.

This disclosure was based on a bank account in the name of "Jimmy Gore" held at the garnishee Dixie Bank; . . .no other disclosure was made of any other account at the said bank—although, without dispute, the defendant debtor Gore held another bank account with the garnishee Dixie Bank entitled "Diamond M" . . . . The signator card for this account was signed—like the first account—by "Jimmy Gore" as sole signator and owner of the account. The . . . Bank had failed to discover and list the latter account in its answer due to an error in its records search. . . . Dixie Bank garnished or put a hold on the disclosed bank account upon its service of the above answer, but failed to take the same action with reference to the omitted bank account. . . .

Chase secured the service of a second writ of garnishment on the . . . Bank[,] which . . . referred to the defendant as "Jim (Jimmy) Gore or any business entities or accounts in which he has an interest or over which he has signatory authority." This writ was issued on February 17, 1984. . . . Again, the answer failed to disclose the existence of the omitted bank account . . . .

On April 13, 1984, subsequent to the filing of a reply to the above-stated answer, the . . . Bank filed . . . an amended answer [which disclosed the Diamond M account with a balance of $275 at the time of the July 1983 garnishment and a balance of $65.63 at the time of the February 1984 garnishment].

Unfortunately . . . Gore deposited a total of $13,870.61 in the above omitted bank account, and then withdrew most of it, between the time the first writ of garnishment was served . . . and the time the amended answer was served. . . .

The cause was tried below as a non-jury matter. . . . The trial court thereupon entered a final judgment in garnishment in favor of the garnishor creditor Chase and against the garnishee Dixie Bank in the amount of $13,870.61. The . . . Bank appeals.

II . . .

Fla. Stat. Ann. §77.06(1) (1983) . . . establishes the extent of a garnishee's liability to the garnishor for debts owed by the garnishee to the defendant debtor: "(1) Service of the writ [of garnishment] shall make garnishee liable for all debts due by him to defendant . . . at the time of the service of the writ or at any time between the service and the time of his answer." Upon filing its answer to a writ of garnishment, the garnishee is further required to garnish or retain any deposit of the defendant debtor which the garnishee holds. However, the amount of monies or credits so garnished may not exceed twice the amount owed by the defendant debtor to the garnishor creditor as specified in the writ of garnishment. Finally, the garnishee is fully protected from any suit [by Gore] for funds reported in its answer and garnished where the garnishee has a good faith doubt as to whether such funds should be reported and retained.

Obviously, this statutory scheme contemplates full disclosure in the garnishee's answer of all debts owed by the garnishee to the defendant debtor and a simultaneous garnishment of said funds so as to fully protect the garnishor creditor . . . . The statutory scheme cannot tolerate incomplete answers wherein only some of the debts owed are disclosed and garnished. If such answers were permissible, as the garnishee Dixie Bank contends, there would be little incentive to file complete answers; moreover, undisclosed funds would plainly remain ungarnished and could be spirited away by the defendant debtor—all to the detriment of the garnishor creditor and contrary to entire purpose of the statutory scheme.

It therefore follows that under §77.06(1), the garnishee is liable to the garnishor creditor (a) for all debts which the garnishee owes to the defendant debtor at the time the writ of garnishment is filed, and (b) for all such similar debts incurred by the said garnishee between service of the said writ and the time the garnishee serves an answer thereto disclosing all such debts owed and properly garnishes all the debtor's funds held by the garnishee. Specifically, we conclude that the term "answer" in the above statute means a *complete* answer revealing all debts owed by the garnishee to the defendant debtor. Cases in other jurisdictions have reached an identical, if not harsher result, based on similar-type garnishment statutes. . . .

III . . .

Affirmed.

NOTES ON GARNISHMENT

1. The basics. Garnishment is an independent action against a third party who owes money to the judgment debtor. The most common garnishees are banks and employers; bank accounts and wages are attractive sources of payment. The garnishee can defend on the ground that it doesn't owe the judgment debtor. It cannot question whether the judgment debtor owes the judgment creditor; that has been determined by the judgment. If the garnishee answers that it does owe the judgment debtor, judgment is entered against the garnishee, it pays the judgment creditor, and its liability to the judgment debtor is discharged.

2. The risks to the garnishee. As *Dixie Bank* illustrates, the garnishee can incur double liability or worse if it ignores or mishandles the garnishment. In many states, a garnishee that fails to answer at all becomes liable for the entire judgment against the judgment debtor—$48,000 in *Dixie Bank*. An example is Webb v. Erickson, 655 P.2d 6 (Ariz. 1982), where a writ of garnishment was served on homeowners who had sold their houses and owed real estate commissions to Erickson. A homeowner who understood the document could arrange to have the title company at the closing pay the commission to Erickson's creditor. The actual homeowner ignored the summons, let his commission be paid to Erickson, and became liable for the entire sum due to Erickson's creditor. The homeowner pleaded various extenuating circumstances and succeeded in getting the matter reopened—seven years after the original judgment against Erickson. It was not at all clear that he would be able to escape liability on remand. In Butler v. D/Wave Seafood, 791 A.2d 928 (Me. 2002), it was a bank that failed to respond on time and got stuck with liability for the entire debt.

When the garnishee disputes his liability to the judgment debtor (rarely an issue for banks), garnishment can turn into a full-scale lawsuit. When there is no dispute, the garnishee might be thought indifferent between paying his own creditor or paying his creditor's creditor. In practice, he is not indifferent; there is some expense and annoyance to being sued in garnishment, even if there is no real dispute, and there is the risk of failing to adequately respond. But banks have turned garnishment into a profit opportunity: They charge a fee for the garnishment, a fee for each bounced check that results from the garnishment, and interest and fees if they choose to lend the judgment debtor money to cover the resulting shortage of cash.

3. The hardships on the judgment debtor. Garnishing wages or bank accounts gets a debtor's attention. Debtors often respond by paying if they can. But sometimes they file for bankruptcy. A bankruptcy petition automatically stays all efforts to collect debts outside the bankruptcy court, so it terminates the garnishment order. Often, the debtor does nothing, because he can't pay and can't afford or doesn't know how to file for bankruptcy. A simple consumer bankruptcy can cost as much as $2,000 in filing fees, attorneys' fees, and fees for mandatory credit counseling.

Garnishing wages is so effective for creditors because it imposes so much hardship on debtors and their families. Congress tried to respond in the Consumer Credit Protection Act, which limits wage garnishment to 25 percent of a worker's take-home pay or the amount by which her weekly take-home pay exceeds 30 times the minimum hourly wage, whichever is less. 15 U.S.C. §1673. An exception authorizes garnishment of up to 65 percent for support of a spouse or dependent child. State restrictions on wage garnishment also have exceptions for child support. Debtors who weren't making it financially on full pay often spiral into much worse financial trouble on 75 percent of their pay. But the small amounts withheld after the exemptions may barely cover the interest. In states that permit contract interest rates to accrue on the judgment, garnishment for credit card debt and the like can continue for months or years without significantly reducing the judgment.

4. The risk to exemptions. Money in small bank accounts is often exempt because it is recently received wages, Social Security benefits, or some other source of exempt income. But consumers often don't know about their exemptions or don't know how to claim their exemptions, and banks feel no obligation to assert exemptions for their depositors or even to inquire. No doubt much exempt cash is seized in garnishment.

More generally, consumer debtors often fail to understand the legal papers served on them either before or after judgment, or fail to assert their rights in response to those papers. Some courts have held that due process requires that the summons inform judgment debtors of their exemptions and how to claim them. Cases are collected in Dorwart v. Caraway, 966 P.2d 1121, 1129-1138 (Mont. 1998). The essence of due process is notice and hearing, and it is an easy inference to hold that the notice must be in plain English. It goes considerably further to require that the notice advise defendants of their potential defenses. That may be good consumer protection policy, but is it required by due process in an adversary system? In an analogous context, involving the right to return of property held as evidence, the Supreme Court unanimously held that due process does not require the state to give "individualized notice of state-law remedies which . . . are established by published, generally available state statutes and case law." City of West Covina v. Perkins, 525 U.S. 234, 241 (1999).

Consumer debtors are of course entitled to notice of the proceedings against them. They do not always get even that. In one case, the Second Circuit approved certification of a class action alleging a conspiracy to buy consumer debt, submit false affidavits that process had been served, and obtain default judgments in every case. Sykes v. Mel S. Harris & Associates, 780 F.3d 70 (2d Cir. 2015). The district court then approved a $60 million settlement. 2016 WL 3030156 (S.D.N.Y. 2016). Mel S. Harris is a law firm; other defendants were a process-serving company and a publicly traded finance and asset-management company that allegedly bought the debt and obtained the judgments.

5. A legislative response. New York now requires the judgment creditor to send the bank two forms for claiming any applicable exemptions, with the address of the bank and the address of the creditor already filled in. The bank is required to send these forms to its depositor, by first-class mail. The forms are prescribed by statute, are written in plain English, and list the exempt sources of cash. If the debtor uses the forms to claim that some or all of the cash in the account is exempt, she must sign under penalty of perjury, and she is encouraged, but not required, to attach supporting documentation. The claim of exemption is controlling on the bank unless the judgment creditor files an objection, in which case the dispute is to be set for hearing within seven days. Judgment creditors who object without reasonable basis are liable for actual damages and attorneys' fees. N.Y. C.P.L.R. §5222-a. It seems unlikely that judgment debtors are regularly returning the form and responding to objections, but we don't know the answer to that question. Banks receiving garnishment orders are not liable for failing to send the forms. Cruz v. TD Bank, N.A., 2 N.E.3d 221 (N.Y. 2013).

6. A regulatory response. The United States now pays most federal benefits electronically, and the electronic label on most benefits that federal law exempts from garnishment now begins with XX: for example, XXSOC SEC. Banks are now required to search for that code and to protect from garnishment either the amount of any exempt benefit deposited within the sixty days preceding the search, or the balance in the account on the day of the search, whichever is less. The labeling of deposits is explained in Garnishment of Accounts Containing Federal Benefit Payments, 76 Fed. Reg. 9939, 9941 (Feb. 23, 2011); the bank regulation is Garnishment of Accounts Containing Federal Benefit Payments, 31 C.F.R. §212.1 *et seq.*

7. The reach of garnishment. New York has held that garnishment of assets in the hands of a New York bank does not reach foreign branches, or implicitly, out-of-state branches, of that bank. Motorola Credit Corp. v. Standard Chartered Bank, 21 N.E.3d 223 (N.Y. 2014). The court thought that such liability risked subjecting banks to inconsistent regulation and orders, and that it was impractical for a bank to search all its branches worldwide. The dissenter thought the rule obsolete in light of modern computers, and that any risks of inconsistent regulation or double liability could be addressed case by case.

The underlying judgment was entered in 2003 ($2.1 billion compensatory) and 2006 ($1 billion punitive). Defendants have vigorously, and apparently successfully, resisted all collection efforts. They are subject to arrest orders in the United States and the United Kingdom and have been convicted of bank fraud in Turkey, but they appear to have kept their substantial assets safe. The underlying judgment is described in section 3.A.1.

8. A safety deposit box twist. Luz Salcedo invested and lost over $1 million with Felix Rodriguez. She claimed fraud and breach of fiduciary duty, and later successfully sued Rodriguez's widow, obtaining a judgment for $895,000. As part of her effort to collect, she served a writ of garnishment on Wells Fargo Bank. Wells Fargo disclosed two bank accounts with a collective balance of about $2,000 as well as a safe deposit box in the name of the widow and her son-in-law and daughter. The trial court issued an order requiring Wells Fargo to pay the amounts from the two accounts and to make the safe deposit box available for inspection; it ordered the bank to hold the property in the box pending further order of the court. Five days after Wells Fargo received the court order, the son-in-law and daughter were given access to the box. When counsel for Salcedo showed up at the branch to inventory what was in the box, bank officials told her the contents had been removed and the account closed. The appeals court held that Wells Fargo could be liable under Florida's garnishment statute for the value of the contents of the box if Salcedo could prove the contents belonged to the widow and prove their value. Salcedo v. Wells Fargo Bank, 223 So. 3d 1099 (Fla. Ct. App. 2017). If she cannot prove what the widow had in the box, Wells Fargo may be off the hook despite its obvious fault. Banks have records of how much money passed through accounts, but they have no idea what is stored in safe deposit boxes.

NOTES ON OTHER MEANS OF COLLECTING

1. What if a solvent defendant won't pay? Execution and garnishment are the basic means of collecting judgments. Many judgment debtors have no or few non-exempt assets, so these tools are of limited utility. And sometimes solvent defendants go to great lengths to avoid paying judgments, either hiding or transferring assets. When they do, litigation to collect a judgment may be longer and more complex than the battle to get the judgment in the first place.

An extreme example is Angiodynamics, Inc. v. Biolitec AG, 880 F.3d 596 (1st Cir. 2018). Biolitec, Inc. ("BI"), a U.S. based subsidiary of a German corporation, sold medical equipment to Angiodynamics, Inc. ("AGI"), and promised to indemnify AGI for any patent infringement claims. AGI settled patent infringement claims arising from its sales of BI's equipment, and then sued BI in New York under the indemnification clause and got a $23-million judgment. Then it sued in Massachusetts, alleging that the German corporate parent had looted more than $18 million from BI to render the company judgment proof. AGI then went to federal court, and got a TRO and then a preliminary injunction barring the German parent from merging with an Austrian subsidiary. AGI alleged that U.S. judgments are unenforceable in Austria and that the merger was being done to avoid collection. The First Circuit upheld a preliminary injunction. 711 F.3d 248 (1st Cir. 2013).

Defendants completed the merger anyway. The district court ordered the merger to be undone, and issued a warrant for the arrest of BI's CEO and fines of $1 million for the first month, then $2 million for the next month, then $4 million for the following month, and then $8 million per month thereafter until the merger was undone. At the time of oral argument in the First Circuit, the fines were at $160 million and growing (another example of a court not thinking through the consequences of growing fines exponentially). The First Circuit upheld the contempt order, but remanded with directions to cap the fines at some total amount. "[W]e expect that the district court will make good on its promise to reassess the fine amount if Defendants come into compliance with the preliminary injunction." 780 F.3d 420, 428 (1st Cir. 2015).

By 2018, the district court had reduced the fines to $70 million plus interest, the First Circuit had sided with AGI on BI's fifth appeal, the district court had imposed new sanctions of up to $1 million per month for BI's failure to provide adequate answers to AGI's discovery requests seeking to find U.S. assets, 305 F. Supp. 3d 300 (D. Mass. 2018), and a sixth appeal was pending. 880 F.3d 596. The district court noted that the CEO's arrest "warrant is still outstanding. Someday, perhaps, it may result in his well-deserved apprehension." 305 F. Supp. 3d at 304.

2. Complicated intangible property. Execution is clumsy but workable with respect to tangible property. Garnishment effectively reaches simple money debts owed to the judgment debtor. Both remedies break down in more complicated situations Most wealth in modern economies is intangible, and many intangibles are held by trustees, custodians, nominees, and other sorts of third parties. Corporate stock may be represented by certificates or by electronic records, usually the latter, and defendant may have shares registered in the name of his broker, his bank, his brother-in-law, or the trustee for his pension plan.

Consider Knapp v. McFarland, 462 F.2d 935 (2d Cir. 1972). Knapp tried to collect her New York judgment against McFarland by levying on a half-million-dollar Treasury bill in possession of Chemical Bank in New York. Chemical held it as custodian for Security National Bank of Washington, D.C. Security acquired it as escrow agent for the proceeds of the sale of an apartment building in Arlington, Virginia. Defendant McFarland owned an undescribed interest in the apartment building; the extent of his interest was the subject of litigation in a Virginia state court. Chemical initially responded that it had never heard of McFarland and could not identify the property the sheriff was trying to levy on. After further investigation, it reported that it had identified McFarland and his Treasury bill, but that Security Bank had a security interest in it.

3. Creditor's bills. The common law courts largely refused to get involved in such problems. Execution was available only for land and tangible property within the jurisdiction. If the common law writs were inadequate to collect the judgment, but the judgment creditor believed the defendant had hidden or intangible assets, he could file a creditor's bill in equity. Today, most of the relief traditionally available in a creditor's bill is available on postjudgment motion.

4. Postjudgment discovery. One important remedy derived from the old creditor's bill is postjudgment discovery. The judgment creditor can ask about the judgment debtor's assets by taking his deposition or serving interrogatories. He can also get discovery from third parties who know about the judgment debtor's assets. The debtor himself may be uncooperative. Unsophisticated or defiant debtors often ignore the discovery notice. The full array of contempt sanctions, including coercive imprisonment, is available against judgment debtors who ignore a court order compelling discovery. Judgment debtors who respond to discovery sometimes lie. Or they may hide their assets very cleverly and then tell the truth, hoping the creditors won't ask the right questions.

In some states, this discovery can be conducted electronically. Judgment creditors in New York can serve "an information subpoena" on any person, posing written questions to be answered by return mail. N.Y. C.P.L.R. §5224(a)3. If the target of the subpoena agrees, the questions can be submitted electronically. §5224(a)4. This has made it possible for collection agencies to send electronic lists of all their judgment debtors to every bank in New York, asking each bank to electronically compare the list to its list of depositors. The practice, and its results, are described in Lucette Lagnado, *Cold-Case Files: Dunned for Old Bills, Poor Find Some Hospitals Never Forget*, Wall St. J. (June 8, 2004).

When a bank reports a match, the "attorney for the judgment creditor as officer of the court" serves a restraining notice under §5222(a). The notice freezes the account, up to twice the amount that the notice states is due, for a year. §5222(b). The notice can also be served electronically. §5222(g). The process slows down to first-class mail for the notice to the judgment debtor explaining how she can claim her exemptions, described in the previous set of notes.

The procedure is so cheap that it makes it worthwhile to troll repeatedly for debtors on old judgments. As the *Journal* story summarizes: "Collectors in New York once had to laboriously track down each delinquent debtor's branch bank, asking one bank after another in the debtor's neighborhood to search its files. . . . [But now] 'it is basically a blitz—you blitz all the banks,'" quoting the director of a collection agency. Judgments should not go unpaid because of the expense of collection procedures; more efficient procedures are surely to be desired. Agencies collecting child support can troll for bank accounts as easily as agencies collecting credit card debt. But it will be a challenge to make the procedures for protecting exemptions work as efficiently as the electronic means of finding accounts, and some states with similar provisions for electronic discovery have nothing like New York's procedures for protecting exemptions.

5. Turnover orders. If postjudgment discovery reveals assets readily subject to execution or garnishment, the judgment creditor can proceed with traditional remedies. If discovery reveals less accessible assets, the creditor needs another tool. In many situations, it is possible to reach assets in the hands of a third party by serving a writ or notice ordering the third party to turn over the asset. Collecting from investment securities requires physical possession of any certificate or "legal process upon the securities intermediary" who holds the security for the debtor. UCC §8-112(c). The creditor "is entitled to aid from a court of competent jurisdiction, by injunction or otherwise," in reaching the security. UCC §8-112(e). The New York court held that a New York court can order a bank to turn over assets held in Bermuda if New York has personal jurisdiction over the bank. Koehler v. Bank of Bermuda Ltd., 911 N.E.2d 825 (N.Y. 2009). The vote was 4-3; the dissenters accused the majority of creating world-wide garnishment jurisdiction in New York.

6. Freeze orders. A variation available in some states is an injunction against transferring property. N.Y. C.P.L.R. §5222. The injunction may run against the judgment debtor himself, or against a third party in possession of some of the judgment debtor's property. The injunction does not create a lien that gives the judgment creditor priority over other creditors. But it does subject the third party to liability if he fails to retain the judgment debtor's property. The injunction is mainly useful to freeze the status quo while waiting for the sheriff to levy.

7. Receivers. Perhaps the most powerful collection remedy for ordinary judgments is the appointment of a receiver to collect defendant's assets. Receivers are principally a prejudgment remedy, and we will study them primarily in that context (in section 9.B.3). But in most states, a receiver can also be appointed after judgment if it appears that a receiver could reach assets that cannot be reached by more ordinary collection methods. In some states the creditor must first try execution and have the writ returned unsatisfied; in others, it is sufficient to show that execution would be futile.

A good example is First National State Bank v. Kron, 464 A.2d 1146 (N.J. Super. 1983). Kron was a CPA with an active practice and a luxurious lifestyle. He kept no records, sent no bills, and had no assets. Or so he claimed. From time to time his clients paid him cash, and the cash was always dissipated before the bank could find out about it. After five years of unsuccessful collection efforts, the court appointed a receiver in aid of execution. Another example is Sommer v. Maharaj, 888 N.E.2d 891 (Mass. 2008), where defendants concealed assets and defied court orders for years.

How will the receiver find the assets? A receiver—typically a lawyer or a business person—has some clear advantages over a sheriff. But what advantages does he have over the plaintiff? The receiver is no panacea. But the receiver as a representative of the court might be more likely to get cooperation and information from third parties. The court's order usually vests the receiver with title to defendant's property, and that may be of some help in gaining possession. It is contempt of court to interfere with the receiver's possession, and the receiver can seek turnover orders. In addition, the receiver's expenses are chargeable to the property if it is ever found. In *Sommer*, the receiver induced mutual funds to freeze accounts while he litigated his right to the funds, and substantial litigation expenses were charged to the receiver, and thus paid with assets collected from defendants, instead of being borne by plaintiffs. These facts are explained in somewhat more detail at 843 N.E.2d 649 (Mass. App. Ct. 2006).

A receiver may be able to sell defendant's assets in an organized way, or sell his whole business as a going concern, getting much more than a series of execution sales of separate assets by competing judgment creditors. Thus receivership is sometimes used as an insolvency proceeding, to liquidate a debtor's assets and divide the proceeds among the creditors. This use of receivership has been largely replaced by bankruptcy. Some liquidations still occur in receivership proceedings, but except in unusual cases, any party can move the case to the bankruptcy court by filing a petition.

8. Setoff. In a wide range of circumstances where parties owe each other offsetting debts, the side that is not being paid may decide to "set off" the offsetting debts. If you have a loan from your bank and a deposit at your bank, the bank can set off the deposit and apply it to the loan. Less likely, if the bank fails and your deposit exceeds the limits on deposit insurance, you can set off your loan against your lost deposit. Either way, the smaller of the two obligations is eliminated, and the larger obligation is reduced to the amount of the difference between the two. This is relatively straight-forward, but it has some important wrinkles. First, it has to be fit into the priority scheme with all the other attempts to collect from bank deposits.

Second, exemption laws often make property exempt from "legal process" or some such phrase. The banks argue that setoff involves no legal process, so they can seize exempt property from depositors in payment of debts. Or they argue that depositors waived their exemptions and agreed to set off when they signed the forms to open their account. The Supreme Court has held that setoff is not "legal process" within the meaning of 42 U.S.C. §407(a), which exempts Social Security payments from creditors. Washington State Department of Social & Health Services v. Guardianship Estate of Keffeler, 537 U.S. 371 (2003). Other courts interpreting other exemption laws, and even other courts interpreting §407(a) in other contexts, have come to differing conclusions. For example, banks in California can set off against exempt deposits in an account to collect overdrafts and overdraft fees incurred in that account, but cannot set off an "independent" debt that did not arise out of that same account. Miller v. Bank of America, 207 P.3d 531 (Cal. 2009).

Students take warning: The United States can collect your student loans by with-holding your Social Security benefits—and there is no statute of limitations! Lockhart v. United States, 546 U.S. 142 (2005). The government can generally collect debts by setoff, and whatever the reach of the exemption for Social Security benefits, student loans are an exception to that exemption, and student loans are also an exception to the general ten-year statute of limitations on collection of debts owing the federal government.

9. Harassment. One traditional creditor response to judgment-proof debtors is to threaten or harass them until they pay. With respect to consumer debt, most of these techniques are barred by the Fair Debt Collection Practices Act, 15 U.S.C. §1692 *et seq.* Any deception of the debtor is also a violation. Attorneys representing creditors are subject to the Act, and thus liable for actual and statutory damages plus attorneys' fees. Heintz v. Jenkins, 514 U.S. 291 (1995).

But most of the Act applies only to "debt collectors," a term that does not include the original lender. 15 U.S.C. §1692b. And in Henson v. Santander, 137 S. Ct. 1718 (2017), the Supreme Court unanimously held that purchasers of defaulted debt who later attempt to collect the debt are not "debt collectors" for purposes of the pro-tections of the FDCPA. The holding may have been correct as a matter of statutory interpretation, but it means that the entire debt-collection industry can exempt itself from the Act by simply buying the defaulted debt rather than undertaking to collect it for a fee. Much of the industry consists of companies that buy defaulted debt, but the prevailing understanding had been that companies were exempt only if they bought the debt before default.

Some states have laws against harassment that apply to creditors exempt from the federal law; some do not. In states where original lenders are relatively free to harass debtors, bankruptcy filings are somewhat higher, but default rates are not much dif-ferent. That is, the right to harass some debtors more intensely does not appear to extract much in the way of additional payments, but it does drive some debtors to file for bankruptcy.

10. Judgment proofing. Many judgments are uncollectible by any means; debtors without assets that can be reached for collection are said to be judgment proof.

Most individuals and many businesses are judgment proof, but no one has any very clear idea how many. Professor LoPucki thinks the number may be high and growing. Lynn M. LoPucki, *The Death of Liability*, 106 Yale L.J. 1 (1996). Many individuals have no savings and no significant nonexempt assets. Many small businesses have no unencumbered assets; their largest lender has a security interest in everything.

For larger and more successful businesses, cheap computing power makes it ever easier to put assets in the hands of corporate entities different from the entity that uses the assets in activities that might generate liability. Obvious examples include parent-subsidiary relationships, equipment leasing, and contracting out ancillary services and even primary production. Affluent individuals can accumulate assets in retirement plans, spendthrift trusts, and foreign accounts.

LoPucki argues that as more and more large businesses and wealthy individuals shelter assets from their creditors, doing so becomes more socially acceptable, and the law tends to accommodate the desire to do it. His thesis is controversial; there are elaborations, responses, and rejoinders in multiple articles at 107 Yale L.J. 1363 (1998), 51 Stan. L. Rev. 147 (1998), and 52 Stan. L. Rev. 1 (1999). We do know that some states are competing for trust business by allowing people to convey assets into spendthrift trusts for their own benefit, or by making spendthrift trusts good even against ex-spouses. These developments are surveyed in Rachel Emma Silverman, *States Court Family-Trust Business*, Wall St. J. (June 22, 2006).

If LoPucki is right and the problem becomes sufficiently serious, the political pendulum may eventually swing the other way; legislators and judges could respond with more aggressive doctrines for piercing corporate veils and sham transactions, expanded use of fraudulent transfer law, compulsory liability insurance, and other efforts to make liability enforceable. Or they may not.

NOTE ON BANKRUPTCY

Many debtors respond to pressure from creditors by filing for bankruptcy. The Bankruptcy Code is long, complex, and the subject of a whole separate course. But you should not think of it as something completely apart from the ordinary collection process. All litigators ought to know something about bankruptcy. Bankruptcy is a large branch of the law of remedies — the ultimate limitation on remedies.

Bankruptcy is defendant's trump card. The mere filing of a petition automatically stays all efforts to collect debts outside of bankruptcy. 11 U.S.C. §362. Creditors who have collected money through execution, garnishment, postjudgment motion, or any other means not in the ordinary course of business, must usually return all they collected in the last 90 days before bankruptcy. §547. The same section invalidates any judgment liens or execution liens acquired in the last 90 days. The debtor in bankruptcy may turn over all his nonexempt assets to a court-appointed trustee and receive a discharge of all his debts, or make partial payments under a court supervised plan.

The threat of bankruptcy hangs over all collection efforts, affecting the tactical calculations of both debtors and creditors. A creditor may do better to accept late payments, or partial payments, if the debtor is willing to make them, rather than force the debtor into bankruptcy with aggressive collection efforts. But the creditor also has to worry that some other creditor will force a bankruptcy. If that happens, he would fare better if he had been more aggressive three months earlier.

NOTES ON COLLECTING MONEY FROM THE GOVERNMENT

1. Governments that are not immune but do not pay. Governments are often immune from damage suits. When they are not immune, they usually pay judgments voluntarily. But what should a court do when a government refuses to pay a judgment from which it is not immune? In nineteenth century cases involving municipal bonds, the Supreme Court ordered payment of cash from municipal treasuries, but it never questioned the exemption of tangible property "held for public uses." Meriwether v. Garrett, 102 U.S. (12 Otto) 472, 501 (1880). Collection of judgments against domestic governments requires a remedy other than execution. For a careful exploration of some of the modern problems, see Michael W. McConnell and Randal C. Picker, *When Cities Go Broke: A Conceptual Introduction to Municipal Bankruptcy*, 60 U. Chi. L. Rev. 425 (1993).

2. A federal remedy? Evans v. City of Chicago was a long-running litigation that illustrates the usual method for paying judgments. Under Illinois law, municipalities are liable for their torts, and obligated to pay the judgments, but they are immune from execution. Chicago appropriated $4.5 million each year to pay tort judgments, but judgments accumulated more rapidly. The city paid all judgments under $1,000 immediately, and it paid the rest in the order they accrued, with interest at 6 percent. In September 1979, with market interest rates much higher than 6 percent, the city was paying judgments entered in October 1975.

The Seventh Circuit initially held that the discrimination against judgments over $1,000 was irrational and violated equal protection, and that the delay in payment took property without due process; it ordered the city to pay judgments immediately. 689 F.2d 1286 (7th Cir. 1982). A different set of judges eventually vacated that judgment, finding no federal right to payment of a judgment on a state law claim. 10 F.3d 474 (7th Cir. 1993).

3. A state remedy? Meanwhile, an Illinois trial court found another way to collect judgments against municipalities: It awarded a tort victim title to the city hall and a city-owned industrial park. The appellate court returned the city hall but not the industrial park, which was apparently not in operation. Estate of DeBow v. City of East St. Louis, 592 N.E.2d 1137 (Ill. App. Ct. 1992). The lead opinion said that the city hall was essential to government, and therefore exempt from execution, but that the industrial park was not. One judge would have let plaintiff keep both properties; one would have given both properties back to the city.

The city had also attempted to pay the judgment by issuing bonds, payable to plaintiff's estate through 2004. The estate in the case caption is a form of guardianship; plaintiff's injuries required permanent custodial care. East St. Louis is one of the most impoverished cities in the country; it doesn't have money to pick up garbage, let alone to pay tort judgments.

4. Funding the cost of structural injunctions. The judgments in *Evans* and *DeBow* were ordinary money judgments. The problem is somewhat different when the court is trying to get the state to raise the money to implement a structural injunction. Those orders are usually written in terms of conditions to be achieved or reforms to be implemented, and not in terms of a specific amount of money. That makes them easily subject to the process of bargaining and partial compliance described by Professor Diver in section 9.A.1, and that process usually blunts head-on collisions with the contempt power. But sometimes an order is sufficiently specific to create the direct collision that courts and defendants try to avoid. The most extreme example is Missouri v. Jenkins, 495 U.S. 33 (1990) (*Jenkins II*), discussed in Notes on Paying for the Remedy in section 4.A.4, where the Court ordered the school district to raise taxes beyond the limits imposed by state law.

5. The need for an appropriation. One recurring feature of these cases is the triangular relationship between the federal court, the state executive, and the state legislature. Even if there is money, state law requires an appropriation before that money can be spent. Fortunately, legislatures often appropriate large sums to the general purposes of a department. Thus, the executive has some discretion, and courts can order that this discretion be used to remedy violations.

But what if the legislature focuses on the specific item and denies the appropriation? An example is Hook v. Arizona Department of Corrections, 107 F.3d 1397 (9th Cir. 1997), where the legislature expressly prohibited any payment for the fees or expenses of masters appointed by federal courts. The court of appeals held that because the masters had been found necessary to enforce the Constitution, the federal court order overrode the state statute, and the Eleventh Amendment was no barrier because the funds were needed to secure prospective compliance. Citing a "continuous history of noncompliance," it also affirmed coercive contempt fines of $10,000 for each day the state officials refused to pay the masters' bills.

The court in *Hook* relied squarely on the Supremacy Clause to override the state-law need for an appropriation. In Halderman v. Pennhurst State School & Hospital, 673 F.2d 628 (3d Cir. 1982) (en banc), the court relied heavily on the defendant official's complicity; she had implicitly invited the appropriations rider prohibiting payment of the master. The court also suggested that the governor should have item vetoed the rider.

What result if the legislature overrode the veto? That happened in Delaware Valley Citizens' Council v. Pennsylvania, 678 F.2d 470 (3d Cir. 1982). The court held the Commonwealth of Pennsylvania in contempt and cut off federal highway funds as a sanction. Pennsylvania could be named as a defendant because the United States was a plaintiff.

One district court held the governor in contempt for not using his best efforts to get the money from the legislature. The court of appeals reversed. It thought that courts should not try to raise large sums of money to reform institutions; rather, they should give the state the choice of reforming the institution or closing it. New York State Association for Retarded Children v. Carey, 631 F.2d 162 (2d Cir. 1980).

2.   *Coercive Collection of Money*

IN RE MARRIAGE OF LOGSTON

469 N.E.2d 167 (Ill. 1984)

RYAN, Chief Justice: . . .

Eugene Logston appeals from orders of the circuit court of St. Clair County that were issued during proceedings instituted by his former wife, Kate Logston. To enforce the maintenance provision of their dissolution-of-marriage judgment, Kate initiated contempt proceedings against Eugene. . . . [T]he trial court determined a maintenance arrearage, entered judgment for that amount, and found Eugene in contempt of court for his failure to pay. . . .

Eugene . . . claimed that all of his monthly income—which consists of social security, a private pension, and a disability insurance benefit—is exempt from judgment under Ill. Rev. Stat. ch. 110, ¶12-1001 (1983). The statute he cited exempts specific personal property, as well as a debtor's right to receive certain types of income, from "judgment, attachment or distress for rent." . . . [T]he trial court rejected this defense . . . .

Eugene and Kate Logston were married in 1966, and they resided together until eight months before their marriage was dissolved in January 1981. No children were born during the marriage. At the time of the divorce, Eugene was fifty-two years old and had been retired, due to poor health, for four years. Kate was fifty years old and had not worked since 1974.

Just before the dissolution of marriage, the Logstons owned their marital home, the house next door, and one vacant lot. Their total equity in the real estate was $42,000. They also owned stock valued at $800, automobiles, and various home furnishings. Kate had no income, and Eugene received a total of $813.32 per month in payments from social security, a private pension, and disability insurance. . . .

Kate was awarded the stock, but she retained no interest in Eugene's right to receive pension or disability benefits. Instead, Eugene was ordered to pay her $221.50 per month as maintenance . . . . [T]he parties agreed that Kate would pay $21,000 to Eugene . . . for quitclaim deeds conveying to her his interest in the [real] property. Kate was allowed to deduct from the $21,000 certain sums that Eugene owed her, so her actual payment to him was $16,887.

From December 1980 through May 1983, Eugene paid no maintenance to Kate. However, in August 1981, the trial court found a $1,993.50 arrearage . . . . The court reduced this amount to judgment, and, during the next year, a total of $1,937.40 was paid to Kate through garnishment proceedings against Eugene's disability insurer. When the court issued the May 1983 order from which Eugene now appeals, the total arrearage had grown to $4,707.60, with Eugene being ordered to either pay $4,043.10 within thirty days or serve a jail sentence of not more than six months.

At the time of the hearing, Eugene was still unable to work. He had remarried, and his new wife taught school but would soon retire. For the present, however, she earned a net monthly income from teaching of $1,457, plus an average of $85 per month from part-time work. Eugene resided with her in a house that she owned.

Eugene's petition, as well as his answers to interrogatories, indicate that his income had decreased since his divorce from Kate. However, further examination during the hearing disclosed that his monthly income actually had increased since the dissolution of marriage and now totaled $922.44.

Eugene's financial statement indicates that . . . he owned no real estate but did possess a small amount of cash and $500 of equity in a motorcycle. He had owned a 1978 Chevrolet truck, valued at under $3,000, but had signed the title over to his present wife to help her obtain a loan for a recreational vehicle. Concerning the $16,887 that Kate paid him for his interest in their real estate, he testified that he used about $5,500 to repay debts and spent the remainder during a trip to California.

The financial statement shows that Eugene reported monthly expenses of $80 for rent; $185 for utilities; $365 for automobile expenses; $150 for food; $70 for clothing and laundry; and $160 for recreation, gifts, hobbies, and the costs of volunteer work. The statement also lists monthly obligations on installment contracts which total $816.47. During Eugene's testimony at the hearing, it became apparent that some monthly expenses that he had listed on his written financial statement were costs shared with his present wife, rather than expenses that he alone incurred each month. His testimony revealed that the $816.47 in monthly installment obligations represented payments on an automobile, a motorcycle, a recreational vehicle, and a $7,500 loan obtained to remodel his wife's kitchen. The trial judge and both parties' counsel questioned Eugene about these expenses, but his responses failed to clarify whether he actually paid each of these amounts each month or whether, instead, his wife shared or fully paid the installment debts. Eugene testified to extensive health problems. However, his responses to cross-examination revealed that health insurance fully paid his hospital expenses, and that Medicare paid a portion of his other medical and dental costs.

When Kate Logston testified, she was unemployed and had not worked since her divorce. . . . She still owned the two houses; her invalid mother lived with her in one, and for the other she received $350 per month in rent. . . . [H]er mother received a $600 monthly pension, which was available to help Kate pay expenses. Because her mother required extensive care, Kate could not obtain a job that would require her to leave home for more than a few hours at a time. . . .

We first address ¶12-1001 and the question whether Eugene may use the exempt status of his income as a defense to the contempt order. . . .

Paragraph 12-1001 indeed refers to each source of Eugene's income:

> The following personal property, owned by the debtor, is exempt from judgment, attachment or distress for rent: . . .
>> (g) The debtor's right to receive:
>>> (1) a social security benefit . . .
>>> (3) a disability, illness, or unemployment benefit . . .
>>> (5) a payment under any pension plans or contracts, to the extent necessary
>> for the support of the debtor and any dependent of the debtor . . .

Ill. Rev. Stat. ch. 110, ¶12-1001 (1983). Since Eugene's social security, pension, and disability insurance benefits are clearly listed in the statute, we must decide whether the language protects against a contempt order issued to enforce a maintenance obligation. . . .

Exempt property is that which is free from liability to processes such as seizure and sale, or attachment, to satisfy debts. Legislative intent is unambiguous insofar as ¶12-1001 "exempts" specified property from certain proceedings against the debtor.

The legislature's intent is not so clear, however, with respect to its use of the word "judgment." Standing alone as a legal term, "judgment" has a well-settled definition. It is a court's official decision with respect to the rights and obligations of the parties to a lawsuit. A judgment, of course, may require one party to pay money to another. This money judgment, however, only states that a party must pay a particular sum. The judgment does not specify the income or property from which the judgment debtor must satisfy the obligation.

If the judgment goes unpaid, it may be enforced through the remedy of execution, whereby as much of the debtor's property may be taken and sold as is necessary to satisfy the obligation. Until the execution process begins, however, "[n]o judgment shall bind the goods and chattels of the person against whom it is entered." Ill. Rev. Stat. ch. 110, ¶12-111 (1983). Thus, while a money judgment concerns the parties' rights and obligations, it cannot of itself attach to a particular item of the judgment debtor's property.

In this way, a money judgment differs from attachment and distress for rent, processes from which ¶12-1001 also exempts a debtor's property. Attachment is a remedy by which a defendant's property is secured and held to satisfy a debt that the plaintiff hopes to prove, while distress for rent denotes a landlord's right to seize a tenant's property in lieu of unpaid rent. Since attachment and distress for rent are both proceedings against property, the legislature's intent is clear insofar as ¶12-1001 exempts certain property from these processes. But with respect to a money judgment, which concerns property only indirectly, the legislative purpose is more obscure. . . .

[A]ll property of the debtor was subject to execution at common law. American legislatures viewed the debtor with more compassion, however, and, as a result, all fifty States now have enacted personal property exemption statutes. In 1843, the Illinois legislature adopted the predecessor to ¶12-1001. . . . As the policy underlying that early enactment, this court cited "the humane principle, that a creditor should not wholly deprive the husband and father of the means of supporting his family, usually helpless in themselves, and preventing them from becoming a public charge." Good v. Fogg, 61 Ill. 449, 451 (1871). Much the same purpose is attributed to exemption legislation today . . . .

From 1843 until quite recently, the Illinois personal property exemption statute underwent occasional changes but maintained the same basic format. It allowed the debtor to keep certain named items, such as clothing and family pictures, as well as specified dollar amounts of other personalty. . . . [T]he statute exempted property from "levy and sale on any execution, writ of attachment, or distress for rent.". . .

In 1978, however, during an overall effort to modernize Illinois statutes, . . . the legislature abolished the use of common law writs in Illinois practice. Certified copies of orders and judgments for the payment of money would now replace documents such as writs of execution and attachment.

Consequently, the legislature amended a series of civil practice statutes to eliminate all references to writs. One such amendment affected the personal property exemption statute, so that property which before was exempt from "execution, writ of attachment and distress for rent," now was exempt from "judgment, attachment or distress for rent.". . .

[Illinois exemptions were expanded in 1981.] After amendment, ¶12-1001 no longer exempted only a few personal possessions and finite amounts of other personalty. It now also exempted the debtor's right to receive certain types of income, such as the social security, pension, and disability insurance benefits that are at issue in the case at bar. . . .

Illinois, like the other forty-nine States, has long regarded contempt as an appropriate sanction for wilful failure to pay alimony or child support. This procedure is authorized throughout the Illinois Marriage and Dissolution of Marriage Act, which refers often to contempt as a means of enforcing its provisions, e.g., Ill. Rev. Stat. ch. 40, ¶505(b) (1983) (child support). We believe it unlikely that the legislature, with neither express nor other evidence of intent, meant to limit this long-standing use of the contempt power when it enacted the amendments to the exemption statute that are discussed above. . . .

Finally, . . . we consider a recently enacted statutory scheme which provides our courts with a new tool for enforcing maintenance and support awards. Under the new legislation, courts may order that the income of a nonpaying former spouse be withheld at the source and paid instead to the party to whom support is owed. Ill. Rev. Stat. ch. 40, ¶706.1(F) (1983). Significantly, this enactment applies to "any form of periodic payment to an individual, regardless of source, including, but not limited to: wages, salary, . . . disability, annuity, and retirement benefits, and any other payments, made by any person, private entity, federal or state government." ¶706.1(A)(4). This provision took effect on January 1, 1984, but courts may apply it to collect an arrearage that accumulated before the effective date. ¶706.1(A)(1)(a), (A)(2).

The new scheme would subject to withholding orders Eugene Logston's income from his General Motors pension and from his disability benefits. It indeed would be anomalous to construe the personal property exemption statute as protecting

Eugene from a contempt order, when his arrearage can now be collected from the very income on which he bases his exemption argument. The new statute also provides that any other State or local laws which limit or exempt income *shall not apply.* ¶706.1(A)(4)(e). . . .

[W]e hold that ¶12-1001 is not a defense to the order which held Eugene in contempt for nonpayment of maintenance. The fact that the trial court also entered judgment for the maintenance arrearage does not alter this result. Whether execution on that judgment may be had against exempt personal property is not at issue here. We conclude only that the contempt order may be enforced. . . .

We next address [Eugene's] second argument, that because he is unable to meet the maintenance obligation, his failure to pay is not wilful.

The power to enforce an order to pay money through contempt is limited to cases of wilful refusal to obey the court's order. The noncompliance with an order to pay maintenance constitutes prima facie evidence of contempt. . . . [O]nce the prima facie showing is made, the burden shifts to the defendant, who may then defend by showing that he is unable to pay. . . .

It is undisputed that Eugene Logston never has voluntarily paid maintenance. . . . This court has described the burden of proof that a defendant must meet to rebut the prima facie showing:

> He who seeks to establish the fact that his failure to pay is the result of lack of funds must show with reasonable certainty the amount of money he has received. He must then show that that money has been disbursed in paying obligations and expenses which, under the law, he should pay before he makes any payment on the decree for alimony. It is proper that he first pay his bare living expenses; but whenever he has any money in his possession that belongs to him and which is not absolutely needed by him for the purpose of obtaining the mere necessaries of life, it is his duty to make a payment on this decree.

Shaffner v. Shaffner, 72 N.E. 447, 449 (1904). We are not satisfied that Eugene has met the requirements described above.

The record shows Eugene's monthly income with reasonable certainty. However, the evidence he presented is conflicting and incomplete with regard to his monthly disbursements. We cannot discern how much he actually pays each month for necessities such as rent and medical care. Nor can we tell whether he diverts some monthly income to payments for nonessential items, such as the recreational vehicle or the improvements to his wife's kitchen. We do know, however, that he spends $160 each month for recreation, gifts, hobbies, and the costs of volunteer work. We also know that during the period that the $4,043.10 arrearage here accumulated, Eugene spent a lump sum of cash in excess of $11,000 on a trip to California. We regard none of these expenditures as the "bare living expenses" that may be paid before the maintenance obligation is met. . . .

[T]he trial court neither abused its discretion nor reached a decision contrary to the manifest weight of the evidence when it rejected Eugene's defense of inability to pay and found him in wilful contempt of court. . . .

One final matter merits our attention. When a party is found in civil contempt of court, . . . the contempt order is coercive in nature. The court seeks only to secure obedience to its prior order. Since the contempt order is coercive rather than punitive, the civil contemnor must be provided with the "keys to his cell." That is, he must be allowed to purge himself of contempt even after he has been imprisoned. Accordingly, imprisonment for a definite period of time is improper in this situation.

The orders from which Eugene Logston appeals do not comport with these principles. The March 1983 order sentences him to not more than six months in jail, but allows him to purge himself of contempt and avoid this sentence by paying the arrearage within thirty days of the date of the order. The May 1983 order, issued on the denial of Eugene's motion for reconsideration, is silent as to the jail sentence but provides that Eugene may purge himself by paying the arrearage within thirty days of the date of the May order. Neither order provides for Eugene's release from jail if he should pay the arrearage after he is incarcerated. On remand, the contempt order should be revised to correct this problem. . . .

The circuit court is affirmed with respect to its finding of contempt . . . . The cause is remanded. . .for further proceedings consistent with this opinion. . . .

NOTES ON COLLECTING FAMILY SUPPORT

1. Family support as a special case. In the usual means of collecting money judgments, defendant is not ordered to pay. Family support is different: The court orders defendant to pay, and it can enforce the order with the contempt power. Unlike most other creditors, children have no capacity to support themselves, and the legal system is far more aggressive about collecting child support than about collecting ordinary debts. But the problem is intractable; courts may go too far in some ways and not far enough in others, and much child support still goes uncollected. What are the advantages and disadvantages of ordering defendant to pay and sending him to jail if he doesn't?

2. The impossibility defense. Do you think it's possible for Eugene Logston to comply with the order to pay $4,043 in 30 days? (A dollar in 1984 would be worth $2.46 in 2018.) It is more common to deal with support arrearages with installment plans. The Texas statute on child support arrearages requires monthly payments that will eliminate the arrearages over two years, or monthly payments 20 percent greater than the regular monthly payment—whichever is greater—but not to exceed 50 percent of defendant's disposable income. Tex. Family Code §158.003-158.004. The arrearages bear interest at 6 percent, §157.265, and many defendants can never catch up. Would it be possible for Eugene to comply with court-ordered installments large enough to catch up on his obligations?

What is the significance of the fact that it would have been possible for him to pay if he had paid the much smaller amount due each month, or if he had not blown $11,000 on a trip to California? Those offenses might have been contempt of court, and he may be subject to punishment in criminal contempt for having committed them. But should they be a basis for coercive civil contempt? Is the wasted $11,000 relevant to deciding whether it is now possible for him to comply with the injunction?

Inability to pay is a defense to both civil and criminal contempt, although coercive contempt should focus on present ability and criminal contempt on past ability. Judges commonly state in open court the stern standard announced in *Logston*, but effective enforcement of such a standard has been rare. The current Texas statute provides that a parent pleading inability to pay must prove that he cannot pay, that he has no property that could be sold or mortgaged to raise the money, that he has attempted unsuccessfully to borrow the money, and that he knows of no source from which the money could be borrowed or legally obtained. Tex. Family Code §157.008(c).

The Michigan Supreme Court set forth a non-exhaustive list of factors to consider to determine impossibility in a child support case:

whether the defendant has diligently sought employment; whether the defendant can secure additional employment, such as a second job; whether the defendant has investments that can be liquidated; whether the defendant has received substantial gifts or an inheritance; whether the defendant owns a home that can be refinanced; whether the defendant has assets that can be sold or used as loan collateral; whether the defendant prioritized the payment of child support over the purchase of nonessential, luxury, or otherwise extravagant items; and whether the defendant has taken reasonable precautions to guard against financial misfortune and has arranged his or her financial affairs with future contingencies in mind, in accordance with one's parental responsibility to one's child.

People v. Likine, 823 N.W.2d 50, 70-71 (Mich. 2012).

Sometimes ability to pay is clear. Consider Melamed v. Melamed, 50 N.E.3d 669 (Ill. App. Ct. 2016). Ex-husband claimed he could not pay the full amount of child support demanded by his wife given that he was unemployed. The court found his claims not credible. Ex-husband controlled an investment account at Morgan Stanley worth over $2 million and regularly made withdrawals from it to support his lifestyle with multiple unmortgaged properties and expensive cars. There are many more defendants with modest incomes. And at all income levels, defendants often have weak money management skills; spending restraint that is entirely possible may be unlike anything defendant has ever accomplished.

3. Litigating ability to pay. Can ability to pay be litigated with reasonable fairness and accuracy and at reasonable cost in proceedings where defendant's liberty is at stake? What should the court examine in determining ability to pay? Is it enough to know defendant's assets and income flow? What if his expenses exceed his income? Doesn't the court have to assess the legitimacy of those expenses? Otherwise, a defendant who is making payments on a Rolls Royce isn't able to pay his child support. There is no way to avoid these inquiries, but they lead to endless wrangling over ability to pay, with courts reviewing personal budgets line by line. The Texas courts have said that a defendant must "reduce to the absolute minimum the expenditures for himself and the children in his home," if that is necessary to pay support for other children outside the home. Ex parte Kollenborn, 276 S.W.2d 251, 254 (Tex. 1955). Under that standard, one appellate court rejected a mother's claims of inability to pay because she had not explained why it was necessary to live by herself in a $160-a-month apartment or maintain a car that required a $106 monthly payment and $40 a month in gas. Ondrusek v. Ondrusek, 561 S.W.2d 236, 238 (Tex. Civ. App. 1978). Multiply by 4.01 to get 2018 dollars.

4. Due process. A defendant at risk of incarceration in a civil contempt proceeding to collect child support is not entitled to court-appointed counsel. But he is entitled to other procedural safeguards. Turner v. Rogers, 564 U.S. 431 (2011). The Court suggested notice to defendant that ability to pay is a crucial issue, a form to elicit financial information, an opportunity at a hearing to respond to questions about his financial status, and an express finding by the court that defendant has the ability to pay. The Court said that other safeguards would be acceptable if they provided as much protection as these four safeguards provide in combination.

Justices Thomas, Scalia, and Alito, and Chief Justice Roberts, would not have reached any question other than the right to counsel, and Thomas and Scalia seemed to think that the Court's procedural safeguards were a bad idea. They emphasized that deadbeat dads often have hidden income that is revealed only by the threat of going to jail. Turner had held eight jobs in three years, which made it difficult for wage withholding orders to keep up, and he had sold drugs for two years while paying no child support. *Id.* at 460 n.6 (Thomas, J., dissenting). Both the majority and the dissent emphasized that the plaintiff in the case was a single mom who was also poor and unrepresented by counsel. The Court reserved the question of cases in which plaintiff was a government agency.

An empirical study of the effect of the Court's four safeguards indicates that they have not accomplished much, at least in South Carolina. Elizabeth G. Patterson, *Turner in the Trenches: A Study of How Turner v. Rogers Affected Child Support Contempt Proceedings*, 25 Geo. J. Poverty. L. & Pol'y 75 (2017). Both before and after *Turner*, nearly 70% of indigent or unemployed child-support obligors were held in contempt and sent to jail.

5. Limiting expenses by prohibiting marriage. A Wisconsin statute took the obligation to minimize unnecessary expenses to its logical conclusion: It provided that a parent obligated to support minor children not in his custody could not marry without permission of a court. Permission could be granted only if the applicant was in compliance with the child support order and could show that the existing children were not likely to become public charges. The Supreme Court held the statute an unconstitutional burden on the right to marry. Zablocki v. Redhail, 434 U.S. 374 (1978).

6. Limiting expenses by prohibiting reproduction. There was some talk in *Zablocki* about how the statute didn't really serve the legislative purpose, because couples denied marriage licenses could conceive illegitimate children. So Wisconsin attempted to prohibit further reproduction by noncustodial parents who weren't supporting their children. State v. Oakley, 629 N.W.2d 200, *amended on rehearing*, 635 N.W.2d 760 (Wis. 2001).

a. No new children. Oakley was the father of nine children by four women; he pled no contest to three counts of intentionally refusing to pay child support, and agreed that four additional counts could be considered at sentencing. He was sentenced to three years in prison, plus five years' probation, with the probation condition that he "cannot have any more children unless he demonstrates that he had the ability to support them and that he is supporting the children he already had." 629 N.W.2d at 203. The planned method of enforcement was apparently that if he fathers a child without permission, he would be returned to prison for the remainder of the five-year term.

The majority upheld the probation condition, emphasizing that the offense was intentional refusal to pay, not inability to pay. But the probation condition, at least as paraphrased by the majority, was no reproduction without ability to pay. Is that condition constitutional? If the condition were that he not intentionally refuse to pay, would that condition be constitutional? Doesn't *Zablocki* mean that there are constitutional limits on the power to regulate debtors' lives, even in child support cases? State regulation of reproduction is deeply alarming, associated with totalitarian regimes. But isn't there also something wrong with a constitutional right to produce unlimited numbers of children that someone else must support? It seems unlikely that Oakley's paternities are carefully planned; if he is unable to avoid fathering children, could the state order him sterilized?

b. No sex without permission. The probation condition in a later Wisconsin case ordered defendant not to have sex with any woman until his probation agent was "convinced" that he would either "accept responsibility for any offspring" or use contraception, and that he had informed his prospective partner of his record of not paying child support. The court upheld these conditions. State v. Henriksen, 2004 WL 2533875 (Wis. Ct. App. 2004).

c. Reasonable steps to avoid further children. An Ohio trial court ordered a defendant convicted of five felonies for failure to pay child support to "make all reasonable efforts to avoid impregnating a woman during the [five-year] community control period or until such time that [defendant] can prove to the Court that he is able to provide support for his children he already has and is in fact supporting the children or until a change in conditions warrant[s] the lifting of this condition." An Ohio appellate court reversed to give the defendant a chance to raise constitutional arguments against this condition. State v. Anderson, 2018 WL 603714 (Ohio Ct. App. Jan. 29, 2018).

7. Maximizing income. Is it enough to examine expenses? What about the possibility of getting more income?

a. Among the poor. Consider Johansen v. State, 491 P.2d 759, 767-769 (Alaska 1971):

> Appellant is an Alaskan Native born in the Native village of Ekuk and raised in the nearby Native fishing village of Dillingham. . . . [H]e is uneducated. Appellant's experience is sharply limited. His whole life, with the exception of four years in the military, has been spent in the village. His only occupation has been fishing, except for some very limited experience as a waiter in Dillingham working a few nights a month as work was available. He has been trained for no other occupation but fishing.
>
> Appellant's last good fishing season, when he cleared $3,200, was in 1965, before his divorce. Since that time he has cleared no more than $700 in any year because of poor fishing conditions. . . .
>
> [W]e cannot agree with the trial judge's suggestion that appellant leave his home in Dillingham and seek employment in an urban community, such as the city of Anchorage. There is no indication from the record that such a move would hold a promise of success within appellant's inherent but unexercised capabilities. Rather, it seems that it would be a gamble, based on little more than hope, that an untrained person could earn more in an urban environment doing an undetermined job than he could in his home locality at his life-long occupation.
>
> We need not close our eyes to the serious problem of unemployment in the city of Anchorage [or to] the wide ranges of difference between life in rural Alaska and life in the city. . . .
>
> We hesitate now to adopt a rule allowing a superior court to force a man to move from one community to another, in the process renouncing his life-long occupation to seek an undetermined one, on the penalty of being found in contempt for failure to do so. In short, leaving Dillingham to seek employment elsewhere would be outside the reasonable effort we require of a father in such cases. . . .
>
> On the other hand, we hold there is a jury question as to the existence of a lawful excuse for non-compliance with the child support order while the appellant resides in Dillingham. In Houger v. Houger, 449 P.2d 766, 770 (Alaska 1969), we spoke of a father's primary and continuing obligation to support his children and of the fact that the inability of a father to engage in his chosen trade may not excuse him from that obligation. We said:
>
> > But there may be other kinds of work which appellee could engage in despite any disability he may have. . . . [T]here is no room for professional or occupational pride where the duty of child support is involved.
>
> We adhere to *Houger* and hold that in a contempt action such as we have here, the father will not be permitted to succeed on the defense of having a legitimate reason or excuse for not complying with an order of child support where he has not made a reasonable effort to employ his earning capacity in directions other than the one he has chosen as his chief means of livelihood.

Should it matter that there was high unemployment in Anchorage? If it were more likely that moving to Anchorage would lead to higher income, should Johansen have to go? Or should courts not intrude into some lifestyle choices? Even if a child is going hungry?

b. Among the voluntarily poor. What if Johansen were a professional capable of earning a substantial income, but he quit work and became penniless to avoid paying child support or alimony? Faced with that situation, courts have ordered support based on earning capacity rather than earnings. An example is Milazzo-Panico v. Panico, 929 A.2d 351 (Conn. App. Ct. 2007), where defendant was working informally for his father for irregular and unreported pay and substantial assets had disappeared. The California court overruled a line of cases prohibiting such orders. Moss v. Superior Court, 950 P.2d 59 (Cal. 1998). It said that holding a parent in contempt for failure to seek or accept work is not involuntary servitude, because the parent retains complete choice of employer, occupation, and location. The court also said that child support is not a debt within the meaning of the state constitutional ban on imprisonment for debt.

The court went further in Lopez v. Ajose, 2005 WL 1160191 (N.Y. Sup. Ct. 2005), *aff'd in relevant part*, 824 N.Y.S.2d 113 (App. Div. 2006). Defendant was a graduate of Columbia Law School; the amount of child support was set while he was a first-year associate at a New York law firm. But he never made more than token payments, and he lost that job when it took him four tries to pass the New York bar exam. When he finally passed, he did not apply for admission to the bar and instead enrolled in divinity school. The court held him in contempt, ordered him to apply for bar admission and get a job, and said that if he still wanted to go to divinity school, he could go to night school. Contempt for switching from a higher paying to a lower paying profession is far more intrusive than contempt for refusing to work at all, and especially when the lower paying occupation is specially protected by the state and federal free exercise clauses. But the judges in this case may also have thought defendant was just a scofflaw, and that the interest in divinity school was less than sincere.

8. What if friends or relatives can pay? Consider In re MH, 662 S.W.2d 764, 768 (Tex. Ct. App. 1983), a probation revocation case. Defendant was a 15-year-old unwed mother who had been ordered to attend school and pay restitution as conditions of probation. Her father was in prison and her mother was unemployed. The court rejected her defense of inability to pay, in part because her mother could have paid a little. Should the daughter be imprisoned because the mother didn't pay?

In these probation revocation cases, Texas has since shifted to the state the burden of proving that failure to pay was intentional. In re JM, 133 S.W.3d 721 (Tex. Ct. App. 2003). That might have helped MH. But in most jurisdictions, inability to pay remains an affirmative defense to contempt, with the burden of proof on defendant.

9. The empirical evidence. Whatever the difficulties, coercing payment collects more child support. In Dane County, Wisconsin, where contempt remedies were available but had to be pursued by the custodial parent, about half of all child support was collected in the first year after it was ordered. That declined to about a quarter in the sixth year. By contrast, in Genesee County, Michigan, where a public agency vigorously pursued child support and jailed parents who failed to pay, 67 percent was collected in the first year and 72 percent in the sixth year. The data are from separate studies by different scholars; they are reported in David L. Chambers, *Men Who Know They Are Watched: Some Benefits and Costs of Jailing for Nonpayment of Support*, 75 Mich. L. Rev. 900, 923, 926 (1977). Professor Chambers found that hardly anyone was so poor that the threat of jail didn't induce him to pay more. David L. Chambers, *Making Fathers Pay* 118-119 (Univ. Chicago Press 1979).

10. New forms of coercion. These traditional means of collecting child support have been greatly augmented by federal legislation that requires states (as a condition of accepting certain federal funds) to create a vast array of enforcement mechanisms. 42 U.S.C. §651 *et seq.* All states have enacted a version of the Uniform Interstate Family Support Act to comply with these federal mandates.

State courts, and a state administrative agency responsible for child support enforcement, must direct that child support be collected through wage withholding payable directly from the employer to the state agency, which then distributes the money to the custodial parent. §666(b). States must require employers to report all new hires, §653a(2)(b), and fine employers who retaliate against employees subject to wage-withholding orders required by the statute. §666(b)(6)(D). The enforcement agency must have in place 19 procedures set out in §666(a), some for establishing paternity but most for collection, including authority to suspend driver's licenses and professional and occupational licenses. The agency must have data-match programs with financial institutions, so that the state can identify accounts opened by parents who owe child support. The Act makes Social Security and tax records available to locate parents who change jobs and disappear. §653(b), 26 U.S.C. §6103(*l*)(6). Parents more than $2,500 in arrears cannot get a new passport and may have their existing passport revoked, 42 U.S.C. §652(k); this provision has been upheld against constitutional attack. Weinstein v. Albright, 261 F.3d 127 (2d Cir. 2001). A federal Office of Child Support Enforcement oversees all the state agencies; its website is *www.acf.hhs.gov/programs/cse.*

We have relied on Laycock's Texas colleague Jack Sampson to explain how these means of collection have worked. Wage withholding and public enforcement have dramatically increased the amount of child support collected, but it is far from solving the problem. The expertise and aggressiveness of the state agency matters; Texas improved collections many fold when it moved the job from the welfare department to the Attorney General. Wage withholding is relatively ineffectual against the self-employed, the unemployed, and the casually or irregularly employed; these groups may include a third of all parents owing child support. It is common in middle-class divorces for the custodial parent to agree not to send the wage withholding order to the paying parent's employer, so long as payments are current. But she has a signed court order if she needs it.

When the noncustodial parent falls behind in payments, the full range of old and new remedies is available: money judgment with execution, garnishment, and the other collection devices; contempt; and belatedly delivering the wage withholding order. Once the custodial parent has to go to court, either through the state agency or, less commonly, with a private attorney, she may as well ask for the full range of remedies. So contempt litigation of the sort illustrated in *Logston* has not been eliminated, and it is still the remedy of choice against the one-third of defendants hard to reach through wage withholding. An example, with a lawyer jailed for contempt for not paying her child support, is In re Hammond, 155 S.W.3d 222 (Tex. Ct. App. 2004). Revocation of licenses is a form of coercion that might be much cheaper to administer than imprisonment, and therefore more easily used and more credible as a threat. Some states have reported good success collecting child support and student loans in this way.

11. Displacing other creditors. Routine wage withholding for child support means less wage garnishment for other creditors. States must grant priority to wage withholding for child support over any other legal process against the same wages. 42 U.S.C. §666(b)(7). But the Consumer Credit Protection Act, described in the Notes on Garnishment in section 9.B.1, limits garnishment for matters other than child or spousal support to 25 percent of the worker's take-home pay. A child support order will take up all or most of that 25 percent, displacing prior garnishment orders and limiting or precluding future ones.

NOTES ON COERCING THE PAYMENT OF MONEY IN OTHER CONTEXTS

1. Victim restitution laws. The other important context in which we order defendants to pay is in the sentencing of convicted criminals. Defendants are often ordered to pay full or partial compensation to their victims; these payments are referred to as restitution, although they are nearly always measured by the victim's loss and the criminal's ability to pay, and not by the criminal's gain. The payments are usually made a condition of probation; if defendant fails to pay, probation can be revoked and defendant sent to prison. In Bearden v. Georgia, 461 U.S. 660 (1983), the Court held that the Constitution requires that inability to pay be recognized as a defense.

Bearden appears to be widely flouted; there are widespread reports of jailing defendants for failure to pay fines and fees, and more recently, class actions challenging the practice. See, e.g., Neil L. Sobol, *Charging the Poor: Criminal Justice Debt and Modern-Day Debtors' Prisons*, 75 Md. L. Rev. 486 (2016); UCLA Institute for Research on Labor and Employment, *Get to Work or Go to Jail: Workplace Rights Under Threat* (2016), available at http://www.labor.ucla.edu/publication/get-to-work-or-go-to-jail/ [https://perma.cc/5WF7-48N7]. The UCLA study also reports widespread incarceration for contempt among low-income and minority fathers unable to pay child support.

2. Informal collection through the criminal laws. Apart from victim restitution laws, there is widespread informal use of criminal prosecution to coerce payment of money. It is fairly common for a potential defendant to compensate his victim in exchange for an agreement not to press the prosecution. The agreement is not binding on the prosecutor, and she may be annoyed, but at least for minor offenses, she is not likely to proceed with an uncooperative complaining witness.

For some crimes the informal procedure is institutionalized and the prosecutor cooperates. The most notable example is bad checks. Originally, the prosecutor would bring charges, defendant would pay the check, and the prosecutor would drop the case. The practice is now institutionalized, and more abusive. In Texas, the legislature authorized prosecutors to charge a collection fee. Tex. Crim. Proc. Code art. 102.007.

California's version of the practice is authorized by statute and described in Cal. Penal Code §1001.60 *et seq.* and in Breazeale v. Victim Services, Inc., 878 F.3d 759 (9th Cir. 2017). A bad check is not criminal without intent to defraud, but even so, California courts were reportedly "inundated" with bad check cases. The statute authorizes prosecutors to divert these cases to the private program after reviewing each case to determine that there is probable cause to believe a crime has been committed and to consider several discretionary factors going to the choice between prosecution and diversion. Diverted defendants can escape prosecution if they pay the check, pay some fees, and complete a check writing class. Plaintiffs in *Breazeale* allege that the private company now running the program in many counties imposes unlawful fees, makes false threats, and sends deceptive letters, all in violation of the Fair Debt Collection Practices Act.

Congress has authorized the practice with additional safeguards. 15 U.S.C. §1692p. The private company must make certain disclosures, principally about the right to dispute the bad check, but apparently need not disclose that it is not really the prosecutor. And some categories of checks are excluded from such programs, including post-dated checks to payday lenders and checks that bounced because the bank debited an account without notice to the depositor.

The Standing Committee on Ethics and Professional Responsibility of the American Bar Association has said that such programs are widespread, and that it is unethical for prosecutors to participate unless a lawyer from the prosecutor's office has reviewed the case file to determine whether a crime has been committed and prosecution is warranted, or reviewed the dunning letter to ensure that it complies with the Rules of Professional Conduct. Formal Opinion 469, http://www.americanbar.org/content/dam/aba/administrative/professional_responsibility/aba_formal_opinion_469.authcheckdam.pdf [https://perma.cc/G3XT-L4W4] (2014). The Committee said that prosecutors who authorize such letters without individualized review violate Model Rules 8.4(c), which prohibits "conduct involving dishonesty, fraud, deceit or misrepresentation," and Model Rule 5.5(a) on "assisting another" in the unauthorized practice of law. These issues are distinct from the more general issue considered in note 4—whether it is ethical for an attorney who does nothing deceptive to use the criminal process in aid of efforts to collect a civil obligation.

3. Outside counsel for the state. The Supreme Court unanimously approved a superficially similar but actually quite different practice in Sheriff v. Gillie, 136 S. Ct. 1594 (2016). Ohio hires outside counsel to collect debts owed to state agencies. These outside lawyers use the Attorney General's letterhead, but identify themselves as debt collectors, sign as "special counsel" or "outside counsel," and give the private law firm's contact information in a signature block and in instructions on responding to the letter. And none of the collection letters at issue in the Supreme Court threatened criminal prosecution. The Court held that this use of the Attorney General's letterhead was not misleading under the Fair Debt Collection Practices Act.

4. Ethical obligations of attorneys. The American Bar Association's Code of Professional Responsibility provided that "a lawyer shall not present, participate in presenting, or threaten to present criminal charges solely to obtain an advantage in a civil matter." Was the prosecutor implicitly exempt? What if the victim's lawyer told him to take the check to the prosecutor? There is no corresponding rule in the ABA's Model Rules of Professional Conduct adopted in 1983. The deletion has been controversial; some states retained the prohibition, and the ABA Ethics Committee apparently believes that it is implicit in more general ethical rules. Cases and ethics opinions are collected in *Restatement (Third) of the Law Governing Lawyers* §98, Reporter's Note *f* (Am. Law. Inst. 2000). Victims' rights statutes in general, and provisions for restitution in criminal cases in particular, increasingly treat criminal prosecution as an alternative remedy for victims. In light of these laws, and the statutory fee for criminal check collection, can it plausibly be extortion to use the criminal remedy? To threaten to use the criminal remedy?

5. Imprisonment for debt. A third distinct means of coercing payment is imprisonment for debt. Imprisonment for debt at common law was about as inflexible a remedy as can be imagined. The remedy was exclusive if elected; a creditor could not imprison his debtor and also levy on the debtor's property. The debtor could not be released unless he paid in full or the creditor relented. If the creditor relented, he had no further remedy. And inability to pay was no defense. Poor debtors could languish indefinitely with no hope of ever being able to pay. But friends and family would sometimes ransom a debtor, and imprisoning a wealthy debtor with hidden or intangible assets might coerce payment. Coercing the wealthy was a real benefit in a system that refused to levy on intangibles. But the costs in human suffering were enormous; it seems likely that many insolvents were imprisoned for every solvent recalcitrant.

Imprisonment for contract debt has been constitutionally prohibited in most states. But some version of imprisonment for tort debt, or for reckless or intentional torts, remains on the books in many places, little used and of doubtful constitutionality. Modern debt imprisonment is illustrated in Landrigan v. McElroy, 457 A.2d 1056 (R.I. 1983). Plaintiff had a $42,000 judgment for assault and battery, with execution twice returned unsatisfied. Under the Rhode Island statute, imprisoned debtors could be released by executing a "poor debtor's oath." Contract debtors could sign the oath immediately; tort debtors had to wait six months. Relying on the same cases the Supreme Court relied on in *Bearden,* the court held that all debtors are constitutionally entitled to a preincarceration hearing on ability to pay. It seems clear that these same cases would give Eugene Logston a constitutional defense to coercive contempt if it is no longer possible for him to pay. In Kinsey v. Preeson, 746 P.2d 542 (Colo. 1987), the court held imprisonment for tort debt flatly unconstitutional, without regard to ability to pay.

6. Professional and driver's license suspensions. Twenty states suspend people's professional or drivers licenses if they fall behind on student loans. Without the ability to drive a car, many people cannot get to work, making their debt situation much worse. The practice is reviewed in Jessica Silver-Greenberg, Stacy Cowley, & Natalie Kitroeff, *When Student Loan Bills Mean You Can No Longer Work,* N.Y. Times (Nov. 18, 2017). The Ninth Circuit has rejected constitutional attacks on suspending the driver's license of debtors with large amounts of unpaid taxes. Franceschi v. Yee, 887 F.3d 927 (9th Cir. 2018). The law targets the 500 taxpayers with the largest delinquencies each year; Franceschi was an attorney who had filed no state tax return and paid no state taxes for 18 years.

7. Money judgments enforcing federal statutes. In McComb v. Jacksonville Paper Co., 336 U.S. 187, 193-195 (1949), where the district court had ordered defendant to pay the minimum wage required by the Fair Labor Standards Act, 29 U.S.C. §201 *et seq.,* the Court said that the order could be enforced with the contempt power. From this beginning, there has grown a wide-ranging and vaguely defined doctrine that when plaintiff is a government agency, enforcing a law to protect the public interest, the court can enforce a money judgment with the contempt power and can ignore state exemption laws. The practice is also applied to consent decrees for money. An example is Securities & Exchange Commission v. Solow, 682 F. Supp. 2d 1312 (S.D. Fla. 2010), enforcing an order to disgorge profits from securities fraud.

8. Modern provisions for coercion in ordinary civil cases. Legislatures unhappy with the ineffectiveness of traditional collection methods have begun to authorize more coercive measures in ordinary cases. New York authorizes courts to order defendants to pay installments out of income, including exempt income in excess of "the reasonable requirements of the judgment debtor and his dependents," and in cases where there appears to be hidden income. N.Y. C.P.L.R. §5226. The procedure is explained in Balanoff v. Niosi, 791 N.Y.S.2d 553 (App. Div. 2005), where an attorney sought to recover unpaid fees out of a former client's award of maintenance from her former husband. If aggressively used, such statutes would bring to ordinary debt collection all the difficulties of child support enforcement. The statutes are used, but perhaps courts are not so aggressive in enforcing them.

The Oklahoma court struck down use of the contempt power to enforce orders to pay judgments in installments out of nonexempt income; the court said it violated the state prohibition on imprisonment for debt. Lepak v. McClain, 844 P.2d 852 (Okla. 1992). *Lepak* effectively overrules a decision upholding the statute, Freeman v. Heiman, 426 F.2d 1050 (10th Cir. 1970). *Freeman* collects older cases upholding such statutes in other states. Oklahoma has since reaffirmed its adherence to the traditional rule that the contempt power is available to collect child support and alimony. Sommer v. Sommer, 947 P.2d 512 (Okla. 1997). And it used the contempt power to coerce a divorced spouse to pay the credit card debt assigned to him by the divorce decree, treating this as part of the support obligation. Stepp v. Stepp, 955 P.2d 722 (Okla. 1998). This is a recurring problem; division of debt between the spouses does not release either spouse from the creditors' claims. A Texas case goes the other way, holding that debt assigned to one spouse by a divorce decree is just a debt, not enforceable by contempt. In re Henry, 154 S.W.3d 594 (Tex. 2005).

9. Turnover orders. Most jurisdictions authorize courts to order defendants to turn over assets: any nonexempt asset under 735 Ill. Comp. Stat. 5/2-1402(c)(1) or Tex. Civ. Prac. & Rem. Code §31.002, or "money or other personal property" under N.Y. C.P.L.R. §5225(a). The Texas provision expressly states that turnover orders against debtors are enforceable with the contempt power. If the assets are beyond the jurisdiction but defendant is before the court, the court may coerce defendant to turn over the assets. Many of the older cases are collected in United States v. Ross, 196 F. Supp. 243 (S.D.N.Y. 1961). Ross was the sole shareholder of a Bahamas corporation; the court ordered him to endorse and deliver all the shares of stock to a receiver. The court of appeals affirmed the order with a modest modification to take account of Bahamian law. 302 F.2d 831 (2d Cir. 1962).

Orders to turn over particular assets differ from an order to pay money. The turnover order is aimed at specific property that is known to have been in defendant's possession. It may be hard to know whether he still has it, but that inquiry is narrowly focused. It does not lead to a full review of defendant's income, expenses, and lifestyle. That is why turnover orders are much more widely used than orders to pay.

10. Criminal fines and court costs. Many jurisdictions try to finance their criminal justice system with fines and costs levied against defendants. Some charge fees for spending time in jail. These practices can put low-income defendants in an endless cycle of criminal debt. The ACLU settled a case against Sherwood, Arkansas for practices in its "hot check" court. The suit alleged that this court "systematically incarcerated misdemeanor offenders for failing to pay their fines, without first questioning whether the defendants had the ability to make payment. The court also added new penalties and fines, including being jailed, against the offenders." Daniel Gill, *Arkansas "Debtors' Prison" Case Settles with New Court Procedures*, 86 U.S.L.W. 652 (Nov. 16, 2017). A news report at the time of the lawsuit tracked the story of Chris Drennan, who bounced a check for a tank of gas when he was 17. Two decades later, he had paid over $5,000 and he still owed money; interest, fines, and late fees accumulated faster than his payments. Victoria Price, *Sherwood Hot Check Court Continues After Lawsuit*, KARK.com (Aug. 25, 2016), http://www.kark.com/news/local-news/sherwood-hot-check-court-continues-after-lawsuit/540366531 [https://perma.cc/W2CB-AK75]. To settle the ACLU's case, the judge and city agreed, among other terms, to stop jailing defendants who cannot afford to pay fines, to stop revoking drivers' licenses for failing to pay fines, and to advise all defendants of their right to counsel, including a public defender at no cost.

Practices like Sherwood's are widespread. Nationally, more than 7 million people may have lost their driver's licenses because of traffic debt. Justin William Moyer, *More Than 7 Million People May Have Lost Driver's Licenses Because of Traffic Debt*, Washington Post (May 19, 2018). There is ongoing litigation over Virginia's law requiring courts to "suspend forthwith" the driver's license of any person who fails pay fines, court costs, or criminal restitution. See Stinnie v. Holcomb, 2018 WL 2337750 (4th Cir. May 23, 2018), giving plaintiffs another chance to allege subject matter jurisdiction after a district court dismissal.

As Professor Birckhead explains:

> Across the United States, even seemingly minor criminal charges trigger an array of fees, court costs, and assessments that can create insurmountable debt burdens for already struggling families. Likewise, parents who fall behind on their child support

payments face the risk of incarceration, and upon release from jail, they must pay off the arrears that accrued, which hinders the process of reentry. Compounding such scenarios, criminal justice debt can lead to driver's license suspension, bank account or wage garnishment, extended supervision until debts are paid, additional court appearances or warrants related to debt collection and nonpayment, and extra fines and interest for late payment. When low-income parents face such collateral consequences, the very act of meeting the most basic physical and emotional needs of their children becomes a formidable challenge, the failure of which can trigger the intervention of Child Protective Services, potential neglect allegations, and further court hearings and fees. For youth in the juvenile court system, mandatory fees impose a burden that increases the risk of recidivism. In short, for families caught within the state's debt-enforcement regime, the threat of punishment is an ever-present specter, and incarceration always looms.

Tamar R. Birckhead, *The New Peonage,* 72 Wash. & Lee L. Rev. 1095, 1096 (2015). For more, see Christopher D. Hampson, *The New American Debtors' Prison,* 44 Am. J. Crim. L. 1 (Fall 2016).

11. Should we coerce the payment of debts? Is coercive collection worth the cost? Collecting child support may be especially burdensome, because it involves an obligation that accrues monthly for many years rather than a single judgment for a fixed amount. But even allowing for that, one may question whether society should invest the same resources, or impose the same burdens on defendants, to collect ordinary judgments.

Is compensation for crime as compelling a claim as child support? Or are the victim rights laws justified on different grounds? The objections to coercing defendants to pay money are that coercion imposes hardship and risk of error. Are those impositions justified in the case of convicted criminals? Is it more productive to impose these hardships than to impose ordinary prison sentences?

Most of these cases involve defendants without substantial assets, who at most could pay a little more each month. What about the defendant who appears to be wealthy but has concealed his assets? Is coercion more appropriate there?

12. The effect of bankruptcy. With respect to the two major grounds for coercion, Congress has mostly amended the bankruptcy laws to avoid providing a haven. Debts for alimony, child support, or spouse support are not dischargeable in either form of bankruptcy. 11 U.S.C. §§523(a)(5), 1328(a)(2). A crime victim's civil claim for damages is in principle a dischargeable debt, but most crimes are covered by one or more of a patchwork of exceptions. 11 U.S.C. §523(a)(2), (4), (6), (9). Payments under a victim restitution order included in a criminal sentence are not dischargeable, by express statutory provision if federal law authorizes restitution, §523(a)(13), or if the debtor completes a plan of partial payments under Chapter 13 of the Bankruptcy Code, §1328(a)(3), and by free-wheeling statutory interpretation in at least some other cases.

Section 523(a)(7) makes nondischargeable a "fine, penalty, or forfeiture," payable "to and for the benefit of a governmental unit," that "is not compensation for actual pecuniary loss." So restitution to the crime victim would seem to be plainly outside the section as not "for the benefit of a governmental unit," and doubly precluded if it is calculated on the basis of the victim's "actual pecuniary loss." No problem, according to Kelly v. Robinson, 479 U.S. 36 (1986), which held that criminal restitution ordered by a state court is not dischargeable. Bankruptcy courts had never interfered with the judgments of criminal courts, and the Court did not believe Congress had meant to change that. But In re Towers, 162 F.3d 952 (7th Cir. 1998), distinguished *Kelly* on the ground that there the crime was welfare fraud and the state was the victim; restitution for the benefit of private victims is dischargeable. *Towers* is more faithful to statutory text, but the *Kelly* opinion was plainly written to cover private victims as well as governmental victims. In re Verola, 446 F.3d 1206 (11th Cir. 2006), notes a circuit split over *Towers*, and reads *Kelly* as making all criminal restitution orders nondischargeable.

MORE NOTES ON THE IRREPARABLE INJURY RULE

1. Are injunctions harder to enforce? One argument for the irreparable injury rule is that injunctions impose a greater burden on the court, because they have to be enforced over time. How persuasive is that now that you know something about enforcing injunctions and collecting damages? Certainly coercion can be difficult, but the "one-time transfer of money" isn't so simple either. Consider the five years of wrangling in First National State Bank v. Kron, in note 7 of Notes on Other Means of Collecting, and the seven years in Webb v. Erickson, in note 2 of Notes on Garnishment. Both cases arose out of simple promises to pay. In *Kron*, the receiver was just beginning to look for assets; in *Webb*, the garnishment had just been remanded for a new trial. There was no prospect of payment any time soon in either case. Judgments expire after 10 or 20 years, but a diligent plaintiff can repeatedly revive a judgment before it expires. Thus, money judgments can be kept alive forever unless discharged in bankruptcy.

Of course, a chapter that illustrates the enforcement of decrees and collection of judgments with appellate cases tends to overemphasize the cases where enforcement and collection are difficult. Some defendants write a check, just as some defendants promptly obey injunctions. It is a mistake to focus only on the hardest cases. But it is a worse mistake to compare the hardest and most publicized injunction cases to the simplest collection cases.

2. Institutional defendants. The strongest examples for the argument that damage judgments are easier to enforce are suits against large institutional defendants. Such a defendant cannot very well hide itself or its assets; it may as well pay. It may be quite able to drag its heels in response to a structural injunction. But the irreparable injury rule is irrelevant to structural injunctions; damages are never adequate in those cases. Any attempt to make damages adequate would involve terribly difficult valuation problems, and enormous liability to large classes of plaintiffs. Massive damage judgments for the harm of segregated schools or bad prison conditions are not much improvement over structural injunctions.

3. Avoiding imprisonment for debt. The strong policy against imprisonment for debt continues, and that is a reason not to order natural persons to pay money. But is that a reason for the irreparable injury rule? If we really wanted to minimize the number of judgments that might eventually lead to imprisonment for debt, wouldn't that be a reason to prefer specific relief and avoid money judgments?

3. Preserving Assets Before Judgment

IN RE HYPNOTIC TAXI, LLC
543 B.R. 365 (Bankr. E.D.N.Y. 2016)

CARLA E. CRAIG, Chief United States Bankruptcy Judge.

[This case involved three loans totaling $31.5 million from Citibank to corporations owned and controlled by Evgeny Freidman. Freidman personally guaranteed each loan, and each loan was secured by taxi medallions owned by the corporations.

A taxi medallion is a permit to operate a taxi within a jurisdiction. They are typically limited in number, and in cities like New York they can be very valuable. But their value has plummeted in response to unlimited competition from Uber and similar companies.

All three loans were in default, and Citibank sued Freidman in state court on his personal guarantees. Citibank obtained an order allowing it to seize the taxi medallions. On July 14, 2015, the Appellate Division granted a stay of that order on condition that defendants post a $50 million bond. No bond was posted, and on July 22, 2015, the debtor corporations filed these chapter 11 bankruptcy cases in the Eastern District of New York. . . . The commencement of these bankruptcy cases automatically stayed enforcement of the Seizure Order. 11 U.S.C. § 362(a).

Citibank sought in the bankruptcy proceeding to attach all of Freidman's assets. Its principal target was not the taxi medallions, but Freidman's real estate. Each property was owned by a separate legal entity; the court variously refers to the Residences, the Investment Entities (meaning real estate held for investment), and the Real Estate Entities (including both the Residences and the Investment Entities.)]

B. THE TRANSFERS

In April 2015, after Citibank commenced the State Court Action . . . Freidman sought the advice of a trust and estates lawyer, Michael Zimmerman, to whom he had been referred by his long time lawyer in other matters, Ellen Walker. At trial, Freidman acknowledged that he was motivated to consult Zimmerman "for trust and estate and tax purposes . . . and for liability purposes." Zimmerman similarly testified that Freidman came to him for estate planning and asset protection. This consultation led to the creation of four separate trusts, the Kelly Funding Trust and the Birkin Funding Trust, both located in the Cook Islands, the Evelyn Funding Trust, located in Belize, and the Lindy Funding Trust, located in Nevis.

Into the Trusts, governed by substantially similar trust documents, Freidman placed his interests in LLCs and corporations owning all of his personal residences and investment real estate holdings in the United States ("Real Estate Entities"). . . . The total value of Freidman's interests in the Real Estate Entities exceeds $60 million.

The purpose of these transfers goes to the heart of Citibank's application for an order of attachment. . . .

C. THE PROCEEDINGS IN THIS COURT

On November 5, pursuant to C.P.L.R. §6210, Citibank moved by order to show cause for a temporary restraining order and order of attachment, seeking to restrain any transfer of assets in which Freidman has an interest and to restrain any further transfer of assets transferred by Freidman to the Trusts. . . . On November 17th, an Order of Attachment and an Amended TRO were entered in favor of Citibank. On November 19th, the Order of Attachment was stayed pending a hearing. On November 30th, an evidentiary hearing was held on Citibank's motion for an order of attachment at which Mr. Zimmerman, the lawyer who drafted the Trusts, testified, along with one of the original trustees of the Kelly Trust. . . . Freidman also testified, providing testimony that, on the whole, lacked credibility.

LEGAL STANDARD

"Prejudgment attachment is a provisional remedy to secure a debt by preliminary levy upon the property of the debtor in order to conserve that property for eventual execution." DLJ Mortgage Capital, Inc. v. Kontogiannis, 594 F. Supp. 2d 308, 318 (E.D.N.Y. 2009). Fed. R. Civ. P. 64, made applicable in adversary proceedings by [Federal Rule of Bankruptcy Procedure] 7064, permits a federal court to issue an order of attachment in the manner provided by the law of the state in which the federal court sits.

Under C.P.L.R. §6212(a), for an order of attachment to be granted or confirmed, a plaintiff is required to show, by affidavit and other written evidence, (1) that there is a cause of action and that it is probable that the plaintiff will succeed on the merits; (2) that one of the grounds for attachment provided in C.P.L.R. §6201 exist; and (3) that the amount demanded from the defendant exceeds all counterclaims known to the plaintiff.

Section 6201, as relevant here, provides:

> An order of attachment may be granted in any action, except a matrimonial action, where the plaintiff has demanded and would be entitled, in whole or in part, or in the alternative, to a money judgment against one or more defendants, when: . . .
>
> 3. the defendant, with intent to defraud his creditors or frustrate the enforcement of a judgment that might be rendered in plaintiff's favor, has assigned, disposed of, encumbered or secreted property, or removed it from the state or is about to do any of these acts; . . .

C.P.L.R. §6201(3).

Section 6201 provides that an order of attachment "may" be granted, and for this reason, courts have held that fulfillment of the requirements of Section 6201 is a necessary but not a sufficient condition for granting an order of attachment. In addition, it is necessary to show there is a need for the order of attachment.

DISCUSSION

A. IS CITIBANK ENTITLED TO AN ORDER OF ATTACHMENT?

To determine whether an order of attachment is appropriate in this proceeding, each prong of §6212(a) will be analyzed separately.

1. That there is a cause of action, and that it is probable that the plaintiff will succeed on the merits. . . .

Whether or not given effect as law of the case, [New York state trial court] Justice Oing's finding, implicit in the issuance of the Seizure Order, that it is probable that Citibank will succeed on the merits, is correct. It is clear that Citibank has made a showing of probability of success which meets the requirements in §6212(a).

To establish probability of success on the merits under §6212(a), a plaintiff must show that it is more likely than not that it will succeed on the merits of its claim. This requires "proof stronger than that required to establish a prima facie case." *Kontogiannis*, 594 F. Supp. 2d at 319. However, in evaluating whether this standard has been met, a court must afford the plaintiff the benefit of all legitimate inferences than can be drawn in plaintiff's favor. . .

It is clear that the showing of likelihood of success required for an order of attachment is met. Freidman does not dispute the basic fact that the Loans were advanced and have not been repaid, and that he guaranteed the Loans. . . .

2. That one of the grounds for attachment provided in section 6201 exist.

The second requirement for obtaining an order of attachment under CPLR 6212(a) is that one or more grounds for attachment provided in §6201 exist. . . . Because "[f]raudulent intent is rarely susceptible to direct proof," courts look to "badges of fraud" to establish actual intent. In re Kaiser, 722 F.2d 1574, 1582 (2d Cir. 1983). However, "[f]raudulent intent is not lightly inferred; allegations raising a mere suspicion of fraud are insufficient to sustain attachment on this ground." Algonquin Power Corp. v. Trafalgar Power Inc., 2000 WL 33963085, at *11 (N.D.N.Y. 2000) (citations omitted).

Because "[f]raudulent acts are as varied as the fish in the sea," any list of the "badges of fraud" would be non-exhaustive. *Kaiser*, 722 F.2d at 1583. However, six telling badges of fraud are:

(1) the lack or inadequacy of consideration;
(2) the family, friendship or close associate relationship between the parties;
(3) the retention of possession, benefit or use of the property in question;
(4) the financial condition of the party sought to be charged both before and after the transaction in question;
(5) the existence or cumulative effect of a pattern or series of transactions or course of conduct after the incurring of debt, onset of financial difficulties, or pendency or threat of suits by creditors; and
(6) the general chronology of the events and transactions under inquiry.

In this case all six of these badges of fraud are present. Each will be examined in turn.

1. The lack or inadequacy of consideration.

The transfer of Freidman's interests in the Real Estate Entities to the Trusts was a gratuitous transfer; this badge of fraud is unquestionably present.

2. The family, friendship or close associate relationship between the parties.

The beneficiaries of the Trusts are Freidman, his children, and his parents. This badge of fraud is unquestionably present as well.

3. The retention of possession, benefit or use of the property in question.

The evidence establishes the presence of this badge of fraud.

First of all, Freidman has structured the Trusts so that he reserves the right to continue to use the properties, including the Residences, owned by the Real Estate Entities he transferred to the Trusts. . . .

In addition, Freidman maintains management control over and use of the Investment Properties [the real estate held for investment] in the same manner as he did prior to the transfer to the Trusts. . . .

Confronted with the fact that he seems to have maintained total control over the Investment Properties, Freidman testified that he is "in the process" of handing over control. When asked, "So in the meantime until all those violations, et cetera, get cleaned up you're in charge of the accounts; right?" Freidman evaded the questions and explained that he was very interested in the Trusts because they are for the benefit of his children, and reiterated that he was "working diligently to hand over control," though five and half months had already elapsed since the properties were transferred to the Trusts. . . .

4. The financial condition of the party sought to be charged both before and after the transaction in question.

It is not necessary to find that Freidman was rendered insolvent by these transfers in order to conclude that the transfers were made with intent to defraud creditors or to frustrate the enforcement of a judgment. What is telling is that, by these transfers, Freidman appears to have sought to convey all of his property against which a judgment creditor could readily execute.

Freidman maintains that his Statement of Financial Condition dated June 30, 2015 ("2015 SFC") demonstrates that even after the transfers he was in robust financial shape. The 2015 SFC lists a net worth of almost $130 Million. However, even a cursory analysis shows that, notwithstanding this purported net worth, Freidman retains few assets from which a potential judgment creditor might readily recover. . . .

Of the purported net worth of $130 million shown on the 2015 SFC, $85 million is ascribed to closely held entities owning taxi medallions. Freidman's equity in closely held entities owning New York City taxi medallion rights . . . is listed on the 2015 SFC as approximately $70 million of the $85 million total equity attributable to taxi medallions. It is clear, therefore, that value attributable to entities owning taxi medallions listed on the 2015 SFC is dependent on the market value of the NYC Medallions. Furthermore, because the NYC Medallions are heavily encumbered (Freidman's reported $70 million of equity in NYC Medallions is the result of subtracting $185 million in encumbrances from $255 million total value listed on the 2015 SFC), any decline in the market value of the NYC Medallions will effect Freidman's equity disproportionally. For example, if the value of the NYC Medallions were to decline by 10%, or $25.5 million, Freidman's equity would decline by over one-third.

NYC Medallions are illiquid. Very few NYC Medallions actually trade. The last transfer of corporate unrestricted medallions, the type of medallion at issue here, with a price reported, before Freidman's June 2015 SFC, occurred in March, 2015. Given the lack of a liquid market for these assets, it is not possible to readily determine the market value of a New York City taxi medallion.

According to Defendants, whatever the market value of a single medallion, if a creditor were to execute on Freidman's interests in the Medallion Collateral and sell the medallions as a group into the market, there is no telling where the bottom would be. . . .

The second major source of value listed on the 2015 SFC is Freidman's interest in closely held taxi cab management companies, which are listed as worth $34,880,000. Here, again, it is highly doubtful that these assets would actually be a significant source of recovery to a creditor seeking to execute on a judgment. Freidman's testimony on this topic can only be described as self-contradictory, evasive and unconvincing. . . .

The other assets listed in Freidman's 2015 SFC are Swiss bank accounts totaling over $2 million, and two residences in France worth a total of $14 million. It is not clear what, if anything, the Swiss bank accounts currently contain; when Freidman was asked at the hearing, "the cash in Switzerland, is that still there now?" he replied "I'd have to check. I did not check before." In any event, such property, like the residences in France, would be difficult for a creditor seeking to enforce a New York judgment to reach.

Thus, it appears that Freidman has transferred substantially all of his assets available for execution by a judgment creditor to the Trusts. . . .

5. The existence or cumulative effect of a pattern or series of transactions or course of conduct after the incurring of debt, onset of financial difficulties, or pendency or threat of suits by creditors, and 6. the general chronology of the events and transactions under inquiry.

Though fraudulent intent is rarely susceptible to direct proof, much can be inferred from the chronology of events. Citibank began this action in March 2015, and Freidman commenced the process of creating the Trusts in April. . . . In May, pressure on Freidman intensified when Justice Oing issued the [order permitting Citibank to seize the taxi medallions.] Then, in the middle of June, Freidman conveyed all his assets on which a judgment creditor would be able to execute to the four Trusts, registered in three different offshore locations. As Trustees, Freidman appointed his business attorneys, who do not appear to have undertaken any action, or to have been apprised of any responsibility they had in that capacity. Furthermore, it does not appear that after the transfers Freidman relinquished the use of the properties owned by the Real Estate Entities or relinquished control of the Investment Property bank accounts.

Freidman asserts that he undertook these transfers simply for estate planning purposes, a proposition that strains credulity. From the perspective of an inquiry into the presence of the badges of fraud, it is difficult to imagine a more arresting chronology. These transfers occurred against the background of a suit by Citibank to recover in excess of $40 million dollars, and [a claim by Capital One] which resulted in a judgment of almost $8.5 million dollars. It is impossible to conclude that the timing of the transfers is merely coincidence.

Events after the TRO was issued by this Court strongly support the inference that Freidman undertook the transfers to the Trusts with the aim of frustrating judgment creditors. After this Court issued the TRO on November 5, 2015, Freidman fired the Trustees located in New York in order to appoint foreign trustees in Moscow, in a transparent attempt to further insulate the assets he placed in the Trusts from the reach of his creditors. Freidman's testimony to the contrary is totally lacking in credibility and is directly contradicted by the deposition testimony of Ellen Walker, Freidman's lawyer and an original trustee of all four Trusts . . .

Freidman's denial that he directed the Trustees to submit resignation letters so that he could appoint foreign trustees is utterly lacking in credibility. . . .

In short, the badges of fraud are numerous and glaring, and C.P.L.R. §6201(3) is satisfied.

3. That the amount demanded exceeds all known counterclaims.
. . . The fact that Citibank does not concede the counterclaims are just is sufficient to allow Citibank to satisfy this requirement, consistent with the fact that an order of attachment is a provisional remedy. . . .

4. The need for the attachment.
Having established that the statutory requirements are met, it is necessary to consider whether there is a need for an order of attachment. The need for attachment has been amply demonstrated by the overwhelming evidence that Freidman made transfers to the Trusts in an effort to strip himself of assets a judgment creditor could readily execute on . . .

Accordingly, the order of attachment is granted. . . .

B. WHAT ASSETS CAN CITIBANK ATTACH?
1. Can an order of attachment issued in this proceeding reach property transferred by Freidman to the Trusts?
Defendant maintains that property transferred to the Trusts cannot be reached by an order of attachment against Freidman because he no longer has an interest in that property. As a general matter, an order of attachment may not reach property in which the defendant does not have an interest. . . . Where, as in this case, intent to

hinder, delay or defraud creditors is shown, a different rule applies. Section 278 of the N.Y. Debt. & Cred. Law provides:

> 1. Where a conveyance or obligation is fraudulent as to a creditor, such creditor, when his claim has matured, may, as against any person except a purchaser for fair consideration without knowledge of the fraud at the time of the purchase, or one who has derived title immediately or mediately from such a purchaser,
>   a. Have the conveyance set aside or obligation annulled to the extent necessary to satisfy his claim, or
>   b. Disregard the conveyance and attach or levy execution upon the property conveyed.

N.Y. Debt. & Cred. Law §278. Thus, section 278(b) expressly states that in the case of a fraudulent transfer, property can be attached in the hands of a third party (other than a bona fide purchaser, an exception not relevant here). . . .

2. Is it necessary that the Trusts be joined as defendants in this proceeding before the property transferred to the Trusts can be attached?

[Cases cited by Defendant] do not stand for the proposition that property may not be attached in the hands of a non-party, but rather that a non-party claiming an interest in property that has been attached is entitled to seek relief from the order of attachment. This remedy is explicitly provided in C.P.L.R. §6223: "[p]rior to the application of property or debt to the satisfaction of a judgment, the defendant, the garnishee or any person having an interest in the property or debt may move, on notice to each party and the sheriff, for an order vacating or modifying the order of attachment." §6223(a). Furthermore, were the Trusts to bring such a motion, the burden to demonstrate the entitlement to an order of attachment would remain on the Plaintiff. §6223(b).

3. Is Citibank required to identify the assets it seeks to attach?

Freidman argues that an order of attachment must state with specificity what property is to be attached. However, C.P.L.R. §6211(a), which prescribes the contents of an order of attachment, contains no such requirement:

> [An order of attachment] shall specify the amount to be secured by the order of attachment including any interest, costs and sheriff's fees and expenses, be indorsed with the name and address of the plaintiff's attorney and shall be directed to the sheriff of any county or of the city of New York where any property in which the defendant has an interest is located or where a garnishee may be served. The order shall direct the sheriff to levy within his jurisdiction, at any time before final judgment, upon such property in which the defendant has an interest and upon such debts owing to the defendant as will satisfy the amount specified in the order of attachment.

Therefore, "It is not necessary for the order of attachment to describe the property to be attached." 12 Weinstein, Korn & Miller, *New York Civil Practice* ¶6211.05 (2015). This rule is of long standing . . .

Furthermore, "[i]f the order does specify certain property, the sheriff is not prohibited from levying upon any other property when it is necessary to do so to secure enough property to guarantee the availability of the amount set forth in the attachment order." *Id.*

Accordingly, Plaintiff's motion is not deficient because it seeks to attach all of Freidman's property and all the property which he transferred to the Trusts.

CONCLUSION

For all of the foregoing reasons, the stay, entered on November 19, 2015, of the order of attachment entered on November 17, is lifted, and Citibank is authorized to attach the Real Estate Entities transferred by Freidman to the Trusts. Citibank is directed to submit an order consistent with this decision.

NOTES ON ATTACHMENT

1. Freidman's other problems. By 2018, Citibank's action against Freidman was far from his only problem. Freidman, known as "the Taxi King," was a personal friend and business partner of Michael Cohen, President Trump's personal lawyer. Freidman had been accused of failing to pay over more than $5 million in taxes he collected from New York City passengers. He faced five felony counts, each of which could carry up to 25 years in prison. He instead pled guilty to one count of evading $50,000 in taxes and will face no jail time if he cooperates with state and federal prosecutors. Danny Hakim, William K. Rashbaum, & Vivian Wang, *Michael Cohen's Business Partner Agrees to Cooperate as Part of Plea Deal*, N.Y. Times (May 22, 2018). Freidman, a lawyer, has also been disbarred. In the Matter of Evgeny A. Freidman, A Suspended Attorney, 72 N.Y.S.3d 825 (App. Div. 2018). In 2017, he served 28 days in a Chicago jail for criminal contempt in an unrelated case, and he has been accused of sexual harassment of an assistant and domestic abuse of his ex-wife. Jillian Jorgensen & John Annese, *"Taxi King" of NYC Serving 28-Day Jail Sentence for Defying Judge's Order*, N.Y Daily News (Dec. 15, 2017); Ken Kurson, *Derailed by Uber, Deposed New York Taxi King Gets Sued in Chicago*, N.Y. Observer (May 16, 2016).

And of course, the value of New York City taxi medallions has declined precipitously with the advent of ride-sharing services such as Uber. This is especially disastrous for those who bought medallions on credit when the price was high, or borrowed money against that value, and now owe all that debt despite the drop in value. At least five taxi drivers holding New York medallions have committed suicide as the value of the medallions has plummeted from as high as $1 million to $175,000. Nikita Stewart and Luis Ferré-Sadurní, *Another Taxi Driver in Debt Takes His Life. That's 5 in 5 Months*, N.Y. Times (May 27, 2018).

The bankruptcy court has issued a long series of follow-on orders involving defendant's efforts to vacate the attachment and Citibank's successful motion for summary judgment on Freidman's liability on the loans.

2. Preserving defendant's assets. Usage varies from state to state, but attachment generally refers to a preliminary garnishment or seizure of assets before judgment. The primary purpose is to preserve plaintiff's access to defendant's assets, and most of the grounds for attachment are variations on the theme that assets may be about to disappear. The statute relied on in *Hypnotic Taxi*, N.Y. C.P.L.R. §6201(3), is typical. Federal Rule 64, also relied on in *Hypnotic Taxi*, merely authorizes federal district courts to use the state attachment rules.

3. Attachment to acquire jurisdiction. *Hypnotic Taxi* illustrates the standard grounds of disappearing assets. The New York statute also contains lesser grounds, drafted when attachment of assets was an independent means of acquiring jurisdiction over defendant. N.Y. C.P.L.R. §6201(2) authorizes attachment against defendants who reside within the state but "cannot be personally served despite diligent efforts." Evading service might be some evidence of intent to secrete assets, but the principal function of this clause is to substitute attachment for personal service.

More troubling is §6201(1), which authorizes attachment against any "nondomiciliary residing without the state, or . . . a foreign corporation not qualified to do business in the state." The attachment does not confer jurisdiction unless the defendant has minimum contacts with the state, Shaffer v. Heitner, 433 U.S. 186 (1977), and depriving out-of-state defendants of their property before judgment, simply because they are from out of state and with no showing that they are likely to remove the assets, is almost certainly an unconstitutional burden on interstate commerce. Compare Bendix Autolite Corp. v. Midwesco Enterprises, 486 U.S. 888 (1988), invalidating a rule that deprived out-of-state defendants of any protection from statutes of limitation. A New York court refused to read the statute literally; it held that attachment under §6201(1) is available only if jurisdiction cannot be obtained by any other means. J.V.W. Investment Ltd. v. Kelleher, 837 N.Y.S.2d 650 (App. Div. 2007). In *J.V.W.*, a Bahamian court had appointed a receiver to collect defendant's assets, and the receiver conceded jurisdiction in the New York courts. So the holding is narrow. But the logic would seem to confine §6201(1) to cases where defendant cannot be found or is avoiding service. If defendant is subject to service under the long-arm act, attachment would be unnecessary, and if the long-arm act is unavailable because defendant has no minimum contacts with the jurisdiction, attachment should be ineffective.

4. Attachment without grounds. In Maine and Massachusetts, attachment issues on a showing that it is "more likely than not" that plaintiff will recover judgment in an amount equal to or greater than the amount of the attachment plus any liability insurance. Me. R. Civ. P. 4A(c); Mass. R. Civ. P. 4.1(c). There is no need to show a risk of dissipation, unless plaintiff seeks an ex parte attachment without notice to defendant. Me. Rule 4A(g); Mass. Rule 4.1(f). A striking example is Clay Corp. v. Colter, 2012 WL 6928132 (Mass. Super. Ct. 2012), issuing a $1.5 million prejudgment attachment in a case where two consumers allegedly defamed an auto dealership. The Appeals Court reduced the amount to $700,000, but otherwise affirmed. http://www.ma-appellatecourts.org/display_docket.php?dno=2012-J-0350 [https://perma.cc/8UE4-E2RF].

The Connecticut attachment statute was typical with respect to attachment of goods, but it was like the Maine and Massachusetts rules with respect to attachment of real estate: It authorized prejudgment attachment without any showing that assets were about to disappear or of any other exigent circumstances. The attachment issued on affidavits, without notice to the owner of the property, and without requiring plaintiff to post a bond. The owner of attached real estate remained in possession, but she could not sell or borrow against her property, and suffering the attachment was an act of default under most mortgages. The owner could move to vacate the attachment, but it was not clear what standards applied to such a motion.

The Second Circuit struck down the statute, holding that prejudgment attachment is unconstitutional in the absence of extraordinary circumstances plus a bond. Pinsky v. Duncan, 898 F.2d 852 (2d Cir. 1990), *aff'd on other grounds as* Connecticut v. Doehr, 501 U.S. 1 (1991). A unanimous Supreme Court held only that a preattachment hearing was required, citing a line of cases requiring hearings before property is seized. The Court did not decide whether exigent circumstances must be shown at the hearing; rather, it considered lack of exigent circumstances as a factor that reduced the state's interest in avoiding the delay of a hearing.

5. The impact on defendants. It is not clear what impact the attachments in *Hypnotic Taxi* would have on Freidman, given all the other problems he faced. It would end his ability to borrow against the real estate, but by the time of the court's opinion, probably no one would lend to him anyway. Consider the impact on an ongoing business when a creditor attaches the bank account with the operating funds, or the inventory available for sale, or the equipment used to manufacture or deliver the product. Attachment can push a debtor into bankruptcy even before plaintiff has proved his claim. Should plaintiffs be permitted such power without strong evidence of fraudulent intent?

Attaching plaintiffs must also post a bond, and in most states their liability for wrongful attachment is not limited to the amount of the bond. Is the risk of liability for wrongful attachment a sufficient deterrent to unjustified attachments? In the next principal case, that issue is further explored in the analogous context of receiverships.

6. Priorities. Another consequence of attachment is to establish priority in the assets from the date of the prejudgment attachment instead of from a postjudgment execution or garnishment. Attachment creates a lien on the attached assets, and the 90-day period for invalidating preferential liens runs from that point. In re Wind Power Systems, 841 F.2d 288 (9th Cir. 1988). It is usually better to get the 90 days running before trial rather than after. But bankruptcy tactics are not grounds for attachment in any state. Whatever the attachment creditor's motives, the motion for attachment must be based on the statutory grounds.

7. Distinguishing replevin. Attachment is a near cousin to replevin. The difference is that in replevin, the plaintiff has some preexisting claim to the particular property replevied. Either he owns it and defendant is wrongfully in possession, or plaintiff has a security interest in it and is entitled to his collateral. Attachment is a more invasive remedy, because it can reach any nonexempt assets defendant owns.

NOTES ON PREJUDGMENT FREEZE ORDERS

1. Freezing the assets in place. Plaintiffs sometimes ask for an injunction ordering defendants and their banks not to transfer any of the assets described in the motion. Such an injunction is commonly called a freeze order, because it attempts to freeze the assets in place. Unlike attachment, a freeze order does not create a lien on the frozen assets. Compare the postjudgment freeze orders described in Notes on Other Means of Collecting, in section 9.B.1.

An example is National Credit Union Administration Board v. Jurcevic, 867 F.3d 616 (6th Cir. 2017). Stan and Bara Jurcevic had a joint account at a credit union where Stan Jurcevic got $1.5 million in personal loans. A credit union officer was later discovered taking bribes in exchange for issuing loans and the credit union itself turned out to be insolvent. The National Credit Union Administration Board sued Stan Jurcevic for fraudulent practices in connection with obtaining his loans. The district court issued an order freezing the Jurcevics' assets pending trial, except for living expenses. The Sixth Circuit affirmed the freeze order, reviewing the order under the standard for issuing preliminary injunctions described in section 5.B.1. In addition to finding that the Board was likely to succeed on the merits in its suit, the court found that "Jurcevic had other creditors, a history of underhanded financial conduct, and a rapidly evaporating pool of assets . . . The Board thus established that the absence of a freeze risked harm, perhaps even of the irreparable variety." *Id.* at 622.

2. Distinguishing defendant's general assets from assets in which plaintiff claims a property right. Some courts refuse to grant prejudgment freeze orders, on the theory that they are attempts to bypass the attachment statutes and get many of the same benefits on a lesser showing. Other courts have granted such injunctions on strong showings of propensity to hide the assets. Many of the cases draw a distinction between claims to specific property and claims for damages; plaintiff is far more likely to get a freeze order if he asserts a property interest in the property to be frozen. Some of the cases are collected in Douglas Laycock, *The Death of the Irreparable Injury Rule* 77 & nn.31-37 (Oxford Univ. Press 1991).

3. *Grupo Mexicano.* Pretrial freeze orders are creatures of state law. Federal law does not authorize courts to issue a preliminary injunction, in an action for money damages, preventing the defendant from transferring assets in which no lien or equitable interest is claimed. Grupo Mexicano de Desarrollo, S.A. v. Alliance Bond Fund, Inc., 527 U.S. 308 (1999). The insolvent Mexican defendant was using its few remaining assets to pay Mexican creditors to the exclusion of U.S. creditors. The assets were in Mexico, beyond the attachment power of U.S. courts, but defendant had consented to jurisdiction in New York, and the federal court there preliminarily enjoined further dissipation of assets.

The Supreme Court reversed. The majority believed that owners of property have a substantive right to be free of interference by an unsecured creditor before judgment. It distinguished cases of persons asserting equitable claims to the attached property, such as lien holders, trust beneficiaries, and even defrauded investors seeking rescission, and it denied that this distinction had been affected by the merger of law and equity.

Two other possibilities for future argument: If this rule protects a substantive right, the existence or nonexistence of that right should be governed by state law in a diversity case, and perhaps even in a federal question case, because the law of property would still be state law. *Grupo Mexicano* was a diversity case, but the state-law issue had not been raised below, and the Court declined to consider it. *Id.* at 318 n.3. The Court also noted that such injunctions might be available in suits to prevent or set aside fraudulent transfers. *Id.* at 324 n.7. This was not such a suit, because the assets were being distributed for value—reducing the claims of other creditors.

The Court expressly declined to decide whether prejudgment freeze orders were a good idea, but the majority was plainly more skeptical than the dissent. The problem is how to screen the allegations of creditors, so that freeze orders are genuinely reserved for cases in which defendant is dissipating assets and do not become abusive weapons in the hands of every creditor inclined to use them. The Court said that the analogous English practice, the *Mareva* injunctions (named for Mareva Compania Naviera v. International Bulkcarriers [1975] 2 Lloyd's Rep. 509 (C.A.)), had been heavily used, citing an article claiming a thousand applications per month. The dissenters would have relied on trial judges to screen allegations and, more plausibly, on the preliminary injunction bond to deter abusive applications.

4. The English experience. *Mareva* injunctions are now called "freezing injunctions" after a procedural reform. E-mail exchanges with English solicitors, and an article on the practice, suggest that the English bar views the current law as appropriately flexible and as reasonably balanced between the legitimate interests of plaintiffs and defendants. The targets are most commonly foreign entities or businesses that are already defunct; an operating business is often allowed to continue to transfer assets in ordinary course of business, including for legal fees. For a broad assessment, see the opening paragraph of Paul McGrath, *The Freezing Order: A Constantly Evolving Jurisdiction*, 31 Civ. Just. Q. No. 1, at 12 (2012).

W.E. ERICKSON CONSTRUCTION, INC. v. CONGRESS-KENILWORTH CORP.

445 N.E.2d 1209 (Ill. App. Ct. 1983)

JIGANTI, Justice:

This is an interlocutory appeal from an order appointing a receiver of a corporation that operates a water slide as an amusement business. The defendants . . . (collectively Congress-Kenilworth) claim that the trial court was in error when it appointed a receiver on the petition of the plaintiffs . . . (collectively Erickson).

Erickson filed an action seeking a money judgment for breach of a construction contract. It also sought to impose a constructive trust on the defendants' interest in the real estate and during the litigation requested that a receiver be appointed or that injunctive relief be granted. The complaint alleged that "Plaintiffs . . . *fear* that said monies generated by the project *will be diverted.* . . ." (Emphasis added.) No underlying facts were alleged. This allegation and the finding on the issue are the focal point of this appeal.

The facts relating to Erickson's alleged fear of diversion were adduced at a four-day evidentiary hearing before the trial court which began on May 26, 1982. The evidence showed that Erickson, a general contractor, was hired to construct a public amusement consisting of a concrete water slide for Congress-Kenilworth for a total cost not to exceed $535,000. Work commenced on April 15, 1981. The contract provided that Erickson was to apply for monthly progress payments and that Congress-Kenilworth was required to pay Erickson within thirty days of application. On June 16, 1981, when the project was 60% completed, Erickson applied for a payment in the amount of $246,958 which it did not receive. Since Congress-Kenilworth was seeking financing, the parties then agreed that Congress-Kenilworth would deliver the deed to the real estate to Erickson and that Erickson would use this deed as security for additional interim financing. Congress-Kenilworth's stockholders' resolution of June 20, 1981, authorizing this deed stated that the assignment was made to guarantee payment of the indebtedness owed to the plaintiff and to ensure payment and completion of the project for opening on July 3, 1981. The . . . beneficial interest was assigned to Elmhurst National Bank as additional security for financing obtained by Erickson.

The season for the use of the water slide runs from approximately the 4th of July to Labor Day. The project was opened to the public on the 4th of July. On July 9, 1981, . . . the three principal stockholders of Congress-Kenilworth . . . filed articles of incorporation for a separate corporation to be known as Thunder Mountain Rapids Corp. The designated purposes of Thunder Mountain Rapids Corp. were identical to those set forth in the articles of incorporation of Congress-Kenilworth. In addition, all bank accounts standing in the name of Congress-Kenilworth were closed; all gross revenues were collected by Thunder Mountain Rapids and deposited in its accounts; and a written management contract was entered into between Congress-Kenilworth and Thunder Mountain Rapids. The contract was requested but not produced at trial. There is no further evidence in the record as to the terms of the contract. The record also reveals that Thunder Mountain Rapids owns 80% of Congress-Kenilworth and a church owns the other 20%.

Because no subsequent arrangements had been made to pay Erickson, a meeting between the parties was held on July 14, 1981. A letter drafted by Congress-Kenilworth's attorney acknowledged Congress-Kenilworth's indebtedness to Erickson in the amount of $550,000 and informed Erickson that "within thirty days or less we expect to pay you in full." The letter enclosed a partial payment in the amount of

$50,000. Another payment of $85,000 was made to Erickson on August 20, 1981. Both payments were made by Thunder Mountain Rapids Corp. It is not clear from the record but all of the parties accept the fact that Erickson was paid an additional $15,000 bringing the total paid on its contract to $150,000.

It is at this juncture that an unusual event occurred. Sometime in August, 1981, the parties learned that the Department of the Army owned the real property conveyed by Congress-Kenilworth to Erickson and that the water slide was an encroachment. Congress-Kenilworth subsequently entered into a lease with the Army.

At the hearing, Erickson's evidence further established that the gross revenues of the project in 1981 were approximately $224,000. It was stipulated that the books and records of Congress-Kenilworth, which were available to Erickson, correctly reflected the results of the operation. At the time of the hearing, there was nothing remaining of the income from the 1981 operation which concluded on Labor Day of 1981. The 1982 season was just beginning. According to the defendants' evidence which was undisputed, the revenue from the slide was given to Erickson. Also, Adams testified that he and Stafford [two of the principal stockholders] did not take a salary but were reimbursed a total of $25,000 for expenses which they had incurred before the slide was opened. This evidence was also undisputed. . . .

The court appointed a receiver after finding that the security given to Erickson, the deed to the real estate, was worthless; that the future proceeds from the slide constituted a special fund; and that hundreds of thousands of dollars were passing through Thunder Mountain Rapids Corp. while Congress-Kenilworth alleged that they could not pay because they did not have any assets. The court made no findings specifically relating to diversion, malfeasance or misfeasance on the part of the defendants.

The facts related above must be measured against the stringent legal requirements for the appointment of a receiver and the rationale for such stringency. The requirements are set out in Bagdonas v. Liberty Land & Investment Co., 140 N.E. 49, 52 (Ill. 1923):

> Application for the appointment of a receiver is addressed to the sound legal discretion of the court. It is a high and extraordinary remedy. The power is not arbitrary, and should be exercised with caution, and only where the court is satisfied there is imminent danger of loss if it is not exercised. The general rule is that the applicant must show, first, that he has a clear right to the property itself or has some lien upon it, or that the property constitutes a *special fund* to which he has a right to resort for the satisfaction of his claim; and, second, that the possession of the property by the defendant was obtained by fraud, or that the property itself, or *the income arising from it, is in danger of loss from neglect, waste, misconduct or insolvency.*

(Emphasis added.)

The rationale as to why a court should only sparingly apply the remedy of a receiver is also enunciated . . . in *Bagdonas.* . . . [W]hen a court exercises its equitable powers and appoints a receiver, it deprives the legal owner of possession. . . . Consequently, the court should only exercise its discretion and appoint a receiver "when the necessity therefor . . . clearly appears." *Id.* . . .

Under *Bagdonas,* . . . there are two requisites for the imposition of a receiver. Erickson had to first prove that there was a special fund. We believe that this requirement was met when Erickson presented evidence to show that it was given a warranty deed as security for additional financing. When this security failed, the court could properly impose an equitable lien on behalf of Erickson because there existed a mutual mistake as to the validity of the deed. Mutual mistake involving improvements on the land of another is a basis for the imposition of an equitable lien. Thus the equitable lien served as the source for the creation of a special fund.

The second requirement for the extraordinary remedy of the appointment of the receiver is that the income arising from the special fund is in danger of loss from neglect, waste, misconduct or insolvency. To comport with this requirement, the plaintiff alleges a fear of diversion. We believe the evidence does not support the necessary showing to meet the second requirement.

At the hearing, Erickson established the following facts. By way of stipulation, it established that the books and records of the defendants correctly reflected the results of the operation of the business. It established that the books and records showed an income of approximately $224,000 and that Erickson received a payment of $150,000 out of this income. Of the $150,000 payment to Erickson, $135,000 came directly from Thunder Mountain Rapids Corp. In addition, Erickson neither argued nor attempted to prove that the management agreement could be considered the source of a fear of diversion. The simple fact that such an agreement existed was not sufficient evidence to support such an inference. Because Erickson did not inquire into the reasons for the establishment of the management agreement in the hearing, there is no evidence in the record to support an inference that the management agreement was forged for nefarious purposes or to support an inference that Erickson was, or would be, deprived of any proceeds because of the agreement. Therefore, all that Erickson was able to show at the hearing is what it had alleged in its complaint. Erickson had a speculative fear that the money would be diverted. A speculative fear is not legally sufficient to support the drastic remedy of the appointment of a receiver. For the above reasons, we reverse and remand the decision of the trial court. . . .

ROMITI, P.J., and JOHNSON, J., concur.

NOTES ON RECEIVERSHIP

1. The aftermath. On remand, there was a 22-day trial on multiple issues, including alleged defects in the construction of the waterslide, the amount due to Erickson under the cost-plus construction contract, and the expenses of the receivership. Both sides appealed, first to the appellate court and then to the state supreme court. 503 N.E.2d 233 (Ill. 1986). The supreme court held that Erickson had substantially performed and was entitled to be paid, with remaining disputes about the amount to be determined by further proceedings on remand. But Congress-Kenilworth was entitled to recover its attorneys' fees for successfully opposing the receivership ($16,000), and on its counterclaim for damages caused by the receivership. These damages were alleged to be $67,000, but disputed items in that amount were to be determined on remand.

The opinion is not perfectly clear, but the $67,000 appears to have been a personal liability of plaintiff, to be offset against the judgment for the price of construction. The $16,000 appears to have been treated as an expense of the receivership, collectible out of receivership assets, which would of course simply be the profits of the waterslide during the period of the receivership. Defendant would be collecting its attorneys' fees out of its own assets; if defendant remained solvent, it is not clear what difference this award of fees would have made. If defendant were insolvent, the difference was this: The court awarded the attorneys' fees a higher priority in the receivership assets than plaintiff's equitable lien to secure the price of construction.

2. The uses of receivership. Receivership may be thought of as a very sophisticated form of attachment. You wouldn't want the sheriff to seize a waterslide; the receiver of a business must be prepared to run it. Ideally, receivers are businesspeople with experience in the industry. Often, they are lawyers. Too often, they are friends of the judge.

Sometimes, a receiver is appointed before judgment simply to find and collect the assets, much like the postjudgment use of receivers described in the Notes on Other Means of Collecting, in section 9.B.1. An example is In re McGaughey, 24 F.3d 904 (7th Cir. 1994), where such a receiver was appointed to collect the assets of a lawyer who owed more than $3 million to the IRS, and who was dissipating assets and giving evasive answers to questions about his assets.

3. Preliminary relief for plaintiffs who claim property rights. A prejudgment receiver manages the property for the court, preserving it for delivery to the true owner once the court decides who the true owner is. In *Erickson*, plaintiffs' claim of ownership grows out of the equitable lien; more commonly, plaintiff claims an ownership interest from the beginning of the dispute. Prejudgment receivership is not available for ordinary creditors in most jurisdictions. An illustration is Owens v. Gaffken & Barriger Fund LLC, 2009 WL 773517 (S.D.N.Y. 2009), denying a receiver to investors in a mutual fund where their only stated grounds for a receivership was fear that assets would be dissipated before they could litigate and collect their claims for damages. Shareholders can sometimes get receivers appointed for the corporations they own shares in, but the judge thought that this claim was just an unsecured claim for money. Plainly, he also thought that no receiver was needed on the facts.

Plaintiffs don't always win when a receiver is appointed; the true owner may turn out to be the defendant. Because it is a preliminary remedy based on a showing of probabilities, much of receivership practice is analogous to preliminary injunction practice. Plaintiff must post a bond, and receivership orders are immediately appealable.

4. Co-owners of a business. One common receivership plaintiff is the part owner of a business suing his co-owners. The litigants are investors in a common enterprise, and one side feels oppressed. Neither side trusts the other to manage the business, and the side that is not in control seeks a receiver. But it's not enough that they aren't getting along; the assets must be in danger. Usually, the charge is that defendant is misappropriating or dissipating assets. Sometimes the charge is that the business is paralyzed by the parties' antagonism, and that it will suffer severe losses unless someone is appointed with power to run it. For a simple illustration, see Poulakidas v. Charalidis, 386 N.E.2d 405 (Ill. App. Ct. 1979), involving a falling out between the owners of a seafood restaurant.

5. A more complicated example. For a bigger business with a far more complex situation, see Adelman v. CGS Scientific Corp., 332 F. Supp. 137 (E.D. Pa. 1971). Adelman had sold his company to CGS, receiving cash and CGS stock. CGS had hired him to run his former company as an independent division. Then it was discovered that CGS had systematically misstated its earnings and inflated the value of its stock. Adelman sued for rescission of his deal; public stockholders filed a class action for securities fraud. CGS notified Adelman that he would be fired when his one-year contract expired.

Adelman feared that CGS would strip his division of cash and other assets, or so integrate it with the rest of the company that rescission would be impossible. He asked that a receiver be appointed to run the division, and that he be the receiver. The court obviously would not appoint one of the litigants as receiver, but it did appoint a receiver with the limited power of resolving disputes between CGS and Adelman's division. The court called this receiver a custodian.

Think about how this order would work out. If CGS and Adelman literally couldn't agree on anything, the custodian would wind up managing the division. More likely, CGS took little interest in the division's day-to-day operation. The most common disputes might have been over cash flow between the division and the rest of the company. Those disputes would go to the custodian instead of to the court. The custodian could devote much more time to such disputes than the court could. He could gather information more easily. He would be less dependent on adversarial submissions by the parties; he could go directly to the company's records, its bureaucracy, and its data management personnel. He could hire his own staff. He couldn't make all the problems go away, but he would have a better chance of solving them than the judge alone.

The loan agreements between CGS and its banks provided that if a receiver were appointed over any part of CGS's business, and if the appointment were not vacated within 60 days, CGS would be in default on its loans. The rationale of such clauses is that a company deserves a chance to get a receiver summarily dismissed if some disgruntled plaintiff convinces an overactive judge to appoint one, but that if he hasn't been dismissed in 60 days, there is probably something to plaintiff's claim. The trial judge tried to evade this clause by calling the receiver a custodian. But CGS soon convinced him that there was at least a substantial argument that a custodian would trigger the clause. Then he appointed the custodian for 59 days and set the case for trial at the end of that time, thus imposing a day and night schedule on the litigants and their lawyers.

6. Secured creditors. Receivership is also available for secured creditors whose collateral is in danger of dissipation, and for other plaintiffs with a claim to specific property. Perhaps the most common use of receivership is in foreclosing mortgages on rental buildings. If it appears that the value of the building is not sufficient to pay the debt, and that it will not be possible to collect the deficiency by execution on the debtor's other assets, the court can appoint a receiver to collect the rents pending foreclosure. Some courts say that for the receiver to be given full power to manage the building, there must be "something more"—fraud, dissipation of assets, failure to maintain the building, or the like. An example with a clear opinion is Canada Life Assurance Co. v. LaPeter, 563 F.3d 837 (9th Cir. 2009), involving a receiver for a shopping mall.

As you might expect, courts vary widely in the strictness with which they enforce these standards. In some places, a receiver is a routine step in most commercial mortgage foreclosures. At the other end of the spectrum, some states with strong debtor protection legislation let the debtor keep the rents through foreclosure and even through the statutory redemption period. Those states will appoint a receiver only if the debtor is damaging the property. A good example of that approach is Home State Bank v. Johnson, 729 P.2d 1225 (Kan. 1986).

7. Federal agencies. When top management is involved in the fraud, the receiver may displace them completely. It is little wonder that receivership has become one of the Securities and Exchange Commission's favorite remedies in cases of serious fraud. Turning the company over to a receiver and ousting suspected wrongdoers makes it much harder for the wrongdoers to alter or destroy records or to divert assets to their personal use. That creates time for the investigation to proceed in a systematic way. The receiver can investigate in much less cumbersome fashion than ordinary discovery or the SEC's subpoena power. His expenses come out of the company's budget instead of the SEC's budget.

In addition, the court appointing the receiver will generally enjoin the company's creditors from suing in other courts. Claims good against the company will still be good against the receiver. But the stay allows those claims to be consolidated and handled in an orderly fashion. A leading case is SEC v. Wencke, 622 F.2d 1363 (9th Cir. 1980). The Small Business Administration uses receiverships for similar purposes when one of its loans gets entangled with fraud. An example is United States v. Acorn Technology Fund LP, 429 F.3d 438 (3d Cir. 2005).

The receivership may end with liquidation, reorganization, or the company being turned over to newly elected management. But receivership is no panacea. Investors are still likely to lose lots of money. The receiver cannot create assets out of nothing; at best, she can prevent further dissipation. The remedy remains expensive and harsh. It tends to freeze the company and the willingness of others to do business with it. And there is always the risk that plaintiff and the court will make a mistake and oust honest management.

8. Other law enforcement uses. Receivers are occasionally used for law enforcement purposes in other contexts; a persistently malfunctioning corporate or governmental entity can be placed in receivership as a last resort. An example is State v. Valley Road Sewerage Co., 712 A.2d 653 (N.J. 1998), approving a receiver for a persistently polluting sewer system owned by a persistently money-losing company.

9. Receiver's certificates. Receivers have a useful power to borrow money or pay claims by issuing receiver's certificates, which are usually nonrecourse debt secured by a lien on the receivership property. If the funds are used to preserve the property, these certificates get priority over existing liens. Litigated examples include City of Chicago v. Kideys, 617 N.E.2d 162 (Ill. App. Ct. 1993), emphasizing that certificates create no personal liability and that the receiver must look to the property for payment of her fees and expenses, and Battista v. Federal Deposit Insurance Corp., 195 F.3d 1113 (9th Cir. 1999), rejecting a claim that certain claimants were entitled to be paid in cash instead of certificates. The underlying issue in *Battista* was that the certificates were not likely to be paid in full; the demand for cash was an attempt to avoid sharing pro rata with other creditors. The Eleventh Circuit agreed with *Battista* in Placida Professional Center, LLC v. Federal Deposit Insurance Corporation, 512 F. App'x 938, 951–952 (11th Cir. 2013).

Bankruptcy courts and trustees have a similar power to grant prior liens for new money. 11 U.S.C. §364. The bankruptcy option is more commonly used in the modern cases; bankrupt businesses hoping to reorganize regularly borrow money to keep operating in bankruptcy.

NOTES ON NE EXEAT

1. How it works. Perhaps the most extraordinary prejudgment remedy is ne exeat—in England called ne exeat regno (let him not go out from the kingdom), but in the United States called ne exeat republica (let him not go out from the republic). Ne exeat begins with an injunction not to leave the jurisdiction. An example is United States v. Shaheen, 445 F.2d 6 (7th Cir. 1971). At a time when the government was claiming $450,000 in back taxes, Shaheen sold his house, mortgaged an adjacent lot, shipped his household goods to London, and flew to London with his wife and daughter. The government could find only nominal assets in the United States, except for trust assets that the trustee refused to turn over. When Shaheen returned to the United States for a hearing on an unrelated criminal charge, the government obtained ex parte a writ of ne exeat, forbidding Shaheen to leave the Northern District of Illinois.

If that were all, the writ would be ineffective. There is no way to stop defendant from leaving the jurisdiction if he is at large within it, and once he leaves, he's beyond the court's contempt power. The court solved that problem by ordering Shaheen to post a $450,000 bond. When he refused to post the bond, he was imprisoned. The bonding requirement turns ne exeat into a form of bailable imprisonment for debt, available before or after judgment.

The court of appeals reversed. Drawing on the procedure for preliminary injunctions, the court required the government to show probable success on the merits, and that the tax could not be collected without the writ. The court found the government's showing insufficient. On a motion to quash, Shaheen had testified that publicity from his difficulties with the government had destroyed his financial consulting business, that he was moving to London to start over, that he had voluntarily returned for all court appearances, that three of his children lived in the United States, that most of his assets were held in trust in the United States, and that he wanted to prove that he owed no additional tax.

The government got the writ on similar facts in United States v. Lipper, 1981-1 U.S. Tax Cases (CCH) ¶9330 (N.D. Cal. 1981), where defendant made the mistake of bragging that he was going to France before the IRS could do anything about it. Lipper was required to post a bond of $370,000 and to surrender his passport. In United States v. Mathewson, 1993-1 U.S. Tax Cases (CCH) ¶50,152 (S.D. Fla. 1993), the court confined defendant to his house, with limited exceptions, and put an electronic monitor around his ankle.

For cases enforcing the bond, see Coursen v. Coursen, 252 A.2d 738 (N.J. Super. Ct. App. Div. 1969), and National Automobile & Casualty Insurance Co. v. Queck, 405 P.2d 905 (Ariz. Ct. App. 1965).

2. Private plaintiffs. Ne exeat is available to private litigants with equitable claims to money or property. It is still used very occasionally, mostly but not exclusively in divorce litigation. The older cases are collected in Elkay Steel Co. v. Collins, 141 A.2d 212 (Pa. 1958). *Elkay* upheld use of the writ in a suit to recover property taken from plaintiff by fraud and forgery.

3. Child custody disputes. Family court judges commonly order parents not to take children out of the state without permission, or condition custody on residence within an area approved by the court. But these orders are usually just part of the custody decree; they are rarely enforced with ne exeat's bonding requirement.

Both approaches are illustrated in In re People ex rel. B.C., 981 P.2d 145 (Colo. 1999), a bitter custody dispute between an American grandmother and a Jordanian father. The custody decree provided that the father could take B.C. to Jordan on vacation but could not permanently remove her from Colorado. The father left B.C. in Jordan, returned to the United States, and was convicted of international parental kidnapping. The grandmother had the father cited for contempt of the earlier custody order, but the court kept postponing the contempt hearing. With the father's release from prison approaching, the grandmother asked for a writ of ne exeat, to be enforced by a bond, lest the father flee the country to avoid the contempt proceedings. The trial court denied that motion; the state supreme court reversed, in an opinion describing ne exeat and its uses, and remanded for consideration of the merits. With B.C. half a world away, and an overworked trial judge with no energy for the case, the grandmother's chances of accomplishing anything useful did not look good.

The Supreme Court enforced a Chilean right of ne exeat in Abbott v. Abbott, 560 U.S. 1 (2010). The issue was whether a law that prohibited the custodial parent from taking the child out of the country created "rights of custody" in the other parent under the Hague Convention on the Civil Aspects of International Child Abduction. The Court said yes, which means the United States presumptively must return the child to Chile. Three dissenters thought the Chilean ne exeat created no rights of custody, but merely protected the noncustodial parent's "rights of access" to the child, which would get a lower level of protection under the Convention.

4. An overactive judge. Compare the underactive judge in *B.C.* with the overactive judge in In re Marriage of Gurda, 711 N.E.2d 339, 345-346 (Ill. App. Ct. 1999). The husband was a ground service worker at United Airlines, and he had hidden assets from his wife. After asking a few questions about whether he was eligible for free travel, the trial judge sua sponte (on his own motion) ordered defendant to surrender his passport to the court. The wife had not asked for that relief, and no one had offered any evidence that he was about to leave the country. No surprise here; the appellate court reversed.

CHAPTER

10

More Ancillary Remedies: Attorneys' Fees and the Costs of Litigation

A. FEE-SHIFTING STATUTES

CITY OF RIVERSIDE v. RIVERA
477 U.S. 561 (1986)

Justice BRENNAN announced the judgment . . . and delivered an opinion in which Justices MARSHALL, BLACKMUN, and STEVENS join. . . .

I

Respondents, eight Chicano individuals, attended a party . . . at the . . . home of respondents Santos and Jennie Rivera. A large number of unidentified police officers, acting without a warrant, broke up the party using tear gas and, as found by the District Court, "unnecessary physical force." Many of the guests . . . were arrested. The District Court later found that "[t]he party was not creating a disturbance . . . ." Criminal charges . . . were . . . dismissed for lack of probable cause.

[R]espondents sued the city of Riverside, its Chief of Police, and 30 individual police officers . . . for allegedly violating their First, Fourth, and Fourteenth Amendment rights. The complaint, which also alleged numerous state-law claims, sought damages and declaratory and injunctive relief. . . . [T]he District Court granted summary judgment in favor of 17 . . . officers. . . . The jury returned a total of 37 individual verdicts in favor of the respondents and against the city and 5 individual officers, finding 11 violations of §1983, 4 instances of false arrest and imprisonment, and 22 instances of negligence. Respondents were awarded $33,350 in compensatory and punitive damages: $13,300 for their federal claims, and $20,050 for their state-law claims.[1]

---

1. [Plaintiffs dropped their request for an injunction, with the explanation that the courts tend to refuse injunctions because they assume that defendants will obey the law.] The District Court's response to this explanation is significant:

> [I]f you [respondents] had asked for [injunctive relief] against some of the officers I think I would have granted it. . . . I would agree with you that there is a problem about telling the officers that they have to obey the law. But if you want to know what the Court thought about some of the behavior, it was—it would have warranted an injunction.

Respondents also sought attorney's fees and costs under 42 U.S.C. §1988. [The district court awarded $245,456.25, based on 1,946.75 attorney hours at $125 per hour and 84.5 law-clerk hours at $25 per hour.]

Petitioners appealed only the attorney's fees . . . .

[T]he Court of Appeals affirmed. . . . 763 F.2d 1580 (9th Cir. 1985). . . .

II

A

In Alyeska Pipeline Service Co. v. Wilderness Society, 421 U.S. 240 (1975), the Court reaffirmed the "American Rule" that, at least absent express statutory authorization to the contrary, each party to a lawsuit ordinarily shall bear its own attorney's fees. In response to *Alyeska*, Congress enacted the Civil Rights Attorney's Fees Awards Act of 1976, 42 U.S.C. §1988, which authorized the district courts to award reasonable attorney's fees to prevailing parties in specified civil rights litigation. While the statute itself does not explain what constitutes a reasonable fee, both the House and Senate Reports accompanying §1988 expressly endorse the analysis set forth in Johnson v. Georgia Highway Express, Inc., 488 F.2d 714 (5th Cir. 1974). *Johnson* identifies 12 factors to be considered in calculating a reasonable attorney's fee.[3]

Hensley v. Eckerhart, 461 U.S. 424 (1983), . . . stated that "[t]he most useful starting point for determining . . . a reasonable fee is the number of hours reasonably expended . . . multiplied by a reasonable hourly rate." *Id.* at 433. This figure, commonly referred to as the "lodestar," is presumed to be the reasonable fee contemplated by §1988. . . .

Hensley emphasized that "[w]here a plaintiff has obtained excellent results, his attorney should recover a fully compensatory fee," and that "the fee award should not be reduced simply because the plaintiff failed to prevail on every contention . . . ." *Id.* at 435.

B . . .

The District Court . . . found that "[t]he amount of time expended by counsel in conducting this litigation was reasonable and reflected sound legal judgment under the circumstances." The court also determined that counsel's excellent performances in this case entitled them to be compensated at prevailing market rates, even though they were relatively young when this litigation began. . . .

The court [also] determined that "it was never actually clear what officer did what until we had gotten through with the whole trial," so that "[u]nder the circumstances of this case, it was reasonable for plaintiffs initially to name thirty-one individual defendants . . . ." . . .

---

3. These factors are: (1) the time and labor required; (2) the novelty and difficulty of the questions; (3) the skill requisite to perform the legal service properly; (4) the preclusion of employment by the attorney due to acceptance of the case; (5) the customary fee; (6) whether the fee is fixed or contingent; (7) time limitations imposed by the client or the circumstances; (8) the amount involved and the results obtained; (9) the experience, reputation, and ability of the attorneys; (10) the "undesirability" of the case; (11) the nature and length of the professional relationship with the client; and (12) awards in similar cases.

III

Petitioners, joined by the United States as amicus curiae, maintain that *Hensley*'s lodestar approach is inappropriate . . . where a plaintiff recovers only monetary damages. . . . [P]etitioners and the United States submit that attorney's fees in such cases should be proportionate to the amount of damages a plaintiff recovers [and] modeled upon the contingent-fee arrangements commonly used in personal injury litigation. . . . [A]ssuming a 33% contingency rate, this would entitle respondents to recover approximately $11,000 in attorney's fees. . . .

A . . .

[W]e reject the notion that a civil rights action for damages constitutes nothing more than a private tort suit benefiting only the individual plaintiffs. . . . Unlike most private tort litigants, a civil rights plaintiff seeks to vindicate important civil and constitutional rights that cannot be valued solely in monetary terms. See Carey v. Piphus, 435 U.S. 247, 266 (1978). . . . Regardless of the form of relief he actually obtains, a successful civil rights plaintiff often secures important social benefits that are not reflected in nominal or relatively small damages awards. . . . [T]he District Court found that many of petitioners' unlawful acts were "motivated by a general hostility to the Chicano community," and that this litigation therefore served the public interest:

> The institutional behavior involved here . . . had to be stopped and. . .nothing short of having a lawsuit like this would have stopped it. . . . [T]he improper motivation which appeared as a result of all of this seemed to me to have pervaded a very broad segment of police officers in the department.

. . . Because damages awards do not reflect fully the public benefit advanced by civil rights litigation, Congress did not intend for fees in civil rights cases . . . to depend on obtaining substantial monetary relief. Rather, Congress made clear that it "intended that the amount of fees awarded under [§1988] be governed by the same standards which prevail in other types of equally complex Federal litigation, such as antitrust cases and *not be reduced because the rights involved may be nonpecuniary in nature.*" S. Rep. No. 94-1011 at 6 (1976), reprinted in 1976 U.S. Code Cong. & Admin. News 5908 (emphasis added). . . . The Senate Report specifically approves [of reported] cases [where] counsel received substantial attorneys' fees despite the fact the plaintiffs sought no monetary damages. Thus, Congress recognized that reasonable attorney's fees under §1988 are not conditioned upon and need not be proportionate to an award of money damages. . . .

B . . .

Congress enacted §1988 specifically to enable plaintiffs to enforce the civil rights laws even where the amount of damages at stake would not otherwise make it feasible for them to do so . . . .

[I]t is highly unlikely that the prospect of a fee equal to a fraction of the damages respondents might recover would have been sufficient to attract competent counsel.[10] Moreover, since counsel might not have found it economically feasible to expend the

---

10. . . . We reject the United States' suggestion that the prospect of working nearly 2,000 hours at a rate of $5.65 an hour, to be paid more than 10 years after the work began, is "likely to attract a substantial number of attorneys."

amount of time . . . necessary to litigate the case properly, it is even less likely that counsel would have achieved the excellent results . . . obtained here. . . . It is precisely for this reason that Congress enacted §1988.

IV . . .

[W]e have held that a civil rights defendant is not liable for attorney's fees incurred after a pretrial settlement offer, where the judgment recovered by the plaintiff is less than the offer. Marek v. Chesny, 473 U.S. 1 (1985).[11] . . .
    Affirmed.

Justice POWELL, concurring in the judgment. . . .
    On its face, the fee award seems unreasonable. But I find no basis for this Court to reject the findings made and approved by the courts below. . . .

II . . .

Where recovery of private damages is the purpose of a civil rights litigation, a district court, in fixing fees, is obligated to give primary consideration to the amount of damages awarded as compared to the amount sought. In some civil rights cases, however, the court may consider the vindication of constitutional rights in addition to the amount of damages recovered. In this case, for example, the District Court made an explicit finding that the "public interest" had been served by the jury's verdict . . . .[3] . . .
    Section 1988 was enacted because existing fee arrangements were thought not to provide an adequate incentive to . . . represent plaintiffs in unpopular civil rights cases. I therefore find petitioners' asserted analogy to personal injury claims unpersuasive . . . .

    Chief Justice BURGER, dissenting. . . .
    [I]t would be difficult to find a better example of legal nonsense than . . . attorney's fees . . . at $245,456.25 for the recovery of $33,350 damages.
    The two [attorneys'] total professional experience when this litigation began consisted of Gerald Lopez' 1-year service as a law clerk to a judge and Roy Cazares' two years' experience as a trial attorney in the Defenders' Program of San Diego County. . . .
    [N]o private party would ever have dreamed of paying these two novice attorneys $125 per hour in 1975, which . . . would represent . . . nearly . . . $250 per hour . . . today [and $600 in 2018.] . . .

    Justice REHNQUIST, with whom Justices BURGER, WHITE, and O'CONNOR join, dissenting. . . .
    [T]he . . . finding that respondents' attorneys "reasonably" spent 1,946.75 hours to recover . . . $33,350 is clearly erroneous . . . .

11. Thus, petitioners could have avoided liability for the bulk of the attorney's fees . . . by making a reasonable settlement offer in a timely manner. . . . "The government cannot litigate tenaciously and then be heard to complain about the time necessarily spent by the plaintiff in response." Copeland v. Marshall, 641 F.2d 880, 904 (D.C. Cir. 1980) (en banc).

3. It probably will be the rare case in which an award of *private damages* can be said to benefit the public interest to an extent that would justify the disproportionality between damages and fees reflected in this case.

Respondents filed . . . 256 separate claims allegedly arising out of the police breakup of a single party. . . . Respondents ultimately prevailed against only the city and 5 police officers . . . . No . . . injunctions were ever issued . . . , nor was the city ever compelled to change a single practice or policy. . . .

The court approved almost 209 hours of "prelitigation time," . . . 197 hours of . . . conversations between respondents' two attorneys, . . . 143 hours for preparation of a pretrial order, [and] 45.50 hours . . . to wait in a . . . hotel room for a jury verdict . . . [while] co-counsel was . . . employed . . . less than 40 minutes . . . from the courthouse. . . .

[T]he award of a "reasonable" attorney's fee under §1988 means a fee that would have been deemed reasonable if billed to affluent plaintiffs by their own attorneys. This . . . principle was stressed in the legislative history of §1988, and by this Court in *Hensley*: ". . . Hours that are not properly billed to one's *client* also are not properly billed to one's *adversary* . . . ." 461 U.S. at 434. . . .

[An attorney cannot reasonably bill more than $10,000 for researching the title to a $10,000 piece of property, no matter how complex the title history. The client would be better off paying $10,000 for a worthless deed. Similarly in litigation,] where the prospective recovery is limited, it is exactly this "billing judgment" which enables the parties to achieve a settlement; any competent attorney, whether prosecuting or defending [an] action for $10,000, would realize that the case simply cannot justify a fee in excess of the potential recovery . . . . All of these examples illuminate the point made in *Hensley* that "the important factor" in determining a "reasonable" fee is the "results obtained." 461 U.S. at 434. The very "reasonableness" of the hours expended . . . by a plaintiff's attorney necessarily will depend, to a large extent, on the amount that may reasonably be expected to be recovered if the plaintiff prevails. . . .

If the litigation is unnecessarily prolonged by the bad-faith conduct of the defendants, or if the litigation produces significant, identifiable benefits for persons other than the plaintiffs, then the purpose of Congress in authorizing attorney's fees under §1988 should allow a larger award of attorney's fees than would be "reasonable" where the only relief is the recovery of monetary damages by individual plaintiffs. Nor do we deal here with a case such as Carey v. Piphus, in which the deprivation of a constitutional right necessarily results in only nominal pecuniary damages. See S. Rep. at 6 (fee awards under §1988 should "not be reduced because the rights involved may be nonpecuniary in nature"). . . .

I agree . . . that the importation of the contingent-fee model to govern fee awards under §1988 is not warranted . . . . But I do not agree with the plurality if it means to reject the kind of "proportionality" that I have . . . described. . . . One may agree with all of the glowing rhetoric . . . about Congress' noble purpose . . . without concluding that Congress intended to turn attorneys loose to spend as many hours as possible to prepare and try a case that could reasonably be expected to result only in a relatively minor award of monetary damages. . . .

I would reverse . . . and remand . . . for recomputation of the fee award in light of both *Hensley* and the principles set forth in this opinion.

NOTES ON THE AMERICAN RULE

1. Attorneys' fees and the rightful position. One might suppose that successful plaintiffs should always recover attorneys' fees under the rightful-position principle.

If the successful plaintiff in Justice Rehnquist's $10,000 lawsuit has to pay $3,000 to his attorney, he has not been restored to the position he would have occupied but for the wrong. The analysis is no different in injunction cases. If he must spend $3,000 to avoid $10,000 in harm, he winds up $3,000 worse off. Plaintiff's practical problem is most severe when the amount at stake is small. But whatever the ratio of fees to judgment, plaintiff is undercompensated if he has to pay his own attorneys' fees.

American law has never viewed the matter that way. Attorneys' fees are viewed as an ancillary remedy, separate from the merits, unavailable unless specifically authorized by statute or rule. This doctrinal structure is similar in federal law and in most states.

The Supreme Court recently emphasized that only a "specific and explicit" provision in a statute or contract can override the American Rule. Baker Botts L.L.P. v. ASARCO LLC, 135 S. Ct. 2158, 2164 (2015). The Court appeared to say that most fee-shifting statutes easily meet this test. The provision at issue, as applied to the expense of litigating a fee petition in bankruptcy, did not.

Oklahoma legislators accidentally repealed the American Rule in nearly all civil cases with a poorly-drafted provision in a bill to amend statutes of limitations. Debra Cassens Weiss, *Oklahoma Unintentionally Adopts Loser-Pays System for Attorney Fees in Civil Cases*, ABAJournal.com. (May 18, 2017). The provision caused an uproar, and the legislature undid it before it took effect. William W. Savage, III, *Back to Normal: OK Legislature Restores American Rule*, Nondoc.com, May 25, 2017, https://nondoc.com/2017/05/25/oklahoma-legislature-restores-american-rule/ [https://perma.cc/NH4V-D4FX].

2. Reasons for the American Rule. Why do we tolerate such a substantial deviation from the usual rule that plaintiff is to be restored to his rightful position? The Court has said that "one should not be penalized for merely defending or prosecuting a lawsuit," that the poor would be especially discouraged by the risk of liability for the other side's fees, and that fee litigation is burdensome to the courts. Fleischmann Distilling Corp. v. Maier Brewing Co., 386 U.S. 714, 718 (1967). The fear of deterring litigation is the most important of these reasons. Many plaintiffs can't pay their own attorneys and are able to proceed at all only because of contingent fee arrangements. These plaintiffs simply couldn't litigate if there were any substantial risk of liability for defendant's fees, which often are fixed hourly rates at high-cost firms. The city's fees surely would have bankrupted the Riveras. Serious claims as well as frivolous ones would be deterred.

3. The rest of the world. Losers pay some or all of winners' attorneys' fees in all but a handful of the world's other nations. John Henry Merryman, David S. Clark, & John O. Haley, *The Civil Law Tradition* 1026 (Michie 1994). The result does not change when common law nations are included. Thomas D. Rowe, Jr., *The Legal Theory of Attorney Fee Shifting: A Critical Overview*, 1982 Duke L.J. 651, 651.

4. A litigation explosion? Talk of a litigation explosion brought suggestions that we make losing litigants liable for fees, but there has been little general move in that direction. It is easy to collect stories of frivolous lawsuits, but it is hard to show that Americans are generally too quick to litigate. Professor Galanter's survey of empirical studies suggests that modern American litigation rates are not high when compared to the number of grievances resolved some other way, litigation rates in some other countries, or litigation rates at earlier times in our own history. Marc Galanter, *Reading the Landscape of Disputes: What We Know and Don't Know (and Think We Know) About Our Allegedly Contentious and Litigious Society*, 31 UCLA L. Rev. 4 (1983). And see the current data on case filings in Notes on the Empirical Debate, in section 2.G.2.

NOTES ON EXCEPTIONS TO THE AMERICAN RULE

There are many substantial exceptions to the American Rule. Common law tort cases, including personal injury litigation, are the largest remaining domain of the pure American Rule.

1. Statutory exceptions. More than 200 federal statutes and almost 4,000 state statutes authorize awards of attorneys' fees. And more such statutes have been enacted since these were counted. The federal count is from Henry Cohen, Congressional Research Service, *Awards of Attorneys' Fees by Federal Courts and Federal Agencies* (2008), available at www.fas.org/sgp/crs/misc/94-970.pdf [https://perma.cc/F29Z-G5VW]; the state count is from Susan M. Olson, *How Much Access to Justice from State "Equal Access to Justice Acts"?* 71 Chi.-Kent L. Rev. 547, 552-553 (1995). Collectively, these statutes account for a large fraction of civil litigation. Many of these statutes are based on the private-attorney-general theory illustrated in *Rivera*: Fees will encourage plaintiffs to enforce the statute.

a. Two-way partial fee shifting. Alaska has the most extensive fee provision, providing for two-way partial fee shifting in all cases unless the court otherwise directs. Alaska R. Civ. P. 82. There is a presumptive fee schedule, which is plainly not intended to be fully compensatory. For example, it authorizes 20 percent of the first $25,000 and 10 percent of the rest of the judgment in cases that go to trial and result in a monetary award, and 30 percent of the "prevailing party's reasonable actual attorney's fees" in cases that go to trial and end in nonmonetary relief or a judgment for defendant. The court "shall" award fees on the basis of this schedule unless it finds, according to a list of ten factors and any "other equitable factors deemed relevant," that "a variation is warranted." One of the listed factors is the risk that an award "may be so onerous to the non-prevailing party that it would deter similarly situated litigants from the voluntary use of the courts."

An empirical study of the Alaska rule is reported in Susanne Di Pietro and Teresa W. Carns, *Alaska's English Rule: Attorney's Fee Shifting in Civil Cases*, 13 Alaska L. Rev. 33 (1996). Alaska lawyers generally support the rule. Fee awards are few—only in cases that go to judgment, and only in about half of those—and generally modest. A common form of postjudgment settlement is for the winner to waive the fee claim in exchange for the loser waiving an appeal. "[T]he three most apparent effects of Rule 82 were that it (1) discouraged some middle class parties from filing cases that either wealthy or poor plaintiffs would file, (2) discouraged some suits (or defenses) of questionable merit and (3) encouraged litigation in strong cases that might otherwise settle." *Id.* at 84. But all of these effects were modest. A more recent study found that the fee provision does not deter potential litigants. Douglas C. Rennie, *Rule 82 & Tort Reform: An Empirical Study of the Impact of Alaska's English Rule on Federal Civil Case Filings*, 29 Alaska L. Rev. 1 (2012).

b. The Equal Access to Justice Act. The Equal Access to Justice Act mandates fees against the United States in nontort civil actions where the prevailing party is a business with fewer than 500 employees and net worth under $7 million, an individual with net worth under $2 million, or a tax-exempt charitable organization. 28 U.S.C. §2412(b). But fees cannot be awarded if the court finds "that the position of the United States was substantially justified or that special circumstances make an award unjust," and fees are capped at below market rates. 28 U.S.C. §2412(d)(1)(a). There is a similar provision for fees in administrative agency proceedings, 5 U.S.C. §504, and more than 30 states had similar laws as of 1995. Olson, 71 Chi.-Kent L. Rev. at 556-557.

Despite the limitation to cases where government's position is not substantially justified, fees are awarded in nearly half of all social security cases and a majority of veterans' benefit cases. The great bulk of awards under the Act are modest amounts for claims under these two programs. Astrue v. Ratliff, 560 U.S. 586, 600 nn.1-2 (2010) (Sotomayor, J., concurring).

In Windsor v. United States, 570 U.S. 744 (2013), the government continued to enforce the Defense of Marriage Act, refusing to recognize same-sex marriages, even though it also argued that the law was unconstitutional. The First Circuit held that this litigation strategy was substantially justified, refusing to award fees in parallel litigation presenting the same issues. McLaughlin v. Hagel, 767 F.3d 113 (1st Cir. 2014). Had the government simply started recognizing marriages, it would have violated and failed to enforce the law on the basis of "a novel legal theory while simultaneously precluding judicial review of that novel theory." *Id.* at 117-118.

Courts are split over whether the question of substantial justification looks at the government's conduct claim-by-claim or as a whole. The D.C. Circuit said the former, Air Transportation Association of Canada v. FAA, 156 F.3d 1329 (D.C. Cir. 1998), and a Ninth Circuit panel said the latter, an issue that will now be reconsidered en banc. Ibrahim v. Department of Homeland Security, 878 F.3d 703 (9th Cir. 2017) (granting en banc review).

c. Other examples. Other fee statutes have diverse and sometimes puzzling rationales. An Arizona statute gives courts discretion to award full or partial attorneys' fees to the prevailing party in cases of express or implied contract, but not in tort. Ariz. Rev. Stat. Ann. §12-341.01(A). Texas *mandates* fees to prevailing plaintiffs in contract cases. Texas Civ. Practice & Remedies Code Ann. §38.001; Ventling v. Johnson, 466 S.W.3d 143, 154 (Tex. 2015). It merely *authorizes* fees to prevailing parties in declaratory judgment actions. *Id.* §37.009.

2. The bad-faith-litigation exception. Courts assert inherent power to award fees to punish bad-faith litigation. Chambers v. NASCO, 501 U.S. 32 (1991). These fees are not limited by the American Rule, and a federal court can award them in a diversity case even if the state court would not award fees for the same misconduct.

The court can also award fees against the lawyer instead of his client. The leading federal case is Roadway Express, Inc. v. Piper, 447 U.S. 752 (1980), where attorneys filed a class action without consulting their clients; failed to answer interrogatories, produce their clients for depositions, or file briefs; and ignored orders from the court. The Court did this as a matter of inherent power; Congress then codified the practice in 28 U.S.C. §1927.

In *Chambers*, the Court affirmed an award of all of plaintiff's attorneys' fees, where defendant had engaged in a pervasive course of bad-faith litigation. But in Goodyear Tire & Rubber Co. v. Haeger, 137 S. Ct. 1178 (2017), the Court said that the normal award should be only those fees that were the but-for consequence of the other side's violations. It applied this rule even though it did not question the lower courts' view that Goodyear's misconduct was "egregious." Goodyear withheld test results showing that the tire at issue overheated when driven at highway speeds; plaintiffs had requested all test results "early and often." *Id.* at 1184-1185. Other cases had gone to trial even though those test results were produced, so the Court could not infer that the case would have immediately settled, or that all litigation expenses after the first request for test results flowed from the dishonest responses.

Justice Kagan's unanimous opinion said that this rule followed, "pretty much by definition," from the nature of compensation. Anything more would be punishment and would require criminal-procedure style protections, citing contempt-of-court cases that appeared in Chapter 9, including United Mine Workers v. Bagwell. On remand, the district court reinstated $2 million of the original $2.7 million award. 2018 WL 1182551 (D. Ariz. Mar. 7, 2018).

The Fourth Circuit affirmed $150,000 in sanctions imposed on lawyers who persistently litigated the authenticity of a contract even though one of them had a copy of that contract on his laptop. Six v. Generations Federal Credit Union, 891 F.3d 508 (4th Cir. 2018). The sanctions were payable to defendant to compensate for additional fees incurred in responding to the bad-faith litigation. The court relied both on §1927 and on the district court's inherent authority, and the opinion detailed the lawyers' misconduct. It is impossible to see how the lawyers expected to get away with this. They were simultaneously attacking the contract's interest rate as usurious while denying the contract's existence to avoid its arbitration clause.

3. The contempt-of-court exception. Toledo Scale Co. v. Computing Scale Co., 261 U.S. 399 (1923), is generally cited for the rule that a court may assess fees for willful disobedience of a court order. Cases that say it more clearly are collected in Annotation, 43 A.L.R.3d 793 (1972 & Supp.). The power to award fees in contempt proceedings is discretionary; successful plaintiffs are not entitled to fees as of right.

4. The contract exception. Courts will enforce contractual provisions for reasonable attorneys' fees. Adhesion contracts routinely provide that the party without bargaining power will pay the stronger party's attorneys' fees if the stronger party sues to enforce the contract. Statutes in California, Oregon, and Washington provide that if a contract provides for fees for one party, then either party can recover fees if it prevails, and this reciprocal right to fees cannot be waived in the contract. See, e.g., Cal. Civ. Code §1717(a).

5. The family-law exception. It is common to award fees in divorce. One spouse may pay the other's fees as part of the property division, or pursuant to the obligation to support the children and dependent spouse, or in a more recent development, simply to ensure that each spouse can be adequately represented. A leading case for the property-division theory is Carle v. Carle, 234 S.W.2d 1002 (Tex. 1950), reaffirmed in Tedder v. Gardner Aldrich, LLP, 421 S.W.3d 651 (Tex. 2013).

There is a substantial discussion of the adequate-representation theory, ultimately affirming a refusal to award fees on the facts of that case, in Edelman v. Edelman, 61 P.3d 1 (Alaska 2002). Illinois directs courts to make interim fee awards sufficient "to enable the petitioning party to participate adequately in the litigation," if it finds that one spouse has sufficient funds to pay fees and the other does not. 750 Ill. Comp. Stat. 5/501(c-1)(3). Florida has a similar provision. Fla. Stat. Ann. §61.16. In Rosaler v. Rosaler, 226 So. 3d 911 (Fla. 2017), the wife made numerous false allegations of domestic violence, sexual abuse, and illegal drug use. The court still awarded fees to the wife, but it reduced the award because of this litigation misconduct and also because the thousand hours billed by her attorneys appeared to be far more than the case required.

6. The collateral-litigation exception. When defendant's wrong involves plaintiff in collateral litigation, plaintiff can recover the expenses of that litigation, including attorneys' fees, as consequential damages. Common examples include malicious prosecution and false arrest. In TXO Production Corp. v. Alliance Resources Corp., 509 U.S. 443 (1993), a slander of title case described in section 3.A.2, the only actual damages were attorneys' fees incurred to defend title to the disputed property. "Collateral litigation" may be a misnomer, because other collateral legal expenses are also recoverable. In Welch v. Kosasky, 509 N.E.2d 919 (Mass. App. Ct. 1987), plaintiffs recovered the fees paid to lawyers who recovered antique silver that had been stolen and fenced; the lawyers apparently recovered the silver by investigation and negotiation and not by litigation.

The Seventh Circuit interpreted Illinois law to allow fees for collateral litigation only if the defendant caused the commencement of the collateral litigation. It is not enough that the defendant increased the expense of collateral litigation that had already begun or would have been filed anyway. Webb v. Financial Industry Regulatory Authority, Inc., 889 F.3d 853 (7th Cir. 2018). Judge Ripple, dissenting in part, thought that the majority had merely described the most common fact pattern and the one that had appeared in all the Illinois cases. But he thought that no Illinois case precluded fees as damages for the increased expense of collateral litigation.

7. The private-attorney-general exception. *Alyeska* squarely rejects a judicially created exception for private litigants who enforce public policy, but that decision is not binding with respect to state-law claims. Several states award fees on a private-attorney-general theory, mostly for state constitutional claims; several others have expressly refused to do so. Some of the cases are collected in State Board of Tax Commissioners v. Town of St. John, 751 N.E.2d 657, 660-661 & nn.6-7 (Ind. 2001).

8. The common-fund exception. When a case creates a common fund in which others will share, plaintiff and her attorney are entitled to fees from the fund. This exception is explored in section 10.B.

9. Procedure. The view that attorneys' fees are generally a collateral matter has procedural consequences that are a trap for unwary litigators. A federal judgment is final and appealable when it is final on all issues except attorneys' fees. Budinich v. Becton Dickinson & Co., 486 U.S. 196 (1988). The merits and the fee award thus become separate final judgments, requiring separate notices of appeal, and becoming separate cases in the court of appeals. To avoid litigating fees while the merits appeal is pending, district courts commonly stay the filing of a fee petition until completion of all appeals on the merits. This sensible solution is illustrated in Friends of the Earth, Inc. v. Laidlaw Environmental Services (TOC), 528 U.S. 167, 195 (2000), where its legitimacy was apparently uncontested. In the absence of such a stay, the fee petition is generally due 14 days after judgment on the merits. Fed. R. Civ. P. 54(d)(2). *Budinich* is fully applicable to claims for fees based on a contract. In Ray Haluch Gravel Co. v. Central Pension Fund, 571 U.S. 177 (2014), plaintiff unsuccessfully argued that a contractual fee award was part of the merits because the liability was on the contract; the Court emphasized the desirability of a uniform rule. The contract at issue was a collective-bargaining agreement, governed by federal common law; the case probably also applies to ordinary contract litigation in federal court under the diversity jurisdiction. Of course, most claims for contractual fee awards will arise in state court and be governed by state law.

Some states have similar procedures; others handle fee awards quite differently. In Texas, the usual practice is to prove attorneys' fees at trial and have the jury award them by special verdict or in response to interrogatories. The practice is illustrated in Holland v. Wal-Mart Stores, Inc., 1 S.W.3d 91 (Tex. 1999).

NOTES ON ONE-WAY FEE SHIFTING

1. Express provisions for one-way fee shifting. It is easy enough to make plaintiffs whole without discouraging them from suing. The solution is to award attorneys' fees to prevailing plaintiffs but not to prevailing defendants.

Some statutes explicitly authorize fees only to prevailing plaintiffs. Federal examples are the antitrust laws, 15 U.S.C. §15, the Fair Labor Standards Act, 29 U.S.C. §216(b), and the Truth in Lending Act, 15 U.S.C. §1640(a)(3). Some statutes authorize fees to all prevailing plaintiffs and authorize fees to prevailing defendants only on a showing akin to malicious prosecution. An example is the Texas Deceptive Trade Practices Act, which awards fees to defendants when the action "was groundless in fact or law or brought in bad faith, or brought for the purpose of harassment." Tex. Bus. & Com. Code Ann. §17.50(c).

2. Statutes interpreted to provide for one-way fee shifting. Some statutes that are facially neutral have been construed to favor plaintiffs. The most notable examples here are the federal civil rights laws. The statute at issue in *Rivera*, which applies to a wide range of civil rights and civil liberties litigation against local governments and state and local officials, provides that "the court, in its discretion, may allow the prevailing party . . . a reasonable attorney's fee" 42 U.S.C. §1988(b). The principal statute on employment discrimination has identical language. 42 U.S.C. §2000e-5(k). The Supreme Court has held that prevailing plaintiffs under these statutes should recover fees as a matter of course, unless special circumstances make an award unjust. Albemarle Paper Co. v. Moody, 422 U.S. 405 (1975). But prevailing defendants recover fees only when plaintiff's claim was "frivolous, unreasonable, or groundless, or . . . plaintiff continued to litigate after it clearly became so." Christiansburg Garment Co. v. Equal Employment Opportunity Commission, 434 U.S. 412, 422 (1978). Bad faith is not required.

The Supreme Court of Idaho refused to follow this rule, on the ground that it was a decision about judicial discretion. "Although the Supreme Court may have the authority to limit the discretion of lower federal courts, it does not have the authority to limit the discretion of state courts where such limitation is not contained in the statute." James v. City of Boise, 351 P.3d 1171, 1192 (Idaho 2015). The Supreme Court summarily and unanimously reversed, quoting Justice Story's opinion in Martin v. Hunter's Lessee, 14 U.S. (1 Wheat.) 304 (1816), which first explained why Supreme Court interpretations of federal law must necessarily be binding in state courts. James v. City of Boise, 136 S. Ct. 685 (2016).

3. The Court's explanation. Why should the Court exercise its discretion so differently for prevailing plaintiffs and prevailing defendants when the statute speaks neutrally of prevailing parties? The Court's answer was that prevailing plaintiffs vindicate federal policy, and losing defendants are adjudicated wrongdoers. But prevailing defendants protect only their own purse, and losing plaintiffs didn't do anything wrong. *Christiansburg* thus shares the prevailing view that most losing litigation is not wrongful. The Court feared that liability for defendant's fees would deter "all but the most airtight claims" if the threshold of liability were set too low. 434 U.S. at 422.

4. Elaborating the explanation. One-way fee shifting epitomizes the American policy of encouraging litigation. Plaintiffs can finance litigation that would be meritorious but prohibitively expensive if they had to pay their own lawyers. They can recover full compensation instead of compensation minus their attorneys' fees. And they don't have to worry much about liability if things go badly. Should we generalize one-way fee shifting? Or is this strong medicine, to be used only in certain kinds of claims?

One-way fee shifting is most common and most valuable where it enables plaintiffs of modest means to pursue claims with modest stakes. Harold J. Krent, *Explaining One-Way Fee Shifting*, 79 Va. L. Rev. 2039 (1993). Tort reformers keep urging two-way fee shifting to deter weak claims. But one-way fee shifting has been included in thousands of statutes on the strong intuition that the statutes would be unenforceable under either the American Rule or two-way fee shifting. Game-theory models unsurprisingly suggest that one-way fee shifting makes the law more enforceable, and more surprisingly, that two-way fee shifting actually inhibits settlement. See Keith N. Hylton, *Fee Shifting and the Predictability of the Law*, 71 Chi.-Kent L. Rev. 427 (1995); Eric Talley, *Liability-Based Fee-Shifting Rules and Settlement Mechanisms Under Incomplete Information*, 71 Chi.-Kent L. Rev. 461 (1995).

5. Repeat players and one-shotters. Professor Galanter's analysis of repeat players and one-shotters casts much light on the debate over attorneys' fees. Marc Galanter, *Why the "Haves" Come Out Ahead: Speculation on the Limits of Legal Change*, 9 Law & Soc'y Rev. 95, 107, 150 (1974). Repeat players have many advantages in litigation, and there have been repeated empirical confirmations of Galanter's larger hypothesis: Repeat players win lawsuits far more often than one-shotters. Some of those studies are collected in Herbert M. Kritzer and Susan Silbey, eds., *In Litigation Do the "Haves" Still Come Out Ahead* (Stanford Univ. Press 2003). Some scholars have noted that in high-stakes litigation such as mass torts, the rise of large, well-capitalized networks of plaintiff's firms appears to have leveled the playing field. See, e.g., Samuel Issacharoff & Robert H. Klonoff, *The Public Value of Settlement*, 78 Fordham L. Rev. 1177 (2009). But Galanter's account is probably still accurate for a wide range of one-on-one and smaller stakes litigation.

A defendant like Walmart is a repeat player; it is in court over and over in cases about employment, personal injury, and false imprisonment. If it has to pay a plaintiff's attorney on occasion, it can spread that loss over many cases. With rare exceptions, each plaintiff is in court only once. Her risk of paying Walmart's lawyer is all-or-nothing; there are no other cases to even things out. Most litigants can be classified as one-shotters or repeat players. Consider Galanter's table:

Figure 10-1
A Taxonomy of Litigation by Strategic Configuration of Parties

Initiator, Claimant

	One-Shotter	**Repeat Player**
One-Shotter (Defendant)	Parent v. Parent (custody) Spouse v. Spouse (divorce) Family v. Family Member (insanity commitment) Family v. Family (inheritance) Neighbor v. Neighbor Partner v. Partner **OS v. OS** **I**	Prosecutor v. Accused Finance Co. v. Debtor Landlord v. Tenant I.R.S. v. Taxpayer Condemnor v. Property Owner **RP v. OS** **II**
Repeat Player (Defendant)	Welfare Client v. Agency Auto Dealer v. Manufacturer Injury Victim v. Insurance Company Tenant v. Landlord Bankrupt Consumer v. Creditors Defamed v. Publisher **OS v. RP** **III**	Union v. Company Movie Distributor v. Censorship Board Developer v. Suburban Municipality Purchaser v. Supplier Regulatory Agency v. Firms of Regulated Industry **RP v. RP** **IV**

6. Designing policy on attorneys' fees. If there is to be one-way fee shifting, should it generally favor plaintiffs? The party with the fewest financial resources? One-shotters? What about cases of one-shotter versus one-shotter and repeat player versus repeat player? Should we have a different rule for each cell of Galanter's table? Could you write a statute codifying such a rule, or would the courts have to work it out case by case? What about the Illinois divorce statute directing courts to use fee awards to enable each side "to participate adequately in the litigation." 750 Ill. Comp. Stat. 5/501(c-1)(3). Is that a workable standard? Or is it tolerable only in divorce?

7. Making lawyers pay? If a legislature were to seriously consider two-way fee shifting, should the liability be placed on the lawyers for one-shotters, and not on the clients? Are the lawyers repeat players who could spread the risk? What about small firms with little capital, or legal-aid offices? A number of academics have proposed two-way fee shifting to lawyers. See, e.g., Deborah R. Hensler & Thomas R. Rowe, *Beyond "It Just Ain't Worth It": Alternative Strategies for Damage Class Action Reform*, 64 L. & Contemp. Probs. 137, 152-159 (Spring/Summer 2001). For a rebuttal from an attorney who would bear the risk, see Marc I. Gross, *Loser-Pays—Or Whose "Fault" Is It Anyway: A Response to Hensler-Rowe's "Beyond 'It Just Ain't Worth It,'"* 64 L. & Contemp. Probs. 163 (Spring/Summer 2001).

8. Other interpretations for other statutes. The civil rights laws are the best-known model for fee shifting, but they are not always the model for interpreting similar language in other statutes.

a. The Copyright Act. The Copyright Act provides that the court "may . . . award a reasonable attorney's fee to the prevailing party as part of the costs," 17 U.S.C. §505, language indistinguishable from the civil rights provision construed in *Christiansburg*. But the Court rejected one-way fee shifting under the Copyright Act. Fogerty v. Fantasy, Inc., 510 U.S. 517 (1994). The Court said that civil rights cases often involve impecunious plaintiffs suing defendants with far more resources, but that in copyright cases, both plaintiffs and defendants "run the gamut from corporate behemoths to starving artists." *Id.* at 524.

The Court also rejected presumptive two-way fee shifting. Rather, it said that trial courts should exercise their discretion "in light of the considerations we have identified," 510 U.S. at 534, and that this discretion should be exercised evenhandedly between plaintiffs and defendants.

More recently, the Court held that "the objective reasonableness" of the losing party's position is "an important factor" but "not the controlling one." Kirtsaeng v. John Wiley & Sons, Inc., 136 S. Ct. 1979, 1988 (2016). A court deciding whether to award fees must consider all the relevant circumstances. These were not specified, but the Court gave two examples: litigation misconduct while litigating an otherwise reasonable claim or defense, and the need to deter repeated infringement or repeated and overaggressive claims, even if in the particular case the repeat offender's position was reasonable.

b. The Patent Act. The Patent Act provides that "[t]he court in exceptional cases may award reasonable attorney fees to the prevailing party." 35 U.S.C. §285. The Court held that "an 'exceptional' case is simply one that stands out from others with respect to the substantive strength of a party's litigating position (considering both the governing law and the facts of the case) or the unreasonable manner in which the case was litigated." Octane Fitness, LLC v. Icon Health & Fitness, Inc., 134 S. Ct. 1749, 1756 (2014).

The Court described the copyright provision construed in *Fogarty* as "similar," 134 S. Ct. at 1756 n.6, although that provision does not use the word "exceptional." The Patent Act provision had originally read the same way; the word "exceptional" was added in 1952, and the Court said the amendment was intended to clarify the original intent, not to actually change anything. And the courts of appeals are applying *Octane*'s standard to the Lanham Act on trademark infringement. Tobinick v. Novella, 884 F.3d 1110 (11th Cir. 2018) (collecting cases).

c. The removal statute. The removal statute provides that courts "may" award fees against defendants who remove state cases to federal court, if the federal judge sends the case back to state court for lack of federal jurisdiction. 28 U.S.C. §1447(c). Here, the Court held that fees should generally be awarded only if "the removing party lacked an objectively reasonable basis for seeking removal." Martin v. Franklin Capital Corp., 546 U.S. 132, 141 (2005). In Rosenbloom v. Jet's America, Inc., 277 F. Supp. 3d 1072 (E.D. Mo. 2017), the district court determined that defendants had an objectively reasonable, but ultimately incorrect, argument for removing the case to federal court based on diversity jurisdiction. It remanded the case to state court but denied plaintiff's motion for fees.

NOTES ON THE AMOUNT OF THE JUDGMENT AS A CONSTRAINT ON ATTORNEYS' FEES

1. Sorting out the arguments in *Rivera*. In considering *Rivera*, it is important to distinguish three arguments. One is the prevailing-party issue: that plaintiffs filed many claims and prevailed on only a few. Two is a calculation issue: that the inexperienced lawyers were paid too much and spent more hours than needed to win the case. Three is that the sum at stake was too small to justify the hours needed—that the task was not worth doing. This last presents a fundamental question about statutory policy.

2. The abandoned request for an injunction. If plaintiffs had recovered $33,000 and the court had enjoined similar police misconduct, would the dissenters have recognized that plaintiffs had enforced "non-pecuniary" rights that justified a fee award? The foolish decision to drop their request for an injunction probably cost them the trouble and delay of full review in the Supreme Court.

3. Nominal damages. Would the rights at issue have been "non-pecuniary" if plaintiffs had requested only nominal damages? See Farrar v. Hobby, 506 U.S. 103, 115 (1992), holding that when plaintiff recovers only nominal damages, "the only reasonable fee is usually no fee at all." Professors Eaton and Wells argue that the *Farrar* rule defeats the purpose of fee shifting:

> the need to assure attorney's fees for the establishment of constitutional wrongs will be especially great when provable damages are low. Thus, the effect of the "low award, low fee" rule is to subvert the essential purpose of §1988 by discouraging §1983 litigation in the very set of cases in which the greatest need exists to encourage suits to vindicate constitutional guarantees and deter their violation.

Thomas A. Eaton & Michael Lewis Wells, *Attorney's Fees, Nominal Damages, and Section 1983 Litigation*, 24 Wm. & Mary Bill Rts. J. 829, 834 (2016).

Courts have continued to award fees in some cases with only nominal damages, based on three factors suggested in Justice O'Connor's opinion for the fifth vote in *Farrar*. A good illustration is Mercer v. Duke University, 401 F.3d 199 (4th Cir. 2005). Women have no statutory right to participate in single-sex contact sports, but *Mercer* establishes the principle that if they are allowed to participate, they are entitled to equal treatment. Plaintiff received only nominal damages, but her precedent paved the way for thousands of female place kickers in high schools, and a handful in colleges, and she recovered $350,000 in attorneys' fees.

4. The cases since *Rivera*. Since *Rivera*, courts have continued to approve fees in excess of damages, although some of these cases say that the amount of the damages is a reason for awarding less than the full lodestar. Examples include Tuf Racing Products, Inc. v. American Suzuki Motor Corp., 223 F.3d 585, 592-593 (7th Cir. 2000), affirming $137,000 in damages and $391,000 in fees in a case tried under the Illinois Motor Vehicle Franchise Act, 815 Ill. Comp. Stat. 710/1 *et seq.*, and Foley v. City of Lowell, 948 F.2d 10, 18-21 (1st Cir. 1991), a police brutality case with a ten-day trial, a $30,000 verdict, and a $110,000 fee award.

Perhaps more striking is Anderson v. AB Painting and Sandblasting, Inc., 578 F.3d 542 (7th Cir. 2009), where plaintiff sought $51,000 in fees for recovering $6,500 in past-due pension contributions and interest. The district court found that request disproportionate and awarded $10,000 in fees. The court of appeals, saying that it's an abuse of discretion to rely on proportionality in this way, vacated and remanded for a new determination of fees.

> Because Congress wants even small violations of certain laws to be checked through private litigation and because litigation is expensive, it is no surprise that the cost to pursue a contested claim will often exceed the amount in controversy. That is the whole point of fee-shifting—it allows plaintiffs to bring those types of cases because it makes no difference to an attorney whether she receives $20,000 for pursuing a $10,000 claim or $20,000 for pursuing a $100,000 claim.

Id. at 545.

And consider Rodriguez v. County of Los Angeles, 892 F.3d 776 (9th Cir. 2018), a case involving five prisoners who were injured during "cell extractions" at the Los Angeles County Men's Central Jail. After protracted litigation, including a month-long trial, a jury found that the Los Angeles Sheriff's Department and individual employees violated plaintiffs' civil rights under both state and federal law. The jury awarded $740,000 in compensatory damages and $210,000 in punitive damages.

The trial court awarded $5.3 million in attorneys' fees under California law. The Ninth Circuit affirmed.

> In accordance with state law, the district court based its decision on the substantial financial risk that appellees' counsel assumed in investing $3.4 million of attorney time in a contingency case; the difficulty of representing prisoners with the Men's Central Jail's highest security classifications, in an excessive force action against high-ranking jail officials, all the while facing "aggressive opposition" from appellants; and the opportunity costs the years-long litigation in this case required. The court expressly noted that it had considered the burden to California's taxpayers that the fee award would represent, and found that the award was justified given the factors described above and the importance of civil rights suits in protecting the public against abuses at the hands of "large or politically powerful defendants."

Id. at 809.

5. The policy argument. The ultimate argument in these cases is whether violations of rights are worth remedying if their dollar value is small in proportion to the cost of litigation. The problem is most acute in cases where damages are inevitably small, such as most consumer cases and constitutional cases without serious consequential damages. But severe beatings and loss of a business franchise are hardly small claims to the victims. Wouldn't the dissenters' position in *Rivera* mean that repeat-player defendants could litigate every case to the point that it was uneconomical for plaintiffs' bar to pursue it? How many hours do you suppose the city spent to defend *Rivera*?

Consider State Farm Fire & Casualty Co. v. Palma, 555 So. 2d 836 (Fla. 1990), where State Farm treated the case as a national test of whether a certain medical procedure was covered by its policies. There was much more at stake for State Farm than for the individual insured, but the precedent was as valuable to policy holders collectively as it was to State Farm. State Farm's counsel spent 731 hours; plaintiff's counsel spent 650. Plaintiff recovered $600 for the treatment, and her lawyer recovered $253,500 in fees.

In high-profile cases, government defendants are often under political pressure that precludes settlement even when litigation is not legally or economically justified. Can the dissenters' position deal with that?

6. The Prison Litigation Reform Act. The Prison Litigation Reform Act limits *Rivera* and §1988 in prisoner litigation. In "any action brought by a prisoner . . . in which attorney's fees are authorized under section 1988 . . . a portion of" any damages awarded, "not to exceed 25 percent . . . shall be applied to satisfy the amount of attorney's fees awarded against the defendant." 42 U.S.C. §1997e(d). Defendant pays the rest of the fee, but if "a monetary judgment is awarded," the fee is capped at 150 percent of the judgment. The courts of appeals have rejected constitutional challenges to these provisions; the cases are collected in Parker v. Conway, 581 F.3d 198, 203 (3d Cir. 2009). In *Rodriguez*, the court held that the PLRA did not limit fees for litigating the state law claim. 892 F.3d at 808.

The Supreme Court has held that "not to exceed 25 percent" means 25 percent, unless a smaller fraction of the prisoner's judgment would entirely satisfy the fee award. Murphy v. Smith, 138 S. Ct. 784, 786 (2018). Justice Sotomayor dissented for the four liberals. The average damage judgment in a successful prisoners' civil rights case is only about $4,000, so the difference between 25 percent and some smaller percentage is likely to be significant only to the prisoner. *Murphy* was the unusual case of permanent physical injuries, a $307,000 judgment, and a $108,000 fee award.

NOTES ON THE PREVAILING-PARTY REQUIREMENT

1. Partially prevailing parties. Section 1988 and many other fee provisions authorize fees to a "prevailing party." What about a partially prevailing party? Hensley v. Eckerhart, 461 U.S. 424 (1983), said that unrelated claims should be treated as separate lawsuits, with fees only for hours spent on successful claims. But the Court acknowledged that most litigation involves related claims and found it unrealistic to separate them. The court said that if plaintiffs prevailed on most of their claims, it might be reasonable to award fees for all the hours spent, but that if plaintiffs prevailed on few of their claims, compensation for all the hours spent would be excessive. Did plaintiffs in *Rivera* prevail on most of their claims? Did they really have 256 claims, or one claim with a lot of factual detail?

2. Partially prevailing defendants. In Fox v. Vice, 563 U.S. 826 (2011), the Court faced the problem of defendants entitled to fees because some, but not all, of plaintiff's claims were frivolous. The Court unanimously announced a but-for standard: Defendant can recover those fees that would not have been incurred but for the frivolous claims. So if frivolous and non-frivolous claims are factually related, defendants can recover no fees for work that would have been done even if the frivolous claim had not been filed.

3. The requirement of relief on the merits. "The touchstone of the prevailing party inquiry must be the material alteration of the legal relationship of the parties in a manner which Congress sought to promote in the fee statute." Texas State Teachers Association v. Garland Independent School District, 489 U.S. 782 (1989).

Plaintiff can achieve a big legal win without getting any personal benefit or altering his own legal relationship with defendant. In Hewitt v. Helms, 482 U.S. 755 (1987), the lawsuit led to reform of the prison's disciplinary procedures, but plaintiff did not benefit from these reforms because he had been paroled before they were implemented, and he recovered no damages because the law had not been clearly established before his lawsuit. He got no fees.

The Fourth Circuit bizarrely held that plaintiffs were not prevailing parties where they got an injunction ordering defendants to comply with the law in the future, but no damages for the past. Lefemine v. Wideman, 672 F.3d 292 (4th Cir. 2012). The idea seemed to be that the injunction gave them only what they were already entitled to under the First Amendment. But all injunctions (with the arguable exception of the prophylactic terms of prophylactic injunctions) enforce pre-existing rights that defendant had been violating. The Supreme Court unanimously vacated and remanded. Lefemine v. Wideman, 568 U.S. 1 (2012).

4. Prevailing defendants. A defendant can prevail on grounds other than the merits. CRST Van Expedited, Inc. v. Equal Employment Opportunity Commission, 136 S. Ct. 1642 (2016). The EEOC sued CRST on behalf of some 250 female employees, alleging sexual harassment. The district court dismissed the pattern-and-practice claim on the merits, and dismissed all the individual claims on a variety of other grounds—statute of limitations, failure to investigate and attempt settlement as the statute requires, and as a sanction for discovery abuse. The court of appeals revived only two individual claims.

The Court thought it obvious that CRST was a prevailing party. Given the *Christiansburg* rule, discussed above, the question presumably becomes whether it was frivolous, unreasonable, or groundless to contend that these claims had been adequately investigated and mediated and filed within the limitations period, or frivolous, unreasonable, or groundless to contend that the EEOC had adequately responded to discovery.

5. Consent decrees. A consent decree is enough to make plaintiff a prevailing party and to support a subsequent fee petition. Maher v. Gagne, 448 U.S. 122 (1980).

6. Other settlements, catalysts for reform, and *Buckhannon*. Lower courts had long awarded fees for "catalytic" claims that triggered "voluntary" reform. But the Court repudiated the catalyst theory in Buckhannon Board & Care Home, Inc. v. West Virginia Department of Health & Human Resources, 532 U.S. 598 (2001). In *Buckhannon*, the legislature responded to the lawsuit by repealing the challenged law. The Court refused to award fees. It said that without an enforceable judgment on the merits, either litigated or a consent decree, plaintiff is simply not a "prevailing party" eligible for fees. The four dissenters thought that plaintiff also prevails when defendant surrenders before judgment.

Buckhannon means that plaintiffs must insist on injunctions or declaratory judgments even after defendant surrenders. Recall that voluntary cessation of challenged conduct does not preclude relief if there is a risk of resumption. See United States v. W.T. Grant Co., reprinted in section 4.A.1. But in *Buckhannon*, the trial court had held the case moot, finding no evidence that the legislature might reenact the statute.

The emerging view in the courts of appeals is that it is enough if the court retains jurisdiction to enforce a settlement agreement, whether or not that agreement is formally entered as a consent decree. The court "may 'expressly retain jurisdiction over enforcement of the agreement' in an order of the court, or it may 'incorporate . . . the terms of that agreement' in such an order." Hendrickson v. United States, 791 F.3d 354, 359-360 (2d Cir. 2015).

7. Preliminary relief. What if a preliminary injunction accomplishes one of plaintiff's principal purposes in the lawsuit, and the case ultimately becomes moot, in part because of the beneficial effects of the preliminary injunction? Several circuits have held that this can make plaintiff a prevailing party, because the preliminary injunction is a court-ordered change in the relationship between the parties. The Fourth Circuit disagrees. The cases are collected in Dearmore v. City of Garland, 519 F.3d 517, 521-522 (5th Cir. 2008).

The Ninth Circuit has held that a preliminary injunction based on a finding of probable success on the merits, followed by a settlement that permanently protects the rights temporarily protected by the preliminary injunction, makes the plaintiff a prevailing party entitled to fees. Higher Taste, Inc. v. City of Tacoma, 717 F.3d 712 (9th Cir. 2013). The court noted that other cases had distinguished preliminary injunctions designed merely to preserve the status quo, without a preliminary finding on the merits, and declined to decide whether such injunctions should be treated differently from injunctions issued based on the merits.

8. The effects of *Buckhannon*. A survey of public interest organizations is reported in Catherine R. Albiston and Laura Beth Nielsen, *The Procedural Attack on Civil Rights: The Empirical Reality of Buckhannon for the Private Attorney General*, 54 UCLA L. Rev. 1087 (2007). This article is more anecdotal than empirical, but the scholars got similar responses from both liberal and conservative organizations. They offer examples of "strategic capitulation," in which defendants litigate until they face an imminent risk of adverse judgment and then surrender, avoiding fee liability. Cases are harder to settle, because defendants can no longer settle without submitting to a judgment. It is harder to get attorneys in firms to assist with cases, because they are less likely to recover fees. The strongest cases are less attractive, because defendant is more likely to change its illegal practice without a formal settlement.

9. The reach of *Buckhannon*. *Buckhannon* applies only to statutes authorizing fee awards to prevailing parties. Some of the environmental statutes authorize fees whenever "appropriate." ERISA, which protects employee fringe benefits, says that "the court in its discretion may allow a reasonable attorney's fee and costs of action to either party." 29 U.S.C. §1132(g)(1). The Court has held that each of these formulations can support fee awards to partially prevailing parties, but not to losing parties. Ruckelshaus v. Sierra Club, 463 U.S. 680 (1983); Hardt v. Reliance Standard Life Ins. Co., 560 U.S. 242 (2010).

The National Childhood Vaccine Injury Act creates a no-fault compensation system for persons injured by covered vaccines. Claimants are paid from a government fund. The Act prohibits attorneys from charging any fee to claimants. Instead, it provides that the court "shall" award attorneys' fees to prevailing plaintiffs, and that it "may" award fees to losing plaintiffs if "the petition was brought in good faith and there was a reasonable basis for the claim for which the petition was brought." 42 U.S.C. §300aa-15(e)(1)(B). The Supreme Court unanimously enforced this unusual statute according to its terms. Sebelius v. Cloer, 569 U.S. 369 (2013). The plaintiff filed a claim after new medical research linked her muscular sclerosis to the hepatitis B vaccine; the Federal Circuit held that the earlier lack of medical information did not excuse her failure to file suit before the statute of limitations expired. Probably her argument for the right to file late was made in good faith and had a reasonable basis; that issue was left for the trial judge on remand. For more on tolling statutes of limitations, see section 11.E.

Dictum in *Ruckelshaus* suggested that it would be "appropriate" to award fees to a plaintiff whose lawsuit induced defendant to comply prior to judgment. 463 U.S. at 686 n.8. This footnote has survived in the lower courts, Ohio River Environmental Coalition, Inc. v. Green Valley Coal Co., 511 F.3d 407 (4th Cir. 2007), and *Hardt* gives a boost to that position. The Freedom of Information Act provides that a plaintiff has "substantially prevailed," and is therefore eligible for fees, if he gets a judgment, a consent decree, or "an enforceable written agreement," or if his claim is "not insubstantial" and he gets "a voluntary or unilateral change in position by the agency." 5 U.S.C. §552(a)(4)(E)(ii).

10. State law. Some states have adopted *Buckhannon* as a matter of state law; California and New Jersey have squarely rejected it. Graham v. DaimlerChrysler Corp., 101 P.3d 140 (Cal. 2004); Mason v. City of Hoboken, 951 A.2d 1017 (N.J. 2008).

NOTES ON CALCULATING THE LODESTAR

1. Vocabulary. "Lodestar" is probably an unfortunate term. It has nothing to do with attorneys pursuing great quantities of gold; it refers to a guiding star. The "lode" in lodestar and the "lode" that means a vein of ore come from two completely different Middle English words.

"Lodestar" in the context of attorneys' fees, and the emphasis on reasonable hours times a reasonable hourly rate to which the word refers, is most prominently associated with Lindy Brothers Builders, Inc. v. American Radiator & Standard Sanitary Corp., 487 F.2d 161 (3d Cir. 1973). Johnson v. Georgia Highway Express, quoted in footnote 3 of *Rivera*, got lip service through the much of the 1980s, but *Lindy Brothers* has been far more influential in the Supreme Court. Less than a week after the plurality in *Rivera* cited *Johnson* as authoritative, a majority rejected it as unworkable in Pennsylvania v. Delaware Valley Citizens' Council for Clean Air, 478 U.S. 546, 563 (1986). Only Justice Stevens joined both opinions.

2. The hourly rate. What is a reasonable hourly rate? This is mainly a question of fact; what is the market rate for attorneys with comparable skills and experience? The early cases in the lower courts assumed that the court should choose an hourly rate in the abstract and then adjust the fee to allow for individual factors. But since Blum v. Stenson, 465 U.S. 886 (1984), the Supreme Court has insisted that most facts about the lawyer and the case be considered in setting the hourly rate.

Its most recent opinion says that "enhancements" (upward adjustments) to the lodestar should be "rare and exceptional," Perdue v. Kenny A., 559 U.S. 542, 552 (2010), and only where there is "specific evidence that the lodestar fee would not have been 'adequate to attract competent counsel.'" *Id.* at 543. The Court's examples involved unusual expense, unusual delay, or an inadequate hourly rate selected after failing to consider all the factors that should have been relevant. Enhancements must be based on objective factors subject to appellate review and not the trial judge's impressionistic assessment of the quality of the representation. The Court vacated an enhancement of 75 percent above the lodestar and remanded the case for further proceedings consistent with its opinion. Four dissenters accepted the "rare and exceptional" standard but would have affirmed; they thought the case *was* rare and exceptional, and they seemed more prepared to allow enhancements based on exceptional outcomes or the exceptional quality of the representation.

There can be no upward adjustment to take account of the fact that getting paid at all in a fee-shifting case is generally contingent on winning. City of Burlington v. Dague, 505 U.S. 557 (1992). That startling proposition is taken up in section 10.B.

3. Reasonable hours. What hours count toward the lodestar? Hours spent unnecessarily or inefficiently do not count, although it is very hard for courts to make informed decisions about this. Petitioning lawyers are supposed to exercise "billing judgment" and eliminate such hours themselves. Hours that cannot be proved do not count; it is important to keep detailed and contemporaneous time records. Courts will award fees based on "reconstructed" time accounts, but lawyers relying on such reconstructions will rarely recover for all their time. An example is Mallinson-Montague v. Pocrnick, 224 F.3d 1224, 1233-1236 (10th Cir. 2000).

Most judges justifiably feel they have more important things to do than review time sheets line by line; even with good time records, they often make gross adjustments based on an overall impression of the reasonableness of time and fees. Judicial instincts on these matters vary widely, so results vary with the judge assigned to the case. One indicator of reasonableness is what a defendant spent to defend. This number is usually available through discovery or an open records act, but some courts have refused discovery on grounds of relevance or on the view that fee litigation should be tightly contained. Some of the conflicting cases are collected in Cohen v. Brown University, 1999 WL 695235 (D.R.I. 1999).

Trial judges can get away with impressionistic gross adjustments to claimed fees as long as nobody appeals. But if someone does appeal, the courts of appeals find it difficult to meaningfully review such adjustments. The Ninth Circuit described such gross adjustments as "an unfortunately common mistake," complaining that its "requirement that district courts show their work is frequently forgotten." Padgett v. Loventhal, 706 F.3d 1205, 1208-1209 (9th Cir. 2013). It remanded for the judge to explain what he had done. On remand, a new judge awarded slightly less in fees and explained why. 2015 WL 1520827 (N.D. Cal. 2015). But the court of appeals ordered yet another remand, to resolve a dispute over who was entitled to fees; plaintiff had changed law firms in the middle of the case. 722 F. App'x 608 (9th Cir. 2018).

4. Fee contracts. Another recurring calculation issue was the effect of a fee agreement on the statutory fee award. It is now settled that the two calculations are wholly independent of each other. The statutory fee award is not limited by the fee agreement, Blanchard v. Bergeron, 489 U.S. 87 (1989), and plaintiff's liability under the fee agreement is not limited to the amount of a statutory reasonable fee, Venegas v. Mitchell, 495 U.S. 82 (1990). But don't forget that the law of professional responsibility requires an attorney's fees to be "reasonable." ABA Model Rule of Professional Conduct 1.5.

5. Plaintiff's evidence. A lawyer seeking fees should provide evidence of actual rates that real clients have paid for her work. If she has no such cases, because all her work is on percentage fees, or because she is a legal-aid or public-interest lawyer, she should offer evidence of actual rates paid to lawyers in the same community with similar skill, experience, and reputation. Either way, but especially in the second case, she should offer evidence of her own skill, experience, and reputation. A recurring theme in the cases is that lawyers who bill high hourly rates should bill fewer hours. Too many hours of research belie the claim to be a specialist in the field; too many hours on procedural details belies the claim to be an experienced litigator, and so on.

Evidence of how much time was spent doing what, evidence of the lawyer's usual billing rate, and much of the justification for that rate have to go in the lawyer's own affidavit. It is also important to have at least one well-respected lawyer attest to the petitioning lawyer's reputation and the reasonableness of the fee request. It is awkward to file an affidavit explaining what a great lawyer you are. If you do not find it awkward, you are probably at high risk of overstating your case, asking for too much, and drawing an award that sharply reduces your request and an opinion that reduces your reputation.

6. Defendant's response. On the defense side, there are now lawyers and consulting firms that specialize in auditing legal bills for duplication, overstaffing, excessive time, time where the task is not adequately described, partners doing work that could have been done by associates or paralegals, and similar defects. You can raise the same kinds of questions without an auditing firm. Defense lawyers challenging fee petitions tend to forget how many hours they forced plaintiffs to spend responding to marginal motions and arguments.

B.   ATTORNEYS' FEES FROM A COMMON FUND

IN RE CABLETRON SYSTEMS, INC. SECURITIES LITIGATION
239 F.R.D. 30 (D.N.H. 2006)

SMITH, District Judge.[1] . . .

V. THE SETTLEMENT AND PLAN OF ALLOCATION . . .

B. ATTORNEYS' FEES

[This was a class action for securities fraud, which settled for $10.5 million. Class counsel then petitioned for fees and expenses, to be paid out of the settlement fund before any distribution to the class members. No class member objected to the settlement or to the requested fees or expenses; three class members opted out.]

Plaintiffs' counsel represent that they have spent more than seven years . . . prosecuting and settling this case on a wholly contingent basis. Plaintiffs' counsel argue that the 30% fee, which in this case means approximately $3.15 million, is "fair, reasonable, and appropriate," approximates what counsel would have received had the private market determined the fee, and is within the range of attorneys' fees that courts in the First Circuit have awarded in similar high-risk class action cases. Additionally, counsel seek $915,414.01 in "reasonable, necessary, and directly related" expenses, "all of which are the sorts of expenses for which 'the paying, arms' [sic] length market' reimburses attorneys."[11] . . .

Plaintiffs' counsel first argue that the fees awarded in class actions should approximate the one-third contingency fees normally contracted for in the private marketplace in non-class action cases. . . .

Next, Plaintiffs' counsel outline several factors specific to this case to support their fee request: they point out that the $10.5 million Cabletron settlement "is vastly greater than the $5.8 million median recovery for all §10(b) class actions that have settled since the passage of the Private Securities Litigation Reform Act [PSLRA]"; that its "skill and efficiency" in prosecuting an extremely complex securities class

---

1. Of the District of Rhode Island sitting by designation.
11. The Court challenged numerous expenses contained in Plaintiffs' original submission. As a result, Plaintiffs modified their reimbursement request to reflect the removal of various questionable items such as multiple filing fees and premiums on administrative expenses. The amount described in this Order is the amended request.

action against defense counsel with "a national reputation . . . in securities class action litigation" should bolster its claim; and that in shouldering a huge risk of non-payment for more than seven years, it has served the public interest by providing recovery for small individual claimants who would otherwise have "lack[ed] the resources to litigate a case of this magnitude."

Finally, Plaintiffs argue that a lodestar/multiplier analysis as a cross-check on the [percentage-of-the-fund] method reveals that the requested 30% award is reasonable. In this case, Plaintiffs' numerous lawyers collectively logged 22,397 hours of professional time for an aggregate lodestar of $8,057,300.50. Thus, Plaintiffs argue that the $3.15 million requested is less than half of the attorneys' cumulative lodestar and further proof that the request is reasonable.

VI. METHODOLOGY FOR DETERMINING ATTORNEYS' FEES

A. PERCENTAGE OF FUND OR LODESTAR?

In In re Thirteen Appeals, 56 F.3d 295, 307 (1st Cir. 1995), the Court of Appeals made clear that a district court has the discretion to award fees in a common fund case "either on a percentage of the fund basis [POF] or by fashioning a lodestar." The POF method, simply put, establishes a percentage of the settlement, to be deducted from the common settlement fund, to compensate the attorneys for their efforts. The POF method has emerged in the last decade-plus as the preferred method . . . in common fund cases. . . . The lodestar method, which held sway in the 1970s and 1980s, has fallen into disuse in recent years. . . . In either case, the fee award is deducted from the common settlement fund.

The Third Circuit's 1985 Task Force Report describes many of the problems inherent in the lodestar approach, including, to name a few, increased judicial workload; inconsistent application; potential for manipulation; reward of wasteful and excessive attorney effort; disincentive to settle early; and confusion and lack of predictability in setting fee awards. 108 F.R.D. 237 (1985).

The POF method is preferred in common fund cases because "it allows courts to award fees from the fund 'in a manner that rewards counsel for success and penalizes it for failure.'" In re Rite Aid Corp. Securities Litigation, 396 F.3d 294, 300 (3d Cir. 2005), quoting In re Prudential Insurance Co. Sales Practice Litigation, 148 F.3d 283, 333 (3d Cir. 1998). This is something the lodestar method cannot do.

While most courts have shifted away from the lodestar approach toward the POF method, it is now common practice to use the lodestar as a cross-check on the POF award. Recently, the argument has been made that using the lodestar cross-check is not merely a good practice but an "ethical imperative." *See* Vaughn R. Walker & Ben Horwich, *The Ethical Imperative of a Lodestar Cross-Check: Judicial Misgivings about "Reasonable Percentage" Fees in Common Fund Cases*, 18 Geo. J. Legal Ethics 1453 (2005).[12] The Court is persuaded . . . that the better approach to awarding attorneys' fees is the POF method. A lodestar cross-check may also be useful; however, it is unclear to this Court where the precise lines of "reasonableness" would be drawn if the lodestar cross-check [were] mandatory (Is .5 too low? Is 2.5 too high?). This Court is not required to decide whether the cross-check is an ethical imperative, nor to define the

---

12. Another recent paper, Theodore Eisenberg & Geoffrey P. Miller, *Attorney Fees in Class Action Settlements: An Empirical Study*, 1 J. Empirical Legal Stud. 27 (2004), appears to reject the lodestar cross-check as a tool for determining reasonableness of a fee award. . . .

parameters of lodestar reasonableness; rather, it is sufficient to conclude that when the lodestar cross-check is applied to the fee award in this case, it raises no reasonableness concerns.

B. DETERMINING THE REASONABLENESS OF THE FEE
1. Methodology . . .

Plaintiffs' counsel rely primarily upon numerous examples in which district courts have awarded fees in [the 30%] range. . . . [H]owever, these examples do not accurately reflect actual experience (or the marketplace) in any statistically significant way; rather, they are merely anecdotal examples. . . . [T]his Court rejects the common practice of reflexively awarding 30% (and calling this market-based). . . .

With no adversary to challenge Plaintiffs' proposal, the Court has been left to fend for itself in crafting an approach for assessing reasonableness. . . . As a starting point, it is important to recall that in determining reasonableness, the district court acts as a fiduciary to the class.

a. Multi-Factor Approach

The first common approach to determining the fee award is to apply a multi-factor test. This approach has been adopted, in varying forms, by the Second, Third, Fourth, Fifth, Sixth and Eleventh Circuits. Within this group, the Second, Third and Sixth Circuits utilize six or seven factors, while the others largely employ the twelve factor analysis contained in the seminal lodestar case of Johnson v. Georgia Highway Express, Inc., 488 F.2d 714, 717-719 (5th Cir. 1974). The approach of the Second, Third and Sixth Circuits appears to simplify and synthesize the *Johnson* factors; in contrast, the Eleventh Circuit expands upon them with five factors to be considered in addition to the twelve *Johnson* factors. . . .

All of the tests include a comparison to the lodestar (time and labor), some consideration of complexity and difficulty of the case, the quality of representation, and the benefit obtained for the class as reflected by the size of the fund, as well as an accounting for the risk associated with the contingency nature of the case. The Third Circuit and the three *Johnson* Circuits specifically include a comparison to awards in similar cases. The Third Circuit and Eleventh Circuit also look to whether there are objections to the fee award.

b. 25% Benchmark

The . . . Ninth Circuit . . . applies a benchmark of 25% from which a deviation is permitted upon consideration of various case specific factors. The Eighth Circuit and the District of Columbia Circuit have not specifically endorsed an approach, but have pointed to "benchmark" percentage ranges to justify reasonableness of particular fee awards. This approach, of course, has the appeal of simplicity and consistency. More importantly, it appears to recognize the reality that most district judges, utilizing a multi-factor approach and looking back at a case from the vantage point of years of hindsight, really have no idea whether a fee award should be 20, 25, or 30%. Instead, the judge picks a percentage that intuitively seems correct and argues back to it using the various factors as justification. The Ninth Circuit's benchmark rejects this in favor of a presumptively reasonable figure.

c. Market Mimicking Approach

The Seventh Circuit has adopted a third method for analyzing reasonableness: the "market mimicking approach." This method is designed to award a fee that is the "market price for legal services, in light of the risk of nonpayment and the normal rate of compensation in the market" at the outset of the case. In re Synthroid Marketing Litigation, 264 F.3d 712, 718 (7th Cir. 2001). The Seventh Circuit opines that reasonableness is not an ethical or philosophical question, and "it is not the function of judges in fee litigation to determine the equivalent of the medieval just price. It is to determine what the lawyer would receive if he were selling his services in the market rather than being paid by court order." In re Continental Illinois Securities Litigation, 962 F.2d 566, 568 (7th Cir. 1992). . . . The Seventh Circuit has fundamentally rejected the multi-factor "consider everything" approach by emphasizing that it "assures random and potentially perverse results." A "list of factors without a rule of decision is just a chopped salad." 264 F.3d at 719.

The Seventh Circuit, however, has also acknowledged that its approach presents particular challenges when a fee award is determined at the completion of the case. . . . [N]o definitive source exists for determining what the market would have yielded had a fee arrangement been negotiated at the outset. Obviously, hindsight [adds information that] simply cannot be known up front . . . .

[T]he multi-factor approach . . . proves unprincipled. Any method of analysis that can equally support a fee award of 16%, 20%, 25%, 30% or 33 1/3%,

> is not a rule of law or even a principle. Instead, it allows uncabined discretion to the fee awarding judge. A judge who likes lawyers and remembers the hazards of practice can be generous; a judge who cares more about public reaction or who never used contingent fees in practice can be stingy. It is difficult to contradict the judge's statement about the case's complexity or lack thereof, the difficulties of discovery, the quality of lawyering, etc. These are all highly subjective judgments.

Nilsen v. York County, 400 F. Supp. 2d 266, 277 (D. Me. 2005). . . .

[T]he POF method directly aligns the interests of the attorneys and the interests of the class (the higher the recovery for the class, the higher the percentage for the attorneys). Applying a multi-factor analysis to the percentage, which could result in adjustments downward for any number of reasons, chips away at this alignment of interests. Further, the multi-factor analysis leads to the consumption of significant attorney and judicial resources, effectively the same considerations responsible for the rejection of the lodestar approach in favor of the POF method. . . .

This Court . . . concludes that the best way to determine the reasonableness of a fee award is to assess what the fee arrangement would have been had it been determined by an open, competitive process at the outset of the case.[18] In spite of the limitations associated with a market based analysis, it is apparent to this Court that this approach is far more preferable than a subjective multi-factor approach, or a blindly applied fixed percentage. . . .

This Court has identified two sources of information. The first is research data analyzing fee awards in other class action . . . cases . . . . The second is the group of class action cases in which courts have set the fee at the beginning of the case by a competitive process. From this information, it is possible to estimate what the fee award would have been in this case had it actually been negotiated in advance. By combining the conclusions drawn from these two data sources, the Court is able to

---

18. . . . [I]t has been argued that, in this context, judges have become the market. See Judith Resnik, *Money Matters: Judicial Market Interventions Creating Subsidies and Awarding Fees and Costs in Individual and Aggregate Litigation*, 148 U. Pa. L. Rev. 2119, 2129 (2000). . . .

arrive at a POF fee award that is well grounded in market-based information and is, therefore, reasonable.

2. Applying the Methodology

In the last twelve years, there have been several comprehensive studies evaluating fee awards in class action cases. [These studies variously found that the average fee in all common-fund class actions was 18.4%, or 24% to 30%, and that the average fee in securities class actions was 32%, 32%, or 26.2%. Eisenberg and Miller, *supra* note 12, reviewed all the studies and concluded that the median fee in securities class actions is 25% and the median fee in non-securities common fund cases is 20%.]

[I]f one views past awards as reflective of the market, and if one assumes that the analysis should be limited to the subset of securities cases . . . , and if one credits . . . Eisenberg and Miller . . . , then it is fair to conclude that 26% is the fee Plaintiffs would have negotiated with their attorneys, prior to the commencement of this action *if* they were limited to an across-the-board percentage fee structure.[20] . . .

[However, when] parties are able to negotiate freely *before* a case is filed, or early in the case, then fee arrangements are much more tailored.

This Court has surveyed the published opinions in cases that utilized a competitive approach to arrive at a fee structure at the outset of a case. . . . Several observations are readily apparent from this information. First, the POF attorney fee awards are generally lower than the across-the-board POF fee awards discussed above. . . . Second, the majority of the fee structures resulting from an early competitive process are more complicated and nuanced than the typical post-settlement, POF awards. Significantly, these fee structures are tailored to the actual risk/reward evaluation of each case. Third, the competitive fee structures uniformly reflect a downward scaling as the settlement fund increases.

[The court detailed the winning bids from seven class actions in which class counsel's fees had been set by auction early in the case. It recognized that there were other such cases, but in these seven, the data were readily available. In six of the seven cases, the percentage declined as the recovery increased, e.g., 24% of the first $1 million, 20% of the next $4 million, 15% of the next $10 million, and 12% of any amount over $15 million. In two of these bids, there was no additional fee for any recovery over $25 million.

In one bid, the percentage increased if the case took more than a year to settle. In two bids, the percentage increased if the case continued past a motion to dismiss, and again if it continued past summary judgment, or to trial, or to an appeal from a final judgment. One bid combined these features, with the percentage increasing at the one-year mark and again if the case went to trial. In each of these four bids, the percentage at each stage declined as the amount of recovery increased.

As applied to the $10.5 million *Cabletron* settlement, the winning bids produced total fees of 7.5%, 8.07%, 12.86%, 14.38%, 17.38%, 22.86%, and 25.48%. The firm that had bid 7.5% successfully petitioned for 18% after the case settled. The court did not comment on the range of these bids or on the range of results in the empirical studies it summarized.]

Although not perfect, it is plain from the experience of the judges who have utilized competitive bidding that it generates lower POF fee arrangements from highly

---

20. . . . [A] 26% figure seems quite close to what counsel in this case have in the past perceived to be the market rate when it was forced to compete [citing two cases where the court set fees by auction and the plaintiffs' firm in *Cabletron* had submitted bids].

respected counsel, returning substantial value to the class without sacrificing quality of representation.

This Court has no doubt that had a fee arrangement been negotiated in advance in this case, and if a competitive bid process had been used, then the negotiated fee would have been considerably less than 26%. How much less is very difficult to assess ten years after the commencement of the action . . . .

[A]pplication of the formulas derived from the bidding cases . . . yields a mean award of 17%. The mean award derived from the various studies discussed in this decision is 26%. . . . [A] reasonable percentage in this case shall be calculated by averaging the 17% figure from the market-based cases with the 26% figure derived from the various studies. Therefore, this Court finds that, in light of all the circumstances, a fee award on a POF basis of 21.5%, or $2,257,500 is reasonable.[28]

In other cases currently pending before this Court, a similar application of market-based information will be used to set a reasonable fee; in future cases this Court intends to utilize a competitive process to set the attorneys' fee at the outset of the litigation. . . .

NOTES ON THE COMMON-FUND RULE

1. Distinguishing common-fund from statutory fee awards. The securities laws do not provide for fee shifting. So in *Cabletron*, the *class* paid plaintiffs' attorneys' fees; the fee is taken out of what defendant owes the class. It is this feature that makes fee awards in common-fund cases fundamentally different from fee-shifting cases like *Rivera*.

Class actions under statutes with fee-shifting provisions can be handled either way, but are usually treated as common-fund cases. The parties can settle for an unallocated lump sum that includes the damage claims and the fee claims. Then class counsel can ask the court to award reasonable fees out of the recovery, as in *Cabletron*. An example that addresses the choice is Staton v. Boeing Co., 327 F.3d 938, 963-972 (9th Cir. 2003).

2. Fees from common funds as restitution. So far, the common-fund rule is just a special case of restitution. The lawyer has conferred a substantial benefit on all the class members, and they would be unjustly enriched if they were allowed to retain the benefit without paying the costs of producing it. Are the lawyer and client who confer the benefit mere volunteers, and the class members mere incidental beneficiaries of their litigation? That does not seem to be a plausible description. Class members are intended beneficiaries, the attorneys' conduct is authorized by the court, and there are generally so many beneficiaries that it would be impossible to contract with them. If the recovery is in cash, there is no doubt that each class member benefits even after her share of attorneys' fees is deducted. See Charles Silver, *A Restitutionary Theory of Attorneys' Fees in Class Actions*, 76 Cornell L. Rev. 656 (1991), and *Restatement (Third) of Restitution and Unjust Enrichment* §29 (Am. Law Inst. 2011).

3. Common funds without a class. The common-fund rule is more controversial where no class is certified. Consider Sprague v. Ticonic National Bank, 307 U.S. 161 (1939), where plaintiff successfully sued to recover trust funds from an insolvent bank, asserting priority over ordinary depositors and other general creditors.

---

28. Applying the lodestar of $8,057,300.50 to this figure yields a lodestar multiplier of slightly less than .3.

Fourteen other trusts were similarly situated, and their beneficiaries recovered on the strength of Sprague's precedent. Sprague was allowed to collect pro rata shares of her attorneys' fees from the other trust funds. Was it impossible for her or her attorney to contract with the other 14?

An example with bigger stakes is In re Diet Drugs, 582 F.3d 524 (3d Cir. 2009), which involved a coordinated group of class actions and settlements that gave class members multiple opportunities to opt out to pursue individual claims as both the class members' medical problems and the litigation developed. Plaintiffs who opted out benefited from the class settlement, because of the multiple chances to opt out and because of issue preclusion on some issues. Plaintiffs who opted out were required to contribute a small percentage of their ultimate recovery to an account for compensation of class counsel. *Id.* at 532-533. In effect, the class and individual recoveries were treated as separate components of a larger, interconnected fund.

Similar fee awards are common in cases coordinated by the Judicial Panel on Multidistrict Litigation. These are typically large numbers of individual cases with similar claims, consolidated for pretrial proceedings in a single federal court. Judges often call these "quasi-class actions." But they are not class actions, and Professor Silver thinks they are not restitutionary. Charles Silver & Geoffrey P. Miller, *The Quasi-Class Action Method of Managing Multi-District Litigations: Problems and a Proposal*, 63 Vand. L. Rev. 107, 120-130 (2010). Contract is not merely possible, but common. Every plaintiff has a contract with his lawyer, and there are often contracts among lawyers for coordination of efforts and division of fees. Individual plaintiffs have viable claims and often feel more harmed than benefited by being forced into the Multidistrict Litigation. Absent class members are mere passive beneficiaries, free-riding on the efforts of class counsel, but individual plaintiffs and their lawyers in the Multidistrict Litigation do important work that increases the value of the whole pool of consolidated cases.

4. Noncash benefits. What if there is no cash fund, but only a noncash benefit? Consider Mills v. Electric Auto-Lite Co., 396 U.S. 375 (1970), and Hall v. Cole, 412 U.S. 1 (1973). *Mills* was a suit challenging misleading proxy statements. The Court held that all shareholders would benefit from the litigation, and that a fee award against the defendant corporation would in effect be borne by the benefiting shareholders. Similar fee awards are common in shareholder derivative suits. *Hall* was a suit against a union for retaliating against a dissident member. The Court held that the union and all its members would benefit from this vindication of union members' rights of free speech, and that an award of attorneys' fees against the union would in effect be borne by the benefiting members. It is inherent in these noncash cases that defendant pays the fees, because cash fees cannot be taken out of a noncash benefit to the class.

The Court in these cases talked about "common benefit" rather than "common fund," but it rested both sets of cases on the same underlying idea: that the beneficiaries of the litigation would be unjustly enriched if they were not required to contribute to the attorneys' fees required to produce the benefit.

5. Taking the idea beyond its rationale? Doesn't it seem likely that many of the "beneficiaries" in *Hall* wished there were a way to make the dissident plaintiff shut up? And that many of the beneficiaries in *Mills* were not much interested in more accurate or more thorough proxy statements? Both *Hall* and *Mills* violate a central principal of restitution law: that the court will not make recipients pay for unsolicited benefits that might have been unwanted. These cases would be much better explained as making the wrongdoer pay. And perhaps there is no other way to make the underlying substantive laws in these cases enforceable. The results are settled, and *Mills* is followed in the *Restatement (Third) of Restitution* §29 illus. 15.

6. Drawing a line. In Alyeska Pipeline Service Co. v. Wilderness Society, 421 U.S. 240 (1975), plaintiffs' lawsuit improved the environmental safety of the Alaska pipeline, which runs 800 miles across federal lands from Prudhoe Bay to Valdez. Who were the beneficiaries in *Alyeska*? The whole population of the United States, because the government owned the land? Those who care about the environment? Those who hunt, fish, and backpack in the Alaskan wilderness?

Alyeska was owned by eight big oil companies with 20 percent of the domestic market. Is there any theory under which their customers were the beneficiaries of plaintiffs' suit? Is there any theory under which those customers benefited in proportion to their use of defendants' petroleum products? The Court rejected Justice Marshall's theory that a fee award in *Alyeska* could be based on a common benefit.

7. Reaffirming the rule. The Court reaffirmed the common-fund rule in Boeing Co. v. Van Gemert, 444 U.S. 472 (1980). The issue was whether attorneys' fees could be collected from money due to class members who failed to file claims. The Court said yes; these absent class members were legally entitled to the money, and that entitlement was a benefit, even if they never claimed it. This makes sense in a litigated case such as *Van Gemert*. But settlements are much more common, and settling counsel may value a fund highly even if it is foreseeable that few class members will actually file claims. The resulting issues are considered in section 10.C.

NOTES ON CONTINGENCY ENHANCEMENTS

1. Fee awards as contingent fees. In most fee-award litigation, whether fee shifting or common fund, the potential fee award is the client's only realistic prospect of paying his attorney. Actual payment of a lawyer's fee is therefore contingent on success, which makes these contingent-fee cases whether payment is based on the lodestar, a percentage, or any other method. The risk of nonpayment is a factor in all the multifactor circuits. In lodestar cases, courts recognized the risk of nonpayment by awarding "contingency enhancements," also called "risk multipliers"—the court multiplies the lodestar by some number greater than one to account for the risk of nonpayment.

2. Ignoring the market. In City of Burlington v. Dague, 505 U.S. 557 (1992), the Supreme Court flatly rejected contingency enhancements in statutory fee-shifting cases. It held that contingency enhancements are inconsistent with the prevailing-party requirement, because they are a disguised way of paying the lawyer for cases he lost. It rejected the argument that contingency enhancements actually pay the lawyer for the risks of accepting the cases he won. No lawyer would fail to adjust his rate depending on whether the fee was fixed or contingent. *Dague* is thus a dramatic departure from the Court's emphasis on market rates. Is it a defensible departure?

3. The reach of *Dague*. Federal courts have decided that *Dague* does not apply in common-fund cases, which is why the lawyers are still talking about risk multipliers in *Cabletron*. There is a good opinion on that point in Cook v. Niedert, 142 F.3d 1004, 1015 (7th Cir. 1998). *Dague* is not binding in state-law cases, and some states continue to award contingency enhancements in statutory fee-shifting cases. An example is Ketchum v. Moses, 17 P.3d 735, 740-746 (Cal. 2001). New Jersey reaffirmed its commitment to contingency enhancements in Walker v. Giuffre, 35 A.3d 1177 (N.J. 2012).

4. How big a multiplier? The Court in *Dague* worried that if contingency enhancements were based on the risk of losing, courts would award the biggest enhancements in the cases that seemed riskiest at the beginning, making lawyers indifferent between strong cases and weak cases. The market does not set contingent fees that way. Most contingent-fee lawyers have a standard percentage; they simply reject cases that are too weak to take for that fee. Studies of fee practices are collected in Charles Silver, *Unloading the Lodestar: Toward a New Fee Award Procedure*, 70 Tex. L. Rev. 865, 912 n.175 (1992).

Moreover, no court enhanced fees by the reciprocal of the original chance of success; that was a straw man invented in *Dague*. Courts assessed the risks of individual cases mostly to avoid overcompensating lawyers for presumed risks that were actually small. Most of the contingency-enhancement decisions proceeded case by case, but Florida developed a clear rule that the multiplier is capped at 2.5 times the lodestar in fee-shifting cases, and at 5 times the lodestar in common-fund cases, no matter how long the original odds. Kuhnlein v. Department of Revenue, 662 So. 2d 309, 315 (Fla. 1995). In Rodriguez v. County of Los Angeles, the jail-brutality litigation described in note 4 of Notes on the Amount of the Judgment as a Constraint on Attorneys' Fees, the trial court used a multiplier of 2.0 given the substantial risks involved in the litigation.

5. Small risk of nonpayment? Goldberger v. Integrated Resources, Inc., 209 F.3d 43 (2d Cir. 2000), awarded a $2.1 million lodestar in a common-fund case with a $54 million settlement, rejecting counsel's claim to 25 percent of the recovery. The *Goldberger* court thought substantial percentages of recovery were based on the false premise that "there is a substantial contingency risk in every common fund case." *Id.* at 52. In fact, the risk in securities fraud cases was often modest, because most cases settle. Plaintiff's counsel in *Goldberger* had said that losses were "few and far between" and that they achieved "a significant settlement" in 90 percent of their cases. *Id.* He was probably bragging about the significance of some of those settlements, but certainly some cases are strong from the beginning. *Goldberger* arose out of Michael Milken's junk bond frauds in the late 1980s; the key facts had been established by the criminal cases, and solvent defendants were available. It was a safe prediction that this case would settle on favorable terms. But even the strongest cases become risky if they go to trial.

NOTES ON COMPETING APPROACHES TO CALCULATING FEE AWARDS

1. The choices. The most fundamental debate over the amount of fee awards has been whether to use the lodestar or a percentage of the recovery as the starting point. The Supreme Court requires the lodestar in federal fee-shifting cases, but each circuit in common-fund cases, and each state in all cases, has had to choose. The common-fund cases are collected in Annotation, 56 A.L.R. 5th 107 (1998 & Supp.). Florida adheres to the lodestar, even in common-fund cases, on the ground that it is more objective and produces more consistent results. Kuhnlein v. Department of Revenue, 662 So. 2d 309 (Fla. 1995). The clear trend is to percentage of recovery in common-fund cases, but most circuits still recognize trial-court discretion to choose either method. The American Law Institute has strongly endorsed percentage of recovery where workable, recognizing that it may be unworkable in cases with only injunctive or declaratory relief. *Principles of the Law: Aggregate Litigation* §3.13 (2010). Recent innovations include auctions and negotiations at the beginning of the case.

The Supreme Court of California reviewed the whole debate at length and decided that California courts may use percentage of recovery, rejecting the argument that percentage of recovery grants too much to lawyers and takes that money away from class members. Lafitte v. Robert Half International Inc., 376 P.3d 672, 686 (Cal. 2016). The court said that there are "recognized advantages of the percentage method," but it did not appear to prohibit the lodestar and it did not address whether the percentage method can be used when there is no common fund from which the award is to be made.

2. Percentage of recovery. Percentage of recovery has no relation to the work required; it may produce fees that are absurdly small, as in *Rivera*, or absurdly large, as in In re Cendant Corp. Securities Litigation, 109 F. Supp. 2d 285, 292 (D.N.J. 2000), *vacated*, 264 F.3d 201 (3d Cir. 2001). In *Cendant*, the proposed fee came out to nearly $11,000 an hour when first awarded, in a case where defendants had disclosed the fraud before any plaintiff hired a lawyer. In In re Visa Check/Mastermoney Antitrust Litigation, 297 F. Supp. 2d 503 (E.D.N.Y. 2003), a fee request based on 18 percent of the cash part of the settlement came out to 9.7 times the lodestar. The judge found this request "absurd" and "fundamentally unreasonable"; he "reject[ed] it entirely." *Id.* at 522-523. He did his own calculation from scratch and awarded a little more than a third of the request. The court of appeals affirmed. Wal-Mart Stores, Inc. v. Visa U.S.A., Inc., 396 F.3d 96 121-124 (2d Cir. 2005).

With megafund recoveries, small changes in the percentage can make huge differences in the fee. In In re Washington Public Power Supply System Securities Litigation, 19 F.3d 1291 (9th Cir. 1994), where the settlement was $687 million, the court used the lodestar because "the size of the fund magnified beyond all reasonable limits the margin of error inherent in a percentage fee award." *Id.* at 1297. *Cendant* and *Visa Check* used percentage of recovery with settlements in the billions, but they used single-digit percentages to achieve reasonable outcomes.

3. The lodestar cross-check. The Third Circuit has "recommended" that district courts compare the results of percentage of recovery "with an abbreviated calculation of the lodestar amount," reducing the percentage to a reasonable multiplier of the lodestar. *Cendant*, 264 F.3d at 285. It has also suggested, based on a survey of cases, that one to four times the lodestar is an appropriate range. In re Diet Drugs, 582 F.3d 524, 545 n.42 (3d Cir. 2009). The American Law Institute endorsed the lodestar cross-check, especially where the value of the settlement is uncertain. *Aggregate Litigation* §3.13.

4. Lodestar. The lodestar has its own problems, including the difficulties of calculation already discussed. Judges hate reviewing time sheets in an adversarial posture. More important, the lodestar encourages lawyers to run the meter, and it discourages early exploration of settlement before significant fees have accrued—although early settlements are scarce for other reasons anyway. The lodestar also distorts settlement incentives late in the case; there inevitably comes a point at which class counsel has spent so many hours that the risk of not being compensated for those hours far exceeds the value of being compensated for additional hours. At that point, it is hard to reject a settlement in which the class receives little and the lawyer receives a large fee based on her hours. John C. Coffee, Jr., *Understanding the Plaintiff's Attorney: The Implications of Economic Theory for Private Enforcement of Law Through Class and Derivative Actions*, 86 Colum. L. Rev. 669, 717-718 (1986).

5. Setting fees in advance. *Cabletron* collects the results of efforts to establish the fee by auction at the beginning of the case. Other judges have tried negotiation at the beginning of the case. The goal is to avoid both the problems of the lodestar and the seeming arbitrariness of picking a percentage of recovery after the fact. Auctions and negotiations have been used only in cases with a prospect of substantial recovery, and in that context, they tend to produce staggered percentage-of-recovery fee structures, with the percentage changing as a function both of the amount recovered and the stage of litigation at which it is recovered.

6. Auctions. Auctions avoid some of the old problems and create new ones:

> One persistent criticism is that courts generally identify the "lowest" bid submitted by an "adequate" bidder and appoint that bidder as lead counsel, without performing the cost/quality weighing in the way that a real client would. Another fear is that because auctions do not reward the attorneys who discover legal violations, they may reduce lawyers' incentives to seek out and disclose illegality. . . . [B]ids in large, potentially high-recovery, cases are likely to be quite complex and it may be difficult for courts to assess their relative costs to the class. This risk is especially strong in cases where the bids consist of a complicated set of alternate fees that vary depending on the size of the recovery and the stage of the proceedings at which the recovery is obtained. In such situations, a court cannot assess which bid is the cheapest without first assessing the likely amount of recovery. Additionally, if there are too few bidders, the degree to which an auction will actually simulate the market is questionable. Finally, there is a risk that auctions could result in a "winner's curse," systematically selecting bidders who overestimate the odds or amount of a likely recovery. Such a "winning" bidder might then find itself litigating an unprofitable case, which may then give it an incentive to settle early and cheaply.

Cendant, 264 F.3d at 259-260.

7. The attorney-client relationship. Equally important, auctions sever the attorney-client relationship. The class representative does not get to select his own counsel but must accept the lawyer who wins the auction. This may be only a theoretical problem if the class representative is unsophisticated, has a small stake, and is just a figurehead controlled by his lawyer. But it is a serious problem if the attorney-client relationship is real.

8. The Private Securities Litigation Reform Act. The PSLRA, enacted in 1995, relies on the attorney-client relationship to address the problem in securities fraud suits. The key provision is 15 U.S.C. §78u-4 in the Securities Exchange Act and 15 U.S.C. §77z-1, the substantially identical provision in the Securities Act. These sections create a rebuttable presumption that the willing class member with the largest financial stake should be the class representative. This class member "shall, subject to the approval of the court, select and retain counsel to represent the class." §78u-4(a)(3)(B)(v). The court retains responsibility for approving any fee award, which "shall not exceed a reasonable percentage of the amount of any damages and prejudgment interest actually paid to the class." §78u-4(a)(6). This provision was aimed at large lodestar awards in cases with modest or nominal settlements.

The Third Circuit held in *Cendant* that "courts should accord a presumption of reasonableness to any fee request submitted pursuant to a retainer agreement that was entered into between a properly-selected lead plaintiff and a properly-selected lead counsel." 264 F.3d at 282. The statute never says that, but this is a reasonable inference from the statutory plan of relying on sophisticated lead plaintiffs with substantial stakes to represent the class in dealings with class counsel. The court also held that the statute generally precludes fee auctions in securities cases, with exceptions only where no responsible lead plaintiff emerges, or where the lead plaintiff repeatedly negotiates unacceptably generous fee agreements that the court refuses to approve. *Id.* at 273-277. The Ninth Circuit emphatically agreed that the power to retain counsel under the PSLRA belongs to the lead plaintiff, not to the court. Cohen v. United States District Court, 586 F.3d 703 (9th Cir. 2009). Judicial proponents of auctions argue that the PSLRA does not preclude auctions, because any time the lead plaintiff refuses to accept the best bid, it has failed to represent the class. Some of those opinions are collected in 264 F.3d at 260 n.45.

The ideal under the PSLRA is a sophisticated lead plaintiff, typically a pension plan or a mutual fund, with enough at stake to give it strong incentives to negotiate the smallest fee with the best law firm. Early in the case, the court reviews that retainer agreement and approves it as fair to the class, or if necessary, approves it subject to the lead plaintiff and its law firm renegotiating or accepting certain amendments. At the end of the case, fees are paid pursuant to the retainer agreement, subject to class members' right to object, but with a strong presumption that the negotiated fee does not exceed a reasonable percentage of the fund.

Sometimes it works out that way, and sometimes not. An empirical study shows that government pension plans negotiate smaller fees than other class representatives (including other institutions). Here's the bad news: The effect disappears if counsel contributed $15,000 or more to the campaign fund of the politician who supervises the pension fund. Stephen J. Choi, Drew T. Johnson-Skinner, and A.C. Pritchard, *The Price of Pay to Play in Securities Class Actions*, 8 J. Empirical L. Stud. 650 (2011). This is consistent with a more recent study concluding that the "available evidence raises suspicion that at least some class action law firms are buying lead counsel status with campaign contributions, i.e., lawyers are paying to play. Not surprisingly, government officials receiving campaign contributions appear to be less vigorous overseers of class action counsel." Stephen J. Choi & Adam C. Pritchard, *Lead Plaintiffs and their Lawyers: Mission, Accomplished, or More to Be Done?*), in Research Handbook on Representative Shareholder Litigation (Elgar Publishing, forthcoming), http://ssrn.com/abstract=2971155 (2017 draft).

A research team reviewed the case files in all 434 securities class actions that settled in federal court from 2007 through 2012. Lynn A. Baker, Michael A. Perino, & Charles Silver, *Is the Price Right? An Empirical Study of Fee-Setting in Securities Class Actions*, 115 Colum. L. Rev. 1371 (2015). A negotiated fee agreement was mentioned in only 41 of the motions to be appointed lead plaintiff and only 21 of the orders appointing lead plaintiffs. An agreement appeared in only 74 of the motions for fee awards. The authors conclude that fees in most cases are being set after the settlement by the same methods used before the PSLRA was enacted.

Judges awarded less than the fees requested in only 62 cases. Fee requests were smaller, and judges were notably less likely to award less than the amount requested, where there was a negotiated fee agreement. The authors found no evidence that lodestar cross checks accomplish anything. And despite the requirement of appointing the plaintiff with the largest claim, the lead plaintiff was an individual in 46 percent of these cases. They collect other empirical studies of fee awards in class actions in footnote 3.

9. Delay. Another problem with auctions and negotiated fees is delay. No plaintiff's lawyer can do any serious work until lead counsel is appointed, and that has taken as much as a year in some cases. Jill E. Fisch, *Aggregation, Auctions, and Other Developments in the Selection of Lead Counsel under the PSLRA*, 64 L. & Contemp. Probs. 53, 62-63 (Spring/Summer 2001). This is a problem even with the procedure for selecting the lead plaintiff under the Securities Reform Act; the problem is worse with an auction.

10. An example. The remarkable facts in *Cendant* reveal something of the potential and hazards of these methods. Lead plaintiffs were the New York and California state pension funds. They negotiated a fee agreement with their preferred lead counsel. The district judge conducted an auction and attracted 12 bids for various parts of the case. These bids are set out in redacted form in In re Cendant Corp. Litigation, 191 F.R.D. 387 (D.N.J. 1998); for a more readable version of the winning bid, see 264 F.3d at 224 n.4. After selecting the winning bidder, the court gave lead plaintiffs' counsel a chance to match the bid, which it did. That preserved the lawyer-client relationship, but as a regular practice it would surely discourage other firms from bidding.

The district court rejected two bids as unrealistically low and therefore not in the interest of the class, commenting that the lowest bid made no sense unless the final recovery "is in the billions." 191 F.R.D. at 391. The subsequent settlement was in fact $3.2 billion. The court of appeals said the district court, knowing what it knew at the time, did not err in rejecting the low bids. If the court had found error, could there be any remedy after the fact?

Three billion dollars is an extraordinarily large settlement, but less so when you realize that as the fraud was disclosed over a period of several months in 1998, the stock dropped from $41 to $6 with 860 million shares outstanding. This very crude measure implies $30 billion in lost value to investors. The stock quickly rebounded to 20; that equally crude but more conservative number implies $18 billion in lost value.

The fee under the agreement negotiated by lead plaintiffs would have been $187 million; the fee under the "lower" bid selected by the district court was $262 million. This crossover was a function of the huge settlement; the selected bid would have been cheaper in the settlement range the court thought more likely.

Because the auction should never have been held, the court of appeals limited the fee to the amount in the original agreement; with expenses, this was about 6 percent of the settlement. Even so, the court remanded for determination whether this exceeded a reasonable percentage of the fund, suggesting that the district court might think of the lodestar as a floor and the agreement as a ceiling. 264 F.3d at 285-286. On remand, lead counsel and lead plaintiffs negotiated a fee of $55 million, or about 1.7 percent of the settlement, which the court approved after considering objections. 243 F. Supp. 2d 166 (D.N.J. 2003).

11. Big cases without megafunds. Megafund cases are rare, despite their high profile. Even in smaller cases, the most visible fee awards still involve many hours and large fees. Consider *Rivera*, with a substantial trial and 1,947 reported hours. In Blum v. Stenson, 465 U.S. 886 (1984), legal-aid lawyers spent 809 hours to file a complaint and one set of interrogatories and brief a motion for class certification and summary judgment. Experience matters; tasks that take many hours the first time you do them take a small fraction of that time the tenth time you do them. Even with experience, complex and novel issues take lots of hours, and they can arise in a legal-aid practice as well as in an elite firm. Professional incentives are at work as well as economic ones; good lawyers in high-stakes cases try to take whatever extra steps might make the difference. These extra hours are a form of insurance, worth expending even if they have a negative expected value, because they reduce the risk of total defeat. Settlement is cheaper, and it also eliminates the risk of total defeat, but sometimes settlement is impossible.

12. Ordinary cases. The cases with large numbers of hours are not so rare as megafunds, but they are rare enough. Most cases are routine, and many lawyers underprepare rather than overprepare. One survey found that the median number of lawyer hours spent on an "ordinary" case is 30.4. Only 12 percent of cases took more than 120 hours, but the big cases raised the mean to 72.9 hours. Only 2 percent of cases in the sample took more than 2,200 hours; these were excluded from analysis as "extraordinary." Cases with less than $1,000 in controversy were also excluded. David M. Trubek, Austin Sarat, William L.F. Felstiner, Herbert M. Kritzer, & Joel B. Grossman, *The Costs of Ordinary Litigation*, 31 UCLA L. Rev. 72, 80-81 & n.17, 90 (1983). If the average case takes 30 to 70 hours, we shouldn't make broad policy judgments about attorneys' fees on the basis of cases like *Cabletron* and *Cendant*, or even *Blum*. We may need different rules for different kinds of cases.

The economics of individual civil rights and consumer cases are very different from the economics of securities fraud class actions. Success rates are modest; monetary recoveries tend to be modest even when success is achieved. Percentage of recovery would produce tiny fees, or none at all in injunction cases. Auctions would draw few bidders, and the bids would be competing hourly rates. Whether or not the lawyer was wisely selected, plaintiff has often developed a personal relationship with him. Fee negotiations with plaintiff are illusory, because plaintiff generally can't pay; fee negotiations with defendant, early in the case when defendant is insisting it has no liability, are unrealistic.

Many of these cases end in the trial court, but a few become test cases of some important proposition in the appellate courts. The generalist litigators who often handle the case in the trial court may retain specialists in the court of appeals or the Supreme Court, and this may be entirely reasonable, but no early fee negotiation is likely to have provided for that. How best to handle the large class actions is an important and fascinating problem. But in ordinary cases, there may be no good alternative to the lodestar.

13. Social Security cases. The Supreme Court got a small-scale version of this debate in Gisbrecht v. Barnhart, 535 U.S. 789 (2002). In suits to collect back benefits under the Social Security Act, the Act authorizes "a reasonable fee . . . not in excess of 25% of the . . . past-due benefits." 42 U.S.C. §406(b)(1)(A). The question was what the limitation to "a reasonable fee" adds to the 25 percent cap. The context is not fee awards, but price regulation; the client pays the fee.

Attorneys uniformly contract for the 25 percent maximum. The Court said that these agreements should be tested for reasonableness. An agreement might be unreasonable if the lawyer's delay had increased the amount of back benefits (because more benefits accrue each month) or "if the benefits are large in comparison to the amount of time counsel spent on the case." 535 U.S. at 808. The court may require time records, "not as a basis for satellite litigation, but as an aid to the court's assessment of the reasonableness of the fee yielded by the fee agreement." *Id.* This is what *Cabletron* calls the "lodestar cross-check."

Justice Scalia dissented. He thought the reasonableness of a contingent fee could be assessed before the case began, but not after the results were known. For after-the-fact fee setting, the lodestar is the only measure of reasonableness. He ridiculed the majority's approach as standardless.

The Court has now agreed to decide whether the 25 percent cap applies to the total representation, or only to representation before a court, allowing the attorney to charge an additional fee for representation in the administrative processes of the Social Security Administration. Wood v. Commissioner of Social Security, 861 F.3d 1197 (11th Cir. 2017), *cert. granted as* Culbertson v. Berryhill, 138 S. Ct. 2025 (2018).

14. Dissenting views. Much of the law in this area is aimed at the risk that lawyers will charge excessive fees. This is the point of having judges review fees in the first place, and it is certainly the point of the lodestar cross-check, of auctions, and of appointing sophisticated class representatives to negotiate fees. The instinct is strong that a standard percentage of a megafund recovery is a windfall to the lawyers.

But there is also an argument that lawyers are not paid enough, clearly stated in Myriam Gilles and Gary B. Friedman, *Exploding the Class Action Agency Costs Myth: The Social Utility of Entrepreneurial Lawyers*, 155 U. Pa. L. Rev. 103 (2006), and in John C. Coffee, Jr., *Understanding the Plaintiff's Attorney: The Implications of Economic Theory for Private Enforcement of Law Through Class and Derivative Actions*, 86 Colum. L. Rev. 669 (1986). Gilles and Friedman (a law professor and a class-action lawyer) argue that compensating class members with small claims is irrelevant, and that overcompensating lawyers is also irrelevant. The only thing that matters in class actions is to force defendants to internalize the costs of their illegal activity. It is irrelevant whether defendants pay class members or class counsel, but class counsel will work harder, and extract larger settlements, if more is paid to counsel. Gilles and Friedman especially condemn the lodestar cross-check, because it puts a de facto cap on fees. They say that once that cap is reached, class counsel has no incentive to work for a larger settlement. Judge Easterbrook expressed similar concerns in In re Synthroid Marketing Litigation, 264 F.3d 712, 718 (7th Cir. 2001), explicitly assuming that "no sane lawyer" would consider the interests of his client instead of considering only his fees. So much for professional responsibility in a world of law and economics.

Reducing percentages as recoveries get larger avoids fees that seem absurdly high, but Professor Coffee argues that this is backwards. The first dollars are the easiest to win; the last dollars require the most skill and effort, and carry the greatest risk. Both Coffee and Gilles and Friedman argue that the class attorney has inadequate incentive to litigate, because what is at stake for her is only a small fraction of what is at stake for the class. If she is profit maximizing, she will turn down socially valuable cases, and she will settle cases sooner and for less than what a profit-maximizing class would settle them for.

15. Empirical studies. Empirical studies of class action settlements are collected in Brian T. Fitzpatrick, *An Empirical Study of Class Action Settlements and Their Fee Awards*, 7 J. Empirical Legal Stud. 811 (2010). Professor Fitzpatrick attempted to collect every federal class action settlement, reported or unreported, in 2006 and 2007. He found 668 class settlements, 40 percent arising under the securities laws, and the rest under a wide variety of other laws.

Sixty-nine percent of fee awards were based on percentage of recovery, 12 percent on the lodestar, and 20 percent on other methods. This "other" category presumably includes all the auctions and negotiated fees and all the judges who didn't explain their method. Fees varied from 3 percent to 47 percent of the settlement, and the percentage awarded (however it may have been calculated) was strongly and inversely correlated with the amount of the settlement. The most common percentages were 25 percent to 35 percent, but the mean and median were 25 percent. Because the smallest percentages were awarded in the largest cases, the total fees as a percentage of the total settlements were only about 15 percent: 13 percent in 2006 and 20 percent in 2007. The difference is explained by a $6.6 billion settlement in 2006, arising out of a massive fraud by Enron, a utility company that pioneered markets for trading energy like investment securities.

16. An editorial comment. The incentives of the lawyers and the class cannot be fully aligned unless they become partners, with the lawyers buying half the claim and the class bearing half the costs of unsuccessful litigation, including the cost of half the lawyers' time. That obviously is not going to happen. Failing that, alignment of interests can carry us only so far; judicial review and the lawyer's sense of duty to her client will have to do some of the work.

NOTES ON COSTS

1. Awarding and denying costs. Federal Rule 54(d) provides that "costs—other than attorney's fees—should be allowed to the prevailing party." State rules are similar, and courts rarely deny costs. When costs are limited or denied, the most common reasons are tactics that needlessly inflate costs or prolong the litigation, or the losing party's indigence. Indigence cases are collected in Rivera v. City of Chicago, 469 F.3d 631 (7th Cir. 2006). Cases supporting a broader range of reasons are collected in Association of Mexican-American Educators v. California, 231 F.3d 572, 591-593 (9th Cir. 2000), affirming a refusal to award costs where the litigation was of great public importance, the costs were very large ($231,000), and plaintiffs had serious claims and some success, despite being unsuccessful on the whole. Costs are generally taxed administratively by the clerk, but there is a fair amount of litigation, especially in trial courts.

2. Disparities in wealth. There is a circuit split on whether courts have discretion to deny costs because of an enormous wealth disparity between the prevailing and losing parties. In Moore v. CITGO Refining & Chemicals Co., 735 F.3d 309 (5th Cir. 2013), the court said there is no such discretion; the cases are collected in the dissent. The court recognized discretion for indigent litigants, but these losing litigants were well-paid individuals, far from indigent.

In Chevron Corporation v. Donziger, 2018 WL 1137119, *10 (S.D.N.Y. Mar. 1, 2018), the court assumed that Steven Donziger's wealth was "very small" compared to Chevron's net equity of $146.7 billion, but it refused to deny Chevron's motion for costs on this basis. After adjustments, it assessed costs of over $740,000 against Donziger. The facts of the underlying case were spectacular. Donziger attempted to extort billions of dollars from Chevron by "foisting fraudulent evidence on an Ecuadorian court, coercing Ecuadorian judges, illegally writing all or much of the Ecuadorian court's purported decision, and then procuring the signature of an Ecuadorian judge on a $19 billion judgment against Chevron that the co-conspirators had written, in part by the promise of a $500,000 bribe." *Id.* at *1.

3. Except where a statute otherwise provides. Rule 54(d) is explicitly subject to contrary statutes; it would be subject to contrary statutes even if it didn't say so. The Fair Debt Collection Practices Act provides: "On a finding by the court that an action under this section was brought in bad faith and for the purpose of harassment, the court may award to the defendant attorney's fees reasonable in relation to the work expended and costs." 15 U.S.C. §1692k(a)(3). The Court held that this language does not provide "otherwise" than Rule 54(d) — that is, it does not require bad faith as a condition to awarding costs — because it does not state a rule for the case in which a plaintiff files a good-faith claim and loses. Marx v. General Revenue Corp., 568 U.S. 371 (2013). The Court viewed the bad-faith language as limiting the provision for attorneys' fees, and as not intended to implicitly change the quite different rule for costs. Justices Sotomayor and Kagan dissented.

Defendant in *Marx* claimed $7,779 in costs for a case with a one-day trial; these consisted of witness fees, witness travel expenses, and the court reporter's fees for deposition transcripts. The trial court allowed $4,543 of this. The district court opinion is unreported, so we get no details. We note the amounts because even $4,543 is significant for a plaintiff who was unable to pay her student loans and was complaining about unfair debt collection practices.

4. What is included? Taxable costs are generally a small fraction of attorneys' fees, but as *Mexican-American Educators* illustrates, they can be worth fighting over in substantial litigation. In the Exxon Valdez litigation, Exxon requested nearly $70 million in costs, consisting mostly of the cost of a supersedeas bond posted while it repeatedly appealed multibillion-dollar awards of punitive damages. The judgment was eventually reduced to $500 million (see section 3.A.1), but the court refused to award costs, holding that each side had succeeded in substantial part. In re the Exxon Valdez, 568 F.3d 1077 (9th Cir. 2009).

Taxable costs in federal court include fees of the clerk, marshal, court reporter, and witnesses; printing costs; the cost of copying documents "necessarily obtained for use in the case"; and fees for court-appointed experts and interpreters. 28 U.S.C. §1920. As the cost of Exxon's supersedeas bond illustrates, the lower courts do not treat this statutory list as exclusive — even though the Supreme Court has said that it *is* exclusive. Crawford Fitting Co. v. J.T. Gibbons, Inc., 482 U.S. 437, 442-443 (1987).

5. Interpreters. The Court has held that the fees of "interpreters" includes only those who translate oral speech, and does not include the fees of those who translate documents. Taniguchi v. Kan Pacific Saipan, Ltd., 566 U.S. 560 (2012). This holding was based on the alleged plain meaning of "interpreters" as distinguished from "translators." *Taniguchi* is also being cited for the proposition that taxable costs have a "narrow scope," and "are limited to relatively minor, incidental expenses[.]" *Id.* at 573.

6. Electronic discovery. The Fourth Circuit has held that the costs of searching and extracting electronic files, making them searchable, indexing metadata, and preparing the files for conversion to non-editable TIFF or PDF files, all in response to allegedly overbroad discovery requests, are not taxable as "the costs of making copies of any materials where the copies are necessarily obtained for use in the case." Only the final steps of converting the files to TIFF or PDF and copying to compact disks for delivery to the plaintiff constituted "making copies." These final steps cost $218; the earlier steps cost $111,000. Country Vintner, LLC v. E & J Gallo Winery, Inc., 718 F.3d 249, 250 (4th Cir. 2013). The court analogized the search and preparation costs to the cost of searching physical files and extracting paper documents, which also is not taxable. A similar decision in the Federal Circuit also allows the cost of producing a mirror image of the original hard drive, a step that is often necessary to preserve metadata in the documents to be produced. CBT Flint Partners, LLC v. Return Path, Inc., 737 F.3d 1320 (Fed Cir. 2013).

But if the losing litigant specified details of how electronic information should be provided, the Ninth and Federal Circuits have held that the cost of complying with those specifications is taxable. In re Online DVD-Rental Antitrust Litigation, 779 F.3d 914 (9th Cir. 2015); *CBT Flint Partners,* 737 F.3d at 1330.

7. Expert-witness fees. Allowable witness fees are the statutory fees required by 28 U.S.C. §1821 — $40 per day plus expenses. Absent express statutory provision, an expert witness's actual fees cannot be recovered as costs, *Crawford,* or as attorneys' fees, West Virginia University Hospitals, Inc. v. Casey, 499 U.S. 83 (1991). *Casey* collects 34 statutes that authorize recovery of expert-witness fees; the Civil Rights Act of 1991 added the principal employment discrimination statutes to the list. 42 U.S.C. §§1988(c), 2000e-5(k).

The Court refused expert-witness fees under the Individuals with Disabilities Education Act, 20 U.S.C. §1415(i)(3). Arlington Central School District v. Murphy, 548 U.S. 291 (2006). This would be a routine application of *Crawford* and *Casey,* except that the conference report approved by both the House and Senate said expressly and unambiguously that expert-witness fees were to be included in the award of attorneys' fees, and the statute itself directed a study of the "fees, costs, and expenses" awarded to prevailing parties and of the hours spent by "attorneys and consultants." But the majority said that neither legislative history nor the study provision gave sufficiently clear notice to government defendants when the text of the fee-award provision used language that had been construed not to include expert-witness fees.

C.   ETHICAL ISSUES IN FEE AWARDS

EVANS v. JEFF D.
475 U.S. 717 (1986)

Justice STEVENS delivered the opinion of the Court.

The Civil Rights Attorney's Fees Awards Act of 1976 . . . provides that "the court, in its discretion, may allow the prevailing party . . . a reasonable attorney's fee" in enumerated civil rights actions. 42 U.S.C. §1988. In Maher v. Gagne, 448 U.S. 122 (1980), we held that fees may be assessed against state officials after a case has been settled by the entry of a consent decree. In this case, we consider . . . whether attorney's fees *must* be assessed when the case has been settled by a consent decree granting prospective relief to the plaintiff class but providing that the defendants shall not pay any part of the prevailing party's fees or costs. We hold that the District Court has the power, in its sound discretion, to refuse to award fees.

I

The petitioners are the Governor and other public officials . . . responsible for the education and treatment of children who suffer from emotional and mental handicaps. Respondents are a class of such children who have been or will be placed in petitioners' care. . . .

The factual allegations in the complaint described deficiencies in both the educational programs and the health care services provided respondents. . . . The complaint prayed for injunctive relief and . . . costs and attorney's fees, but it did not seek damages.

On the day the complaint was filed, the District Court . . . appoint[ed] Charles Johnson as [plaintiffs'] next friend for the sole purpose of instituting and prosecuting the action. At that time Johnson was employed by the Idaho Legal Aid Society . . . .

[O]ne week before trial, petitioners presented respondents with a new settlement proposal. As respondents themselves characterize it, the proposal "offered virtually all of the injunctive relief [they] had sought in their complaint." The Court of Appeals . . . noted that the proposed relief was "more than the district court in earlier hearings had indicated it was willing to grant." 743 F.2d 648, 650 (9th Cir. 1984). . . . [H]owever, petitioners' offer included a provision for a waiver by respondents of any claim to fees or costs. . . . Johnson ultimately determined that his ethical obligation to his clients mandated acceptance of the proposal. The parties conditioned the waiver on approval by the District Court.[5] . . .

Johnson filed a written motion requesting the District Court to approve the settlement "except for the provision on costs and attorney's fees," and to allow respondents to present a bill of costs and fees. . . [T]he District Court approved the settlement and denied the motion . . . .

The Court of Appeals . . . invalidated the fee waiver and left standing the remainder of the settlement . . . .

The court added that "[w]hen attorney's fees are negotiated as part of a class action settlement, a conflict frequently exists between the class lawyers' interest in compensation and the class members' interest in relief." *Id.* at 651-652. "To avoid this conflict," the Court of Appeals relied on Circuit precedent which had "disapproved simultaneous negotiation of settlements and attorney's fees" absent a showing of "unusual circumstances." *Id.* at 652. . . .

II . . .

Rule 23(e) wisely requires court approval of . . . any settlement of a class action, but the power to approve or reject a settlement negotiated by the parties . . . does not

---

5. . . . In addition, the entire settlement agreement was conditioned on the District Court's approval of the waiver provision. . . .

authorize the court to require the parties to accept a settlement to which they have not agreed. Although changed circumstances may justify a court-ordered modification of a consent decree . . . , and the District Court might have advised petitioners and respondents that it would not approve their proposal unless one or more of its provisions was deleted or modified, Rule 23(e) does not give the court the power . . . to modify a proposed consent decree and order its acceptance over either party's objection. . . . The District Court could not enforce the settlement on the merits and award attorney's fees anymore than it could, in a situation in which the attorney had negotiated a large fee at the expense of the plaintiff class, preserve the fee award and order greater relief on the merits. The question we must decide, therefore, is whether the District Court had a duty to reject the proposed settlement. . . .

Although . . . we recognize Johnson's conflicting interests between pursuing relief for the class and a fee for the Idaho Legal Aid Society, we do not believe that the "dilemma" was an "ethical" one in the sense that Johnson had to choose between conflicting duties under the prevailing norms of professional conduct. Plainly, Johnson had no *ethical* obligation to seek a statutory fee award. His ethical duty was to serve his clients loyally and competently.[14] Since the proposal to settle the merits was more favorable than the probable outcome of the trial, Johnson's decision to recommend acceptance was consistent with the highest standards of our profession. . . .

The defect, if any, in the negotiated fee waiver must be traced not to the rules of ethics but to the Fees Act.[15] . . .

The question this case presents, then, is whether the Fees Act requires a district court to disapprove a stipulation seeking to settle a civil rights class action under Rule 23 when the offered relief equals or exceeds the probable outcome at trial but is expressly conditioned on waiver of statutory eligibility for attorney's fees. . . . [W]e are not persuaded that Congress has commanded that all such settlements must be rejected by the District Court. Moreover, on the facts of record in this case, we are satisfied that the District Court did not abuse its discretion by approving the fee waiver.

III . . .

Congress bestowed on the "prevailing *party*" . . . a statutory eligibility for a discretionary award of attorney's fees in specified civil rights actions. It did not prevent the party from waiving this eligibility anymore than it legislated against assignment of this right to an attorney, such as effectively occurred here. Instead, Congress enacted the fee-shifting provision as "an integral part of the remedies necessary to obtain" compliance with civil rights laws, S. Rep. No. 94-1011 at 5 (1976), 1976 U.S. Code Cong. & Admin. News 5913, to further the same general purpose—promotion of respect for civil rights—that led it to provide damages and injunctive relief. The statute and its legislative history nowhere suggest that Congress intended to forbid *all* waivers of attorney's fees—even those insisted upon by a civil rights plaintiff in exchange for some other relief to which he is indisputably not entitled—anymore than it intended

14. Generally speaking, a lawyer . . . must not allow his own interests, financial or otherwise, to influence his professional advice. Accordingly, it is argued that an attorney is required to evaluate a settlement offer on the basis of his client's interest, without considering his own interest in obtaining a fee; upon recommending settlement, he must abide by the client's decision whether or not to accept the offer.

15. Even state bar opinions holding it unethical for defendants to request fee waivers . . . are bottomed ultimately on §1988. For the sake of completeness, it should be mentioned that the bar is not of one mind on this ethical judgment.

to bar a concession on damages to secure broader injunctive relief. Thus, while it is undoubtedly true that Congress expected fee shifting to attract competent counsel to represent citizens deprived of their civil rights, it neither bestowed fee awards upon attorneys nor rendered them nonwaivable or nonnegotiable; instead, it added them to the arsenal of remedies available to combat violations of civil rights, a goal not invariably inconsistent with conditioning settlement on the merits on a waiver of statutory attorney's fees. . . .

[A] general proscription against negotiated waiver of attorney's fees in exchange for a settlement on the merits would itself impede vindication of civil rights, at least in some cases, by reducing the attractiveness of settlement. . . .

Most defendants are unlikely to settle unless the cost of the predicted judgment, discounted by its probability, plus the transaction costs of further litigation, are greater than the cost of the settlement package. If fee waivers cannot be negotiated, the settlement package must either contain an attorney's fee component of potentially large and typically uncertain magnitude, or else the parties must agree to have the fee fixed by the court. . . .[23]

The adverse impact of removing attorney's fees and costs from bargaining might be tolerable if the uncertainty introduced into settlement negotiations were small. But it is not. The defendants' potential liability for fees in this kind of litigation can be as significant as . . . their potential liability on the merits. . . . See, e.g., *Rivera*. . . .

The unpredictability of attorney's fees may be just as important as their magnitude when a defendant is striving to fix its liability. . . . [D]efendant's liability for his opponent's attorney's fees in a civil rights action cannot be fixed with a sufficient degree of confidence to make defendants indifferent to their exclusion from negotiation. It is therefore not implausible to anticipate that parties to a significant number of civil rights cases will refuse to settle if liability for attorney's fees remains open, thereby forcing more cases to trial, unnecessarily burdening the judicial system, and disserving civil rights litigants. Respondents' own waiver of attorney's fees and costs to obtain settlement of their educational claims is eloquent testimony to the utility of fee waivers in vindicating civil rights claims.[29] We conclude, therefore, that it is not necessary to construe the Fees Act as embodying a general rule prohibiting settlements conditioned on the waiver of fees in order to be faithful to the purposes of that Act.[30]

IV

The question remains whether the District Court abused its discretion in this case by approving a settlement which included a complete fee waiver. . . .

[R]espondents . . . suggest that the court's authority to pass on settlements, typically invoked to ensure fair treatment of class members, must be exercised in accordance with the Fees Act to promote the availability of attorneys in civil rights cases.

---

23. It is unrealistic to assume that the defendant's offer on the merits would be unchanged by redaction of the provision waiving fees. . . .

29. Respondents implicitly acknowledge a defendant's need to fix his total liability when they suggest that the parties to a civil rights action should "exchange information" regarding plaintiff's attorney's fees. . . . Apparently, some parties have circumvented the rule against simultaneous negotiation in one Circuit by means of tacit agreements of this kind. . . .

30. The Court is unanimous in concluding that the Fees Act should not be interpreted to prohibit all simultaneous negotiations of a defendant's liability on the merits and his liability for his opponent's attorney's fees. . . .

Specifically, respondents assert that the State of Idaho could not pass a valid statute precluding the payment of attorney's fees in settlements of civil rights cases to which the Fees Act applies. From this they reason that the Fees Act must equally preclude the adoption of a uniform state-wide policy that serves the same end, and accordingly contend that a consistent practice of insisting on a fee waiver as a condition of settlement in civil rights litigation is in conflict with the federal statute authorizing fees for prevailing parties, including those who prevail by way of settlement.[31] Remarkably, there seems little disagreement on these points. Petitioners and the amici who support them never suggest that the district court is obligated to place its stamp of approval on every settlement in which the plaintiffs' attorneys have agreed to a fee waiver. The Solicitor General, for example, has suggested that a fee waiver need not be approved when the defendant had "no realistic defense on the merits," or if the waiver was part of a "vindictive effort . . . to teach counsel that they had better not bring such cases."

We find it unnecessary to evaluate this argument, however, because the record . . . does not indicate that Idaho has adopted such a statute, policy, or practice. Nor does the record support the narrower proposition that petitioners' request to waive fees was a vindictive effort to deter attorneys from representing plaintiffs in civil rights suits . . . .

In light of the record, respondents must—to sustain the judgment in their favor—confront the District Court's finding that the extensive structural relief they obtained constituted an adequate *quid pro quo* [literally, something for something] for their waiver of attorney's fees. The Court of Appeals did not overturn this finding. . . . Only by making the unsupported assumption that the respondent class was entitled to retain the favorable portions of the settlement while rejecting the fee waiver could the Court of Appeals conclude that the District Court had acted unwisely.

What . . . this settlement illustrates is that the Fees Act has given the victims of civil rights violations a powerful weapon that improves their ability to employ counsel, to obtain access to the courts, and thereafter to vindicate their rights by means of settlement or trial. For aught that appears, it was the "coercive" effect of respondents' statutory right to seek a fee award that motivated petitioners' exceptionally generous offer. Whether this weapon might be even more powerful if fee waivers were prohibited in cases like this is another question,[34] but it is in any event a question that Congress is best equipped to answer. . . . [W]e shall rely primarily on the sound discretion of the district courts to appraise the reasonableness of particular class-action settlements on a case-by-case basis . . . . In this case, the District Court did not abuse its discretion in upholding a fee waiver which secured broad injunctive relief, relief greater than that which plaintiffs could reasonably have expected to achieve at trial.

The judgment of the Court of Appeals is reversed. . . .

---

31. . . . National staff counsel for the American Civil Liberties Union estimates that requests for fee waivers are made in more than half of all civil rights cases litigated. See Bill Winter, *Fee Waiver Requests Unethical: Bar Opinion*, 68 A.B.A.J. 23 (1982).

34. We are cognizant of the possibility that decisions by individual clients to bargain away fee awards may, in the aggregate and in the long run, diminish lawyers' expectations of statutory fees in civil rights cases. If this occurred, the pool of lawyers willing to represent plaintiffs in such cases might shrink, constricting the "effective access to the judicial process" for persons with civil rights grievances which the Fees Act was intended to provide. H.R. Rep. No. 94-1558 at 1 (1976). That the "tyranny of small decisions" may operate in this fashion is not to say that there is any reason or documentation to support such a concern at the present time. Comment on this issue is therefore premature at this juncture. We believe, however, that as a practical matter the likelihood of this circumstance arising is remote.

Justice BRENNAN, with whom Justices MARSHALL and BLACKMUN join, dissenting. . . .

Because today's decision will make it more difficult for civil rights plaintiffs to obtain legal assistance, a result plainly contrary to Congress' purpose, I dissent. . . .

II . . .

Congress might have awarded attorney's fees as simply an additional form of make-whole relief, the threat of which would "promote respect for civil rights" by deterring potential civil rights violators. If this were the case, the Court's equation of attorney's fees with damages would not be wholly inaccurate. However, the legislative history of the Fees Act discloses that this is not the case. . . .

Congress did not [authorize fee awards] solely, or even primarily, to confer a benefit on . . . aggrieved individuals. Rather, Congress sought to capitalize on the happy coincidence that encouraging private actions would, in the long run, provide effective public enforcement of [the law]. . . .

III . . .

Congress' primary purpose was to enable "private attorneys general" to protect the public interest by creating economic incentives for lawyers to represent them. The Court's assertion that the Fees Act was intended to do nothing more than give individual victims of civil rights violations another remedy is thus at odds with the whole thrust of the legislation. . . .[4] . . .

Having concluded that the Fees Act merely creates another remedy to vindicate the rights of individual plaintiffs, the Court asks whether negotiated waivers of statutory attorney's fees are "invariably inconsistent" with the availability of such fees as a remedy for individual plaintiffs. Not surprisingly, the Court has little difficulty knocking down this frail straw man. But the *proper* question is whether permitting negotiated fee waivers is consistent with Congress' goal of attracting competent counsel. . . .

A

Permitting plaintiffs to negotiate fee waivers in exchange for relief on the merits actually raises two related but distinct questions. First, is it permissible under the Fees Act to negotiate a settlement of attorney's fees simultaneously with the merits? Second, can the "reasonable attorney's fee" guaranteed in the Act be waived? As a matter of logic, either of these practices may be permitted without also permitting the other. . . .

[T]he Court's discussion conflates the different effects of these practices . . . .

B

1

It seems obvious that allowing defendants in civil rights cases to condition settlement of the merits on a waiver of statutory attorney's fees will diminish lawyers' expectations

---

4. The Court seems to view the options as limited to two: either the Fees Act confers a benefit on attorneys, . . . or the Fees Act confers a benefit on individual plaintiffs, who may freely exploit the statutory fee award to their own best advantage. It apparently has not occurred to the Court that Congress might have made a remedy available to individual plaintiffs primarily for the benefit of the *public*. . . .

of receiving fees and decrease the willingness of lawyers to accept civil rights cases. Even the Court acknowledges "the possibility . . . ." *Ante* n.34. . . .

[N]umerous courts and commentators have recognized that permitting fee waivers creates disincentives for lawyers to take civil rights cases and thus makes it more difficult for civil rights plaintiffs to obtain legal assistance.

But it does not require a sociological study to see that permitting fee waivers will make it more difficult for civil rights plaintiffs to obtain legal assistance. It requires only common sense. Assume that a civil rights defendant makes a settlement offer that includes a demand for waiver of statutory attorney's fees. The decision whether to accept or reject the offer is the plaintiff's alone, and the lawyer must abide by the plaintiff's decision.[8] . . . The plaintiff . . . has no real stake in the statutory fee and is unaffected by its waiver. Consequently, plaintiffs will readily agree to waive fees if this will help them to obtain other relief they desire. As summed up by the Legal Ethics Committee of the District of Columbia Bar:

> Defense counsel . . . are in a uniquely favorable position when they condition settlement on the waiver of the statutory fee: They make a demand for a benefit that the plaintiff's lawyer cannot resist as a matter of ethics and one in which the plaintiff has no interest and therefore will not resist.

Op. No. 147, reprinted in 113 Daily Washington Rptr. 389, 394 (1985). . . .

[F]rom the lawyer's standpoint, things could scarcely have turned out worse. He or she invested considerable time and effort in the case, won, and has exactly nothing to show for it. Is the Court really serious in suggesting that it takes a study to prove that this lawyer will be reluctant when, the following week, another civil rights plaintiff enters his office and asks for representation? . . .

[O]nce fee waivers are permitted, defendants will seek them as a matter of course, since this is a logical way to minimize liability. . . . [D]efense counsel would be remiss *not to* demand that the plaintiff waive . . . fees. A lawyer who proposes to have his client pay more than is necessary to end litigation has failed to fulfill his fundamental duty zealously to represent the best interests of his client. . . .[12] . . .

Because making it more difficult for civil rights plaintiffs to obtain legal assistance is precisely the opposite of what Congress sought to achieve by enacting the Fees Act, fee waivers should be prohibited. We have on numerous prior occasions held that "a statutory right conferred on a private party, but affecting the public interest, may not be waived or released if such waiver or release contravenes the statutory policy." Brooklyn Savings Bank v. O'Neil, 324 U.S. 697, 704 (1945) (holding right to liquidated damages under Fair Labor Standards Act nonwaivable). This is simply straightforward application of the well-established principle that an agreement which is contrary to public policy is void and unenforceable.

8. The attorney is, in fact, obliged to advise the plaintiff whether to accept or reject the settlement offer based on his independent professional judgment, and the lawyer's duty of undivided loyalty requires that he render such advice free from the influence of his or his organization's interest in a fee. . . .

12. The Solicitor General's suggestion that we can prohibit waivers sought as part of a "vindictive effort" to teach lawyers not to bring civil rights cases . . . is thus irrelevant. Defendants will seek such waivers in every case simply as a matter of sound bargaining. Indeed, the Solicitor General's brief suggests that this will be the bargaining posture of the United States in the future.

2

This all seems so obvious that it is puzzling that the Court reaches a different result. The Court's rationale is that, unless fee waivers are permitted, "parties to a significant number of civil rights cases will refuse to settle." This is a wholly inadequate justification for the Court's result.

First, . . . encouraging settlements is desirable policy. But it is *judicially* created policy, applicable to litigation of any kind and having no special force in the context of civil rights cases. The *congressional* policy . . . is . . . to create incentives for lawyers to devote time to civil rights cases . . . . [A] *judicial* policy favoring settlement cannot possibly take precedence over this express *congressional* policy. . . .

The fact that fee waivers may produce some settlement offers that are beneficial to a few individual plaintiffs is hardly "consistent with the purposes of the Fees Act," if permitting fee waivers fundamentally undermines what Congress sought to achieve. Each individual plaintiff who waives his right to statutory fees in order to obtain additional relief for himself makes it that much more difficult for the next victim of a civil rights violation to find a lawyer willing or able to bring *his* case. . . .

I find particularly unpersuasive the Court's apparent belief that Congress enacted the Fees Act to help plaintiffs coerce relief to which they are "indisputably not entitled." . . . [T]his is an unfortunate cost of a statute intended to ensure that plaintiffs can obtain the relief to which they *are* entitled. And it certainly is not a result we must preserve at the expense of the central purpose of the Fees Act.

Second, even assuming that settlement practices are relevant, the Court greatly exaggerates the effect that prohibiting fee waivers will have on defendants' willingness to make settlement offers. . . . [I]t is a prohibition on simultaneous negotiation, not a prohibition on fee waivers, that makes it difficult for the defendant to ascertain his total liability at the time he agrees to settle the merits. . . . [T]he Court's numerous arguments about why defendants will not settle unless they can determine their total liability at the time of settlement are simply beside the point. . . .

The Court asserts, without factual support, that requiring defendants to pay statutory fee awards will prevent a "significant number" of settlements. It is, of course, ironic that the same absence of "documentation" which makes comment on the effects of *permitting* fee waivers "premature at this juncture," *ante* n.34, does not similarly affect the Court's willingness to speculate about what to expect if fee waivers are *prohibited.* Be that as it may, I believe that the Court overstates the extent to which prohibiting fee waivers will deter defendants from making settlement offers. Because the parties can negotiate a fee (or a range of fees) that is not unduly high and condition their settlement on the court's approval of this fee, the magnitude of a defendant's liability for fees in the settlement context need be neither uncertain nor particularly great. Against this, the defendant must weigh the risk of a nonnegotiated fee to be fixed by the court after a trial. . . . Thus, powerful incentives remain for defendants to seek settlement. Moreover, the Court's decision last Term in Marek v. Chesny, 473 U.S. 1 (1985), provides an additional incentive for defendants to make settlement offers, namely, the opportunity to limit liability for attorney's fees if the plaintiff refuses the offer and proceeds to trial.

All of which is not to deny that prohibiting fee waivers will deter some settlements; any increase in the costs of settling will have this effect. . . .

C

I would, on the other hand, permit simultaneous negotiation of fees and merits claims, since this would not contravene the purposes of the Fees Act. Congress determined that awarding prevailing parties a "reasonable" fee would create necessary—and sufficient—incentives for attorneys to work on civil rights cases. Prohibiting plaintiffs from waiving statutory fees ensures that lawyers will receive this "reasonable" statutory fee. . . .

IV

Although today's decision will undoubtedly impair the effectiveness of the private enforcement scheme Congress established for civil rights legislation, I do not believe that it will bring about the total disappearance of "private attorneys general.". . . [S]everal Bar Associations have already declared it unethical for defense counsel to seek fee waivers. Such efforts are to be commended and, it is to be hoped, will be followed by other state and local organizations concerned with respecting the intent of Congress and with protecting civil rights.

In addition, it may be that civil rights attorneys can obtain agreements from their clients not to waive attorney's fees. Such agreements simply replicate the private market for legal services (in which attorneys are not ordinarily required to contribute to their client's recovery[21]), and thus will enable civil rights practitioners to make it economically feasible—as Congress hoped—to expend time and effort litigating civil rights claims. . . .

NOTES ON ETHICAL PROBLEMS IN FEE-SHIFTING CASES

1. The underlying problem. Most cases are settled, and settlement of fee claims involves an inherent conflict of interest for the attorney. Defendants care about the total cost of the settlement; apart from any desire to punish the plaintiff's bar, they have no reason to care how much goes to the lawyer and how much to her client. Once defendant decides how much it is willing to pay, every dollar for the lawyer comes out of her client's pocket. Temptations arise in both directions: The client can sell out the lawyer for a better settlement on the merits, or the lawyer can sell out the client for a better fee.

In some individual cases, the conflict may be no worse than in any other attorney-client relationship. Settlement negotiations in individual fee-shifting cases can award a lump sum to the client, and the client and attorney can divide the sum according to their fee agreement. The lawyer may take advantage of the client in this division, but that risk is always present, and the fee-shifting rules do not aggravate it.

The risk is aggravated if the lawyer negotiates one sum for the client and a separate sum for himself. And this can be necessary if the lawyer agrees to work for an assignment of the fee award. This benefits the client by providing free representation if the case is unsuccessful, but it complicates settlement negotiations by requiring that the fee award be separated from the merits. The problems are further aggravated in class actions. The class can't agree to a fee, and the lawyer must negotiate both a class recovery and her own fee award.

---

21. One of the more peculiar aspects of the Court's interpretation of the Fees Act is that it permits defendants to require plaintiff's counsel to contribute his compensation to satisfying the plaintiff's claims. In ordinary civil litigation, no defendant would make—or sell to his adversary—a settlement offer conditioned upon the plaintiff's convincing his attorney to contribute to the plaintiff's recovery. . . . Thus, rather than treating civil rights claims no differently than other civil litigation, the Court places such litigation in a quite unique—and unfavorable—category.

2. Simultaneous negotiation. Two circuits tried to require that class counsel negotiate the class recovery, get that approved by the court, and then negotiate attorneys' fees. Mendoza v. United States, 623 F.2d 1338, 1352-1353 (9th Cir. 1980); Prandini v. National Tea Co., 557 F.2d 1015 (3d Cir. 1977). *Jeff D.* overruled these cases; simultaneous negotiation is *Jeff D.*'s whole premise. Even so, the Third Circuit did not entirely give up: "[T]here exists a special danger of collusiveness when the attorney fees, ostensibly stemming from a separate agreement, were negotiated simultaneously with the settlement," and courts should be alert to this danger when they review settlements and proposed fee awards. In re Community Bank, 418 F.3d 277, 308 & n.25 (3d Cir. 2005). A West Virginia court, relying on the discussion of collusion in *Community Bank*, wrote that it is "a good practice for counsel to defer discussion of fees at least until after negotiations of the substantive terms of the settlement are concluded, and to maintain a record that demonstrate[s] this chronology." Bibb v. Monsanto Co., 2013 WL 358886, *139 (W. Va. Cir. Ct. 2013).

The New Jersey court abandoned its long-standing ban on simultaneous negotiation, but reaffirmed its ban on fee waivers. Pinto v. Spectrum Chemicals & Laboratory Products, 985 A.2d 1239 (N.J. 2010). Six public-interest law firms as amici supported this result, arguing that the ban on simultaneous negotiation, if taken seriously, made settlement impossible.

Completely separate negotiation would solve the problem if it worked, but it requires a very cooperative defendant. Defendants generally won't settle unless they know the bottom line. If the lawyer for the class steadfastly refuses to discuss fees, it is likely that the case won't settle, or that it will settle for a sum that leaves room for defendant's worst fears of what the fee award might be. Neither result is in the interest of the clients. And there is no good way for the court to police the negotiation process. Suppose defendant says he's willing to spend $100,000 to get rid of this case. Plaintiff's lawyer may understand that if she settles for $80,000 and requests a $20,000 fee, she'll get no fight on the fee.

3. What does *Jeff D.* hold? *Jeff D.* holds only that trial courts are not required to reject settlements that contain fee waivers, and that it is not an abuse of discretion to approve when the settlement gives the class more relief than it could have obtained at trial and defendant does not demand fee waivers in every case. Apparently, trial courts have discretion to approve or reject fee waivers. Does the opinion give any further guidance on the exercise of that discretion? Would a fee waiver be improper if the class got less than it could have obtained at trial? If defendant demands fee waivers in three-quarters of its cases? Whatever the limits of *Jeff D.*'s holding, it is hard to find cases rejecting settlements because of fee waivers.

If acceptance of the settlement is solely up to the clients, and if the lawyer's interest is not to be considered, why should settlements ever include a fee? ABA Model Rule of Professional Conduct 1.2(a) states without qualification: "A lawyer shall abide by a client's decision whether to settle a matter." Is this rule just a mistake as applied to statutory fee awards?

4. The consequences of *Jeff D.* The public-interest bar feared universal fee waivers in the wake of *Jeff D.* That hasn't happened, but the right to counsel in fee-shifting cases has been undermined and bargaining power has shifted to defendants. Two small-scale studies got similar results from structured interviews with plaintiffs' civil rights attorneys. Daniel Nazer, Note, *Conflict and Solidarity: The Legacy of Evans v. Jeff D.*, 17 Geo. J. Legal Ethics, 499 (2004), reports on 10 interviews with lawyers around the country in not-for-profit agencies. Julie Davies, *Federal Civil Rights Practice in the 1990's: The Dichotomy Between Reality and Theory*, 48 Hastings L.J. 197 (1997), reports on 35 interviews with lawyers in both for-profit and not-for-profit practices in the San Francisco area.

a. Defendants' responses. There were few reports of outright demands for fee waivers. Plaintiffs' lawyers interviewed could only speculate about why defendants are not more aggressive, but the explanation may be that plaintiffs' bar has found effective responses. What has become routine is that defendants make lump-sum settlement offers that include both merits relief and fees.

b. Ethics opinions. Ethics committees have generally conformed their views to *Jeff D.*, and some of the earlier opinions holding it unethical to demand fee waivers have been withdrawn. The California ethics committee concluded that defense counsel may ethically demand fee waivers in every case and that plaintiff's counsel must transmit such offers to the client and explain the client's right to waive attorneys' fees. State Bar of California Standing Committee on Professional Responsibility and Conduct, Formal Opinion 2009-176 (2009), available at https://www.calbar.ca.gov/Portals/0/documents/ethics/Opinions/2009-176.pdf [https://perma.cc/4GU6-WPB2]. That opinion says that only one ethics opinion since *Jeff D.* has found an ethical barrier to demanding fee waivers: Los Angeles County Bar Association Formal Opinions, Opinion 445 (1987), available at http://www.lacba.org/docs/default-source/ethics-opinions/archived-ethics-opinions/op_445.pdf [https://perma.cc/MNH4-R2G7]. Bar-association ethics opinions are generally only advisory.

c. Resistance from the plaintiff's bar. Some members of the plaintiff's bar made their own ethical judgments and decided that in most circumstances they could refuse to waive fees. One experienced civil rights litigator told Laycock that he refuses to discuss the possibility of fee waivers; his explanation to defense lawyers is simply, "You're saying your kid goes to college and my kid doesn't." Some of Professor Davies's interviewees made similar statements.

A lawyer can discuss the problem with an individual client who is a competent adult. Some are grateful to their lawyer and refuse to consider fee waivers; some are happy to throw their lawyer overboard to get a recovery for themselves. Lawyers representing children, incompetents, or a class can't even have the conversation. Both Davies and Nazer report lawyers carefully screening clients on this basis, especially for important test cases that are likely to accumulate large fees. Especially at the not-for-profit agencies, the goal is to find a client who cares about the cause, and who can be educated to understand the agency's role in that cause and the importance of fee awards to sustaining the agency. Such a client is much less likely to be bought off with a cash settlement and a fee waiver.

d. Assigning fees to the lawyer. Some public-interest lawyers drafted contracts in which clients agreed at the beginning not to waive fees, or in which they assigned their right to fees to their lawyer. But the general rule is that any delegation of the client's settlement authority is revocable. *Restatement (Third) of the Law Governing Lawyers* §22 (Am. Law Inst. 2000). And the Ninth Circuit has held that a contract assigning the client's right to a fee award to his lawyer is void under California law. Pony v. County of Los Angeles, 433 F.3d 1138, 1142-1145 (9th Cir. 2006). *Jeff D.* suggested that the client could make such an assignment; so did Venegas v. Mitchell, 495 U.S. 82, 88 (1990). But *Pony* reads these comments to apply only to assigning the right to pursue a claim for fees after the client chooses to assert it—not to assigning the substantive right to fees at the beginning of the case.

Under state fee-shifting statutes in California, the right to fees belongs to the lawyer and not to the client. Flannery v. Prentice, 28 P.3d 860 (Cal. 2001). But this allocation of rights did not appear to help the lawyers protect their right to fees. The right to a federal fee award belongs to the client, not to the lawyer. In Astrue v. Ratliff, 560 U.S. 586 (2010), the Court held unanimously that the government can offset the fees against debts the client owes the government.

Professor Carle sees an attorney-client fee agreement as at least a partial solution to the issue.

> Following *Venegas*, many courts have upheld plaintiffs' obligations in public interest cases to pay attorneys' fees to lawyers, separate and apart from amounts covered under fee-shifting statutes. . . . [T]he Court views plaintiffs' rights to statutory attorneys' fees and their contractual obligations to their lawyers as two separate questions. The plaintiff may contract to pay her lawyer a fee related to her monetary recovery. If she does, she must fulfill that promise, regardless of whether she has collected—or waived the right to—statutory attorneys' fees from the defendant.

Susan D. Carle, *The Settlement Problem in Public Interest Law*, 29 Stan. L. & Pol'y Rev. 1, 28-29 (2018).

e. Other contractual solutions. Other contractual solutions try to create financial incentives for the client not to waive the fee. These solutions are mostly used by lawyers in private practice; restrictions flowing from their tax-exempt status make them risky or unavailable for not-for-profit agencies.

Lawyer and client can agree to a contingent fee of one-third of the total recovery, including both the merits award and the fee award. In a suit for an injunction, or where fees are large in proportion to the damages awarded, such an agreement badly undercompensates the lawyer and overcompensates the client. But it reduces the risk of a total fee waiver; a client who gets to keep two-thirds of a fee award is unlikely to waive it. Such arrangements are considerably more attractive to lawyers when there is a prospect of substantial damages. So lawyers now evaluate civil rights cases as they do tort cases, refusing those with modest damages. "[I]f the cop doesn't beat the guy up enough then no one's going to bring the case." Nazer, 17 Geo. J. Legal Ethics at 537, quoting an interviewee. Of course, this removes much of the promise of *Rivera*.

A variation is for lawyer and client to agree to a contingent fee that is reduced by the amount of any fee award. This gives the client a financial stake in a fee award at least large enough to cover the client's liability for the contingent fee.

f. Lump-sum settlements. Lump-sum settlement offers appear to have become standard. Plaintiff's lawyers report a variety of techniques for breaking the lump sum into a merits component and a fees component as the negotiations continue, but defendants remain focused on the bottom line and in the end, both components must be settled simultaneously.

There is no reason in principle that a lump-sum settlement could not be large enough to cover both damages and fees. But there is the *Rivera* problem: If the damages are small in proportion to the cost of litigation, a standard contingent fee agreement will undercompensate the lawyer. And there is the *Jeff D.* problem: If the lump sum offers substantial compensation to the client, the client can accept it even if it places zero value on the fee claim.

The zero-sum nature of the conflict between attorney and client with lump sum settlements came into stark relief in Ellis v. Commissioner of the Department of Industrial Accidents, 37 N.E.3d 681 (Mass. App. Ct. 2015). James Ellis, an attorney, represented a number of clients with workers' compensation claims. Insurance companies would often settle these cases on a lump sum basis; Ellis would claim attorneys' fees and expenses out of the lump sum payment. State administrative law judges reviewed the allocation of expenses and fees, and sometimes made downward adjustments of Ellis's claimed expenses on grounds that they were unsupported by record evidence. Downward adjustment of fees benefited Ellis's clients but hurt Ellis.

   The appeals court rejected Ellis's arguments that administrative law judges lacked power under state law to review the claimed expenses. The court explained the importance of such review:

> Once the insurer agrees to payment of a sum certain lump sum settlement, the insurer has little incentive to scrutinize the attorney's fees and expenses submitted by the employee's attorney. Further, the injured employee would be placed in an awkward position, if called upon to contest the fees and expenses of the attorney who has represented that employee through the settlement process. Thus, it is the impartial administrative judge who stands as the overseer to the fairness and propriety of the lump sum settlement and the fees and expenses incorporated therein.

Id. at 685.

   g. Unjust enrichment? Professor Silver has argued that with or without a contract, clients are unjustly enriched if their lawyers waive fees. Charles Silver, *A Restitutionary Theory of Attorneys' Fees in Class Actions,* 76 Cornell L. Rev. 656, 709-715 (1991). The California court in *Flannery* relied on unjust enrichment as one of several reasons for holding that the right to fees belongs to the lawyer. But *Flannery* announced a default rule, subject to change by a fee agreement, and either an actual fee agreement or the obvious possibility of negotiating a fee agreement would generally displace any claim for unjust enrichment in cases with individual clients. A clear fee agreement is not just a possibility, but an ethical duty; the client is entitled to know what the representation will cost.

   5. Idaho reneges. Think about the *Jeff D.* settlement from Idaho's perspective. Attorneys' fees would have to be paid immediately in cash, but relief to the class could be paid in empty promises. This is a quite general problem in structural injunction cases. *Jeff D.* has been settled repeatedly, with three consent decrees and additional subsidiary agreements along the way, but the state never provided the money to implement the consent decrees and it sought and received repeated extensions of deadlines. The court of appeals consistently held that the fee waiver does not apply to fees incurred in postwaiver efforts to enforce the consent decree. Jeff D. v. Kempthorne, 365 F.3d 844, 855 (9th Cir. 2004); Jeff D. v. Andrus, 899 F.2d 753, 765 (9th Cir. 1989).

   In 2000, an angry district judge credibly threatened contempt sanctions, and for a time, the pace of progress seemed to improve. The parties negotiated an implementation plan with 50 recommendations and with action items under each recommendation. Apparently in the midst of this negotiation, the state moved to vacate the entire decree unless plaintiffs proved that it was still needed to end a constitutional violation. So much for giving the children more than the Constitution required in exchange for the waiver of attorneys' fees. In the wake of Frew v. Hawkins, described in the Introductory Notes to section 4.B, the court of appeals had no trouble rejecting the state's motion to modify or vacate the decree on this ground. 365 F.3d 844.

   Emphasizing that an order must be "both specific and definite" to support a finding of contempt, Jeff D. v. Kempthorne, 2007 WL 461471, *3 (D. Idaho 2007), and requiring clear and convincing evidence of a substantial failure to comply, not based on a "good faith and reasonable interpretation of the judgment," *id.* at *3, *53, the court found Idaho officials in contempt with respect to 21 action items. Later in the year, the court found that defendants had "substantially complied" with the 21 action items, and that "having made significant efforts to substantially comply with their promises," state officials were entitled to have the consent decree vacated. Jeff D. v. Kempthorne, 2007 WL 3256620, *5 (D. Idaho 2007).

Four years later, the Ninth Circuit reversed, holding that the district court applied the wrong legal standard to determine whether to vacate the decree. Rather than require plaintiff to prove by clear and convincing evidence that Idaho officials had violated the decree and that they had not done so in good faith or with a reasonable basis for believing they were in compliance, the district court should have put the burden on defendants to prove that they were in substantial compliance with the decrees or that changes in facts or law made it no longer equitable to give the judgment prospective application. Jeff D. v. Otter, 643 F.3d 278 (9th Cir. 2011).

After more than three decades of resistance and delay, can a brief period of substantial compliance possibly justify any confidence that defendants will continue to comply without continued judicial supervision? Whatever the answer to that question, it is clear that the plaintiff class did not get what it was promised in exchange for the fee waiver.

6. Lawyers selling out clients. *Jeff D.* authorizes simultaneous negotiation, fee waivers, and trading off fees for other relief. Doesn't it inevitably follow that other relief will sometimes be traded off for fees? Can the lawyer for the class do anything more than sensitize herself to the risks and bend over backward to protect the clients instead of herself? Can she structure negotiations in ways that reduce the risk? Does defense counsel have an ethical obligation not to exploit class counsel's dilemma? Or does the duty of zealous advocacy obligate defense counsel to exploit the dilemma if he can?

NOTES ON ETHICAL PROBLEMS IN COMMON-FUND CASES

1. The underlying problem. Ethical problems take a different form in common-fund cases. There, the parties negotiate a lump sum to cover the damages. There is no conflict at this stage, because defendant won't be liable for fees in addition. Then plaintiff's lawyer petitions the court for fees. Now the problem is obvious: Nobody represents the class, and the court approves a fee petition without benefit of any adversarial probing. The problem arises whether the damage judgment was litigated or settled, and whether fees are sought as a lodestar or a percentage of recovery. Conceivably, an individual class member with a large enough stake may come forward to object to the fee petition, but that is rare to nonexistent. In In re Fine Paper Antitrust Litigation, 751 F.2d 562 (3d Cir. 1984), one of the lawyers for the class blew the whistle on the excessive fees claimed by many of the others—but he might have done this only because the lawyers could not agree on how to divide the fees. Some judges take seriously the idea that they become fiduciaries for the class at this stage; others clearly do not.

2. Common-fund fees cannot be negotiated with defendant. The Ninth Circuit has rejected a class settlement in which plaintiff and defendant negotiated a fee based on the common-fund theory. Staton v. Boeing Co., 327 F.3d 938 (9th Cir. 2003). Class counsel settled an employment discrimination claim for $6.5 million in cash to the class, plus injunctive relief that the court characterized as "largely precatory" but that counsel valued at $3.65 million, plus $4.05 million to class counsel as attorneys' fees. *Id.* at 944-945. The parties characterized this as an award of 28 percent of a common fund that consisted of the cash to the class, the cash to counsel, and the value of the injunctive relief. *Id.* at 966.

The court said it is permissible to negotiate a lump sum that includes both merits relief and fees, and for counsel to then petition the court for a common-fund fee award—even in cases such as this one where plaintiffs could have sought a lodestar award under the fee-shifting provisions of the employment discrimination laws. But the majority held that plaintiff and defendant cannot negotiate the fee to be awarded out of a common fund; they can negotiate only the total amount, and class counsel must petition the court for any award based on the common-fund theory. No one represented the class in this negotiation of common-fund fees between class counsel and defendant. And defendant's need to know the bottom line, which justified simultaneous negotiation of fees and merits in *Jeff D.*, did not justify simultaneous negotiation here; defendant already knew the bottom line.

In Nunez v. BAE Systems San Diego Ship Repair Inc., 292 F. Supp. 3d 1018 (S.D. Cal. 2017), plaintiff and defendant agreed that 25 percent of the settlement would go to fees, subject to court approval, and that if the court awarded less than 25 percent, that would not disturb the settlement on the merits. A federal district court distinguished *Staton* and rejected a class member's objections to this agreement.

3. The reverse auction. Multiple class actions in multiple jurisdictions can move the conflict of interest forward to the settlement of the merits. If some of the cases are in state court and cannot be removed, it is impossible to consolidate them all. Then parallel class actions can proceed until one is tried or settled, leaving the other plaintiffs at the head of empty classes. Defendant can exploit that risk to achieve enormous settlement leverage. In Lurie v. Canadian Javelin Ltd., 443 N.E.2d 592 (Ill. 1982), a state class action was left with 12 class members and a $3,000 settlement when another representative of the original class settled a federal case. Professor Coffee calls this the reverse auction—defendant can direct a huge award of attorneys' fees to the plaintiffs' lawyer who accepts the smallest settlement for the class. John C. Coffee, Jr., *Class Wars: The Dilemma of the Mass Tort Class Action*, 95 Colum. L. Rev. 1343 (1995). Judicial review of class settlements is supposed to police this, but that review is sometimes not very energetic, and if there are multiple cases pending, defendants and settling counsel have some capacity to shop for a court that will approve the settlement. One way to avoid the reverse auction is coordination among the lawyers and among the state and federal judges, outside the formal procedural rules. An example is In re Diet Drugs, 582 F.3d 524 (3d Cir. 2009). An attempted statutory solution is discussed in note 9.

4. Reversionary settlements. Some settlements provide that unclaimed funds revert to defendant. If many class members do not file claims, the nominal value of the fund may greatly exceed what is actually distributed to the class, and this may be foreseeable when the settlement is negotiated. An example is Waters v. International Precious Metals Corp., 190 F.3d 1291 (11th Cir. 1999), where counsel received one-third of a $40 million settlement fund, but the class filed just under $6.5 million in claims. So the fee was double the amount actually distributed to the class, and the remaining $20 million reverted to defendant.

Masters v. Wilhelmina Model Agency, Inc., 473 F.3d 423 (2d Cir. 2007), follows *Waters* and similar cases. But *Masters* is less troubling, because the district court had already rejected the idea of returning unclaimed funds to defendant. That court would determine on remand whether to increase the distribution to class members who did file claims, or to make a cy pres distribution, discussed in note 5.

The Seventh Circuit rejected such a settlement in Pearson v. NBTY, Inc., 772 F.3d 778 (7th Cir. 2014). Plaintiffs' claim was that defendants fraudulently advertised that a dietary supplement called glucosamine could cure joint problems. The settlement provided that consumers could recover $3 for each bottle of pills they bought, up to a maximum of four bottles, or $5 a bottle for up to ten bottles if they had receipts. Class counsel valued this provision at over $14 million, on the assumption that all class members would file claims. But the settlement website seemed to imply that receipts or other documentation were required for all claims, and it threatened prosecution for inaccurate claims. Only 30,000 claims were filed, for a total of $865,000.

Class counsel sought $4.5 million in attorneys' fees, which defendants did not oppose. The district court awarded $2 million, reasoning that this was less than 10 percent of a $20 million settlement: $14 million in damages, plus $4.5 million in fees, plus the $1.5 million cost of notifying class members.

Judge Posner's opinion harshly condemned the settlement as the fruit of collusion between class counsel and defendants. He argued that the website and various other terms of the settlement seemed designed to minimize claims, that attorneys' fees and notice were a cost rather than a benefit to the class, and that the fees awarded were more than double the money actually paid to the class.

The Sixth Circuit rejected *Pearson* as inconsistent with Boeing Co. v. Van Gemert, 444 U.S. 472 (1980), described in Note 7 following *Cabletron*, which upheld a fee award based on the total judgment in a litigated case, without regard to how many class members failed to file claims. Gascho v. Global Fitness Holdings, LLC, 822 F.3d 269 (6th Cir. 2016). Judge Clay dissented, relying in part on *Pearson*.

5. Cy pres settlements. Some class actions cumulating many modest claims end in cy pres settlements, in which the class members get nothing but defendant pays attorneys' fees and contributes to a charity—preferably one that serves the needs of class members and people like them. Sometimes this is a legitimate response to the expense of finding class members or of distributing very small recoveries to a great many class members. Cy pres is troubling when distribution to the class is feasible and the money goes to charity instead; it is more troubling when the money goes to the class counsel's law school or some other charity unrelated to the class. Cy pres settlements are explored in more depth in Chapter 12.

6. Coupon settlements. Some of the worst abuses were scrip settlements, where the lawyers got cash but the class members got coupons for discounts on future purchases of defendant's products. A well-developed example, and not the worst such case, is the General Motors truck litigation. From 1973 to 1987, GM mounted fuel tanks on the side of many of its truck models. Plaintiffs' lawyer in a reported wrongful death case claimed that 240 people had been burned to death in these trucks. General Motors Corp. v. Moseley, 447 S.E.2d 302, 306 (Ga. Ct. App. 1994). There were multiple class actions on behalf of uninjured truck owners. GM removed most of the state cases to federal court; then the federal cases were transferred to the Eastern District of Pennsylvania. In re General Motors Corp. Products Liability Litigation, 55 F.3d 768, 779 (3d Cir. 1995).

GM and some of the class lawyers soon proposed to settle the case for certificates worth $1,000 on the purchase of a new GM truck. The certificates were transferable only with the truck for which they were issued, and they expired in 15 months. Objecting class members argued that these certificates were worthless to anyone who did not want another GM truck, and that in fact the settlement was a giant marketing promotion for GM. The settlement did not provide for recall or repair of any trucks. In a 49-state class action, the Third Circuit rejected this proposed settlement. *Id.* at 804-819. The Supreme Court of Texas rejected a similar settlement for a separate Texas class. General Motors Corp. v. Bloyed, 916 S.W.2d 949, 955-957 (Tex. 1996).

The trial courts had awarded class counsel $9.5 million in the federal case, and $9 million in the much smaller Texas case, with no opposition from GM. Both figures were based on a percentage of the alleged value of the certificates. GM had provided a common fund consisting of cash and certificates with the cash portion intended for the attorneys. Both appellate courts vacated the fee awards and remanded for further consideration.

Promptly after the two remands, GM and a different class counsel announced a nationwide settlement in a long dormant Louisiana case. The certificates had a longer life, but reduced value after the initial 15 months. In addition, GM agreed to fund a safety research program. The Third Circuit held that it was powerless to interfere. 134 F.3d 133 (3d Cir. 1998). The state appellate court initially rejected the settlement on procedural grounds. White v. General Motors Corp., 718 So. 2d 480 (La. Ct. App. 1998). The trial court again approved the settlement, and no further appeals by objectors are reported. GM successfully appealed the trial court's approval of a mechanism to broker the certificates, which would have made them easier to sell for cash, on the ground that GM had never agreed to that. 775 So. 2d 492 (2000), *modified on reh'g*, 782 So. 2d 9 (La. Ct. App. 2001). The last opinion in the case is White v. General Motors Corp., 835 So. 2d 892 (La. Ct. App. 2002). The court prohibited, as inconsistent with the settlement agreement, further attempts by plaintiffs' counsel to create a working secondary market in the settlement certificates. The fee award in the Louisiana case was $26,075,000, and counsel for the remaining objectors were included in the fee award, thus buying off their objections. Robert B. Gerard & Scott A. Johnson, *The Role of the Objector in Class Action Settlements—A Case Study of the General Motors Truck "Side Saddle" Fuel Tank Litigation*, 31 Loy. L.A. L. Rev. 409, 422-423 (1998).

7. Settlements that take money from the class. An even worse settlement is an unreported Alabama case with a nationwide class, Hoffman v. BancBoston Mortgage Corp. The claim had to do with defendant's treatment of mortgage borrowers' escrow accounts. In addition to principle and interest, borrowers pay monthly sums toward property taxes and insurance; the lender holds these amounts in escrow and pays the taxes and insurance when they come due. The settlement resulted in credits to the escrow accounts, ranging from zero to $8.76, representing interest on unnecessarily large amounts held in escrow. The settlement also resulted in attorneys' fees debited to the accounts in amounts that were much larger, based on an award of 28 percent of the surplus amount held in the account—even though there was absolutely no dispute that account balances belonged to class members and that they would have recovered the excess balances in the ordinary course of paying down their mortgage. Class member Dexter Kamilewicz was credited with $2.19 and debited $91.33. The calculations that produced this and even more bizarre results are explained in Susan P. Koniak and George M. Cohen, *Under Cloak of Settlement*, 82 Va. L. Rev. 1051, 1057-1068 (1996). Koniak and Cohen also report several similar settlements in other escrow cases around the country.

Kamilewicz sued in federal court in Chicago, where class counsel resided, alleging that the Alabama court lacked personal jurisdiction and that class counsel had committed malpractice. The Seventh Circuit held that it had no jurisdiction over a collateral attack on a state court judgment. Kamilewicz v. Bank of Boston Corp., 92 F.3d 506 (7th Cir. 1996). Class counsel then sued Kamilewicz and his lawyers, in Alabama, for malicious prosecution. The claim against Kamilewicz was dismissed for lack of personal jurisdiction. Ex parte Kamilewicz, 700 So. 2d 340 (Ala. 1997). His lawyers settled for court costs and got out of Alabama.

The Vermont Supreme Court, in a case filed by the state attorney general, held that the Alabama court lacked jurisdiction over 900 Vermont class members and that the judgment was not binding on them. The court found inadequate representation and inadequate notice; it characterized *Hoffman* as a defendant class action in which lawyers sought fees from class members who stood to incur liability rather than receive a remedy. State v. Homeside Lending, Inc., 826 A.2d 997 (Vt. 2003).

8. Settlements not worth the dough. An Australian teenager measured his Subway Footlong sandwich and it was only 11 inches long. He published the photo on

Facebook, the post went viral, and class action lawsuits followed soon thereafter. Subway's unbaked bread loaves are of uniform length, but there is no way to avoid some loaves that bake up a little short. Customers get the same amount of meat and cheese even if the bread is a bit less than 12 inches. That meant that the plaintiffs could not prove damages in the consolidated multidistrict litigation emerging from the Facebook post.

Plaintiffs then sought an injunction and the parties agreed to a settlement which, among other things, would require each restaurant to post a sign indicating that Subway cannot guarantee that each sandwich will bake to exactly 12 inches or greater. The agreement provided $525,000 in attorneys' fees and a $1,000 "incentive payment" to each class representative; these payments are a common part of class settlements. The district court approved the settlement and the fees, but the Seventh Circuit reversed. Judge Sykes, quoting an earlier Seventh Circuit opinion, wrote that a "class settlement that results in fees for class counsel but yields no meaningful relief for the class 'is no better than a racket.'" In re Subway Footlong Sandwich Marketing and Sales Practice Litigation, 869 F.3d 551, 556 (7th Cir. 2017). "The injunctive relief approved by the district court is utterly worthless. The settlement enriches only class counsel and, to a lesser degree, the class representatives." *Id.* at 557.

9. The Class Action Fairness Act. Congress attempted to address some of the problems with consumer class actions in the Class Action Fairness Act of 2005, codified at 28 U.S.C. §§1332, 1453, and 1711 *et seq.* It creates federal jurisdiction over class actions with more than $5 million in controversy and one or more class members with citizenship diverse from one or more defendants. State class actions that satisfy these requirements may be removed to federal court on motion of any defendant, even if one or more defendants reside in the state where the action is pending. The notice of removal need only allege that the amount in controversy exceeds $5 million, and it need not include evidentiary submissions. Dart Cherokee Basin Operating Co., LLC v. Owens, 135 S. Ct. 547 (2014).

Once in federal court, related class actions may be transferred for pretrial purposes to a single district judge. 28 U.S.C. §1407. From the perspective of class members, the Act has the potential to eliminate reverse auctions in cases where it applies, but at the expense of moving these cases from state courts to federal courts that, given the current political alignment, are often less plaintiff friendly.

Other sections of the Act provide that percentage-of-recovery fees in coupon settlements must be based on the coupons actually redeemed, not on the coupons distributed; that in class actions against financial institutions, state or federal bank supervisors shall be notified of any proposed settlement; and that proposed settlements resulting in a net loss to any class member may be approved "only if the court makes a written finding that nonmonetary benefits to the class member substantially outweigh monetary loss." 28 U.S.C. §1713. Defendants generally supported the Act, and the plaintiff's bar opposed it, which indicates its perceived central tendency. For an excellent symposium on early experience with the Act, see *Fairness to Whom? Perspectives on the Class Action Fairness Act of 2005*, 156 U. Pa. L. Rev. 1439 (2008).

10. Coupons again. Despite CAFA, some cases still settle with coupons, and class counsel have sought fees based on the lodestar instead of a percentage of the value of the coupons redeemed. 28 U.S.C. §1712(a) provides that in a coupon settlement, "the portion of any attorney's fee award to class counsel that is attributable to the award of the coupons shall be based on the value to class members of the coupons that are redeemed."

A divided Ninth Circuit held that the lodestar method is impermissible in a coupon settlement, and that fees must be based on percentage-of-recovery. In re HP Inkjet

Printer Litigation, 716 F.3d 1173 (9th Cir. 2013). The Seventh Circuit disagreed, engaging in an extensive statutory analysis of the words "attributable to" in §1712(a). In re Southwest Airlines Voucher Litigation, 799 F.3d 701, 707 (7th Cir. 2015).

In *Southwest Airlines*, plaintiffs sued over the airline's failure to honor some old free-alcoholic-drink coupons sent to the airline's business customers. The settlement agreement got plaintiffs new drink coupons and provided for $3 million in attorneys' fees. The agreement contained both "clear sailing" and "kicker" clauses. "Southwest agreed not to contest a fee request not exceeding $3 million (clear-sailing), and any reduction from the requested fee (roughly $1.35 million in this case) bene- fits Southwest rather than the class (the kicker)." *Id.* at 712. The Seventh Circuit expressed "deep skepticism" about these provisions, *id.*, but approved the district court's $1.65 million lodestar calculation, which included a multiplier of 1.5 for good results. Key to the court's approval of the amount was the court's determination that the plaintiff class got full relief.

The court rejected class counsel's argument that it was entitled to the full $3 mil- lion, and it added a lengthy footnote, which seems an appropriate place to end this unit on ethical issues in seeking attorneys' fees. The brief for plaintiffs' lawyers had spliced together parts of two sentences from an earlier opinion, sentences separated by more than two pages and 1,150 words. The phony quote said more or less the opposite of what each of the two sentences said in context. *Id.* at 713 n.4.

Of course, the attorneys sought additional fees on remand to cover the cost of the appeal and the additional proceedings in the district court. The attorneys asked for an additional $1,365,882, which would have brought fees back up to the settlement cap of $3 million. The district court instead agreed to award an additional $455,294, a decision it later reversed because of failure to give notice to the plaintiff class.

It was then revealed that the settlement had been misrepresented and that the class had not obtained full relief. The attorneys agreed to reduce the additional amount of fees to $200,000, and Southwest agreed to triple the number of drink coupons dis- tributed (but only to those class members who had already filed claims), in exchange for an objecting class member giving up his remaining objections. The objector then requested $80,000 of the fees awarded to class counsel, which the district court denied. In re Southwest Airlines Voucher Litigation, 2017 WL 5295372 (N.D. Ill. Nov. 13, 2017). The court of appeals reversed, holding that the objector was entitled to fees because he had benefited the class by increasing the number of coupons and reducing the fees to class counsel. 898 F.3d 740 (7th Cir. 2018).

CHAPTER

11

Remedial Defenses

A. UNCONSCIONABILITY AND THE EQUITABLE CONTRACT DEFENSES

JAMES v. NATIONAL FINANCIAL, LLC.

132 A.3d 799 (Del. Ct. Ch. 2016)

LASTER, Vice Chancellor.

Defendant National Financial . . . is a consumer finance company that operates under the trade name Loan Till Payday. In May 2013, National loaned $200 to plaintiff Gloria James (the "Disputed Loan"). National described the loan product as a "Flex Pay Loan." In substance, it was a one-year, non-amortizing, unsecured cash advance. . . .

I. FACTUAL BACKGROUND . . .

A. HARDWORKING BUT POOR

James is a resident of Wilmington, Delaware. From 2007 through 2014, James worked in the housekeeping department at the Hotel DuPont. In May 2013, when she obtained the Disputed Loan, James earned $11.83 per hour. As a part-time employee, her hours varied. On average, after taxes, James took home approximately $1,100 per month [or about 115 percent of the federal poverty line. She had been employed more or less continuously since age 13. She was laid off at the hotel when it reduced its part-time staff at the end of 2014.]

B. JAMES' USE OF CREDIT

James is undereducated and financially unsophisticated. She dropped out of school in the tenth grade because of problems at home. Approximately ten years later, she obtained her [general equivalency diploma, treated as equivalent to finishing high school.

In 2007, she enrolled in a night class to learn medical billing and coding, but work and childcare pressures eventually forced her to drop out.] James thought she received a grant to attend the program, but after dropping out she learned she actually had taken out a student loan. She eventually repaid it.

James does not have a savings account or a checking account. She has no savings. She uses a Nexis card, which is a pre-paid VISA card. [She repeatedly borrowed from various finance companies at high interest rates to meet essential expenses such as groceries and rent.]

Before the Disputed Loan, James had obtained five prior loans from National. James believed that she repaid those loans in one or two payments. The payment history for the loans shows otherwise. [Despite her repayment difficulties, National sent her repeated text messages soliciting her for further loans.]

C. THE DISPUTED LOAN

On May 7, 2013, James needed money for food and rent. She went to National's "Loan Till Payday" storefront operation . . . in Wilmington . . . .

Ed Reilly, National's general manager . . . happened to be working in the store . . . when James came in for a loan.

James told Reilly that she wanted to borrow $200. . . .

After reviewing her transaction history, Reilly offered to loan James $400 rather than $200. The $400 would have represented almost 40% of James' after-tax monthly income. Reilly offered that amount because National has a policy of loaning borrowers up to 40% of their after-tax monthly income, regardless of their other expenditures. National only checks to "make sure they're positive on payday."

James declined the offer of $400. She only wanted $200, and she did not believe she could repay $400.

James thought she was getting a payday loan with a block rate of "$30 on $100." As James understood it, this meant she would pay $60 to borrow the $200.

Lenders developed the block rate concept to describe the finance charge for a traditional payday loan, which was a single-payment loan designed to be repaid on the borrower's next payday. National's trade name—Loan Till Payday—embodies this concept. Because the loan was technically intended to be outstanding only for a single block of time, payday loan companies described the finance charge by identifying the dollar amount per $100 borrowed that the customer would owe at the end of the period. A block rate of "$30 on $100" meant that a customer who borrowed $100 would repay $130 on her next payday.

In May 2013, . . . National was no longer making traditional payday loans. Effective January 1, 2013, the General Assembly . . . impose[d] limits on payday loans. 5 Del. Code §§2227, 2235A, 2235B, & 2235C.

In response to the Payday Loan Law, National recast its payday loans as non-amortizing installment loans that were structured to remain outstanding for seven to twelve months. The Payday Loan Law only applied to loans designed to be outstanding for sixty days or less, so by making this change, National sidestepped the law. Throughout this litigation, National insisted that it no longer made payday loans.

Despite shifting to longer-dated installment loans, National continued to frame its finance charges using a block rate. National adhered to this practice for a simple reason: It made a high cost loan product sound cheaper than it was . . . . Although National's customers eventually saw an [Annual Percentage Rate] on the loan agreement, National's employees followed a practice of telling customers that the APR had "nothing to do with the loan." As National pitched it, the APR was "irrelevant" unless the customer kept the loan outstanding for an entire year; if the customer only planned to keep the loan outstanding for a few weeks, National's employees said that the APR "means nothing."

When James obtained the Disputed Loan, she focused on the block rate and the concept of $30 in interest per $100 borrowed, just as National intended. She thought she would have to pay back $260. She told Reilly that she would repay the loan in two payments of $130 each. She planned to pay $130 on her next payday of May 17, 2013, and another $130 on May 31. . . .

The repayment schedule did not reflect either the two repayments that James wanted to make or the two repayments that Reilly entered in [her loan record]. The Loan Agreement instead contemplated twenty-six interest-only payments of $60 each, followed by a balloon payment comprising a twenty-seventh interest payment of $60 plus repayment of the original $200 in principal. The total amount of interest was $1,620. According to the Loan Agreement, the APR for the loan was 838.45%. Using Reilly's planned repayment schedule, the APR was 1,095%.

James signed the Loan Agreement, and Reilly gave her a check. From the time James walked into the store, the whole process took about twenty minutes.

[The next day, James broke her hand at work. She was off for a week before being allowed to return on light duty two to three days a week. National refused to give any accommodation because of her injury, and inexplicably suggested that she increase her bi-weekly payment. National tried debiting James's Nexis account, and soon left messages for her employer and sent her texts demanding payment. James eventually repaid National $197.

She filed this lawsuit as a class action, alleging that the loan terms were unconscionable and that National's disclosure of the APR was erroneous and violated the Truth-in-Lending Act, 15 U.S.C. §1601 *et seq.* (TILA). She sought rescission of her loan, an injunction against further collection efforts, a declaratory judgment that the loan was unconscionable, and minimum statutory damages under TILA. The court denied class certification. It noted, but did not rely on, conflicting and polarized research on high-interest loans to low-income borrowers.]

II. LEGAL ANALYSIS . . .

B. UNCONSCIONABILITY

The doctrine of unconscionability stands as a limited exception to the law's broad support for freedom of contract. . . .

[C]ountervailing principles . . . prevent an indisputably important and salutary doctrine from operating as a tyrannical absolute. One such ground is unconscionability, traditionally defined as a contract "such as no man in his senses and not under delusion would make on the one hand, and no honest or fair man would accept, on the other." Tulowitzki v. Atlantic Richfield Co., 396 A.2d 956, 960 (Del. 1978). It would be difficult to improve on Chancellor Allen's incisive summary of the interplay between the core concept of contractual freedom and the residual protection against unconscionability:

> The right of competent persons to make contracts and thus privately to acquire rights and obligations is a basic part of our general liberty. This ability to enter and enforce contracts is universally thought not only to reflect and promote liberty, but as well to promote the production of wealth. . . .
> It is a general rule, recited by courts for well over a century, that the adequacy or fairness of the consideration that adduces a promise or a transfer is not alone grounds for a court to refuse to enforce a promise or to give effect to a transfer. . . . But as standard as that generalization is, it has not precluded courts, on occasion, from striking down contracts or transfers in which inadequacy of price is coupled with some circumstance that amounts to inequitable or oppressive conduct. That is, the "rule" that courts will not weigh consideration or assess the wisdom of bargains has not fully excluded the

opposite proposition, that at some point, courts will do so even in the absence of actual fraud, duress or incapacity.

Ryan v. Weiner, 610 A.2d 1377, 1380-1381 (Del. Ct. Ch. 1992). [*Ryan* traced the doctrine's long history and noted its codification, most prominently in Uniform Commercial Code §2-302.]
Delaware's version of Section 2–302 states:

(1) If the court as a matter of law finds the contract or any clause of the contract to have been unconscionable at the time it was made the court may refuse to enforce the contract, or it may enforce the remainder of the contract without the unconscionable clause, or it may so limit the application of any unconscionable clause as to avoid any unconscionable result.

(2) When it is claimed or appears to the court that the contract or any clause thereof may be unconscionable the parties shall be afforded a reasonable opportunity to present evidence as to its commercial setting, purpose and effect to aid the court in making the determination.

6 Del. Code §2–302. Although technically limited in scope to sales of goods, Delaware decisions have applied Section 2–302 more broadly.

This estimable pedigree does not mean that the doctrine of unconscionability will be invoked freely. "Unconscionability is a concept that is used sparingly." Ketler v. PFPA, LLC, 132 A.3d 746, 748, (Del. 2016). . . .

Whether a contract is unconscionable is determined at the time it was made. . . .

This court has identified ten factors to guide the analysis of unconscionability. *See* Fritz v. Nationwide Mutual Insurance Co., 1990 WL 186448 (Del. Ct. Ch. 1990). . . . Although this opinion uses the ten *Fritz* factors, it analyzes them in a different order and under two broader headings: substantive unconscionability and procedural unconscionability.

An agreement is substantively unconscionable if the terms evidence a gross imbalance that "shocks the conscience." Coles v. Trecothick, 32 Eng. Rep. 592, 597 (Ch. 1804). In more modern terms, it means a bargain on terms "so extreme as to appear unconscionable according to the mores and business practices of the time and place." Williams v. Walker-Thomas Furniture Co., 350 F.2d 445, 450 (D.C. Cir. 1965) (quoting 1 Arthur L. Corbin, *Corbin on Contracts* §128 (West 1963)).

[P]rocedural unconscionability examines the procedures that led to the contract with the goal of evaluating whether seemingly lopsided terms might have resulted from arms'-length bargaining. Courts focus on the relative bargaining strength of the parties and whether the weaker party could make a meaningful choice. The concept is "broadly conceived to encompass not only the employment of sharp bargaining practices and the use of fine print and convoluted language, but a lack of understanding and an inequity of bargaining power." 1 E. Allan Farnsworth, *Farnsworth on Contracts* §4.28, at 583-584 (3d ed., Aspen 2004).

The two dimensions of unconscionability do not function as separate elements of a two prong test. The analysis is unitary, and "it is generally agreed that if more of one is present, then less of the other is required." *Id.*

1. Factors Relating to Substantive Unconscionability
Six of the *Fritz* factors relate to . . . substantive unconscionability. They are:

- A significant cost-price disparity or excessive price.
- The denial of basic rights and remedies.

- Penalty clauses.
- The placement of disadvantageous clauses in inconspicuous locations or among fine print trivia.
- The phrasing of disadvantageous clauses in confusing language or in a manner that obscures the problems they raise.
- An overall imbalance in the obligations and rights imposed by the bargain. . . .

a. A Threshold Indication of Unfairness . . .

"Inadequacy of consideration does not of itself invalidate a bargain, but gross disparity in the values exchanged may be an important factor in a determination that a contract in unconscionable. . . ." *Restatement (Second) of Contracts* §208, cmt. *c* (Am. Law Inst. 1981). "Such a disparity may also corroborate indications of defects in the bargaining process. . . ." *Id.* "[A]n unreasonably high or exorbitant price at the very least is a factor to be considered in determining whether a particular provision is harsh and whether one party has in fact been imposed upon by another party in an inequitable or unconscionable manner." 8 *Williston on Contracts* §18:15 (4th ed., Lawyers Coop 2015).

In this case, there are obvious indications of unfairness. The Loan Agreement called for finance charges of $1,620 for a $200 loan, resulting in a disclosed APR of 838.45%. That level of pricing shocks the conscience. . .

iii. Fundamental Unfairness

The economic terms of the Disputed Loan are so extreme as to suggest fundamental unfairness. . . . The finance charges incurred over the course of the loan are so high that no rational borrower would agree to pay them, unless under duress or operating under a misapprehension of fact. The first *Fritz* factor is satisfied.

b. Contract Provisions Suggesting Unfairness

The next four *Fritz* factors focus on contract provisions that can contribute to a finding of unfairness. . . . The more general question is whether the contract provisions evidence "[a]n overall imbalance in the obligations and rights imposed by the bargain." Specific provisions might not be unconscionable in isolation or under different circumstances, yet still may contribute to a finding of unconscionability in a given case. . . .

National imposed onerous financial terms and gave itself the right to collect unilaterally from James any amount it wished, up to the full amount of the loan plus fees and charges [by directly debiting her Nexis card or any other accounts]. National ensured that in any challenge to the Disputed Loan, James would not be able to represent a class. She would have to challenge National alone, . . . where the amount in question would make the representation economically irrational for a lawyer unless he could recover his fees from National. Moreover, unless James opted out of the arbitration provision within sixty days—something that no customer other than James has ever done—then James would have to challenge the Disputed Loan in . . . National's chosen forum. Taken as a whole, for purposes of the *Fritz* factors, the Loan Agreement evidences "[a]n overall imbalance in the obligations and rights imposed by the bargain."

2. Factors Relating to Procedural Unconscionability

The next four *Fritz* factors shed light on . . . procedural unconscionability. They are:

- Inequality of bargaining or economic power.
- Exploitation of the underprivileged, unsophisticated, uneducated, and illiterate.

- The use of printed form or boilerplate contracts drawn skillfully by the party in the strongest economic position, which establish industry-wide standards offered on a take it or leave it basis to the party in a weaker economic position.
- The circumstances surrounding the execution of the contract, including its commercial setting, its purpose, and actual effect. . . .

[T]hese factors help a court test the degree to which a seemingly disproportionate outcome could have resulted from legitimate, arms'-length bargaining. The first and second factors plumb this issue by considering the extent to which the parties to the agreement were capable of bargaining at arms'-length. A court rarely will intervene when the contracting parties are both commercial entities or otherwise sophisticated. By contrast, a court may be more concerned where the contracting process involved significant inequalities of bargaining power, economic power, or sophistication, particularly between a business and a consumer. An aggravated version of this scenario arises when one of the parties is an individual who is underprivileged, uneducated, or illiterate.

The third and fourth factors similarly contribute by examining the degree to which actual bargaining took place. The third factor considers whether the agreement is a contract of adhesion. The fourth factor takes into account the contracting environment, including the commercial setting and the purpose and effect of the disputed agreement.

Together, these factors weigh an initial showing of unfairness against the bargaining dynamic. If the contract resulted from legitimate negotiation, then a court should not intervene. . . . But if the contract appears fundamentally unfair and there are valid reasons to suspect that the outcome did not result from legitimate negotiation, then a different picture emerges.

a. The Attributes of the Parties . . .
i. National

National specializes in providing high interest loans to underprivileged consumers who are cash-constrained and lack alternative sources of credit . . . [It generates free cash flow of about $1 million per year.]

National's owner and its personnel are sophisticated and knowledgeable. . . .

ii. James

James is unsophisticated and undereducated. . . . Evidencing her lack of financial sophistication, she believed that the financial aid she received for the [medical billing] program was a grant. It was actually a loan that she struggled to pay back. . . .

James' perception of the financial charge for the Disputed Loan reflected a similar short-term focus. . . . James did not understand how interest accrued, and she did not understand what would happen upon default.

James [over]estimated her likelihood of repaying the Disputed Loan quickly. . . .

James is also underprivileged. . . .

These factors favor a finding of unconscionability.

b. A Take–It–or–Leave–It, One–Sided Form Agreement

The next *Fritz* factor asks directly whether there was actual bargaining involved.

"[A] contract of adhesion is not unconscionable per se, and . . . all unconscionable contracts are not contracts of adhesion." *Restatement (Second) of Contracts* §208, Reporter's Note, *a.* . . .

All else equal, the fact that an agreement is a contract of adhesion makes it relatively more likely that the agreement will be found unconscionable. [It] is not sufficient, standing alone, to render an agreement unconscionable.

The Loan Agreement is a contract of adhesion. It was [a] form agreement, drafted by National, and provided to James on a take-it-or-leave-it basis. James had no ability to negotiate the terms of the Loan Agreement. . . .

c. The Bargaining Environment

The final *Fritz* factor considers the "[t]he circumstances surrounding the execution of the contract." . . . .

i. The Commercial Setting

[James was given standardized forms in a small storefront and was told where to sign.] Those were not ideal conditions, but they were not inherently oppressive. . . .

A more problematic issue is that National's employees denigrate the importance of the APR while describing the interest rate in simplistic ways that are designed to mislead customers. . . .

ii. Lack of Meaningful Choice

A more significant aspect of the circumstances surrounding the Loan Agreement was James' lack of a meaningful choice. . . .

iii. The Purpose and Effect of the Loan Agreement

Perhaps the most critical aspect of the bargaining environment was the purpose and effect of the Loan Agreement, which was to evade the Payday Loan Law. . . .

3. Balancing the Factors

All of the *Fritz* factors point in favor of a finding of unconscionability, albeit to varying degrees. The most telling factors include (i) the economic terms of the Disputed Loan, which support a *prima facie* case of substantive unconscionability, (ii) the purpose and effect of the installment loan structure in circumventing the Payday Loan Law and the Five Loan Limit [the new law provided that no consumer could receive more than five short-term loans in a single year, and each renewal counted as a new loan], and (iii) the exploitation of an underprivileged, undereducated, and financially vulnerable person. Secondary factors include (a) the use of a contract of adhesion, (b) the overall imbalance of rights and obligations, and (c) National's practices when describing the block rate finance charge versus the APR, which present a misleading picture of the cost of credit.

On balance, the Loan Agreement is unconscionable. No one would borrow rationally on the terms it contemplated unless that person was delusional, mistaken about its terms or a material fact, or under economic duress.

4. The Remedy for the Unconscionable Agreement

Because the Loan Agreement is unconscionable, it is voidable. The proper remedy is to declare it invalid.

Declaring the Loan Agreement invalid is likewise appropriate because National sought to use an interest-only, non-amortizing, installment loan to evade the Payday Loan Law. . . . "[E]quity regards substance rather than form." Monroe Park v. Metropolitan Life Insurance Co., 457 A.2d 734, 737 (Del. 1983). . . . In substance, the Disputed Loan was a payday loan designed to roll over twenty-six times, which contravened the Five Loan Limit.

National loaned James $200. James has repaid National $197. As a consequence of rescinding the Loan Agreement, James owes National another $3. . . .

James also asked for a permanent injunction barring National from collecting on similar loans it made to other customers. That relief is too broad to be granted in the current case and would embroil this court in on-going oversight of National's business.

[James also proved at trial that National violated the Truth-in-Lending Act. She could not recover actual damages because she did not rely on the incorrect APR. But TILA also allows attorneys' fees and statutory damages of twice the amount of the finance charge. Twice the stated finance charge was $3,240; the court netted out the $3 still owed on the loan, and gave judgment for $3,237.]

III. Conclusion

The Disputed Loan is invalid. Judgment is entered in favor of James in the amount of $3,237. Pre- and post-judgment interest on this amount will accrue at the legal rate, compounded quarterly, beginning on [the date of the loan.] James is awarded her attorneys' fees and costs. . . .

NOTES ON THE REACH OF EQUITABLE DEFENSES

1. The origins of unconscionability. It was an equitable defense—a defense developed by the equity courts before the merger—that a contract was unconscionable The refusal to enforce unconscionable contracts was rooted in the idea that a suit in equity was an appeal to the king's conscience; recall too, that the early chancellors were usually bishops.

2. Enjoining suits at law. Fraud was an equitable defense with similar roots in an appeal to conscience. The law courts refused to hear fraud defenses in suits on promises under seal. But the debtor could file his own suit in equity and prove the fraud there, and the equity court would enjoin the creditor from suing on the instrument at law or from enforcing his judgment if he already had one. Conflict between the two courts culminated in the historic clash of 1616, in which King James I permanently established equity's power to enjoin proceedings at law. These events are reviewed in Mark Fortier, *Equity and Ideas: Coke, Ellesmere, and James I*, 51 Renaissance Q. 1255 (1998), and John P. Dawson, *Coke and Ellesmere Disinterred: The Attack on the Chancery in 1616*, 36 Ill. L. Rev. 127 (1941).

3. Relief confined to equity, The chancellors did not take all equitable defenses as seriously as they took fraud. That a contract was unconscionable was a defense in equity, and thus a ground for denying specific performance, but it was not a ground for enjoining a suit at law. That tradition survived into modern times. Campbell Soup Co. v. Wentz, reprinted on a different issue in section 5.A.1.b, refused specific performance on grounds of unconscionability but permitted recovery of liquidated damages. That result might have made sense in *Campbell* as a compromise, leaving Campbell to the undercompensatory liquidated-damage clause without denying it relief altogether.

But does it make any sense in the run of cases? Consider *Campbell* without the liquidated-damage clause. Would it make any sense to say the court will *not* order the Wentzes to sell $90 carrots for $30, but it *will* levy a $60 damage judgment against them if they refuse? Is one order any harsher than the other? How often do you suppose a postmerger court that considered a contract too unconscionable to specifically enforce actually awarded full expectancy damages? The Uniform Commercial Code codified unconscionability and made it a defense at law as well as in equity in contracts for the sale of goods. §2-302.

4. Other defenses good only in equity? It is often said that there are other defenses to specific performance that are not defenses to damage actions. Common examples are inadequate consideration, unilateral mistake, and ambiguous terms. Some cases put the burden of proof on plaintiff, and emphasize that specific performance is a discretionary remedy. One finds statements such as the following: "Specific performance will be decreed only if it is clearly established that the contract is just, reasonable, and free from misapprehension or misrepresentation." Lannon v. Lamps, 399 N.E.2d 712, 716 (Ill. App. Ct. 1980).

There are plenty of cases on both sides of these propositions. Compare *Lannon*, refusing to specifically enforce a long-term lease against two feeble octogenarians, with Bliss v. Rhodes, 384 N.E.2d 512, 515 (Ill. App. Ct. 1978), specifically enforcing a contract to sell a farm owned by a depressed drunk. Both transactions were at prices far below market; both cases cited Illinois Supreme Court cases in support of their holdings.

5. A rationale? The most plausible rationale for defenses confined to equity is that courts can easily compromise an award of damages, but cannot easily compromise on specific performance. Emily L. Sherwin, *Law and Equity in Contract Enforcement*, 50 Md. L. Rev. 253 (1991); Edward Yorio, *A Defense of Equitable Defenses*, 51 Ohio St. L.J. 1201 (1990). Courts can compromise on damages by awarding reliance instead of expectancy, by finding consequential damages too remote or uncertain, by accepting defendant's estimate on valuation questions, or by letting the jury nullify the rights of overreaching plaintiffs. Such techniques let a court shave the damages without having to acknowledge that it is doing so because it disapproves of plaintiff's conduct. Is this capacity for concealment a good thing or a bad thing?

These techniques of compromise are relatively unavailable with a specific performance decree. The result is that specific performance cases are full of talk about conscience and discretion, overtly introducing discretion to match the discretion that is inherent in the more flexible process of measuring damages. The idea that damages are more flexible than specific performance flouts the conventional wisdom. But isn't it right?

NOTES ON UNCONSCIONABLE CONTRACTS

1. The remedies in *James*. James sued to rescind the contract, a remedy explained more fully in section 8.B.3.b. Rescission undoes the contract as though it never happened. James has to repay the full $200 principal that she borrowed. National has to give back the full amount of the interest payments it collected, but that relief is subsumed in the Truth-in-Lending remedy of twice the finance charge. Prejudgment and postjudgment interest aim to give James the full value of the money she paid to National a few years earlier. James had $200 of National's money, and rescission would normally require her to pay reasonable interest on that, but the court dispensed with that on these facts.

The court also awarded attorneys' fees of $331,024.50. 2016 WL 3226434 (Del. Ct. Ch. 2016). Each side ordinarily bears its own attorneys' fees, and that would have been true in a simple suit for rescission. James recovered fees under a statutory provision in the Truth-in-Lending Act, and alternatively because of National's bad faith litigation. In addition to the frivolous motion to compel arbitration, National violated discovery orders and concealed evidence. Notes on Exceptions to the American Rule, in section 10.A, explains these two sources of authority to award fees.

The court declined to issue an injunction. James did not intend to borrow again from National, so she was not at risk of further harm from National, and the court had denied class certification.

2. Flexible remedies for unconscionable conduct in contracting? UCC §2-302, quoted in *James*, provides flexible remedies, authorizing courts to refuse to enforce unconscionable contracts in whole or in part. The *Restatement (Second) of Contracts* §208 is nearly identical. But courts have been cautious. "[T]he traditional remedy for a claim of unconscionability is to deny enforcement of the relevant contract[.]" Oneida Indian Nation v. County of Oneida, 617 F.3d 114, 138 (2d Cir. 2010). "[M]ost courts have found that Section 2-302 does not provide authority to award damages for use of an unconscionable contract or clause." 1 William D. Hawkland, UCC Series §2-302:5 (West June 2018 Update). Professor Beh calls unconscionability remedies "meager." Hazel Glenn Beh, *Curing the Infirmities of the Unconscionability Doctrine*, 66 Hastings L.J. 1011, 1022 (2015).

Unlike *Campbell*, where the Wentzes raised unconscionability as an affirmative defense against Campbell's claim to specific performance, the plaintiff in *James* used unconscionability to seek affirmative relief against a defendant who drafted an unconscionable contract. That's not unusual, but some courts say it can't be done. A federal court applying Alabama law dismissed a claim for a declaratory judgment declaring a contract unconscionable because, it said, unconscionability is available only as an affirmative defense. Camp v. Telco Alabama Credit Union, 2013 WL 2106727, *5 (N.D. Ala. 2013). That appears to be the Alabama rule, but it seems clearly wrong; declaratory plaintiffs often assert what would otherwise be defenses, as in all the principal cases in section 7.A.

The court refused to dismiss a similar claim in In re Checking Overdraft Litigation, 694 F. Supp. 2d 1302 (S.D. Fla. 2010). In both cases, bank customers complained about allegedly unconscionable bank fees. The banks took the fees directly from the customers' accounts, so they would never have filed a lawsuit for unpaid fees. The district court in *Checking Overdraft* held that plaintiffs could ask for a declaration that the fees were unconscionable. And both courts held that plaintiffs could potentially recover for unjust enrichment: If the court held the fees unconscionable, it would be unjust for the banks to keep them. *Camp* managed to reach this result by a circuitous route: The bank's defense to the unjust enrichment claim was that a valid contract provided for the fees. Plaintiffs' reply to that defense was that the contract was unconscionable, and that seemed enough like an affirmative defense to the contract that the court allowed the claim to proceed.

3. Procedural and substantive unconscionability. *James*'s analytic structure of procedural and substantive unconscionability is standard; its more specific 10-part test is not. There are various formulations of how procedural and substantive unconscionability relate to each other but, as *James* says, it is usually thought of as a sliding scale between the two. Blackrock Capital Investment Corp. v. Fish, 799 S.E.2d 520, 528 (W. Va. 2017). The sliding scale, whether explicit or implicit, seems almost inevitable in practice. In a survey of 148 federal cases, courts that found one form of unconscionability usually found both. When the court found substantive unconscionability alone, it always invalidated the clause, but it did so only occasionally when it found procedural unconscionability alone. Larry A. DiMatteo and Bruce Louis Rich, *A Consent Theory of Unconscionability: An Empirical Study of Law in Action*, 33 Fla. St. U.L. Rev. 1067(2006).

4. The economic viability of the lawsuit. Suppose National had not engaged in bad faith litigation tactics and there were no statutory right to attorneys' fees. It is hard to see how a lawyer could have brought this case as a suit by a single individual over $3,000. Provisions for attorneys' fees are common in consumer-protection statutes, but they are not part of the common law of contracts or UCC §2-302. For an argument that attorney fees should be available in consumer unconscionability cases, see Stephen E. Friedman, *Giving Unconscionability More Muscle: Attorneys Fees as a Remedy for Contractual Overreaching*, 44 Ga. L. Rev. 317 (2010).

NOTES ON ARBITRATION CLAUSES

1. The arbitration clause in *James*. Companies that engage in many more or less identical transactions using the same form contract use arbitration clauses to prevent class actions. National's contract said that any claims James might have had could be resolved only in an individual arbitration. The clause covered regulatory claims, such as her Truth-in-Lending Act claim, as well as claims on the contract. But she had 60 days to opt out of that arbitration clause, and she did. Why would National give her that option? National no doubt drafted the 60-day opt-out clause to support an argument that its arbitration clause was not unconscionable because borrowers had a choice—secure in the knowledge that hardly any of them would get legal advice and opt out within 60 days.

2. The battle over arbitration. The most important line of unconscionability cases in the early 2000s concerned arbitration clauses. Many cases, including decisions of the supreme courts of California, New Jersey, and Washington, held that arbitration clauses are unconscionable when they leave consumers or employees with no viable remedy for otherwise sound legal claims. Cases are collected in Scott v. Cingular Wireless, 161 P.3d 1000 (Wash. 2007).

The Supreme Court largely brought these cases to a halt in a series of decisions under the Federal Arbitration Act, 9 U.S.C. §1 *et seq.* It held that the Act preempts state unconscionability law, because that law had been disproportionately applied to arbitration clauses—or because arbitration clauses with class action waivers were disproportionately unconscionable. AT&T Mobility LLC v. Concepcion, 563 U.S. 333 (2011). And it held that there can be no class arbitration unless the arbitration clause provides for class arbitration. Stolt-Nielsen S.A. v. AnimalFeeds International Corp., 559 U.S. 663 (2010). Of course the clauses never so provide; their principal point is to prevent class actions.

Subsequent decisions have rejected every effort to find a way around these cases. The dissenters say the goal of the Arbitration Act was less expensive resolution of claims, not an immunity bath that prevents claims from being resolved at all. The majority says that the Act favors the absence of litigation when claims are not viable individually.

3. Other grounds for holding arbitration clauses unconscionable. The California court held that unconscionability review of arbitration clauses survives *Concepcion* where the alleged ground of unconscionability is something other than a class action waiver. Sanchez v. Valencia Holding Co., 353 P.3d 741 (Cal. 2015). The Ninth Circuit came to a similar conclusion in Chavarria v. Ralphs Grocery Co., 733 F.3d 916 (9th Cir. 2013). The arbitration clause in *Chavarria* was procedurally unconscionable because it was imposed on all employees as a condition of keeping their jobs, and substantively unconscionable because it allowed the employer to choose the arbitrator and required the employee to pay half the cost of arbitration. The employer represented that the fees for an arbitrator would range from $7,000 to $14,000 per day.

4. What's left? These cases raise an important remedies issue: What workable remedies are left for small claims? But that issue is not really about remedial defenses, and we will put it aside after one more telling example.

Buyers of Fitbit fitness trackers filed a putative class action, alleging that the tracker gives inaccurate heartbeat information. Fitbit's contract requires individual arbitration of all claims. The court granted Fitbit's motion to compel arbitration as to all but one plaintiff; that one had opted out of the arbitration clause. McLellan v. Fitbit, Inc. 2017 WL 4551484 (N.D. Cal. Oct. 11, 2017).

Meanwhile, another customer, Kate McLellan, alleged a $162 claim before an arbitrator, intending to test the enforceability of the arbitration clause. The cost to file a claim before Fitbit's designated tribunal, the American Arbitration Association, was $750. Fitbit offered to settle the case for more than $2,800, but McLellan refused.

When the case got to federal court, Fitbit's lawyer told the judge that a "claim that is $162—an individual claim—is not one that any rational litigant would litigate." Alison Frankel, *Fitbit Lawyers Reveal "Ugly Truth" About Arbitration, Judge Threatens Contempt*, Reuters (June 1, 2018), available at https://www.reuters.com/article/legal-us-otc-fitbit/fitbit-lawyers-reveal-ugly-truth-about-arbitration-judge-threatens-contempt-idUSKCN1IX5QM. Of course that is what plaintiffs' lawyers have said all along: that the very point of these clauses is to leave customers with no remedy anywhere. The judge was not amused, and he ordered Fitbit to pay McLellan's attorneys' fees as a sanction for misconduct. McLellan v. Fitbit, Inc., 2018 WL 3549042, *6 (July 24, 2018). The court explained:

> Fitbit would like to treat this incident as a misunderstanding, but it is much more than that. It moved McLellan's claims out of court and then undertook a course of conduct intended to shut her out of arbitration as well. It abandoned that plan at an early stage only because McLellan was diligent in sounding the alarm, and the Court expressed its concerns in plain terms at the hearing. Fitbit's conduct has multiplied the proceedings in this case for no good reason and at the expense of plaintiffs' and the Court's resources. It has also bolstered the perception that arbitration is where consumer lawsuits go to die. While the merits of that view can be debated, it's no surprise that many people, including judges, are skeptical about arbitration agreements in light of situations like this one. Fitbit's conduct undermines the public's confidence in getting a fair shake when arbitration is compelled.

Id. at *1.

B.   UNCLEAN HANDS AND *IN PARI DELICTO*

PINTER v. DAHL
486 U.S 622 (1988)

[Pinter was an oil and gas producer who agreed to locate and acquire oil leases, drill wells on the leases on behalf of Dahl and other investors, and operate the wells. Dahl invested $310,000 of his own money and then induced 11 friends to invest about $7,500 each. When the wells turned out to be worthless, Dahl and the other investors sued Pinter under §12(1) of the Securities Act, 15 U.S.C. §77*l*(a), seeking rescission on the ground that the investments had never been registered with the Securities and Exchange Commission.

The duty to register with the SEC depended on whether the securities had been sold as part of a public offering or as a private placement with a small group of sophisticated investors. The parties had relied on the private placement rules, but the lower courts held that the transaction did not qualify under those rules.

Pinter also alleged the defense of *in pari delicto* against Dahl—that Dahl could not recover because he was as much at fault as Pinter. The district court rejected this defense without discussing it. The court of appeals believed that *in pari delicto* should not apply to a strict liability violation. 787 F.2d 985 (5th Cir. 1986).]

Justice BLACKMUN delivered the opinion of the Court. . . .

II

The equitable defense of *in pari delicto*, which literally means "in equal fault," is rooted in the common-law notion that a plaintiff's recovery may be barred by his own wrongful conduct. See Bateman Eichler, Hill Richards v. Berner, 472 U.S. 299, 306 & nn.12, 13 (1985). Traditionally, the defense was limited to situations where the plaintiff bore "at least substantially equal responsibility for his injury," *id.* at 307, and where the parties' culpability arose out of the same illegal act. Contemporary courts have expanded the defense's application to situations more closely analogous to those encompassed by the "unclean hands" doctrine, where the plaintiff has participated "in some of the same sort of wrongdoing" as the defendant. See Perma Life Mufflers, Inc. v. International Parts Corp., 392 U.S. 134, 138 (1968). In *Perma Life*, however, the Court concluded that this broadened construction is not appropriate in litigation arising under federal regulatory statutes. Nevertheless, in separate opinions, five Justices recognized that a narrow, more traditional formulation should be available in private actions under the antitrust laws.

In *Bateman Eichler*, the Court addressed the scope of the *in pari delicto* defense in the context of an action brought by securities investors . . . alleging that . . . defendants had induced the plaintiffs to purchase large quantities of stock by divulging false and materially incomplete information on the pretext that it was accurate inside information. . . . The Court . . . conclud[ed] that "the views expressed in *Perma Life* apply with full force to implied causes of action under the federal securities laws." 472 U.S. at 310. Accordingly, it held that the *in pari delicto* defense is available "only where (1) as a direct result of his own actions, the plaintiff bears at least substantially equal responsibility for the violations he seeks to redress, and (2) preclusion of suit would not significantly interfere with the effective enforcement of the securities laws and protection of the investing public." *Id.* at 310-311. The first prong of this test captures the essential elements of the classic *in pari delicto* doctrine. The second prong, which embodies the doctrine's traditional requirement that public policy implications be carefully considered before the defense is allowed, ensures that the broad judge-made law does not undermine the congressional policy favoring private suits as an important mode of enforcing federal securities statutes. Applying this test to the §10(b) claim before it, the Court concluded that in such tipster-tippee situations, the two factors precluded recognition of the *in pari delicto* defense.

[The Court rejected the Fifth Circuit's view that *in pari delicto* should not apply to strict liability violations, or that it should apply only when plaintiff's wrongdoing was intentional or willful. The doctrine is designed to deter illegal behavior, and strict liability violations should also be deterred.]

B

Under the first prong of the *Bateman Eichler* test, . . . a defendant cannot escape liability unless, as a direct result of the plaintiff's own actions, the plaintiff bears at least substantially equal responsibility for the underlying illegality. The plaintiff must be an active, voluntary participant in the unlawful activity that is the subject of the suit. . . . Unless the degrees of fault are essentially indistinguishable or the plaintiff's responsibility is clearly greater, the *in pari delicto* defense should not be allowed, and the plaintiff should be compensated. Refusal of relief to those less blameworthy would frustrate the purpose of the securities laws; it would not serve to discourage the actions of those most responsible for organizing forbidden schemes; and it would sacrifice protection of the general investing public in pursuit of individual punishment.

In the context of a private action under §12(1), the first prong of the *Bateman Eichler* test is satisfied if the plaintiff is at least equally responsible for the actions that render the sale of the unregistered securities illegal — the issuer's failure to register the securities before offering them for sale, or his failure to conduct the sale in such a manner as to meet the registration exemption provisions. As the parties and the Commission agree, a purchaser's knowledge that the securities are unregistered cannot, by itself, constitute equal culpability, even where the investor is a sophisticated buyer who may not necessarily need the protection of the Securities Act. . . . Although a court's assessment of the relative responsibility of the plaintiff will necessarily vary depending on the facts of the particular case, courts frequently have focused on the extent to which the plaintiff and the defendant cooperated in developing and carrying out the scheme to distribute unregistered securities. In addition, if the plaintiff were found to have induced the issuer not to register, he well might be precluded from obtaining §12(1) rescission.

Under the second prong of the *Bateman Eichler* test, a plaintiff's recovery may be barred only if preclusion of suit does not offend the underlying statutory policies. The primary purpose of the Securities Act is to protect investors by requiring publication of material information thought necessary to allow them to make informed investment decisions concerning public offerings of securities in interstate commerce. The registration requirements are the heart of the Act . . . .

[W]here the §12(1) plaintiff is primarily an investor, precluding suit would interfere significantly with effective enforcement of the securities laws and frustrate the primary objective of the Securities Act. . . . Because the Act is specifically designed to protect investors, even where a plaintiff actively participates in the distribution of unregistered securities, his suit should not be barred where his promotional efforts are incidental to his role as an investor. Thus, the *in pari delicto* defense may defeat recovery in a §12(1) action only where the plaintiff's role in the offering or sale of nonexempted, unregistered securities is more as a promoter than as an investor.

Whether the plaintiff in a particular case is primarily an investor or primarily a promoter depends upon a host of factors, all readily accessible to trial courts. These factors include the extent of the plaintiff's financial involvement compared to that of third parties solicited by the plaintiff; the incidental nature of the plaintiff's promotional activities; the benefits received by the plaintiff from his promotional activities; and the extent of the plaintiff's involvement in the planning stages of the offering (such as whether the plaintiff has arranged an underwriting or prepared the offering materials). We do not mean to suggest that these factors provide conclusive evidence of culpable promotional activity, or that they constitute an exhaustive list of factors to be considered. The courts are free, in the exercise of their sound discretion, to consider whatever facts are relevant to the inquiry.

C . . .

The District Court's findings in this case are not adequate to determine whether Dahl bears at least substantially equal responsibility for the failure to register the oil and gas interests or to distribute the securities in a manner that conformed with the statutory exemption, and whether he was primarily a promoter of the offering. The findings indicate, on the one hand, that Dahl may have participated in initiating the entire investment, and that he loaned money to Pinter and solicited his associates' participation in the venture, but, on the other hand, that Dahl invested substantially more money than the other investor-respondents, expected and received no commission for his endeavors, and drafted none of the offering documents. Furthermore, the District Court made no findings as to who was responsible for the failure to register or for the manner in which the offering was conducted. Those findings will be made on the remand of this case for further proceedings. . . .

IV

The judgment . . . is vacated, and the case is remanded for further proceedings consistent with this opinion. . . .

Justice KENNEDY took no part in the consideration or decision of this case. [The dissenting opinion of Justice STEVENS is omitted.]

NOTES ON UNCLEAN HANDS AND IN PARI DELICTO

1. Two defenses. *In pari delicto* is closely related to unclean hands. The unclean hands defense is based on a maxim of equity: "He who comes into equity must come with clean hands." If plaintiff's hands were not clean—if he were guilty of inequitable conduct, whether or not that conduct was illegal or tortious—it was said that he could not get relief in equity. The unclean hands defense was historically said to be available only in equity, and jurisdictions continue to divide on whether unclean hands can be a defense to suits at law. The cases are collected in T. Leigh Anenson, *Limiting Legal Remedies: An Analysis of Unclean Hands*, 99 Ky. L.J. 63 (2011), and T. Leigh Anenson, *Treating Equity Like Law: A Post-Merger Justification of Unclean Hands*, 45 Am. Bus. L.J. 455, 467-471 (2008).

Whatever the status of unclean hands, *in pari delicto* is available at law in suits for damages. The Court in *Pinter* carefully distinguishes the two defenses; to protect enforcement of the statutory policy, it says that *in pari delicto* is narrower than unclean hands. The distinctions among substantive claims may be more important than the distinction between the two defenses. Is there any reason to deny injunctive relief for misconduct by plaintiff that would not be sufficient to deny damages or rescission?

2. Unclean hands. The best treatment of unclean hands may still be Zechariah Chafee, Jr., *Coming into Equity with Clean Hands*, 47 Mich. L. Rev. 877, 47 Mich. L. Rev. 1065 (1949). His thesis is

> that the clean hands doctrine does not definitely govern anything, that it is a rather recent growth, that it ought not to be called a maxim of equity because it is by no means confined to equity, that its supposed unity is very tenuous and it is really a bundle of rules relating to quite diverse subjects, that insofar as it is a principle it is not very helpful but is at times capable of causing considerable harm.

Id. at 878. The notes that follow explore some of these objections to the conventional wisdom. For a modern doctrinal overview, collecting many cases, see Nakahara v. NS 1991 American Trust, 718 A.2d 518 (Del. Ct. Ch. 1998).

3. The controversy—and a leading example. The essence of what troubles some observers is that these defenses allow defendant to get away with his wrongful conduct, and they provide at best a haphazard remedy for plaintiff's wrongful conduct. Consider Precision Instrument Manufacturing Co. v. Automotive Maintenance Machinery Co., 324 U.S. 806 (1945). Plaintiff's employee invented a wrench and filed a patent application. Defendants filed a wholly false patent application claiming to have invented the same wrench sooner. When plaintiff discovered the perjury, defendants settled the case by assigning their application to plaintiff. Plaintiff received patents on both applications without ever disclosing the perjury in the assigned application.

Defendants then began to manufacture a new wrench, allegedly infringing plaintiff's patents and violating the settlement agreement. Plaintiff sued for both legal and equitable relief. Without distinguishing the claims, the Supreme Court said plaintiff was barred by unclean hands, because it had failed to disclose the perjury to the patent office, and because it had benefited from the perjury by securing a patent based on the perjured application.

Did the doctrine do harm in *Precision Instrument*? Certainly it was an extreme application. The Court refused to compare defendants' wrongdoing to plaintiff's. It invalidated not only the patents based on the perjured application, but also the patent based on the legitimate application. The decision let defendants profit from their theft of plaintiff's invention. But the decision also made it legal for any member of the public to manufacture the wrench; this creates at least the possibility that the wrench would have to be sold at a competitive rather than a monopoly price. Is the decision justified by this public benefit?

4. Rewriting *Precision Instrument*. Eventually the Court dropped the unclean hands rationale and announced a substantive rule of patent law: Patents procured by fraud are invalid. Walker Process Equipment, Inc. v. Food Machinery & Chemical Corp., 382 U.S. 172 (1965). But *Precision Instrument* is still the leading Supreme Court opinion on unclean hands. Does it survive the *in pari delicto* decisions in *Pinter, Bateman Eichler*, and *Perma Life Mufflers*?

5. No honor among thieves? Some of the cases say that a court will not "serve as referee in an accounting between coconspirators." Lawler v. Gilliam, 569 F.2d 1283, 1292 (4th Cir. 1978). This is reminiscent of the Highwayman's Case (Everet v. Williams), decided in 1725 and unofficially reported in 9 L.Q.R. 197 (1893). Plaintiff alleged a partnership for highway robbery and defendant's failure to account for the partnership profits. The chancellor dismissed the bill for "scandal and impertinence" and fined the solicitors for contempt of court.

In Hartman v. Harris, 810 F. Supp. 82 (S.D.N.Y. 1992), *aff'd*, 996 F.2d 301 (2d Cir. 1993), a father sued his son for half the proceeds of the sale of a rare seventeenth-century bronze statue. The father appears to have acquired the statue innocently, but by the time of the sale, both father and son knew the statue was stolen property. The son kept the entire proceeds, and the court dismissed the father's complaint on the ground that any agreement with respect to the proceeds was an illegal contract. In another example, a bankrupt company that organized a Ponzi scheme sued its aiders and abettors under the Racketeer Influenced and Corrupt Organizations Act, 18 U.S.C. § 1961 *et seq.* The court invoked *in pari delicto* to dismiss the claim. Official Committee of Unsecured Creditors v. Edwards, 437 F.3d 1145 (11th Cir. 2006).

Compare Couri v. Couri, 447 N.E.2d 334 (Ill. 1983). Plaintiff sought an accounting of the profits of the family grocery business. One reason the accounting was so difficult was that for 20 years the family had kept phony books to evade taxes. The court allowed an accounting anyway. Is that consistent with the Highwayman's Case?

6. Wrongdoer or victim? In Republic of Iraq v. ABB AG, 768 F.3d 145 (2d Cir. 2014), Iraq brought claims against multiple defendants who allegedly conspired with its then-President Saddam Hussein to corrupt a humanitarian program known as the Oil-for-Food Programme. Defendants circumvented Iraq's economic sanctions by purchasing oil at below-market rates through the Programme, paying additional fees imposed by the Hussein regime, and delivering substandard humanitarian aid in return. The court applied *Bateman Eichler* to bar Iraq's RICO claim, finding equal fault and imputing the former government's fault to Iraq itself. The dissenter thought this ruling was perverse.

> The *in pari delicto* defense is founded on the twin premises that "courts should not lend their good offices to mediating disputes among wrongdoers . . . [and] that denying judicial relief to an admitted wrongdoer is an effective means of deterring illegality." *Bateman Eichler*, 472 U.S. at 306-307. Yet here it functions to release defendants of liability for conduct that, if true, constituted a clear violation of U.S. law and subversion of U.S. policy, and to deprive the ultimate victims of the defendants' conduct of any remedy.

Id. at 174 (Droney, J., dissenting in part).

7. Must the wrongdoing be directed at defendant? Some cases say plaintiff is not barred unless his wrongdoing was directed at defendant. One place this matters is in a large set of cases arising out of fraudulent transfers. A distressed debtor transfers property to a friend or relative to keep it from her creditors. When the coast is clear, she asks for the property back, and the recipient says no. In Beelman v. Beelman, 460 N.E.2d 55 (Ill. App. Ct. 1984), plaintiff and her husband fraudulently transferred their house to his brother to save it from a tax lien. After her husband died and the IRS went away, plaintiff asked for the house back. When her brother-in-law refused, the court imposed a constructive trust. It said plaintiff wasn't barred by unclean hands, because her fraud on the IRS was not directed at her brother-in-law.

Is that the right result? If the court had let the brother-in-law keep the property, would that deter fraudulent transfers? If the result is sound, what about the rationale? Wouldn't the rationale also allow relief in the Highwayman's Case? Fraudulent transfer cases are collected in Annotation, 6 A.L.R.4th 862 (1981 & Supp.).

8. Recovering the fruits of plaintiff's wrong? Another formulation of the unclean hands rule is that the court will not aid a plaintiff whose claim had its inception in the plaintiff's own wrongdoing, whether the victim is the defendant or a third party. That covers the fraudulent transfer cases, because the inequitable conduct (fraudulently transferring the property) is part of the source of plaintiff's claim (asking for it back). This was the rationale for letting defendant keep the fraudulently transferred property in Kauffman-Harmon v. Kauffman, 36 P.3d 408 (Mont. 2001).

A somewhat more precise formulation is that equity will not help a litigant "in securing or protecting gains from his wrongdoing." Niner v. Hanson, 142 A.2d 798, 804 (Md. 1958). Does that help? Aren't the fraudulent transfer plaintiffs attempting to recover the fruits of their fraud against their creditors? The highwayman plaintiff was plainly trying to recover the fruits of his crime. The *Couri* plaintiff was trying to recover some legitimate profits from the sale of groceries and some illegitimate profits from tax fraud.

9. Conduct related to the litigation. The bare minimum requirement is that "plaintiff's improper conduct relates in some significant way to the claim he now asserts." Salzman v. Bachrach, 996 P.2d 1263, 1269 (Colo. 2001). This excludes wholly irrelevant past misconduct; without that, "only those leading pristine and blameless lives would ever be entitled to equitable relief." *Id.*

10. Comparative fault. Another approach is to ask whether defendant is more culpable than plaintiff. *Precision Instrument* refused to consider comparative fault, but *Pinter* goes the other way with *in pari delicto*, and so do most unclean hands cases.

A lawyer who stole money from his client was much more at fault than the client, a medical marijuana dispensary in California whose entire business was illegal under federal law. Northbay Wellness Group, Inc. v. Beyries, 789 F.3d 956 (9th Cir. 2015). The marijuana client's unclean hands did not bar it from asserting its otherwise straightforward claim that the attorney's debt for the stolen money was not dischargeable in bankruptcy.

The New York court held that *in pari delicto* barred a corporation which engaged in fraud from suing its outside financial auditor for professional malpractice in negligently failing to detect the fraud. Kirschner v. KMPG LLP, 938 N.E.2d 941 (N.Y. 2010). These cases often come after management has been booted out and new management, sometimes a bankruptcy trustee or receiver, tries to recover from those who did business with the corrupt old guard. Three dissenters thought the case gave too much protection to those who helped facilitate bad conduct.

A federal court relying on *Kirschner* held that *in pari delicto* prevented the bankrupt brokerage house MF Global from suing its outside auditor for participating in a scheme to unlawfully transfer customer funds to the firm's own account. But the doctrine did not bar MF Global from suing on a claim that it innocently relied on the auditor's negligent advice regarding a different aspect of its business. MF Global Holdings Ltd. v. PriceWaterhouseCoopers LLP, 57 F. Supp. 3d 206 (S.D.N.Y. 2014).

And consider In re Silver Leaf, L.L.C., 2005 WL 2045641 (Del. Ct. Ch. 2005), where plaintiff and defendant formed an LLC to market a vending machine that would dispense hot French fries. The initial prototype didn't work, and a second version couldn't be manufactured at commercial scale. But the LLC's affiliate kept issuing shares, raising more than $40 million from the public. The court ordered the LLC dissolved, holding that the company had become a fraud and that neither side was entitled to a remedy to break a 50-50 corporate deadlock.

In many of these cases, the original wrongdoing was a conspiracy between the parties who become plaintiff and defendant in the unclean hands case. Should it matter who took the initiative in the original conspiracy? Should it matter that they both tried to cheat some third party, but now defendant has committed a second wrong by trying to cheat the plaintiff? On that theory, wasn't the defendant highwayman more culpable than the plaintiff highwayman?

Should it matter if either party has tried to make amends? In the fraudulent transfer cases, a plaintiff who eventually paid her creditor looks less culpable than one who waited till the statute of limitations barred the debt.

11. Protecting the third-party victim? In some of these cases, there is a readily identifiable victim of the fraudulent conduct. That victim is not a party and may have given up on any hope of a remedy. Why not notify the victim instead of arguing over which of the coconspirators should keep the fruits of the conspiracy?

An apparently rare example of this approach is Adams v. Manown, 615 A.2d 611 (Md. 1992). Plaintiff had gotten his bankruptcy discharge in 1989, without disclosing substantial loans to his live-in girlfriend; the girlfriend's obligation to repay him would have been an asset available to his creditors. After his discharge, he sued to collect the loans from the now ex-girlfriend. The court directed the trial judge to notify the bankruptcy trustee. If the bankruptcy trustee declined to proceed, the trial court should reenter its original judgment for plaintiff. A similar Connecticut case reached opposite results on both issues: The court assumed that the bankruptcy trustee would not find it worthwhile to proceed, and it held the bankrupt's claim barred by unclean hands. Thompson v. Orcutt, 777 A.2d 670 (Conn. 2001).

12. The big picture. Is the unclean hands defense the same as saying two wrongs make a right? Denying relief may help deter wrongs like plaintiff's, but it only encourages wrongs like defendant's. Shouldn't courts ask whether denying relief to plaintiff is a sensible remedy for the earlier wrong, either in the sense that it moves the parties closer to their rightful position or in the sense that it furthers relevant substantive policies? Is that the direction in which *Pinter* is moving?

C.   ESTOPPEL AND WAIVER

1.   *Equitable Estoppel*

GEDDES v. MILL CREEK COUNTRY CLUB, INC.
751 N.E.2d 1150 (Ill. 2001)

[Plaintiffs owned an agricultural and landscaping business on 16 acres that bordered the fifth hole of defendants' golf course. Plaintiffs alleged trespass and nuisance, because golf balls continually landed on their property. Plaintiffs claimed to have collected 2,128 golf balls on their property during the 1996 and 1997 seasons, and to have abandoned use of significant portions of their property. Plaintiffs sought actual and punitive damages and an injunction closing the fifth hole.

The golf course had been developed by Sho-Deen, Inc., and its president, Kent Shodeen, who also owned Mill Creek Country Club. The course was part of a planned unit development covering 1,450 acres. The development was ten years in the planning, much of that time devoted to negotiations with plaintiffs and other neighbors.

The original plan provided for the rear lawns of single-family residences to adjoin plaintiffs' western boundary. These houses would face the fairway. Plaintiffs objected to the houses and eventually agreed to the fairway instead. Shodeen testified that it would not be possible to change the fifth hole because of all the approvals required from government agencies.

The fairway was 300 feet wide, running at an angle to plaintiffs' property, not pointing toward the property, and separated from the property by a 40-foot rough. Defendants claimed that the golf course actually increased the value of plaintiffs' property.

The trial and appellate courts ruled for defendants without reaching any issue of estoppel. Defendants continued to make their estoppel argument, invoking the rule that an appellee can rely on any ground that is in the record and supports the judgment.]

Justice FREEMAN delivered the opinion of the court . . . .

Defendants invoke the doctrine of equitable estoppel. Defendants claim that plaintiffs, by their conduct, are estopped from bringing their action. According to defendants, plaintiffs chose the fairway over other options that Sho-Deen presented to them and made other requests that Sho-Deen granted. Sho-Deen, at great expense, redesigned the development plan to accommodate plaintiffs. The agreement between plaintiffs and Sho-Deen, which contains several references to a golf course and a specific reference to the fairway, memorializes plaintiffs' requests. Defendants argue that plaintiffs' conduct prevents them from maintaining this action. . . .

The general rule is that where a person by his or her statements and conduct leads a party to do something that the party would not have done but for such statements and conduct, that person will not be allowed to deny his or her words or acts to the damage of the other party. Equitable estoppel may be defined as the effect of the person's conduct whereby the person is barred from asserting rights that might otherwise have existed against the other party who, in good faith, relied upon such conduct and has been thereby led to change his or her position for the worse.

To establish equitable estoppel, the party claiming estoppel must demonstrate that: (1) the other person misrepresented or concealed material facts; (2) the other person knew at the time he or she made the representations that they were untrue; (3) the party claiming estoppel did not know that the representations were untrue when they were made and when they were acted upon; (4) the other person intended or reasonably expected that the party claiming estoppel would act upon the representations; (5) the party claiming estoppel reasonably relied upon the representations in good faith to his or her detriment; and (6) the party claiming estoppel would be prejudiced by his or her reliance on the representations if the other person is permitted to deny the truth thereof.

Regarding the first two elements, the representation need not be fraudulent in the strict legal sense or done with an intent to mislead or deceive. Although fraud is an essential element, it is sufficient that a fraudulent or unjust effect results from allowing another person to raise a claim inconsistent with his or her former declarations. The following corollary must be remembered:

> Estoppel may arise from silence as well as words. It may arise where there is a duty to speak and the party on whom the duty rests has an opportunity to speak, and, knowing the circumstances, keeps silent. It is the duty of a person having a right, and seeing another about to commit an act infringing upon it, to assert his right. He cannot by his silence induce or encourage the commission of the act and then be heard to complain.

Bondy v. Samuels, 165 N.E. 181, 186 (Ill. 1929).

The question of estoppel must depend on the facts of each case. The party claiming estoppel has the burden of proving it by clear and unequivocal evidence.

Applying these principles to this case, we conclude that defendants' estoppel defense is meritorious. . . . Plaintiffs, by their conduct, induced or encouraged defendants to design and build the fifth hole. For plaintiffs to assert these claims now would be inequitable and damage defendants.

Plaintiffs attempt to avoid the consequences of their conduct with Sho-Deen. Initially, plaintiffs claim in their reply brief that they "never *requested* that the golf course be located next to their property." (Emphasis added.) This is beside the point. The record clearly and unequivocally shows that plaintiffs knowingly *agreed* to the placement of the fairway. The original concept plan provided for single-family residences to adjoin the western boundary of the property. Sometime during the following two years, Sho-Deen and plaintiffs agreed on the placement of the fifth hole fairway next to plaintiffs' property. The record contains unrebutted testimony that, prior to signing the formal agreement, Larry Geddes informed a county development planning committee meeting of his work with Shodeen and asked the board not to alter any of the proposed plans as they related to him. Finally, plaintiffs signed the 1994 agreement, which refers throughout to a golf course, and once specifically to "the golf course fairway that borders the Geddes' western property line."

Acknowledging that they agreed to the placement of the fifth hole adjacent to their property, plaintiffs contend that their decision was not a knowing one. In their reply brief, plaintiffs argue that "the agreement is silent as it relates to golf balls," and "the concept of golf balls is never addressed in the 1994 agreement." Plaintiffs testified that when they signed the agreement, and during the construction of the golf course, they knew nothing about the game of golf. They had no idea of the number of errant golf balls that would enter their property.

This contention lacks merit. That golfers do not always hit their golf balls straight is a matter of common knowledge . . . . This condition is as natural as gravity or ordinary rainfall. . . .

Defendants knew it. . . . [P]laintiffs also knew it. This is evidenced by the agreement provision that plaintiffs' property be surrounded by an eight-foot-high fence with landscaping that includes trees over that height. Even assuming that plaintiffs did not know of this fact of life, they reasonably should have. Plaintiffs cannot avoid the reasonable results of their conduct.

Regarding the third element of equitable estoppel, defendants did not know, either at the time of the agreement or during the construction of the fifth hole, that plaintiffs would act in a manner contrary to the agreement. Fourth, plaintiffs, of course, expected that Sho-Deen would perform all of the provisions of the 1994 agreement. Plaintiffs' promise not to protest the construction of the golf course, specifically the fifth hole, was conditional on Sho-Deen's compliance with the agreement.

Fifth, defendants reasonably relied upon plaintiffs' conduct to their detriment. All agreements between adults should be entered into thoughtfully. This admonition takes on increased significance in the context of a planned unit development . . . . The creation of the golf course, specifically the fifth hole, required considerable negotiation with many public and private parties, including plaintiffs. Sho-Deen obtained their approval and, based thereon, built the fifth hole.

Regarding the sixth element of equitable estoppel, defendants would be prejudiced if plaintiffs were permitted to deny their conduct. Initially, the original concept plan had residences adjoining the fifth hole on the east, between the fairway and plaintiffs' property. The record contains unrebutted evidence that there would have been approximately 14 of these lots, and Shodeen would have charged an additional $15,000 for each lot because it would have adjoined the fairway. Thus, Sho-Deen lost approximately $210,000 in lot "premiums" by placing these residences elsewhere. Additionally, the record contains evidence that Sho-Deen incurred other costs in relocating the fifth hole, e.g., $25,000 for re-engineering the area.

Not only did Sho-Deen incur costs in relocating the fifth hole, it now would be problematic to move it or close it. . . . If Sho-Deen now moved or closed the fifth hole, it could be liable for violating the PUD agreement with other lot owners.

"An injunction will be refused where the complainant has actively encouraged defendant to undertake the work and then has silently, without protest, permitted defendant to go ahead with the work in disregard of the right of complainant." *Bondy*, 165 N.E. at 187. In this case, plaintiffs are equitably estopped from bringing their claims. . . .

CONCLUSION . . .

[T]he judgment of the appellate court is affirmed. . . .

NOTES ON EQUITABLE ESTOPPEL

1. The rule. The essence of equitable estoppel is one party's detrimental reliance on the other's earlier statement or conduct. There are six-part formulations, as in *Geddes*, four-part formulations, as in In Re Langlois/Novicki Variance Denial, 175 A.3d 1222, 1227-1228 (Vt. 2017); three-part formulations, as in Atlas Van Lines, Inc. v. Dinosaur Museum, 368 P.3d 121, 125 (Utah Ct. App. 2016); and even one-sentence formulations, as in the first sentence of this paragraph and in Plymouth Foam Products, Inc. v. City of Becker, 120 F.3d 153, 156 (8th Cir. 1997). All lead to substantially the same results. The Utah formulation may be the best combination of brevity and clarity: an act or statement inconsistent with the right later asserted, reliance, and injury. The whole doctrine is surveyed in T. Leigh Anenson, *The Triumph of Equity: Equitable Estoppel in Modern Litigation*, 27 Rev. Litig. 377 (2008).

The *Geddes* formulation is common but somewhat misleading in its reference to concealing "facts," and to knowing that the representations were "untrue" when made. When the issue is what plaintiff wanted or intended, it doesn't matter what the truth was. Whether or not plaintiffs intended to choose the fairway over the houses, they acted as though they had, and that is what matters. It doesn't matter whether they lied or changed their mind or just got confused. If they are now saying something different from what they said before, and if defendants relied on what they said before, they are estopped to change their position.

2. Law and equity. Equitable estoppel originated in equity but has long been fully assimilated to law and available in suits for damages as well as in suits for injunctions. An example that takes note of the question is Brooks v. Cooksey, 427 S.W.2d 498, 503-504 (Mo. 1968).

3. Estoppel and contract. What does estoppel add to the parties' contract? Perhaps on these facts the contract would have been enough. But estoppel adds the whole course of dealing between the parties: The evidence is not confined to the words of the written agreement, and the golf course does not have to worry about contract formalities. The contract referred to the fairway's location but apparently it did not expressly make the location of the fairway part of the agreed exchange. In the contract, plaintiffs promised not to "protest the development," which most naturally refers to the planning commission, the zoning board, and the like; the contract did not explicitly release future claims for trespass and nuisance arising after the development was completed. Sensible contract interpretation might protect the golf course, but estoppel fit better. Estoppels can arise informally, from oral representations or even from silence, with nothing that looks like an enforceable contract.

4. But I didn't know. Of course it would matter if what plaintiffs said before had been induced by defendants' own misrepresentations or withholding of information. Plaintiffs also hoped to avoid estoppel if, even without any fault on the part of the golf course, there were essential facts that they simply hadn't known. That is the point of arguing that they knew nothing about golf, and that is why the court says that basic information about golf is readily available and they must be held to have known it. It's entirely possible that they believed the fence, the trees, and the 40-foot rough would be sufficient to protect them from golf balls. But when there is as much reliance as there was here, should it matter what they knew? Sometimes courts say that the party to be estopped had to know; sometimes, as in the next note, they say it doesn't matter what he knew.

5. Estoppel and fraud. Equitable estoppel is closely related to fraud. All frauds give rise to estoppels and may be relied on defensively. But fraud is also a tort; it gives rise to a claim for damages. The usual distinction is that fraud requires intentional or reckless misrepresentation, but negligent or even inadvertent misrepresentations can give rise to an estoppel. Even good-faith representations that become untrue because of changing circumstances can create an estoppel. An example is People v. Kinion, 454 N.E.2d 625, 629 (Ill. 1983). A privately retained attorney had his client declared indigent so that the county would pay her psychiatric witnesses. But he told the court that he would continue to represent her without demanding attorneys' fees from the county. He thought that defendant had enough assets to pay him but not enough to pay the experts in addition. Relying on the attorney's representation, the court appointed him instead of the public defender. When it turned out that the defense cost more than defendant could pay, the attorney petitioned for an award of fees from the county. The court held him estopped to seek fees.

In Petrella v. Metro-Goldwyn-Mayer, Inc., 134 S. Ct. 1962 (2014), the Court wrote that the "gravamen of estoppel, a defense long recognized as available in actions at law, is misleading and consequent loss." The context was plaintiffs misleading potential defendants into believing that no lawsuit would be filed. *Petrella* is more fully described in Notes on the Relationship Between Laches and Statutes of Limitation in section 11.D.

6. Estoppel and expectancy. Estoppel is only a defense; the golf course could not sue anyone for estoppel. But one way to think of estoppel is that it is the golf course's remedy for the plaintiffs' misleading conduct. Is it an appropriate remedy? There is a certain intuitive justice in estoppel: You said it, you're stuck with it. But sometimes estoppel seems to give more than is needed to right the wrong. More precisely, the court holds the estopped party to what he said and awards the misled party what she came to expect on the basis of the misrepresentation. In CIGNA Corp. v. Amara, 563 U.S. 421 (2011), the Court described estoppel as an "equitable remedy" that "'operates to place the person entitled to its benefit in the same position he would have been in had the representations been true.'" *Id.* at 441.

Consider United States v. Georgia Pacific Co., 421 F.2d 92 (9th Cir. 1970), where the government appeared to abandon a long-term contract to eventually acquire a privately owned forest, and Georgia-Pacific bought the forest and invested substantial sums in forest management. Then the government reasserted its claim. Reliance damages might have made Georgia-Pacific whole, but the remedy was to hold the government to its abandonment of the contract. Was that an expectancy remedy for a reliance injury?

7. Parenthood by estoppel. Many cases hold that one who assumes the role of parent can be estopped to deny that he is the parent. These cases typically arise after termination of a sexual relationship between one of the biological parents and the estopped nonparent. Some courts treat the child's affection for the nonparent as a form of detrimental reliance; more, recognizing the limits of what future relationship they can enforce, say that only financial harm is relevant. Cases are collected in B.E.B. v. R.L.B., 979 P.2d 514 (Alaska 1999).

An Arizona statute codifies the fairly common rule that a man is at least rebuttably presumed to be the parent of his wife's child. In McLaughlin v. Jones in and for County of Pima, 401 P.3d 492 (Ariz. 2017), the court held that this statute applies to same-sex couples. After Kimberly and Suzan married, Kimberly bore a child by an anonymous sperm donor. The couple signed a co-parenting agreement declaring Susan to be the child's "co-parent" and guaranteeing access to the child if the marriage dissolved. After Suzan filed for divorce, Kimberly denied her visitation rights. The court held that the statutory presumption could not constitutionally be applied only to opposite-sex couples. And Kimberly could not rebut the statutory presumption; she was "equitably estopped from rebutting Suzan's presumptive parentage." *Id.* at 502.

8. Other estoppels. Promissory estoppel is an extension of equitable estoppel; plaintiff is allowed to recover because he relied on defendant's promise. Claim and issue preclusion are sometimes referred to as estoppel by judgment; the usage survives more commonly in the phrase "collateral estoppel." Judicial estoppel arises when a litigant takes a position in court inconsistent with a position she successfully asserted earlier in the same or a related matter.

NOTES ON ESTOPPEL AGAINST THE GOVERNMENT

1. The traditional rule. The traditional rule is that the government cannot be estopped. The leading modern case was Federal Crop Insurance Corp. v. Merrill, 332 U.S. 380 (1947). The government insured plaintiff's wheat, but when the crop was lost it refused to pay, because the variety of wheat that Merrill planted was uninsurable under a regulation published in the *Federal Register.* The court of appeals held the government estopped to deny coverage, but the Supreme Court reversed. There were four dissents. Justice Jackson thought that if any farmer read the *Federal Register,* "he would never need crop insurance, for he would never get time to plant any crops." *Id.* at 387.

2. The governmental/proprietary distinction again. The lower federal courts resisted the rule. One escape route was the distinction between governmental and proprietary activities, which we first encountered in section 6.A.1 on sovereign immunity. The distinction is unworkable, because many government activities can't be classified either way. Was the crop insurance program proprietary, because it was an ordinary insurance contract? Or governmental, because the market had failed to provide adequate crop insurance and government was solving an important social and economic problem? The *Merrill* majority said it didn't matter, that the government was immune from estoppel in all its activities. "Government is not partly public or partly private," depending on the activity. 332 U.S. at 383.

3. Further resistance in the lower courts. For a time the lower courts held that the government could be estopped even in its governmental capacity when it was guilty of "affirmative misconduct," a phrase that crystallized in United States Immigration & Naturalization Service v. Hibi, 414 U.S. 5, 6 (1973). The courts of appeals developed a thriving government estoppel jurisprudence, punctuated by occasional reversals from the Supreme Court. Finally, in Office of Personnel Management v. Richmond, 496 U.S. 414 (1990), the Court announced an absolute rule:

> Whether there are any extreme circumstances that might support estoppel in a case not involving payment from the Treasury is a matter we need not address. As for monetary claims, it is enough to say that this Court has never upheld an assertion of estoppel against the Government by a claimant seeking public funds. In this context there can be no estoppel, for courts cannot estop the Constitution.

Id. at 434. The Court principally relied on the Appropriations Clause: "No Money shall be drawn from the Treasury, but in Consequence of Appropriations made by Law." U.S. Const., art. I, §9, cl. 7. Plaintiff was not eligible for benefits, and erroneous advice from a government official was not an appropriation made by law.

4. Policy arguments. *Richmond* also invoked the traditional policy arguments against estopping the government.

a. Preventing deliberate waivers by the executive. One is that the rule protects against misconduct by the executive. Dishonest officials might conspire with private citizens to promise benefits that the government would then have to pay. Or estoppel might permit the executive to override legislation. Consider Doris v. Police Commissioner, 373 N.E.2d 944 (Mass. 1978). A Massachusetts statute required police officers to live within ten miles of the city that employed them. The statute was not enforced for a long time, and some 200 Boston police officers lived more than ten miles from the city limits. Then the police commissioner sent them all letters threatening to begin enforcement proceedings in ten days. The 200 officers argued that prior nonenforcement had led them to believe the statute was a "dead letter" and had induced them to buy homes beyond the ten-mile limit. The court held the city not estopped.

Is that the right result? If so, is widespread nullification different from errors in individual cases? Is *Doris* special because the statute regulated the executive, which might have had an interest in letting it become a dead letter?

b. Protecting the stream of free advice. *Richmond* also relied on Professor Braunstein's argument that if the government is held responsible for its advice, it will give less advice. That will make everyone worse off, but especially the ordinary citizen who can't afford private advice. Michael Braunstein, *In Defense of a Traditional Immunity—Toward an Economic Rationale for Not Estopping the Government*, 14 Rutgers L.J. 1 (1982). He thinks that most government advice is accurate, and that we're better off letting the victims live with the mistakes than chilling the source of advice. He cites the example of the Federal Reserve Board, which quit giving informal staff interpretations of the Truth in Lending Act after Congress made reliance on such interpretations a defense in private litigation.

It is easy to see how the government can quit giving free legal advice to banks. But is it feasible to cut off the informal opinions that field officers give in government transactions with the public? Is the government likely to instruct Social Security employees, for example, to take applications and refuse to answer questions?

5. Morals and justice? Should *Geddes* come out the other way if plaintiff were a local government? Courts commonly say that estoppel is designed "to prevent a party from taking an unconscionable advantage of his own wrong while asserting his strict legal right." Avanta Federal Credit Union v. Shupak, 223 P.3d 863, 872 (Mont. 2009). The Ninth Circuit once said that government resisting what would otherwise have been a clear case of estoppel sought an "exemption from . . . morals and justice." *Georgia-Pacific*, 421 F.2d at 103. The government understandably fears being bound by the mistakes of every GS-7 bureaucrat. But is such a plea any more persuasive when made by the government than when made by Microsoft or Citibank?

2. *Waiver*

CARR-GOTTSTEIN FOODS CO. v. WASILLA, LLC

182 P.3d 1131 (Alaska 2008)

MATTHEWS, Justice. . . .

[The court mostly refers to the tenant as CG Foods, and to the landlord as CG Properties. They had similar names because the tenant bought the business from the landlord, but they were wholly independent of each other. Wasilla, LLC, was an affiliate of the landlord.

The tenant operated a supermarket in the Wasilla Shopping Center, and an Oaken Keg liquor store in a satellite building in the same shopping center. The supermarket lease said that the premises would be used as "a general food supermarket," and that the premises could not be subleased without the landlord's consent. The liquor store was owned by Oaken Keg Spirit Shops, a wholly owned subsidiary of the tenant, and covered by a separate lease.

In 1996, after the liquor store lease expired, the tenant moved the liquor store into the supermarket. The landlord did not object, and its property management subsidiary did the necessary electrical work. After the move, the liquor store's sales figures were reported to the landlord monthly, to be used in calculating the rent.

In 1998, the landlord borrowed money and mortgaged the Wasilla Shopping Center. The landlord's general manager signed a sworn statement for the lender that the leases in the shopping center were not in default.

In 1999, Safeway bought the tenant. Before closing this transaction, Safeway requested estoppel certificates from the landlord declaring that the tenant was not in default on its lease. The landlord did not say that the tenant was in default, but neither did it sign the certificates.

In February 2002, the landlord wrote Safeway that it considered the liquor store to be a breach of the supermarket lease. The landlord then sued Safeway, CG Foods, and Oaken Keg for an injunction against operating the liquor store inside the supermarket and for damages from past operations. The trial judge found that CG Foods had breached the sublease clause (because Oaken Keg was a separate entity) and that it had breached the clause limiting use of the property to a "general food supermarket." The landlord's damage theory was that Oaken Keg would have renewed the lease on the satellite building if it had not moved to the supermarket, and that since the move, the landlord had collected lower rents for other uses of the satellite building.

The jury found $270,000 in damages. But sitting as an advisory jury on an equitable issue, the jury also found that the landlord was estopped from complaining about the breach. The trial judge rejected the jury's finding on estoppel, concluding that there was no "unambiguous statement or action" inconsistent with the landlord's claim and no reliance by the tenants.]

IV. DISCUSSION . . .

B. WAIVER . . .

When a party to a contract is aware of conduct on the part of the other party that constitutes a breach and fails to protest the breach while continuing to perform the contract, that party may be held to have waived its right to rely on the breach in subsequent litigation. The seminal case in Alaska on contract waiver is Milne v. Anderson, 576 P.2d 109 (Alaska 1978). In *Milne* we stated:

> Waiver is generally defined as "the intentional relinquishment of a known right." However, waiver is "a flexible word, with no definite, and rigid meaning in the law. . . . A waiver can be accomplished either expressly or implicitly. An implied waiver arises where the course of conduct pursued evidences an intention to waive a right, or is inconsistent with any other intention than a waiver, or where neglect to insist upon the right results in prejudice to another party. To prove an implied waiver of a legal right, there must be direct, unequivocal conduct indicating a purpose to abandon or waive the legal right, or acts amounting to an estoppel by the party whose conduct is to be construed as a waiver.

Milne, 576 P.2d at 112.

In later cases we added an objective gloss to this formulation. "[N]eglect to insist upon a right," we have said, may result in an implied waiver, or an estoppel, when "the neglect is such that it would convey a message to a reasonable person that the neglectful party would not in the future pursue the legal right in question." Anchorage Chrysler Center, Inc. v. DaimlerChrysler Corp., 129 P.3d 905, 917 n.35 (Alaska 2006). . . .

Milne . . . purchased land and buildings from the Andersons. His offer contained language to the effect that all furnishings and fixtures on the premises would be included in the purchase. The Andersons, who resided outside Alaska, wrote in some exceptions to the offer specifying furnishings that they would retain. These terms were communicated to Milne's attorney but not, evidently, to Milne, and the warranty deed did not contain them. Later Mr. Anderson returned to Alaska and removed some personal property from the premises. Milne observed him doing this, asked what he was doing, but made no protest. Sometime later a bank official asked Milne to initial his approval to the language that the Andersons had added. Milne refused, but made no complaint to the Andersons. Later Milne borrowed $4,000 from Mrs. Anderson in exchange for an unsecured promissory note. He made payments for awhile and then defaulted. When the Andersons' attorney sent him a demand letter, Milne did not claim that he was offsetting the balance of the note because of the property that had been removed from the premises. But he took that position at the trial of the suit to collect on the note. He also claimed that he had made certain utility payments before he took possession of the premises and these payments, too, should be offset. The trial court held that Milne had waived his right to claim these offsets. On appeal we affirmed . . . .

In Altman v. Alaska Truss & Manufacturing Co., 677 P.2d 1215 (Alaska 1983), we [applied] *Milne* [to] a lease. The property involved was owned by the State of Alaska and leased under a long-term lease to Altman. Altman in turn had subleased part of the property to Alaska Truss & Manufacturing (ATM). . . . A clause in the sublease provided that if the state increased its rate on the primary lease, the sublease rent would be increased by the same percentage. On December 15, 1974, the state increased its rent by approximately 500 percent. This increase occurred in a period during which Altman [and] ATM . . . were [negotiating the] rent for a five-year renewal of the sublease. . . . Although Altman was seeking a rent increase, he did not advise ATM . . . of the 500-percent increase in the state's rent until September 1976, and even then he did not state that he intended to enforce the escalation provision. Rather, he relied on the increased rent as a reason why ATM . . . should agree to an increase. It was only in 1978 when Altman filed suit that he notified ATM . . . that he intended to enforce the rent escalation clause. The superior court held that Altman had impliedly waived his right to enforce the escalation provision. . . . [W]e affirmed . . . :

> . . . Altman's conduct in never insisting upon his right to enforce the escalation provision was inconsistent with any other intention than a waiver of his right; furthermore, his neglect to insist upon his right resulted in prejudice to ATM. . . . [T]he superior court properly held that Altman is estopped from enforcing, and has waived his right to enforce, the escalation provision of the sublease.

Id. at 1223.

In at least two other cases we have held that a landlord has waived its right to rely on potential lease breaches by conduct amounting to acquiescence. Thus in Fun Products Distributors, Inc. v. Martens, 559 P.2d 1054 (Alaska 1977), a tenant gave notice of lease renewal that was untimely [and signed by only one of the two tenants].

Thereafter . . . [f]or some three years the landlord [accepted rent payments and] gave no notice that it considered the option to renew ineffective. The trial court held that the option to renew the lease was not effectively exercised and that the tenancy had become a month-to-month tenancy. . . . [T]his court reversed [on the ground that the landlord had waived any defects in the notice of renewal].

In Dillingham Commercial Co. v. Spears, 641 P.2d 1 (Alaska 1982), the lessee sought to exercise a purchase option in the lease. The lessor resisted on a number of grounds, one of which was that nearly every payment of rent over the nine-year history of the lease had been made late. The landlord had accepted the late payments without objection but argued that a non-waiver clause preserved her right to object to the late payments. The clause provided: "Only waivers in writing executed by Landlord shall be effective. No delay or omission on the part of Landlord in exercising any of its rights shall operate as a waiver of such right or any other right." *Id.* at 7. We observed that if literally applied, this clause "would permit the landlord to accept late payment and still assert default of the lease." But we found that the non-waiver clause did not preclude the defense of waiver and that the superior court had correctly concluded that the landlord's "long acquiescence constituted a waiver of her right to claim a default for [the tenant's] late payments of rent." *Id.* at 7-8.

Based on the above principles . . . , the course of conduct of CG Properties in this case constituted implied waiver as a matter of law. . . . CG Properties had full knowledge of the relocation, and facilitated it, and also had full knowledge of the continued sales of liquor by the Oaken Keg store from within the supermarket premises. CG Properties' general manager . . . upon learning of the relocation made a conscious decision not to protest it, preferring a wait-and-see approach in order to be able to select the most economically favorable choice as events unfolded. . . . Meanwhile, [he] signed a sworn statement that "there are no defaults" in connection with the leases in the shopping center in order to obtain a large loan for CG Properties. In addition, at the time of Safeway's acquisition of CG Foods, Safeway sought information and a certificate as to whether CG Foods was in default on the lease. CG Properties had a duty to declare itself on that subject, but did not claim that a default existed. Instead it maintained its non-committal stance.

These acts—except for the statement made to obtain the loan—prejudiced CG Foods and Safeway. Timely notice that the relocation violated the lease would have afforded CG Foods the opportunity to reconsider its position. It could have declined to make the move—thus saving the expense of altering the supermarket premises—or sought to amend the lease. Further, if Safeway had been told that CG Foods was in breach of its lease in the Wasilla Center—and had a potential six-figure liability to CG Properties—it could have declined to purchase CG Foods, offered a lower price, or sought a bond to protect it against potential damages. Because of CG Properties' failure to claim that the relocation breached the lease, CG Foods and Safeway had no occasion to pursue these options.[34]

This combination of acquiescence and assistance in the relocation, consciously declining to declare a breach, even upon request, and prejudice is inconsistent with

---

34. Preserving the opportunity to cure defects in performance and opening the way to settlement negotiations are two of the interests that underlie the statutory waiver provision of Alaska Stat. §45.02.607(c)(1) [UCC §2-607(3)(a)]. . . .

any conclusion other than that CG Properties waived its right to claim that the lease was breached.[35]

C. THE NON-WAIVER CLAUSE APPLIES ONLY TO FUTURE BREACHES.

The non-waiver clause on which CG Properties relies states:

> The failure of either party to insist in any one or more instances upon the strict performance of any one or more of the . . . terms . . . of this Lease . . . shall not be construed as a waiver or relinquishment for the future . . . of the right to exercise such right [or] remedy.

Under this clause, CG Properties' failure to insist on strict performance of the lease on one occasion does not waive its right to insist on strict performance on a future occasion. . . . Thus, the non-waiver clause means that Safeway could not, in reliance on CG Properties' failure to insist on strict performance of the lease in connection with the Oaken Keg relocation, in the future move some other business onto the supermarket premises in violation of the use and sublease clauses. But nothing in the clause suggests that the waiver of these clauses as to the Oaken Keg move would be ineffective.

V. CONCLUSION . . .

[W]e REVERSE . . . and REMAND . . . for further proceedings consistent with this opinion.

BRYNER, Justice, not participating.

NOTES ON WAIVER

1. Waiver and estoppel. *Geddes* is an estoppel case; *CG Foods* is a waiver case. Is there any difference between them? Couldn't each opinion have been written under the other doctrine?

Estoppel arose in equity, waiver in the common law of contracts. Estoppel emphasized reliance and prejudice; waiver emphasized the intentional relinquishment of a

---

35. . . . [A]uthorities [from other states] and our own cases suggest . . . that the traditional verbal formulation for implied waiver is not as demanding as it sounds. What the cases have in common is knowledge on the part of the party charged with waiver of facts giving rise to a right to assert a breach (or claim a contract benefit as in *Altman*), unreasonable delay in asserting a breach (or claiming a benefit), and acceptance of continued performance. Frequently there is also prejudice — often because failure to protest deprives the other party of an opportunity to cure — even if prejudice is not discussed. Little or no attention is paid to whether the party charged with waiver actually intended to relinquish a known right. At least one respected text recognizes the problems with the traditional formulation. The text says of the "voluntary and intentional relinquishment of a known right" definition that

> there are few, if any, more erroneous definitions known to the law. For one thing, waiver is far more multifaceted than this definition would allow for. Moreover, even as far as it goes, it is totally misleading. It strongly implies that the waiving party intends to give up a right. In reality, many, if not most waivers are unintentional and frequently do not involve a "right" that the party is aware of.

Joseph M. Perillo, *Calamari & Perillo on Contracts* §11.29, at 458 (5th ed., West 2003).

known right. But each doctrine has spread out both in its range of application and in the bases on which it will be found, until the two defenses are substantially overlapping. General statements must be taken with caution; the real content of these defenses varies with context.

2. Is reliance required? Some cases say emphatically that waiver is essentially a unilateral act and that reliance is not required. An example is Best Place, Inc. v. Penn American Insurance Co., 920 P.2d 334 (Haw. 1996), one of many cases holding that when an insurance company continues to investigate a claim, or offers to pay part of it, it waives its right to later reject the claim on the ground that the proof of claim was filed late. The insurance context no doubt matters in these cases; so does the view that the late-filing defense is something of a technicality if no information has gone missing in the meantime.

Other cases distinguish express waivers that are truly knowing and intentional from waivers that are implied from conduct and possibly inadvertent. An example of this approach is Hanover Insurance Co. v. Fireman's Fund Insurance Co., 586 A.2d 567 (Conn. 1991), holding that Fireman's had not by its silence waived a contractual one-year time limit on filing suit. The letter in which Fireman's should have mentioned the time limit but did not was mailed after the time limit had expired, so the court found no reliance. If Fireman's had explicitly stated that it would not rely on the time limit, this would be an express waiver and the court implies that no reliance would be required. But reliance was required for a waiver from silence. "[I]mplied waivers and estoppels by conduct are so similar that they are nearly indistinguishable." *Id.* at 573.

3. Should reliance be required? A waiver without reliance is like a gift: The beneficiary of the waiver gets something for nothing. The Alaska court is surely right in footnote 35 when it says that "[f]requently there is . . . prejudice . . . even if prejudice is not discussed." But sometimes prejudice is very hard to find. In a case like *Hanover Insurance*, where defendant allegedly waived the deadline after the deadline had expired, could plaintiff claim it relied by continuing to spend money on hopeless litigation that it would have abandoned if defendant had just pointed out the time limit? Or might the court reasonably assume that plaintiff would have litigated anyway and attacked the time limit on some other ground?

Might waiver without reliance make sense as a way of avoiding litigation over attenuated reliance questions? If so, when? Only when the waiver is truly knowing and intentional? Only when the right waived is not very important?

4. Late payments. Creditors regularly accept late payments for substantial periods before giving up on a debtor and "accelerating"—declaring all future payments immediately due and payable. The debtor often argues that the earlier acceptance of late payments precludes the creditor from insisting on prompt payment now. Courts regularly hold that sellers have waived their right to accelerate for payments no later than the ones that have been accepted. But creditors can usually reclaim the right to prompt payment, and to acceleration as a remedy, by telling the debtor that they will insist on it henceforth. Both these propositions are illustrated in Foundation Property Investments, LLC v. CTP, LLC, 186 P.3d 766 (Kan. 2008).

5. Antiwaiver clauses. Contracts often provide that failure to enforce rights with respect to some payments or obligations doesn't waive those rights with respect to other payments or obligations. *Foundation Property* suggests that an unambiguous clause to this effect would have been enforced. But the greater the gap between such a clause and the actual course of dealing, the more likely a court is to construe it not to apply to the facts. Or, as the court put it in General Electric Capital

Corp. v. Bio-Mass Tech, Inc., 136 So. 3d 698, 703 (Fl. Dist. Ct. App. 2014), "[a]n antiwaiver clause itself can be waived." What happened to the antiwaiver clause in *CG Foods*?

6. What conduct is inconsistent with the claimed right? Conduct is often ambiguous. Is it clearly inconsistent with a known right to investigate an insurance claim after receiving a late proof of loss? Maybe the adjuster just didn't notice the dates at first. Maybe her practice is to waive proof of loss where coverage is clear, but not to waive where she has any doubt about the claim. In Van Independent School District v. McCarty, 165 S.W.3d 351 (Tex. 2005), a fired maintenance worker claimed that the school board had held a hearing on his appeal and thereby waived his failure to file a notice of appeal within seven days of his discharge. The court found no waiver, and it said its holding might benefit employees:

> District policy allowed the parties to waive time deadlines "by mutual consent." Reasonable board members might want to grant such consent only in cases that appear to have merit. If any inquiry along those lines waives the deadline . . . then no board will ever do it, and all extensions will be denied.

Id. at 353-354.

And then there is Richardson v. Richardson, 218 S.W.3d 426 (Mo. 2007), where an ex-wife did not waive her right to spousal support by hiring a hit man to kill her ex-husband. If she had succeeded, her right to support would have ended by the terms of the divorce decree. But the attempt to murder was not an "unequivocal attempt to relinquish" her right to support while her ex-husband lived. *Id.* at 430. Might unclean hands have been a better argument? The case was influenced by a clause in the agreed divorce decree, expressly authorized by Missouri law, that prohibited modification of the decree in response to events after the divorce.

7. Procedural waivers. Perhaps the most common use of the waiver idea is in procedure. Courts regularly say that litigants waived a claim, defense, or procedural right by not asserting it at the proper time. The rationale here is clearly that the court and the other litigants relied by continuing the litigation; the courts will not retry a case to correct an error that could have been corrected when it was made. For the most part there is no pretense that these waivers are knowing or intentional. Inadvertence is just as binding. The Supreme Court has repeatedly suggested that these waivers be called "forfeitures," because they do not involve "intentional relinquishment . . . of a known right." See Kontrick v. Ryan, 540 U.S. 443, 458 n.13 (2004).

8. Waiver of defenses. The insurance cases in note 2 illustrate one other point about equitable defenses. Not only are they not exclusively equitable, they aren't exclusively defenses. Plaintiffs in those cases argue that the defendant has waived a defense. In section 11.E.3, we will see cases on whether defendants are estopped to assert the statute of limitations. Defendants who seek any kind of relief can be barred by unclean hands.

In Sickler v. Sickler, 878 N.W.2d 549 (Neb. 2016), an ex-husband was held in contempt of court for not paying $37,234.84 to his ex-wife from their joint retirement account, in accordance with a decree issued 14 years earlier. Defendant argued laches, but plaintiff argued defendant's unclean hands. The court held that the ex-husband could not assert laches or "any other equitable defense," because he willfully depleted the retirement account during the 14-year period, and consequently did not have clean hands. *Id.* at 564.

NOTES ON WAIVER BY THE GOVERNMENT

1. Waiver by the government. Even if the government can't be estopped, can it waive its rights? Some courts say yes, but only if the official who waived the rights had authority to do so.

Consider Cinciarelli v. Reagan, 729 F.2d 801 (D.C. Cir. 1984). Cinciarelli was a colonel in the Marine Corps Reserve. He was appointed to a five-year tour of active duty under a written agreement. A regulation provided that such agreements could not be offered to colonels, but the regulation was frequently ignored. The Commandant of the Marine Corps promulgated the regulation; he also approved the agreement with Cinciarelli. But the Marines reneged when Cinciarelli was promoted to general. There were no more slots for active-duty generals, and all such slots were reserved for career officers anyway. The Marines sent Cinciarelli back to reserve status, and he sued for five-years' pay as a general. The case eventually settled for $365,000, and then Cinciarelli asked for attorneys' fees under the Equal Access to Justice Act, described in Notes on Exceptions to the American Rule in section 10.A.

His right to fees turned on whether the government's litigation position was "substantially justified." The court held that it was not:

> Though the law is clear that the government is not bound by the unauthorized acts of its agents, the law in this circuit is equally clear that . . . when a government official has authority to waive the regulations allegedly violated, "we look instead to the standards of waiver that would govern between private parties." Molton, Allen & Williams, Inc. v. Harris, 613 F.2d 1176, 1179 (D.C. Cir. 1980). Thus when, in the course of making an agreement, an official with power to waive a regulation that would bar the agreement acts in a way that signals to a private party an objective intent to waive the regulation, and the private party relies on that behavior, the government official is estopped from voiding the agreement on the basis of the regulation.

Id. at 807-808. Note the mixture of estoppel and waiver.

2. Which officials have authority? How does the court know which government employees have authority to waive regulations? In *Cinciarelli* the government apparently conceded that the Commandant had authority. In *Molton,* the court found authority in regulations of the defendant agency, the Federal National Mortgage Association (better known as Fannie Mae). One regulation said the agency could "alter or waive" any requirements; another said that the agency's loan officers could do anything the agency could do. *Molton,* 613 F.2d at 1178. And the court thought it was in the agency's interest to grant such power to its loan officers. The agency buys and sells mortgages in the open market, and market conditions often change rapidly; granting authority to field officers enabled the agency to act more efficiently in a fluctuating market. That helped prove that the loan officer really had authority to waive regulations, even though his waiver disadvantaged the government on this particular occasion.

3. Procedural waivers. Not even the Supreme Court has been reluctant to hold the government to procedural defaults in litigation. Thus, in Steagald v. United States, 451 U.S. 204, 209-211 (1981), the court held that the government had waived its right to claim that defendant had no expectation of privacy in a house where it had found incriminating evidence.

D.   LACHES

ARIZONA LIBERTARIAN PARTY v. REAGAN
189 F. Supp. 3d 920 (D. Ariz. 2016)

DAVID G. CAMPBELL, United States District Judge. . . .

I. BACKGROUND

Plaintiffs are the Arizona Libertarian Party ("AZLP") and Michael Kielsky, the party's chairman and a candidate for public office. Defendant Michele Reagan is the Arizona Secretary of State . . . , the state officer responsible for administering elections . . . . Plaintiffs seek to enjoin the enforcement of certain portions of Ariz. Rev. Stat. §§16–321 and 16–322 . . . .

[A] candidate who wishes to have her name printed on a primary ballot must . . . file a valid nomination petition with the Secretary by a specified deadline. The petition must contain a minimum number of signatures from the relevant jurisdiction. The required number of signatures varies depending on the office sought. The purpose of the signature requirement is "to ensure that candidates have 'adequate support from eligible voters to warrant being placed on the ballot.'" Jenkins v. Hale, 190 P.3d 175, 176 (Ariz. 2008).

[In 2015, Arizona amended the statutes about who could sign petitions and the required number of signatures. The changes made it more difficult for Libertarians to get on the ballot.]

The deadline by which candidates must submit nomination petitions this year is June 1, 2016. The deadline by which candidates must file as write-in candidates is July 21, 2016. The primary election is scheduled for August 30, 2016. . . .

Plaintiffs ask the Court to require the Secretary to place their candidates on the primary election ballot if, by the June 1, 2016 deadline, they submit nomination petitions containing the number of signatures . . . required before [the 2015 amendment].

II. LACHES

"Laches—unreasonable and prejudicial delay—requires denial of injunctive relief, including preliminary relief." Arizona Public Integrity Alliance Inc. v. Bennett, 2014 WL 3715130, at *2 (D. Ariz. 2014). Over the last 25 years, the Arizona Supreme Court has repeatedly cautioned that litigants should bring election challenges in a timely manner or have their requests for relief denied on the basis of laches.

Laches applies when there is both unreasonable delay and prejudice. "In the context of election matters, the laches doctrine seeks to prevent dilatory conduct and will bar a claim if a party's unreasonable delay prejudices the opposing party or the administration of justice." Id. at *2. To determine whether delay was unreasonable, a court considers the justification for the delay, the extent of the plaintiff's advance knowledge of the basis for the challenge, and whether the plaintiff exercised diligence in preparing and advancing his case.

To determine whether delay has prejudiced a defendant, a court considers only prejudice that stems from the plaintiff's delay in bringing suit, not difficulties caused by the fact of having been sued. Defendants are entitled to reasonable time to consider and develop their case, including "the opportunity to develop and present their own evidence, hire an expert, or prepare their cross-examination," Mathieu v. Mahoney, 851 P.2d 81, 84-85 (Ariz. 1993).

To determine whether delay has prejudiced the administration of justice, a court considers prejudice to the courts, candidates, citizens who signed petitions, election officials, and voters. As Arizona cases have noted, "[t]he real prejudice caused by delay in election cases is to the quality of decision making in matters of great public importance." Sotomayor v. Burns, 13 P.3d 1198, 1200 (Ariz. 2000). Unreasonable delay can prejudice the administration of justice "by compelling the court to steamroll through . . . delicate legal issues in order to meet" election deadlines. Lubin v. Thomas, 144 P.3d 510, 512 (Ariz. 2006). "Late filings 'deprive judges of the ability to fairly and reasonably process and consider the issues . . . and rush appellate review, leaving little time for reflection and wise decision making.'" *Sotomayor*, 13 P.3d at 1200.

In Arizona Public Integrity Alliance v. Bennett, the Alliance and four voters sought to enjoin the Secretary of State from enforcing [a] statutory requirement that candidates' nomination petitions contain a certain number of signatures from voters in at least three counties. The plaintiffs had begun seriously examining the constitutionality of the county-distribution requirement in December 2013. In the 2014 primary election cycle, nomination petitions were due by May 28, challenges to the petitions were due by June 11, and early primary voting was set for July 28. On May 2, 2014, the plaintiffs provided notice to the state that they intended to seek an injunction, but they did not do so until May 15. The court set an accelerated briefing schedule and a hearing for May 29.

The court found that the plaintiffs had unreasonably delayed in bringing their suit because the plaintiffs had been considering a constitutional challenge since December 2013 and could have relied on sworn affidavits instead of waiting to file suit until after receiving their certified voting records. The plaintiffs' unreasonable delay prejudiced the defendant because he did "not respond on the merits for inability to marshal facts and authorities in the short time left." 2014 WL 3715130 at *3. The court concluded that "[h]ad Plaintiffs filed suit promptly, a motion for preliminary injunction could have been briefed and decided without unreasonable burden on the Defendant, the Court, and the election process." *Id.* at *2. The court held that the plaintiffs' request for preliminary injunctive relief was barred by laches.

This case has followed almost the same timeline. [The statutory amendment] became effective on July 3, 2015. In late August, Plaintiff Kielsky told State Election Director Eric Spencer that the AZLP intended to challenge the constitutionality of the new law. Plaintiffs were therefore aware of the underlying basis for their challenge by August 2015.

Despite this knowledge, Plaintiffs did not file their complaint until April 12, 2016, and did not file their "emergency" motion for a temporary restraining order until May 12, 2016, less than three weeks before the June 1 deadline for nomination petitions. As a result, the Court has been forced to set an expedited briefing schedule and hold a hearing on Plaintiffs' motion only eight days before the deadline.

Plaintiffs argue that their delay was justified by the Secretary's unreasonable delay in releasing the 2016 petition signature requirements on March 21, 2016. The Court is not persuaded. First, the Secretary did not delay unreasonably. As defense counsel noted during oral argument, the Secretary was required by statute to use the March

1, 2016 voter registration data to calculate the primary election signature require-ments. Second, Plaintiffs' own complaint and exhibits show that they had access to the necessary information months ago. Plaintiffs' complaint attaches charts detailing the 2012 and 2014 petition signature requirements for Maricopa County.

Plaintiffs also cited the Secretary's January 2016 voter registration statistics. Even a cursory examination of this data reveals that [the statutory amendment] significantly increased the number of signatures AZLP candidates must obtain to secure a place on the primary ballot. This evidence fully supports the claims made by Plaintiffs in this case—that AZLP members are required to obtain an unconstitutionally high percentage of signatures from AZLP members, or to seek signature from non-AZLP voters. Plaintiffs were not required to wait for the March 21, 2016 numbers before asserting these arguments. Plaintiffs have not provided an adequate justification for their delay.

The Secretary argues, with some persuasive force, that Plaintiffs' unreasonable delay prejudiced her "ability to fully develop facts and arguments for the Court to assess in ruling on whether to grant" Plaintiffs' request for preliminary injunctive relief. Laches is designed to protect a defendant from this precise type of prejudice.

More importantly, Plaintiffs' delay has prejudiced the administration of justice. Plaintiffs' delay left the Court with only 18 days before the petition-submission dead-line to obtain briefing, hold a hearing, evaluate the relevant constitutional law, rule on Plaintiffs' motion, and advise the Secretary and the candidates which statutory petition requirement applies. What is more, signature gathering is well under way. Nomination petitions are due next week. Candidates who have been collecting sig-natures under the current law could be greatly disadvantaged by any injunctive relief that changes the rules at the last minute.

In summary, the Court finds that Plaintiffs unreasonably delayed seeking prelimi-nary relief. The Court also finds that the delay prejudiced Defendant and the admin-istration of justice. The Court therefore will apply the doctrine of laches.

In some cases, laches requires dismissal of the entire claim, while in others it justi-fies only the denial of expedited relief. Plaintiffs challenge a signature requirement that will continue to apply in future elections if it is not invalidated by a court or revised by the Legislature. This is different than a challenge to a ballot proposition [that] will either be passed or defeated in the election. The Court therefore con-cludes that laches should bar only Plaintiffs' request for emergency relief. The merits of the case may continue without the prejudice caused by the late-filed request for that relief.

IT IS ORDERED that Plaintiffs' emergency motion for a temporary restraining order and preliminary injunction is denied. . .

NOTES ON LACHES

1. Laches and the other equitable defenses. *Arizona Libertarian Party* sets out the two essential elements of laches: unreasonable delay and prejudice. The requirement of prejudice to defendant emphasizes the close link between laches and estoppel. The emphasis in laches is on delay; the emphasis in estoppel is on misleading. But the difference is attenuated when defendant is misled by plaintiff's silence.

The similarity of estoppel, waiver, and laches is more apparent in some contexts than in others. Recall Whitlock v. Hilander Foods in section 5.A.2. The footings for defendants' retaining wall encroached on plaintiff's property. Plaintiff delayed filing suit while defendant built its wall, perhaps because defendant misled him about compensation; the court remanded for further consideration of defendant's laches argument. Suppose the ultimate determination is that plaintiff waited too long. It would be entirely plausible to say plaintiff was estopped by his silence and barred by laches, and that he had waived his rights. His apparent acquiescence would probably shift the balance of equities on the undue hardship defense as well.

Estoppel, waiver, and laches are conceptually distinct despite their overlap, and you should learn the separate elements of each. Even within the area of overlap, the facts generally fit one of the three defenses better than the other two.

2. Prejudice and preventive injunctions. Claims for immediate relief are unusual laches cases in that the argument is that the case is moving too fast, depriving defendant of time to prepare a defense and the court of time to decide. But even here, the essential claim is that plaintiff moved too slowly. For other interesting examples of ballot litigation, compare McCarthy v. Briscoe, 429 U.S. 1317 (1976) (Powell, Circuit Justice), ordering the name of Senator Eugene McCarthy placed on the presidential ballot in Texas, with Fishman v. Schaffer, 429 U.S. 1325 (1976) (Marshall, Circuit Justice), refusing to order the name of Gus Hall placed on the presidential ballot in Connecticut. McCarthy was a hero of the movement that opposed the Vietnam War; Hall was the perennial candidate of the Communist Party. The two orders came down on September 30 and October 1, 1976.

The Hall plaintiffs had complained about the Connecticut rule four years before and could have sued at any time in the interim; the Texas law had not been enacted until September 1, 1975. The Connecticut ballots had already been printed; the Texas ballots had not been. There was no time left for either candidate to demonstrate support by circulating petitions. But McCarthy had qualified for the ballot in many other states, and Justice Powell assumed that he had as much support in Texas as elsewhere.

3. Reliance. More commonly, laches is about events alleged to be too far in the past. The claim of prejudice is different from that in the emergency relief cases, and if the claim is barred, permanent relief is barred along with preliminary relief.

The most obvious form of prejudice is detrimental reliance on the lack of any legal challenge to one's conduct. The country club in *Geddes*, in section 11.C, could have argued laches. But estoppel fit better; plaintiffs may not have delayed unduly after the golf balls began landing on their property.

4. Lost evidence. The other common form of prejudice is lost evidence. In Gull Airborne Instruments, Inc. v. Weinberger, 694 F.2d 838 (D.C. Cir. 1982), an unsuccessful bidder on a government contract challenged the eligibility of the successful bidder. Plaintiff filed suit only after 40 months of unsuccessfully pursuing administrative remedies. In the meantime, the contracting officer had died. The district court dismissed for laches; the court of appeals reversed. The court of appeals thought the written record should sufficiently document the reasons for the contracting officer's decision. A written record is better than a witness for some things. But what about explaining the contracting officer's exercise of discretionary judgment? Wasn't the government prejudiced despite having the written record?

Would the contracting officer's death have been sufficient prejudice if plaintiff had delayed suit for five years for no good reason? What if plaintiff had delayed for six months, for no reason except that it took plaintiff's lawyers that long to get around to drafting the complaint, and the contracting officer dropped dead a week before his deposition? What if plaintiff's lawyers got to the complaint in only two months, but during those two months the government had foreseeably incurred $10 million in liability to the successful bidder? Doesn't laches inevitably require the court to balance the reasonableness of the delay against the severity of the prejudice?

5. Third parties? In election cases, the public can suffer when election laws are changed at the last minute. In *Arizona Libertarian Party*, candidates and others had been collecting signatures in reliance on the new rules. They too would face prejudice if the court changed the rules in the middle of the election season.

In *Gull Airborne*, the successful bidder had performed so slowly that nothing had been delivered to the government by the time plaintiff filed suit, and the court of appeals believed that the government had incurred no liability either in restitution or on the contract. Assuming that's right, doesn't it just transfer the reliance loss from the government to the successful bidder? Should this harm to a third party count in the balance?

6. Speculating at defendant's expense. Another form of prejudice is a plaintiff who awaits the outcome of uncertain events, leaving the risk of loss on the defendant, but sues to capture all the gains if things go well. The more volatile the value of the matter in dispute, the sooner any claim will be barred. One classic citation is Twin-Lick Oil Co. v. Marbury, 91 U.S. 587 (1875), an early case involving oil wells:

> Property worth thousands to-day is worth nothing to-morrow; and that which would to-day sell for a thousand dollars as its fair value, may, by the natural changes of a week or the energy and courage of desperate enterprise, in the same time be made to yield that much every day. The injustice, therefore, is obvious, of permitting one holding the right to assert an ownership in such property to voluntarily await the event, and then decide, when the danger which is over has been at the risk of another, to come in and share the profit.

Id. at 592-593.

For a more prosaic example, see Fitzgerald v. O'Connell, 386 A.2d 1384 (R.I. 1978), granting specific performance of a contract to sell an undeveloped residential lot in Newport. The lot increased in value from $500 to $2,800 over a ten-year period, but for much of the ten years, plaintiff's delay was excused by defendant's inability to perform. The court thought the appreciation in the possibly unexcused period was unremarkable.

A less conventional example came out of the infamous presidential election of 2000, between Republican George W. Bush and Democrat Al Gore, which culminated in an aborted recount in Florida. The better-known part of that controversy involved disputes over ambiguously marked punch-card ballots. But there was also a second issue. Each county designed its own ballot, and in most counties, the names of presidential candidates extended over two pages. Palm Beach County listed presidential candidates on two facing pages, with arrows pointing toward holes between the two pages where a voter could punch out her choice of candidate. The arrows did not line up well and many voters appeared to vote for a candidate other than their real choice. Most prominently, many elderly Jewish voters voted for minor party candidate Pat Buchanan, an extremely conservative critic of Israel and "the Jewish lobby."

After the election, Gore supporters sued to have the election redone in the county because of the confusing ballot. The courts refused, finding that the ballot substantially complied with Florida law. That explanation was questionable as a matter of substantive election law, but a better explanation would have been laches: The ballot was available for public inspection before the election, and no one objected then. Allowing a do-over after the election would have given litigants an option: If we win, we win, but if we lose, we get a do-over.

Another form of prejudice was that a do-over would not have been the same as the original election. Everyone would know that the national results now hung on the

Palm Beach revote. There were thousands more voters who voted for minor party candidates than the difference between Bush and Gore. Those voters could change their votes during a revote. Voters who had not voted the first time could turn out the second time, unless the court barred them from voting. For a fuller description of the Florida debacle, see Richard L. Hasen, *The Voting Wars* 11-40 (Yale Univ. Press 2012).

The Supreme Court may have limited this doctrine in Petrella v. Metro-Goldwyn-Mayer, Inc., 134 S. Ct. 1962 (2014), a dispute over copyright in a movie, more fully described in the next set of notes. There was evidence that plaintiff delayed filing suit because the movie did not make any money until a remake was re-released in 2005. MGM attempted to portray this delay as plaintiff speculating at its expense; it had taken all the risk and invested large sums to make the new version. But the Court thought there was nothing untoward in waiting to see if the harms from infringement would justify the cost of litigation.

7. Unreasonable delay. The other element of laches is unreasonable delay. This is partly a function of how much time has passed, and partly a function of the reasons for the delay. Perhaps the most common reason is that plaintiff didn't know she had a claim. If she didn't know and had no reason to know, delay is not unreasonable. If defendant is a fiduciary in whom plaintiff reposed trust and confidence, plaintiff has no duty of inquiry until something happens that ought to arouse her suspicions. But many unsophisticated plaintiffs lose their claims because they aren't sufficiently diligent.

In Wanlass v. General Electric Co., 148 F.3d 1334 (Fed. Cir. 1998), plaintiff claimed not to have known that one of GE's electric motors infringed his patent. The majority said that GE's sales and advertising of the motor were open and notorious, that plaintiff could have easily checked for infringement, and that his ignorance of his claim was not excusable. The dissenter thought the court had placed on small inventors an unreasonable duty to police a crowded marketplace; there were many competing motors, and he had inspected earlier GE models and found them non-infringing. If plaintiff knows or should know the facts, further delay is unexcused whether or not he knows the law or figures out the consequences of putting law and facts together.

Courts have also said that poverty or inability to find a lawyer does not justify delay. "[P]overty, by itself, is never an excuse for laches purposes," although it is a factor to be considered when there is some other "legally cognizable excuse." Hall v. Aqua Queen Manufacturing, Inc., 93 F.3d 1548, 1554 (Fed. Cir. 1996). Similar cases are collected in Artrip v. Ball Corp., 2014 WL 7336212, *4 (W.D. Va. 2014).

NOTES ON THE RELATION BETWEEN LACHES AND STATUTES OF LIMITATIONS

1. Statutes of limitations. The conventional statute of limitations, taken up in section 11.E, creates a fixed time in which suit must be filed. Time begins to run when the cause of action accrues, and the suit is barred when time runs out. It is possible to precisely identify the very last day on which suit can be filed. There are defenses, exceptions, and arguments about how to count that make statutes of limitations much less precise than this simple description suggests. But limitations analysis always begins, and often ends, with a fixed period that runs from the day the cause of action accrues.

2. The origins of laches. Laches is quite different from statutes of limitations, and it is important to know the relationship between the two rules. The chancellors originally took the position that statutes of limitations applied only to actions at law.

Laches was the equitable substitute for statutes of limitations, and the sole time limit on suits in equity. Thus, it was possible for suits in equity to be filed decades after the events giving rise to the claim if plaintiff's delay was excused or defendant could not show prejudice. That is still the rule in actions subject only to laches, but there are fewer and fewer of those. Breach of trust was the most important example, but most states now apply statutes of limitations to claims for breach of trust.

A modern example is Mailloux v. Town of Londonderry, 864 A.2d 335, 341-342 (N.H. 2004), an environmental cleanup case. Defendant was the town, which had acquired a junkyard when the owner failed to pay taxes; as the quantity of junk grew, it had covered three acres of plaintiff's adjoining property. The case is rather dubious on its facts. Plaintiff had known the junkyard was encroaching in 1988, although the problem was small at that time. He sent the junkyard's owner a letter asking him to remove all encroachments, but he didn't check on compliance until he prepared to sell his property in 2002. The court said it was reasonable not to have checked, apparently because the property was somewhat inaccessible, and that the town was not prejudiced by the 14-year delay in filing suit, although the extent of the problem had grown substantially in the meantime.

3. Integrating laches and limitations. When an equitable claim is subject to a statute of limitations, laches is irrelevant unless it bars the claim before the limitations period expires, as in *Arizona Libertarian Party*. The Supreme Court's most important statement on this issue is Petrella v. Metro-Goldwyn-Mayer, Inc., 134 S. Ct. 1962 (2014), a copyright suit over the movie *Raging Bull*. MGM acquired the rights to the screenplay from the author, Frank Petrella, in 1976. The original copyright expired in 1991, but it could be renewed for an additional 67 years. And under a curious provision of the Copyright Act, the renewal rights belonged to Petrella's heirs, notwithstanding Petrella's attempt to assign those rights to MGM.

Paula Petrella, the heir, renewed the copyright and notified MGM of her claim in 1991, but she did not file suit until 2009. The statute of limitations was three years, running separately from each act of infringement. Petrella sought MGM's profits from sales in 2006 and later, and an injunction against further distribution of the movie. The Ninth Circuit held that the entire claim, and all remedies, were barred by laches. 695 F.3d 946 (9th Cir. 2012). The Supreme Court reversed.

The opinion says many things, some with full explanations and some without. By barring all remedies for sales prior to 2006, the three-year statute of limitations fully protected most of MGM's alleged reliance. For sales in 2006 and after, MGM would get credit for its contributions to making and promoting the movie, citing Sheldon v. MGM, reprinted in Section 8.B.2. Laches cannot be applied to bar a suit for legal remedies filed within the period of a congressionally enacted statute of limitations; this statement is quite general but perhaps not quite absolute and universal. But estoppel might bar legal remedies within the statute of limitations if a plaintiff intentionally misleads a potential defendant into thinking there will be no lawsuit and defendant detrimentally relies.

And laches might completely bar some or all equitable remedies in extraordinary circumstances. The Court cited two examples from the lower courts, each involving a demand for destruction of valuable tangible property created while plaintiff delayed—books published; houses built, sold, and occupied. More routinely, MGM's reliance could also be taken into account in crafting injunctive relief and in calculating MGM's profits from the infringement; the Court treated restitution of profits as equitable for this purpose. But the lower courts should closely examine MGM's alleged reliance, and among other things, take account of the protection MGM might have received by suing Petrella for a declaratory judgment.

4. The Federal Circuit foiled again. The Federal Circuit convened en banc to decide whether *Petrella* required a change in its rule that laches can bar a claim to damages for patent infringement before the six-year limitations period has run. And it decided, 6-5, that no change was required. SCA Hygiene Products Aktiebolag SCA Personal Care, Inc. v. First Quality Baby Products, LLC, 807 F.3d 1311 (Fed. Cir. 2015). The Supreme Court reversed. 137 S. Ct. 954 (2017). It is hard to see any reason why laches in patent cases should be different from laches in copyright cases, and the Court rejected the argument that laches was implicitly codified in the Patent Act.

5. Preventive injunctions. Preventive injunctions in short-lived disputes raise problems that statutes of limitations cannot handle. It would be crazy to say that the claim in *Arizona Libertarian Party* could be filed any time up to three years after the election, or even three years after the statutory amendment. If the injunction is to prevent the wrong from happening, plaintiff has to seek the injunction far enough in advance to make prevention possible, and general statutes of limitations are irrelevant. Because the injunction is an equitable remedy, nothing in *Petrella* is at odds with *Arizona Libertarian Party*.

6. A Supreme Court example. The Court unanimously held that plaintiffs had waited too long to challenge a gerrymander in time for the 2018 election. Benisek v. Lamone, 138 S. Ct. 1942 (2018). The allegedly gerrymandered districts were drawn in 2011; the complaint was filed in 2016. A federal statute required that a three-judge court be assembled; then there were discovery disputes; and of course the law was complex and unsettled. The plaintiffs said a preliminary injunction should be issued by August 18, 2017 to allow time for drawing new districts; the three-judge court denied relief on multiple grounds on August 24, commenting that each member of the panel had made the case a priority. It held that plaintiffs had not shown probable success on the merits, and it stayed further proceedings pending decision in another gerrymandering case in the Supreme Court.

The Supreme Court thought it entirely reasonable to have stayed proceedings to wait for the other case. But its opinion affirming the lower court emphasized that plaintiffs had waited too long. It said that "a party requesting a preliminary injunction must generally show reasonable diligence," citing Fishman v. Schaffer in note 2 on laches above. The Court did not invoke laches, although that seems clearly to be what it meant. Instead, invoking its version of the traditional four-part test for preliminary injunctions from Winter v. Natural Resources Defense Council in section 5.B.1, the Court said that plaintiffs' delay counted against them in the balance of the equities, and that the public interest in orderly elections counted against them. Denying relief with respect to 2018 does not necessarily deny relief with respect to 2020.

7. Reparative injunctions. Any time defendant completes a threatened wrong, plaintiff may seek a reparative injunction to undo the wrong. Sometimes that would be impractical, but often it is not impractical. Should it be irrelevant whether plaintiff unreasonably delayed suit? If delay creates problems that are prejudicial but not insuperable, doesn't it matter who is responsible for the delay? Laches speaks directly to those concerns; mootness, impracticality, and statutes of limitations do not.

8. Continuing violations. Some cases involve not a single wrong but continuing violations over time, raising knotty issues at the intersection of laches and statutes of limitations. Consider NAACP v. NAACP Legal Defense & Educational Fund, Inc., 753 F.2d 131 (D.C. Cir. 1985). The NAACP Legal Defense and Educational Fund continues to use the initials of the National Association for the Advancement of Colored People, even though the two organizations have been completely separate since 1957. If the Fund's use of those initials is trademark infringement, it was infringement in 1957, and in 1982 when the Association filed suit, and it would still be infringement in 2018. To use the initials in 1982 was a new violation, on which the statute of limitations had just begun to run. See Klehr v. A.O. Smith Corp., the next principal case. If delay is measured from each violation, the Fund's reliance on the status quo will never be protected.

The court held the NAACP barred by laches. It had known about the continuing violation for years and had not filed suit, and meanwhile the Fund had built up substantial public recognition of its name. But *Petrella* says that laches applies only to equitable remedies. Would it make any sense to say that the NAACP can never get an injunction because of laches, but it can get damages for all future use of the initials? To avoid that result, the explanation might have to be that estoppel bars the damage claims. Many cases find estoppel from silence when there was a duty to speak. *Petrella* describes estoppel in terms of "intentionally misleading representations," but it does not explicitly require such statements as the only way to show estoppel.

The NAACP might have difficulty proving actual damages. But the Lanham Act also authorizes courts to award "such sum as the court shall find to be just," without regard either to plaintiff's actual damages or defendant's profits. 15 U.S.C. §1117(a). And the Court has held that a similar provision in the Copyright Act creates a legal remedy, triable to a jury. Feltner v. Columbia Pictures Television, 523 U.S. 340 (1998). Can defendant argue to the jury that plaintiff's long delay makes any award unjust?

E.   STATUTES OF LIMITATIONS

1.   *Continuing Violations*

KLEHR v. A.O. SMITH CORP.
521 U.S. 179 (1997)

Justice BREYER delivered the opinion of the Court. . . .

I

The Racketeer Influenced and Corrupt Organizations Act (RICO) . . . makes it a crime "to conduct" an "enterprise's affairs through a pattern of racketeering activity." 18 U.S.C. §1962(c). The phrase "racketeering activity" is a term of art defined in terms of activity that violates other laws, including more than 50 specifically mentioned federal statutes . . . . §1961(1). The word "pattern" is also a term of art defined to require "at least two acts of racketeering activity, . . . the last of which occurred within ten years . . . after the commission of a prior act of racketeering activity." §1961(5).

. . . [C]ivil RICO permits "[a]ny person injured in his business or property by reason of a violation" of RICO's criminal provisions to recover treble damages and attorney's fees. §1964(c). Marvin and Mary Klehr, the petitioners here, are dairy farmers. They filed this civil RICO action on August 27, 1993, claiming that [respondents] (whom we shall simply call "Harvestore"), had committed several acts of mail and wire fraud, thereby violating RICO and causing them injury. Their injury, they said, began in 1974, when Harvestore sold them a special "Harvestore" brand silo, which they used for storing cattle feed. The Klehrs alleged that they bought the silo in reliance on Harvestore's representations, made through advertisements and a local dealer, that the silo would limit the amount of oxygen in contact with the silage, thus preventing moldy and fermented feed, and thereby producing healthier cows, more milk, and higher profits. The representations, they claim, were false; the silo did not keep oxygen away from the feed, the feed became moldy and fermented, the cows ate the bad feed, and milk production and profits went down. They add that Harvestore committed other acts—consisting primarily of additional representations made to them and to others and sales made to others—over a period of many years after 1974.

Harvestore, pointing out that the Klehrs had filed suit almost 20 years after they had bought the silo, moved to dismiss the lawsuit on the ground that the limitations period had long since run. [RICO has no statute of limitations, but the Court had earlier held it subject to the four-year statute in the Clayton Antitrust Act.] The Klehrs could not file suit, Harvestore said, unless their claim had accrued within the four years prior to filing, i.e., after August 1989, or unless some special legal doctrine nonetheless tolled the running of the limitations period or estopped Harvestore from asserting a statute of limitations defense.

The Klehrs responded by producing evidentiary material designed to support a legal justification for the late filing. Essentially they claimed that Harvestore had covered up its fraud—preventing them from noticing the silo's malfunction—for example, by means of an unloading device that hid the mold by chopping up the feed instantly as it emerged; through continued dealer misrepresentations; with advertisements that tried to convince farmers that warm, brown, molasses-smelling feed was not fermented feed, but good feed; and even by hanging on the silo itself a plaque that said:

> "DANGER
> DO NOT ENTER
> NOT ENOUGH OXYGEN
> TO SUPPORT LIFE"

Not until 1991, say the Klehrs, did they become sufficiently suspicious to investigate the silo, at which time, by opening the silo wall and chopping through the feed with an ice chisel, they discovered "mold hanging all over the silage.". . .

II

A

We shall first discuss the Third Circuit's accrual rule—the "last predicate act" rule—for it is the only accrual rule that can help the Klehrs. . . . For purposes of assessing the rule's lawfulness, we assume, as do the Klehrs, that this rule means that as long as Harvestore committed one predicate act within the limitations period (i.e., the four years preceding suit), the Klehrs can recover, not just for any added harm caused them by that late-committed act, but for all the harm caused them by all the acts that make up the total "pattern." We also assume that they can show at least one such late-committed act. Finally, we note that the point of difference between the Third Circuit and the other Circuits has nothing to do with the plaintiff's state of mind or knowledge. It concerns only the accrual consequences of a late-committed act. . . .

[T]he Third Circuit's rule is not a proper interpretation of the law. . . . Because a series of predicate acts (including acts occurring at up to 10-year intervals) can continue indefinitely, such an interpretation, in principle, lengthens the limitations period dramatically. It thereby conflicts with a basic objective — repose — that underlies limitations periods. Indeed, the rule would permit plaintiffs who know of the defendant's pattern of activity simply to wait, "sleeping on their rights," as the pattern continues and treble damages accumulate, perhaps bringing suit only long after the "memories of witnesses have faded or evidence is lost," Wilson v. Garcia, 471 U.S. 261, 271 (1985). . . .

Second, the Third Circuit rule is inconsistent with the ordinary Clayton Act rule, applicable in private antitrust treble damages actions, under which "a cause of action accrues and the statute begins to run when a defendant commits an act that injures a plaintiff's business." Zenith Radio Corp. v. Hazeltine Research, Inc., 401 U.S. 321, 338 (1971). . . .

The Clayton Act helps here because it makes clear precisely where, and how, the Third Circuit's rule goes too far. Antitrust law provides that, in the case of a "continuing violation," say, a price-fixing conspiracy that brings about a series of unlawfully high priced sales over a period of years, "each overt act that is part of the violation and that injures the plaintiff," e.g., each sale to the plaintiff, "starts the statutory period running again, regardless of the plaintiff's knowledge of the alleged illegality at much earlier times." 2 Phillip Areeda & Herbert Hovenkamp, *Antitrust Law* ¶338b at 145 (Aspen, rev. ed. 1995). But the commission of a separate new overt act generally does not permit the plaintiff to recover for the injury caused by old overt acts outside the limitations period.

Similarly, some Circuits have adopted a "separate accrual" rule in civil RICO cases, under which the commission of a separable, new predicate act within a 4-year limitations period permits a plaintiff to recover for the additional damages caused by that act. But, as in the antitrust cases, the plaintiff cannot use an independent, new predicate act as a bootstrap to recover for injuries caused by other earlier predicate acts that took place outside the limitations period. Thus, the Klehrs may point to new predicate acts that took place after August 1989, such as sales to other farmers or the printing of new Harvestore advertisements. But that fact does not help them, for . . . they have not shown how any new act could have caused them harm over and above the harm that the earlier acts caused. Nor can the presence of the new act help them recover for the injuries caused by pre-1989 acts . . . .

[The Court declined to review the lower courts' holding that even under the most generous version of the discovery rule, the Klehrs reasonably should have discovered their claim before 1989 and that no jury could find otherwise. The Klehrs also claimed that Harvestore had fraudulently concealed their cause of action. The Court held that to invoke that exception to the statute of limitations, the Klehrs must have exercised reasonable diligence; it declined to review the lower courts' holding that as a matter of law, they had not done so. The discovery rule and fraudulent concealment are taken up in the next two principal cases.]

NOTES ON CONTINUING VIOLATIONS

1. Multiple theories for avoiding statutes of limitations. The Klehrs offered three independent theories in their attempt to escape the statute of limitations: continuing violation, the discovery rule, and fraudulent concealment. Each is sometimes discussed in terms of defining when the cause of action accrues and sometimes in terms of "tolling" — suspending the running of — the statute of limitations on a cause of action that has already accrued. This alternative vocabulary occasionally creates confusion, but the two ways of describing the rules do not appear to generate different results.

2. Continuing violations and RICO. *Klehr* is a good statement of continuing violation doctrine, a doctrine that has caused a surprising amount of confusion in the lower courts. But the Klehrs' claim of continuing violation was unusually weak, and really an artifact of RICO. The allegedly fraudulent sale of the silo was a one-time event; it is only the statutory element of a pattern of violations that made the Klehrs' continuing violation claim even arguable.

3. More typical continuing violations. In more conventional cases, the violation is a continuing course of conduct. Perhaps the classic example is Hanover Shoe, Inc. v. United Shoe Machinery Corp., 392 U.S. 481, 502 n.15 (1968). Hanover filed suit in 1955, alleging that United's restrictive system of distributing shoe machinery violated the antitrust laws. United argued that the claim was barred by limitations because it had applied the challenged policy to Hanover since 1912. Should United be able to continue its illegal conduct forever because no one challenged it during World War I? Should Hanover be able to collect 40 years of damages with prejudgment interest? The Court thought it obvious that Hanover could sue, but that it could recover only those damages suffered within the period of limitations.

Hanover Shoe noted not only that defendant continuously violated the antitrust laws, but also that these violations "inflicted continuing and accumulating harm." *Id.* There are three distinct requirements tucked into that formulation: The violation must continue, the harm must continue, and the continuing violation must cause the continuing harm.

4. "Discrete acts." The logic of the continuing-violation cases is that each new violation triggers a new limitations period. What the Court calls the "separate accrual rule" in *Klehr* is often called the "discrete acts" rule, and sometimes called the day-by-day rule, because if the violation is continual and not just intermittent, a new claim accrues daily. Emphasizing many accruals of separate causes of action clarifies the theory but exaggerates the problem of calculating damages. A single cut-off date is established by counting back from the day plaintiff filed suit. In *Klehr*, that cut-off date was August 27, 1989. The parties had to allocate all damages to violations from the period before that date or violations from the period after that date, but they did not have to allocate day by day within the two periods.

5. Cumulative violations. The Third Circuit's last-predicate-act rule in *Klehr* was the RICO version of an alternative understanding: that the statute of limitations does not begin to run on any part of a continuing violation until the violation ends. The Court flatly rejects this idea in *Klehr*, and it would be ridiculous in *Hanover Shoe*. But even the Supreme Court has accepted it on facts that we will call "cumulative violations."

a. Hostile environment claims. In National Railroad Passenger Corp. v. Morgan, 536 U.S. 101 (2002), plaintiff offered evidence of many incidents of racial discrimination and harassment throughout his five years with the railroad. The court of appeals held that plaintiff could recover for all the incidents, because a jury could find that they were all closely related, involving the same individual wrongdoers and the same pattern of harassing conduct.

The Supreme Court reversed only in part. With respect to "discrete" discriminatory acts, the Court unanimously applied the separate-accrual rule. The claim for each discriminatory act was barred 300 days after it occurred. But, the Court said, "Hostile environment claims are different in kind from discrete acts. . . . A hostile work environment claim is composed of a series of separate acts that collectively constitute one 'unlawful employment practice.'" *Id.* at 116-117. As long as the hostile acts that created the hostile environment are sufficiently related, plaintiff may recover for the entire hostile environment, including the part that happened more than 300 days before plaintiff filed. But such claims may be barred by laches if plaintiff delays unreasonably and defendant is prejudiced. Four dissenters argued that the acts creating the hostile environment should also be divided into those that occurred within and without the 300-day limit.

The kind of violation illustrated by the hostile environment claim does not yet have an accepted name for limitations purposes. Some judges are saying that these, and only these, are continuing violations, but that phrase has long been used to also describe violations with a long series of discrete acts. For now, cumulative violation will have to do.

The Court repeatedly distinguished the two kinds of violations in Petrella v. Metro-Goldwyn-Mayer, Inc., 134 S. Ct. 1962 (2014). With respect to the many acts of alleged copyright infringement in that case, the Court variously referred to "the separate-accrual rule," "[s]eparately accruing harm," "discrete acts, each independently actionable," and "separately accruing wrongs." With respect to the cumulative violations illustrated by *Morgan*, it variously referred to "harm from past violations that are continuing," "conduct cumulative in effect," and "hostile-work-environment claims, cumulative in effect and extending over a long time." *Id.* at 1969-1970 & 1975, nn.6-7, n.16. The Court acknowledged that laches could bar claims within the period of limitations applicable to the latter category, conduct cumulative in effect. But laches could not bar legal relief for separate wrongs within the statute of limitations.

b. Drawing the line. The line between discrete-acts continuing violations and cumulative violations is explored in Rodrigue v. Olin Employees Credit Union, 406 F.3d 434, 440-448 (7th Cir. 2005). Over a period of seven years, the credit union paid 269 insurance reimbursement checks on endorsements forged by an embezzler in Dr. Rodrigue's office. The embezzler went to prison; the doctor sued the credit union. Applying Illinois law, the court held that each check was a discrete act with its own three-year limitations period; the embezzlement scheme was not a single cumulative violation. Illinois had found cumulative violations in a wife's claim for intentional infliction of emotional distress based on 11 years of emotional abuse by her ex-husband, Feltmeier v. Feltmeier, 798 N.E.2d 75 (Ill. 2003), and in a medical malpractice case where plaintiff claimed that "a continuous course of negligent treatment" had caused her injury. Cunningham v. Huffman, 609 N.E.2d 321, 326 (Ill. 1993). But in Belleville Toyota, Inc. v. Toyota Motor Sales U.S.A., Inc., 770 N.E.2d 177 (Ill. 2002), where a car dealer complained that Toyota arbitrarily manipulated its system for allocating cars to dealers and discriminated against the plaintiff, the court said that each delivery of new cars triggered a new limitations period. The Seventh Circuit had no difficulty concluding that each embezzled check from Rodrigue's office was more like a discrete delivery of cars than like a course of medical treatment or emotional abuse.

6. Pay discrimination. Another good example of a discrete-acts continuing violation is pay discrimination, where victims get another discriminatory check every pay period. But the Court has not always seen it that way.

a. *Bazemore*. In Bazemore v. Friday, 478 U.S. 385 (1986), black employees sued for pay discrimination. Defendant argued that for years the employees had gotten raises greater than or equal to those of whites. Those raises had been added to a base of pay rates set before the civil rights laws, when black employees were paid much less than white employees, and any remaining difference in pay was the residual consequence of that old discrimination. The Supreme Court unanimously disagreed; it held that each paycheck was a new violation, and that plaintiffs could sue for all pay periods within the limitations period.

b. *Ledbetter.* The Supreme Court sharply limited *Bazemore* in Ledbetter v. Goodyear Tire & Rubber Co., 550 U.S. 618 (2007). In plaintiff's job category, Goodyear conducted annual performance reviews and then set salaries on the basis of merit. Plaintiff proved that this process had long discriminated against women, with the result that her pay was now far lower than that of men with similar experience doing the same work. But she did not prove any discrimination in the decisions setting the most recent pay raises. The Court held that each "pay-setting decision" was a "discrete act," and if discriminatory, a discrete violation. *Id.* at 621. Subsequent unequal paychecks were not new discriminatory acts, but merely the present consequence of past discriminatory decisions.

The Court distinguished *Bazemore* as a case where the employer maintained "a discriminatory pay structure." *Id.* at 637. What does that mean? Maybe it is the number of victims, or the openness of the discrimination, that makes a pay "structure" discriminatory. There is no way to tell from the opinion; the distinction is wholly unexplained.

Justice Ginsburg dissented for four. She feared that the Court had insulated systemic pay discrimination. Suppose that each year, the men get a slightly larger raise than Ledbetter. In year 1, the pay difference would be small, and the reasons for the difference might be unclear. If Ledbetter does not sue, that decision becomes insulated from judicial review. If she sues and loses for lack of proof, the finding of no discrimination in year 1 becomes binding. Either way, the events of year 1 are legally insulated when she sues over a similar small disparity in year 2. Even if her pay eventually becomes egregiously less than that of similarly situated men, there might never be a time when she can successfully sue.

c. Legislative correction. Congress overruled *Ledbetter* with the Lilly Ledbetter Fair Pay Act of 2009, which amended the principal federal employment discrimination statues to provide that "with respect to discrimination in compensation," a violation occurs "each time wages, benefits, or other compensation is paid." See, e.g., 42 U.S.C.A. §2000e-5(e)(3)(A). A separate two-year limit on back pay, 42 U.S.C. §2000e-5(e)(3)(B), would still apply. The curious history of this provision—of how one key remedy came to have a time limit independent of the statute of limitations—is reviewed in Douglas Laycock, *Continuing Violations, Disparate Impact in Compensation, and Other Title VII Issues*, 49 L. & Contemp. Probs. 53, 57 (Autumn 1986).

d. Claims of disparate impact. In Lewis v. City of Chicago, 560 U.S. 205 (2010), plaintiffs challenged a discriminatory civil-service exam. The court of appeals held that the statute of limitations ran from when the test results were announced, not from when the results were later applied to individual hiring decisions. 528 F.3d 488 (7th Cir. 2008). The Supreme Court unanimously reversed. In *Ledbetter* and similar cases, plaintiffs had alleged disparate treatment—that the employer intentionally treated employees differently on the basis of race or sex. The violation occurred when the employer acted with the prohibited intent, and on the Court's view, that intent existed only when the discriminatory decisions were first made, and not when they were repeatedly implemented. But *Lewis* was a disparate impact claim, challenging the unjustified discriminatory effects of the test. When Congress belatedly codified disparate impact liability, it said that plaintiff proves an unlawful employment practice by showing that an employer "uses" an employment practice that has disparate impact on a protected minority group. And the city "uses" its practice every time it makes new hires based on the test.

7. Constructive discharge. If an employer discriminates by subjecting an employee to intolerable working conditions, and the employee resigns, the resignation is treated as a constructive discharge for which the employee can sue. The Supreme Court held that the very short statute of limitations (even shorter for federal employees) runs from the date the employee gives notice of his resignation, and not from the last discriminatory act in the series of acts that provoked the resignation. Green v. Brennan, 136 S. Ct. 1769 (2016). The Court invoked the general rule that limitations begins to run when the plaintiff "can file suit and obtain relief." *Id.* at 1776. That requires that all events essential to the cause of action have happened. Plaintiff could not sue for constructive discharge until he actually resigned; it was not enough that he had adequate grounds to resign.

8. Continuing duties. In the absence of repeated wrongful acts, plaintiff can sometimes succeed by showing a continuing duty to perform some act that was never done. A good example is Russo Farms, Inc. v. Vineland Board of Education, 675 A.2d 1077 (N.J. 1996). Improper siting and construction of a school building caused flooding on plaintiff's land; plaintiff sued the school board for maintaining a nuisance and sued the architect for negligence. The nuisance claim alleged a continuing violation, because if the nuisance could be abated, state law imposed a continuing duty to do so. The negligence claim alleged only continuing harm from a one-time violation; the architect had completed his work and had no continuing duty at the site. "For there to be a continuing tort there must be a continuing duty." *Id.* at 1091.

The Employee Retirement Income Security Act provides that suits against plan administrators for breach of fiduciary duty must be filed within six years of "the last action which constituted a part of the breach," or "in the case of an omission the latest date on which the fiduciary could have cured the breach[.]" 29 U.S.C. §1113(1). In Tibble v. Edison International, 135 S. Ct. 1823 (2015), employer included in its retirement plan six retail mutual funds, with high fees charged to employees, when it could easily have included institutional versions of the same funds with much lower fees. But the employees sued more than six years after some of the funds were selected. The Court noted that trustees have a duty to periodically review all of a trust's investments for appropriateness; it unanimously concluded that the statute ran from the last breach of that duty to review.

9. Continuing injuries are not enough. Many wrongs inflict continuing harm, but they are not continuing violations because the wrong is finished immediately. The sale of the Klehrs' silo is an example (unless RICO changes something); the ordinary personal injury case is a simpler example. A claim for negligent driving accrues when defendant's negligence first causes injury, even if plaintiff's damages continue to accrue for years.

10. The Establishment Clause. In Tearpock-Martini v. Borough of Shickshinny, 756 F.3d 232 (3d Cir. 2014), the borough erected a directional sign advertising and pointing to a Baptist church. The sign was in the public right of way in front of plaintiff's residence, and she claimed that the sign violated the Establishment Clause. The claim was eventually rejected on the merits. 196 F. Supp. 3d 457 (M.D. Penn. 2016). But our focus is on Pennsylvania's two-year statute of limitations, which applied by analogy (see the next set of notes).

Plaintiff sued more than two years after the sign was installed. The Third Circuit held that the continued presence of the sign was not a continuing violation, but merely a continuing effect of the only alleged violation, which occurred when the sign was installed. This seems clearly wrong, and in a way that illuminates the distinction. If there were a constitutional violation, it was not a small bit of construction, but the borough's endorsement of the church. And if the sign were an unconstitutional endorsement, it was such an endorsement every day the sign remained. There is a decision going the other way in Gonzales v. North Township, 800 F. Supp. 676 (N.D. Ind. 1992), *rev'd on other grounds*, 4 F.3d 1412 (7th Cir. 1993), and scores of cases that should have come out the other way if the Third Circuit were right.

Recognizing what it called "the long standing apparent exemption of Establishment Clause claims" from statutes of limitations, the court held that it would be "inconsistent with federal law or policy" to apply Pennsylvania's statute of limitations to the claim. *Tearpock-Martini*, 756 F.3d at 239. The traditional rationales for limitations periods had "no persuasive force in this context," because plaintiff challenged "a still-existing monument that communicates anew an allegedly unconstitutional endorsement of religion by the government each time it is viewed." *Id.* And that is exactly why the court should have said that plaintiff had alleged a continuing violation.

11. Laches and estoppel. Why aren't suits to enjoin continuing violations barred by laches or estoppel? Although the point is rarely articulated, courts implicitly distinguish legitimate and illegitimate reliance. Defendants could not acquire a right to monopolize the shoe machinery industry, or to discriminate against black workers, in the way that the Legal Defense Fund could acquire the right to use the initials of the NAACP, or defendant in Whitlock v. Hilander Foods could acquire the right to have its footings extend into plaintiff's property. Can you articulate the basis for such distinctions? Or do we just have to know it when we see it? One key difference is the role of consent: Property owners commonly authorize the use of a trademark or an encroachment on land. No one authorizes discrimination or monopolies, although a plaintiff could presumably agree not to sue about it.

NOTES ON LIMITATIONS OF FEDERAL CLAIMS

1. Federal statutes of limitation—and their absence. RICO has no statute of limitations; the Court had to choose one. It chose the antitrust laws, because of certain modest similarities between the statutes. Congress does enact statutes of limitations, but frequent congressional enactment of claims with no stated limitations period has been far more visible. The courts have always rejected the implication that there is no limitations period, and the results have been chaotic.

2. Borrowing the analogous state statute. For a long time, the dominant solution was to apply the state statute of limitations for the most nearly analogous state-law claim. This practice produced huge amounts of wasted litigation; each federal circuit had to decide, for each state in the circuit, which statute of limitations was most nearly analogous to each claim that could be brought under each of the many statutes without an express limitations period.

3. Judicial efforts to simplify. Beginning in the mid-1980s, the Supreme Court tried to impose an easily applied nationwide rule for each federal statute, abandoning the search for the particular state limitations period most analogous to the facts of the particular federal claim. A good example is Owens v. Okure, 488 U.S. 235 (1989), reaffirming the choice of the personal injury statute of limitations for §1983 actions, and choosing the general or residual statute in states that have special statutes of limitations for certain intentional torts. This approach has slowly reduced and simplified the litigation.

In another line of cases, the Court has looked to analogous federal statutes of limitations that might apply nationwide. RICO's choice of the antitrust statute is an example. But the Court has also said that reference to the analogous state statute of limitations remains the norm, and that reference to an analogous federal statute of limitations is exceptional. North Star Steel Co. v. Thomas, 515 U.S. 29 (1995).

4. The congressional effort to simplify. Congress finally addressed the problem prospectively, providing a four-year statute of limitations for all civil actions arising under federal statutes enacted after December 1, 1990. 28 U.S.C. §1658(a). Inexplicably, Congress refused to do anything about all the federal statutes already on the books.

5. Tolling rules. Federal courts traditionally borrowed only the number of years from state statutes of limitations, applying federal law to tolling rules of the sort at issue in *Klehr.* Holmberg v. Armbrecht, 327 U.S. 392, 395-396 (1946). But more recent cases ignore *Holmberg*, arguing that it makes no sense to mix and match tolling rules from one statute with a number of years from some other statute. These cases are collected in Justice Scalia's concurring opinion in *Klehr.* 521 U.S. at 199-200. *Holmberg* has not been overruled, but it is in serious jeopardy.

6. State claims in federal court. All the discussion in these notes is about federal claims. If plaintiff sues in federal court on a state claim, all the elements of state limitations law apply. Guaranty Trust Co. v. York, 326 U.S. 99 (1945). The next principal case is an example.

2. The Discovery Rule

DEBIEC v. CABOT CORP.
352 F.3d 117 (3d Cir. 2003)

Before BECKER, RENDELL and AMBRO, Circuit Judges.

BECKER, Circuit Judge.

These personal injury and wrongful death cases . . . stem from the deaths of four people, all of whom worked at and/or lived near the defendants' beryllium plant in Reading, Pennsylvania. Each of the deaths was traceable to Chronic Beryllium Disease. [The court also refers to the disease as CBD or as berylliosis. The district court granted summary judgment for defendants, holding that the statute of limitations had run and that no reasonable jury could find that any of the plaintiffs had exercised due diligence to discover the cause of their illness.]

II. LEGAL STANDARD

A.

[I]n this diversity action we look to Pennsylvania law . . . .

Pennsylvania has a two year statute of limitations for personal injury and wrongful death actions. 42 Pa. Cons. Stat. §5524(2). The question before us is, at what point did the plaintiffs' claims accrue? Generally, a claim accrues "as soon as the right to institute and maintain a suit arises," Pocono International Raceway, Inc. v. Pocono Produce, Inc., 468 A.2d 468, 471 (Pa. 1983), which, in most tort actions, is at the moment the injury is sustained. In order to "'ameliorate the sometimes harsh effects of the statute of limitations," however, Pennsylvania courts have crafted an exception to this rule for situations in which a party, through no fault of his or her own, does not discover her injury until after the statute of limitations normally would have run. Bohus v. Beloff, 950 F.2d 919, 924 (3d Cir. 1991), quoting Cathcart v. Keene Industrial Insulation, 471 A.2d 493, 500 (Pa. Super. Ct. 1984). Latent disease cases often implicate this . . . "discovery rule," which tolls the statute. In this type of case, "the statute of limitations begins to run . . . when the plaintiff knows, or reasonably should know: (1) that he has been injured, and (2) that his injury has been caused by another party's conduct." *Cathcart*, 471 A.2d at 500. The burden is on the party claiming the benefit of the discovery rule to prove that she falls within it.

In order to take advantage of the discovery rule, a plaintiff must have exercised "due diligence" in investigating her physical condition. *Bohus*, 950 F.2d at 924. We have explained that "[t]he 'polestar' of the discovery rule is not the plaintiff's actual knowledge, but rather 'whether the knowledge was known, or through the exercise of diligence, knowable to [the] plaintiff.'" *Id.* at 925. The Pennsylvania Supreme Court has described the required diligence in this setting as follows:

> Reasonable diligence is just that, a reasonable effort to discover the cause of an injury under the facts and circumstances present in the case. . . . [T]here are few facts which diligence cannot discover, but there must be some reason to awaken inquiry and direct diligence in the channel in which it would be successful. This is what is meant by reasonable diligence.

Cochran v. GAF Corp., 666 A.2d 245, 249 (Pa. 1995). The Court stressed that "[r]easonable diligence is an objective, rather than a subjective standard. . . ." *Id.*

B. . . .

[Plaintiffs] rely on a line of Pennsylvania cases, starting with Trieschock v. Owens Corning, 511 A.2d 863 (Pa. Super. Ct. 1986), [holding] that a plaintiff cannot be charged with having more information than his doctors have about his condition. The defendants counter that *Trieschock* and its progeny are no longer good law.

[But the Third Circuit had followed *Trieschock* in *Bohus*, and in the absence of an intervening decision in the Pennsylvania Supreme Court, *Bohus* was binding on the panel.]

In . . . *Bohus* this Court held that a plaintiff's reliance on a doctor's assurances is reasonable as long as the plaintiff retains confidence in the doctor's professional abilities. In other words, a doctor's assurances that a plaintiff does not have a particular injury may toll the statute of limitations until that "point in time when a patient's own 'common sense' should lead her to conclude that it is no longer reasonable to rely on the assurances of her doctor." 950 F.2d at 930. . . .

[A] definitive diagnosis of an injury is not necessary to start the statute running; and . . . a definitive negative diagnosis may be sufficient in some cases to overcome the fact that the claimant harbored suspicions that she had a particular injury. . . .

III. APPLICATION OF THE LEGAL STANDARD

A. DEBIEC

[Mrs. Debiec lived all her life near the beryllium plant. She first experienced difficulty breathing in 1976; she died in 2000, at age 57. In 1978, her doctor diagnosed sarcoidosis, a lung disease of unknown origin. He did not change that diagnosis until after her autopsy.]

The defendants contend that the statute of limitations on Mr. Debiec's claim began to run "no later than July 22, 1992," the date of the public EPA hearing at which he spoke about his suspicion that his wife had berylliosis. . . . The suit was filed on May 29, 2001.

[Defendants] urge that by the time she visited Dr. Shuman in . . . 1980, Debiec was aware that her lung condition might be caused by exposure to an environmental pollutant, possibly beryllium. In addition, Mr. Debiec had undertaken significant research into the cause of his wife's ailment, and had received correspondence . . . informing him that beryllium was one known cause of [her symptoms]. Defendants also draw our attention to Mrs. Debiec's brother-in-law John's research paper linking sarcoidosis to berylliosis, and to Michael Debiec's speech at the EPA meeting in July 1992, in which he discussed the possible links between sarcoidosis and beryllium. Finally, the defendants rely on [a research report by the federal Agency for Toxic Substances and Disease Registry (ATSDR), known to the Debiecs], which advised that CBD could "masquerade" as sarcoidosis.

Defendants urge that this information was more than sufficient to put Debiec on notice that she had an injury for which redress might be available, and argue that Debiec simply failed to use reasonable diligence to investigate her claims. . . .

In *Cochran* [a suit against asbestos manufacturers for the wrongful death of a cancer victim], the plaintiff was told he had cancer, and was told to stop smoking, but was apparently not told that his smoking had caused his cancer. Cochran himself came to that mistaken conclusion. In the case at bar, Debiec was told she had sarcoidosis, not CBD, and that it was very unlikely that her ailment had been caused by exposure to beryllium. Cochran knew he had an ailment whose origin could be discovered, but he chose not to take the necessary steps to make this discovery. Debiec was told that the cause of her ailment was not beryllium and therefore she did not have the same incentives as Cochran to pursue further research on her condition. Therefore, while we agree that *Cochran* creates a fairly high bar for what qualifies as reasonable diligence, we do not think it dooms Debiec's case.

Debiec . . . relies heavily on Burnside v. Abbott Laboratories, 505 A.2d 973 (Pa. Super. Ct. 1985), a case [filed by women who suffered damage to their reproductive organs caused by their mothers taking a drug called DES during pregnancy. One of the plaintiffs, Ann Lynch, suspected DES and consulted a lawyer, but was told by two doctors that DES was not the cause of her problems.]

We believe that Debiec's situation more closely resembles the facts of *Burnside* than those of *Cochran*. Like Lynch in *Burnside*, Debiec's personal physician told her there was little or no reason to suspect that her condition was related to exposure to beryllium, and, like Lynch, it was family members who advised Debiec of the potential connection between her ailments and the toxic compound at issue. Indeed, it is safe to say that there was more public information available about the link between DES and Lynch's symptoms than there was linking beryllium and Debiec's symptoms. The only fact that may significantly distinguish *Burnside* from the case at bar is that Lynch sought a second medical opinion and Debiec did not. We are not, however, prepared to hold that reasonable diligence requires a plaintiff who has received a definitive diagnosis to seek a second opinion to determine the cause of her injuries. . . .

[W]hile at some point her husband and brother-in-law suspected that her condition was beryllium-related, Mrs. Debiec did not agree. . . . Mrs. Debiec told [her husband] that he was "crazy" for pursuing the idea that she may have had berylliosis. . . .

On the basis of these facts, particularly the fact that Mrs. Debiec had confidence in Dr. Shuman, who told her she did not have berylliosis . . . and who consistently diagnosed her as suffering from sarcoidosis, we conclude that reasonable minds could differ on the question whether Debiec employed reasonable diligence in pursuing the cause of her injury. Therefore, it was error for the District Court to hold, as a matter of law, that the statute of limitations had run on Debiec's claim.

B. RUSSO

Defendants argue that the statute of limitations began to run on Mary Russo's claim by April 12, 1999, the date on which Russo read a newspaper article linking the Reading beryllium plant to incidence of lung disease. The District Court agreed, holding that the fact that Russo had started to clip newspaper articles on the link between lung disease and the Reading plant meant that she suspected that her illness was beryllium-related in early 1999 and that therefore the statute of limitations had begun to run at that point. Russo urges that the statute did not begin to run until June 25, 1999, the day she received [test results] confirming that she had CBD. This suit was filed on May 24, 2001. . . .

[W]hatever suspicions Russo may have had on the basis of the articles in the *Eagle*, neither of Russo's physicians, certainly more credible and persuasive sources of medical information than the *Eagle*, endorsed her theories. Dr. Bell flatly stated that he did not believe Russo's condition was related to beryllium. Russo testified that when she raised the issue with Bell, he told her "[i]t's so long ago, Mary . . . it can't be that . . . ." Dr. Mengel, less enthusiastically perhaps, endorsed this diagnosis. Indeed, he did not alter his diagnosis until [test results], which Russo herself requested, demonstrated that she was suffering from CBD. . . .

On the basis of these negative diagnoses, we conclude that the District Court erred in ruling that reasonable minds could not disagree about whether Russo had pursued her claim with sufficient diligence.

C. REESER (EXECUTRIX OF THE ESTATE OF GENEVA BARE)

In granting summary judgment, the District Court noted that by the mid-1990s Bare had asked one of her doctors about the possibility that she had CBD, knew that she had lung disease, knew about emissions from the nearby plant, and "yet she took no further action." Reeser counters that it was not clear that Bare's condition was beryllium-related until an autopsy was performed after her death on November 2, 2000. The suit was filed on June 6, 2001.

The facts here are certainly close. It is clear that Bare's doctors were discussing among themselves the possibility that she had CBD, but Reeser stated that they never shared their suspicions with Bare. . . . Bare's daughter, Mrs. Forry . . . stated that at some point her mother had asked a doctor if berylliosis was a possibility, a question that had been prompted by an article Bare had read in the local paper. Forry testified that the doctor had "put off" this question and told Bare that the test for berylliosis was unreliable, but it does not appear that he ruled out the possibility. This testimony hurts Reeser's case because it suggests that Bare knew about the possibility that she had CBD in the mid-1990s and that she did not pursue this possibility by getting the relevant tests. But [when] pressed on whether this event might have happened in the late rather than the mid-1990s, Forry said "It could have. I just don't remember. I honestly don't."

Defendants' argument rests on Forry's testimony; absent the conversation between Bare and her doctor, there is little reason to think that Bare suspected that she had berylliosis until directly before her death. . . . Because Forry cannot remember when the key conversation took place, reasonable minds could differ about whether Bare pursued her claim with reasonable diligence. Therefore that question is for a jury to decide. . . .

[E]ven if that conversation took place more than two years before Reeser filed suit, there is still the possibility that reasonable minds could differ on the question whether Bare exercised due diligence in pursuing her claim. [Her doctor told her that he didn't think she had CBD and that] "the test wasn't really accurate." On the basis of this conversation, a reasonable person in Bare's situation could easily have surmised that further investigation . . . would be unavailing . . . .

D. BRANCO

Plaintiff John Branco argues that he justifiably relied on a negative result from a CBD test in deciding not to file suit. We are, however, persuaded that Branco should have suspected as early as 1995, and certainly by May 1997, that he suffered from CBD, and that the tests which followed, negative though they were, cannot support tolling in light of the doctor's warnings that the tests were technically unsatisfactory and that Branco should undergo further testing, and in the absence of assurance from his physicians that he did not have a beryllium-related disease.

Branco worked at the defendants' plant for thirty-three years . . . and lived nearby most of his life. In May 1995, Branco visited his doctor complaining of shortness of breath . . . . One month later, he received a packet of information from the Department of Health and Human services [warning that he was at risk for CBD]. . . . [T]he mailing also included a summary of [a government study's] findings, and a [statement] that "[t]he main symptoms of chronic beryllium disease are shortness of breath while exercising or walking, cough, fatigue, weight loss, or chest pain." [T]hese warnings were sufficient to put Branco on notice that he was at risk of contracting CBD.

By May 1997, Branco's shortness of breath had progressed to the point that he was admitted to the hospital. At that time he was advised he had mild berylliosis. [This diagnosis was repeated several times through the summer.]

These visits culminated in a September 1997 referral to Dr. Milton Rossman [for testing]. These tests were negative. . . . Critically, however, Rossman cautioned that "the positive controls of the lung cells did not respond . . . and therefore this is a technically unsatisfactory study. . . ."

The information provided to Branco from the test results was hardly a definitive negative diagnosis for CBD. At most, those studies "[could not] confirm [CBD]." This is not the same as ruling out the defendants' plant as the cause of the injury. Indeed, [Dr. Rossman] "recommended that Mr. Branco [repeat the tests]." Moreover, unlike the other plaintiffs dealt with in this opinion, Branco was never assured by his physician that he did not have a beryllium-related disease (and indeed he was advised that he did).

Unfortunately, the testing was physically difficult for Branco. . . . Branco was already very ill at this point and . . . he understandably did not want to endure a second round of tests which would make him sicker still. Yet Branco's poor health cannot justify equitable tolling, the purpose of which is to safeguard potential plaintiffs against causes of action they had no means of discovering. Here, even after the testing, Branco knew it was possible he had CBD, so if he considered further testing infeasible, the proper recourse was to file suit.

In sum, we think the June 1995 HHS warnings and the May 1997 advice that he had berylliosis were sufficient to put Branco on notice that he might have CBD, and to start the running of the statute of limitations. We do not believe that reasonable minds can differ on this point in the absence of assurance from his physicians that he did not have a beryllium-related disease.

IV. Conclusion . . .

The judgments of the District Court will . . . be reversed as to Debiec, Russo, and Reeser and their cases will be remanded. The judgment regarding John Branco will be affirmed.

Ambro, Circuit Judge, . . . dissenting in part.

I. Introduction . . .

"[R]eliance upon the word of one physician when the patient's own common sense should lead to a different conclusion is unreasonable." *Bohus*, 950 F.2d at 925. . . .

[I]f a plaintiff had symptoms of lung disease, and had reason to believe the defendants' beryllium plant caused that injury—whether the information was obtained from a doctor, medical study, government letter, or possibly a media story—the statute of limitations began to run. Pennsylvania's discovery rule tolled the limitations period only if a physician definitively informed a plaintiff that she did not have an illness caused by beryllium . . . *and* common sense did not make her reliance unreasonable. . . .

I join fully the majority's opinion as to John Branco, concur in the result reached as to Geneva Bare and Mary Russo, and dissent as to Jane Debiec. . . .

II. APPLICATION OF PENNSYLVANIA LAW TO DEBIEC CASE

The majority examines Jane Debiec's health history at great length but, in doing so, disproportionately relies . . . on the diagnosis of her treating physician, Dr. John Shuman. . . .

[The work of Mrs. Debiec's husband and brother-in-law gave her ample reason to suspect that beryllium caused her illness.]

[Whether she] agreed with her husband is not relevant. . . . Layer upon layer of strong evidence compiled by Mr. Debiec and his brother . . . demanded [that] Mrs. Debiec exercise reasonable diligence to investigate further. A "diligent investigation may require one to seek further medical examination as well as competent legal representation," *Cochran*, 666 A.2d at 249, and Mrs. Debiec sought neither.

I agree with the majority that usually a claimant may rely on the assurances of her doctor instead of the suspicions of her spouse. But that is not what happened here. There is no evidence that, in the twenty years after Dr. Shuman first told Mrs. Debiec it was unlikely her sarcoidosis was caused by beryllium, he ever reiterated this opinion in response to an inquiry based on the growing body of evidence to the contrary. . . . Mrs. Debiec chose to ignore [her husband's] information and engaged in no further investigation. . . . Although Dr. Shuman never altered his original diagnosis, in later years, when sources such as the ATSDR were advising that CBD may masquerade as sarcoidosis, Mrs. Debiec no longer could ignore that the defendants' beryllium plant may have been the cause of her injury. Indeed, even if we ignore all the [other] warnings . . . the ATSDR report . . . alone triggered the . . . limitations period . . . .

III. OTHER PLAINTIFFS . . .

I concur . . . in the result reached as to Mary Russo, but I believe her case is closer than the majority acknowledges. Contrary to the majority's factual analysis, Mrs. Russo's doctors never definitively diagnosed her as not having CBD, much less did they dispel her concern that the defendants' plant was the cause of her injury. Dr. Bell diagnosed her with idiopathic pulmonary fibrosis of an unknown nature, and told her it was unlikely her illness was due to her *employment* at the facility five decades ago. Dr. Mengel confirmed this diagnosis. But there is no evidence any doctor told Mrs. Russo her injury was not caused by her many years of living and working near the defendants' plant, as she evidently suspected. According to Mrs. Russo, "I wasn't happy with that" explanation. "It bothered me because I heard people that didn't even work there had this. . . ." Mrs. Russo's suspicion of nonoccupational CBD was derived from information she received from her local newspaper. While her doctors may not have shared her concern, these articles gave Mrs. Russo adequate information for her to propose to them that she undergo a medical procedure that in the end confirmed her suspicions were correct. Ultimately, however, I do not believe the facts are so clear that reasonable minds cannot differ as to when the limitations period began. Although the March 29, 1999, and April 12, 1999, newspaper articles provide some persuasive evidence Mrs. Russo had notice of the cause of her injury prior to May 29, 1999 — two years before she filed suit — this is too slim a reed on which to rest entirely a finding that her suit is time barred. . . .

NOTES ON THE DISCOVERY RULE

1. The choices. The time in which plaintiff must sue can run from the date of defendant's wrongful act, the date of injury, or the date the wrong is or should have been discovered. In a car wreck, or an assault and battery, all three dates are the same. For Jane Debiec, the wrongful act began when she was born and continued much of her life, ending when and if defendant cleaned up its emissions. The injury began insidiously and was first noticed in 1976. She perhaps should have discovered the claim in the 1990s, or perhaps no one could discover it until her autopsy in 2000. Statutes of limitation typically run from the date of injury or the date the wrong should have been discovered, depending on the jurisdiction and the cause of action.

2. The discovery rule. The discovery rule applies an objective standard of reasonableness to plaintiffs' subjective knowledge. What did each of them know, and when did she know it? When did she know enough that she should have investigated and discovered the tort?

3. Discovering causation. The focus in *Debiec* is on plaintiff's knowledge of causation. Some diseases, like the DES injuries in *Burnside* (discussed in *Debiec*), have causes that no one would ever suspect without the benefits of medical research. In *Debiec*, the cause is easy to suspect but much harder to confirm. In simpler cases, the likely cause is apparent from the injury. An example is White v. Peabody Construction Co., 434 N.E.2d 1015, 1020-1021 (Mass. 1982). Plaintiffs were tenants of a public housing project that leaked water from the beginning. They didn't sue until the Housing Authority completed an investigation and officially blamed the construction company. The court said it should have been obvious that widespread leaks in a new building must result from defective design or construction, so plaintiffs could have sued immediately.

4. Discovering fraud. Congress codified the discovery rule for claims of securities fraud; in most cases, suit must be filed within "2 years after the discovery of the facts constituting the violation," or within five years of the violation, whichever is earlier. 28 U.S.C. §1658(b)(1)(2). The Court interpreted this provision in Merck & Co. v. Reynolds, 559 U.S. 633 (2010), and the opinion offers a good overview of many debates about the discovery rule. Merck's blockbuster drug for chronic pain, Vioxx, turned out to cause heart attacks, and Merck eventually settled hundreds of products liability suits with patients who took the drug. Merck v. Reynolds was a class action by Merck's investors alleging that Merck did not disclose the drug's risks to them.

The case was filed shortly after the media reported an academic study and declining Vioxx sales. There had been many partial disclosures more than two years before, including research reports, an FDA warning, lawsuits by patients, and widespread media coverage. But all the coverage emphasized the tentative nature of the findings and Merck's continued defense of the drug, and none of these stories had any effect on Merck's stock price. Securities fraud requires knowing misrepresentation or failure to disclose, and the misrepresentation or nondisclosure must be material to a reasonable investor.

The Court held first that "'discovery' as used in this statute encompasses not only those facts the plaintiff actually knew, but also those facts a reasonably diligent plaintiff would have known." *Id.* at 648.

Second, for purposes of §1658(b), the Court rejected what it called the "inquiry notice" standard. Pennsylvania law is that the statute runs from the time at which plaintiffs were "on notice that a wrong has been committed and that [they] need investigate." *Debiec.* But under §1658(b), the statute does not run from the time when a diligent plaintiff would have *begun* to investigate. It runs only from the time that such a plaintiff's investigation would have succeeded—when she would have discovered the facts constituting the violation.

And third, "the facts constituting the violation" include Merck's mental state. Plaintiffs must have been able to discover not just that there were problems with Vioxx, but that Merck knew about material problems and that it misrepresented or failed to disclose those problems. Facts that show a statement was false do not necessarily show that the securities issuer *knew* the statement was false. Securities defendants make much of that proposition at the merits stage; they must also live with its consequences for statutes of limitations. In the Court's view, nothing disclosed more than two years before the lawsuit should have led diligent plaintiffs to discover that Merck knew its statements about Vioxx were false.

5. Discovering the evidence. The statute runs from when plaintiff discovers her claim, not when she later discovers the evidence to prove it. Here's a harsh example: Plaintiff recognized her symptoms in a news story about a drug and its side effects. She went to four doctors in search of a diagnosis, all of whom erroneously said she did not have the relevant disease. The statute ran from the newspaper story, not from her positive diagnosis three years later. Vaught v. Showa Denko K.K., 107 F.3d 1137, 1140-1143 (5th Cir. 1997). Is that result consistent with the Pennsylvania rule in *Debiec?* With the federal rule in *Merck?*

6. Discovering the law. The discovery rule tolls the statute of limitations until plaintiff knows enough facts; it is irrelevant whether she knows the law. Limitations runs even if she has never heard of tort law, and even if existing tort law precludes her claim and the law is later changed to permit a claim. Jolly v. Eli Lilly & Co., 751 P.2d 923 (Cal. 1988). There is a similar decision in Menominee Indian Tribe v. United States, 136 S. Ct. 750 (2016), rejecting the tribe's argument that limitations should be tolled because filing suit appeared futile until a Supreme Court decision in 2005.

7. Discovering that it was wrong. A recurring issue that provokes disagreement is claims of childhood sexual abuse, where plaintiff says she didn't know the sexual contact was wrongful or didn't know that it was harmful. Without the discovery rule, the statute would usually run from the age of majority, typically 18; the question is whether failure to understand the wrong at that age tolls the statute further. Conflicting cases and legislative responses are collected in S.V. v. R.V., 933 S.W.2d 1, 20-22 (Tex. 1996). For more recent examples, see Koe v. Mercer, 876 N.E.2d 831 (Mass. 2007), and Annotation, 9 A.L.R.5th 321 (1993 & Supp.)

8. Recovered memories? The sexual abuse cases have given rise to another issue that is even more troubling: Should the discovery rule apply where plaintiff claims that she repressed all memory of the tort until she discovered her memories, in psychotherapy or otherwise? *S.V.* and the Annotation in note 7 also collect conflicting cases, statutes, and literature on this issue. *S.V.*, 933 S.W.2d at 15-20. An extreme example is Johnson v. Johnson, 701 F. Supp. 1363 (N.D. Ill. 1988), where plaintiff complained about childhood sexual abuse in letters written as an adult. But she said she didn't remember the abuse until she recalled it in psychotherapy, and that she didn't remember the letters. Her psychiatrist diagnosed multiple personality disorder, and attributed the letters to a different personality. How is a court supposed to adjudicate such claims?

A more recent Illinois case held a claim of childhood sexual abuse could go forward based on an allegation that the victim "was unable to recognize the sexual abuse was wrong or harmful or that he had been injured as a result of the abuse, 'due to the fact that he had . . . repressed and suppressed any memory of the abuse taking place,' and that he only recognized his injuries when the memories returned in 2011 [when he was 33]." Horn v. Goodman, 60 N.E.3d 922, 925 (Ill. App. Ct. 2016).

When the Pennsylvania court rejected tolling for claims of repressed memory, it wondered how anyone could defend against a 20-year-old claim, with no corroborating evidence, based solely on plaintiff's allegedly refreshed memory. Dalrymple v. Brown, 701 A.2d 164 (Pa. 1997). A concurring opinion took note of the serious scientific debate about the reliability of repressed memory evidence, expressing doubt that such evidence should be admissible in any event. *Id.* at 233 (Newman, J., concurring). Accumulating studies show that it is remarkably easy to implant false memories in people, and that the best techniques for doing so are substantially the techniques commonly alleged to unlock repressed memories. The research is surveyed in Elizabeth F. Loftus, Maryanne Garry, and Harlene Hayne, *Repressed and Recovered Memory*, in *Beyond Common Sense: Psychological Science in the Courtroom* 177 (Eugene Borgida & Susan T. Fiske, eds., Blackwell 2008). They conclude that "repressed memory appears to be a notion that lacks credible empirical support," and that "[o]nly 22% of psychological scientists believe that there is evidence to support the notion of repression." *Id.* at 189-190.

Some legislatures have enacted extremely long statutes of limitations for the sexual abuse cases. In 2018, Michigan enacted legislation providing that an individual has ten years to "recover damages sustained because of criminal sexual conduct." M.C.L.A. §600.5805(6). Oklahoma law stipulates that suits for childhood sexual abuse can be brought until the victim's 45th birthday. 12 Okla. Stat. §95. These laws do not solve the difficulty of litigating what happened so long after the alleged events, but they do eliminate most of the litigation about what plaintiff knew and when she knew it.

9. Some claims and not others. The discovery rule does not apply to all statutes of limitations. It has been most common with respect to torts that are not always obvious, such as fraud, products liability, and professional malpractice; the last two make it a target for tort reformers. It is more common for consumer plaintiffs than for commercial plaintiffs. It is much less common in contract cases; for an opinion exploring why that is, see Via Net v. TIG Insurance Co., 211 S.W.3d 310 (Tex. 2006).

10. Codification. Judges developed the discovery rule and other exceptions to statutes of limitations. Some statutes now codify some or all of these exceptions, and they often bungle the job.

An example is TRW v. Andrews, 534 U.S. 19 (2001). A billing clerk used plaintiff's Social Security number to obtain credit based on plaintiff's credit history. Plaintiff knew nothing of the wrong until she was turned down for a mortgage. She then alleged that the defendant credit bureau had facilitated the fraud by its neglect of various security standards required by the Fair Credit Reporting Act, 15 U.S.C. §1681 *et seq.* This would seem to be a classic case for the discovery rule; the wrong's impact on plaintiff was necessarily delayed until she made a new credit application of her own. Only a frequent check of her credit records would enable a victim to discover identity theft as it happens. Unfortunately, the Act codifies a variant of the fraudulent concealment rule, and the Court held, unanimously, that express enactment of one tolling rule excluded all the others.

11. Statutes of repose. Some statutes enact an absolute time limit on suit, with no exceptions; others codify the discovery rule but add an absolute outside limit. These absolute limits are often called statutes of repose. These statutes can sometimes bar a claim before it exists. An example is Ohio Rev. Code Ann. §2305.10, which provides that no suit for product liability can be brought more than ten years after the first sale of the product. Discovery is irrelevant; when the injury occurs is irrelevant. Such statutes have generally but not universally been upheld; the products cases are collected in Annotation, 30 A.L.R.5th 1 (1995 & Supp.). The court upheld Ohio's statute of repose prospectively, but struck it down as applied to injuries suffered before it was enacted. Groch v. General Motors Corp., 883 N.E.2d 377 (Ohio 2008).

Cutting off a few victims altogether is a lot easier than reducing jury verdicts for everyone. But is it fair to extract all the savings from a few of the victims?

12. Don't call them statutes of limitations. The Supreme Court has held that statutes of repose are different enough from statutes of limitations that a federal statute preempting state statutes of limitations does not preempt state statutes of repose. CTS Corp. v. Waldburger, 134 S. Ct. 2175 (2014). The federal statute was aimed at environmental toxins with long latency periods, so this interpretation most likely defeats the statutory purpose. And the vocabulary for the two kinds of statutes was unfamiliar and unsettled in 1986, when the federal statute was enacted. But the vocabulary has become much more settled in the meantime. Justices Ginsburg and Breyer dissented.

13. Class actions. If one set of plaintiffs files a class action, the statute of limitations is tolled for all members of the alleged class. American Pipe & Construction Co. v. Utah, 414 U.S. 538 (1974). Class members do not have to all file their own lawsuits in case something goes wrong with the class action. But this rule too does not apply to statutes of repose. California Public Employees' Retirement System v. ANZ Securities, Inc., 137 S. Ct. 2042 (2017). And it does not apply to subsequent class actions; only individual claims can take advantage of *American Pipe*. China Agritech, Inc. v. Resh, 138 S. Ct. 1800 (2018). *ANZ Securities* was 5-4 on the usual ideological lines, but *China Agritech* was unanimous on the result and 8-1 on the rationale. The Court feared that successive class actions, each tolling limitations for as long as it lasted, could toll the statute indefinitely until plaintiffs finally found a district judge willing to certify a class.

14. "Jurisdictional" time limits. Sometimes courts say that what appears to be a statute of limitations is really a substantive limit on the underlying right, or a limit on the court's jurisdiction, and therefore not subject to the discovery rule or any other tolling doctrine. Sometimes this was clearly the legislative intent, as in statutes of repose. More often, the distinction seems metaphysical at best and wrongheaded at worst. In a series of cases, the Supreme Court tried to clarify this confusing usage. "Clarity would be facilitated if courts and litigants used the label "jurisdictional" not for claim-processing rules, but only for prescriptions delineating the classes of cases (subject-matter jurisdiction) and the persons (personal jurisdiction) falling within a court's adjudicatory authority." Kontrick v. Ryan, 540 U.S. 443, 454-455 (2004).

The Court said the proper question was "whether the time restrictions . . . are in such emphatic form as to preclude equitable exceptions." *Id.* at 458. The Court has returned to the theme in several subsequent cases. But it waffled in Bowles v. Russell, 551 U.S. 205 (2007), where it held that the time for filing a notice of appeal is jurisdictional, and in John R. Sand & Gravel Co. v. United States, 552 U.S. 130, 133-134 (2008), where it held that the statute of limitations for suing the United States in the

Court of Federal Claims is jurisdictional. Each of these decisions was guided by long-standing precedent.

In Henderson v. Shinseki, 562 U.S. 428 (2011), a mentally ill war veteran missed the deadline for appealing a denial of veterans' benefits. In a unanimous opinion by Justice Alito, the Court said that "[f]iling deadlines . . . are quintessential claim-processing rules." *Id.* at 435. "Congress is free to attach the conditions that go with the jurisdictional label to a rule that we would prefer to call a claim-processing rule." *Id.* Congress need not use "magic words," but it must give a "'clear' indication" that it wanted a time limit to be treated as jurisdictional. *Id.* at 436, 439. Congress had not clearly stated any intent to subject veterans to a time limit with jurisdictional consequences.

The Court offered a further clarification, in a unanimous opinion by Justice Ginsburg, in Hamer v. Neighborhood Housing Services, 138 S. Ct. 13 (2017). A statutory rule governing the transfer of a case from one federal court to another is jurisdictional, citing Bowles v. Russell on notice of appeal, but no provision of a federal rule of procedure is jurisdictional, because only Congress can expand or contract the jurisdiction of the federal courts. Federal Rule of Appellate Procedure 4 imposes tighter limits than the statute on extensions of time for filing notice of appeal, but those tighter limits are not jurisdictional.

The Court has granted a cert petition that seeks to recreate the whole mess, arguing that claims processing rules can be mandatory and not subject to equitable tolling. Lambert v. Nutraceutical Corp., 870 F.3d 1170 (9th Cir. 2017), *cert. granted*, 138 S. Ct. 2675 (2018). Federal Rule 23(f) says that a party has 14 days to file a request for permission to appeal an order granting or denying class certification. This is shorter than, and different from, the usual 30-day period to file a notice of appeal. Under *Hamer*, this rule cannot be jurisdictional, because it appears in the Federal Rules rather than a statute. But petitioner argues that it is mandatory and not subject to tolling, not even by a motion to reconsider the order denying class certification. If claims processing rules can be held not subject to tolling, then the Court's distinction between jurisdictional and claims processing rules will have come to naught.

15. The Tort Claims Act. The Court applied a rebuttable presumption of equitable tolling, derived from earlier cases, to the time limits in the Federal Tort Claims Act. United States v. Kwai Fun Wong, 135 S. Ct. 1625 (2015). Four conservative justices dissented, invoking the contrary interpretation of the Tucker Act and the rule that waivers of sovereign immunity must be construed narrowly.

3. Fraudulent Concealment

KNAYSI v. A.H. ROBINS CO.

679 F.2d 1366 (11th Cir. 1982)

Before TJOFLAT, HILL and ANDERSON, Circuit Judges.

JAMES C. HILL, Circuit Judge.

Appellants Anita and Ed Knaysi filed suit against appellee A.H. Robins . . . seeking recovery of damages resulting from injuries to Anita Knaysi allegedly caused by her use of the Dalkon Shield intrauterine device . . . . Mrs. Knaysi became pregnant after insertion of the Dalkon shield and in the first trimester suffered a spontaneous septic abortion of twin fetuses. [The Knaysis' sued, alleging] that Robins was aware from test results that the effectiveness of the device in preventing pregnancy was lower than it advertised and from both test results and the reports of physicians that

occur with the Dalkon Shield in place, no harm would result if the Shield was not removed. This brochure contains no reference to septic abortion. Nonetheless, an individual who had a septic abortion and read the brochure might be convinced that the Dalkon Shield could not have caused the abortion and might therefore be lulled into not bringing suit against Robins.

I will assume, arguendo, that Mrs. Knaysi's physician received and read Robins' October 1972 brochure. There is absolutely nothing in the record, however, that even suggests that the physician believed what the brochure said or relied on it in any way. More importantly, nothing suggests that the brochure lulled the physician, and in turn the Knaysis, into a state of inaction vis-à-vis Robins. Without the critical link between the alleged misrepresentation and the Knaysis' failure to bring this suit within the limitations period, the Knaysis cannot prevail. . . .

Since the Knaysis failed to raise a material issue of fact . . . , Robins . . . is entitled to . . . summary judgment . . . .

NOTES ON FRAUDULENT CONCEALMENT

1. No discovery rule in *Knaysi*. In New York, Mrs. Knaysi's causes of action accrued when the shield first began to damage her body, whether or not she could have known about it. There was no discovery rule.

a. The court. The Court of Appeals reaffirmed that doctrine in Martin v. Edwards Laboratories, 457 N.E.2d 1150 (N.Y. 1983), a case in which the Dalkon Shield caused permanent sterility. In both *Knaysi* and *Martin*, there were noticeable symptoms shortly after the onset of injury. But New York had also applied its accrual rule in cases of slow-onset disease that produce no symptoms for years. In Schwartz v. Heyden Newport Chemical Corp., 188 N.E.2d 142 (N.Y. 1963), plaintiff was given a radioactive substance in 1944 that caused cancer diagnosed in 1957. The court held that the radiation must have begun to do damage as soon as it entered the body, so that the claim was barred long before the injury was noticeable.

b. The legislature. The New York legislature overruled many of these cases in 1986. Actions for personal injury caused by the latent effects of exposure to substances may be brought within three years of the date at which plaintiff discovered the injury or should through reasonable diligence have discovered the injury. N.Y. C.P.L.R. §214-c.2. The "injury" means only the "physical condition" of which plaintiff complains; the statute begins to run even if she has no idea what caused the injury. Wetherill v. Eli Lilly & Co, 678 N.E.2d 474 (N.Y. 1997). There is a narrow exception for cases affected by new scientific discoveries three to five years after plaintiff should have discovered the injury.

c. The judicial response. The New York court has adhered to its traditional doctrine in cases not subject to the new statute, including loss-of-consortium claims by the spouse of the person exposed, and claims for repetitive stress injuries, excluded on the ground that a computer keyboard is not a "substance" within the meaning of the act. Blanco v. American Telephone & Telegraph Co., 689 N.E.2d 506, 509 (N.Y. 1997).

d. A plaintiff win. As these cases illustrate, the New York Court of Appeals has historically been defense oriented with respect to statutes of limitations. But it went the other way in a case about wrongful birth, a claim for the extraordinary expenses of raising a child born disabled as a result of medical negligence. The New York statute of limitations for medical malpractice says that the statute runs from the date of the malpractice. But the court held that when the malpractice results in a wrongful birth, the statute runs from when the child is born. B.F. v. Reproductive Medicine

Associates, 92 N.E.3d 766 (N.Y. 2017). The holding was not based on the discovery rule, but on the view that the parents had nothing to sue for—that no cause of action accrued—until the child was born with disabilities.

2. Vocabulary. Fraudulent concealment is distinct from the discovery rule, and mostly important where no discovery rule applies. Some courts inevitably confuse the two rules, and there is some blurring when courts reduce the fraud element of fraudulent concealment. New York adds to the risk of confusion by using a different vocabulary from most of the rest of the country. When defendant conceals the existence of the cause of action, most courts describe that as fraudulent concealment. When defendant induces plaintiff to forbear suing on a known cause of action, he may be estopped to plead limitations. New York follows the same two rules, but treats them as two branches of equitable estoppel.

3. Concealing a product-liability claim. The judges in *Knaysi* do not seem to disagree over the applicable legal standard. Is there anything to Judge Tjoflat's view that plaintiff hasn't shown enough to get to the jury?

a. General claims of safety. Robins distributed lots of literature claiming that the shield was "safe." Should that count? Another panel of the Eleventh Circuit said those advertisements might have fraudulently induced women to use the shield, but they were irrelevant to whether Robins fraudulently concealed its liability from women who had already been injured by the shield. Sellers v. A.H. Robins Co., 715 F.2d 1559 (11th Cir. 1983), *reh'g granted*, 732 F.2d 1129 (11th Cir. 1984). No order or opinion on rehearing is reported; probably the case settled.

Sellers distinguished *Knaysi* on the ground that Alabama law is different from New York law. At least at the big picture level, that was not true; both states recognized fraudulent concealment and neither recognized the discovery rule. The real source of disagreement between the two panels was over the relevance of general claims of safety not directed at the particular injury plaintiff suffered. If general advertising claims are enough, won't most plaintiffs in products cases be able to show fraudulent concealment?

b. General claims that touch on plaintiff's specific injury. Robins also made a specific claim that the shield would do no harm if left in during pregnancy. Tjoflat says that isn't enough because there is no evidence Knaysi or her doctor relied on it. What further proof might he be looking for? Plaintiffs should have put in an affidavit from her doctor; maybe the lawyer overlooked it, or maybe the doctor had nothing helpful to say. What if Robins created such an air of safety about its product that no one's suspicions were ever aroused, and women and their doctors never wondered? Isn't that the most effective form of concealment?

4. Requiring more than the violation. One view of the concealment requirement is that defendant is entitled to the protection of limitations unless he does something in addition to the underlying wrong. An example is Ross v. Louise Wise Services, Inc., 868 N.E.2d 189 (N.Y. 2007), where an adoption agency concealed histories of mental illness in the genetic parents, but did nothing further during the limitations period to conceal what it had done (or not done). In addition, nearly all courts subscribe to the view that mere silence is not fraudulent concealment. Except for fiduciaries, defendants have no duty to disclose their wrongdoing.

The wrong in products liability is selling a defective product. Advertising the product is not an element of the wrong; it is a legally distinct act. But few products can be sold without advertising; realistically, Robins did nothing but sell its product. Should that matter? Should it matter whether Robins believed its product was safe? Should "fraudulent concealment" require Robins to conceal a wrong it knows it committed?

5. Withdrawing the product. One other piece of the Dalkon Shield story is curiously missing from *Knaysi*. In May 1974 Robins warned physicians that the shield might cause septic abortions. In June 1974, under pressure from the Food and Drug Administration, it withdrew the product from the market. The Ninth Circuit held that these acts necessarily ended any fraudulent concealment. Sidney-Vinstein v. A.H. Robins Co., 697 F.2d 880 (9th Cir. 1983). But not until 1984 did Robins recommend that women already using the shield have it removed. Mary Williams Walsh, *A.H. Robins Begins Removal Campaign for Dalkon Wearers—Company Offers to Pay Costs of Procedure and Exams, Seeks No Lawsuit Waiver*, Wall St. J. (Oct. 30, 1984). In the interim, Robins continued to issue statements asserting that the shield was safe and effective. The Ninth Circuit apparently thought the earlier disclosures made these claims irrelevant.

Is that the right result? Aren't safety claims after 1974 more culpable—more "fraudulent"—than safety claims before 1974? On the other hand, must Robins waive the statute of limitations unless it admits liability to the world? If it isn't fraudulent concealment to deny plaintiff's allegations in court, why is it fraudulent concealment to deny them out of court? Should we distinguish general claims of safety from false denials of specific facts?

6. Due diligence? A few courts have held that limitations are tolled by fraudulent concealment whether or not plaintiff is diligent, but that is plainly the minority view. *Klehr* held that at least in civil RICO and antitrust actions, fraudulent concealment does not excuse plaintiff's duty of due diligence. Thus, limitations generally runs from the time plaintiff should have known she had a cause of action, even if defendant continues to conceal it. Does that help reconcile the dilemmas explored in notes 4 and 5? Should a diligent plaintiff proceed despite denials, once she has enough information? What if defendant's denial is supported by a false but convincing explanation? Note that in *Klehr* as in *Knaysi*, the fraud and concealment consisted of continuing to promote and advertise an allegedly defective product.

7. Codification. Like the discovery rule, fraudulent concealment doctrine is sometimes codified and sometimes judicially implied. Legislators sometimes codify it even in statutes of repose.

NOTES ON ESTOPPEL TO ASSERT LIMITATIONS

1. The general rule. Estoppel to assert limitations is simply a special case of the general equitable estoppel rules; any representation that induces plaintiff to refrain from suit might suffice. The most common examples are promises to pay plaintiff's claim, McAllister v. Federal Deposit Insurance Corp., 87 F.3d 762 (5th Cir. 1996), and promises not to assert limitations if settlement negotiations fall through after the statute expires, Annotation, 43 A.L.R.3d 756 (1972 & Supp.). The mere pendency of promising settlement discussions is not enough. McAdam v. Grzelczyk, 911 A.2d 255 (R.I. 2006).

2. A Supreme Court example. The leading federal case on estoppel to assert limitations is Glus v. Brooklyn Eastern District Terminal, 359 U.S. 231 (1959). Plaintiff was an employee with an industrial disease, suing under the Federal Employers Liability Act, 45 U.S.C. §51 *et seq.* The FELA has a three-year statute of limitations, but the employer repeatedly told Glus he had seven years to sue. The Court held that these facts could give rise to an estoppel, and that whether it was reasonable to rely on a misrepresentation of law was a jury question.

3. Estoppel by duress. Another variation, most commonly seen in sexual abuse cases, is estoppel by duress, where defendant threatens the victim with further harm if he discloses the wrongful conduct. Cases are collected in Murphy v. Merzbacher, 697 A.2d 861 (Md. 1997).

In One Star v. Sisters of St. Francis, 752 N.W.2d 668 (S.D. 2008), plaintiffs sued a boarding school in 2004, alleging that they were sexually abused from 1960 to 1971. They asserted estoppel by duress, but the court found that the "exception generally requires a showing that the duress be continuous," originating at a time within the statute of limitations. *Id.* at 683. Because plaintiffs did not identify facts suggesting that the duress began during their schooling and persisted for the subsequent decades, they could not successfully assert estoppel by duress.

A more unusual example is Manker v. Manker, 644 N.W.2d 522 (Neb. 2002), where a woman discovered that 14 years before, her husband had managed to get a divorce without her knowledge. He then deterred her from suing for a share of the "marital" property by threatening that the IRS would come after them for back taxes, and that he would lose his job, if she revealed that they were not really married.

NOTES ON THE POLICY CHOICES IN STATUTES OF LIMITATIONS

1. The victims. Many people know little of courts and lawyers and nothing of statutes of limitations. They arrive in the lawyer's office far too late, after some person or event has forcefully brought to their attention information they had known long before, or after they acquire the name of a lawyer through some chance encounter. Even with the discovery rule, the test of diligence is largely objective, and some people are not able to meet it. There is much to be said for the view that no claim should be barred except on the merits.

2. The defendants. Statutes of limitations balance these hardships against the hardships that delayed claims inflict on defendants and the courts. The most common concern is loss of evidence and fading memories. At the extreme, in some of the cases of adults claiming that they were sexually abused as a child, the accused abuser and everyone who supervised him or worked with him is dead, and the only surviving witness is the plaintiff, who is free as a practical matter to remember, embellish, or reconstruct events, or even just make things up.

This leads to another theme in the cases: the suspicion that many old claims are fabricated. If the alleged events really happened, plaintiff would have sued right away. Years later, the complaint might look like a reconstruction of reality, a product of recent imagination and the likelihood that contrary evidence has been lost. But statutes of limitations bar valid claims as well. Indeed, "that is their very purpose." United States v. Kubrick, 444 U.S. 111, 125 (1979).

3. Categorical balancing. These competing interests are mostly balanced by category, not case by case. The presence or absence of actual prejudice to defendant is irrelevant to limitations and to the tolling doctrines. The claims in *Debiec* all depended on medical files and research on beryllium; they might have been no harder to try in 2003 than they would have been in 1992. Or maybe the plaintiffs' deaths deprived defendant of an opportunity to have its own tests or medical examinations done. Such arguments about prejudice would matter to laches but not to limitations.

Generalizations about categories of cases sometimes guide legislative and judicial decisions about limitations. Thus, contract claims generally have longer statutes of limitations than tort claims, and written contracts generally have longer statutes of limitations than oral contracts. Sometimes these generalizations seem to make sense;

sometimes not. If one is worried about fabricated claims, an oral contract is much more suspicious than a serious injury. Sometimes the legislature is pursuing other goals altogether; a short statute of limitations is a good way to sabotage a statute.

Variations in statutes of limitations mean that sometimes a claim is barred under one legal theory but not under other legal theories. For example, breach of warranty is a contract claim; products liability is a tort claim. The contract claim will usually have a longer statute of limitations, but limitations will run from the date of sale, not the date of injury, and the discovery rule is likely to be unavailable. In general, any lawyer faced with a limitations problem should consider whether there is some way to plead the claim that will put it under a more favorable statute.

4. Inability to sue. Nearly all statutes of limitations have explicit or implicit exceptions for people who lack capacity or ability to sue. Minors, mental incompetents, and prisoners are the most common examples. There was no mention of the possibility that imprisonment might toll limitations in the two extraordinary cases that follow. The applicable statutes were those of New York and Illinois respectively; these decisions turned on state law rather than federal.

Davino Watson is a U.S. citizen held for deportation for three years, without a lawyer, by Immigration and Customs Enforcement. He repeatedly told everyone he encountered that he was a citizen, and he obtained the documents to prove it. ICE officers contacted his father to verify his claims, but reached the wrong Hopeton Watson and concluded that the son's claims were phony.

When the son was finally cleared and released, he sued for false imprisonment. The court held that his suit was barred by the two-year statute of limitations, which ran while he was imprisoned. The statute ran from when the false imprisonment ended, but that happened the first time he appeared before an immigration judge. After that, the imprisonment was pursuant to legal authority and no longer false. After that, his only claim was for malicious prosecution, but while the agents' acts were grossly negligent, they were not malicious. Watson v. United States, 865 F.3d 123 (2d Cir. 2017). Chief Judge Katzmann dissented.

The court relied on Wallace v. Kato, 549 U.S. 384 (2007), where a murder suspect was arrested without probable cause. The Court said the statute ran on his claim for false imprisonment from when he first appeared before a magistrate.

5. No outside limit? Statutes of repose are troubling, especially when they cut off claims before they arise, or before it was even possible for plaintiff to know about the claim. But without some outside limit, bizarre things can happen.

a. The King Ranch. The Chapmans are descendants of a half-owner of the King Ranch, the surviving portions of which are larger than Rhode Island. In 1883, the executor of the ancestral Chapman settled a quiet title suit with the ancestral King, accepting payment for a quarter of the ranch and conceding that she was not entitled to the other quarter she claimed. Her descendants sued in 1995, alleging that King had hired Chapman's lawyer, and that that lawyer had entered into the settlement fraudulently and without disclosing to Chapman either the true facts or his conflict of interest. The court of appeals had been willing to let this case go to trial, Chapman v. King Ranch, Inc., 41 S.W.3d 693 (Tex. Ct. App. 2001), but the state supreme court was not. 118 S.W.3d 742 (Tex. 2003). The court found no evidence of extrinsic fraud on the court, which it defined very narrowly, and it said that fraud or conflict of interest by the attorney didn't count.

b. Native American land claims. The usual context for litigation over ancient land claims is American Indian treaty claims. Damage claims for treaty violations are subject to no statute of limitations, County of Oneida v. Oneida Indian Nation, 470 U.S. 226, 240-244 (1985), but claims for equitable relief can be barred by laches. City of

Sherrill v. Oneida Indian Nation, 544 U.S. 197 (2005). The Court feared that the tribe's argument might also support claims to dispossess owners of land that had been held and governed by non-Indians for nearly 200 years.

c. Racial wrongs. Other cases barring ancient claims include *Alexander v. Oklahoma*, 382 F.3d 1206 (10th Cir. 2004), a suit for damages caused by a 1921 riot in which a white mob in Tulsa destroyed a black neighborhood and killed many black citizens; and *In re African-American Slave Descendants Litigation*, 471 F.3d 754 (7th Cir. 2006), a suit on behalf of the estates of slaves for restitution of the profits of corporations that owned, traded, or financed slaves.

6. Don't rely on any of this. Tolling rules are litigation rules, not planning rules. You can rarely be sure that they apply or what they will accomplish if they do apply. Missing the statute of limitations is one of the most common forms of legal malpractice. It is not necessary to file early and often, but it is only prudent to file early.

CHAPTER

12

Fluid-Class and Cy Pres Remedies

IN RE PHARMACEUTICAL INDUSTRY AVERAGE
WHOLESALE PRICE LITIGATION

588 F.3d 24 (1st Cir. 2009)

Before LYNCH, Chief Judge, TORRUELLA and HOWARD, Circuit Judges.
  LYNCH, Chief Judge. . . .

I.

This . . . is . . . one case of a series of class actions alleging [that] pharmaceutical companies fraudulently inflated a figure known as the "average wholesale price" (AWP) between 1991 and 2003 . . . .

Insurers used AWPs to decide how much to reimburse providers when patients obtained drugs, which in turn affected patients' co-payments. [The published AWP was a fictional list price that did not reflect substantial discounts offered to doctors. Some drugs are sold directly to doctors, because they have to be injected, or administered in some more complex way, in a doctor's office. To induce doctors to prescribe their drugs, drug companies told doctors they could keep the difference between the discounted price they actually paid and the much higher reimbursement they would receive on the basis of the AWP.] Consequently, Medicare, insurers, and patients allegedly overpaid by many millions of dollars for critical treatments based on manipulated AWPs.

[Classes of patients sued under the consumer-protection statutes of the several states. The subclass in this appeal consisted of patients who purchased Zoladex through Medicare Part B and who paid part of the cost themselves. Zoladex is a drug for prostate cancer, manufactured by defendant AstraZeneca. Medicare paid 80 percent of the AWP; patients owed a co-payment of 20 percent of the AWP. Most patients had supplemental insurance that paid 80 percent of their 20 percent, leaving the patient to pay 20 percent of 20 percent, or 4 percent, of the AWP. Patients with supplemental insurance that paid all of the 20 percent co-payment were excluded from the class. Insurers filed similar claims for their share of the overpayment either individually or in separate classes.]

After months of intense litigation and negotiation, AstraZeneca and the Zoladex subclass reached a final settlement in May 2007, on the eve of trial. [The settlement calculated damages to all class members with supplemental insurance on the assumption that they had actually paid 4 percent of the overcharge. The opinion is not perfectly clear, but damages to class members without supplemental insurance were apparently calculated on the assumption that they had paid 20 percent of the overcharge. The AWP was expensive; some individual class members would recover hundreds or thousands of dollars under the settlement.] The plaintiffs' expert had calculated [that] the class's damages were $31,128,851. In the settlement, AstraZeneca agreed to pay $24 million in total compensation to all class members or, for deceased class members, to their spouses or the legal representatives of their estates. In an effort to achieve a comprehensive settlement, the parties also agreed [that] AstraZeneca would pay the consumers from nine states who had previously been excluded from the class. [These states had originally been excluded because their consumer-protection statutes did not create a private cause of action.] If the amount of submitted claims exceeded $24 million, class members' recovery would be reduced proportionally.

AstraZeneca also promised to pay all costs of distributing this money as well as $8.7 million in attorneys' fees and costs, representing about one-third of the settlement amount. The parties agreed [that] AstraZeneca would pay fees and costs separately and not deduct [those costs] from the class members' $24 million recovery.

The parties expected [that] a large portion of the total sum AstraZeneca was willing to pay would go unclaimed. . . . [M]any class members were elderly, had died, or could die soon, and not all of them could be found. The parties addressed this issue through two mechanisms.

First . . . [c]lass members only had to submit relatively minimal proof of when they took Zoladex. Then, based on a formula created by the plaintiffs' expert, class members would receive compensation for *double* their actual losses. . . .

Second, the parties agreed to create a fund, called a cy pres fund, that would pay any amount remaining (after payout to the claimants) of the $24 million to "mutually acceptable charitable organizations funding cancer research or patient care" that the court would approve in the future. The parties capped the cy pres amount at $10 million if not all of the $24 million was paid out. . . .

The district court granted preliminary approval of the settlement. In the preliminary approval the court certified an expanded class that included the residents in [the] nine states who were previously excluded.

[After preliminary approval of a class settlement, the class is notified of the proposed settlement and given an opportunity to object. The court then holds a "fairness hearing" before finally approving or disapproving the settlement. One class representative, Joyce Howe, suing on behalf of her husband's estate, objected to the settlement. Howe's individual claim was unusual, because her husband's supplemental insurance had paid only 50 percent of the 20 percent co-payment.]

Class counsel reported [at the fairness hearing] that they expected $14 million of the $24 million settlement to go unclaimed. Under the proposed settlement, up to $10 million of those leftover funds would be distributed through cy pres. The district judge agreed with Howe that more money should go to the plaintiffs rather than to the cy pres fund. She instructed the parties that the settlement should pay *treble* damages to those plaintiffs who had the strongest claims. . . . [Patients with the strongest claims were treated with Zoladex between 1997 and 2003. Earlier claims faced serious difficulties with statutes of limitations; later claims challenged less egregious misconduct, because the scheme changed after Congress changed the Medicare reimbursement policy in 2003.]

The court . . . accepted class counsel's justification for calculating damages for class members with supplemental insurance based on the average . . . coverage, even if some members' insurance covered less than 80 percent of the Medicare co-payment. Class counsel reported that Howe's attorney had identified no plaintiff other than Howe who had different supplemental coverage, the plaintiffs' expert had reaffirmed that 80 percent coverage fairly approximated the class's supplemental insurance, and those few with different coverage would still be compensated beyond their losses [because their damages as estimated by the formula would be trebled.

The court also rejected Howe's proposal to send equal checks to every class member. That method had been used for some drugs that were prescribed in varying dosages and taken for varying periods of time, which made more precise calculations of individual damages "prohibitively expensive."] Zoladex, by contrast, is taken at regular dosages at regular intervals. With information about when a plaintiff started Zoladex and whether the plaintiff had supplemental insurance, it was easy to calculate a Zoladex plaintiff's actual damages.

The parties amended the proposed settlement agreement to address the court's instruction to increase the payout to class members. . . .

On October 2, 2008, the district court approved the amended settlement, subject to two further qualifications. First, the court instructed the parties to adjust the settlement to pay [1997-2003] plaintiffs treble damages, then, if money remained, to pay treble damages to all class members pro rata. If money was still left over, the parties agreed the remaining money would be distributed to charity through cy pres. Second, it reduced the attorneys' fees to 30 percent of the recovery. . . .

The parties once more amended the settlement agreement to reflect the court's instructions. . . . The plaintiffs' expert predicted in February 2009 that, even with class-wide treble damages, class members would claim only about $17.2 million, leaving about $6.8 million of the $24 million settlement left over for charity. [In case that prediction was wrong, the cy pres distribution was still capped at $10 million.]

It is this amended settlement that the district court approved . . . .

II. . . .

"A district court can approve a class action settlement only if it is fair, adequate and reasonable," City Partnership Co. v. Atlantic Acquisition LP, 100 F.3d 1041, 1043 (1st Cir. 1996), "or (in shorthand) 'reasonable,'" National Association of Chain Drug Stores v. New England Carpenters Health Benefits Fund, 582 F.3d 30, 44 (1st Cir. 2009). If the parties negotiated at arm's length and conducted sufficient discovery, the district court must presume the settlement is reasonable. "[T]he district court enjoys considerable range in approving or disapproving a class action settlement, given the generality of the standard and the need to balance [a settlement's] benefits and costs." Id. at 45. . . .

Howe argues the settlement is unreasonable because it creates a cy pres fund . . . .

A. THE DISTRICT COURT DID NOT ABUSE ITS DISCRETION . . .
Appellate courts review a district court's conclusion that a settlement . . . is reasonable for abuse of discretion. . . . We find no abuse of discretion.

1. The Cy Pres Distribution
This circuit has not had occasion to consider whether settlement agreements in class actions may establish cy pres funds. Other circuits have approved agreements that provide for cy pres funds, particularly those negotiated at arm's-length by the parties.

A cy pres distribution results from application of a legal doctrine that courts have imported into class actions from trusts and estates law. In trusts and estates law, cy pres, taken from the Norman French expression *cy pres comme possible* ("as near as possible"), "save[s] testamentary gifts that otherwise would fail" because their intended use is no longer possible. In re Airline Ticket Commission Antitrust Litigation, 307 F.3d 679, 682 (8th Cir. 2002). Courts permit the gift to be used for another purpose as close as possible to the gift's intended purpose.

In class actions, courts have approved creating cy pres funds, to be used for a charitable purpose related to the class plaintiffs' injury, when it is difficult for all class members to receive individual shares of the recovery and, as a result, some or all of the recovery remains. The use of a cy pres fund sometimes "prevent[s] the defendant from walking away from the litigation" without paying a full recovery because of practical obstacles to individual distribution. Mirfasihi v. Fleet Mortgage Corp., 356 F.3d 781, 784 (7th Cir. 2004); *see also* 3 Alba Conte & Herbert B. Newberg, *Newberg on Class Actions* §10:15, at 513 (Thomson West, 4th ed. 2002) ("[T]he cy pres . . . distributions serve the objectives of compensation for the class (albeit in an indirect manner), access to judicial relief for small claims, and deterrence of illegal behavior.").

Court-mandated cy pres distributions, as opposed to court-approved settlements using cy pres, are controversial. But "courts are not in disagreement that cy pres distributions are proper in connection with a class settlement, subject to court approval of the particular application of the funds." 4 Conte & Newberg §11:20 at 28. . . .

Courts have approved cy pres funds in settlements in at least two circumstances. First, cy pres settlement funds have been approved when it is economically infeasible to distribute money to class members. Distribution of all funds to the class can be infeasible, for example, when class members cannot be identified, when the class changes constantly, or when class members' individual damages—although substantial in the aggregate—are too small to justify the expense of sending recovery to individuals. In these cases, some courts have permitted the parties to create a cy pres fund *in lieu of* a class payout. That is not our situation.

Second, courts have allowed parties to establish cy pres funds when money remained from the defendant's payout after money for damages had been distributed to class members. This situation often arises because some class members never claimed their share. Among other solutions, courts have approved giving money unclaimed after payout to class members to charities related to the plaintiffs' injuries. This kind of cy pres fund is at issue in this case.

Although unusually timed, the cy pres fund in this case, contrary to Howe's argument, is not taking damages away from the class members. The settlement permits all plaintiffs to claim and be paid their damages—indeed *treble* their damages—before any money is paid to charity through cy pres. This process is like other, routinely approved cy pres distributions. See, e.g. Powell v. Georgia-Pacific Corp., 119 F.3d 703, 705-706 (8th Cir. 1997) (refusing, after money in a settlement fund remained, to distribute the rest to class members because "neither party ha[d] a legal right" to the unclaimed funds). It would elevate form over substance to require the parties to wait until after all claims are paid before reaching an agreement as to how to distribute any remaining money to charity.

Howe nevertheless insists that the class members are entitled to receive any remaining money. She argues that, when deciding how to allocate remaining money, the primary consideration is whether it is economically infeasible to distribute the remaining proceeds to all claimants. Howe relies on and, in our view, Howe misunderstands the American Law Institute's . . . recent draft . . . discussing the appropriateness of cy pres distributions in settlements. *See Principles of the Law of Aggregate Litigation* §3.07 (Am. Law Inst. Proposed Final Draft 2009). . . .

The district court's actions in this case were entirely congruent with the proposed draft's purposes. The ALI's proposed draft expresses a policy preference, when settlement money remains, for redistributing that money to class members to ensure they recover their losses. The ALI was concerned that cy pres funds are often inappropriate because "few settlements award 100 percent of a class member's losses, and thus it is unlikely in most cases that further distributions to class members would result in more than 100 percent recovery." §3.07 cmt. *b.* The ALI also believed "that in most circumstances distributions to class members better approximate the goals of the substantive laws than distributions to third parties that were not directly injured by the defendant's conduct." *Id.*

The district court shared these concerns. The court ultimately insisted that the settlement pay class members treble damages before any money is distributed through cy pres. This set the benchmark well above the ALI's hope that class members might receive 100 percent recovery.

And the court recognized that the cy pres fund serves the goals of civil damages by ensuring [that] AstraZeneca fairly pays for the class's alleged losses. We asked at oral argument why AstraZeneca would be willing to pay a total sum more than the treble damages for each class member. Counsel for Plaintiff Townsend replied that the plaintiffs had insisted on AstraZeneca paying a larger sum to better represent the losses of the entire class, including those class members who would never claim their recovery. . . .

III.

The approval of the settlement is *affirmed.*

NOTES ON CLASS ACTIONS FOR DAMAGES

1. The role of class actions. Class actions for damages attempt to aggregate many individual claims into one class claim that can be adjudicated collectively. Very often, the individual claims are so small that no one could afford to litigate them individually. Claims of a few dollars each obviously fit this description, but given the expense of litigation and the complexity of the claims, the Zoladex claims of a few hundred or a few thousand dollars face the same problem. If the claims cannot be litigated on a class basis, they generally go away. This is why defendants are generally eager to avoid class actions and why some courts held class action waivers in mandatory arbitration clauses unconscionable. See the Notes on Arbitration Clauses in section 11.A. As explained there, the Supreme Court has held many of these unconscionability claims preempted by the Federal Arbitration Act, leaving consumers and employees with no economically viable way to band together to seek damages.

2. The limits of class actions. Of course, the aggregation of claims in a class action is only partial. Class actions achieve great economies of scale, but the claims of individual class members must eventually be addressed, and that is usually expensive.

a. Notice. Class members who can be identified with reasonable effort are entitled to individual notice. Fed. R. Civ. P. 23(c)(2)(B); Eisen v. Carlisle & Jacquelin, 417 U.S. 156 (1974). Another mailing is needed to distribute the funds from a settlement or judgment to the members of the class. Individual notice is expensive, and occasionally, if the individual claims are very small but the class members are mostly identifiable, the cost of notice may exceed the amount in controversy.

b. Calculating damages. Damages must ultimately be determined for each member of the class. If this requires an individual hearing for each class member, the class action becomes unmanageable. There is enormous pressure to find a way of measuring damages that does not require hearings but relies on information in defendants' files or information that can be reported on a simple claim form that class members can complete without the help of a lawyer. That often means reducing damage calculations to a formula or an approximation.

3. The parties' incentives. The parties' incentives depend on the size of the individual claims and the stage of the litigation.

a. Plaintiffs. If the claims are too small to litigate individually, the class will not be compensated unless the court certifies a class action and the court or the parties find a way to decide the case, administer the claims, and distribute the funds at an affordable cost. So the class as a whole has powerful incentives to find cost-effective ways of determining individual damages. Approximations and estimates are much better than nothing. Perhaps even more important to incentives, if the claims do not succeed on a class basis, the attorneys for the class will not get paid. And in practice, the attorneys for the class are making most of the decisions.

Class members whose claims are disadvantaged by the compromises necessary to make the class action manageable have incentives to complain about those compromises. And lawyers who are involved in the case but are not the lead lawyers for the class have incentives to file objections in hopes that, when the objections are settled, they will get a bigger share of the fees. So Joyce Howe complained that the settlement assumes that everyone's supplemental insurance paid 80 percent of the Medicare co-payment, but her supplemental insurance paid only 50 percent. Maybe she was really upset about that, or maybe her lawyer was really upset that the other class representative had negotiated a settlement without much help from him. Neither Howe nor her lawyer really wanted to defeat class certification or prevent an eventual settlement; neither would have gotten paid without a settlement or a successful trial. But they were willing to attack the settlement in hopes of getting it modified to achieve a larger payout for themselves.

If the individual claims are large enough to litigate individually, more class members are likely to object to the settlement, and some class members will want to opt out of the class and pursue their case individually. Defendants don't want to pay the class and also have to deal with large numbers of individual cases, so they often reserve the right to walk away from the settlement if too many class members opt out.

b. Defendants. If the claims are too small to litigate individually, defendants don't have to pay anybody (except their own lawyers), unless the case is certified as a class action. So defendants fight class certification with every available argument, including the argument that damages cannot be determined without thousands of individual hearings. Plaintiffs respond that damages can be determined, closely enough, with simple and inexpensive procedures. The Second Circuit has held that damages cannot be calculated on a class-wide basis over defendant's objection. McLaughlin v. American Tobacco Co., 522 F.3d 215 (2d Cir. 2008).

Once a class has been certified—or once serious settlement discussions begin—defendants' incentives change. Now defendants want the class settlement to finally dispose of all similar claims that could be brought against them; they want everyone to be included in the class and bound by the settlement, and no one left out and free to sue separately. This means that both sides now have strong incentives to find a cost-effective way to determine damages. These changing incentives on the defense side are why, in the *Average Wholesale Price* litigation, victims in nine states were initially excluded from the class and then restored to the class.

If claims of individual class members are large enough to litigate individually, defeating class certification will not make the claims go away. So with larger claims, defendants may prefer from the beginning to include all possible claimants in the class and to achieve one global settlement at the lowest possible cost.

4. Approximating damages to individual class members. Is there a problem with approximating damages? Joyce Howe gets paid as though her supplemental insurance covered 80 percent of the Medicare co-payment, when it actually covered only 50 percent. Maybe the parties could have addressed that with one more line on the claim form. But every additional mailing is expensive; if no one raised this issue before the claim form was mailed, it is not in the interest of the class as a whole to send a supplemental claim form with one more question.

This is a settlement; approximations are justified in part by the consent of the parties. Joyce Howe did not consent, but a class representative has consented for her. The court has appointed the class representative and his lawyers to act as fiduciaries for the class, and class members have been given an opportunity to opt out. This standard explanation is somewhat complicated here by the fact that Joyce Howe was also a class representative. But with or without that unusual fact, class settlements are imposed on objecting class members without their consent. If every class member could veto the settlement by withholding consent, hold-out problems might be insuperable; every class member could potentially demand a side payment as the price of her consent.

Some lawyers try to extract such payments by routinely objecting to class settlements. A federal judge has described such conduct as "reprehensible," but held that it is not racketeering under federal law, Edelson PC v. The Bandas Law Firm PC, 2018 WL 723287 (N.D. Ill. Feb. 6, 2018), and it is not abuse of process under Illinois law, 2018 WL 3496085 (N.D. Ill. July 20, 2018).

The treble damages in *Average Wholesale Price* are also a departure from individual calculation of damages. Some of the state consumer-protection statutes at issue provide for single damages, some for double damages, some for treble damages. Some provide no private cause of action. Varying the payout by state to take account of these differences would not have required hearings and probably would have been manageable. A uniform damages formula simplified a bit (some patients no doubt moved interstate while taking Zoladex), treble damages for everybody gave more money to the class and less to charity, and once defendant had committed $24 million, it was not affected by changes in the distribution formula.

5. Coming full circle. We began the course with Hatahley v. United States, in section 2.A, where the government slaughtered the Navajos' horses. The court of appeals refused to let the district court approximate damages, even for emotional distress. This holding did not make the claims go away, but it made it considerably more expensive for the plaintiffs to prove their claims, and that litigation burden helped shift bargaining leverage to the government. The case eventually settled for less than a quarter of what the district judge had awarded before the government's appeal.

Hatahley was not a class action; it was a simple joinder of the claims of many plaintiffs. It was a litigated case, not a settlement. And the court of appeals had obviously lost confidence in the district judge. Should *Hatahley*'s requirements for individual proof of damages apply to class action settlements? Even if the result is that most class actions become impossible, and potential defendants realize that they have effective immunity for taking small sums from each of many people? Did the court of appeals go too far in *Hatahley* even on the facts before it?

NOTES ON FLUID-CLASS RECOVERIES AND CY PRES DISTRIBUTIONS

1. Leftover class funds. Some of the settlement money in *Average Wholesale Price* will not be paid to class members at all. It will be given to charity. What is the justification for that? Is it just that this is a settlement and the parties agreed to it?

Such distributions are common in class actions. *Average Wholesale Price* illustrates the most common practice: Notices are sent to all class members who can be found, inviting them to file claims. But many cannot be found, and many who are found do not respond, either because they do not understand the instructions, cannot find the (usually minimal) records needed to prove their claim, or don't think their small claim is worth the effort. So after the filed claims are paid (in full in *Average Wholesale Price*, but more commonly, only in part), there is money left over. What to do with it?

If the amount left over is very small per class member, the cost of a second distribution to class members may be prohibitive. Sometimes the class members who can be found have been fully compensated and have no viable claim to a further distribution. Sometimes the court or defendants take the view that the class members' entitlement is determined by the settlement, not by what their rightful position would have been if they had proved their claims at trial. On that view, the class members who filed claims have been fully compensated, even if they have gotten only a small fraction of their provable damages.

Recall the law-and-economics idea (in note 6 following *Hatahley*) that it is of secondary importance whether damages are paid *to victims*; the important thing is that defendants have to pay. That is the key to deterrence. And here, where distribution to victims is difficult or impossible, that idea is actually implemented.

2. Fluid-class recoveries. A more focused, more complicated idea arose in some early class actions where it appeared that any distribution to the class would be impossible. The idea was to spend the money for the benefit of the class, or a proxy for the class. So in antitrust or rate-regulation cases where defendants overcharged for a product or service, damages might be calculated on a class-wide basis and defendants might be required to sell the same product or service at a discounted price until the amount of the settlement had been consumed in discounts. These discounts would not necessarily go to the class members who had paid the overcharges, and certainly there would be no relationship between any class member's earlier damages and his subsequent discounts. But some of the class members who had paid the overcharges would benefit from the subsequent discounts, and at least the class that received the discounts would be similar to the class that paid the overcharges. There was a class of all the consumers of the product or service, even if membership in that class was fluid.

The fluid-class recovery in this sense appears to have been talked about much more than it was ever implemented. It was actually ordered at least once, in a case about regulated bus fares. Bebchick v. Public Utilities Commission, 318 F.2d 187, 203-204 (D.C. Cir. 1963). The most famous fluid-class recovery case was Eisen v. Carlisle & Jacquelin, 479 F.2d 1005 (2d Cir. 1973), *vacated on other grounds*, 417 U.S. 156 (1974). The court of appeals emphatically rejected fluid-class recoveries in litigated cases; the Supreme Court did not reach the issue. *Eisen* largely killed the fluid-class recovery in cases litigated to judgment; perhaps it was impractical in any event. But the idea survived, evolved into a simpler form, and flourished in class action settlements.

3. Cy pres distributions. The idea of the fluid class has been extended by analogy to expenditures that benefit people like the class members, or serve some interest related to the theory of the class action, or sometimes, just do some unrelated public good chosen by class counsel or even defendant. There is no bright line along this continuum; these solutions are sometimes described in terms of fluid class and more often in terms of cy pres.

Cy pres is most plausible when payments have been distributed to individual class members based on the original settlement formula and when the amount left over will be consumed, or nearly so, by the cost of a second distribution. But the practice grew, first to include larger amounts of unclaimed funds and then to include settlements where everything went to the lawyers and to charity and nothing went to the class. Examples of this evolution are collected in Superior Beverage Co. v. Owens-Illinois, Inc., 827 F. Supp. 477, 478-479 (N.D. Ill. 1993), where the court held a grant competition to dispose of the unclaimed settlement fund. Purely cy pres settlements, with nothing for the class, are collected in In re Microsoft Corp. Antitrust Litigation, 185 F. Supp. 2d 519, 523 (D. Md. 2002), where Microsoft proposed to create a foundation to provide technology to schools. Fluid-class and cy pres cases of all sorts are collected in Judge Weinstein's massive opinion in Schwab v. Philip Morris USA, Inc., 449 F. Supp. 2d 992, 1250-1272 (E.D.N.Y. 2006), *rev'd as* McLaughlin v. American Tobacco Co., 522 F.3d 215 (2d Cir. 2008).

Charities have hired lawyers to seek money from settlements. Legal charities have been popular for distributions supervised by lawyers and judges; some legal-aid societies have come to expect, and to rely on, regular distributions from unclaimed class action settlements. Illinois has provided by statute that unclaimed funds in state class actions must go to legal services providers, except that in settlements, 50 percent may go to other charities "if the court finds there is good cause to approve such a distribution as part of a settlement." 735 Ill. Comp. Stat. 5/2-807(b).

After a period of growth, cy pres settlements have come under more scrutiny, with some courts insisting on maximizing the distribution to the class and on a tighter link between the class and any cy pres distribution. The district court's insistence on treble damages to the class in *Average Wholesale Price* is an example. In both *Average Wholesale Price* and *McLaughlin*, the courts of appeals cited the American Law Institute's statement encouraging distributions to the class. And now the Supreme Court is poised to weigh in.

4. Appeals courts start reining in broad cy pres remedies. Courts of appeals are adopting the ALI standards and enforcing them vigorously. Some of the cases are collected in In re BankAmerica Corp. Securities Litigation, 775 F.3d 1060 (8th Cir. 2015).

> Because the settlement funds are the property of the class, a *cy pres* distribution to a third party of unclaimed settlement funds is permissible "*only* when it is not feasible to make further distributions to class members" . . . except where an additional distribution would provide a windfall to class members with *liquidated*-damages claims that were 100 percent satisfied by the initial distribution.

Id. at 1064, quoting *Principles of the Law of Aggregate Litigation* §3.07 cmt. *a* (Am. Law Inst. 2010). Paying out 100 percent of the amount due under a settlement formula is not the same as paying 100 percent of a class member's actual damages. Where a cy pres distribution is permitted, *BankAmerica* said that the court must identify the next-best recipient that most closely approximates the class. It is not clear who that would be for a nationwide class of investors.

In an example of the 100-percent-satisfied branch of the doctrine, the First Circuit has approved an $11.4 million cy pres distribution out of a $40-million settlement, where those class members who filed claims had already received full payment of their estimated damages. In re Lupron Marketing and Sales Practices Litigation, 677

F.3d 21 (1st Cir. 2012). Lupron is a cancer drug, and the cy pres distribution went to cancer centers for research on the cancers treated with Lupron.

The Third Circuit joined the trend, and may have toughened the emerging requirements, in In re Baby Products Antitrust Litigation, 708 F.3d 163 (3d Cir. 2013). Plaintiffs' expert estimated that Toys R Us and its co-conspirators had inflated the price of certain baby products by 18 percent. The settlement refunded 20 percent of the purchase price, trebled under the antitrust laws, to any customers with some documentary evidence that they had purchased one of the products from Toys R Us. The settlement paid $5 to anyone who claimed to have purchased one of the products but had no evidence. Few claims with documentary evidence were filed, with the result that $3 million went to the class, $14 million to counsel, and $18.5 million to cy pres.

The court of appeals was troubled by those proportions. It approved cy pres settlements in principle, but vacated the district court's approval of this settlement. Noting that some of the products cost up to $300, so that 20 percent trebled would be $180, the court thought that the reason consumers failed to file claims must have been that the documentation requirements were too stringent. It remanded without suggesting what lesser documentation requirements might be feasible. The court also said that cy pres distributions are less valuable than distributions to the class and should be discounted for purposes of awarding attorneys' fees.

5. Some examples. Does it make sense to give the unclaimed portion of the Zoladex settlement to cancer research? Why not prostate-cancer research in particular? Is patient care as good as research? It might be harder to target patient care to a particular cancer.

Consider some other examples. What is a good cy pres distribution, and what is a bad one? Does it make any difference how closely the cy pres recipient is linked to the class?

a. Race discrimination. In Powell v. Georgia-Pacific Corp., 119 F.3d 703 (8th Cir. 1997), there was more than a million dollars in unclaimed funds and accrued interest from a class action alleging employment discrimination against black workers. The court approved a scholarship fund for black students from the six counties where most of the class members had lived, to be administered by defendant for ten years, with any remaining money to be contributed to the United Negro College Fund.

b. Travel agents. In a nationwide class action alleging a price-fixing conspiracy to hold down the fees paid to travel agents, the court first rejected a cy pres distribution to charitable and educational institutions in Minneapolis; local charities did not fit the national scope of the case. In re Airline Ticket Commission Antitrust Litigation, 268 F.3d 619, 625-626 (8th Cir. 2001). After a remand, the court rejected a distribution to the National Association for Public Interest Law because it had nothing to do with the theory of the case or the interests of class members. 307 F.3d 679 (8th Cir. 2002). The court directed that the money be distributed first to travel agencies in Puerto Rico and the Virgin Islands, which were subject to the conspiracy but not included in the class, and that any remaining funds be distributed to a recipient that "must relate, as nearly as possible, to the original purpose of the class action and its settlement." Id. at 684. Is there a travel-agent charity?

c. Male flight attendants. Wilson v. Southwest Airlines, Inc., 880 F.2d 807 (5th Cir. 1989), arose from a successful class action on behalf of males who applied for flight attendant and ticket agent jobs at a time when Southwest was promoting itself as the love airline, with sexy flight attendants in boots and hot pants, and with its principal hub at Love Field in Dallas. The only remnant of that highly successful but illegal campaign is Southwest's stock-market symbol, LUV. No charity served any approximation of Texas males rejected for flight attendant jobs, and the class members who filed claims had been fully compensated. The court rejected any distribution to charity, used some of the money to pay additional fees to plaintiffs' counsel, and returned the rest to defendant.

d. Unrelated charities. Cases going the other way, giving unclaimed funds to charities wholly unrelated to the class, are collected in Jones v. National Distillers, 56 F. Supp. 2d 355, 358-359 (S.D.N.Y. 1999). *Jones* gave the remnants of a securities fraud settlement to a legal-aid society.

e. Fashion models. Fears v. Wilhelmina Model Agency, Inc., 2005 WL 1041134 (S.D.N.Y. 2005), was an antitrust class action alleging that model agencies conspired to hold down the fees paid to fashion models. After hearing from many interested charities, the district court awarded the leftover money to hospital programs focused on eating disorders, ovarian cancer, and heart disease in women, and to the Legal Aid Society. The judge expressly sought out charities benefiting women, apparently thinking of models as female even after recognizing that 40 percent of the class was male. See *id.* nn.14-15.

The class appealed, arguing that those who had filed claims (about 5% of the class) should be paid treble damages under the antitrust laws, even though the settlement had not provided for that. The court of appeals vacated the order for further consideration. Masters v. Wilhelmina Model Agency, Inc., 473 F.3d 423 (2d Cir. 2007). The trial judge reinstated his original award, in a careful opinion that doubted his authority to increase the distribution to class members and doubted the justice of distributing so much more to so few. Fears v. Wilhelmina Model Agency, Inc., 2007 WL 1944343 (S.D.N.Y. 2007). This time class counsel appealed, arguing that the money should be used to increase the fee award. The court of appeals vacated again, 315 Fed. Appx. 333 (2d Cir. 2009), and the district court, in another substantial opinion, again reinstated his original order. 2009 WL 2958396 (S.D.N.Y. 2009).

f. AOL subscribers. Without disclosing that it was doing so, AOL, once a leading provider of internet access before the rise of broadband, added advertising at the end of every e-mail message sent by any of its 66 million subscribers. Damages were unquantifiable; unjust enrichment was $2 million, which would have been less than 3 cents per class member. The case settled for a promise of repeated disclosures at six-month intervals, with a right to opt out of having advertising attached to one's e-mails, and charitable contributions of $110,000, principally directed to the Legal Aid Foundation of Los Angeles, the Boys and Girls Clubs of Santa Monica and Los Angeles, and the Federal Judicial Center.

The court of appeals disapproved, because two of the charities were local but the class was national, and because none of the charities had anything to do with the underlying claims. The court rejected the parties' argument that the class was so diverse that no more appropriate charity was available. "The parties should not have trouble selecting beneficiaries from any number of non-profit organizations that work to protect internet users from fraud, predation, and other forms of online malfeasance." Nachshin v. AOL, LLC, 663 F.3d 1034, 1041 (9th Cir. 2011). And if no such charity could be found, the district court was instructed to consider giving the money to the government.

g. Securities fraud. Additional cases are collected in In re Bankamerica Corp. Securities Litigation, 775 F.3d 1060 (8th Cir. 2015). The court held that no cy pres distribution is permitted if an additional distribution to the class is feasible, and that where a cy pres distribution is permitted, the court and counsel must search diligently for a charity that serves the interests of the class. A legal aid society could not receive any cy pres distribution when there were organizations devoted to securities fraud as their issue, "such as the SEC Fair Funds." *Id.* at 1067. Fair Funds are created from judgments or settlements in SEC enforcement litigation and are to be distributed to victims of the fraud that triggered the SEC lawsuit; Fair Funds can also accept contributions. 15 U.S.C. §7246.

6. The Supreme Court steps in, in a case where plaintiffs recovered nothing. The Supreme Court has agreed to consider the issue in a case where the entire settlement was cy pres. In re Google Referrer Header Privacy Litigation, 869 F.3d 737 (9th Cir. 2017), *cert. granted* as Frank v. Gaos, 138 S. Ct. 1697 (2018). Any page you go to from a list of Google search results gets the URL for the last website you were on before you made the search (the "referrer" page). Class plaintiffs alleged that this practice violates the Stored Communications Act and was also a breach of contract.

The case settled for $8.5 million and better disclosures of Google's practices; the practices themselves were not changed. The settlement set aside $3.2 million for attorneys' fees, administrative costs, and incentive payments to the class plaintiffs. The remaining $5.3 million was to be allocated to grants to promote internet privacy at Harvard, Stanford, Carnegie-Mellon, Chicago-Kent, the World Privacy Forum, and AARP (formerly and more informatively known as the American Association of Retired Persons). No cash went to any class member other than the named plaintiffs, who each got $5,000 for their time and trouble. Class counsel had graduated from the law schools at Harvard, Stanford, and Chicago-Kent, and Google had previously made charitable contributions to three of the recipients as well as hundreds of other charities.

Both the district court and the court of appeals approved the settlement. There were 129 million class members, so a distribution would come to 4 cents per class member (except that the cost of cutting and mailing the 129 million checks would have cost much more than $5.3 million). The small size of the settlement was justified by "the shakiness of the plaintiffs' claims." *Id.* at 742. Judge Wallace, dissenting, agreed that a cy pres settlement was appropriate but disapproved of nearly half the settlement going to class counsel's alma maters.

7. Escheat. Another obvious model for disposition of unclaimed funds is escheat, or giving the money to the government. The general rule is that unclaimed property escheats to the state where the property is located or where the owner is last known to have resided. Delaware v. New York, 507 U.S. 490, 498-499 (1993). Where money is paid into federal court, its rightful owner has been determined, and the money remains unclaimed for five years, the "court shall cause such money to be deposited in the Treasury in the name and to the credit of the United States." 28 U.S.C. §2042. There it will be held for the true owner, if he ever shows up, or for a state with a stronger claim to escheat the funds. United States v. 8.0 Acres of Land, 197 F.3d 24, 29-30 (1st Cir. 1999). The government can use the money until or unless someone else claims it. But choosing charities is more fun for judges and lawyers, and it is probably a greater motivation to settlement. Courts have held §2042 discretionary as applied to unclaimed funds in class actions. Some of these cases are collected in *Jones,* 56 F. Supp. 2d at 358. The Seventh Circuit invoked §2042 with respect to unclaimed settlement funds in In re Folding Carton Antitrust Litigation, 744 F.2d 1252 (7th Cir. 1984). The order provoked defiance and evasion by the parties and the district judge. For the aftermath, see Houck ex rel. United States v. Folding Carton Administration Committee, 881 F.2d 494 (7th Cir. 1989).

8. Suits against the federal government. Attorney General Jeff Sessions has forbidden attorneys representing the federal government to enter into any form of cy pres settlement. Memorandum for All Component Heads and U.S. Attorneys, https://www.justice.gov/opa/press-release/file/971826/download (June 5, 2017) [https://perma.cc/Z5RK-DXF2].

NOTES ON AFFIRMATIVE ACTION AS A FLUID-CLASS REMEDY

1. Court-ordered hiring goals. The most widespread exception to the general rejection of litigated fluid-class recoveries was generally not recognized as such. Every circuit ordered numerical goals as a remedy for employment discrimination. In these cases, employers who discriminated against earlier minority job applicants were ordered to prefer future minority job applicants. Most of these decrees resulted from settlements, but many of them were litigated, especially in the early years of discrimination law. A substantial opinion that cites many of the others is Association Against Discrimination in Employment, Inc. v. City of Bridgeport, 647 F.2d 256 (2d Cir. 1981).

Most of the cases spoke in general terms about eliminating the effects of discrimination. The effect to be eliminated was the racial composition of the employer's workforce, not any effect on an individual plaintiff. The cases mostly took this for granted, but there was a square statement in Justice Blackmun's dissent in Firefighters Local Union No. 1784 v. Stotts, 467 U.S. 561 (1984):

> In determining the nature of "appropriate" relief under §706(g) [42 U.S.C. §2000e-5(g)], courts have distinguished between individual relief and race-conscious class relief. . . . [A]n individual plaintiff is entitled to an award of individual relief only if he can establish that he was the victim of discrimination. That requirement grows out of the general equitable principles of "make whole" relief; an individual who has suffered no injury is not entitled to an individual award. . . .
>
> In Title VII class-action suits, the Courts of Appeals are unanimously of the view that race-conscious affirmative relief can also be "appropriate" under §706(g). . . . Because the discrimination sought to be alleviated by race-conscious relief is the classwide effects of past discrimination, rather than discrimination against identified members of the class, such relief is provided to the class as a whole rather than to its individual members. The relief may take many forms, but in class actions it frequently involves percentages . . . that require race to be taken into account when an employer hires or promotes employees. The distinguishing feature of race-conscious relief is that no individual member of the disadvantaged class has a claim to it, and individual beneficiaries of the relief need not show that they were themselves victims of the discrimination for which relief was granted.

Id. at 612-613.

2. Hiring goals compared to other fluid-class remedies. The reasons for "race-conscious class relief" were substantially the same as the reasons for attempting fluid-class recoveries in other contexts. It was often impractical to identify individual victims of discrimination. They had typically found another job by the time the litigation was over, or they could not be found at all. A court that wanted to create an immediate and substantial minority representation in the employer's workforce couldn't do it merely by reinstating identifiable victims. It was also much easier to police compliance with a numerical goal than to police compliance with an order not to discriminate in future hiring. Are these cases consistent with the general rejection of fluid-class recoveries in class actions for damages? Does the difference between damages and injunctions reconcile the cases?

3. Affirmative action and the nature of remedies. The comparison to fluid-class recoveries makes clear that much of the great national debate over affirmative action was really a debate over the nature of remedies. Proponents of hiring goals saw them as a remedy for widespread and longstanding discrimination. Opponents were generally willing to give identifiable victims of identifiable discrimination back pay, reinstatement with seniority, and anything else needed to make them whole (subject to statutes of limitation that are often unusually short). But these opponents thought that hiring goals or other forms of affirmative action granted preferences based on race rather than victimization.

4. *Hatahley* **again.** The district court in *Hatahley* treated the Indians' loss as a loss to the group as a whole; the court of appeals insisted on individual damage determinations. The court of appeals' decision reflects our legal system's traditional view that courts grant remedies to particular plaintiffs for particular wrongs. To change that practice as a general matter would require a wholly different law of remedies, and perhaps a wholly different role for courts in the constitutional scheme. Close attention to the litigants' rightful positions distinguishes remedial redistribution from legislative redistribution. Court-ordered affirmative action and the heyday of free-wheeling structural injunctions were notable exceptions; cy pres settlements are an exception today. But *Eisen*'s emphatic rejection of fluid-class recoveries, in 1973, illustrates the strength of the tradition even in an era when judges were more willing to be aggressive on behalf of plaintiffs.

5. **Hiring goals as an exception to the general rule.** Courts can create an exception or two without abandoning the system. Were the discrimination cases an appropriate exception? On one view they were a highly suspect exception: If the only exception from a fundamental general principle is granted on the basis of race, critics will say that is race discrimination.

From another perspective, the race cases were a highly appropriate exception: Pervasive racial discrimination has had cumulative effects on its victims and their descendants, and only a tiny portion of those effects will ever be remedied by traditional litigation. The beneficiaries of hiring goals might not have been discriminated against by defendant, but nearly all of them were adversely affected by discrimination by somebody. Most obviously, one reason simple nondiscrimination often fails to produce racial balance is that the states have always provided better education to whites than to blacks and other minorities. *Hatahley* also prefigured this argument: One reading of the district judge's opinion was that the Navajo had suffered many other wrongs, and he was going to remedy as much as he could.

6. **Remedies at whose cost?** Assuming that the beneficiaries of a racial hiring order deserved preference because of some past discrimination by someone else, why should *defendant* remedy that discrimination? Perhaps the answer was that he couldn't complain because he had discriminated and most of his victims couldn't be identified. That still left a harder question: The burden of a hiring goal fell on new applicants. What were they guilty of besides their ethnicity? Often they were new entrants to the workforce, young and powerless. They didn't design the discriminatory school system. Was it enough that some of them presumably benefited from it? Were the burdens of race-conscious hiring a rough-and-ready form of restitution from third-party beneficiaries of a wrong? Were they acceptable on the ground that whites would have less trouble than others getting a job somewhere else? Don't be too sure: The burden would tend to fall on the least qualified whites.

If all of this was just, it must be on the theory that gross approximations were good enough and substantial errors in individual cases had to be tolerated. Were the approximations good enough? We know that hiring goals gave benefits to people who had not been discriminated against by that employer; we know that confining relief to identifiable victims of particular employers would leave most discrimination wholly irremediable. Is there any way to know which set of errors was greater? Did courts get more people closer to their rightful position by ordering hiring goals or by insisting on individual proof?

7. Limits. Many courts would not order numerical goals in *promotions* if the burden would fall on a small and identifiable group of whites. The *Bridgeport* case in note 1 is a good example. Even more striking, courts generally refused to displace incumbents to make room even for identifiable victims of discrimination. See *Stotts*, 467 U.S. at 579 n.11. This was so even though the incumbents' union was often complicit in the adjudicated discrimination and the incumbents had likely benefited from it. A finding that a particular minority applicant had been discriminatorily rejected was also a finding that some incumbent had been discriminatorily hired. It might even be possible to identify the very incumbent who was hired on the day the victim was rejected. It didn't matter. Even when a company demoted a victim on discriminatory grounds and gave her job to someone else, most courts would not displace the beneficiary. An example is Spagnuolo v. Whirlpool Corp., 717 F.2d 114, 119-122 (4th Cir. 1983). Victims could recover lost pay while they waited for a position to open.

Don't these cases give identifiable victims too little relief? If the courts were so scrupulous about the rights of identifiable incumbents, why were they so cavalier about the rights of applicants? One answer is that the applicant had not relied on a job with the particular employer but incumbents had. Another is that identifiable incumbents often appeared in court as real human beings, with lawyers to represent them. Future applicants were usually unrepresented abstractions.

8. The Supreme Court cases. The Supreme Court addressed court-ordered hiring goals in Local 28 of the Sheet Metal Workers v. Equal Employment Opportunity Commission, 478 U.S. 421 (1986). Four justices said that courts could order "racial preferences" as a remedy, but not in "the majority" of cases. *Id.* at 475-476. They thought such remedies would be appropriate in cases of "particularly longstanding or egregious discrimination" where the alternative was "endless enforcement litigation," *id.* at 448, where "necessary to dissipate the lingering effects of pervasive discrimination," *id.* at 476, and perhaps in other situations, but not "to create a racially balanced work force," *id.* at 475.

The plurality gave content to "lingering effects of pervasive discrimination." It said that the union's reputation for discrimination would discourage minorities from even applying, and that its informal recruiting processes would reach whites much more effectively than minorities. Neither of these effects of past discrimination was likely to end until "a substantial number" of nonwhite workers had become union members. *Id.* at 477. Justice Powell concurred in the result with respect to "cases involving particularly egregious conduct," where he thought an order to quit discriminating was an insufficient remedy. *Id.* at 483. Four dissenters would have vacated the hiring goals.

The Court also upheld a temporary 50 percent promotion quota for the Alabama Department of Public Safety. United States v. Paradise, 480 U.S. 149 (1987). Again the history of discrimination was long and egregious, and again the Court failed to produce a majority opinion.

9. Hiring goals without a fluid class? Suppose that court-ordered numerical goals are now limited to egregious discrimination like that in *Sheet Metal Workers* and *Paradise*. Does this use of numerical goals depend on the fluid-class-recovery notion? Does it view minority applicants as substitute beneficiaries of a remedy that cannot be effectively delivered to earlier victims? Or can this use of goals be defended as part of a preventive remedy for minority workers who, because of defendant's egregious past discrimination, will be deterred from applying in the future unless other minorities are hired now?

10. Other arguments about affirmative action. Remedies law is only one perspective from which to consider the debate over affirmative action, and court-ordered hiring plans were only one small subset of all affirmative action plans. Employers and universities can implement affirmative action plans for reasons of their own, without having to justify judicial power to order such a plan against an unwilling defendant. Arguments that voluntary affirmative action plans are a remedy for past discrimination may invoke a looser, more political concept of remedy, related only by analogy to judicial remedies and judicial definitions of the rightful position. Important arguments about the meaning of the Constitution and the civil rights laws, about the wisdom of affirmative action, about the nature of racial justice, and about the doubtful legitimacy of public institutions with whole racial groups unrepresented are beyond the scope of these notes. But those arguments are also essential to a full understanding of affirmative action.

11. Why the past tense? This set of notes is largely written in the past tense, not because the cases with court-ordered hiring goals have been overruled, but because they have mostly faded away. There is less discrimination than in the past, and while much discrimination remains, most of it is more subtle and harder to prove. The courts have become far less sympathetic to civil rights remedies, and far more sympathetic to claims challenging affirmative action as a form of reverse discrimination. The Bridgeport Fire Department, having lost discrimination suits by blacks in the 1980s, lost a discrimination suit in the 2000s by whites challenging its continued efforts to avoid excluding minority applicants. Ricci v. DeStefano, 557 U.S. 557 (2009). *Ricci* is formally consistent with earlier cases, but it aggressively applies the limits in those cases and raises questions about a wide range of efforts to hire or promote more minorities.

NOTES ON PARTLY IDENTIFIABLE VICTIMS

1. Victims of employment discrimination. In the fluid-class-recovery and affirmative action cases, the victims are often impossible to identify. In another important set of cases, the victims can be partly identified. A good example is Hameed v. International Association of Iron Workers, 637 F.2d 506 (8th Cir. 1980). The union's apprentice program had wholly excluded black applicants. When the Civil Rights Act of 1964 banned employment discrimination, the union dropped its explicit racial barrier and adopted a new system for selecting apprentices. The new system had 12 criteria, many tending to unnecessarily exclude minorities. The court of appeals eventually held that the new selection system was also illegal. But by that time, the system had been in use for many years. What remedy for applicants denied admission under the new system?

Hameed presents a common problem in discrimination litigation. Plaintiffs are identifiable victims in the sense that we know they were rejected and that discriminatory selection criteria were used. But plaintiffs are not identifiable in the sense that we know they would have been admitted to the apprentice program but for the discrimination. We don't know what criteria the union would have used if it had not used the illegal criteria. Ordering the union to devise a legal selection method, and then applying that method retroactively to see which of the plaintiffs would have been selected, is not very attractive.

In cases where the employer or union had nondiscriminatory selection criteria but didn't apply them to minorities, it is theoretically possible to reconstruct the rightful work history of every applicant and employee. But in practice, this effort often bogs down in "a quagmire of hypothetical judgments." Pettway v. American Cast Iron Pipe Co., 494 F.2d 211, 260 (5th Cir. 1974). "To assume that employee #242 would have been promoted in three years to such-and-such job instead of employee #354 is so speculative as to unfairly penalize employee #354." *Id.* at 262 n.152. The task is more manageable in individual actions, where the court can focus on a few individual plaintiffs and decide that they would or would not have been hired, promoted, or admitted. An example is Hopwood v. Texas, 236 F.3d 256 (5th Cir. 2000), where a university proved that four white plaintiffs would not have been admitted to law school even in the absence of affirmative action.

2. Pro rata back pay. One remedy in cases like *Hameed* and *Pettway* has been pro rata back pay. The basic technique is to determine how much the group of discrimination victims would have earned but for discrimination. Then, all class members who had a chance to be selected share in that award pro rata. An example is United States v. City of Miami, 195 F.3d 1292 (11th Cir. 1999). Where the employer's workforce is small and the legitimate hiring and promotion criteria relatively clear, the preferred remedy is to reconstruct actual work histories and award back pay to the plaintiff who would have gotten the job.

Should the courts deny relief to partly identifiable victims because no plaintiff can show it's more likely than not that he would have been selected but for discrimination? Note that these plaintiffs can show a lot more than the beneficiary of a numerical goal. Any minority applicant may benefit from a goal, no matter how clear it is that he wasn't around at the time of the discrimination being remedied. Plaintiffs in *Hameed* and similar cases were the targets of the discrimination being remedied, and it's nearly certain that but for the discrimination, some of them would have been hired or admitted. As long as the employer does not have to pay for the same vacancy more than once, isn't a pro rata payment to all the potential victims the best approximation of the rightful position?

3. The chance to be fairly considered. Maybe no one can show that she lost a job, but all plaintiffs lost the opportunity to be fairly considered. That opportunity may be valued as the pay plaintiff would have earned if selected, discounted by the risk of not being selected. Should we think of pro rata back pay as the value of the lost chance to be fairly considered? An example of that approach is Alexander v. City of Milwaukee, 474 F.3d 437, 449-451 (7th Cir. 2007). Is that explanation easier to reconcile with the traditional focus on the rightful position?

4. Loss of chance. Thinking of these cases in terms of loss of chance shows that they are essentially similar to cases from other contexts. Toxic torts often involve large numbers of people exposed to a toxin, with a disease that could have been caused by that exposure or could have occurred naturally. Consider Allen v. United States, 588 F. Supp. 247 (D. Utah 1984), *rev'd on other grounds*, 816 F.2d 1417 (10th Cir. 1987). The government conducted nuclear tests in the open air, and two decades later, the cancer rate went up in communities downwind from the test site. Some of these cancers would have happened anyway. The judge tried to decide each case on a more-likely-than-not standard. Might he have partially compensated every cancer based on the odds that it was caused by the testing? Would that have been better or worse?

Loss of chance can arise in situations with only one possible victim. The doctrine is most commonly used in cases of medical malpractice—usually failure to diagnose—that reduces plaintiff's chances of surviving an illness that might well have killed him anyway. More than 20 states have adopted loss of chance in this context; about 15 have rejected it. Smith v. Providence Health & Services—Oregon, 393 P.3d 1106, 1114 (Or. 2017); Matsuyama v. Birnbaum, 890 N.E.2d 819, 828 n.23 (Mass. 2008).

5. The big picture. Remedies have to be strong enough to work, and accurate enough to be just. Requiring too much precision defeats a remedy in all but the simplest cases. Requiring too little can compensate the undeserving and impose liability on the innocent. As with so many questions, the challenge is to find the right solution in the middle, one that appropriately divides the unavoidable risk of error between plaintiffs and defendants.

APPENDIX

Present Value Tables

Present value tables are useful in determining the present value of a worker's lost income or the present value of the income produced by a capital asset. The example here is taken from Rufus Wixon, *Accountant's Handbook* 29.58-29.59, fig. 25 (4th ed. 1960). It shows the present value of $1 at interest rates ranging from 1 to 6 percent over periods from 0 to 100 years. If you read across the row for any period, to the column for any interest rate, you will find the present value of $1 at that time and interest rate. Some examples:

The present value of $1 paid immediately—period 0—is $1; that is true at any interest rate. The present value of $1 paid in one year is 99.009901 cents at an interest rate of 1 percent, or 94.339623 cents at an interest rate of 6 percent. The present value of $1 paid in thirty years is 74.192292 cents at an interest rate of 1 percent, or 17.411013 cents at an interest rate of 6 percent.

For larger amounts, simply multiply. Thus, the present value of $10,000 to be paid in thirty years is $7,419.23 at an interest rate of 1 percent, or $1,741.10 at an interest rate of 6 percent.

To calculate the present value of a stream of income, you have to treat each year separately. Find the value of the first year's income, the second year's income, and so on to the end of the expected stream. Then add up the present value of each year's income to get the present value of the whole stream of income.

If you want to work with interest rates higher than 6 percent, you can use periods of less than a year. For example, ten years at 12 percent is equal to 20 six-month periods at 6 percent.

Present Value of 1 at Compound Interest

Value for period n and interest rate $i = \dfrac{1}{(1 + i)^n} = (1 + i)^{-n}$

Periods	1%	1.25%	1.5%	1.75%	2%	2.25%	2.5%
0	1.	1.	1.	1.	1.	1.	1.
1	0.99009901	0.98765432	0.98522167	0.98280098	0.98039216	0.97799511	0.97560976
2	0.98029605	0.97546106	0.97066175	0.96589777	0.96116878	0.95647444	0.95181440
3	0.97059015	0.96341833	0.95631699	0.94928528	0.94232233	0.93542732	0.92859941
4	0.96098034	0.95152428	0.94218423	0.93295851	0.92384543	0.91484335	0.90595064
5	0.95146569	0.93977706	0.92826033	0.91691254	0.90573081	0.89471232	0.88385429
6	0.94204524	0.92817488	0.91454219	0.90114254	0.88797138	0.87502427	0.86229687
7	0.93271805	0.91671593	0.90102679	0.88564378	0.87056018	0.85576946	0.84126524
8	0.92348322	0.90539845	0.88771112	0.87041157	0.85349037	0.83693835	0.82074657
9	0.91433982	0.89422069	0.87459224	0.85544135	0.83675527	0.81852161	0.80072836
10	0.90528695	0.88318093	0.86166723	0.84072860	0.82034830	0.80051013	0.78119840
11	0.89632372	0.87227746	0.84893323	0.82626889	0.80426304	0.78289499	0.76214478
12	0.88744923	0.86150860	0.83638742	0.81205788	0.78849318	0.76566748	0.74355589
13	0.87866260	0.85087269	0.82402702	0.79809128	0.77303253	0.74881905	0.72542038
14	0.86996297	0.84036809	0.81184928	0.78436490	0.75787502	0.73234137	0.70772720
15	0.86134947	0.82999318	0.79985150	0.77087459	0.74301473	0.71622628	0.69046556
16	0.85282126	0.81974635	0.78803104	0.75761631	0.72844581	0.70046580	0.67362493
17	0.84437749	0.80962602	0.77638526	0.74458605	0.71416256	0.68505212	0.65719506
18	0.83601731	0.79963064	0.76491159	0.73177990	0.70015937	0.66997763	0.64116591
19	0.82773992	0.78975866	0.75360747	0.71919401	0.68643076	0.65523484	0.62552772
20	0.81954447	0.78000855	0.74247042	0.70682458	0.67297133	0.64081647	0.61027094
21	0.81143017	0.77037881	0.73149795	0.69466789	0.65977582	0.62671538	0.59538629
22	0.80339621	0.76086796	0.72068763	0.68272028	0.64683904	0.61292457	0.58086467
23	0.79544179	0.75147453	0.71003708	0.67097817	0.63415592	0.59943724	0.56669724
24	0.78756613	0.74219707	0.69954392	0.65943800	0.62172149	0.58624668	0.55287535
25	0.77976844	0.73303414	0.68920583	0.64809632	0.60953087	0.57334639	0.53939059
26	0.77204796	0.72398434	0.67902052	0.63694970	0.59757928	0.56072997	0.52623472
27	0.76440392	0.71504626	0.66898574	0.62599479	0.58586204	0.54839117	0.51339973
28	0.75683557	0.70621853	0.65909925	0.61522829	0.57437455	0.53632388	0.50087778
29	0.74934215	0.69749978	0.64935887	0.60464697	0.56311231	0.52452213	0.48866125
30	0.74192292	0.68888867	0.63976243	0.59424764	0.55207089	0.51298008	0.47674269
31	0.73457715	0.68038387	0.63030781	0.58402716	0.54124597	0.50169201	0.46511481
32	0.72730411	0.67198407	0.62099292	0.57398247	0.53063330	0.49065233	0.45377055
33	0.72010307	0.66368797	0.61181568	0.56411053	0.52022873	0.47985558	0.44270298
34	0.71297334	0.65549429	0.60277407	0.55440839	0.51002817	0.46929641	0.43190534
35	0.70591420	0.64740177	0.59386608	0.54487311	0.50002761	0.45896960	0.42137107
36	0.69892495	0.63940916	0.58508974	0.53550183	0.49022315	0.44887002	0.41109372
37	0.69200490	0.63151522	0.57644309	0.52629172	0.48061093	0.43899268	0.40106705
38	0.68515337	0.62371873	0.56792423	0.51724002	0.47118719	0.42933270	0.39128492
39	0.67836967	0.61601850	0.55953126	0.50834400	0.46194822	0.41988528	0.38174139
40	0.67165314	0.60841334	0.55126232	0.49960098	0.45289042	0.41064575	0.37243062
41	0.66500311	0.60090206	0.54311559	0.49100834	0.44401021	0.40160954	0.36334695
42	0.65841892	0.59348352	0.53508925	0.48256348	0.43530413	0.39277216	0.35448483
43	0.65189992	0.58615656	0.52718153	0.47426386	0.42676875	0.38412925	0.34583886
44	0.64544546	0.57892006	0.51939067	0.46610699	0.41840074	0.37567653	0.33740376
45	0.63905492	0.57177290	0.51171494	0.45809040	0.41019680	0.36740981	0.32917440
46	0.63272764	0.56471397	0.50415265	0.45021170	0.40215373	0.35932500	0.32114576
47	0.62646301	0.55774249	0.49670218	0.44246850	0.39426809	0.35141809	0.31331294
48	0.62026041	0.55085649	0.48936170	0.43485848	0.38653761	0.34368518	0.30567116
49	0.61411921	0.54405579	0.48212975	0.42737934	0.37895844	0.33612242	0.29821576
50	0.60803882	0.53733905	0.47500468	0.42002883	0.37152788	0.32872608	0.29094221
55	0.57852808	0.50497892	0.44092800	0.38512970	0.33650425	0.29411528	0.25715052
60	0.55044962	0.47456760	0.40929597	0.35313025	0.30478227	0.26314856	0.22728359
65	0.52373392	0.44598775	0.37993321	0.32378956	0.27605069	0.23544226	0.20088557
70	0.49831486	0.41912905	0.35267692	0.29688670	0.25002761	0.21065309	0.17755358
75	0.47412949	0.39388787	0.32737599	0.27221914	0.22645771	0.18847391	0.15693149
80	0.45111794	0.37016679	0.30389015	0.24960114	0.20510973	0.16862993	0.13870457
85	0.42922324	0.34787426	0.28208917	0.22886242	0.18577420	0.15087528	0.12259463
90	0.40839119	0.32692425	0.26185218	0.20984682	0.16826142	0.13498997	0.10835579
95	0.38857020	0.30723591	0.24306699	0.19241118	0.15239955	0.12077719	0.09477073
100	0.36971121	0.28873326	0.22562944	0.17642422	0.13803297	0.10806084	0.08464737

2.75 %	3 %	3.5 %	4 %	4.5 %	5 %	6 %
1.	1.	1.	1.	1.	1.	1.
0.97323601	0.97087379	0.96618357	0.96153846	0.95693780	0.95238095	0.94339623
0.94718833	0.94259591	0.93351070	0.92455621	0.91572995	0.90702948	0.88999644
0.92183779	0.91514166	0.90194271	0.88899636	0.87629660	0.86383760	0.83961928
0.89716573	0.88848705	0.87144223	0.85480419	0.83856134	0.82270247	0.79209366
0.87315400	0.86260878	0.84197317	0.82192711	0.80245105	0.78352617	0.74725817
0.84978491	0.83748426	0.81350064	0.79031453	0.76789574	0.74621540	0.70496054
0.82704128	0.81309151	0.78599096	0.75991781	0.73482846	0.71068133	0.66505711
0.80490635	0.78940923	0.75941156	0.73069021	0.70318513	0.67683936	0.62741237
0.78336385	0.76641673	0.73373097	0.70258674	0.67290443	0.64460892	0.59189846
0.76239791	0.74409391	0.70891881	0.67556417	0.64392768	0.61391325	0.55839478
0.74199310	0.72242128	0.68494571	0.64958093	0.61619874	0.58467929	0.52678753
0.72213440	0.70137988	0.66178330	0.62459705	0.58966386	0.55683742	0.49696936
0.70280720	0.66095134	0.63940415	0.60057409	0.56427164	0.53032135	0.46883902
0.68399728	0.66111781	0.61778179	0.57747508	0.53997286	0.50506795	0.44230096
0.66569078	0.64186195	0.59689062	0.55526450	0.51672044	0.48101710	0.41726506
0.64787424	0.62316694	0.57670591	0.53390818	0.49446932	0.45811152	0.39364628
0.63053454	0.60501645	0.55720378	0.51337325	0.47317639	0.43629669	0.37136442
0.61365892	0.58739461	0.53836114	0.49362812	0.45280037	0.41552065	0.35034379
0.59723496	0.57028603	0.52015569	0.47464242	0.43330179	0.39573396	0.33051301
0.58125057	0.55367575	0.50256588	0.45638695	0.41464286	0.37688948	0.31180473
0.56569398	0.53754928	0.48557090	0.43883360	0.39678743	0.35894236	0.29415540
0.55055375	0.52189250	0.46915063	0.42195539	0.37970089	0.34184987	0.27750510
0.53581874	0.50669175	0.45328563	0.40572633	0.36335013	0.32557131	0.26179726
0.52147809	0.49193374	0.43795713	0.39012147	0.34770347	0.31006791	0.24697855
0.50752126	0.47760557	0.42314699	0.37511680	0.33273060	0.29530277	0.23299863
0.49393796	0.46369473	0.40883767	0.36068923	0.31840248	0.28124073	0.21981003
0.48071821	0.45018906	0.39501224	0.34681657	0.30469137	0.26784832	0.20736795
0.46785227	0.43707675	0.38165434	0.33347747	0.29157069	0.25509364	0.19563014
0.45533068	0.42434636	0.36874815	0.32065141	0.27901502	0.24294632	0.18455674
0.44314421	0.41198676	0.35627841	0.30831867	0.26700002	0.23137745	0.17411013
0.43128391	0.39998715	0.34423035	0.29646026	0.25550241	0.22035947	0.16425484
0.41974103	0.38833703	0.33258971	0.28505794	0.24449991	0.20986617	0.15495740
0.40850708	0.37702625	0.32134271	0.27409417	0.23397121	0.19987254	0.14618622
0.39757380	0.36604490	0.31047605	0.26355209	0.22389589	0.19035480	0.13791153
0.38693314	0.35538340	0.29997686	0.25341547	0.21425444	0.18129029	0.13010522
0.37657727	0.34503243	0.28983272	0.24366872	0.20502817	0.17265741	0.12274077
0.36649856	0.33498294	0.28003161	0.23429685	0.19619921	0.16443563	0.11579318
0.35668959	0.32522615	0.27056194	0.22528543	0.18775044	0.15660536	0.10923885
0.34714316	0.31575355	0.26141250	0.21662061	0.17966549	0.14914797	0.10305552
0.33785222	0.30655684	0.25257247	0.20828904	0.17192870	0.14204568	0.09722219
0.32880995	0.29762800	0.24403137	0.20027793	0.16452507	0.13528160	0.09171905
0.32000968	0.28895922	0.23577910	0.19257493	0.15744026	0.12883962	0.08652740
0.31144495	0.28054294	0.22780590	0.18516820	0.15066054	0.12270440	0.08162962
0.30310944	0.27237178	0.22010231	0.17804635	0.14417276	0.11686133	0.07700908
0.29499702	0.26443862	0.21265924	0.17119841	0.13796437	0.11129651	0.07265007
0.28710172	0.25673653	0.20546787	0.16461386	0.13202332	0.10599668	0.06853781
0.27941773	0.24925876	0.19851968	0.15828256	0.12633810	0.10094921	0.06465831
0.27193940	0.24199880	0.19180645	0.15219476	0.12089771	0.09614211	0.06099840
0.26466122	0.23495029	0.18532024	0.14634112	0.11569158	0.09156391	0.05754566
0.25757783	0.22810708	0.17905337	0.14071262	0.11070965	0.08720373	0.05428836
0.22490511	0.19676717	0.15075814	0.11565551	0.08883907	0.06832640	0.04056742
0.19637679	0.16973309	0.12693431	0.09506040	0.07128901	0.05353552	0.03031434
0.17146718	0.14641325	0.10687528	0.07813272	0.05720594	0.04194648	0.02265264
0.14971726	0.12629736	0.08998612	0.06421940	0.04590497	0.03286617	0.01692737
0.13072622	0.10894521	0.07576590	0.05278367	0.03683649	0.02575150	0.01264911
0.11414412	0.09397710	0.06379285	0.04338433	0.02955948	0.02017698	0.00945215
0.09966540	0.08106547	0.05371187	0.03565875	0.02372003	0.01580919	0.00706320
0.08702324	0.06992779	0.04522395	0.02930890	0.01903417	0.01238691	0.00527803
0.07598469	0.06032032	0.03807735	0.02408978	0.01527399	0.00970547	0.00394405
0.06634634	0.05203284	0.03206011	0.01980004	0.01225663	0.00760449	0.00294723

TABLE OF CASES

Italic type indicates principal cases.

TABLE OF STATUTES, RULES, CONSTITUTIONS, TREATIES, RESTATEMENTS, AND MORE

TABLE OF SECONDARY AUTHORITIES

Italic type indicates principal extracts.

Abraham, Kenneth S. & Jeffries, John C. Jr. Punitive Damages and the Rule of Law: The Role of Defendant's Wealth, 18 J. Legal Stud. 415 (1989), 238

Akerlof, George. The Market for Lemons, 84 Q.J. Econ. 488 (1970), 24

Albiston, Catherine R. & Nielsen, Laura Beth. The Procedural Attack on Civil Rights: The Empirical Reality of Buckhannon for the Private Attorney General, 54 UCLA L. Rev. 1087 (2007), 936

Allen, Michael P. Of Remedy, Juries, and State Regulation of Punitive Damages: The Significance of Philip Morris v. Williams, 63 N.Y.U. Ann. Surv. Am. L. 343 (2008), 253

Amdur, Spencer E. & Hausman, David. Nationwide Injunctions and Nationwide Harm, 131 Harv. L. Rev. F. 49 (2017), 287

Amsterdam, Anthony G. Criminal Prosecutions Affecting Federally Guaranteed Civil Rights: Federal Removal and Habeas Corpus Jurisdiction to Abort State Court Trial, 113 U. Pa. L. Rev. 793 (1965), 620

Anderson, Alan. Local Black History Chronology, available at www.sumtercountyhistory.com/history/BlackHx.htm, 313

Anderson, Roy Ryden. A Look Back at the Future of UCC Damages Remedies, 71 SMU L. Rev. 185 (2018), 40

Anderson, Roy Ryden. Damages for Sellers Under the Code's Profit Formula, 40 Sw. L.J. 1021 (1988), 38

Anderson, Roy Ryden. Failure of Essential Purpose and Essential Failure on Purpose: A Look at Section 2-719 of the Uniform Commercial Code, 31 Sw. L.J. 759 (1977), 70

Anenson, T. Leigh. The Triumph of Equity: Equitable Estoppel in Modern Litigation, 27 Rev. Litig. 377 (2008), 989, 996

Anenson, T. Leigh. Treating Equity Like Law: A Post-Merger Justification of Unclean Hands, 45 Am. Bus. L.J. 455 (2008), 989

Ardia, David S. Freedom of Speech, Defamation, and Injunctions, 55 Wm. & Mary L. Rev. 1 (2013), 137

Areeda, Phillip & Hovenkamp, Herbert. Antitrust Law (Aspen, rev. ed. 1995), 1017

Aristotle. Nicomachean Ethics (Walter M. Hatch trans., 1879), 323

Avraham, Ronen. An Empirical Study of the Impact of Tort Reforms on Medical Malpractice Settlement Payments, 36 J. Legal Stud. S183 (2007), 199

Avraham, Ronen. Database of State Tort Law Reforms (5th), https://ssrn.com/abstract=902711 (2014), 193

Avraham, Ronen. Putting a Price on Pain-and-Suffering Damages: A Critique of the Current Approaches and a Preliminary Proposal for Change, 100 Nw. U. L. Rev. 87 (2006), 204

Avraham, Ronen & Yuracko, Kimberly. Torts and Discrimination, 78 Ohio St. L.J. 661 (2017), 163

Baker, Lynn A., Perino, Michael A. & Silver, Charles. Is the Price Right? An Empirical Study of Fee-Setting in Securities Class Actions, 115 Colum. L. Rev. 1371 (2015), 915

Baker, Tom. Liability Insurance as Tort Regulation: Six Ways That Liability Insurance Shapes Tort Law in Action, 12 Conn. Ins. L.J. 1 (2005), 166

Baker, Tom. Medical Malpractice and the Insurance Underwriting Cycle, 54 DePaul L. Rev. 393 (2005), 196

Baker, Tom, Holland, Eric & Klick, Jonathan. Everything's Bigger in Texas: Except the Medmal Settlements, 2 Conn. Ins. L.J. 1 (2016), 194

Baldus, David, MacQueen, John C. & Woodworth, George. Improving Judicial Oversight of Jury Damages Assessments: A Proposal for the Comparative Additur/Remittitur Review of Awards for Nonpecuniary Harms and Punitive Damages, 80 Iowa L. Rev. 1109 (1995), 212

Baude, William. Foreword: The Supreme Court's Shadow Docket, 9 N.Y.U. J. of L. & Liberty 1 (2015), 481

Baude, William. Is Qualified Immunity Unlawful?, 106 Cal. L. Rev. 45 (2018), 513

Baumer, David & Marschall, Patricia. Willful Breach of Contract for the Sale of Goods: Can the Bane of Business Be an Economic Bonanza?, 65 Temple L. Rev. 159 (1992), 45-46

Beerman, Jack Michael. Qualified Immunity and Constitutional Avoidance, 2009 Sup. Ct. Rev. 139, 511

Beh, Hazel Glenn. Curing the Infirmities of the Unconscionability Doctrine, 66 Hastings L.J. 1011 (2015), 984

Berger, Robert S. The Mandamus Power of the United States Courts of Appeals: A Complex and Confused Means of Appellate Control, 31 Buff. L. Rev. 37 (1982), 308

Birckhead, Tamar R. The New Peonage, 72 Wash. & Lee L. Rev. 1095 (2015), 897-898

Bishop, William. The Choice of Remedy for Breach of Contract, 14 J. Legal Stud. 299 (1985), 406

Black, Bernard, Silver, Charles, Hyman, David A. & Sage, William M. Stability, Not Crisis: Medical Malpractice Claim Outcomes in Texas, 1988-2002, 2 J. Empirical Legal Stud. 207 (2005), 199

LeDuff, Charlie. For 28 Cows and Precious Water, a Man's Got to Sit in Jail, N.Y. Times (May 9, 2004), 810

LeDuff, Charlie. Rancher Has Change of Heart, N.Y. Times (May 13, 2004), 810

Lewis, Neil A. Federal Jury Acquits McDougal On One Charge and Is Split on 2, N.Y. Times (Apr. 13, 1999), 812

Mangalindan, Mylene. EBay Is Ordered to Pay $30 Million in Patent Rift, Wall St. J. (Dec. 13, 2007), 447

McHugh, Margaret. Mom Embraces Her Daughter After Long Global Custody Battle, Newark Star-Ledger (Nov. 2, 2002), 808

Metcalf, Andrew. White Flint Property Draws Another Lawsuit as Amazon Decision Looms, Bethesda Magazine (Apr. 2, 2018), 429

Metcalf, Andrew. White Flint Property Owners to Pay Lord & Taylor After Lengthy Legal Battle, Bethesda Magazine (Mar. 28, 2017), 429

Morgenson, Gretchen. Adviser Jailed Since 2000 Pleads Guilty in Securities Fraud Case, N.Y. Times (Aug. 18, 2006), 811

Moyer, Justin William. More Than 7 Million People May Have Lost Driver's Licenses Because of Traffic Debt, Wash. Post (May 19, 2018), 897

Mufson, Steven, BP's Big Bill for the World's Largest Oil Spill Reaches $61.6 Billion, Wash. Post, (July 14, 2016), 112

Navy Settles Lawsuit Over Whales and Its Use of Sonar, N.Y. Times (Dec. 29, 2008), 453

Norton, Ron. People Column, St. Louis Post-Dispatch (Feb. 19, 1996), 416

Onishi, Norimitsu. Jury Clears Man, 70, of Abuse Charges, N.Y. Times (May 1, 1997), 527

Price, Victoria. Sherwood Hot Check Court Continues After Lawsuit, KARK.com (Aug. 25, 2016), 897

Sandomir, Richard. Raiders Lose Lawsuit Against N.F.L., N.Y. Times (May 22, 2001), 458

Savage, Charlie. A Onetime "Person of Interest" Moves a Step Closer to Public Exoneration, N.Y. Times (Aug. 2, 2008), 811

Savage, Charlie. White House Unblocks Twitter Users Who Sued Trump, But Appeals Ruling, N.Y. Times (Jun. 5, 2018), 614

Savage, William W., III. Back to Normal: OK Legislature Restores American Rule, Nondoc.com, May 25, 2017, 924

Schwartzman, Paul. Blind to His Faults: She Spurned Him, He Maimed Her, and They Lived Happily Ever After, Sort Of, Wash. Post (June 6, 2007), 528

Selk, Avi. A Treasure Hunter Found 3 Tons of Sunken Gold — and Can't Leave His Jail Cell Until He Says Where It Is, Wash. Post (Dec. 14, 2016), 8

Silver-Greenberg, Jessica, Cowley, Stacy & Kitroeff, Natalie. When Student Loan Bills Mean You Can No Longer Work, N.Y. Times (Nov. 18, 2017), 896

Silverman, Rachel Emma. States Court Family-Trust Business, Wall St. J. (June 22, 2006), 882

Stanton, Sam & Walsh, Denny. Major Progress Cited in Prison Inmate Care, Sacramento Bee (Dec. 20, 2014), 343

Stewart, Nikita & Ferré-Sadurní, Luis. Another Taxi Driver in Debt Takes His Life. That's 5 in 5 Months, N.Y. Times (May 27, 2018), 905

Wall St. J. (Clifford Olson story) (Jan. 27, 1982), 221

Walsh, Mary Williams. A.H. Robins Begins Removal Campaign for Dalkon Wearers—Company Offers to Pay Costs of Procedure and Exams, Seeks No Lawsuit Waiver, Wall St. J. (Oct. 30, 1984), 1038

Weiser, Benjamin. Judge's Approval Is Sought in 2 Lawsuits From 9/11, N.Y. Times A19 (Mar. 5, 2010), 156

Wollan, Malia. California Asks Removal of Prison Overseer, N.Y. Times (Jan. 29, 2009), 341

Wright, Scott W. Living with Pain, Austin American-Statesman (Sept. 21, 1990), 185

Nielson, Aaron L. & Walker, Christopher J. The New Qualified Immunity, 89 S. Cal. L. Rev. 1 (2015), 512

Nimmer, Melville B. & Nimmer, David. Nimmer on Copyright (Matthew Bender 1996), 702-704

North Carolina Occupational Safety and Health Annual Comparison Report October 2015-September 2016, 527

Note, Defendant Class Actions, 91 Harv. L. Rev. 630 (1978), 849

Olson, Susan M. How Much Access to Justice from State "Equal Access to Justice Acts"? 71 Chi.-Kent L. Rev. 547 (1995), 925

Oppenheimer, David Benjamin. Martin Luther King, Walker v. City of Birmingham, and the Letter from Birmingham Jail, 26 U.C. Davis L. Rev. 791 (1993), 829

Ostrom, Brian et al. A Step Above Anecdote: A Profile of the Civil Jury in the 1990s, 79 Judicature 233 (1996), 226

Paik, Myungho, Black, Bernard, & Hyman, David A. The Receding Tide of Medical Malpractice Litigation: Part 1—National Trends, 10 J. Empirical Legal Stud. 612 (2013), 199

Palmer, George E. Law of Restitution (Little Brown 1978), xxiv, 699, 719, 730, 746, 748

Parillo, Nicholas R. The Endgame of Administrative Law: Governmental Disobedience and the Judicial Contempt Power, 113 Harv. L. Rev. 685 (2018), 802

Parker, Wendy. The Decline of Judicial Decisionmaking: School Desegregation and District Court Judges, 81 N.C. L. Rev. 1623 (2003), 365

Schlanger, Margo. Civil Rights Injunctions Over Time: A Case Study of Jail and Prison Court Orders, 81 N.Y.U. L. Rev. 550 (2006), 344, 363

Schlanger, Margo. Jail Strip-Search Cases: Patterns and Participants, 71 L. & Contemp. Probs. 65 (Spring 2008), 209

Schlanger, Margo. Trends in Prison Litigation, as the PLRA Enters Adulthood, 5 UC Irvine L. Rev. 153 (2015), 344

Schoenbrod, David S. The Measure of an Injunction: A Principle to Replace Balancing the Equities and Tailoring the Remedy, 72 Minn. L. Rev. 627 (1988), 306

Schwartz, Alan. Proposals for Products Liability Reform: A Theoretical Synthesis, 97 Yale L.J. 353 (1988), 202

Schwartz, Alan. The Case for Specific Performance, 89 Yale L.J. 271 (1979), 409

Schwartz, Joanna C. How Qualified Immunity Fails, 127 Yale L.J. 2 (2017), 513

Schwartz, Joanna C. Police Indemnification, 89 N.Y.U. L. Rev. 885 (2014), 513

Schwartz, Joanna C. The Case Against Qualified Immunity, 93 Notre Dame L. Rev. 1797 (2018), 513-514

Scott, Robert E. & Triantis, George G. Embedded Options and the Case Against Compensation in Contract Law, 104 Colum. L. Rev. 1428 (2004), 43

Sebok, Anthony. What Did Punitive Damages Do?, 78 Chi.-Kent L. Rev. 163 (2003), 225

Sharkey, Catherine M. Federal Incursions and State Defiance: Punitive Damages in the Wake of Philip Morris v. Williams, 46 Willamette L. Rev. 449 (2010), 252

Sharkey, Catherine M. Punitive Damages as Societal Damages, 113 Yale L.J. 347 (2003), 255

Sharkey, Catherine M. Unintended Consequences of Medical Malpractice Damages Caps, 80 N.Y.U. L. Rev. 391 (2005), 200

Shavell, Steven. Specific Performance Versus Damages for Breach of Contract: An Economic Analysis, 84 Tex. L. Rev. 831 (2006), 413

Sherwin, Emily L. Law and Equity in Contract Enforcement, 50 Md. L. Rev. 253 (1991), 983

Siegel, Stephen A. Injunctions for Defamation, Juries, and the Clarifying Lens of 1868, 56 Buff. L. Rev. 655 (2008), 438, 439

Silver, Charles. A Restitutionary Theory of Attorneys' Fees in Class Actions, 76 Cornell L. Rev. 656 (1991), 944, 967

Silver, Charles. Unloading the Lodestar: Toward a New Fee Award Procedure, 70 Tex. L. Rev. 865 (1992), 947

Silver, Charles & Miller, Geoffrey P. The Quasi-Class Action Method of Managing Multi-District Litigations: Problems and a Proposal, 63 Vand. L. Rev. 107 (2010), 945

Smith, George P. Re-Validating the Doctrine of Anticipatory Nuisance, 29 Vt. L. Rev. 687 (2005), 295

Sobol, Neil L. Charging the Poor: Criminal Justice Debt and Modern-Day Debtors' Prisons, 75 Md. L. Rev. 486 (2016), 894

Speiser, Stuart M. Recovery for Wrongful Death 2d (Lawyers Co-op 1975), 152

Speiser, Stuart M. Recovery for Wrongful Death, Economic Handbook (Lawyers Co-op 1970), 155

Stein, Jacob A. Stein on Personal Injury Damages (3d ed., Clark Boardman Callaghan 1997 & Supp.), 193

Stephens, Hugh W. The Texas City Disaster, 1947 (Univ. of Texas Press 1997), 530

Sterk, Stewart E. Property Rules, Liability Rules, and Uncertainty About Property Rights, 106 Mich. L. Rev. 1285 (2008), 391

Sullivan, Teresa A., Warren, Elizabeth & Westbrook, Jay Lawrence. As We Forgive Our Debtors (Oxford Univ. Press 1989), 870

Swedloff, Rick and Huang, Peter H. Tort Damages and the New Science of Happiness, 85 Ind. L.J. 553 (2010), 172

Symposium, Fairness to Whom? Perspectives on the Class Action Fairness Act of 2005, 156 U. Pa. L. Rev. 1439 (2008), 982

Talley, Eric. Liability-Based Fee-Shifting Rules and Settlement Mechanisms Under Incomplete Information, 71 Chi.-Kent L. Rev. 461 (1995), 930

Thomas, Tracy A. The Continued Vitality of Prophylactic Relief, 27 Rev. Litig. 99 (2007), 302

Thomas, Tracy A. The Prophylactic Remedy: Normative Principles and Definitional Parameters of Broad Injunctive Relief, 52 Buff. L. Rev. 301 (2004), 306-307

Threedy, Debora. United States v. Hatahley: A Legal Archaeology Case Study in Law and Racial Conflict, 34 Am. Indian L. Rev. 1 (2010), 15

Todres, Jacob L. Tax Malpractice Damages: A Comprehensive Review of the Elements and the Issues, 61 Tax Law. 705 (2008), 142

Trubek, David M. et al. The Costs of Ordinary Litigation, 31 UCLA L. Rev. 72 (1983), 951

UCLA Institute for Research on Labor and Employment, Get to Work or Go to Jail: Workplace Rights Under Threat (2016), 894

Ulen, Thomas S. The Efficiency of Specific Performance: Toward a Unified Theory of Contract Remedies, 83 Mich. L. Rev. 341 (1984), 406

Van Hecke, M.T. Equitable Replevin, 33 N.C. L. Rev. 57 (1954), 393

INDEX